S0-DQR-830

Q-R Volume 16

The World Book Encyclopedia

www.worldbook.com

The World Book Encyclopedia

© 2022 World Book, Inc. All rights reserved. This volume may not be reproduced in whole or in part in any form without prior written permission from the publisher.

For information on other World Book publications, visit our website at **www.worldbook.com** or call **1-800-WORLDBK (967-5325).** For information about sales to schools and libraries, call **1-800-975-3250 (United States); 1-800-837-5365 (Canada).**

World Book, Inc.
180 North LaSalle Street
Suite 900
Chicago, Illinois 60601
USA

About the SPINESCAPE®

Dinosaurs roamed Earth for about 160 million years. Even though these animals died out millions of years ago, they have fascinated people ever since they were first described in the early 1800's. And scientists continue to discover new species and learn more about these fantastic creatures and the world in which they lived. Featured on *The World Book Encyclopedia* 2022 Spinescape® is a *Giganotosaurus,* one of the largest meat-eating dinosaurs that ever lived. Its saw-edged, daggerlike teeth could easily slice flesh. It weighed approximately 8 tons (7.3 metric tons), measured about 45 feet (14 meters) in length, and stood about 15 feet (4.6 meters) tall at the hips. The **Dinosaur** article in the 2022 edition of *The World Book Encyclopedia* has been fully revised to reflect the most recent findings in the field of paleontology. Highlights include an in-depth look into the life cycle of a dinosaur and detailed descriptions of many important dinosaur groups. The article features realistic illustrations of dinosaurs in their natural habitats as well as a detailed family-tree graphic depicting dinosaur origins and relationships over time.

2022 SPINESCAPE® photo credit: © Damir G. Martin

WORLD BOOK, the GLOBE DEVICE, and SPINESCAPE® are registered trademarks or trademarks of World Book, Inc.

Copyright © 2021, 2020, 2019, 2018, 2017, 2016, 2015, 2014, 2013, 2012, 2011, 2010, 2009, 2008, 2007, 2006, 2005, 2004, 2003, 2002, 2001, 2000, 1999, 1998, 1997, 1996, 1995, 1994, 1993, 1992, 1991, 1990, 1989, 1988, 1987, 1986, 1985, 1984, 1983 by World Book, Inc.
Copyright © 1982, 1981, 1980, 1979, 1978 by World Book-Childcraft International, Inc.
Copyright © 1977, 1976, 1975, 1974, 1973, 1972, 1971, 1970, 1969, 1968, 1967, 1966, 1965, 1964, 1963, 1962, 1961, 1960, 1959, 1958, 1957 by Field Enterprises Educational Corporation.
Copyright © 1957, 1956, 1955, 1954, 1953, 1952, 1951, 1950, 1949, 1948 by Field Enterprises, Inc.
Copyright 1948, 1947, 1946, 1945, 1944, 1943, 1942, 1941, 1940, 1939, 1938 by The Quarrie Corporation.
Copyright 1937, 1936, 1935, 1934, 1933, 1931, 1930, 1929 by W. F. Quarrie & Company.
The World Book, Copyright 1928, 1927, 1926, 1925, 1923, 1922, 1921, 1919, 1918, 1917 by W. F. Quarrie & Company.
Copyrights renewed 1990, 1989, 1988, 1987, 1986, 1985, 1984, 1983 by World Book, Inc.
Copyrights renewed 1982, 1981, 1980, 1979, 1978 by World Book-Childcraft International, Inc.
Copyrights renewed 1977, 1976, 1975, 1974, 1973, 1972, 1971, 1970, 1969, 1968, 1967, 1966, 1965, 1964, 1963, 1962, 1961, 1960, 1959, 1958 by Field Enterprises Educational Corporation.
Copyrights renewed 1957, 1956, 1955, 1954, 1953, 1952, 1951, 1950 by Field Enterprises, Inc.

International Copyright © 2022, 2021, 2020, 2019, 2018, 2017, 2016, 2015, 2014, 2013, 2012, 2011, 2010, 2009, 2008, 2007, 2006, 2005, 2004, 2003, 2002, 2001, 2000, 1999, 1998, 1997, 1996, 1995, 1994, 1993, 1992, 1991, 1990, 1989, 1988, 1987, 1986, 1985, 1984, 1983 by World Book, Inc.
International Copyright © 1982, 1981, 1980, 1979, 1978 by World Book-Childcraft International, Inc.
International Copyright © 1977, 1976, 1975, 1974, 1973, 1972, 1971, 1970, 1969, 1968, 1967, 1966, 1965, 1964, 1963, 1962, 1961, 1960, 1959, 1958, 1957 by Field Enterprises Educational Corporation.
International Copyright © 1957, 1956, 1955, 1954, 1953, 1952, 1951, 1950, 1949, 1948 by Field Enterprises, Inc.
International Copyright 1948, 1947 The Quarrie Corporation.

Library of Congress Cataloging-in-Publication Data

Title: The World Book Encyclopedia
Description: Chicago, IL: World Book Inc., [2022] | Includes index.
Identifiers: LCCN 2021041068 | ISBN 9780716601227 (set)
Subjects: LCSH: Encyclopedias and dictionaries.
Classification: LCC AE5 .W55 2022 | DDC 031--dc23
LC record available at https://lccn.loc.gov/2021041068

Printed in the United States of America by LSC Communications, Willard, Ohio
1st printing November 2021

Qq

Q is the 17th letter of the alphabet used for the modern English language. It is also used in a number of other languages, including French, German, and Spanish.

In English, the sound of *Q* is spelled with *QU,* and it sounds like *KW,* as in the words *quick* and *sequel. Q* can also represent a *K* sound, as in *unique.* This pronunciation is found with words of French origin. In English, *Q* only occurs without *U* in a few words. Nearly all of those words are of Arabic origin, and many are proper names, such as *Qatar* and *Iraq.*

Scholars believe the letter *Q* evolved from an Egyptian *hieroglyph* (pictorial symbol) that represented a baboon. Hieroglyphs were adapted to be used for a Semitic language by around 1500 B.C. The alphabet for this Semitic language—the earliest known alphabet—is called Proto-Sinaitic. By 1100 B.C., an alphabet for another Semitic language, Phoenician, had evolved from Proto-Sinaitic. See **Semitic languages.**

The Phoenician letter that can be traced to the Egyptian baboon hieroglyph is the 19th letter of the Phoenician alphabet, *qop,* which was the Phoenician word for *monkey.* The Phoenicians used the letter to represent the beginning sound of *qop,* a sound something like a *K.* However, this sound was made farther back in the mouth than an English *K,* with the back of the tongue touching the *uvula.* The uvula is a piece of flesh that hangs from the back of the roof of the mouth. Around 800 B.C., when the Greeks adapted the Phoenician alphabet, they did not have such a sound, but they kept *qop* for a time and called it *qoppa,* using it for the *K* sound.

The Etruscans adopted the Greek alphabet about 700 B.C. They used three letters for the *K* sound—*C, K,* and *Q* (when before *U*). When the Romans adopted the alphabet from the Etruscans by around 650 B.C., they used *QU* for the sound *KW.* Peter T. Daniels

See also **Alphabet; C; K.**

WORLD BOOK map and illustrations

Development of the letter *Q*

Seafarers and traders aided the transmission of letters along the coast of the Mediterranean Sea.

The Latin alphabet was adopted by the Romans from the Etruscans around 650 B.C. The Romans used the combination *QU,* which had a *K* sound in Etruscan, to make the sound *KW.*

The Etruscan alphabet was adopted from the Greek about 700 B.C. The Etruscans adapted their letter *Q* from one of the Greek dialects that used the letter *qoppa.*

Faster ways of writing letters developed during Roman times. Curved, connected lines were quicker than imitations of the *inscriptional* (carved) forms of Roman letters. These inscriptional forms of the Roman letters were retained as capital letters. The modern form of the small letter *q* was set by around A.D. 800.

A.D. 300 — 1500 — Today

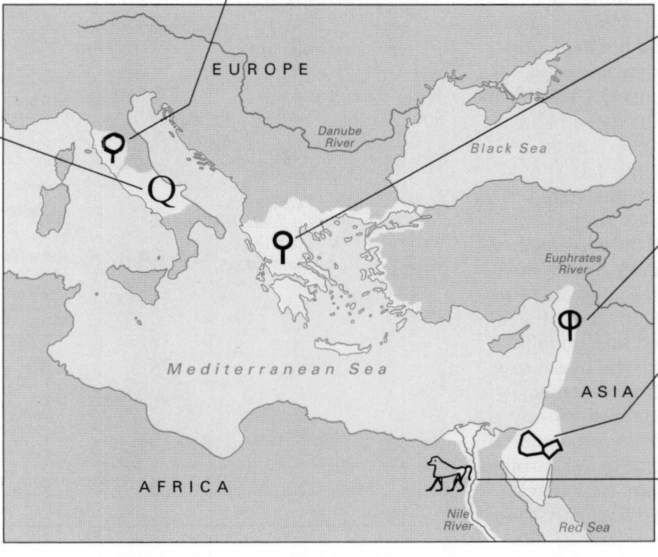

The Greek alphabet evolved from the Phoenician by around 800 B.C. The Greek letter *qoppa,* which was adapted from *qop,* was used in certain dialects of Greek, but it dropped out of the dialect used for classical texts by around 500 B.C.

The Phoenician alphabet had evolved from the Proto-Sinaitic by around 1100 B.C. The Phoenician letter *qop* was used for a sound similar to *K.*

A Proto-Sinaitic alphabet for a Semitic language evolved from Egyptian hieroglyphs by around 1500 B.C. The Proto-Sinaitic letter that came from the baboon hieroglyph was *qop.*

The Egyptians, about 3000 B.C., drew a hieroglyph representing a baboon.

EUROPE
Danube River
Black Sea
Euphrates River
Mediterranean Sea
ASIA
AFRICA
Nile River
Red Sea

Qadhāfī, *guhd DAH fee,* **Mu'ammar Muhammad al-,** *moo ahm MAHR moo HAM uhd ahl* (1942-2011), headed Libya's government from 1969 to 2011. He came to power after he led a military overthrow of Libya's monarchy. He held the rank of colonel and was commander in chief of the Libyan armed forces. Other spellings of his name include Gadhafi, Kaddafi, and Qaddafi.

In 2011, antigovernment protests led to an armed rebellion against Qadhāfī's rule. Qadhāfī ordered the Libyan military to attack the rebels, killing thousands. The United Nations (UN) responded with a resolution calling for "all necessary measures" to protect Libyan civilians. Air strikes led by United States, French, and British warplanes then hit Libyan military positions. As fighting continued, the North Atlantic Treaty Organization (NATO) took over the military operations aimed at protecting civilians. By August, rebel forces controlled most of the country, including Tripoli, Libya's capital. On October 20, Qadhāfī was killed in his hometown of Surt (also spelled Sirte). For details, see **Libya** (History).

Qadhāfī was an outspoken, radical leader with a strong belief in Arab unity under the religion of Islam. He encouraged strict obedience to Islamic laws. He also supported unifying the countries of Africa. From February 2009 to January 2010, Qadhafi served as chairman of the African Union, an organization that promotes cooperation among African nations. He aided revolutionaries and terrorists in many parts of the world. Leaders of many countries, especially Western countries, denounced him for interfering in other nations' affairs.

Qadhāfī was born near the town of Surt. He attended the Libyan Military Academy in Benghāzī and the Royal Military Academy at Sandhurst, England. Malcolm C. Peck

Qa`ida, *KY ih duh,* **Al-,** also spelled al-Qaida and al-Qaeda, is a terrorist organization that supports the activities of Muslim extremists around the world. Its founder and leader was Osama bin Laden, a Saudi-born millionaire (see **Bin Laden, Osama**). United States special forces troops killed bin Laden on May 2, 2011, in Pakistan (May 1 in the United States). *Al-Qa`ida* is an Arabic term that means *the base.* The United States has blamed al-Qa`ida for the Sept. 11, 2001, attacks against the World Trade Center in New York City, New York; and the Pentagon Building near Washington, D.C. Al-Qa`ida also is believed to have aided other attacks against U.S. targets, including the 1998 bombings of U.S. embassies in Kenya and Tanzania. Al-Qa`ida believes that governments of Muslim countries that fail to follow Islamic law should be overthrown. Al-Qa`ida also considers the United States to be a primary enemy of Islam.

In 1979, bin Laden reportedly joined the *mujahideen,* the Muslim resistance movement fighting against the Soviet occupation of Afghanistan. He founded al-Qa`ida in the late 1980's to resist the Soviets. During the 1990's, al-Qa`ida expanded its goals. It opposed foreign influence in Muslim countries and called for the overthrow of Muslim governments allied to the United States.

In 1996, bin Laden and other al-Qa`ida leaders moved to Afghanistan. There, they lived under the protection of the Taliban, a conservative Islamic group that controlled most of the country. After the September 2001 attacks, the United States and its allies launched a military campaign that drove the Taliban from power later in 2001.

Since the fall of the Taliban, U.S. and allied forces have searched for al-Qa`ida leaders in Afghanistan, Iraq, and elsewhere. Many of the leaders have been captured or killed. United States officials accused one of those killed, Abu Musab al-Zarqawi, of leading a resistance movement against U.S.-led coalition forces in Iraq.

The coalition invaded Iraq in 2003, overthrew the government of Saddam Hussein, and then remained in Iraq until 2011. The main resistance group—called al-Qa`ida in Iraq—was blamed for suicide bombings, kidnappings, and hostage beheadings. In 2014, al-Qa`ida cut ties with the Iraqi group, which became known as the Islamic State, or the Islamic State in Iraq and Syria (ISIS).

In 2015, a branch of al-Qa`ida called al-Qa`ida in the Arabian Peninsula (AQAP) claimed responsibility for an attack on a newspaper in Paris, France. The group also fought government and rival rebel forces in Yemen, where AQAP was based. Al-Qa`ida created a strong presence in war-torn Syria as well. Al-Qa`ida in the Islamic Maghreb, a branch based in Algeria, launched attacks in nearby Mali in 2015 and Burkina Faso in 2016. In the early 2020's, al-Qa`ida and its affiliated groups remained active in areas of conflict in Asia and Africa.

Christine Moss Helms

See also **Afghanistan** (Recent developments); **Islamic State; September 11 terrorist attacks; Taliban.**

Qatar, *KUHT uhr* or *KAH tahr* or *GAH tahr,* is a small Arab country in southwestern Asia. It occupies a peninsula that juts from eastern Arabia into the Persian Gulf. Doha is Qatar's capital and largest city.

Qatar

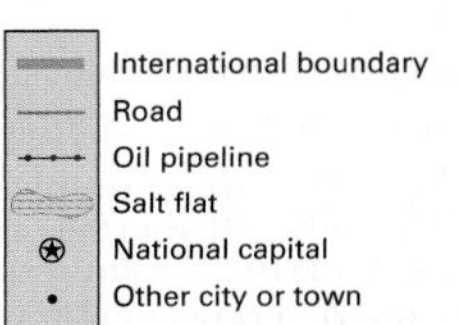

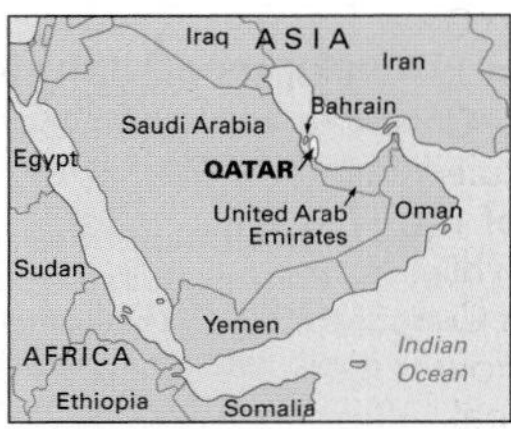

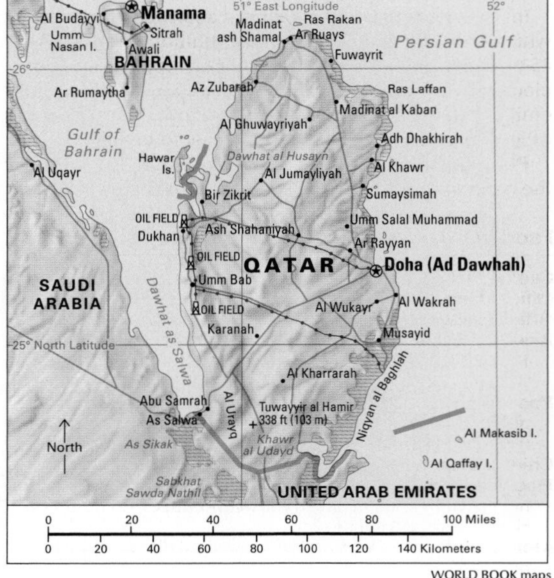

WORLD BOOK maps

© Robert Azzi, Woodfin Camp, Inc.

Doha is the capital and largest city of Qatar. Examples of the city's traditional Islamic architecture are shown here. But much of Doha has a modern appearance.

Over two-thirds of Qatar's people were born in other countries. The native-born are called Qataris. Until the 1940's, most Qataris worked tending camels, fishing, or diving for pearls. Today, most work in cities or oil fields.

Qatar's economy depends largely on oil and natural gas. Since the 1950's, the government has earned much income from oil exports and used it to develop Qatar. Qatar ranks among the richest nations in terms of average income per person. The government provides free education, free health care, and housing for the poor.

Qatar became a protectorate of the United Kingdom in 1916. It gained full independence in 1971.

Government. Qatar is an *emirate.* An *emir* (prince) rules the country according to a provisional constitution of 1970. The emir is a member of the al-Thani family, which has ruled Qatar since the mid-1800's. He appoints a Council of Ministers and an Advisory Council. The government allows no political parties. A central Municipal Council, elected by the people, provides advice on municipal services.

In 2003, Qataris voted in favor of a new constitution, which took effect in 2005. The Constitution establishes a 45-member parliament in which 30 members are to be elected by the people and 15 are to be appointed by the emir. It allows both men and women to vote and hold office. Parliamentary elections have yet to be held.

People. Oil was found in Qatar in 1939. By the 1950's, the oil industry was providing more jobs than had ever been available in Qatar before. As a result, thousands of people moved to Qatar from other Arab countries.

Arabs make up most of Qatar's population. Arabic is the official language, but many business executives and government officials use English with people from other countries. Islam is the state religion. Most people live in or near Doha in modern houses or apartments.

The government requires children from the ages of 6 to 16 to go to school. Almost all adults can read and write.

Land and climate. Most of Qatar's land is stony desert. Barren salt flats cover the south. Summer temperatures sometimes rise above 120 °F (49 °C), but the winter is cooler. Qatar seldom gets more than 4 inches (10 centimeters) of rain a year. Qatar has little natural water. It must distill most of its drinking water, which comes from the sea. The people grew few crops until the late 1950's, when the government dug wells.

Economy. Oil is Qatar's most important product and chief export. The export of petroleum and petroleum products provides most of Qatar's income. The government encourages the growth of other industries to reduce Qatar's dependence on oil. The government owns and operates the oil wells and refineries; flour mills; a fishing fleet; and plants that produce cement, fertilizers, petrochemicals, plastics, and steel.

Agriculture plays a small role in Qatar's economy, and the country must import most of its food. Qatar also imports chemicals, machinery, and transportation equipment. The country's chief trading partners include China, India, Japan, South Korea, and other Asian countries.

Doha has a port and an international airport. Roads link Doha to the rest of Qatar and to Saudi Arabia and the United Arab Emirates. The government finances a satellite TV station called Al-Jazeera that broadcasts throughout much of the world.

History. People have lived in what is now Qatar for thousands of years. Before oil was discovered, they made a living by raising camels, fishing, or pearl diving.

The people of Qatar had no strong government until the late 1700's, when the Wahhābis, an Islamic sect from Saudi Arabia, took control of the country. During the mid-1800's, *sheiks* (Arab chiefs) of the al-Thani family became the leaders of Qatar's tribes. The Ottomans extended their territory to Qatar during the late 1800's. In 1916, Qatar became a British protectorate.

Oil was discovered in Qatar in 1939. But World War II began that year and delayed oil exportation until 1949.

Qatar became an independent nation in 1971. In 1972, Khalifa bin Hamad al-Thani, the deputy ruler, became emir after peacefully overthrowing his cousin, Emir Ahmad bin Ali al-Thani. In the mid-1970's, the government took ownership of Qatar's petroleum industry.

After Iraq invaded Kuwait in August 1990, Qatar allowed the United States and its allies to use a Qatari air force base to attack the Iraqi forces. Qatar also took part in air and ground attacks to liberate Kuwait in early 1991. In 1995, Crown Prince Hamad bin Khalifa al-Thani peacefully overthrew his father, Khalifa bin Hamad al-Thani, to become emir. The new ruler had long served as defense minister. In 2013, he handed power to his son, Crown Prince Tamim bin Hamad al-Thani.

In 2017, Bahrain, Egypt, Saudi Arabia, and the United Arab Emirates cut diplomatic ties with Qatar because of

Facts in brief

Capital: Doha.
Official language: Arabic.
Official name: State of Qatar.
Area: 4,473 mi² (11,586 km²). *Greatest distances*—north-south, 115 mi (185 km); east-west, 55 mi (89 km). *Coastline*—235 mi (378 km).
Population: *Estimated 2022 population*—2,809,000; density, 628 per mi² (242 per km²); distribution, 99 percent urban, 1 percent rural. *2015 census*—2,404,776.
Chief products: Petroleum and petroleum products.
Flag: The left third is white with a vertical series of points on the right side. The right two-thirds is maroon. See **Flag** (picture: Flags of Asia and the Pacific).
Money: *Basic unit*—Qatar riyal. One hundred dirhams equal one riyal.

its alleged support of terrorism and its close ties with Iran. They also imposed a blockade on Qatar. The blockade caused damage to both Qatar's economy and Arab unity. After extended negotiations, the four countries restored diplomatic ties with Qatar in 2021.

Mamoun H. Fandy

See also **Doha; Organization of the Petroleum Exporting Countries; Persian Gulf War of 1991.**

Qin dynasty, *chihn,* also spelled Ch'in, was a Chinese *dynasty* (family of rulers) that governed from 221 B.C. to 206 B.C. The dynasty began after Shi Huangdi, ruler of the state of Qin, conquered rival states to the east. He later extended his rule to southeastern China. The dynasty maintained complete control over areas where, previously, local Chinese chiefs had much power.

Shi Huangdi made local rulers move to his new capital at Xianyang (near present-day Xi'an) and appointed local administrators responsible to him. He banned most books to try to silence critics, promote obedience, and blot out knowledge of the past. He built walls that connected with older border walls to keep invaders out. This wall building marked the start of the Great Wall of China. He standardized weights and measures, currency, and the Chinese script. He gave his country a lasting ideal—national unity. The name *China* came from his dynasty's name.

Shi Huangdi died in 210 B.C., and his son proved to be a weak ruler. Rebellions began in 209 B.C., and the Qin dynasty soon collapsed. The Han dynasty then gained control of China. Grant Hardy

See also **Great Wall of China; Legalism; Shi Huangdi.**

Qing dynasty. See **China** (History); **Manchus.**

Qom, *kum* (pop. 1,229,964), is a city in north-central Iran. It lies on the western edge of a vast desert called the Dasht-e Kavir (see **Iran** [political map]). Qom, also spelled Qum, has long been a spiritual center for Shī`ite Muslims, members of the Shī`ah branch of Islam.

The city has ancient origins. Alexander the Great, a Macedonian general, destroyed Qom in the 300's B.C. But the city became prosperous again during the rule of the Sasanian dynasty in Persia (now Iran) from the A.D. 200's to the 600's. In the early 800's, Fatimah bint Musa ibn Jafar—sister of Imām Alī al-Rida ibn Musa, a Shī`ite leader—died in Qom. A shrine was built to her. During the rule of the Safavid dynasty from 1501 to 1722, Qom was promoted as a destination for *pilgrimages* (religious journeys). The Iranian tribal wars of the 1700's destroyed parts of Qom. But the Qajar dynasty, which ruled from 1794 to 1925, restored shrines, sanctuaries, and libraries.

In the mid-1900's, Qom became an important center of opposition to the government of Shah Mohammad Reza Pahlavi. Ayatollah Ruhollah Khomeini, the leader of the Islamic Revolution of 1979 that overthrew the shah, made Qom his home. Rudi Matthee

Quadruplets. See **Multiple birth.**

Quail is the name of many kinds of small-sized birds found throughout much of the world. Quail live on every continent except Antarctica. People commonly hunt these birds for sport or food.

Most adult quail grow 8 to 12 inches (20 to 30 centimeters) long. Males are shades of brown or gray and may have patterns of reddish-brown, blue, white, or black feathers. Most females are patterned in shades of brown, tan, or gray. These colors help protect quail from *predators* (hunting animals) by making the birds hard to see when they sit in a pasture or woodland.

Leonard Lee Rue, NAS

The mountain quail lives in the mountains of the Pacific Coast States and the Baja Peninsula of Mexico.

During fall and winter, quail live in groups called *coveys.* Depending on the kind of quail, a covey may range from fewer than 10 birds to more than 100. The covey helps protect its members from foxes, hawks, owls, and human hunters. When such a predator approaches a covey, the quail squawk loudly and fly in all directions. This behavior often confuses the predator. The covey breaks up in spring, and males and females form pairs for the nesting season. Quail often eat insects and seeds.

A well-known *species* (kind) of quail in North America is the northern bobwhite. These birds live chiefly in the middle and eastern parts of the continent and in Mexico. During the spring, they build their nests on the ground and conceal them with grass. Females lay 8 to 16 eggs, which hatch in about three weeks.

The California quail lives in western North America. It has grayish coloring with a teardrop-shaped feather rising from the forehead. Many California quail inhabit foothills and mountain valleys and migrate to and from the highlands by walking. Others nest and raise their young in residential areas of even large cities.

Other kinds of North American quail include the Gambel's quail, mountain quail, and Montezuma quail. The mountain quail ranks as the largest quail, measuring from 10 ½ to 11 ½ inches (26.7 to 29.2 centimeters) long and weighing about 8 ounces (230 grams). The Montezuma quail is the smallest, measuring 8 to 9 ½ inches (20 to 24 centimeters) long. All these birds live in western and southwestern areas of the continent. The common quail inhabits much of Europe and Africa. Its European populations migrate chiefly to northern Africa and the Middle East. The blue-breasted quail lives in Asia, Australia, and the Pacific Islands. In June 2006, the Manipur bush-quail was rediscovered in India. Scientists believed this quail had become extinct in the 1920's. Edward H. Burtt, Jr.

Scientific classification. New World quail belong to the New World quail family, Odontophoridae. Most other quail are in the family Phasianidae. The northern bobwhite is *Colinus virginianus.* The California quail is *Callipepla californica,* the Gambel's quail is *C. gambelii,* the mountain quail is *Oreortyx pictus,* and the Montezuma quail is *Cyrtonyx montezumae.* The common quail is *Coturnix coturnix,* and the blue-breasted quail is *C. chinensis.* The Manipur bush-quail is *Perdicula manipurensis.*

See also **Bird** (pictures); **Grouse; Partridge.**

Quakers is the popular name for members of the Religious Society of Friends. Quakerism developed in England in the 1600's. Today, a majority of its followers live in Kenya. England, Bolivia, and the United States also have large Quaker populations. Smaller Quaker groups exist in most other parts of the world.

Quakers have been known throughout their history for their humanitarian activities. They reject war and stress peace education. They have pioneered in supporting the ministry of women and in removing barriers to racial equality. They also have been among the leaders in prison reform and the humane treatment of people with mental illness. The high quality of Quaker schools and colleges also has been widely recognized.

History. George Fox of England, a founder of Quakerism, began preaching in 1647. Fox believed that the Inner Light of Christ dwelt in the hearts of all people and that the inner experience of Christ resulted in outward actions that challenged religious and civic authorities. The Inner Light is the presence of God. The word *Quaker* was originally meant as an insult to Fox, who told an English judge to "tremble at the Word of the Lord." The judge called Fox a "quaker." See **Fox, George.**

During the early decades of Quakerism, its followers often were imprisoned for long periods of time. The movement survived because of the organizational skills and creative compassion of the Englishwoman Margaret Fell. Fell maintained communication with desperate imprisoned Quakers. She offered pastoral care through her letters and dispensed practical aid for those in need.

In 1681, a Quaker, William Penn, received a charter from the king of England to establish the colony of Pennsylvania. Penn hoped to make the colony a haven for the persecuted English Quakers and other people who disagreed with the established church. Penn gave the colony a constitution that was a model for safeguarding religious liberties. See **Penn, William.**

Worship. Quakers practice a distinctive form of worship. They regard all life as sacramental and observe no special sacraments. They gather for periods of group silence, waiting for God to exercise power upon their lives. They expect God to lay on them "the burden of the world's suffering," and they accept the responsibility to respond. Anyone who feels he or she has been given a message during the silence may speak. Some Quaker gatherings include periods of programmed worship, such as scripture reading, hymns, and sermons.

Business. Quaker business is conducted at regular meetings guided by a *clerk.* The clerk introduces a concern and listens to attendees' views and suggestions. Then the clerk presents for group consideration a *minute* that combines the attendees' comments and seeks to address the concern. No votes are taken, but the process continues until all present are satisfied that their positions have been heard and considered.

The loose organizational structure of the Religious Society of Friends has always given a great deal of liberty to its regional Yearly Meetings. The Friends World Committee for Consultation, based in London, is a communications center for many of the world's Quakers.

Mary Van Vleck Garman

Related articles in ***World Book*** include:

American Friends Service Committee
Dyer, Mary
Hicks, Edward
Marriage (Wedding ceremonies)
Mott, Lucretia Coffin
New Jersey (English control)
Pacifism
Pennsylvania (picture: A Quaker meeting house)
Prison (Early prison reform)
Whittier, John Greenleaf
Woolman, John

Quanah, *KWAH nuh* (1845-1911), was a leader of the Comanche Indians. He led them against white settlers to stop the slaughter of buffalo in the tribe's homeland in Texas. In 1875, he surrendered to the United States Army, and his band moved to a reservation near Fort Sill, in what is now southwestern Oklahoma. Quanah encouraged his people to get an education and to farm the land. He also persuaded the Comanche to increase their income by leasing pastureland to white ranchers. Quanah obtained full U.S. citizenship for every member of his band. He served as a judge on the reservation's court and, by 1890, had become head of all the Comanche.

Quanah was born near what is now Lubbock, Texas. He was the son of a Comanche chief and Cynthia Ann Parker, a white captive. He was also called Quanah Parker. The name Quanah comes from the Comanche *kwaina,* meaning *fragrant.* He died on Feb. 23, 1911.

Jeffrey P. Shepherd

Quanta. See **Photon; Quantum mechanics.**

Quantrill, *KWAHN trihl,* **William Clarke** (1837-1865), led a Confederate guerrilla band during the American Civil War (1861-1865). He was born on July 31, 1837, in Canal Dover, Ohio. In 1857, he went to Kansas and started farming. The next year, he rode west and became a gambler. He returned to Kansas in 1859 and taught school. Quantrill was accused of stealing cattle and horses and of killing several people but escaped arrest.

At the start of the Civil War, Quantrill formed a band of guerrilla troops. He led his men on raids against Union supporters in Kansas and Missouri. Quantrill's band was mustered into Confederate service in 1862 but continued to operate independently. On Aug. 21, 1863, he and his men burned most of Lawrence, Kansas, and killed about 150 people. Quantrill was killed on June 6, 1865, during a raid in Kentucky. Thomas L. Connelly

Quantum field theory is a set of basic ideas that physicists use to explain the laws of nature. The two most important of those ideas are: (1) interactions between objects are transmitted by *fields,* and (2) those interactions obey the principles of *quantum mechanics.*

A field is an influence that an object creates in the region around it. For example, a magnet creates a *magnetic field* in the space around it. This field, in turn, can make another magnet move. Magnets interact by means of the *magnetic force;* the field transmits the force.

Consider a magnetic field created by a bar magnet. Suppose a compass lies far from the magnet. If the compass is far enough away, the bar magnet's field will be too weak to affect the compass needle, a small magnet itself. Now, imagine that the compass comes closer to the bar magnet. At a certain point, the field will make the compass needle rotate by a measurable amount.

An *electric field* transmits the *electric force* between electrically charged objects. Electric fields and magnetic fields usually occur together, so they are usually referred to jointly as *electromagnetic fields.* Other kinds of fields transmit three major forces: (1) the *strong force,* which holds particles called *quarks* together in protons, neutrons, and other objects; (2) the *weak force,* which is responsible for certain kinds of radioactivity; and (3) the *gravitational force,* by which all types of objects are attracted to one another.

The fundamental principle of quantum mechanics is that energy transmitted by fields comes in packets or bundles. Physicists refer to the packets as *field particles.* Each kind of field particle has a name. For example, the field particles of electromagnetic energy are known as *photons.* Visible light is a form of electromagnetic energy, and so its field particles are photons. Michael Dine

See also **Photon; Quantum mechanics; Standard Model.**

Quantum mechanics, *KWAHN tuhm,* is a branch of physics that describes the structure and behavior of matter. It has replaced *classical mechanics,* a group of older theories, as a description of the smallest known units of matter and their activity. The older theories are still adequate for describing and predicting the behavior of objects that we ordinarily encounter in our daily lives.

Classical mechanics is based on physical laws described by two physicists and mathematicians, Isaac Newton of England and James Clerk Maxwell of Scotland. Newton explained his laws of motion and gravitation in *Philosophiae naturalis principia mathematica (Mathematical Principles of Natural Philosophy),* published in 1687. In 1864, Maxwell described electric and magnetic phenomena in a series of equations. Several scientists helped establish quantum mechanics from 1900 to the late 1920's.

Quantum mechanics describes several objects and phenomena that seem strange and are difficult to understand. Among these are *quanta,* or "chunks" of energy; the *wave-particle duality* of matter; and the *uncertainty principle,* which limits what we can know about objects.

Quanta of energy. Before quantum mechanics was developed, physicists considered atoms to be made up of solid particles. In addition, scientists had found that light has properties of waves. For example, they had observed that light can spread around an obstacle.

Scientists knew that visible light is one form of electromagnetic radiation. Physicists also understood the relationship between the energy of electromagnetic waves and their *wavelength* (distance between successive wave crests). The greater the energy of a wave, the shorter its wavelength. See **Electromagnetic waves.**

Physicists commonly refer to all kinds of electromagnetic radiation as *light,* except when it is important to mention a specific kind of radiation. The remainder of this article follows that practice.

Emission of quanta. The German physicist Max Planck found the first failure of classical mechanics in 1900. Scientists had measured the amounts of energy in different wavelengths of light *emitted* (sent out) from the surfaces of certain hot objects. According to classical mechanics, the tiny vibrating objects that emit light from the surfaces, now known as molecules and atoms, can emit continuous amounts of energy. But Planck showed that the measured emissions cannot be explained if the energy is emitted continuously. He said that, instead, the energy is emitted in "chunks," which came to be called quanta. *Quantum* is the singular of *quanta.*

Quantum nature of light. The German-born physicist Albert Einstein extended Planck's ideas in a series of scientific papers starting in 1905. One of Einstein's ideas was that light consists of quanta, later called *photons.*

Quantized orbits. By 1911, scientists knew that an atom is made up of a positively charged nucleus surrounded by negatively charged electrons. But positively charged objects attract negatively charged objects. Scientists could not explain why electrical attraction does not make the electrons spiral into the nucleus.

In 1913, the Danish physicist Niels Bohr offered an explanation. He said that electrons in atoms can change their energy only by absorbing or emitting quanta. According to Bohr's explanation, electrons can occupy only certain orbits around the nucleus. When an electron absorbs a quantum, the electron moves quickly to an orbit farther from the nucleus. When an electron emits a quantum, the electron jumps to a closer orbit. But when an electron reaches its closest possible orbit, it cannot plunge into the nucleus.

Wave-particle duality refers to the fact that light and parts of atoms have properties of both particles and waves. In 1923, American physicist Arthur H. Compton showed that photons have a property of particles called *momentum*—that is, a total amount of motion. For slowly moving particles, momentum equals *velocity* (speed in a given direction) times *mass* (amount of matter). Photons have zero mass but still possess momentum.

In 1924, Louis de Broglie, a French physicist, proposed that subatomic particles, such as electrons, are associated with waves. Experiments later showed that he was correct. As he suggested, electrons can bend around obstacles, and they can display wave shapes known as *interference patterns* and *diffraction patterns.*

Quantum mechanics now describes an electron as a wave—but a wave with an unusual interpretation. The wave serves to locate the electron, but the electron must always be measured as a whole particle. Specifically, the *square* of the height of the wave at a given point in space corresponds to the probability that the electron is at that point. (The square of the height equals the height multiplied by itself.)

The uncertainty principle. In 1927, German physicist Werner Heisenberg discovered a general characteristic of quantum mechanics, the *uncertainty principle.* According to this principle, it is impossible to precisely describe both the location and the momentum of a particle at the same time. For example, if you describe a particle's location with much precision, you must give its momentum in terms of a broad range of numbers.

The uncertainty principle affects attempts to measure a particle's location and momentum. Suppose you want to measure the position of an electron precisely. To do so, you force the electron to absorb and then re-emit a photon so that a light detector can "see" the electron. You know the precise location of both the photon source and the light detector. But even so, the photon's momentum spoils your attempt: The absorption of a photon by the electron changes the electron's momentum. That is, the photon "bumps the electron off course." The electron is therefore proceeding in a new direction when it re-emits the photon. Thus, your detection of the re-emitted photon cannot enable you to determine where the electron was when it absorbed the initial photon. Frank Wilczek

Related articles in *World Book* include:

Atom	Bohr, Niels	Born, Max

De Broglie, Louis Victor	Momentum	Quantum field theory
Einstein, Albert	Motion	Schrödinger, Erwin
Heisenberg, Werner	Newton, Sir Isaac	Standard Model
Light (Photons)	Photon	String theory
Maxwell, James Clerk	Physics (Quantum theory)	Supersymmetry
	Planck, Max K. E. L.	

Quarantine occurs when people, animals, or plants are isolated or their movements are restricted to prevent the spread of infection. The period of quarantine depends on the time needed to stop the spread of a particular disease. The word *quarantine* comes from the Latin *quadraginta,* meaning 40. In early times, officials held a ship outside of port for 40 days if they suspected it carried infection among its passengers or freight.

All people entering a country are subject to quarantine. The officer in command of a ship or airplane is required to report illnesses or deaths on board to officials at the port of entry. People infected with certain diseases may be detained, placed in isolation, or denied entry. In the United States, the Centers for Disease Control and Prevention (CDC) is the agency responsible for developing and enforcing quarantine regulations. Quarantine regulations in Canada are administered by the Public Health Agency of Canada. The World Health Organization, an agency of the United Nations, helps national health agencies develop quarantine laws.

Harmful insect pests and disease organisms have been brought into the United States and Canada by diseased plants and animals. Both nations have laws that provide for the inspection of all plants and animals entering the country. Local areas may be quarantined to prevent the spread of such animal diseases as foot-and-mouth disease, which affects livestock. Alan R. Hinman

Related articles in *World Book* include:

Epidemic	Insect (Insect control)	Plant quarantine
Fumigation		Sanitation

Quark, *kwawrk,* is one of the three families of particles that serve as "building blocks" of matter. The other two families are the leptons and the fundamental, or gauge, bosons. Quarks are *elementary particles*—that is, they have no known smaller parts.

There are six types of quarks, each of which carries a fraction of an electric charge. Three of the quarks, called *down* (or *d), strange* (or *s),* and *bottom* (or *b),* have ⅓ unit of negative charge. The other three—the *up* (or *u), charm* (or *c),* and *top* (or *t)*—have ⅔ unit of positive charge.

A quark is almost always combined with one or two other quarks. *Composite particles* made up of quarks are known as *hadrons.* These include protons and neutrons, which form the nuclei of atoms.

There are two main kinds of hadrons—(1) baryons and (2) mesons. A baryon is a three-quark combination. A proton is a baryon consisting of two *u* quarks and one *d,* while a neutron is a baryon made up of two *d*'s and one *u.* A meson is made up of a quark and an *antiquark.* Antiquarks are the antimatter equivalents of quarks, opposite in electric charge and certain other properties. In addition, scientists have found evidence of rare, short-lived hadrons made up of four or five quarks.

Quarks have no measurable size. Physicists call them "pointlike." The *t* quark is the heaviest known elementary particle. Its mass is about 190 unified atomic mass units, almost as heavy as an entire atom of gold. The lightest quark, the *u,* has about 35,000 times less mass than the *t.*

The *s, c, b,* and *t* quarks are much heavier than the *u* and *d.* The heavy quarks do not exist in ordinary matter. They break down into lighter particles in less than a billionth of a second. Physicists must create *s, c, b,* and *t* quarks with devices called *particle accelerators.*

Two California Institute of Technology physicists, the American Murray Gell-Mann and Russian-born George Zweig, independently proposed the first theory of quarks in 1964. The original theory required only *u, d,* and *s* quarks to build all known hadrons. In the late 1960's and early 1970's, experiments showed that protons and neutrons contain parts much smaller than they are, and that these parts carry fractional charges. Discoveries in 1974, 1977, and 1995 proved the existence of the *c, b,* and *t,* in that order. Robert H. March

See also **Boson; Gluon; Hadron; Lepton; Psi particle.**

Quarles, *kwawrlz,* **Benjamin Arthur** (1904-1996), was an African American historian. He wrote many books about African Americans and their role in United States history. His books include *Frederick Douglass* (1948), *The Negro in the Civil War* (1953), *The Negro in the American Revolution* (1961), and *The Negro in the Making of America* (1964). Quarles was born on Jan. 23, 1904, in Boston. He became professor of history at Dillard University in 1939 and was dean of Dillard from 1946 to 1953. He served as head of the department of history at Morgan State College from 1953 to 1974. Quarles died on Nov. 16, 1996. Robert A. Pratt

Quarrying, *KWAWR ee ihng,* is a method of mining a deposit that lies at the surface. This method is commonly used to dig out large slabs or blocks of stone called *dimension stone.* The stone is removed from a large pit called a *quarry.* Quarries have nearly vertical walls that in some cases can be 1,000 feet (300 meters) high. Dimension stone cut from quarries includes flagstone, granite, limestone, marble, sandstone, and slate. It is used mainly as a building material and for flooring and decorative wall coverings. Quarrying is not a common method of mining because only limited amounts of dimension stone are used each year. William Hustrulid

See also **Mining** (Quarrying).

Quart is a unit of volume and capacity for both dry and liquid substances in the inch-pound system of measurement. This system is used in the United States. The liquid quart equals ¼ of a gallon. It equals 0.946 liter in the metric system. The dry quart equals 1/32 of a bushel. It equals 1.101 liters. Quarts are divided into two pints. See also **Weights and measures.** Richard S. Davis

Quarter is a United States coin worth 25 cents, or a quarter of a dollar. The government issued the first quarters in 1796. The Washington quarter was first minted in 1932, the 200th anniversary of George Washington's birth. His head appears on one side, and an eagle is on the other side. Quarters of several other designs were used before the Washington quarter. In 1999, the government began issuing quarters that replaced the eagle with one of 50 designs that each commemorates a U.S. state. In 2010, the U.S. mint began issuing a series of quarters with designs depicting 56 different national parks and other national sites on the back.

Until 1965, quarters contained 90 percent silver and 10 percent copper. Because of a shortage of silver, the Coinage Act of 1965 eliminated silver from the coin.

Since then, it has consisted of a layer of copper between layers of a copper-nickel mixture. Burton H. Hobson

Quartz, *kwawrts,* is a common mineral that occurs in many types of rock. Quartz is a form of *silica,* a chemical compound of silicon and oxygen. Its chemical formula is SiO_2. Quartz is one of the most abundant minerals in the *continental crust,* the part of Earth's rocky outer layer that lies beneath the continents. It makes up about 12 percent of the rock found there. Quartz is an extremely stable mineral. It is abundant in most beach sands because its grains do not dissolve easily in water. Quartz crystals often line rock cavities called *geodes.*

Quartz appears in many kinds of rock. Quartz crystals form as granite solidifies from *magma* (molten rock). Quartz also occurs in *metamorphic rocks,* rocks whose mineral composition has been changed by heat and pressure. Underground waters sometimes deposit dissolved silica as quartz. This quartz can cement grains of sand to form a rock called *sandstone.* Heat and pressure can transform sandstone that consists almost entirely of quartz into a hard rock called *quartzite.* White veins of quartz often line or fill fractures in rock.

Quartz that forms in underground cavities sometimes develops into clumps of large six-sided crystals with smooth faces. Common varieties are white or colorless, but traces of metallic elements or other impurities can result in a variety of colors. Quartz crystals have a glassy or greasy *luster* (shine). They break along smoothly curving surfaces. Quartz, one of the hardest minerals, defines a 7 on the Mohs hardness scale, a ranking of mineral hardness used by geologists. Quartz scratches glass easily and cannot be scratched by a knife blade.

Types. Geologists divide quartz into many different varieties based on the size and color of its crystals. They usually separate these varieties into two major groups: (1) coarse crystalline and (2) cryptocrystalline.

Coarse crystalline varieties of quartz have crystals that can be seen with the unaided eye. Geologists have found crystals of the colorless variety, called *rock crystal quartz,* that measure up to 3 feet (1 meter) long. Colored varieties include the gems *amethyst,* which is purple, and *citrine,* which is yellowish. *Rose quartz* is pinkish, *milky quartz* is white, and *smoky quartz* is gray.

Cryptocrystalline quartz varieties have crystal grains that can be seen only under a microscope. *Chalcedony,* a variety with *fibrous* (fiberlike) crystals, can replace wood fibers to form petrified wood. *Chert,* an abundant form of quartz, breaks into angular pieces or flakes with smooth surfaces. *Flint,* a dark variety of chert, gives off sparks when struck. *Onyx* is a black quartz with parallel bands of white, yellow, or gray. *Jasper* is a reddish or orangish quartz often found in the presence of iron or manganese. A variety called *agate* has colored bands.

Uses. Quartz is a major part of sands and gravels used in cement, concrete, and sandpaper. Manufacturers melt unusually pure quartz sands into glass for windows and containers. Large, well-formed quartz crystals serve as lenses in certain microscopes and telescopes.

When a quartz crystal is squeezed, it can develop a slight positive electric charge on one side and a slight negative electric charge on the opposite side. This effect, called the *piezoelectric effect,* generates a voltage across the crystal. When a voltage is applied to such a crystal, the reverse effect occurs and the crystal expands and contracts in certain directions. Quartz clocks and watches use piezoelectric quartz crystals to measure time. A small alternating voltage causes the quartz crystal to vibrate at a certain frequency. The clock or watch counts the vibrations to record the passing of seconds, minutes, and hours. Piezoelectric quartz crystals have converted vibrations into electrical signals in such devices as microphones and transformed electrical signals into vibrations in such devices as radios and radar.

Manufacturers produce large, nearly perfect crystals of quartz in special furnaces. These crystals are used in electrical and optical devices. Mark Cloos

Related articles in ***World Book*** include:

Agate	Geode	Quartzite
Amethyst	Jasper	Sand
Chalcedony	Mineral (pictures)	Sandstone
Flint	Onyx	Silica
Gem (pictures)	Piezoelectricity	

Quartzite, *KWAWRT syt,* is a rock composed chiefly of the mineral quartz. The quartz occurs both as individual grains and as the cementing material that holds the grains together. Quartzite, one of the hardest rocks, is a common type of metamorphic rock (see **Metamorphic rock**). It forms when heat and pressure change the grains in quartz sandstone. In this process, called *recrystallization,* quartz grains become so firmly bonded that any breaks that occur in quartzite go through the grains rather than pass around them. John C. Butler

Quasar, *KWAY sahr* or *KWAY zahr,* is an extremely luminous object at the center of some distant galaxies. Quasars can resemble stars in our own galaxy in photographs. For this reason, they are sometimes called *quasi-stellar* (nearly starlike) objects. But they are actually among the most distant objects detected in the universe. The light from the farthest quasars traveled 13 billion *light-years* to reach Earth. A light-year is the distance light travels in a year, about 5.88 trillion miles (9.46 trillion kilometers). Some quasars shine a trillion times brighter than the sun. The word *quasar* is short for *quasi-stellar radio source.* Scientists applied this term to the first type of quasar identified.

Scientists determine the distance to a quasar by measuring the quasar's *redshift.* Redshift is a shift in the wavelengths of light given off by an astronomical object. The light shifts toward the longer, or red, wavelengths of the spectrum. The more distant an object is, the larger its redshift. All quasars have large redshifts (see **Redshift**).

Quasars give off tremendous energy in the form of visible light, ultraviolet light, infrared rays, X rays, gamma rays, and in many cases, radio waves. They also release high-speed jets made up of positively charged particles called *protons* and negatively charged particles called *electrons.* Radiation from quasars takes billions of years to reach Earth. For this reason, the study of quasars can yield information about the early history of the universe.

Quasars were first identified in 1963 by a group of astronomers at the Palomar Observatory, near San Diego. Since then, astronomers have discovered thousands of quasars. They think each quasar is powered by a giant *black hole* at the center of a galaxy. A black hole is a region of space whose gravitational pull is so strong that nothing can escape it (see **Black hole**). The central black hole in a quasar produces energy by swallowing clouds of gas from the surrounding galaxy.

The *mass* (amount of matter) of the central black hole tends to be about 0.5 percent of the mass of all the stars in the surrounding bulge at the center of the quasar galaxy. Scientists use this relationship to try to determine how galaxies and their central black holes formed in the early universe. Most astronomers agree that the black holes were created after the universe's first stars exploded in events called *supernovae* (see **Supernova**).

Quasars rank as the most luminous objects in a more general category of galaxy centers called *active galactic nuclei* (AGN). Two less luminous types of AGN are *blazars* and *Seyfert galaxies.* However, many astronomers have proposed that the different types of AGN may not be different objects. This theory suggests that the observed differences between AGN are due to the angle from which astronomers on Earth see the objects. For example, a blazar may be an AGN with one jet pointing directly at Earth, and a Seyfert may be an AGN that is observed from the side of the jets. Jane C. Charlton

See also **Astronomy** (Finding quasars and pulsars).

Quasicrystal is a solid made up of atoms arranged in an orderly pattern that differs from the pattern in a crystal. In a crystal, the atomic structure is composed of a single type of atom cluster called a *unit cell.* The unit cell repeats throughout the structure so that the distance between the centers of the unit cells is the same throughout. A quasicrystal is composed of two or more kinds of unit cells. The unit cells repeat with different spacings between the different types of unit cells. The ratio of the spacings is an irrational number—that is, a number that cannot be expressed as a fraction (see **Rational number**).

Bell Laboratories

Quasicrystals have shapes that are impossible in crystals. For example, these quasicrystals have five-sided faces.

Both crystals and quasicrystals display *symmetry*—that is, it is possible to rotate their atomic structure by certain angles and have the structure appear identical to the first view. However, because quasicrystals have more than one shape of unit cell, they have types of symmetry that are impossible in crystals. For example, many quasicrystals have fivefold symmetry, meaning that they look the same after every one-fifth rotation around a circle. Crystals cannot have this type of symmetry because it is not possible to pack together a single shape of unit cell so that there is both fivefold symmetry and equal distance between the unit cells. Physicists discovered quasicrystals in 1984. The only known natural quasicrystals were found in Russia. They are believed to be the remains of a meteorite. Paul Joseph Steinhardt

See also **Symmetry.**

Quayle, Dan (1947-), served as vice president of the United States from 1989 to 1993, during the term of President George H. W. Bush. Quayle represented Indiana in the U.S. Senate from 1981 to 1989. He previously had served two terms in the U.S. House of Representatives.

© R. Maiman, Sygma

Dan Quayle

Early life. James Danforth Quayle was born on Feb. 4, 1947, in Indianapolis. He graduated from DePauw University in Greencastle, Indiana, in 1969 with a degree in political science. In 1974, he received a law degree from Indiana University in Indianapolis. While attending law school at night, Quayle worked in the offices of the governor and attorney general of Indiana and directed the state's Inheritance Tax Division. From 1974 to 1976, he was associate publisher of *The Huntington Herald-Press,* a paper owned by his family.

In 1972, Quayle married Marilyn Tucker of Indianapolis. They had three children: Tucker Danforth, the oldest; Benjamin Eugene; and Mary Corinne, the youngest.

Political career. Quayle was elected to the United States House of Representatives in 1976 and in 1978 from a district in northeastern Indiana. In the House, he had a consistently conservative voting record. In 1980, Quayle won election to the U.S. Senate, defeating Democratic Senator Birch E. Bayh, Jr. Quayle was reelected in 1986. He served on the Senate's Budget, Armed Services, and Labor and Human Resources committees.

In 1988, the Republican National Convention nominated Quayle for vice president at Bush's request. The selection sparked controversy. Much of it centered on charges that Quayle had used family influence to get into the Indiana National Guard in 1969, thereby avoiding the draft and possible combat in the Vietnam War (1957-1975). Quayle's experience and accomplishments were also questioned. In the 1988 election, Bush and Quayle defeated their Democratic opponents, Governor Michael S. Dukakis of Massachusetts and Senator Lloyd Bentsen of Texas. Questions concerning Quayle's capabilities persisted throughout his term, but Bush defended his vice president. Quayle also received support from the conservative branch of the Republican Party.

As vice president, Quayle traveled throughout the United States and to other countries to promote the Bush administration's policies. He also headed the National Space Council and the Council on Competitiveness. As head of the competitiveness council, Quayle sought to end government regulations he considered harmful to U.S. economic efficiency. But critics claimed many of the regulations were needed for environmental protection and other purposes.

In 1992, Bush and Quayle again became Republican nominees. But they were defeated by the Democratic candidates, Governor Bill Clinton of Arkansas and Senator Al Gore of Tennessee. Quayle briefly sought the Republican presidential nomination for the 2000 election but withdrew after attracting little support. Quayle's son Ben represented an Arizona district in the U.S. House of Representatives from 2011 to 2013. Lee Thornton

© Nicolas McComber, iStockphoto

Montreal, Quebec's largest city, viewed from the Lachine Canal in winter

Quebec

Quebec, *kwih BEHK,* or in French, *kay BEHK,* is the largest province of Canada in area. In addition, it has more people than any other province except Ontario. Most of Quebec's people have French ancestors, and many of the people in this group speak only French. Montreal is the largest city in Quebec. The capital of the province is also named Quebec, but it is often called Quebec City.

The strong French influence makes Quebec quite different from the rest of Canada. For example, about 75 percent of the people are Roman Catholics. Many Quebec schools teach the Roman Catholic religion, and most schools teach students in French. The province's older buildings are French in architecture. Beautiful French-style homes can still be seen in the countryside. Almost every village has a Catholic church, and crosses and shrines stand by the roadsides. Nevertheless, Quebec also has churches and temples of many other denominations and religions. Although the majority of people speak French, the government provides its services in both French and English.

The early French settlers in the Quebec region were interested chiefly in the fur trade. Rapid economic growth during the late 1800's and 1900's placed Quebec among the great industrial regions of North America. Factories and mills use the power provided by hydroelectric plants on Quebec's many rivers. Quebec is a leading producer of hydroelectric power in North America.

Quebec produces about 25 percent of all of the goods manufactured in Canada. The Montreal area ranks second to the Toronto area among the leading manufacturing centers of Canada. Important products manufactured in Quebec include processed foods, aircraft, and chemicals. The province is one of the leading producers of paper in Canada. Quebec ranks first among the Canadian provinces in the production of aluminum.

The province's vast natural resources provide its industries with huge supplies of valuable raw materials. The far northern wilderness of Quebec has vast deposits of iron ore, one of the province's leading mineral prod-

© All Canada Photos/Alamy Images

Norman-style house on the Île d'Orléans

Interesting facts about Quebec

WORLD BOOK illustrations by Kevin Chadwick

The Cathedral-Basilica of Mary, Queen of the World, in downtown Montreal, is a reproduction of St. Peter's Basilica in Vatican City. The cathedral covers about one-fourth the area of St. Peter's. It was dedicated in 1870.

Cathedral

The Haskell Opera House in Rock Island, Quebec, has performances on a stage in Canada while the audience watches from seats in the United States. North of the U.S.-Canadian boundary line is Rock Island. To the south is Derby Line, Vermont. Many other buildings in the area were built before the international boundary was firmly established. In some houses, meals are prepared in Canada and served in the United States.

Joseph-Armand Bombardier of Valcourt helped to launch the sport of snowmobiling when his company began mass-producing sled-sized snowmobiles in 1959. Bombardier began building his first snowmobile in 1922, when he was only 15 years old.

Snowmobiles

ucts. Quebec also is a leading producer of gold, silver, titanium, and zinc. Forests cover about half of the province. They provide balsam firs, spruces, and other trees for Quebec's great paper industry.

The Saint Lawrence River Valley and the rolling Eastern Townships, south of the river, have rich soils. Quebec ranks among North America's leading producers of dairy cattle, hogs, and milk, and leads in the production of maple syrup.

Quebec's great St. Lawrence River is one of the most important waterways in North America. The word *Quebec* came from the Algonquian word *kebec,* meaning *the place where the river narrows.* Originally, it described only the place where the St. Lawrence River narrowed and where the French explorer Samuel de Champlain founded Quebec City in 1608. It was the first permanent European settlement in Canada. The British used the name *Quebec* to describe a larger area after they defeated the French and confirmed possession of the French North American colonies in the 1763 Treaty of Paris.

© Jiawangkun, Shutterstock

The Port of Quebec on the St. Lawrence River, Quebec City

Quebec in brief

Symbols of Quebec

The provincial flag was adopted in 1948. The provincial coat of arms, adopted in 1939, combines the emblems of France, the United Kingdom, and Canada. The three *fleurs-de-lis* represent the coat of arms of the French kings. The British lion stands across the center. The three maple leaves symbolize Canada.

Provincial flag

Provincial coat of arms

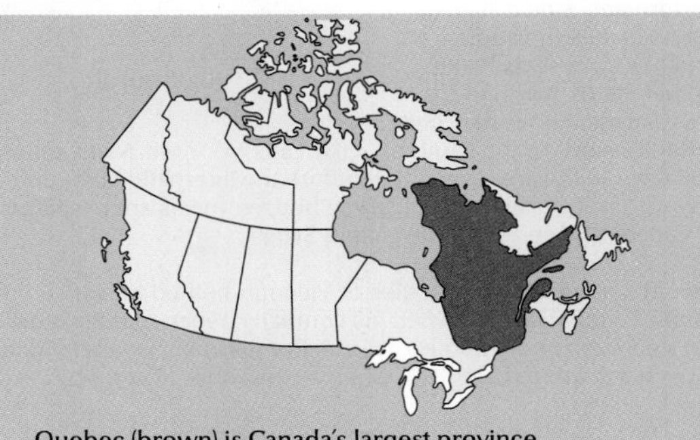

Quebec (brown) is Canada's largest province.

The Parliament Building is in Quebec City, the capital from 1608 to 1841 and since 1867. From 1841 to 1867, Quebec was part of the Province of Canada, which had several capitals.

General information

Entered the Dominion: July 1, 1867, as one of the original four provinces.
Provincial abbreviation: QC (postal).
Provincial motto: *Je Me Souviens.*

Land and climate

Area: 595,391 mi² (1,542,056 km²), including 68,312 mi² (176,928 km²) of inland water.
Elevation: *Highest*—Mont d'Iberville, 5,420 ft (1,652 m) above sea level. *Lowest*—sea level.
Record high temperature: 104 °F (40 °C) at Ville Marie on July 6, 1921.
Record low temperature: -66 °F (-54 °C) at Doucet on Feb. 5, 1923.
Average July temperature: 61 °F (16 °C).
Average January temperature: 0 °F (-18 °C).
Average yearly precipitation: 37 in (94 cm).

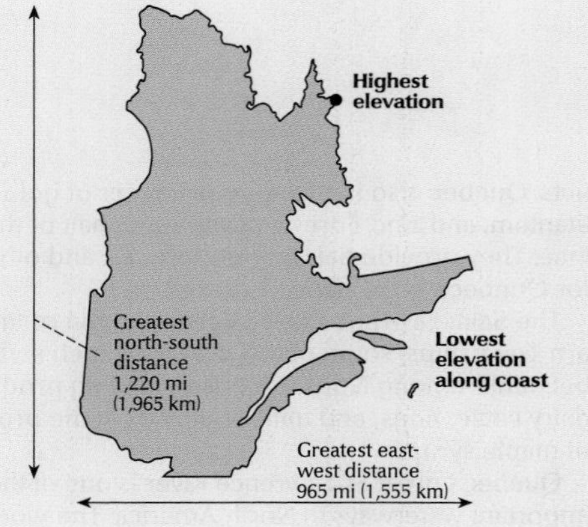

Important dates

1534 Jacques Cartier reached the Gulf of St. Lawrence and claimed the Quebec region for France.

1608 Samuel de Champlain established Quebec City, the first permanent European settlement in Canada.

1763 The Treaty of Paris gave Quebec to Britain.

1867 Quebec became one of the original four provinces on July 1.

Bird
Snowy owl

Tree
Yellow birch

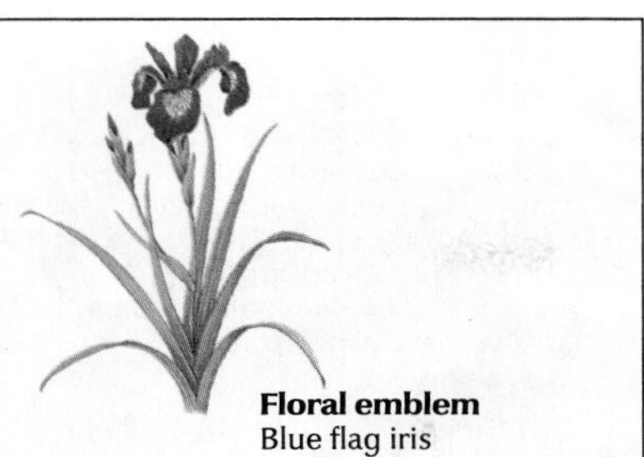

Floral emblem
Blue flag iris

People

Population: 8,164,361 (2016 census)
Rank among the provinces: 2nd
Density: 14 persons per mi² (5 per km²), Canada average 10 per mi² (4 per km²)
Distribution: 81 percent urban, 19 percent rural

Largest cities and towns*

Montreal	1,704,694
Quebec	531,902
Laval	422,993
Gatineau	276,245
Longueuil	239,700
Sherbrooke	161,323

*2016 census.
Source: Statistics Canada.

Population trend

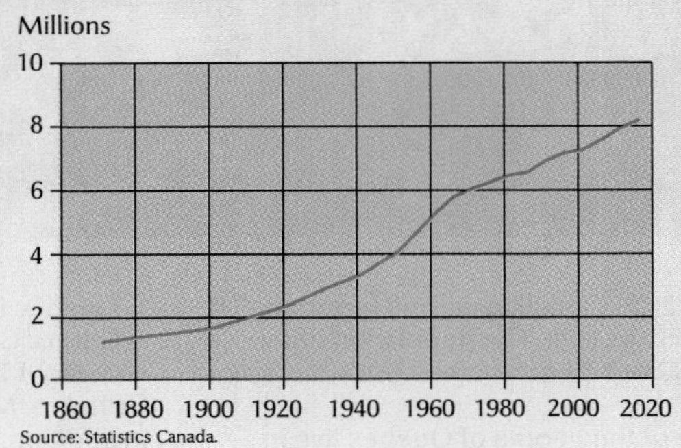

Year	Population
2016	8,164,361
2011	7,903,001
2006	7,546,131
2001	7,237,479
1996	7,138,795
1991	6,895,963
1986	6,540,276
1981	6,438,403
1976	6,234,445
1971	6,027,764
1966	5,780,845
1961	5,259,211
1951	4,055,681
1941	3,331,882
1931	2,874,662
1921	2,360,510
1911	2,005,776
1901	1,648,898
1891	1,488,535
1881	1,359,027
1871	1,191,516

Source: Statistics Canada.

Economy

Chief products

Agriculture: beef and dairy cattle, chickens, corn, hogs, maple products, soybeans, vegetables.
Manufacturing: chemicals, fabricated metal products, machinery, paper products, primary metals, processed foods and beverages, transportation equipment, wood products.
Mining: gold, iron ore, nickel, zinc.

Gross domestic product

Value of goods and services produced in 2018: $439,375,000,000.* *Services* include community, business, and personal services; finance; government; trade; and transportation and communication. *Industry* includes construction, manufacturing, mining, and utilities. *Agriculture* includes agriculture, fishing, and forestry.

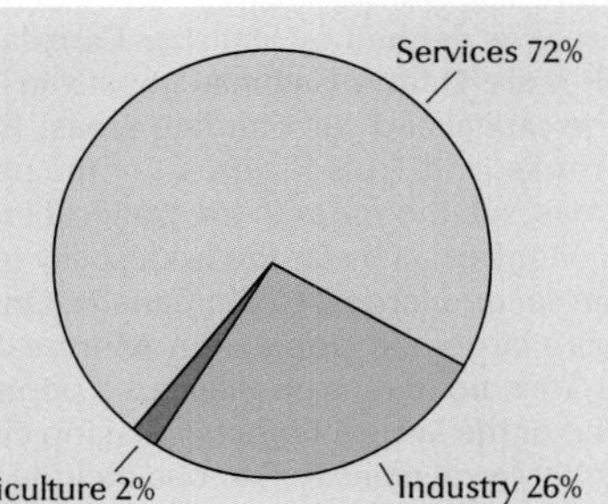

*Canadian dollars.
Source: Statistics Canada.

Government

Provincial government

Premier: term of up to 5 years
Members of the National Assembly: 125; terms of up to 5 years

Federal government

Members of the House of Commons: 78
Members of the Senate: 24

Sources of information

Quebec's website at https://www.quebec.ca provides a gateway to much information on the province's government, history, and economy.

In addition, the website at https://www.quebecoriginal.com provides information about tourism.

1912 Quebec nearly doubled in size by acquiring territory east of Hudson Bay.

1963 The provincial government bought all privately owned electric power companies.

1974 The Quebec legislature made French the province's official language.

1980 Quebec's first referendum on sovereignty took place.

1995 Quebec voters narrowly defeated another referendum on sovereignty.

People

The Montreal International Jazz Festival is one of Quebec's most popular annual events. Each summer, more than 2 million people attend the festival, which features thousands of performers from around the world.

© Hemis/Alamy Images

Population. The 2016 Canadian census reported that Quebec had 8,164,361 people. The population of the province had risen about 3 percent over the 2011 figure of 7,903,001.

About 80 percent of the people of Quebec live in urban areas. About half live in the metropolitan area of Montreal. Quebec has five other Census Metropolitan Areas as defined by Statistics Canada in the 2016 census. They are Ottawa-Gatineau (mostly in Ontario), Quebec (the capital and surrounding areas), Saguenay, Sherbrooke, and Trois-Rivières. For the population of these areas, see the *Index* to the political map of Quebec.

Montreal is by far the largest city in Quebec, and it is the second largest city in Canada. Only Toronto, Ontario, has a larger city population. Montreal also ranks second to Toronto in metropolitan area population. Montreal is one of the largest French-speaking cities in the world. Other large cities of Quebec include Gatineau, Laval, Longueuil, and Quebec City. For more information, see the articles on Quebec cities listed in the *Related articles* at the end of this article.

Most of Quebec's people are French Canadians. Nearly all are descendants of the settlers who came to the Quebec region during the 1600's and 1700's, when Quebec was a French colony. Quebec came under British rule in 1763, but not many British settlers arrived until the early 1800's. The British had a great deal of economic and political power. However, the French Canadians continued to follow their own ways of life.

People of British descent form a significant minority in Quebec. There are also about 87,000 First Nations people (American Indians) and about 10,000 Inuit (formerly called Eskimos). Another 30,000 people have some First Nations ancestry. French is the only tongue spoken by over half of the people of Quebec. It is the province's official language. About 40 percent of the population speaks French and English.

Ninety percent of Quebec's population was born in Canada. In the early 2000's, significant sources of immigrants have included Algeria, China, Colombia, France, Haiti, and Morocco.

Quebec is home to members of all the world's major religions. Christians form a large religious majority, and about 75 percent of Quebec's people are Roman Catholics. Many Jews and Muslims also live in Quebec. In addition, there are Buddhists, Hindus, and Sikhs. Over 10 percent of Quebecers claim no religious affiliation.

Schools. During the 1600's, Roman Catholic missionaries from France established the first schools in the

Population density

Most of Quebec's people live in the southern part of the province. Montreal, Quebec's largest city, is there. The vast northern areas have few settlements.

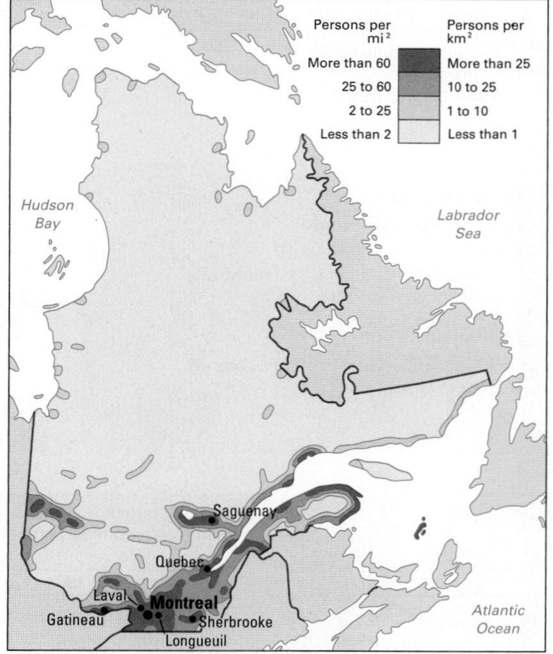

WORLD BOOK map; based on the *National Atlas of Canada*

Quebec region. The missionaries taught First Nations and white children. Priests and nuns provided the only formal schooling in Quebec for many years.

British colonists began arriving during the late 1700's. They were mainly Protestants and wanted their own schools. In 1801, the colonial authorities set up a system of free, nondenominational schools. For the most part, the French Catholics opposed these schools. In 1829, the government began to subsidize Catholic parish and township schools. In 1846, the colony established a system of denominational schools run by Catholic and Protestant school boards.

Until 1964, a superintendent of education headed Quebec's educational system. That year, the provincial government created the cabinet post of minister of education to oversee schools. It also created the independent Superior Council of Education, which advises the government in all educational matters.

In 1998, Quebec's school system was reorganized on the basis of language. French, English, and First Nations school boards replaced Catholic and Protestant ones. However, students may still take classes on religion.

Parents may send their children to private schools, some of which receive government funds. Private schools must follow the same basic regulations that public schools do. Children must attend school from the ages of 6 to 16.

Libraries. Canada's first library was established in Quebec City in the 1630's. Université Laval (Laval University), McGill University, Université du Québec à Montréal (University of Quebec at Montreal), and Université de Montréal (University of Montreal) have outstanding libraries.

The Bibliothèque et Archives nationales du Québec (National Library and Archives of Quebec), in Montreal, is a major provincial library. The Library of the National Assembly is in Quebec City.

Museums. Quebec is home to hundreds of museums. The Montreal Museum of Fine Arts includes collections of Canadian paintings and decorative arts. The Château Ramezay Museum, built in 1705 for Governor Claude de Ramezay in Montreal, houses a fine historical museum. The Musée d'Art Contemporain de Montréal (Montreal Museum of Contemporary Art) exhibits works completed since 1939.

The McCord Museum of Canadian History contains art, photographs, textiles, and other items that document the history of Canada and Quebec. The Musée National des Beaux-Arts du Québec (Quebec National Fine Arts Museum), in Quebec City, features works by Quebec artists since the 1600's.

Exhibits at the Musée de la Civilisation (Museum of Civilization) in Quebec City concentrate on aspects of human civilization and culture. The Canadian Museum of History (Musée Canadien de l'Histoire) in Gatineau is one of Canada's national museums. The Canadian Centre for Architecture in Montreal has a collection of books, drawings, photographs, prints, and architectural archives.

Universities and colleges

This table lists the universities and colleges in Quebec that grant bachelor's or advanced degrees and are members of Universities Canada.

Name	Mailing address
Bishop's University	Sherbrooke
Concordia University	Montreal
HEC Montreal	Montreal
McGill University	Montreal
Montréal, Université de (University of Montreal)	Montreal
Polytechnique Montréal	Montreal
Québec, Université du (University of Quebec)	*
Sherbrooke, Université de (University of Sherbrooke)	Sherbrooke
Université Laval (Laval University)	Quebec

*For campuses, see **Quebec, University of.**

© Marc Robitaille, Université Laval

Laval University, in Quebec City, was established as the Seminary of Quebec in 1663 by Bishop François de Laval. In 1852, the Roman Catholic school was granted a royal charter as Laval University. The Pavillon Louis-Jacques-Casault, *shown here,* was named for a French Canadian priest who served as superior of the seminary and rector of the university.

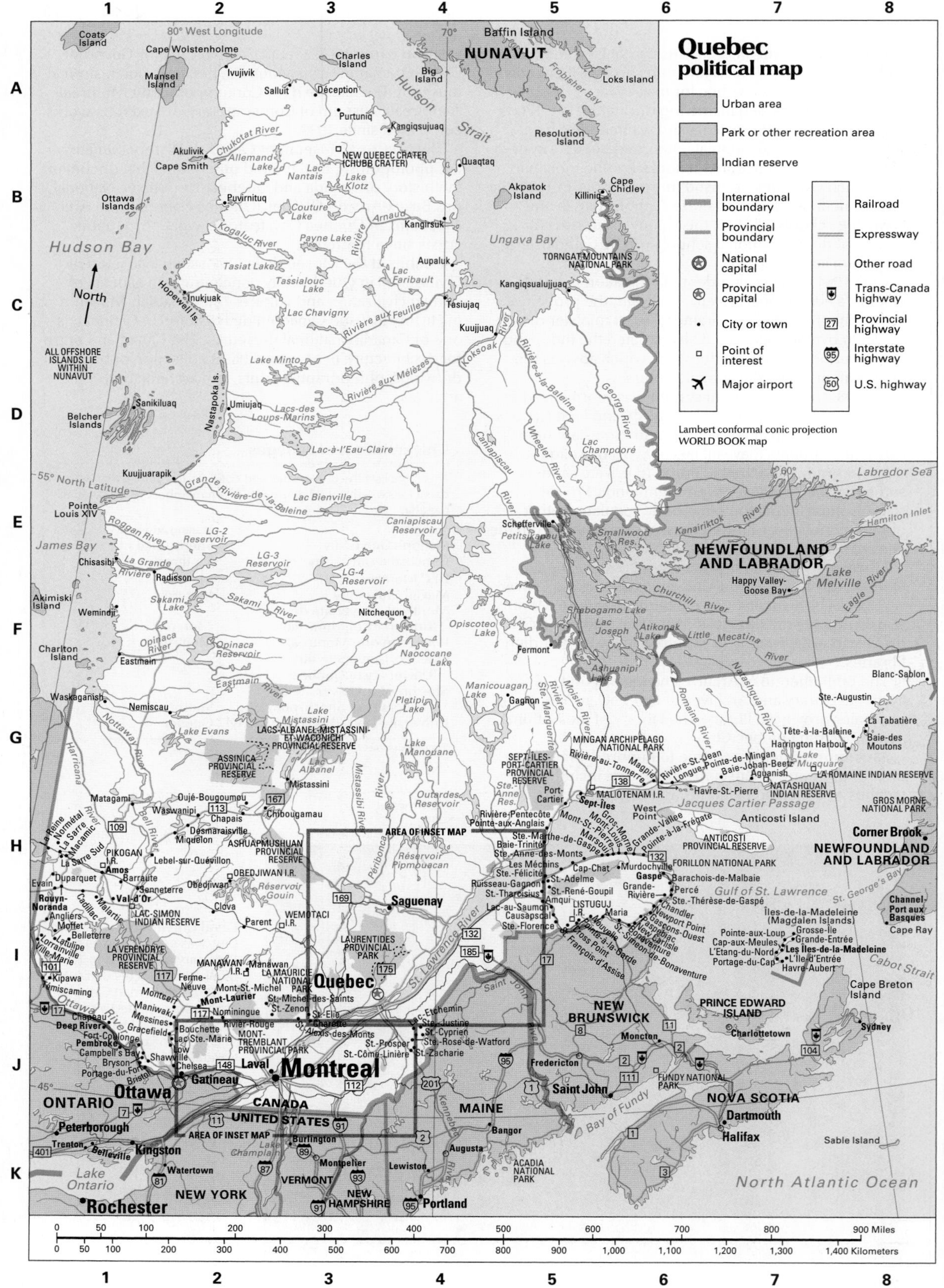

Quebec
political map
Urban area
Park or other recreation area
Indian reserve
International boundary
Provincial boundary
National capital
Provincial capital
City or town
Point of interest
Major airport
Railroad
Expressway
Other road
Trans-Canada highway
Provincial highway
Interstate highway
U.S. highway
Lambert conformal conic projection
WORLD BOOK map
1
2
3
4
5
6
7
8
A
B
C
D
E
F
G
H
I
J
K
80° West Longitude
70°
55° North Latitude
60°
45°
North
Coats Island
Cape Wolstenholme
Mansel Island
Ivujivik
Salluit
Charles Island
Déception
Big Island
Baffin Island
NUNAVUT
Frobisher Bay
Loks Island
Purtuniq
Kangiqsujuaq
Hudson Strait
Resolution Island
Akulivik
Cape Smith
Chukotat River
Allemand Lake
NEW QUEBEC CRATER (CHUBB CRATER)
Quaqtaq
Lac Nantais
Lake Klotz
Akpatok Island
Cape Chidley
Killiniq
Ottawa Islands
Puvirnituq
Couture Lake
Arnaud
Kangirsuk
Hudson Bay
Kogaluc River
Payne Lake
Rivière
Ungava Bay
Aupaluk
TORNGAT MOUNTAINS NATIONAL PARK
Tasiat Lake
Lac Faribault
Tassialouc Lake
Kangiqsualujjuaq
Hopewell Is.
Inukjuak
Lac Chavigny
Rivière aux Feuilles
Tasiujaq
Kuujjuaq
Koksoak River
Rivière-à-la-Baleine
ALL OFFSHORE ISLANDS LIE WITHIN NUNAVUT
Lake Minto
Rivière aux Mélèzes
Nastapoka Is.
George River
Sanikiluaq
Umiujaq
Belcher Islands
Lacs-des Loups-Marins
Wheeler River
Caniapiscau
Lac Champdoré
Lac-à-l'Eau-Claire
Kuujjuarapik
Grande Rivière-de-la-Baleine
Labrador Sea
Pointe Louis XIV
Lac Bienville
Caniapiscau Reservoir
Schefferville
Petitsikapau Lake
Smallwood Res.
Kanairiktok River
Hamilton Inlet
Roggan River
LG-2 Reservoir
James Bay
LG-3 Reservoir
Chisasibi
La Grande Rivière
Radisson
LG-4 Reservoir
NEWFOUNDLAND AND LABRADOR
Happy Valley-Goose Bay
Lake Melville
Eagle River
Akimiski Island
Sakami Lake
Sakami River
Churchill River
Wemindji
Nitchequon
Shabogamo Lake
Lac Joseph
Atikonak Lake
Opiscoteo Lake
Little Mecatina River
Charlton Island
Opinaca River
Opinaca Reservoir
Fermont
Eastmain
Naococane Lake
Ashuanipi Lake
Blanc-Sablon
Eastmain River
Manicouagan Lake
Gagnon
Waskaganish
Nemiscau
Lake Mistassini
Pletipi Lake
Ste. Marguerite
Moisie River
Romaine River
Natashquan River
Ste.-Augustin
Nottaway River
Lake Evans
LACS-ALBANEL-MISTASSINI-ET-WACONICHI PROVINCIAL RESERVE
La Tabatière
Harricana
ASSINICA PROVINCIAL RESERVE
Lac Albanel
Lake Manouane
MINGAN ARCHIPELAGO NATIONAL PARK
Tête-à-la-Baleine
Baie-des Moutons
Harrington Harbour
Mistassini River
SEPT-ÎLES-PORT-CARTIER PROVINCIAL RESERVE
Rivière-au-Tonnerre
Magpie
Rivière-St.-Jean
Longue-Pointe-de-Mingan
Baie-Johan-Beetz
Aguanish
Lake Musquaro
LA ROMAINE INDIAN RESERVE
Mistassini
Ste.-Anne Res.
Havre-St.-Pierre
NATASHQUAN INDIAN RESERVE
Matagami
Oujé-Bougoumou
Outardes Reservoir
Port-Cartier
MALIOTENAM I.R.
Sept-Îles
Jacques Cartier Passage
GROS MORNE NATIONAL PARK
Waswanipi
Chapais
Chibougamau
Rivière-Pentecôte
Pointe-aux-Anglais
West Point
Anticosti Island
La Reine
Normétal
La Sarre
Macamic
Désmaraisville
Miquelon
ASHUAPMUSHUAN PROVINCIAL RESERVE
AREA OF INSET MAP
Ste.-Marthe-de-Gaspé
Baie-Trinité
Ste.-Anne-des-Monts
Mont-St.-Pierre
Gros-Morne
Mont-Louis
Marsoui
Grande-Vallee
Pointe-à-la-Frégate
ANTICOSTI PROVINCIAL RESERVE
Corner Brook
NEWFOUNDLAND AND LABRADOR
La Sarre Sud
PIKOGAN I.R.
Amos
Lebel-sur-Quévillon
Péribonca
Réservoir Pipmuacan
Les Méchins
Cap-Chat
Murdochville
FORILLON NATIONAL PARK
Evain
Duparquet
Barraute
OBEDJIWAN I.R.
Obedjiwan
St.-Félicité
St.-Adelme
Gaspé
Barachois-de-Malbaie
Rouyn-Noranda
Senneterre
Réservoir Gouin
Ruisseau-Gagnon
St.-René-Goupil
St.-Tharcisius
Grande-Rivière
Percé
Gulf of St. Lawrence
St. George's Bay
Val-d'Or
Cadillac
Malartic
Clova
Saguenay
Amqui
LISTUGUJ I.R.
Ste.-Thérèse-de-Gaspé
Angliers
Moffet
Belleterre
LAC-SIMON INDIAN RESERVE
Parent
WEMOTACI I.R.
Lac-au-Saumon
Causapscal
Ste.-Florence
Maria
Chandler
Newport Point
Gascons-Ouest
Îles-de-la-Madeleine (Magdalen Islands)
Channel-Port aux Basques
Latulipe
Lorrainville
Ville-Marie
LAURENTIDES PROVINCIAL PARK
St. Lawrence River
Paspebiac
New Carlisle
Bonaventure
Pointe-aux-Loup
Grosse-Île
Grande-Entrée
Cape Ray
LA VERENDRYE PROVINCIAL RESERVE
MANAWAN I.R.
Manawan
LA MAURICIE NATIONAL PARK
St.-François-d'Assise
Cross Point
Pointe-à-la-Garde
St.-Siméon-de-Bonaventure
Cap-aux-Meules
L'Etang-du-Nord
Les Îles-de-la-Madeleine
L'Île-d'Entrée
Portage-du-Cap
Havre-Aubert
Cabot Strait
Kipawa
Témiscaming
Ferme-Neuve
Mont-St-Michel
Mont-Laurier
Quebec
Saint John
Cape Breton Island
Ottawa River
Montcerf
Maniwaki
Messines
Nominingue
St.-Michel-des-Saints
St.-Zenon
NEW BRUNSWICK
PRINCE EDWARD ISLAND
Sydney
Chapeau
Deep River
Fort-Coulonge
Pembroke
Gracefield
Bouchette
Lac Ste.-Marie
Rivier-Rouge
Mont-Tremblant Provincial Park
St.-Elie
Charette
Lac-Etchemin
Ste.-Justine
St.-Alexis-des-Monts
St.-Cyprien
Ste.-Rose-de-Watford
Moncton
Charlottetown
Campbell's Bay
Bryson
Portage-du-Fort
Bristol
Low
Shawville
Chelsea
Gatineau
Laval
Montreal
St.-Prosper
St.-Côme-Linière
St.-Zacharie
Fredericton
FUNDY NATIONAL PARK
Ottawa
ONTARIO
CANADA
UNITED STATES
MAINE
Saint John
Bay of Fundy
NOVA SCOTIA
Dartmouth
Halifax
Peterborough
AREA OF INSET MAP
Bangor
Kennebec River
Sable Island
Trenton
Belleville
Kingston
Burlington
Lake Champlain
Augusta
Montpelier
Lewiston
ACADIA NATIONAL PARK
Lake Ontario
Watertown
VERMONT
NEW HAMPSHIRE
North Atlantic Ocean
NEW YORK
Rochester
Portland
0
50
100
200
300
400
500
600
700
800
900 Miles
0
50
100
200
300
400
500
600
700
800
900
1,000
1,100
1,200
1,300
1,400 Kilometers

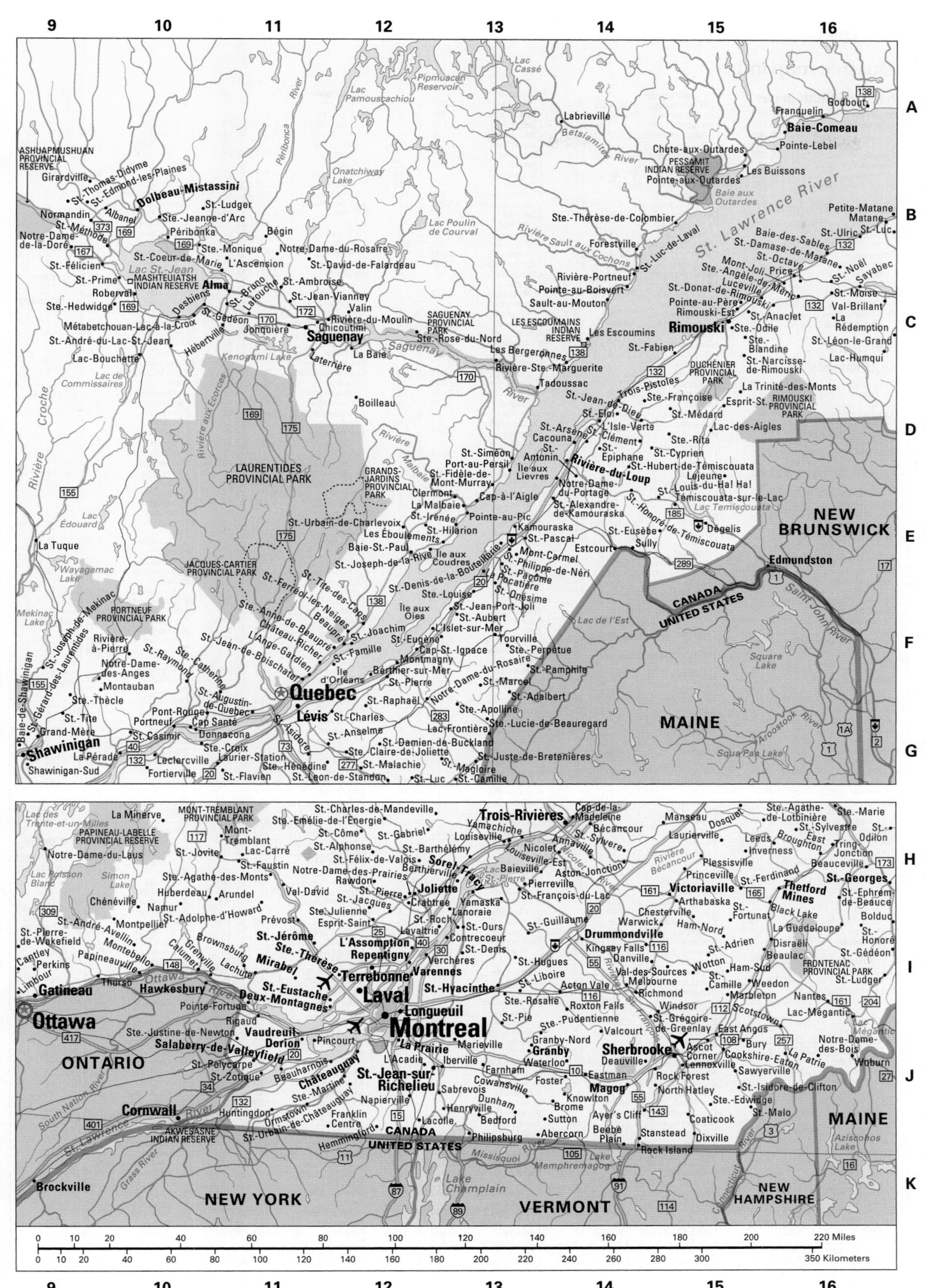

9
10
11
12
13
14
15
16
A
B
C
D
E
F
G
H
I
J
K
Lac Cassé
Pipmuacan Reservoir
Lac Pamouscachiou
Péribonca River
Labrieville
Betsiamites River
Franquelin
Godbout
Baie-Comeau
Pointe-Lebel
Chute-aux-Outardes
PESSAMIT INDIAN RESERVE
Pointe-aux-Outardes
Les Buissons
Baie aux Outardes
St. Lawrence River
ASHUAPMUSHUAN PROVINCIAL RESERVE
Girardville
St.-Thomas-Didyme
St.-Edmond-les-Plaines
Dolbeau-Mistassini
Onatchiway Lake
Normandin
St.-Méthode
Albanel
St.-Ludger
Ste.-Jeanne-d'Arc
Notre-Dame-de-la-Doré
Péribonka
Bégin
Lac Poulin de Courval
Ste.-Thérèse-de-Colombier
Petite-Matane
Matane
St.-Ulric
St.-Luc
Ste.-Monique
St.-Coeur-de-Marie
L'Ascension
Notre-Dame-du-Rosaire
St.-David-de-Falardeau
Rivière Sault aux Cochons
Forestville
St.-Luc-de-Laval
Baie-des-Sables
St.-Damase-de-Matane
St.-Octave
St.-Félicien
Lac St.-Jean
St.-Prime
MASHTEUIATSH INDIAN RESERVE
Roberval
Alma
St.-Bruno
Desbiens
Labrecque
St.-Ambroise
Rivière-Portneuf
Mont-Joli
Price
Ste.-Angèle-de-Mérici
St.-Noël
Sayabec
Luceville
Ste.-Hedwidge
St.-Gédéon
St.-Jean-Vianney
Valin
Pointe-au-Boisvert
St.-Donat-de-Rimouski
St.-Moïse
Sault-au-Mouton
Pointe-au-Père
Rimouski-Est
Val-Brillant
Métabetchouan-Lac-à-la-Croix
Hébertville
Jonquière
Rivière-du-Moulin
Chicoutimi
SAGUENAY PROVINCIAL PARK
LES ESCOUMAINS INDIAN RESERVE
St.-Anaclet
La Rédemption
St.-André-du-Lac-St.-Jean
Saguenay
Ste.-Rose-du-Nord
Les Escoumins
Rimouski
Ste.-Odile
Lac-Bouchette
Kenogami Lake
Laterrière
La Baie
Saguenay River
Les Bergeronnes
St.-Fabien
Ste.-Blandine
St.-Léon-le-Grand
Rivière-Ste.-Marguerite
St.-Narcisse-de-Rimouski
Lac-Humqui
Lac de Commissaires
Tadoussac
DUCHÉNIER PROVINCIAL PARK
Trois-Pistoles
La Trinité-des-Monts
Croche Rivière
Boilleau
St.-Jean-de-Dieu
Ste.-Françoise
Esprit-St.
RIMOUSKI PROVINCIAL PARK
St.-Éloi
St.-Médard
Rivière aux Écorces
L'Isle-Verte
Lac-des-Aigles
St.-Arsène
St.-Clément
Cacouna
Ste.-Rita
St.-Antonin
St.-Épiphane
St.-Cyprien
LAURENTIDES PROVINCIAL PARK
St.-Siméon
Port-au-Persil
GRANDS-JARDINS PROVINCIAL PARK
Rivière Malbaie
St.-Fidèle-de-Mont-Murray
Île aux Lievres
Rivière-du-Loup
St.-Hubert-de-Témiscouata
Lejeune
Notre-Dame-du-Portage
St.-Louis-du-Ha! Ha!
Clermont
Cap-à-l'Aigle
La Malbaie
St.-Alexandre-de-Kamouraska
Témiscouata-sur-le-Lac
Lac Témiscouata
St.-Irénée
Pointe-au-Pic
St.-Honoré-de-Témiscouata
NEW BRUNSWICK
Lac Édouard
St.-Urbain-de-Charlevoix
St.-Hilarion
Kamouraska
Dégelis
Les Éboulements
St.-Pascal
St.-Eusèbe
La Tuque
Baie-St.-Paul
Île aux Coudres
Mont-Carmel
Estcourt
Sully
Wayagamac Lake
JACQUES-CARTIER PROVINCIAL PARK
St.-Joseph-de-la-Rive
St.-Denis-de-la-Bouteillerie
St.-Philippe-de-Néri
St.-Pacôme
Edmundston
La Pocatière
St.-Tite-des-Caps
Ste.-Louise
St.-Onésime
CANADA
UNITED STATES
Mekinac Lake
St.-Joseph-de-Mekinac
PORTNEUF PROVINCIAL PARK
St.-Ferréol-les-Neiges
Île aux Oies
St.-Jean-Port-Joli
Lac de l'Est
Saint John River
Ste.-Anne-de-Beaupré
Beaupré
St.-Aubert
Rivière-à-Pierre
St.-Gérard-des-Laurentides
Château-Richer
St.-Joachim
L'Islet-sur-Mer
Tourville
St.-Jean-de-Boischatel
L'Ange-Gardien
St.-Eugène
Ste.-Perpétue
St.-Raymond
Ste.-Catherine
Ste.-Famille
Cap-St.-Ignace
Square Lake
Notre-Dame-des-Anges
Montmagny
Berthier-sur-Mer
Île d'Orléans
Notre-Dame-du-Rosaire
St.-Pamphile
Montauban
St.-Pierre
St.-Marcel
Baie-de-Shawinigan
Ste.-Thècle
St.-Augustin-de-Québec
Quebec
St.-Raphaël
Ste.-Adalbert
St.-Tite
Pont-Rouge
Lévis
St.-Charles
Ste.-Apolline
Grand-Mère
Portneuf
Cap Santé
St.-Isidore
Lac-Frontière
Ste.-Lucie-de-Beauregard
MAINE
Shawinigan
St.-Casimir
Donnacona
St.-Anselme
St.-Damien-de-Buckland
Aroostook River
La Pérade
Ste.-Croix
Laurier-Station
Ste.-Claire-de-Joliette
Squa Pan Lake
Leclercville
St.-Juste-de-Bretenières
Shawinigan-Sud
Fortierville
St.-Flavien
Ste.-Hénédine
St.-Malachie
St.-Léon-de-Standon
St.-Magloire
St.-Luc
St.-Camille
Lac des Trente-et-un-Milles
La Minerve
MONT-TREMBLANT PROVINCIAL PARK
St.-Charles-de-Mandeville
Trois-Rivières
Cap-de-la-Madeleine
Manseau
Dosquet
Ste.-Agathe-de-Lotbinière
Ste.-Marie
PAPINEAU-LABELLE PROVINCIAL RESERVE
Mont-Tremblant
Ste.-Émélie-de-l'Énergie
St.-Côme
St.-Gabriel
Yamachiche
Louiseville
Bécancour
Ste.-Sylvère
Laurierville
Leeds
St.-Sylvestre
East Broughton
St.-Odilon
Notre-Dame-du-Laus
St.-Jovite
Lac-Carré
St.-Alphonse
St.-Barthélémy
Nicolet
Annaville
Inverness
Tring-Jonction
St.-Faustin
St.-Félix-de-Valois
Sorel-Tracy
Louiseville-Est
Rivière Bécancour
Plessisville
Beauceville
Lac Poisson Blanc
Simon Lake
Ste.-Agathe-des-Monts
Notre-Dame-des-Prairies
Berthierville
Lac St.-Pierre
Baieville
Aston-Jonction
Princeville
St.-Ferdinand
St.-Georges
Rawdon
Pierreville
Nicolet River
Huberdeau
Arundel
Val-David
St.-Pierre
Joliette
St.-François-du-Lac
Victoriaville
Thetford Mines
St.-Ephrem-de-Beauce
Chénéville
Namur
St.-Jacques
Crabtree
Yamaska
Arthabaska
Black Lake
Bolduc
St.-Adolphe-d'Howard
Prévost
Ste.-Julienne
Lanoraie
Chesterville
St.-Fortunat
St.-André-Avellin
Montpellier
Esprit-Saint
St.-Roch
Ham-Nord
La Guadeloupe
St.-Honoré
St.-Pierre-de-Wakefield
Montebello
Brownsburg
St.-Jérôme
Lavaltrie
St.-Ours
St.-Guillaume
Drummondville
Warwick
St.-Adrien
Disraëli
Grenville
L'Assomption
Contrecoeur
Kingsey Falls
Ste.-Gédéon
Cantley
Perkins
Papineauville
Calumet
Ste.-Thérèse
Repentigny
Verchères
St.-Denis
Danville
Beaulac
Limbour
Lachute
Mirabel
Terrebonne
Varennes
St.-Hugues
Val-des-Sources
Wotton
Ham-Sud
FRONTENAC PROVINCIAL PARK
Thurso
Ottawa River
St.-Liboire
Melbourne
St.-Camille
Weedon
St.-Ludger
Gatineau
Hawkesbury
St.-Eustache
Laval
St.-Hyacinthe
Acton Vale
Richmond
Marbleton
Nantes
Deux-Montagnes
Ste.-Rosalie
Roxton Falls
Windsor
Scotstown
Ottawa
Pointe-Fortune
Longueuil
Lac-Mégantic
Rigaud
St.-Pie
Ste.-Pudentienne
St.-Grégoire-de-Greenlay
East Angus
Ste.-Justine-de-Newton
Vaudreuil-Dorion
Montreal
Valcourt
Notre-Dame-des-Bois
Pincourt
La Prairie
Marieville
Granby-Nord
Sherbrooke
Bury
Salaberry-de-Valleyfield
Granby
Ascot Corner
Cookshire-Eaton
La Patrie
ONTARIO
St.-Polycarpe
Beauharnois
L'Acadie
Iberville
Farnham
Waterloo
Deauville
Lennoxville
Woburn
St.-Zotique
Châteauguay
St.-Jean-sur-Richelieu
Foster
Eastman
Rock Forest
Sawyerville
Ste.-Martine
Cowansville
Magog
North Hatley
St.-Isidore-de-Clifton
Sabrevois
Knowlton
Ste.-Edwidge
Napierville
Dunham
Brome
Cornwall
Huntingdon
Ormstown
Franklin Centre
Henryville
Bedford
Sutton
Ayer's Cliff
Coaticook
St.-Malo
MAINE
St.-Urbain-de-Châteauguay
Lacolle
Stanstead
AKWESASNE INDIAN RESERVE
Hemmingford
CANADA
Philipsburg
Abercorn
Beebe Plain
Dixville
Aziscohos Lake
UNITED STATES
Rock Island
Missisquoi River
Lake Memphremagog
Connecticut River
South Nation River
Grass River
Brockville
Lake Champlain
NEW YORK
VERMONT
NEW HAMPSHIRE
0
10
20
40
60
80
100
120
140
160
180
200
220 Miles
220
240
260
280
300
350 Kilometers

Quebec map index

Metropolitan areas

Montreal ... 4,098,927
Ottawa-Gatineau ... 1,323,783 (991,726 in Ontario; 332,057 in Quebec)
Quebec ... 800,296
Saguenay ... 160,980
Sherbrooke ... 212,105
Trois-Rivières ... 156,042

Census divisions*†

Francheville ... 153,030 ..I 3
Le Saguenay-et-son-Fjord ... 167,549 ..B 11
Minganie-Le Golfe-du-Saint-Laurent ... 11,323 ..H 6
Nord-du-Québec ... 44,561 ..E 3
Sept-Rivières-Caniapiscau ... 39,322 ..H 6

Territory equivalents*†

Gatineau ... 276,245 ..I 9
La Tuque ... 15,059 ..E 9
Laval ... 422,993 ..I 12
Les Îles-de-la-Madeleine ... 12,475 ..I 7
Lévis ... 143,414 ..G 11
Longueuil ... 415,347 ..I 12
Mirabel ... 50,513 ..I 11
Montreal ... 1,942,044 ..J 12
Quebec ... 569,717 ..G 11
Rouyn-Noranda ... 42,334 ..H 1
Shawinigan ... 49,349 ..G 9
Sherbrooke ... 161,323 ..J 15

Regional county municipalities*†

Abitibi ... 24,639 ..H 1
Abitibi-Ouest ... 20,538 ..H 1
Acton ... 15,594 ..I 13
Antoine-Labelle ... 35,243 ..I 2
Argenteuil ... 32,389 ..I 10
Arthabaska ... 72,014 ..H 15
Avignon ... 14,461 ..I 15
Beauce-Sartigan ... 52,406 ..I 16
Beauharnois-Salaberry ... 64,320 ..J 11
Bécancour ... 20,404 ..H 14
Bellechasse ... 37,233 ..G 12
Bonaventure ... 17,660 ..I 6
Brome-Missisquoi ... 58,314 ..J 13
Charlevoix ... 12,997 ..E 12
Charlevoix-Est ... 15,509 ..D 13
Coaticook ... 18,497 ..J 15
D'Autray ... 42,189 ..H 12
Deux-Montagnes ... 98,203 ..I 11
Drummond ... 103,397 ..I 14
Joliette ... 66,550 ..H 12
Kamouraska ... 21,073 ..E 13
La Côte-de-Beaupré ... 28,199 ..E 11
La Côte-de-Gaspé ... 17,117 ..H 6
Lac-Saint-Jean-Est ... 52,741 ..C 10
La Haute-Côte-Nord ... 10,846 ..B 13
La Haute-Gaspésie ... 11,316 ..H 6
La Haute-Yamaska ... 88,306 ..J 13
La Jacques-Cartier ... 43,485 ..F 11
La Matapédia ... 17,925 ..C 16
La Mitis ... 18,210 ..C 16
La Nouvelle-Beauce ... 36,785 ..J 4
La Rivière-du-Nord ... 128,170 ..I 11
L'Assomption ... 124,759 ..I 12
La Vallée-de-la-Gatineau ... 20,182 ..I 2
La Vallée-de-l'Or ... 43,226 ..H 2
La Vallée-du-Richelieu ... 124,420 ..I 13
Le Domaine-du-Roy ... 31,285 ..H 3
Le Granit ... 21,462 ..I 16
Le Haut-Richelieu ... 117,443 ..J 13
Le Haut-Saint-François ... 22,335 ..J 15
Le Haut-Saint-Laurent ... 22,454 ..J 11
L'Érable ... 23,425 ..H 15
Le Rocher-Percé ... 17,282 ..I 6
Les Appalaches ... 42,346 ..H 16
Les Basques ... 8,694 ..D 14
Les Collines-de-l'Outaouais ... 49,094 ..I 9
Les Etchemins ... 16,536 ..J 4
Les Jardins-de-Napierville ... 27,870 ..J 12
Les Laurentides ... 45,902 ..H 11
Les Maskoutains ... 87,099 ..I 13
Les Moulins ... 158,267 ..I 12
Les Pays-d'en-Haut ... 41,877 ..H 11
Les Sources ... 14,286 ..I 15
Le Val-Saint-François ... 30,686 ..I 14
L'Île-d'Orléans ... 7,082 ..F 12
L'Islet ... 17,798 ..F 13
Lotbinière ... 31,741 ..G 11
Manicouagan ... 31,027 ..G 5
Marguerite-D'Youville ... 77,550 ..I 12
Maria-Chapdelaine ... 24,793 ..H 3
Maskinongé ... 36,316 ..H 13
Matane ... 21,301 ..B 16
Matawinie ... 50,435 ..I 3
Mékinac ... 12,358 ..I 3
Memphrémagog ... 50,415 ..J 14
Montcalm ... 52,596 ..I 12
Montmagny ... 22,698 ..F 12
Nicolet-Yamaska ... 23,159 ..H 13
Papineau ... 22,832 ..I 10
Pierre-De Saurel ... 51,025 ..H 13
Pontiac ... 14,251 ..I 1
Portneuf ... 53,008 ..F 10
Rimouski-Neigette ... 56,650 ..C 15
Rivière-du-Loup ... 33,958 ..D 14
Robert-Cliche ... 19,125 ..H 16
Roussillon ... 171,443 ..J 12
Rouville ... 36,536 ..J 13
Témiscamingue ... 15,980 ..I 1
Témiscouata ... 19,574 ..E 15
Thérèse-de-Blainville ... 157,103 ..I 12
Vaudreuil-Soulanges ... 149,349 ..J 11

Cities, towns, and other populated places

Abercorn ... 334 ..J 13
Acton Vale ... 7,656 ..I 14
Akulivik ... 633 ..B 2
Alma ... 30,776 ..C 11
Amos ... 12,823 ..H 1
Amqui ... 6,178 ..H 5
Angliers ... 303 ..I 1
Annaville ... H 14
Armagh* ... 1,488 ..G 12
Arthabaska ... H 15
Aston-Jonction ... 424 ..H 14
Ayer's Cliff ... 1,047 ..J 14
Baie-Comeau ... 21,536 ..A 16
Baie-de-Shawinigan ... G 9
Baie-des-Sables ... 628 ..B 16
Baie-d'Urfé* ... 3,823 ..J 12
Baie-St.-Paul ... 7,146 ..E 12
Baie-Trinité ... 407 ..H 5
Barraute ... 1,968 ..H 1
Beaconsfield* ... 19,324 ..J 12
Béarn* ... 690 ..I 1
Beauceville ... 6,281 ..H 16
Beauharnois ... 12,884 ..J 12
Beaulac [-Garthby] ... 905 ..I 16
Beaupré ... 3,752 ..F 12
Bécancour ... 13,031 ..H 14
Bedford ... 2,560 ..J 13
Beebe Plain ... K 14
Belleterre ... 313 ..I 1
Beloeil* ... 22,458 ..I 12
Berthier-sur-Mer ... 1,555 ..F 12
Berthierville ... 4,189 ..H 13
Blainville* ... 56,863 ..I 12
Blanc-Sablon ... 1,112 ..F 8
Bois-des-Fillon* ... 9,636 ..I 12
Boisbriand* ... 26,884 ..J 3
Bonaventure ... 2,706 ..I 6
Boucherville* ... 41,671 ..I 12
Brome ... 296 ..J 14
Bromont* ... 9,041 ..J 13
Brossard* ... 85,721 ..I 12
Brownsburg-Chatham ... 7,122 ..I 11
Bryson ... 697 ..J 1
Campbell's Bay ... 744 ..J 1
Candiac* ... 21,047 ..J 13
Cap-à-l'Aigle ... E 13
Cap-Chat ... 2,476 ..H 5
Cap Santé ... 3,400 ..G 10
Carignan* ... 9,462 ..J 12
Carleton-sur-Mer* ... 4,073 ..I 5
Causapscal ... 2,304 ..I 5
Chambly* ... 29,120 ..J 12
Chambord* ... 1,765 ..H 4
Champlain* ... 1,735 ..G 9
Chandler ... 7,546 ..I 6
Chapais ... 1,499 ..H 2
Chapeau ... J 1
Charette ... 953 ..J 3
Charlemagne* ... 5,913 ..I 12
Châteauguay ... 47,906 ..J 12
Château-Richer ... 4,126 ..F 11
Chelsea ... 6,909 ..I 3
Chénéville ... 764 ..H 10
Chertsey* ... 4,696 ..I 3
Chibougamau ... 7,504 ..H 3
Chisasibi Indian Reserve* ... 4,872 ..E 1
Chute-aux-Outardes ... 1,563 ..A 15
Clermont ... 3,085 ..E 13
Coaticook ... 8,698 ..J 15
Compton* ... 3,131 ..J 15
Contrecoeur ... 7,887 ..I 13
Cookshire [-Eaton] ... 5,393 ..J 15
Côte-St.-Luc* ... 32,448 ..I 12
Cowansville ... 13,656 ..J 13
Crabtree ... 3,958 ..H 12
Danville ... 3,826 ..I 14
Daveluyville* ... 965 ..H 15
Dégelis ... 2,863 ..E 15
Delson* ... 7,457 ..J 12
Desbiens ... 1,028 ..C 10
Deschaillons-sur-St.-Laurent* ... 909 ..G 10
Deux-Montagnes ... 17,496 ..I 12
Disraëli ... 2,336 ..I 16
Dixville ... 696 ..K 15
Dolbeau-Mistassini ... 14,250 ..B 10
Dollard-des-Ormeaux* ... 48,899 ..I 12
Donnacona ... 7,200 ..G 10
Dorval* ... 18,980 ..I 12
Drummondville ... 75,423 ..I 14
Dunham ... 3,432 ..J 13
Duparquet ... 666 ..H 1
East Angus ... 3,659 ..J 15
East Broughton ... 2,199 ..H 16
East Farnham* ... 554 ..J 13
Eastmain ... 866 ..F 1
Eastman ... 1,843 ..J 14
Esprit-Saint ... 341 ..I 12
Estérel* ... 196 ..I 11
Farnham ... 8,909 ..J 13
Fassett* ... 431 ..I 10
Ferme-Neuve ... 2,706 ..I 2
Fermont ... 2,474 ..F 5
Forestville ... 3,081 ..B 14
Fort-Coulonge ... 1,433 ..J 1
Fortierville ... 669 ..G 10
Fossambault-Sur-le-Lac* ... 1,960 ..F 11
Franquelin ... 313 ..A 16
Gaspé ... 14,568 ..H 6
Gatineau ... 276,245 ..I 9
Godbout ... 265 ..A 16
Gracefield ... 2,462 ..J 2
Granby ... 66,222 ..J 13
Grande-Rivière ... 3,408 ..H 6
Grande-Vallée ... 1,057 ..H 6
Grenville ... 1,711 ..H 6
Gros-Mécantina* ... 428 ..G 8
Ham-Nord ... 869 ..I 15
Hampstead* ... 6,973 ..I 12
Hébertville-Station* ... 1,311 ..C 11
Hemmingford ... 755 ..J 12
Henryville ... 1,406 ..J 13
Howick* ... 778 ..J 12
Hudson* ... 5,185 ..I 11
Huntingdon ... 2,444 ..J 11
Inukjuak ... 1,757 ..B 4
Inverness ... 899 ..H 15
Ivujivik ... 414 ..A 2
Joliette ... 20,484 ..H 12
Joutel* ... G 1
Kamouraska ... 616 ..E 13
Kangiqsualujjuaq ... 942 ..C 5
Keyano* ... E 2
Kingsey Falls ... 1,947 ..I 14
Kirkland* ... 20,151 ..I 12
Kuujjuaq ... 2,754 ..C 5
Kuujjuarapik ... 686 ..E 2
Lac-au-Saumon ... 1,450 ..I 5
Lac-Bouchette ... 1,196 ..C 10
Lac-Brome* ... 5,495 ..J 3
Lac-Carré ... H 11
Lac-des-Aigles ... 512 ..D 15
Lac-des-Écorces* ... 2,734 ..I 2
Lac-Etchemin ... 3,822 ..J 4
Lachute ... 12,862 ..I 11
Lac-Mégantic ... 5,654 ..I 16
Lacolle ... 2,596 ..J 12
Lac-St.-Joseph* ... 260 ..F 11
Lac-Simon Indian Reserve ... 1,380 ..I 2
La Guadeloupe ... 1,707 ..I 16
La Malbaie ... 8,271 ..E 13
L'Ancienne-Lorette* ... 16,543 ..G 11
L'Ange-Gardien ... 5,464 ..F 11
La Patrie ... 768 ..J 16
La Pêche* ... 7,863 ..I 9
La Pocatière ... 4,120 ..E 13
La Prairie ... 24,110 ..J 12
La Reine ... 339 ..H 1
La Romaine Indian Reserve ... 977 ..G 7
Larouche ... 1,486 ..C 11
La Sarre ... 7,282 ..H 1
L'Ascension* ... 791 ..I 2
L'Assomption ... 22,429 ..I 12
La Tabatière ... G 8
La Tuque ... 11,001 ..E 9
Laurier-Station ... 2,573 ..G 11
Laurierville ... 1,346 ..H 15
Laval ... 422,993 ..I 12
Lavaltrie ... 13,657 ..I 13
Laverlochère* ... 675 ..I 1
Lawrenceville* ... 635 ..J 14
Lebel-sur-Quévillon ... 2,187 ..H 2
Leclercville ... 473 ..G 10
L'Épiphanie* ... 5,493 ..I 12
Léry* ... 2,318 ..J 12
Les Bergeronnes ... 661 ..C 14
Les Éboulements ... 1,331 ..E 13
Les Îles-de-la-Madeleine ... 12,010 ..I 7
Lévis ... 143,414 ..G 11
L'Île-Perrot* ... 10,756 ..I 11
L'Isle-aux Allumettes* ... 1,334 ..J 1
L'Islet* ... 3,827 ..F 13
L'Isle-Verte ... 1,294 ..D 14
Listuguj Indian Reserve ... 1,241 ..I 5
Longueuil ... 239,700 ..I 12
Lorraine* ... 9,352 ..I 12
Lorrainville ... 1,272 ..I 1
Louiseville ... 7,152 ..H 13
Macamic ... 2,751 ..H 1
Magog ... 26,669 ..J 14
Malartic ... 3,377 ..H 1
Maliotenam Indian Reserve ... 1,542 ..G 5
Manawan Indian Reserve ... 2,060 ..I 2
Mandeville* ... 2,189 ..G 12
Maniwaki ... 3,853 ..I 2
Manseau ... 816 ..H 15
Marbleton ... I 15
Maria ... 2,615 ..I 5
Marieville ... 10,725 ..J 13
Marsoui ... 275 ..H 6
Mascouche* ... 46,692 ..I 12
Mashteuiatsh Indian Reserve ... 1,957 ..C 10
Maskinongé* ... 2,319 ..H 13
Massueville* ... 529 ..I 13
Matagami ... 1,453 ..H 1
Matane ... 14,311 ..B 16
McMasterville* ... 5,698 ..I 12
Melbourne ... 1,063 ..I 14
Mercier* ... 13,115 ..J 12
Métabetchouan [-Lac-à-la-Croix] ... 3,985 ..C 10
Métis-sur-Mer* ... 587 ..I 11
Mirabel ... 50,513 ..I 11
Mont-Carmel ... 1,127 ..E 13
Mont-Joli ... 6,281 ..C 16
Mont-Laurier ... 14,116 ..I 2
Mont-Royal* ... 20,276 ..I 12
Mont-St.-Gregoire* ... 3,077 ..J 13
Mont-St.-Hilaire* ... 18,585 ..I 12
Mont-St.-Michel ... 503 ..I 2
Mont-St.-Pierre ... 155 ..H 6
Mont-Tremblant ... 9,646 ..H 11
Montebello ... 983 ..I 10
Montmagny ... 11,255 ..F 12
Montreal ... 1,704,694 ..J 3
Montréal-Est* ... 3,850 ..I 12
Montréal-Ouest* ... 5,050 ..J 12
Murdochville ... 651 ..H 6
Napierville ... 3,899 ..J 12
Natashquan Indian Reserve ... 835 ..G 7
Neuville* ... 4,392 ..G 1
New Carlisle ... 1,388 ..I 6
New Richmond* ... 3,706 ..I 6
Newport* ... 733 ..H 6
Nicolet ... 8,169 ..H 14
Noranda, see Rouyn-Noranda
Normandin ... 3,033 ..B 9
Normétal ... 808 ..H 1
North Hatley ... 632 ..J 14
Notre-Dame-de-l'Île-Perrot* ... 10,654 ..J 11
Notre-Dame-de-Lourdes* ... 2,783 ..H 12
Notre-Dame-des-Pins* ... 1,594 ..H 16
Notre-Dame-des-Prairies ... 9,273 ..H 12
Notre-Dame-du-Bon-Conseil* ... 1,557 ..J 3
Notre-Dame-du-Laus ... 1,558 ..H 9
Notre-Dame-du-Mont-Carmel* ... 5,751 ..C 9
Notre-Dame-du-Rosaire ... 392 ..B 11
Nouvelle ... 1,659 ..I 5
Obedjiwan Indian Reserve ... 2,019 ..H 2
Ormstown ... 3,595 ..J 11
Otterburn Park* ... 8,421 ..I 12
Papineauville ... 2,101 ..I 10
Parc Mailloux* ... D 14
Parc Rémillard* ... J 13
Paspébiac ... 3,164 ..I 6
Percé ... 3,103 ..H 6
Pessamit Indian Reserve ... 2,256 ..B 15
Philipsburg ... K 13
Pierreville ... 2,143 ..H 13
Pincourt ... 14,558 ..J 11
Plaisance* ... 1,088 ..I 10
Plessisville ... 6,551 ..H 15
Pohénégamook* ... 2,582 ..E 14
Pointe-au-Pic ... E 13
Pointe-aux-Outardes ... 1,332 ..B 15
Pointe-Calumet* ... 6,428 ..I 12
Pointe-Claire* ... 31,380 ..I 12
Pointe-des-Cascades* ... 1,481 ..J 12
Pointe-Lebel ... 1,918 ..A 16
Pont-Rouge ... 9,240 ..G 10
Port-Cartier ... 6,799 ..H 5
Portage-du-Fort ... 234 ..J 1
Portneuf ... 3,187 ..G 10
Port-St.-François* ... H 13
Prévost ... 13,002 ..I 11
Price ... 1,759 ..C 16
Princeville ... 6,001 ..H 15
Puvirnituq ... 1,779 ..B 2
Quaqtaq ... 403 ..B 4
Quebec ... 531,902 ..I 3
Radisson ... F 1
Rawdon ... 11,057 ..H 12
Repentigny ... 84,285 ..I 12
Richelieu* ... 5,236 ..I 13
Richmond ... 3,232 ..I 14
Rigaud ... 7,777 ..I 11
Rimouski ... 48,664 ..C 15
Ripon* ... 1,542 ..I 10
Rivière-à-Pierre ... 584 ..F 10
Rivière-au-Tonnerre ... 279 ..G 6
Rivière-du-Loup ... 19,507 ..D 14
Rivière-Rouge ... 4,322 ..I 2
Roberval ... 10,046 ..C 10
Rock Island ... K 14
Rosemère* ... 13,958 ..I 12
Rougemont* ... 2,755 ..I 13
Rouyn-Noranda ... 42,334 ..H 1
Roxton Falls ... 1,305 ..I 14
Saguenay ... 145,949 ..C 11
St.-Adelme ... 692 ..H 5
St.-Adelphe* ... 922 ..I 3
St.-Adrien ... 522 ..I 15
St.-Alban* ... 1,198 ..G 10
St.-Alexis-de-Matapédia* ... 500 ..I 5
St.-Alexis-des-Monts ... 2,981 ..J 3
St.-Alphonse-de-Granby* ... 3,094 ..J 13
St.-Alphonse-Rodriguez* ... 3,162 ..I 3
St.-Amable* ... 12,167 ..I 12
St.-Ambroise ... 3,781 ..C 11
St.-Ambroise-de-Kildare* ... 3,856 ..H 12
St.-Anaclet-de-Lessard* ... 3,071 ..C 15
St.-Andre-Avellin ... 3,749 ..I 10
St.-Andre-d'Acton* ... I 14
St.-Andre-du-Lac-St.-Jean ... 467 ..C 10
St.-André-Est* ... I 11
St.-Anicet* ... 2,626 ..J 11
St.-Anselme ... 3,938 ..G 12
St.-Antonin ... 4,049 ..D 14
St.-Arsène ... 1,230 ..D 14
St.-Augustin ... 445 ..G 8
St.-Augustin-de-Desmaures* ... 18,820 ..F 10

© Pierdelune, Shutterstock

Mingan Archipelago National Park Reserve in northeastern Quebec consists of many islands, islets, and reefs shaped by erosion and the movement of glaciers. The park's features include *monoliths* (large stone blocks) like those shown here, stone arches and pillars, cliffs, and caverns.

St.-Barnabé*......1,196 ..H 13
St.-Barthélémy...1,934 ..H 13
St.-Basile*........2,631 ..G 10
St.-Basile-le-Grand*.......17,059 ..I 12
St.-Benjamin*......987 ..H 16
St.-Benoît-Labre*.........1,630 ..C 16
St.-Boniface......4,832 ..G 9
St.-Bruno-de-Montarville*..26,394 ..I 12
St.-Camille.........529 ..G 13
St.-Camille-de-Lellis*........752 ..J 4
St.-Césaire*.......5,877 ..I 13
St.-Charles-Borromée*...13,791 ..H 12
St.-Christophe-d'Arthabaska*.........3,021 ..H 15
St.-Chrysostome*..........2,645 ..J 12
St.-Colomban*...16,019 ..I 11
St.-Côme.........2,193 ..H 12
St.-Côme-Linière........3,239 ..J 4
St.-Constant*....27,359 ..J 12
St.-Cuthbert*.....1,862 ..H 13
St.-Cyrille-de-Wendover*....4,723 ..I 14
St.-Damase*......2,473 ..I 13
St.-Damien-de-Buckland......1,956 ..G 12
St.-Denis-de-Brompton*....4,054 ..J 12
St.-Denis [-De La Bouteillerie].....517 ..I 13
St.-Dominique*...2,553 ..I 13
St.-Donat..........876 ..C 15
St.-Donat-de-Montcalm*...........H 11
St.-Elie [-de-Caxton]........1,836 ..I 3
St.-Elzéar*........2,400 ..I 1
St.-Ephrem-de-Beauce....2,400 ..H 16
St.-Épiphane.......827 ..D 14
St.-Étienne-des-Grès*......4,541 ..G 9
St.-Eugène.......1,126 ..F 13
St.-Eustache....44,008 ..I 12
St.-Fabien........1,837 ..C 15
St.-Fabien-de-Panet*........954 ..F 12
St.-Félicien......10,238 ..C 10
St.-Félix-de-Valois.........6,305 ..H 12
St.-Ferdinand....2,076 ..G 11
St.-Fidèle-de-Mont-Murray..........E 13
St.-Flavien........1,618 ..G 11
St.-François-d'Assise.........644 ..I 5
St.-François-du-Lac.........1,965 ..H 13
St.-François-Xavier-de-Brompton*....2,273 ..I 14
St.-Gabriel........2,640 ..H 12
St.-Gabriel-de-Brandon.......2,635 ..H 12
St.-Gédéon.......2,085 ..I 16
St.-Georges.....32,513 ..H 16
St.-Georges-de-Cacouna.......1,803 ..D 14
St.-Gérard-Majella*.........242 ..I 12
St.-Germain-de-Grantham*.....4,917 ..I 14
St.-Gilles*........2,525 ..G 10
St.-Grégoire-de-Greenlay...........I 15
St.-Grégoire-le-Grand*..............J 13
St.-Guillaume....1,476 ..I 13
St.-Hilarion.......1,127 ..E 12
St.-Hippolyte*....9,113 ..I 11
St.-Hugues........1,327 ..I 13
St.-Hyacinthe....55,648 ..I 13
St.-Isidore........2,608 ..G 11
St.-Isidore-de-Clifton........695 ..J 15
St.-Jacques........3,971 ..H 12
St.-Janvier*..............I 11
St.-Jean-Baptiste*.......3,107 ..J 13
St.-Jean-Baptiste-de-Nicolet*...........H 14
St.-Jean-de-Boischatel............F 11
St.-Jean-de-Matha*........4,450 ..H 12
St.-Jean-sur-Richelieu.....95,114 ..J 12
St.-Jérôme.......74,346 ..I 11
St.-Joachim.......1,441 ..F 12
St.-Joseph-de-Beauce*....4,858 ..H 16
St.-Joseph-de-Sorel*......1,642 ..H 13
St.-Joseph-du-Lac*........6,687 ..I 11
St.-Jovite..............H 11
St.-Lambert*.....21,861 ..I 13
St.-Lambert-de-Lauzon*....6,647 ..G 11
St.-Lazare*.......19,889 ..J 11
St.-Léon-de-Standon.......1,127 ..G 12
St.-Léon-le-Grand..........953 ..C 16
St.-Léonard-d'Aston*.......2,331 ..H 14
St.-Léonard-de-Portneuf*...1,145 ..G 10
St.-Liboire........3,062 ..I 13
St.-Liguori*.......1,943 ..H 12
St.-Lin-Laurentides*.........20,786 ..I 12
St.-Louis-de-Gonzague*....1,481 ..J 4
St.-Louis-du-Ha! Ha!.........1,292 ..E 14
St.-Ludger.........1,071 ..B 10
St.-Marc-des-Carrières*.....2,911 ..G 10
St.-Marc-sur-Richelieu*.....2,172 ..I 13
St.-Martin*.......2,477 ..I 16
St.-Mathias-sur-Richelieu*.....4,531 ..J 13
St.-Maurice*......3,286 ..H 14
St.-Maxime-du-Mont-Louis*...1,134 ..H 6
St.-Michel*.......3,186 ..J 12
St.-Moïse..........580 ..C 16
St.-Narcisse*.....1,832 ..C 9
St.-Narcisse-de-Rimouski........961 ..C 15
St.-Noël............398 ..C 16
St.-Octave-de-Dosquet*.............G 15
St.-Odilon-de-Cranbourne*..1,374 ..H 16
St.-Omer*..........277 ..I 5
St.-Ours..........1,669 ..I 13
St.-Pamphile.....2,400 ..F 13
St.-Pascal.........3,468 ..E 13
St.-Patrice-de-Beaurivage*...1,036 ..J 4
St.-Patrice-de-la-Rivière-du-Loup*......D 14
St.-Paul-d'Abbotsford*...........2,890 ..J 13
St.-Philippe*......6,320 ..J 13
St.-Philippe-de-Néri..........832 ..E 13
St.-Pie.............5,607 ..J 13
St.-Pierre...........276 ..H 12
St.-Pierre-de-Sorel*................H 13
St.-Prime.........2,753 ..C 10
St.-Raphaël.......2,390 ..G 12
St.-Raymond....10,221 ..F 10
St.-Rémi*.........8,061 ..I 12
St.-René-de-Matane*.........965 ..B 16
St.-Roch-de-l'Achigan*.....5,147 ..I 12
St.-Sauveur*.....10,231 ..H 11
St.-Séverin*........846 ..J 3
St.-Siméon.......1,227 ..D 13
St.-Sulpice*.......3,439 ..I 12
St.-Sylvestre.....1,019 ..H 16
St.-Thomas*......3,249 ..H 12
St.-Tite...........3,673 ..G 9
St.-Ulric..........1,585 ..B 16
St.-Urbain........1,373 ..E 12
St.-Victor*........2,448 ..H 16
St.-Zénon........1,120 ..I 3
St.-Zotique.......7,934 ..J 11
Ste.-Adèle*......12,919 ..H 11
Ste.-Agathe-de-Lotbinière.....1,168 ..H 15
Ste.-Agathe-des-Monts....10,223 ..H 11
Ste.-Angèle-de-Monnoir*......1,823 ..J 13
Ste.-Anne-de-Beaupré.......2,880 ..F 12
Ste.-Anne-de-Bellevue*......4,958 ..I 12
Ste.-Anne-de-Sorel*......2,771 ..H 13
Ste.-Anne-des-Monts.....6,437 ..H 5
Ste.-Anne-des-Plaines*.......14,421 ..I 12
Ste.-Catherine*..17,047 ..J 12
Ste.-Catherine-de-la-Jacques-Cartier*........7,706 ..F 11
Ste.-Croix........2,516 ..G 10
Ste.-Élisabeth*....1,459 ..H 12
Ste.-Emélie-de-l'Énergie...1,567 ..H 12
Ste.-Famille........938 ..F 12
Ste.-Félicité......1,065 ..H 5
Ste.-Geneviève-de-Batiscan....1,006 ..G 9
Ste.-Geneviève-de-Berthier*...2,280 ..H 12
Ste.-Hedwidge.....846 ..C 10
Ste.-Hélène-de-Kamouraska*....918 ..E 13
Ste.-Hénédine....1,271 ..G 12
Ste.-Jeanne-d'Arc..........1,050 ..B 10
Ste.-Julie*........29,881 ..I 12
Ste.-Julienne.....9,953 ..H 12
Ste.-Justine.......1,820 ..J 4
Ste.-Louise.........671 ..F 13
Ste.-Madeleine*....2,233 ..I 13
Ste.-Madeleine-de-Rigaud*...........I 12
Ste.-Marguerite*...1,078 ..H 11
Ste.-Marie.......13,565 ..H 16
Ste.-Marie-de-Monnoir*.............J 13
Ste.-Marthe-sur-le-Lac*....18,074 ..J 11
Ste.-Martine......5,461 ..J 12
Ste.-Mélanie*.....2,989 ..H 12
Ste.-Monique......501 ..B 10
Ste.-Perpétue......959 ..F 13
Ste.-Petronille*...1,033 ..F 11
Ste.-Sophie*.....15,690 ..I 11
Ste.-Thérèse....25,989 ..I 12
Ste.-Victoire-d'Arthabaska*.........H 15
Salaberry-de-Valleyfield....40,745 ..J 11
Salluit............1,483 ..A 3
Sault-au-Mouton...... ..C 14
Schefferville.......155 ..E 5
Scotstown..........472 ..I 16
Scott*............2,352 ..I 4
Senneterre......2,868 ..H 1
Senneville*.........921 ..I 12
Sept-Îles.........25,400 ..G 5
Shawinigan.....49,349 ..G 9
Shawville........1,587 ..J 2
Shefford*.........6,947 ..J 13
Sherbrooke....161,323 ..J 15
Sorel-Tracy.....34,755 ..H 13
Stanstead........2,788 ..K 14
Stanstead Plain*..........J 14
Stoke*............2,955 ..I 14
Stoneham-et-Tewkesbury*..8,359 ..F 11
Stukely-Sud*.....1,058 ..J 14
Sutton............4,012 ..J 13
Tadoussac.........799 ..D 13
Taschereau*.......963 ..H 1
Tasiujaq............369 ..C 4
Témiscaming....2,431 ..I 1
Témiscouata-sur-le-Lac......4,910 ..E 15
Terrebonne....111,575 ..I 12
Thetford Mines........25,403 ..H 16
Thurso...........2,818 ..I 10
Tingwick*........1,410 ..I 15
Tourelle*..................H 5
Tring-Jonction...1,401 ..H 16
Trois-Pistoles....3,246 ..D 14
Trois-Rivières.....134,413 ..H 14
Umiujaq............442 ..D 2
Upton*...........2,092 ..I 13
Val-David........4,917 ..H 11
Val-des-Sources.......6,786 ..I 15
Val-d'Or.........32,491 ..H 1
Valcourt.........2,165 ..J 14
Varennes.......21,257 ..I 12
Vaudreuil-Dorion.......38,117 ..J 11
Vaudreuil-sur-le-Lac*.....1,341 ..I 11
Verchères.......5,835 ..J 12
Victoriaville.....46,130 ..H 15
Ville-Marie.......2,584 ..I 1
Warden*...........363 ..J 14
Warwick.........4,635 ..I 14
Waterloo.........4,410 ..J 14
Waterville*.......2,121 ..J 14
Weedon.........2,670 ..I 15
Wemindji................F 1
Wemotaci Indian Reserve.......1,213 ..I 3
Westmount*....20,312 ..I 12
Windsor.........5,419 ..I 14
Wotton...........1,430 ..I 15
Yamachiche.....2,830 ..H 13
Yamaska.........1,687 ..H 13

*Not on map. Key shows general location.
†Type of census division. Census divisions administer services to a group of municipalities.
Source: 2016 census. Places without populations are unincorporated.

Visitor's guide

Quebec attracts tens of millions of tourists annually, including many from the United States. Probably no other Canadian province is so rich in places of historical interest. Vacationers find the charm of Old France as they wander through the winding cobblestone streets of historic Quebec City. Every year, pilgrims visit the many religious shrines.

The rugged Gaspé Peninsula attracts artists, hikers, and mountain climbers. The Eastern Townships have lovely lakes, mountains, and rolling farmland. Many tourists take canoe trips down the rushing rivers of the Laurentian Mountains. Sports fans visit Montreal to see the Canadiens of the National Hockey League and the Alouettes of the Canadian Football League. In winter, thousands of skiers from all parts of Canada and the United States speed down Quebec's fine ski trails. Cross-country skiing, hockey, ice skating, snowmobiling, and snowshoeing are also popular.

On June 24, French Canadians honor their patron saint, Saint Jean-Baptiste (Saint John the Baptist). The province observes this legal holiday, called La Fête Nationale du Québec (Quebec National Day), with lively festivities and art and music events. Major festivals that attract many tourists annually include the Festival International de Jazz de Montreal (Montreal International Jazz Festival); the Festival Juste pour rire (Just for Laughs Festival), a comedy festival in Montreal; the Carnaval de Québec (Quebec Winter Carnival), in Quebec City; and the Festival d'été de Québec (Quebec Summer Festival), a music festival in Quebec City.

© Denis Roger, Shutterstock

Percé Rock off the coast of the Gaspé Peninsula

Places to visit

Following are brief descriptions of some of Quebec's many interesting places to visit:

Bonaventure Island, off the Gaspé Peninsula near Percé, is one of the largest water-bird refuges that people can visit. Hundreds of thousands of birds nest on the island during the summer months.

Île d'Orléans is an island in the middle of the St. Lawrence River near Quebec City. About 7,000 French Canadians live on the island the year around. Old Norman-style houses, churches, and chapels attract visitors to the island.

Mount Royal Park, in Montreal, is a lovely wooded area. The top of Mount Royal, which is 763 feet (233 meters) high, offers a magnificent view of Montreal and the St. Lawrence. For more information, see **Montreal** (Cultural life).

Percé Rock, about 200 feet (60 meters) off the Gaspé coast, rises 290 feet (88 meters) straight out of the water. The rock is about 1,560 feet (475 meters) long and 300 feet (90 meters) wide.

Quebec City, founded in 1608, is known as the cradle of French civilization in North America. The Citadel, a walled fortress, overlooks the city. Another major landmark of Quebec City is a district called Place Royale. The area includes a number of houses dating from the 1600's and 1700's and the Notre-Dame-des-Victoires Church, completed in 1688. The church stands on the former site of the first settlement of the French explorer Samuel de Champlain. See **Quebec** (City).

Sainte-Anne-de-Beaupré, in Montmorency County, is a Roman Catholic shrine where miracles are said to have occurred. See **Sainte-Anne-de-Beaupré.**

Parklands and historic sites. Quebec has three of Canada's national parks—Forillon, La Mauricie, and Mingan Archipelago—and one of Canada's national marine parks—Sanguenay-St. Lawrence Marine Park. The province also has a number of national historic sites, including Fort Chambly and Fort Lennox. For more information, visit the website of Parks Canada at https://www.pc.gc.ca/en. See **Canada** [table: National parks and park preserves in Canada]. In addition, Quebec has a number of provincial parks that it calls *parcs nationaux* (national parks). They include large areas of the Canadian Shield and Gaspé Peninsula. The website of the Société des établissements de plein air du Québec (Society of Outdoor Recreation Establishments of Quebec, also known as Sépaq), the Quebec government agency that manages parks, at http://www.sepaq.com provides information on the province's parks and wildlife areas.

Quebec Winter Carnival in Old Quebec City

© Hemis/Alamy Images

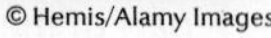

© Derek Caron, Masterfile

The Basilica of Sainte-Anne-de-Beaupré

© JHVEPhoto, Shutterstock

Migratory bird sanctuary on Bonaventure Island

Land and climate

Land regions. Quebec has four main land regions: (1) the Canadian Shield, (2) the St. Lawrence Lowland, (3) the Appalachian Region, and (4) the Hudson Bay Lowland.

The Canadian Shield is a vast, horseshoe-shaped region. It covers almost half of Canada and dips into the Northern United States. In Quebec, this rough, rocky plateau lies north of the St. Lawrence Lowland and Appalachian regions, and covers about nine-tenths of the province. It includes the North Shore, which extends along the St. Lawrence River from the Saguenay River to Labrador.

Through the ages, the Canadian Shield was scraped by glaciers. Much of its soil was worn away by wind and water. In many sections, the ancient rocks have no soil. Most of the region has remained a wilderness of forests, lakes, rivers, and streams. Treeless tundras with mosses and lichens cover the northern part of the Canadian Shield (see **Tundra**). The region has little land that can be farmed, but it has a variety of great mineral deposits.

Mont d'Iberville (called Mount Caubvick in Newfoundland), the highest point in Quebec, rises 5,420 feet (1,652 meters) in the northeastern part of the Canadian Shield. The Laurentian Mountains, or Laurentides, form the southeastern edge of the Canadian Shield in Quebec. Some of the province's highest ranges rise in the Laurentides Provincial Park and Mont Tremblant Provincial Park areas. See **Canadian Shield**.

The St. Lawrence Lowland consists chiefly of the St. Lawrence River Valley and the Montreal Plain. It includes Anticosti Island and islands in the river's mouth. The lowland is about 10 miles (16 kilometers) wide near Quebec City, and broadens to about 100 miles (160 kilometers) at Montreal. The plain lies less than 500 feet (150 meters) above sea level, but is broken by some rocky hills. Eight hills called the Monteregians rise in the southwestern part of the lowland. The best known is Mount Royal, which is 763 feet (233 meters) high. It overlooks Montreal.

The fertile soil of the St. Lawrence Lowland supports most of Quebec's farming. The many cities and towns in the St. Lawrence River Valley make it one of the most heavily populated regions of Canada.

The Appalachian Region is the northeastern extension of the Appalachian Mountains of the Eastern United States. It extends from Vermont along the province's southeastern boundary. This region consists of three main sections: (1) the Eastern Townships, between the St. Lawrence River Valley and the Canadian-United States border; (2) the South Shore, which extends along the mouth of the St. Lawrence from the Eastern Townships to the Gaspé Peninsula; and (3) the Gaspé Peninsula, north of New Brunswick. The land is broken by lakes, mountains, and streams.

In the gently rolling Eastern Townships, the Sutton Mountains form an extension of the Green Mountains of Vermont. The South Shore has two separate areas. The Piedmont Region along the St. Lawrence estuary is a rich farming area, and the inland plateau has thick forests. The Gaspé Peninsula is also heavily forested. Mountain ranges in the interior of the peninsula make transportation between the northern and southern coasts difficult. See **Gaspé Peninsula**.

The Hudson Bay Lowland extends into Quebec from Ontario. In Quebec, it covers a small strip of land south of James Bay.

Coastline. Water forms most of Quebec's boundaries. The province has a coastline of 8,558 miles (13,773 kilometers), including bays, inlets, and offshore islands. The main bodies of water that surround Quebec are James and Hudson bays on the west, Hudson Strait and Ungava Bay on the north, and the Gulf of St. Lawrence on the southeast and south.

North of the Gulf of St. Lawrence, the coastline is uneven. Many bays cut into the land, and rocks rise along the water's edge. To the south, along the Gaspé Peninsula, the coastline is more regular. The waters along the northern and western coasts usually remain frozen from the end of December to May.

Map index

Land regions of Quebec

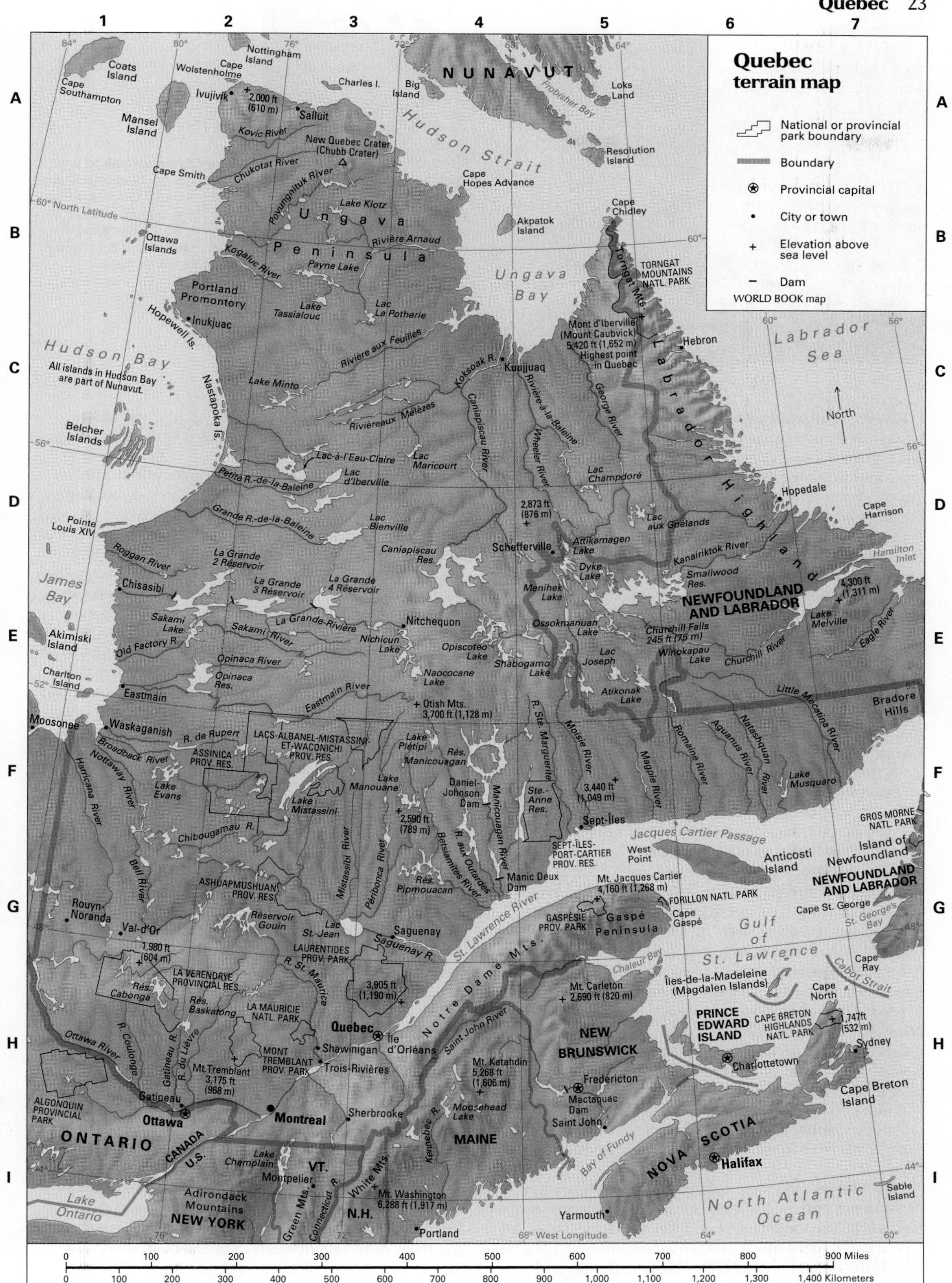

Quebec
terrain map
National or provincial park boundary
Boundary
Provincial capital
City or town
Elevation above sea level
Dam
WORLD BOOK map
NUNAVUT
Hudson Strait
Ungava Peninsula
Ungava Bay
Hudson Bay
All islands in Hudson Bay are part of Nunavut.
James Bay
Labrador Sea
Labrador Highland
NEWFOUNDLAND AND LABRADOR
Mont d'Iberville (Mount Caubvick) 5,420 ft (1,652 m) Highest point in Quebec
TORNGAT MOUNTAINS NATL. PARK
Kuujjuaq
Schefferville
Chisasibi
Eastmain
Waskaganish
Nitchequon
Sept-Îles
Anticosti Island
Gaspé Peninsula
Gulf of St. Lawrence
St. Lawrence River
Saguenay
Quebec
Trois-Rivières
Shawinigan
Montreal
Ottawa
Gatineau
Sherbrooke
Rouyn-Noranda
Val-d'Or
ONTARIO
NEW BRUNSWICK
NOVA SCOTIA
PRINCE EDWARD ISLAND
MAINE
NEW YORK
VT.
N.H.
Halifax
Charlottetown
Fredericton
North Atlantic Ocean
0 100 200 300 400 500 600 700 800 900 Miles
0 100 200 300 400 500 600 700 800 900 1,000 1,100 1,200 1,300 1,400 Kilometers

© Jean Hubert, Alamy Images

The Canadian Shield is a rough, rocky land region covering most of Quebec. Relatively few people live in this region, which has large mineral deposits but is largely unsuitable for farming.

Rivers, waterfalls, and lakes. Inland waters in Quebec cover 71,000 square miles (184,000 square kilometers). Quebec has a greater total area of fresh water than any other province. Its many rivers help make it a leading producer and exporter of hydroelectric power in Canada and the United States.

Quebec's principal river is the St. Lawrence. The river enters Quebec at the point where the province, New York, and Ontario meet. It then flows northeast into the Gulf of St. Lawrence. Long before the French explorer Jacques Cartier sailed up the St. Lawrence in 1535, First Nations people used the river. Since then, this important trade route has influenced the life and development of Quebec and Canada. Its importance increased greatly in 1959, when the St. Lawrence Seaway was completed. The seaway allows large oceangoing ships to travel up the river and to the Great Lakes. See **Saint Lawrence River; Saint Lawrence Seaway.**

All the other important rivers in Quebec flow into the St. Lawrence. Most of them, including the Saguenay, St. Maurice, and Ottawa, rise in the Canadian Shield and join the St. Lawrence from the north or northwest. The Ottawa River marks much of Quebec's border with Ontario, to the west. The main rivers south of the St. Lawrence include the Chaudière, Richelieu, and St. Francis.

Rivers flowing east, north, or west into James Bay, Hudson Bay, Hudson Strait, and Ungava Bay drain more than half the province. Many of them are more than 200 miles (320 kilometers) long. Many of these rivers are used to produce hydroelectric power.

Most of Quebec's rivers have waterfalls and rapids. Many of the rapids, such as Rapide Blanc on the St. Maurice River and Rapide des Quinze on the Ottawa River, are the sites of hydroelectric power dams. The best-known falls include Shawinigan Falls, which drops 146 feet (45 meters) on the St. Maurice River; 114-foot (35-meter) Joffre Falls on the Chaudière River; and 251-foot (77-meter) Montmorency Falls on the Montmorency River.

Beautiful lakes lie throughout Quebec. More than 20 of them cover over 100 square miles (260 square kilometers) each. The Canadian Shield has the largest lakes, of which 840-square-mile (2,180-square-kilometer) Lake Mistassini is the biggest. Other lakes in this region include Lac-a-l'Eau-Claire, Lac St.-Jean, and Lakes Bienville, Caniapiscau, and Minto. Lakes Mégantic and Memphremagog, just north of Maine, are famous among fishing enthusiasts.

Plant and animal life. Forests cover about 319,000 square miles (825,000 square kilometers), about 55 percent of Quebec's land. The southern part of the Canadian Shield has important stands of balsam fir and spruce, Quebec's most valuable trees. Maples, pines, and white and yellow birches also grow there. Small stands of balsam, birch, black and white spruce, dwarf aspen, and willow trees grow in northern Quebec. Mosses and lichens grow west of Ungava Bay and Hudson Strait. The Appalachian Region has thick stands of timber. Most of Quebec's maple trees grow in the Eastern Townships. Forest wildflowers include bellworts, bloodroots, dogtooth violets, spring beauties, squirrel corn, and trilliums. Buttercups, daisies, and prairie strawberries and raspberries grow on Quebec's prairies.

Beavers, foxes, martens, minks, muskrats, and seals are the most numerous fur-bearing animals in Quebec. There are many caribou in the north, but their population has declined significantly since the 1990's. Bears are found throughout the province. Large numbers of deer, moose, and raccoons live in the southern regions. Game birds include black ducks and geese. Fish in the waters off Quebec include cod, herring, and redfish. In addition, crabs, lobsters, and scallops live in these waters. Fish in Quebec's inland rivers and lakes include bass, pike, muskellunge, salmon, and trout.

Climate. Quebec's climate varies greatly. The average annual temperature ranges from 44 °F (7 °C) in the far south to 17 °F (–8 °C) in the far north.

Quebec's winters are long and cold. The average January temperature in the north is about –11 °F (–24 °C). In July, the average temperature there is 52 °F (11 °C). In southern Quebec, the average January temperature is about 10 °F (–12 °C). Summers are warm, but short. The average July temperature is 68 °F (20 °C).

In southern Quebec, *precipitation* (rain, melted snow, and other forms of moisture) averages about 40 inches (102 centimeters) a year. The north receives about 24 inches (60 centimeters) annually. Most places in Quebec get from 70 to 140 inches (178 to 356 centimeters) of snow yearly, most of it between late November and mid-March.

Economy

Many early settlers of Quebec earned their living by farming, fishing, or fur trading. Logging became important in the early 1800's, manufacturing grew in the mid-1800's, and mining began to develop during the early 1900's. Service industries have grown rapidly in importance since the mid-1900's. The development of Quebec's economy has been boosted by the province's natural resources, which include rivers well suited to shipping and hydroelectric power.

Today, service industries combine to account for the largest portion of Quebec's *gross domestic product* (GDP)—the total value of goods and services that are produced in the province in a year. Quebec has a higher GDP than any province except Ontario.

Average monthly weather

Montreal						Quebec City					
	Temperatures °F High	Low	°C High	Low	Days of rain or snow		Temperatures °F High	Low	°C High	Low	Days of rain or snow
Jan.	19	1	-7	-17	17	Jan.	19	3	-7	-16	17
Feb.	25	5	-4	-15	14	Feb.	25	7	-4	-14	14
Mar.	34	18	1	-8	14	Mar.	34	18	1	-8	14
Apr.	52	32	11	0	13	Apr.	48	32	9	0	13
May	64	43	18	6	14	May	64	43	18	6	12
June	73	52	23	11	13	June	72	52	22	11	14
July	79	57	26	14	13	July	77	57	25	14	16
Aug.	77	55	25	13	12	Aug.	75	55	24	13	13
Sept.	68	46	20	8	11	Sept.	66	48	19	9	13
Oct.	54	36	12	2	14	Oct.	52	37	11	3	14
Nov.	41	27	5	-3	16	Nov.	39	27	4	-3	15
Dec.	27	12	-3	-11	17	Dec.	27	12	-3	-11	19

Natural resources of Quebec include rich soils and vast mineral deposits. The province also has great forests, much wildlife, and plentiful supplies of water.

Soil. The St. Lawrence Lowland has the province's richest soils. They are composed chiefly of *sediments* (material that settles to the bottom of liquid). The sediments were deposited by the sea and various lakes and streams that covered the region after the most recent ice age, which ended about 11,500 years ago. The soils include clays, loams, sands, and silts.

Material deposited by the ice age glaciers, and some lake sediments, cover most of the Appalachian Region. These soils include clays, limestone and slate loams, sands, and sandy loams. Stony soils occur in much of the Eastern Townships. The Gaspé Peninsula has sandy soils broken by boulders. Heavy loams occur on the southern shores of the peninsula.

Granites, schists, and other stone are found in most of the Canadian Shield. Most of the soil covering is thin and not suitable for agriculture. A rock and clay soil covers the Hudson Bay Lowland.

Minerals. The Canadian Shield has some of the world's largest deposits of metallic minerals. Vast iron ore deposits lie along the central part of the Labrador border and near Ungava Bay. Most copper deposits are in the Chibougamau and Rouyn-Noranda areas. Lead and zinc are found on the Gaspé Peninsula. Northern Quebec also has nickel deposits.

The most important gold-bearing ore deposits are located near Rouyn-Noranda and Val-d'Or. This area also has deposits of uranium and zinc. Another rich mining territory lies west and northwest of Montreal. This area

Average January temperatures

There is a wide range of temperatures in Quebec during winter. The area along the southern border is the mildest.

Degrees Fahrenheit / Degrees Celsius: Above 14 / Above -10; 5 to 14 / -15 to -10; -4 to 5 / -20 to -15; -13 to -4 / -25 to -20; Below -13 / Below -25

Atlantic Ocean; Kuujjuaq; Schefferville; Eastmain; Sept-Îles; Saguenay; Quebec; Montreal

Average July temperatures

The southwestern area has the warmest summers. The temperature decreases sharply toward the far north.

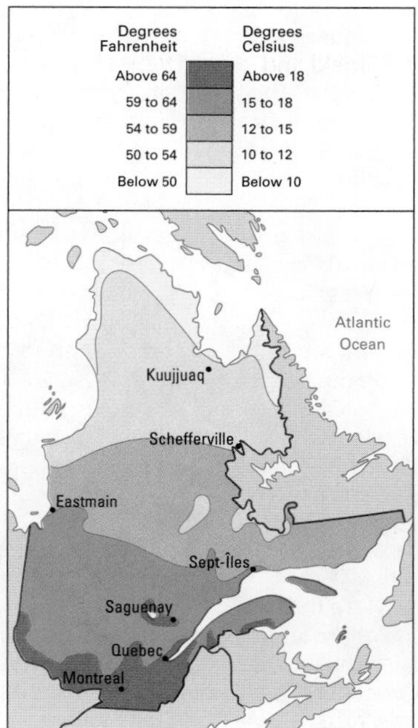

Average yearly precipitation

Quebec's precipitation is heaviest in the southeastern section. The province becomes steadily drier northward.

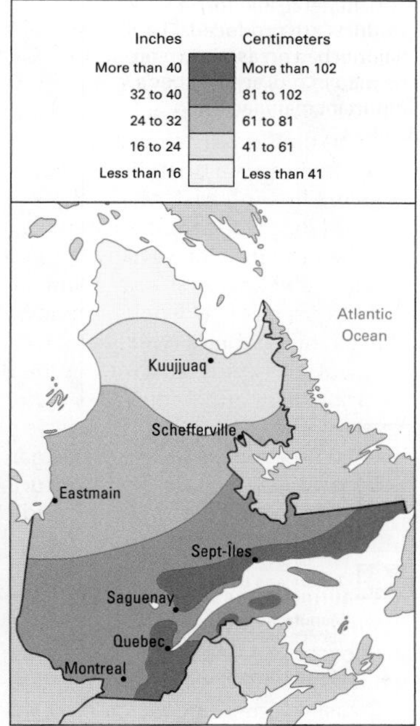

WORLD BOOK maps; based on the *National Atlas of Canada.*

Quebec economy

Agriculture

Cash receipts	$8,886,546,000
Rank among Canadian provinces	4th
Distribution	62% livestock, 38% crops
Farms (2016)	29,000
Farm acres/hectares (2016)	8,103,247/3,279,267
Rank among Canadian provinces	5th
Farmland	2% of Quebec

Leading products

1. Dairy (ranks 1st in Canada)
2. Hogs (ranks 1st in Canada)
3. Hens and chickens (ranks 2nd in Canada)
4. Corn (ranks 2nd in Canada)
5. Soybeans (ranks 3rd in Canada)

Other products: apples, blueberries, cattle, eggs, floriculture and nursery products, maple products, vegetables.

Fishing

Commercial catch	$342,289,000
Rank among Canadian provinces	5th

Leading catches

1. Crabs (ranks 2nd in Canada)
2. Lobsters
3. Shrimp (ranks 3rd in Canada)
4. Halibut

Other catches: clams, flatfishes, Greenland turbot, herring, scallops, sea cucumbers, sea urchins, whelk.

Figures are for 2018.
Dollar amounts are in Canadian dollars.
Source: Statistics Canada, Fisheries and Oceans Canada. (Continued on page 27)

General economy

Gross domestic product (GDP)* (2018)	$439,375,000,000
Rank among Canadian provinces	2nd
Unemployment rate (2019)	5.1% (Canada avg: 5.7%)

*Gross domestic product is the total value of goods and services produced in a year and is in Canadian dollars.
Source: Statistics Canada.

Production and workers by economic activities

Economic activities	Percent of GDP produced	Employed workers: Number of people	Employed workers: Percent of total
Community, business, & personal services	26	1,586,500*	37*
Finance, insurance, & real estate	18*	240,300	6
Trade, restaurants, & hotels	14	930,400	22
Manufacturing	14	488,200	11
Transportation & communication	7	397,500	9
Government	7	247,900	6
Construction	6	249,600	6
Utilities	4	26,600	1
Agriculture	2†	55,900	1
Mining	2	39,300†	1†
Total	100	4,262,200	100

*Includes figures from establishments that manage other companies.
†Includes figures from forestry and fishing.
Figures are for 2018.
Source: Statistics Canada.

Economic map of Quebec

This map shows the economic uses of land in Quebec and where the province's leading farm, mineral, and forest products are produced. The major urban areas (shown on the map in red) are Quebec's important manufacturing centers.

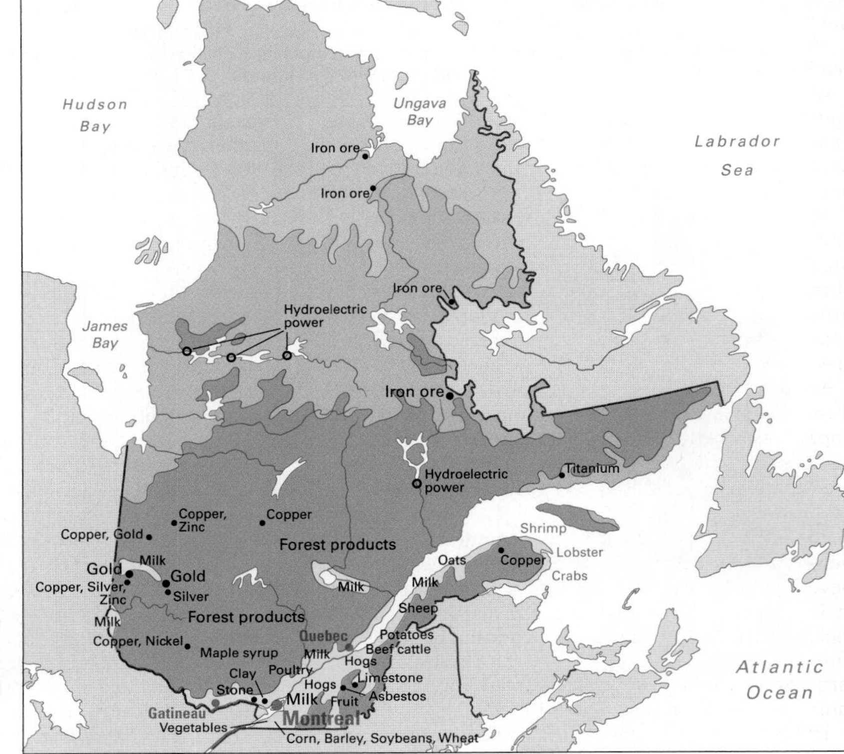

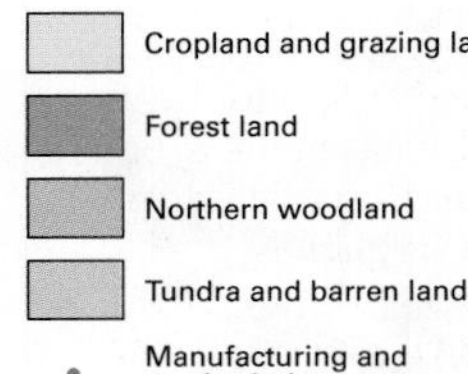

WORLD BOOK map

Mining

Mineral production	$9,986,901,000
Rank among Canadian provinces	2nd
Crude oil and equivalents	*
Natural gas (million cubic feet †)	3,309
Rank among Canadian provinces	5th

*No significant mining of this product in Quebec.
†One cubic foot equals 0.0283 cubic meter.

Leading products

Copper (ranks 3rd in Canada), diamonds (ranks 3rd in Canada), gold (ranks 2nd in Canada), iron ore (ranks 1st in Canada), nickel (ranks 2nd in Canada), sand and gravel, stone (ranks 2nd in Canada), zinc (ranks 2nd in Canada).

Electric power

Hydroelectric	98.9%
Petroleum	0.3%
Natural gas	0.1%
Other	0.7%

Manufacturing

Value added by manufacture*	$61,887,352,000
Rank among Canadian provinces	2nd

Leading products

1. Food and beverage products
2. Transportation equipment
3. Primary metals
4. Fabricated metal productss
5. Chemicals
6. Wood products
7. Machinery

Other products: computer and electronic products, paper products, petroleum and coal products, plastic and rubber products.

*Value added by manufacture is the increase in value of raw materials as they become finished products.

Figures are for 2017, except for the mining figures, which are for 2018.
Dollar amounts are in Canadian dollars.
Source: Statistics Canada.

has deposits of a great variety of minerals, including feldspar, granite, graphite, kaolin, magnesite, mica, molybdenum, and silica.

Service industries account for most of Quebec's gross domestic product and employment. These industries are concentrated in the Montreal and Quebec City metropolitan areas.

Montreal ranks second to Toronto among Canada's leading financial centers. Such major banks as the Bank of Montreal, the National Bank of Canada, and the Royal Bank of Canada have large operations in the city. Montreal is also the home of three of Canada's largest universities: Concordia University, McGill University, and the University of Montreal. Several of the world's largest engineering research companies are based in Montreal.

Most provincial and local government employees work in the Montreal and Quebec City areas. Université Laval (Laval University) is in Quebec City. Several federal agencies have headquarters in the Gatineau area. The Fédération des Caisses Desjardins du Québec, an organization that supports credit unions, has headquarters in Lévis, across the St. Lawrence River from Quebec City.

Manufacturing. The province's vast raw materials and hydroelectric power have helped industries develop. Quebec's factories, mills, and refineries account for about 25 percent of the value of Canada's total industrial production. Most of Quebec's production occurs in the Montreal area, which ranks second only to the Toronto area among Canada's manufacturing centers.

Montreal is a major center of Canada's aerospace industry. Such leading aerospace companies as Bell Helicopter Textron, Bombardier Aerospace, Pratt and Whitney Canada, and Rolls-Royce Canada employ many in the Montreal area. The city also produces pharmaceutical products.

Food-processing plants are concentrated in the area between Montreal and Quebec City. Quebec produces beverages, dairy products, and meat. Leading beverages include beer, coffee, soft drinks, and tea. Dairy products include cheese, milk, and yogurt. Pork and poultry are important meat products. The industry also turns out large amounts of baked goods, canned fruits and vegetables, livestock feed, and snack foods.

The province produces most of Canada's aluminum. Aluminum plants along the Saguenay and St. Lawrence rivers and a steel plant in Contrecoeur account for most of Quebec's primary metals production. Quebec is also one of the leading provinces in the production of paper.

Agriculture. Farmland covers a small portion of Quebec's land area, mostly in the St. Lawrence Lowland. Livestock products account for the majority of the province's farming production.

Dairy production accounts for the largest part of Quebec's farm income. Quebec ranks among the leading provinces and states in milk production and in the number of dairy cattle. Most of Quebec's dairy farms are in the far south. Much of the milk goes into manufacturing butter, cheese, ice cream, powdered milk, and yogurt. The farmers sell most of the rest of the milk for drinking.

Hogs are the most valuable meat animals raised in Quebec. Farmers in the rural areas surrounding Montreal and Quebec City keep the largest number of hogs. Most of the beef cattle and poultry are raised in the southern part of the province. Only Ontario raises more chickens and eggs than Quebec. Quebec farmers also keep sheep and turkeys.

Nearly all farmers in the province grow some vegetables. Important vegetables include broccoli, cabbage, carrots, green beans, lettuce, onions, peas, potatoes, and sweet corn. Growing ornamental plants also has become an important activity. Apples, one of Quebec's most important fruit crops, are grown chiefly in the Montreal area. Farmers also raise blueberries, cranberries, raspberries, and strawberries.

Corn is Quebec's leading field crop, and Quebec is one of Canada's leading corn producers. Most of the corn is grown in the far southern part of the province. Farmers in Quebec also grow barley, oats, soybeans, and wheat. Much of the grain is used as livestock feed.

Quebec leads the provinces and states in the production of maple products. Over half of the world's maple syrup, sugar, and taffy comes from Quebec.

Mining. Gold, iron ore, and nickel are among the leading mineral products of Quebec. Quebec is Canada's second leading gold-producing province. Only Ontario produces more gold. Gold mines operate around Rouyn-Noranda and Val-d'Or. Most of the gold ore also contains silver. The Fermont area near the Labrador border supplies most of Quebec's iron ore. Nickel is mined in the Ungava Peninsula.

Quebec is a large producer of titanium. Quebec's titanium is obtained from ilmenite ore in the Lake Allard area, north of Havre-St.-Pierre. Titanium is a metal that is highly resistant to corrosion and heat. It is used in the production of paint and many other items.

Quebec is Canada's only producer of niobium, and a leading producer of copper, diamonds, silver, and zinc. Quebec's other mined products include clays, limestone, peat, salt, and sand and gravel.

Forestry. Quebec is a leading timber-producing area in North America. Balsam firs, jack pines, and spruce provide much of the province's timber. The most productive forests in Quebec lie in a broad belt that extends west from Sept-Îles to the Ontario border. Much of the timber in Quebec is used by the paper industry.

Fishing. Crabs and lobsters are Quebec's most valuable catches. They account for most of the province's total fishing income. Other important catches include Greenland turbot and shrimp.

Electric power and utilities. Quebec is a leading producer of hydroelectric power in North America. The province produces hydroelectric power more cheaply than most other regions in North America because it has great water resources.

Hydroelectric plants supply almost all of Quebec's electric power. Much of the rest comes from petroleum. Quebec's hydroelectric plants are managed primarily by Hydro-Québec, a government corporation. The major hydroelectric plants lie on the La Grande and Manicouagan rivers. Hydro-Québec sells surplus electric power to neighboring Canadian provinces and U.S. states.

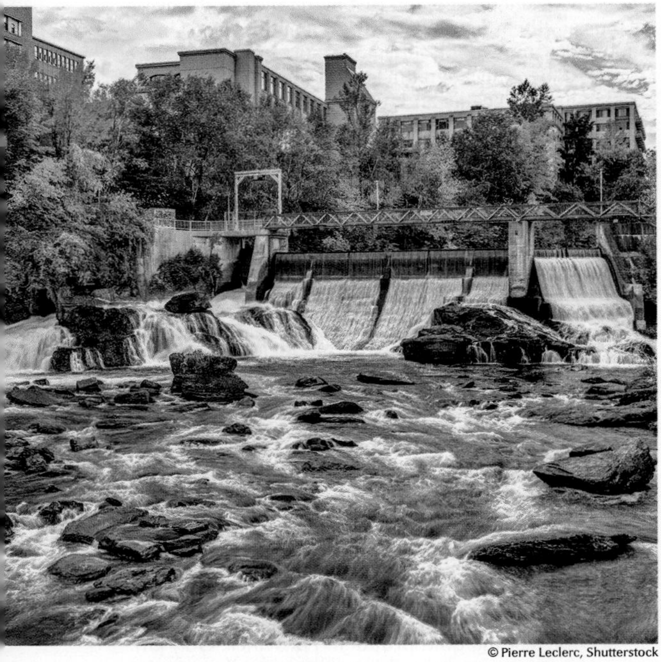

© Pierre Leclerc, Shutterstock

Hydroelectric plants supply almost all of Quebec's electric power. The Frontenac Power Station in Sherbrooke, *shown here,* is Quebec's oldest operating hydroelectric power station.

Transportation. Quebec's first major road was the Chemin du Roi (King's Highway), built between Montreal and Quebec City in the 1730's. Today, Quebec's system of roads includes limited-access superhighways called *autoroutes,* secondary highways, and local roads. Montreal is the hub of the province's highway network.

Canada's first major canal, the Lachine Canal, bypassed the Lachine Rapids on the St. Lawrence River near Montreal. It opened in 1825 and closed in 1970, after ships began using the new South Shore Canal.

Montreal is at the gateway to the St. Lawrence Seaway, which leads to the Great Lakes. Sorel is at the head of a waterway leading south to New York City. The Richelieu and Ottawa rivers, like the St. Lawrence Seaway, have canal systems. Most of Quebec's chief ports, such as Baie-Comeau, Bécancour, Montreal, Port-Cartier, Quebec City, Sept-Îles, Sorel, and Trois-Rivières, lie along the St. Lawrence River. These ports are accessible by boat all year long.

A 15-mile (24-kilometer) railroad, the first in Canada, began operating between Laprairie and Saint-Jean in 1836. In the 1800's, Montreal was the headquarters for Canada's major railroad companies, including the Grand Trunk and the Canadian Pacific. Today, Quebec's railroads are mainly in the St. Lawrence Lowland and the Appalachian Region. Other lines reach the mining areas to the north and connect Quebec with Ontario and the United States.

Quebec has two international airports. They are the Montreal-Pierre Elliott Trudeau International Airport and the Jean Lesage International Airport at Quebec City. The province also has several domestic airports and many landing facilities for helicopters and seaplanes.

Communication. Quebec has many daily newspapers. Most of them are printed in French. Publishing in the province began in 1764 with the founding of the *Quebec Gazette* in Quebec City. This paper was published in French and English until 1842, when it changed to English only. In 1884, the paper merged with the *Quebec Chronicle-Telegraph,* which is still published.

A French printer, Fleury Mesplet, came to Montreal with Benjamin Franklin in 1776. The two men published propaganda material for the 13 American Colonies during the American Revolution (1775-1783). In 1778, Mesplet began publishing *La Gazette du Commerce et Littéraire, pour la Ville et District de Montréal,* now the English-language Montreal newspaper *The Gazette.*

Le Journal de Montréal is the newspaper with the largest daily circulation in Quebec. Other large Montreal newspapers include *La Presse, Le Devoir,* and *The Gazette.* Quebec City's two daily newspapers are *Le Journal de Québec* and *Le Soleil.*

In 1919, the Canadian Marconi Company made the first radio broadcast in Canada, from Montreal. Its station, CFCF, began regular broadcasts in 1920. The government-owned Canadian Broadcasting Corporation (now called Canadian Broadcasting Corporation/Radio-Canada) introduced television broadcasting in the province in 1952. Station CBFT of Montreal began broadcasting that year, chiefly in French. Today, Quebec has dozens of radio and television stations. Most TV stations broadcast in French. Cable and satellite TV systems service most Quebec communities and provide access to major U.S. and English-language Canadian networks.

Lieutenant governor of Quebec represents the British monarch, Canada's official head of state, in the province. The lieutenant governor is appointed by Canada's *governor general in council*—that is, the governor general acting with the advice and consent of the federal Cabinet. The position of lieutenant governor is largely ceremonial.

Premier of Quebec is the actual head of the provincial government. Quebec, like Canada itself, has a parliamentary form of government. The premier is an elected member of the National Assembly. The person who serves as premier is usually the leader of the majority party in the Assembly.

The premier presides over the Executive Council. The council includes other ministers chosen by the premier from among the majority party's members in the legislature. The ministers direct about 20 departments of the government. The council resigns if it loses the support of a majority of the legislature.

Legislature. Quebec has a one-house legislature called the National Assembly. Each of its 125 members is elected from an electoral district and serves a term of up to five years. If the lieutenant governor, on the advice of the premier, calls for an election before five years have passed, all Assembly members must run again for office. The legislature meets at least once a year.

The premiers of Quebec

	Party	Term
Pierre-J.-O. Chauveau	Conservative	1867-1873
Gédéon Ouimet	Conservative	1873-1874
C.-B. de Boucherville	Conservative	1874-1878
Henri-G. Joly	Liberal	1878-1879
J.-Adolphe Chapleau	Conservative	1879-1882
J.-Alfred Mousseau	Conservative	1882-1884
John Jones Ross	Conservative	1884-1887
L.-Olivier Taillon	Conservative	1887
Honoré Mercier	Liberal	1887-1891
C.-B. de Boucherville	Conservative	1891-1892
L.-Olivier Taillon	Conservative	1892-1896
Edmund J. Flynn	Conservative	1896-1897
F.-Gabriel Marchand	Liberal	1897-1900
S.-Napoléon Parent	Liberal	1900-1905
Lomer Gouin	Liberal	1905-1920
L.-Alexandre Taschereau	Liberal	1920-1936
Adélard Godbout	Liberal	1936
Maurice Duplessis	Union Nationale	1936-1939
Adélard Godbout	Liberal	1939-1944
Maurice Duplessis	Union Nationale	1944-1959
J.-Paul Sauvé	Union Nationale	1959-1960
Antonio Barrette	Union Nationale	1960
Jean Lesage	Liberal*	1960-1966
Daniel Johnson	Union Nationale	1966-1968
Jean-Jacques Bertrand	Union Nationale	1968-1970
Robert Bourassa	Liberal*	1970-1976
René Lévesque	Québécois	1976-1985
Pierre Marc Johnson	Québécois	1985
Robert Bourassa	Liberal*	1985-1994
Daniel Johnson	Liberal*	1994
Jacques Parizeau	Québécois	1994-1996
Lucien Bouchard	Québécois	1996-2001
Bernard Landry	Québécois	2001-2003
Jean Charest	Liberal*	2003-2012
Pauline Marois	Québécois	2012-2014
Philippe Couillard	Liberal*	2014-2018
François Legault	Coalition Avenir Québec	2018-

*Since 1955, the Quebec Liberal Party has had no official ties with the federal Liberal Party.

Quebec formerly had a two-house legislature. The lower house was called the Legislative Assembly and the upper house the Legislative Council. But in 1968, the Legislative Council was abolished, and the Legislative Assembly became the National Assembly.

Courts. The highest court in Quebec is the Court of Appeal, which hears cases in Quebec City and Montreal. Decisions of the Court of Appeal can be appealed to the Supreme Court of Canada. The Quebec Superior Court meets in the major cities of 36 judicial districts. The federal government appoints all judges of the Court of Appeal and the Superior Court. The judges may hold office until the age of 75, but they become semi-retired at age 65. The lower courts of Quebec include the Court of Quebec, which has more than 300 judges, and the municipal courts. Provincial authorities appoint the judges of these courts.

Quebec is the only province in which judges do not decide civil cases chiefly on the basis of *common law.* Under the common-law system, developed in England, rulings are determined by previous court decisions and by the customs of the people. In Quebec, judges decide civil cases mainly on rules in the Civil Code, which has its origins in the Code Napoleon, also called the Napoleonic Code. The judges can disregard the decisions of other judges in similar cases. In criminal matters, the courts follow a federal criminal code. Because of Quebec's unique legal system, Canada's constitution requires that three of the nine judges on the Supreme Court of Canada come from Quebec.

Local government. The first level of local government in Quebec consists of *cantons* (townships), *cantons-unis* (united townships), parishes, towns, and villages. These are governed by a mayor and at least six council members, all elected by the people. Also, Quebec has many regional county municipalities (RCM's).

Claude Mathieu, Collection National Assembly of Quebec

Quebec's National Assembly meets in the National Assembly Chamber in Quebec City. Following British tradition, members of the governing and opposition parties sit facing one another.

Each RCM covers a certain area of the province and contains a number of the first-level local government units. A council made up of the mayors of the communities that fall within an RCM govern that RCM. RCM's are responsible for such matters as land-use planning, land assessment, and emergency measures. Some of Quebec's largest cities, including Montreal and Quebec City, do not come under the authority of an RCM.

Revenue. Taxes account for about 60 percent of the province's *general revenue* (income). Quebec is the only province that collects provincial personal income taxes, instead of having the federal government collect them. Corporate profits and retail sales are also taxed.

Quebec's government receives about 20 percent of its revenue from federal-provincial tax-sharing arrangements. Most of Quebec's other revenue comes from license and permit fees and from the sale of liquor. The sale of liquor in Quebec is under government control.

Politics. One of four political parties controlled Quebec's government from the time Quebec became a province in 1867 until 2018. These parties were the Conservative, Liberal, and Union Nationale parties, and the Parti Québécois (PQ).

The Conservatives held power for the first 30 years, except for two brief administrations under the Liberals. In 1896, Wilfrid Laurier, a Liberal from Quebec, became Canada's first French-Canadian prime minister. His victory helped bring the Liberals to power in Quebec in 1897.

The Union Nationale party, led by Maurice Duplessis, governed during much of the 1930's to 1950's. It supported *autonomy* (self-rule) for the province.

Power shifted between the Liberal and Union Nationale parties from 1960 to 1976, and then between the Parti Québécois and the Liberal Party. In 2018, the center-right Coalition Avenir Québec (CAQ), which had been formed in 2011, won control of Quebec's government.

History

Early days. People first settled in the Quebec region several thousand years ago, after the glaciers of the last ice age had disappeared. When the first Europeans arrived, Inuit (formerly called Eskimos) and several First Nations peoples were living there. The Inuit lived in the far north, chiefly west of Ungava Bay and along Hudson Bay. The Innu First Nations people lived in the south and eastern parts of Quebec. Those who lived in the eastern part were often called the Naskapi. Some Innu lived toward the south, between the St. Maurice River and present-day Sept-Îles. The French called them *Montagnais* (mountaineers). The Cree lived between the Innu and Inuit lands and south of James Bay. Other First Nations peoples included the Algonquin, Maliseet (also called Wolastoqiyik), and Mi'kmaq.

The beginning of European settlement. In 1534, the French explorer Jacques Cartier sailed into what is now the Gulf of St. Lawrence and claimed the Quebec region for France. This region became the base of France's colonial empire in North America, called New France. In 1608, the French explorer Samuel de Champlain established the first permanent colony at Quebec City, beginning nearly 150 years of French rule. Some 30,000 French people migrated to New France between 1608 and 1759. But only about 10,000 to 12,000 stayed there permanently. In 1759, the British defeated the French in the Battle of Quebec, also called the Battle of the Plains of Abraham. The Treaty of Paris of 1763 gave control of Quebec to Britain (now the United Kingdom).

In 1791, the British divided Quebec into two colonies—Upper Canada (now southern Ontario) and Lower Canada (now southern Quebec). English settlers formed a majority in Upper Canada and French people made up a majority in Lower Canada. Following armed rebellions in both colonies in 1837-1838, the Act of Union of 1840 united Upper and Lower Canada into the Province of Canada. For more on the early history of Quebec, see **Canada, History of; New France.**

Early years as a province. The British North America Act of 1867 created the Dominion of Canada with four provinces (see **British North America Act**). The Province of Canada became the provinces of Ontario and Quebec. The other provinces of the Dominion were New Brunswick and Nova Scotia. French, in addition to English, was recognized as one of Quebec's two official languages. The act gave Quebec direct control over its education and civil law. However, it also guaranteed the education rights of Canada's two major religious groups—Catholics and Protestants. In Quebec, the Protestant, English-speaking minority received provincial funds for its schools. But Quebec's French Canadians soon discovered that French Canadians in some other provinces were prevented from using public funds to establish Roman Catholic, French-language schools.

Relations between French and English Canadians grew worse after the *Métis* (people of mixed white and First Nations ancestry) of Saskatchewan rebelled in 1885. Louis Riel, a French, Catholic Métis, was their leader. Riel was convicted of treason and hanged later that year. Many French Canadians considered Riel a hero who had been unjustly killed. Many English Canadians regarded him as a traitor. See **North West Rebellion.**

Tension between the French- and English-speaking Canadians rose again in 1899. That year, the United Kingdom went to war against the Boers in South Africa. Many French Canadians opposed fighting in the Anglo-Boer War of 1899-1902. Some English-speaking Canadians considered it Canada's duty to send troops to aid the British.

Sir Wilfrid Laurier of Quebec, Canada's first French-Canadian prime minister, spent government funds to equip volunteers and send them to South Africa, where they joined the British army. This policy angered many people in Quebec, especially Laurier's former ally Henri Bourassa. Bourassa objected to providing support for the United Kingdom and held that Canadians should be loyal first to Canada. See **Laurier, Sir Wilfrid.**

About 1900, a period of rapid industrialization began in Quebec. In 1912, Quebec nearly doubled in size. Its northwestern boundaries were extended to Hudson Bay and Hudson Strait. Interest in the region's natural resources grew, and Quebec and the colony of Newfoundland disputed the Quebec-Labrador boundary. The British Privy Council settled the dispute in 1927 in fa-

Historic Quebec

British forces captured the city of Quebec in 1759. This victory enabled Britain to obtain nearly all of France's territory in Canada in the 1763 Treaty of Paris.

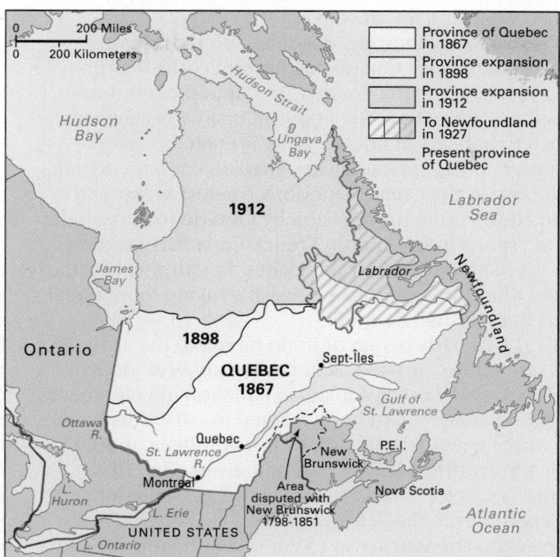

Quebec expanded northward to the Hudson Strait between 1867 and 1912. In 1927, part of northeastern Quebec became part of Newfoundland (now called Newfoundland and Labrador).

The Expo 67 world's fair took place in Montreal as part of Canada's centennial celebration.

WORLD BOOK illustrations by Richard Bonson, The Art Agency

Important dates in Quebec

1534 Jacques Cartier reached the Gulf of St. Lawrence and claimed the Quebec region for France.

1608 Samuel de Champlain established Quebec City, the first permanent European settlement in Canada.

1663 King Louis XIV of France made the Quebec region a royal province.

1759 The British captured Quebec City during the French and Indian War.

1763 Britain acquired Quebec by the Treaty of Paris.

1774 The British Parliament approved the Quebec Act, extending Quebec's borders and establishing French-Canadian political and religious rights.

1791 The Constitutional Act divided Quebec into the colonies of Upper Canada and Lower Canada.

1841 The Act of Union joined Upper Canada and Lower Canada under one government.

1867 The British North America Act created the Dominion of Canada, forming the province of Quebec.

1912 Quebec nearly doubled in size by acquiring territory east of Hudson Bay.

1927 The British Privy Council set the present Quebec-Labrador boundary.

1963 The provincial government bought all privately owned electric power companies.

1974 The Quebec legislature made French the only official language of the province.

1976-1985 The Parti Québécois, a separatist political party, controlled the provincial legislature.

1990 The Meech Lake accord, a constitutional amendment that would have recognized Quebec as a distinct society, failed to pass all 10 provincial legislatures.

1995 Quebec voters narrowly rejected a referendum proposal that called for independence for Quebec.

vor of Newfoundland. However, Quebec never has formally recognized the border.

World War I. Tensions again developed between English and French Canadians during World War I (1914-1918). At first the country was united behind the war effort, but soon some English Canadians accused French Canadians of not enlisting. French Canadians pointed out that most English Canadian volunteers had been born in the United Kingdom. Matters worsened when courts upheld a decision by Ontario to abolish the use of French in its schools. French Canadians asked why they should fight for the United Kingdom when the United Kingdom's supporters were denying them equal rights in their own country.

In 1917, Canada began drafting men into the army. In 1918, the army was used to put down antidraft riots in Quebec City. A French-Canadian battalion of volunteers, the 22nd Battalion, had been formed in 1914. This battalion, which eventually included some draftees, fought in France from 1915 until the end of the war. Two of its members were awarded the Victoria Cross, the highest military honor in the British Empire.

Between the wars. After World War I, industry continued to expand rapidly. More people from rural areas found work in the cities. Until this time, many had been moving to Ontario or the United States.

Many French-Canadian leaders resented the industrial expansion, which was controlled by the English Canadians and Americans. The French Canadians feared that their language and culture would not survive in the cities, where English was the main language used in business. But the people accepted this threat because the new industry offered an improved living standard.

World War II. During World War II (1939-1945), Quebec was of great value to the Allies. The province had a large labor force, plentiful electric power, and huge deposits of asbestos, copper, and zinc. Quebec's industrial production nearly tripled.

Tension between French and English Canadians developed again during the war. In 1944, the federal government, under the Liberal Party, set up a military draft for service overseas, despite promises to Quebecers that it would not do so. Partly as a result, Quebec voters elected the Union Nationale party to power in 1944. The new government, under Premier Maurice Duplessis, emphasized French-Canadian political rights in Quebec and opposed control by the federal government.

Postwar Quebec. The economic growth in Quebec that followed World War II extended into the 1950's and 1960's. In 1950, mines near Havre-Saint-Pierre began to produce ilmenite, a titanium ore. In 1954, an asbestos fiber mill that was then the largest in the world opened in the town of Asbestos. In 1960, huge asbestos deposits were discovered in the Ungava Peninsula.

In 1960, the Liberal Party won control of Quebec's government. Jean Lesage became premier and served from 1960 to 1966. This period often is called Quebec's *Quiet Revolution* because of its many reforms and the secularization of such social service institutions as hospitals and schools. To *secularize* means to separate from religious influence. A new labor code made it easier to form trade unions. A new Ministry of Education was established, and it increased the number of high schools, colleges, and universities. A major symbol of the Quiet Revolution was putting hydroelectric power production under Quebec government control, under the slogan "Maîtres chez nous" ("Masters in our own house").

During the 1960's, Quebec and other provinces became dissatisfied with joint federal and provincial social programs and division of taxes. Quebec exercised the provinces' right to withdraw from these programs and to administer its share of taxes without federal supervision. Quebec then gained control of its pension plans, social security programs, and student loans.

The 1960's also saw a surge of nationalist feelings among French-speaking Quebecers. A number of them wanted Quebec to *secede* (withdraw) from the Canadian confederation and form a separate nation. Some Quebecers used demonstrations to promote secession, and a few extremists used bombings. In 1968, many separatist groups joined forces and formed the Parti Québécois (PQ). René Lévesque, a former Quebec Liberal cabinet minister, led the party.

The late 1900's. In 1970, members of the *Front de Liberation du Québec* (FLQ), a revolutionary separatist group, kidnapped British Trade Commissioner James R. Cross and Quebec Labor Minister Pierre Laporte. Canadian Prime Minister Pierre Trudeau suspended civil liberties and sent thousands of federal troops to Quebec cities to protect public officials and buildings. Provincial police arrested about 450 people. Laporte was later murdered, and four FLQ members were convicted of the crime. Trudeau and Quebec authorities allowed Cross's kidnappers to go to Cuba in return for his release.

In 1974, the National Assembly adopted French as Quebec's only official language. This act promoted French-language instruction in schools and made French Quebec's chief language of business and government.

In the 1976 general election, the Parti Québécois won control of the government. Lévesque became premier. In 1977, the legislature adopted the Charter of the French Language, also called Bill 101. The charter established deadlines and fines to help enforce the program to make French the chief language of Quebec. But the Supreme Court of Canada later ruled that parts of the charter were unconstitutional.

In a 1980 *referendum* (direct public vote), Lévesque's government asked voters for authority to negotiate a *sovereignty association* with the rest of Canada. Such an association would give Quebec political independence but maintain its economic ties to Canada. Voters rejected the proposal.

In 1981, proposed changes in Canada's constitution upset many French-speaking Quebecers. They felt the proposals would not help preserve and promote Quebec's French character. In 1982, the proposals became part of a revised constitution that was accepted by all provincial legislatures except Quebec.

Lévesque resigned as party leader and premier in the autumn of 1985, and the PQ was defeated in elections in December. Former Premier Robert Bourassa of the Liberal Party again became premier and held the position until 1994.

In April 1987, at Meech Lake, Quebec, Prime Minister Brian Mulroney and all the provincial premiers developed a plan for a new constitutional amendment. The amendment provided for Quebec to be recognized as a distinct society within Canada. Mulroney and the provincial leaders approved the proposed amendment, known as the Meech Lake Accord, in June 1987. The accord became a divisive issue across Canada.

To take effect, the accord had to be ratified by all 10 provinces by June 23, 1990. However, Newfoundland (now called Newfoundland and Labrador) withdrew its support for the accord, and Manitoba failed to ratify it. Many Quebecers then began to demand more independence. In 1992, fundamental changes to the national government were again under consideration, primarily to keep Quebec part of Canada. Among the possible changes was the transfer of certain federal powers to the provinces. But voters in Quebec and five other provinces voted against the changes in an October referendum.

The separatist Parti Québécois won a majority of seats in 1994 legislative elections. PQ leader Jacques Parizeau became premier. In October 1995, the Quebec government held a referendum on independence for Quebec. The proposal was narrowly defeated, with 50.58 percent voting against independence. Parizeau then resigned as premier and PQ leader and was replaced by Lucien Bouchard.

In late 1995 and early 1996, the Canadian Parliament passed resolutions aimed at promoting national unity. In 1996, the federal government asked the Supreme Court of Canada to decide if Quebec had a right to secede on its own. The court ruled that it did not. The federal government then passed the Clarity Act, setting out rules governing any future referendum on independence.

The early 2000's. In 2001, Bernard Landry replaced Bouchard as Parti Québécois leader and as premier. Under Premiers Bouchard and Landry, the provincial government had many disputes with the federal government, led by Liberal Prime Minister Jean Chrétien. In 2003, the provincial Liberal Party, led by Jean Charest, won control of Quebec's government. The Liberals remained in power until 2012.

In the spring of 2012, Montreal was the center of massive student demonstrations against university tuition increases. Opposition to the increases helped defeat Quebec's Liberal government in fall elections. The PQ was elected, and party leader Pauline Marois became Quebec's first woman premier. The PQ lost the 2014 general election to the Liberals, and Philippe Couillard became premier. In 2018, the center-right Coalition Avenir Québec (CAQ) won a majority in Quebec's legislature. The party supported stronger policies to protect Quebec's French language and culture. François Legault, the party's leader, succeeded Couillard as premier.

In the early 2000's, Quebec's government faced public anxiety about the cultural values of recent immigrants and how those values might affect Quebec's French character. During this time, the government, under several different administrations, proposed legislation to ban the wearing of religious symbols by people providing or receiving public services. In 2019, Quebec's legislature passed a controversial *secularism* law banning certain public employees from wearing religious symbols, such as Muslim headscarves, Jewish skullcaps, and Christian crosses. Secularism is the idea that religion should remain separate from politics and government.

Alan Gordon

Related articles in *World Book* include:

Biographies

Abbott, Sir John Joseph Campbell
Bourassa, Henri
Brock, Sir Isaac
Carleton, Sir Guy
Cartier, Sir George Étienne
Cartier, Jacques
Champlain, Samuel de
Charest, Jean
Chrétien, Jean
Drummond, William Henry
Garneau, Marc
Laurier, Sir Wilfrid
Laval de Montmorency, Saint François Xavier de
Léger, Jules
Lévesque, René
McGill, James
Montcalm, Marquis de
Mulroney, Brian
Papineau, Louis Joseph
Saint Laurent, Louis Stephen
Scott, F. R.
Taché, Sir Étienne-Paschal
Trudeau, Pierre Elliott
Turner, John Napier
Vanier, Georges-Philias
Verchères, Marie Madeleine Jarret de
Wolfe, James

Cities

Gatineau
Laval
Montreal
Quebec
Sherbrooke

History

Acadia
Bloc Québécois
British North America Act
Canada, History of
French and Indian wars
Innu Indians
Mohawk Indians
Parti Québécois
Quebec, Battle of
Quebec Act
United Empire Loyalists
War of 1812

Physical features

Anticosti
Canadian Shield
Gaspé Peninsula
Gulf of Saint Lawrence
Hudson Bay
James Bay
Lake Champlain
Ottawa River
Saguenay River
Saint Lawrence River

Outline

Additional resources

Level I

Craats, Rennay. *Quebec.* Weigl Educational Pubs., 2016.
Rodger, Marguerite. *Quebec.* Scholastic Canada, 2009.
Rowe, Percy, and Coster, Patience. *Montreal.* World Almanac Lib., 2005.

Level II

Courville, Serge. *Quebec: A Historical Geography.* UBC Pr., 2008.
Dickinson, John A., and Young, B. J. *A Short History of Quebec.* 4th ed. McGill-Queen's Univ. Pr., 2008.
Gossage, Peter, and Little, J. I. *An Illustrated History of Quebec.* Oxford, 2012.
Linteau, Paul-André. *The History of Montréal.* Baraka Bks., 2013.

© Songquan Deng, iStockphoto

Quebec, the capital of the province of Quebec, possesses the charm of an old European city. The Château Frontenac, a castlelike hotel built in the 1890's, is a Quebec landmark. It rises dramatically from Upper Town, the walled portion of Old Quebec City.

Quebec, *kwih BEHK,* or, in French, *kay BEHK,* is the capital of the province of Quebec and the oldest city in Canada. In French, the name is spelled with an accent—*Québec.* To distinguish the city from the province, it is often called Quebec City in English. The French explorer Samuel de Champlain founded the city in 1608. Quebec ranks as an important Canadian port and tourist center. It is built on and around Cap Diamant (Cape Diamond), a high cliff rising above the Saint Lawrence River. Quebec lies at the point where the St. Charles River flows into the St. Lawrence. There, the St. Lawrence narrows to about ½ mile (0.8 kilometer). The city's name comes from an Algonquian word meaning *the river narrows here.*

Quebec is the only surviving walled city in North America north of Mexico. But most of the present-day city lies outside the walls. Quebec's many churches, old stone houses, and crooked cobblestone streets give it the charm of an old European city. The Fairmont Château Frontenac, a castlelike hotel with towers, red brick walls, and a steep copper roof, rises dramatically from the edge of Cap Diamant.

The city has been called the *Cradle of New France* because it served as the base of early French explorers and missionaries in North America. Quebec also has the nickname *Gibraltar of America* because of the Citadel, a huge fort on the cliffs above the St. Lawrence River. (The nickname refers to Gibraltar, a historically strongly fortified site that overlooks the strait that links the Atlantic Ocean and the Mediterranean Sea.) In 1759, British troops defeated the French on the Plains of Abraham, west of the Citadel. In 1763, the Treaty of Paris, which ended the French and Indian War, gave Canada to Britain (now also called the United Kingdom).

The city

Quebec City covers 175 square miles (453 square kilometers). The Quebec metropolitan area, which includes Lévis on the south shore of the St. Lawrence, spreads over 1,316 square miles (3,409 square kilometers). The city has an old section that makes up about 4 square miles (10 square kilometers). The old section, in turn, has two parts, Upper Town and Lower Town.

The Citadel, one of Quebec's most famous landmarks, overlooks the rest of the city from a height of 347 feet (106 meters). It stands on the highest point of Cap Diamant. The cape drops sharply toward the St. Lawrence River but slopes more gradually to the St. Charles River in the northeast. Massive walls and cannons surround the fort and its 140 acres (57 hectares) of parade ground. The British completed the Citadel in 1832 to protect Quebec from possible invasion by the United States.

Upper Town lies north of the Citadel atop Cap Diamant. A stone wall, begun in the 1600's but rebuilt and modified in the 1700's and 1800's, encircles Upper Town. The wall averages 35 feet (11 meters) in height and has four entrance gates.

Most of Quebec's best hotels, luxury shops, monuments, parks, and fine restaurants are in Upper Town. Just outside the city walls is the Grande Allée (Great Way), a road lined with popular shops, restaurants, and nightclubs. It leads from one of the city gates, past Quebec's provincial Parliament buildings, toward fashionable residential areas.

The Dufferin Terrace, a planked walkway 60 feet (18

Facts in brief

Population: *City*—531,902. *Metropolitan area*—800,296.
Area: *City*—175 mi² (453 km²). *Metropolitan area*—1,316 mi² (3,409 km²).
Altitude: 162 ft (49 m) above sea level at City Hall.
Climate: *Average temperature*—January, 10 °F (−12 °C); July, 66 °F (19 °C). *Average annual precipitation* (rainfall, melted snow, and other forms of moisture)—48 in (123 cm).
Government: Mayor-council. *Terms*—4 years each for the mayor and the 37 other council members.
Founded: 1608. Incorporated as a city in 1832.

meters) wide, extends along the cliffs from the Citadel to the Château Frontenac. The terrace offers excellent views of Lévis, across the St. Lawrence, and of the Beaupré Coast and the Isle of Orleans downstream.

Lower Town, northeast of Upper Town, includes the business and industrial districts of Quebec. It lies 19 feet (6 meters) above sea level on a strip of land between the rivers and the cliffs of Cap Diamant. Lower Town has many large stores and some factories. A number of its homes date back to the 1700's and 1800's. Some of the area's oldest streets are extremely narrow. Sous-le-Cap measures only 8 feet 10 inches (2.69 meters) at its narrowest point and is one of the narrowest streets in North America.

A square called Place Royale is Lower Town's best-known landmark. The Notre-Dame-des-Victoires Church there has an altar built to look like a fort. This church, completed in 1688, stands on the site once occupied by Samuel de Champlain's first settlement, the Habitation.

The people

About 95 percent of Quebec City's people were born in Canada. The vast majority have French ancestors, and many of the rest have English, Irish, or Scottish ancestors. The majority of the people are Roman Catholic. About 95 percent of Quebecers speak French, the province of Quebec's official language.

The deterioration of old neighborhoods in Lower Town has been a major problem, causing a lack of adequate housing. However, the city has implemented a major renewal program in the core of several of these neighborhoods, particularly Saint Roch.

The economy

Industry and commerce. Hundreds of manufacturing companies operate in the Quebec area. Most of the industrial sites are along the St. Charles River and in industrial parks along the Autoroute de la Capitale. Leading industries include shipbuilding, papermaking, and the manufacture of *electrooptical* products, such as optical scanning equipment and components and testing equipment for fiber-optic communication systems. The science of electrooptics deals with relationships between light and electricity. Tourism also is important to the city's economy. The port of Quebec handles millions of tons of goods yearly. Its chief exports are grain, ore, and pulp and paper.

Transportation. Quebec's harbor stays open the year around and can handle oceangoing ships. The waterfront extends 6 miles (10 kilometers) along both the east and west sides of the cape and into the mouth of the St. Charles River. A ferry crossing and two bridges link Quebec to the south shore of the St. Lawrence River. Railroad passenger trains and rail freight lines serve

City of Quebec

Quebec is the capital of the province of Quebec. It serves as an important shipping and manufacturing center. This map shows the southeastern section of the city, which includes Quebec's major points of interest.

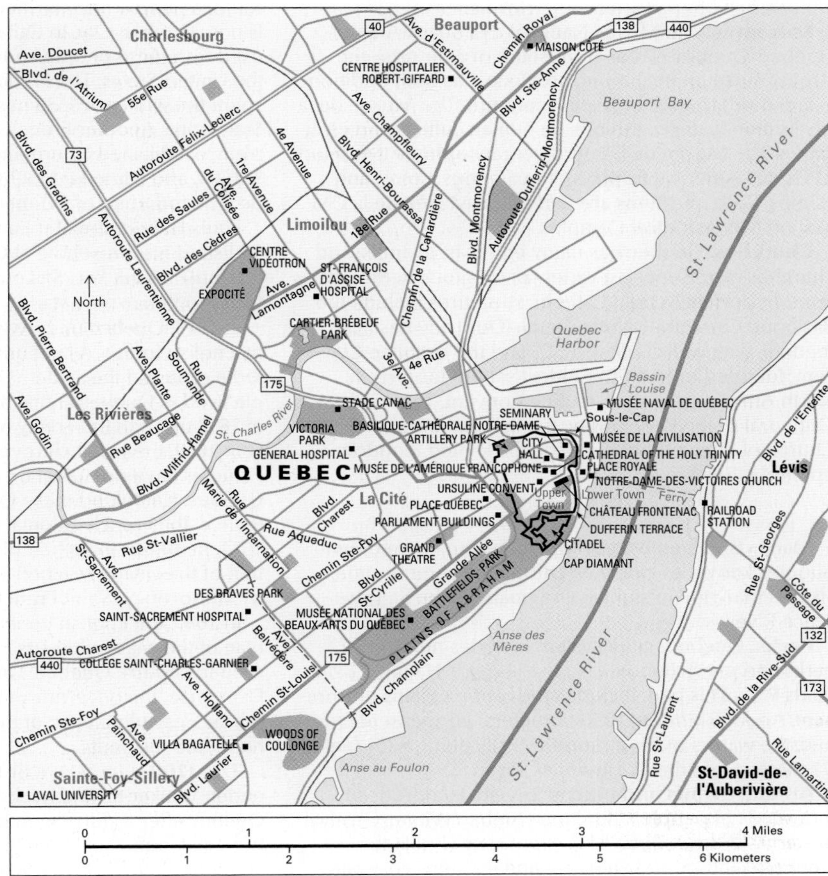

City boundary

Old city wall

Expressway

Main road

Other road

Railroad

Point of interest

Park

WORLD BOOK maps

the city. Commercial airlines use the Jean Lesage International Airport, which lies 10 miles (16 kilometers) west of the heart of the city. A public transit system provides local bus transportation.

Communication. Two daily French-language newspapers, *Le Journal de Québec* and *Le Soleil,* serve Quebec. The city has several radio and television stations, most of which broadcast in French. A few stations broadcast in English.

Education

Schools. The city of Quebec has both French-language public schools and English-language public schools. Université Laval (Laval University) and a campus of the University of Quebec are also in the city. Université Laval was founded in 1852.

Libraries. Quebec's public library system, the Bibliothèques de la Ville de Québec, has branches throughout the city. The libraries of the provincial legislature and Université Laval also have large collections of books.

Cultural life

The arts. Cultural activity in Quebec centers around the Grand Théâtre de Québec. The Orchestre Symphonique de Québec (Quebec Symphony Orchestra), the Opéra de Québec, and a local drama company perform there. In addition, the Capitole de Québec (Quebec Capitol) theater and the Palais Montcalm (Montcalm Palace) concert hall offer a variety of performances.

Museums. The Musée National des Beaux-Arts du Québec (Quebec National Museum of Fine Arts), the largest museum in Quebec province, has both traditional and modern paintings and sculpture. The Musée de la Civilisation features exhibits on human culture and civilization. The Musée de l'Amérique francophone (Museum of French America) displays old paintings, coins, and stamps. Both museums are part of the Musée de la Civilisation Museological Complex.

Churches. Quebec has many basilicas, chapels, and churches representing a variety of religious denominations. Important Roman Catholic structures include the Basilique-Cathédrale Notre-Dame (Our Lady Basilica-Cathedral), with walls built in 1647, and the Ursuline Convent, founded in 1639. The oldest school for girls in North America is at the Ursuline Convent. The Anglican Cathedral of the Holy Trinity, the first cathedral of the Church of England built outside the United Kingdom, opened in 1804.

Recreation

Many visitors enjoy touring Quebec in horse-drawn buggies known as *calèches.* During the summertime, visitors may ride in sightseeing boats on the St. Lawrence River.

Parks. Quebec's park system includes hundreds of parks and playgrounds. Also in the city is National Battlefields Park. This park includes the historic Plains of Abraham. About 6 ½ miles (10.5 kilometers) northeast of Quebec, the waters of Montmorency Falls plunge 251 feet (77 meters) into the St. Lawrence River.

Annual events and places to visit. Hundreds of thousands of people attend the Quebec Winter Carnival or Carnaval de Québec. This event lasts almost three weeks in January and February and includes costume balls, dog-sled and ice-canoe races, parades, and street dancing. The Festival D'Été de Québec (Quebec Summer Festival) in July features top performers from many parts of the world. The Grande Foire de Québec (Great Quebec Fair), a provincial fair held in August, features agricultural and industrial exhibits.

Many visitors attend the changing-the-guard ceremony that is held in the Citadel each summer day. During this colorful ceremony, soldiers from the Royal 22nd Regiment wear elaborate British uniforms and march to military music and commands.

Government

Quebec City has a mayor-council form of government. The people elect a mayor and 21 other members of the City Council, the city's legislative body. Borough councils provide local services in each of Quebec's six *boroughs* (administrative divisions). The Executive Committee makes decisions about city operations and prepares Quebec's annual budget and municipal bylaws. The committee consists of the mayor, two vice-chairs, and seven councilors. Taxes on businesses, property, and sales provide most of Quebec's revenue. Quebec also receives grants and loans from the federal and provincial governments.

History

Early days. Algonquian- and Iroquoian-speaking First Nations people once farmed and hunted in the area that is now Quebec City. In Canada, the term *First Nations* is used to refer to people known as Native Americans in the United States. The French explorer Jacques Cartier spent the winter of 1535 near the Iroquoian village of Stadacona. Another French explorer, Samuel de Champlain, established a permanent settlement there on July 3, 1608, and named it Quebec (see **Champlain, Samuel de** [The founding of Quebec]).

Louis Hébert, the first European to farm in Canada, established his household at Quebec in 1617. In 1620, Champlain built Fort St. Louis on the site where the Château Frontenac now stands.

In 1628, Quebec underwent the first of several attacks by English forces. A fleet under the command of David Kirke captured the settlement in 1629. Fewer than 60 people lived in Quebec at that time. France regained Quebec in 1632 through the Treaty of Saint-Germain-en-Laye.

In 1659, the Jesuit clergyman now known as Saint François Xavier de Laval de Montmorency arrived in Quebec. He helped make Quebec the center of New France, the French colonial empire in North America. In 1674, he became the first bishop of Quebec. The population of the village reached 547 in 1666. See **Laval de Montmorency, Saint François Xavier de.**

In 1690, the English general Sir William Phips, a Bostonian of the Massachusetts Bay Colony in New England, tried to capture Quebec. Louis de Buade, Comte de Frontenac, the governor general of New France, headed the successful defense of the city. At that time, Quebec had 1,500 residents.

The 1700's. In 1711, a British fleet under Admiral Hovenden Walker turned back from a planned attack on Quebec after a storm wrecked many of the ships on the Isle-aux-Oeufs reef in the St. Lawrence River. However, in September 1759, after a two-month siege, General

James Wolfe's British troops defeated French forces under the Marquise de Montcalm in the Battle of Quebec on the Plains of Abraham. The French surrendered Quebec five days later (see **Quebec, Battle of**). By 1760, the city's population had grown to 7,900. The Treaty of Paris, which ended the French and Indian War in 1763, gave Canada to the British.

In 1775, during the American Revolution, American troops led by General Richard Montgomery and Colonel Benedict Arnold attacked Quebec. They suffered a disastrous defeat on New Year's Eve. General Montgomery was killed during the invasion.

The British colonies of Upper and Lower Canada (now the southern parts of the provinces of Ontario and Quebec) were formed in 1791. Quebec City became the capital of Lower Canada at that time.

The 1800's. Through the years, Quebec City became increasingly important as an industrial port and a center of government. Business people took advantage of Quebec City's nearby forests and its river location and developed lumber and shipbuilding industries.

Quebec received a city charter in 1832. In 1841, Upper and Lower Canada united to form the Province of Canada. Quebec City twice served as capital of the Province of Canada, from 1851 to 1855 and from 1859 to 1865. When the Dominion of Canada was established in 1867, the area that had been Lower Canada became the province of Quebec. Quebec City was named the capital of the province. The city's population stood at almost 60,000 that year.

During the mid-1800's, the Montreal Harbour Commission deepened the St. Lawrence River from Quebec City to Montreal. As a result, Quebec City's importance as a port declined sharply. Montreal, closer to the heart of the continent and connected by canal and railroad to the Great Lakes, took much of Quebec City's trade. At about the same time, iron ships began replacing wooden vessels, which hurt Quebec's lumber and shipbuilding industries.

The 1900's. The early 1900's brought further industrialization to Quebec City. By 1911, Quebec City had 80,000 people. During World War I (1914-1918), the Canadian government enacted a military draft. Many people in Quebec City opposed the draft, and major riots broke out in the city in the spring of 1918. During World War II (1939-1945), Quebec City's factories expanded to manufacture war materials. The increased labor demand helped raise the population to 164,016 by 1951. Twice during the war, in 1943 and 1944, British Prime Minister Winston Churchill and United States President Franklin D. Roosevelt met in Quebec City. They conferred at the Château Frontenac and the Citadel about important war matters.

In 1970, the Quebec Urban Community was formed to deal with area problems and to promote tourism and industrial development. It consisted of Quebec City and 12 suburbs and had a council made up of mayors and other community representatives. In the early 1970's, Quebec City annexed four suburbs and its area increased from 8 square miles (21 square kilometers) to 34 square miles (89 square kilometers).

Since the 1970's, several hotels have been built in the area near the Parliament buildings. The city has become a popular convention destination. In 1996, a $125-million convention center was completed at Place Quebec, which is opposite the Parliament buildings. This project included a 600-room hotel and convention facilities.

In 1985, the Historic District of Old Quebec became the first urban district in Canada to be designated a UNESCO World Heritage Site. Such sites are places of unique cultural or natural importance, as designated by the United Nations Educational, Scientific and Cultural Organization.

The early 2000's. In January 2002, Quebec merged with 12 other communities to form an enlarged city of Quebec, which replaced the Quebec Urban Community. In January 2006, two of the merged communities—L'Ancienne-Lorette and Saint-Augustin-de-Desmaures—became separate municipalities. Before the 2002 expansion, Quebec City covered just 36 square miles (93 square kilometers). Following the 2006 demergers, it covered 175 square miles (454 square kilometers), its current area. Alan Gordon

See also **Champlain, Samuel de; French and Indian wars** (The French and Indian War); **Quebec** (province).

Quebec, *kwih BEHK,* **Battle of,** in 1759, helped bring an end to the French empire in North America. The Treaty of Paris of 1763 gave almost all French territory in what is now eastern Canada and in the region east of the Mississippi River to Britain (now the United Kingdom).

About 2 million British colonists were living along the eastern seaboard of North America when the Seven Years' War began in Europe in 1756 (see **Seven Years' War**). About 60,000 French lived in North America, mostly in what is now eastern Canada. Skirmishes between the British and French occurred for two years before war actually broke out. The British wanted to expand westward, but a chain of French forts west of the Appalachian Mountains blocked their move. In 1755, the British began an unsuccessful campaign to expel the French from these forts. The French responded by encouraging their American Indian allies to raid the frontiers of the British colonies. In 1756, the Marquis de Montcalm took command of French troops and began a successful assault on Britain's major American forts. He captured Fort Oswego in 1756 and Fort William Henry in 1757. In 1758, Montcalm overwhelmingly defeated a larger British force that had attacked Fort Ticonderoga.

In 1758, however, the British seized Louisbourg, a fortress on Cape Breton Island that was the center of French power in the area. The British assembled a huge fleet of ships and set sail for the city of Quebec in May 1759. The 250 ships carried 8,000 soldiers under the command of General James Wolfe.

Bombardment of Quebec. The strongly fortified city stood on heights dominating the St. Lawrence River. Montcalm defended Quebec with about 14,000 soldiers. British troops landed on the Île d'Orléans, 5 miles (8 kilometers) east of Quebec, in June. Other forces occupied Pointe Lévis on the south bank. For nearly a month, the British and French exchanged fire, with no results. On July 31, Wolfe launched an attack on Beauport, on the north shore east of Quebec, opposite Pointe Lévis. Under Montcalm and General François de Lévis, French, French Canadian, and American Indian soldiers repelled the British forces.

In August and September, Wolfe's men burned the towns and farms beneath Quebec to force Montcalm to initiate an attack. But Montcalm himself refused to engage in battle. With the winter approaching, Wolfe decided to strike from the Plains of Abraham, a plateau west of the city. Starting on September 1, Wolfe's soldiers moved upriver in naval vessels and on foot.

The attack on Quebec began during the cloudy, calm night of Sept. 12-13, 1759. The tide bore British flatboats to the Anse au Foulon, a bay from which a path rose steeply to the Plains of Abraham. One boatload of men climbed silently and surprised an enemy guard. By dawn, about 4,500 British regulars were ranged for battle. Montcalm had expected an attack at Beauport. He quickly moved about 4,000 troops to meet the enemy. They arrived around 10 o'clock that morning.

The French advanced too quickly and began firing at long range, with little effect. The British held their fire until the French were within 120 feet (37 meters). Then the British fired, reloaded, fired again, and charged with bayonets and swords. The French retreated in disorder. Wolfe was mortally wounded in the first shots. Montcalm, who had been trying to rally his men, was wounded about the same time. His soldiers took him back to Quebec, where he died the next day. The Battle of Quebec had lasted just 15 minutes. Jean-Baptiste Ramezay, the king's lieutenant at Quebec, surrendered Quebec to General George Townshend on September 18.

The French nearly recaptured Quebec in April 1760, when they defeated the British at Sainte Foy, near the previous battle site. However, France failed to regain Quebec because the last of its Atlantic fleet had been destroyed in 1759, at the Battle of Quiberon Bay on the French coast. Without naval reinforcements, the French retreated to Montreal, where they surrendered to the British in September 1760. The Treaty of Paris reduced all French possessions in North America to two small islands off the coast of Newfoundland, St.-Pierre and Miquelon. In 1908, the sites of the battles of Quebec and Sainte Foy became the National Battlefields Park.

Fred W. Anderson

Related articles in ***World Book*** include:

Acadia	Montcalm, Marquis de
Canada, History of (picture)	Murray, James
French and Indian wars (The French and Indian War)	Wolfe, James

Quebec, University of, called the Université du Québec in French, is Canada's largest university network. It includes universities based in Gatineau, Montreal, Rimouski, Rouyn-Noranda, Saguenay, and Trois-Rivières. It also includes the National Institute for Scientific Research and the National School of Public Administration, both based in Quebec City, and the School of Higher Technology in Montreal. All courses are in French. The Tele-University, part of the University of Quebec at Montreal, offers distance learning programs. The government of Quebec established the University of Quebec system in 1968. Its administrative offices are in Quebec City. Critically reviewed by the University of Quebec

Quebec Act, *kwih BEHK,* was a law passed by Britain (now also called the United Kingdom) in 1774 to calm tensions in Quebec. At that time, Quebec, though a British colony, had a largely French, Roman Catholic population. The act formally granted political rights and religious freedom to Catholic French Canadians in the colony.

After the Seven Years' War (1756-1763), Britain had taken control of Quebec from France. During the next 10 years, cultural and political tensions developed as the British attempted to bring Quebec under British laws. These laws severely limited the rights of Catholics. The Quebec Act retained British criminal law but guaranteed the use of French civil law in Quebec. It restored to the Catholic clergy in Quebec rights and privileges they had enjoyed when Quebec was a French colony. In addition, it enlarged Quebec to include much of present-day Ontario, Quebec, and the midwestern United States.

The Quebec Act angered many British colonists in both Quebec and the 13 American Colonies. British merchants in Quebec felt persecuted by the act. American colonial leaders felt that it was an assault on American freedoms and rights. The Quebec Act became known as one of the Intolerable Acts (see **Intolerable Acts**), which the Americans used to help justify the American Revolution (1775-1783). John C. Walsh

Quebec Conference, *kwih BEHK,* was a meeting at which Canadian leaders proposed a plan for forming a united Canada. It was held in the city of Quebec from Oct. 10 to Oct. 27, 1864. At that time, eastern Canada consisted of five self-governing colonies of the United Kingdom—the Province of Canada, New Brunswick, Newfoundland, Nova Scotia, and Prince Edward Island. The Hudson's Bay Company, a fur-trading firm, controlled most of western Canada. British Columbia and Vancouver Island were two British colonies on the Pacific coast.

Three chief factors made union desirable: (1) The United Kingdom felt that Canadians could better defend themselves if they united. (2) Union could aid economic growth. (3) Union might help end friction between Canada's French- and English-speaking groups.

The delegates to the Quebec Conference, now called the Fathers of Confederation, proposed a federal union of all the eastern colonies under a central government. They also made provision for future admission of the western territories. Within two years, the Province of Canada, New Brunswick, and Nova Scotia agreed to the plan. The Province of Canada was divided into the provinces of Quebec and Ontario. Quebec, Ontario, New Brunswick, and Nova Scotia were the provinces when the British North America Act formed the Dominion of Canada on July 1, 1867. José António Brandão

See also **Confederation of Canada.**

Quechan Indians, *kweh CHAHN,* also called the Yuma Indians, live along the Colorado River in southeastern California and southwestern Arizona. Traditionally, the Quechan lived in villages, in airy houses made from branches or reeds plastered with mud. They cultivated corn, beans, squash, and melons in the fertile soils created by the flooding each spring of the Colorado River. They also fished; gathered wild beans, seeds, and nuts; and made pottery and baskets. Dreams played an important role in their religion.

About 1540, Spanish explorers probably became the first white people to encounter the Quechan. In 1780, the Spanish built two settlements in Quechan territory, near what is now Winterhaven, California. To protect their homeland, the Quechan attacked and destroyed the settlements in 1781. For years, the Quechan remained independent of government control. But in 1852, the United States Army established Fort Yuma, also near what is now Winterhaven. In 1884, the U.S. government set up the Fort Yuma Reservation, and the Indians agreed to live there. The reservation lies in California and Arizona and includes the sites of the destroyed settlements and of the fort. Today, Quechan living on the reservation grow large amounts of vegetables for sale.

Victoria D. Patterson

Queen, the insect. See **Ant** (Life in an ant colony); **Bee; Insect** (Family life); **Termite.**

Queen is the title of a woman who rules a kingdom in her own right, or who is the wife of a king. If she rules in her own right, she is called a *queen regnant.* She has the same powers that a king would have, depending on the constitution of the country she rules.

If the queen is the wife of the king, she is called a *queen consort.* The mother of the ruling monarch is the *queen mother,* and the widow of a king is a *queen dowager.* Each of these queens has her own household. But none can exercise any official power in the government.

Kings or queens of the United Kingdom and other constitutional monarchies have few powers of government. But they can refuse the advice of the prime minister, and they can influence public opinion.

Robert E. Dowse

For names of queens, see names of individuals; for example, **Elizabeth II.** See also **Coronation; King; Prince consort; Royal Household of the United Kingdom.**

Queen, Ellery, was the pen name of two cousins, Frederic Dannay and Manfred B. Lee, who became successful detective-story writers. Ellery Queen is also the name of their chief fictional character. They also published under the name of Barnaby Ross.

Lee was born on Jan. 11, 1905, and Dannay was born on Oct. 20, 1905. They were both born in New York City. They became full-time writers soon after they won a detective-story contest in 1928. The story became their first Ellery Queen novel, *The Roman Hat Mystery* (1929). The early Ellery Queen novels especially are great examples of the cleverly plotted mystery puzzle. In 1941, Dannay and Lee founded *Ellery Queen's Mystery Magazine,* which publishes original detective fiction and reprints detective fiction classics. As editor and anthologist, Ellery Queen made a major contribution to the popularity of mystery fiction in the United States. Lee died on April 3, 1971. Dannay died on Sept. 3, 1982. David Geherin

Queen Anne's lace. See **Wild carrot.**

Queen Charlotte Islands. See **Haida Gwaii.**

Queens. See **New York City** (The city; Queens).

Queensland is Australia's second largest state in area. Western Australia is the largest. Queensland occupies the entire northeastern part of the continent. The Great Barrier Reef is one of the wonders of Queensland. It is the largest group of coral reefs in the world. Queensland is known as Australia's *Sunshine State* because of its pleasantly warm winters and long hours of sunshine. Brisbane is its capital and largest city (see **Brisbane**).

Land and climate. The eastern section of Queensland is rugged and mountainous. The Great Dividing Range runs in a north-south direction through this section. The state's highest peak is 5,287-foot (1,611-meter) Mount Bartle Frere. For detailed maps, see **Australia.**

Most of Queensland's rivers flow south and west from the Great Dividing Range. Cooper Creek and the Diamantina River flow southwest to Lake Eyre in central Australia. Dense forests cover the state's coastal mountain ranges. Mangrove thickets, where the spreading roots of mangrove trees catch and hold soil, occur along the coast.

Farther south, the Warrego and Condamine rivers flow southward and join the Darling River in New South Wales. Forests, including subtropical rain forests, grow on the mountain slopes of southern Queensland. Central and western Queensland have vast grazing areas. *Artesian wells,* which tap ground water that is under pressure, provide this region with water for livestock (see **Artesian well**).

Temperatures in Queensland average 65 °F (18 °C) in July and 90 °F (32 °C) in January. Rainfall on the eastern coast is heavy, especially in the north, where it averages 160 inches (406 centimeters) a year. In the extreme west, as little as 6 inches (15 centimeters) of rain falls in a year.

People. The 2016 Australian census reported that Queensland had 4,703,793 people. Most of Queensland's people were born in Australia, New Zealand, or the United Kingdom. About half of the people live in the capital, Brisbane. Gold Coast is Queensland's second largest city. Aboriginal and Torres Strait Islander people make up about 4 percent of the state's population.

Primary school education is free and compulsory. There are 10 universities in Queensland. The University of Queensland, the oldest university in the state, began holding classes in Brisbane in 1911. Various technical and secondary schools receive government support.

Economy. Queensland depends on mining and agriculture for much of its wealth. The chief crops include sugar cane and cereal crops such as sorghum and wheat. Many kinds of tropical fruits thrive on the coast. Apples, citrus fruits, cotton, grapes, peanuts, and tomatoes are also grown. The state raises about half of Australia's beef cattle. Sheep raising is also important.

Queensland is rich in bauxite, coal, copper, gemstones, magnesite, natural gas, petroleum, silver, and tin. Queensland manufactures aluminum; chemicals; fabri-

© Australian Picture Library

Queensland has a booming cattle industry. The state raises about half of Australia's beef cattle, mostly on large cattle ranches called *stations,* such as Tonkoro Station, *shown here.*

cated metal products; food products, including meat and processed sugar; and machinery.

WORLD BOOK map
Location of Queensland

Government. The British monarch, on the advice of the Queensland government, appoints a governor as the chief executive for the state. This position is largely ceremonial, however. The state Parliament has most of the governing power in Queensland. The Parliament has a single assembly consisting of 93 members who serve four-year terms. The governor has an Executive Council made up of the ministers of government departments. In Queensland, as in the rest of Australia, all citizens 18 years of age or older must vote.

History. The English navigator James Cook explored the coast of Queensland in 1770 and took possession of the region, calling it New South Wales. The first settlement in Queensland was a *penal* (prison) colony, established on Moreton Bay in 1824. After 1840, free settlers began to establish farms and settlements in Queensland.

Queensland was a part of New South Wales until 1859, when it became a separate colony. In 1867, the discovery of gold brought a rush of immigrants to Queensland. In January 1901, Queensland and the other Australian colonies became states when they united to form the Commonwealth of Australia. Desmond Houghton

See also **Daintree rain forest; Great Barrier Reef.**

Quemoy, *kih MOY,* is the name of a group of islands about 5 miles (8 kilometers) off the coast of China, in the Taiwan Strait. Quemoy is also the name of the largest island in the group. The Chinese call this island Kinmen, also spelled *Jinmen.* For the location of Quemoy, see **Taiwan** (map).

The Quemoy islands have a population of about 139,000 and an area of 59 square miles (152 square kilometers). The Chinese Nationalist government continued to control the islands after the Chinese Communists conquered mainland China in 1949. The Chinese Communists bombarded the islands with artillery fire in 1954 and 1958. Occasional shelling, first with explosive shells and then in the 1970's with shells that dropped propaganda leaflets, continued until an official cease-fire was announced in 1979. Parris H. Chang

Querétaro, *keh REHT uh roh,* is a state in central Mexico. One of the country's smaller states in area, it covers 4,420 square miles (11,449 square kilometers). At the time of the 2020 census, Querétaro had a population of 2,368,467. The state capital is also named Querétaro. The northeastern part of the state lies in the Sierra Madre Oriental mountain range, and the southwestern part is in Mexico's Central Plateau region. Most of Querétaro has a *temperate* (moderate) and dry climate, with seasonal rainfall from June to October.

Querétaro has a diverse economy. Industries in the state produce automobile parts, paper, processed foods, and textiles. Agriculture contributes significantly to the economy, and tourism also generates some revenue. Northern Querétaro has mines that produce gold, opals, silver, and other metals.

The Otomí Indians lived in what is now Querétaro before Spain colonized the area in the 1500's. Today, the state is home to their descendants. The Otomí founded the capital city before the Spaniards arrived. Querétaro became one of the original states of Mexico in 1824. Emperor Maximilian, who ruled Mexico from 1864 to 1867, established his court in the capital during the final year of his reign. The Mexican Constitution of 1917 was drafted at a convention in Querétaro city. In 1929, the capital hosted the first convention of the National Revolutionary Party. This party, now known as the Institutional Revolutionary Party (Partido Revolucionario Institucional, or PRI), governed Mexico continuously for 70 years.

Jürgen Buchenau

Quesnay, *keh NAY,* **François,** *frahn SWAH* (1694-1774), was a French economist who made some of the earliest contributions to the development of economics. He headed a group of economic writers called the *physiocrats.* The physiocrats believed that natural laws direct economic activity, and they tried to discover these laws. They devised early forms of economic *models,* charts or sets of formulas showing the relationships between various parts of a nation's economy.

Quesnay developed the idea that wealth flows continuously between producers and consumers. He and his followers considered land the only source of wealth. Only agriculture, they believed, could yield products of greater value than the resources used for production. In a chart called the *Tableau Économique* (1758), Quesnay traced the relationships between different economic classes, such as farmers and merchants. He showed how the wealth created by agricultural production circulates throughout the economy.

Quesnay was born on June 4, 1694, in Méré, France, near Paris. Before taking up economics, he studied medicine and served as the personal physician of King Louis XV of France. Quesnay died on Dec. 16, 1774.

Barry W. Poulson

See also **Physiocrats.**

Question mark. See **Punctuation.**

Quetzal, *keht SAHL,* is a brilliantly colored bird of Central and South America. There are several *species* (kinds) of quetzals. The head, back, and chest of the resplendent quetzal of Central America are glittering emerald-green. The underparts are crimson. The head has a wide crest of golden-green, hairlike feathers. The upper tail feathers are enormously developed and form a train about 2 feet (61 centimeters) long. The brown and buff-colored female has no long tail feathers. The quetzal's feet are small and weak. The bird sits quietly for long periods on a perch in dense forest. The quetzal builds its nest in a hole in a tree.

Ancient Maya chiefs used the long tail feathers of the quetzal as a symbol of authority. One of the legends about this bird says that it loves freedom too much to survive captivity. The quetzal is the national bird of Guatemala, and the bird appears on that nation's coat of arms. John W. Fitzpatrick

Scientific classification. Quetzals are in the trogon family, Trogonidae. The resplendent quetzal is *Pharomacrus mocinno.*

See also **Bird** (picture: Birds of Central and South America).

Quetzalcóatl. See **Aztec** (Religion); **Mythology** (Aztec mythology; picture); **Orozco, José Clemente** (picture).

Quevedo, *kay VAY doh,* **Francisco de** (1580-1645), was the leading Spanish humanist of the 1600's. He wrote extensively on social, political, religious, and aesthetic problems of Spanish Renaissance life. His works include *Life of the Swindler* (written about 1605 and published in 1626), a cruelly ironic picaresque novel; *Visions* (1627), a satirical prose portrait of Spanish society; and hundreds of poems on moral and sentimental themes.

Quevedo expressed his political beliefs in the *Politics of God* (1626) and other works. He modeled his beliefs on the life and teachings of Jesus Christ and contrasted them with the harsh realities of Spanish court intrigue. Quevedo's theological and philosophical essays generally reflect an ascetic and stoic point of view.

Quevedo was born in Madrid on Sept. 17, 1580. His bitter satires caused him much personal trouble. He was jailed from 1639 to 1643 as the supposed author of verses ridiculing corruption in the court of King Philip IV. Quevedo died on Sept. 8, 1645. Harry Sieber

Quezon City, *KAY sawn* (pop. 2,936,116), is the largest city in the Philippines. It lies just northeast of Manila. For location, see **Philippines** (map). The city is named for Manuel Luis Quezon, first president of the Commonwealth of the Philippines. As a whole, Quezon City has one of the lowest poverty levels in the Philippines. The Ateneo de Manila University and the main campus of the University of the Philippines are in the city.

The Philippine government purchased the land where Quezon City now stands in 1939. The land was part of a private estate and was bought chiefly to serve as a residential area. Many Filipinos moved to the city from Manila after World War II ended in 1945. In 1948, the government officially transferred the capital from Manila to Quezon City. But Manila again became the official capital in 1976.

Quezon City is part of the Manila metropolitan area, which in turn is part of the National Capital Region. Several federal government agencies are in Quezon City.

James Putzel

Quicksand is a soft mass of wet sand that yields easily to pressure. It usually forms on the bottoms of streams and on sand flats along seacoasts. Quicksand behaves like a fluid because water flowing through the sand grains forces them apart and prevents them from settling. In this *quick* condition, the sand loses its firmness and cannot support heavy weight. Thick layers of quicksand can trap and even kill people or animals that sink into them.

People caught in deep quicksand must remain calm. They should fall flat on their back with arms stretched out at right angles to the body. In this position, the body should float on the sand. The person should roll slowly off the area of quicksand to firm ground. Mark Cloos

Quicksilver. See **Mercury** [element].

Quill. See **Feather; Pen; Porcupine.**

Quillwort. See **Plant** (Lycophytes).

Quilt is a cloth bedcover. A quilt consists of two layers of cloth filled with an *interlining* of a soft, insulating material, such as cotton, down, or wool. The layers are fastened by tiny stitches that run in plain rows or in decorative designs. Many beautifully decorated quilts are considered outstanding examples of folk art.

The top layer of a quilt is often decorated with colorful geometric forms or pictures of animals, buildings, people, and plants. Designs may commemorate historic events or important family occasions. A quilt design can be created in several ways. In a *pieced quilt,* the top layer consists of many different pieces of cloth sewed together in a design. An *appliquéd quilt* has cutout designs sewed onto one large piece of cloth (see **Appliqué**). *Cord quilts* and *trapunto-stuffed quilts* feature a raised design that is made by cotton cording or padding inserted between the top and bottom layers of cloth.

Baltimore Album Quilt (about 1847-1850); the Baltimore Museum of Art, gift of Dr. William Rush Dunton, Jr., Baltimore

An appliquéd quilt has cutout designs sewed onto a large piece of cloth. This one, made in Maryland, has an embroidered picture of Baltimore's Washington Monument in the third row.

The technique of quilting originated in prehistoric times. Quilting in the United States began during colonial days, when immigrants began practicing the quilting skills they learned in Europe. Quilters frequently made quilts together at social gatherings that were called *bees.*

Colonial quilters mainly made pieced quilts from scraps of linen and wool they saved because cloth was scarce. During the 1800's, a variety of cotton materials became readily available and quilting developed into an art form. During the mid-1800's, *album quilts* became popular. Many album quilts bear verses, quotations, and the quilters' signatures in needlework or ink. These quilts were often presented as gifts to a guest of honor at a quilting bee. *Crazy quilts* were popular in the late 1800's. Most often, they consisted of randomly placed pieces of silk of various sizes, colors, and shapes. Traditional patterns were also used.

Today, quilting styles have been revived by needlework artists who often gather to exchange ideas and practice their craft. Quilters still use traditional patterns and techniques, but with a fresh approach that produces unusual designs. Dena S. Katzenberg

Quince, *kwihns,* is a type of attractive shrub or small tree that is closely related to apple and pear trees. The common quince has numerous large, pinkish-white flowers and twisted branches. Its fragrant, fuzzy fruit is round to pear-shaped and is golden-yellow. The fruit grows up to 3 inches (7.6 centimeters) in diameter and bears many seeds in its core. Botanists call this type of fruit a *pome.* The fruit of the common quince is hard, has an acid taste, and is almost never eaten fresh. It is used in marmalades and jellies, often in combination with other fruits.

The common quince can be grown from cuttings or by *grafting* (joining) a quince seedling to another plant. Buds from pear trees sometimes are grafted to quince rootstocks to produce dwarf pear trees (see **Pear** [Raising pears]). The common quince has been cultivated since ancient times and was originally grown in central Asia. It is rarely grown commercially in the United States.

Eric Crichton, Bruce Coleman Ltd.

The hard, golden-yellow quince puckers the mouth when tasted raw, but it has a delightful flavor when it is cooked.

Another type of quince, the Japanese *flowering quince,* is a thorny shrub with showy red blossoms. It bears a sour fruit that grows up to 1 ½ inches (3.8 centimeters) in diameter. John A. Barden

Scientific classification. Quinces belong to the rose family, Rosaceae. The common quince is *Cydonia oblonga.* The flowering quince is *Chaenomeles japonica.*

Quinceañera, *keen say ah NYAIR ah,* is a coming-of-age celebration for girls around their 15th birthday. It is celebrated in many Latin American countries, including Colombia, Cuba, Ecuador, Guatemala, Mexico, and Peru; and in Puerto Rico and among Latino American communities in the United States.

The term *quinceañera* comes from the Spanish words for *fifteen* and *years.* Many historians believe the quinceañera tradition originated in ancient Aztec society. During the 1500's, following the Spanish conquest of Mexico and Central America, the ancient ritual was adapted to Christianity. The tradition grew in popularity throughout Latin America during the 1800's.

Quinceañera customs vary somewhat among countries. The celebration typically is structured much like a wedding. It has both religious and nonreligious elements. For the ceremony, the honored girl, who is also called the quinceañera, is dressed in formal adult attire, such as a ball gown, and attended by several *damas* (female attendants) and *chambelanes* (young male escorts). Together, they walk up the aisle of a church and celebrate a special service, often a Mass of thanksgiving, with family and friends. During the ceremony, the quinceañera is presented with symbolic gifts from her parents and selected *padrinos* (godparents). Gifts often include a Bible, a rosary, a *tiara* (small crown), and jewelry that has religious significance.

Several other rituals are performed at a banquet or party that follows the religious ceremony. Some of the activities include a formal dance by the quinceañera and her father, followed by a group dance with her damas and chambelanes. In some places, it is also customary for the quinceañera to receive her symbolic last doll, and to change into a pair of high-heeled shoes. All of these rituals and gifts emphasize the quinceañera's change in status from a girl into a *señorita* (young woman), and acknowledge her as an adult member of the community. Cesáreo Moreno

See also **Rite of passage.**

Quinine, *KWY nyn* or *kwih NEEN,* is a drug made from the bark of the cinchona tree. Quinine was once the only known treatment for malaria. It reduces the fever of malaria, and, especially when used with other drugs, can cure some types of the disease.

Beginning in the mid-1940's, when supplies of quinine became scarce because of World War II (1939-1945), synthetic drugs, such as chloroquine, mefloquine, and primaquine, were developed to treat malaria. These drugs are generally less dangerous to use than quinine. However, in Southeast Asia and many other regions, types of malaria have developed that are resistant to synthetic drugs. As a result, physicians in those areas are again using quinine. They have found that quinine can help save the lives of people infected with multidrug-resistant forms of the disease.

Quinine is also used to relieve nighttime leg cramps. Many physicians prescribe the drug *quinidine* to treat and correct certain disorders of heart rhythm. Quinidine has the same chemical formula as quinine and differs from quinine only in the way its atoms are arranged. Physicians believe that both drugs, particularly quinine, may cause abnormalities in unborn children. For this reason, pregnant women should not take quinine and quinidine without first consulting a physician.

Cinchona trees first grew along the eastern slopes of the Andes Mountains in South America. In the early 1600's, Spanish explorers and missionaries found that the American Indians of the region used the bark of the trees as medicine.

The trees began to die out during the mid-1800's, but other cinchona trees were planted in India and Indonesia, especially Java. Most of the quinine used today comes from Indonesia. Frank Welsch

See also **Alkaloid; Cinchona; Malaria** (Treatment and prevention).

Quinoa, *KEE noh ah* or *KEEN wah,* is a grain plant native to the Andes Mountains of South America. For centuries, quinoa has been one of the chief foods of Andean Indians. It has been called the "mother grain" of the Inca because of its importance to the ancient Inca civilization. Most quinoa is still grown in South America, though it was introduced into the United States during the 1980's.

Quinoa is typically cultivated at high elevations. It requires cool temperatures and grows well in relatively poor soil. The quinoa grows from 3 to 6 feet (0.9 to 1.8 meters) tall. It bears large clusters of seeds at the tips of its stalks. The leaves of the quinoa are shaped like a goose's foot.

Quinoa seeds are cooked and eaten whole like rice. They may be ground into flour and made into breads, tortillas, and pastas. The seeds also may be popped like corn or added raw to soups and hot breakfast cereals. The leaves of the quinoa are cooked and eaten like spinach. They also may be used as feed for livestock. Both the seeds and the leaves of the quinoa are rich in protein and other nutrients. Stephen G. Diver

Scientific classification. The scientific name of the quinoa plant is *Chenopodium quinoa.*

Quintana Roo, *keen tahn uh ROH,* is a state on the Yucatán Peninsula in southeastern Mexico. Quintana Roo covers 19,387 square miles (50,212 square kilometers). At the time of the 2020 census, the population was 1,857,985. Most of Quintana Roo's people live in a few coastal cities. The capital is Chetumal (formerly Payo Obispo).

For many years, the state economy was based on agriculture and fishing. In the 1970's, the Mexican government launched a campaign to promote tourism. Today, many tourists visit the Riviera Maya, a strip of hotels and resorts along the state's Caribbean coast. Clear, warm water and extensive coral reefs have made the Riviera a popular destination for snorkelers and scuba divers. The southern part of the state has many impressive ruins from the Maya civilization. Inland from the coast, agriculture is the chief economic activity.

The area that is now Quintana Roo was once part of the state of Yucatán. In 1847, a Maya peasant rebellion known as the Caste War broke out in Yucatán. Thousands of rebels fled to the forests and coastal areas of what is now Quintana Roo. The rebels established the town of Chan Santa Cruz (present-day Felipe Carrillo Puerto). Over time, they spread to smaller villages. They controlled the area until 1901, and it became a territory of Mexico in 1902. The government named the territory after Andrés Quintana Roo, a Yucatán-born statesman who supported Mexican independence. In 1974, the territory became a state. Terry Rugeley

Quintuplets are five babies born to the same mother at one time. See **Multiple birth.**

Quirinal Hill, *KWIHR uh nuhl,* is the northernmost of the famous seven hills of Rome. It was named for the god Quirinus. Evidence of the ancient settlement of the Sabines has been found on this hill. There were many famous temples on the hill, including the oldest shrine of the god Jupiter. Julius Caesar had large gardens on the edge of the hill, and the emperor Constantine built a famous public bath there. In the A.D. 1500's, a large palace and garden were built on the hill for the Roman Catholic popes. These were later used by the kings of Italy. The palace now serves as the official residence and offices of the president of the Italian Republic. David I. Kertzer

See also **Sabines.**

Quirinus. See **Mythology** (Roman divinities).

Quisling, *KWIHZ lihng,* **Vidkun** (1887-1945), was a Norwegian traitor of World War II (1939-1945). The word *quisling* came to stand for *traitor* because of his aid to German occupation forces.

Vidkun Abraham Lauritz Jonssøn Quisling was born on July 18, 1887, in Fyresdal, Norway. He served in Norway's army and its diplomatic corps. From 1931 to 1933, he was minister of defense. In 1933, Quisling formed the National Unity Party, a political party modeled on Germany's Nazi Party.

When Germany invaded Norway in 1940, Quisling briefly assumed power. The Germans took control of the Norwegian government, and in 1942 they installed Quisling as a puppet leader. After the war, he was convicted on charges of treason. Quisling was executed on Oct. 24, 1945. Norman J. W. Goda

Quito, *KEE toh,* is the capital of the Republic of Ecuador. The municipality of Quito has a population of 1,607,734. A municipality may include rural areas as well as the urban center. The city lies almost on the equator, 9,350 feet (2,850 meters) above sea level in the Andes Mountains. For location, see **Ecuador** (map).

The name *Quito* comes from the word *Quitus,* the name of an ancient people who lived in Ecuador. The Inca civilization established a regional capital at what is now Quito, but the city fell to Spanish conquerors in 1534. The Spaniards ruled Quito until 1822. During colonial times, the Quito region prospered as a center for weaving and the production of ponchos. But the textile industry collapsed during a wave of epidemics in the 1690's. Colonial Quito also functioned as a center for trading and shipping agricultural products, for religious activity by the Roman Catholic Church, and as the seat of colonial government for what is now Ecuador. In addition, the city was a great center of religious art in a tradition known as the Quito School, which combined indigenous and European characteristics. In 1822, General Antonio José de Sucre defeated the Spaniards in the Battle of Pichincha on a mountain slope overlooking Quito. The victory helped Ecuador secure its independence from Spain.

Isolated in the Andes Mountains, Quito developed a culture distinct from other parts of Ecuador. The city tends to be more conservative and traditional than coastal locations such as the international port of Guayaquil. Beginning in the 1950's, Latin America experienced great population growth, and many migrants have flooded into Quito. A more modern section has developed north of the colonial city center. Many recent

Shostal

Quito lies high in the Andes Mountains. The city's skyline is a blend of old tile-roofed buildings and modern skyscrapers.

immigrants live in poor neighborhoods surrounding the Quito area. Ronn Pineo

See also **Ecuador** (picture).

Quixote, Don. See **Don Quixote.**

Quoll is a small, spotted mammal that lives in the forests of New Guinea and Australia, including Tasmania. Quolls are *marsupials*—that is, the females give birth to extremely immature young that complete their development attached to the mother's nipples. There are several *species* (kinds) of quolls.

Quolls have brown or black fur with white spots. The *tiger quoll,* the largest meat-eating marsupial on the Australian continent, grows up to 4 feet (1.2 meters) long, including the tail. The animal may weigh more than 13 pounds (6 kilograms). Quolls eat chiefly insects but also feed on birds, mice, and small lizards.

The female quoll normally has five to eight young, which attach themselves firmly to nipples within a pouch on her belly. The young leave the pouch after about three or four months. However, they may cling to the mother's fur for a few more weeks. Quolls are threatened by destruction of their habitat and by introduced species, such as the cane toad. Michael L. Augee

Scientific classification. Quolls make up the genus *Dasyurus.*

WORLD BOOK illustration by Colin Newman, Bernard Thornton Artists

The eastern quoll lives in forests in the southeastern part of mainland Australia and on the island of Tasmania.

Quorum. See **Parliamentary procedure** (Holding meetings).

Quota system. See **Immigration** (Immigration to the United States).

Qur'ān, *ku RAHN* or *ku RAN,* is the sacred book of the Muslims. It is also spelled *Quran* or *Koran.* The name *Qur'ān* means *a recitation* or *something to be recited,* presumably in worship.

Muslims believe the angel Gabriel revealed the Qur'ān to the Prophet Muhammad a little at a time. The revelations began about A.D. 610 and continued until Muhammad's death in 632. Muhammad's followers, who wrote down the revelations, collected them into the book that is now known as the Qur'ān. The standard text of the Qur'ān was formed during the reign of the *caliph* (leader) Uthmān ibn Affān, who ruled from 644 to 656. Muslims consider the Qur'ān to be the words of God, and in no sense the composition of Muhammad. They believe that the earthly book, bound between covers, is a copy of an eternal book that is kept in heaven.

The Qur'ān consists of verses grouped into 114 chapters. The chapters vary in length from a few lines to over 200 verses. Much of the Qur'ān is written in rhymed Arabic prose. Muslims believe that the rich, forceful language of the text is humanly unmatchable, and a miracle that confirms Muhammad's prophethood.

Teachings. The central teaching of the Qur'ān is that there is only one God. The word for God in Arabic is *Allah.* Allah is the creator of the universe and requires *Islam* (submission) to himself. Allah, in his mercy, sent the Qur'ān as a guide for humanity. Another important teaching concerns the prophets who have been God's messengers to different peoples. The Qur'ān mentions the prophets Abraham, Moses, Jesus, and many others. It describes Muhammad as the last of the prophets.

The Qur'ān speaks of a day of judgment when people shall stand before God to account for their lives. It contains many teachings to regulate Muslim daily life. It requires daily prayers, and stresses charity and brotherly love among Muslims. The Qur'ān teaches that one should be humble, temperate, brave, and just.

Influence. The Qur'ān is one of the most widely read books in the world. Its teachings formed the basis of the great Islamic civilization of the past, and it guides and inspires millions of Muslims. The Qur'ān is the final authority in matters of faith and practice for all Muslims. It is the highest authority for Islamic law.

Most Muslims have been taught and have memorized at least parts of the Qur'ān. Thus, even illiterate Muslims possess and prize the text. The reverence for the holy book is so great that many Muslims learn the entire work by heart. People have preserved and passed on the art of properly reciting the Qur'ān through the years.

For hundreds of years, Muslims refused to translate the Qur'ān into other languages. They thought they should preserve the words of God in their original form. But in the early 1900's, Muslims began to translate the Qur'ān into Eastern and Western languages.

Richard C. Martin

See also **Islam; Muhammad.**

Qutb, *KOO tuhb,* **Sayyid,** *SAH yihd* or *SAY yihd* (1906-1966), was an Egyptian scholar, writer, and activist. He followed a strict approach to Islam and rejected modern interpretations of Islamic law. Qutb believed that all laws governing human life must be based in God's word as revealed by the Qur'ān, the sacred book of Islam. Qutb condemned governments and societies that did not function in strict agreement with Islamic teaching. He wrote that Muslims had a duty to wage *jihad* (holy war) against enemies of what he considered true Islam.

Most Muslim scholars regard Qutb's ideas as extreme and not representative of mainstream Muslim thought. Since Qutb's death, however, his ideas have influenced radical Islamic organizations in Afghanistan, Egypt, the Palestinian territories of the Gaza Strip and West Bank, and elsewhere.

Qutb was born on Oct. 8, 1906, in the village of Musha, near Asyut, Egypt. After graduating from Dar al-Ulum, a teachers' training college, in 1933, Qutb worked for Egypt's Ministry of Education. During the 1930's and 1940's, he wrote poetry, novels, and literary criticism. In the 1950's, he began calling for the creation of an Islamic state in Egypt. In 1954, he was arrested twice for his membership in the Muslim Brotherhood, a fundamentalist Muslim organization. Qutb was released in 1964, but he was soon rearrested and accused of plotting against the government. He was hanged on Aug. 29, 1966. John C. M. Calvert

R is the 18th letter of the alphabet used for the modern English language. It is also used in a number of other languages, including French, German, and Spanish. The *R* sound occurs in such words as *run, very, far, hurry,* and *purr.*

A *dialect* is a variation of a language used by a group of speakers. In certain English dialects—especially some spoken in the United States, the United Kingdom, and Australia—the letter *R* is not pronounced after a vowel.

Scholars believe the letter *R* evolved from an Egyptian *hieroglyph* (pictorial symbol) that represented a head. Hieroglyphs were adapted to be used for a Semitic language by around 1500 B.C. The alphabet for this Semitic language—the earliest known alphabet—is called Proto-Sinaitic. By 1100 B.C., an alphabet for another Semitic language, Phoenician, had evolved from Proto-Sinaitic. See **Semitic languages.**

The Phoenician letter that can be traced to the Egyptian head hieroglyph is the 20th letter of the Phoenician alphabet, *resh.* The Phoenicians used the letter to represent the beginning *R* sound of *resh,* which was their word for *head.* Around 800 B.C., when the Greeks adapted the Phoenician alphabet, *resh* became *rho,* which was used for the same sound.

When the Etruscans adopted the Greek alphabet about 700 B.C., they continued to form *rho* as the Greeks had, much as a modern *P* is formed. This created no confusion, as *P* itself was formed like a shepherd's crook. The Romans adopted the alphabet from the Etruscans by around 650 B.C., however, and they began to write a *P* in the shape of the modern *P.* This meant that *P* and *R* began to look alike. A small tail was then added to *R* to distinguish the two letters. Peter T. Daniels

See also **Alphabet; P.**

WORLD BOOK map and illustrations

Development of the letter *R*

Seafarers and traders aided the transmission of letters along the coast of the Mediterranean Sea.

The Latin alphabet was adopted by the Romans from the Etruscans around 650 B.C. The Roman letter *R* had a tail added to it to prevent its being confused with the letter *P,* which in its modern version is similar in form.

The Etruscan alphabet was adopted from the Greek about 700 B.C. Because Etruscan was written right to left, the Etruscan letter faces the opposite direction from the Greek.

Faster ways of writing letters developed during Roman times. Curved, connected lines were faster to write than imitations of the *inscriptional* (carved) Roman letters. The inscriptional forms of the letters developed into capital letters. The curved forms developed into small letters. The form of most small letters, including *r,* was set by around A.D. 800.

A.D. 300 1500 Today

The Greek alphabet evolved from the Phoenician by around 800 B.C. The Greek letter *rho,* which was adapted from *resh,* was more rounded at the top and faced the opposite direction from the Phoenician letter. By 500 B.C., Greek was written from left to right, opposite from Phoenician.

The Phoenician alphabet had evolved from the Proto-Sinaitic by around 1100 B.C. The Phoenician letter *resh* looked something like a triangle with a tail.

A Proto-Sinaitic alphabet for a Semitic language evolved from Egyptian hieroglyphs by around 1500 B.C. The Proto-Sinaitic letter that came from the head hieroglyph was a diamond shape with a tail.

The Egyptians, about 3000 B.C., drew a hieroglyph that represented a head.

℞ is a symbol used on prescriptions written by doctors. It is generally accepted as representing the Latin word *recipe,* which means *take.* ℞ is traceable to ♃, the sign of Jupiter, which was placed on ancient prescriptions to appeal to that god for favorable action of the medicine. A more recent explanation of the cross at the end of the letter *R* is that it represents a period. Edward J. Shahady

Ra. See **Re.**

Rabat, *rah BAHT* (pop. 577,827), is the capital of Morocco. Rabat is in the northern part of the country. It is on the Atlantic coast at the mouth of the Bou Regreg, a shallow river (see **Morocco** [map]). The Bou Regreg separates Rabat from the city of Salé.

Rabat is divided into old and new sections. The old section, called the *medina,* is in the northern part of the city. It has small, white, flat-roofed houses and several *mosques* (Muslim houses of worship). The new section spreads out around the medina. It has broad streets and modern European-style buildings. The royal palace is in this part of Rabat. The two sections of the city are connected by Avenue Mohammed V, the main business street. Hassan Tower, the *minaret* (prayer tower) of an incomplete mosque, stands on a bluff overlooking the Bou Regreg. Nearby is the tomb of Mohammed V, the first ruler of independent Morocco.

Rabat is chiefly a government and administrative center. It has textile and cork-processing industries. It also produces asbestos products, bricks, cement, and flour. Craftworkers in the city make baskets, carpets, leather goods, tapestries, and other handicrafts.

Mohammed V University was founded in Rabat in 1957. Rabat's Archaeological Museum exhibits objects from prehistoric and Roman times.

The Romans occupied the site of present-day Rabat in the first century after Christ. Ruins of Roman buildings stand in southeastern Rabat. The Berber leader Abd al-Mu'min and his grandson Abu Yusuf Ya`qub al-Mansur established the present city in the 1100's. In 1912, France established a protectorate over most of Morocco. The French made Rabat their headquarters. When the protectorate ended in 1956, Rabat became the capital of the independent nation of Morocco. Kenneth J. Perkins

See also **Morocco** (picture).

Rabbi, *RAB eye,* is the title given to an ordained Jewish minister. The word is Hebrew and means *my master* or *my teacher.* The title of rabbi was popularized in the Mishnah, an important book of Jewish law compiled about A.D. 200.

Many influential leaders of medieval Jewish communities were rabbis. They wrote books and helped people with their religious and worldly concerns, and they frequently represented Jewish communities to non-Jewish groups. They often judged civil and religious legal cases. Some of the most famous rabbis were also doctors.

Today, the role of the rabbi has changed. The main responsibilities of rabbis are to preach, counsel, officiate at religious services, teach, and conduct important personal and community celebrations. Some also serve as authorities on Jewish law.

Despite the importance of ordination to become a rabbi, no uniform course of study is required for all rabbis. Students may attend seminaries or special schools called *yeshivas.* Seminaries teach a variety of subjects, including the Bible and Talmud, and Jewish philosophy, history, and literature. Yeshivas concentrate mainly on teaching the Talmud. The major American schools also train future rabbis in teaching, preaching, and caring for the needs of their congregations. Individual rabbis may train and certify their students as rabbis. B. Barry Levy

See also **Judaism** (The rabbi).

Rabbit is a furry animal with long ears and a short, fluffy tail. Wild rabbits live throughout the world in all climates. Tame varieties of rabbits make excellent pets.

Rabbits are closely related to hares. Rabbits and hares look similar and are often mistaken for one another. Some rabbits and hares are misnamed. For example, the *Belgian hare* is a rabbit, and the *jack rabbit* is a hare. Rabbits and hares can be told apart most easily at birth. Newborn rabbits have no fur and are blind and helpless. Newborn hares have fur and their eyes are open. Also, mother rabbits shelter their young in a soft, fur-lined nest. Mother hares do not make nests for their young.

Kinds of rabbits

Biologists classify rabbits into 10 groups called *genera* and into many *species* within the genera. Numerous species, such as the *volcano rabbit* of Mexico, have become rare. The most widespread rabbits are *cottontails* and *European rabbits.* Domestic rabbits are tame varieties of European rabbits.

Cottontails are wild rabbits of North America and parts of Central and South America. Most species have fluffy white fur on the underside of the tail. Perhaps the most common species is the eastern cottontail. Cottontails inhabit fields, prairies, marshes, and swamps—wherever they can find bushes or clumps of tall grass in which to hide. They may also live in wooded areas bordering open country.

European rabbits originally lived in southern Europe and northern Africa, and on some western Mediterranean islands. From these places they spread throughout Europe. People brought European rabbits to many other parts of the world, including Australia, New Zealand, and South America. Rabbits have often become pests in these regions. The animals reproduce quickly in areas where they have few natural enemies, and they can present a threat to plant life.

Domestic rabbits are raised for their meat and fur, for use in scientific research, and as pets. People around the world eat rabbit meat, which is tasty and nutritious. Rabbit breeds raised commercially for meat include the Californian and New Zealand. Many people raise other breeds for meat in small backyard "rabbitries."

Artificial furs have largely replaced rabbit fur in clothing. However, people still raise the Angora rabbit for its long fur, which is spun into a soft, warm yarn. Rabbit fur is also used in making stuffed toys.

The use of rabbits in research laboratories requires great numbers of highly similar animals, which only large commercial breeders can provide. The Californian, Florida White, and New Zealand White are breeds frequently used in laboratories.

Many of the more than 40 rabbit breeds are raised for show or as pets. Popular show breeds include the Californian, Dutch, Holland Lop, Mini Rex, Netherland Dwarf, and Satin. Judges rate rabbits on such features as size and shape, and the quality and color of the fur. Favorite pet breeds include the Netherland Dwarf, Dutch,

Robert J. Ellison, NAS

A young cottontail sits motionless to escape hunters, but hops away quickly if they come near.

Holland Lop, and Mini Lop. The ears of the English Lop may grow more than 2 feet (60 centimeters) long.

The body of a rabbit

Wild rabbits have brownish fur that mixes white, light brown, gray, dark reddish-brown, and black hairs. Domestic rabbits may be black, brown, gray, white, or even spotted in various combinations of these colors.

An adult cottontail rabbit grows about $21\frac{1}{2}$ inches (55 centimeters) long and can weigh up to 6 pounds (2.7 kilograms). European rabbits may be somewhat smaller. Domestic rabbits can grow larger than wild rabbits. The White Flemish Giant, the largest breed of rabbit, weighs up to 17 pounds (8 kilograms). The smallest species of rabbit, the volcano rabbit, measures only about 12 inches (30 centimeters). Female rabbits, called *does,* tend to grow larger than males, called *bucks.* In most species, the tail of a rabbit measures about $\frac{3}{5}$ to $2\frac{3}{4}$ inches (1.5 to 7 centimeters) long and is covered with soft, fluffy fur.

Rabbits generally move in a hopping motion using their long, powerful hind legs. This motion enables them to travel quickly. A rabbit's hind legs have long toes hidden beneath a thick cushion of fur. The toes are webbed to keep them from spreading when the rabbit jumps.

Linda Shuping, Winsome Rabbitry

A Lop rabbit has floppy ears that may be more than 2 feet (0.6 meter) long. The Lop is a favorite pet breed.

A rabbit's eyes are on the side of its head, toward the back. As a result, the animal can see better to the side than forward. A rabbit's keen sense of smell helps alert it to danger. But rabbits rely mostly on their hearing. They may move their long, sensitive ears together or one at a time to catch sounds from any direction. The ears also keep the rabbit cool in hot weather by giving off heat.

Rabbits' teeth grow continually throughout their lives. Their chisellike front teeth, the *upper incisors* and *lower incisors,* resemble those of rodents. Unlike rodents, rabbits have two pairs of upper incisors. One pair is directly behind the other. Rabbits use the incisors to gnaw and clip off plants. They then chew their food with sideways movements of the lower jaw, which grinds the food and helps wear down the ever-growing teeth.

The life of a rabbit

Rabbits have many natural enemies and can protect themselves mainly by hiding or running from danger.

Hans Reinhard, Bruce Coleman Inc.

An angora rabbit is raised for its fur. The long white hairs are plucked from the animal's coat and spun into soft yarn.

Jane Burton, Bruce Coleman Inc.

Belgian hares are raised for show. The Belgian hare is not really a hare but is a breed of European rabbit.

The skeleton of a rabbit

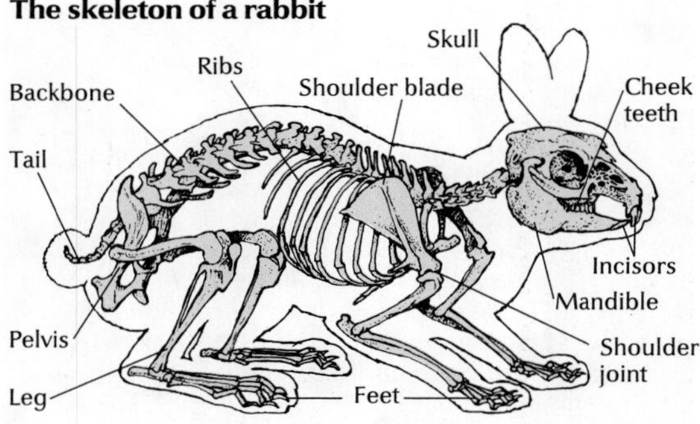

WORLD BOOK illustration by John D. Dawson

Although pet rabbits may live as long as 10 to 15 years, wild rabbits rarely survive beyond 6 years of age.

Homes. Cottontail rabbits spend most of the daylight hours resting in shallow depressions in the ground called *forms.* In cold weather underneath deep snow, a cottontail may take over another wild animal's abandoned burrow and make a network of connected paths called *runs.* Cottontails live mostly solitary lives, but they share territory with others and come together for mating. The *pygmy rabbit* constructs its own burrow.

European rabbits live in large colonies and will warn one another about danger by making loud thumps with their hind feet before running off. They share vast underground burrows called *warrens.* Warrens may be dug up to 10 feet (3 meters) underground and have several entrances and exits. They consist of interconnecting tunnels, living chambers, and nesting chambers where females give birth to and nurse their babies.

Food. Most rabbits eat and play from dusk to dawn, and spend the day resting and sleeping. In spring and summer, rabbits eat green leafy plants, including clover, grass, and herbs. In winter, they eat the twigs, bark, and fruit of bushes and trees. Rabbits sometimes damage crops because they nibble the tender sprouts of beans, lettuce, and other vegetables.

The plant foods that rabbits eat are hard to digest. To get the most nutrients from these foods, rabbits pass the plant matter through their digestive system more than once. Rabbits produce two kinds of solid wastes: moist pellets, which they swallow again and redigest, and solid pellets, which are true wastes.

Young. Because wild rabbits often die before reaching maturity, they must produce many young to survive. A female rabbit usually has four to five young at a time, and she may give birth several times a year. Female cottontails may bear about four litters of young per year.

A female cottontail rabbit carries her young, called *kits,* inside her body for 26 to 30 days before giving birth. The mother keeps the newborns in a nest she has dug in the ground. She lines the nest with fur pulled from her chest with her teeth. The mother stays near the nest and covers the kits with grass and fur to keep them warm. Kits develop a coat of soft fur around 10 days after birth.

About two weeks after birth, the kits leave the nest and hide in long grass and leaves. The mother nurses her young for only a few weeks. Some females start their own families when less than 6 months old.

Enemies. People rank as the greatest enemies of rabbits. Every year, hunters kill millions of rabbits for sport and for food. Farmers kill rabbits to protect crops. Human beings also kill rabbits by destroying the animals' natural habitats. Other rabbit enemies include coyotes, foxes, weasels, snakes, hawks, and owls.

Rabbits usually try to hide from enemies. If a rabbit is in the open, it may sit still, unnoticed, and wait for the foe to go away. If the enemy comes too close, the rabbit flees. A frightened rabbit can leap 10 feet (3 meters) or more and can travel as fast as 25 miles (40 kilometers) an hour. But it tires quickly. It tries to confuse its enemy by zigzagging. It sometimes circles back and follows its own trail for a while, and then leaps off in another direction. It may dive into a burrow or into brush to escape.

Wild rabbits often die from the disease *tularemia,* also known as *rabbit fever.* Tularemia can spread to people who handle sick rabbits (see **Tularemia**).

Pet rabbits

Many people keep domesticated rabbits as pets. All rabbits initially avoid human contact. Rabbit owners must use frequent, gentle handling to teach their pets not to fear people. Owners also need to provide proper cages, food, and medical care for these animals.

Handling. Never pick up a rabbit by the ears. Lifting it that way can cause pain and injury to the rabbit. Instead, grasp the animal by the scruff of the neck with one hand and support its rear quarters with the other hand. You can also hold a rabbit against your body by using the crook of the supporting arm's elbow to cover the animal's head. Use both hands to restrain its rump and rear legs. Rabbits scratch or sometimes bite people who have not restrained them properly. They can also break their own backs or legs if allowed to struggle too much.

Cage. You can buy a *hutch* (rabbit cage) at a pet store, or you can build one. Rabbits may be housed outdoors or indoors as long as they have good ventilation. Elevate outdoor hutches to prevent predators from reaching the rabbits and to help keep the rabbits healthy. Outdoor hutches must also protect rabbits from rain, wind, direct sunlight, extreme cold and heat, and wild animals.

When constructing a hutch, use cleanable materials that are strong enough to withstand a rabbit's chewing. Such materials include wire mesh, sheet metal for roofing, and hardwood framing. Make the hutch large enough for the rabbit to move freely. Provide food and water bowls that the animal cannot tip over and cannot chew. Rabbits can also learn to drink water from *siphons* (sucking tubes). Rabbits should have safe, indestructible toys and chew sticks to prevent boredom. Remove uneaten food and waste from the hutch each day and clean the hutch thoroughly at least three times a week. Rabbits kept indoors can learn to use a litter box.

Male rabbits may fight with one another and even kill baby rabbits. Owners should house them individually.

Food. Rabbits have sensitive digestive systems. They do best when their diets consist mainly of high-quality commercial rabbit pellets. Supplement the main diet with hay or straw to provide fiber. Fiber helps prevent hairballs and other serious intestinal problems. Owners can also feed rabbits small amounts of bread, tender tree growths, and such fruits and vegetables as apples, cabbage, cauliflower, leaf lettuce, spinach, and turnips.

Do not give your rabbit all the day's food at once. Two meals each day help prevent boredom. Provide water and a *mineral block* at all times. Mineral blocks, also called *salt licks,* are blocks of salt injected with other minerals that the animal needs.

Health. Owners must brush pet rabbits at least once a week, especially when the animals *molt* (shed their hair). Molting occurs about once a year. Long-haired breeds, such as the Angora, must be brushed every day. Excess hair licked off by the rabbit can cause a hairball to form in the stomach. During brushing, examine the rabbit for ear mites, fur mites, and fleas. Consult a veterinarian if you find such parasites.

Trim your rabbit's toenails if they do not wear down naturally. The animal also may need its teeth trimmed by a veterinarian if the teeth have grown irregularly. Signs of bad teeth include drooling and lack of appetite.

Rabbits not used for breeding should undergo *neutering* (removal of some of the sex organs) between 4 and 6 months of age. Female neutering, called *spaying,* removes the ovaries and uterus and prevents uterine cancer, a common cause of death among does. Male neutering, called *castration,* can make bucks less aggressive.

Owners should not ignore any signs of illness in rabbits because the animals often die quickly from disease. Signs of disease include diarrhea, runny eyes, sneezing, and loss of appetite. Terri McGinnis

Scientific classification. Rabbits are in the rabbit and hare family, Leporidae. Cottontails make up the genus *Sylvilagus.* The scientific name of the eastern cottontail is *S. floridanus.* European and domestic rabbits are genus *Oryctolagus.* The volcano rabbit makes up the genus *Romerolagus.* The pygmy rabbit is *Brachylagus idahoensis.*

See also **Hare; Jack rabbit.**

Rabbit fever. See **Tularemia.**

Rabelais, *RAB uh LAY* or *ra BLEH,* **François,** *frahn SWA* (1494?-1553?), a French humanist, wrote the comic narrative "Gargantua and Pantagruel." Begun in 1532 with *Pantagruel,* the series comprises five books. Gargantua and his son Pantagruel are giants with enormous appetites. In the work, Rabelais used laughter to question and examine the most important institutions of his time. For example, the comic descriptions of Gargantua's education actually satirize the educational methods of the time and express Rabelais's own ideas on the subject. Although famous for the earthy quality of his humor, Rabelais wrote earnestly about many subjects.

Rabelais was born near Chinon in the province of Touraine. He became a Franciscan friar in 1520. He practiced and lectured on medicine from 1532 to 1546.

Pantagruel is a continuation of an anonymous popular work, *Chronicles of the Giant Gargantua,* published earlier in 1532. While preserving its popular tone, Rabelais added much learned material and showed extraordinary gifts as a satirist and storyteller. *Pantagruel* was condemned for obscenity by the Sorbonne, the theological college of the University of Paris. In 1534, Rabelais published *Gargantua,* his own version of the episodes preceding *Pantagruel.* The Sorbonne also condemned this book, which introduces a mischievous monk, Frère Jean.

In 1546, Rabelais published *Book Three,* which the Sorbonne condemned for heresy. He published *Book Four* in two parts, in 1548 and 1552. He may have written only parts of *Book Five,* which appeared in 1562 and 1564, after his death.

With his linguistic creativity, Rabelais invented many words, some of which remain in the French language. His verve, his optimism, his delightful storytelling, and his ability to become involved in both fun and ideas have made him one of the greatest and most loved French writers. Mary B. McKinley

See also **French literature** (The Renaissance); **Humanism.**

Rabies, *RAY beez,* is an infectious disease that destroys the nerve cells of part of the brain and almost always causes death. Human beings and most other mammals can get the disease. The word *rabies* is Latin for *rage* or *fury.* The disease probably received its name because infected animals often become excited and attack any object or animal in their way. Because one of the symptoms of rabies is an inability by the infected animal to swallow water, the disease is sometimes called *hydrophobia,* which means *fear of water.*

Cause. Rabies is caused by a virus known as a *rhabdovirus.* Most mammals can carry this virus, which usually lives in the nerve cells and glands of the *host* (carrier). The rabies virus can be carried in the salivary glands for long periods of time. If the host bites another animal or a human being, or if some of its infected saliva enters an open wound, the victim may get rabies. Dogs, cats, and wild animals are common sources of infection for people. Research indicates that rabies virus can also enter mucous membranes, such as those lining the nose and eyes. People and other mammals can develop rabies after breathing the air in caves that house large numbers of bats, which may carry the virus.

When rabies virus enters the body, it travels along nerves to the spinal cord and up to the brain, producing inflammation. Symptoms of the disease generally develop about 10 days to 7 months after exposure.

Symptoms in human beings. Among the first symptoms are pain, burning, or numbness at the site of the infection. The victim complains of headaches and is extremely restless. Muscle spasms make the throat feel full, and swallowing becomes difficult. Later, the patient may have convulsions. After a day or two, a quiet period can occur, which can progress to unconsciousness and, finally, death. Symptoms generally last from 2 to 12 days.

Symptoms in animals. The development of rabies in animals follows the same pattern as in people. During the period of excitation, the animal may wander great distances. It vocalizes almost constantly, often becomes aggressive, and will attack without reason. The disease then usually progresses to paralysis of the jaw and throat muscles, followed by general paralysis and death. Some animals with rabies never show signs of excitation but only of paralysis. This form of the disease is sometimes called *dumb rabies.* Some animals that recover from rabies continue to carry and spread the virus.

Treatment. The first step in treating a person bitten by any animal should be to wash the wound with soap and water. The animal should either be caged and watched for signs of rabies, or killed and its brain tissue tested for rabies virus. If either procedure indicates the presence of rabies, a doctor should begin preventive treatment at once. If the animal cannot be found, the doctor may follow such treatment as a safety measure.

Standard preventive treatment in the United States consists of one injection of antirabies globulin followed by five injections of rabies vaccine. Vaccinating all dogs and cats against rabies is an important means of controlling the disease. Lawrence D. McGill

See also **Pasteur, Louis.**

Rabin, *rah BEEN,* **Yitzhak,** *YIHTS hahk* (1922-1995), was prime minister of Israel from 1974 to 1977 and from 1992 until his death. On Nov. 4, 1995, he was assassinated in Tel Aviv, Israel. A right-wing Israeli university student who opposed Rabin's policies confessed to the murder.

Rabin was born in Jerusalem on March 1, 1922. He was Israel's first native-born prime minister. Previous prime ministers were born in Europe. In 1941, during World War II, Rabin joined the *Palmach,* a unit of the Jewish underground army in Palestine. He was deputy commander of the Palmach in 1948 during the first Arab-Israeli war. Rabin headed Israel's defense forces from 1964 to 1967. He planned the strategy in a 1967 war in which the Israelis defeated the Arabs and occupied the Arab lands of the Gaza Strip and West Bank.

© Johnson, Gamma/Liaison
Yitzhak Rabin

From 1968 to 1973, Rabin was ambassador to the United States. A Labor Party member, he was elected to Israel's parliament in 1973. He became Labor Party head and prime minister in 1974, and held those posts until 1977. He was minister of defense from 1984 to 1990.

Rabin again became Labor Party head in February 1992. Elections in June brought the party to power, and Rabin became prime minister again. He appointed himself minister of defense. In 1993, Rabin's government and the Palestine Liberation Organization (PLO) signed an agreement that included the start of a plan for self-government for, and Israel's withdrawal from, the Gaza Strip and West Bank. Israel and the PLO also agreed to try to work out their conflicts. Rabin, Israeli foreign minister Shimon Peres, and PLO leader Yasir Arafat shared the 1994 Nobel Peace Prize for their peace efforts. Also in 1994, talks between Rabin and King Hussein I of Jordan led to a peace treaty ending a state of war that had technically existed between their countries since 1948.

Bernard Reich

See also **Israel** (Recent developments).

Rabinowitz, Solomon. See **Sholem Aleichem.**

Raccoon is a furry animal that has a bushy, ringed tail and a band of black hair around its eyes. This black hair looks like a mask. Raccoons, which are often called *coons,* belong to the same family as coatis, kinkajous, and ringtails. Raccoons live in North America and South America. There are two main species, the northern raccoon and the crab-eating raccoon. The northern raccoon lives in Canada, the United States, and Central America. The crab-eating raccoon lives in Costa Rica, Panama, and South America. Several kinds of raccoons live on tropical islands.

The body of a raccoon. The northern raccoon measures from 24 to 42 inches (61 to 107 centimeters) long, including its tail. Most raccoons weigh from 8 to 20 pounds (3.6 to 9 kilograms), though some males may weigh more than 40 pounds (18 kilograms). Male raccoons usually grow larger than females.

A raccoon has coarse, long hair that is generally gray in color, but sometimes tinged with yellow or brown. Northern raccoons and crab-eating raccoons both have pale brown or gray underfur. But a crab-eating raccoon has shorter hair and thinner underfur.

The tail of both the northern and the crab-eating raccoon may grow as long as 15 inches (38 centimeters). Most raccoon tails have from five to seven rings. Both main species possess a pointed snout and long, flexible fingers. Raccoons have strong, sharp claws, which help them climb. They can handle objects almost as skillfully as monkeys can.

The life of a raccoon. Raccoons live both on the ground and in trees. They live alone or in small family groups. Each raccoon has a *home range.* Most raccoons in good *habitats* (living areas) have home ranges of about 100 to 250 acres (40 to 100 hectares). Male raccoons may roam up to 10 miles (16 kilometers). Within its home range, the raccoon mates, finds its home, and

A raccoon has a "mask" of black hair around its eyes. This furry mammal eats fish and frogs that it catches in rivers and streams.

The feet of a raccoon

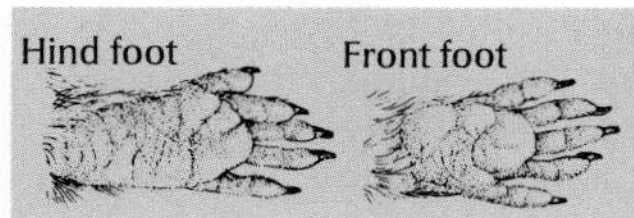

Raccoon tracks

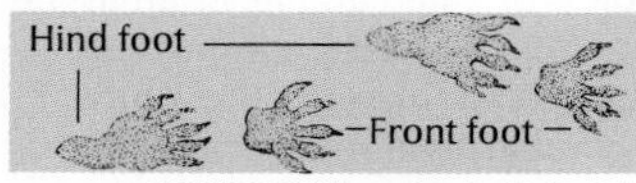

WORLD BOOK illustrations by Marion Pahl

Hans Reinhard, Bruce Coleman Ltd.

searches for food. Raccoons usually hunt for food at night and stay in their dens during the day. They walk like bears, with all four feet flat on the ground, and are good swimmers.

Raccoons in captivity may live 15 years or more because they have a constant food supply and are not attacked by enemies. But most raccoons in their natural habitats probably live less than 5 years.

Raccoons that inhabit wooded areas have their dens in hollow logs, stumps, or trees. They may also make their homes in abandoned barns or farmhouses. In marshy, treeless areas, raccoons nest in high grass, or they may take over abandoned muskrat dwellings.

Both northern and crab-eating raccoons eat crabs. Their other food includes crayfish, frogs, fish, and other freshwater animals. Raccoons also eat acorns, birds' eggs, corn, fruits, nuts, seeds, and such small land animals as grasshoppers and mice.

Many people think raccoons "wash" their food because they frequently dunk food in water before eating it. But experiments show that the animals dunk food that is already clean or wet as often as they dunk dirty or dry food. This habit of dunking food in water seems much more common among raccoons in captivity than those in their natural environment. Some scientists say captive raccoons are simply imitating the way they would pull fish or other animals from rivers and streams. For these reasons, scientists do not believe that the animals actually wash their food.

Raccoons in the southern United States and South America remain active the year around. In colder areas of the northern United States and Canada, raccoons sleep for long periods during the winter, but they do not hibernate. During true hibernation, an animal's heart rate and temperature decrease greatly. On mild winter days, a raccoon may wake up and leave its den to search for food. Raccoons in such colder areas prepare for winter by eating extra food during the fall. They store up a layer of fat under their skin, and this fat keeps them alive during the long winter sleep.

Northern raccoons mate once a year between January and June. About nine weeks after mating, the female has from one to eight babies. Most females give birth to three or four young each year. Newborn raccoons have no mask around their eyes or rings on their tail. Their eyes do not open until about 20 days after birth. The mother raccoon protects her young and does not even let the father near them. The babies stay in the den from 8 to 10 weeks. They then follow their mother when she searches for food. The mother teaches her young to feed and protect themselves. They may stay with her until the beginning of winter, when they find their own dens.

People and raccoons. Native Americans hunted raccoons for their furs. After the arrival of Dutch, English, and French fur traders, the Native Americans exchanged pelts for guns and other items. North American colonists made the pelts into caps, overcoats, and sleigh robes. They also used the furs as money before paper currency was established. The settlers traded pelts for such items as flour and sugar. During the 1830's and 1840's, the Whig Party in the United States used the raccoon as its emblem.

During the 1920's, long-haired raccoon furs—especially overcoats—again became popular. Today, fashion designers sometimes make coats out of raccoon furs that have had the long hairs plucked out. The pale-brown underfur remaining is called *sheared raccoon.*

Raccoon hunts remain a favorite sport in some rural areas of North America. People use dogs to chase the animals until the raccoons jump up into trees to escape. Hunters sometimes roast and eat the raccoons that are caught in a hunt.

People can train raccoons easily, and some attempt to keep them as pets. But after raccoons reach the age of about 1 year, they often bite and scratch. Raccoons also have been known to carry rabies.

Raccoons can become a serious nuisance if they break into chicken houses and kill poultry. They also damage corn crops by breaking the stalks of the plant and eating the growing corn.

John H. Kaufmann and Arleen B. Kaufmann

Scientific classification. Raccoons belong to the raccoon family, Procyonidae. The scientific name for the northern raccoon is *Procyon lotor.* The crab-eating raccoon is *Procyon cancrivorus.*

See also **Coati; Fur; Kinkajou; Panda; Ringtail.**

Raccoon dog. See **Fox** (Raccoon dogs).

Raceme, *ray SEEM* or *ruh SEEM,* is a type of flower cluster. A raceme has a single central stem that bears several flowers, each on a stalk, in a spiral arrangement. The central stem is called the *peduncle.* The stalk bearing each flower is called a *pedicel.* Each flower bud of a raceme forms above a small modified leaf called a *bract.* The flowers of a raceme develop in a spiral pattern, with the lowest flowers on the peduncle developing first. Flowers continue to develop at the tip of the peduncle as it grows. This type of flowering is called an *indeterminate inflorescence.* Such plants as the hyacinth and the lily-of-the-valley produce flowers in racemes.

Joseph E. Armstrong

See also **Inflorescence.**

Racer is the name of a group of harmless, fast-moving snakes of the United States. Racers usually measure about $3\frac{1}{2}$ feet (107 centimeters) long, but they sometimes grow nearly 6 feet (1.8 meters) long.

There are several varieties of racers. The *northern black racer* is found from southern Maine to central Alabama. The skin of its back is glossy and slaty-black. The belly of the northern black racer is bluish-gray, and the chin and throat are white. A bluish variety of racer, called the *blue racer,* is found between the Great Lakes and the Ohio River. A mottled variety of racer found in Louisiana is known as the *buttermilk snake.* Racers live chiefly in the eastern United States. Varieties found west of the Mississippi Valley have tan to olive coloration on their backs.

Racers often climb trees to reach birds' nests and eat the eggs and young birds. They also eat insects, frogs, small mammals such as mice, and other snakes. Some people believe racers kill large rattlesnakes, but racers never attack other snakes of their own size. When cornered, they defend themselves by biting. But they prefer to run away. D. Bruce Means

Scientific classification. Racers are members of the common snake family, Colubridae. The scientific name for the northern black racer is *Coluber constrictor constrictor.*

See also **Snake** (picture: Eastern yellow-bellied racer).

© Michal Heron, Woodfin Camp, Inc.

Human beings resemble one another in many essential ways. However, people also differ from one another. The youngsters in this photo exhibit variations in skin color and hair color. Today, most experts avoid classifying people into races based on such variable physical characteristics.

Human races

Races, Human. All human beings are descended from people who lived hundreds of thousands of years ago. Thus, we all share a common ancestry. This means that all people living today are related to one another. But even though we are all related, we do not all look alike. Our bodies have different sizes and shapes, our skins have varying shades, our eyes differ in color and shape, our lips and noses have different shapes, and our hair has different colors and textures.

Most anthropologists believe that human beings originated in Africa and gradually spread throughout the world (see **Prehistoric people** [Migration from Africa]). They have observed that groups of people who have lived in certain parts of the world for many thousands of years tend to differ from groups living in other parts of the world. Living in regions with differing environments is one reason human beings have developed different appearances. For example, people whose ancestors lived for many generations in northern parts of the world—such as northern Europe or northern Japan—tend to have light-colored skin. People who come from places near the equator, such as central Africa or southern India, tend to have dark-colored skin. People who come from places between those two environmental extremes tend to have medium-colored skin. For information on how skin colors result from adaptations to the environment, see the *Climatic adaptations* section of this article.

In some instances, we observe that certain physical traits tend to cluster in a group. For example, we might associate blond hair, blue eyes, and fair skin with people from Denmark, Norway, and Sweden. We also might associate red hair, green eyes, and a freckled complexion with people from Ireland. However, many people in these four countries actually have brown hair, brown eyes, and light brown skin. This example shows some of the problems facing human biologists who attempt to classify human beings into races.

Biologists define a race as a subdivision of a plant or animal *species.* The members of the same species resemble one another in many essential ways. Most importantly, they can breed with one another and produce fertile offspring. Members of different species usually cannot interbreed and produce fertile offspring. Grizzly bears and black bears, for example, are closely related North American bears. Despite their similarities, grizzly bears and black bears do not interbreed. Therefore, they belong to different species.

Many plant and animal species can be subdivided

Alan Swedlund, the contributor of this article, is Professor Emeritus of Anthropology at the University of Massachusetts at Amherst.

into groups that differ from one another. These groups are often called *subspecies.* Among grizzly bears, for instance, biologists observe distinct physical differences from region to region. They group grizzly bears into subspecies based on these differences.

All living human beings belong to the subspecies *Homo sapiens sapiens.* But like those of the grizzly bear, human populations differ from one region to another. Scholars have used these differences to classify people into various races. They have devised racial categories for human beings according to such physical characteristics as the color of the skin, the color and texture of the hair, and the shape of the eyes.

But some people assigned to the same race—and even some members of the same family—have widely differing features. Over the years, scientists have disagreed over how many races of human beings can be devised, and over which individuals belong to what race. For this reason, many anthropologists and biologists have come to believe that the assignment of a racial label to any group of people is arbitrary and thus open to argument.

For many years, most scholars believed that "pure" races of human beings existed some time in the prehistoric past. According to these scholars, the "pure" human races developed in complete isolation from one another, and the members of each race exhibited physical characteristics that the members of other races did not possess.

Today, however, most *physical anthropologists* (scientists who study the physical differences and prehistoric development of human beings) doubt that "pure" races ever existed. They point out that people have probably always taken mates from outside their own population as well as from within. They also note that as transportation and communication have become easier, populations have blended more and more. For these reasons, the biological definition of race does not describe human populations well. Most anthropologists now avoid classifying people into races. Instead, they try to learn more about human diversity by studying how human traits vary throughout the world.

Despite the lack of a scientifically valid racial classification system, people generally consider those who "look different" from themselves to be members of a different race. As a result, the concept of race remains important in a sociological sense. Societies continue to divide their members into "races"—though the criteria and labels used may vary from society to society.

The idea of race has often been misunderstood, and the term has sometimes been misused on purpose. The biological concept of race has often been confused with culture, language, nationality, or religion. Differences in physical appearance have led some people to mistakenly conclude that members of different groups are born with differences in intelligence, talents, and moral standards. Race has also been a major basis of *discrimination*—that is, the treatment of other groups as inferior to one's own group. For more information, see the *World Book* articles on **Minority group, Racism,** and **Segregation.**

This article describes some racial classification systems that have been used over the years and discusses alternative approaches to the study of human variation. It also describes how the physical characteristics of human beings change, and it discusses the social significance of race.

Systems of racial classification

Physical differences among human beings have long been recognized, and many of these differences have been used throughout history as bases of racial classification. Obvious physical characteristics, such as size, build, skin color, eye form, hair form, and nose shape, were the main criteria of early classifications of race, with skin color considered most important.

Since the beginning of recorded history, scholars have classified human beings in different ways, and the number of categories recognized by each system varied. The development of racial classification systems was influenced by three important theories: (1) the three-race theory, (2) evolutionary theory, and (3) the geographical-race theory.

The three-race theory. Ancient Egyptians, Greeks, and Romans knew about dark-skinned, curly-haired peoples that lived in Africa. They also knew about the so-called "yellowish-skinned" peoples of Asia, most of whom had folds of skin that extended from their eyelids over the inner corners of their eyes. Limited knowledge of the peoples of the world at this time suggested the existence of three races—European, or "white"; African, or "black"; and Asian, or "yellow." These groups eventually became known as Caucasoid, Negroid, and Mongoloid, respectively. For many years, scholars attempted to classify all human populations in terms of these three races, or some variation of the three. They believed that all people belonged to one of a limited number of racial types. They also believed that the traits of each race were fixed and unchanging.

The major period of European overseas exploration, which began in the late 1400's, provided increased contacts with peoples of different cultures. By the 1800's, it became evident that much of the world's population did not easily fit into the three-race system. For example, as Europeans came into contact with more and more Asian peoples, they realized that the skin of the people they had classified as Mongoloids was not really yellow, but that it varied from very dark to very light brown. They also discovered that the *epicanthic fold*—the inner eyefold thought to characterize Mongoloids—was rare in some Asian populations but present in some of the native peoples of southern Africa and North America. Lip form and hair form were also found to vary across the traditional racial groupings.

Evolutionary theory. The view that human beings could be classified into races based on fixed physical characteristics began to change dramatically as biologists came to accept the theory of evolution. During the 1700's, most biologists believed that all plant and animal species remained the same from generation to generation. However, geologists of the early 1800's found fossils of animals and plants that were not the same as living species, thus providing evidence that species were not fixed.

Even though scientists could now see that species could change, they did not know how evolution worked. It was the idea of *natural selection* as the mechanism for evolution that helped scientists understand how organ-

The three-race theory

For many years, scholars classified all human populations into one of three races—Caucasoid, Negroid, or Mongoloid. These three illustrations show the physical characteristics that were believed to typify the members of each race.

Typical Caucasoid traits were believed to include fair skin and fine, light-colored hair that was either straight or wavy. Blue eyes, a narrow nose, and fairly thin lips were also considered Caucasoid traits.

Typical Negroid traits were believed to include dark brown or black skin and coarse, kinky black hair. Brown eyes, a broad nose, and thick lips were also thought to characterize Negroids.

WORLD BOOK illustrations by Nathan Greene

Typical Mongoloid traits were believed to include yellowish skin and coarse, straight black hair. A fold of skin across the inner corner of the eye was thought to characterize Mongoloids.

isms could change over many generations. This idea, set forth by the British naturalist Charles R. Darwin in his book *The Origin of Species* (1859), states that populations of organisms can change over generations as they adapt to their physical environment. This new understanding of the processes of evolution through natural selection, when applied to human populations, showed that many of the supposedly "fixed" traits that had been used to identify races were actually adaptations that had evolved over time in response to environmental conditions. See **Evolution; Darwin, Charles R.**

Scientists saw that widely separated groups could develop similar characteristics as a result of adapting to similar environments, even if they shared no recent ancestral relationship. For example, the Quechua, a people who live in the Andes Mountains of South America, and the Sherpas, a people of the Himalaya in Asia, are only remotely related. However, they have many similar physical characteristics as a result of prolonged adaptation to living in their high mountain environments.

As they came to understand evolutionary theory, experts began to see the difficulty of trying to use adaptable traits to fit people into just a few major races. Physical anthropologists began to search for *nonadaptive,* or *neutral,* traits—that is, physical characteristics that would persist even if a population moved to a different environment. They viewed race as something fixed and unchanging and wanted to discover traits that were also unchanging. Anthropologists compared many traits and physiological processes of people living in different environments, including blood groups and rates of respiration, circulation, and metabolism. These comparisons are discussed later in this article, in the section on *How human populations develop and change.*

The geographical-race theory. In an effort to reconcile the theory of evolution with the observed variations among the world's populations, some anthropologists developed a new system of racial classification during the 1950's. They divided human beings into large categories called *geographical races.* These races were collections of populations that exhibited similar characteristics. One popular classification system recognized nine geographical races: (1) African, (2) American Indian, (3) Asian, (4) Australian, (5) European, (6) Indian, (7) Melanesian, (8) Micronesian, and (9) Polynesian.

In general, the geographical races extended throughout major continental areas and large island chains. But they did not correspond exactly to the continents. For example, the European geographical race included populations throughout Europe, in the Middle East, and north of the Sahara in Africa. It also included descendants of these populations in other parts of the world, such as the "whites" of North America and Australia.

Geographical races were believed to exist because of the isolation caused by such natural barriers as oceans, mountains, and deserts. The idea was that these barriers separated groups of people for many thousands of years, allowing the populations to evolve in different directions. India, for example, is partly isolated from the rest of Asia by the Himalaya. According to the geographical-race theory, this isolation permitted the Indian geographical race to develop separately from the Asian geographical race.

Anthropologists used the term *local races* to describe

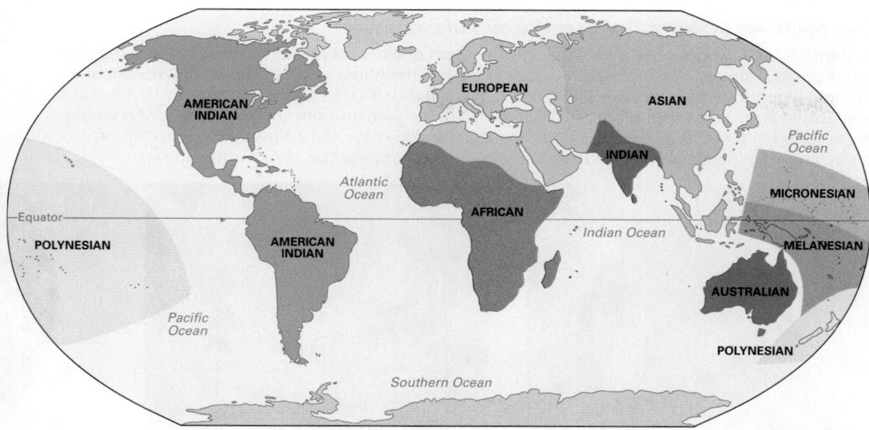

The geographical-race theory

Geographical races were believed to exist because of the isolation created by oceans, mountains, and deserts. This map shows the races that were recognized by one popular classification system.

WORLD BOOK map

distinct subcategories of geographical races. Some local races had millions of members. For example, the Northwest European local race included the populations of Scandinavia, Germany, Belgium, Luxembourg, the Netherlands, the United Kingdom, and Ireland. It also included peoples who emigrated—or whose ancestors emigrated—from those areas. Local races containing much smaller numbers of people included the Sami (formerly known, to outsiders, as Lapps) of extreme northern Europe and the Basques, who live in northern Spain and southwestern France.

Some anthropologists used the term *microraces* to describe the subpopulations that existed within local races. But microraces—and even local races—could not always be clearly defined. Within a given geographic area, the members of different subpopulations often intermarried, so the physical features used to define these groups blended together.

This expanded and detailed classification system represented an important change in the view of human races. The geographical-race system took into account the theory of evolution as well as heredity, recognizing that populations are shaped by their environment. However, many anthropologists believed that it did not eliminate the problems of the older systems. Because members of different races could possess the same physical characteristics, the racial criteria could not be clearly identified.

Alternatives to racial classification

In the past, scholars based racial classifications on clusters of physical characteristics that supposedly represented the "typical" member of that race. But many of the individuals categorized in a particular race did not reflect all the characteristics attributed to that race. In addition, the scholars who constructed classification systems did not always agree on which traits—or how many—should be considered.

To see the problems involved in defining races by means of "typical" characteristics, consider skin color. A pigment called *melanin* determines skin color. Melanin is formed by cells called *melanocytes* in the upper layers of the skin. All human beings have about the same number of melanocytes. However, the melanocytes of dark-skinned people produce more melanin than do those of light-skinned people. The amount of melanin produced in each person's skin is determined mainly by heredity.

Skin color has been used as an important classifying characteristic in all racial systems. For example, a light brown skin color was considered "typical" for the members of the European geographical race. But some members of the European race had skin that was far lighter than the "typical" color, and others had skin that was much darker. Similarly, the members of the African geographical race "typically" had brownish-black skin. But again, many individuals who were classified in this race had skin that was lighter or darker than the "typical" shade.

To further confuse matters, some of the darker-skinned members of the European geographical race had skin as dark as some of the lighter-skinned members of the African geographical race. In view of these complications, it has become extremely difficult to assign people to a race based solely on skin color.

Increasing the number of identifying traits only added more problems. The shape and fullness of the lips, for example, varied widely among people who were considered members of the same race. Furthermore, lip shape demonstrated the same kind of overlap among members of supposedly different races as did skin color.

These problems have led many anthropologists to conclude that classification based on physical characteristics is not scientifically valid and serves no useful purpose. They find the study of human variation to be more productive than the assignment of racial labels. As a result, they have adopted alternate approaches to traditional systems of racial classification. Chief among these alternatives are (1) the clinal approach and (2) the population approach.

The clinal approach. The geographical distribution of a physical characteristic can be shown on a map by zones called *clines.* Clines are formed by drawing lines to connect points of the same or similar frequency. For example, in the case of skin color, each cline includes

The problem of skin color in racial classification

According to the geographical-race theory, members of different races can possess the same physical characteristics. For example, the Kuwaiti woman in the photograph would be classified in the European geographical race. But skin color varies widely within each racial group. Thus, the skin of the Kuwaiti woman is more similar in color to that of the woman from southern Chad, who would be assigned to the African geographical race. But the skin color of the Kuwaiti woman is quite different compared with the woman from Norway, who belongs to the same European race.

© Jacques Jangoux from Peter Arnold

Woman from southern Chad

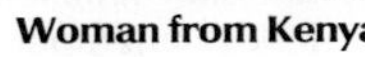

© Martha Cooper from Peter Arnold

Woman from Kenya

© Gerd Ludwig, Woodfin Camp, Inc.

Woman from Togo

© Gerard, Photo Researchers

Woman from Norway

© Blaine Harrington, The Stock Market

Woman from Germany

© Peter Turnley, Corbis

Woman from Kuwait

locations at which populations demonstrate the same average skin color. As variations from dark to light are plotted on a map, certain distribution patterns begin to emerge. A clinal distribution does not associate specific traits with traditional racial categories, nor does it associate different traits with one another. For example, skin color and blood type would be plotted on separate maps and show different patterns of distribution.

The clinal approach has been used extensively to examine the worldwide distribution of blood types. Scientists classify human blood into groups according to proteins on the membranes of the red blood cells. The presence or absence of these proteins is determined by heredity. Studies show differences in the frequencies of some blood groups throughout the world.

The best-known blood-group system is called the ABO system. In this blood-group system, type O is the most common. Type O is followed by types A, B, and AB. Other systems that are used in comparing blood-group frequencies include the Kell, Kidd, Lutheran, MNS, P, and Rh systems. See **Blood** (Blood groups).

Clines of blood-type distribution help anthropologists consider possible explanations for the geographic variations they observe. For instance, clinal mapping shows that central Asia has the lowest frequencies of type O blood. One possible explanation for this has to do with the deadly epidemic disease bubonic plague—a disease that has long been present in central Asia. The surface proteins that characterize type O red blood cells resemble the surface proteins found on the infectious bacteria that cause bubonic plague. Normally, the body can produce disease-fighting chemicals that recognize and attack cells that carry the bubonic-plague surface proteins. But if a person has type O blood, the body is less likely to make these disease-fighting substances because they would damage its own red blood cells. During a plague epidemic, central Asians with type O blood would have been at greater risk of dying from the disease than were those with other blood types. Over the centuries, this disadvantage could have led to the comparatively low frequency of type O blood in central Asia.

The population approach is used to study patterns of variation among human populations. Anthropologists define a population as a group of similar people who are more likely to mate with one another than with outsiders. Anthropologists using the population approach investigate clusters of physical traits but make no assumptions about race on the basis of those clusters. Instead, they see each population as the product of a unique set of circumstances, including adaptation, genetic change, isolation, and history of migration. These researchers then attempt to explain the similarities and differences among the populations. They do not try to fit the populations into racial categories.

The population approach assumes that groups of people who have lived in similar environments for a long period will demonstrate similar adaptations. This can happen even if the location of these similar environments is far apart. For example, populations living at very high altitudes must adjust to extreme conditions. Temperatures can get extremely hot during the day and very cold at night. Also, the air pressure is so low that less oxygen is available, making breathing more difficult. Throughout the world, populations living at high altitudes show specific traits in response to similar environmental conditions. For instance, their lungs can hold more air than those of people at lower altitudes, enabling them to inhale more oxygen with each breath.

How human populations develop and change

The characteristics studied by physical anthropologists—such as eye color, nose shape, blood type, body height, and susceptibility to genetic diseases—are determined by both heredity and the environment. The inherited aspects of a trait are determined by tiny biochemical structures in cells, called *genes.* Genes contain chemical instructions for the formation of hereditary characteristics. Children inherit half their genes from their father and half from their mother. The underlying genetic makeup of a trait is called the *genotype.* The actual appearance of the trait is called the *phenotype.* The phenotype results from the environment and heredity.

Members of the same population of human beings tend to have more genes in common than do members of different populations. Closely related populations also share more genes than do distantly related groups, just as cousins have more genes in common than do members of different families. All the genes in a population are called the group's *gene pool.* The degree to which a gene is present in a population is called the *gene frequency.* For more information on how characteristics are inherited, see **Heredity; Cell; Gene.**

Scientists have shown that the gene pools of human populations can change over time. The presence of some genes increases, while the presence of other genes declines. As gene frequencies change, the frequencies of physical characteristics in a population may also change. Such changes can result from a number of different factors, including (1) natural selection, (2) mutation, (3) genetic drift, (4) the founder effect, and (5) migration and gene flow.

Natural selection is the process that enables some organisms or individuals to live and reproduce while others do not survive. Those who reproduce pass their genetic characteristics on to their offspring. Natural selection is the force that drives Darwinian evolution. For example, certain individuals within a population might possess a genetic characteristic that provides resistance to a local disease. As a result, those individuals tend to survive longer and to produce more offspring than the other members of the population. Moreover, their children who inherit the favorable characteristic will likewise tend to live longer and leave more descendants. Over time, individuals who possess the favorable trait

A clinal map shows the geographical distribution of a physical characteristic. Zones called *clines* indicate where the trait occurs with similar frequency. This map shows the distribution of a trait called the *B allele* in the ABO system of blood classification. People with the B allele have type A or type AB blood. It is more common in eastern Europe than in western Europe.

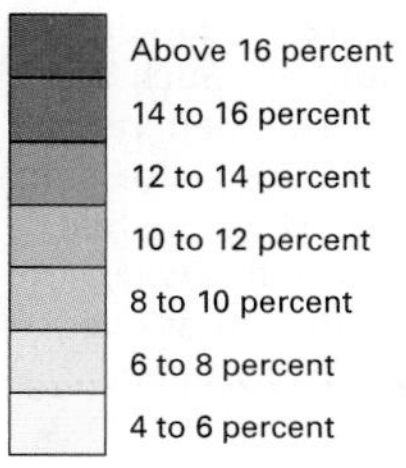

WORLD BOOK map

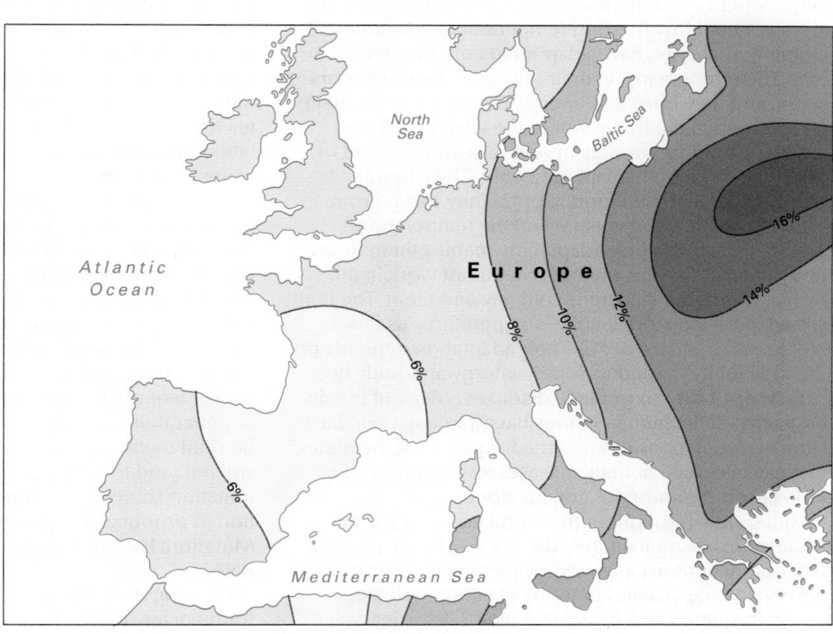

will tend to outnumber those who do not, and the gene frequencies of the population will have changed.

As a result of natural selection, a population that lives in a certain area for many generations tends to exhibit distinctive genetic traits or clusters of traits. Scientists have shown that differences in skin color, body build, and other physical characteristics represent adaptations to environmental factors. See **Natural selection.**

Climatic adaptations. The genetic makeup of populations may change over time to adjust to climate. For example, dark and light skin and eye color represent adaptations to different amounts of sunlight. The color of our skin, hair, and eyes is determined by the pigment melanin. The amount of melanin in the skin, hair, and eyes can differ greatly from one person to another. Large amounts of melanin in the skin help protect it from sunburn and reduce the risk of skin cancer. Dark pigment in the eyes improves vision in bright sunlight. Therefore, dark skin and dark eyes represent adaptations of people whose ancestors have lived for many generations in sunny climates.

Sunlight also affects skin color in another way. Our bodies need vitamin D to help us absorb calcium. The absorption of sunlight enables our bodies to make vitamin D. In climates with long winter nights, it can be difficult for our bodies to absorb the sunlight needed to make enough vitamin D. People whose ancestors have lived in these climates for generations have adapted to reduced sunlight by developing light-colored skin that will absorb the little sunlight that is available. Therefore, skin colors in humans result from adaptations to the environments in which our ancestors have lived.

Human populations also differ in response to cold. Among Inuit (formerly known, to outsiders, as Eskimos), for instance, the body maintains a high temperature by burning large amounts of fat and protein. It also keeps large amounts of blood flowing to the arms, legs, fingers, and toes, to prevent frostbite. Aboriginal Australians, who live in a generally warm climate but traditionally slept in below-freezing temperatures with little clothing or shelter, have adapted to cold in a different way. The temperature in their legs and feet drops during sleep, and they burn less energy. But their bodies maintain warmth in the trunk, where the vital organs are.

The Aboriginal peoples of Australia and the Inuit of the Arctic have both adapted to cold. The Aboriginal peoples had a limited food supply. They had no extra food to burn for body heat when the temperature dropped. Instead, their adaptation enables them to save body energy. But this method would not work in the Arctic, where the climate is cold day and night. The Inuit are adapted to extreme cold—temperatures as low as -40 to -60 °F (-40 to -51 °C). Their adaptation depends on the availability of food to supply energy and body heat.

Susceptibility to genetic diseases. Many of the diseases that afflict human beings have some genetic basis. Human populations differ in the frequency of the genes that cause certain genetic diseases and disorders. For this reason, a number of genetic diseases are distributed differently throughout the world and affect some populations more than they do others. The fact that certain populations are plagued by particular genetic diseases can be explained in terms of natural selection.

The frequency of a hereditary blood disorder called *sickle cell anemia* varies widely in different populations. Individuals who inherit the sickling gene from both parents suffer from sickle cell anemia. Most cases of this disease are fatal. *Carriers*—people who inherit the defective gene from only one parent—may have almost no problems or experience only mild symptoms. But they can transmit the abnormal gene to their children. See **Sickle cell anemia.**

Scientists have found that carriers of the sickling gene have a higher resistance than noncarriers to *malaria,* a dangerous disease transmitted by certain mosquitoes. Sickle cell anemia is a rare disorder, but it occurs more often among populations of western Africa, the Middle East, southern Europe, and the Caribbean, most of whom live in areas threatened by malaria. Thus, the sickling gene—despite its negative effects—represents an important advantage for people in these areas.

Another genetic disease, *cystic fibrosis,* is more common among European populations and their descendants than among other populations. This rare and incurable disease affects the lungs and other organs. Like sickle cell anemia, cystic fibrosis results from the inheritance of a disease-causing gene from both parents. Carriers of the gene do not contract cystic fibrosis, but they can pass it on to their offspring. Some scientists believe that carriers are more resistant than other individuals to *tuberculosis,* an infectious disease affecting the lungs. Tuberculosis swept through Europe from the 1700's to the early 1900's. People who acted as carriers of the cystic fibrosis gene may have been more likely to survive these epidemics, which would explain the relatively high frequency of the cystic fibrosis gene in these populations. See **Cystic fibrosis.**

Mutation. A mutation is a change in genetic material. A changed gene often produces a different inherited trait that can be passed on to future generations. Mutations result from a chemical change in *DNA* (deoxyribonucleic acid), the chief chemical compound of genes. Mutations may also result from a change in the number or arrangement of *chromosomes,* the threadlike structures that contain the genes. Scientists know of many agents that can cause mutations, such as certain types of radiation, chemical treatments, and heat, but they cannot tell in advance which genes or chromosomes will mutate or how the trait controlled by that gene or chromosome will change.

Many mutations are harmful, causing mental or physical disorders. But other mutations are neutral, and some are favorable. A favorable mutation may provide the raw material for natural selection by making a person better suited to the environment. For example, a mutation that enhances the body's ability to make vitamin D from sunlight would be advantageous to a person living in the Far North, where Earth receives less sunlight. Such beneficial genes will increase in frequency from generation to generation. On the other hand, individuals possessing harmful mutations may be selected against, so the trait will not tend to increase in a population. In this way, mutation sometimes works together with natural selection to produce changes in gene frequencies. See **Mutation; Heredity** (Sources of genetic variation); **DNA; RNA.**

Genetic drift refers to chance fluctuations in the gene frequencies of a population from generation to generation. The genes of each generation represent only a sample of the previous generation's gene pool. As a result, the gene frequencies of each generation of individuals tend to vary randomly within the limitations of the preceding generation's gene pool. The smaller the population, the stronger the impact of these fluctuations is likely to be. Such changes are not likely to have much effect in very large populations, but they can lead to significant genetic changes in small populations.

The founder effect. When a small number of people from a large population establish a new population in a different place, it is unlikely that the founders represent the full range of diversity in their parent population's gene pool. When these founders produce offspring, a smaller, more limited gene pool is created. This phenomenon is called the *founder effect.* In future generations, the members of a population influenced by the founder effect are likely to resemble one another more closely than they do the members of the larger, more diverse parent population.

The founder effect may explain the increased incidence of certain traits or diseases in a population. For example, a hereditary brain disorder called *Tay-Sachs disease* occurs mainly among children from Jewish families of eastern European ancestry. People with one Tay-Sachs gene do not have the disease but may transmit the gene to their children. Children who inherit the gene from both parents have the disease. The Jews of eastern Europe made up a small population with a limited gene pool, so the incidence of the disease remains higher among their descendants than in other populations. See **Tay-Sachs disease.**

A similar limitation on a population's gene pool may occur if the genes of one person or family in a small population are passed to a large number of offspring. For example, if one man in a small, isolated group married several women and fathered many children, his genes would appear in future generations with more frequency than would the genes of other members of the population.

Bettmann

Migration can lead to changes in the gene frequencies of populations over time. This photograph shows newly arrived European immigrants on Ellis Island, a United States immigration station in New York Harbor, about 1900.

Migration and gene flow. When migration occurs between separate populations, new genes or combinations of genes are likely to be introduced into each group through interbreeding. As a result, the gene pool of each group comes to include genes from the gene pools of the other populations. In this manner, migration may cause the gene frequencies of populations to change over time. In modern times, easy access to transportation has greatly increased gene flow.

Since earliest times, people have moved from one place to another and have chosen mates from other groups. The greatest amount of gene flow occurs between populations that live next to one another. Mixture may also occur as a result of various cultural practices. Throughout history, such practices as exploration, colonization, bride capture, and enslavement have brought individuals of various genetic makeups together. The result in many cases has been change in the gene frequencies of the populations affected by these practices.

The social significance of race

As we have seen, most physical anthropologists have abandoned the idea of classifying human beings into biological races. In many societies, however, people continue to identify themselves and others as members of a particular race, often based on skin color. Thus, whatever its shortcomings on a biological basis, racial classification remains an important sociological factor. Social scientists must recognize the way a society defines racial categories if they hope to understand human behavior. It would, for instance, be difficult to analyze American society without taking into account the commonly used division of that society into "white," "black," "Hispanic," and other races. Yet these categories themselves reveal problems with the concept of race. "White" and "black" represent categories traditionally used to identify biological races. But "Hispanic" refers to the language group of Spanish-speaking people, not to any one biological group. Unfortunately, many social distinctions between races result from racial prejudice and misunderstanding.

Race and ethnic or national identity. The biological concept of race is sometimes confused with the idea of ethnicity or nationality. People identify themselves as members of certain ethnic or national groups based on certain geographical, cultural, or religious characteristics. However, these identifications are not based on physical differences. For instance, people sometimes incorrectly speak of the "Arab race," the "German race," the "Irish race," or the "Jewish race." But these labels refer to ethnicity or nationality and have nothing to do with the biological concept of race.

Race and discrimination. History includes many episodes in which the members of one group of people deemed themselves superior to another group. Such beliefs were long used to rationalize the enslavement and persecution of people viewed as inferior. For example, the ancient Romans viewed the Germanic tribes as a "race" of *barbarians*—that is, non-Romans—who were barely human. Europeans who settled in America claimed superiority over the American Indians in order to justify their expansion into the New World. During the 1930's, the leaders of Nazi Germany preached that Germans belonged to the "superior Aryan race," and that Jews and all other non-Aryan peoples were inferior.

Experts have not discovered any scientific basis for such claims of superiority. But many people still view other groups in terms of *stereotypes.* That is, they have oversimplified, preconceived, and generalized beliefs about the members of these groups. At various times, for example, certain groups have been described as dirty, dishonest, sly, humorless, or dull. These judgments have often been confused with racial traits, though they have nothing to do with the biological concept of race. Many such judgments have nothing to do with culture either, but only with the opinions or prejudices of those who make them. Discrimination can result from these stereotypes. As a result of these beliefs, members of minority groups in many societies have fewer educational and job opportunities than do members of the majority group.

The belief that some groups are more intelligent than others has been used to justify discrimination. Scientists have shown that a person's intelligence is partly inherited and partly determined by the environment. The use of intelligence to compare groups of people is extremely difficult, because few such comparisons can be considered equal. A better-educated group, for example, will score higher on tests that measure education. Groups that value mathematical skills or technical ability will do better on tests involving such skills.

Many experts believe it is impossible to design an intelligence test that is not influenced by a person's experiences. Nevertheless, scientists are trying to develop *culture-fair* or *culture-free* tests that reduce the effects of cultural differences on test scores.

The differences among human beings make the world a fascinating place in which to live. But when people focus on differences, they often fail to appreciate how alike all humans are. Most distinctions that people make between themselves and others have much more to do with culture than with biology.

Alan Swedlund

Related articles. See the separate ***World Book*** articles listed under "People" at the end of **Africa** and **Asia**. See also:

Aboriginal peoples of Australia
Adaptation
Africa (People)
African Americans
Aleuts
Asia (People)
Dayaks
Europe (People)
Evolution
Heredity
Indian, American
Inuit
Latin America (People)
Māori
North America (People)
Pacific Islands (People)
Prehistoric people (The origin of *Homo sapiens*)
Racial profiling
Racism

Outline

I. Systems of racial classification
A. The three-race theory
B. Evolutionary theory
C. The geographical-race theory

II. Alternatives to racial classification
A. The clinal approach
B. The population approach

III. How human populations develop and change
A. Natural selection
B. Climatic adaptations
C. Susceptibility to genetic diseases
D. Mutation
E. Genetic drift
F. The founder effect
G. Migration and gene flow

IV. The social significance of race
A. Race and ethnic or national identity
B. Race and discrimination

Rachel, *RAY chuhl,* in the Old Testament, was the favorite wife of Jacob. Jacob served Rachel's father, Laban, seven years in order to win her, and his love was so great, "they seemed to him but a few days" (Genesis 29:20). But Laban tricked Jacob and gave him Rachel's older sister, Leah, instead. Jacob married Rachel a week later, but had to work another seven years for her. Rachel's first child, Joseph, became his father's favorite. At the end of a journey from Mesopotamia to Canaan, Rachel died after giving birth to Benjamin. Canaan was roughly an area that extended from east of the Jordan River to the Mediterranean Sea.

Rachel was considered the ancestress of the northern Israelite tribes of Ephraim and Manasseh, which claimed descent from Joseph. A century after the Assyrians deported part of the tribes in 722 or 721 B.C., Jeremiah described Rachel as mourning over her lost children (Jeremiah 31:15). J. Maxwell Miller

See also **Jacob.**

Rachmaninoff, *rahk MAH nuh NAWF,* **Sergei Vassilievich,** *sehr GAY vahs SEE lyuh vihch* (1873-1943), was a Russian composer and conductor and one of the greatest pianists in history. His compositions generally carry the late Romantic style of Russian composer Peter Ilich Tchaikovsky into the early 1900's. Even Rachmaninoff's last works from the 1930's are hardly affected by modern trends. His music is strongly influenced by the chants and church bells of the Russian Orthodox Church. These musical influences appear in Rachmaninoff's severely simple melodies and rich, full keyboard sounds. He combined these native Russian materials with his own passion and intensity of expression.

Rachmaninoff gained his greatest international reputation for his piano compositions. His most famous work is the Prelude in C-sharp minor for piano. He composed it in 1892, when he was 19 years old. The second (1901) of his four piano concertos shows the melancholy lyricism of his mature style and his skillful writing of virtuoso piano compositions. His other work for piano and orchestra is the *Rhapsody on a Theme of Paganini* (1934).

Rachmaninoff's major works for orchestra are his three symphonies (1897, 1908, and 1936), the symphonic poem *The Isle of the Dead* (1909), *Symphonic Dances* (1941), and the choral symphony *The Bells* (1913). The composer based *The Bells* on a Russian translation of the poem by the American author Edgar Allan Poe.

Rachmaninoff's main works for solo piano appear in the collections *Moments musicaux* (1896), two sets of *Preludes* (1903, 1910), and two sets of *Études-tableaux* (1911, 1917). He also wrote over 80 songs, all to Russian texts, for solo voice and piano accompaniment. He composed three operas, but none is widely performed.

Rachmaninoff was born on April 1, 1873, on his family estate near Velikiy Novgorod. In 1885, he entered the Moscow Conservatory to study piano and begin courses in composition, orchestration, and counterpoint. He completed his piano studies at the conservatory in 1891. He graduated in composition the next year, winning the highest award for his one-act opera *Aleko.*

In 1902, Rachmaninoff married his cousin Natalya Satina. He was conductor of the Bolshoi Opera in Moscow from 1904 to 1906 and made his first tour of the United States in 1909 as a pianist and conductor. Rachmaninoff left Russia with his wife and two daughters in 1917.

Eventually, he settled in the United States late in 1918.

In America, Rachmaninoff concentrated on concert performances rather than composing. He gained enormous popularity in America and Europe for his compositions and as a piano soloist. He lived in Switzerland for much of the 1930's but returned to the United States in the late 1930's. He died in the United States shortly after he received his American citizenship. Edward V. Williams

Racial profiling is the act of targeting a person for criminal investigation primarily because of racial or ethnic characteristics. This practice is based on an assumption that people of color or ethnic minorities are more likely to commit crimes than other people. This assumption is common among people with racially prejudiced beliefs. But racial profiling, also known as *ethnic profiling,* is generally regarded as a violation of the civil rights of minority groups. Charges of racial profiling commonly involve automobile stops by law enforcement officers. However, people have also claimed to be targets of racial profiling at other times—for example, while walking on city streets or while shopping in stores or malls.

In the United States, many legal experts regard racial profiling to be a violation of certain constitutional protections, including the prohibition against unreasonable searches and seizures. The U.S. Supreme Court has limited the degree to which police officers may use racial profiles. According to the court, the police must demonstrate that the racial profile, along with other information, justifies a reasonable suspicion that the person is engaged in criminal activity.

In 2001, terrorists destroyed the World Trade Center in New York City and part of the Pentagon Building near Washington, D.C. Because the terrorists involved were believed to be Arab Muslims, the investigation focused on individuals of that background. Many critics argued that U.S. investigators and law enforcement officers engaged in racial profiling in the months following the attack. The U.S. Department of Justice said that it did not tolerate racial profiling against Arab Americans.

Kenneth B. Nunn

Racial segregation. See **Segregation.**

Racine, Jean, *ruh SEEN, zhahn,* (1639-1699), ranks among the greatest French playwrights. Racine wrote during the French Classical Age. He followed the classical rules for composition, including the use of a single concentrated plot. The outstanding feature of Racine's art is its simplicity. He used a limited vocabulary and his plots contain little explicit action. He said his artistic ideal was "to construct something out of nothing."

Most of Racine's important plays are tragedies. Many of his tragic heroes and heroines follow a pattern. They are victims of violent passions and try unsuccessfully to force their wills on others. In the process, most of them cause the death of those they love. They finally recognize their illusions and accept the misery of the human condition as unavoidable. In this respect, Racine is close in spirit to the Greek playwright Sophocles. Racine's tragedies have much in common with the descriptions of tragedies in Aristotle's literary essay, *Poetics.* Both Racine and his rival Pierre Corneille wrote in 12-syllable couplets, but Racine's style often is more severe.

Racine was born in La Ferté-Milon, near Meaux, and was educated by the strict Jansenist religious sect. He showed promise of a literary career at an early age. In 1664, Racine staged *La Thébaïde,* his first tragedy to be produced. It met with little success. His next play, *Alexandre* (1665), received considerable acclaim.

With the production of *Andromache* (1667), Racine became known as one of the greatest dramatists of his time. His next seven plays are masterpieces. They are *Les Plaideurs* (1668), his only comedy; and the tragedies *Britannicus* (1669), *Bérénice* (1670), *Bajazet* (1672), *Mithridate* (1673), *Iphigénie* (1674), and *Phaedra* (1677). In 1677, Racine retired from the stage. Later, he wrote *Esther* (1689) and *Athalie* (1691), tragedies based on stories from the Bible. Racine died on April 21, 1699. Carol L. Sherman

See also **Drama** (Neoclassical playwrights); **French literature** (The Classical age).

Racing is a contest of speed. People compete in running, swimming, and walking races. Such sports as horse racing and automobile racing involve people riding animals or operating machines. Trained animals compete against one another in dog racing and pigeon racing. Some races are among the world's most popular spectator sports, attracting millions of people each year.

Racing includes both individual and team competition. In some races, winners are determined only by the fastest time. In others, the winner is the individual who finishes first. Some races last only a few seconds. Some other races are very long and test endurance as well as speed. A well-known example is the marathon, a running race of 26 miles 385 yards (42.2 kilometers). Some ocean yacht races and bicycle road races last for weeks.

Racing events have been popular throughout human history. A footrace was the only event in the first recorded Olympic Games held in ancient Greece in 776 B.C. More recently, racing has contributed to improvements in design and performance in airplanes, bicycles, and automobiles. William F. Reed

Related articles in *World Book* include:

Automobile racing
Bicycle racing
Bobsledding
Canoeing (Canoe racing)
Dog racing
Harness racing
Homing pigeon
Horse racing
Ice skating (Speed skating)
Iceboating
Kart racing
Motorboat racing
Motorcycle
Olympic Games
Roller skating
Rowing
Sailing (Sailboat racing)
Skiing
Swimming
Track and field
Walking

Racism is the belief that human beings can be divided into races and that members of some races are inferior to members of other races. People who believe in racism are called *racists.* They claim that members of their own race are mentally, physically, morally, or culturally superior to those of other races. Because of this, racists feel they deserve special rights and privileges. Racism in most countries has been directed mainly by the majority population group against ethnic minority groups. These minorities have faced discrimination in such areas as housing, education, and employment.

Although no scientific proof supports racist claims, racism is widespread and has caused major problems throughout the world. Racism is most often used to justify the creation of political or economic systems that encourage or maintain the domination of one racial group over another. Claims of racial superiority have supported discrimination, segregation, colonialism, slavery, and even mass murder.

Racism is a form of *prejudice.* Many people tend to

consider their own appearance and behavior as normal and therefore desirable. They may distrust or fear people who look or act different. People often view other groups in terms of *stereotypes.* That is, they have oversimplified, preconceived, and generalized beliefs about the members of these groups.

Types of racism. Sociologists distinguish between individual and institutional racism. *Individual racism* refers chiefly to the prejudicial beliefs and discriminatory behavior of individuals in relation to other ethnic groups. It is based on racial assumptions of superiority and inferiority. Individual racism is often conscious and intentional. When a person is influenced by racist assumptions but is unaware of this influence, it is considered *unconscious racism.*

Institutional racism refers to the policies that restrict the opportunities of minorities in communities, schools, businesses, and other group settings. Institutional racism may or may not be intentional, but it can produce harmful results. For example, a company may hire only college graduates for work that does not require a college degree. But if a smaller number of Black people than white people possess college degrees, this company policy would limit the opportunities available to Black people.

Another example of institutional racism is the reported use of *racial profiling* in law enforcement. Racial profiling refers to the practice of using skin color as a basis for stopping people for police encounters, such as traffic checks. In the United States, some states have passed laws against the practice.

Systemic racism is institutional racism that has become manifest in many areas of society over many generations. It can be manifested, for example, as patterns of residential segregation; as a high presence of minorities in the criminal legal system; or as differences in public-school budgets, in access to higher education, in career opportunities, in wages, and in banks' lending policies in regard to people of different races.

Systemic racism occurs as a cycle with interrelated parts that reinforce one another. For example, racial discrimination can lead to minorities living in poor residential areas. Low tax revenues in such areas can result in poorly funded local schools. Students who attend such schools may have limited opportunities to attend college or get a good job. It can be extremely difficult for minorities to escape such a cycle.

In a way, systemic racism is like a deeply rutted trail for racist thoughts, actions, and institutions. As more "wagons" travel the trail, the ruts grow deeper and it becomes more difficult to travel outside of them. Thus, racial prejudice, discrimination, economic and social inequalities, and injustice persist and thrive. This dynamic supports a system in which one racial group in a society dominates others.

Environmental racism, also called *environmental injustice,* results when individual or institutional racism produces harmful environmental effects on a group. Environmental racism can occur, for example, when members of a minority group are forced to live near a toxic waste dump due to a lack of housing elsewhere.

History. The idea of *biological determinism* became widespread in Europe during the 1700's. Biological determinism is the idea that a person's biological makeup determines his or her intelligence and behavior. This belief led to the development of racism as Europeans began to spread out around the world.

From the 1700's to the early 1900's, Europeans gained control of large parts of Asia and Africa. These colonialists justified their domination on the grounds that people with darker skin color had to be "civilized" by the "superior" white people. By the mid-1900's, most colonialism had ended, but its effects on the world are still felt today. For details, see **Africa** (History) and **Asia** (Results of colonialism; The spread of Communism).

From the 1600's to the mid-1800's, many white people in the United States held Black people in slavery. The enslaved people were freed during the 1860's, but segregation and discrimination against Blacks continued. In the 1960's, the U.S. government passed laws designed to give equal opportunities to Black people. Even so, racial problems—which began with slavery and were fostered by discrimination and segregation—continue to plague the United States.

Genocide is the deliberate and systematic mistreatment or extermination of an entire people. It is the most extreme result of racial hatred. Genocide was widely practiced by European settlers against the local peoples in Africa and the Americas. Adolf Hitler, the ruler of Nazi Germany, preached that Germans belonged to the "superior Aryan race," and that Jews and other non-Aryans were racially inferior. Hitler's racist beliefs led to the murder of millions of Jews and others during the 1930's and 1940's. See **Jews** (Beginnings of Nazi persecution).

In the late 1940's, the government of South Africa established a racial policy called *apartheid,* one of the world's most complete systems of racial separation. It called for separate institutions for white and nonwhite people and reserved about 85 percent of the nation's land for the white minority. In 1991, South Africa repealed the last of the laws that formed the basis of apartheid. See **Apartheid; South Africa** (Racial and ethnic groups; Ways of life; Apartheid).

The science of race. Groups, as well as individuals, differ. But there is no scientific evidence to support claims of superiority or inferiority based on these differences. Social scientists emphasize that no two groups have exactly the same environment. As a result, many group differences are largely the result of different environments.

Scientists have long debated the relative importance of heredity and environment in determining differences among people. Most anthropologists today reject the idea that human beings can be divided into races based on biological differences alone. Instead, race is understood to be a complex concept that involves many other factors, such as environment and social behavior. For a discussion of these ideas, see **Intelligence** (The roles of heredity and environment) and **Races, Human** (Race and discrimination).

Kenneth B. Nunn

Related articles in *World Book.* For discussions of racism against minority groups in the United States, see **African Americans; Asian Americans; Hispanic Americans;** and **Indian, American.** See also the following articles:

Anti-Semitism
Apartheid
Ethnic group
Genocide
Hate crime
Minority group
Oriental Exclusion Acts
Prejudice
Races, Human
Racial profiling
Segregation
Slavery
Stereotyping

Racketeering is any of several types of illegal activities usually associated with organized crime groups, such as the Mafia. There are three main types of rackets: (1) protection rackets, (2) labor rackets, and (3) business rackets. In a protection racket, an organization uses threats, also called *extortion,* to force businesses to pay it money. In a labor racket, the offenders steal union funds or use a union's power to force companies to give them money. In a business racket, a firm tries to prevent other businesses from competing against it.

In the United States, racketeering is prohibited under RICO, a section of the federal Organized Crime Control Act of 1970. RICO is an abbreviation of the section's title, "Racketeer Influenced and Corrupt Organizations Act." Under RICO, people convicted of racketeering can be given up to 20 years in prison for each offense.

After RICO took effect, a number of U.S. states and many other countries adopted similar laws. The countries with such laws include Belgium, Germany, Italy, and South Africa. Howard Abadinsky

Rackham, Arthur (1867-1939), an English artist, won wide recognition for his illustrations for children's books. His illustrations were filled with such figures as gnomes, elves, witches, and fairies, as well as with kindly human beings.

Rackham drew and painted these figures with delicacy and rich detail. He made such details as wood grain, tree bark, and lines in faces and hands important parts of the whole design. He even gave his trees personalities. Rackham's imaginative and skillful pictures brought to life the characters in many favorite stories, including *Rip Van Winkle* (1905), *Peter Pan in Kensington Gardens* (1906), *Alice's Adventures in Wonderland* (1907), *Mother Goose, the Old Nursery Rhymes* (1913), *Some British Ballads* (1919), and *The Arthur Rackham Fairy Book* (published in 1950, after his death).

Rackham was born on Sept. 19, 1867, in London. He became interested in drawing when he was a boy and entered the Lambeth School of Art in 1884. He supported himself by working in an insurance office from 1885 to 1892. Rackham first gained recognition for his illustrations in an edition of *Grimm's Fairy Tales* that was published in 1900. He died on Sept. 6, 1939.

Marilyn Fain Apseloff

From *Alice's Adventures in Wonderland* by Lewis Carroll. Illustrated by Arthur Rackham. All rights reserved. By permission of Viking-Penguin Inc.

A Rackham illustration from 1907 shows the artist's detailed style. In this scene from *Alice's Adventures in Wonderland,* Alice and the Gryphon listen to the Mock Turtle's sad life story.

Racquetball is a fast, exciting game in which the players hit a ball with a short racket (or racquet) that resembles a small tennis racket. They play with a hollow rubber ball about the size of a tennis ball. Most racquetball games are played on indoor courts that are 20 feet (6.1 meters) high, 40 feet (12.2 meters) long, and 20 feet wide. The game can be played with one or two players on a side. In cutthroat racquetball, three players compete against each other.

A racquetball game starts with a *serve.* The server stands between the *service line* and the *short line* with the receiver standing behind the short line. In doubles play, the server's partner stands in the *service box* with his or her back to the wall. The server drops the ball on the floor and hits it on the first bounce. The ball must strike the front wall and rebound behind the short line. The players or teams then take turns hitting the ball. Each player must return the ball before it bounces twice on the floor. A player can return the ball by hitting it against any wall or the ceiling. But the ball must strike the front wall before it touches the floor.

The server or serving team scores points if an opponent fails to return the ball properly. The side continues the serve after each point until it makes an error on its serve or fails to win the point. The other side then serves. Originally, games were played to 21 points. Most games now go to 15 points. The first side to win either two or three games wins the match.

The American Amateur Racquetball Association governs the sport at the amateur national level. The International Racquetball Tour governs professional play.

Critically reviewed by the American Amateur Racquetball Association

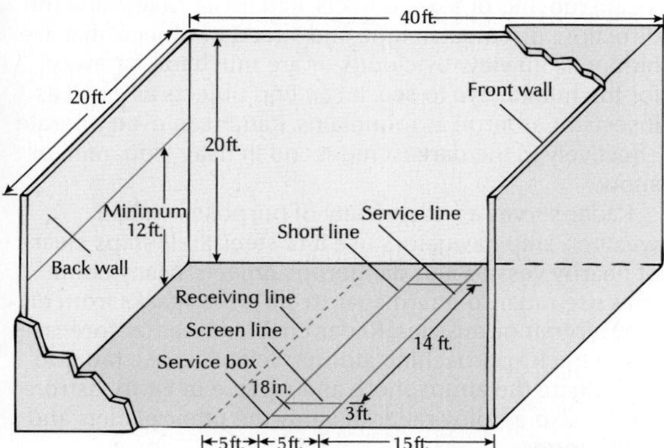

WORLD BOOK diagram by Lisa Wilkinson

A racquetball court has four walls. The server stands between the *short line* and the *service line.* During the serve, the ball must hit the front wall and bounce behind the short line. The opponent waits for the serve behind the *receiving line.*

© Fotogrin/Shutterstock

Radar helps control ship traffic in harbors and seaports. Harbor masters follow the movements of all ships in a harbor on a radar display that provides a maplike picture of the harbor. By means of radio communication, harbor masters can guide ships into and out of a port safely in any weather.

Radar

Radar is an electronic instrument used to detect and locate moving or fixed objects. Radar can determine the direction, distance, height, and speed of objects that are hidden from view by clouds or are much too far away for the human eye to see. It can find objects as small as insects or as large as mountains. Radar can even operate effectively in the darkest night and in heavy fog, rain, or snow.

Radar serves a wide variety of purposes. In bad weather, ship navigators use it to steer their ships clear of nearby vessels and dangerous objects. Many countries use radar to guard against surprise attacks from enemy aircraft or missiles. Radar enables weather forecasters to track approaching storms. Scientists use radar to investigate the atmosphere and surface of Earth. Astronomers also employ radar to study the other planets and their moons.

The word *radar* comes from *ra*dio *d*etection *a*nd *r*anging. Almost every radar set works by sending radio waves toward an object and receiving the waves that are reflected from the object. The time it takes for the reflected waves to return indicates the object's *range*—how far away it is. The direction from which the reflected waves return tells the object's location.

Radar sets vary greatly in size and shape, but they all have the same basic parts. Every set has a transmitter to produce radar waves and an antenna to focus them and send them out. In most types of radar, the same antenna collects the waves bounced back from an object. The reflected waves, commonly called *echoes,* are strengthened by a receiver so they can be seen on a *display.* The typical radar display resembles the picture tube of a television set. It shows the echoes as spots of light or as a color image of the object observed.

The uses of radar

In aviation. Radar contributed greatly to aviation safety both at airports and in airplanes. Air traffic near large airports is extremely heavy. *Air traffic controllers* at major airports used radar to direct the continuous flow of incoming and outgoing planes. Radar enabled the controllers to prevent collisions by selecting the safest routes for pilots to follow. Radar also enabled controllers to direct landings from the ground when bad weather made approach lights and runways difficult for pilots to see.

Most modern aircraft now have technology called Automatic Dependent Surveillance-Broadcast (ADS-B). ADS-B uses signals from Global Positioning System (GPS) satellites to safely communicate with air traffic controllers and other airplanes.

In ship navigation. Radar is widely used as a navigation aid on all kinds of boats and ships, from small pleasure craft to huge oil tankers. When visibility is poor, a ship's radar can spot other vessels, reefs, and icebergs in time to prevent an accident. Radar is especially useful in fog. When a ship is close to shore, the navigator can determine the position of the vessel by the radar echoes from special reflector buoys, islands, and other landmarks.

Harbor masters use radar to control ship traffic in crowded seaports. They follow the movements of all ships in a harbor on a radar display that provides a maplike picture of the harbor. By means of radio communication, harbor masters can guide ships into and out of a port safely in any weather.

Coast guard stations keep track of vessels in their vicinity through radar observations. Coast guards also use radar to search for ships that have been reported missing.

In the military. Radar has a variety of military uses. The major uses include (1) air defense, (2) missile defense, (3) space surveillance, (4) intelligence gathering, (5) range instrumentation, and (6) weapon fire control.

Air defense requires long-range radar that can detect and track approaching enemy aircraft at great distances and so give the earliest possible warning. Vast networks of radar stations form the heart of most nations' air defense systems. The North Warning System, a network of radar stations across northern North America, is designed to alert the United States and Canada to an airborne attack from the north. Australia, China, Russia, and the United States also have built huge *over-the-horizon radar* stations to detect attacks coming from any direction.

In addition to land radar stations, Israel, the United Kingdom, the United States, and several other countries use aircraft equipped with radar for protection against surprise air attacks. Airborne radar can spot low-flying enemy bombers that may escape detection by ground-based radar.

Missile defense consists of radar networks like those used for early warning of hostile aircraft. However, more powerful radar is needed to detect guided missiles because they fly faster and much higher than planes. For example, the main radar network developed by the United States for missile defense is the Ballistic Missile Early Warning System (BMEWS). This system has installations in Alaska, Greenland, and England. Its radar units can spot long-range missiles as far as 3,000 miles (4,800 kilometers) away. Another major United States radar network operates under the Sea-Launched Missile Defense (SMD) program. Its radar stations guard the eastern and western coasts of the United States against missiles launched from enemy submarines and from surface vessels.

Space surveillance involves the use of extremely powerful radars to detect and track artificial satellites and other objects put into orbit around Earth. For this purpose, the United States operates the Space Surveillance Network (SSN). The U.S. Air Force coordinates the network, which includes about 20 sites around the world that use radars and satellites to track other satellites and space debris. Each day, the SSN observes the locations of thousands of orbiting objects. Data from these observations can help identify *reconnaissance satellites,* which are used for spying.

Intelligence gathering. Government agencies and the

© DeltaOff/Shutterstock

Boats and ships use radar as a navigation aid, especially to avoid obstacles when visibility is poor. Some smaller vessels, such as the yacht shown here, use a compact radar set with an antenna that rotates.

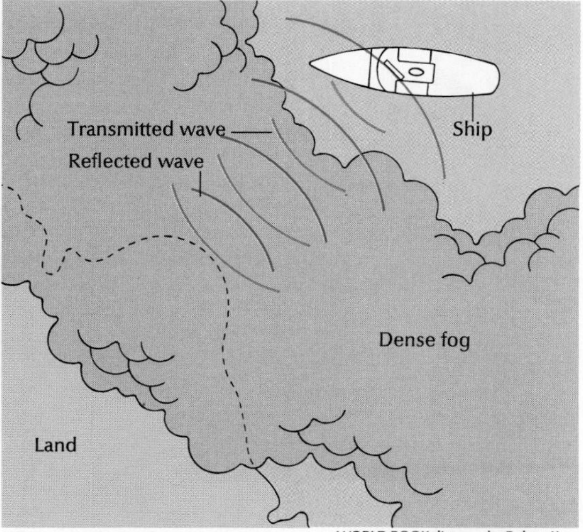

WORLD BOOK diagram by Robert Keys

Radar aids navigation by enabling a ship's navigator to detect land, reefs, or other vessels during poor weather conditions. This diagram shows how radar waves can penetrate dense fog, returning echoes that indicate a land mass.

Radar is vital to the defense of the United States and Canada. Powerful BMEWS radars warn against long-range missiles. Radars of the North Warning System detect aircraft approaching from the north, and over-the-horizon radars protect against attack from other directions. The United States Air Force (USAF) Spacetrack Network keeps track of artificial satellites orbiting Earth.

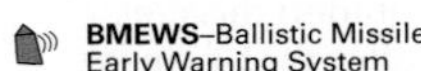

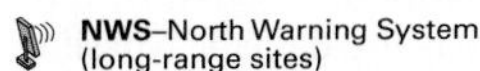

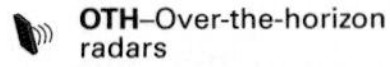

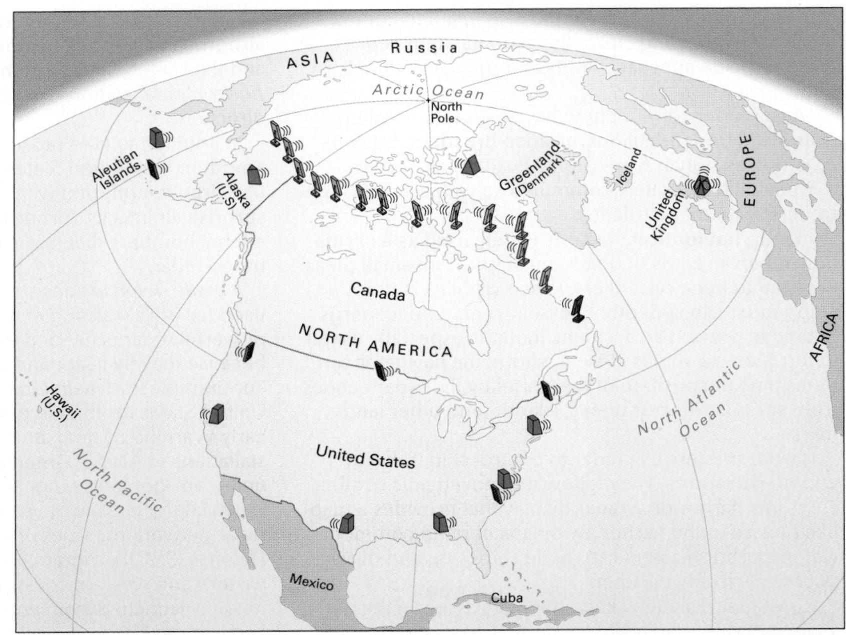

WORLD BOOK map

military use radar to collect information about preparations other countries might be making for war. A *mapping radar* in a plane can produce detailed maps of the ground and show military installations and equipment. Other types of radar provide information about another country's missile systems by monitoring its missiles during test firings.

Range instrumentation. Radar is often used at rocket test ranges to check the performance of military equipment. For example, *range instrumentation radars* can accurately track the flight of a new missile. If the missile does not perform as well as expected, the tracking data might help the designer determine what went wrong.

Weapon fire control. Radar can locate objects so precisely that it is used to aim and fire many kinds of weapons. Radar controls the firing of antiaircraft guns on tanks and warships. It directs guided missiles from jet fighters and from land-based launching sites. In addi-

U.S. Air Force

U.S. Air Force

A long-range radar has a huge dome, *left,* which houses an antenna structure, *right,* that stands about 65 feet (20 meters) high. The radar shown here is part of the North Warning System, which protects the United States and Canada from attack from the north.

tion, planes with radar bombsights can drop bombs accurately on targets at night or in bad weather.

In controlling automobile speed and traffic. Police in many countries use radar to enforce speed laws by checking the speed of motor vehicles on streets and highways. Their portable radar sets can detect speeding vehicles up to $\frac{1}{2}$ mile (0.8 kilometers) away.

In weather observation and forecasting. Radar has an important role in short-term forecasting of local weather conditions. Radar echoes can be detected from raindrops and ice particles in clouds up to 250 miles (400 kilometers) away. Meteorologists use storm surveillance radars to monitor developing weather conditions and to map regions of heavy precipitation. They can estimate precipitation rates and accumulations by measuring the strength of reflected radar signals. Storm echoes from weather radars are displayed on weather segments of television news broadcasts and on Internet Web sites that feature weather reports. The weather services of many countries operate national radar networks to monitor precipitation.

Most weather surveillance radars can measure the wind speeds and airflow patterns inside storms. Radar data help save lives by providing early warnings of weather dangers. These dangers include heavy rain; hail; *wind shear,* a sudden change in wind direction or speed; and *mesocyclones,* rotating columns of air that usually produce tornadoes. Weather services often issue tornado warnings on the basis of radar data alone, before anyone has actually sighted a tornado.

Data from short-range weather radar systems at airports provide immediate warnings to help pilots avoid aviation weather hazards. Even shorter-range weather radars on board many airplanes give pilots a maplike view of thunderstorms as they fly between airports.

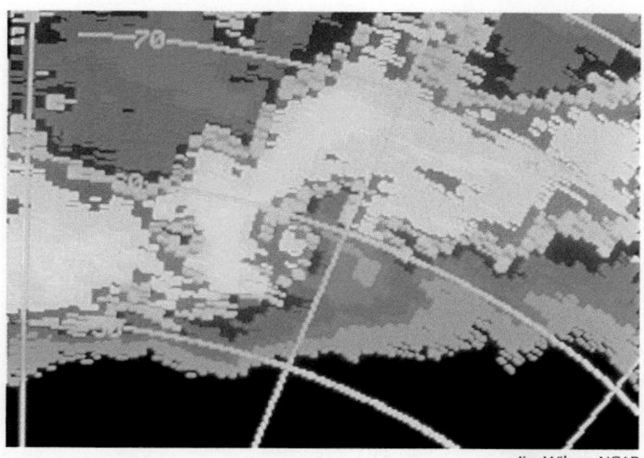

Jim Wilson, NCAR

Weather radar can detect the formation and movement of storms by registering echoes bounced off raindrops and ice particles. This display shows a tornado forming in Oklahoma.

Meteorologists use *wind-profiling radars* to gather information on wind speed and direction at various altitudes up to about 59,000 feet (18,000 meters). Computers can use this information to generate forecasts covering several days.

In space travel. The first step in a mission into space is to launch a spacecraft into orbit around Earth. During the launch, mission controllers use a system of ground-based radars and other radio equipment to track the vehicle. As soon as the spacecraft enters orbit, the radars measure the orbit's size and shape. Using the measurements, computers calculate when the craft's remaining rocket engines should be fired and for how long to

How radar helps police catch speeders

Police radar uses the *Doppler effect* to detect speeding vehicles. A radar antenna mounted on the outside of a police car, *bottom left,* launches a continuous radio wave of a certain frequency. When this wave strikes a moving car, it is reflected at a different frequency, as shown in the diagram. The radar set measures the frequency difference to find the car's speed and records it, *bottom right.*

WORLD BOOK diagram by Robert Keys

Milt and Joan Mann

Jet Propulsion Laboratory

A radar image of a volcano on Venus was made by a computer using data from a scan by the space probe Magellan. Heights in the image are exaggerated 10 times to show detail.

send the vehicle from Earth orbit into outer space.

Spacecraft designed to land on the moon or on another planet carry *landing radar.* This instrument measures the altitude of the spacecraft above the landing site and the rate of descent. Such information is used to regulate the engines of the craft so that it lands at the correct speed. If the vehicle descends too fast, it will crash. If it lands too slowly, it will burn too much fuel. Radar is also used to select stable, level landing sites for spacecraft.

A mission may call for a spacecraft to dock with another space vehicle. The astronauts in the spacecraft locate the other vehicle with radar. They then use the radar data to adjust the direction and speed of their own craft to perform the docking maneuver.

In scientific research. Scientists rely on radar in conducting various kinds of studies. Meteorologists employ radars to study how clouds affect climate and climate change. Special *cloud radars* detect the tiny water droplets and ice crystals that make up clouds, as well as the precipitation they form.

Scientists use high-powered radars to investigate Earth's upper atmosphere. At altitudes of 60 miles (100 kilometers) and higher, the air reflects radio waves. This air is in a part of the upper atmosphere known as the *ionosphere.* In this region, the sun's radiation is so strong that it breaks air molecules into electrically charged particles called *electrons* and *ions.* As a result, the ionosphere can be studied by radar from Earth's surface. Radar observations help scientists determine the temperature of the upper atmosphere and the kinds of gases in the air. Radar observations also indicate how fast winds blow at such high altitudes during different periods of the day.

Radar equipment and techniques contribute much to the study of the solar system. Astronomers have made radar observations of the moon, the sun, and the planets closest to Earth. They have even collected radar echoes from several of Jupiter's largest satellites. Such radar observations provide extremely accurate measurements of the distances to these objects. They also show how rapidly the objects rotate. Astronomers have obtained detailed radar maps of the moon and Mars by recording radio waves bounced off their surfaces. By using the same technique, astronomers have succeeded in penetrating the thick clouds that surround Venus and discovered enormous mountains and valleylike features on its surface. See **Telescope** (Radio telescopes).

Zoologists depend on radar to trace the flight patterns of birds that migrate at night or that are too small to be seen from the ground. Radar can also be used to measure and map currents on the ocean surface. Such information is useful for research in marine biology and for planning offshore oil-drilling projects.

Geologists and engineers use *ground-penetrating radar* to detect underground features and objects within about 50 feet (15 meters) of the surface. They pull the small, boxlike antenna of such a radar across the terrain. The radar can detect soil layers and such buried objects as pipelines, archaeological artifacts, and land mines.

How radar works

Radar sets differ in design and purpose, but they all operate on the same general principles. All radars produce and transmit signals in the form of *electromagnetic waves*—that is, related patterns of electric and magnetic energy. These electromagnetic waves include radio waves and light waves. A true radar transmits radio waves. But similar instruments commonly called *optical radars* or *laser radars* send out light waves. These instruments are also known as *lidars,* from *li*ght *d*etection *a*nd *r*anging.

When the transmitted waves strike an object, they are reflected. Some of the reflected waves return to the set along the same path on which they were sent. This reflection closely resembles what happens when a person shouts in a mountain valley and hears an echo from a nearby cliff. In this case, however, sound waves are reflected instead of radio waves or light waves.

The waves transmitted by radar have a definite frequency. The frequency of such a wave is measured in units called *megahertz* (MHz). One megahertz equals 1 million *hertz* (cycles per second). Radio waves have lower frequencies than light waves have. Most radars that transmit radio waves operate at frequencies of about 3 to 300,000 MHz. Optical radars operate at much higher frequencies. Some generate light waves with frequencies up to 1 billion MHz.

In many cases, radar sets designed for different purposes operate at different frequencies. Radars that transmit at lower frequencies are more effective than high-frequency radars in penetrating clouds, fog, and rain and so are widely used on planes and ships. On the other hand, high-frequency radars provide precise direction measurements with much smaller antennas than those used by lower-frequency radars. Optical radars are especially useful for surveying rough terrain where distant points have to be measured between such objects as large rocks and trees. Over-the-horizon radars use relatively low-frequency radio waves between 3 and 30 MHz. These waves reflect from the ionosphere and can reach beyond the horizon to detect ships, planes, and ocean surface currents at great distances. Ground-penetrating radars also use low frequencies. Radars of the North Warning System use relatively high-frequency radio waves called *microwaves,* which pass through the ionosphere.

Radar sets also differ in how they transmit signals. On this basis, they are usually classified into two general types: (1) pulse radar and (2) continuous-wave radar. Pulse radar is the more common type.

Pulse radar sends out signals in powerful bursts, or pulses, of waves. These pulses last only a few millionths of a second. A pulse radar set usually has only one antenna, which alternately transmits the pulses and receives their echoes.

The distance to an object is found by measuring the time it takes a radar wave to reach the object and return. Radar waves, like all other electromagnetic waves, travel at the speed of light—186,282 miles (299,792 kilometers) per second. Therefore, a radar wave that returns after two seconds would have traveled 372,564 miles (599,584 kilometers)—186,282 miles to the object and 186,282 miles back. Using a measurement of the time required for the round trip, a pulse radar automatically calculates the distance to the object.

The antenna focuses the transmitted energy and sends out the pulses of waves in a narrow beam, enabling the set to determine an object's direction. Only an object within the area of the beam can reflect the waves. Thus the direction from which the waves are reflected to the antenna indicates the location of the object.

Pulse radar can track an object by transmitting signal pulses and measuring the object's distance and direction at regular intervals. It also can be used to make radar maps. Radar maps are produced by scanning a beam of pulses over an area and plotting the strength of the echoes from each direction. The echoes appear on the radar display screen as spots or as images of various colors and brightnesses and are stored as *digital* (numeric) data by a computer. Such objects as buildings, bridges, and mountains produce especially bright images because they produce strong echoes.

If an object in the radar beam is moving, the frequency of reflected waves differs from that of the transmitted waves. An object moving away from the antenna will return waves with a lower frequency, and an approaching object will cause a shift to a higher frequency. This phenomenon is called the *Doppler effect,* and the frequency change is known as a *Doppler shift.* The faster a tracked object is moving, the greater the Doppler shift. Special electronics in some pulse radar systems can indirectly measure the Doppler shift to determine the speed of a moving object. Modern storm surveillance and wind-profiling radars are pulse Doppler systems.

Continuous-wave radar, or *CW radar,* sends out its energy continuously rather than in short bursts. It uses one antenna for transmitting and another for receiving the reflected waves. CW radar directly measures Doppler shift, but not the distance to the moving object. The military uses CW radar to check the speed of incoming aircraft, and the police use it to watch for speeding automobiles on the highway. It is also used in baseball stadiums to clock the speed of pitches.

A more complex form of CW radar is *frequency-modulated continuous-wave* radar, or *FM-CW radar.* In addition to transmitting continuously, FM-CW radar rapidly increases or decreases the transmitted frequency of its signal at regular intervals. This feature enables FM-CW radar to determine the distance to a moving or stationary object. By the time the signal reaches an object and returns, the transmitter's frequency will have changed. The difference between the frequency of the

Goodyear Aerospace Corporation

Radar mapping can be done from an airplane. The radar map of Flagstaff, Arizona, shown here was made from an altitude of about 40,000 feet (12,000 meters). The city appears as a cluster of yellow images. The enormous landform to the left of the city is Elden Mountain.

How pulse radar works Pulse radar is the most widely used type of radar. This diagram shows the principal parts of a typical pulse radar set and illustrates how it detects a distant object.

WORLD BOOK diagram by Robert Keys

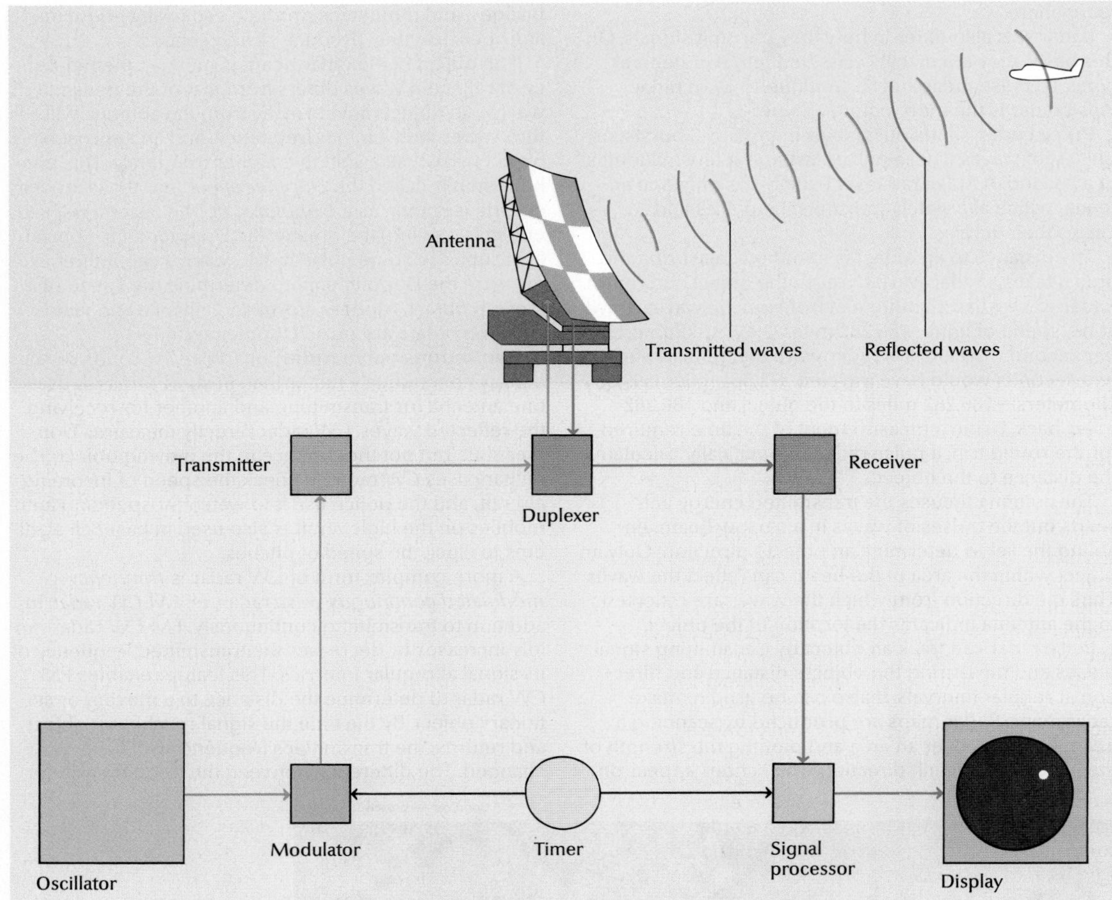

Transmitting radar waves. The oscillator of a pulse radar set generates a low-power electric signal of a constant frequency. A modulator turns the transmitter on and off, causing the transmitter to produce short bursts of electromagnetic waves. The transmitter produces these high-power waves by amplifying the electric signal generated by the oscillator. A duplexer routes the waves from the transmitter to an antenna. After the waves have been released through the antenna, the duplexer connects the receiver to the antenna, which then collects the waves reflected from an object.

Receiving reflected waves. The switching action of the duplexer enables the receiver to pick up the echoes collected by the antenna. The receiver amplifies the reflected waves and filters out much of the accompanying noise and interference. A signal processor takes the incoming waves from the receiver and combines them, which improves their quality. A display shows the echoes as spots of light or as an image of the object detected. A timer automatically turns the signal processor and the modulator on and off at the right time and so coordinates the operations of the radar set.

echo and that of the transmitter is measured, and the measurement is used to calculate the distance from the antenna to the object. The farther away an object is, the greater the difference in frequency.

Like pulse radar, FM-CW radar is used for mapping and tracking. It also serves as an altimeter for airplanes.

The parts of a radar set

Radar sets vary widely in size. A set's size depends mainly on its use. For example, the sets used by motorcycle police to detect speeding cars can be held in the hand and may weigh less than 2 pounds (0.9 kilogram). Many of the huge radar units used to study planets and other distant objects occupy large buildings. One radar unit is built into a valley and has an antenna that measures 1,000 feet (305 meters) in diameter.

Although radar sets differ in size, most have similar parts. These parts include (1) the oscillator, (2) the modulator, (3) the transmitter, (4) the duplexer, (5) the antenna, (6) the receiver, (7) the signal processor, (8) the display, and (9) the timer.

The oscillator is a device that generates a low-power electric signal of a constant frequency. This frequency determines the operating frequency of a radar set.

The modulator. In pulse radar, the modulator is an electronic switch that rapidly turns the transmitter on and off. It causes the transmitter to produce short pulses of waves. In FM-CW radar, the modulator varies the frequency of the continuously transmitted wave.

The transmitter serves as an amplifier. It takes the low-power electric signal generated by the oscillator and produces a high-power electromagnetic wave. For example, the transmitter of a pulse radar used in air traffic control may produce wave pulses with a peak power of several million watts.

The duplexer makes it possible to transmit and receive using the same antenna. It routes the electromagnetic waves from the transmitter to the antenna and prevents them from flowing into the receiver. The powerful waves from the transmitter would damage the sensitive receiver if they flowed into it. After the waves have been released through the antenna, the duplexer connects the receiver to the antenna. This switching action enables the receiver to pick up incoming echoes.

The antenna sends out radar waves in a narrow beam. It also collects the reflected echoes. Most modern radar units have a duplexer, and so they use the same antenna for transmitting and receiving.

The most common type of antenna consists of a horn attached to the front of a large reflecting dish called a *reflector.* The horn sends out the radar waves, and the reflector focuses them into a narrow beam. The antenna rotates so that the beam sweeps around the radar station, scanning for objects in all directions.

Other types of antennas are used in radar sets that operate either at extremely low frequencies or at extremely high frequencies. Radars that transmit low-frequency radio waves have an antenna made of metal tubes or rods. Such antennas resemble the outdoor aerials of TV sets. A device called a *laser* generates the intense beam of light used by an optical radar. In such a radar, lenses control the size of the transmitted beam and capture the light waves returning from the target.

An antenna generally transmits wave pulses for much briefer periods than those during which it receives reflected waves. In typical weather radars, for example, the antenna transmits pulses for only about one-millionth of a second and then receives waves for about one-thousandth of a second.

The receiver takes the weak echoes collected by the antenna and greatly amplifies them. It is so sensitive that it can easily detect echoes of less power than a millionth of a millionth of a watt. The receiver also filters out much of the noise and other interference picked up by the antenna.

The signal processor. In most radar sets, the incoming waves from the receiver pass through a signal processor before going to the display. The signal processor performs different tasks in radars used for different purposes. In many radar units, it blocks out echoes from large, fixed objects and allows only echoes from small, moving targets to reach the display. By doing so, the signal processor enables the operator of a radar set to see an airplane, for example, even though the echoes from the plane arrive at the same time as much stronger echoes from a mountain. A computer serves as the signal processor in most modern radars.

The display presents radar operators with information obtained about an object. Some sets have a simple display. The portable Doppler radars used by the police, for example, have a meter that indicates the speed of a vehicle. But most radar sets have a more complex display that consists of a computer screen or some other type of display screen. Such a display can present radar data in several forms. The most common form is the *Plan Position Indicator,* generally called the PPI.

The PPI provides a circular, maplike picture of the area scanned by the radar beam. The center of the picture corresponds to the location of the radar set. The screen has a compass scale around its edge for direction readings. The screen might also have geographical landmarks and rings spreading out from the center of the picture to mark distance in miles or kilometers. Radar echoes appear as bright or colored spots. The position of a spot with respect to the compass scale shows the direction of the object. The distance of the spot from the center indicates how far away the object is. The speed of a moving object can be determined by noting the time it takes a spot to travel a certain distance on the radar screen, or it can be measured using its Doppler shift and displayed instantaneously, without waiting for the spot to travel.

Other display presentations show the elevation of an object. Such a presentation is used with radar sets designed to help direct aircraft landings.

The timer ensures the smooth, efficient operation of a radar set. This device automatically turns other major parts of the radar set on and off at precisely the right time. The timer does so by sending control signals to the various parts of the system in the proper sequence.

The development of radar

The theories and experiments of many scientists led to the development of radar. James Clerk Maxwell, a British mathematician and physicist, made the first major contribution. During the 1860's, Maxwell said that there existed then-undiscovered kinds of electromagnetic waves that travel at the speed of light. He also proposed that devices might be developed to generate such waves. In the late 1880's, Heinrich R. Hertz, a German physicist, proved Maxwell's ideas correct by producing radio waves. In addition, Hertz demonstrated that such waves could be reflected from solid objects.

Hertz's discovery promoted widespread efforts to find ways of using radio waves for communication. Some scientists realized that radio waves might also be used for detecting distant objects. However, little research could be done until basic radio equipment was developed. Devices for sending and receiving radio signals over long distances became available by the early 1900's.

The first uses of radar. In 1925, two American physicists, Gregory Breit and Merle A. Tuve, bounced short radio pulses off the ionosphere. They determined the height of the ionosphere by measuring the time taken by the reflected signals to return. Many scientists consider this experiment to have been the first practical use of radar.

Scientists also began experimenting with radio echoes to detect airplanes and ships. Much of the early work in this area was done by Robert A. Watson-Watt, a Scottish engineer and physicist. In 1935, he and a team of British scientists refined the pulse techniques used in ionospheric studies to locate aircraft at distances up to about 17 miles (27 kilometers).

The growing threat of a world war stimulated efforts to improve radar technology during the late 1930's. Before World War II began in 1939, the British had built a chain of radar stations along the east and south coasts of England for defense against air and sea attacks. By 1940, the United States was producing pulse-type radar for tracking planes and for controlling antiaircraft guns. Germany also had similar kinds of radar by about the same time. Japan and the Soviet Union developed radar-warning systems a few years later.

Advances during World War II. The radar sets available at the beginning of the war proved extremely valuable for military operations. As a result, scientists were urged to develop even better equipment.

American and British radar experts cooperated closely during the war and produced important advances. The British were working to improve a special kind of vacuum tube called the *magnetron*. By late 1939, their version of the magnetron could generate pulses of microwave energy at high enough power levels to be used in radar systems. In 1940, the British turned their version over to the Americans for further development and manufacturing.

The magnetron contributed greatly to the development of modern radar. This vacuum tube generates *microwaves*—that is, short radio waves with frequencies of more than 1,000 MHz. These high-frequency waves can be concentrated into narrow beams without the use of a huge radar antenna. Microwaves thus made it possible to design radar units small enough for aircraft, patrol boats, and mobile ground stations. In one of the earliest applications of airborne radar, Allied forces located German submarines from a distance as they surfaced.

Before the war ended in 1945, both the Allies and the opposing Axis forces had developed methods of making enemy radar less effective. In one widely used method, planes on bombing missions dropped countless numbers of metal foil strips called *chaff*. Each strip reflected radio signals like a radar target. The bombers filled the air with so many strips that enemy radar operators had difficulty recognizing echoes from the planes.

In another countermeasure, planes and ships carried high-powered radio transmitters. These transmitters produced enough interference to prevent enemy radar from receiving echoes from the planes and ships. Engineers also designed equipment that received pulses from enemy radar and sent them back at an increased power level after a short pause. As a result, false targets appeared on the display of the enemy radar and drew attention from the real targets.

Continued progress. During the early 1950's, American scientists worked on a type of vacuum tube called the *klystron*. They succeeded in developing a high-powered klystron, which is well-suited for radars that require a constant microwave frequency from one pulse to the next. This development helped increase the accuracy of radar. Scientists also worked to improve radar sensitivity. By the late 1960's, they had designed receivers that produced little internal noise, which interferes with the reception of faint echoes.

The rapid development of the computer after World War II contributed much to radar technology. Computers make effective signal processors. They can analyze echoes efficiently at high speeds and present the information obtained in a form useful to radar operators.

Radar also benefited from the invention of the transistor in 1947 and of related solid-state electronic devices during the 1950's and 1960's. These devices enabled engineers to build lighter and more reliable radar sets. In addition, engineers used a solid-state device called a *phase shifter* to develop a new kind of radar. This radar, known as a *phased array radar,* moves its signal beam electronically rather than by rotating an antenna. Phased

© PhotoStock-Israel/Alamy Images

An optical radar is used to survey terrain and construction sites where distant points must be accurately measured. The device works by measuring the reflection of light waves it transmits in an extremely narrow beam.

array radars are especially useful when a signal beam must be moved rapidly from one target to the next.

In the late 1960's, physicists perfected the laser. Their work led to the development of optical radars, also called *lidars,* which operate at the high frequencies of laser light. Such instruments require only a small antenna to send out an extremely narrow signal beam.

Radar in the future. Researchers today are seeking ways to reduce the size and production costs of microwave radars. Pocket-sized radar units could be widely used as aids for blind people and as collision-warning devices in cars. Radars on orbiting satellites could provide worldwide measurements of precipitation and cloud conditions. Special *polarimetric radars* will be able to identify objects by shape, enabling scientists to distinguish between rain, snow, and swarms of insects, for example. Microwave navigation radars built into a single artificial satellite might one day track ship and aircraft traffic over most of Earth. Brooks E. Martner

Related articles in *World Book* include:

Airport	North Warning System	Rangefinder
Doppler effect	Radio	Watson-Watt, Sir Robert A.
Guided missile	Rain (Measuring rainfall)	Weather (Measuring the weather)
Laser		
Microwave		
Navigation		

Outline

I. The uses of radar
- A. In aviation
- B. In ship navigation
- C. In the military
- D. In controlling automobile speed and traffic
- E. In weather observation and forecasting
- F. In space travel
- G. In scientific research

II. How radar works
- A. Pulse radar
- B. Continuous-wave radar

III. The parts of a radar set
- A. The oscillator
- B. The modulator
- C. The transmitter
- D. The duplexer
- E. The antenna
- F. The receiver
- G. The signal processor
- H. The display
- I. The timer

IV. The development of radar

Questions

What are some uses of radar in scientific research?
Why was the magnetron important in the development of radar?
How does pulse radar find the distance to an object?
What is a Plan Position Indicator?
What are some military uses of radar?
What is the special feature of phased array radar?
How does radar help weather forecasters?
What is a Doppler shift? How is it used?
Why is radar an effective aid in ship navigation?
What is a duplexer? Why is it important?

Radcliffe-Brown, A. R. (1881-1955), a British anthropologist, helped develop British social anthropology during the 1920's. He argued that human societies should be studied the same way that a naturalist studies plants and animals.

Alfred Reginald Radcliffe-Brown was born on Jan. 18, 1881, in England. He graduated from Cambridge University. In 1937, he became the first professor of social anthropology at Oxford University. He died on Oct. 24, 1955. John W. Burton

Radcliffe College was a private liberal arts college for women in Cambridge, Massachusetts, with close ties to Harvard University. Radcliffe was founded as the Harvard Annex in 1879. At that time, the school delegated to the Harvard faculty the responsibility for the instruction of its students. The name Radcliffe College was adopted in 1894.

Radcliffe was a separate institution designed to advance society by educating women. By the mid-1970's, however, women students began to be admitted jointly to Harvard and Radcliffe, although Radcliffe remained an independent college for undergraduate women. In 1999, Radcliffe College and Harvard University merged. On the Radcliffe campus, the Radcliffe Institute for Advanced Study was established, offering advanced scholarship and research with a focus on women, gender, and society. The institute inherited Radcliffe College's famous Arthur and Elizabeth Schlesinger Library on the History of Women in America. The library houses the papers of many notable women, including the women's rights leader Susan B. Anthony; the chef Julia Child; the author Shirley Graham Du Bois, wife of the civil rights leader W. E. B. Du Bois; and the aviator Amelia Earhart. The institute's Web site at http://www.radcliffe.edu offers more information.

Critically reviewed by the Radcliffe Institute for Advanced Study

See also **Harvard University.**

Radford, Arthur William (1896-1973), an admiral in the United States Navy, served from 1953 to 1957 as chairman of the Joint Chiefs of Staff. Radford was born on Feb. 27, 1896, in Chicago. He graduated from the United States Naval Academy in 1916 and served during World War I (1914-1918) and World War II (1939-1945). Radford won recognition as an expert on naval aviation and aircraft-carrier warfare. He was commander in chief of the U.S. Pacific Fleet from 1949 to 1953. Radford died in Bethesda, Maryland, on Aug. 17, 1973.

Adrian R. Lewis

Radian is a metric unit used to measure angles. Engineers and scientists frequently measure angles in radians because the unit simplifies many of their calculations. Navigators, surveyors, and most other people measure angles in degrees. One radian equals an angle of 57.29578 degrees.

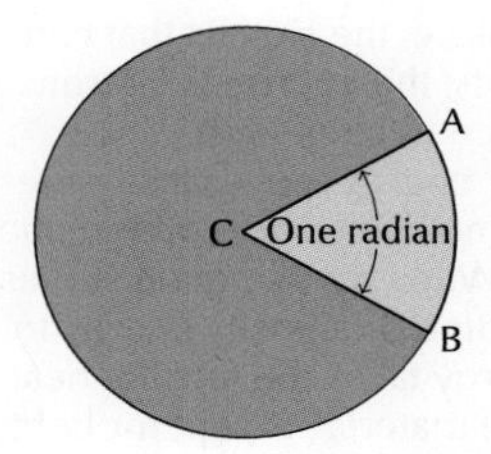

WORLD BOOK diagram

A radian. To draw an angle that equals 1 radian, first measure the radius of a circle. On the circumference of the circle, measure an arc that is the same length as the radius. In this diagram, the arc AB equals the radius. Connect the ends of the arc with the center of the circle. The angle between lines AC and BC equals 1 radian.

An angle of 1 radian is formed between two radii of a circle if they mark off an arc equal to the length of the radius of the circle. Circles and arcs may represent angles and may be measured in radians. For example, the circumference of a circle equals 2 times *pi* (π) times the radius of the circle. Thus, there are 2π radians in a circle.

Colin C. Graham

See also **Degree.**

Radiant energy. See **Sun** (Energy output).

Philippe Plailly/SPL, Photo Researchers

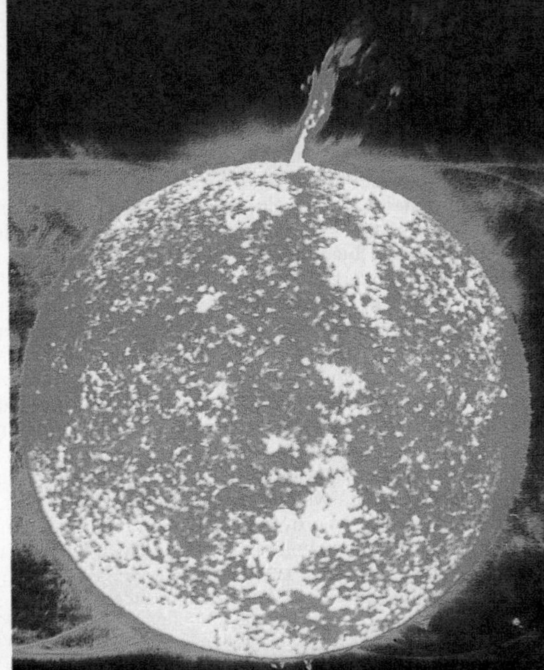
NASA

Radiation is a vital form of energy. Artificially produced radiation has many uses in medicine and other fields. A medical worker handles radioactive iodine, *left,* with special gloves through a protective shield. All life on Earth depends on natural radiation from the sun, *right.*

Radiation

Radiation is energy given off in the form of waves or tiny particles of matter. Radiation is found throughout the universe. It comes in many forms. Most people have heard of X rays, gamma rays, and radiation from nuclear reactors. These kinds of radiation are often mentioned as possible health hazards. X rays and gamma rays also have valuable uses in scientific research. But there are many other forms of radiation. The most familiar is probably the light we see, for example from the sun or a flashlight. The sun's ultraviolet rays, which cause suntan and sunburn, are another form of radiation. Other examples include heat from a fireplace, the signals that carry radio and television broadcasts, the intense light from a laser, and the microwaves used to cook food.

Radiation occurs whenever energy moves from one place to another. Atoms and molecules give off radiation to dispose of excess energy. When the radiation strikes a substance, it may transfer some or all of its energy to the substance. Often, the energy takes the form of heat, raising the temperature of the material. Except for light, most kinds of radiation are invisible.

There are two chief types of radiation. One type is called *electromagnetic radiation.* It consists only of energy. The other type is known as *particle radiation* or *particulate radiation.* It consists of tiny bits of matter.

There are many sources of electromagnetic radiation. All materials that have been heated give off such radiation. The sun produces electromagnetic radiation from nuclear reactions in its core. This energy heats the sun's outer layer until the hot gases glow, giving off light and other radiation. This solar radiation travels through space to Earth and other planets.

Particle radiation comes from radioactive elements. Radium, uranium, and many other heavy elements found in rocks and soil are naturally radioactive. In addition, scientists can create radioactive forms of any element. They do this by bombarding the element with *atomic particles,* the tiny bits of matter that make up atoms.

All life on Earth depends on radiation. But some forms of radiation can be dangerous if not handled properly. Doctors use X rays, for example, to locate and diagnose hidden diseases. But X rays also can damage cells, causing them to become cancerous or die. Light from the sun enables plants to grow and warm Earth. But sunlight also causes sunburn and skin cancer. Doctors use gamma radiation to treat disease by killing cancer cells. But gamma rays are also thought to cause birth defects. Nuclear power plants produce electric energy. But the same facilities create radioactive waste that can kill living things if not properly handled.

Uses of radiation

In medicine, radiation and radioactive substances are used for diagnosis, treatment, and research. X rays, for example, pass through muscles and other soft tissue. However, they are stopped by dense materials. This property enables doctors to use X rays to find broken bones and to locate cancers in the body. Doctors also look for certain diseases by injecting a radioactive substance. To find the disease, they monitor the radiation given off as the substance moves through the body.

In communication. Communication systems use forms of electromagnetic radiation to carry information. Variations in the radiation represent changes in the sound, pictures, or other information being sent. For example, a human voice can be sent as a radio wave or microwave by making the wave vary to correspond to variations in the voice.

In science, researchers use radioactive atoms to determine the age of materials that were once part of a living thing. The age of such materials can be estimated by measuring the amount of radioactive carbon they contain. This process is called *radiocarbon dating.* Environmental scientists use radioactive atoms known as *tracer atoms* to identify the pathways taken by pollutants through the environment.

Radiation is used to determine the composition of materials in a process called *neutron activation analysis.* In this process, scientists bombard a sample of a substance with particles called *neutrons.* Some of the atoms in the sample absorb neutrons and become radioactive. The scientists can identify the elements in the sample by studying the radiation given off.

In industry, radiation has many uses. Food processing plants use doses of radiation to kill bacteria on certain foods, thus preserving the food. Radiation is used to make plastics because it can cause molecules to link together and harden. Industry also uses radiation to look for flaws in manufactured materials, a process called *industrial radiography.*

Nuclear power plants obtain energy from *nuclear fission.* Nuclear fission is the splitting of the nucleus of an atom into the nuclei of two lighter elements. Fission releases large amounts of radiation, producing heat. The heat is used to turn water into steam. This steam powers a turbine that produces electric energy.

The opposite process is called *nuclear fusion.* It occurs when the nuclei of two lighter elements join to form the nucleus of a heavier one. Fusion, like fission, releases vast amounts of radiation. Fusion creates the heat and light of the sun and other stars. It also creates the explosive force of the hydrogen bomb. Scientists are working to harness fusion to produce electric energy.

In military operations, radio waves are used in radar systems to locate aircraft and ships. Microwaves and laser light have been used both for communication and to guide "smart" missiles to their targets. Heat-sensing devices for night detection rely on the infrared radiation—that is, the heat—given off by living bodies.

Radiation and radioactivity

Scientists distinguish radiation from *radioactivity,* a property of some types of matter. Radioactivity results from changes in the nuclei of the atoms that make up such matter. These changes cause the matter to release certain forms of radiation.

To understand radiation and radioactivity, it helps to know the structure of an atomic nucleus. The nucleus of the most common *isotope* (form) of hydrogen consists of a single *proton.* A proton is a particle with a positive electric charge. All other nuclei consist of at least one proton and one *neutron.* A neutron is a particle with no charge. The most common form of helium, for example, has two protons and two neutrons in the nucleus.

In certain circumstances, an atom can change the number of protons and neutrons in its nucleus. This change is accomplished by giving off or taking in atomic particles or bursts of energy—that is, by giving off or taking in radiation. Any change in the number of protons in the nucleus produces an atom of a different element.

Radioactive atoms spontaneously release radiation to take on a more stable form. The process of giving off atomic particles is called *radioactive decay.* As radioactive elements decay, they change into different isotopes of the same element or into other elements until they finally become stable and nonradioactive.

Radioactive decay takes place at different rates in different elements and isotopes. The rate of decay is measured by the *half-life.* The half-life is the length of time taken for half the atoms in a sample to decay. For example, the half-life of cesium 137, a radioactive isotope of cesium, is about 30 years. This fact means that after about 30 years, only half the atoms in a sample of cesium 137 will remain undecayed. After about 60 years, about a fourth of the original cesium 137 remains. After another 30 years, only an eighth remains, and so on. The half-life of radon 222 is about 3.8 days. Half-lives vary from fractions of a second to billions of years.

Electromagnetic radiation

Electromagnetic radiation consists of electric and magnetic energy. Every electrically charged body is surrounded by an *electric field.* This field is the region where the body's electric force can be felt. Every magnetic body is surrounded by a similar region known as a *magnetic field.* An electric current or a changing electric field creates a magnetic field. Likewise, a changing magnetic field creates an electric field. Electric and magnetic fields act together to produce electromagnetic radiation.

Electromagnetic radiation moves through space as a wave. However, it also has properties of particles. Atoms release electromagnetic radiation in the form of a tiny packet of energy called a *photon.* Like a particle, a photon occupies a fixed amount of space. Like a wave, however, a photon has a definite *frequency* and *wavelength.* A wave's frequency is the number of times each second that the wave passes through one cycle. The wavelength is the distance the wave travels in the time it takes to pass through one cycle.

The energy of a photon varies according to the frequency and wavelength. If the radiation has a high frequency and a short wavelength, its photons have high energy. If the radiation has a low frequency and a long wavelength, its photons have low energy.

In a vacuum, all electromagnetic radiation moves at the speed of light—186,282 miles (299,792 kilometers)

Outline

Kinds of electromagnetic radiation

Electromagnetic radiation travels through space in waves, which vary in *frequency* (how quickly a wave passes through a cycle) and *wavelength* (how far the wave travels during one cycle). The kinds of radiation range in wavelength from short gamma rays to long radio waves.

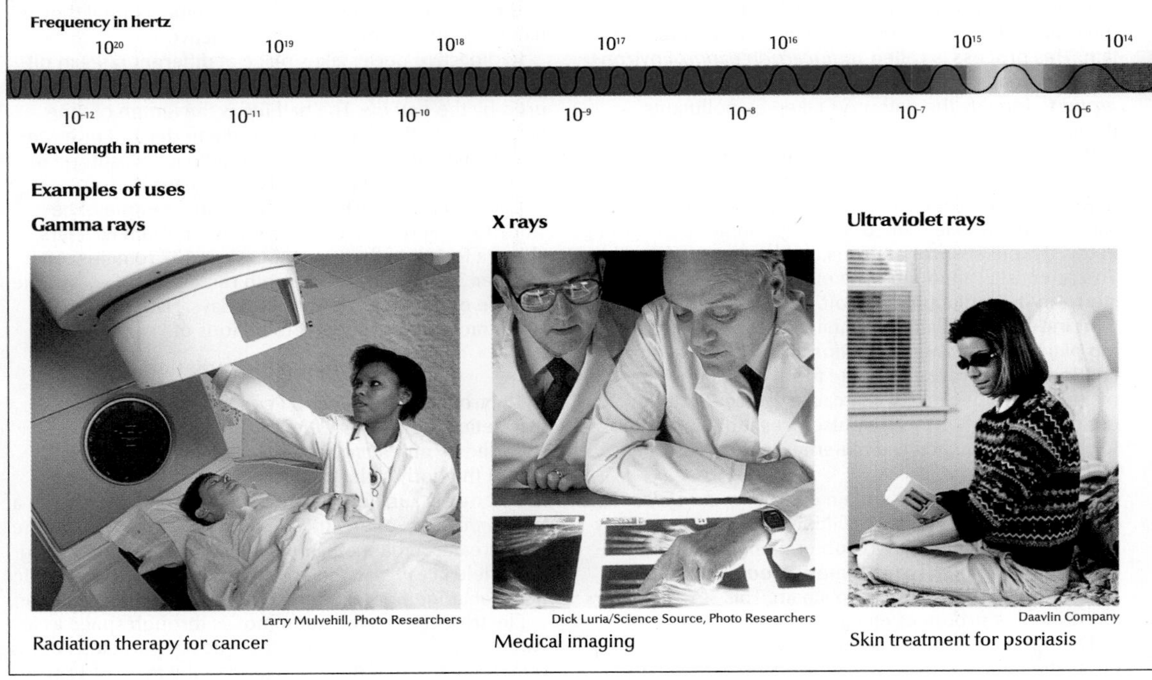

Larry Mulvehill, Photo Researchers
Radiation therapy for cancer

Dick Luria/Science Source, Photo Researchers
Medical imaging

Daavlin Company
Skin treatment for psoriasis

per second. The various kinds of radiation differ, however, in their frequency and wavelength. They are classified according to an arrangement called the *electromagnetic spectrum.* In order of increasing wavelength, the kinds of electromagnetic radiation are: gamma rays, X rays, ultraviolet rays, visible light, infrared rays, microwaves, and radio waves. Gamma rays and X rays are high-energy forms of radiation. Radio waves, on the other end of the spectrum, have relatively low energy.

Particle radiation

Particle radiation includes protons, neutrons, and negatively charged *electrons.* These three types of tiny particles serve as the building blocks of an atom. All types of particle radiation have both mass and energy. Most such radiation travels at high speeds but slower than the speed of light. A type of particle called a *neutrino,* however, has an undetermined mass and travels at or near the speed of light.

We usually think of protons, neutrons, and electrons as particles. But scientists have discovered that they also behave like waves. These waves, called *matter waves,* have wavelengths. The faster a particle is moving, the shorter its wavelength. Thus, particle radiation, like electromagnetic radiation, has characteristics of both particles and waves. There are four common types of particle radiation: (1) alpha particles, (2) beta particles, (3) protons, and (4) neutrons.

Alpha particles consist of two protons and two neutrons. They are identical with the nuclei of helium atoms. Alpha particles have a positive electric charge. The mass of an alpha particle is about 7,300 times that of an electron. Alpha particles are given off by the nuclei of some radioactive atoms. Most alpha particles eventually gain two electrons to become atoms of helium gas.

Beta particles are generally electrons. Most beta particles form when a radioactive nucleus creates and releases an electron. In the process, a neutron in the nucleus changes into a proton and a beta particle is released.

Most beta particles are negatively charged. But some are positively charged particles called *positrons.* Positrons are produced when an atom changes a proton into a neutron. Positrons are a form of *antimatter.* Antimatter is a type of matter that resembles ordinary matter but with electric charge or certain other properties reversed. When a positron collides with a negatively charged electron, the two particles destroy each other. The collision produces two or three gamma ray photons. This process is called *pair annihilation.*

Two other small particles, neutrinos and *antineutrinos,* accompany beta radiation. When a nucleus produces a positron, it also releases a neutrino. When a nucleus releases a negatively charged beta particle, it also gives off an antineutrino, the antimatter equivalent of a neutrino.

Protons and neutrons can also be released from some radioactive nuclei. Each of these particles has a mass about 1,850 times that of an electron. The mass of a neutron is slightly larger than the mass of a proton. Neutron radiation is more common than proton radiation, which rarely occurs naturally on Earth.

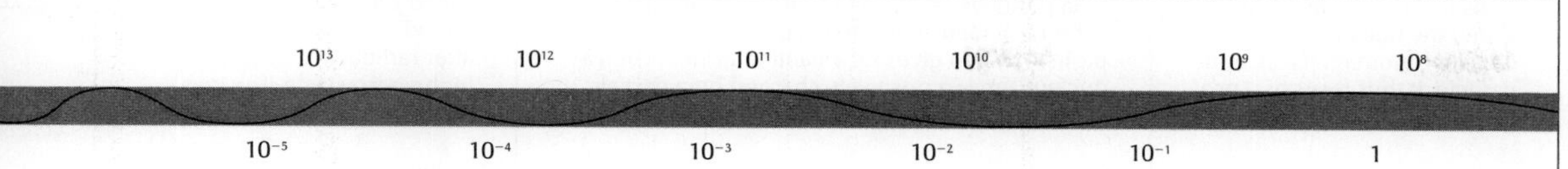

Infrared rays

Aaron Haupt, Frazier Photolibrary

Heating and cooking

Microwaves

H. Gans, The Image Works

Microwave cooking

Radio waves

David R. Frazier

Television broadcasting

WORLD BOOK illustrations by Hans & Cassady, Inc.

Sources of radiation

Natural sources of radiation include the sun, other stars, and naturally radioactive elements. There are also many artificial sources of radiation.

The sun and other stars give off both electromagnetic and particle radiation. This radiation results from the fusion of hydrogen nuclei in the star. The hydrogen changes into helium, releasing a large amount of energy. This process produces electromagnetic radiation across the entire spectrum. Besides visible light, a star gives off everything from radio waves to high-energy gamma radiation. The gamma radiation, however, is produced when new elements form deep in the core of the star. It does not reach Earth directly.

Stars also produce alpha and beta particles, protons, neutrons, and other forms of radiation. The high-energy particles released by stars are called *cosmic rays.* The sun puts on brief displays called *solar flares,* bathing Earth in cosmic rays. These rays are strong enough to interfere with communications and electrical service lines.

Naturally radioactive substances. Many elements have isotopes that are naturally radioactive. Most naturally radioactive substances belong to one of three sequences of change called *radioactive decay series.* They are: (1) the uranium series, (2) the thorium series, and (3) the actinium series. In each of these series, heavy isotopes decay into various lighter isotopes by giving off radiation until they eventually become stable. Different isotopes of an element have the same number of protons in their nuclei but a different number of neutrons.

The uranium series begins with uranium 238, the heaviest isotope of uranium. It has 92 protons and 146 neutrons. After losing an alpha particle—which consists of 2 protons and 2 neutrons—the nucleus has 90 protons and 144 neutrons. It is no longer uranium but a radioactive isotope of thorium. Scientists call this process of changing into another element *transmutation.* The thorium, in turn, breaks down in several steps to radium 226. The radium 226 decays into radon, a naturally occurring radioactive gas. Radon may become a health hazard if it accumulates in certain buildings, especially poorly ventilated ones. The series continues until the isotope becomes a stable form of lead.

The thorium series begins with thorium 232, an isotope of thorium. The actinium series begins with uranium 235, another isotope of uranium. These two series also end with lead.

A fourth group of naturally radioactive substances includes a variety of materials that do not belong to a radioactive series. Cosmic radiation striking Earth's atmosphere makes many of these elements. Such elements include carbon 14, potassium 40, and samarium 146. Carbon 14 and potassium 40 are also present in the human body.

Artificial radioactive substances are made by human activities, such as the fission that takes place in nuclear weapons and nuclear reactors, or in laboratories. When fission splits a nucleus, it releases several types of radiation, including neutrons, gamma radiation, and beta particles. Fission also produces new radioactive atoms called *fission products.* For example, atomic

Particles given off by radioactive atoms

Alpha particles consist of two protons and two neutrons that act as one particle. When the nucleus of a radioactive atom emits an alpha particle, it thus loses two protons and two neutrons.

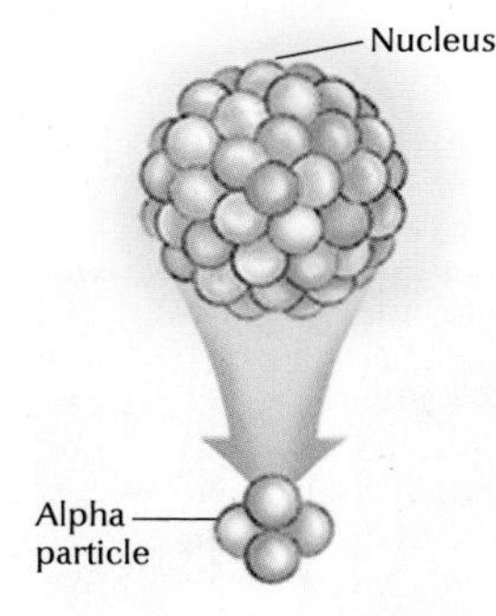

Beta particles are high-speed electrons emitted from the nuclei of certain radioactive elements. Beta particles can be either negative or positive. When a nucleus emits a negatively charged beta particle, it also gives off an antineutrino. When a nucleus emits a positively charged beta particle, called a *positron,* it also gives off a neutrino.

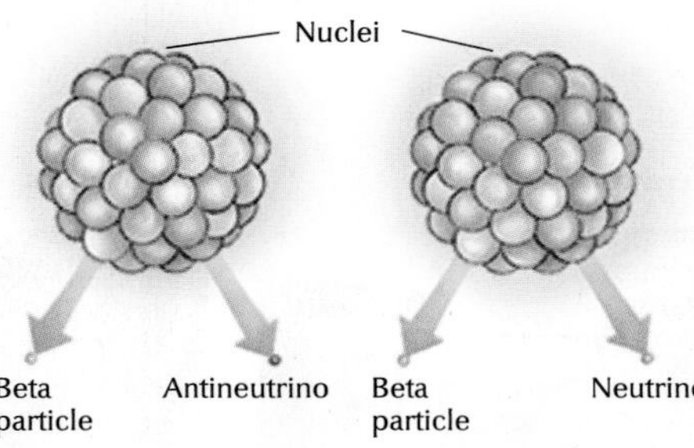

Gamma rays are particles of electromagnetic energy called *photons.* Gamma rays are released when a nucleus, after radioactive decay, is in a high-energy state. The rays travel at the speed of light.

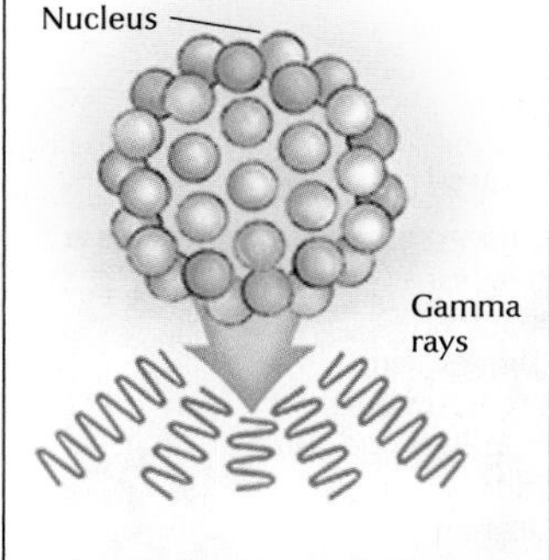

WORLD BOOK illustration by Sarah Woodward

bomb tests in the 1950's and 1960's covered Earth with a fission product called cesium 137, a radioactive isotope of cesium. Used fuel from nuclear power plants also contains many fission products, such as plutonium 239, strontium 90, and barium 140. This used fuel, called *nuclear waste,* remains radioactive and dangerous for thousands of years.

In addition, nuclear plants create new radioactive elements known as *activation products.* Activation products form when the pipes and other materials in a nuclear reactor absorb neutrons and other types of radiation, becoming radioactive.

Many other types of radiation are created by human activities. Physicists use powerful devices called *particle accelerators* to speed up the movement of electrically charged particles, including electrons, protons, and entire nuclei. The physicists then bombard stable, nonradioactive atoms with beams of these high-speed particles. The resulting collisions produce new radioactive atoms. Such experiments help scientists learn more about the structure and properties of atoms.

Causes of radiation

Within an atom, electrons are confined to regions called *electron shells.* The shells lie at various distances from the nucleus, according to how much energy the electrons have. Electrons with less energy travel in inner shells. Electrons with more energy are in outer shells. Protons and neutrons in the nucleus are also arranged according to their energy levels in layers known as *nuclear shells.* All the protons, neutrons, or electrons in a shell have almost the same amount of energy.

Just as water always seeks its lowest possible level, electrons seek the state of lowest energy. When an elec-

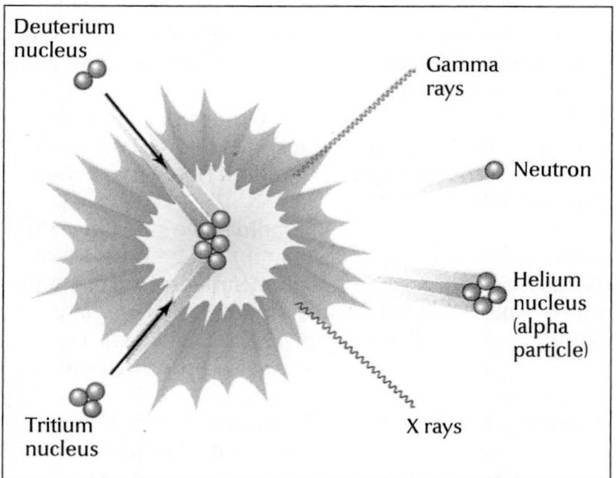

WORLD BOOK illustration by Mark Swindle

Nuclear fusion releases large amounts of radiation. Fusion occurs when the nuclei of two lightweight elements join to form the nucleus of a heavier one. In this example, nuclei of deuterium and tritium unite and form a helium nucleus.

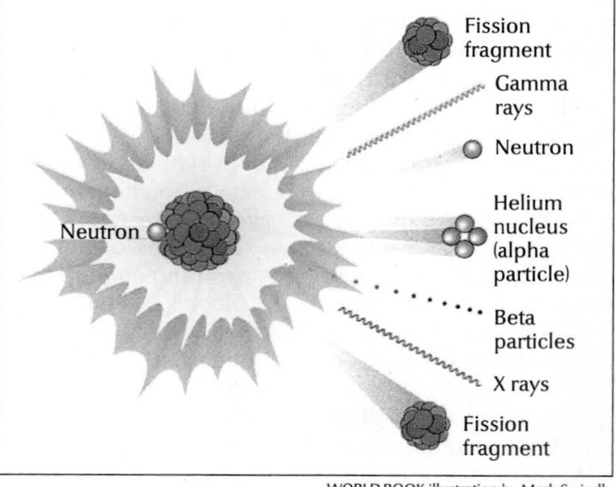

WORLD BOOK illustration by Mark Swindle

Nuclear fission releases several types of radiation, including neutrons, alpha and beta particles, gamma rays, and X rays. Fission involves using a neutron to split a nucleus of a heavy element, such as uranium, into two fission fragments.

tron shifts from an outer shell to one closer to the nucleus, the electron releases a packet of energy. This packet, a photon, escapes from the atom. The energy of the photon equals the difference in energy between the electron's original shell and the new one. If the energy difference is small, the atom will give off visible light, infrared radiation, or both. Light bulbs produce light in this way. If the energy difference is large, the atom might produce X rays.

When a proton or neutron moves from one nuclear shell to another, the nucleus releases gamma radiation. Most atoms that release particle radiation in the course of radioactive decay also produce gamma radiation. This happens because their protons and neutrons are shifting into new shells. The radiation produced by nuclear reactions also results from protons, neutrons, and electrons moving to new shells. In nuclear fission, for example, the particles are moving to the shells of new nuclei created when a nucleus splits into two smaller nuclei.

Electromagnetic radiation also is produced if an electrically charged particle changes direction, speed, or both. A particle that enters an electric or magnetic field, for example, slows down and changes course. As a result, the particle releases radiation. X rays are produced whenever electrons suddenly slow down. For example, electrons give off X rays when they collide with atoms of metal inside an X-ray machine. Electrons also produce X rays if they pass near a large nucleus. The negatively charged electrons are attracted by the positively charged nucleus. As the electrons change direction, they produce X rays called *bremsstrahlung (BREHM shtrah lung). Bremsstrahlung* is a German word that means *braking radiation.*

Effects of radiation

Radiation produces two main effects in atoms or molecules: (1) *excitation* and (2) *ionization.* In excitation, an atom or molecule absorbs energy from radiation, moving its electrons to higher-energy shells. In most cases, the excited atom can hold the extra energy for only a fraction of a second. Then it releases the energy as a photon, falling back to a state of lower energy. In ionization, the radiation transfers enough energy to the electrons that they leave the atom. Atoms that have lost electrons become positively charged particles called *positive ions.* The electrons may then join other atoms.

Excitation and ionization also affect living tissues. The body's cells contain molecules, many of which are held together by electrons. When radiation excites or ionizes the molecules, chemical bonds may be broken and the shape of a molecule change. These changes can disrupt normal chemical processes in cells, causing the cells to become abnormal or die.

The hereditary material in living cells is in the form of a molecule called DNA (deoxyribonucleic acid). If radiation affects DNA, it may cause a permanent change called a *mutation.* In rare cases, these mutations may pass on undesirable traits to offspring. Even low-energy photons, particularly ultraviolet light from the sun, may damage cells by excitation. If damage is severe, the cell may become cancerous or die while trying to divide. The damage depends on the radiation's ionizing ability, the dose received, and the type of tissue involved.

Ionizing ability. Radiation may be classified as *ionizing* or *nonionizing.* Ionizing radiation is the most dangerous. Some types of ionizing radiation have enough energy to directly strip electrons from any atoms near their path. Such radiation includes alpha and beta particles and protons. Other types of ionizing radiation must first transfer energy to an atom. These types include X rays, gamma radiation, and neutron radiation. The added energy then causes the atom to lose an electron.

Nonionizing radiation consists of photons with too little energy to cause ionization. Radio waves, microwaves, infrared radiation, and visible light are all nonionizing radiation. Each will cause only excitation.

Dose. Scientists use two systems for measuring the amount, or *dose,* of radiation absorbed. The older system, still sometimes used, measures doses in units called *rads. Rad* stands for *r*adiation *a*bsorbed *d*ose. One rad is produced when 1 gram of material absorbs 100 *ergs.* An erg is an extremely small unit of energy. The newer and more commonly used system was introduced in 1975. It measures dosage in units called *grays,* named after the British scientist Louis H. Gray. One gray equals 100 rads or 1 *joule* per kilogram of material. A

WORLD BOOK illustration by Mark Swindle

Radioactive decay

A radioactive decay series is the process by which a radioactive atom releases radiation and changes into different forms of the same element or into other elements. The uranium series, shown at the right, begins with uranium 238. Losing an alpha particle, the atom changes into radioactive thorium 234. The series continues through many more steps of decay until the atom becomes a stable form of lead.

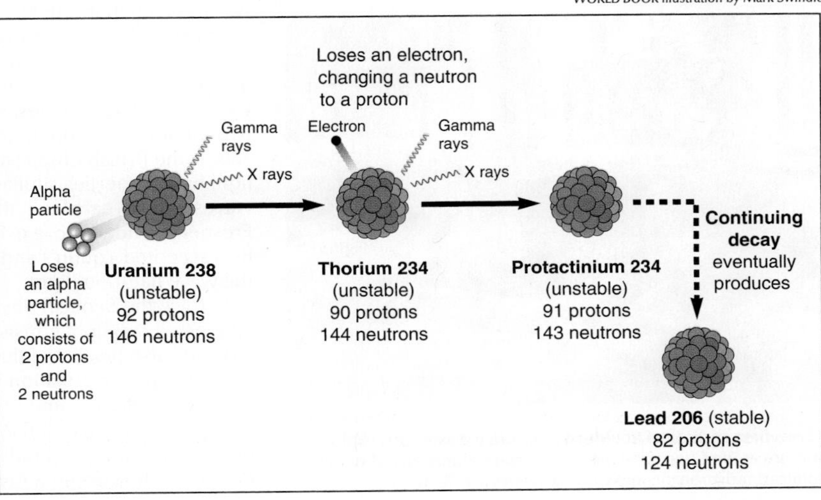

joule is a unit of energy. It equals 10 million ergs.

Different types of radiation produce different effects at the same dose. To account for this, scientists have developed a measure called the *radiation weighting factor.* This factor indicates how much the radiation damages living tissue compared with an equal dose of gamma rays or X rays. For example, a dose of alpha particles causes about 20 times as much damage as the same dose of X rays. Thus, alpha particles have a radiation weighting factor of 10. X rays, gamma radiation, and beta particles have a radiation weighting factor of 1. Neutrons range from 2 to 20, depending on their energy.

Multiplying the dose by the radiation weighting factor gives a measure of damage called the *equivalent dose.* If the dose is given in rads, the dose equivalent will be in *rems. Rem* stands for *r*oentgen *e*quivalent in *m*an. One rem is the amount of radiation that causes the same effect on a human being as 1 rad of gamma rays or X rays. If the dose is in grays, the equivalent dose will be in *sieverts.* Sieverts are named for the Swedish scientist Rolf M. Sievert. One sievert equals 100 rems. Grays and sieverts are part of the metric system of measurement.

Large single doses cause a combination of effects often called *radiation sickness.* Doses above roughly 0.70 sievert damage the parts of the body that produce blood cells. Death can result from infections and hemorrhaging within a few months to a few weeks depending on the dose. At doses above about 6 sieverts, the cells lining the digestive tract die and bacteria in the intestines invade the bloodstream. Death often occurs within a few weeks. At doses of tens of sieverts, the circulatory system collapses and the brain is severely injured leading to death in as little as a few days.

Deaths from radiation sickness are extremely rare. People have only suffered such large doses in reactor accidents, in a few cases where radioactive material was mishandled, and in the 1945 nuclear bombings of Hiroshima and Nagasaki, Japan. The worst reactor accident in history was a 1986 explosion and fire at the Chernobyl nuclear power plant in Ukraine, then part of the Soviet Union. Thirty-one workers died in the accident.

Small single doses. The doses typically encountered in daily life are much smaller. Many scientists believe that the average person is exposed to about 0.003 to 0.004 sievert of radiation per year. About half of this amount comes from breathing radon gas released by radioactive rocks and soil. Medical and dental X rays add another 0.0004 to 0.0008 sievert per year on average. Other sources, such as nuclear power plants and waste disposal sites, typically account for less than 0.0001 sievert per year. Smokers take in much higher doses from radioactive isotopes in smoke.

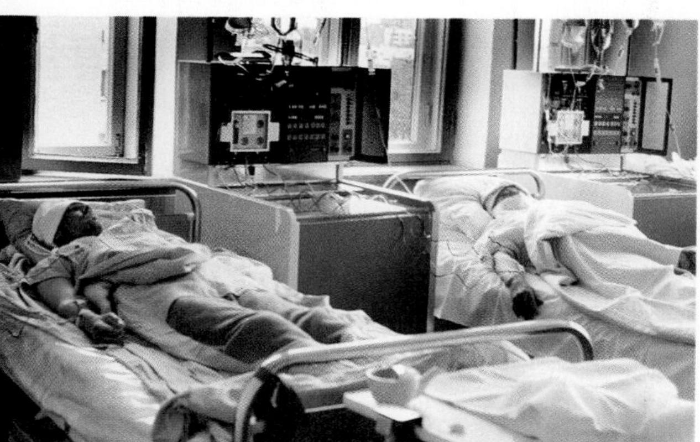

Robert Gale, Sygma

The worst radiation accident in history was a 1986 explosion and fire at the Chernobyl plant in Ukraine. Hundreds of workers suffered radiation sickness, *shown here,* and 31 died.

An accumulation of small doses of radiation increases the risk of developing a condition. However, it does not increase the severity of any resulting condition. The chief risks of repeated small doses of radiation are cancer and birth defects. Extremely small doses do not always produce clear evidence of harmful effects. Some researchers believe that continual exposure to low doses of ionizing radiation are beneficial. They think that such exposure may stimulate repair mechanisms within the cell, protecting against disease. This idea is called *radiation hormesis.*

The International Commission on Radiological Protection (ICRP), a panel of experts from many countries, sets guidelines to protect people from the effects of radiation. It recommends a *maximum permissible dose* (MPD) for radiation workers and the general public. The MPD states the maximum amount of radiation a person should be exposed to over a one-year and a five-year period. Other agencies set similar guidelines, including the National Council on Radiation Protection and Measurements in the United States and the Canadian Nuclear Safety Commission in Canada.

History

Scientists have studied radiation since ancient times. In the 300's and 200's B.C., the Greek philosopher Epicurus wrote of particles "streaming off" the surface of bodies. Euclid, a Greek mathematician of the same time, thought the eye sent out radiation to enable an object to be seen.

Robert Grosseteste, an English bishop and scholar of the 1200's, thought of light as the root of all knowledge. He believed that understanding the laws controlling light would uncover all the laws of nature.

Electromagnetic waves. The composition of light was debated in the 1600's by the followers of the English scientist Sir Isaac Newton and the Dutch physicist Christiaan Huygens. Newton insisted that light consisted of tiny particles. Huygens, on the other hand, suggested it was composed of waves. Scientists argued about these two theories for more than 100 years. Then, in the early 1800's, the British physicist Thomas Young showed that light had properties similar to those of sound and water waves. A few years later, the French physicist Augustin Fresnel provided more evidence. By 1850, most scientists accepted Young's and Fresnel's findings as proof of the wave nature of light.

In 1864, the Scottish physicist James Clerk Maxwell suggested that light consisted of electromagnetic waves. Maxwell also predicted that other, invisible forms of electromagnetic radiation would be discovered. Maxwell's predictions came true with the work of two German physicists, Heinrich R. Hertz and Wilhelm C. Roentgen. Hertz discovered radio waves in the late 1880's, and Roentgen discovered X rays in 1895.

Discovery of radioactivity. In 1896, the French physicist Antoine Henri Becquerel discovered that crystals of a uranium compound would darken photographic plates even if the plates were not exposed to light. He proposed that uranium gave off energy in the form of radiation. Later experiments by the New Zealand-born physicist Ernest Rutherford showed that this radiation consisted of particles he named *alphas* and *betas.*

In 1898, the French physicists Marie and Pierre Curie found another substance that produced radiation. They named it *polonium.* Later that year, with the French chemist Gustave Bémont, they discovered an additional substance that gave off radiation. They named it *radium.* A few years later, Rutherford showed that radioactive substances could change into new elements in the process of transmutation.

The work of Rutherford and the Curies led to great interest in the structure of the atom. Rutherford, his colleagues, and other scientists soon proved that the atom had a nucleus of high mass and positive electric charge surrounded by negatively charged electrons.

The quantum theory. In 1900, the German physicist Max Planck studied radiation from hot objects. He suggested that objects could only *emit* (give off) and absorb this radiation in packets of energy called *quanta.* The name *quanta* was later changed to *photons.* Another German physicist, Albert Einstein, used Planck's theory in 1905 to explain a phenomenon known as the *photoelectric effect.* Earlier scientists had discovered this effect. They found that a bright beam of light striking a metal causes the metal to release electrons. Einstein proposed that the energy supplied by a single photon could free an electron from an atom in the metal. To produce the photoelectric effect, photons act in a localized manner characteristic of particles rather than waves. Thus, Einstein's ideas revived the particle theory of light. Scientists now know that radiation has features of both particles and waves.

The Danish physicist Niels Bohr used the quantum theory in 1913 to explain the structure of the hydrogen atom. Bohr proposed that electrons can have only certain values of energy. He showed that atoms release photons of radiation when their electrons drop from a high-energy level to a lower one. In 1924, the French physicist Louis de Broglie predicted that electrons themselves might act as waves, called *matter waves.*

The nuclear age began in 1942, when the Italian-born physicist Enrico Fermi and co-workers at the University of Chicago produced the first artificial nuclear chain reaction. Since then, many scientists have turned their attention from understanding what causes radioactivity and radiation to finding uses for them. Nuclear weapons based on fission—the atomic bomb—and fusion—the hydrogen bomb—were developed. The first full-scale nuclear power plant began operation in 1956.

Refining the uses of radiation has benefited many scientific fields. For example, researchers have refined the use of radiation in cancer therapy. Early radiation therapies exposed patients to radiation that was less controlled, sometimes damaging healthy parts of the body. Newer methods of radiation therapy, including *intensity modulated radiation therapy* (IMRT), can shape the beam of radiation to target the area of the body that shows cancer. In contrast, doctors increasingly use *total body irradiation,* which exposes the entire body to a low dose of radiation, to prepare patients for bone marrow or stem cell transplants. Medical research has also increased its use of *radioactive tracers.* Such tracers are radioactive atoms that enable researchers to track where molecules travel in the body. Radiation from across the electromagnetic spectrum has also been developed and refined for use in communication, industry, and research.

Jason P. Hayward

Related articles in *World Book* include:

Kinds of radiation

Alpha particle
Beta particle
Cosmic microwave background (CMB) radiation
Cosmic rays
Electromagnetic waves
Gamma rays
Infrared rays
Light
Microwave
Radio (How radio programs are broadcast)
Sun (Energy output)
Ultraviolet rays
X rays

Radioactive substances

Actinide
Actinium
Americium
Astatine
Berkelium
Bohrium
Californium
Curium
Darmstadtium
Dubnium
Einsteinium
Fermium
Francium
Hassium
Lawrencium
Meitnerium
Mendelevium
Neptunium
Nobelium
Pitchblende
Plutonium
Polonium
Promethium
Protactinium
Radiocarbon
Radium
Radon
Roentgenium
Rutherfordium
Seaborgium
Technetium
Thorium
Transuranium element
Uranium

Other related articles

Atom
Cancer (Carcinogens; Cancer treatment)
Chernobyl disaster
Energy
Environmental pollution (Hazardous waste)
Fallout
Fluorescence
Geiger counter
Ion
Irradiation
Isotope
Luminescence
Nuclear energy
Nuclear physics
Nuclear weapon
Particle accelerator
Particle detector
Phosphorescence
Photon
Plasma (physics)
Quantum mechanics
Radiation sickness
Radiochemistry
Radiogeology
Radiology
Subatomic particle
Transmutation of elements

Radiation sickness is the term for a variety of symptoms that follow a person's exposure to damaging amounts of certain types of radiation. The radiation may come from nuclear explosions and the resulting fallout, from medical and industrial uses of *radioisotopes* (radioactive forms of elements), or from such devices as particle accelerators or X-ray machines. Such radiation can *ionize* (give an electric charge to) atoms and molecules in body tissues, causing a series of reactions that results in damage to cells. The main symptoms of radiation exposure are loss of appetite, nausea, vomiting, and fatigue. Additional symptoms include hair loss and loss of the body's ability to fight infection. Exposures to high levels of radiation may cause lasting injury or death.

Some cells are more easily injured by radiation than others. The most sensitive cells are those of the blood-forming bone marrow and of lymphoid tissues. Adult muscle and brain cells are least sensitive to radiation.

Scientists measure radiation exposure in human beings using a unit called the *sievert* (Sv). The sievert has largely replaced another such unit, the *rem.* One sievert is equal to 100 rems. A single exposure of 0.70 sievert (70 rems) or less produces few symptoms. Higher exposures, of 3 to 4 sieverts (300 to 400 rems), cause illness that is fatal for about 50 percent of the people exposed.

Physicians can treat only the symptoms of radiation sickness. Treatment with antibiotics or blood transfusions helps some people exposed to high doses of radiation survive. Ann R. Kennedy

See also **Actinide; Fallout; Radiation** (Effects of radiation).

Radiator is a set of pipes or tubes that gives off heat to its surroundings. Steam or hot-water radiators in homes transfer heat to the air in a room. When warmed, the air next to the pipes expands, becomes lighter, and rises. Cooler air from the room streams in to take its place, creating a constant circulation of air. This process is called *convection,* and certain types of radiators are called *convectors.* Radiators also heat room air by direct *radiation.* See **Heat** (How heat travels).

An automobile radiator works in the same way. Water carries heat from the engine to tubes at the front of the radiator. Air rushing past the tubes absorbs heat from the water and cools it. An engine-driven or electric fan helps move air through the radiator when the car is stopped or moving at low speed.

Evan Powell

See also **Automobile** (The cooling system); **Heating** (Central heating systems).

Radical, in chemistry, is a group of two or more charged or neutral atoms that have at least one unpaired electron. Molecular oxygen, O_2, has two unpaired electrons and is a common radical. Most radicals are extremely reactive and combine with other atoms or radicals to form compounds or ions. However, some radicals, called *free radicals,* may exist for relatively short times unbound to any other group. Radicals play a major role in certain chemical reactions of commercial significance, including the formation of polymers. They are also important in understanding atmospheric reactions caused by sunlight. Mark S. Wrighton

Radical Republican. See **Reconstruction** (The radicals and the moderates).

Radicalism is a political philosophy that emphasizes the need to find and eliminate the basic injustices of society. The word *radicalism* comes from the Latin word *radix,* meaning *root.* Radicals seek what they consider the roots of the economic, political, and social wrongs of society and demand immediate and sweeping changes to wipe them out.

Many people regard radicals as political extremists who tend to use violence in support of their cause. But the political meaning of the word *radical* has changed over time and varies from country to country. For example, in the mid-1900's, radicals in Western Europe were committed to the establishment of socialist states. But in the late 1900's, radicals in Eastern Europe sought to overthrow existing socialist governments. In addition, the radicals of one generation may be seen as conservatives by the next generation.

In Europe, modern radicalism began with the French Revolution (1789-1799), in which radicals executed the king and queen and created a republic. Even though the French republic eventually fell and the monarchy was restored, the French Revolution inspired radicals for years to come. During the 1800's, many European radicals took the French Revolution as their model and tried to establish republics in their own countries.

The term *radical* came into general use in the United Kingdom during the early 1800's. It described reform demands by such political leaders as Charles James Fox. In 1797, Fox demanded what he called "radical reform" to make Britain's political system more democratic. During the 1800's, the British philosopher Jeremy Bentham led a group called "philosophical radicals." He believed all legislation should aim to provide the greatest happiness for the greatest number of people.

Several European radicals established the socialist movement and demanded the total reconstruction of society. During the late 1800's, the movement split into moderate and radical factions. The moderate socialists sought change through gradual reform. The radical socialists insisted that only revolution could reform society. In Russia, the moderates were called Mensheviks and the radicals Bolsheviks. The Bolsheviks seized power in 1917 and set up a Communist government.

In the United States, the followers of Alexander Hamilton, the first secretary of the treasury, opposed the French Revolution. They used the term *radicals* for the pro-French followers of Thomas Jefferson. In the years before and during the American Civil War (1861-1865), radical abolitionists called for the end to slavery. Other radicals demanded cheap land, prohibition of alcoholic beverages, voting reforms, and women's rights.

American radicals, unlike European radicals, have never been able to establish a major political party. However, radicals in the United States have influenced national politics through their writings and speeches. They also have organized third parties that have often gained enough support to force the major parties to pass reform legislation. Such legislation has included the income tax, government regulation of industry, and social welfare programs.

Radicalism became increasingly prominent in the United States during the 1960's and early 1970's. Radicals marched, held rallies, and burned draft records in protest of the Vietnam War (1957-1975). Radical "black power" activists, believing that the goals and tactics of the civil rights movement were too moderate, became more active. Some radical feminists wished to overthrow male-dominated institutions or separate themselves from them. Since the late 1990's, many radicals have opposed *globalization*—that is, the increased connectedness between individuals, businesses, and organizations throughout the world. Many people argue that globalization enables multinational corporations to take unfair advantage of poor countries.

Some radicals support traditionally conservative causes. Such radicals include members of white supremacist groups and those who use violence to oppose abortion.

Around the world today, radicalism takes a variety of forms. Antiglobalization, antiabortion, and white supremacist radicals are active in a number of countries. Other radicals promote a wide range of political, religious, and social causes. In many Muslim countries, for example, Islamic radicals call for new governments based on traditional Islamic teachings. Some radicals in the Middle East and elsewhere oppose the spread of Western values and influence. Tom Mockaitis

See also **Left wing; New Left; Right wing.**

© Shutterstock

© age fotostock/SuperStock

Radio broadcasting originates in a studio and can be heard almost anywhere. A disc jockey at a radio station, *left,* announces and plays recorded music. Many people use portable radios, *right,* to listen to broadcasts.

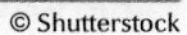

Radio

Radio is one of our most important means of communication. It enables people to send words, music, images, codes, and other signals over long distances. People on ships and in aircraft and spacecraft keep in contact with other people far away on land, air, or sea by using radio. People also use radio to communicate far into space.

The most widespread and familiar use of radio is for the form of one-way communication known as broadcasting. Radio broadcasts feature music; news; discussions; interviews; sports coverage; drama; educational, cultural, and religious programs; and commercial advertising. Many people wake up to clock radios and listen to radio while in their automobiles. Many also enjoy listening to radio programs during their leisure hours. Some people listen to their favorite radio shows on their computers.

Radio broadcasting once had much the same entertainment role as television has today. From the 1920's to the early 1950's, millions of families gathered around their radios every night. They listened to dramas, light comedies, variety shows, live music, and other kinds of programs. This period, which is sometimes called the Golden Age of Broadcasting, ended with the rise of television during the 1950's.

Radio has many uses in addition to broadcasting. People in many occupations use radio for two-way, wireless communication. Scientists send radio waves into the sky to learn about the weather. Telephone companies send messages across the ocean by radio. Many people operate amateur radio stations.

The contributors of this article are Donna L. Halper, Assistant Professor of Communication, Lesley University, Cambridge, Massachusetts; and David W. Matolak, Associate Professor of Electrical Engineering and Computer Science, Ohio University.

Radio works by changing sounds or other signals into radio waves, a form of energy called *electromagnetic radiation.* Radio waves travel through the air and through space. They also go through some solid objects, such as the walls of buildings. A radio receiver changes them back into the original sounds.

Many people contributed to the development of radio, and no one individual can be called radio's inventor. The Italian inventor Guglielmo Marconi sent the first radio communication signals in 1895. Today, radio waves that are broadcast from thousands of stations, along with waves from other sources, fill the air around us continuously.

Uses

Broadcasting ranks as the most familiar use of radio by far. Every day, millions of people throughout the world listen to news, sports, music, and other radio programs that are broadcast for their entertainment and information.

People also use radio in dozens of other ways. Many uses involve *two-way communication,* in which radio equipment is used both to send and to receive messages. In broadcasting and in most two-way communication, radio transmits sounds, such as voice and music. But in other uses, radio sends communication signals other than sounds. Such signals include the radio beams used in navigation and the remote control signals used in operating certain kinds of equipment.

Broadcasting. Most radio broadcasts originate at radio stations. There is at least one radio station in every independent country in the world, and altogether there are tens of thousands of stations.

Some radios are powered by current from electrical outlets. These radios are usually kept in the home, where electrical outlets are readily available. But many radios are powered by batteries. People listen to these

Radio terms

AM stands for *amplitude modulation,* a broadcasting method in which the strength of the carrier waves is varied to match changes in the audio-frequency waves.
Amplitude is the strength of a wave.
Audio-frequency waves are electric or sound waves that fall within the range of human hearing, typically 20 to 20,000 hertz.
Automatic Frequency Control (AFC) is an electric circuit in an FM receiver that automatically remains locked on to the frequency of the selected transmission.
Bandwidth is the frequency range occupied by a transmitter signal.
Broadcast band is a group of radio frequencies. One band is for AM broadcasting, and one is for FM broadcasting.
Call letters are the initials that identify a radio station, such as station KRKO in Everett, Washington.
Carrier waves are radio waves that "carry" the sounds of a program by being combined with audio-frequency waves.
Channel is the radio frequency assigned to a station.
Detector is an electronic circuit that recovers the portion of a radio signal that represents the program.
Digital Audio Broadcasting (DAB) is a system for transmitting sound and other information as a numeric code.
FM stands for *frequency modulation,* a broadcasting method in which the frequency of the carrier waves is varied to match changes in the audio-frequency waves.
Frequency is the number of complete cycles per second of an electric wave.
Ground waves consist of the radio waves that spread along the ground away from a broadcasting antenna.
Ham is a name for the operator of an amateur radio station.
Hertz is a unit used to measure frequency. One hertz equals one cycle per second.
Kilohertz means 1,000 hertz.
Line-of-sight refers to the direct line in which radio waves travel. Waves in the FM band travel this way, without "bending" over mountains or the curve of Earth.
Live broadcast consists of sounds made at the moment of the broadcast, without having been prerecorded.
Long-wave band is the frequency band ranging from 148 to 283.5 kilohertz. It is used for radio broadcasts in Europe and in parts of Asia and northern Africa.
Medium-wave band is the frequency band ranging from 535 to 1,705 kilohertz used for AM radio broadcasts throughout the world.
Megahertz means 1 million hertz.
Multiplexing means sending two or more signals on a shared channel, as in stereophonic transmissions.
Network is an organization that provides radio programming for a group of stations that belong to it. It also refers to a collection of radio transmitters and receivers that communicate with one another.
Oscillator is an electrical device that produces an electric or electromagnetic signal at a desired frequency. It may use mechanical vibrations or electronic means to produce the signal.
Podcast is a digital audio or video recording that is available on the Internet. Many podcasts are recordings of programs that were initially broadcast on radio or TV.
Prerecorded means recorded on phonograph records, tapes, or audio compact discs for broadcast at a later time.
Radio data system (RDS) is an FM-based method for transmitting data along with an audio program.
Radio waves are electromagnetic waves in the radio frequency band.
Satellite radio is a system that uses satellites to broadcast many channels of coded digital audio signals to special radio receivers. Companies typically offer satellite radio service by subscription.
Selectivity is a radio's ability to pick a desired radio signal from among the many received by the antenna.
Short-wave band is the frequency band ranging from 3 to 30 megahertz. It is used worldwide for radio broadcasts and other services.
Sky waves consist of the radio waves that come from a transmitting antenna and go into the sky.
Stereophonic sound comes from at least two radio speakers to match as closely as possible the sounds people would hear with their two ears.
Stream means to send audio or video data over the Internet.
Superheterodyne is a tuning method in which the desired incoming radio station signal is converted to an intermediate frequency before a detector recovers the signal.
Webcast is a broadcast made on the World Wide Web.

radios almost everywhere—in homes and yards, at beaches and picnics, and even while strolling down the street. In addition, nearly all automobiles have a radio.

In some parts of the world, radios provide the people with one of the few links they have to the world outside their village or town. In some places, there is no electric power and batteries are too scarce or expensive for people to buy them. People in such communities sometimes use a special wind-up radio that requires no other source of power. Many people do not own radios, and they listen to radio programs in public gathering places instead.

Two-way communication. Two-way radio provides communication in an almost endless variety of jobs—whenever there is a need for wireless contact between one point and another. Some of the most important of these uses are in (1) public safety, (2) industry, (3) defense, and (4) private communication.

In public safety. Police officers and firefighters use two-way radios in their patrol cars and fire engines. They also carry small, portable two-way radios called *walkie-talkies.* They use these radios to get directions from their headquarters and to communicate with one another (see **Walkie-talkie**). Airplanes and ships use two-way radios for safe operation and for rescue missions. Special ambulance teams use radio to help save lives after rushing to the scene of an accident. These specialists radio the details of a victim's condition to a doctor in a hospital. The doctor then directs the emergency treatment of the victim by radio.

In industry. Two-way radio has become a standard tool of the transportation industry. Taxi drivers receive radioed instructions on where to pick up customers. Airplane pilots receive landing and take-off instructions by radio. Ships, trains, and many trucks and buses are equipped with two-way radios.

Radio also helps save time, money, and work in many other industries. Construction workers use it to communicate from street level to the top of a skyscraper. With the aid of two-way radio, farmers, ranchers, and lumber workers receive information when they need it and get equipment delivered where they want it.

In defense, radio plays a key role by linking a country's defense units. Military personnel use radio equipment in planes and tanks and on ships. Large communications centers and handy walkie-talkies help provide instant contact between military units.

In private communications. Many licensed radio operators called *hams* send and receive long-distance messages by radio as a hobby. Children play with walkie-talkies that broadcast over short distances. Many people use two-way radios in such places as cars and pleasure boats. One popular type of radio used by private citizens for short-distance, two-way communication is called *citizens band radio.* Radio signals also enable people to communicate using portable cellular telephones and through wireless local area networks.

Other uses. Radio waves can carry many more kinds of information than just sounds. Radio signals make possible the operation of navigational aids, remote control devices, and data transmission equipment. In addition, radio has several highly specialized uses.

Navigation. Radio beams made up of special navigation signals help airplane pilots stay on the proper flying course. Many ships have devices for mapping their position with the aid of signals radioed from shore. Airplanes and ships also rely on radar—a special form of radio—for their safe operation (see **Radar**).

Remote control by radio can be used to guide the flight of a model airplane or a real plane that has no pilot. Radio-controlled devices also direct railroad cars in switching yards. In addition, radio-controlled devices do such jobs as opening garage doors or changing television channels (see **Remote control**).

Data transmission. Radio equipment can send large quantities of information at great speeds. Data transmission usually occurs between one electronic device and another. For example, radio equipment on the ground may transmit data to a computer in a spacecraft orbiting Earth.

Special uses. Criminals and law enforcement officials sometimes use hidden radio devices called *bugs* to listen in on conversations in attempt to gather information. High-energy radio waves cook food in microwave ovens.

Radio programming

Radio programming varies from country to country. In most countries, a majority of programs broadcast are designed for entertainment. The rest provide some type of information. Advertisements are broadcast during and between the programs of commercial stations. Noncommercial stations, also called *educational* or *public* stations, have few or no commercials. Radio stations compete with one another for listeners. Most stations choose programs to appeal to a specific audience, called a *target demographic.* For example, stations in the United States that play rock music try to attract teenage and young adult listeners.

Entertainment. Recorded music is the chief kind of radio entertainment. Most stations specialize in one kind of music, such as rock, classical, country, or jazz. Some stations broadcast several kinds of music.

Most radio stations that broadcast music have *disc jockeys* who introduce and comment on the music. They play an important role. Commercial stations try to hire disc jockeys whose announcing styles and personalities appeal to the station's largest audience.

Additionally, entertainment programs include comedy shows, serials, and plays that are performed live or recorded in a studio by actors. Some plays are written especially for radio.

Information. Programs that provide information include newscasts, talk shows, and live broadcasts of sports events. Newscasts are broadcast at regular times—every half-hour or hour on some stations. In addition, radio stations present on-the-spot news coverage of such events as political conventions, disasters, and speeches by national leaders. Radio stations also broadcast such specialized news as weather forecasts, traffic reports, and stock market information. Other information features include public service announcements about community events and government services. A few stations broadcast only news.

Talk shows present discussions on a variety of topics and interviews with people from many professions. Each show has a host who leads the discussion or does the interviewing. The subject of a program may be a current political topic, such as an election or a government policy, or it may deal with a social issue, such as crime, pollution, poverty, racism, or sexism. Many talk shows allow listeners to take part in the program. Listeners are invited to telephone the station to ask questions or give their opinions about the topic.

Sports events, like news, have always been an important part of radio programming. Sports announcers try

© Richard Hutchings, Photo Researchers

An airplane pilot radios the control tower for instructions. During flight, radio beams help pilots stay on course.

© Paul David Drabble, Alamy Images

A soldier uses a handheld two-way radio called a *walkie-talkie* to communicate with a military unit.

© Alex Segre, Alamy Images

A police officer uses a walkie-talkie to communicate with other officers. Emergency personnel also use walkie-talkies.

to capture a game's action and excitement for the listeners. Games in many professional sports, such as baseball, basketball, cricket, football, hockey, and soccer, are broadcast locally on radio. Radio stations also broadcast many college and some high school sports contests. Stations that broadcast only sports and discussions of sports are also popular.

How radio programs are broadcast

Radio stations are places where radio broadcasts begin. The *studio* is the part of the radio station from which programs are broadcast. It is soundproofed so that no outside sounds can interfere with the broadcasts. Many studios have two separate areas—the *main studio* and the *control room.* The main studio is the place where the performers do their jobs. The control room contains the equipment needed to prepare and broadcast programs. This equipment includes the *control board,* a panel with the switches, knobs, buttons, and other devices used to regulate the sounds of the broadcasts. A large window in the wall between the main studio and the control room enables people in each area to see one another.

Putting a show on the air involves such jobs as researching current events, script writing, announcing, and controlling the broadcasting equipment. Some shows have a producer who contacts guests and helps prepare interviews. At a small station, the same person may write scripts, announce, play recordings, and even operate the controls. A large station has a staff that plans programs, including the writing of news and other scripts. An announcer may use a script or may simply *adlib* (speak without a script).

During the Golden Age of Broadcasting, the production of some radio programs was a complex process involving many people. Writers wrote scripts for comedies, dramas, and variety shows. A director guided actors and actresses, who stood around a microphone reading their lines. An announcer introduced the show, closed it, and read the commercials. Sound-effects specialists created such sounds as thunder, footsteps, creaking doors, and galloping horses. An orchestra played appropriate music. Most radio stations were in hotels, and many radio shows were broadcast *live* (while they were being performed). These shows were often performed on the stage of a hotel ballroom or a theater-like studio in front of an audience.

Today, the production of most radio programs is less complicated. Only a small number of radio shows are broadcast in front of a live studio audience. Most shows today take place in the radio studio, where only the on-air staff is heard. New technology has even enabled some radio hosts to broadcast directly from their homes. Most programs consist of conversation and recorded music. In addition, many radio stations use computers to do much of the work formerly done by people, such as operating technical equipment, recording program information, and even running the control board. Automation saves money by reducing the number of employees needed to run the station.

From sound waves to electric waves. A radio program consists of speech, music, and other sounds. These sounds may either be live or *prerecorded.* Prerecorded sounds are not broadcast when first produced. Most are stored on tapes or audio compact discs (CD's) and broadcast later. Almost all the music and commercials heard on radio are prerecorded.

To understand how radio broadcasting works, it is necessary to know what sound is. All sounds consist of vibrations. The number of vibrations each second is the *frequency* of the sound. For example, the sound of a person's voice consists of vibrations of the air that are caused by the person's vibrating vocal cords. The faster the vocal cords vibrate, the higher the frequency. The slower the vocal cords vibrate, the lower the frequency. Sound travels through the air in the form of waves called *sound waves.*

During a live radio broadcast, a microphone picks up speech and other sounds that make up the program. When sound waves enter the microphone, they cause an electric current that runs through the microphone to vary. The variations in the current form electric *audio-frequency waves* that match the program's sound waves. Prerecorded sounds are also changed into audio-frequency electric waves before being broadcast.

From electric waves to radio waves. The electric waves representing the live and prerecorded sounds of the program travel over wires to the control board. A technician uses switches on the control board to select, adjust, and mix the material to create the *program signal* that will be broadcast. The program signal travels from the control board to the transmitter, either by wire or by a special beam of radio waves.

Low-power transmitters may be in the studio. High-power transmitters are generally far away from the studio, at the site of the *transmitting antenna,* the device that sends radio waves through the air. Special types of radio waves called *microwaves* are sometimes used to send the program signal from the studio to a distant transmitter in a narrowly focused "beam."

In the transmitter, the program signal is combined with electric waves called *radio-frequency waves.* Radio-frequency waves have a much higher frequency than do the audio-frequency waves that make up the program signal. Radio-frequency waves are also known as *carrier waves* because they "carry" the program signal from the transmitter to radios. Carrier waves are used because they travel through the atmosphere better than the original audio-frequency waves can. The frequency of the carrier waves produced in the transmitter is the station's *broadcast frequency*—that is, the frequency to which a radio must be tuned to hear that station.

Transmitting radio waves. After the program signal is combined with the carrier waves, the transmitter *amplifies* (strengthens) the combined radio signal and sends it to the antenna. The antenna then broadcasts the radio signal through the air.

Radio waves travel at the speed of light. This speed is 186,282 miles (299,792 kilometers) per second. By contrast, sound waves move through the air at the speed of only about ⅕ mile (0.3 kilometer) per second.

Most radio broadcasts are transmitted in one of two ways, depending on how the carrier waves and program signal are combined. These two kinds of radio transmission are *amplitude modulation* (AM) and *frequency modulation* (FM). In AM band transmission, the *amplitude* (strength) of the carrier waves is varied to match changes in the program signal coming from the radio studio. In FM band transmission, the amplitude of the carrier waves remains constant. But the frequency of the carrier waves is varied to match changes in the program signal. The radio wave signal properties described here depend on the carrier frequencies used by the AM and FM broadcasting systems.

Transmitting AM band signals. An AM antenna sends out two kinds of radio waves—*ground waves* and *sky waves.* Ground waves spread out horizontally from the transmitting antenna. They travel through the air along Earth's surface and follow the curve of Earth for a short distance. Sky waves spread up into the sky. When they reach a layer of the atmosphere called the *ionosphere* or the *Kennelly-Heaviside layer,* they are reflected down to Earth (see **Ionosphere**). AM broadcasts are thus reflected beyond Earth's curve. The ionosphere rises at night and so reflects AM waves farther than it does during the day. As a result, radios can receive broadcasts from distant stations more clearly at night.

Transmitting FM band signals. An FM radio antenna sends out waves that travel in the same directions as AM waves, but FM waves that travel skyward are not reflected. Instead, they pass through the atmosphere and go into space. The FM waves that spread horizontally travel in what is called *line-of-sight.* This means that FM waves cannot be received farther than the horizon as seen from the antenna.

Transmitting short-wave signals. Many broadcasting stations operate in the short-wave bands. Short-wave broadcasts travel over long distances. In some sparsely populated areas, only short-wave broadcasts can be received. Generally, programs transmitted by short-wave stations are addressed to audiences far away.

Most short-wave broadcasting stations transmit on several frequencies to ensure worldwide reception at different times of the day and year. Programs consist mainly of international and national news, commentaries, interviews, music and other cultural programs, sports events, radio plays, and language courses. The governments of some countries block short-wave broadcasts during periods of political unrest.

The ionosphere reflects short waves best when the solar activity is greatest. Thus, short-wave transmissions travel farther during the day than at night. They also travel farther in the winter, when the sun is farther away. However, eruptions on the sun's surface called *solar flares* may disturb the ionosphere enough to interfere with communication or even cause blackouts of short-wave reception.

Digital audio broadcasting (DAB). Beginning in the early 1990's, several countries began experimenting with digital audio broadcasting (DAB). For DAB broadcasts, sound is *sampled* by taking thousands of segments of sound per second and translating each into *digital* (numeric) code. The digital data are compressed by eliminating parts of the signal that do not change from sample to sample, and the signal is transmitted.

DAB can deliver sound of the same quality provided by a compact disc. DAB can also deliver data services. Some AM and FM radio transmitters must be modified to broadcast DAB. Special receivers are required to receive DAB.

One form of digital audio broadcasting is *satellite radio.* Satellite radio systems use satellites to broadcast more than 120 channels of coded digital audio signals directly to special radio receivers or to ground-based *repeaters* that rebroadcast the signals. Computer chips (circuits) in the receivers decode the signals to produce high-quality audio signals. The satellites may be in either a *geostationary orbit,* remaining in a constant position relative to Earth, or a circular or *elliptical* (oval-shaped) orbit around Earth. Companies typically offer satellite radio service by subscription. Some offer adapters that allow conventional radios to receive satellite radio signals.

Webcasting and podcasting. In the mid-1990's, some radio stations began transmitting, or *webcasting,* over the Internet. Radio stations carry computer signals to and from the Internet via wireless *local area networks* (LAN's). LAN's are small networks that connect computers in one office, school, or building. Stations may *stream* their programming—that is, simultaneously broadcast into the air and onto the Internet. Stations may also *podcast,* or release a digital audio recording on the Internet.

Broadcasting power and frequency. Another factor that influences the distance a radio program can be

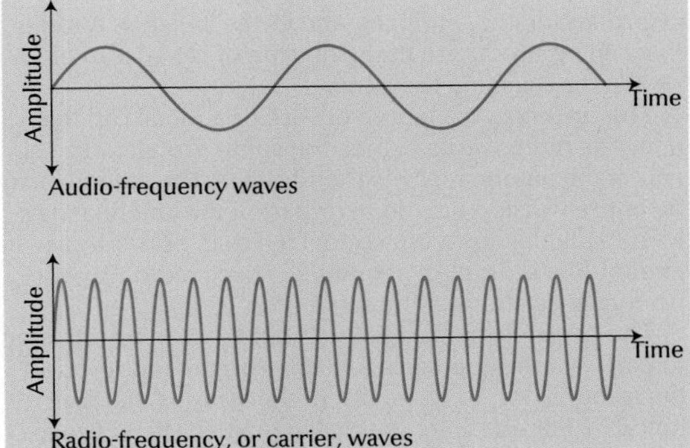

Broadcast waves are a combination of two kinds of electric vibrations. Audio-frequency waves represent voice and other sounds. Radio-frequency waves "carry" audio waves after being combined with them in one of the ways shown at the right.

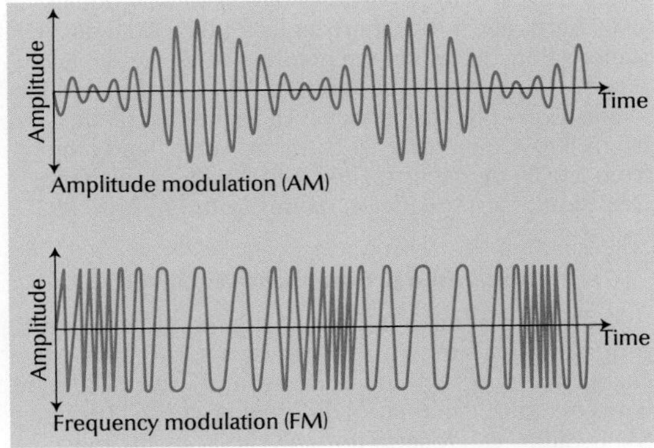

WORLD BOOK diagrams by Mark Swindle

AM and FM. In AM, the *amplitude* (strength) of the radio-frequency waves is varied to match the audio waves. In FM, the *frequency* (number of vibrations per second) of the radio-frequency waves is varied to match the audio waves.

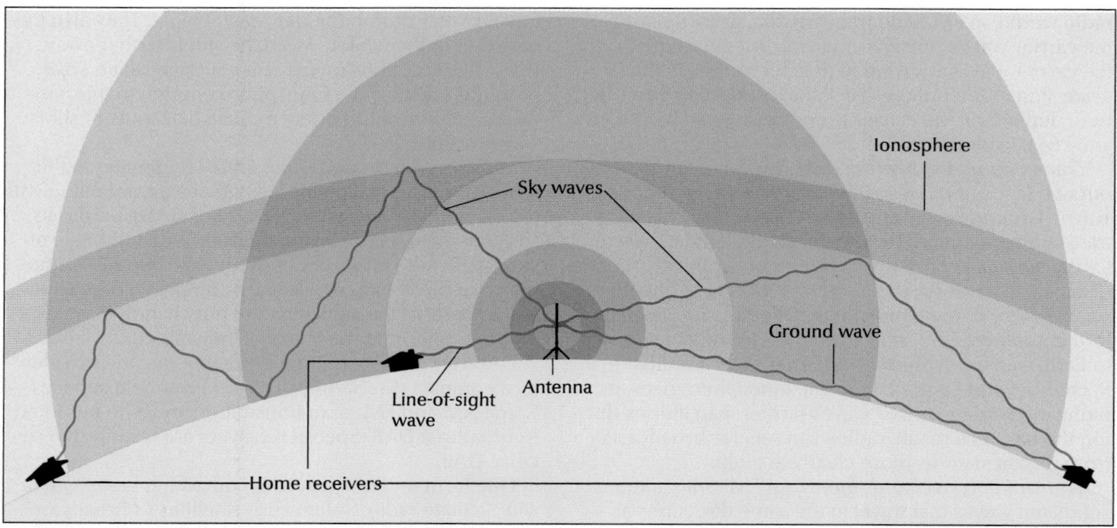

WORLD BOOK diagram by Sally Wayland

Radio waves. An AM antenna radiates *ground waves,* which may extend a short distance beyond the horizon, and *sky waves,* which bounce off the ionosphere and may also bounce off Earth. An FM antenna radiates *line-of-sight waves,* which cannot be detected beyond the horizon.

broadcast is the power of the transmitter. The strongest AM stations have a power of 50,000 watts. They can be heard far away, especially at night when reflected waves travel farther. For example, 50,000-watt stations in Chicago can be heard at night by listeners in Florida, about 1,000 miles (1,600 kilometers) away. The weakest AM stations operate at 250 watts and usually serve only one or two towns.

The power of FM stations ranges from 100 watts, which can broadcast about 15 miles (25 kilometers), to 100,000 watts, which can broadcast about 65 miles (105 kilometers). Some noncommercial FM educational stations operate at as little as 10 watts and reach an area of only a few miles or kilometers.

Each station broadcasts on a different *channel,* also called an *assigned frequency.* The use of different carrier frequencies keeps stations from interfering with one another's broadcasts. Frequency is measured in units called *hertz* (cycles per second). One kilohertz equals 1,000 hertz, and 1 megahertz equals 1,000,000 hertz. AM stations transmit within the medium-wave band, which ranges from 535 to 1,705 kilohertz. FM stations transmit within a very high frequency (VHF) band that ranges from 88 to 108 megahertz. The short-wave band ranges from 3 to 30 megahertz. The L-band, within which most DAB signals are broadcast, ranges from 1,452 to 1,492 megahertz.

How radio programs are received

Radios detect radio-frequency signals, separate the program signals from the carrier waves, and then change the program signals into sound waves. Different types of radios can receive different broadcast bands. Many radios can receive both AM and FM, the most popular broadcast bands. *Multiband radios* can pick up AM, FM, and other bands, such as police, marine, aviation, and short-wave bands.

One of the simplest radio receivers is the *crystal radio.* This type of receiver uses an electronic device called a *crystal rectifier* to detect changes in the strength of an AM signal. These changes in signal strength represent the program's original sound waves. A crystal radio works on just the power of the radio waves it receives and needs no electric power source. However, a listener must use earphones because a crystal radio can produce sound only at a low volume. Furthermore, this type of radio does not receive FM broadcasts well. Because of such limitations, most radios made today are electrically powered.

The electric power for a radio can come from batteries or from an electrical outlet in a house or other building. A typical radio that runs on household power has a component called a *power transformer* that lowers the household voltage to the level the radio requires.

The main parts of an electrically powered radio include (1) the antenna, (2) the tuner, (3) the intermediate-frequency amplifier and detector, (4) the audio-frequency processor and amplifier, and (5) the speaker. A radio that can receive more than one type of signal also has a switch for selecting the band.

The antenna is a length of wire or a metal rod that converts radio waves in the atmosphere to electrical signals at the antenna *terminal* (end point). The antenna may be entirely inside the radio, or part of the antenna may be outside the radio but connected to it, as is the case in automobile radios. An antenna receives radio waves from many stations at the same time.

The tuner is the part of the radio that can be adjusted to particular frequencies. A display on the radio shows the frequencies, or channels, of the stations that may be tuned in. For example, station WQAM in Miami broadcasts on a frequency of 560 kilohertz. To tune in WQAM, a listener selects number 560 (abbreviated as 56 or 5.6 on some radio displays).

Today, most radio receivers use the *superheterodyne* tuning method because of the advantages it offers. The

Main parts of an AM/FM transistor radio

Emerson Radio Corp. (WORLD BOOK photo)

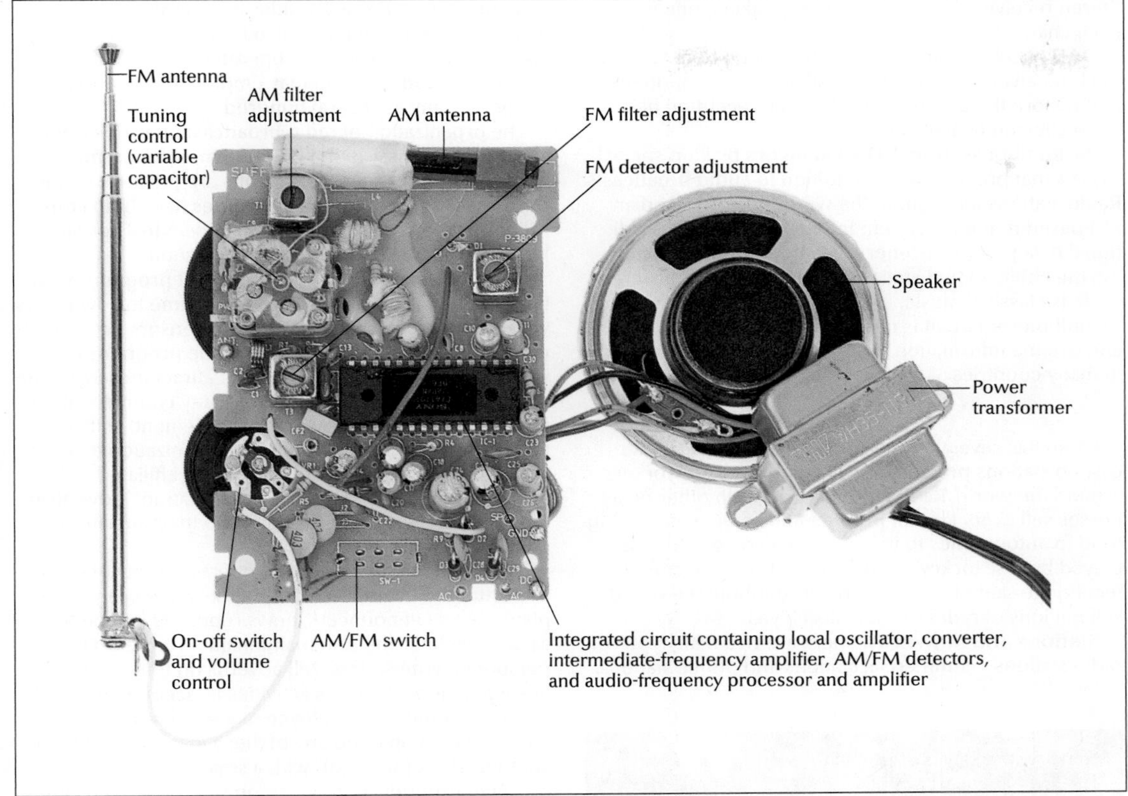

tuner of a superheterodyne radio consists of three main parts: (1) an amplifier, (2) a local oscillator, and (3) a mixer/converter. The amplifier strengthens the antenna signal. The local oscillator generates a signal of a specific frequency, which the mixer/converter combines with the amplified antenna signal. The combined signal, called the *intermediate frequency,* contains a particular radio program. When a listener adjusts the tuning control, the local oscillator frequency changes and a different radio program is selected to be on the intermediate frequency. The intermediate frequency is 10.7 MHz for FM and 455 KHz for AM. Use of the same intermediate frequency to process many radio frequencies simplifies the radio's design. It also allows for improved *selectivity*—that is, the radio's ability to pick a desired radio signal from among the many received by the antenna.

The intermediate-frequency amplifier and detector receive the intermediate-frequency signal produced by the tuner. The amplifier strengthens the signal, which then enters the detector. The detector removes the intermediate-frequency components from the signal and leaves only the *audio-frequency signal*—the part that represents the program.

The audio-frequency processor and amplifier strengthen the audio-frequency portion of the signal. Volume, bass, and treble controls can be used to adjust the loudness and tone of the sound before it goes to the speaker.

The speaker is the final link between the broadcasting studio and the listener. It changes the electrical signal back into sound waves that represent the original program sounds. The basic parts of a speaker are a magnet and a coil of wire called the *voice coil.* The voice coil is attached to a cone, which is usually made of paper. The electric current from the amplifier passes through the coil and exerts varying push and pull against the magnet's field. The cone vibrates in time with the electric current flowing through the coil. The cone's vibrations create sound waves that match those that first went into the microphone or were recorded earlier, and the original program sounds come out of the speaker.

Stereophonic receivers can detect *stereophonic,* or *stereo, multiplex* signals. These signals are formed by sending two separate audio-frequency signals on a single carrier frequency at the same time. The two audio-frequency signals are called the *right channel* and the *left channel.* Stereo multiplex signals better re-create for the listener the sensation of hearing live sounds than do *monophonic* signals, which transmit only one channel.

Both stereo and monophonic receivers have a superheterodyne circuit. However, stereo receivers have an additional circuit called a *demultiplexer.* This circuit changes the multiplex signal back into its original left and right channels. The two parts of the signal then enter separate audio-frequency processors and amplifiers. Stereo receivers have at least two speakers, one for each channel.

DAB receivers are required to pick up DAB signals. Such receivers recombine a DAB signal's components and restore the original sound even if reception has been affected by interference.

Radio data system (RDS) receivers pick up special signals that provide data in addition to audio broadcasts. Radio stations throughout the world have adopted an FM-based multiplex system for such signals. The additional data provide listeners with new features, including the ability to find stations based on type of program, such as classical music, rock and roll, or news. A special demultiplexer circuit is needed in the radio to receive and use the information. RDS radios are popular in cars in many countries.

The radio industry

Radio has several important industrial roles. Broadcasting stations provide jobs for thousands of workers around the world. Radio commercials help other businesses sell every kind of product and service—from dog food to automobiles to insurance. The recorded music played by disc jockeys is often an important factor affecting the sale of music. Stores throughout the world sell millions of radio receivers each year.

Stations and networks. There are two main types of radio stations—commercial stations and public stations. Commercial stations, which are owned by private companies, make profits from advertisements. Public stations are funded at least partly by the government. However, in some countries, public stations also take advertisements. Some countries also have nonprofit radio stations, many of which are operated by educational institutions. A radio station may employ only a few workers or as many as several hundred.

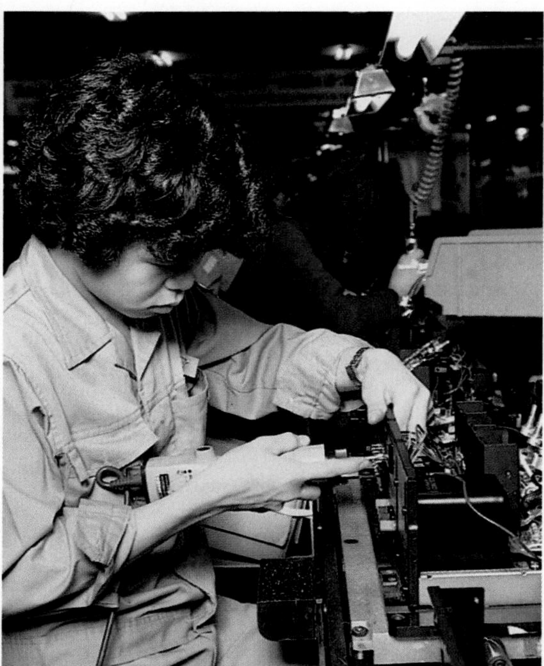

Cameramann International, Ltd.

The manufacture of radios provides job opportunities for a variety of skilled workers, from technicians to electronics engineers. The technician shown here is assembling radio parts.

The organization of radio broadcasting varies from country to country. In the United States, for example, almost all commercial radio stations are privately owned businesses. Most European countries have both commercial stations and nonprofit stations. Most countries have at least one commercial radio station.

Commercial radio stations broadcast programs to attract listeners. They sell broadcasting time to advertisers who want to reach these listeners. Sponsors pay the stations for time during and between the programs to advertise their products. Stations that attract the largest audiences receive the highest fees. Many commercial stations have an *affiliation* (working agreement) with a national *network.* A network is an organization that provides some of the programming for its affiliated radio stations. It may also sell some of the stations' advertising time. Networks send radio signals to their affiliates using communications satellites.

Careers. The radio industry offers a variety of career opportunities. Stations and networks need program planners and announcers, news reporters and newscasters, technicians, and maintenance workers. Other personnel write scripts, sell advertising time, and work in such general business activities as accounting and public relations. An employee of a small radio station may be called on to do any of these jobs at one time or another. Therefore, a job with a small station provides excellent experience for a person starting a radio career. Most people who hold a key job at a large station first gained experience by working at small stations.

Employees of large stations or networks generally specialize in one of four kinds of work. These kinds of work are (1) programming, (2) engineering, (3) sales, and (4) general administration.

The programming department is headed by a program director. This department includes journalists who gather the news and write news reports and other material to be broadcast. Other members of the programming department include announcers, copywriters, and production personnel. The engineering department includes the technicians who operate and maintain the broadcasting equipment. Members of the sales department are responsible for selling broadcasting time to sponsors. The general manager of the station or network heads the department of general administration and has overall responsibility for the organization's operation. The general administration department includes accountants, secretaries, and other office workers.

Careers outside of broadcasting are available to people trained in the operation and repair of radio equipment. Many people skilled in radio repair go into business for themselves.

Government regulation of radio

The government of every country regulates the use of radio in some way. Without regulation, radio stations and other radio users would broadcast signals that would interfere with one another and make it impossible for communications to be understood. Another reason for regulation is to ensure that stations adhere to the terms of their broadcast licenses. Many governments regulate radio in a way that enables them to use the medium to promote their own ideas and policies. They also effectively prevent the broadcast of ideas that government leaders oppose.

Many nations have private and government-owned stations. In most other countries, the government owns all the stations. In the United States, the federal government does not control any radio stations that broadcast to the general public.

In general, a country allows radio broadcasters the same degree of freedom it allows its citizens. Most democratic countries allow wide freedom in broadcasting. Many totalitarian governments severely regulate and censor broadcasting for political purposes.

In the United States, the Federal Communications Commission (FCC) regulates all nonmilitary communication by radio. The FCC assigns frequencies and call letters for various types of radio operations, including broadcasting, amateur radio operation, and marine and aviation radio. In addition, the FCC issues licenses to stations and certain other users of transmitting equipment. The FCC does not censor radio programs or tell stations what programs they should broadcast. But it can impose a fine on or revoke the license of a station that violates broadcasting rules.

The Canadian Broadcasting Corporation/Radio-Canada (CBC/Radio-Canada) provides the programs for the government stations in Canada. The Canadian Radio-television and Telecommunications Commission supervises government and private stations. In the United Kingdom, the British Broadcasting Corporation (BBC) regulates the government-owned stations. The Office of Communications (commonly called Ofcom), a government agency, regulates privately owned stations.

History

The development of radio in the late 1800's revolutionized communication. At that time, people had two other means of quick, long-distance communication—telegraph and telephone. But the signals sent by both these devices had to travel through wires. As a result, telegraph and telephone communication was possible only between places that had been connected by wires. Radio signals, on the other hand, passed through the air. Thus, radio enabled people to communicate quickly between any two points on land, at sea, and—later—in the sky, and even in space.

Radio broadcasting, which began on a large scale during the 1920's, caused major changes in the everyday lives of people. It brought a tremendous variety of entertainment into the home for the first time. It also enabled people to learn about news developments as they happened or shortly afterward.

Early development. Radio, like many other inventions, developed from the theories and experiments of many people. Joseph Henry, a professor at the College of New Jersey (now Princeton University), and a British physicist, Michael Faraday, discovered one of the first important ideas in the early 1830's. Both men had experimented with electromagnets. Separately, they each developed the theory that a current in one wire can produce a current in another wire, without the wires being connected. This idea is called the *induction theory.*

In 1864, the Scottish physicist James Clerk Maxwell helped explain the induction theory by suggesting the existence of electromagnetic waves that travel at the speed of light. During the late 1880's, the German physicist Heinrich Hertz conducted experiments that proved Maxwell's theory.

Nikola Tesla, an American inventor from Austria-Hungary, has been credited with the invention of the radio, based on his early patents for radio communications equipment. In 1891, he invented the Tesla coil, a type of high-frequency transformer. This device is a vital component of radio transmitters.

In 1895, Guglielmo Marconi, an Italian inventor, combined earlier ideas and his own ideas and sent the first radio communication signals through the air. He used electromagnetic waves to send telegraph code signals a distance of more than 1 mile (1.6 kilometers). In 1901, Marconi's radio equipment sent code signals across the Atlantic Ocean from England to Newfoundland (now Newfoundland and Labrador), Canada.

During the early 1900's, electrical engineers developed devices called *vacuum tubes* that could be used to detect and to amplify radio signals. Lee De Forest, an American inventor, created a vacuum tube called a *triode* in 1906. This tube became the key element in radio reception.

There are many claims for the first broadcast of human speech over the air. Most historians give credit to Reginald A. Fessenden, a Canadian-born physicist. In 1906, Fessenden spoke by radio from Brant Rock, Massachusetts, to ships offshore in the Atlantic Ocean. The American inventor Edwin H. Armstrong did much to improve radio receivers. In 1918, he developed the superheterodyne circuit. In 1933, he discovered how to make FM broadcasts.

Culver

Guglielmo Marconi invented a way of sending telegraph signals by radio in 1895. His invention helped lead to the development of broadcasting. This photograph shows him with some of his wireless equipment.

The first practical use of the "wireless," as radio was then called, was for ship-to-ship and ship-to-shore communication. Radio helped save the lives of thousands of victims of sea disasters. The first sea rescue involving the use of radio took place in 1909, after the S.S. *Republic* collided with another ship in the Atlantic Ocean. The *Republic* radioed a call for help that brought rescuers who saved almost all the passengers.

Dozens of new uses were soon found for radio. By the 1930's, airplane pilots, police officers, and military personnel were using radio for wireless communication.

The start of broadcasting. Experimental radio broadcasts began about 1910. In that year, Lee De Forest produced a radio program from the Metropolitan Opera House in New York City. The program starred the famous opera singer Enrico Caruso.

Many people consider radio station WWJ (then known as 8MK), in Detroit, the first commercial radio station. It began regular broadcasts on Aug. 20, 1920. Others claim the distinction for station KDKA in Pittsburgh. KDKA grew out of an experimental station that began in 1916 in Wilkinsburg, a suburb of Pittsburgh. KDKA's broadcast of the 1920 U.S. presidential election results on Nov. 2, 1920, is generally considered the beginning of professional broadcasting, even though 8MK also broadcast the election. The first license to broadcast regularly went to station WBZ in Springfield, Massachusetts. The U.S. government issued the license on Sept. 15, 1921.

Network broadcasting began as early as October 1921. At that time, WJZ in New York City and WGY in Schenectady, New York, broadcast the World Series. The two stations formed a simple network connected by telephone lines. Network broadcasting—or, as it was called, *chain broadcasting*—soon included stations across the United States. The Radio Corporation of America (RCA) formed the National Broadcasting Company (NBC), which was the first permanent national network, in 1926.

In the 1920's, radio stations began operating in many other countries as well. The British Broadcasting Corporation (BBC) began broadcasting in 1922. Stations began operations in Australia in 1923 and in Japan in 1925.

The Golden Age of Broadcasting began in the United States about 1925 and lasted until the early 1950's. During this period, radio was a major source of family entertainment. Every night, many families gathered in their living rooms to listen to comedies, adventure dramas, music, and other kinds of radio entertainment. Children hurried home from school to hear afternoon adventure shows. In the daytime, millions of people listened to dramas that were called *soap operas* because soap manufacturers sponsored many of them.

Radio brought to the home the music of famous band leaders, including Tommy Dorsey, Duke Ellington, Benny Goodman, Harry James, Guy Lombardo, and Glenn Miller. Exciting radio dramas of the Golden Age included "Buck Rogers in the 25th Century," "Gangbusters," "The Green Hornet," "Inner Sanctum," "Jack Armstrong, the All-American Boy," "The Lone Ranger," "The Shadow," and "Superman." Some radio soap operas were "The Guiding Light," "John's Other Wife," "Just Plain Bill," "Ma Perkins," "One Man's Family," "Our Gal Sunday," and "Stella Dallas."

Radio's famous comedians included Fred Allen, Jack Benny, Eddie Cantor, and Bob Hope. The ventriloquist Edgar Bergen and his dummy, Charlie McCarthy, hosted a weekly comedy program with famous stars as guests. Situation comedies included "Fibber McGee and Molly," "The Great Gildersleeve," "Duffy's Tavern," "Henry Aldrich," and "Our Miss Brooks." The husband-and-wife comedy team of George Burns and Gracie Allen gained fame in radio.

The popularity of "Amos 'n' Andy," a situation comedy, and the impact of a dramatic program called *The War of the Worlds* help illustrate the enormous influence radio entertainment had on people. "Amos 'n' Andy" was broadcast each weekday throughout the 1930's. While the program was being broadcast—from 7:00 to 7:15 p.m. Eastern Standard Time—many movie theaters stopped their films and turned on radios so the audiences could listen to the program. Some stores and restaurants played radios over public address systems so that customers would not miss it. Although "Amos 'n'

Bettmann

A "crystal" radio of the early 1920's worked without batteries or other source of power, but a listener needed earphones to hear it.

Culver

A radio of the mid-1920's was powered by electric energy and had a trumpetlike loudspeaker.

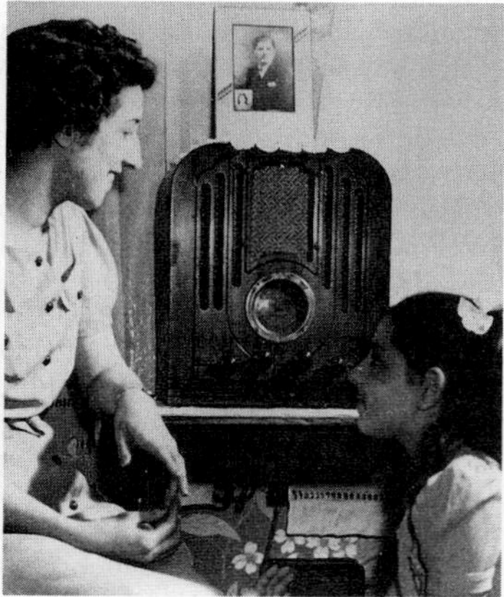

Bettmann

By the early 1940's, radios had become "streamlined." Members of a family often got together to listen to programs.

Andy" was immensely popular, it also became controversial. The actors and actresses on the radio show were whites who portrayed blacks. Many people have criticized the program for portraying African Americans as a stereotyped group to be laughed at. Some people tried to have the show taken off the air.

The War of the Worlds, broadcast on Oct. 30, 1938, was one program in a series of dramas put on by Orson Welles's Mercury Theatre on the Air. The program was adapted from the science-fiction novel of the same name by the British author H. G. Wells. It took the form of on-the-spot news reports describing an invasion of New Jersey by aliens from Mars. The announcer told the radio audience that the show was fictional. Even so, large numbers of listeners believed the invasion was actually taking place, and widespread panic resulted. Thousands of people called the police and other authorities for instructions on what to do. Many people fled their homes, some taking furniture with them. Still others were treated in hospitals for shock.

Some radio news reporters of the Golden Age became almost as well known as the top entertainers. They included Kathryn Cravens; Elmer Davis; Gabriel Heatter; H. V. Kaltenborn; Fulton Lewis, Jr.; Edward R. Murrow; Lowell Thomas; Dorothy Thompson; and Walter Winchell.

Newscasts became especially important during World War II (1939-1945). Millions of people turned to radio every day for latest news on the war. The governments of countries that fought in the war made widespread use of broadcasts to their own and other countries for propaganda purposes. The Voice of America, an agency of the United States government, began broadcasting overseas in 1942 to inform the world of America's role in the war.

Franklin Delano Roosevelt, president of the United States from 1933 to 1945, used radio effectively. He held informal talks called "fireside chats." The talks did much to help Roosevelt gain support for his policies. Earlier presidents, beginning with Woodrow Wilson in 1919, had spoken on radio. However, Roosevelt was the first to fully understand the great force of the medium and the opportunity it provided for taking government policies directly to the people. Other political leaders, including Winston Churchill of the United Kingdom and Charles de Gaulle of France, made use of radio to address their nations.

Also popular and often influential were religious broadcasters. Listeners tuned in to hear sermons and commentary by such religious radio pioneers as the

Brown Bros.

President Franklin Delano Roosevelt broadcast "fireside chats" to the nation during the 1930's and 1940's. These talks helped him gain popular support for his government policies.

NBC

A sound-effects expert used odd-looking equipment to create realistic sounds for Golden Age dramas. This picture shows water being sprayed into a bucket to make the sound of rain.

Culver

George Burns and Gracie Allen were famous radio performers during the Golden Age. The husband-and-wife team starred in a popular weekly situation comedy from 1932 to 1950.

Protestant minister S. Parkes Cadman, the evangelist Aimee Semple McPherson, the rabbi Stephen S. Wise, and the controversial Roman Catholic priest Charles Coughlin.

The Golden Age was also the era of the "radio homemakers," such as Ida Bailey Allen and Mary Margaret McBride. These women hosted daily programs directed at stay-at-home wives and mothers. The programs featured guest experts who gave advice on child-rearing, cooking, health, and other issues. These heavily sponsored shows appealed to women as an important consumer market for broadcasters and advertisers.

Radio since the 1950's. The rise of television in the 1950's ended the Golden Age of radio broadcasting. People turned to TV for comedies, dramas, and variety shows, and these kinds of shows all but disappeared from radio. Many people believed television would cause radio broadcasting to become an unimportant communication medium with a small audience. Instead, radio's audience has continued to grow, in spite of its competition from television.

After the Golden Age of Broadcasting, music became the major form of radio entertainment. Rock music, which was a new form of music in the 1950's, became an important kind of music on radio. Broadcasts of rock music gained many listeners—especially teenagers—for radio. Talk shows and stations that broadcast only news also helped radio gain listeners. Thorough coverage of a topic or news event continues to be an important feature of such programs.

Portable radios also helped increase radio's popularity. Such devices, including tiny *personal radios* with headphones, have made radio a source of individual, rather than family, enjoyment. In addition, automobile radios are now commonplace.

Still another aid to radio's growth has been the development of stereophonic broadcasting. Stereo broadcasts began on a large scale in the 1960's. In 1961, the FCC allowed only FM stations to broadcast in stereo in the United States to help them compete with AM stations. FM's better sound quality enabled it to surpass AM in popularity by the late 1970's. The FCC authorized AM stereophonic broadcasting in 1982.

In the late 1980's and early 1990's, researchers developed *digital audio broadcasting* (DAB), a system that converts sounds to *digital* (numeric) code before transmission. DAB was introduced at a world conference in Spain in 1992. In 1998, the first commercial DAB operation began in the United Kingdom. Because DAB can carry multiple signals, radio programs similar to those broadcast today may be supplemented by images, text, graphics, and other data. For example, information about local traffic problems could be transmitted over a DAB data channel. Drivers might receive this information as text, synthesized speech, or maps. An LCD (liquid crystal display) on the receiver might display the name and composer of any music played, the radio station's telephone number, or an electronic program guide.

The 1990's also saw an increase in the popularity of the "talk radio" format in the United States. Notable radio personalities who have found large, loyal listenerships with this format include the conservative political commentator Rush Limbaugh and the controversial entertainer Howard Stern. Beginning in 2006, Stern helped popularize subscription-based satellite radio when he made a highly publicized move from "terrestrial" (land-based) radio to Sirius Satellite Radio Inc. of New York City.

Satellite radio has now become an important new form of radio. Most satellite radio receivers are portable units mainly for use in automobiles, but equipment is also available for use with a home stereo, a portable radio, or a personal computer. Many models of cars now come equipped with satellite radio receivers. In 2008, the U.S. Department of Justice and the FCC approved a merger of Sirius with the country's other satellite service, XM Satellite Radio Holdings Inc. of Washington, D.C., to create a single satellite radio network in the United States.

In 2006, a coalition of major radio station operators in the United States launched an effort to promote HD Radio—a technology that transmits programs digitally over existing AM and FM frequency bands. In its campaign, the alliance stressed the high-quality sound of HD Radio, as well as the fact that, unlike satellite radio, listeners could tune in to HD Radio for free. Thousands of AM and FM stations now broadcast with HD Radio technology. HD Radio has also become an option in many models of cars. However, a major challenge for HD Radio has been the higher cost of a digital radio compared with a regular AM-FM radio.

Donna L. Halper and David W. Matolak

Important dates in radio

1864	James Clerk Maxwell predicted the existence of electromagnetic waves that travel at the speed of light.
1880's	Heinrich Hertz proved Maxwell's theory.
1895	Guglielmo Marconi became the first person to send radio communication signals through the air.
1906	Reginald A. Fessenden broadcast voice and music by radio.
1909	Passengers of the S.S. *Republic* were saved in the first sea rescue using radio.
1918	Edwin H. Armstrong developed the superheterodyne circuit.
1919	Woodrow Wilson became the first U.S. president to make a radio broadcast. He spoke from a ship to World War I troops aboard other vessels.
1920	Two U.S. stations, WWJ of Detroit and KDKA of Pittsburgh, made the first regular commercial broadcasts.
1922	The British Broadcasting Company, later the British Broadcasting Corporation, made its first broadcast.
c. 1925-1950	Radio was a major source of family home entertainment, during the Golden Age of Broadcasting.
1934	The Telecommunications Act created the Federal Communications Commission (FCC) in the United States.
1947	Scientists at Bell Telephone Laboratories (now part of Lucent Technologies) developed the transistor.
1960	John F. Kennedy and Richard M. Nixon held the first radio and television debates between two U.S. presidential candidates.
1961	Soviet space officials held the first radio talks with a space traveler, cosmonaut Yuri Gagarin.
1960's	Stereophonic radio broadcasting began.
1969	Radio signals carried to Earth the first words spoken by astronauts on the moon.
1982	AM radio stations in the United States began broadcasting in stereo.
1998	The world's first commercial digital audio broadcasting (DAB) service began in the United Kingdom.
1999	Subscription satellite radio broadcasting began.
2004	Internet radio podcasting began.
2006	HD Radio began.

Related articles in *World Book* include:

Biographies

Armstrong, Edwin H.
De Forest, Lee
Hertz, Heinrich Rudolf
Lodge, Sir Oliver J.
Marconi, Guglielmo
Maxwell, James Clerk
Sarnoff, David
Tesla, Nikola

Parts of a radio

Antenna
Headphones
Microphone
Speaker
Transistor

Radio equipment

Cellular telephone
Citizens band radio
Communications satellite
Fax machine
Radar
Radiosonde
Remote control
Telephone (How a telephone works; How a telephone call travels)
Television
Walkie-talkie

Other related articles

Advertising
Airplane (Air navigation)
Australia (picture: Schools of the air)
British Broadcasting Corporation
Canadian Broadcasting Corporation/Radio-Canada
Corporation for Public Broadcasting
Electronics
Federal Communications Commission
Frequency modulation
Grand Ole Opry
Invention
Ionosphere
Journalism (Radio; Radio journalism)
National Public Radio
Public opinion (Radio and television)
Radio, Amateur
Radio Free Europe/Radio Liberty
Radio wave
Railroad (Traffic control)
Reflection
Ship (A ship at sea)
Short waves
Soap opera
Static
Stereophonic sound system
Telescope (Radio telescopes)
Viacom Inc.
Voice of America
Wireless communication

Outline

I. Uses
A. Broadcasting
B. Two-way communication
C. Other uses
II. Radio programming
A. Entertainment
B. Information
III. How radio programs are broadcast
A. Radio stations
B. Putting a show on the air
C. From sound waves to electric waves
D. From electric waves to radio waves
E. Transmitting radio waves
F. Broadcasting power and frequency
IV. How radio programs are received
A. The antenna
B. The tuner
C. The intermediate-frequency amplifier and detector
D. The audio-frequency processor and amplifier
E. The speaker
F. Stereophonic receivers
G. DAB receivers
H. Radio data system (RDS) receivers
V. The radio industry
A. Stations and networks
B. Careers
VI. Government regulation of radio
VII. History

Radio, Amateur, is a popular hobby in which individuals operate small, personal radio stations to communicate with other operators locally and throughout the world. Amateur radio is often called *ham radio,* and operators are frequently referred to as *hams.* Enthusiasts come from all backgrounds, professions, and age groups.

Amateur radio operators may transmit radio signals on designated groups of *bands,* or frequencies, within the radio spectrum. Frequencies are measured in *hertz* (cycles per second). The frequencies most often used for amateur radio are in the middle or high frequency ranges, often called *short wave.* Short wave is useful for long-distance international communication.

Amateur radio differs from a service called *citizens band* (CB) radio. The biggest difference is that, in most countries, amateur radio operation requires a federally approved license while CB is unlicensed. Citizens band also offers fewer frequencies than amateur radio and is more limited in power and range. For more information on CB, see **Citizens band radio.**

Many amateur radio operators enjoy talking to hams in faraway places. Hams send messages using voice and computer signals. Amateurs may use an internationally accepted set of three-letter signals called *Q signals* because they all begin with the letter Q. For example, the signal *QTH?* means "What is your location?" Q signals enable radio operators without a common language to understand each other.

Uses of amateur radio. Hams have long provided voluntary communications in times of emergency. Fires, floods, tornadoes, hurricanes, and other disasters can interrupt telephone service and other means of communication. Hams often work with national and international disaster relief organizations, as well as with local emergency officials. Organized amateur radio groups also routinely provide assistance during such community events as parades, marathons, and bicycle races.

Amateur radio communications use signals relayed via satellite to reach around the world. Many nations have allowed amateur radio satellites to "hitchhike" into orbit during the launch of other satellites. Most amateur radio satellites are called *Oscars.* The word *Oscar* comes from the term *o*rbiting *s*atellite *c*arrying *a*mateur *r*adio. Some schools tune in Oscars to provide students with firsthand experience in space science.

Some hams bounce their signals off the moon to communicate with hams on the other side of the world. Using a device called a *radio modem,* hams may transmit text messages from one computer to another. Some hams even send television pictures over amateur radio frequencies.

Equipment. Some operators enjoy building their own radios from kits, and others purchase commercially manufactured equipment. A complete amateur radio station includes an antenna and a *transceiver,* which combines a transmitter and a receiver in a single unit. By purchasing used equipment, hams can assemble a station for only a few hundred dollars. Operators can also get "on the air" using an even cheaper handheld radio. Sophisticated stations may cost thousands of dollars.

Licenses. In the United States, amateur radio operators are required to earn a Federal Communications Commission (FCC) license. There are three levels of radio licenses: (1) Technician, (2) General, and (3) Amateur Extra. Starting with the Technician level, each license requires greater knowledge and abilities, and grants access to more frequencies.

The Technician class license gives access to amateur radio frequencies above 30 *megahertz* (millions of hertz), enabling licensees to legally communicate within North America. To earn the license, an applicant must pass a written examination on radio theory, FCC regulations, and operating practices.

The General class license grants some operating privileges on all amateur radio bands and the use of all operating modes. Licensees thus can legally communicate with hams throughout the world. To earn the license, an applicant must pass a written examination. Applicants must also have passed the Technician examination.

The Amateur Extra class license grants all available United States amateur radio operating privileges. To earn the license, an applicant must pass a written examination. Licensees must also have passed all the Technician and General class examinations.

Many local clubs offer courses that prepare people to take the license examinations. Prospective hams may also prepare for the exams on their own using a variety of print and Internet-based study guides and tools.

In Canada, a government organization called Industry Canada issues a single license for amateur radio operators. The governments of many other countries offer similar licenses.

Amateur radio organizations. Many amateur radio operators belong to local clubs or national organizations. These clubs and organizations sponsor contests and other events for operators. Many national organizations produce magazines, websites, and other publications related to amateur radio.

The International Amateur Radio Union, with headquarters in Newington, Connecticut, is a federation of amateur radio societies in numerous countries. Newington is also the headquarters of the national organization in the United States, the American Radio Relay League. The Canadian organization is Radio Amateurs of Canada, which is based in Ottawa, Ontario. The amateur radio society in the United Kingdom is the Radio Society of Great Britain, with headquarters in Bedford, England.

WORLD BOOK photo by Odyssey Productions

An amateur radio station may use a transceiver, *shown here.* The operator sends messages by speaking into a microphone and listens to other hams through headphones or a speaker.

History. In 1901, the Italian inventor Guglielmo Marconi and his staff successfully sent and received radio signals across the Atlantic Ocean from England to Newfoundland. Marconi's wireless feat encouraged many eager experimenters to set up their own radio stations and begin communicating with each other over the airwaves.

Amateur radio regulation began in the United States when Congress, believing a law was necessary to prevent radio interference, passed the Radio Act of 1912. Amateur radio operators were restricted to short-wave frequencies because experts thought those frequencies had little potential for development. But hams were soon sending messages between coasts, showing the value of short-wave radio for long-distance transmission.

Amateurs pioneered radio in many ways. In 1919, a ham named Frank Conrad used his station in Wilkinsburg, Pennsylvania, to transmit recorded music for the entertainment of people in the area listening on small crystal radios. Although transmitting music via amateur radio is not permitted today, this early use helped lead to commercial radio broadcasting.

During the late 1930's, a United States amateur radio operator named Grote Reber built the first *radio telescope,* a bowl-shaped antenna that collects radio waves, and received radio noise from outer space. In 1961, the first amateur radio satellite, Oscar 1, was launched. Oscar 1 was also the first nongovernmental, noncommercial satellite. The first direct satellite communication between the Soviet Union and the United States took place via the Oscar 4 amateur radio satellite in 1965.

Critically reviewed by the American Radio Relay League

See also **Marconi, Guglielmo; Morse code; Radio; Short waves.**

Radio control. See **Remote control.**

Radio Free Europe/Radio Liberty (RFE/RL) is a nonprofit corporation that provides international communications service to Central and Eastern Europe, the Balkans, the Caucasus, Central Asia, and the Middle East. It broadcasts in dozens of the languages used in these regions.

The United States established Radio Free Europe/Radio Liberty to oppose attempts by Communist governments of the Soviet Union and Eastern Europe to isolate their citizens from information about the world. During the late 1980's and early 1990's, Communists lost control of nearly all these governments. In 1991, the Soviet Union broke up into a number of independent states. RFE/RL is funded by grants from the United States Congress.

People from the listening areas write and produce most RFE/RL programs. Many of the programs consist of news and news analysis, and they focus on current events in the audience countries. RFE/RL operates many news bureaus in audience countries. Other RFE/RL programs describe cultural and religious activities and offer background information about economic, historical, and political matters.

Radio Free Europe began broadcasting to Eastern Europe in 1950, and Radio Liberty started broadcasting to the Soviet Union in 1953. In 1976, the networks merged and formed RFE/RL, Inc. RFE/RL broadcasting headquarters are in Prague, Czech Republic.

Critically reviewed by Radio Free Europe/Radio Liberty

Radio telescope. See **Telescope** (Radio telescopes).

Radio wave is the longest kind of electromagnetic wave. Other kinds of electromagnetic waves include gamma rays, visible light, and X rays (see **Electromagnetic waves**). A wave can be measured by its *wavelength,* the distance between successive crests or troughs of the wave. Radio waves have wavelengths greater than 0.04 inches (1 millimeter). A wave can also be measured by its *frequency,* the number of wave cycles in a given time. Radio waves have frequencies of less than 300 *gigahertz,* or 300 billion *hertz* (cycles per second). All electromagnetic waves travel at the speed of light, about 186,000 miles (300,000 kilometers) per second.

Radio waves are used in a variety of communication devices. They are used to broadcast radio and television signals. Radio waves are also used by wireless devices, including cell phones, Global Positioning System (GPS) receivers, satellite communication systems, police radios, and wireless Internet devices. Garage door openers and radio-controlled toys also use radio waves. Most radar systems detect objects as varied as airplanes, ships, cars, or clouds by bouncing radio waves off them.

Radio waves are also important in astronomy. In 1932, the American physicist Karl Jansky first detected radio waves from space. Jansky discovered a radio pulse coming from the center of our galaxy. Astronomers have since detected radio waves from planets, *supernovae* (exploding stars), rapidly spinning *pulsars,* and galaxies with supermassive black holes at their centers.

A large *parabolic* (curved) dish serves as the best means of collecting radio waves from space. The American radio engineer Grote Reber built the first radio dish in 1937. One of the world's largest radio dishes, at Arecibo, Puerto Rico, measures 1,000 feet (305 meters) in diameter. Astronomers also use *arrays* (groups of dishes), such as the Very Large Array in New Mexico, to increase the sensitivity of their observations. James C. Lochner

For more information on radio waves and their uses, see the article **Radio** and its list of related articles. See also **Astronomy** (Radio astronomy); **Microwave; Wireless communication.**

Radioactivity. See **Radiation.**

Radiocarbon, or carbon 14, is a radioactive isotope of carbon. It is used to determine the age of fossils and other kinds of ancient objects. In addition, researchers use radiocarbon to study certain biological processes. Radiocarbon has a *relative atomic mass* of about 14 and is heavier than the most common isotope of carbon, which has a relative atomic mass of exactly 12. An isotope's relative atomic mass equals its *mass* (amount of matter) divided by $\frac{1}{12}$ of the mass of an atom of carbon 12.

In nature, radiocarbon forms when high-energy atomic particles called *cosmic rays* smash into the atmosphere of Earth. Cosmic rays cause atoms in the atmosphere to break down into electrons, neutrons, protons, and other particles. Some neutrons strike the nuclei of nitrogen atoms in the atmosphere. Each of these nuclei absorbs a neutron and then loses a proton. In this way, a nitrogen atom becomes a radiocarbon atom.

All living things contain radiocarbon. In the atmosphere, there is about one atom of radiocarbon for every trillion molecules of carbon dioxide gas. Plants absorb radiocarbon from the carbon dioxide in the air. Human beings and other animals take in radiocarbon chiefly from the food provided by plants.

Radiocarbon dating is a process used to determine the age of an ancient object by measuring its radiocarbon content. This technique was developed during the late 1940's by Willard F. Libby, an American chemist. Archaeologists and geologists have used it extensively. They have learned much about prehistoric human beings, animals, and plants that lived up to about 50,000 years ago.

Radiocarbon atoms, like all radioactive substances, *decay* (break down by releasing particles) at an exact and uniform rate. Half the radiocarbon decays, turning back into nitrogen, in about 5,730 years. Therefore, radiocarbon is said to have a *half-life* of that period of time. After about 11,460 years, a fourth of the original amount of radiocarbon remains. After another 5,730 years, only an eighth remains, and so on.

The radiocarbon in the tissues of a living organism decays extremely slowly, however it is continuously renewed as long as the organism continues to live. After the organism dies, it no longer takes in air or food. Therefore, it no longer absorbs radiocarbon. The radiocarbon already in the tissues continues to decrease at a constant rate. This steady decay at a known rate—a half-life of about 5,730 years—enables scientists to determine an object's age.

In one method of radiocarbon dating, scientists burn

Radiocarbon dating

Scientists determine the age of an ancient object by measuring its radiocarbon content. This process is called *radiocarbon dating.* Two methods of radiocarbon dating are described here.

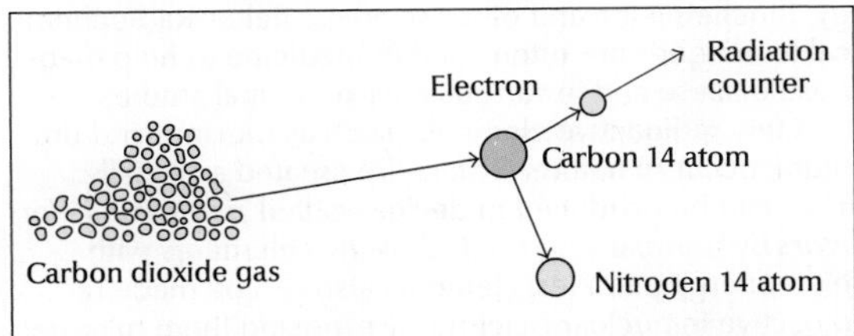

In the traditional method, a piece of the object is burned and converted to carbon dioxide gas. Radiocarbon (carbon 14) atoms in the gas release electrons as the radiocarbon changes into nitrogen 14. *Radiation counters* detect the number of electrons given off, which determines the object's radiocarbon content.

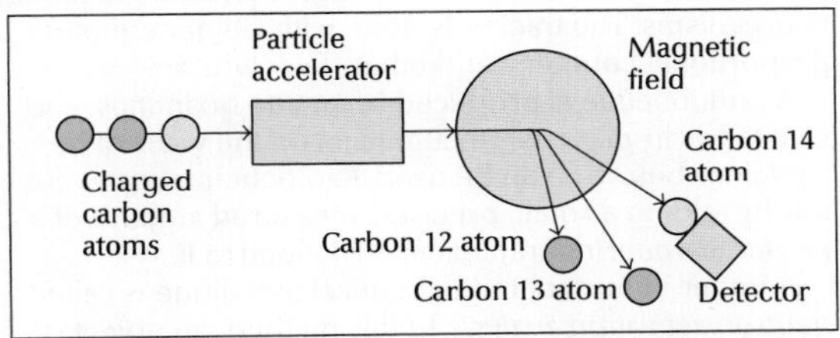

WORLD BOOK diagrams by Arthur Grebetz

In a newer method, a *particle accelerator* fires charged atoms originally from a small piece of the object into a magnetic field. The field deflects and separates the various carbon atoms by their weight. Then a *detector* counts individual carbon 14 atoms to determine the object's radiocarbon content.

a piece of the object and convert it to carbon dioxide gas. The carbon dioxide is purified, and the amount of radiocarbon in the purified carbon dioxide is measured with *radiation counters.* These instruments detect the electrons released by the radiocarbon atoms as the atoms change back into nitrogen atoms. The number of electrons emitted indicates the radiocarbon content.

Another method of radiocarbon dating involves the use of certain types of *particle accelerators* instead of radiation counters (see **Particle accelerator**). An accelerator enables scientists to detect and count directly the individual radiocarbon atoms in an extremely small portion of an object. After scientists measure an object's radiocarbon content, they compare it with the radiocarbon in tree rings whose ages are known (see **Tree** [diagram: How a tree reveals its history]). This technique enables them to compensate for small variations of radiocarbon content in the atmosphere at different times in the past. By doing so, scientists can convert an object's radiocarbon age to a more precise date.

Radiocarbon in biology. Radiocarbon is used as a "tracer" to study various complex biological processes. In such research, scientists substitute a radiocarbon atom for an atom of a carbon molecule. Then they use a radiation counter to trace the path of the radiocarbon atom through a chemical reaction in an organism.

The radiocarbon used as a tracer is produced artificially in nuclear reactors. Artificial radiocarbon was first discovered in 1939 by two American chemists, Martin D. Kamen and Samuel Ruben. Rainer Berger

See also **Archaeology** (Dating).

Radiochemistry is a field of chemistry that involves the study of radioactive elements. It also deals with the production, identification, and use of such elements and their isotopes. Radiochemistry has benefited archaeology, biochemistry, and other scientific fields. Radiochemical techniques are often used in medicine to help diagnose disease and in various environmental studies.

A few radioactive elements, such as thorium and uranium, occur in nature. Others are created artificially. They can be produced in devices called *particle accelerators* by bombarding nonradioactive elements with high-energy particles. Elements also can be made radioactive in nuclear reactors by exposing them to large numbers of neutrons.

The isotopes of radioactive elements are called *radionuclides* or *radioisotopes.* They are widely used as *tracers* in certain kinds of research, especially the study of complex biological processes. This type of study involves tracing radionuclides through chemical reactions in organisms. The tracing is done with Geiger counters, proportional counters, and other detection devices.

A radionuclide is produced in minute quantities, and so it tends to *plate out* (accumulate) on the walls of its container before it can be used. Radiochemists prevent this by adding a small, precisely measured amount of a *carrier element* (nonradioactive element) to it.

Another important radiochemical technique is called *neutron activation analysis.* In this method, an object is exposed to neutrons, causing some of the elements in the object to become radioactive. These elements then emit radiation of certain energies. One of the uses of this method is the verification of the authenticity of old paintings. The paint used in old works of art differs in composition from the paint in recent paintings, and so it gives off different radiations. Raymond P. Borkowski

Radiogeology is the science that deals with the relation of radioactivity to geology. Geologists can determine the age of rocks, fossils, and other objects by measuring the radioactive elements in them.

The earth, the waters of the oceans, the air we breathe, and all living things contain small amounts of radioactivity. This radioactivity is caused by (1) the radioactive elements uranium and thorium, and their decay products; (2) radioactive potassium; (3) small amounts of less abundant radioactive elements, such as samarium and rubidium; and (4) radiocarbon, which forms when high-energy particles called *cosmic rays* strike nitrogen in the earth's atmosphere.

The rocks of the earth's surface contain an average of five parts of uranium per million parts of rock. Uranium has been in the earth since the earth was formed. It decays over time to become lead and helium. The rate at which a radioactive isotope decays is measured by its *half-life*—that is, the time required for half the atoms in the isotope to decay into another isotope. Lead isotope 206 is formed from uranium isotope 238, which has a half-life of about $4\frac{1}{2}$ billion years. Lead-207 is formed from uranium-235, which has a half-life of 700 million years. Scientists can measure the amounts of these isotopes in a rock sample and then calculate the rock's age from the ratio of lead-206 to uranium-238, the ratio of lead-207 to uranium-235, and the ratio of lead-206 to lead-207. Similar calculations can be made using other radioactive isotopes.

On the basis of lead-to-uranium ratios, scientists estimate that the age of the solar system is about $4\frac{1}{2}$ billion years. This figure agrees with the ages of meteorites and the oldest moon rocks as measured by the decay of other radioactive elements.

The decay of long-lived radioactive isotopes is like a great clock that measures time in millions or billions of years. The clock also has a "second hand" that measures time in thousands of years. This is radiocarbon, which has a half-life of 5,700 years. Analysis of radiocarbon content makes it possible to determine the age of wood, bone, and other once-living materials.

G. Brent Dalrymple

See also **Radiation; Radiocarbon.**

Radioisotope. See **Isotope; Radiochemistry.**

Radiolaria. See **Protozoan** (Sarcodines).

Radiological warfare. See **Chemical-biological-radiological warfare.**

Radiology, *ray dee AHL uh jee,* is the field of medicine that uses X rays and other means to create images of structures and processes inside the body. These images aid in diagnosis and treatment of diseases and other disorders. Radiology includes the use of such imaging techniques as computed tomography (CT), fluoroscopy, magnetic resonance imaging (MRI), and positron emission tomography (PET). Medical procedures that involve *ultrasound* (high-frequency sound waves) are also part of radiology. Doctors who specialize in radiology are called *radiologists.*

Radiological imaging techniques help doctors to diagnose disorders by providing a view of the patient's bones, organs, and other internal structures. For example, a *radiograph* (X-ray picture) of the leg can reveal a

Custom Medical Stock Photo

Radiologists use X rays and other techniques to create images of the body. The radiologists in this photograph are examining an X-ray picture during a surgical operation.

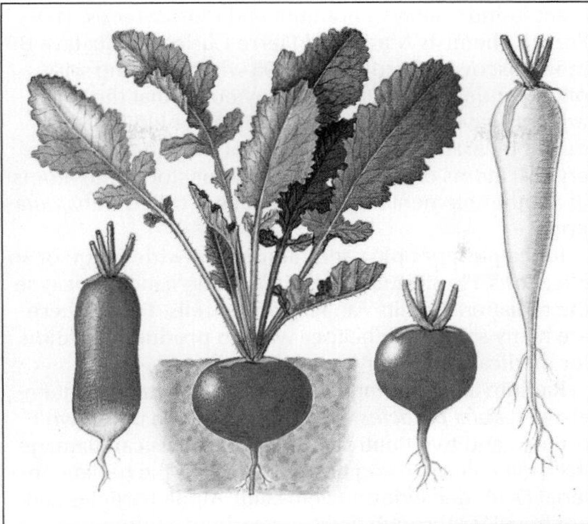

WORLD BOOK illustration by Jill Coombs

Radishes are plants that have crisp, sharp-tasting roots. This illustration shows several varieties of radishes. They are, *from left to right,* the French Breakfast, the Cherry Belle, the Scarlet Globe, and the White Icicle.

fractured bone. A CT scan of the brain can detect a tumor or blood clot. In examinations of certain organs, including the intestines and the urinary tract, the radiologist may give a substance called a *contrast agent* to the patient. The contrast agent may be a barium mixture given orally to coat the lining of the bowel so it is more visible. A contrast agent made of an iodine mixture may be injected into a blood vessel to study arteries or veins.

Radiological procedures also aid in the treatment of certain disorders. For example, doctors use fluoroscopy, CT, or ultrasound imaging to guide *catheters* (small tubes) into a patient's body. This technique is used to drain obstructed ducts in the urinary tract and for many other treatments. P. Andrea Lum

Related articles in ***World Book*** include:

Computed tomography
Fluoroscopy
Magnetic resonance imaging
Positron emission tomography
Ultrasound
X rays

Radiosonde, *RAY dee oh SAHND,* is an instrument that meteorologists use to take *soundings* (measurements) of the upper air. A radiosonde consists of devices that measure temperature, relative humidity, and air pressure, combined with a radio transmitter. The measuring devices and transmitter are in a small, lightweight box carried aloft by a balloon filled with helium or hydrogen.

The radio transmits the information recorded by the measuring instruments to ground stations. In addition, a radio direction finder tracks the radiosonde to determine the speed and direction of the wind at various levels of the atmosphere.

Donald T. Acheson

See also **Balloon** (Sounding balloons); **Weather** (Weather balloons, airplanes, and ships).

Radiotelephone. See **Cellular telephone.**

Radiotherapy. See **Cancer** (Radiation therapy).

Radish is a plant grown for its fleshy root. The roots, also called *radishes,* are crisp and sharp-tasting. People eat radishes raw in salads or as an appetizer.

There are many *cultivars* (varieties) of radishes. Some have a round or oblong shape, and others resemble icicles in form. They range in weight from less than 1 ounce (28 grams) to more than 2 pounds (1 kilogram). Their colors include white, red, yellow, pink, purple, black, and a combination of red and white.

Radishes grow best in cool weather. They can withstand frost. The plants are ready for harvest 20 to 60 days after planting, depending on the cultivar. Many people plant radishes in their home gardens.

Albert Liptay

Scientific classification. The radish's scientific name is *Raphanus sativus.*

Radisson, *ra dee SAWN,* **Pierre Esprit,** *pyair ehs PREE* (1640?-1710), was a French explorer and fur trader. He and his brother-in-law, Médard Chouart, Sieur des Groseilliers, were among the first white people to explore the areas around and south of Lake Superior.

Born in France, Radisson moved to what is now Canada as a boy. Mohawk warriors captured him around 1651, but he escaped about two years later. Radisson and Groseilliers explored the Lake Superior area in 1659-1660. After quarreling with the French over fur-trading rights, the pair went to England in 1665. They persuaded some English merchants to fund a trading expedition to Hudson Bay. This trip led to the creation of the Hudson's Bay Company, an English fur-trading firm, in 1670. Radisson and Groseilliers worked for the firm from 1670 to 1675, then went to France. About 1682-1683, Radisson returned to Hudson Bay as a supporter of French interests in the region. But in 1684, he transferred his loyalty to the English. Radisson lived in London from 1687 until his death. Germaine Warkentin

See also **Groseilliers, Médard Chouart, Sieur des; Minnesota** (Exploration); **Wisconsin** (European exploration and settlement).

Radium, *RAY dee uhm,* is a radioactive metallic element found mainly in uranium and thorium ores. The French chemists Marie and Pierre Curie and Gustave Bémont discovered radium in 1898 while working with pitchblende, a uranium ore. They noted that the ore *emitted* (gave off) more radiation than could be produced by uranium alone. Their work led to the discovery that atoms of one element can transform into atoms of another element through a process called *transmutation.*

In the past, people used radium in a wide range of applications. Physicians used it in treating cancer because the radiation it emits can kill cancer cells. Today, there are many safer and cheaper ways to produce radiation for medical and other uses.

Radium atoms going through transmutation emit energetic *alpha particles,* tiny particles made up of two protons and two neutrons. These particles can damage the molecules in living tissue, including the genetic material DNA (deoxyribonucleic acid). Alpha particles cannot travel far through tissue, so radium seldom poses a serious health risk unless it accumulates in the body. In the early 1900's, manufacturers used radium in fluorescent paint applied to watch and instrument dials. This practice eventually stopped because many workers who applied the paint developed bone cancer. The painters often used their lips to straighten the bristles of radium-contaminated paintbrushes and thus developed harmful accumulations of the radioactive material.

Radium behaves chemically like calcium and tends to travel to the parts of the body where calcium is found—the bones. There, radiation from radium can kill the cells that produce red blood cells or can produce cancers in the bone marrow. Dangerous exposure to radium is rare because little radium persists in the environment.

Properties. Pure radium is silver-white. Its chemical symbol is Ra, and its *atomic number* (number of protons in its nucleus) is 88. Radium has 33 known *isotopes.* Different isotopes of an element have the same number of protons but different numbers of neutrons. The most common and stable isotope of radium is called radium 226 because it has an *atomic mass number* (total number of protons and neutrons) of 226. Radium 226 has a *half-life* of 1,599 years—that is, because of radioactive decay, only half the atoms in a sample of radium 226 will still be atoms of that isotope after 1,599 years. Radium melts at 700 °C and boils at 1140 °C. It has a density of 5 grams per cubic centimeter at 20 °C.

How radium forms and breaks down. Radium 226 forms during the radioactive decay of uranium 238. The uranium atom emits two alpha particles, eventually becoming an atom of thorium 230. That atom then emits an alpha particle to become an atom of radium 226. Radium 226 decays by emitting an alpha particle, producing the radioactive gas radon 222. Douglas John Crawford-Brown

Related articles in ***World Book*** include:

Curie, Marie Skłodowska
Curie, Pierre
Pitchblende
Radiation (Naturally radioactive substances)
Radon
Transmutation of elements

Radon, *RAY dahn,* is a radioactive chemical element that occurs naturally as a gas. The gas is produced by the radioactive *decay* (breakdown) of radium, a metallic element found in nearly all soil and rocks. Radon gas is colorless and odorless. It is classified as a *noble gas,* or an *inert gas,* because its atoms do not combine readily with other atoms. Radon gas may become a health hazard in certain buildings.

The main sources of radon in buildings are the soil and rocks beneath basements. Minor sources of radon include water that comes from wells and building materials such as granite and gypsum that come from the ground. Some areas have a high concentration in the ground.

The gas seeps from soil and rocks into water and air. Radon may enter a basement through cracks or other openings. If the building is in a high-radon area, the gas may build up inside to an unhealthy level.

Radon decay. Radon atoms decay by giving off a form of radiation that is called an *alpha particle.* When a radon atom decays, it becomes an atom of the radioactive element polonium. Further decay produces atoms of other elements. Atoms produced by one or more decays of what were originally radon atoms are called *radon daughters,* also known as radon *progeny* (children).

How radon affects health. Radon daughters cling to airborne dust particles and can catch in the lungs when people breathe them. When well water contains high levels, faucets or showers may release radon and its daughters into the air. Some radon may also enter the body when people drink water which contains the gas.

Alpha particles released by radon and its daughters in the body disrupt the normal genetic or chemical processes of living cells, causing cells to grow abnormally or to die. Over time, such damage to cells may lead to cancer.

During the 1960's and 1970's, studies of uranium miners, who breathed large amounts of radon in the air of mines, showed unusually high rates of lung cancer. Smokers who are exposed to high radon levels are also at increased risk of developing lung cancer. The United States Environmental Protection Agency (EPA) estimates that radon may cause as many as 10 percent of cancer deaths in the country.

Protection against radon. Test kits to check the radon levels in homes are available from stores and mail-order sources. The EPA recommends corrective action if the radioactivity due to radon exceeds 4 *picocuries* per liter of air (4 pCi/L). A picocurie is one-trillionth of a *curie,* a unit of radioactivity. The EPA estimates that 6 percent of U.S. homes exceed 4 pCi/L.

Contractors use several methods to lower radon levels in houses. Some of these techniques prevent radon from entering the home. Others reduce the level of the radon after it has entered. For example, a technique known as soil suction draws radon from below the house. The radon is then vented through a pipe or pipes to the air above the house.

In 1988, Congress passed the Indoor Radon Abatement Act to help reduce the threat from radon. The act set a goal of reducing radon until all home air was as pure as outdoor air. In outdoor air, the radioactivity due to radon is usually less than $\frac{1}{2}$ pCi/L.

Chemical properties. Radon's chemical symbol is Rn. Its *atomic number* (number of protons in its nucleus)

is 86. The *atomic mass number* (total number of protons and neutrons) of its most stable *isotope* (form) is 222. Radon freezes at −71 °C and boils at −61.7 °C. Friedrich E. Dorn, a German chemist, discovered radon in 1900.

Douglas John Crawford-Brown

Raeburn, *RAY buhrn,* **Sir Henry** (1756-1823), was the leading Scottish portrait painter of his day. He painted straightforward portraits that captured the character of the subject. Most of his subjects were fashionable and upper-class Scottish people. Many of his portraits show strong color contrasts and dramatic lighting effects.

Raeburn was born on March 4, 1756, in Edinburgh. He lived there most of his life. He was largely a self-taught artist. In 1785, he met Sir Joshua Reynolds, an English portrait artist. Though influenced by Reynolds's style, he painted in a more Romantic manner. Douglas K. S. Hyland

Quentin McAdam (about 1810), an oil painting on canvas; Yale Center for British Art, Paul Mellon Collection

A Raeburn portrait shows the bold brushstrokes and dramatic lighting effects that are typical of the Scottish painter's style.

Raffia, *RAF ee uh,* is a fiber made from the leafstalks of some kinds of palm trees. One of these palms, the *Raphia ruffia,* grows abundantly on Madagascar's northeastern coast. Another, the *Raphia taedigera,* grows on the islands of Japan. Madagascar's residents make clothes from raffia fiber and weave baskets, mats, and small fancy bags from it. Raffia was once used in greenhouses to protect plants from cold and to tie buds and grafts. But today, artificial fibers are often used for these purposes. Raffia is used in schools for weaving baskets and other products. Robert A. Barnhardt

See also **Basket making.**

Raffles, Sir Thomas Stamford (1781-1826), a British colonial administrator, was the founder of modern Singapore. Singapore was then a thinly inhabited island, but Raffles recognized its potential importance to trade. Today, it is one of the world's busiest ports.

Raffles was born on July 6, 1781, on the merchant ship *Ann* off Port Morant in Jamaica. At the age of 14, he entered the service of a British trading company called the East India Company. The company sent him to Penang, Malaya (now Malaysia), in 1805 as an assistant secretary.

In 1811, Raffles accompanied a British military expedition to the island of Java (now part of Indonesia). The Dutch had controlled Java until Emperor Napoleon I of France annexed the kingdom of Holland in 1810. The British, who were at war with Napoleon, occupied Java without a struggle. They appointed Raffles lieutenant governor. In that post, he abolished forced labor and introduced trial by jury and other reforms. The United Kingdom returned Java to Dutch control in 1816, and Raffles went back to England. There, he wrote a two-volume *History of Java* (1817) and received a knighthood.

Raffles returned to Asia in 1818, serving as lieutenant governor of Bengkulu, Sumatra (now part of Indonesia), from 1818 to 1824. In 1819, he signed a treaty with Temenggong Abdul Rahman, the local chief of Singapore, and Sultan Hussein, the ruler of Johor (now part of Malaysia). The treaty gave the British East India Company rights to establish a trading station on Singapore and helped to limit Dutch influence in the area. By making Singapore a duty-free port, Raffles attracted ships wishing to exchange cargo. Singapore became a thriving center of trade.

Raffles was one of the few Europeans of his time to study the language, history, and culture of the Malays. He was a noted naturalist, and he founded the London Zoological Society in April 1826. Raffles died on July 5, 1826. Alan W. Cafruny

See also **East India Company; Java; Singapore** (History).

Rafflesia, *ra FLEE zhuh,* is the name of a small genus of plants which have huge flowers but no leaves or stems. The flowers grow as parasites on the stems and roots of several Cissus shrubs in Southeast Asia.

The giant rafflesia bears the largest flowers known. They can grow more than 3 feet (90 centimeters) wide.

Kjell B. Sandved, Photo Researchers

The giant rafflesia produces the world's largest known flowers. They can grow more than 3 feet (90 centimeters) wide.

The stamens and pistils of the rafflesia grow on separate flowers. The flowers have five wide, fleshy lobes and usually have a bad odor. This odor attracts flies and beetles, which pollinate the flowers. Thomas B. Croat

Scientific classification. Rafflesias make up the genus *Rafflesia.* The giant rafflesia is *Rafflesia arnoldii.*

See also **Flower** (picture: The rafflesia).

Rafsanjani, *ruhf sehn JAN ee,* **Ali Akbar Hashemi,** *AH lee AHK bahr HASH uh mee* (1934-2017), served as president of Iran from 1989 to 1997. He succeeded Ali Khamenei, who became Iran's spiritual leader after the death of Ayatollah Ruhollah Khomeini. Rafsanjani was considered a moderate president. He was succeeded by Mohammad Khatami in 1997.

© Eslami Rad, Gamma/Liaison

Hashemi Rafsanjani

Rafsanjani was born on Aug. 25, 1934, in a village near Kerman in eastern Iran. He became a follower of Khomeini in the 1950's, while studying theology in Qom.

During the 1960's and 1970's, Rafsanjani participated in a campaign organized by Iran's clergy against the government of Shah Mohammad Reza Pahlavi. In 1979, Khomeini became the chief political figure of Iran after his followers had overthrown the shah. Khomeini appointed Rafsanjani to the Revolutionary Council, which governed Iran until 1980. Rafsanjani was elected to parliament in 1980 and served as its speaker until 1989. During the 1980's, he also was minister of the interior and acting commander in chief of the armed forces.

After stepping down as president in 1997, Rafsanjani became chairman of Iran's Expediency Council, which rules on disputes between parliament and Iran's Council of Guardians. In 2005, Rafsanjani ran again for president, but lost. He died on Jan. 8, 2017. Michel Le Gall

Raft is one of the simplest kinds of watercraft. It may be made of logs lashed together with ropes, or of any other material that floats. Rafts are usually square or rectangular. Poles, paddles, or sails can be used to help propel a raft across the water. Sometimes river and ocean currents alone move a raft to its destination. Most modern rafts used for recreational purposes are inflatable and are made of nylon fabric coated with a synthetic rubber called *neoprene* (see **Rafting**).

Early people built rafts of logs, bundles of reeds, or inflated animal skins lashed together with vines or twisted animal hides. Such rafts provided a means of using the currents of waterways for transportation. A raft drifting with a river's current could carry passengers and goods downstream to the sea. For this reason, ancient seaports were frequently located at the mouths of rivers, where they could easily receive goods from areas farther inland. During the 1800's, *flatboats* (large rafts) served as an important means of transportation on the Ohio and Mississippi rivers (see **Flatboat**).

In 1947, Thor Heyerdahl of Norway and five companions drifted on the balsa-wood raft *Kon-Tiki* for about 4,300 miles (6,920 kilometers). They sailed from Peru to the Tuamotu Islands in the central Pacific (see **Heyerdahl, Thor**). In 1963 and 1964, 70-year-old William Willis of the United States sailed for 10,850 miles (17,461 kilometers) on the *Age Unlimited,* a steel pontoon raft. He went from Peru to Australia—with a stop in the Samoa Islands for repairs—in 204 days. Octavia N. Cubbins

Rafting is an outdoor recreational activity in which small groups of people float down a river on rafts. Rafting provides an opportunity to enjoy scenic wilderness areas in a fresh way. Many people enjoy the adventure and challenge of rafting on rivers that have *white water* (rapids). A raft trip can last for hours, or it can be combined with a camping trip that lasts for days.

Most rafts are inflatable, 12 to 16 feet (3.7 to 5 meters) long, and made of nylon fabric coated with *neoprene* (synthetic rubber). The shape resembles a rectangle with rounded corners. Most crews consist of six people, who sit on the sides of the raft and steer it with paddles. The raft is one of the oldest forms of transportation. But rafting did not become a popular leisure-time activity until the 1960's. Critically reviewed by the American Rafting Association

Ragtime is a type of rhythmic music that was highly popular in the United States around 1895 to 1915. Ragtime (from "ragged time"), or simply *rag,* probably

Phil Degginger from E. R. Degginger

Rafting on *white water* (rapids) is an exciting challenge. The crew uses paddles to steer the craft through the swirling waters. A raft trip can last for hours, or it can be combined with a camping trip that lasts for days.

developed from military marches and from music that accompanied minstrel show dances.

Ragtime is characterized by melodies that are highly syncopated (irregularly accented) combined with accompaniments that have regular accents. Ragtime pieces also have clear-cut thematic sections. Rags were played either on piano or by small bands with various combinations of instruments and became an early influence on jazz.

Although improvised rags were common in the early years, formally composed versions soon became widely published. Among the earliest published rags were Tom Turpin's "Harlem Rag" (1897) and Scott Joplin's "Maple Leaf Rag" (1899). Joplin became known as the "King of Ragtime." Other important ragtime composers included Joseph F. Lamb and James Scott.

Thomas W. Tunks

See also **Jazz** (The roots of jazz); **Joplin, Scott; Popular music** (Ragtime, jazz, and blues).

Ragweed is the name of several weeds that grow in the United States and Canada. These weeds grow along roadsides, and in pastures, fields, and vacant lots. Many people are allergic to ragweed pollen. It is produced in great amounts and spread by the wind. People who are allergic to ragweed pollen may get symptoms of hay fever when there are about 25 grains of pollen per cubic yard (33 grains per cubic meter) of air. The air may contain more pollen than this when the plants bloom.

The *common ragweed,* also called *bitterweed* and *hogweed,* is a coarse annual plant with finely divided leaves. It usually grows 1 to 3 feet (30 to 91 centimeters) high. Its small, hard fruit has short, sharp spines near the end. *Giant ragweed,* sometimes called *kinghead,* is also an annual. It commonly grows 3 to 6 feet (0.9 to 1.8 meters) tall but may grow to 10 feet (3 meters). Its leaves usually are divided into three broad parts. *Perennial ragweed* grows from long, spreading roots. It looks something like the common ragweed but its fruit has blunt *tubercles* (small projections) instead of spines.

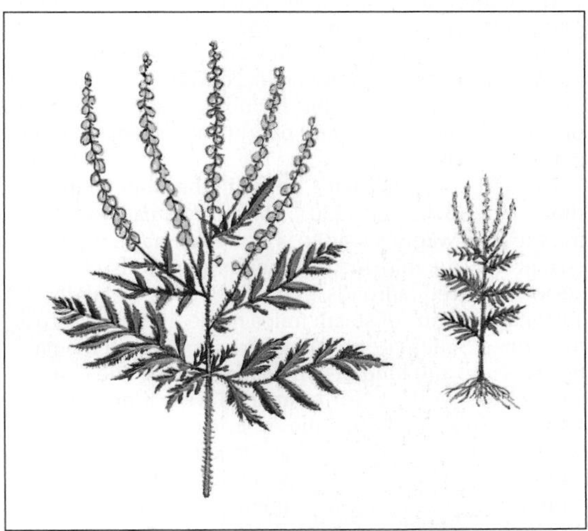

WORLD BOOK illustration by James Teason

The common ragweed usually grows 1 to 3 feet (30 to 91 centimeters) high. Ragweed sprouts quickly along roadsides and in fields. Many people are allergic to ragweed pollen.

Ragweed grows quickly in any untended spot. It is so ordinary looking and its flowers are so inconspicuous that efforts to eliminate it have failed.

Anton A. Reznicek

Scientific classification. Ragweeds are in the composite family, Compositae. The scientific name for the common ragweed is *Ambrosia artemisiifolia.* The giant ragweed is *A. trifida.* Perennial ragweed is *A. psilostachya.*

See also **Hay fever.**

Raikes, Robert (1735-1811), an English publisher, first developed Sunday schools on an extensive scale. Many children in his home city, Gloucester, worked six long days in the factories and had no chance for education. He opened his first Sunday school there in 1780. Sunday schools helped train children in reading and arithmetic as well as in the Bible, because there were no public schools. Before Raikes died, his system had spread throughout England. He was born in Gloucester on Sept. 14, 1735. He died on April 5, 1811.

F. A. Norwood

John H. Gerard, DPI

The Virginia rail is a swift, slender bird that lives in marshes. The rail's coloring helps it blend into the vegetation.

Rail is the common name of a family of birds that live in grassy marshes throughout most of the world. They run swiftly over the mud, seeking worms, insects, snails, floating seeds, and plant sprouts to eat. Rails vary in length from 5 to 25 inches (13 to 64 centimeters). They have long, narrow bodies, short wings and tails, long legs and toes, and loose plumage of mixed black, gray, and brown feathers. A rail's shape helps it slip through reeds and grasses. The expression "thin as a rail" may come from their appearance. Rails migrate long distances. However, the birds are seldom seen in flight except when chased from cover. They build nests of grasses on the ground or among rushes over water. They lay from 6 to 15 buffy-white eggs that are speckled with reddish-brown.

The rails most common in Europe are the *water rail* and the *corn crake,* which frequents fields. The *king rail, yellow rail, black rail, clapper rail, Virginia rail,* and *sora* (or *sora rail)* are found in America. The clapper rail is hunted in the southern United States.

James J. Dinsmore

Scientific classification. Rails make up the rail family, Rallidae.

See also **Coot; Gallinule.**

Gamma/Liaison

One of the world's fastest passenger trains is France's TGV *(train à grande vitesse).* The TGV travels between Paris and other cities in France and Belgium at speeds of 200 miles (320 kilometers) per hour or more. Trains once carried most of the passenger traffic between cities. But today more people use cars or airplanes, and most railroads get most of their income from hauling freight.

Railroad

Railroad is one of the most important means of transportation. Every day, thousands of trains speed along railroad tracks throughout the world. Some trains carry passengers. Others haul coal, grain, lumber, machinery, and other products on which people depend. Only ships carry heavier cargoes for longer distances. And only airplanes provide a faster means of public transportation than do railroads. A freight train can haul thousands of tons of goods across a continent. Some of the fastest wheeled passenger trains can operate at more than 200 miles per hour (mph), or 320 kilometers per hour (kph). Magnetic levitation trains, or *maglevs,* float above their tracks and can travel even faster. In many parts of the world, railroads are also called *railways.*

Railroads use a two-railed track to guide trains of cars along a permanent route. Trains therefore are not steered, unlike airplanes, automobiles, and ships. Powerful diesel-electric or electric locomotives move most trains along the track. However, older steam locomotives still haul a few trains in some parts of the world, such as China and India.

Almost every country has at least one railroad. The world's longest rail line is in Russia. It extends about 5,600 miles (9,000 kilometers) and connects Moscow and Vladivostok. Laid end-to-end, the tracks of the world's main railroad routes would stretch about 680,000 miles (1,100,000 kilometers)—about three times the distance from Earth to the moon.

William L. Withuhn, the contributor of this article, is Curator of Transportation at the Smithsonian Institution.

The word *railroad* may refer not only to a method of transportation, but also to an organization that provides rail transportation. In many countries, a government agency or government-owned corporation operates the railroads. In other countries, including the United States, private companies own and operate all or most of the main railroads.

The first public railroads began in the United Kingdom in the 1820's and 1830's. They used steam locomotives to haul wagons loaded with freight or passenger coaches. By the mid-1800's, other countries also had steam-powered railroads. In the late 1800's and early 1900's, thousands of steam trains made their way across the United States countryside, carrying most of the nation's freight and long-distance passengers. The first railroad across western North America was completed in 1869 and so helped open the American West to settlers.

Over the years, railroads have faced ever-increasing competition from other forms of transportation. In most countries, the central government supports the railroads. But in a few countries, including the United States, freight railroads get little government aid. Private railroads generally face greater financial risks than do government-owned ones.

How railroads serve the public

Railroads provide two main types of service: (1) passenger service and (2) freight service. The importance of each type of railroad service varies from country to country.

Passenger service. Railroads operate two main types of passenger trains: *commuter trains* and *intercity trains.* Commuter trains carry passengers between large cities and the surrounding suburbs. A majority of these trains are made up of a locomotive and a number of *coaches.* Coaches provide seats for passengers but do not ordinarily offer any extra services, such as meals or refreshments. Intercity trains make longer runs than most commuter trains do. The longest intercity runs cover great distances and take several days to complete. As a result, many intercity passenger trains have special cars, such as *dining cars* and *sleeping cars,* in addition to coaches.

Since the 1940's, the number of rail passengers has declined sharply in many industrial countries, as more and more people travel by automobile and airplane. For example, railroads in the United States now carry less than 1 percent of all intercity passenger traffic. In some countries, however, passenger trains have not faced such strong competition from other forms of transportation. People in China, India, Japan, and most European countries still rely heavily on trains for intercity transportation. Even in the United States, thousands of people who live in suburban areas ride commuter trains into major cities.

Commuter trains. A majority of rail passengers ride commuter trains. Each working day, these trains carry great numbers of suburban residents to and from work in such large cities as London and New York City. Commuter trains also serve many other cities throughout the world, including Berlin, Chicago, Johannesburg, Moscow, New Delhi, Paris, São Paulo, Tokyo, and Toronto. Some intercity trains also serve commuters.

It takes up to 1,000 automobiles to carry as many commuters as one commuter train can carry. Commuter trains thus help relieve rush-hour traffic jams on city highways. By reducing the number of automobiles in use, commuter trains help conserve fuel. They also help reduce air pollution caused by exhaust fumes.

Intercity trains. Some countries have unusually fast, efficient intercity passenger trains. The world's fastest intercity passenger trains operate in China, France, Japan, South Korea, and Taiwan. Some of the fastest of these trains can travel more than 200 mph (320 kph) between stops. They may average more than 175 mph (282 kph). In addition, high-speed trains serve cities in Germany, the United Kingdom, and other European countries. Some of the Japanese and European high-speed trains offer a number of luxury services, including gift shops, telephones, and meals served at the passengers' seats.

© Shutterstock

A commuter train carries passengers between cities and suburbs. Many commuter trains have double-deck coaches.

Photo Trends

Refrigerator cars are equipped to keep fruits, vegetables, and meats at the right temperature.

Michael K. Nichols, Magnum

Container shipping speeds the loading and unloading of freight trains. The containers are large boxes loaded with freight. The double-stack car, *shown here,* can carry two large containers. A crane is about to stack the container at the rear on top of the container in the car.

Some Canadian intercity trains, called *Corridor Trains,* also provide luxury service. One of these trains carries passengers between Toronto and Montreal—a 335-mile (539-kilometer) journey—at an average speed of about 80 mph (130 kph).

In the early 1900's, there were thousands of passenger trains in the United States, linking almost all U.S. cities. Today, only about 125 daily intercity trains serve the entire country. The only high-speed trains operating in the United States are *Acela Express* trains. They serve a number of cities in the northeastern United States and can reach a speed of 150 mph (240 kph).

Freight service. In a large number of countries, a majority of the income earned by railroads comes from hauling freight. Railroads provide the most inexpensive method of land transportation over long distances. Trains are used extensively to carry such bulk goods as chemicals, coal, grain, iron ore, and petroleum. They also carry such manufactured goods as automobiles and television sets, and such agricultural products as fruits, vegetables, and meats. Some of the cars on a freight train are empty cars being moved to various points for reloading.

Railroads use a large number of types of cars and freight-handling equipment. Bulk materials, such as coal and ores, travel in open cars with *hatches* (doors) underneath. Such cars can be emptied quickly through these doors. Powdered materials, such as cement, travel in cars that are pressurized steel containers. The cars are loaded and unloaded using air pressure that pumps the material in or out through pipes. Chemicals, gasoline, milk, and other liquids are carried in tank cars. Refrigerated cars transport fruits, vegetables, and meats. Special railroad cars with two or three decks are used to carry automobiles.

The longest freight trains have 200 or more cars. In the United States, a typical freight train has around 80 cars and carries approximately 5,000 tons (4,500 metric tons) of goods.

Railroads in many countries carry more freight today than ever before. However, railroads haul a smaller share of the total freight traffic than in the past. For example, in 1929, railroads handled almost 75 percent of all the freight carried between U.S. cities. Today, they carry approximately 40 percent of all intercity commercial freight.

To attract more customers, railroads in a large number of countries have tried to improve their freight service. In the 1950's, for example, railroads in the United States introduced *piggyback* service—the use of flatcars to carry truck trailers loaded with freight. Piggyback service attracted shippers because one train could carry many truck trailers for a fraction of what it cost to haul them individually by highway. Today, railroads in the United States carry hundreds of thousands of truck trailers each year.

Another type of service uses flatcars to haul large containers loaded with freight. The containers are transferred to the flatcars from specially designed ships or trucks (see **Containerization**). The *Freight operations* section of this article discusses other improvements in freight service.

What makes up a railroad

A railroad consists basically of a track along which locomotives pull trains of cars. The track is made up of

Railroad passenger routes

This map shows the major railroad passenger routes in North America. Amtrak, a semipublic corporation created in 1970, provides most of the passenger service in the United States. In Canada and Mexico, passenger service exists along with freight service on many minor routes not shown on the map. The cities shown are important rail passenger terminals.

Amtrak route

Other passenger railroad

0 500 Miles
0 500 Kiometers

WORLD BOOK map

Atchison, Topeka and Santa Fe Railway

Diesel-powered trains make up the backbone of U.S. railroads. Many diesel locomotives consist of several power units at the head of the train, all under the control of one engineer.

two steel rails fastened lengthwise to a series of wooden or concrete *crossties,* called *sleepers* in some countries. The wheel-and-axle assemblies on locomotives and cars are specially designed to run on the track. Each wheel has a *flange* (raised edge) around its rim. The flanges on each pair of wheels guide the wheels along the track. *Switches*—short movable rails—are built into a track where it meets other tracks. By turning a switch, a train can be made to run from one track to another. A railroad also includes signal and communications systems to control train traffic, stations to handle passengers and freight, *yards* to make up trains, and *shops* to repair locomotives and cars.

Rolling stock is a term that refers to railroad locomotives and cars.

Locomotives. Most trains are pulled by a locomotive at the head of the train. But some locomotives push as well as pull. These locomotives are especially useful on commuter lines because they eliminate the need to turn a train around for a return trip at the end of a run.

Locomotives can be classified into two groups by the work they do. *Road locomotives* haul freight or passenger trains. *Switching locomotives,* sometimes called *shunting locomotives* or *switch engines,* move cars from track to track in rail yards.

Almost all locomotives can also be classified into three groups according to how they are powered. *Diesel-electric locomotives* use oil-burning diesel engines to turn electric generators. The electric power produced by the generators runs the motors that turn the locomotive's wheels. *Electric locomotives* work much as diesel-electrics do. But instead of producing their own electric power, they get it from wires suspended above the track or from an electrified third rail. *Steam locomotives* burn coal or fuel oil to produce steam. The force of the steam powers the locomotive.

A few trains are hauled by two other kinds of locomotives. *Gas-turbine electric locomotives* use the force of hot gases to run turbines, which in turn operate electric generators. Power produced by the generators runs the locomotives. *Diesel-hydraulic locomotives* use diesel engines to produce energy that is transmitted to the driving mechanisms by means of fluids under pressure. See **Locomotive** and **Electric railroad**.

Railroads in most industrial countries operate both diesel-electric and electric locomotives. Almost all locomotives operated by U.S. railroads are diesel-electric. No large, commercial U.S. railroads use steam locomotives. Steam locomotives are still used in a few parts of China and India.

Passenger and freight cars. Railroad cars are grouped in two general categories, passenger cars and freight cars. Each car has a *coupler* at each end. This device links the cars together. Cars also have *air brakes,* which are connected to a master control in the locomotive (see **Brake** [Air brakes]).

On most passenger trains, the cars consist mainly of coaches. A typical coach has seats for 50 to 90 passengers. Double-deck coaches on commuter trains seat from 150 to 170 people. Some passenger-train cars, such as club cars or lounge cars, provide card tables, refreshments, or other services that are not generally available on coaches. Other passenger-train cars include baggage

Pulse Electronics, Inc.

An end-of-train device, mounted next to a coupler (yellow), senses the train's motion and monitors the air pressure for the brakes. A radio transmits data to the locomotive cab.

cars, dining cars, and sleeping cars.

Freight cars differ in shape and size according to the freight they are designed to haul. They range from boxcars for carrying general freight to specially designed cars for new automobiles. Many newer freight cars are longer and have been designed to carry different kinds of freight. For example, piggyback cars are flatcars designed to carry truck trailers.

Since the early 1980's, railroads have eliminated *cabooses,* which once commonly served as the end cars on freight trains. Monitoring devices called *end-of-train devices* now perform duties once handled by crew members riding in the caboose.

Railroad companies are exploring the idea of *integral trains* for use in freight transport. An integral train consists of cars permanently coupled in units of various lengths. The train moves as a unit to its destination and back.

Railroads have greatly improved the safety of railroad cars over the years. One of the chief improvements has been to reduce the danger from overheated *journal boxes,* also called *axle boxes.* On older cars, each end of an axle turns on solid surfaces enclosed in an oil-filled journal box. On modern cars, the use of roller bearings rather than solid surfaces at the ends of axles has practically eliminated overheated axles, called "hotboxes." Railroads have electronic devices called *hotbox detectors* installed at various points alongside railroad tracks. As trains pass by, the devices detect any hotboxes. This information is transmitted to a control station. The station radios the train crew to stop the train and to remove cars with hotboxes.

Railroad cars with built-in power units do not need a locomotive. Such cars, sometimes called *railcars,* may be diesel-electric, electric, or gas-turbine electric.

Some railcars are equipped to carry passengers. These cars have seats and windows located behind the power unit. Some passenger railcars haul one or more passenger cars to form *railcar trains.* Well-known railcar trains include the Docklands Light Railway of London.

Some self-propelled cars are designed for use in railroad maintenance. Each carries equipment to do a particular job along a railroad line. For example, some have track-laying machinery or machinery for inspecting or repairing tracks. Others carry such equipment as snowplows or weed cutters.

Tracks. The rails and crossties that make up railway track are laid along a *roadbed*—that is, land that has been prepared as a foundation for the track. The roadbed follows the route planned for a railroad. *Main-line* routes link major cities. *Branch lines* extend between main lines and various places not served by main lines, such as small communities or mining sites. Many main lines consist of two or more tracks laid side by side. Such *multiple tracks* enable trains to travel in opposite directions on the same line at the same time. Single-track lines must be equipped with *sidings* at various points along the route. A siding is a short track alongside a main or branch line to which one of two meeting trains is switched until the other train passes.

The track and roadbed, together with such other railway structures as tunnels and bridges, are sometimes referred to as the *roadway.* In addition to the roadway, railways own a certain amount of land on both sides of

Kinds of railroad cars These illustrations show major kinds of passenger and freight cars. Not all the illustrations are drawn to the same scale.

WORLD BOOK illustrations by Art Grebetz

Amtrak Superliner: Double-deck, long-distance coach carries 75 passengers on two levels; baggage on lower level; 85 feet (26 meters) long.

Amtrak Viewliner: Single-level sleeping car contains 12 sleeping compartments, including 2 deluxe bedrooms and 1 handicapped-accessible deluxe bedroom; 85 feet (26 meters) long.

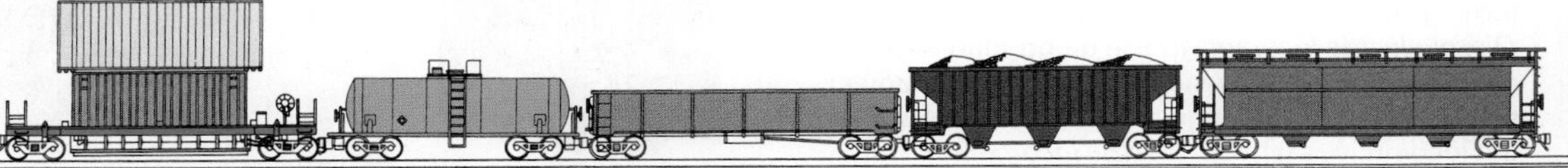

Double-stack container car: Hauls general freight in stacked containers; 51 feet (16 meters) long.

Tank car: Carries oil and other liquids; 50 feet (15 meters) long.

Gondola car: Hauls metal products and bulk freight; $52\frac{1}{2}$ feet (16 meters) long.

Open-top hopper car: Hauls such bulk freight as coal; length varies.

Covered hopper car: Protects bulk freight from the weather; 54 feet (16.5 meters) long.

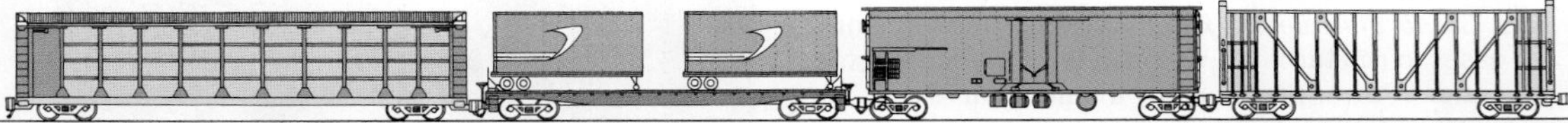

Enclosed rack car: May have two or three enclosed decks for transporting vehicles safely; holds up to 18 automobiles; 90 feet (27 meters) long.

Piggyback flatcar: Common flatcar can hold two truck trailers or containers; 92 feet (28 meters) long.

Refrigerator car: Cooled car; hauls fresh and frozen produce and meats; 60 feet (18 meters) long.

Center-beam car: Has open sides for carrying lumber and other large goods; 73 feet (22 meters) long.

the roadway. This land and the roadway make up a railroad's *right of way.*

The crossties and rails. Most crossties, or *ties,* are spaced about 21 inches (53 centimeters) apart. The ties average about 3,000 per mile (1,900 per kilometer). There are two types of ties—wood ties and concrete ties.

When wood ties are used, two steel *tie plates* are placed on top of each tie, one plate near each end of the tie. Each plate has a wide groove that is shaped to hold the bottom of the rail. Steel spikes are driven through holes in the plates. The spikes hook over the bottom of the rail and keep it firmly fastened to the tie.

Concrete ties do not have plates and spikes. Instead, plastic pads replace the plates, and two steel bolts with spring clips hold the base of the rail firmly to the tie.

The spikes or bolts must be the same distance apart on each tie so that they hold the rails the same distance apart all along the track. This uniform distance between rails is called the *gauge.* Every country has a *standard gauge* for all its main rail lines. In addition, a majority of countries have this same standard gauge for most branch lines. In this way, any locomotive or car can travel on almost any track in the country. However, the standard gauge varies from country to country. Australia, Canada, Mexico, the United States, and most European nations have a standard gauge of 4 feet 8 $\frac{1}{2}$ inches (1.44 meters).

In the United States, steel mills produce rails in 39-foot (12-meter) or 78-foot (24-meter) lengths. Little new track is laid, and so new rails are used mainly to replace existing track. Much existing track consists of 39-foot lengths of rail joined end to end by pieces of steel called *joint bars* or *fishplates.* The joint bars are fastened to the rails by bolts that pass through holes in the bars and in the sides of the rail.

Railroads in the United States have replaced most of the old short-length rail with new lengths of rail. A majority of this rail measures about $\frac{1}{4}$ mile (0.4 kilometer) long. Shorter rail lengths are welded together to make the $\frac{1}{4}$-mile lengths. Welded rails have fewer gaps and so produce a smoother ride than do rails joined in many places. Such continuous rail is also easier for railroad work crews to maintain.

The roadbed and route. In building a roadbed, civil engineers use special instruments and machinery to make the land as smooth and level as possible. This process is called *grading.* Most roadbeds are then covered with a layer of *ballast,* which consists of such materials as gravel or crushed stone. Ballast holds the ties in place and so helps keep the track stable. Ballast also helps distribute the weight of passing trains and gives them a degree of cushioning. Trains thus ride more easily than they would over bare ground. Ballast also promotes drainage of rain water and slows the growth of weeds.

Before constructing the roadbed, engineers plan a route with the least possible *grade* and *curvature.* Grade refers to the steepness of the land. Curvature refers to the number and sharpness of curves along the route. The ideal railroad route lies across perfectly flat land. Track laid along such a route has little or no grade or curvature. Freight trains can easily carry heavy loads along the track, and passenger trains can travel at top speed. Steep grades, on the other hand, make it difficult for a train to carry heavy loads or travel at a high speed. If a route passes through hilly or mountainous country, engineers lay track around steep grades instead of over them. The track thus has many curves. Curves reduce a train's speed but do not prevent it from carrying heavy loads.

A route through a mountain range might require so many curves that travel along the route would be extremely slow. Engineers therefore sometimes build railroad tunnels through mountains. They also construct railroad bridges to span chasms and rivers. Tunnels and bridges are also built to extend railroad routes under or across bays and other bodies of water.

Freight operations

Freight trains are assembled in *classification yards,* also called *sorting yards* or *marshaling yards,* at various railroad terminals. A terminal may also have facilities for loading and unloading cars and for repairing locomotives and cars. After trains of freight cars arrive at a classification yard, the cars are sorted into groups according to their destinations. All the cars in a group must be headed for destinations along the same route or along branches of this route. After a locomotive has been coupled to such a group of cars, the cars become a freight train. Cars headed for destinations off the main route must be switched to other trains along the way.

In the past, railroad freight shipments frequently met long delays at classification yards. They also met delays at *interchanges*—that is, at rail junctions where cars are

Train wheels and tracks

Trains ride on *flanged* wheels. A flange is a rim on a wheel's inner edge that guides the wheel along the track. The track consists of two rails supported by *ties.* On wood ties, steel *tie plates* are spiked to the ties. A groove in the plates helps hold the rails in place. The ties are anchored in *ballast* (gravel or crushed stone). On concrete ties, steel rail clips hold the rails to the ties. The clips fit through steel parts that are bolted to the ties.

WORLD BOOK diagrams by Linda Kinnaman

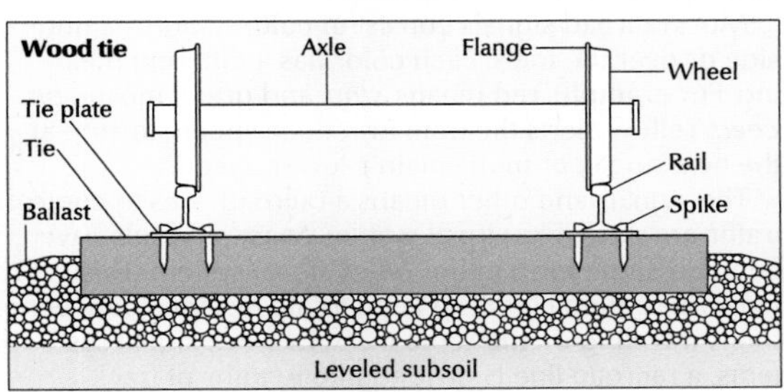

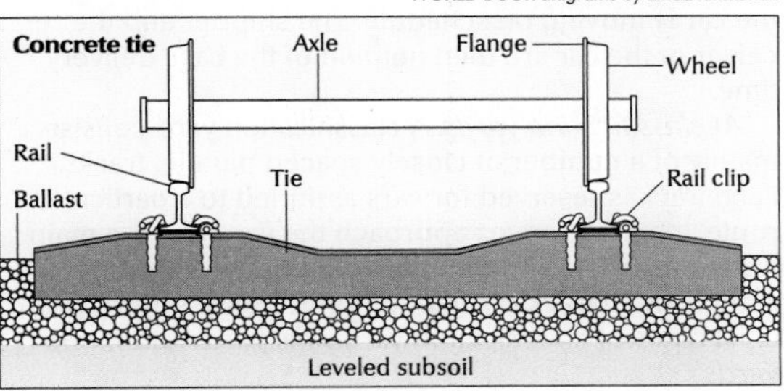

Jon Bentz, West Stock

A unit train is a freight train whose cars all carry the same kind of freight and are all headed for the same destination. This unit train is made up of open-top hopper cars loaded with coal.

switched from one railroad to another.

To speed freight shipments, railroads have improved their freight-handling methods in three main ways. First, they have consolidated and modernized classification yards. Second, they have simplified the work performed at interchanges. Third, and perhaps most important, the railroads have developed computer systems for planning and monitoring their operations. In one such system, the computer generates a specific "trip plan" for each car. As the car moves in trains from its origin to its destination, its plan is checked continually to see that the car is moving on schedule. The shipper and the receiver of the car are then notified of the car's delivery time.

At classification yards. A classification yard consists mainly of a number of closely spaced parallel tracks. Each track is reserved for cars assigned to a particular route. Incoming trains approach the yard along a main track at one end. Newly assembled trains leave the yard along a main track at the other end. There are two principal types of classification yards: *flat yards* and *hump yards.*

Flat yards are the older type of classification yard. In these yards, switching locomotives haul cars from incoming trains onto the proper tracks, from which departing trains are made up. A switching locomotive must travel back and forth many times to make up a train. In addition, the track switches and car brakes in these yards are operated by hand. The work requires many employees and proceeds only as fast as the workers can do their jobs. As a result, classification often takes a long time.

Hump yards speed the work of classification. These yards make use of gravity. In hump yards, switching locomotives push incoming trains along a single track to the top of a low hill, or *hump.* On the other side of the hump, the track branches out into a number of classification tracks. As each car reaches the top of the hump, it is uncoupled and the proper track switches are opened. Devices called *retarders* control the car's speed, and the car rolls down the hump onto its assigned track. The retarders regulate a car's speed so that it meets the other cars on its track with just enough force to engage its coupler. Operators in a control tower use computers to control most of the yard operations.

At interchanges. Automated hump yards help speed interchange by *preblocking* cars on a freight train—that is, by arranging all the cars on the train into groups according to their final destination. Cars on such a *block train* do not have to be reclassified at interchanges or yards.

Unit trains further reduce the number of switchings or eliminate switching entirely. Unit trains have a single type of freight car loaded with a single type of freight, such as coal or wheat. The cars all have the same destination and remain together until they reach it. Many unit trains make regular nonstop runs between the same two terminals—for example, between a coal mine and an electric power plant. Some unit trains change or add locomotives when they change from one rail line to another.

Trains of flatcars carrying highway trailers or freight containers are called *intermodal trains.* Such trains require their own specialized yards. Special flatcars carry containers stacked two high. Heavy forklifts or other lifting machines pick up the containers and trailers. Trucks carry the containers between the yard and their final destinations over highways. Use of containers greatly speeds freight movement.

Traffic control

Railroads use signals and various other means to control train traffic. The chief purpose of traffic control is to prevent accidents. But it also helps make railroad operations speedier and more efficient.

Most railroad signals consist of colored lights alongside or over the track. Each color has a different meaning. For example, red means *stop,* and green means *proceed.* Yellow alerts the train to reduce speed, to stop at the next signal, or to maintain a lower speed.

The signals and other means a railroad uses to control traffic are part of its signal system. Most railroads have adopted some form of the *block signal* system. This system is designed chiefly to keep a safe distance between trains traveling on the same track. In block signal systems, a railroad line is divided into lengths of track

How freight trains are made up

Freight trains are made up at *classification yards,* which consist mainly of groups of parallel tracks. Each track is reserved for cars that will make up a particular train. Most large classification yards are *hump yards,* which use a low hill, or *hump,* in sorting cars onto the proper tracks.

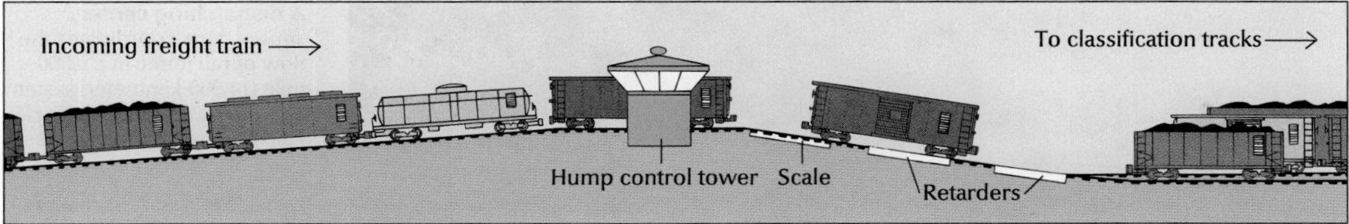

WORLD BOOK diagram

The hump has a single track up one side, *left.* Partway down the other side, the track branches out into the classification tracks. A switch engine pushes an incoming train up the hump. As each car reaches the top, it is uncoupled and the proper switches are opened. The car is weighed and rolls onto its assigned track. Most hump yards are automated.

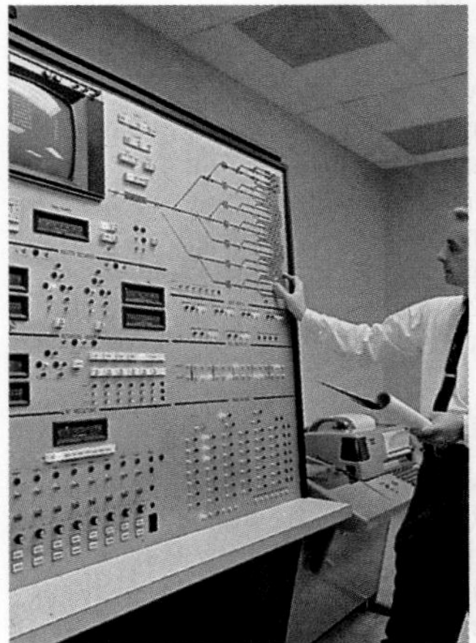

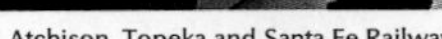

Atchison, Topeka and Santa Fe Railway

Atchison, Topeka and Santa Fe Railway

© Shutterstock

Sorting cars. A computer, *left,* uses information about each car's destination and weight to open the switches leading to the car's assigned track and to operate *retarders* in the downhill track, *center.* The retarders slow the car so that when it reaches the classification tracks, *right,* it is traveling just fast enough to couple automatically with the car ahead on the proper track.

called *blocks.* Most blocks range from 1 to 2 miles (1.6 to 3.2 kilometers) long. Only one train may be in a block at a time. Colored-light signals control entry to the block. When a train is in the block, the signals warn other trains to stop. No train may proceed from one block to the next without an all-clear signal. Block signals may be either *automatic* or *manual* (hand-operated).

Automatic block signal systems are the most common type of block systems used today. In an automatic block system, the signals are operated by an electric current, also called a *track circuit,* that flows through the rails. A train entering a block short-circuits this current, causing the signal that guards the block to turn red. As soon as the train leaves the block, the signal returns to yellow, meaning "all clear." Many automatic block systems also have *interlocking* controls. Interlocking controls set multiple track switches at one time to ensure a safe path for the train to follow through complex junctions.

A remotely controlled signal system is called Centralized Traffic Control (CTC). Signals and switches on the line are controlled from a central dispatch station. This station has one or more electronic diagrams that show the present location of every train on a line. CTC operators study the diagrams to decide how to route the trains as safely, speedily, and efficiently as possible. The operators direct train traffic by setting the necessary signals and switches. Modern forms of CTC, with advanced computers and safety systems, are referred to as *centralized dispatching.* Such dispatching makes it possible for railroads to use single tracks efficiently for two-way traffic. If two trains are headed toward one another on the same track, a dispatcher switches one of the trains to a siding until the other passes. CTC also makes use of interlocking controls.

In the United States, the federal government requires automatic block systems on all tracks where passenger trains travel at 60 mph (97 kph) and over and where freight trains travel at 50 mph (80 kph) and over.

Manual block signal systems require operators at various points along the line to control the signals. Each operator is responsible for the movement of trains

Trans Pix from CSX Corporation

A dispatching center, *shown here,* coordinates the flow of rail traffic in a 9,000-mile (14,500-kilometer) system. This center at Jacksonville, Florida, has illuminated displays that cover the walls of a circular building. Dispatchers seated at consoles talk by radio with train crews throughout the system.

within one or two blocks and informs other operators by telephone whether a block is occupied or clear. The possibility of human error makes manual signal systems less reliable than automatic systems.

Some manual block systems have interlocking controls. These controls ensure that switches in complex combinations can only be set safely. They also give signals to approaching trains to prevent derailment or collision.

Other train controls. A large number of railroads are experimenting with *advanced train control systems,* also known as *positive train control,* to improve safety and efficiency. In addition to signal lights alongside their tracks, some railroads have signals providing the same information on panels in their locomotives. These signals may also work in connection with safety devices. One such device is the *automatic train stop* (ATS). The ATS puts on a train's brakes automatically if the engineer fails to notice a stop signal. Another safety device, called *automatic train control* (ATC), automatically controls a train's speed. If the engineer fails to notice a caution signal, the ATC puts on the brakes to slow the train to the required speed. The device also stops the train if necessary.

Many railroads use advanced communications systems to help control the movement of trains. Two-way radio systems on trains enable crew members to communicate from one end of the train to the other. Train crews also use two-way radio systems to communicate with distant dispatching centers. Railroads trace the exact locations of their trains and of individual cars by using *transponders* (electronic transmitting devices) as tags. Track-side equipment sends and then receives radio signals from the transponders. Satellite-based tracking of trains using the Global Positioning System (GPS) also helps railroads improve train control (see **Global Positioning System**).

Railroad systems

In the United States. The United States has about 450 railroad companies. All but two of the major railroad companies are owned by private investors. The exceptions are the Alaska Railroad, which is owned by the Alaska state government, and Amtrak Corporation, a passenger railroad financed by the United States government.

Categories of railroads. The federal government *categorizes* (classes) U.S. railroads as either *line-haul* or *switching and terminal.* Line-haul companies own the nation's main rail lines. Switching and terminal companies own tracks and other facilities in and around certain large railroad stations and classification yards. The largest U.S. line-haul companies in terms of miles of track operated include the Burlington Northern Santa Fe; CSX Corporation; Norfolk Southern Corporation; and the Union Pacific Railroad.

Automatic block signaling

Automatic block signals allow trains to follow one another safely on the same track. The track is divided into *blocks* about 1 to 2 miles (1.6 to 3.2 kilometers) long. An electric current flows through the rails and is short-circuited when a train is in a block. The short circuit causes the signal for that block to turn red and the preceding block signal to turn yellow. Other signals show green. A train may proceed through a green signal but must slow down at a yellow signal and stop at a red one.

WORLD BOOK diagram, adapted courtesy of Westinghouse Air Brake Company and Pulse Electronics, Inc.

Occupied block
Stop signal

Unoccupied block
All-clear signal

Unoccupied block
Caution signal

Occupied block
Stop signal

The United States government further classifies railroads according to *operating revenue* (money earned from operations). Companies whose operating revenue is $250 million or more a year are *Class I railroads.* Only a small number of line-haul companies and Amtrak fall in this group. Firms with operating revenue between $20 million and $250 million are *Class II railroads.* Companies whose operating revenue is less than $20 million are *Class III railroads.* Some Class II and Class III railroads are owned by Class I railroads. Some Class I railroads are owned by conglomerates. A large number of Class I railroads have resulted from the *merger* (union) of smaller railroads.

Many railroads have been formed from line segments sold by other railroads because they were unprofitable. They include *short line railroads,* which have from a few to several hundred miles or kilometers of track, and larger companies called *regional railroads.*

Cooperation among railroads. The Association of American Railroads, an organization sponsored by the railroads, deals with matters of concern to the entire industry. Its membership includes railroads in Canada and Mexico as well as in the United States.

Railroad companies also cooperate with one another in various other ways. For example, a majority of rail routes in the United States are owned by separate companies. Much of the freight traffic handled by a railroad originates on lines owned by other companies. In the past, every company required that its own locomotives and train crews be used on all trains run on its tracks. Today, a number of railroads share the use of their lines. Each of these companies operates *run-through trains* over lines owned by the other companies. A run-through train changes only its crew when it moves to another line.

Railroad workers range from dispatchers and switch operators to salespeople and clerks. Many railroad jobs require training in electronics, computer operations, marketing, and other fields.

Perhaps the best-known railroad jobs are those of the train crew. Most crews consist of a *conductor* to supervise the train's operation, an *engineer* to run the locomotive, and possibly a *brakeman* to uncouple cars and do various other tasks. In the days of steam locomotives, a *fireman* tended the locomotive boiler.

Rail unions. United States railroad workers belong to about 15 different labor unions. One of the most important is the United Transportation Union. Some of the unions include only railroad workers, but others also include workers in other industries. The Brotherhood of Locomotive Engineers, founded in 1863, is the oldest labor union in the United States.

Over the years, the rail unions and the railroads have agreed to certain *work rules.* Unions have generally opposed changing most work rules, but they have agreed to change certain rules to improve safety. The Railway Labor Act, passed by Congress in 1926, establishes the rules for settling railroad labor disputes (see **Railway Labor Act**).

The role of the federal government. The Surface Transportation Board (STB), an independent government body, regulates some of the economic activities of railroads in the United States. For example, a railroad must receive board approval to merge with another railroad. The Federal Railroad Administration (FRA) sets railroad safety standards and inspects locomotives, cars, tracks, and signal systems. Both the FRA and the STB are part of the United States Department of Transportation. Amtrak operates as a semipublic corporation partly financed by the federal government. The Department of Transportation and Amtrak work with Congress and local governments to decide Amtrak's routes and the number of trains on each route.

Railroad finances. The United States federal government provides less financial aid for railroads than it does for any other form of transportation. In 1980, deregulation of U.S. railroads began, and many pricing controls were removed. Since that time, the major railroads have become profitable.

The railroads have become more competitive with other forms of transportation. A large number of railroads have speeded up freight shipments and improved service by operating container trains and unit trains. In addition, railroads have increased their ability to handle a variety of freight. They earn much of their income by hauling bulk cargoes, such as coal and grain. However, many railroads have redesigned equipment so that they can handle more manufactured goods. The use of freight cars designed to carry new automobiles has proved especially successful. The railroads' share of new-automobile shipments has risen from about 10 percent in the 1950's to about 50 percent today. Manufactured goods account for a growing share of freight railroad income.

In Canada. Canada has two major freight railway systems. Both systems, the Canadian National Railway Company (CN) and the Canadian Pacific Railway Company (CPR), are privately owned. Both systems own and operate extensive rail lines across the southern half of Canada. CN has a line as far north as the Northwest Territories. Both systems also operate lines in the United States. Canada's major passenger railway is VIA Rail Canada, a government-funded company. A number of smaller, privately owned railroads also operate in Canada.

Two agencies of the Canadian government—Transport Canada and the Canadian Transportation Agency—regulate Canadian railways. These agencies operate within the Ministry of Transport, Infrastructure, and Communities. They set and enforce rail safety standards and make decisions on requests by railroads to drop unprofitable schedules or abandon unprofitable track.

In other countries. The majority of countries have a single national railroad system, which the government owns and operates. Some countries have a number of small, privately owned railroads in addition to the national railroad.

Most of the world's railroads make little or no profit. In most countries, the government provides the additional funds needed to keep the railroads running. These governments believe the services the railroads provide are worth the additional money. Other governments have *privatized* their railroads—that is, they have sold them to private companies.

In Latin America. Mexico has a large railroad network. It is made up of several privately owned companies. Some Central American countries have short lines that operate in coastal regions. Railroads in Peru and Bolivia were originally built to carry materials mined from the

Andes Mountains. The railroads are the world's highest, rising to nearly 19,700 feet (6,000 meters) above sea level. Argentina's railroad system links to those of Uruguay and Paraguay. The vast majority of Brazil's extensive railroad system is less than 300 miles (500 meters) from the coast.

In Australia and New Zealand. Australia's main-line rail systems were all publicly owned until the late 1900's. However, many of these systems are now privately owned. Many of Australia's railroad lines use the standard gauge of 4 feet 8 ½ inches (1.44 meters). However, other railroad lines, such as those that operate in Queensland's sugar plantations, use other gauges. New Zealand's private system of railroads uses a narrow gauge of 3 feet 6 inches (1.07 meters). Ferries carry rail vehicles between the North Island and South Island of New Zealand.

Leading countries in railroad transportation

Passenger service

Country	Passenger-miles*	Passenger-kilometers*
China	893,908,000,000	1,438,606,000,000
India	719,035,000,000	1,157,174,000,000
Japan	164,120,000,000	264,125,000,000
Russia	82,879,000,000	133,381,000,000
France	58,982,000,000	94,923,000,000
Germany	53,304,000,000	85,785,000,000
United Kingdom	43,712,000,000	70,348,000,000
United States	38,613,000,000	62,142,000,000
Italy	31,694,000,000	51,006,000,000
Egypt	25,375,000,000	40,837,000,000

Freight service

Country	Ton-miles†	Ton-kilometers†
Russia	1,782,176,000,000	2,601,928,000,000
United States	1,729,633,000,000	2,525,217,000,000
China	1,571,820,000,000	2,294,814,000,000
India	505,847,000,000	738,523,000,000
Canada	241,467,000,000	352,535,000,000
Brazil	183,360,000,000	267,700,000,000
Kazakhstan	150,638,000,000	219,927,000,000
Ukraine	127,635,000,000	186,344,000,000
South Africa	95,892,000,000	140,000,000,000
Germany	58,224,000,000	85,005,000,000

Length of track‡

Country	Miles	Kilometers
United States	182,412	293,564
China	81,400	131,000
Russia	72,798	117,157
Canada	48,425	77,932
India	42,579	68,525
Argentina	22,939	36,917
Germany	20,872	33,590
Australia	20,718	33,343
Brazil	18,548	29,850
France	18,417	29,640

*A passenger-mile is one passenger carried 1 mile. A passenger-kilometer is one passenger carried 1 kilometer.
†A ton-mile is 1 ton carried 1 mile. A ton-kilometer is 1 metric ton carried 1 kilometer.
‡Mainline routes, not counting double tracks, sidings, or branch lines.
Figures are for 2019 or most recent year available.
Sources: U.S. Bureau of Transportation Statistics; International Union of Railways; U.S. Central Intelligence Agency.

In Asia. China's railroad system is concentrated in the densely populated eastern part of the country. The system includes the longest high-speed rail service in the world. This service stretches about 1,200 miles (1,900 kilometers) from the northeastern capital of Beijing to Guangzhou, a major city in the southeast. Because China has little of the petroleum needed to run diesel locomotives, it has historically operated mainly steam locomotives. Many modern Chinese trains are electric. In India, millions of people ride passenger trains every day. The railroad system is important to the support of India's tremendous freight traffic. Most of India's trains run on a gauge of track 5 feet 6 inches (1.68 meters) wide.

In Japan, a higher percentage of people ride the train daily than in any other country. Many trains run on a gauge of 3 feet 6 inches (1.07 meters). The country's high-speed Shinkansen—also known as "bullet trains"—travel on standard-gauge track.

In Europe, most countries use standard-gauge track. The exceptions are Finland and Russia, which use a gauge of 5 feet (1.52 meters), and Spain and Portugal, which use a gauge of 5 feet 6 inches (1.68 meters).

European governments typically operate the railroad systems. Many European railroads cooperate to improve train service between countries, and a number of trains move freely across national boundaries. Several European countries, including France, Germany, Italy, and the United Kingdom, operate high-speed trains. Such trains also carry passengers and freight between the United Kingdom and France through the Channel Tunnel.

In Africa. South Africa has Africa's best railroad system. The system primarily handles freight, but it has many passenger trains, including the famous *Blue Train.* The system operates on a gauge of 3 feet 6 inches (1.07 meters). It links to a rail line in Namibia and to one in Zimbabwe through Botswana. A good network of tracks links parts of northern Africa. Rail lines in other parts of the continent are mainly single-track routes that are used to ship freight from mines and farms to seaports that handle international trade.

History

Several European countries had a few primitive railroads as early as the mid-1500's. However, these railroads were used mainly to bring up wagonloads of coal or iron ore from underground mines. The mining railroads consisted of two wooden rails that extended down into the mines and across the mine floors. Laborers or horses pulled wagons with *flanged* wheels—that is, wheels made with a protective rim—along the rails. The wagons moved more easily along the rails than they did over the rutted or muddy entrances and floors of the mines.

In the early 1700's, English coal-mining companies began building short wooden railroads to carry coal aboveground as well as underground. Horses pulled the trains of wagons along the rails. In the mid-1700's, workers began nailing strips of iron to the wooden rails to make them last longer. English ironmakers also began making all-iron rails. The rails were flanged to carry wagons with ordinary wheels. By the end of the 1700's, ironmakers were producing all-iron rails without flanges. These rails carried wagons with flanged wheels.

Invention of the locomotive. Meanwhile, inventors had been developing the steam engine. About 1800, the English inventor Richard Trevithick experimented with the first engines capable of using high-pressure steam. Trevithick mounted one of the engines on a four-wheeled undercarriage designed to roll along a track. In 1804, Trevithick used this vehicle to pull 10 tons (9 metric tons) of iron, 70 men, and 5 wagons along 9 $\frac{1}{2}$ miles (15 kilometers) of track. Trevithick's invention thus became the world's first successful railroad locomotive. Soon, other English inventors had also built successful locomotives.

An English railway engineer named George Stephenson constructed the world's first public railroad, the Stockton and Darlington, which opened in 1825. The line operated between the towns of Stockton and Darlington, a distance of about 20 miles (32 kilometers). It was the first railroad to run steam freight trains on a regular schedule. Stephenson's second railroad opened in 1830. It ran 30 miles (48 kilometers) from Liverpool to Manchester. It was the first railroad to run steam passenger trains on a regular schedule.

Stephenson also originated the idea that a country's railroads should all have a standard gauge. The gauge he selected for the railroads he built—4 feet 8 $\frac{1}{2}$ inches (1.44 meters)—corresponded to the length of the axles on many horse-drawn wagons. This gauge was eventually adopted by most European railroads and then by railroads in other parts of the world.

Developments in the United States. A few horse-powered railroads began operating in the eastern United States in the early 1800's. In 1815, an American engineer named John Stevens obtained a charter from the state of New Jersey to build a steam-powered railroad across the state. Although Stevens could not raise enough money for this project, he still wanted to apply steam locomotion to railway track. He constructed a circular track near his estate in Hoboken, New Jersey, and built a small steam-powered wagon to run on it. In 1825, this vehicle made a successful run.

In the late 1820's, the Delaware and Hudson Canal Company of Pennsylvania decided to build a railroad. In 1829, the company ran an English-built locomotive along a section of wooden track. This locomotive, called the *Stourbridge Lion,* became the first full-sized locomotive to run on a track in North America.

In 1830, the Baltimore and Ohio Railroad began service over 13 miles (21 kilometers) of track between Baltimore and Ellicott's Mills (now Ellicott City). The railroad's first cars were drawn by horses. These horse-powered cars were the first railroad cars in the United States to carry passengers. The Baltimore and Ohio also experimented with a car equipped with sails. In the summer of 1830, New York manufacturer Peter Cooper built a steam-powered locomotive, later called the *Tom Thumb,* for the Baltimore and Ohio. However, it was too small for regular service. In 1831, the railroad began regular passenger service with a locomotive called the *York.*

Meanwhile, the West Point Foundry of New York had built a steam locomotive for the South Carolina Canal and Railroad Company. In 1830, this locomotive, called the *Best Friend of Charleston,* pulled a train of cars along 6 miles (10 kilometers) of track. This event marked the first run of a steam-powered train in the United States. The *Best Friend* began making regular runs between Charleston and Hamburg, South Carolina, in 1831. The South Carolina Canal and Railroad Company thus became the first U.S. railroad to provide regular steam-powered passenger and freight service.

The number of locomotives and railroads multiplied rapidly in the United States after 1830. Historic first runs of locomotives included those of the *De Witt Clinton* on the Mohawk and Hudson Railroad in New York in 1831; the *John Bull* on the Camden and Amboy Railroad in New Jersey in 1831; *Old Ironsides* on the Philadelphia, Germantown, and Norristown Railroad in Pennsylvania in 1832; and the *Pontchartrain* on the Pontchartrain Railway in Louisiana in 1832. By 1835, more than 200 railroad charters had been granted in 11 states, and over 1,000 miles (1,600 kilometers) of track had been laid.

Meanwhile, builders were developing locomotives especially suited to the eastern United States, where roadbeds had many curves. These locomotives had an independent wheeled undercarriage called a *leading truck.* The leading truck was attached to the locomotive by a *center pin,* which allowed the truck to swivel. A truck gave a locomotive more flexibility on curves. Most of the new locomotives had a four-wheeled truck and four driving wheels. These eight-wheeled locomotives, known as the *American-type,* became the most popular type of U.S. locomotive during the second half of the 1800's.

Canada's first steam-powered railway, the Champlain and St. Lawrence Railroad, was started in the province of Quebec. The line opened for business as a horse-powered railroad in July 1836, and began steam-powered service later that year. The railway operated between the towns of Laprairie and Saint-Jean, a distance of about 16 miles (26 kilometers). Other small railroads began operating in Canada soon after 1836.

Expansion in the United States. Railroads were under construction in all states east of the Mississippi River by 1850. Most of the lines were concentrated in the Northeast, and many of them ran only short distances. A network of lines radiated from Boston, New York City, and Philadelphia. Railroads also linked cities in the Southeast.

Competition for trade spurred railroad construction in the East. By the early 1850's, four railroads had built rail lines that enabled them to haul freight between the Great Lakes region and the East Coast. New York's Erie Railroad opened between Piermont and Dunkirk on Lake Erie in 1851. In 1853, 10 small railroads along the Erie Canal merged to form the New York Central Railroad, which provided service between Albany and Buffalo. By 1852, the Pennsylvania Railroad and the Baltimore and Ohio had opened lines to the Ohio River, one of the most important trade routes in the country. The large railroads took over many smaller lines and so expanded rapidly.

During the 1850's, railroad lines connected Chicago with the Mississippi River, which was a major trade route. The Baltimore and Ohio reached St. Louis on the Mississippi in 1857. Both Chicago and St. Louis thrived as transportation centers.

In 1850, Congress began granting federal land to develop railroads. Government leaders knew that railroads

The "Lightning Express" Trains (about 1863), a lithograph by Currier & Ives

Powerful steam locomotives hauled passengers and freight throughout the United States as rail transportation became a nationwide industry during the last half of the 1800's.

would help attract settlers to undeveloped regions of the Midwest and the South. The railroad companies kept some of the land for right of way and sold the rest to help pay railroad construction costs. The first grant helped build the Illinois Central Railroad from the Great Lakes at Chicago to Cairo, Illinois. Settlers poured into the area along the route after the railroad's completion. The success of the experiment persuaded Congress to grant federal lands for railroad development in the western United States. In return, all U.S. railroads agreed to carry government troops and property at half the standard rates and United States mail at four-fifths the standard rates. These rates remained in effect until the mid-1940's.

The railroads continued to expand during the 1860's. They played a major role in the American Civil War (1861-1865) by moving troops and supplies to battle. The South was at a disadvantage because it had far fewer railroad tracks and locomotives than the North had. After the war, iron and steel railroad bridges were built across such major rivers as the Ohio, the Mississippi, and the Missouri.

The first transcontinental rail lines. In the early 1860's, the United States government decided to extend rail lines across the country. The proposed route roughly followed the 42nd parallel from Omaha, Nebraska, to Sacramento, California. Eastern rail lines were to be extended westward from Chicago to meet the new railroad at Omaha. Congress passed the Pacific Railroad Act in 1862. The act gave two companies responsibility for building the railroad. The Union Pacific was to start laying track westward from a point near Omaha. The Central Pacific Railroad was to lay track eastward from Sacramento. Congress granted both railroads large tracts of land and millions of dollars in government loans.

Work began on the Central Pacific track in 1863 and on the Union Pacific in 1865. The railroads faced the gigantic task of crossing the rugged Rockies and the towering Sierra Nevada. To obtain skilled labor, the Central Pacific hired thousands of Chinese immigrants to work on the railroad. Thousands of European immigrants and former Civil War soldiers worked on the Union Pacific. On May 10, 1869, the tracks of the two railroads finally met at Promontory, Utah. North America became the first continent to have a rail line from coast to coast.

By the end of the 1800's, the United States had five transcontinental rail lines. The Canadian Pacific Railway completed Canada's first transcontinental line in 1885. It extended from Montreal, Quebec, to Vancouver, British Columbia. The completion of these rail lines opened vast regions of the continent to town development, farming, and trade.

Worldwide development. Railroad building spread rapidly, first in England and then throughout Europe. By 1870, most of Europe's major rail systems had been built. Other lines were built in the late 1800's and early 1900's. Some of these lines required that tunnels be blasted through the Alps to connect France, Switzerland, and Italy. The *Orient Express,* one of the most famous European passenger trains, began operation between Paris, France, and Istanbul, Turkey, in 1883.

As they had done for the western United States, rail-

Important dates in railroading

1804 Richard Trevithick of England invented the steam locomotive.

1825 The Stockton and Darlington Railway, built in England by George Stephenson, became the first railroad to offer regularly scheduled steam-powered train service.

1831 The South Carolina Canal and Railroad Company began the first regularly scheduled steam-powered train service in the United States.

1836 The Champlain and St. Lawrence Railroad began operating Canada's first regularly scheduled steam-powered trains in Quebec.

1850 Congress made the first federal land grants for the development of U.S. railroads.

1859 The first Pullman sleeping car went into service between Chicago and Bloomington, Illinois.

1869 The world's first transcontinental rail line was completed across the United States.

1885 The first transcontinental rail line across Canada was completed.

1887 Congress passed the Interstate Commerce Act to control certain economic practices of U.S. railroads.

1893 The American steam locomotive *No. 999* made the world's first 100-mph (160-kph) run.

1895 The Baltimore and Ohio Railroad started the world's first electric main-line service in Baltimore.

1925 The first commercial diesel-electric locomotive in the United States began service as a switch engine.

1934 The Burlington *Zephyr,* the first streamlined passenger train powered by a diesel-electric locomotive, began service in the United States.

1964 Japanese passenger trains began operating between Tokyo and Osaka at speeds up to 130 mph (209 kph).

1970 Congress authorized the creation of Amtrak to operate U.S. intercity passenger trains.

1980 The Staggers Rail Act eased some of the regulations imposed by the Interstate Commerce Act.

1990's Many countries privatized their railroad systems, including Mexico, the Netherlands, and the United Kingdom.

2003 A transcontinental rail line spanning Australia from north to south was completed.

Union Pacific Railroad

The meeting of two railroads at Promontory, Utah, in 1869 marked the completion of the world's first transcontinental rail line. Officials of the Central Pacific and Union Pacific railroads drove in the last spike.

roads opened up other parts of the world to development and trade. Argentina and Brazil developed rapidly after they built extensive rail networks in the late 1800's. Railroads were also built across South America's towering Andes Mountains. One such railroad, the Central Railway of Peru, was begun in 1870. It is the world's highest standard-gauge railroad, climbing to more than 3 miles (5 kilometers) above sea level.

Also in the late 1800's, France, Germany, and the United Kingdom built railroads in their African and Asian colonies. The United Kingdom, for example, helped construct nearly 25,000 miles (40,200 kilometers) of railroad track in India during the late 1800's. Russia started work on its 5,600-mile (9,000-kilometer) Trans-Siberian railroad in 1891 and completed it in 1916. The Trans-Siberian is the world's longest continuous railroad line. Australia started building a railroad across its southern plains in 1912. This line, completed in 1917, extends 1,108 miles (1,783 kilometers) from Port Pirie to Kalgoorlie.

Engineering improvements. Beginning about the 1870's, railroads started to use steel for rails and cars. Steel rails last up to 20 times longer than iron rails, and so they gradually replaced iron rails. Early freight and passenger cars were made largely of wood. All-steel passenger cars were first put into regular service in 1907 and gradually replaced most wooden cars. All-steel freight cars had replaced most wooden freight cars by the late 1920's.

Several important inventions after the mid-1800's helped improve railroad safety. In 1869, the American inventor George Westinghouse patented a railroad air brake. The brake automatically stopped a train if air pressure was lost. In 1873, an American amateur inventor named Eli Janney patented an automatic car coupler. Before Janney's invention, coupling had to be done manually. Many brakemen and switchmen lost fingers or hands while coupling cars. But fail-safe air brakes and automatic couplers were not widely used until after 1893. That year, Congress passed the Railroad Safety Appliance Act, which required air brakes and automatic couplers on all trains.

The building of electric telegraph lines in the mid-1800's made block signaling possible. Manual block systems became common before the end of the 1800's. American engineer William Robinson patented the track circuit used in automatic block signaling in 1872. In 1887, American inventor Granville T. Woods patented an *induction telegraph.* This system allowed communication between stations and moving trains by sending a signal through the track.

Meanwhile, more and more people traveled by train. The railroads themselves did much to attract passengers. In 1867, an American businessman named George Pullman organized the Pullman Palace Car Company. The company manufactured a sleeping car that Pullman had designed. Other sleeping cars were already in use, but Pullman's car improved greatly on the others. By 1875, about 700 Pullman sleeping cars were in service. Railroads also introduced luxurious parlor cars and elegant dining cars.

Designers gradually increased the power and speed of steam locomotives. By the 1890's, many trains easily reached speeds of 50 to 70 mph (80 to 113 kph). In 1893, a train pulled by the American steam locomotive called *No. 999* was the first to exceed 100 miles (160 kilometers) per hour.

In 1879, Werner von Siemens, a German inventor, introduced the first functional electric train. In 1895, the Baltimore and Ohio Railroad became the first U.S. railroad to provide electric main-line service. It operated an electric train through a $3\frac{1}{2}$-mile (5.6-kilometer) tunnel under the city of Baltimore. Many European railroads electrified their main lines after 1900. But almost all U.S. railroads continued to use steam locomotives.

Regulation and control of U.S railroads. A financial panic in 1873 cut deeply into the profits of U.S. railroads. Financial leaders battled for control of the richest companies. Dishonest promoters made fortunes selling worthless railroad stock. The companies themselves fought bitterly for freight business. Some railroads combined to eliminate competition and raise prices, also called *rates.* Others offered bargain rates to favored shippers. These and other unfair practices led Congress to pass the Interstate Commerce Act in 1887. The act set up guidelines to regulate competition between railroads and to ensure reasonable railroad rates. The act also established the Interstate Commerce Commission (ICC). For more information, see **Interstate commerce** (The Interstate Commerce Act).

The United States entered World War I in 1917. In December 1917, the federal government took over wartime control of U.S. railroads. The war ended in November 1918, but the government kept control of the railroads until after Congress passed the Esch-Cummins Act of 1920. This legislation, also called the Transportation Act, increased the ICC's control over railroad rates. It also encouraged railroads to merge if mergers would increase their operating efficiency. The government returned the railroads to private control in March 1920.

The 1920's and the Great Depression. Railroads in the United States made record profits during the 1920's. Up to 80 percent of long-distance freight and passengers moved by rail. But there were signs of approaching trouble. Automobiles, buses, and trucks began carrying traffic once carried by trains. Disputes with labor also troubled the railroads during the early 1920's. The Railroad Shopmen's strike of 1922 was one of the largest strikes in U.S. history. Labor disputes led Congress to pass the Railway Labor Act in 1926. The act set up means to settle disputes.

Like most other industries, the railroads lost huge sums of money during the Great Depression of the 1930's. Many companies went into bankruptcy. But others spent large sums of money to win back passenger business with sleek, new diesel-electric trains.

Diesel-electric locomotives were more fuel-efficient and much easier to maintain than steam locomotives. The first commercial diesel-electric locomotive in the United States began service in 1925. It was used as a switch engine. The stainless steel *Zephyr,* the world's first streamlined passenger train powered by a diesel-electric locomotive, began regular service on the Burlington railroad in 1934. It traveled between Denver and Chicago and could maintain an average speed of 78 mph (125 kph). No other train had ever maintained so high a speed over such a long, nonstop run. Also in 1934, a streamlined, aluminum-bodied passenger train, the Union Pacific's *City of Salina,* began operation. Other railroads soon put diesel trains into service. These trains included the Santa Fe's *Super Chief* and the New York, New Haven, and Hartford's *Comet.* The Santa Fe put the first regularly scheduled diesel-electric freight trains into service in 1940.

Economic recovery—and decline. After the United States entered World War II in 1941, the nation's railroads handled more traffic than ever before. Rubber and gasoline rationing limited highway travel. Passenger and freight trains ran day and night, and almost every train was packed to capacity. During the war, the government left the railroads under private control.

After the war ended in 1945, railroads in many countries faced financial difficulties. Much railroad equipment was nearly worn out from overuse. During the late 1940's and early 1950's, the world's railroads spent billions of dollars to replace worn-out equipment. At the same time, they faced serious competition from other forms of transportation. In the 1950's, most industrialized countries phased out steam locomotives in favor of more economical diesel-electric models.

In 1958, Congress passed legislation enabling railroads to discontinue hundreds of unprofitable passenger runs. But some railroads continued to lose money during the 1960's.

Until 1970, the U.S. government required U.S. railroads to provide intercity passenger service even though most passenger trains lost money year after year. To relieve the railroads of this financial burden, the government formed Amtrak in 1970. This semipublic corporation, partly financed by the federal government, took over the operation of almost all U.S. intercity passenger trains in 1971 (see **Amtrak**).

Although the formation of Amtrak helped U.S. railroad companies reduce their losses, the financial condition of some railroads—especially those in the Northeast—continued to worsen. The Railroad Reorganization Act of 1973 was designed to help reverse the huge losses of several railroads and to guarantee continued rail service. In 1976, six bankrupt Northeastern railroads were reorganized by the federal government as a private corporation called the Consolidated Rail Corporation (Conrail). At first, the federal government was Conrail's chief stockholder, but the government sold its stock to private investors in 1987.

Railroads today. In 1980, Congress passed the Staggers Rail Act, which was designed to help railroads increase their profits. The law greatly reduced regulation of prices and various other aspects of railroad operations. It helped railroads become more competitive with other forms of transportation, and the financial health of major U.S. railroads improved dramatically in the 1990's. During the 1990's, railroad services were privatized in many countries to improve competition and profitability. Mexico, the Netherlands, and the United Kingdom were among the countries that had railroad services transferred from public to private control.

In 1998, the United States government authorized the breakup of Conrail, which had by that time become profitable. CSX Corporation and Norfolk Southern Corporation purchased Conrail's holdings.

Australia completed a north-south transcontinental railroad in 2003. The line extends 1,851 miles (2,979 kilometers), from Adelaide in South Australia to Darwin in the Northern Territory.

Today, many people view railroads as essential to relieving highway traffic congestion. Many also point out the environmental benefits of trains, which produce a much lower amount of pollution per traveler than automobiles do. Some railroads are looking to high-speed trains to replace airplanes for travel over distances up to about 500 miles (800 kilometers). William L. Withuhn

Related articles. See the *Transportation* section of the various state, province, country, and continent articles. See also:

Biographies

Baldwin, Matthias William
Brady, Diamond Jim
Cooper, Peter
Gould, Jay
Henry, John
Hill, James Jerome
Jones, Casey
Long, Stephen Harriman
Pullman, George Mortimer
Stanford, Leland
Stephenson, George
Stephenson, Robert
Stevens, John
Stevens, Robert Livingston
Trevithick, Richard
Vanderbilt, Cornelius
Westinghouse, George

Other related articles

Amtrak
Andes Mountains
Brake (Air brakes)
Channel Tunnel
Credit Mobilier of America
Diesel engine
Electric railroad
Elevated railroad
Europe (pictures: High-speed trains; The Industrial Revolution)
Freight
Industrial Revolution (picture)
Interstate commerce
Iowa (The coming of the railroads)
Locomotive
Magnetic levitation train
Monorail
National Mediation Board
New Hampshire (Places to visit; picture: Mount Washington Cog Railway)
Pullman Strike
Railway Labor Act
Tennessee (Places to visit)
Transcontinental railroad
Transit
Transportation
Trans-Siberian Railroad
Tunnel (Railroad tunnels)
United States, History of the (picture: Railroads and steamboats)
Western frontier life in America

Outline

I. How railroads serve the public
- A. Passenger service
- B. Freight service

II. What makes up a railroad
- A. Rolling stock
- B. Tracks

III. Freight operations
- A. At classification yards
- B. At interchanges

IV. Traffic control
- A. Automatic block signal systems
- B. Manual block signal systems
- C. Other train controls

V. Railroad systems
- A. In the United States
- B. In Canada
- C. In other countries

VI. History

Questions

What is a *flange?* What does it do?
Who built the first public railroad? When did it open?
When was the first transcontinental rail line completed?
What is a *piggyback car?* A *siding? Ballast?*
How did World War II affect U.S. railroads?
How did the railroads of the 1500's operate?
How does ownership of U.S. railroads differ from that in most other countries?
What is railroad *gauge? Standard gauge?*
What is a *classification yard?* A *flat yard?* A *hump yard?*
How are trains on the same track kept safely apart?

Additional resources

Level I

Balkwill, Richard. *The Best Book of Trains.* Kingfisher, 1999.
Cefrey, Holly. *High Speed Trains.* Children's Pr., 2001.
Evans, Clark J. *The Central Pacific Railroad.* Children's Pr., 2003.
Houghton, Gillian. *The Transcontinental Railroad.* Rosen Central, 2003.

Level II

Jane's World Railways. Jane's, published annually.
Middleton, William D. *Metropolitan Railways: Rapid Transit in America.* Ind. Univ. Pr., 2003.
Solomon, Brian. *The Heritage of North American Steam Railroads.* Reader's Digest, 2001.
Stover, John F. *American Railroads.* 2nd ed. Univ. of Chicago Pr., 1997. *The Routledge Historical Atlas of the American Railroads.* Routledge, 1999.
Welsh, Joe. *The American Railroad.* MBI Pub., 1999.

Railroad, Electric. See Electric railroad.

Railroad, Elevated. See Elevated railroad.

Railroad, Model, is a small railroad that copies the appearance and operation of a full-sized railroad. Model railroading is the hobby of building and operating model railroads. It is a favorite pastime for thousands of people.

A model railroad can include all the major features of a real railroad, such as locomotives, cars, switches, signals, stations, and bridges. In addition, model railroaders can build miniature towns and natural scenery as settings. Model railroad cars, engines, and other equipment can be bought ready-made. However, a majority of model railroad enthusiasts enjoy designing and assembling their own systems. They build models from kits or make them from parts and raw materials. Model railroaders lay down tracks according to their own layout designs, and they wire their railroads to operate in a realistic way.

Model railroading offers a variety of activities in addition to modelmaking, such as carpentry, wiring electrical circuits, and making scenery. Model railroaders can concentrate on building only those parts of the system that they enjoy most, because the other parts can be purchased ready-made.

Model railroading differs from the hobby of operating toy trains. Model railroads are made to represent real trains in accurate detail. In building their systems,

Model Railroader

Railroad models are divided into two categories, *toy trains* and *model trains.* Each category is built to *scale,* which is the comparison between its size and the size of a real train. Most toy trains are built to *O* scale, *right.* The most popular model train scales are *HO, center,* and *N, left.*

model railroaders copy as closely as possible the appearance and operation of a real railroad. Toy trains are larger than most model trains, and they are built to withstand rougher handling. Toy trains do not have much of the fine detail and realism that model trains have. Toy train enthusiasts may put together large and highly complicated railroad systems. However, most toy locomotives, cars, and other equipment are purchased completely assembled.

Scale and size. Railroad models are built to *scale.* The scale is the comparison between the size of the model and the full-sized railroad, called the *prototype.* In the most common model railroad scale, called *HO,* each part of the model is $\frac{1}{87}$ the size of the prototype. HO uses a *gauge* (track width) of 16.5 millimeters, or about $\frac{5}{8}$ inch. This represents the standard track gauge of 4 feet 8 $\frac{1}{2}$ inches (1.44 meters) on a real railroad.

The most popular scale after HO is *N* scale, in which models are $\frac{1}{160}$ the size of the prototype. N scale models run on N gauge tracks that are 9 millimeters, or about $\frac{1}{3}$ inch wide. Most toy trains are built in *O* scale, which is $\frac{1}{48}$ the size of the prototype. They run on O gauge tracks that are 1 $\frac{1}{4}$ inches (3.2 centimeters) wide.

A layout built in N scale will take up less space than the same layout in HO scale. But a modeler can build an N scale layout in a larger space and devote more of that space to scenery and buildings. A model railroad may cover as little as 9 to 12 square feet (0.8 to 1.1 square meters). Many are built on tabletops made from a plywood sheet measuring 4 feet (1.2 meters) wide and 8 feet (2.4 meters) long. Bigger systems can occupy most or all of a basement or attic. The largest scale is *G* scale. It is $\frac{1}{22.5}$ of the prototype and is often used outdoors in *garden railways.* The smallest is *Z* scale, $\frac{1}{220}$ the size of the prototype, and it can operate on a small layout.

Track can be purchased in short sections or in longer flexible strips. Sectional track comes in straight or curved pieces, which are put together to form the desired layout. Sectional model railroad track resembles toy train track. But model railroad track has more ties per section so it looks more realistic. Flexible track, often called *flextrack,* comes in either 3-foot or 1-meter strips. The strips can be put down either straight or curved to fit the layout design. Some model railroaders buy rails separately and spike them down by hand on individual wooden ties for greater realism.

Most model railroads use the two rails to carry electrical current to and from the locomotive. The rails form the sides of an electrical circuit, and the locomotive completes the circuit through its wheels and motor. Some model railroads represent prototypes of electrically powered trains. Some of these models are powered through an overhead wire, as in a trolley car. Other models receive power through an outside third rail, as in the elevated and subway trains operating in many cities.

Toy trains have a third rail running down the middle of the tracks. This rail and the side rails carry current to and from the toy train locomotive.

Locomotives for model railroads are purchased already assembled, or they are built from kits. Their power comes from household current that first passes through a separate electrical unit called a *power pack.* The power pack reduces the voltage of the household current from 110 volts to 12 volts. It also changes the type of current from *alternating current,* which continually reverses direction, to *direct current,* which flows in one direction. Most toy trains use alternating household current. The current first passes through a transformer that reduces the voltage. Both power packs and transformers include switches by which the operator controls the speed and direction of the locomotive.

Most model locomotives are made in one of two engine prototypes—steam or diesel.

Steam locomotives are especially popular with model railroad enthusiasts, though they are no longer used on real railroads. A great variety of steam locomotives were custom built for different railroad companies. Each steam locomotive prototype has unique features that model builders value. Many hobbyists enjoy building steam locomotives because the locomotives have many visible moving parts. In a steam locomotive model, the motor is usually located in the firebox behind the boiler. A set of gears connects the motor to the axles of the large drive wheels.

Diesel locomotives are simpler in appearance and easier to build than steam models. They are popular with hobbyists who want to create a more modern looking system. Diesel locomotive models have a more standard appearance than steam locomotives, but they have a variety of paint and lettering designs that represent the different railroad companies. Most diesel locomotive models have the motors in the middle of the body. The wheels are mounted on swiveling pieces called *trucks* attached to the bottom of the body. Gears connect the motor to the wheels of the locomotive. Many diesel models use two or more locomotive units to copy the makeup of real diesel locomotives. One of the model units might be a *dummy,* without motor or gears, which will still create the appearance of the real locomotive but at less expense.

Cars for model railroads usually come in kits that can be assembled with a few simple tools. Most are made of plastic pieces that snap together. More challenging kits, called *craftsman kits,* include a combination of materials, such as wood, metal, and plastic. The pieces of the model must be cut to size and fitted together. In many kits, the cars are already painted with the designs of prototype railroads. In others, the model builders paint the cars themselves with their own designs. Some model builders combine parts from two or more kits, a practice that is called *kitbashing.*

Buildings and scenery. Much of the realism of a model railroad depends on how creatively the builder designs the scenery of the system. The builder may send the train over a complicated route through tunnels and small towns, over rivers and highways, and into freight yards or passenger terminals.

There are a variety of kits for making buildings. Buildings can also be constructed from raw materials. Hobbyists build most scenery by shaping screen wire or cardboard webbing into the contours of hills, valleys, streams, and other landforms. They cover this shell with plaster. Builders then apply paint and texture materials to represent earth and grass, and add miniature trees and shrubs to complete the landscape.

Other systems and equipment can be as simple or complex as the builder wishes. The basic wiring system for a model railroad allows only one train to run at a time. More complicated wiring permits several trains to run at once. Signals reproduce the functions of their prototype systems and add additional realism. Sound effects systems re-create the sounds of steam and diesel locomotives. Some hobbyists build working models of such equipment as drawbridges and coal dumpers. However, such accessories are more common in toy

Model Railroader

Lifelike scenery adds realism and variety to a model railroad layout. Hobbyists can create scenes depicting a highly detailed miniature town, *shown here.*

train systems. Advanced model railroaders may operate their railroad systems by radio control or by computer.

History. Model railroading became a well-known hobby as a result of the model railroads shown at the Century of Progress Exposition in Chicago during 1933 and 1934. Public interest in these models encouraged manufacturers to produce model railroad kits and parts. In 1935, model railroad hobbyists and manufacturers organized the National Model Railroad Association to establish uniform standards for tracks, wheels, and other model railroad equipment.

Hundreds of thousands of adults operate model railroads as a hobby. Many belong to model railroad clubs. Members of clubs work as a group to build larger and more elaborate model railroads than they could do as individuals. Andy Sperandeo

Additional resources

Level I

Basic Model Railroading: Getting Started in the Hobby. Kalmbach, 1999.

Goodman, Michael E. *Model Railroading.* Crestwood Hse., 1993.

Souter, Gerry and Janet. *Classic Toy Trains.* MBI Pub., 2002.

Level II

Amos, Roger S. *Complete Book of Model Railway Electronics.* 2nd ed. Haynes, 1998.

Freezer, Cyril J. *The Model Railway Manual: A Step-by-Step Guide to Building a Layout.* Haynes, 1994.

Simmons, Norman. *Railway Modelling.* 8th ed. Patrick Stephens, 1998.

Railroad Retirement Board (RRB) is a United States government agency that administers a retirement pension system for retired railroad employees, their spouses, and their survivors. It also administers an unemployment-sickness benefit system, together with a reemployment service. The board was established by the Railroad Retirement Act of 1935. The president appoints the three members of the board, with the consent of the Senate. The national headquarters of the RRB are located in Chicago.

Critically reviewed by the Railroad Retirement Board

Railroad worm. See **Apple maggot; Insect** (picture: The gorgeous colors).

Railway is the term used in the United Kingdom and other Commonwealth countries for a railroad. See **Railroad.**

Railway brotherhoods were unions of railroad workers in the United States and Canada. Many persons used the term for the "big four" railroad labor unions. These were the Brotherhood of Locomotive Engineers, the Brotherhood of Locomotive Firemen and Enginemen, the Brotherhood of Railroad Trainmen, and the Order of Railway Conductors and Brakemen. In 1969, the latter three unions merged with the Switchmen's Union of North America to form the United Transportation Union. This union has about 160,000 members.

Railroad unions did not develop as other unions did. They started as insurance agencies for their members. Insurance companies considered railroading so hazardous that they would not insure the workers. Locomotive engineers formed the first brotherhood in 1863. They were followed by the railway conductors in 1868, the firemen and engineers in 1873, and the railroad trainmen in 1883.

The railway brotherhoods did not operate in the same way as other labor unions. The railroads were subjected to strict government controls, and the unions usually used collective bargaining, rather than strikes, to achieve their goals. The brotherhoods remained independent of the organized labor movement until the late 1950's. Then the trainmen and the firemen and enginemen groups joined the American Federation of Labor and Congress of Industrial Organizations (AFL-CIO).

Robert C. Post

Railway Labor Act is a United States federal law that deals with labor disputes between railroad and airline companies and their employees. Its main purpose is to prevent strikes that might endanger the economy or create a national emergency.

The act was designed to bring about settlements through negotiation, mediation, arbitration, or, if necessary, through the investigation and recommendations of an emergency fact-finding board appointed by the president. The act has no provision that can force the parties to reach an agreement. However, it does require that employees not strike for a period of 60 days after the appointment of a fact-finding board. If the employees reject the board's recommendations, they are then free to go on strike after the 60 days.

Two federal agencies administer the Railway Labor Act. The three-member National Mediation Board can invoke the act on its own or upon the request of employers or employees. The board also handles disputes concerning railroad and airline employee representation and negotiation of new contracts. The 36-member National Railroad Adjustment Board decides disputes involving grievances or the interpretation of existing agreements. This board has jurisdiction only over railroads and their employees.

The Railway Labor Act was passed by Congress in 1926, and it has since been amended several times. The original act applied only to railroads. The railway industry received early congressional attention because its unions were strong, and it was feared that a series of railroad strikes might be dangerous for the nation's economy. In 1936, the act was amended to make it apply also to labor relations between airlines and their employees.

The Railway Labor Act proved successful in helping avoid major strikes until the early 1940's. In 1941, the railroads prevented a strike by granting wage increases that were much higher than the emergency board's recommendations. It soon became common for companies and unions to reject board recommendations. Since the early 1960's, most railroad and airline strikes have been prevented by emergency actions outside the Railway Labor Act. During a railroad dispute in 1963, Congress passed an emergency measure demanding compulsory arbitration. There has since been increasing pressure for revision of this act, which was once considered a model labor law. David Brody

See also **National Mediation Board; Strike** (Kinds of strikes).

Rain is precipitation that consists of drops of water. Raindrops form in clouds when microscopic droplets of water grow or when particles of ice melt before reaching the ground. Rain falls throughout most of the world. In the tropics, almost all precipitation is rain. But in the inland areas of Antarctica, all precipitation is snow.

Rain is a part of an unending process known as the *hydrologic cycle.* This process begins with the evaporation of water from the surface of the earth—mostly from the ocean. The resulting *water vapor*—the gaseous state of water—then condenses, forming clouds of liquid droplets. Some of the droplets may freeze, forming particles of ice. The droplets and particles then undergo a variety of changes in the clouds. Eventually, however, they fall to the surface as precipitation. Much of the precipitation that falls on continents eventually flows in rivers into the ocean. The process then repeats itself.

When ocean water evaporates, the salt in the ocean water remains in the ocean. As a result, rain and frozen precipitation, such as snow, hail, and sleet, are made up of fresh water. Human beings and most other creatures that live on land depend on the fresh water produced by the hydrologic cycle.

Rain cleans the air by washing away dust and chemical pollutants. But too much rain may cause flooding that destroys property and threatens lives. Heavy rainfall can also damage crops and speed up the loss of soil.

Characteristics of rain

Raindrops vary greatly in their size and in the speed of their fall. The diameter of most raindrops ranges from about 0.02 to 0.25 inch (0.5 to 6.35 millimeters). Rates of fall for these sizes range from $6\frac{1}{2}$ feet (2 meters) per second for the smallest to about 30 feet (9 meters) per second for the largest. *Drizzle* is rain with drops less than about 0.02 inch in diameter and falling speeds of less than about $6\frac{1}{2}$ feet per second.

Raindrops smaller than about 0.04 inch (1 millimeter)

How rain forms Raindrops develop within clouds by means of two processes. The different stages of development occur in overlapping zones, as shown in these greatly simplified diagrams.

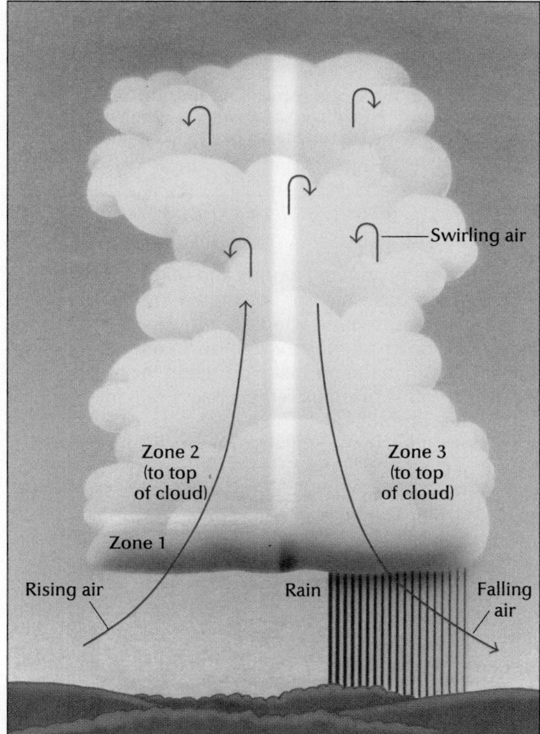

The coalescence process begins at the cloud base, zone 1. There, *water vapor* (the gaseous form of water) condenses on tiny particles called *cloud condensation nuclei*, creating water droplets. In zone 2, droplets grow as more vapor condenses on them. As droplets fall through zone 3, larger ones strike smaller ones and *coalesce* (combine) with them, forming raindrops.

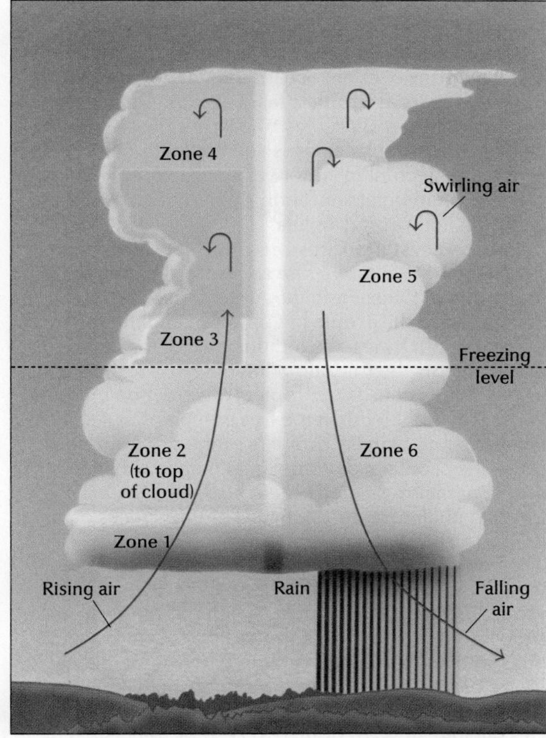

WORLD BOOK diagrams by Leonard E. Morgan

The ice-crystal process begins when water droplets form and grow in zones 1 and 2. A tiny fraction of the droplets freeze in zone 3. In zone 4, water vapor freezes on the frozen droplets, forming snow crystals. As the crystals fall through zone 5, liquid droplets freeze onto them, creating hailstones or ice particles called *graupel.* These objects melt in zone 6 and fall as raindrops.

in diameter are round. Larger drops are somewhat flat, due to the force of the air flowing around them. The largest raindrops alternate between a flattened shape and a stretched-out shape.

Most rain comes from *convective clouds,* in which currents of air usually rise 10 to 100 feet (3 to 30 meters) per second. Within the currents, the air undergoes many sudden changes in speed and direction. Because of the currents, the growing raindrops take complicated paths within the clouds.

It takes about 10 to 30 minutes for rain to form. The time rain takes to fall to the ground depends on the height of the cloud in which it forms and the size of the raindrops. This time ranges from a few seconds for large drops falling from low clouds to about 15 minutes for small drops falling from high clouds. In dry areas, rain from high clouds may not even reach the ground. Instead, it evaporates completely as it falls.

The intensity of rainfall varies widely. Rainfall that is too light to measure is called a *trace* of rain. Rain that falls at a measurable rate of up to 0.10 inch (2.5 millimeters) per hour is a *light rain.* A *moderate rain* falls at a rate of 0.11 to 0.30 inch (2.8 to 7.6 millimeters) per hour. Rain that is even more intense is *heavy rain.*

Acid rain is the term for rain, snow, sleet, or other precipitation that is polluted by such acids as sulfuric acid and nitric acid. The acid in acid rain forms when chemical compounds known as nitrogen oxides and sulfur dioxide react within growing droplets and raindrops. These compounds are released by motor vehicles, factories, and certain power plants. Acid rain pollutes lakes and streams. It also damages buildings and other structures and is suspected of harming forests and soil.

Formation of rain

The "life" of a raindrop begins when molecules of water vapor in a cloud condense on a tiny particle of matter called a *cloud condensation nucleus.* This particle can be a speck of dust or soot. However, it is usually a very tiny droplet known as a *haze droplet.* This consists of a concentrated solution of sea salt or of a chemical compound such as ammonium sulfate or magnesium sulfate. The compound may have formed when gases in the air interacted chemically, or it may have been given off by a motor vehicle or a factory.

Continuing condensation enlarges the droplet, which grows as long as the air is rising. But it will grow by condensation to a diameter of only a few thousandths of an inch—less than 0.1 millimeter, too small to be a raindrop. To become a raindrop, a droplet must undergo one of two processes—(1) the *coalescence process* or (2) the *ice-crystal process.*

The coalescence process produces much of the rain that forms over the oceans and in the tropics. This process occurs as droplets fall. The larger droplets fall faster than the smaller ones. The larger droplets thus collide with the smaller ones and *coalesce* (combine) with them, becoming larger yet. A large droplet that falls 1 mile (1.6 kilometers) through a cloud may coalesce with 1 million small droplets.

The ice-crystal process accounts for much of the rainfall in the two *temperate zones*—(1) the area between the Tropic of Cancer and the Arctic Circle and (2) the area between the Tropic of Capricorn and the Antarctic Circle. In both zones, the temperature of the clouds is usually below the freezing point of water, 32 °F (0 °C).

The clouds consist of droplets of *supercooled water,* water that is colder than the freezing point, but still liquid. But some of these droplets eventually freeze because they contain, or come into contact with, microscopic particles called *freezing nuclei* or *ice nuclei.* Most freezing nuclei are dust particles or tiny specks of plant debris raised by the wind.

When a supercooled droplet freezes, it turns into an ice crystal. The crystal then grows by collecting water vapor. This growth produces the complicated shapes of snow crystals. As a crystal grows, it falls faster and collides with supercooled droplets, which immediately freeze onto it. This process produces soft ice pellets called *graupel* or small hailstones. When these ice particles fall into air warmer than 32 °F, they melt. Such particles produce almost all the raindrops in thunderstorms.

Rain in long-lasting, steady storms forms in a slightly different way. The ice crystals continue to grow by collecting water vapor. The resulting snow crystals may then collide with one another and stick together as snowflakes. Snow crystals and snowflakes become raindrops when they fall into air that is warmer than 32 °F and melt.

Scientists have been trying to develop reliable methods of *cloud seeding* to make more rain fall from clouds. In the technique investigated the most, aircraft drop artificial freezing nuclei into clouds. The usual seeding material has been silver iodide, whose crystals have a structure much like that of ice.

Rainfall distribution

Earth as a whole receives abundant rainfall. If rain fell evenly, all the land would receive about 40 inches (100 centimeters) a year. But rainfall is unevenly distributed over Earth's surface. Distribution is especially uneven over the continents because of mountain ranges. Heavy rain often drenches slopes where the air rises, leaving dry the slopes where the air descends. For example, *southerly winds* (winds from the south) rising over the Himalaya range in Asia deposit 200 to 600 inches (510 to 1,500 centimeters) of rain annually on their southern slopes. But the northern slopes of the range average less than 10 inches (25 centimeters) of rain a year.

Rainfall is generally heavy along the equator because of the high humidity and because surface winds *converge* (come together) there. The convergence causes the air to rise, producing clouds and rain.

Certain regions alternate between rainy and dry seasons because of shifting winds. In regions near the tropics, winds known as *monsoons* blow in one direction in the winter and in the opposite direction in the summer. Monsoon winds bring extremely heavy rain to southern Asia in the summer.

On both sides of the equator, generally along the Tropic of Cancer and the Tropic of Capricorn, are regions where the air usually sinks to the surface. Rainfall is therefore light in those areas, and so deserts have formed in them. Sinking air is responsible for the Sahara and the Kalahari Desert in Africa and a band of deserts in the western and central parts of Australia.

Away from the tropics, the western coasts of large land masses have more rainfall than their central regions. For example, along the west coast of North America, moist winds from the Pacific Ocean produce as

Some rainfall records

Earth's average annual precipitation (including rain, snow, and hail) is about 40 inches (100 centimeters).
Greatest rainfall in the world occurs at Mawsynram, India. An average of about 467.4 inches (1,187 centimeters) of rain falls there yearly.
Least rainfall in the world is recorded at Arica, Chile, a desert town that receives an average of 0.03 inch (0.76 millimeter) a year.
Least rainfall in the United States occurs in Death Valley, California. An average of about 2.2 inches (5.5 centimeters) falls there annually.

Sources: U.S. National Climatic Data Center; *Weather and Climate Extremes,* U.S. Army Corps of Engineers.

World distribution of precipitation

much as 150 inches (381 centimeters) of rain and snow a year. To the east lies the Great Basin, a desert area that covers parts of Oregon, California, Nevada, Idaho, Utah, and Wyoming. The eastern side of North America receives moisture largely from southerly and southwesterly winds from the warm Gulf of Mexico.

Polar regions are dry partly because their cold air cannot hold much water vapor. In addition, relatively little evaporation occurs in those regions, and the wind blows away from the poles.

Measuring rainfall

People measure rainfall with a variety of devices, including simple funnel gauges and sophisticated radar systems.

A funnel gauge consists of a funnel connected to the top of a narrow cylindrical tube. The diameter of the mouth of the funnel is much larger than the diameter of the tube. Rain falls into the funnel and collects in the tube. Markings on the side of the tube indicate the amount of rainfall. This design makes the depth of the rain easy to measure. A small amount of water falling into the mouth of the funnel will fill the tube to a considerable—and easily readable—level.

Radar systems. Networks of gauges can measure rainfall over large regions, such as river basins, states and provinces, and even countries. However, a network can produce an inaccurate result if the rainfall is unevenly distributed across a region.

A radar system can provide a more complete picture of rainfall. In a radar system, an antenna sends out radio waves that reflect from raindrops and return to the antenna. Electronic devices connected to the antenna measure the strength of the returning waves. The strength of the reflection indicates the amount of rainfall—the stronger the waves, the heavier the rainfall.

This method of measurement avoids the limited coverage of gauge networks. However, radar may provide inaccurate results if the raindrops are unusually large or if hail is mixed with the rain. In this case, the radar waves may appear to have been reflected from a storm that is much heavier than the actual storm. A combination of radar and rain gauges usually provides the most accurate results. Charles A. Knight

Related articles. See the *Climate* section of the articles on the continents, countries, states, and provinces. See also:

Acid rain	Desert	Rain gauge
Climate	El Niño	Rainbow
Cloud	Evaporation	Storm
Cloud seeding	Humidity	Water

Rain dance is a ceremony performed by American Indians of the southwestern United States to ask spirits to send rain for their crops. The Indians ask the spirits to send the rain in the proper amounts and at the right times. Indians hold most rain dances during the spring planting season and in the summer while the crops are growing. Each tribe has its own particular ceremonies for bringing rain. For example, participants in the rain ceremony of the Tohono O'odham tribe sing and dance and drink wine made from cactus juice. The Hopi dance with live rattlesnakes in their mouths to encourage the gods to send rain (see **Snake dance**). Michael D. Green

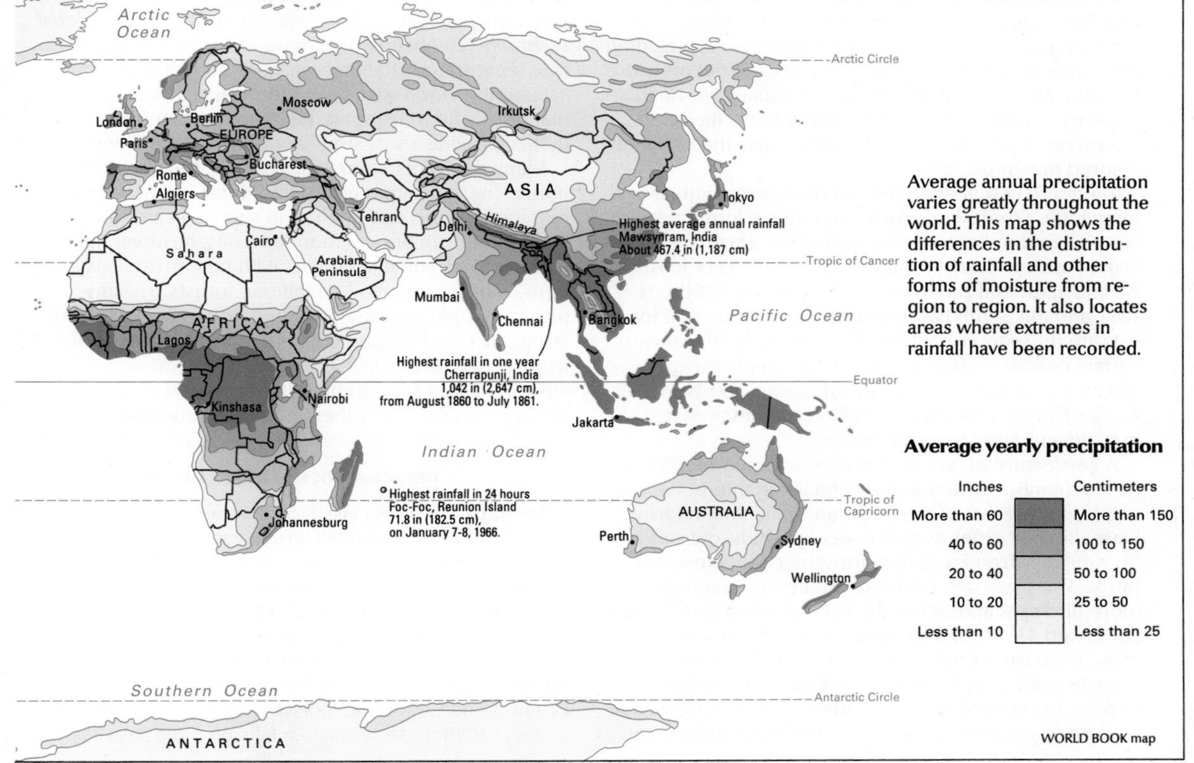

Average annual precipitation varies greatly throughout the world. This map shows the differences in the distribution of rainfall and other forms of moisture from region to region. It also locates areas where extremes in rainfall have been recorded.

© Gerald R. Urquhart, Lyman Briggs College and Department of Fisheries and Wildlife

The tropical rain forest hosts a wealth of plant life, including a dense cover of treetops called the *canopy.* This photograph shows the canopy in the western Amazon rain forest, in Ecuador.

Rain forest

Rain forest is a woodland of tall trees growing in a region of plentiful rainfall. Rain forests include some of the world's richest *ecosystems.* An ecosystem consists of a community of living things and the nonliving things on which they depend.

In a rain forest, rain, temperature, and humidity combine to create excellent conditions for plant growth. The trees of a rain forest often grow to great heights. They support a dense community of nontree plants, including *epiphytes,* which grow on other plants and get moisture from the air. Rain forests support an equally spectacular diversity of animal life, from beautiful butterflies and swarming ants to showy birds-of-paradise and brilliantly colored poisonous frogs.

There are two major types of rain forests: tropical and temperate. Tropical rain forests are those found near Earth's equator, between the Tropic of Cancer and the Tropic of Capricorn. Tropical rain forests occur in Africa, Australia, Central America, South America, Southern Asia, and the South Pacific islands. Temperate rain forests are those found outside the tropics. They appear in certain coastal regions on all the continents except Antarctica, as well as in island nations such as New Zealand. In rare instances, small areas of temperate rain forest occur away from the oceans.

A key feature of rain forests is an amazing *biodiversity,* the richness of variation among living things. For example, some areas of the Peruvian Amazon rain forest have about 10 times as many *species* (kinds) of trees as do similarly sized areas of North American temperate forest. The small rain-forested country of Panama has more bird species than all the United States and Canada combined. Diversity also appears on smaller scales, with over 40 species of epiphytes found growing on the branches of a single tree in Nicaragua. Each epiphyte species has several species of insects, birds, or bats that feed on or pollinate it, further multiplying biodiversity.

Rain forests provide incredible benefits to the planet. South America's Amazon River and rain forest, for example, hold around one-fifth of Earth's fresh water, continuously purifying the water through cycles of rain and evaporation. Rain forest trees also store large amounts of the element carbon, helping to limit levels of carbon dioxide gas in the atmosphere. Excess carbon dioxide can trap heat near Earth's surface, contributing to *global warming*—an observed increase in Earth's average surface temperature. Rain forests have benefited people around the world with such food plants as bananas, mangoes, and pineapples. Rain forest *organisms* (living things) provide a vast supply of potential medicines.

Many different cultures have called the rain forest home. These groups rely on traditional knowledge of rain forest plants and animals to survive in a challenging environment. In the last four centuries, however, new cultures have come in contact with rain forest ecosystems, taking a great toll on the rain forests. In many places, people are rapidly cutting down rain forests for farmland. Less than 50 percent of the area covered by tropical rain forests in 1500 still has trees today. Temperate rain forests are also being destroyed at a rapid pace. Conservationists and others must work together if we are to preserve these vanishing ecosystems.

Characteristics of a rain forest

Climate. Scholars classify an area as rain forest mainly by the amount of rainfall it receives. By definition, a tropical rain forest gets at least 100 inches (250 centimeters) of rain each year. Temperate rain forests receive about 80 inches (200 centimeters) of annual rainfall.

Tropical rain forests generally receive rain the year around, without any long dry periods. The wettest rain forests, such as those near the Andes Mountains in Ecuador and Colombia, receive over 30 feet (9 meters) of rain a year. In these areas, rain falls on most days.

Tropical rain forests have steady temperatures throughout a typical year. They also have high daytime and nighttime temperatures. In the Amazon rain forest, for example, daytime temperatures are typically over 86 °F (30 °C), and nighttime lows are around 75 °F (24 °C).

As large, rain-carrying clouds float by, conditions in a tropical rain forest often change from intense tropical sunshine to overcast clouds to a drenching downpour and back again in short cycles. The ample heat, humidity, and sunlight are ideal for plant growth. Beneath the rain forest *canopy* (the tops of the trees), however, most light is blocked. Plants struggle for light, but fungi thrive.

Soil with high clay content is most common in rain forests. But some areas, including parts of the Amazon, have sandy soils.

With hearty plant growth and a wealth of decaying material from living things, it may seem that rain forest soils should be rich and productive. But in reality, typical rain forest soils have few nutrients. Almost all rain forest soils have scarce nitrogen, phosphorus, and potassium, the key nutrients for plant growth.

Rain forest soils are poor because rain forests recycle nutrients efficiently. When an organism dies, rain forest fungi, bacteria, and small animals break down the dead tissue rapidly. The nutrients and carbon from a decaying tree or dead bird, for example, may never enter the soil. Instead, they are taken up by other living things.

Structure and growth. Tall trees and jungle vines serve as the most visible characteristics of rain forests. But such plants are part of a more intricate structure unique to each individual ecosystem. In the interior of a tall forest, the canopy usually stands between 100 and 130 feet (30 and 40 meters) above the ground. Enormous *emergent* tree species rise above the canopy to heights of 160 to 260 feet (50 to 80 meters). In undisturbed areas, the canopy forms a nearly continuous cover, with the tops of trees fitting together like puzzle pieces.

When a tree falls, a complex cycle of plant growth begins. This cycle helps maintain the structure of the forest. It also contributes to diversity, by encouraging the growth of trees with different lifestyle strategies. There are three kinds of tree of particular importance to growth and structure: (1) pioneers, (2) shade-tolerant hardwoods, and (3) sun-lovers.

Pioneer species grow rapidly and are often first to colonize a new sunny spot. But they are typically short-lived. Pioneer species can grow as much as 16 feet (5 meters) in a single year. They have soft trunks and grow poorly in shade.

Shade-tolerant hardwoods, on the other hand, spend years to decades waiting in the *understory*, a shady area below the canopy. They grow slowly until a break in the treetops gives them a chance to reach the canopy. Once they reach the canopy, they can live for centuries. They are supported by their thick wood and strong branches.

The third group, called sun-lovers or *heliophiles*, falls somewhere in between. They rely heavily on canopy openings for light. The sun-lovers grow at a moderate rate and are strong enough to live for long periods.

Trees form only a small part of the rain forest structure. Epiphytes, vines, and woody *lianas* hang from the trees, often weaving multiple trees together. Palms are typically not as tall as the hardwoods and form multiple levels of the rain forest structure, from a lower treetop level called the *sub-canopy* to the understory. Woody shrubs and *herbaceous* (non-woody) plants dominate the understory.

Plant life of all sizes, from tiny mosses to enormous trees, makes up the majority of a rain forest's living tissue, called *biomass*. Flowering trees dominate inland

© Bildagentur Zoonar GmbH/Shutterstock

Temperate rain forests occur outside the tropics. Ferns, mosses, and other plants of the *understory* (forest floor) appear in this photograph of Horseshoe Falls, a waterfall in a temperate rain forest in the Catlins region of New Zealand.

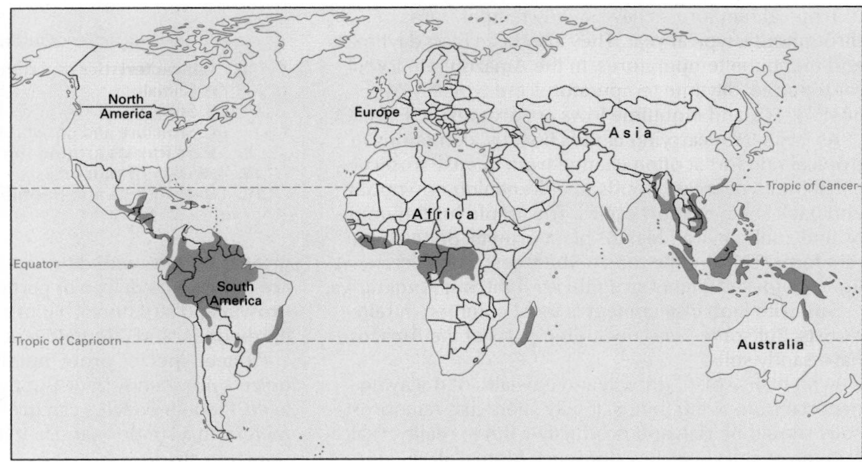

WORLD BOOK map

Tropical rain forests of the world

The largest rain forests occur in tropical parts of the Americas, Asia, and Africa. Smaller areas of rain forest exist on many Pacific Islands and in parts of Australia's northeastern coast. These forests lie chiefly near the equator, in regions that receive some of the world's heaviest rainfall.

tropical rain forests, whereas some island rain forests feature a large diversity of such cone-bearing *gymnosperm* plants as *Araucaria* and cycads. Temperate rain forests have a large number of cone-bearing trees.

Mosses and similar plants of ancient ancestry are incredibly important in temperate rain forests, making up much of the understory. Mosses today play a small role in tropical forests. Prehistoric tropical rain forests, on the other hand, were dominated by mosses and by giant, treelike club mosses, which made up the canopy.

Ferns are another ancient group of plants that play a major role in rain forests. They may grow along the ground, as dangling epiphytes perched on tree branches, and even as enormous tree ferns with hard trunks. Such tree ferns can reach heights of more than 65 feet (20 meters). Ferns reproduce using tiny spores and can *disperse* (scatter) over great distances. Some modern *fossil fuels* come from the remains of ancient rain forests with many tree ferns. Fossil fuels are fuels such as coal, oil, and natural gas developed from the remains of ancient living things.

Gymnosperms, such as firs, spruces, and pines, make up the majority of trees in temperate rain forests. But they play only minor roles in most tropical rain forests. Some tropical forests of the Pacific Islands, however, rely heavily on such distinctive gymnosperms as the Norfolk Island pine.

Dicots make up the majority of the biomass in tropical rain forests. Dicots are flowering plants with two *cotyledons* (leafy parts within each seed). Most large trees are dicots, including such giants as the kapok of Africa and the American tropics. The *legumes* are particularly important in tropical rain forests. Legumes are relatives of the pea. They grow in a vast variety of forms from small plants to giant woody vines to enormous emergent trees. Legumes can capture nitrogen from the air and turn it into a usable form with the aid of bacteria. This ability enables legumes to dominate many rain forest regions, where nitrogen is scarce in the soil.

Monocots are also important in rain forests. Monocots are flowering plants with one cotyledon. More kinds of orchids grow in the rain forest than any other type of plant. Because of their small size, however, orchids make up only a tiny fraction of rain forest biomass. Other monocots with spectacular flowers are the bird-of-paradise plant, the *Heliconia,* and the ginger family. Palms are an important monocot in tropical rain forests. The widely diverse Araceae family of plants, which includes dumb cane, peace lily, *Philodendron,* and *Pothos,* appears in both ground-growing and climbing forms.

Animals. An astonishing number of animal species live in rain forests. Millions of species of *arthropods* (animals with jointed legs and no backbone) make their home in tropical rain forests. Most are insects, with beetles contributing the greatest number of species. Some beetles, such as Goliath and Hercules beetles, dwarf most other insects. Dung beetles play an important role by moving nutrient-rich *dung* (solid waste) dropped by larger animals, helping to fertilize the rain forest.

Beetles are the most diverse rain forest animals, but ants are often considered the most important. Ants serve an incredible variety of functions in rain forests. Massive swarms of army ants raid the forest floor to catch prey. They can overwhelm and consume nearly any insect or other small animal in their path. Acacia tree ants live on acacia trees, getting all that they need from the tree. In return, the ants fend off such intruders as grasshopper pests and vines that compete for sunlight.

Other arthropods, such as spiders, scorpions, millipedes, and even land-dwelling crabs, make their home in tropical rain forests. Such strange, unique groups as the velvet worms—which somewhat look like many-legged slugs—inhabit rain forests as well.

Both rivers and lakes form important parts of tropical rain forests. Such rain forest waters are home to the majority of Earth's freshwater fish species. Tropical fish are not limited to rivers and lakes. They may enter the rain forests during floods, when, for example, large piranha relatives such as the pacu eat fruits fallen from trees. Some rain forest species, such as walking catfish, are known to crawl over land using their front fins. Freshwater stingrays are among the few *cartilaginous fishes*—that is, fish with a skeleton made of cartilage instead of bone—found outside the oceans. Amazonian stingrays are most closely related to stingrays of the Pacific Ocean. This and other evidence suggests that the Amazon was connected to the Pacific Ocean million of years ago, before the Andes Mountains arose.

Rain forests also house more types of land *vertebrates* (animals with backbones) than do any other ecosystems. Among amphibians, frogs are incredibly diverse, with land-living, water-living, and tree-living forms found in the rain forest. Brightly colored poisonous frogs are found in the rain forests of the American tropics, of Madagascar, and even of Australia. These frogs make up three distinct groups that *evolved* (developed over time) independently. All three groups use bright colors to warn away *predators* (hunting animals) and typically get their toxins from foods they eat. Salamanders are one of the few groups that are less diverse in the tropics.

Thousands of reptiles live in the rain forests. They include a wide variety of lizards, snakes, and turtles. Some reptiles have bizarre adaptations for rain forest living. The chameleon, for example, can change colors by altering the structure of its skin cells, with different colors serving as social signals to other chameleons or as camouflage. The basilisk lizard can run on the surface of water. Rain forests are home to the world's largest snakes, including the pythons of Asia and Africa and the anacondas and boas of the Americas. Some *venomous* (poisonous) snakes include the deadly king cobras of Asia, the spectacular vipers of Africa, the aggressive fer-de-lance of the American tropics, and a number of deadly Australian species. Among turtles, the mata mata of the Amazon and Orinoco river systems is notable for its fringed head, which is easily camouflaged among fallen leaves. The majority of the world's *crocodilians* (crocodiles, caimans, and related animals) are found in tropical rain forest waters.

Rain forest birds come in all sizes and colors and fulfill a great range of ecological roles. Some birds help control insects, others disperse seeds, and still others serve as *top predators* (hunting animals at the top of the food chain). New World tanagers have magnificent coloration. Birds-of-paradise feature bizarre plumages. Other well-known rain forest birds include parrots and toucans. Parrots are found in all tropical rain forests. Most parrots specialize in eating seeds and aid in seed dispersal. In the Americas, hummingbirds have evolved as important plant pollinators. They appear to favor the color red, leading to more red flowers in the rain forests that hummingbirds inhabit. Many tropical bird species nest in hollows in trees, rather than among the branches. The limited number of such hollows is thought to limit populations of some tropical bird species. Tropical rain forests also attract a wide range of migratory birds wintering far from their nesting grounds.

Around half of the mammal species in a tropical rain forest are bats, ranging from tiny insect-eaters to the enormous flying foxes, which eat fruit. Flying foxes can have wingspreads up to 6 ½ feet (2 meters). Like birds, bats help to control insects and disperse seeds. Some bat species even serve as pollinators. Large, white rain forest flowers often serve to attract pollinating bats.

Although less diverse than the bats, nonflying mammals remain ecologically important in the rain forest. Large mammals are the least numerous, but they play an outsize role due to their size and strength. In African and Indian rain forests, for example, elephants can uproot trees, making room for new growth. Such large seed-eaters as tapirs serve as the only species that can crack hard nuts. Mammals that live in the rain forest trees include such primates as monkeys and lemurs as well as tree-dwelling *marsupials* (pouch-bearing mammals) in Australia. Rain forests are home to the world's smallest primates, including the pygmy marmoset of the Amazon and the Philippine tarsier, each less than 6 ½ inches (17 centimeters) in length. Some mammals—including

Rain forest life includes an astonishing variety of colorful animals and plants. More kinds of birds, flowers, insects, mammals, and reptiles live in the rain forests than in any other region. Biologists believe millions more rain forest species remain undiscovered. As a result of human activities, including deforestation, many species may become extinct before scientists can discover them.

© Dirk Ercken, Shutterstock

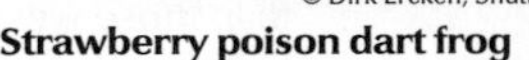

Strawberry poison dart frog

© Erik Zandboer, Shutterstock

Flying fox

© Morley Read, Shutterstock

Army ant

© Edwin Verin, Shutterstock

Philippine tarsier

© Shutterstock

Bird-of-paradise flower

© Rich Carey, Shutterstock

Deforestation threatens some of the world's most important rain forests. This photograph shows workers and heavy machinery clearing rain forest in Borneo to make room for an oil palm plantation.

pumas, tigers, and white-tailed deer—live in both temperate and tropical regions. These mammals are generally smaller in the tropics, perhaps because they have less need of mass to conserve body heat.

Ecology. Many features of rain forests help to enable a great diversity of species to live close together. For example, the structural diversity of plants, ranging from small plants of the understory to giant trees, creates a variety of places for organisms to live. Many species live their entire lives in the forest canopy, never even touching the ground.

Many rain forest species have developed relationships with other species that benefit both, called *mutualisms.* Such relationships contribute to diversity. A tree such as *Dipteryx oleifera,* for example, sometimes called the giant tropical almond, is home to many species, feeds many species, and relies on a whole host of species to survive and reproduce. Like other legumes, *Dipteryx* trees make use of *Rhizobium* bacteria to capture nitrogen from the air. The trees also rely on fruit-eating bats and such birds as great green macaws to pick their fruits, dispersing the seeds. They rely on mammals, such as agoutis, to further disperse the seeds that birds and bats drop to the forest floor. At least thirteen different kinds of bees help pollinate *Dipteryx* trees. All these species live on, around, or with the help of one tree, and there are around 16,000 tree species in the Amazon alone.

For a land ecosystem to be productive, it must have access to water and to energy from sunlight. The abundance of water and sunlight in tropical rain forests makes them the most productive land ecosystems on Earth. High productivity enables rapid tree growth, a high level of interdependence among species, and the capture of great quantities of carbon in tree trunks.

Rain forests around the world

Rain forests exist on all continents with tropical regions, but their characteristics differ greatly from continent to continent. Distinct major regions are the New World tropics or Neotropics—which includes the North and South American tropics and the Caribbean region—and the African, South Asian, Southeast Asian, and Australian tropics. The wettest rain forests typically occur at the windward base of mountain chains. In such areas, warm, moist air cools as it rises into the mountains, dropping much of its moisture as rain.

In the Neotropics, the Amazon rain forest is one of the largest continuous land ecosystems. The only forests larger are the vast boreal forests of Canada and northern Asia. The Amazon is more diverse than the rain forests of Central America or the Brazilian Atlantic Forest.

Legume trees dominate neotropical rain forests. These forests also have many large palm species. Neotropical rain forests are more common on the Atlantic side, where easterly winds blow moist, warm air off the Atlantic Ocean. The Amazon, however, stretches nearly the width of South America from the Atlantic Ocean to the Andes mountains, near the Pacific Ocean.

In Asia, easterly winds bring rain from the Pacific Ocean, watering tropical rain forests in Southeast Asia. The islands of the South Pacific and such mainland countries as Vietnam, Thailand, and Myanmar are home to incredibly diverse rain forests. Scholars divide the South Pacific rain forests into two distinct types along a boundary known as the Wallace Line. It is named for the British naturalist Alfred Russel Wallace, who first described it. Islands east of the Wallace line, such as New Guinea and Sulawesi, have different groups of species than those west of the line, such as Borneo and the Philippines. Southeast Asian rain forests are dominated by trees from a family called the Dipterocarps, but they also have a high diversity of palms and other trees.

The Indian subcontinent has rain forests on the western coast of India and on the eastern side in Bangladesh and extreme east India. The forests of the eastern side are ecologically similar to southeast Asian rain forests. But the rain forests in the Western Ghats region are different. Both regions feature Asian elephants and have the Bengal tiger as a top predator. But they differ in terms of plants, birds, bats, and other living things.

The tropical rain forests of Africa are found in a fairly narrow band stretching along the equator from the Gulf of Guinea in the Atlantic Ocean to the center of the continent. The Congo Basin houses a vast rain forest sometimes called the Amazon of Africa. Africa and South America were once much closer together, and as a result their rain forests share many common features. Legume trees, for example, are important in both regions. But African rain forests have many unique life forms, including lowland gorillas and forest elephants.

Australia's tropical rain forests are limited to a thin band along the eastern coast of the continent. They share some common features with the southeast Asian rain forests, but the only native mammals in Australia's rain forests are marsupials and bats.

The major temperate rain forests are found near coasts and mountains in New Zealand, Tasmania, Japan, northern Europe, South Africa, and the Pacific Coast of the Americas. A few small temperate rain forests are found inland in places where moist winds rising into mountains drop heavy annual rainfall.

History of rain forests

Ever since land plants grew large enough to form forests, rain forests have been an important ecosystem. The first land forests appeared during the Devonian Period, about 420 million to 360 million years ago. During the Carboniferous Period, about 360 million to 300 million years ago, rain forests covered much of Earth's land surface. Plants of these ancient rain forests differed greatly from rain forests today. Treelike club mosses and ancient horsetails dominated the forests of the Carboniferous period. *Invertebrates* (animals without backbones) ruled the rain forests. Many of these invertebrates grew much larger than their modern counterparts. Dragonflies with wingspreads of 28 inches (70 centimeters) or more patrolled the skies, long before the development of birds. Scorpions up to 28 inches in length served as top predators. Most land vertebrates were somewhat similar to modern amphibians.

By the late Carboniferous Period, the first cone-bearing gymnosperm plants appeared. They became important forest elements in the Permian, Triassic, and Jurassic periods, from about 300 million to 145 million years ago. Flowering plants evolved late in the Jurassic Period, about 200 million to 145 million years ago. By the Cretaceous Period, about 145 million to 65 million years ago, rain forests began to resemble their modern forms, dominated by such flowering plants as woody dicot trees and a variety of monocot families. The global climate was much warmer, and tropical rain forest vegetation covered much of Earth's land, including North America as far north as what is now Colorado.

At the end of the Cretaceous Period, the last dinosaurs and many other species died out. Around that time, animals associated with modern rain forests began to appear. Primates became more widespread. Tapirs, sloths, and anteaters first evolved and later became more diverse. Up until the Pleistocene Epoch, about 3 million to 10,000 years ago, these groups were much more diverse than they are today. Giant ground sloths, about 20 feet (6 meters) in length, roamed the Amazon. These and other gigantic seed-eating mammals may have been important seed dispersers for trees that still exist today. Such trees have seeds too large to be dispersed through digestion by modern animals.

The movement of the continents has played a major role in the history of rain forests. Around 105 million years ago, a *supercontinent* (giant land mass) known as West Gondwana split into what are now Africa and South America. The two gradually moved farther and farther apart. Most modern rain forest organisms did not exist at the time. But many evolved around 50 million to 60 million years ago, when the two continents were much closer than they are today. The closeness made it easier for organisms from one continent to disperse to the other. As the continents moved farther apart, this exchange of organisms declined, resulting in some unique distinctions. For example, hummingbirds originated in South America relatively recently and are therefore not present in Africa.

A major event in rain forest history occurred much more recently and helps explain why the American rain forests are so diverse. Around 3 million years ago, moving plates lifted what is now Panama above the water, creating a bridge between the previously separate North and South America. Species that had evolved on one continent could suddenly migrate to the other, enriching the diversity of species in that new land. Cichlid fishes, poison frogs, parrots, hummingbirds, and modern sloths expanded northward from South America. Meanwhile, pit vipers, peccaries, and big cats migrated into South America. The interchange was probably even more dramatic among plant and insect species.

Rain forests and people

Cacao, the plant that gives us chocolate, is a small tree that grows in the rain forest understory. It is native to South America. Chili peppers, black pepper, mangoes,

© Martin Shields, Alamy Images

Ecotourism involves the use of environmentally and socially responsible tourism to promote conservation. In this photograph, a guide leads ecotourists on a walking tour of the rain forest.

bananas, and passion fruit are just a few other important food plants from the rain forest. Humans *domesticated* (developed into crops) these plants from their rain forest ancestors. Many popular nuts, including cashews and Brazil nuts, originated in tropical rain forests.

Native cultures. Such groups as the Yanomami of South America, the Dayaks of Southeast Asia, and the Mbuti of central Africa have lived in rain forests for centuries. They make their living by hunting, fishing, collecting forest products, and farming.

Many more cultures lived in the rain forests of Africa, Asia, and the Americas in the past. Little is known of some of these peoples, in part because the wet conditions in a rain forest speed the breakdown of *artifacts,* tools and other items made by people. Small native groups practiced both hunting and gathering and small-scale farming in the rain forest. Some of these cultures made use of *slash-and-burn* agriculture, cutting down and burning wild plants to clear and fertilize crop fields. When a crop field grew poor through years of farming, the forest was allowed to reclaim it.

A more widespread early rain forest culture was the Maya of what are now Mexico, Guatemala, Honduras, and Belize. The Maya had one of the most advanced cultures of their time. Their civilization spanned from about 1000 B.C. to 1697 A.D., when the Spanish conquered their last independent city. The Maya used irrigation systems to grow such crops as corn, beans, and squash on a large scale. Amazing pyramids in Petén, Palenque, and Tikal stand as reminders of their greatness.

Threats to rain forests. Human interactions with rain forests have changed dramatically since around 1500. At that time, European settlers began to explore and expand into rain forests. They often extracted large quantities of forest products and established low-productivity agricultural systems, such as cattle ranching. Such practices have resulted in a great loss of rain forests.

Current deforestation is threatening some of the most important tropical rain forests in the world. In Indonesia, the expansion of oil palm plantations has created devastating forest loss. In the Amazon, much forest has been lost to increased soy production. In the past, agricultural deforestation was limited by the availability of human labor to work farms. However, modern soy production relies on large machines instead of human workers, and oil palm requires less human labor than traditional crops.

The rain forest could regenerate the small parcels of land cleared by traditional agriculture. But today, the combined effects of deforestation and pollution produce a much greater setback. Particularly damaging practices include oil drilling, chemical-intensive agriculture, and the use of mercury in gold mining. These practices have introduced extreme pollution to previously pristine areas, harming plants, animals, and people. Unlike the cutting of trees, from which a rain forest can recover in a few decades, the impacts of chemical pollution are much longer lasting.

Oil drilling is especially problematic in rain forests. In countries such as Ecuador and Venezuela, foreign oil companies have extracted crude oil for several decades, producing heavy pollution in the process. Historically, few measures have been taken in rain forest areas to minimize spills and other damage. In the 1970's and 1980's, spills and contamination were common. Such issues led to heavy contamination of rain forests and created great health problems for native populations.

The industrial scale farming of such crops as banana and pineapple also harm rain forests. Plantations of these crops can extend for thousands of acres or hectares, covering entire watersheds. Banana and pineapple plantations depend heavily on pesticides to control pests. The result is pollution of both land and waterways, affecting the entire food web.

Saving rain forests. At the same time that rain forests are rapidly being destroyed, researchers are discovering amazing things about them. The biodiversity of rain forests may be 10 to 20 times as high as once thought. Among this wealth of life forms—if they can be saved—may be species that can improve the lives of people. The medicine quinine, for example, is made from the bark of South America's cinchona tree. It is used to treat the disease malaria. Quinine was one of the first rain forest medicines adopted worldwide. Healers from traditional cultures have used a wide variety of other rain forest plants for centuries to treat everything from toothache to snakebite. Medicines derived from such plants may someday save or improve millions of lives.

Conservationists are developing new ways to protect rain forests ecosystems. Many of these hold great potential for reversing our damaging relationship with rain forests.

Ecotourism is an increasingly important approach to protecting rain forests. Ecotourism is environmentally and socially responsible tourism that promotes the conservation of natural areas. The income brought by visitors can help native people, serving as a healthful alternative to destructive economic activities such as deforestation and mining. Ecotourism can also provide education for visitors and increase their awareness of the beauty and importance of rain forests. National parks have been created in some areas to protect forests and serve as ecotourism destinations.

Conservationists are exploring other sustainable uses of the rain forest. As they grow, trees collect carbon in their trunks. Reforesting in the tropics is therefore an attractive means of removing excess carbon dioxide from the atmosphere. Conservationists are also working to promote less damaging, more sustainable agriculture. Activists have called for a reduction of the impact of oil palm farming by pressuring food companies to replace palm oil in their products. Gerald R. Urquhart

Related articles in *World Book* include:

Rain forest animals

Cuscus	Loris	Parrot	Tarsier
Flying lemur	Mandrill	Sloth	Titi
Gorilla	Okapi	Tamarin	Toucan
Lemur	Orangutan	Tapir	

Rain forest plants

Anthurium	Cinchona	Litchi	Rattan
Baobab	Ebony	Mahogany	Rosewood
Brazil nut	Epiphyte	Mango	Rubber
Brazilwood	Kapok	Orchid	Sapodilla
Cacao	Kola nut	Palm	Tamarind
Cashew	Liana	Rafflesia	Teak

Rain forest peoples

Dayaks	Pygmies	Yanomami Indians

Other related articles

Amazon rain forest
American Samoa, National Park of
Daintree rain forest
Deforestation
El Yunque National Forest
Forest (Tropical rain forest)
Jungle
Olympic National Park

Additional resources

Corlett, Richard T., and Primack, R. B. *Tropical Rain Forests.* 2nd ed. Wiley-Blackwell, 2011.
Hunter, Nick. *Rain Forests.* Raintree, 2014. Younger readers.

Rain gauge is an instrument used to measure the amount of rain that falls in a certain place during a specific period. The National Weather Service uses a rain gauge that is shaped like a cylinder and has a removable cover. Inside the cylinder is a long narrow tube, where the rainfall is measured. The top of the tube is connected with a funnel. The rain falls into the funnel and flows into the tube. The mouth of the funnel has an area 10 times that of the tube. Therefore, if an inch (2.5 centimeters) of rain falls into the funnel, it would fill 10 inches (25.4 centimeters) of the tube. The rain in the tube is measured by a "ruler." With this ruler, a depth of 10 inches gives a reading of 1 inch of rainfall. Rain gauges that use the metric system measure in millimeters.

If the rainfall is so heavy that the water in the tube overflows, this extra rain flows into the space between the outside of the cylinder and the tube. After the rain in the tube is measured, it is poured out and the extra rain is placed in the tube and measured. The total rainfall equals the sum of these two measurements. A gauge is usually placed on the ground away from buildings and trees to ensure accuracy.

Some rain gauges can record the amount and the rate of rainfall. A *tipping bucket rain gauge* has a small bucket that tips and empties after it fills with rain. Each tip of the bucket activates an electrical switch that records the amount of rain. A *weighing rain gauge* collects water in a bucket that stands on a platform attached to a scale. As the bucket fills, the weight of the rain water pushes down the platform. This movement is recorded on a tape and processed by a computer.

Some rain gauges can be used to measure snowfall. However, the gauges do not provide accurate measurements when they are used for this purpose.

David D. Houghton

Rain tree, also called *monkey pod,* is a shade tree that grows in tropical climates. Rain trees have short, stout trunks and long spreading branches. The canopies of some rain trees measure more than 100 feet (30 meters) across. The trees are called *rain trees* in part because moisture often drips from them. Some of this "rain" is really a discharge from cicadas feeding on the trees.

Rain trees have pink and white flowers that grow in clusters. The seeds are held in long, brown pods.

A freshly cut rain tree has moist wood that is easy to carve and keeps its shape as it dries. The wood has a golden to dark brown color and is used to make bowls, trays, furniture, and paneling.

The tree is native to Central America and northern South America. In the United States, it is grown in Hawaii and Florida. Christopher W. Dick

Scientific classification. The rain tree's scientific name is *Samanea saman.*

Rainbow is a circular arc of colors that appears in the sky after it rains. A rainbow appears when raindrops are illuminated by sunlight. A rainbow is not a physical object. Rather, it is a pattern of light.

A rainbow may spread across the entire sky. The ends of such a rainbow may seem to rest on the earth. Not all rainbows form complete arcs, however. A rainbow cannot appear in a part of the sky where there is no rain.

No two people ever see exactly the same rainbow. You are at the center of the rainbow you see. A person standing next to you would be at the center of a different rainbow. A different set of raindrops forms each rainbow.

How to find a rainbow. A rainbow in the form of a complete arc attracts our attention. Sometimes, however, only patches of a rainbow are visible. Knowing when and where to look will help you find them.

Rainbows are most likely to appear toward the end of the day. The best time for a rainbow is a hot summer day, when a thunderstorm brings rain in the late afternoon. To find a rainbow, turn your back to the sun. Next, locate your *antisolar point.* The antisolar point will lie in the direction of the shadow of your head. Scan the sky in an arc about 42° above the antisolar point. A rainbow at this location is called a *primary rainbow.* It will be red on its outer edge and violet on its inner edge—with many other colors in between.

© Shutterstock

Rainbows appear in the sky when sunlight illuminates raindrops. Occasionally, as shown here, a dim *secondary rainbow* will appear above a bright *primary rainbow.* The colors in a secondary rainbow appear in reverse order of those in the primary rainbow.

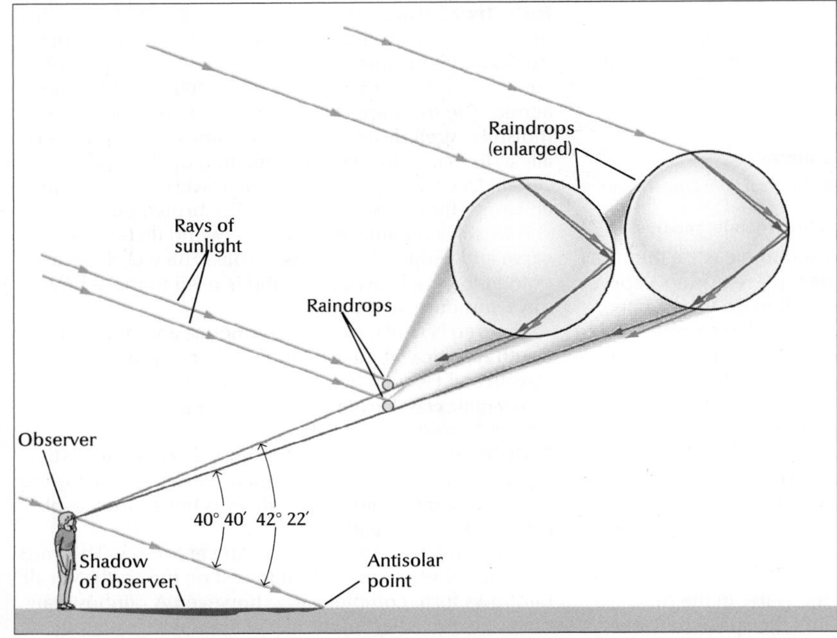

WORLD BOOK diagram by Precision Graphics

A rainbow forms when raindrops bend and reflect sunlight, *as shown here.* As this light bends, it breaks up into rays of various colors—red and violet as shown and, between them, orange, yellow, green, and blue. The rays reflect off the inner surface of the drops, then bend again as they exit the drops. As a result, a rainbow appears about 42° above an observer's *antisolar point,* the point directly opposite the sun. The rainbow's outer edge is red, and its inner edge is violet.

If you scan about 9° above this rainbow, you may see a less bright *secondary rainbow* with its color order reversed. Between the rainbows will be a relatively dark region called *Alexander's dark band.*

How rainbows appear. To understand some of the general features of rainbows, it helps to pretend that sunlight can be divided into many parallel rays. The rays are uniformly spaced when they arrive at the surface of a raindrop. It also helps to know about the wave nature of light, and how a prism bends sunlight.

The wave nature of light. Light is a form of energy that behaves in some ways like waves. Light waves have a range of *wavelengths.* A wavelength is the distance between any point on one wave and the corresponding point on the next wave. Visible light of different wavelengths appears as different colors. Light with the longest wavelengths appears red. Light with the shortest wavelengths appears violet.

Sunlight has a mixture of wavelengths. We see this mixture as white light. People often specify the colors in sunlight, from the longest wavelength to the shortest, as red, orange, yellow, green, blue, and violet. Other people also mention the color indigo, which is closely related to blue, between blue and violet. All these colors shade into their neighboring colors, however, and each shading is itself a color. Nature produces many more colors than people have ever named.

How a prism bends sunlight. When light passes through a prism, the light is *refracted* (bent). Light of a given wavelength bends at only one angle. Therefore, when sunlight—with its mixture of wavelengths—passes through a prism, it separates into a rainbowlike band of colors. Light with the longest wavelengths bends the least and appears red. Light with the shortest wavelengths bends the most and appears violet.

How droplets form a rainbow. When uniformly spaced rays of white light enter a raindrop, the raindrop acts as a prism. Thus, each ray of white light is separated into many rays corresponding to all the colors in sunlight. Each ray of colored light bends at a different angle.

Some of the rays of colored light reflect once off the inside surface of the raindrop, then exit the drop. As they exit, they bend again. The exiting rays are highly concentrated at angles of about 42° relative to the paths of entry of the original rays of white light.

Such concentrations of rays exit from many raindrops. These rays reach an observer who is scanning the sky about 42° above the antisolar point. As a result, the observer sees a primary rainbow with its colors in the following order, from outer edge to inner edge: red, orange, yellow, green, blue, violet.

Other rays of colored light reflect twice off the inside surface of raindrops. The rays exit the drops concentrated at angles of about 51°. Thus, an observer sees a secondary rainbow at about 51° above the antisolar point.

Other kinds of bows. People sometimes use the term *rainbow* to refer to colored arcs formed in sea spray or the spray of waterfalls, garden hoses, or lawn sprinklers. You may see such bows even when the sun is high in the sky. Craig F. Bohren

See also **Color** (The relationship between color and light); **Light** (The spectrum of light sources); **Prism.**

Rainbow Bridge National Monument, in southern Utah, has one of the world's best-known natural bridges. This bridge is 290 feet (88 meters) high and has a 275-foot (84-meter) span. There are two hiking trails to the bridge. The area was established as a national monument in 1910. See also **Utah** (Places to visit [picture]).

Rainbow for Girls is an international organization for girls from the ages of 11 through 20. Its official name is International Order of the Rainbow for Girls. Rainbow for Girls was originally created for Masonic daughters and their friends. Masons belong to one of the oldest and largest fraternal organizations in the world. But today any girl who is interested in joining Rainbow for Girls may join. An applicant must submit a petition to a local chapter, called an *assembly.* Once the petition is accepted, the assembly conducts a ballot to vote an applicant into their group.

Although members do not have to be Christian, Rainbow for Girls encourages church membership and reverence for the Bible. It also encourages patriotism, love of family, and service to the community. Assemblies raise funds for charitable causes and sponsor recreational and cultural outings for their members.

The organization was founded in McAlester, Oklahoma, in 1922 by W. Mark Sexson, an American clergyman and Mason. Today, Rainbow for Girls has hundreds of thousands of active members worldwide. The organization's central governing board, the Supreme Assembly, issues the bylaws for all Rainbow assemblies. Each assembly also has its own advisory board headed by a Mother Adviser. The organization's headquarters are in McAlester. Critically reviewed by Rainbow for Girls

See also **Masonry.**

Rainier, Mount. See **Mount Rainier.**

Rainier III, *ray NEER* (1923-2005), became prince of Monaco in 1949. His full name was Rainier Louis Henri-Maxence Bertrand de Grimaldi. Rainier married actress Grace Kelly in 1956. The birth of their daughter Princess Caroline the next year delighted Monaco. As long as the royal family continues, Monaco remains independent from France. The couple also had a son, Prince Albert, and another daughter, Princess Stephanie Marie Elisabeth. Rainier's wife died in 1982 after a car accident near Monaco. As prince, Rainier provided low-cost housing, expanded schools, and tried to balance the budget of his government. He was born on May 31, 1923, in Monaco. Rainier died on April 6, 2005. Janet L. Polasky

See also **Kelly, Grace; Monaco.**

Rainmaking. See **Cloud seeding.**

Rainy Lake lies on the boundary between Ontario and Minnesota, about 125 miles (201 kilometers) north of Duluth, Minnesota. For location, see **Minnesota** (physical map). It covers about 350 square miles (906 square kilometers) and is shaped roughly like a capital L. Each arm is about 40 miles (64 kilometers) long and from 3 to 8 miles (5 to 13 kilometers) wide. Thousands of islands lie scattered throughout the lake. The longest stretch of open water is only about 1 mile (1.6 kilometers) wide. The Canadian National Railway crosses the lake almost at its center on bridges that link islands.

Spruce and pine cover the rocky shores of Rainy Lake. Many of the trees are cut for paper mills at Fort Frances and International Falls, at the lake's west end. A dam at Fort Frances harnesses water for power. Pike, pickerel, and other fish are caught in Rainy Lake. Whitefish from the lake are sold commercially. Bear, moose, and other wild game roam around the lake. Thomas J. Baerwald

Raisa, *rah EE suh,* **Rosa** (1893-1963), a dramatic soprano, was especially popular for many years with audiences in Italy and Chicago. Born on May 23, 1893, in Białystok, Poland, she fled from there at the age of 14. She went to Italy and studied singing at the Conservatory of Naples. She was trained by opera singer Eva Tetrazzini. Raisa made her European and American opera debuts in 1913. She died on Sept. 28, 1963. Martin Bernheimer

Raisin is a dried grape. The word *raisin* comes from a French term meaning *dry grape.* Varieties of white grapes that have tender skin, rich flavor, and high sugar content are especially suited for making raisins. Raisins are used in puddings, cakes, candies, cookies, and bread. They are also sold as sweets in small boxes.

Raisins have been a food delicacy since ancient times. The Egyptians first discovered that drying fruit preserved it, made it sweeter, and improved its flavor. The Bible mentions that an Israelite brought cheese and raisins to pay his taxes to King David. Wealthy Romans served raisins at feasts.

Spanish missionaries planted grapevines in California in the 1700's. After the Civil War ended in 1865, former gold hunters found that the region of California now called the Central Valley had an ideal climate for producing raisins. The dry, hot summers allowed grapes to ripen, and the low chance of rain after the harvest meant the grapes could be sun-dried in the vineyard. Commercial raisin production began in California in the 1870's.

Today, California leads the world in raisin grape production. It is the only U.S. state that produces raisins commercially. California produces about 670 million pounds (300 million kilograms) annually. Other leading producers include Australia, Greece, Iran, and Turkey.

Varieties. Four main varieties of grapes are used in raisin production. The most common is the Thompson Seedless. Seedless grapes used to make raisins first came from Turkey. In 1872, William Thompson introduced seedless grape cuttings to California. Thompson Seedless now make up over 95 percent of the grapes used to make raisins in California. Other varieties are Muscat of Alexandria, Black Corinth, and Sultana. The Muscat is a large, seed-bearing grape brought to America by Spanish missionaries. Grapes from Black Corinth vines are used to make Zante currants—tiny, seedless raisins used mainly to flavor baked goods. Raisins made from Sultana grapes, which are seedless and have a distinctive flavor, are used mainly in baked goods.

Growing grapes. Almost all the raisins produced in California come from vines grown within 100 miles (160 kilometers) of Fresno. Grapevines start growing there in March, and the fruit is harvested about the first week of September. The vineyards must be irrigated because little rain falls in the area during the period when the vines grow. Vines used for raisins must be spaced far enough apart to allow room for drying the fruit and to permit cultivation. Grapevines begin bearing fruit in three years. With proper care, they may continue to produce fruit for 100 years. About 4 ½ pounds (2 kilograms) of grapes produce 1 pound (0.5 kilogram) of raisins.

Preparation for market. Seedless grapes ripen on the vine until sugars account for more than 20 percent of their weight. The grapes are then harvested by hand or machine and placed on trays of heavy, brown paper between the rows of vines. The fruit may be turned over after about eight days so that grapes on the bottom can dry faster. Because the rows are planted in an east-west direction, the sun can dry the grapes in 10 to 14 days. The raisins are then stored in large bins, called *sweat boxes,* to equalize their moisture content. Next, the fruit is sent to packing houses, where workers stem and grade the raisins by passing them over screens. Machines remove stem caps. A machine whirls the raisins through a fine spray of water to give them a final cleaning. The raisins are then pressed into sealed packages.

Raisins with seeds go through a different process. Muscat raisins are larger and softer than the seedless types after drying. Muscat raisins are passed through the stem-removal machine and are washed in hot water to soften them further. They are then fed between rubber rollers that press the seeds to the surface. A sawtooth roller catches the seeds between its teeth and removes them.

Sun-dried raisins are called *natural raisins.* Most raisins are natural. However, golden seedless or golden raisins, made from Thompson Seedless grapes, are dried in large machines. The grapes are first treated with sulfur dioxide to preserve their golden color.

Because of their high sugar content, raisins need no preservatives to keep them fresh. If raisins are kept cool and stored in a sealed container, they will retain their flavor, color, and nutritional value for up to 15 months. They may also be frozen.

Food value. Raisins are a good source of vitamin A; the B_1 vitamins thiamine and riboflavin; and such minerals as calcium, iron, and potassium. The sugars in raisins give quick energy because the body absorbs them immediately. Larry E. Williams

See also **Grape.**

Raisin River Massacre. See **War of 1812** (Campaigns of 1813).

Rajah, *RAH juh,* is a title taken from the Sanskrit word *rajan,* which means *king.* Ruling princes of native states in India were once the only persons known as rajahs. But under the British Empire, the title of rajah was also given to certain other high-ranking Hindus. Native princes who kept some authority under British rule were called *maharajah* (great king). Jonathan Grant

Rake is a machine used to gather mowed hay and place it in long piles called *windrows.* The windrows are then gathered by a hay loader or baler. The first rakes were wooden hand rakes. People still use hand rakes to rake leaves from lawns. Modern rakes are usually pulled by, or mounted on, a tractor. Rakes can also be used to gather straw, green forage, and seed crops.

The dump rake consists of curved steel teeth mounted on an axle between two wheels. The teeth slide over the ground and rake hay as the machine moves forward. The operator dumps the hay in a windrow by pulling a lever that causes the teeth to lift from the ground.

The side-delivery rake leaves the hay in a continuous windrow at the side of the vehicle carrying the rake. In one type of side-delivery rake, the teeth are attached to cylinders that roll along at an angle to the direction traveled. The teeth just clear the ground as the cylinder rotates. As the machine moves ahead, the teeth brush the hay to the side, leaving it in a windrow. A *dual rake* consists of two side-delivery rakes, which deposit two windrows together at one time.

The *finger-wheel rake* consists of several wheels with spikes on the rim. The wheels are set at an angle to the direction traveled, and move the hay sideways to form a windrow. The *drag-type rake* has no moving parts. It has curved fingers that move the hay to one side, much as a snowplow moves snow. Gerald E. Rehkugler

Ralegh, Sir Walter. See **Raleigh, Sir Walter.**

Raleigh, *RAW lee* or *RAH lee* (pop. 403,892; met. area pop. 1,130,490), is the capital of North Carolina and a center of education, research, and trade. It lies in east-central North Carolina, where the hilly Piedmont region meets the flat, sandy coastal plain (see **North Carolina** [political map]).

The city's chief products include electronic components, processed food, and textiles. Many corporations and federal agencies operate research facilities at Research Triangle Park, a large complex near the city.

Cultural attractions in Raleigh include the North Carolina Symphony and state museums of art, history, and natural sciences. The city is the home of the Carolina Hurricanes of the National Hockey League. Institutions of higher learning in the city include Meredith College, North Carolina State University, St. Augustine's University, Shaw University, and William Peace University. The Andrew Johnson House, the birthplace of the 17th president of the United States, is also in Raleigh.

Tuscarora Indians lived in what is now the Raleigh area before white settlers arrived there. The state legislature founded Raleigh in 1792 after choosing the site for the state capital. The city was named for English soldier and explorer Sir Walter Raleigh, who sent colonizing expeditions to the area in the late 1500's.

Raleigh's chief growth occurred after World War II ended in 1945, especially following the opening of Research Triangle Park in 1959. In 1977, the city finished turning part of its main street into a pedestrian mall called the Fayetteville Street Mall. The State Capitol

Greater Raleigh CVB

Raleigh is the capital of North Carolina and a center of education, research, and trade. Downtown Raleigh, *shown here,* has many high-rise office buildings and hotels.

stands at one end of the mall, and at the other end is a performing arts center, completed in 2001. In 2006, the mall was reopened to vehicle traffic.

Raleigh is the county seat of Wake County. It has a council-manager form of government. Jerry L. Surratt

See also **North Carolina** (Climate; pictures).

Raleigh, *RAW lee* or *RAH lee,* **Sir Walter** (1552?-1618), is one of the most colorful figures in English history. He was a soldier, explorer, writer, and businessman. He spelled his last name Ralegh.

Raleigh was born at Hayes Barton, a family home in Devonshire, and attended Oxford University. He left school before graduating to join a band of gentlemen volunteers who were helping the Huguenots in France (see **Huguenots**). In 1578, he returned to England and joined his half brother, Sir Humphrey Gilbert, on a voyage of discovery and piracy.

Raleigh and Elizabeth I. In 1580, Raleigh became a captain in the army in Ireland. There he distinguished himself by his ruthlessness at the siege of Smerwick. The next year, he went to Queen Elizabeth's court with dispatches (see **Elizabeth I**). There is a famous story about his meeting with Elizabeth. The queen was out walking, and stopped before a large mud puddle. Raleigh removed his coat and placed it over the puddle for her to walk on. It is doubtful that this story is true. But Raleigh did become the queen's favorite. She granted him an estate of 12,000 acres (4,860 hectares) in Ireland. She also gave him trade privileges and the right to colonize in America. In 1585, she made him a knight.

His expeditions. Raleigh became deeply interested in exploration. He sent several expeditions to America, and spent a fortune trying to establish an English colony there. His settlers landed in what is now the state of North Carolina and explored the coast as far as present-day Florida. Raleigh and Elizabeth, who was known as "The Virgin Queen," named much of what is now the eastern United States *Virginia,* in honor of the queen.

Raleigh's first colonizing expedition left Plymouth in April 1585. It established a colony on Roanoke Island in Pamlico Sound. But sickness and fear caused the survivors of this first English colony in North America to go home with Sir Francis Drake in 1586.

In 1587, Raleigh sent a second expedition. A group of 117 colonists, including 17 women, landed on Roanoke Island. On Aug. 18, 1587, the first English child was born in North America (see **Dare, Virginia**). John White, the governor, went back to England for supplies. He was delayed by war with Spain, and when he returned to Roanoke in 1590, the settlers had mysteriously disappeared (see **Lost Colony**).

Raleigh also took part in the victory over the Spanish Armada in 1588. He led other expeditions against Spanish possessions and returned with much booty. During the 1590's, his power reached its height, and he had much influence and many enemies. Raleigh, who was also a poet, obtained a pension for the English poet Edmund Spenser and helped Spenser publish *The Faerie Queene* (see **Spenser, Edmund**). Raleigh also helped introduce the potato plant and tobacco use to Ireland.

His fall. Raleigh lost the queen's favor by marrying one of her attendants. Hoping to recover his position and the money he had spent, Raleigh led an expedition to Guiana, in South America, to search for El Dorado, which was a legendary land of gold. However, the expedition failed.

Oil painting on canvas (1588) by an unknown artist (Granger Collection)

Sir Walter Raleigh tried to establish an English colony in North America. He failed, but his efforts aided later colonists.

Elizabeth died in 1603, and the new king, James I, distrusted and feared Raleigh. The king charged Raleigh with treason and imprisoned him in the Tower of London. There Raleigh lived comfortably for 12 years with his family and servants, and wrote his *History of the World.* Raleigh was released in 1616 to lead an expedition to search for gold in South America. The king ordered him not to invade Spanish territory. However, Raleigh's men attacked the Spaniards. Raleigh's son Wat was killed in the attack, and Raleigh was forced to abandon the project.

Upon his return to England, he was sentenced to death for disobeying orders. Raleigh met his fate bravely Oct. 29, 1618. He joked with the executioner and even gave the signal for the ax to fall. Stephen Greenblatt

Ram. See **Aries; Battering ram; Sheep** (The body of the sheep).

Rama is a popular god in Hinduism. He is the seventh *avatar* (physical form) of the god Vishnu. Rama is usually shown as a king carrying a bow and arrow.

Rama's story is told in many books. A complete version of the story appears in the epic the *Ramayana.* Rama was the oldest of four sons of the king of Ayodhya, and the heir to the throne. One of his father's wives wanted her son Bharata, Rama's half brother, to rule instead. She made the king exile Rama to a forest for 14 years. Rama's wife, Sita, and brother Lakshmana accompanied him.

While in the forest, Sita was abducted by the 10-headed demon Ravana. The demon took Rama's wife to his island kingdom of Lanka (now Sri Lanka). Rama defeated

Ravana in a war and rescued Sita with the aid of troops led by the monkey god Hanuman.

After 14 years of exile, Rama returned to Ayodhya and assumed the throne. He ruled as a righteous king over a land known for peace and prosperity. Today, Ayodhya in northern India is a popular pilgrimage site, with many temples dedicated to Rama. David L. Haberman

See also **Ramayana; Vishnu.**

Ramadan, *ram uh DHAN* or *rahm uh DAHN,* is an Islamic holy month when Muslims may not eat or drink from morning to night. The term *Ramadan* comes from the word *Ramz,* meaning *great heat or burning.* Ramadan is believed to cleanse a person of sins. Muslims are supposed to seek God's forgiveness during Ramadan.

Ramadan is the ninth month of the Islamic year. Because the Islamic calendar is based on lunar months rather than on solar months as the Western Gregorian calendar is, Ramadan falls at different times of the year. Muslims celebrate Ramadan as the month during which the prophet Muhammad received the first of the revelations that make up the Qur'ān, the holy book of Islam.

All Muslims who have reached puberty and are of sound mind must fast. Exceptions include the sick, the elderly, pregnant women, and travelers. But those who are able must make up the missed fast days later. A Muslim who deliberately breaks the fast must atone by fasting for two months or feeding the poor.

Fasting begins at dawn and lasts until sunset. During this time, Muslims cannot eat food or drink beverages, inhale tobacco smoke, or engage in sexual activity. The daily fast is broken by a light meal called the *iftar,* followed by the evening prayer.

Fasting helps Muslims to experience and apply many teachings from the Qur'ān in their daily lives. Such teachings include compassion, self control, and spiritual reflection. Fasting also teaches Muslims to sympathize with those who are less fortunate than they are.

The nights during Ramadan are devoted to special prayers and to recitations from the Qur'ān. During the last 10 days, some Muslims seclude themselves in a mosque to devote time to prayer and religious contemplation. The end of Ramadan is celebrated by a great festival called 'Īd al-Fitr (see **'Īd al-Fitr**). Liyakat Takim

Raman, *RAH muhn,* **Sir Chandrasekhara Venkata,** *CHUHN druh SHAY kuhr uh VEHNG kuh tuh* (1888-1970), an Indian physicist, discovered that when a beam of light passes through a liquid or gas, it scatters and the frequency of some of the scattered light changes. This change, called the *Raman effect,* provides a way to study the structure of the scattering molecules. For his discovery, Raman was knighted in 1929 and received the 1930 Nobel Prize in physics. Raman was born on Nov. 7, 1888, in Trichinopoly (now Tiruchchirappalli). He founded the *Indian Journal of Physics* and the Indian Academy of Sciences. After 1930, Raman mainly studied the structure of crystals. He died on Nov. 21, 1970. Peter Pesic

Ramayana, *rah MAH yuh nuh,* is one of the two great epic poems of India. The other is the *Mahabharata.* Rama, the hero of the *Ramayana,* is a human form of the god Vishnu. In the *Ramayana,* he is the son and heir of an Indian king. Rama serves as a model for Hindu men. He is handsome and brave and a devoted husband. Sita, his beautiful wife, represents the Hindu ideal of devotion to duty and husband.

In the story, Rama lives in the kingdom of Ayodhya in northern India. His father exiles him for 14 years because of a dispute over the throne. The main plot concerns a conflict between Rama and Ravana, a demon-king. Ravana kidnaps Sita and takes her to his kingdom on the island of Lanka (now Sri Lanka). Rama rescues Sita and kills Ravana with an arrow. At the end of Rama's exile, he and Sita return home in triumph, and he becomes king.

The poet Valmiki supposedly wrote the first version of the *Ramayana* in Sanskrit about 500 B.C. or earlier. It has 24,000 couplets. Translated or rewritten versions of the *Ramayana* appear in other Indian languages. The Hindi version, written by the poet Tulsidas (also spelled Tulsi Das) in the late 1500's, became the most popular. The *Ramayana* remains popular today because of its characters, who set high standards for human behavior and in-

© AFP/Getty Images

The end of Ramadan, the Islamic holy month, draws a crowd of Muslims to pray at the Taj Mahal in Agra, India, *shown here.* Muslims celebrate the conclusion of Ramadan with a great festival called 'Īd al-Fitr.

spire devotion to God. Readers also enjoy the beautiful language and exciting plot of the *Ramayana.*

Charles S. J. White

See also **Mahabharata; Rama; Vishnu.**

Rameau, *ra MOH,* **Jean-Philippe,** *zhahn fee LEEP* (1683-1764), was a French composer and musical theorist of the Baroque period. Rameau worked as an organist for about 20 years in several cities before settling in Paris in about 1722. He became famous that year with the publication of a book of music theory called *Treatise on Harmony.* The book became a landmark in the history of harmony and was the first of several works he wrote on harmony.

At the age of 50, Rameau began a new career as an opera composer. He wrote more than 25 operas and opera-ballets, beginning with the opera *Hippolyte and Aricie* (1733). His major opera-ballets included *Les Indes galantes* (1735) and *Les Fêtes d'Hébé* (1739). His operas include *Castor and Pollux* (1737) and *Dardanus* (1739, 1744). Rameau's operas were controversial because of their unconventional use of orchestral color, vivid harmonies, and speechlike singing called recitative. Rameau engaged in a quarrel with the philosopher Jean-Jacques Rousseau, largely over the preferred style of opera. Rameau favored the French style, and Rousseau supported opera in the Italian fashion.

Rameau was born in September 1683, in Dijon. In addition to his theoretical writings and compositions for the stage, he wrote many suites for an early keyboard instrument called the harpsichord. In 1745, Rameau was appointed chamber music composer to King Louis XV. The composer died on Sept. 12, 1764. Joscelyn Godwin

See also **Opera** (French opera).

Rameses II. See **Ramses II.**

Ramie, *RAM ee,* is a perennial plant grown chiefly for its fiber. It is native to Asia and is grown chiefly in India, China, and Taiwan. Ramie is one of the oldest known sources of fiber. There are over 30 known varieties of ramie. The most common kinds come from China and Japan. The thick, broad leaves of the ramie plant are dark green on top, and white and woolly underneath. Growers plant pieces of the roots, which grow into plants in about three months. The stalks grow from 3 to 7 feet (0.9 to 2 meters) high.

In Asia, workers strip the tough ramie fiber from the stalks by hand. The fiber at this stage is often called *China grass.* Then it is washed and dried several times to remove the gums, pectins, and waxes. In the United States, ramie is grown mainly in Florida. Machines harvest it and strip it of its bark and core. Chemicals remove gummy material and impurities from the fiber.

Ramie's strength increases greatly when it is wet, so it is suitable for life rafts, ropes, canvas, and nets. Other uses include surgical dressings, towels, air-conditioning filters, and fabrics. However, synthetic fibers have largely replaced ramie fibers in these products, especially in industrialized nations. Farmers in Central America have used ramie as a high-protein fodder for pigs.

Robert A. Barnhardt

Scientific classification. Ramie is in the nettle family, Urticaceae. It is classified as *Boehmeria nivea.*

Ramjet. See **Jet propulsion** (Ramjet).

Rammohun Roy (1772-1833) was a social and religious reformer in India. He helped change Hinduism in a time when it had come under criticism from India's British colonial rulers, Christian missionaries, and others. Rammohun Roy is sometimes called the father of modern India.

Rammohun Roy sought to change religion and society within Indian traditions by claiming that ancient Hindu writings supported his ideas for reform. For example, he rejected the *polytheism* (belief in many gods) that Hindus practiced at that time. He argued instead that certain Hindu texts supported the belief in one supreme being. He held that Hinduism was an ethical religion and one that was based on reason. Rammohun Roy objected to such traditional Hindu practices as idolatry and suttee, in which a widow was burned along with her dead husband. He also opposed the caste system's rigid structure and strict rules.

Rammohun Roy was born in West Bengal on May 23, 1772. In 1828, he founded the Brahmo Samaj (Society of God). This organization played an important role in reforming Indian society and religion in the 1800's. He died on Sept. 27, 1833. Ian J. Kerr

Ramp, or *wild leek,* is a wild onion that grows in moist woodland areas in the eastern United States. The flat leaves grow from the ground in spring and disappear by summer. Then a leafless flowering stem appears, bearing several greenish-white flowers at its tip. The plant smells and tastes like onions. Some people believe that the Indian word *checagou,* from which the city of Chicago got its name, refers to the smell of the ramp.

Hugh C. Price

Scientific classification. The ramp belongs to the onion family, Alliaceae. Its scientific name is *Allium tricoccum.*

See also **Leek; Onion.**

Rampolla del Tindaro, *rahm POHL lah dehl TEEN dah roh,* **Mariano,** *mah RYAH noh* (1843-1913), Marchese del Tindaro, became a cardinal of the Roman Catholic Church and papal secretary of state in 1887. He shared responsibility for Pope Leo XIII's policy of reconciling French Catholics to their country's republican form of government. His efforts displeased not only the French monarchists, but also Emperor Francis Joseph of Austria-Hungary. The emperor took extraordinary action in 1903, when the College of Cardinals met to elect a new pope. He registered a veto of Cardinal Rampolla. The exact effect of the emperor's veto cannot be known, because popes are elected by secret vote. However, it seems likely that the veto prevented the choice of Rampolla, whose ability was well known.

Rampolla was born on Aug. 17, 1843, at Polizzi, Italy. He was ordained a priest in 1866. During his education at the Vatican seminary, he showed such ability, particularly in Asian languages, that he was chosen for a career in Vatican diplomatic service. Rampolla died on Dec. 16, 1913. Marvin R. O'Connell

Ramsay, *RAM zee,* **Sir William** (1852-1916), was a Scottish chemist who, with English physicist Lord Rayleigh, isolated the rare atmospheric gas argon. Ramsay also discovered helium, neon, krypton, and xenon gases. The five gases are called *noble gases* because they do not readily react with other elements. For this work, Ramsay received the 1904 Nobel Prize in chemistry. His explanation of the nature of these elements led to important ideas about atomic structure. Each of these elements has a separate article in *World Book.*

Statues of Ramses II guarded the Abu Simbel temple near the Nile for more than 3,000 years. Construction of the Aswan High Dam made it necessary to move the temple to higher ground.

© Robert Azzi, Woodfin Camp, Inc.

Ramsay was born on Oct. 2, 1852, in Glasgow. He taught at Glasgow and Bristol, and at University College in London. He was knighted in 1902 and, in 1911, he became president of the British Association for the Advancement of Science. Ramsay died on July 23, 1916.

Bruce R. Wheaton

See also **Element, Chemical.**

Ramses II, *RAM seez,* was one of the most celebrated kings of ancient Egypt. He reigned from about 1279 to 1213 B.C. While young, Ramses served for a time as prince *regent* (substitute ruler) under his father, Seti I. From the fourth year of his own reign, Ramses conducted military campaigns in northern Syria to halt the expansion of the Hittite kingdom. A major battle against the Hittites at Kadesh (also spelled Qadesh) in the fifth year of his reign was indecisive. But the personal bravery of Ramses during the battle was recorded in texts and artwork throughout Egypt and the Egyptian colony of Nubia. By about 1259, Egypt had made a formal peace treaty and developed close diplomatic ties with a weakened Hittite kingdom.

Ramses was a great builder. He constructed a new capital, Per-Ramses (City of Ramses), in the Nile Delta. He continued his father's work on temples at Abydos and Karnak. His building projects appeared throughout Egypt and Nubia. Ramses also built the famous Temples of Abu Simbel, which are dedicated to the worship of him as a living god. Ramses outlived his first dozen heirs. A tomb for some of his sons has undergone some excavation in the Valley of the Kings in central Egypt. His mummy is preserved in the Egyptian Museum in Cairo.

Robert K. Ritner

See also **Abu Simbel, Temples of.**

Ramsey, Alexander. See **Minnesota** (Territorial days; table: The governors of Minnesota).

Ranching usually means raising cattle and sheep on large farms. Some fruit farms and farms that raise such small fur animals as mink are also called *ranches.* So are many places of 5 to 10 acres (2 to 4 hectares) in California. But this article deals with cattle and sheep ranching. For information on *dude ranches,* resorts where tourists experience life in the Old West, see **Dude ranch.**

Cattle and sheep ranches are large because it generally takes many acres of grassland to feed a herd. An average ranch in the western United States covers several thousand acres or several hundred hectares.

Most North American ranches are found in the western United States and Canada. There are some in the Southeastern States along the Gulf of Mexico. Argentina, Australia, Mexico, New Zealand, and some African countries also have large ranches. But Australians and New Zealanders call them *stations.*

Most early American ranchers raised cattle on unfenced land called *open range.* Workers called *cowboys* or *cowhands* herded the cattle. Today, ranchers generally own much of the land in their ranch, and they and members of their family do most of the work. Neighbors help one another when extra help is needed on the ranch. Only the largest ranches employ cowhands.

Life on a cattle ranch centers on raising calves to be sold as *stocker cattle* or as *feeder cattle.* After the animals are fattened, they are called *slaughter cattle.* The fattened stock are shipped to a stockyard, where they are sold and slaughtered for meat. The rancher usually keeps some *heifer* (female) calves to replace older cows.

Ranchers start their year in the fall after selling their calves. They prepare for winter by buying or harvesting a hay crop and such feed grains as barley, corn, oats, or sorghum. When snow covers the ground in the winter, the cattle cannot find food by themselves. Ranchers then carry feed to their cattle in trucks or helicopters, spreading it on the ground for them to eat.

Many of the cows give birth to calves in early spring, and the rancher must watch them closely. If a calf becomes ill, the rancher may move it and its mother from the fields to the ranch headquarters to treat the calf.

A month or two later, when the calves are active and strong, neighbors help the rancher round up the cattle

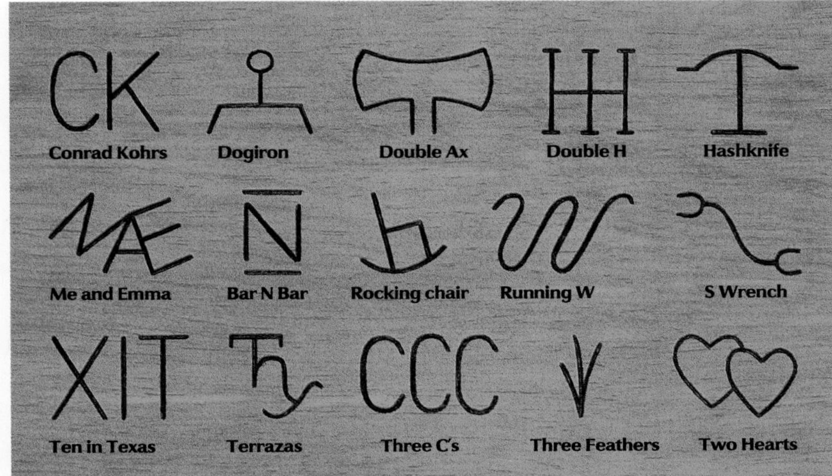

WORLD BOOK illustration by Walter Maslon

Famous ranch brands of the Old West. Branding cattle was very important in the 1800's, when cattle roamed on *open* (unfenced) range. The brand on each animal showed who owned it. Branding also made it difficult for *rustlers* (thieves) to steal cattle and sell them as their own.

and herd them into a small fenced area called a *corral.* There the calves are *branded* (marked) with a hot iron to show who owns them. They may also be ear tagged at this time. They are given medicine to prevent diseases. Male calves may be *castrated* (have their sex glands removed). During the rest of the spring and summer, the herd *grazes* (eats grass) on the range.

The cattle follow a daily routine on the range. They graze very early in the morning, eating rapidly. They chew their food only enough to moisten it and then swallow it. In the middle of the day, the cattle rest in a shady place. The food is returned to their mouths in the form of a *cud,* and they chew it again to aid in its digestion. In late afternoon, most cattle go to the watering hole or stock tank to drink. They then graze until dusk.

During the day, ranchers mend fences, repair machinery, and make sure watering holes store enough water. They also put out blocks of salt mixed with other minerals that the cows can lick, because cattle need such minerals in their diet. In the fall, neighbors help each other round up cattle. Then the calves that are old enough to be *weaned* (taken from their mothers) are sold.

Ranch life once was lonely. But the automobile, truck, and good roads have brought the rancher closer to other people. Most ranch children ride buses to school in nearby towns. Ranch families now live in comfortable homes that have electric power, plumbing, a telephone, and other modern conveniences.

Life on a sheep ranch is different from life on a cattle ranch because sheep produce two crops—lambs and wool. In the spring, crews of workers use power clippers to *shear* (cut off) the sheep's wool, and the rancher sells it. Lambs are usually born in spring. They and the freshly sheared *ewes* (mother sheep) are then branded with paint or are ear tagged. In the fall, most of the lambs are weaned, shipped to feeders or stockyards, and sold for slaughter.

History. Ranching in the United States began in the mid-1800's. Ranchers raised cattle on the open range and hired cowhands to help guard and herd the cattle.

When the cattle were almost ready for slaughter, the ranchers formed big herds and drove them overland to

Werner Stoy, Camera Hawaii; Ernst Peterson, Publix

Life on cattle ranches has changed greatly since they were founded in the 1800's in the American Southwest. Ranchers still use cow ponies occasionally to rope calves and do other work. But now some also use helicopters to check on herds in a ranch's distant areas.

the nearest railroad, in Kansas. A single herd had several thousand cattle and moved from 10 to 15 miles (16 to 24 kilometers) each day. In Kansas, the cattle were sold to buyers who shipped the cattle to the East.

During the 1870's and early 1880's, large ranches developed in the West. One of them, the XIT ranch in northern Texas, was 200 miles (320 kilometers) long, 25 miles (40 kilometers) wide, and had 150,000 cattle. Many cowhands worked on these big ranches, and they lived in buildings called *bunkhouses.* But in the mid-1880's, bad weather killed thousands of cattle and ruined many ranchers. Many big ranches were sold and divided.

Range wars. Some of the best land was *homesteaded.* That is, people moved onto federal land under the terms of the Homestead Act, which gave a person up to 160 acres (65 hectares) of land if the individual promised to live on it and farm it. Homesteaders built fences to protect their crops from cattle. Sheep ranching also began to develop. Sheep ranchers moved sheep from one range to another, and the sheep occasionally grazed on ranges that cattle used. Soon, cattle ranchers, homesteaders, and sheep ranchers began to fight for the land and watering holes. Many of these disputes developed into bloody *range wars.* Unlimited use of the open range ended in 1934. Since then, ranchers have needed permits to graze herds on federal land.

Since the 1940's. Land prices increased in the 1940's, so ranchers had to develop new ways to make their land more productive. They developed more watering holes, cleared brush, planted better grasses for their cattle and sheep to eat, and rotated their animals from one grazing area to another to allow the grass to grow back. Ranchers also began to use new methods of handling livestock with less help. Horses are often still used, but ranchers now also use jeeps, trucks, and even helicopters to get the most production. Doreen H. D. Kinkel

Related articles in *World Book* include:

Australia (Agriculture)
Cattle
Chuck wagon
Cowboy
King Ranch
Sheep
Western frontier life in America (Ranching)

Rand, Ayn, *eyen* (1905-1982), was an American author and social critic. Her books serve mainly as a means of expressing her philosophies. Literary critics tend to see them as marred by a tendency to instruct the reader.

Rand's best-known novels are *The Fountainhead* (1943) and *Atlas Shrugged* (1957). Both present a moral and economic philosophy, called Objectivism, based on individualism and self-interest. These novels express the belief that original ideas are the main force in the world and that creative individuals deserve to profit from their ideas. The heroes represent disciplined, rational people of action who reject organized religion. In *The Fountainhead,* an architect destroys a housing project in which his ideas had been altered. In *Atlas Shrugged,* one of the central characters calls a *mind strike,* during which all creative people withhold their ideas from the rest of the world. The strike reveals that society cannot exist without creative genius.

NYT Pictures
Ayn Rand

Rand was born on Feb. 2, 1905, in St. Petersburg, Russia. She moved to the United States in 1926 and became a U.S. citizen in 1931. Her novels *We the Living* (1936) and *Anthem* (1938) reflect her early life in Russia. Both novels express her revolt against socialist forms of government. She also wrote about her philosophies in such works of nonfiction as *For the New Intellectual* (1961), *The Virtue of Selfishness* (1964), and *Capitalism: The Unknown Ideal* (1966). Rand died on March 6, 1982. Arthur M. Saltzman

RAND Corporation is a nonprofit research organization that studies policy problems of the United States, especially those involving national defense. The U.S. Air Force began Project RAND (*R*esearch *AN*d *D*evelopment) in 1946 to conduct long-range studies of intercontinental warfare by forces other than armies. RAND became an independent corporation in 1948, but the U.S. Department of Defense still finances most of its work.

The RAND Corporation's early work included investigating such subjects as the military and economic strength of Russia and China, and the air defenses of the United States. The organization has also studied international terrorism, nuclear arms control, defense resource management, weapon design, uses of Earth satellites, and military and political conditions around the world. Since 1967, the corporation has increased its research on such nonmilitary issues as children and families, education and the arts, energy and the environment, health and health care, infrastructure and transportation, law and business, population and aging, public safety, and science and technology. Since 1970, it has published the *RAND Journal of Economics,* a peer-reviewed journal.

Most of the RAND Corporation's reports on military matters are secret and are given directly to the Air Force or the Department of Defense. The corporation also operates an Army research center and a graduate program that grants doctor's degrees in policy analysis. The corporation's headquarters are in Santa Monica, California, but it also has offices in Arlington, Virginia; Boston; and Pittsburgh. The RAND Gulf States Policy Institute was established in 2005 to support hurricane recovery and long-term economic development in Alabama, Louisiana, and Mississippi. It has offices in New Orleans and in Jackson, Mississippi. RAND Europe, the European arm of the RAND Corporation, was established in 1992. It has offices in Cambridge, United Kingdom; and in Brussels, Belgium. Allan R. Millett

Randolph, A. Philip (1889-1979), played a leading role in the struggle for black rights from the 1920's through the 1960's. He also became an important figure in the American labor movement. In 1925, Randolph founded the Brotherhood of Sleeping Car Porters (now part of the Transportation Communications International Union), a union he headed until 1968. He became a vice president of the American Federation of Labor and Congress of Industrial Organizations (AFL-CIO) in 1957.

Asa Philip Randolph was born in Crescent City, Florida, on April 15, 1889. He moved to New York City as a young man. He held odd jobs during the day and attended City College of New York at night. A Socialist during World War I (1914-1918), Randolph later believed unions offered African Americans the best hope for a fair wage. A group of Pullman car porters asked him to organize and lead a union for them. In 1941, Randolph threatened a march on Washington, D.C., to demand jobs for blacks in defense industries. The threat was one reason why President Franklin D. Roosevelt set up the Fair Employment Practices Committee. Randolph won the Spingarn Medal in 1942. He was one of the main organizers of the 1963 March on Washington, which protested racial and economic injustice. He died on May 16, 1979. Robert A. Pratt

Wide World
A. Philip Randolph

Randolph, Edmund (1753-1813), a Virginia statesman, presented the famous *Virginia Plan* to the Constitutional Convention in 1787. The plan favored the large states by calling for representation in Congress based on population or the tax contribution made by each state. Randolph refused to sign the Constitution because he thought it would create dangerously powerful presidents. Nevertheless, he supported its adoption at Virginia's ratifying convention.

In 1789, President George Washington appointed Randolph the nation's first attorney general and, in 1794, named him secretary of state. However, Randolph resigned as secretary of state in 1795 after he was unjustly accused of trying to sell diplomatic secrets to France.

Randolph was born on Aug. 10, 1753, near Williamsburg, Virginia, and was educated at the College of William and Mary. During the Revolutionary War in America (1775-1783), he served as then General George Washington's *aide-de-camp* (assistant). Randolph became attorney general of Virginia in 1776 and later served as a member of the Continental Congress and as governor of Virginia. Randolph also was one of Aaron Burr's attorneys when Burr was tried for treason in 1807 (see **Burr, Aaron** [Tried for treason]). Robert A. Becker

Randolph, Edward (1632?-1703), was a British agent in colonial New England. In 1676, he carried royal instructions for the colonial governments to Boston. Curtly treated there, he returned to England and wrote two strongly critical reports. As a result, the British separated New Hampshire from Massachusetts.

Randolph took charge of customs for New England in 1679, and he started the new royal government of New Hampshire the next year. When Massachusetts resisted his authority, he had its charter annulled in 1684. In 1686, Massachusetts and New Hampshire became part of the newly formed Dominion of New England. Randolph served the royal governor of the dominion, Sir Edmund Andros, until 1689, when both were jailed during a rebellion in Boston. Randolph became surveyor general of customs for Britain in North America in 1691. He was born in Canterbury, England. John W. Ifkovic

Randolph, John (1773-1833), was a Virginia politician noted more for his colorful personality than for his achievements. He had a cruel, biting tongue, and was one of the most feared orators of his time. He is also known as John Randolph of Roanoke.

Randolph served a number of terms in the United States House of Representatives, where he became a champion of lost causes and opposed many popular measures. He led the Democratic-Republican Party in the House and supported President Thomas Jefferson's purchase of the Louisiana Territory in 1803. But later, he broke with the president over the intended purchase of Florida. Thereafter, Randolph was almost always in the opposition. He upheld states' rights against expanding federal powers. He opposed the War of 1812 and tariffs on imports. He led Southern opposition to the Missouri Compromise in 1820 and became a bitter enemy of Henry Clay, one of its chief supporters.

Randolph was born on June 2, 1773, in Prince George County, Virginia. He served in the U.S. House of Representatives from 1799 to 1813, 1815 to 1817, 1819 to 1825, and 1827 to 1829. He was a member of the U.S. Senate from 1825 to 1827. James C. Curtis

Randolph, Peyton (1721?-1775), was an American lawyer who served as president of both the First and the Second Continental Congresses in 1774 and 1775. Those two meetings of colonial leaders at first sought fair treatment from Britain for the American Colonies but eventually declared independence. Randolph himself held moderate political views. He persuaded extreme patriots and those with more cautious views to work together.

Culver
Peyton Randolph

Randolph was born in Williamsburg into one of Virginia's most respected families. He graduated from the College of William and Mary and then studied law at the Inns of Court in London. In 1748, Randolph became attorney general of Virginia. That year, he won election to the House of Burgesses, Virginia's legislature. In 1766, he became speaker of the House.

The British governor of Virginia dissolved the House of Burgesses in 1774. Its members then met in a series of revolutionary conventions. Randolph was elected to preside over the conventions in 1774 and 1775. He headed Virginia's delegates to the First and Second Continental Congresses. He was elected as the first president of both meetings. He died in October 1775, five months after the Second Continental Congress began.

James Kirby Martin

See also **Continental Congress.**

Range is an appliance that provides heat for cooking. A range has a cooktop with several heating areas, and one or two ovens. Ranges are sometimes referred to as *cookers* or *stoves,* though the word *stove* properly means an apparatus used for heating. In the United Kingdom and some other countries, the cooktop is called the *hob.* There are two chief kinds of ranges: (1) electric ranges and (2) gas ranges. For information about microwave ovens, see the article on **Microwave oven.**

Electric ranges have *heating units,* in which an electric current generates heat. Most electric ranges have four circular heating units on the cooktop and one or

WORLD BOOK photo by Dan Miller

Amana Refrigeration, Inc.

Ranges cook with gas or electric power. The gas range in which the woman is baking cookies has burners on the cooktop and in the oven beneath it. The electric range shown here has four heating units covered by a smooth ceramic cooking surface.

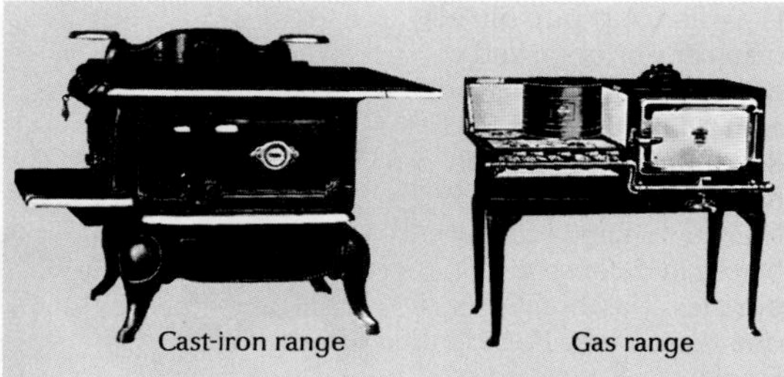

Chambers Corporation, Crown Stove Works

Ranges of the past. A cast-iron range of the late 1800's, *left,* could burn coal, coke, or wood. A 1925 gas range, *right,* had an oven next to the cooktop rather than below it.

more units in each oven. In some ranges, a smooth ceramic surface covers the cooktop units.

Most heating units have an outer surface that consists of a metal tube in two parts. Each part has a spiral shape and encloses a coil of wire. Electric current passes through the coil and heats the coil and the metal tube. An insulating material prevents electric current in the coil from reaching the surface of the tube.

A *magnetic induction cooktop* works only with pans made of magnetic materials, such as iron and steel. The cooktop passes alternating current through metal coils to create an area of magnetic force called a *magnetic field.* The magnetic field creates a current in the pan, heating the pan—and so the food—but not the cooktop.

The amount of heat produced by a heating unit can be regulated easily. Some cooktop units have controls that regulate which one of two possible voltages of electric current is supplied to the coil. The coil becomes hotter at the higher voltage. Controls may also regulate whether both of the coils heat up or whether only one heats up. Another kind of cooktop unit control turns the current on and off at intervals that vary with the heat desired. The longer the current flows through the unit, the higher the heat. Some cooktop units and most oven units are regulated by thermostats (see **Thermostat**).

Some modern ovens are *convection,* or *hot-air, ovens.* In such ovens, blowers circulate hot air around the food. Convection ovens cook faster, more evenly, and at a lower temperature than regular ovens.

Other modern ovens called *halogen ovens* heat food with *halogen lamps,* a type of light bulb that produces great light and heat. Still others use a combination of halogen heat and short radio waves called *microwaves.*

Gas ranges have *burners* on the cooktop and in each oven. A burner mixes air with natural gas, synthetic natural gas, or *LP-gas* (liquefied petroleum gas). The resulting mixture flows through small holes in the burner. The mixture is ignited by a spark produced by a built-in electric device or a *pilot light* near the burner. A pilot light is a small flame that burns continuously.

The heat produced by a burner depends mainly on the amount of gas flowing to it. A valve regulates the gas flow to each burner. Hand-operated valves control most cooktop burners. Thermostats operate the valves of most oven burners and some cooktop burners.

History. The first practical cooking stove was designed in the 1790's by Benjamin Thompson, Count Rumford, a British statesman and inventor. This stove, a boxlike brick structure, had holes in the top to hold pots. Before that time, many people used fireplaces for cooking as well as for heating.

During the 1830's, advances in ironmaking and transportation made cast iron widely available. As a result, iron cookstoves became popular. Most of these early stoves burned wood. In 1855, Robert W. Bunsen, a German chemist, invented the first practical gas burner. In the 1860's, ranges based on Bunsen's burner became popular in cities that had gas piped into homes for use in gaslights. People who lived in rural areas began to use gas ranges after 1910, when gas became available in pressurized containers.

Electric ranges were first sold in 1909. The early electric ranges cooked slowly, and few people bought them. After the modern cooking unit was developed in 1930, electric ranges became popular. Microwave ovens appeared in the mid-1950's. In the early 1980's, convection ovens began to gain popularity. Paul S. Baeder

See also **Baking; Cooking.**

Rangefinder is a device for measuring distances. The military uses rangefinders to determine the distance to a target.

The basis of a military rangefinder is a long tube with eyepieces at the center and an arrangement of lenses and prisms at each end. By adjusting the prisms, the operator can sight the target simultaneously from both ends of the tube. The difference in direction of the two lines of sight is called the *parallactic angle.* This angle will be large at short distances, and small at long distances. The parallactic angle is measured on a dial from which the range in yards can be read directly.

There are two principal types of rangefinders. The operator of a *coincidence* instrument looks through a single eyepiece and sees two distinct images of the target. By turning a knob, the operator can make these two images merge. When this happens, the distance can be read on the range dial. The operator of a *stereoscopic* instrument looks through a pair of eyepieces like binoculars and sees a single image of the target. In addition, the instrument's operator sees a marker that appears to be floating in space near the target. The operator moves a knob until the marker and the target appear to be at the same distance. Then the distance is read on the range dial.

Since World War I (1914-1918), rangefinders have been used in naval gunnery as a part of *director systems* that aim the guns automatically. During World War II (1939-1945), some armies adopted director systems for antiaircraft fire. But radar, which can measure ranges more accurately, largely replaced the rangefinder in World War II.

Since the early 1970's, the armies of many nations have equipped their tanks and other large weapons with *laser rangefinders.* These instruments measure the time needed for a light pulse to travel to and from a target. Laser rangefinders work during the day and at night. Some can measure the distance to a target up to 12 miles (20 kilometers) away. Frances M. Lussier

See also **Photography** (Cameras); **Radar.**

Rangel, *RANG guhl,* **Charles Bernard** (1930-), a New York Democrat, served as a member of the United States House of Representatives from 1971 to 2017. He helped found the Congressional Black Caucus, an organization of African American senators and representatives.

As a representative, Rangel worked to provide federal aid for the poor and for cities. He sponsored programs to redevelop neighborhoods and provide affordable housing. From 2007 to 2010, Rangel served as chairman of the Ways and Means Committee, which oversees government spending. In 2010, the House Ethics Committee resolved to *censure* (formally condemn) Rangel for ethics violations related to tax payments and the funding of trips Rangel took overseas.

Rangel was born on June 11, 1930, in the Harlem section of New York City. He served in the U.S. Army from 1948 to 1952, during which time he fought in the Korean War. He graduated from New York University in 1957 and from St. John's University School of Law in 1960. Rangel was an assistant United States attorney and a member of the New York State Assembly before his election to the U.S. House in 1970. Robert A. Pratt

Ranger, Forest. See **Forest Service; Forestry.**

Rangers are specialized United States Army infantry units. They undergo more intensive training than other infantry. The Rangers were organized in 1942, during World War II, under Colonel William O. Darby. The first regiment of 2,000 men was formed in the United Kingdom. It consisted of volunteers from the American Commando School. About 9 out of 10 of the first regiment died opening up enemy defenses before invasions.

A group called Rogers's Rangers fought with the British and American armies during the French and Indian wars of the 1750's. They developed stealthy, daredevil tactics, which have since been associated with the name *ranger.* Joel Slackman

See also **Commando; Rogers's Rangers.**

Rangers, Texas. See **Texas Rangers.**

Rangoon. See **Yangon.**

Ranjit Singh, *RUHN jiht sihng* (1780-1839), known as the *Lion of the Punjab,* was one of the most important figures in the history of modern India. He became the first Indian ruler to establish a Sikh kingdom (see **Sikhism**).

Ranjit was born on Nov. 13, 1780, in Gujranwala. He was the son of an important chief in the Punjab, a region in northwest India. His father died when he was 12. At first, Ranjit ruled only a small state. But he gradually conquered neighboring areas and resisted the control of the powerful Afghans.

Ranjit expanded to the north and west and made his state the largest in the Indus valley. He wanted to unite all Sikhs in a great nation, but he fell short of his goal. Soon after his death on June 27, 1839, the British took over the Punjab. Patricia Risso

Rank, Military, indicates a person's authority and standing. The terms *rank* and *grade* are usually synonymous, but officers are said to hold rank, and enlisted men and women to hold ratings or grades. Grade also refers to the authorized level of pay. These terms indicate rights, powers, and duties fixed by law. In the United States, Congress creates ranks and grades and regulates appointments and promotions.

Under the Constitution of the United States, the president holds the rank of *commander in chief* of the armed forces. A *commissioned* officer holds a commission granted by the president with the advice and consent of the Senate. A *warrant* officer, a specialist in a particular field, holds a warrant granted by the secretary of the Army, Navy, or Air Force. *Noncommissioned* officers are enlisted personnel who hold their grades based on skill and long service.

A person is appointed to, or commissioned in, a rank or grade. Among people who hold the same grade, length of service and date of appointment to the grade determine who ranks higher. One colonel outranks another if he or she has been in grade one day longer. If a group without a designated commander faces a situation that requires command decisions, the highest ranking person takes command. This person may later have to prove the right to command others.

Rank is a right granted to an officer by law. It cannot be withdrawn except through legal processes. An officer's rank is not a guarantee of the right to exercise command or hold employment, but it normally indicates that the officer will do so. The president or a military superior in the chain of command may relieve an officer of command.

During the 1800's, the Army used the honorary title *brevet* to recognize superior service by officers. The brevet, a temporary rank, gave an officer a rank higher than his regular one. Brevet rank sometimes allowed officers to command other officers of higher regular rank. During and after World War I (1914-1918) and World

Grades for United States armed services personnel

Commissioned officers

Grade	Air Force, Army, and Marine Corps	Navy
O-10	General	Admiral
O-9	Lieutenant general	Vice admiral
O-8	Major general	Rear admiral (upper half)
O-7	Brigadier general	Rear admiral (lower half)
O-6	Colonel	Captain
O-5	Lieutenant colonel	Commander
O-4	Major	Lieutenant commander
O-3	Captain	Lieutenant
O-2	First lieutenant	Lieutenant junior grade
O-1	Second lieutenant	Ensign

Warrant officers

Grade	Army, Marine Corps, and Navy
W-4	Chief (commissioned) warrant officer
W-3	Chief (commissioned) warrant officer
W-2	Chief (commissioned) warrant officer
W-1	Warrant officer

Enlisted personnel

Grade	Air Force	Army
E-9	Chief master sergeant	Sergeant major
E-8	Senior master sergeant	First sergeant; master sergeant
E-7	Master sergeant	Sergeant first class
E-6	Technical sergeant	Staff sergeant
E-5	Staff sergeant	Sergeant
E-4		Corporal; specialist
E-3	Airman first class	Private first class
E-2	Airman	Private 2
E-1	Airman basic	Private

Grade	Marine Corps	Navy
E-9	Sergeant major; master gunnery sergeant	Master chief petty officer
E-8	First sergeant; master sergeant	Senior chief petty officer
E-7	Gunnery sergeant	Chief petty officer
E-6	Staff sergeant	Petty officer first class
E-5	Sergeant	Petty officer second class
E-4	Corporal	Petty officer third class
E-3	Lance corporal	Seaman
E-2	Private first class	Seaman apprentice
E-1	Private	Seaman recruit

War II (1939-1945), army officers held both *temporary* and *permanent* ranks. The permanent rank was normally two or three grades lower than the temporary one.

Promotion to the next higher rank for officers is usually based on length of service in the grade they hold, satisfactory performance of their duties, and a vacancy in the next higher grade. Promotion boards consider officers for promotion. Boards usually consider officers within a certain *zone* (based on their time in grade), but outstanding officers below the zone may be promoted. A person "passed over" for promotion twice while in the zone may be discharged or retired. In wartime, promotions may be given "on the battlefield."

Enlisted men and women must spend some time in a grade before they can be considered for advancement. All the services use both written tests and performance evaluations to determine fitness for promotion.

Rank and pay. Officers and enlisted personnel are paid according to their rank and length of service. Increases are added to minimum basic pay after certain years of service are completed. These increases are called *longevity pay.* Most personnel begin to receive such pay after two years of service. Officers above the rank of major general or rear admiral receive a personal allowance. The armed services also grant *proficiency pay* to people with much needed skills. Allan R. Millett

Related articles in *World Book* include:

Air Force, U.S. (pictures)
Army, U.S. (pictures)
Commission, Military
General
Marine Corps, U.S. (pictures)
Mate
Navy, U.S. (pictures)

Ranke, *RAHNG kuh,* **Leopold von,** *LAY oh pohlt fuhn* (1795-1886), a German historian, persuaded historians to use critical methods and examine history scientifically. He introduced the seminar method of teaching. After 1840, his methods were largely used in teaching German historians. Ranke was born on Dec. 21, 1795, at Wiehe, in Thuringia. His first book, *History of the Romance and Teutonic Nations,* appeared in 1824. His other published works include a three-volume *History of the Popes* (1834-1836), and a nine-volume *World History* (1881-1888) that covers events up to the end of the 1400's. Ranke died on May 23, 1886. See also **History** (History in the universities). Joseph Martin Hernon, Jr.

Rankin, Jeannette (1880-1973), was the first woman to be elected to the United States Congress. A Republican, she served from 1917 to 1919 as congresswoman at large from Montana. In 1940, Rankin was elected to the House of Representatives for one term. She voted against U.S. participation in World War I (1914-1918) and was the only member of the House to vote against entering World War II in 1941. She also opposed U.S. involvement in the Korean War (1950-1953) and the Vietnam War (1957-1975).

Harris & Ewing

Jeannette Rankin

Rankin was born on June 11, 1880, near Missoula, Montana. A statue of her represents Montana in the United States Capitol in Washington, D.C. Rankin died on May 18, 1973. James S. Olson

Ransom, John Crowe (1888-1974), was an American poet, critic, and editor. In his writing, Ransom criticized what he considered a materialistic, spiritually barren society brought about by science and technology. He expressed nostalgia for the rural and feudalistic values he associated with the Old South.

Ransom's poems seem to be quiet and gentle, but they are toughened by his ironic wit, complexity of thought, and awareness of human frailty. Ransom helped lead the New Criticism movement, which emphasized close analysis of the language of a work rather than discussing its author or social significance.

Ransom was born on April 30, 1888, in Pulaski, Tennessee. While teaching at Vanderbilt University, he led a group of conservative Southern writers called the Fugitives. From 1937 to 1958, he taught at Kenyon College. There, he founded and edited the *Kenyon Review,* a literary magazine. Ransom died on July 14, 1974.

Steven Gould Axelrod

Ransome, Arthur (1884-1967), was a British author and journalist. Ransome became best known for his series of children's outdoor adventure novels. The first book, *Swallows and Amazons* (1931), is a classic story about a group of young people camping and sailing. Ransome wrote 11 other novels in the series, ending with *Great Northern?* (1947).

Ransome was born on Jan. 18, 1884, in Leeds, England. He became a free-lance writer of articles and stories at the age of 17. He went to Russia in 1913 and stayed as a correspondent for English newspapers until 1919. In addition to children's books, Ransome wrote books about Russia and fishing. He died on June 3, 1967. *The Autobiography of Arthur Ransome* was published in 1976.

Rap music is a form of popular music that is generally spoken or chanted at a fast pace rather than sung. Rap is performed over musical accompaniment that emphasizes rhythm rather than melody. Often, this accompaniment consists of short segments of previously recorded music combined in new patterns. Rap music often features clever rhymes, word play, and lyrics that are made up on the spot.

The term *rap* is frequently used to mean *hip-hop*, but the second term includes more than just music. Hip-hop is part of a modern urban lifestyle. The term is used to describe a culture with both visual and audio elements, such as clothing, rapping, disc jockeying, break dancing, language, and graffiti. Hip-hop music often is more melodic than pure rap.

The biggest inspiration for rap came from disc jockeys in Jamaica, who would *toast* (talk) over recorded music they played in clubs. The style, known as *dub*, produced popular records that featured disc jockeys talking over instrumental backgrounds and electronic effects. The disc jockey used records on two turntables, switching rapidly between them to mix and match beats. This style was introduced into clubs in New York City, New York, and became a part of the music more regularly heard in the clubs.

American rap music developed in the mid-1970's in New York City. It spread to other urban areas, primarily among African American teenagers. Rap grew in popularity in dance clubs in the late 1970's as disco music began to lose its following among dancers. Rap spread throughout the United States and much of the world.

As with rock music before it, the lyrics of rap and hip-hop music have often been controversial. Some critics see a recurring theme of violence toward women in the songs. The videos of rap and hip-hop artists also have been criticized for violence and strong sexual content.

The first rap hit was "Rapper's Delight" (1979) by the Sugar Hill Gang. "The Breaks" (1980) by Kurtis Blow helped spread rap among a wider audience. Much of early rap expressed a party spirit. But such performers as Public Enemy looked harder at social issues and were often angry and aggressive. A style known as *gangster rap* or *gangsta rap* emphasized gunplay and other outlaw aspects of urban life.

In some variations of rap and hip-hop, artists have returned to the reggae music of Jamaica for inspiration. Mainstream rock artists have tried to incorporate elements of rap into their music by inviting rappers to perform on their records. Popular rap performers have included Bad Bunny, the Beastie Boys, Cardi B, Chance the Rapper, Drake, Dr. Dre, Missy Elliott, Eminem, 50 Cent, Ice-T, Jay-Z, Lil Wayne, Lizzo, Megan Thee Stallion, Nicki Minaj, Queen Latifah, Run-D.M.C., Snoop Dogg, and Kanye West. William McKeen

Related articles in *World Book* include:

Eminem	Rock music (Rap)	Smith, Will
Hip-hop	Shakur, Tupac	West, Kanye
Jay-Z		

Rapanui. See Easter Island.

Rape is the crime of having sexual intercourse with a person against that person's will. It is an act of violence and domination. Women or men may be the victims, although most victims are female.

In most cases of rape, the victim knows the attacker. *Date rape* is the act of having forced sexual intercourse with another person while on a social date. *Marital rape* occurs when a married person forces his or her spouse to have sexual intercourse. *Statutory rape* refers to sexual intercourse with a person who is under the legal age of consent. The age of consent is the age at which the law considers a person fully responsible for his or her sexual actions. In most states of the United States, the legal age ranges from 14 to 18.

Rape is a widely misunderstood crime, and victims often are not believed. There are many myths about rape. The main ones are: (1) it is impossible to rape a resisting woman; (2) men often are falsely accused of rape; (3) some categories of forced sex (date rape or marital rape, for example) are not really rape; (4) boys and men cannot be raped; and (5) the answer "no" to sexual intercourse can mean "yes."

Some experts believe that rape is one of the most underreported crimes. Officials estimate that the actual number of rapes committed may be three or more times the number reported. Many rape victims do not report the crime to police because of shame or fear. Some victims dread the possible humiliation of media publicity or being asked embarrassing questions by the police or, later, in a courtroom.

In a rape trial, unlike other criminal trials, the victim becomes the focus of attention. The victim's life may be placed under intense examination. Defense lawyers routinely have tried to cast doubt on the victim's story by asking about the victim's past sex life or by trying to discredit the victim's character. This focus on the victim, as opposed to the crime and the criminal, increasingly is regarded as unacceptable. Since the 1970's, states across the United States have passed "rape shield" laws that severely restrict the evidence that can be introduced in court regarding the victim's sexual history.

In the United States, only about 2 percent of all people charged with rape are convicted and imprisoned. On average, convicted rapists serve only about half of their original sentence. The low conviction rate results from the difficulty of proving the crime. Some states require evidence from witness accounts or evidence of bodily injury to the victim.

During the 1970's, because of increased alarm about the number of incidents of rape, local communities and feminist groups created crisis centers to offer counseling to rape victims. These centers encourage women to report the crime to the police. Other groups also offer instruction on rape prevention and provide support to victims who prosecute their attackers.

Beginning in the early 2010's, the prevalence of sexual violence in the U.S. military and on U.S. college campuses became an issue of national concern. Previously, sexual assault in the military was not treated as a criminal offense. Victims who reported such incidents faced such retaliation as harassment, ridicule, and demotion. In late 2013, President Barack Obama gave the U.S. Department of Defense one year to show progress in eliminating sexual assaults in the military. In December 2014, the department reported improvement in its handling of sex crimes, prompting more victims to come forward. The department said there was an 8 percent increase in the number of reported rape cases over the past year and the number of sexual assaults had declined to 19,000 annually from 26,000 in 2012.

Also in 2014, the White House Council on Women and Girls issued a report on sexual violence on college campuses. The report said one in five college students are victims of sexual assault, but that only 12 percent reported the crime. In January 2014, President Obama stepped up pressure on colleges and universities to prevent or improve their response to campus rape and sexual assaults. Obama announced a task force to coordinate federal enforcement efforts aimed at preventing such attacks. In May, the U.S. Department of Education released the names of at least 55 colleges and universities that were under investigation for their handling of sexual violence and sexual harassment complaints. In September, the Obama administration launched a public awareness campaign aimed at ending sexual violence on college campuses. The initiative, called "It's on us," urged college men to join the fight against sexual assault. Joanna Bourke

Rape is a flowering herb of the mustard family. Rape plants are grown commercially in Asia, Canada, Europe, New Zealand, and the United States. Some varieties of rape are called *rutabagas* in the United States and *swedes* in Europe. The plants have an edible turniplike root. Farmers grow other varieties of rape as pasture crops. Varieties called *rapeseed* are grown for their oilbearing seeds, which are processed into livestock feed, vegetable oil, and industrial lubricants.

WORLD BOOK illustration by John D. Dawson

The rape plant

Canola is a variety of rapeseed from which canola oil is obtained. Food-processing companies use canola oil to make cooking oil and such products as margarine and salad dressings. Canola oil is popular because it is lowest in *saturated fat* among vegetable oils. Saturated fats seem to increase the amount of *cholesterol* in blood and thus may contribute to heart disease (see **Cholesterol**).

The rape plant grows from about 2 to 6 feet (61 to 183 centimeters) tall. It has slender, branched stems with bluish-green leaves. It bears pale yellow flowers about ½ inch (1.3 centimeters) long.

Some varieties of the plant live only one year. Others live for two years. Richard C. Keating

Scientific classification. All varieties of rape plants belong to either of two species, *Brassica napus* and *B. campestris.*

See also **Canola oil.**

Raphael, *RA fih uhl* or *RAY fee uhl* (1483-1520), was one of the greatest and most influential painters of the Italian Renaissance. His graceful figures and skillful compositions influenced artists up to the early 1900's. The period of his activity is called the *High Renaissance.*

Raphael painted altarpieces, *frescoes* (paintings on damp plaster) of historical and mythological scenes, and portraits. His most popular works include his gentle paintings of the Madonna and Child. Raphael was also an architect. From 1514 until his death, he directed the construction of St. Peter's Basilica in Rome.

His life. Raphael was born on March 28 or April 6, 1483, in Urbino. His real name was Raffaello Sanzio. His father served as court painter to the Duke of Urbino. About 1494, Raphael went to Perugia to study with Perugino, an important painter. Perugino introduced Raphael

Oil painting on wood panel (1504); Brera Gallery, Milan (SCALA)

Raphael's *Marriage of the Virgin* is one of his earliest masterpieces. This painting is particularly noteworthy for its graceful figures and expert use of perspective.

Fresco (1510-1511); The Vatican, Rome (The Art Archive)

Raphael's *School of Athens* shows a gathering of ancient Greek philosophers and scientists in a Roman architectural setting. Standing in the center are Plato, *left,* and Aristotle, *right.* The harmony and balance of the composition are typical of the historical period called the High Renaissance.

to the latest ideas in Italian art and greatly influenced his student's style.

Raphael settled in Florence in 1504. In Florence, Raphael studied the paintings of the great Italian artist Leonardo da Vinci. Leonardo da Vinci's balanced compositions and idealized figures had a strong influence on all Renaissance painters, including Raphael.

Late in 1508, Pope Julius II asked Raphael to work for him in Rome. Julius wanted to rebuild and redecorate Rome to reflect its ancient glory. The pope gathered the most illustrious architects, painters, and sculptors from all parts of Italy. Raphael created his finest work while in the service of Julius and his successor, Pope Leo X. With the assistance of a large workshop, Raphael produced religious paintings, tapestry designs, palace decorations, and portraits. Raphael remained in Rome until he died on April 6, 1520, after a short illness.

His works. A masterpiece of Raphael's early career is the *Marriage of the Virgin* (1504), reproduced on the previous page. It shows the influence of Perugino's sentimental style. However, Raphael's own style can be seen in the dignified figures and the emphasis on perspective. The painting shows a gentle Virgin Mary receiving a ring from an ideally handsome Joseph.

Perhaps Raphael's greatest achievement was the series of frescoes that decorate the pope's private quarters in the Vatican. Raphael painted several of these frescoes in a room called the Stanza della Segnatura. Each wall in the room has an arch to support the curved ceiling. Raphael brilliantly incorporated this architectural feature into his compositions.

Raphael's *School of Athens,* shown above, covers one wall of the Stanza and captures the classical spirit of the High Renaissance. Three painted arches serve as a background for the ancient Greek philosophers and scientists in the front of the scene. In the center of the painting, beneath the arches, stand Plato and Aristotle, the leading philosophers. These powerful and expressive figures were influenced by Michelangelo's paintings on the Sistine Chapel ceiling. But Raphael harmonized and clarified the arrangement of figures in space, achieving the perfect balance for which he is noted.

In his final works, such as *The Transfiguration* in the Vatican, Raphael began to move toward a style of greater emotion and movement that would characterize the next generation of Italian artists.

For other examples of Raphael's works, see the pictures with the articles on **Madonna and Child; Painting; Plato;** and **Renaissance.** Eric M. Zafran

Rapid City (pop. 67,956; met. area pop. 134,598) is the second largest city in South Dakota. Only Sioux Falls has more people. Rapid City is a center of education, health care, tourism, and trade for western South Dakota. It lies just east of the scenic Black Hills, about 25 miles (40 kilometers) from Mount Rushmore National Memorial. For location, see **South Dakota** (political map).

The city's chief industries make cement, computer parts, jewelry, meat products, and particleboard. The city also has a number of customer-service call centers. The South Dakota School of Mines and Technology is in Rapid City. Ellsworth Air Force Base lies nearby.

Sioux Indians lived in the Black Hills before white settlers arrived there. Prospectors founded Rapid City in 1876, during the Black Hills gold rush. They named it after Rapid Creek, which flows through the city.

In 1972, Rapid Creek overflowed. The flood killed 238 people and caused about $165 million in damage. The city then created a *floodway*—a path for drainage of excess water—by clearing land on both sides of the creek. The floodway, 8 miles (13 kilometers) long, involved removal of about 240 businesses and 800 homes. Other projects of the 1970's included a civic center and the Rushmore Mall. The Journey Museum opened in 1997. Its exhibits focus on the history of the Black Hills. Rapid City has a mayor-council government. Ronald Bender

Rappahannock River, *RAP uh HAN uhk,* is a Virginia river. Much fighting in the American Civil War (1861-1865) occurred along this river. It flows from the Blue Ridge Mountains southeast for 185 miles (298 kilometers) into Chesapeake Bay (see **Virginia** [physical map]). The Rapidan River is its main branch. Michael P. O'Neill

Rare earth is a term once used for a series of chemical elements now commonly known as the *lanthanides.* These elements are lanthanum, cerium, dysprosium, erbium, europium, gadolinium, holmium, lutetium, neodymium, praseodymium, promethium, samarium, terbium, thulium, and ytterbium. Scientists called them "rare earth" in part because they were assumed to be present in Earth's crust in only tiny amounts. Later, scientists found some of them to be relatively abundant. For example, many of the rare earths are thousands of times more abundant in Earth's crust than gold. For more information, see **Lanthanide.** David W. Ball

Ras Tafari. See **Haile Selassie I; Rastafarians.**

Raschka, Chris (1959-), is an American illustrator and author of children's books. He won the 2006 Caldecott Medal for his illustrations for *The Hello, Goodbye Window* (2005), written by Norton Juster, an American architect and author. Raschka also won the 2012 Caldecott Medal as illustrator and author of *A Ball for Daisy* (2011). The Caldecott Medal is awarded annually to the best picture book by an American. *The Hello, Goodbye Window* describes a little girl's visit to her grandparents and the magical things she sees through their kitchen window. Raschka decorated the warm-hearted story with richly colored illustrations that suggest lively pictures a child would draw. *A Ball for Daisy* is a wordless story about a dog who loses a red ball, her favorite toy.

Raschka has been praised for his daring subject matter. His first book as an author and illustrator was *R and R: A Story About Two Alphabets* (1990). It deals with tolerance and cultural differences. *Yo! Yes?* (1993) portrays a potential racial confrontation that ends in friendship. *Elizabeth Imagined an Iceberg* (1994) tells how a child copes with a frightening stranger. *The Purple Balloon* (2007) introduces children to the difficult topic of death.

The Hello, Goodbye Window by Norton Juster. Text copyright © 2005 Norton Juster. Pictures copyright © 2005 Chris Raschka. Published by Hyperion Books for Children.

Chris Raschka's richly colored illustrations for *The Hello, Goodbye Window* won the 2006 Caldecott Medal.

Raschka also wrote *Everyone Can Learn to Ride a Bicycle* (2013), *The Cosmobiography of Sun Ra* and *Give and Take* (both 2014), *The Doorman's Repose* (2017), *Side by Side: A Celebration of Dads* and *Mother Goose of Pudding Lane* (both 2019), and *In the City* (2020).

In 2000, Raschka published a series of eight picture books called "Thingy Things." They included *Whaley Whale, Moosey Moose, Sluggy Slug,* and *Wormy Worm.* In 2014, Raschka added several more titles to the series. He has also illustrated books by other authors.

Christopher Raschka was born on March 6, 1959, in Huntingdon, Pennsylvania. He received a B.A. degree from St. Olaf College in 1981. Dan Zeff

Rashi, *RAH shee* (1040-1105), was a French Jewish scholar whose commentaries on the Bible and the Talmud are among the most influential in Judaism. The Talmud is a collection of Jewish religious and civil laws.

Rashi's commentaries are known for their clarity and brevity. He provided meanings for difficult words and phrases and also explored the inner meanings of the texts, such as their ethical and mystical elements.

Rashi's commentaries remain a cornerstone of Jewish study. They have themselves been the subject of hundreds of commentaries, many of which were written by French and German scholars from the 1100's through the 1300's. These scholars were called *tosafists,* from the Hebrew word *tosafot,* meaning *addition* or *supplement.*

Rashi was born as Shlomo Yitzhaqi (Solomon, son of Isaac) in Troyes, France, in 1040. The name Rashi comes from the Hebrew acronym for Rabbi Shlomo Yitzhaqi. Little is known of his early years. After studying in Troyes, Rashi became a traveling scholar, studying and teaching in Worms, Germany, for several years. He eventually returned to Troyes, where he established a religious academy. Rashi also wrote hymns and *responsa,* which are responses to religious questions submitted to him by individuals or Jewish communities. In 1475, Rashi's commentary on the Pentateuch (the first five books of the Bible) became the first Hebrew book to be printed. Rashi died on July 13, 1105. Yaakov Elman

Raskin, Ellen (1928-1984), was an American author and illustrator. She won the 1979 Newbery Medal for her children's novel *The Westing Game* (1978), a mystery about 16 people who compete for a millionaire's fortune by trying to solve a puzzle in his will. Raskin wrote and illustrated many other children's books. She was born on March 13, 1928, in Milwaukee and died on Aug. 8, 1984. Virginia L. Wolf

Raspberry is a thorny bush that grows small, round, tasty fruit. Each fruit, called a *berry,* consists of a cluster of cells called *drupelets* that look like tiny beads. Drupelets are partly hard and partly fleshy and grow around a core called a *receptacle.* The receptacle stays on the bush after the fruit is picked. Most commercially grown raspberries are red, but some are purple, black, white, or yellow. Raspberries are eaten fresh or used to make jams and jellies. Frozen raspberries are also popular.

Raspberries grow best in cool regions of North America and Europe. The countries of eastern Europe produce more than three-fourths of the world's raspberries. In the United States, the leading raspberry-growing states are Oregon and Washington. In Canada, British Columbia ranks first in production.

Growing raspberries. Growers begin new red raspberry bushes from raspberry *suckers* obtained from healthy plants. Suckers are underground shoots that grow from the plants' roots. The suckers are raised in a nursery for one growing season and then transplanted outdoors. In the first growing season after transplanting, they produce only *canes* (stems) and branches. Fruit and flowers develop the next year. Growers produce new black and purple raspberries by bending the plants' tips and covering them with soil. The tips develop roots, which are transplanted the next season. They produce fruit the second growing season after transplanting. Most raspberry plants produce fruit for about six years. The bushes thrive in deep, fertile, well-drained soil.

Various *training systems* are used to grow raspberries. These systems ensure the proper development of the raspberry plants and allow growers to care for them easily. The three most common systems are the *hedgerow, staked hill,* and *trellis* systems. In the hedgerow system, raspberry bushes are planted in rows that are about 3 feet (0.9 meter) apart. Growers using the staked hill system plant the bushes in mounds about 6 feet (1.8 meters) apart. In the trellis system, plants grow on three to five wires attached to stakes. Raspberries are harvested by machine, or they are picked by hand.

WORLD BOOK illustration by Kate Lloyd-Jones, Linden Artists Ltd.

Raspberries are tasty fruits that grow on thorny bushes. Each berry consists of a cluster of tiny, beadlike *drupelets.* Most raspberries are red, but some are purple or black.

Diseases and pests. Raspberries are attacked by a number of diseases, including mosaic disease and other virus diseases, as well as the fungus diseases anthracnose and orange rust (see **Fungal disease; Mosaic disease**). Growers control these diseases by spraying the bushes with fungicides and by clearing patches of dead wood away from the plants. They also destroy the canes after the fruit has been harvested.

Raspberry plants are also attacked by such insects as the crown borer, the cane borer, the raspberry sawfly, and the rose chafer. Growers guard against these pests by spraying the bushes with insecticides. Paul Eck

Scientific classification. The raspberry belongs to the rose family, Rosaceae. The American red raspberry is *Rubus strigosus.* The European red raspberry is *R. icaeus.* The purple raspberry is *R. neglectus,* and the black raspberry is *R. occidentalis.*

Raspe, Rudolph Erich. See **Munchausen, Baron.**

Rasputin, Grigori Efimovich, *rah SPOO tihn, grih GAW rih ih FEE muh vihch* (1871?-1916), was a Siberian peasant, healer, and holy man. He served as an adviser to the last Russian czar, Nicholas II, and may have contributed to the czar's downfall.

Rasputin impressed Russia's church and society leaders with his rural wisdom and religious teachings. In 1905, he met Nicholas and his wife, Czarina Alexandra. Rasputin was able to stop the bleedings of their son, Alexis, who had *hemophilia* (a disease in which blood does not clot normally). Rasputin's standing with the royal couple gave him influence over appointments to church and state offices. Businessmen bribed Rasputin to gain government contracts and favors.

Culver

Grigori Rasputin

During World War I (1914-1918), the widespread resentment of Rasputin's influence over government appointments deepened. Some opponents accused him of being a German spy. A group of supporters of Czar Nicholas feared that the resentment of Rasputin would lead to the czar's overthrow. According to a confession, over the night of Dec. 29-30, 1916 (Dec. 16-17 on the Russian calendar then in use), the group poisoned and shot Rasputin and threw his body into the Neva River. There was no full investigation into his death, and rumors about its circumstances have persisted. The Russian Revolution broke out less than three months later, and Nicholas was deposed.

Rasputin was born in Pokrovskoye, near Tyumen. His date of birth is believed to be Jan. 22, 1871 (Jan. 10 on the old Russian calendar). Andrew Barnes

Rastafarians are members of a religious and political movement that began in Jamaica in the late 1920's. They are perhaps best known as the originators of a musical style called *reggae;* for their use of marijuana (which they call *ganja);* and for wearing their hair in long, rope-like braids called *dreadlocks.*

The name *Rastafarian* comes from *Ras Tafari,* a title held by Emperor Haile Selassie I of Ethiopia from 1916 to 1974. Ethiopia is a country in northeastern Africa. Many early Rastafarians believed Haile Selassie was a god. However, Haile Selassie did not consider himself a god, and when he visited Jamaica in 1966, he was puzzled by Rastafarians who tried to worship him.

Today, Rastafarianism is a worldwide movement. Members live not only in Jamaica but also in the United States, Canada, Australia, New Zealand, South Africa, and many European countries. Although Rastafarians today belong to many races and nationalities, the religion began as a black nationalist movement.

Early Rastafarians taught that all Africans are descendants of the ancient Hebrews. According to this teaching, God made many black Africans the slaves of whites as punishment for disobedience. The Rastafarians believed Haile Selassie would arrange for all people of African descent to return to Africa. After Haile Selassie's death in 1975, Rastafarians changed some of their beliefs. Today, many look forward to a return to African spirituality rather than to actually living in Africa. Stephen D. Glazier

See also **Haile Selassie I; Jamaica** (People); **Reggae.**

Rat is a furry mammal that looks like a mouse but is larger. The smallest kinds of rats grow longer and weigh more than the largest mice. Rats, like mice, beavers, and squirrels, are *rodents.* All such animals have chisellike front teeth especially suited for gnawing.

There are about 120 kinds of rats, of which the best known are the *black rat* and the *brown rat.* Both of these species live in all parts of the world. Most other kinds of rats live in areas not inhabited by people.

Black rats and brown rats rank among the most serious animal threats to people. They carry the germs of several diseases, including plague, food poisoning, and typhus. Rats also damage or destroy crops and other food products, and they kill poultry, lambs, and baby pigs. On the other hand, scientists use rats in research projects that have benefited people.

The word *rat* is often used for any long-tailed rodent that is larger than a mouse. But most of these animals are not true rats. They include the *cotton rat,* the *rice rat,* the *kangaroo rat,* and the *woodrat.*

The body of a rat. All species of rats have a slender, scaly tail and long, sharp claws. But black rats and brown rats differ in several ways besides color.

Black rats grow 7 or 8 inches (18 or 20 centimeters) long, not including their tail, and weigh about 10 ounces (280 grams). The tail is longer than the rest of the body. These rats have large ears, a pointed snout, and soft fur. A black rat's fur may be black, grayish-brown, or smoky-gray. Gray, white, or yellow fur covers the animal's underside. Black rats are also called *roof rats* or *ship rats.*

Brown rats measure from 8 to 10 inches (20 to 25 centimeters) long, not including their tail, and weigh up to 16 ounces (485 grams). The tail is shorter than the rest of the body. Brown rats have small ears, a blunt snout, and coarse fur. They vary in color from brownish-gray to reddish-gray. Other names for the brown rat include *barn rat, gray rat, house rat, Norway rat,* and *sewer rat.*

The life of a rat. Black rats and brown rats originally lived in Asia. They reached Europe by ship or overland. From Europe, they spread to North and South America on ships. More brown rats than black rats live in North America. Some black rats live near coastal seaports in the northern United States, but most dwell in the Gulf states, such as Louisiana and Texas. Brown rats live throughout the United States.

Both black and brown rats live in large groups, with certain rats *dominating* (having control over) others. Most members of both species build a nest in or near buildings. Black rats live in the upper stories of buildings or in trees. Brown rats are found under floors, within walls, in piles of garbage, or in the ground. If the two species live in the same building, black rats usually occupy the upper levels, and brown rats dwell on the ground level. Rats are cautious creatures and generally avoid anything unfamiliar in their environment. They

John Markham, Bruce Coleman Inc.

Rats are small, furry mammals that have plagued human beings for centuries. The black rat, *shown here,* causes disease and widespread property damage in the seaports of North America.

The skeleton of a rat

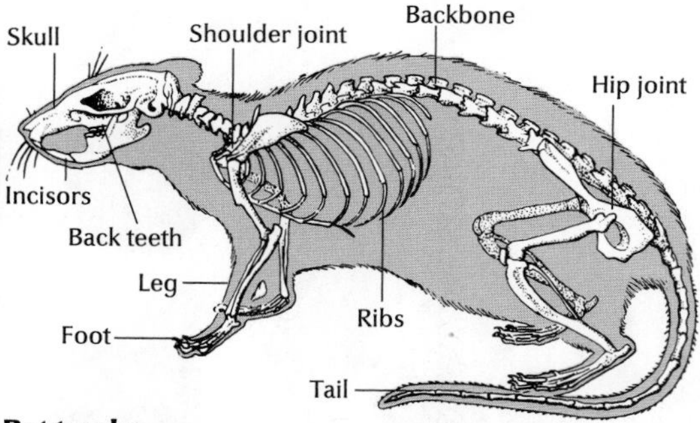

Rat tracks

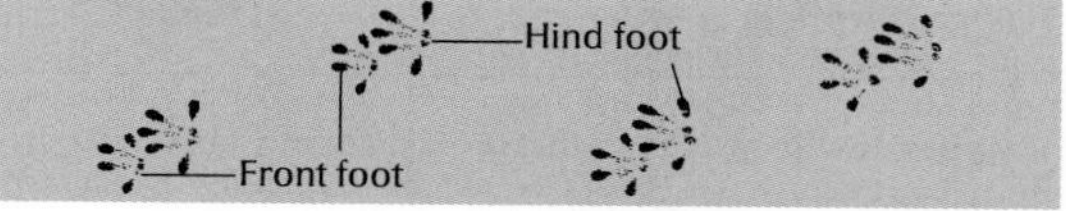

WORLD BOOK illustration by Marion Pahl

have a keen sense of smell and can quickly detect approaching danger.

Both black and brown rats eat almost any kind of plant or animal—even other rats of the same or a different species. The brown rat is fierce and aggressive, compared with the milder black rat. Rats feed mostly at night, and sometimes they band together and attack such animals as chickens and pigs. Most rats live within an area that may be no more than 150 feet (46 meters) in diameter. But if a food shortage occurs, rats may travel long distances in search of food.

Most black and brown rats mate the year around, and the females give birth to three to six litters annually. A female rat carries her young in her body for about three weeks before they are born. Most black rat litters consist of six or seven *pups* (young). Most brown rat litters have eight or nine pups. Newborn rats are blind and deaf. They remain in the nest for about three weeks.

Few rats live more than a year in their natural surroundings because they have so many enemies. Animals that prey on rats include cats, dogs, hawks, owls, snakes, and weasels. In captivity, some rats live more than three years.

Rats and people. Rats thrive in farm and city environments, where they cause damage totaling billions of dollars a year. Both black and brown rats destroy eggs, fruits, stored grain, vegetables, and other foods and attack various farm animals. Rats also cause considerable additional damage by gnawing on such objects as furniture and lead pipes. They sometimes cause fires by chewing the insulation off electric wires. In addition to spreading disease, rats sometimes attack human beings, including babies in cribs. Their bite may cause a disease called ratbite fever.

Some people fight rats by destroying the food sources or homes of the animals. Others kill rats by poisoning, shooting, or trapping them. Rat poisons must be used carefully to prevent accidental poisoning of human beings or of other animals.

Rats may also be controlled by placing specially treated food in areas where they live. Such food contains chemicals called *antifertility drugs.* These drugs make the rats incapable of reproducing.

Domesticated varieties of brown rats, especially the *white rat,* play an important role in many research projects. Researchers use white rats to study disease, drug effects, heredity, nutrition, and learning and other aspects of behavior. They also use rats in the preparation and testing of new drugs. Many zoos maintain colonies of rats as food for snakes and other animals. Some people keep domesticated rats as pets. Clark E. Adams

Scientific classification. Rats belong to the family, Muridae. Black rats are *Rattus rattus.* Brown rats are *R. norvegicus.*

See also **Kangaroo rat; Mole-rat; Mouse; Rodent; Woodrat.**

Additional resources

Hodgson, Barbara. *The Rat.* Ten Speed, 1997.
Marrin, Albert. *Oh, Rats! The Story of Rats and People.* Dutton, 2006. Younger readers.
Sullivan, Robert. *Rats: Observations on the History and Habitat of the City's Most Unwanted Inhabitants.* Bloomsbury Pub., 2004.

Ratchet, *RACH iht,* is a wheel or bar that can move in only one direction. It often consists of a notched wheel and a *pawl* (metal bar hung from a pivot). The pawl is attached to a lever. As the lever is moved, the free end of the pawl locks into a tooth of the wheel, causing the wheel to rotate. A second pawl may be used to prevent the wheel from turning backward while the lever is being returned to begin another stroke.

A mechanical counter is a simple device that uses the ratchet-and-pawl combination. A ratchet-and-pawl mechanism locks a machine, such as a hoisting winch, so that it does not slip. Alva H. Jared

Rate of exchange. See **Exchange rate.**

Ratel, *RAY tuhl,* is a badgerlike animal that lives in Saudi Arabia, India, Nepal, and much of Africa. The ratel is also called the *honey badger* because it often feeds on honey. The ratel is about 2 ½ feet (76 centimeters) long. It has white or dark gray fur on its upper body and black fur on its underside. Ratels have long claws; thick, loose skin that provides protection from stings or bites; and special glands that give off a foul-smelling liquid that helps to discourage the animals' enemies.

Mark N. Brultan, Photo Researchers

The ratel, unlike most fur-bearing mammals, is light on top and dark below, reversing the usual coloration.

Ratels live in holes in the ground, among rocks, or in hollow logs, stumps, or trees. They may travel alone or in pairs. Ratels feed chiefly on honey, insects, small mammals, lizards, and both poisonous and nonpoisonous snakes. They also eat plants, roots, and fruit. The ratel often looks for honey with the assistance of a bird called the *honey guide.* The honey guide's call leads the ratel to a beehive. The ratel then uses its claws to break open the hive, and both animals feed. Gary A. Heidt

Scientific classification. The ratel belongs to the weasel family, Mustelidae. It is classified as *Mellivora capensis.*

Rating, in television. See **Television** (The national networks).

Ratio, *RAY shee oh* or *RAY shoh,* is an ordered pair or set that represents a relationship between numbers or quantities. The numbers in a ratio are called the *terms* of the ratio.

The ratio of two numbers or quantities represented by the letters *a* and *b* may be written as *a:b, (a,b), a/b,* or $\frac{a}{b}$. All fractions and percentages are ratios. The expression "40 percent" may be restated as $\frac{40}{100}$ or 40:100. Two ratios are equal when each term of one ratio can be multiplied by a certain number to produce the terms of the other ratio. The expressions 2:3, 4:6, and 6:9 represent equal ratios. Two equal ratios make up a *proportion* (see **Proportion**).

Ratios may be used to describe a variety of relationships. For example, a ratio may express the relationship between the amounts of two ingredients in a liquid mixture. If a mixture contains 5 gallons of syrup and 15 gallons of water, the relationship, or ratio, of syrup to water is 5:15 or 1:3. A ratio may also indicate the rate at which something occurs, such as the use of gasoline by an automobile. The rate of gasoline use for an automobile that travels 30 miles on a gallon of gas is expressed by the ratio 30:1. Such a ratio may also be stated as "30 miles per gallon." A ratio may also describe the probability of the occurrence of an event. For example, the probability of drawing an ace from a well-shuffled deck of cards is described by the ratio 4:52 or 1:13. The terms of this ratio are derived from the number of aces (4) and the total number of cards (52) in the deck.

Ratio ranks as one of the most widely used mathematical concepts. It plays an important role in the physical sciences, the social sciences, and the arts. In physics, for example, ratio provides a basis for the concepts of speed and acceleration. Thomas E. Kieren

See also **Fraction; Percentage; Trigonometry.**

Rational number, *RASH uh nuhl,* is any number that can be expressed in the form a/b, where *a* is any integer and *b* is any integer except zero. Integers are whole numbers greater than, less than, or equal to zero. Rational numbers include such positive numbers as $3/4$ and $2/3$ and such negative numbers as $-1/3$ and $-5/2$.

Integers are rational numbers because they can be expressed as fractions (a/b). For example, the integers 3 and -5 can be written as the fractions $3/1$ and $-5/1$. *Terminating decimals* and *repeating decimals* are also rational numbers. Terminating decimals are decimals that have a limited number of digits. For instance, .75 is a terminating decimal. When expressed in the form a/b, .75 becomes $3/4$. Repeating decimals repeat the same digit or a series of digits. In the repeating decimal $.\overline{6}$, the digit 6 repeats indefinitely. When expressed in the form a/b, $.\overline{6}$ becomes the fraction $2/3$.

Numbers that cannot be expressed as a/b are called *irrational numbers. Pi* (π), for example, can be written as a decimal with an approximate value of 3.14159. However, the decimal continues indefinitely, does not repeat, and cannot be converted into a fraction. Pi is therefore an irrational number. Thomas E. Kieren

Rationalism, *RASH uh nuh LIHZ uhm,* is an outlook that emphasizes human reason and its ability to answer basic questions and to lead people to happiness and well-being. *Philosophical rationalism,* in the 1600's, stressed the power of reason as opposed to sense experience. René Descartes, Gottfried Leibniz, and Baruch Spinoza developed philosophical systems based on the idea that, through reason, people have direct access to the nature of reality. *Cultural rationalism,* in the 1700's, relied on reason rather than on faith in creating a theory of human beings and their destiny. Voltaire and Thomas Paine were prominent figures in this movement. See also **Enlightenment; Philosophy** (Modern philosophy).

Steven Nadler

Rationing, *RASH uh nihng* or *RAY shuh nihng,* is a system used by a government to distribute scarce products among the people of a country. Rationing is generally used only during a war or some other emergency. During a war, for example, people usually earn more money and so want to buy more products than they did before. But the armed forces need many of these products. Thus, manufacturers cannot produce enough of the products to satisfy the people's demand.

When people want to buy more products than manufacturers can supply, *inflation,* a period of rising prices, usually results. A government can try to fight inflation by using a system of *price controls* to limit the amount of money that manufacturers can charge for their products. Through rationing, the government also tries to assure a fair distribution of the scarce products to all the people.

The two most common types of rationing are *specific rationing* and *point rationing.* Specific rationing uses a coupon for each type of rationed product. The government gives each household a certain number of coupons for the rationed goods. A person must submit the correct coupon and the cash value of each rationed item being purchased. Specific rationing generally is used to control the sale of scarce products that vary little in value and quality, such as gasoline and sugar. To use this rationing system for such goods as meat and clothing, which differ greatly in value and quality, there would have to be coupons for every variety of the products. For such products, the government uses point rationing, giving each rationed item a point value. The government also gives each individual or family a certain number of points to use when buying products with point values.

The stages involved in creating an effective ration program may be difficult to carry out. A large government organization must be set up to decide which products will be rationed and what price controls will be put into effect. Also, laws must be established and enforced to prohibit *black marketing,* the selling of rationed products without proper coupons or points. Black markets operate because people want to buy larger amounts of certain products than the government allows and are willing to pay a high price for the products.

In World War II (1939-1945), the United States and other countries involved in the war rationed a wide variety of products, including automobiles, coffee, sugar, and tires. Today, periods of rationing are common for certain items in short supply in a number of developing nations, including India and Sri Lanka. Gary Jay Dorman

See also **Black market; Price control; World War II** (On the home front).

Rattan, *ra TAN,* is a tough, stringy material. It comes from the reedy stems of different kinds of palms that grow in Africa and southeast Asia. These trees belong to the genus of palms known as *Calamus.* The stems of rattan palms may grow to lengths of more than 500 feet (150 meters). The plants climb over other trees by means of hooks on the stems.

People who live in the countries where these palms grow use the stem to make ropes and mats. American and European countries import the stems. Manufacturers use them to make umbrella handles, walking sticks, furniture, baskets, ship cables, and chair bottoms. Rattan is strong, bends easily, and lasts long. The finest grades of rattan come from the island of Borneo. Other good rattans grow in Malaysia, Myanmar, Sri Lanka, and Sumatra.

Workers prepare the stems for shipment by cutting them into lengths of 5 to 20 feet (1.5 to 6 meters). They remove the leaves and outer covering by pulling the stems through a notch in a tree or board. Some rattan palms have a fruit that can be eaten. The young shoots of others are eaten like vegetables. David S. Seigler

See also **Basket making.**

Rattlesnake is any of a group of snakes with a rattle on the end of the tail. Rattlesnakes have a poisonous substance called *venom,* which they use to kill prey and defend themselves against enemies. They use their rattle to warn enemies to stay away. Sometimes the snakes give no warning sound with the rattle before they bite.

Scientists classify rattlesnakes among the pit vipers. There are about 30 *species* (kinds) of rattlers. All live in the Western Hemisphere from southern Canada to Argentina. Many inhabit the dry region of the southwestern United States and northern Mexico. These include the horned rattlesnake, or sidewinder, and the ridge-nosed rattlesnake. The eastern diamondback rattlesnake, pygmy rattlesnake, and timber rattlesnake inhabit the eastern United States. The northern Pacific rattlesnake lives from southwestern Canada to southern California. One species, the neotropical rattlesnake, occurs from southwestern Mexico to Argentina.

People can easily recognize a rattlesnake by its rattle, which consists of a set of horny pieces loosely joined together. The rattle makes a buzzing sound when shaken. Certain harmless snakes, often mistaken for rattlers, can make a sound by vibrating their tails in dry grass or leaves. But a careful observer can quickly tell whether a snake is a real rattler. The rattlesnake always lifts the end of its tail when it sounds. The harmless snake vibrates its tail back and forth on top of dry leaves or grass.

Rattlesnakes vary in size. The eastern diamondback ranks among the heaviest of venomous snakes, though not among the longest. It gets its name because dark, diamond-shaped blotches edged with yellow cover its body. It rarely measures over 7 $\frac{1}{3}$ feet (2.2 meters) long. Several small species, including the sidewinder, may grow only 2 feet (61 centimeters) long. The ridge-nosed rattlesnake and pygmy rattlesnake are even shorter.

Females of many rattlesnake species can have young by about 3 years of age. The young usually are born in late summer. All rattlesnakes bear live young instead of laying eggs. Newborn rattlers can take full care of themselves and give painful and dangerous bites.

The oldest rattlesnakes, mostly those in captivity, may live up to 30 years. Each year, two to four new segments grow on the rattle, one every time the skin is shed. The segments resemble hollow cones, each one partly fitting over the one behind it. Segments often break off during the snake's life. People can use the number of segments to determine the age of a young rattler. But the snake must retain the original *button,* or end segment, on its rattle. The existence of a button indicates that no segments have yet broken off.

Most rattlesnakes eat birds and small mammals. A few also eat amphibians and reptiles. The snakes destroy rodents and other animals that harm crops. A rattler lies in wait for prey, biting and injecting venom into the prey as it passes by. The snake injects venom through two fangs—long, hollow teeth in its upper jaw. The venom forms in glands behind the eyes. Once the prey succumbs to the venom, a rattlesnake can track the animal by using its tongue tips to detect the prey's scent.

Larger rattlers are among the most dangerous snakes and should be avoided. They do not always rattle before biting. When an angry rattler strikes, its fangs are erected and the mouth is opened wide. The fangs fold back

Some common varieties of rattlesnakes

WORLD BOOK illustrations by Richard Lewington, The Garden Studio

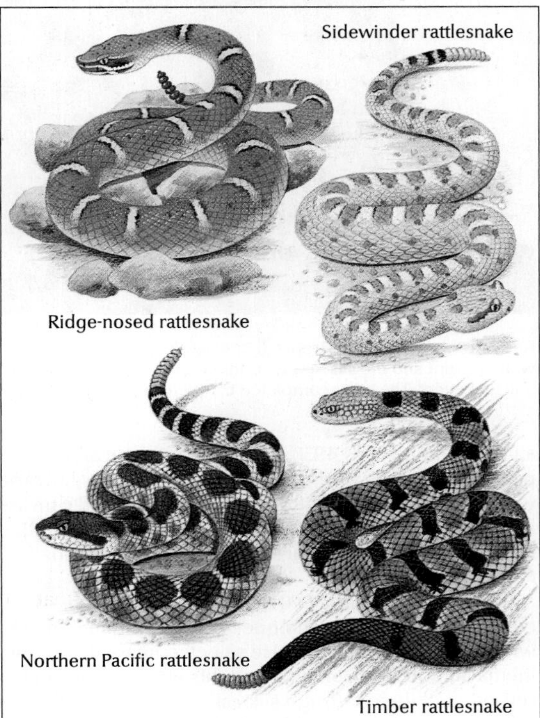

© Shutterstock

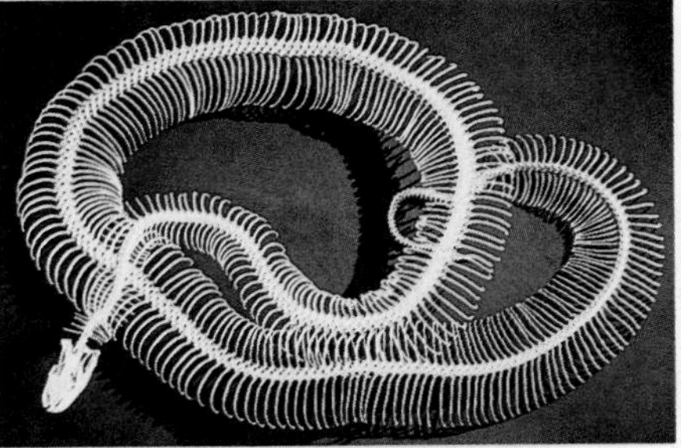
Field Museum, Chicago

© Shutterstock

A rattlesnake has a forked tongue, *left,* that helps it detect odors. Its backbone, *center,* has about 200 flexible joints. The rattle on its tail, *right,* is a set of loosely interlocking segments.

in the mouth when not in use. D. Bruce Means

Scientific classification. Rattlesnakes belong to the viper family, Viperidae. The scientific name of the pygmy rattlesnake is *Sistrurus miliarius.* The ridge-nosed rattlesnake is *Crotalus willardi.* The eastern diamondback is *C. adamanteus,* the sidewinder is *C. cerastes,* the northern Pacific is *C. viridis oreganus,* the timber is *C. horridus,* and the neotropical is *C. durissus.*

See also **Snake** (picture: Some venomous snakes of the world); **Snakebite.**

Rattner, Abraham (1895-1978), was an American painter best known for his religious works. His paintings are noted for their brilliant color and rich texture. They have been compared to stained-glass windows because

Oil painting on composition board (1958); Whitney Museum of American Art, New York City

Rattner's *Song of Esther* shows the artist's use of vibrant colors and geometric forms, which create a stained-glass effect.

of their glowing colors and bold black lines. Rattner often used words and inscriptions in his works. He painted many Biblical themes, including the Crucifixion and the Last Judgment. Rattner developed symbolic themes. For example, he painted a window cleaner removing dirt from a window. This is a symbol of the way God clears human vision to enable people to see the brilliance and beauty of the divine. Rattner was born on July 8, 1895, in Poughkeepsie, New York. He died on Feb. 14, 1978. Pamela A. Ivinski

Ratzinger, Joseph Alois. See **Benedict XVI.**

Rauschenberg, *ROW shuhn burg,* **Robert** (1925-2008), was an American artist famous for experimenting with a variety of materials, techniques, and styles. His search for new forms of expression inspired many artists in the United States and other countries.

Milton Ernst Rauschenberg was born on Oct. 22, 1925, in Port Arthur, Texas. He studied art at Black Mountain College in North Carolina. Rauschenberg first attracted

Nelson-Atkins Museum of Art, Kansas City, Missouri

Rauschenberg's *Tracer* reproduces unrelated realistic images with oil paint and the silk-screen printing process to achieve an unusual effect. The artist completed the picture in 1963.

attention in the early 1950's with all-white and all-black paintings. He then invented the *combine,* an assemblage with everyday objects, often joined with painted canvases. One combine called *Bed* (1955) consists of a real quilt, sheet, and pillow, all splattered with paint. See **Painting** (picture: *Bed).*

Starting in the early 1960's, Rauschenberg experimented with printmaking techniques, often combining them with printing and drawing. He selected images from the media and ordinary objects from his environment and reproduced them through silk-screen printing. Rauschenberg's works, in subject and technique, anticipate the Pop Art movement of the 1960's (see **Pop Art**). His random combinations of imagery illustrate the contradictions of modern life.

In 1966, Rauschenberg cofounded Experiments in Art and Technology (EAT), a project that advanced the incorporation of new interests, such as electric light and motion, in art. From 1985 to 1991, he worked on the Rauschenberg Overseas Cultural Exchange. He visited 10 countries with the goal of promoting world peace through nonpolitical communication. Rauschenberg died on May 12, 2008. David Cateforis

Ravel, *ruh VEHL,* **Maurice,** *moh REES* (1875-1937), was a French composer. Ravel's music is finely crafted, and his piano music is especially brilliant. Many critics classify him as an Impressionist along with Claude Debussy. Indeed, Ravel's piano works *Mirrors* (1906) and

Gaspard de la nuit (1909) fall into the Impressionist category. However, Ravel's music is generally less experimental than Debussy's and relies more on the forms and mannerisms of earlier periods.

Ravel used Classical forms in his early String Quartet (1904) and *Sonatine* for piano (1906) and in his late Piano Concerto in G (1932). *The Tomb of Couperin* (1919) is a Baroque keyboard suite. His orchestral suite *La Valse* (1920) exaggerates the Viennese waltz of the 1800's. A more modern influence, jazz, can be found in portions of the Concerto for Left Hand (1932) for piano.

Ravel was especially known for his skill as an orchestrator. Along with his own compositions, his orchestration in 1922 of Modest Mussorgsky's *Pictures at an Exhibition* is a standard symphonic work. Ravel's works for the stage include the comic opera *The Spanish Hour* (1911) and the ballet *Daphnis and Chloé* (1912).

Joseph Maurice Ravel was born on March 7, 1875, in Ciboure, near the Spanish border. A Spanish influence appears in such works as the orchestral *Spanish Rhapsody* (1907), the opera *The Spanish Hour,* and Ravel's famous ballet music *Boléro* (1928). Ravel died on Dec. 28, 1937. Stewart L. Ross

Raven is a type of large all-black bird that resembles a crow. Ravens live throughout the Northern Hemisphere. The *common raven* and the *chihuahuan raven* are found in North America. The common raven ranges from the Arctic south to Nicaragua in the west and New England in the east. It also lives in the Appalachians as far south as eastern Kentucky and western Virginia. The chihuahuan raven ranges from western Kansas and central Texas west to south-central Arizona.

WORLD BOOK illustration by Trevor Boyer, Linden Artists Ltd.

The raven has black feathers with a purple luster. Ravens are often mentioned in myths and legends as magical birds.

A raven is 22 to 27 inches (56 to 69 centimeters) long and has a wingspread of 36 inches (90 centimeters). Its black feathers have a bluish-green luster on the head, wings, and underparts. Feathers elsewhere have a purplish-blue luster. A raven's voice is a deep, rumbling croak with variations in tone and length that seem meaningful to other ravens. Ravens feed on insects, worms, young birds, frogs, and other small animals. They also eat fruits, grains, and *carrion* (the flesh of dead animals).

Ravens build their nests in late winter on cliffs or in trees. The nest's outer part is made of sticks reinforced with lumps of earth and grass. The deep inner cup is lined with fine strands of wool, hair, and plant fibers.

The female raven lays 3 to 6 spotted eggs that may vary widely in color. The female *incubates* (sits on and warms) the eggs. The eggs hatch after about 18 days. Both parents feed the young. They prepare the food by crushing insects and by removing the hair, feathers, and bones from birds and other small animals. Young ravens can fly at about 6 weeks of age, but the parents continue to care for them for another five months.

The raven is one of the first birds mentioned in mythology. In Norse mythology, the god Odin had two sacred ravens that flew about the world each day and returned at evening to tell him everything they had seen. In American literature, Edgar Allan Poe immortalized the bird in his famous poem "The Raven." Edward H. Burtt, Jr.

Scientific classification. Ravens belong to the genus *Corvus.* The common raven is *Corvus corax.* The chihuahuan raven is *C. cryptoleucus.*

Ravenna, *ruh VEHN uh* (pop. 153,740), is a city in northern Italy, famous for its art treasures and architecture. It is also an agricultural and manufacturing center. A 6-mile (10-kilometer) canal connects Ravenna with the Adriatic Sea. For location, see **Italy** (political map).

Ravenna's Mausoleum of Galla Placidia, built about A.D. 440, is one of the oldest examples of early Christian architecture. It has some of the most beautiful mosaics in Ravenna. The famous churches of San Vitale, Sant' Apollinare Nuovo, and Sant' Apollinare in Classe, built in the 500's, also contain beautiful mosaics.

Ravenna served as the capital of the West Roman Empire from about 402 until the Germanic leader Odoacer seized the empire in 476. Ravenna was part of the Byzantine Empire from about 540 until the 700's. It was one of the Papal States for many years. Ravenna became part of the Kingdom of Sardinia in 1860 and part of the Kingdom of Italy in 1861. Anthony James Joes

See also **Clothing** (picture: Clothing of early Byzantine times); **Mosaic** (pictures: An early Christian mosaic).

Rawlings, Jerry John (1947-2020), was the head of Ghana for all but two years from 1979 to 2001. Rawlings seized control of the government in a military coup in 1979. He was elected president of Ghana in multiparty elections held in 1992 and was reelected in 1996. Ghana's Constitution prevented him from seeking another term in the 2000 presidential election. Rawlings became known for his efforts to end government corruption and to improve the Ghanaian economy.

Rawlings was born in Accra, Ghana's capital, on June 22, 1947. He joined the air force in 1967 and rose through the ranks. He was promoted to flight lieutenant in 1978. Rawlings tried to overthrow Ghana's military government on May 15, 1979. The coup failed, and Rawlings was jailed. But he gained nationwide attention for the speeches against corruption that he made during his trial. On June 4, Rawlings was freed from prison as he and fellow officers staged a successful coup. As head of the government, Rawlings allowed scheduled elections to go ahead as planned. In September 1979, he turned control over to the elected civilian government. Angered by what he saw as continued corruption, however, Rawlings retook control of the government on Dec. 31, 1981. Rawlings died on Nov. 12, 2020. Mark W. DeLancey

Rawlings, Marjorie Kinnan (1896-1953), was an American novelist who wrote about the conflict between people and nature in the Florida backwoods. In 1928, Rawlings left a journalism career to settle on a farm in Cross Creek, Florida. Her hard life there gave her the setting and theme for her novels. *The Yearling,* her best-known novel, won the 1939 Pulitzer Prize for fiction. Set in rural Florida in the 1870's, it tells the story of a 12-year-old boy whose father must kill the boy's pet fawn because the animal was eating the family's scanty crops.

Marjorie Kinnan was born in Washington, D.C., on Aug. 8, 1896. She married Charles Rawlings, also a writer, in 1919. Her other novels include *South Moon Under* (1933) and *Golden Apples* (1935). Her stories were collected in *When the Whippoorwill* (1940). Rawlings humorously described her life in Florida in *Cross Creek* (1942). Her first novel, *Blood of My Blood,* was published in 2002, 74 years after she wrote it. Rawlings died on Dec. 14, 1953. Barbara M. Perkins

Ray is any of a group of nearly 550 species of fishes. These fishes include eagle rays, guitarfish, manta rays, sawfish, skates, stingrays, and electric rays.

Most rays live on the sea floor. They feed on such bottom-dwelling creatures as clams, oysters, shellfish, and certain fishes. Many species of rays dwell in coastal waters, but a few live at great depths. Manta rays live in the upper waters of the open sea and feed on small sea animals and on tiny organisms called *plankton.*

Rays, like sharks, have a boneless skeleton made of a tough, elastic substance called *cartilage.* Rays also resemble sharks in having slotlike body openings called *gill slits* that lead from the gills. However, a ray's gill slits lie under the *pectoral fins* (fins behind the gill openings), and a shark's lie on the sides of its head. Most rays have a flat, disklike body. Among many species, the pectoral fins form large "wings." Guitarfish and sawfish have a more sharklike, torpedo-shaped body.

Ray eggs, unlike those of most other fishes, are fertilized inside the female's body. Skates lay the fertilized eggs. The eggs of all other rays hatch inside the female. She then releases the live young. John E. McCosker

Scientific classification. Rays belong to the orders Myliobatiformes, Pristiformes, Rajiformes, and Torpediniformes.

See also **Electric ray; Fish** (pictures: Fish of coastal waters); **Sawfish; Skate; Stingray.**

Ray, Dixy Lee (1914-1994), was governor of the state of Washington from 1977 to 1981. She had chaired the United States Atomic Energy Commission from 1973 until it was dissolved in 1975. In 1973, when the nation faced serious fuel shortages, President Richard M. Nixon asked Ray to prepare a plan to develop new sources of energy. She proposed a $10-billion research and development program. It included the development of new forms of nuclear power generation and new ways to make gaseous and liquid fuels from coal. Ray also started a campaign to rid nuclear power plants of defects.

Ray was born on Sept. 3, 1914, in Tacoma, Washington. From 1945 to 1972, she served as a marine zoologist on the faculty of the University of Washington. She became an AEC commissioner in 1972. Ray died on March 15, 1994. Robert Gillette

Ray, James Earl. See **King, Martin Luther, Jr.**

Ray, Man (1890-1976), was an American painter, sculptor, photographer, and filmmaker. Early in his career,

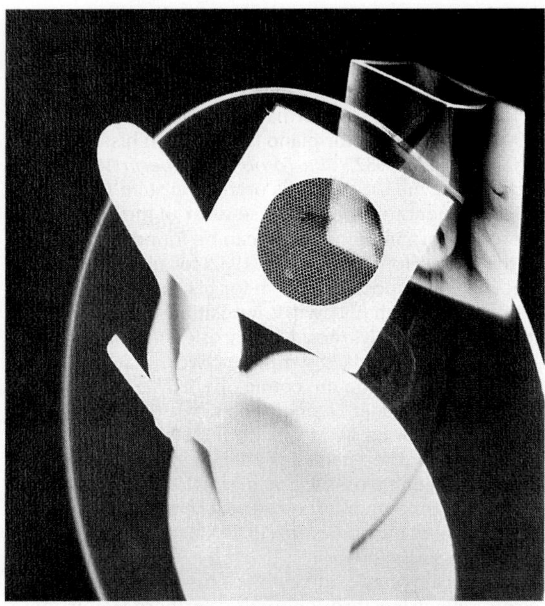

Untitled gelatin-silver print (1927); The Museum of Modern Art, New York City. Abby Aldrich Fund ©The Museum of Modern Art

A Man Ray photo called a *rayograph, shown here,* was made without a camera. Ray placed objects directly on sensitized paper and exposed them to light, producing abstract images.

Ray painted in a fairly realistic style. In 1913, he began to experiment with Cubist and Expressionist styles that were modern at the time. By 1916, he was affiliated with an experimental art movement called Dadaism, which encourages use of unconventional materials and chance occurrences. Ray incorporated found objects, called *ready-mades,* into his Dada sculptures and paintings.

Ray concentrated on filmmaking in the 1920's. Most of his films reflect the style of the Surrealism movement, in which the imagery is inspired by dreams and the subconscious. In the early 1920's, he developed a cameraless technique called *rayograph,* in which objects are placed on photographic paper and exposed to light. Ray continued to work mostly in photography in the 1930's, combining portraiture, nude studies, and abstraction.

Ray was born on Aug. 27, 1890, in Philadelphia. His real name was Emmanuel Radnitzky. He died on Nov. 19, 1976. Deborah Leveton

Ray, Satyajit (1921-1992), was the first internationally famous Indian motion-picture director. He wrote the screenplays for all of his films. Ray gained fame for his Apu trilogy, three films that deal with a poor young man from rural India as he grows into manhood. The films are *Pather Panchali* (1955), *Aparajito* (1956), and *The World of Apu* (1959). The trilogy won acclaim for its realism, humanity, and sensitivity. Ray's other major films include *The Big City* (1963), *The Lonely Wife* (1964), *The Hero* (1966), *The Chess Players* (1977), and *The Stranger* (1991). Ray was born on May 2, 1921, in Calcutta (now Kolkata) and died there on April 23, 1992. Dan Zeff

Rayburn, Sam (1882-1961), a Democrat, served longer as speaker of the United States House of Representatives than any other person. He was speaker from 1940 to 1947, from 1949 to 1953, and from 1955 until his

UPI/Bettmann Newsphotos
Sam Rayburn

death—nearly 17 years. Rayburn also served 49 consecutive years as a member of the House of Representatives.

Samuel Taliaferro Rayburn was born on Jan. 6, 1882, in Roane County, Tennessee. At age 5, he moved to Texas with his family.

He studied at East Texas College and at the University of Texas Law School. He served in the Texas state legislature from 1907 to 1913 and was speaker of the Texas House of Representatives from 1911 to 1913. He was elected to the U.S. House in 1912 and quickly became a leader in Congress, though he seldom made speeches. He presided over the 1952 and 1956 Democratic national conventions.

Alonzo L. Hamby

Raymond, Henry Jarvis (1820-1869), brought political independence and moderation to American journalism through the newspaper he and two associates founded, *The New York Times.* He had two careers, one in journalism, the other in politics. As a journalist, he worked as an assistant to Horace Greeley, editor of the *New York Tribune.* After Raymond helped found the *Times,* they became political and journalistic rivals. The *Times* avoided sensationalism and concentrated on facts, and it soon became a leading newspaper. Raymond held public offices in New York, and served a term as a Republican member of Congress from 1865 until 1867. But he supported President Andrew Johnson's Reconstruction policies and soon lost political power. Raymond was born on Jan. 24, 1820, near Lima, New York. Robert K. Stewart

Rayon is a manufactured fiber produced from wood or cotton. It is widely used to make industrial materials and knit and woven textiles for use in clothing and decorative items. Some rayon fabrics are heat resistant.

How rayon is made. Rayon is manufactured from the cellulose fiber of wood pulp or cotton (see **Cellulose**). Various chemical processes change the cellulose into a thick liquid. This liquid is then forced through extremely small openings in devices called *spinnerets* to form *filaments,* or tiny threads. There are two chief methods for making rayon: the viscose process and the cuprammonium process.

The viscose process is the usual method of making rayon. Sheets of white pulp are first soaked in a solution of sodium hydroxide. They are then put through presses that squeeze out the excess solution. The sheets then pass through shredding machines where they are made into fine pieces called *crumbs.* The crumbs of cellulose are aged at high temperatures for about a day. Aging helps determine what type of yarn will be produced.

After aging, the crumbs are treated with carbon disulfide, which turns them to *cellulose xanthate,* a deep orange substance. Then the crumbs are dissolved in a weak solution of sodium hydroxide, producing *viscose,* a thick, molasseslike solution. The viscose "ripens" for one to two days at a low temperature. After ripening, the solution is pumped to spinning machines and forced through the tiny holes in spinnerets to form filaments.

The cuprammonium process is a method of dissolving cotton cellulose in a copper-ammonia solution. A special spinning process produces yarns of ultrafine *denier,* or weight.

Spinning. All rayon-making centers on the spinneret, which contains a plate with tiny holes. Pumps force the cellulose through these holes. The threadlike cellulose then flows into a chemical bath that hardens the liquid into threads. The threads are twisted together to form rayon yarn. The yarns are woven into fabrics that look like cotton, wool, or spun silk.

Properties of rayon. Viscose and cuprammonium rayons have much the same chemical properties. Both dye easily, and both lose their strength when wet. They regain their original strength when dry. The wet strength of rayon can be considerably improved by varying the chemical bath composition.

History. In 1884, the French inventor and industrialist Hilaire Chardonnet patented the first practical manufactured fiber. He called it *artificial silk.* The fiber was first commercially produced in the United States in 1910. In 1924, it was named *rayon,* the *ray* indicating the sheen of the fiber, and the *on* showing that it was a cottonlike fiber. John H. Cosgrove

See also **Fiber** (Manufactured fibers); **Flannel.**

Razor is a cutting instrument used to remove hair from the skin. There are three chief kinds of razors: (1) safety razors, (2) straight-edged razors, and (3) electric razors.

Safety razors have blades that are shielded by metal or plastic holders. The holders make it hard to be cut deeply while shaving. The blade may have a cutting edge on one side or on both. It may be made of stainless steel, with chromium or platinum edges to prolong sharpness. After the blade becomes dull, it is replaced by a new one. Some razors use two, three, or even four blades, positioned one on top of the other. Other razors have a replaceable metal band that can be unwound to

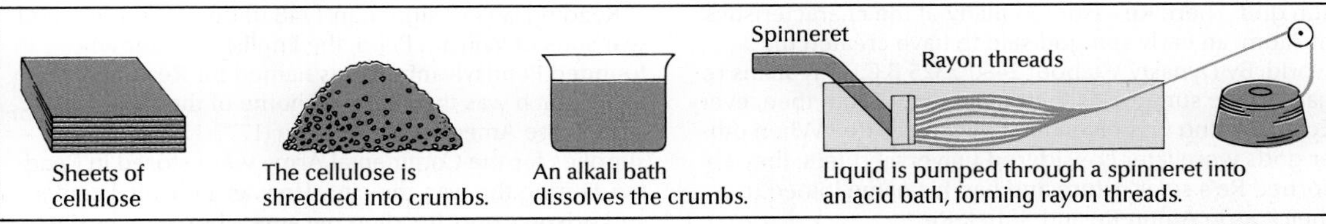

WORLD BOOK diagram

In the viscose process of making rayon, cellulose fibers from wood pulp or cotton are formed into sheets and treated with sodium hydroxide. The cellulose is then shredded into crumbs, treated with carbon disulfide, and dissolved in an alkali bath. Next, pumps force the liquid through the tiny holes of a device called a *spinneret* and into an acid bath to form rayon threads.

expose a fresh cutting edge. Disposable safety razors do not have replaceable blades. These inexpensive razors are thrown away after the blade becomes dull.

Straight-edged razors have specially tempered steel blades about 3 or 4 inches (8 to 10 centimeters) long. The blade has a rounded back and slopes to a fine edge. It is usually fastened by a rivet to a handle. The blade rests in the handle when not in use. It closes like a springless knife. Some of the best blades were formerly made in Sheffield, England, but a number of factories make similarly fine razors.

A good straight razor will last a long time if given good care. The razor wears well if the shaver soaks his face with lather before shaving. When a person shaves, the edge of the blade actually bends, causing it to become dull. The cutting edge should be smoothed with a leather strop before it is used. The blade must be *honed* (sharpened) regularly.

Electric razors are widely used. These little machines are powered by small electric motors. The cutting head passes over the skin and clips the hair. The head may become dull after continued use and may need either sharpening or replacing. The heads of many electric shavers can be adjusted for trimming beards. Some shavers have built-in auxiliary clippers that can trim long hairs and sideburns. Most cutting heads must be cleaned from time to time. Robert Mugnai

RCMP. See **Royal Canadian Mounted Police.**

RDX is a powerful explosive also known as *cyclonite* and *hexogen.* During World War II (1939-1945), RDX was widely used as the chief explosive charge in bombs. It is still an important military explosive and also has wide use in detonators and fuses. RDX is made by the action of nitric acid on hexamethylene-tetramine, a product of formaldehyde and ammonia. Mixing RDX with liquid TNT forms an explosive called *Composition B.* This explosive is more powerful than TNT and has replaced it in most artillery shells. James E. Kennedy

Re, *ray,* also known as Ra, *rah,* was the sun god and the most important god in the mythology of ancient Egypt. He was a popular god often merged with other Egyptian deities. Usually, he is shown as a man with the head of a falcon, crowned with the disk of the sun and the *uraeus,* a cobra symbol. He is also shown as a child rising from a lotus, a falcon, a cat, and a scarab.

There are more myths and legends about Re than about any other Egyptian god. Some tell about the creation of the world and describe his daily rebirth and perilous journey through the sky and the underworld. Other myths tell about Re's ruling on earth as king and about his becoming the father of three pharaohs.

Heliopolis was an early center for the worship of the sun god. There Re assumed many of the characteristics of Atum, an early sun god said to have created the world. By Dynasty V (about 2450-2325 B.C.), Egyptians regarded the sun god as their chief deity. From then, every Egyptian king was given the title "son of Re." When other gods were later considered universal rulers, they absorbed Re's solar nature and had his name joined to theirs, as in Amun-Re and Sobek-Re.

Scott A. Leonard

See also **Amun; Egypt, Ancient** (Gods and goddesses; The New Kingdom); **Mythology** (Egyptian mythology).

REA. See **Rural Electrification Administration.**

Reaction, in physics. See **Rocket** (How rockets work).

Reaction, Chemical. See **Chemical reaction.**

Reactionary. See **Conservatism.**

Reactor, Nuclear. See **Nuclear energy.**

Read, *reed,* **George** (1733-1798), a lawyer and statesman from Delaware, was one of six people who signed both the Declaration of Independence and the Constitution of the United States. At the Constitutional Convention of 1787, Read was a chief spokesman for the interests of small states, such as Delaware. In addition, he supported the establishment of a strong presidency. Read led the movement for *ratification* (approval) of the Constitution by Delaware.

Read was born on Sept. 18, 1733, near North East in Cecil County, Maryland. Soon after his birth, his family moved to New Castle in the Delaware region. In 1754, Read began practicing law in New Castle. He served as attorney general of Delaware from 1763 to 1774 and as a Delaware legislator from 1765 until about 1777.

Read served in the First and Second Continental Congresses from 1774 to 1777. He first voted against the Declaration of Independence, but he eventually signed the document.

Read served as a United States senator from 1789 to 1793. In 1793, he was appointed chief justice of the Delaware Supreme Court. He held this position until his death on Sept. 21, 1798. Barbara E. Benson

Reading, *REHD ihng* (pop. 88,082; met. area pop. 411,442), is a city on the Schuylkill River in southeastern Pennsylvania. The city lies in the heart of the Pennsylvania Dutch region. It is surrounded by fertile valleys that are noted for fruit growing, poultry production, and dairy farming. For the location of Reading, see **Pennsylvania** (political map).

Reading is a center for agriculture-related businesses, including the farming of mushrooms and the production of pretzels and candy. Other products of the city include electronic components and specialty steels. The Reading area is a regional center for banking, insurance, and engineering services.

The city is the home of Albright College and Alvernia University. Kutztown University of Pennsylvania is in the area, and the Berks campus of Pennsylvania State University is also nearby.

The Schuylkill River, the Schuylkill Canal, and the Reading Railroad played an important role in the development of Reading as a regional transportation center in the early 1800's. Today, the city receives rail freight service from the Norfolk Southern Railway. Commuter airplanes link Reading Regional Airport with East Coast airports. An extensive system of highways, including the Pennsylvania Turnpike, serves the area.

Reading was designed in 1748 under the direction of two sons of William Penn, the English Quaker who founded Pennsylvania. It was named for Reading, England, which was the ancestral home of the Penn family. During the American Revolution (1775-1783), military supplies for the Continental Army were stored in Reading. During the war, the city also was a hospital center and prison camp. Reading became a borough in 1783 and a city in 1847.

The city of Reading has a mayor-council form of government. It is the seat of Berks County.

Charles M. Gallagher

WORLD BOOK photo

© Richard Gross, The Stock Market

© David R. Frazier Photolibrary

Reading is important at school, at work, and during leisure time. Students may read information from a computer for a class project. An executive may read a financial report or business plan. People may read magazines on home decorating or many other topics that interest them.

Reading

Reading is the act of getting meaning from printed or written words. It is basic to learning and one of the most important skills in everyday life. Reading provides the key to all kinds of information. It enables us to learn how to build or fix things, to enjoy stories, to discover what other people believe, and to develop ideas and beliefs of our own.

People may read hundreds or thousands of words a day without even looking at a book, newspaper, or magazine. For example, they read their mail, street signs, traffic directions, billboards, the printing on television commercials, package labels, and many other things that contain words.

In the simplest sense, reading means recognizing letters and groups of letters as symbols that stand for particular sounds. The sounds, in turn, form words that express ideas in written or printed form. A broader definition of reading links it more closely with other uses of language and with thinking. According to that definition, reading first depends on a reader's memory and experience to understand what is read. It then involves how well the reader remembers, uses, and reacts to the material.

In most cases, the teaching of reading stresses certain skills, such as word recognition, vocabulary development, and *comprehension* (understanding of reading matter). However, the best way to learn to read may simply be just to read. Adults, especially parents, teachers, and librarians, can help children become good readers by reading to them and by encouraging them to read many kinds of materials—and to read often.

Lawrence O. Picus, the contributor of this article, is Professor of Education at the University of Southern California.

The importance of reading

Reading plays an essential role in the daily lives of most people. People read road signs, maps, recipes, labels on medicine bottles, and directions for operating new appliances. They read and fill out forms to file their income tax, to apply for jobs, and to request credit. The ability to perform such useful activities is sometimes called *functional reading* or *functional literacy.*

A special kind of functional reading, *learner literacy,* has always been important to students. All elementary school subjects, such as mathematics, science, social studies, and spelling, require students to read. In high school and college, learner literacy becomes even more vital. Older students must read to gain an understanding of a wide variety of topics. Learner literacy also requires the ability to read special kinds of materials, including charts, graphs, maps, and tables. People learn throughout their lives, and so such reading skills remain useful after a person has completed school.

Another kind of functional literacy, *workplace literacy,* concerns the ability to read written materials necessary for doing a job. Such materials include manuals on how to operate computers, robots, and other technical devices. In addition, being promoted often involves special training classes and workshops that call for particular reading skills. This is one way that a person's ability to read directly influences job success.

Besides reading in the classroom and on the job, people read books, magazines, and other printed materials for personal information and recreation. Many people read to learn more about their special interests, such as sports, science, current events, history, health, flowers, or painting. Millions of people read novels, adventure stories, biographies, and other books for fun. Recreational reading helps people understand others, takes readers on journeys to unknown parts of the world, and enables them to share the experiences of people throughout history.

As television became a major part of modern life, some experts predicted that people would not need or want to read as much as before. However, books, magazines, and newspapers still fill shelves in bookstores, drugstores, and supermarkets, as well as in libraries. Some experts believe that the information and entertainment provided by TV and related technologies have exposed people to new ideas and interests and so have created additional reasons to read.

Kinds of reading

People differ in reading ability. For example, those who have been reading a long time tend to understand what they read more quickly and more automatically than do new readers. In addition, older readers bring more background experiences to their reading. They can use their experiences to fill in important information that is not clearly stated in the text.

Regardless of age, training, and other experiences, reading abilities and habits vary from person to person. Some people read remarkably fast, while understanding the main points and remembering key examples. Others read at a snail's pace as they try to absorb every word—sometimes without evaluating the worth of the information.

A good reader uses various reading techniques. The technique depends on the type and difficulty of the material, the purpose for reading it, and the reader's own language development and familiarity with the subject.

Reading can be classified into three main kinds: (1) recreational reading, (2) study-type reading, and (3) survey reading. Good readers can easily shift from one kind to another, depending on their purpose for reading and on the material itself.

Recreational reading can provide hour after hour of enjoyment. When reading a story purely for pleasure, most people read at a relaxed, uneven speed. They may skim through a tale until they come to a scene, a description, or even a phrase that is especially pleasing or satisfying. That portion may be read slowly and then reread to be enjoyed, appreciated, or considered.

Study-type reading usually requires the reader to pay close attention to the text. A good reader looks for significant ideas and details. The reader then tries to understand how those ideas and details relate to one another and how they fit into the general topic. Reading speed tends to be slower the first time study-type material is read, and the reader may need to reread portions of the text to understand it fully. Reading speed may be much faster when the material is reviewed.

Survey reading involves covering a large amount of text to get a general idea of its content. In such cases, the person may first skim the material to understand the main point. The reader may then look for details that reinforce or illustrate that point. If the purpose is to find a particular fact or example, the reader may begin by skimming the text. The person may then read some sections carefully to make sure that the desired information has been found.

Shifting among kinds of reading. Most people use different reading techniques for different reading situations. For example, a mystery enjoyed simply for entertainment may be read rapidly. But a classic Russian novel may call for slow, careful reading. Technical texts that could lead to job advancement or that tell how to fix something usually require thoughtful reading.

Good readers can easily shift from one kind of reading to another. For instance, a student collecting information to write a paper might begin surveying articles to see if they fit the topic. One article may lead the student to consider changing the topic, and so the article is studied thoroughly and another topic chosen. While surveying for the new topic, the student looks for information to create an outline. During the survey reading, the student may see an entertaining article and read it for pleasure.

Reading flexibility improves with experience. Beginners may tend to read everything somewhat awkwardly, advancing slowly word by word because they doubt their ability to recognize words. By reading materials that follow their own *language patterns*—that is, familiar words and sentences they use—even beginning readers can read with both speed and understanding. In time, they learn that different reading materials make different demands on their abilities.

How we read

Reading depends first on our *perceiving* (seeing and recognizing) written or printed letters and words. We must then be able to comprehend what we perceive.

Perceiving reading matter. The process of reading begins as our eyes see *visual stimuli*—that is, the printed or written symbols that make up what is to be read. Eye movements across the symbols capture the stimuli. Eye movements called *saccadic movements* take place as our eyes move across a page, pausing briefly to take in groups of words. As our eyes move across a line, they alternately pause and move on. The pauses are called *fixations.* Another type of eye movement, *regression,* occurs when our eyes shift back to reread a word or group of words. To move from one line of type to the next, our eyes use a movement called a *return sweep.* However, good readers are unaware of their eye movements as they read.

Nerve cells in our eyes change the visual stimuli into electrical impulses that travel to the vision center of the brain. The vision center then sends the impulses to the specific areas of the brain responsible for thought organization, memory storage, and reasoning. Those areas identify the printed and written symbols and translate them into meaning. The physical process of reading also includes the storage of the sounds, meanings, and pictorial representations of what we read.

Comprehending what is perceived. Reading involves far more than simply seeing visual stimuli. You must first choose a particular text to satisfy some purpose. That purpose not only determines the selection of the text but also helps you decide which experiences and reading skills to use to comprehend the material. Your purpose may also suggest how you might use any new knowledge or understanding that you gain from the material.

While reading, you draw on numerous ideas and feelings stored in your memory. Those ideas and feelings make up your *background.* You also rely on *verbal memory*—that is, an understanding of how words come together and form more complex ideas.

Your background and verbal memory change and grow with each reading experience. Information in new material blends with your past experiences and may correct misunderstandings, provide fresh knowledge, broaden interests, or help solve problems.

In many cases, readers lack the background and verbal memory needed to comprehend a text quickly and easily. Such readers may use techniques called *word-recognition strategies.* The more experienced a reader becomes, the more automatically the reader applies these strategies to comprehend unfamiliar words.

Readers can use several general types of word-recognition strategies. For example, a reader who does not know the meaning of a particular word may look for *context clues* in the surrounding text. These clues may be either *semantic* or *syntactic.* When using semantic clues, the reader tries to relate the word to other information or illustrations in the material. Semantic clues include comparisons and contrasts, definitions, descriptions, and the placement of new words near familiar words that help explain their meaning. A reader may also rely on syntactic clues—that is, the word's position and grammatical use in the text. For example, deciding whether a word is functioning as a noun, verb, adjective, or adverb can help a reader figure out its meaning.

In a word-recognition strategy called *structural analysis,* a reader uses clues within the word itself to guess what the word means. The reader relies on knowledge of the meanings of prefixes, suffixes, *roots* (word bases), compound words, and inflectional endings such as *ed* and *ing,* and of how they are combined. For example, the adverb *undoubtedly* has the prefix *un,* the root *doubt,* the inflectional ending *ed,* and the suffix *ly.* Knowing the meanings of the parts of the word leads the reader to decide that the word means *without doubt.* Some methods of teaching reading drill students on prefixes, suffixes, and the meaning of Latin and Greek roots. But the best way for readers to add such knowledge to verbal memory is to encounter words made of those parts in text they find meaningful, and to use the words in conversation and writing.

A word-recognition strategy called *phonics* uses the relationships between spoken sounds and letters. The word *phonics* comes from a Greek word meaning *sound.* Many beginning readers are taught to "sound out" a word, which they may then recognize if they have heard it before. In that way, a reader learns to associate printed symbols with spoken sounds. For more information on phonics, see the section *The teaching of reading* in this article. See also **Phonics.**

Readability. Reading success is determined not only by how well a person reads, but also by how readable the material is. Important factors that influence the readability of any printed material include (1) the average number of words in sentences, (2) the number of commonly understood words, (3) the average number of syllables in the words, (4) the number of long complex sentences, (5) the number of abstract ideas, and (6) the use of prepositional phrases.

Textbooks, reference books, newspapers, government publications, and informational brochures for consumers can be written at predetermined grade levels by controlling these factors. A number of formulas have been developed for estimating readability. The approximate reading level of the people who will read the material must be known. However, there is no formula or procedure to predict the attitudes and interests of readers, or to predict their previous knowledge about the subject. These three factors may lead people to read at lower or higher levels than might be predicted by a formula. Today many publishers reject rigid readability formulas, but they continue to design materials to the reading levels of the intended audience.

The teaching of reading

The complexity of the reading process makes it difficult to teach reading by only one method. Instead, most reading teachers use a combination of techniques determined by their own preferences, students' needs, and the instructional materials available. Commonly used teaching programs include (1) the developmental method, (2) the whole-language philosophy, (3) the language-experience method, (4) phonics instruction, (5) sight words and look-and-say instruction, and (6) individualized reading programs.

The developmental method uses a series of textbooks called *basal readers.* They serve as the basic reading materials in many schools. Basal readers gradually introduce the skills considered important for new readers, especially word-recognition strategies. The textbooks also give students opportunities to apply and practice the various skills.

The typical basal reader series consists of textbooks for each level of reading instruction. Publishers of these textbooks try to present stories, essays, and other writings to which children can relate. A book may include selections from award-winning literature and classics. In addition to student textbooks, basal programs provide teacher manuals, student workbooks, tests, and supplementary materials for each grade level. Teachers who use basal readers generally separate the children into groups according to reading abilities and instructional needs. They can then select the teaching materials that most closely match their teaching goals and the students' needs.

In developmental programs, most reading lessons involve answering in writing questions about the assignment and completing workbook pages that enable students to practice concepts presented in the reading lesson. A large number of lessons and activities also focus on the development of comprehension and analytical thinking. In addition, many programs help students determine their purpose for reading and encourage them to select additional reading materials.

Developmental programs are planned in great detail and enable schools to adjust their reading courses for all grade levels. However, some experts believe that the programs emphasize word-recognition strategies over comprehension, especially for beginning readers.

The whole-language philosophy tries to teach children that language is an effective and enjoyable way to communicate. Children learn new words in the reading material itself, where the meanings and uses of the words can be best understood.

The relationships between reading, writing, listening, and speaking are essential to the whole-language philosophy. The method defines writing as speaking in print, reading and listening as means of learning, and writing and reading as two ways of thinking with language. Whole-language teachers introduce children to both oral language and written language at as young an age as possible, sometimes as early as preschool.

The whole-language method states that the best way to learn to read is to read meaningful materials. Whole-language teachers emphasize the purpose for reading and student selection of reading matter. Instead of reading copies of the same textbook, students read materials that reflect their individual interests. They may often choose their own materials from their classroom, school, library, and home collections.

Reading in a whole-language classroom does not follow lessons that foresee reading strategy needs for a particular text. Nor do teachers drill students after reading a particular text on the reading skills used for that text. Instead, practice comes from simply reading more.

Whole-language theory claims that students cannot interpret a text correctly or incorrectly. Teachers encourage students to bring meaning to a text on the basis of their own backgrounds. The teachers assist students in the process by engaging them in conversation, asking thought-provoking questions, and suggesting examples of how they might interpret or respond to the text. A student learns through experience that inappropriate interpretations may lead to unsuccessful applications of what has been read. At the same time, the student learns that fresh, creative interpretations may be effective. Teachers accept any reasonable ideas that result from trying to construct meaning.

Educators who favor the whole-language method believe that reading cannot be analyzed in terms of specific strategies or skills. They argue that such analysis detracts from what reading really and simply is—the attempt of a reader to get meaning from a text. However, other educators believe that children learn reading more effectively through more structured programs that teach various strategies essential to reading.

The language-experience method seeks to develop reading skills by having learners use their own experiences and language abilities. It is based on the belief that "What I can say, I can write. What I can write, I can read." The method helps students understand that written language is simply oral language in printed form. The teacher uses the children's own language patterns and ideas to help them improve skills in reading, writing, listening, and speaking. The method is commonly used in whole-language classrooms and in some developmental programs.

In language experience, beginning readers create their own texts by dictating story ideas to the teacher. The students base the ideas on their own experiences at home or school. The teacher writes the story ideas on a chalkboard or on large sheets of paper, creating what are sometimes called *experience charts.* The teacher

© David Grossman, Alamy Images

Teachers encourage reading development by reading to the children in their classes.

then goes over the experience chart with the class, having individual students read various sentences, reviewing material the class has already learned, or teaching any new words the chart contains. More experienced readers may also write and illustrate the stories themselves to create books for others to read.

Some educators believe that the language-experience method might limit students' learning of different ideas and cultures. But in most cases, teachers soon combine language experience with other methods. Experts who favor language experience believe that it is especially effective in giving children a solid grasp of what reading is—the process of getting meaning from written words.

Phonics instruction teaches children to relate letters to sounds. Phonics is actually a word-recognition strategy that becomes a teaching method only through heavy emphasis. Using phonetic principles, youngsters learn to associate the correct sound with each part of a word and to recognize and pronounce words.

Teachers of phonics assume that children know certain words from hearing them. They also assume that children can learn that the various sounds of spoken language, called *phonemes,* are represented by specific letters and letter combinations, called *graphemes.* Phonics instruction generally begins with teaching the sounds of initial consonants in words and of some vowel sounds. It moves on to consonants at the end of words, additional vowel sounds, and consonant combinations, such as *ch* in *chair* and *sh* in *wish.* Students also learn certain rules for sounding out words. For example, they are taught that when a word contains two vowels and one of them is a final *e,* as in *hole,* the final *e* is silent while the sound of the first vowel is long and so sounds like the name of the letter.

Phonics can be taught in two general ways. *Synthetic,* or *deductive, phonics* deals with the relationships between individual letters and sounds. Children then learn to split graphemes and to blend the phonemes they represent into words. They *synthesize* (sound out) the sounds that form unfamiliar words. Synthetic phonics has helped some people with severe reading problems. But it may limit a reader's ability to quickly grasp the ideas represented by groups of words. In *analytic,* or *inductive, phonics,* children analyze words for their sounds. Instruction begins by teaching the relationships between letters and sounds by referring to words the students know by sight. The teacher may then present other words that begin or end with the same letter and sound. Consonant and vowel combinations are also taught that way. Beginning readers eventually learn to recognize the sounds of new words.

The great irregularity in the relationships between letters and sounds in the English language presents difficulty if reading instruction heavily emphasizes phonics. Many sounds may be spelled in several ways. For example, the words *beat* and *beet, size* and *sighs,* and *eight* and *ate* sound the same but have different spellings and meanings. In addition, the same letters and letter combinations can stand for several sounds. For instance, the word *tear* is pronounced one way if it means to rip and another way if it means a drop of water from the eye. Some phonics instruction tries to deal with such irregularities through numerous complex exceptions to the rules of sounding out words.

A knowledge of phonics enables a person to determine the sounds of many unfamiliar words. Phonics can also help children in the early elementary grades learn to read. But the majority of experts believe that phonics becomes most effective when combined with other methods which stress meaning and comprehension.

Sight words and look-and-say instruction. If a reader recognizes a series of letters as soon as they are seen as a word, it is considered a *sight word.* Such a word communicates its meaning to the reader so fast that the process seems automatic. Sight-word instruction grew out of the assumption that children probably learn to identify words first by either their appearance or the context in which they appear. They learn to recognize the form of many words from simple books, program titles and commercials on television, and labels on various products. The beginning reader must acquire a basic sight vocabulary that includes the words used most frequently in spoken language. The same words also occur often in written language. Children can be helped to recognize basic sight words by practicing them.

Some reading authorities believe that new words can be taught as sight words, without any analysis of the sounds they require. Children learn many common words that way. In the 1930's, an extension of the practice led to a method called *look-and-say instruction* or *whole-word identification.* The technique stresses word recognition. Phonetic principles may unconsciously aid word recognition in the method. Reading teachers no longer emphasize look-and-say learning, but the development of a vocabulary of sight words remains part of the reading instruction in many classrooms.

Individualized reading programs take into account the wide range of reading abilities and needs. Such a program adjusts instruction and reading materials to the reading achievement, interests, and ability of each student. The classrooms and school libraries have books and other reading matter that cover many grade levels and fields of interest. An individualized reading program requires careful supervision by the teacher, who must check each child's progress in skills, attitudes, and interests. Individual children progress as rapidly as they can. These programs may include elements of other teaching methods, such as the whole-language philosophy or the language-experience method.

Computer-assisted instruction may play an important role in individualized reading programs, though it can also supplement other teaching methods. Computer instruction includes text material followed by questions that test the student's comprehension. In addition, word-processor programs enable students to create their own stories. Such programs are also common in language-experience and whole-language classrooms.

Developing good readers

For many years, educators tried to determine *reading readiness*—that is, when children were ready to learn how to read. They believed that visual and listening abilities, personality development, interests and experiences, emotional stability, language achievement, and certain other characteristics indicated reading readiness. The experts generally agreed that by the time boys and girls reached $6\frac{1}{2}$ years of age, the various charac-

Oak Park Elementary Schools (WORLD BOOK photo by Dan Miller)

A visit to the library enables students to select books on subjects that interest them. Reading about topics they enjoy, or want to know more about, helps children develop their reading abilities.

teristics had developed enough for children to learn to read. As a result, most schools offered formal reading instruction to youngsters beginning at that age.

Today, most educators question the idea of reading readiness at precisely age $6\frac{1}{2}$. They point out that being $6\frac{1}{2}$ years old does not automatically assure that a child will profit from reading instruction. Some children do not fully develop the skills traditionally associated with reading readiness until age 8. Others have them by age 4. In addition, many experts now believe that learning to read depends mainly on whether a child can focus the mind on letters and words as symbols of meaning. The development of that capacity has come to be called *emergent literacy*—that is, the beginning of the ability to read. The amount of experience a child has had with oral and written language—rather than the child's age—appears to be a key to emergent literacy.

Research shows that children begin to associate sounds with the symbols they stand for at an early age. Very young children with no reading experience may astound their parents with the first words they read, such as a department store sign announcing "Big Sale." If children who cannot write are asked to write the story they have been telling orally, they tend to scribble in patterns across a page. Such children show an understanding of what writing is and how it is put on a page.

Research thus demonstrates that children begin to understand language from the time they first listen to adults talk to them. Children try, in turn, to express their needs to adults with a variety of sounds. Emergent literacy suggests that children of all ages can learn from language-related experiences. Children's experiences at home and at school greatly influence how well they learn to read.

Learning in the home. At home, parents and other adults can promote the growth of a child's language-related abilities in many ways. First, they should make sure that the child is physically able to read by watching for vision or hearing problems that could be treated or corrected. Adults should also spend much time talking to the young child in an appealing and clear voice. Such attention will likely arouse the youngster's interest in language and provide opportunities to distinguish various sounds and to build vocabulary. Some adults move attractive objects before a baby's eyes to encourage alertness and to exercise developing *motor skills* (controlled movements) of the eyes and head.

As children begin to use language, parents and other adults should try to converse with them. In so doing, grown-ups should respect a child's interests and ideas and be patient with the youngster's attempts to express them. Adults thereby teach the value of language as a means of communication. They also become a chief source of information for a curious child. Adults can help a child grasp basic ideas and how they relate to one another, such as the difference between *up* and *down* and between *under* and *over.*

Letting a child assist with cooking or building something serves as an excellent way to introduce measurements and an understanding of sizes and proportions. In helping sort the laundry, the youngster can learn to group or classify objects. Such activities aid the development of logical-thinking skills and teach the young girl or boy how to follow a sequence of directions.

By reading aloud to a child regularly, an adult can help a child learn to love books and reading. Even a child too young to understand the words will enjoy the closeness of the activity. In selecting reading materials for older children, adults should consider the child's maturity and interests. The youngster can become involved in a story by asking questions or by trying to guess what will happen next. Above all, frequent reading aloud to the child enables the adult to demonstrate the enjoyment that language and reading can provide. Adults can also show how much they like to read by setting aside time to read for their own enjoyment.

Working with the school. Schools build on the language learning begun in the home. Teachers encourage reading development by reading to children, telling them stories, discussing childhood experiences, and providing them with new experiences. Teachers can also give children many opportunities to express themselves orally, and they can write or type simple stories that the children dictate. Reading programs in the early elementary grades stress basic skills essential to gaining independence in recognizing and understanding new words. Such programs also help children use the words in meaningful sentences and develop interests and attitudes toward reading as a satisfying experience.

A child's progress in becoming an independent reader depends heavily on cooperation between parents and teachers. Parents can reinforce the school's reading instruction by learning about their youngster's school experiences. As the child learns to read, adults should continue to show that they view reading as important, enjoyable, and worthwhile. For example, they can read often and regularly themselves. They can also provide interesting and appealing reading matter in the home.

Parents and other adults should find out which topics and school subjects especially interest a child. The information will help them determine how well the school's reading materials serve—or could serve—the youngster's particular interests. Adults themselves may then be led to provide reading matter to which the child would gladly turn. For example, the parent of a teen-ager might mention what a critic said about a new pop singer in a magazine. A copy of the magazine just happens to be on the coffee table, where the teen-ager can later discover it and verify or challenge the critic's comments.

Children who care little about school and perform poorly might not have developed the necessary reading abilities to succeed, or they may simply lack interest in the subjects covered. Forcing a youngster to read seldom provides a lasting solution and almost certainly does not contribute to developing a good reader. However, appealing to the interests of young people and showing how reading can serve them have proved to be successful.

© Superstock

Reading aloud to a child is an enjoyable activity for both the adult and the youngster. In selecting reading materials, adults should consider the child's maturity and interests.

Reading problems

Researchers have long tried to identify the specific reasons that some people do not learn to read as well as others. But the more that researchers have realized how complex the reading process is, the more they have concluded that it is more important to treat the reading problems that arise in an individual child than to find the precise cause of the problems. Some specialists use the term *dyslexia* to cover most reading problems. Narrowly defined, dyslexia refers to an inability to identify the distinguishing characteristics of letters and words. However, such an inability occurs fairly often among inexperienced readers. The term has lost favor with some experts because it came to be used to describe a broad range of reading problems, which led to confusion about its meaning. See **Dyslexia.**

Most specialists prefer the term *reading disability* to describe a lack of the reading development that could be expected in a person with normal vision, normal hearing, and normal or above normal intelligence. Many experts now believe that reading problems have a combination of causes. Many of the causes are so closely interwoven that it is extremely difficult to separate them. In addition, no two readers have exactly the same difficulties. All reading problems should be therefore diagnosed and treated by a specialist. For more information on reading problems, see **Learning disabilities.**

Signs of reading problems. Parents, teachers, and other adults should watch for signs of reading difficulty in children. They should suspect a possible disability if a child dislikes reading, school, and homework. Instead, the child may prefer activities that require little or no use of language. Poor grades and teacher concern may result. The youngster may seek out friends who are not particularly involved or successful at school.

Adults should also consider the possibility of a reading problem if a child has an unusually small vocabulary. A youngster who does not speak well, resists talking with adults, or avoids situations that might involve writing may have trouble understanding both oral language and written language.

Causes of reading difficulties. Reading problems can be classified into four general types. They are (1) aliteracy, (2) failure to concentrate, (3) insufficient experience, and (4) physical disabilities.

Aliteracy means the lack of desire to read. Aliterate people can read, but they tend to avoid the activity. Aliteracy reinforces itself—that is, people who do not read much do not develop their reading skills. People usually dislike doing things they do poorly, and so aliterate people tend to read less and less. Such reinforcement becomes especially true in the classroom, where the aliterate student sits among skilled readers.

A solution to aliteracy lies in capturing the student's interest with attractive, meaningful reading materials. The student who learns obviously beneficial things through reading may become a frequent reader.

Failure to concentrate. To get meaning from reading matter, a person must focus the mind on the text. Almost all readers occasionally fail to understand the text their

Oak Park Elementary Schools (WORLD BOOK photo by Dan Miller)

Reading disabilities require special teaching methods. This teacher is using individualized reading materials to help a student improve her ability to recognize letters and words.

eye movements perceive. Some readers—particularly young ones dealing with assigned material—often try to read that way, as though the process were so automatic as to require no thought. But for comprehension to occur, readers must bring their knowledge and experience to the act of gaining meaning from words. Obviously, comprehension demands paying attention to the topic and what the text appears to say about it.

Readers can work to improve comprehension in several ways. First, they should understand the reason for reading a particular text. Readers should then make assumptions and predictions regarding the text to be read based on such things as its title, author, and structure. While reading, they should summarize and evaluate the material. Consulting other resources—such as a dictionary, another text, or a teacher or other adult—can help clarify difficult material.

Insufficient experience. All readers bring their experiences to the comprehension process. Youngsters from homes where conversation, ideas, and printed materials are valued have a broad base of experience and thus an advantage in developing as readers. Children whose experiences have been limited may have more difficulty with reading. In addition, readers may bring considerable background to some topics but little experience to others.

Adults can help children become successful readers by providing them with many varied experiences, especially language-related experiences. The act of reading itself enriches the child's background, and so experience and reading reinforce each other.

Children who speak a language or dialect that differs from the one used in their school may require language-development programs. Such programs teach that children can learn more than one language or dialect to take part in mainstream society—and still have pride in their own culture. Many schools in the United States teach English as a second language and provide special instruction for children who speak two languages.

Physical disabilities. Inadequate brain development or vision or hearing defects can cause reading difficulties. However, they account for only a small percentage of all reading problems. Adults will almost certainly notice major brain-development abnormalities in a child long before concerns about the youngster's reading abilities arise. Parents may thus already have been receiving help with the child. However, lesser abnormalities may not appear until the child begins to learn to read. Teachers who notice a large difference between a child's expected reading performance and the youngster's actual achievement may recommend that a pediatrician evaluate the child.

A vision or hearing problem does not by itself cause poor reading. However, correction of such a problem aids reading development. Vision or hearing defects may not become obvious until a child takes screening tests at school, but parents or teachers may notice them earlier. Signs of possible vision problems include frequent rubbing or squinting of the eyes, holding pictures and print close to the face or too far away, and complaining of headaches. Children who do not pay attention, who misunderstand directions or ask to have them repeated, or who have unusual speech habits may experience hearing difficulties. In most cases, vision or hearing problems can be corrected with eyeglasses or a hearing aid. But for some children, special help with reading is also necessary.

Reading and society

The way of life in any country reflects in large part the percentage of its people who can read and write—and

Reading Is Fundamental®; illustrated by Tracy Bailey, winner of the RIF National Poster Contest

A poster promoting the joy of reading was created by a schoolgirl for Reading Is Fundamental, one of various groups that work to increase awareness of the importance of reading.

© J. R. Holland, Stock, Boston

Eliminating illiteracy is an important part of the educational program of developing nations. The teacher shown above is teaching students in Libya how to read Arabic.

the percentage who can read and write well. The higher the percentage of literate people, the more technologically, scientifically, and economically advanced the way of life.

Most societies therefore value the ability to read and write well. Skilled readers contribute to creating a prosperous, productive society. At the same time, they themselves enjoy fuller, more satisfying lives.

In every society, some people have only basic reading and writing skills. They can read simple signs, package labels, and similar matter. Such functionally literate people can read and write just enough to get by. That limited ability may be adequate in a remote village of a developing country but not in a major city of a modern industrial nation.

On the other hand, even highly developed nations have functionally illiterate people. They cannot handle the reading and writing that may be required on the job. In addition, these people may be unable to use language well enough in other ways to meet the demands of their society.

Figures on literacy in countries around the world are based on estimates made in each country. Not all countries define literacy in the same way. However, most nations try to describe some basic level of reading and writing ability. In 2000, about 80 percent of the world's population 15 years old or older could read and write. That means more than 1 billion of the world's people were illiterate.

In a number of countries, including Australia, Germany, and Japan, 99 percent or more of the people age 15 or older can read and write. However, functional illiteracy remains a problem in advanced countries. For example, about one-fifth of all adult Americans are functionally illiterate.

Africa, Asia, and Latin America have the greatest percentages of illiterate people. The world literacy rate, however, has been increasing. In Latin America, for example, the literacy rate rose from approximately 70 percent in 1960 to about 88 percent in 2000. See **Literacy** (table: Literacy rates for selected countries).

Lawrence O. Picus

Related articles in ***World Book*** include:

Book	Learning disabilities
Curriculum	Library
Dictionary	Literacy
Dyslexia	Literature for children
Elementary school	Perception
Encyclopedia	Phonics
Guidance	Speed reading
Kindergarten	Study
Language	Vocabulary

Outline

I. **The importance of reading**
II. **Kinds of reading**
 A. Recreational reading
 B. Study-type reading
 C. Survey reading
 D. Shifting among kinds of reading
III. **How we read**
 A. Perceiving reading matter
 B. Comprehending what is perceived
 C. Readability
IV. **The teaching of reading**
 A. The developmental method
 B. The whole-language philosophy
 C. The language-experience method
 D. Phonics instruction
 E. Sight words and look-and-say instruction
 F. Individualized reading programs
V. **Developing good readers**
 A. Learning in the home
 B. Working with the school
VI. **Reading problems**
 A. Signs of reading problems
 B. Causes of reading difficulties
VII. **Reading and society**

Questions

How can teachers encourage reading development?
Why do most people use different reading techniques for different reading situations?
What is *emergent literacy?*
Why has the ability to read well always been important to students?
How can *context clues* help a reader figure out the meaning of a word?
Why do most societies value reading ability?
What is *aliteracy?* How can it be solved?
In the language-experience method of instruction, how do beginning readers create their own texts?
How can parents and other adults promote language development in children at home?
How do the two general types of phonics instruction differ?

Additional resources

Bloom, Harold. *How to Read and Why.* Scribner, 2000.
Cullinan, Bernice E. *Read to Me: Raising Kids Who Love to Read.* Rev. ed. Scholastic, 2000.
Hauser, Jill F. *Wow! I'm Reading! Fun Activities to Make Reading Happen.* Williamson, 2000. Younger readers.
Reynolds, Marilyn. *I Won't Read and You Can't Make Me: Reaching Reluctant Teen Readers.* Heinemann, 2004.
Ruddell, Robert B. *Teaching Children to Read and Write.* 3rd ed. Allyn & Bacon, 2002.
Smith, Frank. *Understanding Reading.* 6th ed. Lawrence Erlbaum, 2004.

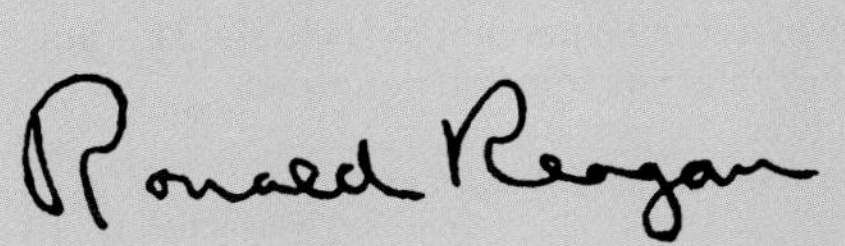

40th president of the United States 1981-1989

Carter
39th president
1977-1981
Democrat

Reagan
40th president
1981-1989
Republican

Bush
41st president
1989-1993
Republican

George H. W. Bush
Vice president
1981-1989

Michael Evans, Gamma/Liaison

Reagan, *RAY guhn,* **Ronald Wilson** (1911-2004), was elected president of the United States in 1980 and won a second term in 1984. Reagan, a Republican, had served two terms as governor of California before he became president. In 1980, Reagan defeated President Jimmy Carter, the Democratic candidate. In 1984, Reagan defeated former Vice President Walter F. Mondale, the Democratic nominee, in a landslide. The president won 525 electoral votes, more than any other presidential candidate in the nation's history. Before Reagan entered politics, he had been an actor nearly 30 years. He appeared in more than 50 movies.

When Reagan became president, the nation faced serious foreign and domestic problems. Relations between the United States and the Soviet Union had reached their lowest point in years following a Soviet invasion of Afghanistan in late 1979 and early 1980. Reagan strengthened the military systems of the United States and its allies in Western Europe. This angered the Soviet Union. The Reagan administration also increased U.S. involvement in Central America. It gave military equipment to troops fighting Communist-supported forces in El Salvador and Nicaragua. In 1987, Reagan and Soviet leader Mikhail Gorbachev signed a treaty that led to a reduction of certain U.S. and Soviet nuclear arms.

At home, Reagan had to deal with high inflation, a recession, and high unemployment. He won congressional approval of large federal income tax cuts to help stimulate the economy. By the end of Reagan's first term, rapid inflation had ended, unemployment had fallen, and the economy had made a strong recovery. But federal expenses so greatly exceeded income that budget *deficits* (shortages) reached record levels.

Reagan was a skillful campaigner and gifted speaker. He stressed such traditional values as work, family, patriotism, and self-reliance. At the age of 69, he was the oldest man up to that time to be elected president. (Donald Trump was 70 upon his election in 2016.) But Reagan looked far younger than his age and was vigorous and athletic. He listed his chief interests as drama, politics, and sports. He enjoyed horseback riding at his weekend ranch, Rancho del Cielo, near Santa Barbara, California.

Bill Boyarsky, the contributor of this article, is a former Los Angeles Times *journalist and the author of* Ronald Reagan: His Life and Rise to the Presidency.

Early life

Boyhood. Reagan was born on Feb. 6, 1911, in Tampico, Illinois. His parents were John Edward Reagan, a shoe salesman, and Nelle Wilson Reagan, a homemaker and occasional shop clerk. When Ronald was a baby, his father nicknamed him Dutch. The boy had one brother, John Neil (1909-1996), nicknamed Moon, who was an advertising executive.

Nelle Reagan loved the theater and took part in many amateur productions. As a result, Dutch became interested in acting at an early age. The Reagans lived in several small towns in western Illinois. Dutch's father moved the family from town to town as he searched for work. Reagan later wrote about his boyhood, "I realize now that we were poor, but I didn't know it at the time."

Education. When Dutch was 9 years old, he and his family settled in Dixon, Illinois, where the boy finished elementary school and went to high school. In high school, he played football and basketball and took part in track and swimming meets. He appeared in several

Sandra Day O'Connor became the first woman justice of the Supreme Court of the United States. Reagan appointed O'Connor during his first term to fill a vacancy created by the retirement of Justice Potter Stewart in 1981.

A terrorist bombing of U.S. Marine headquarters in Beirut, Lebanon, in 1983 killed 241 U.S. troops. They were part of a peacekeeping force sent by the Reagan administration.

The world of President Reagan

The first permanent artificial heart implantation took place at the University of Utah Medical Center in 1982. Surgeons implanted the mechanical heart in 61-year-old Barney Clark, who survived for 112 days after the surgery.

Terrorism became a growing international concern, as political extremists from various countries used such tactics as bombings, hijackings, and kidnappings to call attention to their causes.

A "computer revolution" took hold in the United States during the 1980's. Computers became common in schools, banks, offices, libraries, supermarkets, and other places.

Famine in Africa caused thousands of deaths in the early 1980's, as one of the worst droughts in history spread across Ethiopia and other nations. Worldwide relief efforts included an all-day televised rock music concert, called "Live Aid," that raised millions of dollars for the famine victims in 1985.

A volcanic eruption in Colombia in 1985 triggered mud slides and floods that killed about 25,000 people.

The space shuttle Challenger's destruction in an accident in January 1986 stunned the nation and brought the United States manned space program to a halt. The country mourned the deaths of the seven crew members on board.

South Africa's apartheid system of racial segregation became the target of widespread protests in the United States and elsewhere during the mid-1980's.

The Statue of Liberty centennial was celebrated in New York City in July 1986. The extravaganza included fireworks, parades of ships, and outdoor musical performances.

© Owen Franken, Sygma; © Frank Dougherty, Camera 5

school plays and was elected president of the student council. During the summers, he worked as a lifeguard.

In 1928, following graduation from high school, Reagan entered Eureka College in Eureka, Illinois. He paid his college expenses with a partial scholarship, savings from the lifeguard job, and money he earned washing dishes at a fraternity house. In college, Dutch majored in economics and sociology. He played football, joined the track team, and served as captain of the swimming team. He had leading roles in many college plays and became president of the student body.

Acting career

Motion-picture star. After graduating from Eureka College in 1932, Reagan became a sports announcer for radio station WOC in Davenport, Iowa. That year, he moved to station WHO in Des Moines, Iowa. He broadcast play-by-play accounts of major league baseball games, Big Ten football games, and other sports events.

Important dates in Reagan's life

1911	(Feb. 6) Born in Tampico, Illinois.
1932	Graduated from Eureka College.
1937	Made film debut in *Love Is On the Air.*
1940	(Jan. 25) Married Jane Wyman.
1942-1945	Served in the U.S. Army Air Forces.
1948	Divorced from Jane Wyman.
1952	(March 4) Married Nancy Davis.
1966	Elected governor of California.
1970	Reelected governor of California.
1980	Elected president of the United States.
1984	Reelected president.
2004	(June 5) Died in Los Angeles.

In 1937, Reagan traveled to southern California to report on the spring training season of the Chicago Cubs baseball team. There, he made a screen test for Warner Brothers, one of the largest motion-picture studios. The studio signed him to an acting contract.

Reagan made his film debut in *Love Is On the Air*

Carol M. Highsmith Archive/Library of Congress

Reagan's boyhood home was a modest two-story white frame house in Dixon, Illinois. Reagan, born in nearby Tampico, Illinois, moved to the home with his family when he was 9 years old.

(1937), in which he played a radio announcer. He soon became a star and was known for his roles as a wholesome, likable young man. He portrayed Western heroes in such films as *Santa Fe Trail* (1940), *Law and Order* (1953), and *Tennessee's Partner* (1955). He also played American servicemen in many movies, including *International Squadron* (1941), *The Voice of the Turtle* (1947), and *The Hasty Heart* (1949). In *Knute Rockne—All American* (1940), Reagan played one of his best-known roles, that of college football star George (the Gipper) Gipp. Reagan won praise from critics for his performance as a young man whose legs were amputated in *Kings Row* (1942). In 1965, Reagan used a line he spoke in that film—"Where's the rest of me?"—as the title of his first autobiography. Altogether, Reagan appeared in more than 50 feature films between 1937 and 1964, most of them for Warner Brothers.

Reagan entered the U.S. Army Air Forces in 1942, during World War II. He was disqualified from combat duty because of poor eyesight. Instead, he spent most of the war in Hollywood, where he helped make training films. He was discharged in 1945 as a captain.

Union leader. In 1947, Reagan became president of the Screen Actors Guild (SAG)—now called SAG-AFTRA. SAG was a union that represented film performers. Reagan was elected to five consecutive terms, serving until 1952. During that time, which was a period of strong anti-Communist feeling in the United States, he worked to remove suspected Communists from the movie industry. In 1949 and 1950, he served as chairman of the Motion Picture Industry Council, a public relations organization devoted to improving the public image of the film business.

Reagan served a sixth term as president of SAG in 1959 and 1960. During that period, he led a long, successful strike against the movie studios. The strike won payments to the actors for sales of their old films to television. Part of the money was used for a pension fund.

Family life. Reagan met actress Jane Wyman (1914-2007) while they both were appearing in Warner Brothers films. They were married on Jan. 25, 1940. The couple had a daughter, Maureen Elizabeth (1941-2001), and adopted a son, Michael Edward (1945-). The marriage ended in divorce in 1948.

In 1951, while Reagan was president of SAG, he met actress Nancy Davis (1921-2016). Davis had complained to SAG that she was receiving unwanted Communist literature in the mail. She and Reagan were married on March 4, 1952. The couple had two children, Patricia Ann (1952-) and Ronald Prescott (1958-).

Television star. From 1954 to 1962, Reagan hosted "The General Electric Theater," a weekly dramatic series on television. He also starred in several episodes in the series, which was sponsored by the General Electric Company, a leading manufacturer of electrical products. Between TV appearances, Reagan toured the country as a public relations representative for General Electric. He visited the company's plants and made speeches before chambers of commerce and other civic groups. In his talks, Reagan stressed such conservative ideas as the importance of free enterprise and the dangers of too much government.

From 1962 to 1965, Reagan hosted and performed in a Western series called "Death Valley Days." He also made commercials for the sponsor, United States Borax & Chemical Corporation, a maker of cleaning products.

Culver

A popular movie actor, Reagan appeared in more than 50 feature films from 1937 to 1964. This scene is from *Tennessee's Partner* (1955), one of many Westerns that starred Reagan.

Political career

Entry into politics. Reagan had long taken an active interest in politics. At first, he held liberal views and belonged to the Democratic Party. In the 1948 presidential election, he campaigned for President Harry S. Truman, the Democratic candidate. During the 1950's, Reagan's views became more conservative. He campaigned as a Democratic supporter of several Republican candidates, including presidential nominees Dwight D. Eisenhower in 1952 and 1956 and Richard M. Nixon in 1960. In 1962, Reagan became a Republican.

Reagan first gained nationwide political attention during the 1964 presidential campaign, when he made a stirring TV speech on behalf of the Republican candidate, Barry M. Goldwater. In the speech, Reagan attacked high taxes, wasteful government spending, the growth of government agencies, the rising crime rate, and soaring welfare costs. The speech drew record numbers of contributions for the Goldwater campaign.

Governor of California. Reagan first won public office in 1966, when he was elected governor of California. He defeated the state's Democratic governor, Edmund G. (Pat) Brown, by a landslide.

Reagan began his term as governor in January 1967. Once in office, he worked to slow the growth of government spending. He put a freeze on the hiring of state employees. He also persuaded state lawmakers to pass a welfare reform program. During his campaign, Reagan had criticized high taxes. Upon taking office, however, he found that there was a deficit in the state treasury. Reagan then sponsored three tax increases, one of them the largest in the state's history. But after the tax hikes had produced a surplus in the treasury, Reagan distributed much of the excess money to taxpayers.

Reagan was reelected governor of California in 1970 and served until 1975. As governor, he made major policy decisions himself but relied on others to handle the details.

Presidential candidate. In 1968, Reagan had campaigned briefly for the Republican presidential nomination but did not win. In 1976, he tried again. He attracted much support among conservatives and won many delegates in the South and West. In an attempt to appeal to more liberal and Eastern delegates, he announced that his choice for Vice President would be Senator Richard S. Schweiker of Pennsylvania. Schweiker was known for his liberal Senate record. But Reagan lost the nomination to President Gerald R. Ford by a narrow margin.

Reagan soon began to plan his campaign for the 1980 nomination. By November 1979, when he announced his candidacy, he had a huge lead in the polls over his Republican rivals. Six other Republicans sought the nomination. Reagan's chief opponents were Representative John B. Anderson of Illinois; George H. W. Bush, former U.S. ambassador to the United Nations (UN); and John B. Connally, former governor of Texas.

In February 1980, Reagan won the year's first presidential primary election in New Hampshire. His popularity continued to grow during the spring. In March, he won important primary victories over Connally in South Carolina and over Anderson and Bush in Illinois. By the end of May, Reagan had won 20 of the 24 primaries so far held, and the other Republican candidates had withdrawn from the race. Anderson, however, decided to run as an independent.

In July 1980, Reagan easily won the nomination for President on the first ballot at the Republican National Convention in Detroit. At his request, Bush was nominated for Vice President. The Democrats renominated President Jimmy Carter and Vice President Walter F. Mondale. Anderson chose former Governor Patrick J. Lucey of Wisconsin as his running mate.

The 1980 election. In the presidential campaign, Reagan charged that Carter had failed to deal effectively with inflation and unemployment. During the first half of 1980, the inflation rate was about 15 percent, and about 7 $\frac{1}{2}$ percent of the nation's workers had no jobs. Reagan called for a lowering of the minimum wage in the case of teen-agers to reduce unemployment among young people. To stimulate the economy, he proposed to slash federal income taxes by up to 30 percent. He pledged to boost military spending and to reduce government regulation of business. He also promised to balance the federal budget, claiming that a tax cut would increase economic activity so much that tax revenues would rise, not fall. This emphasis on tax reductions to stimulate business activity was known as the *supply-side theory* of economics.

© Shelly Katz, Black Star

Reagan and his running mate, George H. W. Bush, easily won the 1980 presidential election. They were reelected in 1984.

Reagan's first election

Place of nominating convention	Detroit
Ballot on which nominated	1st
Opponents	Jimmy Carter (Democratic Party) John B. Anderson (independent candidate)
Electoral vote	489 (Reagan) to 49 (Carter) and 0 (Anderson)
Popular vote	43,904,153 (Reagan) to 35,483,883 (Carter) and 5,719,437 (Anderson)
Age at inauguration	69

Carter argued that Reagan's plans would lead to still more inflation. He also questioned whether Reagan could balance the budget, reduce taxes, and increase defense spending all at the same time. In the election, Reagan defeated Carter and Anderson by a wide margin. He received about 44 million popular votes to about 35 million popular votes for Carter and about 5 $\frac{1}{2}$ million for Anderson. Reagan carried 44 states for a total of 489 electoral votes, while Carter carried only 6 states and the District of Columbia for 49 electoral votes.

Reagan's first Administration (1981-1985)

Events at home. Reagan's first major domestic programs dealt with the economy. The President quickly took steps to fulfill his campaign pledges to stop rapid inflation and stimulate business.

Early economic programs. In February 1981, Reagan proposed an economic plan that combined tax cuts with wide reductions in welfare and unemployment programs and in many other areas of the budget. The plan included a large increase in defense spending. Reagan also worked to curb federal agencies that he felt went too far in regulating business. Newspapers and magazines called his economic policies *Reaganomics.*

By August, Congress had approved nearly all of Reagan's proposed tax and spending cuts. The main law, called the Economic Recovery Tax Act of 1981, reduced individual and corporation income taxes by about $33 billion for the 1982 fiscal year, with more cuts scheduled later. It was the largest income tax cut in U.S. history.

Recession and recovery. A recession struck in mid-1981 and ended Reagan's hope for rapid improvement in the economy. The rate of inflation slowed, but thousands of companies went bankrupt and unemployment soared. The rising joblessness contributed to a sharp loss of tax revenue. This decline and increased defense spending helped produce a growing federal budget deficit.

To reduce the deficit, Congress adopted tax increases

totaling about $91 billion in 1982. This was the largest tax increase in U.S. history. The deficit for the 1982 fiscal year, however, reached a record $110.7 billion. By late 1982, about 11 percent of the labor force had no jobs—the highest unemployment rate since 1941.

The economy began to recover rapidly in 1983. But the federal budget deficit reached another record level in the 1983 fiscal year—about $195 billion. The economy thrived in 1984, and the rate of inflation remained low. But the deficit rose rapidly.

Public criticism of many of Reagan's appointments and domestic policies grew steadily. The president's major critics included African Americans, women, and environmentalists. Millions of Americans, especially blacks, suffered from unemployment and reductions in social programs. Numerous blacks charged that the president's policies discriminated against them. Many people claimed Reagan's chief goal was to aid the rich. But a number of wealthy Americans criticized the president for supporting the tax increases. In addition, many business executives objected to the record deficits.

A number of women's groups claimed that Reagan did not name enough women to important government posts. But Reagan became the first president to appoint a woman to the Supreme Court of the United States. In 1981, he chose Sandra Day O'Connor to fill a vacancy on the court. Reagan was the first president to have three women serving in Cabinet-level posts at the same time. These women were Margaret M. Heckler, secretary of health and human services; Elizabeth H. Dole, secretary of transportation; and Jeane J. Kirkpatrick, U.S. representative to the United Nations.

Reagan and Secretary of the Interior James G. Watt came under heavy criticism from conservation and wildlife preservation groups. These groups opposed the administration's efforts to weaken a number of laws designed to protect air and water quality, endangered species, and wildlife refuges. Reagan argued that the laws blocked industrial and mineral development needed to create jobs and help the economy. Continued criticism of Watt led to his resignation in 1983.

Important legislation approved during Reagan's first administration included bills dealing with banking, job training, and Social Security. The Garn-St. Germain Depository Institutions Act of 1982 helped banks and savings and loan associations compete with money market funds for savings (see **Bank** [A boom in money market funds]). The Job Training Partnership Act of 1982 provided job training for unskilled, disadvantaged youths and for needy adults. The Social Security Amendments of 1983 were designed to solve short- and long-term financing problems. One of the amendments raised the system's traditional retirement age (see **Social security** [Financing Social Security]).

An attempted assassination of Reagan occurred in March 1981 in Washington, D.C. Reagan was shot in the chest, but surgeons removed the bullet, and the president made a full recovery. Three other people, including Reagan's press secretary, James S. Brady, also were shot. John W. Hinckley, Jr., of Evergreen, Colorado, was charged with the shooting. In 1982, a jury declared that Hinckley was insane at the time of the attempted assassination and, therefore, found him not guilty of the attempted murder charge. A federal judge later ordered that Hinckley be placed in a mental institution.

Foreign affairs. Reagan showed much political skill when he won a struggle with Congress over his defense program. The plan called for a large build-up of missiles, bombers, and other weapons. Critics charged that the build-up was unneeded and too expensive. Reagan insisted that the Soviet Union held a military advantage over the United States. The United States and the Soviet Union held talks to reduce nuclear arms, but they failed to reach an agreement. Reagan then supplied nuclear missiles to U.S. allies in Western Europe. This action further worsened U.S.-Soviet relations.

The Reagan administration attempted to reduce the level of fighting in Lebanon in the early 1980's. In June 1982, Israel had invaded Lebanon to attack military bases of the Palestine Liberation Organization (PLO). The PLO is the political representative of Palestinians, many of whom fled from Israeli-controlled territory during the Arab-Israeli War of 1948 and became refugees in Lebanon. PLO forces in Lebanon had been attacking settlements in Israel. In August 1982, the United States helped arrange for the withdrawal of PLO units from Lebanon. It later sent several U.S. Marine Corps units to join a peacekeeping force in Lebanon.

In October 1983, explosives set off by a terrorist collapsed a four-story Marine headquarters building at the airport of Beirut, Lebanon's capital. A total of 241 U.S. troops died as a result of the explosion. In early 1984, the level of fighting between Lebanese groups in Beirut increased. In February, the United States began moving its troops stationed in Beirut to offshore ships.

Rebellions in Nicaragua and El Salvador also became a major concern in the early 1980's. Cuba and the Soviet Union were giving war materials to the government of Nicaragua and the rebels in El Salvador. The United States, in turn, sent advisers and arms to the rebels in Nicaragua and the government of El Salvador.

In October 1983, Reagan ordered the invasion of the Caribbean island of Grenada after Grenadian rebels overthrew the island's government. Soldiers from six other Caribbean nations helped defeat the rebels. Reagan said the invasion was needed to protect Americans in Grenada, including almost 600 students at St. George's University School of Medicine. Reagan also said Cuba planned to use Grenada as a military base.

Life in the White House. The Reagans took great pleasure in hosting official receptions and other formal functions in the White House. They created a warm and elegant atmosphere and restored much of the traditional pageantry that President Jimmy Carter had ended. The Reagans brought back the trumpeters who announced the president and the first lady and welcomed foreign visitors. A color guard once again preceded the entrance of the presidential family and its guests of honor. At state dinners, military social aides accompanied members of the official party. The Reagans often sat at separate tables with their own special guests.

The Reagans' children lived in California and New York and occasionally visited the White House. When the Reagans were not entertaining, they sometimes had their meals on trays as they watched television. They both liked to watch movies in the White House theater. Mrs. Reagan took a special interest in supporting activities that called attention to the problems of drug and alcohol abuse among young people. In October 1987, she underwent surgery for breast cancer.

The 1984 election. Reagan and Bush easily won renomination at the 1984 Republican National Convention in Dallas. The Democrats nominated former Vice President Walter F. Mondale for president and Representative Geraldine A. Ferraro of New York for vice president. In the campaign, Reagan stressed the nation's economic growth, the decline in unemployment, and the low rate of inflation. Mondale charged that Reagan's economic policies had greatly favored the wealthy and that the president's foreign policies had increased tension between the United States and the Soviet Union. In the election, Reagan and Bush won in a landslide. For the electoral vote by states, see **Electoral College** (table).

Reagan's second administration (1985-1989)

The president's health became a national concern early in his second term. A cancerous tumor was found in Reagan's colon, and a surgical team removed the tumor on July 13, 1985. Reagan made a rapid recovery.

Domestic affairs. The president hoped to reduce the huge federal budget deficit, but slow economic growth contributed to another record deficit exceeding $200 billion in the 1986 fiscal year. In 1986, Congress followed up on Reagan's request to create a new, simplified tax system that included lower tax rates on individual and corporate income taxes. The tax reform and a thriving economy helped reduce the deficit to $148 billion for the 1987 fiscal year. But after a U.S. stock market crash on Oct. 19, 1987, Reagan and Congress agreed on tax increases for 1988. Most of the increases affected corporations and wealthy individuals. In the mid-1980's, Reagan expanded the Strategic Defense Initiative, a controversial research program designed to develop a space-based missile defense system (see **Strategic Defense Initiative**). The press called the program "Star Wars."

Foreign events. Reagan met with Soviet leader Mikhail Gorbachev several times during his second administration. In Geneva, Switzerland, in 1985, the first

Reagan's second election

Place of nominating convention	Dallas
Ballot on which nominated	1st
Democratic opponent	Walter F. Mondale
Electoral vote	525 (Reagan) to 13 (Mondale)
Popular vote	54,455,075 (Reagan) to 37,577,185 (Mondale)
Age at inauguration	73

Vice president and Cabinet

Vice president	*George H. W. Bush
Secretary of state	Alexander M. Haig, Jr. *George P. Shultz (1982)
Secretary of the treasury	Donald T. Regan *James A. Baker III (1985) *Nicholas F. Brady (1988)
Secretary of defense	*Caspar W. Weinberger Frank C. Carlucci III (1987)
Attorney general	William French Smith Edwin P. Meese III (1985) Richard L. Thornburgh (1988)
Secretary of the interior	James G. Watt William P. Clark (1983) Donald P. Hodel (1985)
Secretary of agriculture	John R. Block Richard E. Lyng (1986)
Secretary of commerce	Malcolm Baldrige, Jr. C. William Verity (1987)
Secretary of labor	Raymond J. Donovan William E. Brock III (1985) Ann Dore McLaughlin (1987)
Secretary of health and human services	Richard S. Schweiker *Margaret M. Heckler (1983) Otis R. Bowen (1985)
Secretary of housing and urban development	*Samuel R. Pierce, Jr.
Secretary of transportation	Andrew L. Lewis, Jr. *Elizabeth H. Dole (1983) James H. Burnley IV (1987)
Secretary of energy	James B. Edwards Donald P. Hodel (1982) John S. Herrington (1985)
Secretary of education	Terrel H. Bell William J. Bennett (1985) *Lauro Cavazos (1988)

*Has a separate biography in *World Book.*

© Dennis Brack, Black Star

Reagan debated Walter Mondale, the Democratic presidential nominee, on national television during the 1984 campaign. In the election, Reagan won in a landslide.

Bill Fitz-Patrick, The White House

Reagan and Soviet leader Mikhail Gorbachev signed a treaty in 1987 that led to reductions of U.S. and Soviet nuclear arms. Reagan met with Gorbachev several times.

David Wells, Gamma/Liaison

Reagan and his wife, Nancy, liked to spend time at their ranch near Santa Barbara, California.

meeting between the two men led to agreements for educational, scientific, and cultural exchanges. The two leaders met again at Reykjavík, Iceland, in 1986. In 1987, Gorbachev visited the United States. During the visit, he and Reagan signed a treaty to eliminate all U.S. and Soviet ground-launched nuclear missiles with ranges of 500 to 5,500 kilometers (310 to 3,420 miles). The treaty took effect in 1988. That year, Reagan met with Gorbachev in the Soviet Union.

Terrorism increased in the mid-1980's, and Reagan acted boldly to combat it. In October 1985, he ordered U.S. Navy jets to intercept an Egyptian airliner carrying a small group of Palestinian terrorists. The terrorists had hijacked the Italian cruise ship *Achille Lauro* and killed an American passenger before surrendering to Egyptian authorities. The U.S. jets forced the airliner to land in Sicily, where the hijackers were arrested. Egypt had planned to give the terrorists to the PLO. In April 1986, a U.S. serviceman was killed and others injured when terrorists bombed a disco in West Berlin. United States officials claimed Libyan agents were involved. Reagan ordered air strikes against military and suspected terrorist centers in the Libyan cities of Tripoli and Benghazi.

The Iran-contra affair. Reagan and his administration lost prestige because of sales of U.S. weapons to Iran and use of the profits to help Nicaraguan rebels, known as *contras.* Both activities were secret operations but became widely known to the public in November 1986.

The arms sales were chiefly designed to win the freedom of Americans who were held hostage by Lebanese terrorists friendly to Iran. Reagan supported the arms sales. At the time, however, the United States had a policy that prohibited the sale of weapons to Iran and other nations considered to be supporters of terrorism. The arms sales led to the release of three hostages.

The transfer of funds to the contras took place in the mid-1980's. Congress had banned military aid to the contras during that period. Reagan said he knew nothing about the fund diversion. Both that action and the arms sales had been carried out by the National Security Council (NSC), a White House advisory agency.

In 1987, televised congressional hearings into what became known as the *Iran-contra affair* revealed deep conflict among members of the Reagan administration. The hearings also exposed attempts by the NSC to deceive Congress about the arms sales and contra aid. Later in 1987, Reagan was strongly criticized in a joint report of the congressional committees investigating the affair. Most committee members blamed Reagan for failing to meet the constitutional obligation to "take care that the laws be faithfully executed" and said he was chiefly responsible for wrongdoing by his aides.

Marine Lieutenant Colonel Oliver L. North, an NSC aide, was the person most involved with the day-to-day management of the undercover operation. In 1989, a federal court convicted North on three charges related to the Iran-contra affair, including altering and destroying documents related to Congress's investigation. But in 1990, an appeals court overturned North's conviction.

During the Iran-contra operations, North worked under national security advisers Robert C. McFarlane and John M. Poindexter. In 1989, McFarlane pleaded guilty of withholding information from Congress during its investigation. In 1990, Poindexter was convicted of conspiracy and of lying to and obstructing Congress in its investigation. An appeals court overturned Poindexter's conviction in 1991. In 1992, Caspar W. Weinberger, Reagan's secretary of defense, was charged with lying to Congress and government investigators in connection with the Iran-contra affair. Later that year, President George H. W. Bush pardoned Weinberger, McFarlane, and several other former federal officials for any crimes they may have committed in relation to the Iran-contra affair.

Persian Gulf conflicts. In 1987, Iran laid mines to disrupt shipping in the Persian Gulf and fired on U.S. vessels and helicopters there. Reagan ordered military responses to these actions and ended U.S.-Iranian trade. In May 1987, two missiles from an Iraqi warplane hit the U.S.S. *Stark,* a warship that was patrolling the gulf. Thirty-seven American crew members were killed. Iraqi officials said the attack was a mistake. In July 1988, the U.S.S. *Vincennes* shot down an Iranian civilian airliner that it mistook for a warplane, killing all 290 people on board.

Later years

In 1990, Reagan gave videotaped testimony in the Iran-contra trial of former national security adviser John Poindexter. But it had little effect on the trial's outcome. Later in 1990, Reagan published his autobiography, *An American Life.* In 1991, the Ronald Reagan Presidential Library opened in Simi Valley, California. It contains documents and other items related to Reagan and his presidency.

In 1994, Reagan revealed that he was suffering from the early stages of Alzheimer's disease. The disease causes an increasing loss of memory and other mental processes. Reagan died on June 5, 2004, at his home in the Bel Air district of Los Angeles. He died of pneumonia complicated by Alzheimer's disease. He is buried on the grounds of the Ronald Reagan Presidential Library.

Bill Boyarsky

Related articles in ***World Book*** include:

Bush, George H. W.   Carter, Jimmy

Iran-contra affair
President of the United States
Republican Party

Outline

I. Early life
A. Boyhood
B. Education

II. Acting career
A. Motion-picture star
B. Union leader
C. Family life
D. Television star

III. Political career
A. Entry into politics
B. Governor of California
C. Presidential candidate
D. The 1980 election

IV. Reagan's first administration (1981-1985)
A. Events at home
B. Foreign affairs
C. Life in the White House
D. The 1984 election

V. Reagan's second administration (1985-1989)
A. Domestic affairs
B. Foreign events

VI. Later years

Additional resources

Arquilla, John. *The Reagan Imprint.* Ivan R. Dee, 2006.
Ehrman, John. *The Eighties: America in the Age of Reagan.* Yale, 2005.
Kengor, Paul, and Schweizer, Peter, eds. *The Reagan Presidency.* Rowman & Littlefield, 2005.
Reeves, Richard. *President Reagan.* Simon & Schuster, 2005.
Time for Kids editors. *Ronald Reagan.* HarperCollins, 2006. Younger readers.
Yager, Edward M. *Ronald Reagan's Journey.* Rowman & Littlefield, 2006.

Real estate is land and all the things permanently attached to it, such as trees, buildings, and minerals beneath the surface. A house is *real estate,* but the rugs and furniture in it are *chattels* (personal property).

The basic real estate vocation is that of a *broker,* who markets real property on behalf of owners. Typically, *salespeople* are associated with and responsible to the broker. A career in real estate usually begins with sales work that may involve long, irregular hours. But success may bring an excellent income.

Millions of people throughout the world are actively employed as real estate brokers or salespeople. Many more people work in building, mortgage finance, and related fields. All states of the United States and all Canadian provinces require real estate agents and brokers to be licensed. Applicants must pass a test on real estate principles. Fields of specialization in real estate include *appraisal, property management,* and *counseling* on such real estate problems as industrial sites and farm purchases and sales. Other specialized fields in real estate are *mortgage lending, financial analysis,* and *market analysis.*

Hundreds of four-year universities and colleges and two-year colleges offer real estate courses for credit. Some universities offer courses leading to a master's degree in real estate. Real estate organizations encourage formal training by offering seminars on such topics as finance, appraisal, and market analysis.

The National Association of Realtors is a professional group of brokers, salespeople, property managers, appraisers, and others engaged in the real estate industry in the United States. The Canadian Real Estate Association is a similar group in Canada. Both associations use the term *Realtor* to designate their active members who subscribe to the Code of Ethics of the association. The term may not lawfully be used by others. John M. Clapp

Related articles in *World Book* include:

Appraisal	Lease	Property
Deed	Lien	Title
Depreciation	Mortgage	Torrens system
Fixture	Primogeniture	Will
Heir		

Realism, in the arts, is the attempt to portray life as it is. To the Realist, the main function is to describe as accurately and honestly as possible what is observed through the senses.

Realism began as a recognizable movement in the arts in the 1700's. By the mid-1800's, Realism was a dominant art form. In part, Realism has been a revolt against Classicism and Romanticism—artistic movements that are characterized by works that idealize life. The works of Classicists show life as being more rational and orderly than it really is. The works of Romanticists portray life as being more emotionally exciting and satisfying than it normally is.

Realists try to be as objective as possible. They try not to distort life by forcing it to agree with their own desires or with the formulas of art. However, in the process of selecting and presenting their material, they cannot help being influenced by what they feel and think. Even the most thoroughgoing Realism, therefore, is the result of observation and personal judgment.

In fiction. Realistic fiction has been primarily a revolt against the sentimentality and melodrama of Romantic idealism. Characters in Realistic fiction tend to be less extraordinary than those in Romantic fiction. Settings are more familiar, styles are plainer, and plots have fewer twists. Most Realistic fiction deals with probable, com-

The Washerwoman (1863), detail of an oil painting on a wood panel; The Louvre, Paris (SCALA/Art Resource)

A Realistic painting by the French artist Honoré Daumier shows ordinary people in everyday surroundings.

Egg tempera painting on canvas (1930); Whitney Museum of American Art, New York City

Realistic art is an attempt to portray life as accurately as possible. The American artist Reginald Marsh painted *Why Not Use the "L"?, shown here,* and other scenes of everyday life in New York City.

monplace events and believable people. Much Realistic fiction presents dreary, and even ugly, subject matter. This sordid quality is especially associated with *naturalism,* an outgrowth of Realism.

The growing popularity of Realism has been more than simply a reaction against the pretty worlds of Romantic fiction. More fundamentally, its popularity has been due to two factors. One is the development of modern science, with its emphasis upon detailed reporting. The other is an increasing desire of writers and readers for a realistic understanding of social problems.

In English literature, Realism first became important in the 1700's with the work of Daniel Defoe. In the 1800's, Realism became much more important in the works of Jane Austen, George Eliot, Thomas Hardy, George Moore, William Makepeace Thackeray, and Anthony Trollope. Honoré de Balzac, Gustave Flaubert, and Stendhal of France; and Leo Tolstoy and Ivan Turgenev of Russia were other outstanding European Realists of the 1800's. See **Russian literature** (The age of Realism).

Henry James, William Dean Howells, and, to some extent, Mark Twain were the first acknowledged Realists in American literature. Stephen Crane, Frank Norris, and Theodore Dreiser were the first American Naturalists. In their fiction, and in that of later writers such as Sinclair Lewis, F. Scott Fitzgerald, Ernest Hemingway, John Steinbeck, and Saul Bellow, Realism became so accepted as to make Romantic fiction seem outdated.

In drama. As in fiction, Realism in drama is an attempt to show life as it is. Realistic drama first developed in Europe as a reaction to the melodramas and sentimental comedies of the early and middle 1800's. It has taken many forms, from the light Realism of the comedy of manners to the heavy tragedy of Naturalism.

Realistic drama first became important in Europe with the plays of Henrik Ibsen of Norway. Ibsen examined the social issues of his time in such plays as *Pillars of Society* (1877) and *A Doll's House* (1879). Anton Chekhov described Russia's fading aristocracy in *The Cherry Orchard* (1904). The English theater was slow to accept Realism. George Bernard Shaw finally brought the movement to life with his long series of witty plays dealing with social problems, starting with *Widowers' Houses* in 1892. In Ireland, John Millington Synge blended Realism and poetry in *Riders to the Sea* (1904). In a similar manner, Sean O'Casey explored the issues of Ireland's struggle for independence from England in *Juno and the Paycock* (1924) and other plays.

Realism did not make a permanent impact on the American theater until the production of Eugene O'Neill's *Beyond the Horizon* in 1920. Since then, most American drama has been realistic.

In painting. Realistic painting developed as a reaction to two influential styles of the early 1800's—Neoclassicism and Romanticism (see **Painting** [The 1800's]). Aspects of Realism can be seen in the work of Spanish painter Francisco Goya in the 1700's. Realism gained dominance in European painting in the 1800's with the work of such French artists as Camille Corot, Gustave Courbet, and Honoré Daumier. The French *impressionists* of the late 1800's developed a modified form of Realism. In their paintings, Realism was narrowed to the brightly lighted but restricted reality that can be seen at a momentary glance (see **Impressionism**).

Leading American Realists of the late 1800's included Thomas Eakins and Winslow Homer. They were followed in the early 1900's by a group called the *Ashcan School* or *The Eight.* This group opposed the sentimentality and academic quality then popular in American art (see **Ashcan School**). It included William Glackens, Robert Henri, and John Sloan. They painted realistic street scenes, portraits, and landscapes. Other Realists include George Bellows, John Steuart Curry, Edward Hopper, Reginald Marsh, and Grant Wood.

Realism today. In fiction and drama, Realism has become so widespread it scarcely has identity as a distinct movement. Common Realistic themes include the importance of upbringing, the oppression of minorities, and the search for values in a hostile world. During the early 1900's, painters began rejecting Realism in favor of nonrepresentational and abstract styles. By the 1980's, Realism was often associated with photography rather than with painting. Lawrence Lipking

There are biographies in *World Book* for most of the authors and painters discussed in this article.

Reaney, *RAY nee,* **James** (1926-2008), was a Canadian poet and playwright. He sought to express the allegorical patterns behind the sights, sounds, and customs of rural Ontario, where he grew up. His plays combine rapidly shifting scenes, organized more by patterns of images than by plot.

Reaney won three Governor General's Awards for poetry for *The Red Heart* (1949), *A Suit of Nettles* (1958), and *Twelve Letters to a Small Town* (1962). The best of his poetry was collected in *Selected Shorter Poems* (1975) and *Selected Longer Poems* (1976). Reaney founded the literary magazine *Alphabet* and was its editor from 1960 to 1971. He also wrote more than 20 plays, including many for children. His play *Wacousta* (1979) is based on an early Canadian novel by John Richardson. Reaney's best dramatic writing is found in the three related plays *Sticks and Stones* (1973), *St. Nicholas Hotel* (1974), and *Handcuffs* (1975). Reaney was born on Sept. 1, 1926, near Stratford, Ontario. He died on June 11, 2008.

Laurie R. Ricou

Reaper is a machine that farmers once used to harvest grain. Horse-drawn reapers took the place of sickles and cradle scythes, which farmers had used for centuries. With a reaper, farmers could harvest larger crops with fewer workers than ever before.

Several reapers were developed during the early 1800's. But none of them became as commercially successful as the reaper developed by the American inventor Cyrus Hall McCormick (see **McCormick, Cyrus Hall**). His reaper had a straight blade linked by gears to a drive wheel. As the wheel turned, the blade moved back and forth and sawed through the stalks of grain. Projecting rods caught and held the stalks while the blade cut through them. The stalks fell onto a platform and a worker raked them onto the ground.

McCormick first offered his reaper for sale in 1840. He continued to improve it, and sales grew. The reaper was well suited for the Midwest, where farmers grew wheat and other small grains on fairly level land. But 8 to 10 workers were needed to bring in the crop. One drove the horse, a second raked the platform, and 6 to 8 workers bound the sheaves. Inventors worked on reducing the number of workers needed.

During the mid-1850's, *self-rake reapers* came into use. On these reapers, a rake swept across the platform. In the early 1870's, the American inventor Sylvanus D. Locke produced a *binder.* This reaper bound the sheaves and dropped them on the ground. By the early 1920's, many farmers used tractors to pull binders. Since the 1920's, reapers have been replaced by combined harvester-threshers that are called *combines* (see **Combine**). R. Douglas Hurt

Reapportionment. See **Apportionment.**

Reason usually has three different meanings. (1) It can signify the mind, or an agency used in thinking. For example, we may ask someone to use reason rather than emotions. (2) Reason also refers to the evidence for a belief, opinion, or judgment. We may demand a reason for a person's belief that someone is a thief. (3) Reason may refer to a process of arriving at a decision or a conclusion. For instance, we may say that a jury was reasoning correctly when it decided a defendant was guilty.

Reasoning can be inductive or deductive. People use *inductive reasoning* when they see a puddle of water and infer that it has rained recently. Inductive reasoning is not conclusive. The evidence only makes the conclusion probable. See **Inductive method.**

People use *deductive reasoning* when they assert that oxygen is present in a place because life is present there and because life requires oxygen. Deductive reasoning shows what else must be true if the initial beliefs are true. See **Deductive method.** Morton L. Schagrin

See also **Fallacy; Geometry** (The study of geometry); **Human being; Logic; Philosophy** (Logic).

Reason, Age of. See **Enlightenment.**

Reasoning. See **Logic.**

Rebate, *REE bayt,* in mercantile law, is a discount, or reduction of the amount to be paid. Giving a certain percentage off for cash is a rebate. Many manufacturers of such items as television sets, household appliances, and automobiles offer rebates to improve sales. Sometimes a rebate is given to obtain favors or good will. It is unlawful for transportation companies to give rebates to shippers. Those who do are subject to heavy fines. See also **Roosevelt, Theodore** (Domestic problems).

Jay Diamond

Rebecca. See **Isaac.**

Rebellions of 1837 were revolts against British rule in the North American colonies of Upper Canada and Lower Canada. Both colonies had an elected Legislative Assembly. But a British governor and a Legislative Council appointed by the British government still had much control over local affairs. The rebel leaders, Louis J. Papineau in Lower Canada and William Lyon Mackenzie in Upper Canada, attempted to win independence for their colonies from the United Kingdom. However, both revolts were easily defeated.

In Lower Canada, French-speaking professionals and small merchants held a majority of seats in the Legislative Assembly. But many of them felt that the Legislative Council favored the interests of Lower Canada's large landowners over those of the colony's French-Canadian, middle-class majority. Papineau was especially concerned with the English-speaking minority's growing opposition to the traditional French civil law and landholding system in the colony. He called for the establishment of an elected Legislative Council, knowing that such a council would protect the interests of the French-Canadian people.

However, the British rejected Papineau's proposal. He then helped organize a French-Canadian protest group called the Sons of Liberty. Increasing tension led to an uprising in late 1837. Armed rebels won a battle with government forces at St. Denis but lost clashes at St. Charles and St. Eustache. Another uprising broke out in late 1838, but British troops quickly crushed it. Altogether, about 8,000 colonists joined the revolt.

In Upper Canada, many members of the Legislative Assembly had difficulty dealing with powerful members of the Legislative Council who belonged to the *Family Compact.* The Family Compact consisted of officials and Anglican religious leaders who supported the policies of the Church of England. But most colonists did not belong to that church and strongly opposed its influence.

In 1837, Mackenzie became convinced that moderate reformist members of the Legislative Assembly had no chance of winning British approval of their proposals for major democratic reforms. He urged the colonists to revolt. In December 1837, several hundred rebels tried to capture government military supplies in Toronto, but they were defeated. Mackenzie fled to the United States. His followers in Canada attracted little support, and the uprising ended late in 1838.

Results. Largely as a result of the uprisings, the British Parliament passed the Act of Union in 1840. This act, which took effect in 1841, united the colonies of Upper and Lower Canada into a single colony, the Province of Canada. Fernand Ouellet

See also **Mackenzie, William L.; Union, Act of.**

Rebus, *REE buhs,* is a word game in which the placement or size of letters, numbers, or words indicates names, phrases, or other words. A rebus can also have pictures, or words and pictures. For example, a picture

Bettmann Archive

Benjamin Franklin used rebuses along with script writing in a short tract called "The Art of Making Money Plenty."

of an eye, followed by "C A," followed by a picture of a dog, could stand for "I see a dog." Or, using words and figures:

stand   you   4   my
I   charged   shoes

could mean "I understand you overcharged for my overshoes." AL could be *altogether* (*A L* together). Will Shortz

Recall enables voters to remove a person from office before a term is completed, and to elect a new public official. A special election is held for this purpose.

Before a recall election can be held, a petition must be filed that has been signed by a certain number of voters. Usually the number must equal from 10 to 25 percent of the votes cast for this particular office during the previous election. The individual in question may give up the office voluntarily. If the individual does not do this, candidates for the office may file petitions in the usual way. The special election then becomes a contest between the new candidates and the officer whose recall is sought. The person receiving the largest vote in the election serves the rest of the term.

The movement to provide for recall of state and local officials came with efforts to provide for more direct popular control over government generally. The modern use of recall in the United States began with the charter of Los Angeles in 1903. Several hundred cities and 19 states have since adopted it. The states include Oregon (1908); California (1911); Colorado, Washington, Idaho, Nevada, and Arizona (1912); Michigan (1913); Louisiana and Kansas (1914); North Dakota (1920); Wisconsin (1926); Alaska (1960); Montana (1976); Georgia (1979); Rhode Island (1992); New Jersey (1993); Minnesota (1996); and Illinois (2010). Virginia permits recall by trial rather than election. The District of Columbia also allows recalls. Some states that use the recall do not apply it to judges. Mayors have often been recalled. The recall of a state officer is unusual. There have been only three gubernatorial recall elections in U.S. history. North Dakota removed a governor by recall in 1921, and California did so in 2003. But in 2012, Wisconsin Governor Scott Walker survived a recall attempt.

People who favor the recall argue that voters should have a direct way of removing an officer whom they consider dishonest, incompetent, or heedless of public opinion. Most state constitutions provide for the removal of an officer by impeachment. But people sometimes wish to remove from office someone who is not guilty of an impeachable offense.

Opponents of recall point out that the practice may be abused. They say that able individuals may be unwilling to take an office from which the voters may later remove them for no fault except the failure to go along with the public sentiment of the moment. Robert Agranoff

Recall, in psychology. See **Memory** (Measuring memory).

Receipt is a written statement showing that one person has paid money to another. It may also be a written statement showing that goods, or property, has passed from the ownership or responsibility of one person to another. The receipt is proof that a transaction has taken place. Three kinds of receipts are *receipts in full, receipts on account* (when some of the amount due is paid), and *receipts to apply on special accounts.*

A receipt should always show whether payment is made in full, on account, or on the special account to which payment is made when there is more than one account between two persons. A receipt should always be given when an account is paid. A bill that has been properly signed and marked *paid* serves as a receipt. A canceled check is also proof of payment. Jay Diamond

Receiver. See **Radio** (How radio programs are received); **Telephone** (How a telephone works); **Television** (Receiving television signals).

Receiver is an individual, a bank, or a trust company appointed by a court to hold, manage, or dispose of property. A receiver may also be called a *trustee* or an *assignee.* The most common reason for appointing a receiver is bankruptcy (see **Bankruptcy**). If a person or company does not have enough assets to cover all debts, the court may name a receiver to protect the people or companies to whom the debts are owed. A receiver also may manage property involved in a lawsuit, such as a mortgage foreclosure.

Receivers are officers of the court. Their authority and actions are limited by the decree appointing them and by the laws of the state and nation. Ordinarily, receivers must have no direct interest in the business or estate they handle. They also must administer the estate in the best interests of all parties concerned. After receivers finish their work, they are discharged by the court.

The court pays receivers for their services. The fees of receivers and the expenses of the receivership must be paid before any other obligations. The court requires receivers to furnish bond. James E. Krier

Recession is a decline in overall business activity. During a nationwide recession, a country suffers a drop in buying, selling, and production and a rise in unemployment. A recession may also hit an industry or a region. Recessions hurt countless people, especially the workers who lose jobs.

Recessions, also known as *contractions,* are part of the *business cycle,* a recurring rise and fall in economic activity. A recession is often defined as a decline in a nation's *gross domestic product* (GDP)—a measure of a nation's output of goods and services—for six consecutive months. But the National Bureau of Economic Research, which decides the beginning and ending dates of a recession in the United States, uses a variety of measures besides the GDP to determine such dates. Generally, the length of recessions is considerably shorter than the length of periods of economic *expansion* (increases in economic activity). Many recessions last less than a year. A deep, long-lasting recession is called a *depression.*

Recession and inflation. Because demand for goods and services is weak during recessions, *inflation* (an increase in prices throughout a nation's economy) is usually low. Sometimes a recession can cause prices in an economy to fall. Prior to World War II (1939-1945), recessions were usually accompanied by *deflation*—that is, declines in the overall price level. Since World War II, recessions have usually resulted in *disinflation,* a reduction in the inflation rate. Some recessions, however—such as those that took place in the United States in the 1970's—were accompanied by an increase in inflation. Such recessions are known as periods of *stagflation.*

Causes of recession. Most recessions occur because the total amount of spending in the economy drops. For example, if sales rise more slowly than usual, businesses may reduce their orders for new goods. The manufacturers that supply the goods cut back on production. They need fewer workers, and so layoffs and unemployment increase. Workers have less money to spend, which further decreases the demand for goods. As this pattern spreads, a recession begins.

Government action may trigger the drop in spending. For example, cuts in government spending could reduce the nation's total spending enough to start a recession. Reduced spending also may result if the government conducts a *tight money* policy, which makes bank loans more expensive and harder to obtain.

People's expectations also play a role in the decline of economic activity. If manufacturers or consumers believe conditions will worsen, they may cut back on their buying. By doing so, they can bring on the slump they were trying to avoid.

Fighting recession. A government tries to end a recession chiefly through its *fiscal policy* and *monetary policy.* Fiscal policy deals with a government's spending and taxing. Monetary policy refers to how a government influences such economic factors as interest rates and the availability of money and loans. To halt a recession, a government may boost its own spending or reduce income taxes. It may implement policies that reduce interest rates so that loans are less expensive and easier to get. These actions aim to give people more money to spend, in the hope that such an increase will also raise demand for goods and services and create more jobs.

Many nations also have built-in stabilizers that work to stimulate the economy without any special government action. One such stabilizer in the United States is unemployment insurance, which provides benefit payments from the government for laid-off workers. Ken Rebeck

Related articles in *World Book* include:

Business cycle
Deflation
Depression
Gross domestic product
Inflation
National Bureau of Economic Research
Unemployment

Recife, *ruh SEE fuh,* in northeastern Brazil, is the capital of the state of Pernambuco (see **Brazil** [political map]). The municipality of Recife has a population of 1,537,704. A municipality may include rural areas as well as the urban center. Recife lies at the mouths of the Capibaribe and Beberibe rivers, partly on the mainland and partly on an island in the Atlantic Ocean.

Recife's factories produce food, beverages, and textiles. Hospitals, port activities, and tourism also are important to Recife's economy. A technology park called Porto Digital employs thousands of people in the fields of information technology and communications. The Suape Port and Industrial Complex, south of Recife, employs tens of thousands of people and includes a shipyard. Recife has several institutions of higher education.

The Portuguese established permanent settlements in the Recife region in 1535. During Dutch invasions of Brazil (1630-1654), Recife was the center of Dutch operations. It became a Brazilian town in 1710 and a city in 1823. J. H. Galloway

Reciprocal trade agreement, *rih SIHP ruh kuhl,* is a pact between two or more nations to lower tariffs or other trade barriers on certain goods or services. Reciprocal trade agreements form the basis of most nations' foreign trade policies.

Most reciprocal trade agreements begin as pacts between two governments to lower tariffs or other trade restrictions. Such pacts are called *bilateral trade agreements.* Since 1947, most bilateral trade agreements have grown to include other countries. That year, 23 countries, including the United States and Canada, signed the General Agreement on Tariffs and Trade (GATT). They received tariff reductions on goods specified in various bilateral trade agreements. The GATT provision that grants the reductions is called a *most-favored-nation clause.* See **General Agreement on Tariffs and Trade.**

As an example of how a reciprocal trade agreement might be arranged, suppose that one nation produces more wheat than it needs—but not enough shoes. Another country produces too many shoes but not enough wheat. The two governments would negotiate a bilateral agreement. The first country would reduce by a certain percentage its tariff on shoes imported from the second country. The second country would similarly reduce its tariff on wheat imported from the first country. Under the most-favored-nation clause of the GATT, each country would extend its tariff reductions to all GATT countries. These nations could then trade under the lower tariff even if they had not signed a trade agreement with that country. Most nations have subscribed to the GATT.

In 1995, the World Trade Organization (WTO) was set up to administer the GATT and to reduce barriers to trade in services and in other areas not covered by the GATT. As a result, the most-favored-nation clause began to be applied to trade in services and other areas.

Reciprocal trade agreements have been an important part of U.S. foreign trade policy since 1934. That year, Congress passed the first Reciprocal Trade Agreements Act. Since then, periodic legislation has allowed the government to continue such trade policies.

Today, some reciprocal trade agreements are designed to encourage economic growth in developing countries. For example, industrial nations may agree to import manufactured products from developing countries at a lower tariff rate than is charged for the same products made by other industrial nations. At the same time, the developing countries may keep their own tariffs high to encourage expansion of their domestic industries. Robert M. Stern

See also **World Trade Organization.**

Reclamation, *REHK luh MAY shuhn,* **Bureau of,** is a United States government agency that works to manage and protect water resources in the Western States. It plans projects that create more efficient use of water for cities and industries, hydroelectric power generation, irrigation, and outdoor recreation. It also works to preserve water quality and to create habitats for fish and other animals that live in water.

The agency was established in 1902. It planned the construction of dams, hydroelectric power plants, reservoirs, and water distribution systems. It also maintained the projects after they were completed. In 1987, the Bureau of Reclamation announced that it would no longer plan such large-scale construction projects.

The original name of the agency was the Reclamation Service. Its name was changed in 1923 to the Bureau of Reclamation, in 1979 to the Water and Power Resources Service, and in 1981 back to its present name. The Bureau of Reclamation is part of the United States Department of the Interior.

Critically reviewed by the Bureau of Reclamation

See also **Irrigation** (History); **Rio Grande Project.**

Recombinant DNA. See **Genetic engineering.**

Reconstruction was the period in United States history that followed the American Civil War (1861-1865). The word also refers to the process by which the Union restored relations with the Confederate States after their defeat. Reconstruction lasted from 1865 to 1877 and was one of the most controversial periods in the nation's history. Scholars still debate its successes and failures.

The American South faced enormous problems in rebuilding itself after the Civil War. Such cities as Atlanta, Georgia, and Richmond, Virginia, lay in ruins. Much of the South's railroad system, as well as its few factories, had been destroyed. The North, on the other hand, had suffered relatively little damage during the war. Farms and industries in the North had prospered.

Political leaders of the North and South faced many difficult questions during Reconstruction. For example, how should the 11 states that had *seceded* (withdrawn) from the Union be readmitted? How, if at all, should the Confederate leaders be punished? What rights should be granted to the approximately 4 million freed slaves, and how should these rights be protected? How should the war-torn South be rebuilt?

Some of the problems were solved during Reconstruction. The Confederate States eventually met various requirements for readmission, and all rejoined the Union by 1870. The U.S. Congress passed laws and proposed constitutional amendments to protect the rights of the former slaves and to give them the vote. Newly formed state governments in the South began to rebuild the ruined regions.

Other problems remained, however. Most Southern whites refused to accept blacks as equals, and blacks continued to be poor and powerless. The Reconstruction governments also failed to win enough support from Southern whites to survive without aid from the North. Most Southern whites considered these governments illegal, and some whites used violence to prevent blacks from voting.

The North gradually lost interest in Reconstruction. In time, Southern whites regained control of their state governments and took away many of the rights that blacks had won during Reconstruction.

Detail of *Back Home: April 1865* (1939), an oil mural on canvas by Tom Lea; Pleasant Hill (Missouri) Post Office

The Reconstruction period followed the American Civil War. It marked the beginning of efforts to rebuild the war-torn South. Thousands of Southerners, such as the ones shown here, faced the problem of finding enough food to stay alive until they could cultivate the land again.

The debate over Reconstruction

Soon after the Civil War began in 1861, Northerners started to debate how the Confederate States should be brought back into the Union. These states were Alabama, Arkansas, Florida, Georgia, Louisiana, Mississippi, North Carolina, South Carolina, Tennessee, Texas, and Virginia. Some Northerners believed these states should be treated as territories. Others insisted that, because secession was illegal, the South still belonged to the Union. Still others declared that the Southern leaders—but not the states—should be punished.

Lincoln's plan. In December 1863, President Abraham Lincoln announced his plan for Reconstruction. This plan offered a pardon to every Southerner who took an oath to support the Union. Lincoln proposed that if 10 percent of a state's voters took the oath, the state could form a new government and adopt a new constitution. The 10 percent would be based on the number of people who had voted in the 1860 presidential election. The state's new constitution had to prohibit slavery.

Early congressional reaction. Many Northerners considered Lincoln's plan too mild. In 1864, Congress proposed that Reconstruction wait until half the voters in a state had taken an oath of loyalty. A national debate then developed over whether Congress or the president should establish Reconstruction policy.

In January 1865, Congress proposed the 13th Amendment to the U.S. Constitution. This amendment called for the abolition of slavery throughout the nation. In March, Congress created the Freedmen's Bureau to protect the interests of Southern blacks. Most blacks had no homes or money. They also lacked education because Southern laws had barred them from receiving instruction. The bureau supervised labor contracts between former slaves and their employers and set up hospitals and schools for blacks in the South. See **Freedmen's Bureau**.

Lincoln was assassinated by John Wilkes Booth on April 14, 1865, as the war was drawing to a close. Vice President Andrew Johnson, a former Democratic U.S. senator from Tennessee, succeeded Lincoln as president. The Republicans had added Johnson to their ticket in 1864 to attract Democratic support.

The start of Reconstruction

Johnson's plan. In May 1865, Johnson announced his own Reconstruction plan. It offered pardons to all Southern whites except the main Confederate leaders and wealthy Confederate supporters. The defeated Southern States were to hold conventions and form new state governments. These governments had to abolish slavery and vow loyalty to the nation in order to qualify for readmission to the Union. Johnson's plan did not offer blacks a role in the process of Reconstruction. The Southern States were to determine that role themselves. During the summer and fall of 1865, new state governments were organized throughout the South under Johnson's plan.

Most Northerners hoped the nation could be reunified quickly. They expected the South to renew its loyalty to the Union, and they insisted that the basic rights of the former slaves be protected. The 13th Amendment was ratified in December 1865.

The black codes. The status of the blacks soon became the most crucial issue of Reconstruction. The state governments established under Johnson's plan passed a series of laws called the *black codes.* One of these codes permitted employers to whip black workers. Other codes allowed states to jail unemployed blacks and hire out their children. See **Black codes**.

Violence against blacks. The former slaves also suffered from attacks by whites. In 1865 and 1866, whites murdered about 5,000 Southern blacks. During race riots in 1866, white mobs killed 46 blacks in Memphis and 34 in New Orleans.

In 1865 or 1866, a secret white organization called the Ku Klux Klan was founded in Tennessee. It grew rapidly and spread terror across the South. Klan members tried to keep blacks from voting or exercising other rights gained during Reconstruction. They threatened, beat, and even murdered many blacks and their white sympathizers. See **Ku Klux Klan**.

The Newberry Library, Chicago

Schools for blacks were opened throughout the South by the Freedmen's Bureau. This federal agency was established in 1865 to help blacks make the change from slavery to freedom. The sketch shown here appeared in *Frank Leslie's Illustrated Newspaper* in 1866.

NPS Photo

The impeachment of President Andrew Johnson took place in 1868. The ticket shown above was required for admission to Johnson's impeachment trial in the United States Senate.

The struggle over Reconstruction

Congress was in recess during the summer and fall of 1865, when Johnson's plan took effect. When Congress reassembled in December, many newly elected Southern congressmen came to Washington, D.C., to take their seats.

Many of the Southern newcomers had been Confederate officials, and few of the others had remained loyal to the Union during the Civil War. The election of such lawmakers, plus the passage of the black codes, helped convince Republicans in Congress that Johnson's plan had failed. Congress, which had a Republican majority, refused to seat any of the Southerners who had been elected from Confederate States. Congress wanted to control Reconstruction, and it started to develop its own policies for the South.

The Radicals and the Moderates. When the Civil War ended, the Republican Party included two main groups. They were the *Radicals* and the *Moderates.*

The Radicals in Congress vigorously demanded a new Reconstruction policy. Their leaders were Senator Charles Sumner of Massachusetts and Representative Thaddeus Stevens of Pennsylvania. The Radicals felt the federal government should take strong action to protect the rights of blacks and loyal whites in the South. They also thought that giving blacks the vote was the only way to establish Southern governments that were loyal to the Union and controlled by Republicans. Some of the Radicals wanted to confiscate the big Southern plantations, divide them into small farms, and give them to the former slaves. See **Stevens, Thaddeus; Sumner, Charles.**

The Moderates made up the largest group of Republicans, and they controlled the party. They agreed with Johnson that the states should decide whether to give blacks the vote. But the Moderates also agreed with the Radicals that the rights of blacks needed greater protection. And they supported the Radicals in demanding that Congress, rather than Johnson, should determine Reconstruction policy.

The Civil Rights Act. Early in 1866, Congress passed the Civil Rights Act, which guaranteed various legal rights of the former slaves. Johnson vetoed the bill because he opposed federal protection of the rights of blacks. Congress then repassed the Civil Rights Act, which was the first major law in U.S. history to be approved over a president's veto.

The 14th Amendment. In June 1866, Congress proposed the 14th Amendment to the Constitution, which gave citizenship to blacks. It also guaranteed that all federal and state laws would apply equally to blacks and whites. In addition, the amendment barred former federal and state officeholders who had supported the Confederacy from holding high political office again.

None of the defeated Southern States had yet been readmitted into the Union, and Congress declared that none could rejoin until it ratified the 14th Amendment. Johnson urged the states to reject the amendment, and all the former Confederate States except Tennessee did so. Tennessee then became the first of the 11 defeated Southern states to be readmitted into the Union. The 14th Amendment was finally ratified by the required number of states in 1868.

The Reconstruction Acts. The stubbornness of Johnson and his Southern supporters helped move the Moderates toward the Radical position. Early in 1867, Congress passed a series of laws called the Reconstruction Acts. These laws abolished the Southern state governments formed under Johnson's plan. They divided all of the states that had seceded from the Union—except Tennessee—into five military districts. A major general commanded each area. Federal troops stationed in each district helped enforce the Reconstruction Acts.

The Reconstruction Acts also outlined the process of readmission for the 10 Southern states that still had not rejoined the Union. Election boards in each state would register as voters all adult black males and all qualified adult white males. The voters would elect a convention, which would adopt a new state constitution. This constitution had to give black men the right to vote. The voters then would elect a governor and state legislature. Finally, the state had to ratify the 14th Amendment.

Johnson vetoed the Reconstruction Acts. But the Republican-controlled Congress easily repassed them over his vetoes.

The impeachment of Johnson. Congress passed another measure in 1867 that challenged Johnson's authority. The Tenure of Office Act prohibited the president from firing Cabinet members and certain other officials without the Senate's approval. Johnson believed that the measure was unconstitutional. In February 1868, he violated the Tenure of Office Act by dismissing Secretary of War Edwin M. Stanton, a supporter of the Radicals. Partly as a result, the Radicals demanded that Johnson be removed from office.

On Feb. 24, 1868, the House of Representatives voted 126 to 47 to impeach the president. About three weeks later, his impeachment trial began in the Senate. On May 16, the Senate voted 35 to 19 to remove Johnson from office. This tally was one vote short of the two-thirds majority required for removal, and Johnson remained president. See **Johnson, Andrew** (Johnson's administration).

In 1869, Congress proposed the 15th Amendment to the Constitution. This amendment, which was ratified by the states in 1870, made it illegal to deny citizens the right to vote because of their race.

The Reconstruction governments

New state governments were established under the Reconstruction Acts. Many Southern whites protested against the acts by refusing to vote in the elections that set up these governments. The Republicans, who had little strength in the South before the Civil War, won control of every new state government.

By 1870, all the former Confederate States had been readmitted to the Union. Alabama, Arkansas, Florida, Louisiana, North Carolina, and South Carolina had met the requirements of the Reconstruction Acts by 1868. Georgia, Mississippi, Virginia, and Texas took longer to ratify the 14th Amendment and were not readmitted until they had ratified the 15th Amendment.

The Republicans in the South consisted of three chief groups: (1) blacks; (2) former Northerners, who became known as *carpetbaggers;* and (3) Southern whites, who were called *scalawags* by their opponents.

Blacks formed the largest group of Southern Republicans. Thousands of blacks voted in the elections to form the new Reconstruction governments. These voters helped the Republicans win power throughout the South. Opponents charged that blacks dominated the new state governments. But no state elected a black governor, and only 17 blacks won election to Congress during Reconstruction. South Carolina, where blacks made up more than half the population, was the only Southern state with a black majority in its legislature.

The carpetbaggers were largely former Union soldiers who had been attracted by economic opportunities in the South. Many carpetbaggers bought cotton land or opened businesses in the cities. More than 60 carpetbaggers won election to Congress, and 9 served as governors. Others included missionaries and teachers who wanted to help blacks. Southern whites made up the term *carpetbagger* to suggest these Northerners could fit all their possessions in a *carpetbag* (suitcase) when they came south. See **Carpetbaggers**.

Most scalawags lived in the hilly areas of the South. They resented the plantation owners who had long dominated Southern politics, and many of them had opposed the Confederacy during the war. See **Scalawags**.

New state programs and policies. The Reconstruction governments established the first public, tax-supported school systems in most states of the South. Only one Southern state, North Carolina, had such a system before the war. Many historians consider the school programs to be the most significant achievement of the new state governments. The states took over the schools established by the Freedmen's Bureau and built many more. Blacks, both young and old, flocked to these schools. At first, many whites refused to attend. Most of the Southern States then attracted white students by segregating the schools by race, even though many laws prohibited this action.

Major economic problems troubled the Southern state governments. Agriculture, the basis of the South's economy before the war, recovered slowly. And few Southerners had enough money to launch new industries. The state governments attempted to fight the South's economic backwardness by offering aid to railroads and various industries. State officials also worked to attract investment money from the North.

The Reconstruction governments opened the political process to Southern blacks. The new governments not only banned racial discrimination, but also guaranteed blacks the right to vote and to hold political office.

White resistance. Most Southern whites refused to support the Reconstruction governments. Many of these Southerners considered the governments illegal because the 14th Amendment prevented many former Southern leaders from holding political office and because some of the governments also took away voting rights from former Confederates. Some whites had land and other property taken from them because they were unable to pay taxes. Corruption in the new governments also angered many whites. A number of Southern legislators accepted bribes from railroad officials. Southern whites were also concerned about rapidly rising taxes and public expenses. But much of the increased state spending was needed to pay for the new schools and other public facilities.

The basic reason for white opposition to the Reconstruction governments was that most Southern whites could not accept the idea of former slaves voting and holding office. Many whites stayed away from elections. Others turned to violence. U.S. Army regiments tried to stop the attacks against blacks and their white sympathizers. But these troops had little success in preventing the Ku Klux Klan and similar groups from terrorizing blacks and keeping them from voting.

The end of Reconstruction

The Republicans lose power. Southern Democrats began to regain control of the South in 1869, when they defeated the Republicans in Tennessee and Virginia. Reconstruction—and Republican control—ended in North Carolina in 1870 and in Georgia in 1871.

The use of violence to keep blacks from voting, despite attempts by President Ulysses S. Grant to stop it, played a large part in the Democratic victories. Also during the early 1870's, many Northerners lost interest in Reconstruction, partly because they were distracted by other issues. These issues included a militant movement pressing for women's right to vote and widespread suffering and labor violence resulting from an economic depression that began in 1873. U.S. troops aiding the Reconstruction governments were gradually withdrawn. Alabama, Arkansas, and Texas came under the control of the Democratic Party in 1874, and Mississippi in 1876.

The 1876 presidential election led to the end of Reconstruction. In this election, Rutherford B. Hayes, the Republican candidate, opposed Democrat Samuel J. Tilden. The outcome depended on disputed returns from the three states that still had Reconstruction governments—Florida, Louisiana, and South Carolina. A compromise, which included agreement to withdraw the remaining federal troops, resulted in Hayes's election as president. Hayes carried out the agreement after he took office in 1877. See **Hayes, Rutherford B.** (The election dispute; The end of Reconstruction).

Effects of Reconstruction

During Reconstruction, the Union was restored and the rebuilding of the South was started. The public school systems that were established in the South had lasting importance for the region.

However, Reconstruction failed to solve the economic problems of either the blacks or the South as a whole. Few blacks acquired land and thus lacked the economic independence that it provided. Many of them turned to sharecropping. They rented small plots from white plantation owners and paid with a portion of their crop. This system gave blacks more independence, but it was an inefficient method of production that weakened the South's agricultural economy. State governments helped develop the South's natural resources and expand its railroad network. But the South long remained the poorest, most backward section of the country.

In politics, Reconstruction made most Southern whites firm supporters of the Democratic Party and created what became known as the "Solid South." For more than 40 years after Reconstruction, no Republican presidential candidate received a majority of the votes in any Southern state.

Reconstruction also failed to bring racial harmony to the South. Whites refused to share important political power with blacks. Blacks set up their own churches and other institutions rather than attempt to join white society. After Reconstruction ended, the blacks gradually lost many of the rights they had gained. By the early 1900's, every Southern state had passed laws limiting voting rights. These laws gave the vote only to males who could pass certain educational tests or pay special taxes called *poll taxes.* Such laws prevented most blacks from voting. See **Grandfather clause; Poll tax.**

The Southern States continued to violate the rights of blacks for many years after the end of Reconstruction. Yet, perhaps the most lasting effect of the period resulted from the 14th and 15th amendments to the Constitution. These amendments established a national system of legal protection of equality before the law. The guarantees of these amendments remained part of the United States Constitution. And, starting in the mid-1900's, the 14th and 15th amendments became the legal basis of the civil rights movement, the struggle of black Americans for equality. Stephen V. Ash

See also **African Americans** (The first years of freedom); **Civil War, American; Constitution of the United States** (Amendments 13, 14, 15); **Force Bill; Grant, Ulysses S.** (Reconstruction policies).

Record player. See **Phonograph.**

Recorder is a type of flute that has a whistle mouthpiece. The instrument consists of a wooden or plastic tube with a row of seven finger holes and a thumb hole. A recorder is held almost vertically, and the holes are covered or uncovered to play different notes. The instrument has a soft, mellow tone. The most popular sizes of recorders are, from smallest to largest, soprano, alto, tenor, and bass.

The recorder was invented during the Middle Ages and has remained basically unchanged. It became popular during the 1500's and 1600's and was an important part of the music of the Renaissance. By the mid-1700's, the modern flute had largely replaced the recorder. Since about 1920, however, a revival of interest has developed in the recorder and in recorder music of the Renaissance and baroque periods of music history.

André P. Larson

Northwestern University (WORLD BOOK photo by Ted Nielsen)

A recorder has a whistle mouthpiece and holes that the musician covers and uncovers to play different notes. The instrument produces a soft, mellow tone. The tenor recorder, *shown in the photo,* is among the largest sizes of recorders.

WORLD BOOK illustration by Bensen Associates

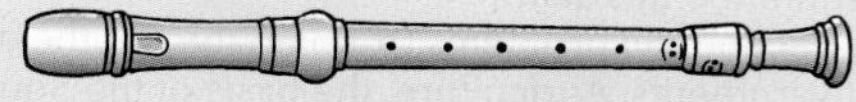

Alto recorder

Recording industry is the group of businesses involved in the production and sale of such sound recordings as vinyl records, compact discs (CD's), and digital music data files. Digital music data files store sound in numeric form. Hundreds of companies in the United States, and many more in other countries, make up the recording industry.

Each year, millions of musical recordings are made and sold throughout the world. Such recordings enable people to listen to a wide variety of musical styles, including classical, country and western, jazz, blues, rap, and rock. They also enable musicians around the world to learn about one another's musical styles, instruments, and songs. A number of spoken-word recordings, such as instructional records, comedy albums, and dramatic readings, are also made and sold. For information on the impact of recordings on musical styles, see **Popular music** (The recording era).

Several companies dominate the manufacture and distribution of popular recordings. These companies, called the "majors," include Sony Music Entertainment, Universal Music Group, and Warner Music Group. Many well-known record companies, such as Atlantic, Elektra, Geffen, Interscope, and Motown, are administered by the larger recording companies. In addition, small independent companies are important in certain segments of the industry, including bluegrass, folk, and gospel music.

Making a musical recording

The procedure used to make a musical recording varies. This section describes how a popular recording, such as a pop song or country performance, is made by a large recording company.

Before recording. Performers who do not write their own music obtain a composition from a composer. Composers protect their interest in a song by copyrighting it and by assigning it to a publisher (see **Copyright**). The publisher promotes the song for the composer.

After an artist has decided to record a song, a copy of it is given to an arranger. The arranger adds instrumen-

De Laubier, Gamma/Liaison

In a recording studio, a vocalist sings while an engineer adjusts sound levels with a mixer and records the performance. A soundproof glass window separates the performing studio from the control room. The engineer hears the singer through speakers in the control room.

tal or vocal parts, changing the music to suit the artist's performing style. An *artist and repertoire* (A & R) executive, who works for the record company, oversees artists and their recordings. The responsibilities of an A & R executive also include listening to demonstration, or "demo," tapes from new artists, deciding which artists to hire, and choosing which songs to record.

In a recording studio. A recording session involves the work of musicians and technicians, and their assistants. These individuals are directed by the recording engineer and the producer. The recording engineer oversees all technical aspects of the recording session, such as choosing the recording equipment and arranging the placement of microphones. The producer makes artistic decisions about the overall sound of the recording based on the tastes of the music-buying public. The producer's duties also include reserving the studio and hiring musicians.

Popular recordings are usually made in two basic steps. First, the song is recorded part by part. Next, the parts are edited and combined into a single performance.

Recording. The singers and the instrumentalists needed for a song are recorded with separate microphones. These recordings may be made with professional *multitrack recorders,* which can record dozens of separate *tracks* (channels of sound). The tracks may be recorded on magnetic tape as *analog* patterns, which are similar to the wave patterns of the original sound. Or they may be recorded as a digital pattern that represents the sound, on digital audiotape or on a computer hard disk. Each musician is usually recorded on a separate track. The tracks can be played back alone or in any combination.

The parts of a popular recording are often recorded at different times. A process called *overdubbing* enables engineers to add one musical part after another. The background sounds of a song, such as drums, rhythm guitars, and bass, are usually recorded first. As the remaining parts are recorded, the other musicians use headphones to listen to and play along with what has already been recorded. Vocal tracks are usually recorded last, though a rough vocal track may be made first to guide the instrumentalists.

The mixdown. Once all the parts have been recorded, the tracks are edited and combined on tape or on a computer's hard disk using a device called a *mixer.* This process, called the *mixdown,* reduces tracks to the required number. Two tracks are needed for stereophonic sound. Surround-sound recordings using a DVD-Audio (digital versatile disc) format require six tracks (see **DVD**).

With a mixer, an engineer can control the overall sound of the song. For example, mistakes in the recording can be corrected by erasing unnecessary or undesirable parts. Various aspects of sound quality, such as loudness and tone, can be adjusted for each track. The mixing engineer can even rearrange vocal and instrumental segments of the recording. The mixing engineer tries to find a sound balance that will work well on home, car, and portable stereo playback systems, and over the radio. Many mixers have computer controls that can "remember" the way in which the engineer has organized and manipulated the tracks. This feature allows engineers to experiment until they achieve the desired sound effects.

More than one version of a recording may be made. Recording companies often remix popular recordings to make them better for dancing.

Mastering refers to the processes used to create copies of the recording for use in the mass production of such products as vinyl records, CD's, and digital music data files.

The mixdown process produces a new recording called the *master.* The sound information on the master is eventually transferred to a number of *production masters,* tapes or digital files that quickly duplicate the information onto blank tapes or discs. Different mastering techniques are required for each type of product. For information on how sound is stored on various products, see **Compact disc; Phonograph; Tape recorder.**

Live recording involves installing portable recording equipment at a concert site. Actual live recordings do not have the excellent sound quality of those made in studios, where an engineer can carefully record the elements of a performance. Most recordings that are labeled "live" are actually combinations of parts from several live performances, often with studio recording enhancement.

Releasing the recording

The release of a new recording is often promoted by a music video or by a concert tour. Traditionally, radio was important in introducing new music to listeners. But today, listeners often use the Internet to discover new music.

A company can release a recording for sale whenever it wishes. Sometimes a company reissues an old recording because the public seems interested in it again. A company may also reissue an old recording to make it available in a different format, or to offer a *remastered* (improved) version of the original recording.

An artist receives a *royalty* payment from the record company for every recording sold. A royalty is a percentage of the price of the recording. Composers and publishers receive *mechanical royalties* for allowing a song to be recorded. The owner of the song's copyright receives a *performance royalty* whenever the music is used on radio or television or in a motion picture. Performance royalties are collected by several large societies, including the American Society of Composers, Authors and Publishers (ASCAP) and Broadcast Music, Incorporated (BMI). See **Copyright.**

The sale and release of *pirated* recordings costs recording companies and artists billions of dollars annually. Pirated products include *bootleg* records made by secretly recording a live performance; records, tapes, and digital data files copied from an original recording without permission; and recordings posted illegally on the Internet. Since the growth of the Internet in the 1990's, music piracy has become a serious threat to the recording industry. See **Piracy.**

Recording industry awards

Several organizations present awards for artistic and commercial achievement within the recording industry. For example, Grammy Awards are given annually by the National Academy of Recording Arts and Sciences (NARAS) for artistic achievement in a broad range of categories. Grammy winners are determined by members of the academy, which includes musicians, engineers, and producers. In Canada, the Canadian Academy of Recording Arts and Sciences (CARAS) gives the Juno Awards yearly.

The Recording Industry Association of America (RIAA) presents awards to artists who sell a specific number of recordings. When 500,000 copies of an album have been sold, an artist receives a *gold record.* A *platinum record* is awarded when sales of an album reach 1 million copies, and a *multi-platinum* record is given for sales of 2 million or more.

History

The history of the recording industry has been dictated by technological developments. In 1877, Thomas Edison invented the phonograph, which could record and play back sounds on tin-wrapped cylinders. Edison's invention was later improved by recording on wax cylinders. By the late 1890's, the flat disc record had been introduced by the Victor Talking Machine Company of Camden, New Jersey. During the mid-1920's, discs became widespread, and cylinder recordings began to disappear. The first discs were made primarily of shellac and played at 78 revolutions per minute (rpm).

Recording tape was invented in the 1940's. As a result, the length of recordings was no longer determined by the wax disc blanks of three or four minutes duration that were being used at the time. The plastic long-playing (LP) record was introduced in 1948. In 1949, the 45-rpm record was introduced. This smaller, less expensive record became an important format for recording companies to promote new songs. Stereo records and recorded tapes were first sold during the 1950's and 1960's. Beginning in the early 1970's, compact cassettes began to compete with LP's as a popular format for prerecorded music.

In the 1980's, music videos became a popular means for promoting songs and artists. CD's were introduced in 1982. By the 1990's, CD's had largely replaced phonograph records; by the late 1990's, CD's had also largely replaced cassettes. By the 2010's, phonograph records began to make a comeback among serious music fans. Manufacturers introduced surround-sound recordings on the DVD-Audio format in 2000.

The growth of the Internet has led to the distribution of music recordings as digital data files. The smaller a data file is, the more quickly and easily it can be transferred over the Internet. Using data compression methods, the size of digital music data files can be reduced. *MP3* is a common compressed music data format. In some cases, a computer user *downloads* (copies) a file before it is played. In other cases, music is *streamed*—that is, it begins to play while the file is being downloaded. In the late 1990's, record labels began using the Internet to sell music. Purchasers can download music files directly to their computer's hard disk. They can then transfer the files into a digital music player or to a device that can record the music on a CD. John Vernon Forbes

Related articles in *World Book* include:

American Society of Composers, Authors and Publishers
Compact disc
Copyright
DVD
Phonograph
Piracy
Popular music
Portable media player
Sony Corporation
Stereophonic sound system
Tape recorder

Recreation is an activity that people voluntarily pursue for personal enjoyment or satisfaction, usually during their free time. Recreation takes a wide variety of forms and occurs in many different places, indoors and outdoors, depending on the preferences of the individual. Since the 1940's, recreation has become a highly visible element in modern life. Higher incomes and improvements in working conditions and transportation have given many people more money, time, and mobility for recreation.

Today, recreation is a major industry. People spend billions of dollars annually on recreational activities. The major categories include video and audio equipment and related services; sports and recreation goods and related services; memberships in clubs, sports centers, parks, theaters, and museums; amusement parks, campgrounds, and related services; admission to spectator events and movies; gambling; magazines, newspapers, and books; pets, pet products, and related services; photography goods and related services; and tours.

Recreation provides enjoyment and relaxation for millions of people, but it may also make an important contribution to an individual's mental and physical health.

Kinds of recreation include media activities, social opportunities, sports and physical activities, hobbies and games, outdoor activities, cultural events, and travel. The most popular form of recreation for many people is watching television. Related media activities include social networking, online shopping, playing video games, and listening to music.

Socializing includes visiting with friends or attending social gatherings. Online dating includes both socializing and media.

Sports includes watching spectator sports, either in person or through media, and participating in such activities as running, tennis, or golf. Walking is the most common form of physical activity.

Hobbies include gardening, reading, driving for pleasure, and interacting with pets. Collecting is a popular hobby, as are card games and online games.

Many people participate in outdoor forms of recreation. The most popular are running, jogging, and trail running; road biking, mountain and BMX biking; bird watching and viewing wildlife; fishing; and hiking.

For many people, attending cultural events is a favorite form of recreation. Such people may attend museum exhibits, theater performances, and concerts.

Individuals travel to visit friends and relatives, sightsee, go to beaches and waterfronts, visit nature areas, go on excursions and cruises, and enjoy theme parks.

Opportunities for recreation. Private businesses, nonprofit service organizations, and government agencies all provide recreational activities. Nonprofit recreation services are offered by boys clubs, scouting organizations, and religious groups. Most local governments have a recreation and parks department responsible for maintaining facilities and offering programs financed by taxes and fees. At the state, provincial, and national levels, recreation is primarily provided through parks.

Karla A. Henderson

Related articles in ***World Book.*** See **Sports** and its list of *Related articles.* See also the *Visitor's guide* section of the state and province articles. Other related articles include:

Amusement park
Camping
Carnival
Circus
Colonial life in America (Recreation)
Cruise ship
Dance
Electronic game
Fair
Game
Handicraft
Hobby
Jogging
Motion picture
Museum
National park
National Park System
National Trails System
Park
Photography
Play
Radio
Reading
Retirement
Safety (Safety in recreation)
Sports car
Storytelling
Television
Theater
Trampoline
World's fair
Zoo

Recreational vehicle (RV) provides temporary living quarters for year-round travel, camping, or recreation. Some RV's have an engine and can be driven. Others are towed by an automobile, a van, or a truck. Still other RV's are carried on the bed of a pickup truck. All can

Popular recreational vehicles

Recreational vehicles provide living quarters for people who are camping or traveling. Many models have a bathroom, kitchen, areas for sleeping, and other facilities of permanent homes.

WORLD BOOK illustrations by Robert Keys and Ronald L. Kempke

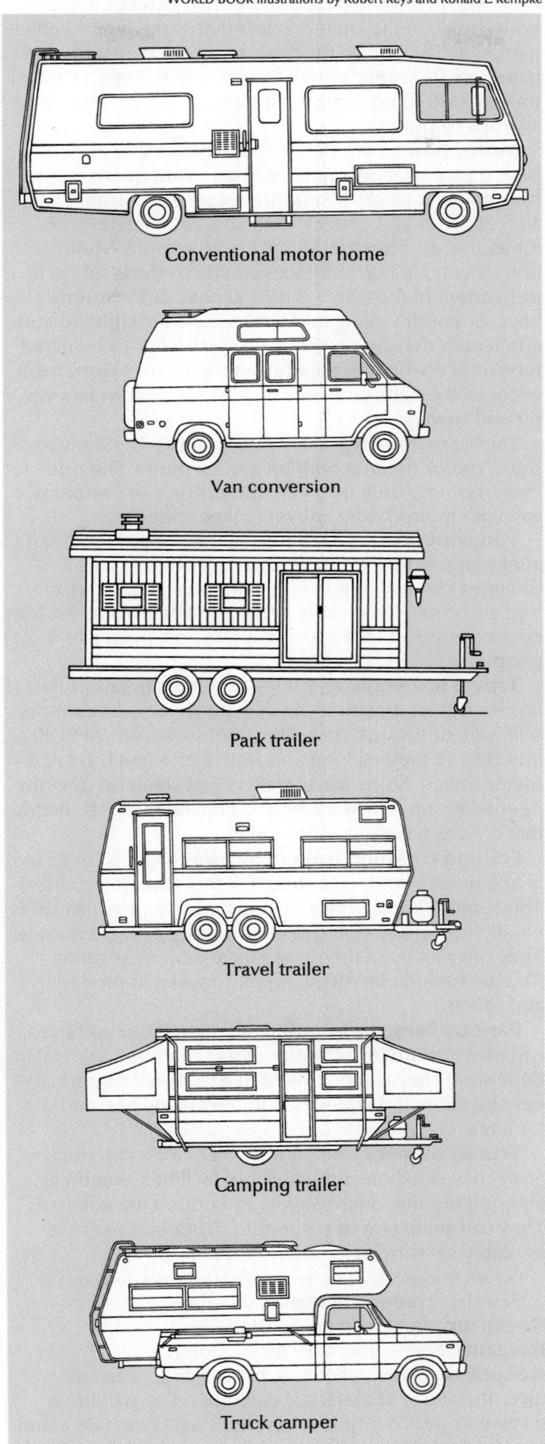

be moved easily and travel almost anywhere on land.

Early models of the recreational vehicle appeared in the 1920's. During the 1960's, recreational vehicles came into wide use as a means of comfortable and economical travel. In the early 1990's, about 10 percent of the households in the United States that had a motor vehicle owned an RV. Today, the basic types of recreational vehicles are (1) motor homes, (2) van conversions, (3) travel trailers, (4) folding camping trailers, (5) park trailers, and (6) truck campers.

Motor homes are motorized vehicles that provide both transportation and temporary living quarters for camping and travel. Motor homes measure from 17 to 40 feet (5.2 to 12.2 meters) long and up to 8 ½ feet (2.6 meters) wide. They can sleep 2 to 10 people. Motor homes contain conveniences similar to those found in permanent homes, including a kitchen, a bathroom, heat, air conditioning, and a television set. Lighting and appliances may be powered by electricity, a 12-volt battery, or propane gas. Separate storage tanks carry fresh water to the bathroom and kitchen and hold waste water and sewage.

There are three types of motor homes. The *conventional motor home* is built on a truck frame. The *mini-motorhome* is built on a van frame. The *van camper* is a van with motor home conveniences added.

Van conversions are vans that have been modified after manufacture for travel and recreational use. Changes may include special windows, carpeting, custom seats, fold-down sofa beds, and a television set. Van conversions can seat 7 to 12 people and sleep 2 to 4 people.

Travel trailers have the same conveniences as motor homes but are towed by a hitch attached to an automobile, van, or pickup truck. They measure from 10 to 40 feet (3 to 12 meters) long and from 6 to 8 feet (1.8 to 2.4 meters) wide. Some travel trailers can sleep up to eight people. A *fifth-wheel trailer* has a raised forward section that creates a two-level floor plan.

Folding camping trailers measure from 10 to 25 feet (3 to 8 meters) long and about 6 ½ feet (2 meters) wide. They unfold into a tentlike enclosure that provides kitchen, dining, and sleeping facilities for up to eight people. They offer many of the same conveniences as other RV's, including electricity, running water, appliances, and toilets.

Park trailers, the largest of all recreational vehicles, can measure up to 400 square feet (37 square meters) in floor area. They can be towed to a seasonal or permanent location and connected to electricity, gas, and water lines.

Truck campers ride on the bed of a pickup truck. Many have kitchen and bathroom facilities, electricity, air conditioning, microwaves, and other conveniences. They can sleep two to six people. Truck campers are available in many sizes and floor plans.

Critically reviewed by the Recreation Vehicle Industry Association

See also **Trailer** (Recreational trailers).

Rectifier. See **Electronics** (Diodes).

Rectum. See **Alimentary canal; Colon.**

Recycling is the collection, processing, remanufacture, and reuse of materials that otherwise would be thrown away. Commonly recycled wastes include aluminum and steel cans, glass containers, newspapers, and office paper. Recycling programs also collect plastics, used motor oil, magazines, and computers, cellular telephones, and other electronic equipment.

Recycling helps conserve raw materials and energy needed to make new products. It also keeps wastes from being buried in landfills, saving scarce landfill space. In addition, recycling helps reduce the pollution that may result from waste disposal.

Some manufacturers purposely design new products to be recycled. They may even sell their products under a leaselike arrangement or exchange program. Such programs encourage the customer to return used items to the manufacturer, which can recycle them.

Use of recycled materials. Recycled wastes provide basic raw materials, sometimes called scrap or *feedstocks,* for manufacturing a variety of products. Recycling has been an important source of feedstocks for the iron and steel industry and for papermaking since the early 1900's. Manufacturers use aluminum from recycled cans to make new cans and other products. Recycled paper is used not only in paper and cardboard but also in such materials as insulation and animal bedding. Manufacturers grind up waste glass and use it to make new glass containers and as a substitute for sand in concrete. Some plastic containers can be melted and molded into new plastic products. Recycled motor oil can be used as industrial fuel oil.

Such *organic waste* as plant material and food scraps can be recycled through *composting.* In this process, the collected waste is allowed to decay into a substance that can be added to soil to improve it.

Collecting materials. Recyclable materials have the most value if they are not mixed with garbage but are sorted before the garbage is sent for disposal. This sorting keeps materials from becoming contaminated, which lowers their usefulness and value. Separating recyclable materials can be more complicated when done at a waste-processing plant. Such special equipment as conveyor belts, screens, and magnets is used to separate large quantities of waste mechanically.

Recyclable materials are collected from consumers mainly through (1) buy-back centers, (2) drop-off centers, and (3) curbside collection programs. Buy-back centers pay people for materials they bring in. People are asked to separate recyclables by type and to separate glass by color. Drop-off centers are usually open longer hours than buy-back centers but do not offer money for the materials. Many communities require residents to participate in curbside collection programs. In these programs, residents of a community separate their materials and put them on the curb by their homes. Trucks pick up the materials and bring them to a central plant for processing. Curbside recycling usually recovers the greatest quantity of materials.

Many businesses and industries also take part in recycling efforts. Offices can recycle such wastes as paper and cardboard. Many countries have laws that require or encourage businesses to purchase products made from recycled materials, such as office paper. These laws provide incentives for businesses to invest in recycling equipment.

Prices paid for recycled waste usually depend on local demand, the quantity that a seller can guarantee to the market, and the degree of contamination of the material. Buyers often reject loads of recyclables that are too dirty.

Recycling is most successful where it is less expensive than other methods of waste management. For example, recycling programs work well in many European countries and in Japan. These areas have ideal conditions for recycling, including high population density, plentiful recyclable materials, low transportation costs, and a shortage of landfill space. Harvey Bryan

Related articles in *World Book* include:

Aluminum (Recycling)
Compost
Conservation (picture)
Environmental pollution
Plastics (Plastics and the environment)
Waste disposal

Red. See Color.
Red Baron. See Richthofen, Baron Manfred von.
Red Beard. See Frederick I.
Red blood cell. See Blood.

Red Cloud (1822-1909) was one of the greatest warriors and chiefs of the Oglala, a band of the Teton Sioux Indians. During the 1860's, Red Cloud and his followers fought to keep the whites out of Sioux territory in what are now Montana, South Dakota, and Wyoming. Some historians have called this struggle Red Cloud's War.

During the 1860's, white settlers began to travel the Bozeman Trail to gold fields in Montana (see **Bozeman Trail**). This trail crossed northeastern Wyoming, a main hunting area of the Sioux. Red Cloud's band continually attacked travelers on the trail. In 1866, to keep the route open, the United States Army built Fort Phil Kearny and Fort Reno in Wyoming and Fort C. F. Smith in Montana. Red Cloud and his allies kept these forts under siege for almost two years.

Smithsonian Institution, Washington, D.C.
Red Cloud

In 1868, the U.S. government agreed to abandon the three forts and not build any more roads through Sioux territory. Because of this victory, Red Cloud has been called the only American Indian who won a war against the U.S. government. He later became an important mediator between his people and white officials. Red Cloud died on Dec. 9, 1909.

Jeffrey P. Shepherd

Red Cross is a worldwide network of organizations whose members work to relieve human suffering. Nearly all countries have Red Cross or Red Crescent societies. Each national society operates its own program. However, Red Cross and Red Crescent workers in all parts of the world are united in their aims. They help relieve human suffering during times of crisis or disaster. Red Cross and Red Crescent organizations have seven fundamental principles that guide their work: (1) humanity, (2) impartiality, (3) neutrality, (4) independence, (5) voluntary service, (6) universality, and (7) unity.

The name Red Cross comes from the flag used by Red Cross organizations. It features a red cross on a white background. The flag honors Switzerland, where the international Red Cross movement was founded in 1863. The Swiss flag is a white cross on a red field. Societies in most Muslim countries use a red crescent on a white field and call themselves Red Crescent societies. In Israel, the society is called the Magen David Adom (MDA) and has a red Star of David on a white field for its flag. In 2006, the international Red Cross and Red Crescent organization formally accepted the MDA. But Israel's symbol is not recognized by international law, and so the MDA uses the red star surrounded by a red diamond or crystal as its symbol outside of Israel. In 2005, the Geneva Conventions—which provide for the humane treatment of civilians, prisoners, and wounded people during wartime—were amended to recognize the red crystal in addition to the red cross and red crescent. See **Flag** (pictures: Flags of world organizations).

The American Red Cross

In the United States, the American Red Cross provides humanitarian services that include disaster relief, biomedical services, health and safety training, community services, and services to military personnel and their families. The American Red Cross is supported by hundreds of thousands of volunteers and tens of thousands of employees.

Disaster services begin long before disaster strikes. American Red Cross workers help communities prevent and prepare for disaster through comprehensive educational programs. The American Red Cross responds every year to tens of thousands of disasters, including house fires, chemical spills, tornadoes, floods, and hurricanes. Relief workers help families recover from tragedy by providing food, clothing, shelter, health care, and counseling.

Biomedical services. The American Red Cross is the primary supplier of blood and blood products in the United States. The organization collects units of blood from millions of donors each year. The Red Cross also conducts research to improve the safety of the nation's blood supply and develop potentially lifesaving medical products.

Health and safety training. The American Red Cross provides health and safety training as part of its mission of emergency prevention and preparedness. Experts in medical and safety fields design the training programs to teach people the skills necessary to respond to an emergency. For example, the Red Cross offers instruction in first aid, including cardiopulmonary resuscitation (CPR) and use of an *automated external defibrillator,* a device to correct abnormal heart rhythms. The organization also provides training in lifeguarding and water safety, HIV/AIDS prevention, and other health and safety issues.

Community services. American Red Cross chapters provide humanitarian services to help people within communities lead safer, healthier, more self-reliant lives. Services include food pantries and home-delivered meals, homeless shelters, school clubs, and nursing home volunteers.

Services to military personnel. The Red Cross helps keep people in touch with family members serving in the U.S. military. The Red Cross locates military personnel and delivers information during times of per-

American Red Cross

Red Cross volunteers are prepared to help when disaster strikes, such as the tornado that destroyed this man's home. Red Cross organizations provide food, clothing, shelter, and medical aid to disaster victims throughout the world.

sonal crisis, such as a death or serious illness, in the family. The organization also arranges emergency financial assistance to help military personnel meet family emergencies. Red Cross workers accompany military forces on missions to provide essential services as well as recreational activities to troops in the field. The Red Cross also offers counseling and assistance to veterans and furnishes trained volunteers to work in military medical facilities and veterans hospitals.

International services. The American Red Cross maintains relations with national societies in other countries and assists the societies in their work. It provides emergency relief, food and sanitation programs, and basic health care to disaster victims in other countries. It also offers training in international humanitarian law and helps reunite families separated by war, disasters, and other emergencies.

Organization. Volunteers and employed staff form the backbone of most Red Cross activities in the United States. Hundreds of Red Cross chapters provide services to communities in every part of the country. Members of Red Cross chapters elect a volunteer board of directors to oversee chapter programs and services. Volunteers also serve on advisory boards for Red Cross blood services regions.

Volunteers and employees work in partnership at all levels of the American Red Cross. They manage local operations and serve on state service councils, on regional and area committees, and at Red Cross national headquarters.

American Red Cross headquarters are in Washington, D.C. A board of governors, made up of volunteers, oversees the organization and develops national policies. The president of the United States appoints the chairperson of the board of governors. Representatives of chapters and blood services regions elect other board members at the organization's annual national meeting. The board selects the chief executive officer and other officers of the American Red Cross.

The Canadian Red Cross

The Canadian Red Cross Society operates thousands of clinics with a network of tens of thousands of volunteers to assist people in communities across the country. The Canadian Red Cross offers a wide variety of services.

Health services. The Red Cross in Canada has pioneered in many nursing projects. It has a number of outpost hospitals and nursing stations that serve remote areas. Hundreds of communities benefit from the free use of sickroom supplies provided by medical equipment loan programs. Registered nurses volunteer to teach basic home nursing.

Until 1998, the National Blood Transfusion Service was a major project of the Canadian Red Cross. In 1998, a new national agency called Canadian Blood Services officially took over collection and distribution of blood in Canada.

The Canadian Red Cross also provides first aid training to teach citizens how to respond to situations involving personal injury or illness. Each year, hundreds of thousands of Canadians benefit from Red Cross swimming and water-safety training programs. Other safety promotion campaigns teach people how to prevent accidents and respond quickly to emergencies.

Community-based services include providing in-home assistance to help elderly or sick individuals maintain their independence and remain in their own home. Other programs help educate children and adults about ways to recognize and prevent domestic abuse.

Disaster services. All provincial divisions of the Canadian Red Cross are prepared to give emergency disaster relief. Their services include the provision of food, shelter, clothing, and medical assistance; registration of disaster victims; and answers to inquiries during the emergency.

The Canadian Red Cross supplies clothing as well as other items to national societies in various countries throughout the world. The organization also sends professional and technical personnel to international disaster areas when it is requested to do so by the International Federation of Red Cross and Red Crescent Societies or the International Committee of the Red Cross. The Canadian Red Cross's tracing and reunion service obtains health and welfare reports on people throughout the world. It also traces missing persons.

Organization. The Canadian Red Cross is governed at all levels by volunteer members. The national headquarters are in Ottawa. To deliver services throughout the country, the Canadian Red Cross is organized into four zones: Western, Ontario, Quebec, and Atlantic. The zones are divided into provincial and territorial divisions. Some divisions are divided further into regional offices, branches, and smaller units, depending on the size of the community and nature of the services provided. There are hundreds of branches, the primary operational units of the Canadian Red Cross, across the nation. Many smaller communities have informal Red Cross units, affiliated with a branch or region, to provide services locally.

The Red Cross in other lands

The American and Canadian Red Cross societies belong to the International Red Cross and Red Crescent Movement, which is made up of national Red Cross and Red Crescent societies in all parts of the world. All member national societies cooperate through the International Federation of Red Cross and Red Crescent Societies (formerly the League of Red Cross Societies), headquartered in Geneva, Switzerland. The federation works to help all national societies develop programs and meet the needs of their citizens.

The International Committee of the Red Cross, also in Geneva, serves as a neutral intermediary during conflicts between nations for the protection of war victims and adherence to the Geneva Conventions. The Geneva Conventions provide guidelines for the protection and humane treatment of wounded soldiers, prisoners of war, and civilian victims of war and civil unrest. The League of Red Cross Societies and the International Committee shared the 1963 Nobel Peace Prize.

The International Committee of the Red Cross, the International Federation of Red Cross and Red Crescent Societies, and the national societies are independent bodies that together make up the International Red Cross and Red Crescent Movement. The International Conference of the Red Cross and Red Crescent is the highest deliberative body of the movement. Delegates from Red Cross and Red Crescent groups and representatives of governments that signed the Geneva Conventions attend the conference about every four years to discuss the Geneva Conventions and world humanitarian problems.

History

Beginnings. Jean Henri Dunant, a Swiss philanthropist, founded the international Red Cross movement. He was touring Italy in 1859 during the Franco-Austrian War. Dunant saw the field at Solferino the day after 40,000 people had been killed or wounded in a battle. Horrified at the suffering of the wounded, he formed a group of volunteers to help them.

In 1862, Dunant wrote a book called *Un Souvenir de Solferino (Recollections of Solferino).* It ended with the plea, "Would it not be possible to found and organize in all civilized countries permanent societies of volunteers who in time of war would give help to the wounded without regard for their nationality?" The appeal won favorable response. On Oct. 26, 1863, delegates from 16 nations and several charitable organizations met in Geneva to discuss Dunant's idea. This conference laid the groundwork for the Red Cross movement and chose the organization's symbol.

Delegates from 15 European nations met in Geneva in August 1864, on invitation from the Swiss Federal Council. Two U.S. observers also attended. Out of this meeting came the First Geneva (or Red Cross) Convention. Later treaties amended and improved it.

In the United States, Congress did not ratify the Geneva Convention for 18 years, fearing foreign entanglements. The American Association for the Relief of Misery on the Battlefields was organized during this time. It adopted the red cross as its emblem. This group disbanded in 1871 because the United States had not yet ratified the Geneva Convention. Clara Barton worked to have the treaty ratified and helped establish the American Association of the Red Cross in 1881. President Chester A. Arthur finally signed the treaty on March 1, 1882. The Senate accepted it a few days later without a dissenting vote. The Red Cross association was later reorganized, and in 1905 Congress granted it a new charter that established the basic organization of today's American Red Cross.

The American Red Cross grew during World War I (1914-1918). It met the welfare needs of rapidly expanding military forces. Red Cross field directors and other workers served troops in the United States and overseas. In 1917, Home Service was set up in many communities to provide a link between military personnel and their families. The Red Cross also organized and equipped 58 base hospitals, 54 of which went overseas. The Junior Red Cross, founded in 1917, gave U.S. schoolchildren a chance to help the war effort.

After the war, the Red Cross aided millions of veterans and helped relieve war-caused suffering in many lands. In the 1920's, the Red Cross established 2,400 public health nursing services throughout the United States.

During World War II (1939-1945), the Red Cross Army-Navy Blood Donor Service collected more than 13 million pints (6,150,000 liters) of blood. Whole blood was flown from the United States to a warfront for the first time during the Korean War (1950-1953). Also during the 1950's, the Red Cross aided refugees of Algerian and Hungarian revolts.

The Red Cross spent nearly $146 million during the 1960's for disaster relief and rehabilitation. The organization provided assistance for survivors of earthquakes in Chile (1960), Yugoslavia (1963), and Alaska (1964). The Red Cross also directed the shipment of $53 million worth of donated food and drugs to Cuba in exchange for the release of about 1,100 prisoners and refugees (see **Cuba** [The Bay of Pigs invasion]).

In the late 1960's and early 1970's, the Red Cross provided hospital and recreational programs for United States armed forces in Vietnam. In 1973, the Red Cross assisted released American prisoners of war. In addition, the organization worked with the U.S. government in 1975 on the resettlement of refugees from Southeast Asia in the United States. Major foreign relief efforts by the American Red Cross followed the earthquakes in Nicaragua in 1972, Guatemala in 1976, and several other nations in the 1980's.

The American Red Cross also took part in the Cambodian refugee relief operation in 1979 and 1980, the medical and food relief effort in Poland in 1982, the drought relief operation in Africa in 1985, and the volcanic eruption effort in Colombia in 1985. In 1990, the Red Cross began refugee relief operations in Jordan as a result of the events that led to the Persian Gulf War of 1991. After the war, it aided Kurdish refugees in camps in Kuwait, Iraq, and Turkey. In 2001, the American Red Cross helped provide relief after floods in Mozambique and Malawi and devastating earthquakes in India. The Red Cross also played a key role in Iraq following a war that began there in 2003. In 2005, the American Red Cross launched a major relief effort after Hurricane Katrina struck New Orleans and other parts of the Gulf Coast. The effort was believed to be the largest response to a natural disaster in the organization's history.

In Canada. George S. Ryerson, an army doctor, founded the Red Cross movement in Canada. He first flew a flag with a red cross on a white background while serving in the Canadian Army Medical Services during the North West Rebellion of 1885. In 1896, Ryerson organized a Canadian branch of the British Red Cross. This branch developed into the Canadian Red Cross Society and was incorporated by an act of the Canadian Parliament in 1909. Critically reviewed by the American Red Cross

See also **Barton, Clara; Dunant, Jean Henri; First aid; Geneva Conventions.**

Additional resources

Moorehead, Caroline. *Dunant's Dream: War, Switzerland and the History of the Red Cross.* Carroll & Graf, 1998.

Pollard, Michael. *The Red Cross and the Red Crescent.* New Discovery Bks., 1994.

Red deer is the common name for a species of deer that lives in forests of Europe, Asia, and northern Africa. There are several subspecies of red deer. Scientists classify the *American elk,* also called *wapiti,* as a subspecies of red deer (see **Elk**).

Red deer have smooth coats that range in color from rich, reddish-brown in summer to grayish-brown in winter. The *hart* (adult male) grows stately, branched antlers that are shed each year. A hart weighs from 250 to 350 pounds (113 to 159 kilograms) and stands 3 ½ to 4 ½ feet (1 to 1.4 meters) high.

Most *hinds* (adult females) are shorter than the harts and have no antlers. American elk are much larger than other red deer. Males may weigh up to 1,000 pounds (500 kilograms). Gregory K. Snyder

Scientific classification. Red deer belong to the deer family, Cervidae. They are *Cervus elaphus.*

See also **Deer.**

Red drum. See **Redfish.**

Red gum. See **Sweet gum.**

Red Jacket (1750?-1830) was a Seneca Indian leader and noted orator. He strongly opposed efforts by whites to force their culture on the Seneca.

Thomas Gilcrease Institute of American History and Art, Tulsa, Oklahoma

Red Jacket

Red Jacket and his tribe aided the British during the Revolutionary War in America (1775-1783). A British officer rewarded him with a red jacket, the source of his name. Red Jacket served as an official spokesman of the Iroquois Confederacy, which included the Seneca, in dealings between the Indians and the United States government after the war. The Seneca leader encouraged his tribe to live in peace with the whites. He also resisted efforts by Christian missionaries, other whites, and even the Seneca prophet Handsome Lake to change some traditional Seneca ways of life.

Red Jacket was born in what is now Seneca County in New York. His Indian name was *Sagoyewatha,* which means *He Keeps Them Awake.* He died of cholera on the Buffalo Creek Reservation in New York. A monument of him stands in Buffalo, New York. Robert E. Powless

Red pepper. See **Cayenne pepper.**

Red River, so named because of the red-colored sediment it carries, forms much of the boundary between Oklahoma and Texas. It is about 1,300 miles (2,090 kilometers) long. The Red River rises in northern Texas. Its north fork has its source east of Amarillo, Texas, and the Prairie Dog Town fork rises south of it. The river flows through southwestern Arkansas and into Louisiana. It joins the Atchafalaya River about 5 miles (8 kilometers) north of Simmesport, Louisiana (see **Louisiana** [terrain map]). See also **Lake Texoma.** Daniel D. Arreola

Red River of the North is a major waterway of the United States and Canada. In Canada, it is known as the Red River. But the full name is used in the United States to distinguish it from the Red River that rises in northern Texas. The Red River of the North flows north 545 miles (877 kilometers) and empties into Lake Winnipeg in the Canadian province of Manitoba. It forms part of Canada's Saskatchewan-Nelson river system. It runs through a level plain that was formerly the bed of Lake Agassiz, a glacial lake (see **Lake Agassiz**). The Red River Valley is one of the richest farming areas in the world.

The Red River of the North is formed by the union of the Otter Tail and Bois de Sioux rivers at Wahpeton, North Dakota, opposite Breckenridge, Minnesota. The Red forms the boundary between North Dakota and Minnesota. The Otter Tail rises in west-central Minnesota, just west of the headwaters of the Mississippi River. The Bois de Sioux begins in Lake Traverse. The Red River flows northward into Lake Winnipeg.

Farmers in the Red River Valley raise wheat, oats, flax,

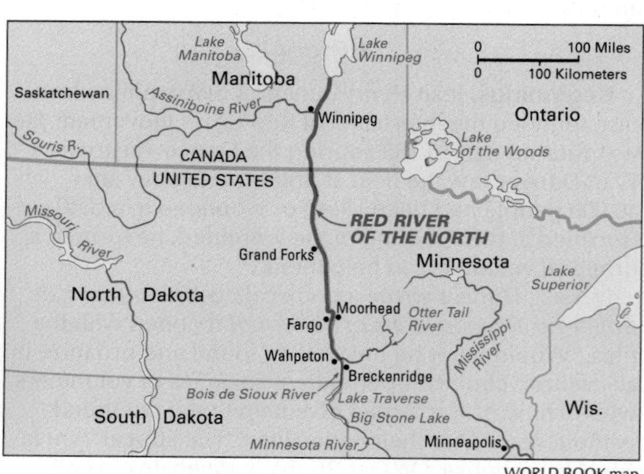

WORLD BOOK map

Location of the Red River of the North

barley, potatoes, sugar beets, sunflowers, hogs, and poultry. Cities along the Red River of the North include Fargo and Grand Forks, in North Dakota; Moorhead, Minnesota; and Winnipeg, Manitoba. Boats carried goods between Winnipeg and Fargo until 1878, when a railway began to serve the valley. Winnipeg is now protected from flooding by the Red River Floodway, a channel that directs the flow of the river around the city. In 1997, severe flooding caused major damage along the river, especially in the Grand Forks area. John S. Brierley

Red River Rebellion occurred in 1869 and 1870, when settlers of the Red River Valley of what is now Manitoba resisted steps to put the valley under Canadian government control. The region had long been governed by the Hudson's Bay Company. The uprising is sometimes called the First Riel Rebellion, after its leader, Louis Riel.

The Hudson's Bay Company had allowed the valley's residents much independence. In 1869, however, the company surrendered its rights in Rupert's Land, including the Red River Valley, to the United Kingdom. The British decided to transfer Rupert's Land to the Canadian government, which paid the company for the land. The Canadian government planned to develop the region for farmers from what is now eastern Canada.

In 1869, the population of the Red River Valley consisted of Indians, settlers, and a few fur traders. Most of the settlers were *Métis* (people of mixed white and Indian ancestry). The settlers farmed land to which they held no formal title. They feared that the transfer of the valley to the Canadian government would threaten their land rights and their distinctive culture.

The revolt. Shortly before the transfer of Rupert's Land to the Canadian government, roadbuilders, surveyors, and officials of all kinds from the east descended upon the valley. One of their chief aims was to divide the land into townships and sections in advance of incoming settlers. This activity angered the residents.

A leader arose among the Métis. He was Louis Riel, a young man of French, Irish, and Indian descent who came from a prominent local family. The Canadian government then sent out William McDougall as the first governor of the new territory. When the Métis heard of McDougall's approach, they determined to prevent him from entering the territory. A group of Métis met McDougall at the border of Rupert's Land and forced him to turn back. Riel then led the Métis in a successful attempt to capture Fort Garry, at what is now Winnipeg, and set up a *provisional* (temporary) government there.

As a result of the rebellion, the Canadian government decided not to take control of the area on Dec. 1, 1869, as it had planned. Early in 1870, a group of Métis with much popular support in the valley decided to negotiate with the Canadian government. But before any negotiations began, settlers loyal to Canada launched an unsuccessful attack on Fort Garry. Riel's provisional government imprisoned several of them. One of the prisoners was an English Canadian named Thomas Scott. The provisional government condemned Scott as a traitor and had him shot. Scott's death inflamed the people of eastern Canada against the provisional government.

End of the conflict. After the killing of Scott, the Canadian government ordered troops under Colonel Garnet Wolseley to the Red River Valley. But before the force could start westward, Riel's provisional government opened negotiations with the government of Canada. The Canadian government agreed to admit the Red River area to the Canadian Confederation as a self-governing province. It also set aside 1,400,000 acres (567,000 hectares) of land for the Métis. But many of the Métis moved westward into what is now Saskatchewan. In addition, the Canadian government refused to pardon Riel for actions taken by the provisional government, including the killing of Scott. As a result, Riel fled to the United States. In 1885, he returned to Canada to lead another Métis uprising, known as the North West Rebellion. But he was captured and hanged for treason later that year. J. M. Bumsted

See also **Manitoba** (History); **Métis; North West Rebellion; Riel, Louis.**

Red Sea is a long, narrow arm of the Indian Ocean that separates the Arabian Peninsula from northeastern Africa. The sea ranks as one of the world's busiest waterways. Much of the trade between Europe and Asia passes through the Red Sea, which is connected with the Mediterranean Sea by the Suez Canal. Scholars are uncertain about the origin of the sea's name. One widely held theory is that the Red Sea is so named because a type of algae forms a reddish-brown scum on its surface during the summer.

The Red Sea covers about 176,000 square miles (456,000 square kilometers), an area larger than the state of California. The sea is about 1,400 miles (2,200 kilometers) long and about 220 miles (350 kilometers) wide at its widest point. Its average depth is 1,765 feet (538 meters). Its deepest point is 9,974 feet (3,040 meters).

At its northern end, the Red Sea branches into the Gulf of Suez on the west and the Gulf of Aqaba on the east. The Sinai Peninsula lies between the two gulfs. The Gulf of Suez, a major offshore oil-producing area, leads into the Suez Canal. The Gulf of Aqaba leads to the Israeli port of Elat and the Jordanian port of Aqaba. At the southern end of the Red Sea, a narrow waterway called the Strait of Bab el Mandeb flows into the Gulf of Aden, which, in turn, leads into the Indian Ocean.

The Red Sea lies in the Great Rift Valley system, a series of valleys that cut through much of eastern Africa and part of southwestern Asia. High cliffs tower above both banks of the sea. In most places, narrow coastal

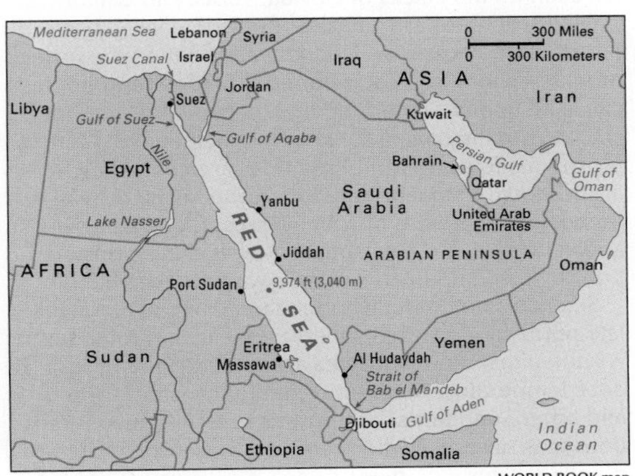

Location of the Red Sea

plains lie between the cliffs and the sea. The Red Sea has large numbers of coral reefs. The reefs, together with irregular currents and strong winds, make navigation in the Red Sea difficult for small vessels.

In summer, the water temperature at the surface of the Red Sea averages 85 °F (29 °C). The waters are among the saltiest in the world. Extreme heat in the region produces a rapid rate of evaporation, resulting in the high salt concentration. Some salt is collected in evaporation pans for local use. Many varieties of fish live in the Red Sea. But the number of fish of each variety is too small to make commercial fishing profitable.

The Red Sea was probably formed millions of years ago when the Arabian Peninsula and the African continent drifted apart. One of the most famous stories in the Bible describes the parting of the waters of the Red Sea, which enabled the Israelites to escape from Egypt (Exodus 14). However, because the Hebrew text actually says "sea of reeds," most modern scholars believe the body of water was actually the marshy lands east of the Nile Delta, well to the north of the Red Sea.

The Red Sea has served as an important trade route since ancient times. Before the opening of the Suez Canal in 1869, goods were transported overland by camel or donkey between the Mediterranean and Red seas. Bernard Reich

Red snapper. See **Snapper.**

Red tape is an unfavorable term used to describe the inefficiency of any large bureaucracy, public or private. The term originated in England during the 1700's. People used red string to tie legal and official documents together. Later, the term came to mean official routine in general. *Red tape* may describe an official's rigid observance of rules and regulations; the routing of requests and orders through channels, resulting in delay; or excessive paperwork associated with the administration of a program. See also **Bureaucracy.** Charles O. Jones

Red tide is a term used for brownish or reddish areas of ocean, river, or lake water. The color comes from the presence of millions of microscopic organisms in the water. The discolored areas may range from less than a few square yards or meters to over 1,000 square miles (2,600 square kilometers). They may last from a few hours to several months. Red tides appear in waters in most parts of the world. In the United States, they are often seen off the coasts of Florida, Texas, and California.

Many red tides are harmless. But some kill fish and other water animals, which then may float on the water or wash ashore in great numbers. The decaying bodies cause an unpleasant odor. Still other red tides do not kill sea life, but they make the shellfish that feed on them poisonous to eat. Harmful red tides are caused by several species of *dinoflagellates* (one-celled organisms). Some dinoflagellates produce a poison that paralyzes and kills fish. Dinoflagellates may also kill fish during red tides by using up nearly all the oxygen in the water.

Scientists do not fully understand why the dinoflagellate population suddenly increases, causing red tides. It is known that dinoflagellates accumulate when the nutrients, temperature, amount of sunlight, water currents, and other conditions in the water suit their needs. Red tides may decrease when other sea organisms eat the dinoflagellates. David L. Garrison

See also **Dinoflagellate; Pfiesteria.**

Red-winged blackbird. See **Blackbird.**

Redbird is the common name for all birds with red or mostly red plumage. In the United States, the name is often applied to the cardinal and occasionally to the scarlet tanager and summer tanager. See also **Cardinal** (bird); **Tanager.**

Redbreast. See **Robin.**

Redbud is the name for a group of trees and shrubs native to Asia, North America, and southern Europe. Redbuds are particularly beautiful early in spring when they are covered with delicate blossoms, each about 1 inch (2.5 centimeters) long. The flowers, which may be pink, purplish-pink, or white, reach full bloom before the leaves appear. Redbud trees have smooth, reddish-brown bark and heart-shaped leaves. The trees bear many seeds in flat, thin pods. The seeds are a valuable source of food for animals.

Redbuds grow best in fertile, sandy soil. Some grow 40 feet (12 meters) high. People cultivate the trees from seeds or from cuttings. Redbuds are widely planted as ornamental trees because of their colorful blossoms and graceful form.

One species of redbud is called the *Judas tree* be-

© Irvin L. Oakes, Photo Researchers

A redbud tree has spreading branches with reddish-brown bark. Gardeners use redbuds as decorative shrubs.

© Thinkstock

Clusters of redbud blossoms cover the tree's branches in the early spring, before the leaves begin to unfold.

cause of the belief that Judas Iscariot, the betrayer of Jesus Christ, hanged himself on this kind of tree. The Judas tree grows in southern Europe and western Asia.

Linda B. Brubaker

Scientific classification. Redbuds make up the genus *Cercis.* The Judas tree is *Cercis siliquastrum.*

See also **Tree** (Broadleaf and needleleaf trees [picture]).

Redcoat. See **Revolution, American.**

Redfish is a name applied to several kinds of fish, but particularly to the *red drum,* also called *channel bass.* This game fish lives along the Atlantic Coast of North America from Massachusetts to northern Mexico. It has a gray skin with a reddish sheen. The fish grows to 5 feet (1.5 meters) long and may weigh up to 75 pounds (34 kilograms), but red drums of more than 40 pounds (18 kilograms) are rare. This popular food fish has been caught in large numbers, and fishery agencies have restricted the catching of red drums in the Gulf of Mexico.

The term *redfish* is also applied to the *California sheephead,* a red fish of southern California. This richly colored fish has a thick, crimson body with blackish-purple fins. It weighs up to 15 pounds (7 kilograms) and is sometimes called the *fathead* because of the fatty lump on its blunt forehead. Its flesh is prized, especially by the Chinese, who dry and salt it. *Redfish* is also the name given in Alaska to the *red salmon,* also called *sockeye salmon* (see **Salmon**).

William J. Richards

Scientific classification. The red drum is *Sciaenops ocellatus.* The California sheephead is *Semicossyphus pulcher.*

Redford, Robert (1937-), is an American motion-picture actor and director. He is known for his good looks and understated acting style. Redford won the 1980 Academy Award as best director for *Ordinary People.* He also directed the films *A River Runs Through It* (1992), *Quiz Show* (1994), *The Legend of Bagger Vance* (2000), and *The Conspirator* (2011). He directed and starred in *The Horse Whisperer* (1998), *Lions for Lambs* (2007), and *The Company You Keep* (2012).

In 1981, Redford founded the Sundance Institute, a nonprofit organization in Park City, Utah. The institute is dedicated to discovering, developing, and training new filmmakers, composers, and playwrights. It is best known for the Sundance Film Festival, an annual motion-picture exhibition and competition. The festival concentrates on independent filmmaking—that is, movies made outside the big-budget, commercially oriented Hollywood film industry.

George Rodriguez, Shooting Star

Robert Redford

Charles Robert Redford, Jr., was born on Aug. 18, 1937, in Santa Monica, California. He first won praise in 1963 in the Broadway comedy *Barefoot in the Park.* He also starred in the film version in 1967. Redford became a movie star as an outlaw in *Butch Cassidy and the Sundance Kid* (1969) and as a successful screenwriter in *The Way We Were* (1973). His other notable films as an actor include *The Candidate* and *Jeremiah Johnson* (both 1972), *The Sting* (1973), *The Great Gatsby* (1974), *Three Days of the Condor* (1975), *All the President's Men* (1976), *The Electric Horseman* (1979), *The Natural* (1984), *Out of Africa* (1985), *Spy Game* (2001), *The Clearing* (2004), *All Is Lost* (2013), *Captain America: The Winter Soldier* (2014), *A Walk in the Woods* and *Truth* (both 2015), *Pete's Dragon* (2016), and *The Old Man & the Gun* (2018).

In 1996, Redford launched the Sundance Channel, a cable television network that airs independent films and original programs. In 2014, the network was rebranded as SundanceTV.

Louis Giannetti

Redgrave, Michael (1908-1985), was a British actor who became known for his roles in the plays of William Shakespeare. Redgrave made more than 50 motion pictures and played a wide variety of parts ranging from comic to tragic. He was also a noted stage director.

In 1934, Redgrave made his stage debut in the play *Counsellor-at-Law.* He began a movie career in 1938 in *The Lady Vanishes,* a famous suspense film directed by Alfred Hitchcock. His other movies include *The Stars Look Down* (1939), *Dead of Night* (1945), *Fame Is the Spur* (1947), *The Browning Version* (1951), *The Importance of Being Earnest* (1951), and *The Loneliness of the Long Distance Runner* (1963).

Michael Scudamore Redgrave was born on March 20, 1908, in Bristol and graduated from Cambridge University. He was knighted in 1959. He married Rachel Kempson, a famous stage actress. Their daughters, Vanessa and Lynn, became noted film and stage actresses. Vanessa Redgrave's daughters, Natasha Richardson and Joely Richardson, also became successful actresses. Michael Redgrave died on March 21, 1985.

John F. Mariani

Redpoll is the name of a group of small songbirds found in North America, Asia, and Europe. Redpolls are 5 to 5 ½ inches (12.7 to 14 centimeters) long. The *common redpoll* has a patch of red feathers on the forehead, a black chin, and whitish underparts, with dark streaks on the sides. The adult male has a rosy-pink breast. The *hoary redpoll,* or *Arctic redpoll,* resembles the common redpoll but is paler in color. Some scientists consider the *lesser redpoll,* which looks much like the common redpoll, to be a third species. However, other scientists consider it a subspecies of the common redpoll.

Redpolls breed in Arctic regions. They build grassy nests on the ground or in small trees or bushes. The females lay from three to seven pale blue eggs. Redpolls eat plant buds, seeds, and insects. In North America,

WORLD BOOK illustration by Trevor Boyer, Linden Artists, Ltd.

The common redpoll has a reddish crown. The adult male has rosy-pink breast feathers.

common redpolls sometimes migrate as far south as the central United States for the winter. Martha Hatch Balph

Scientific classification. The scientific name for the common redpoll is *Acanthis flammea.* The hoary redpoll is *A. hornemanni.* The lesser redpoll is *A. cabaret* if treated as a species, or *A. flammea cabaret* if treated as a subspecies.

Redshift is a stretching of the wavelengths of light or other electromagnetic waves, observed most often in radiation given off by astronomical objects. *Wavelength* is the distance between successive crests of a wave. Redshifts can occur in any type of electromagnetic wave, including radio waves, visible light, and X rays. Most observed redshifts result from two different causes. An object's motion relative to the observer can produce a *Doppler redshift.* A *cosmological redshift* results from the expansion of space between the object and the observer. Astronomers often measure an object's redshift to determine its speed or distance relative to Earth.

The Doppler redshift. The motion of a wave source relative to an observer can cause a change in the wavelength of light, sound, or other waves given off by the object. Consider, for example, a train that whistles as it moves past an observer. As the train approaches, successive waves of sound from the whistle crowd together, resulting in a shorter wavelength and thus a higher observed pitch. As the train moves away, the waves spread out, and the listener hears a lower pitch. Scientists call this shifting in wavelength the *Doppler effect.* See **Sound** (diagram: The Doppler effect).

Light waves given off by an object moving away from an observer will also spread out to longer wavelengths. The wavelength of a light wave determines its color, with red having the longest wavelength of visible light. The light will therefore appear redder, or redshifted, as a result of the object's motion. Likewise, if the object is moving toward the observer, its light waves will crowd together and appear bluer, an effect known as *blueshift.*

Astronomers measure redshifts and blueshifts by arranging light from a cosmic source into a band of wavelengths called a *spectrum.* First, they examine the spectrum for characteristic wavelengths of light produced by specific atoms or molecules. They then compare these wavelengths to those given off by the same atoms or molecules on Earth. Such features may appear redshifted or blueshifted by an amount that depends on the speed and direction of the astronomical object's motion.

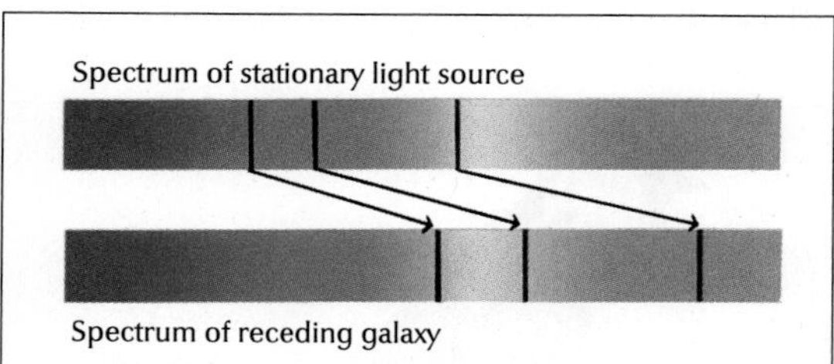

WORLD BOOK diagram by Ernest Norcia

Redshift causes a displacement of lines in the *spectrum* (band of colors) sent out by a galaxy that is *receding* (becoming farther away) from Earth. If the distance between the galaxy and Earth were not changing, those lines would appear in the positions shown in the upper diagram. The cause of the displacement is known as *redshift* because the lines are displaced toward the red end of the spectrum.

Scientists have observed many redshifted and blueshifted objects within our own galaxy, the Milky Way.

Cosmological redshift. Astronomers have found that nearly all cosmic objects far outside the Milky Way have only redshifts—indicating that they are *receding* (becoming farther away) from our galaxy. In 1929, the American astronomer Edwin P. Hubble discovered this effect, which became known as the cosmological redshift. Hubble found that cosmic objects have redshifts in proportion to their distance from our galaxy, a principle called *Hubble's law.* This law can be expressed by the equation $v = H \times d$, where v is the redshift of the object expressed as a rate of recession, H is a fixed number known as the *Hubble constant,* and d is the object's distance from Earth. Astronomers can use Hubble's law to derive an object's distance using its redshift.

The cosmological redshift does not result from the Doppler effect. Instead, it is produced by the expansion of the universe. Most scientists believe that the universe began expanding about 14 billion years ago in a cosmic explosion called the *big bang.* As the universe expands, the distance between most galaxies increases. The wavelength of light also steadily grows as it travels through the expanding space. The farther the radiation travels—that is, the more space it travels through—the more its wavelength stretches. Mario Mateo

See also **Cosmology** (The movement of galaxies); **Electromagnetic waves; Light** (The Doppler effect); **Spectrum.**

Redstart is a group of small woodland birds. The *American redstart* breeds throughout most of North America. The male is black with vivid salmon-red or orange-red markings. The female and young are brown with dull yellow markings. The female lays four or five creamy white eggs. The bird feeds chiefly on insects. The *painted redstart* breeds from the southwestern part of the United States to Central America. The male is black, with a bright red breast and white marks on the wings and tail. The female usually lays three or four eggs. See also **Bird** (picture: Birds of forests and woodlands). Sandra L. Vehrencamp

Scientific classification. Redstarts belong to the wood-warbler family, Parulidae. The American redstart is *Setophaga ruticilla.* The painted redstart is *Myioborus pictus.*

Reduction is a chemical reaction in which a substance gains electrons. The term originally referred to any chemical process in which a substance either combines with hydrogen or loses oxygen. Reduction is the opposite of *oxidation,* a chemical reaction in which a substance gives up electrons. Reduction and oxidation always occur together. These two combined reactions are known as *redox reactions.* See **Oxidation.**

Many kinds of processes involve reduction. For example, metal plating occurs when metal *ions* (electrically charged atoms) in a solution are reduced to form neutral atoms. When a piece of copper is placed in a solution containing silver ions (Ag^+), it slowly becomes coated with silver. In this process, each positively charged silver ion gains an electron given up by a copper atom and becomes electrically neutral. The chemical equation for the reduction of silver is written as follows:

$$Ag^+ + 1e^- \rightarrow Ag.$$

An example of the original meaning of reduction is the combining of nitrogen and hydrogen gases in the production of ammonia (NH_3). Another example is the removal of oxygen from zinc oxide (ZnO) to form metallic zinc. Zinc may be extracted from its ore in this manner.

Cathleen J. Hapeman

See also **Corrosion; Electrolysis.**

Redwood is a common name for several magnificent forest trees. One well-known type, the *coast redwood* or *California redwood,* grows along the west coast of the United States from central California to southern Oregon. It thrives in a narrow, mountainous region facing the Pacific Ocean, rarely more than 50 miles (80 kilometers) inland. Another redwood, the *dawn redwood,* comes from China. A third species, called the *sequoia, big tree,* or *Sierra redwood,* grows in central California. For a discussion of this last species, see **Sequoia.**

The coast redwood is the world's tallest living tree. Adult trees from mature forests typically grow 200 to 300 feet (61 to 90 meters) high, with trunks 8 to 12 feet (2.4 to 3.7 meters) wide. The tallest known redwood, in northern California, stands over 377 feet (115 meters) high. The coast redwood is the state tree of California.

In a typical redwood forest, the massive trees grow close together, shutting out sunlight. Thick summer fog often blankets the forest, and the trees obtain water from this fog. Redwood forests have little underbrush, for few plants can survive in the cool, dim conditions beneath the trees. Tight circles of young redwoods, called *fairy rings,* grow from the roots of many old stumps, completely enclosing them. The lowest branches of mature trees may hang 80 to 100 feet (24 to 30 meters) above the ground. However, the lowest branches of young redwoods grow all the way to ground level.

Bob Fitch, Black Star

The massive trunk of a redwood dwarfs a curious sightseer. Redwoods grow along the West Coast of the United States from central California to southern Oregon.

The coast redwood possesses a range of needle sizes and shapes. Spiky needles from the lower branches grow about 1 inch (2.5 centimeters) long. Smaller, scale-like needles appear on the upper branches. All needles remain on the tree for several years. The tree's oval-shaped cones measure about 1 inch in length. Tightly packed under each scale of a cone are tiny reddish-brown seeds, each about $\frac{1}{16}$ inch (1.6 millimeters) long.

A coast redwood has reddish, deeply grooved bark that measures from 6 to 18 inches (15 to 45 centimeters) thick. This thick bark protects the tree from damage caused by fire. The tree's wood is soft, light red, and weak. However, it is also remarkably resistant to decay, disease, and insects. A coast redwood can live more than 2,000 years.

The dawn redwood is a close relative of the coast redwood. Scientists once believed that dawn redwoods were extinct, knowing them only from fossils. But in 1941, a Chinese forester, Tsou Kan, discovered a large tree growing in a secluded valley in central China. In 1946, two Chinese botanists, Hsen-Hsu Hu and Wan-Chun Cheng, identified this tree as the dawn redwood. Living dawn redwoods have since been found in Sichuan and Hubei provinces of China. Fossils show that the tree once grew in North America as far south as California, as well as in Greenland, Siberia, and Japan.

Unlike coast redwoods, which are evergreens, dawn redwoods are *deciduous trees.* They shed their needles each fall and grow new ones again in the spring. These needles resemble those of coast redwoods, but they are slightly narrower and not as stiff. Dawn redwoods typically stand about 100 feet (30 meters) tall.

Like coast redwoods, dawn redwoods grow readily from seeds. Scientists brought seedling trees from China and planted them in the eastern United States and the Pacific Northwest. Today, dawn redwoods thrive in parks and gardens around the world.

Redwood conservation. Most coast redwood forests receive protection in state and national parks and from conservation organizations. Redwood parks rank among the most visited forests in the United States. The long-term conservation of all redwoods will depend upon incorporating scientific research about the trees with conservation and management plans and policies.

Todd E. Dawson

Scientific classification. Redwoods belong to the baldcypress family, Taxodiaceae. The scientific name of the coast redwood is *Sequoia sempervirens.* The dawn redwood is *Metasequoia glyptostroboides.*

See also **Conifer; Tree** (Broadleaf and needleleaf trees [picture]).

Redwood National Park, in northern California, is in the huge forest of redwood trees along the Pacific Coast from central California to southern Oregon. For location, see **California** (political map). The world's tallest living trees, redwoods that rise more than 370 feet (113 meters) high, are in the park. The park has 37 miles (60 kilometers) of scenic coastline. Three state parks lie within its boundaries. Congress established Redwood National

Park in 1968. For the park's area, see **National Park System** (table: National parks). See also **Redwood.**

Critically reviewed by the National Park Service

Reed is a common name for many kinds of tall, slender grass plants. The word may also refer to the stems of these plants, which are often jointed in many places. The stems may be as slender and fragile as straw, or as thick and sturdy as bamboo. The pith that fills the center of the reed can usually be removed, leaving a hollow, jointed tube. The hollow stems of the reed have been used to make musical instruments.

The reed musical instruments have a mouthpiece with a vibrating strip once made only of reed. Plastic, wood, glass, and metal are now used to make the "reed." Farmers in Europe thatch houses with other types of reeds.

Reeds grow in almost all countries of the temperate and warm regions. They are found in a variety of habitats. Straw is sometimes called reed in the United Kingdom. The American Indians often made the roots, young leaves, and stems of various kinds of reeds a part of their diet. David A. Francko

Reed, John (1887-1920), was an American journalist and revolutionist. He is best known for his book *Ten Days That Shook the World* (1919), an eyewitness account of the Russian Revolution of 1917. He also helped organize the first Communist Party in the United States.

Reed was born on Oct. 22, 1887, in Portland, Oregon. He graduated from Harvard University in 1910 and the next year moved to New York City. He became an editor of *The Masses,* a Socialist journal of politics and culture. Reed gained national attention for his reporting of the revolt led by Pancho Villa of Mexico in 1914. He served as a reporter in Europe later in 1914 and in 1915, during World War I. In 1917, Reed and his wife, the journalist Louise Bryant, went to Russia. Reed became a supporter of V. I. Lenin, leader of a group of Russian Communist revolutionists known as the Bolsheviks. Reed observed the Bolsheviks' victory in the Russian Revolution.

After returning to the United States, Reed helped form the Communist Labor Party. In 1919, he went to Russia on business for the party. While trying to return to the United States, Reed was arrested in Finland and imprisoned for 13 weeks. Then he returned to Russia, and he died there of typhus on Oct. 19, 1920. He was buried in front of the Kremlin in Moscow.

Robert A. Rosenstone

Reed, Thomas Brackett (1839-1902), served as speaker of the United States House of Representatives from 1889 to 1891 and from 1895 to 1899. He was sometimes called *Czar Reed* because of the blunt way he controlled the House. A Maine Republican, Reed served in the House from 1877 to 1899. In 1890, he won adoption of "Reed's Rules," which increased the speaker's power but made the House more effective. The House still uses many of these rules. Reed was born on Oct. 18, 1839, in Portland, Maine. He died on Dec. 7, 1902.

Edward A. Lukes-Lukaszewski

Reed, Walter (1851-1902), a medical officer in the United States Army, helped show how to control typhoid fever and yellow fever. During the Spanish-American War (1898), he directed a commission to study the origin and spread of typhoid fever in Army camps. Experiments showed that flies were the main carriers of the infection and that dust and uncleanliness helped spread it.

In 1900 and 1901, Reed headed a commission to investigate an epidemic of yellow fever among American troops in Cuba. He and the other doctors, including James Carroll and Jesse Lazear, carried on a series of daring experiments. Several doctors, as well as some soldiers, volunteered to be infected by yellow fever germs to study the course of the disease. All of them contracted the disease but survived. Two others, who were not volunteers, became infected accidentally and died as a result. The experiments established that the bite of certain mosquitoes transmits yellow fever. In addition, the experiments showed how the disease might be controlled. See **Yellow fever.**

Reed was born on Sept. 13, 1851, in Gloucester County, Virginia. He studied medicine at the University of Virginia and at Bellevue Hospital Medical College in New York City. He entered the U.S. Army in 1875. Reed died on Nov. 22, 1902. Walter Reed National Military Medical Center Bethesda, in Maryland, is named for him.

Audrey B. Davis

Reef. See **Atoll; Coral reef.**

Reference book. See **Almanac; Atlas; Dictionary; Encyclopedia; Library.**

Referendum. See **Initiative and referendum.**

Reflection is the return of a wave of energy, such as light, heat, sound, or radio, after it strikes a surface. Reflection can be compared to the action of a ball rebounding from a wall. A ball thrown at right angles to the wall will bounce back in the same line. If the ball is thrown along a path that makes less than a right angle with the wall, its path on rebounding will make the same angle with the wall, but on the opposite side of the point where the ball hit the wall. Imagine a line drawn to make a 90-degree angle with the wall at the point where the ball struck. The angle formed by the path of the thrown ball and this line is called the *angle of incidence.* The corresponding angle made by the rebounding ball is known as the *angle of reflection.* These angles are equal.

The principle of reflection has many applications in daily living. A mirror (a glass coated with silver) reflects most of the light that strikes it. The best example of the reflection of sound waves is the echo. Radar uses the reflection of radio waves. Joseph A. Muscari

Related articles in ***World Book*** include:

Echo
Kaleidoscope
Light (Reflection and absorption)
Mirror
Parabola
Radar
Sound (Reflection)
Telescope

Reflex action. If you accidentally touch a hot stove, you jerk away before you have time to think what you are doing. Actions of this kind, which are not planned or decided beforehand, are called reflex actions. Each reflex involves some stimulus that causes a response. In the above example, the hot stove was the stimulus and the jerking away was the response.

Reflex actions are quite common and easy to notice. If light is directed at a person's eye, the pupil of the eye will become smaller. When the light is removed and the person's eye is shaded, the pupil becomes larger again. The light acts as a stimulus, and the reaction of the pupil is the eye's response. Doctors often test a person's reflex actions. Frequently they test the *patellar reflex,* or knee jerk. The patient sits with her or his knees crossed, and the doctor strikes a point just below the kneecap. This causes the patient's foot to kick suddenly.

Scientists call these kinds of reflexes *unconditioned reflexes.* They occur in all normal people and many animals. Unlike most of human behavior, unconditioned reflexes occur with no specific learning or experience. They are considered involuntary acts, because a response always occurs when a stimulus is presented.

How reflex action occurs. Most reflex acts are very complicated. But in the simplest forms, four events are involved. Briefly, these events could be called (1) reception, (2) conduction, (3) transmission, and (4) response. Stimulation is received by *receptors,* or sensitive nerve endings. These may be in the eye, ear, nose, tongue, or skin. Energy from the stimulus is changed into nerve impulses and conducted from the receptor to the central nervous system. From there, the nerve impulses are transmitted to the motor nerves, which control muscle action. The motor nerves conduct the impulses to the muscles and glands, causing them to respond, or act.

Most reflex acts are much more complicated than this. They often involve other parts of the nervous system, such as the brain. Reflex acts are quicker than voluntary acts. You jerk your hand away from a hot stove before you feel pain. You do not have to take the time to decide exactly what you are going to do.

People have many reflex reactions to emotional stimuli. These include changes in blood pressure and respiration. A lie detector measures certain body reactions to emotional stimuli. A person telling a lie usually has small emotional reactions that can be detected because of these reflex reactions. See **Lie detector**.

Conditioned reflex, another kind of reflex action, works by association. For example, a dog's mouth begins to water when the animal smells food. The Russian physiologist Ivan P. Pavlov showed that the flow of saliva—though originally an automatic reaction to the smell of food—can become a conditioned reflex. Pavlov rang a bell each time he brought food to a dog. Eventually, the dog's mouth began to water when Pavlov merely rang the bell—with no food being present. The dog associated the ringing of the bell with the food, just as it associated the odor with the food. Daniel S. Barth

See also **Nervous system**.

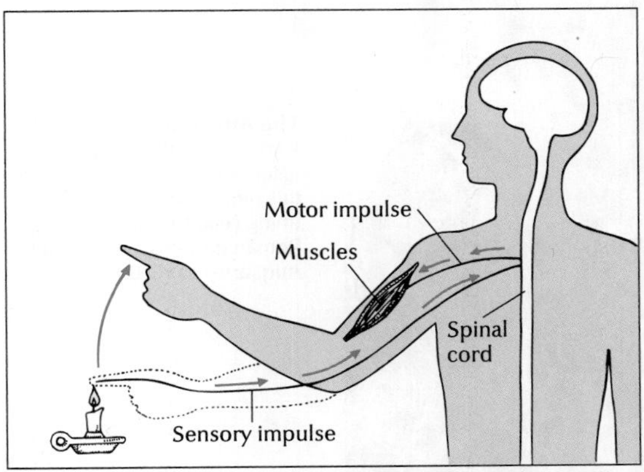

WORLD BOOK diagram by Patricia Wynne

A reflex action occurs automatically. When a person touches a candle flame, impulses travel along a nerve to the spinal cord. The message is relayed to the muscles, which jerk the arm back.

Reform Party was a conservative political party in Canada. Based in Alberta, it gained much support in Canada's Western provinces. The party favored extensive federal budget cuts to reduce the national debt, greater equality among Canada's provinces, and lower immigration. It also supported amending Canada's constitution to provide for an elected and more powerful Senate.

The Reform Party was founded in 1987. Preston Manning, an Alberta business consultant, became its leader. He claimed Canada's traditional parties had lost touch with voters' concerns. The Reform Party received strong support from Alberta's oil industry, which claimed it had been hurt by federal government policies.

In 1989, one Reformer won a seat in Canada's House of Commons. In 1990, a Reformer was appointed to the Canadian Senate. In 1992, the party helped defeat the Charlottetown accord, a set of constitutional amendments proposed by leaders of the federal and provincial governments. The plan included recognizing French-speaking Quebec as a distinct society within Canada. In 1993, Reformers captured 52 House seats. In the 1997 general election, the Reform Party won 60 of 301 House seats—more than any other party except the Liberal Party—and became Canada's official opposition party. In 2000, Reform members voted to dissolve their party and join a new national conservative party called the Canadian Reform Conservative Alliance. The new party was commonly known as the Canadian Alliance. In 2003, the party merged with the national Progressive Conservative Party to form the Conservative Party of Canada. See also **Day, Stockwell; Manning, Preston.** J. L. Granatstein

Reform Party is a political party in the United States that promises to reform national politics. Ross Perot, a wealthy Texas businessman, founded the party in 1995. It quickly became the most successful third party since Theodore Roosevelt's Progressive or "Bull Moose" Party of 1912. But in 2000, arguments over the choice of a presidential candidate divided and weakened the party.

The Reform Party's platform calls for balancing the federal budget, repaying the national debt, and simplifying the nation's tax code. The platform urges stricter laws to regulate campaign financing and limit gifts to officeholders "to ensure that our elected officials owe their allegiance to the people whom they are elected to serve." The party also supports term limits, which would prevent elected officials from serving more than a specified number of terms. For example, U.S. senators would serve no more than two terms, or 12 years. The Reform Party also urges elimination of the U.S. trade deficit. It calls for trade policies that would protect home industries from outside competition, and it opposes free-trade agreements. See also **Perot, Ross.** James I. Lengle

Reformation was a religious movement of the 1500's that led to Protestantism. It had a tremendous impact on social, political, and economic life, and its influences are still felt today. The movement began in 1517 when Martin Luther, a German monk, protested certain practices of the Roman Catholic Church. About 40 years later, Protestantism was established in nearly half of Europe.

Before the Reformation, Europe had been held together religiously by the Catholic Church. After the Reformation, Europe had several large Protestant churches and some smaller Protestant religious groups. All of these churches competed with the Catholic Church—

and with each other—for the faith and allegiance of the people.

Causes of the Reformation

Religious causes. During the late Roman Empire and the early Middle Ages, missionaries had converted many European peoples to Christianity. The pope gradually assumed greater importance and authority in the church and in relation to the secular rulers. In the early 1200's, Pope Innocent III claimed that "Ecclesiastical liberty is nowhere better preserved than where the Roman church has full power in temporal as well as spiritual matters." But about 100 years later, in 1303, King Philip IV of France humiliated Pope Boniface VIII by having him arrested (see **Philip IV** [of France]). The secular rulers were growing in power, and the church was no longer a serious threat to them.

In the 1300's and 1400's, the church suffered several serious setbacks. In 1309, a French pope, Clement V, moved the papacy from Rome to Avignon, a city on the border of France, where it remained for about 70 years. This period was called the *Babylonian Captivity,* in remembrance of the 70 years that the Biblical prophet Jeremiah predicted the Jews would spend as captives in ancient Babylon. In 1378, after Pope Gregory XI moved the papal residence back to Rome, a small group of French cardinals elected another pope, called an *antipope* (see **Pope** [The troubles of the papacy]). For nearly 30 years, there were two popes. After 1409, there was a third pope, who resided in Pisa, Italy. This split caused great confusion in the church. Some Catholic leaders believed that the church should be ruled by church councils rather than by a pope. Such councils met in Constance, Germany, from 1414 to 1418 and in Basel, Switzerland, from 1431 to 1449. The councils called for a "reform in head and members."

Serious abuses also had appeared in the church. The large administrative structure of the church required a great deal of money to finance it. To obtain this money, the church used many devices that hurt its spiritual nature. These devices included selling important positions

Wood engraving of the early 1500's by Jorg Breu the Elder; The Newberry Library, Chicago

The sale of indulgences caused Martin Luther to attack the church. This picture shows three enemies that threatened Germany with financial ruin. Indulgences are represented in the center by an indulgence letter that hangs on the cross in place of Jesus. Greedy merchants are portrayed on the left, and expensive imported foreign fashions are shown on the right.

in the church. In Italy, the popes and higher clergy lived like secular princes. They built lavish palaces and indulged in corrupt financial practices. The religious life of the church suffered. The sacraments were often celebrated mechanically, and the church's spiritual message about God's mercy was weakened by an emphasis on a person's good works.

Critics of the church included the religious reformers John Wycliffe in England, John Hus in Bohemia, and Girolamo Savonarola in Italy. These men protested the abuses but could not stop them. Some thinkers within the church, including Johannes Eckhart and Thomas à Kempis, emphasized a mystical approach to Christianity. But no one could restore the church's spiritual health and moral purity.

Cultural causes. Beginning in the 1300's, a great revival of learning and art called the Renaissance developed in Italy and, to a lesser extent, elsewhere in Eu-

Engraving of the 1500's by M. Herz and G. Köler; Bibliothèque Nationale, Paris

The Augsburg Confession summarized the religious teachings of Martin Luther. In this picture, the confession is being read to Charles V, Holy Roman emperor, at the Diet of Augsburg in 1530.

rope. Between 1300 and 1500, universities more than tripled in number. The Italian author Petrarch pioneered in the revival of classical studies—the literature, history, and philosophy of ancient Greece and Rome. Renaissance humanists believed that by returning to the classics, they could begin a new golden age of culture.

The interest in ancient civilizations encouraged by the Renaissance had an important effect on religion. The study of Hebrew and Greek enabled scholars to read the Holy Scriptures in the languages in which they originally had been written. Also, in studying early Christian times, scholars saw how the church had changed through the centuries. The invention of movable type in Europe in the mid-1400's helped spread learning and criticism through printed books. As a result, an increasing number of people outside the clergy gained an education during the Renaissance and Reformation.

Political causes. During the Middle Ages, the Holy Roman emperor claimed to be the secular head of Christianity within the Holy Roman Empire. Most of the nobility ranked beneath the emperor. But the broad authority of the emperor never really existed, and by the end of the Middle Ages, the empire consisted chiefly of the German territories of central Europe. Even there, the princes of a large number of areas were independent. An imperial *diet* (council), which consisted of the princes and representatives of the nobility and of the cities, helped the emperor govern.

In western Europe, the kings were increasing their power over their own people and against the pope. The monarchies in England, France, and Spain were growing stronger, organizing their finances, and building their armies. Some people regarded the pope as a political leader of a foreign state and opposed his control and influence in their own countries. After the Reformation began, some monarchs broke away from the pope.

Economic causes. During the Middle Ages, Europe had an agricultural economy. Most people were peasants who lived in villages and tilled the soil with simple tools. Beginning in the 1100's, cities began to increase in size, especially in Italy and the Netherlands. Merchants traded woolen cloth, glassware, iron implements, and other manufactured goods for raw materials such as furs, wood, and wool. As the cities grew wealthy and independent, they threw off the control of local lords and prince-bishops. Many turned to kings or the emperor for protection.

Development of the Reformation

Martin Luther. The Reformation began within the Catholic Church itself. On Oct. 31, 1517, Martin Luther, a monk and professor of theology, wrote his Ninety-Five Theses and, according to tradition, posted them on the door of the Castle Church in Wittenberg, Germany. The theses were a series of statements that attacked the sale of *indulgences* (pardon from some of the penalty for sins). Luther later criticized what he considered other abuses in the church.

Luther believed that people could be saved only through faith in Jesus Christ, in whom alone righteousness sufficient for salvation could be found. His view of religion placed a person directly before God, trusting Him and relying on His forgiving grace. Luther taught that God *justifies* human beings. By that he meant that God makes them righteous through His kindness to them. This doctrine of justification by faith in Christ alone was the heart of Luther's belief. It contradicted the church's teaching of grace and good works as a way to salvation.

In January 1521, Pope Leo X excommunicated Luther and declared him a heretic. Emperor Charles V and members of the imperial diet ordered Luther to appear before the diet in Worms, Germany, in April. There, Luther was ordered to *recant* (take back) what he had said and written. Luther replied in a famous speech: "Unless I am convinced by the testimony of the Scriptures or by clear reason (for I do not trust either in the pope or in councils alone, since it is well known that they have often erred and contradicted themselves), I am bound by the Scriptures I have quoted and my conscience is captive to the Word of God. I cannot and I will not retract anything, since it is neither safe nor right to go against conscience."

In May 1521, the emperor signed the Edict of Worms, a document that declared Luther to be an outlaw whom anyone could kill without punishment. However, Frederick the Wise, Prince of Saxony, feared a revolt and protected Luther. Luther continued to lead the Protestant movement until his death in 1546.

The word *Protestant* (one who protests) dates from the diet of Speyer, Germany, in 1529. There, princes who supported Luther protested the anti-Lutheran actions forced on them by the emperor and the Catholic nobility. In 1530, the Lutherans presented the *Augsburg Confession* to the diet of Augsburg, Germany. The main author of the confession was Philipp Melanchthon, Luther's chief colleague in the Reformation. The confession became the basic statement of Lutheran doctrine. In the Peace of Augsburg, signed in 1555, the Lutheran churches were officially recognized in the Holy Roman Empire. Each ruler was allowed to choose the religious faith of his land. See **Augsburg Confession**.

The introduction of Lutheranism into Scandinavia was largely the work of the Swedish and Danish kings. In the 1520's, King Gustav I Vasa of Sweden took over much church property and introduced Lutheranism in Sweden and in Finland, which was then under Swedish control. In 1536, King Christian of Denmark and the National Assembly made Lutheranism the state religion. They also established it in Norway, which was then a Danish province.

Zwingli and the Anabaptists. In Switzerland, Huldreich Zwingli, a priest in Zurich, led the movement for religious reform. Zwingli was an eloquent preacher and a great Swiss patriot. Long after his death in 1531 in a war against Catholic forces, his ideas of reform continued to inspire the Swiss Protestant churches. In 1529, Zwingli and Luther met in Marburg, Germany, to discuss their disagreement over the interpretation of Christ's presence in the Lord's Supper. Luther regarded this sacrament as a means by which God gave people His grace. He believed in a real presence of Christ in the bread and wine. Zwingli considered the sacrament a thanksgiving to God for grace already given in other ways, especially through the Gospel. He believed the bread and wine were powerful symbols of Christ's body and blood. The quarrel between Luther and Zwingli led to the first major split in Protestantism.

In Zurich during the 1520's, a group known as the Swiss Brethren, led by Conrad Grebel, decided that the Scriptures did not teach infant baptism. The Swiss Brethren favored adult baptism and were called Anabaptists (rebaptizers). The Anabaptists were not satisfied with Protestant efforts to reform Christianity, so they withdrew from religious and secular life and formed their own communities. The Anabaptists were the ancestors of the modern-day Amish and Mennonites. The Anabaptists were persecuted by both Catholic and Protestant authorities. See **Anabaptists**.

John Calvin helped establish Protestantism in Geneva, Switzerland. From there, he directed efforts to convert the people of France and other countries of western Europe. Calvin, a refugee from France, had studied law and the classics before becoming a Protestant. He had an iron will and a great gift for organization. Calvin's *Ecclesiastical Ordinances* (1541) established the structure of a *presbyterian* form of church government in which a council of elders rules each church. His influential *Institutes of the Christian Religion,* first published in 1536, offers a clear, systematic presentation of Protestant teachings.

Calvin's followers in France were called Huguenots. They came from all classes of society, including some influential noble families such as the Bourbons. Supported by Spain, France's Catholic kings tried to suppress the Huguenots in a series of religious wars from 1562 to 1598. Beginning on Saint Bartholomew's Day, Aug. 24, 1572, the pro-Catholic party murdered thousands of Huguenots in Paris and the French provinces. But Protestantism survived as a minority religion, even in France. See **Saint Bartholomew's Day, Massacre of.**

In England, as in Scandinavia, the Reformation was established by an act of state. But its success was due in part to anticlericalism among the people. The immediate cause for England's break with the Catholic Church was the refusal of Pope Clement VII to *annul* (cancel) King Henry VIII's marriage to his first wife, Catherine of Aragon. Catherine had borne only one child who survived infancy—a daughter. The king wanted to marry Anne Boleyn in the hope that the marriage would produce a male heir to the throne.

In 1534, Parliament passed the Act of Supremacy, which made the monarch the head of the church in England. Henry VIII remained basically a Catholic. However, Protestantism made great advances under his son, Edward VI. Queen Mary I succeeded Edward in 1553. She restored Catholicism as the state religion of England, and she suppressed the Protestants.

Queen Elizabeth I, who reigned from 1558 to 1603, established a moderate form of Protestantism that became known as Anglicanism. The Thirty-Nine Articles, issued in 1563 and approved by Parliament in 1571, presented the teachings of Anglicanism. Some English people, called Puritans, wanted additional reforms. For example, they opposed Anglicanism because it was *episcopal* (governed by bishops). The Puritans preferred the presbyterian form of church government. Catholicism was officially banned in England. See **England** (The English Reformation).

In Scotland, John Knox introduced Calvin's teachings and presbyterian system. In 1560, the Scots made Protestantism their state religion. England forced Ireland to adopt Protestantism as the state religion, but the Irish people remained loyal Catholics. Protestants colonized northern Ireland, also known as Ulster, and the conflict there between Catholics and Protestants is still a serious problem today.

Results of the Reformation

Religious influences. As a result of the Reformation, Europe was divided between the Catholic countries of the south and the Protestant countries of the north. Many Protestant denominations developed, and they were organized in a variety of ways. In many parts of Europe, this diversity of religious life created the necessity of religious toleration and a respect for the importance of the individual conscience. The Reformation also stimulated reforms within the Catholic Church. The church gained new strength from the middle 1500's into the 1600's in a movement called the Counter Reformation, also known as the Catholic Reformation (see **Counter Reformation**).

Political and social influences. The establishment of state churches, as occurred in England, reflected the growth of nationalism. Lutheran regions tended to be conservative and supported strong central governments. Calvinist areas, where Protestants were often in the minority, tended to support democracy and argued for a citizen's right to oppose tyranny by monarchs.

Luther and other Protestants regarded life in the world as the "sphere of faith's works." They opposed the celibate life of monks and nuns and idealized family life and participation in community activities. The Protestant stress on the holiness of a person's daily life encouraged industriousness, thrifty living, and careful management of material things. This attitude became known as the *Protestant ethic.* It may have contributed to the growth of industry and commerce during the 1700's and 1800's. See **Protestant ethic.**

Protestant leaders also emphasized education. They promoted literacy, an educational curriculum based on ancient Greek and Roman literature, and a high respect for teachers and learning. Steven Ozment

Related articles in ***World Book*** include:

Biographies

Calvin, John
Cranmer, Thomas
Erasmus, Desiderius
Henry VIII
Hus, John
Knox, John
Latimer, Hugh
Luther, Martin
Mary I
Melanchthon, Philipp
Ridley, Nicholas
Tetzel, Johann
Tyndale, William
Wycliffe, John
Zwingli, Huldreich

Reform groups

Albigenses
Anabaptists
Anglican Communion
Huguenots
Lollards
Lutherans
Presbyterians
Puritans
Waldenses

Other related articles

Augsburg Confession
Church and state (History)
Education (The Reformation)
England (The English Reformation)
France (Religious wars)
Germany (The Reformation; The Thirty Years' War)
Nantes, Edict of
Peasants' War
Pope (Renaissance and Reformation)
Protestantism
Schmalkaldic League
Scotland (The Scottish Reformation)
Thirty-Nine Articles
Thirty Years' War
Toleration Act
Worms, Edict of

Reformatory is a correctional institution for lawbreakers over age 18 who do not need maximum security. Reformatories are often used to separate young adult offenders from older prisoners. They provide vocational training, counseling, education, and other improvement programs. State or local government authorities or private agencies operate reformatories in the United States.

Institutions for most lawbreakers under the age of 18 are called *training schools.* Most inmates of training schools are held from 6 to 9 months. Institutions at which youthful offenders stay for a shorter time are called *juvenile detention centers.*

The first reformatories in the United States were established during the early 1800's in New York City, Boston, and Philadelphia. These institutions received some state funds but were mainly supported and operated by private citizens. In 1847, Massachusetts opened the first state-controlled reformatory.

By 1900, reformatories had been established throughout the United States. They originally attempted to reform and educate the youths rather than to punish them. But early reformatories operated much like prisons and lacked effective programs. Anthony P. Travisono

Reformed Church in America is incorporated as the General Synod of the Reformed Church in America, a Protestant organization. The doctrines of the Reformed Church have their origin in the Bible as interpreted through the teachings of John Calvin. The minister, elders, and deacons are collectively designated the *consistory* in each local church, and they run the local churches. A group of churches make up a *classis,* and a group of classes make up a *synod.* The *General Synod* is the highest policy-making assembly of the Church. It consists of delegates from each classis.

The Reformed Church in America is an offspring of the Dutch Reformed Church in the Netherlands. The Reformed Church was organized on Manhattan Island in 1628 by Dutch and Walloon colonists. King William III of England first gave a charter to a congregation of the Reformed Church in 1696.

The Reformed Church founded Queens College (now Rutgers, the State University of New Jersey) in New Brunswick, New Jersey; Hope College in Holland, Michigan; Central College (now Central University of Iowa) in Pella, Iowa; and Northwestern College in Orange City, Iowa. In addition, the Reformed Church has seminaries in New Brunswick, New Jersey, and in Holland, Michigan. Critically reviewed by the Reformed Church in America

Refraction is the bending of a light ray as it travels through the surface of a transparent material. Refraction can distort the apparent size, shape, and location of an object when light travels from one material to another. Refraction will occur only when a light ray travels through a surface at an angle other than a right angle. Different materials bend rays by different amounts.

Refraction occurs because light travels at different speeds in different materials. The speed of light in a vacuum is 186,282 miles (299,792 kilometers) per second. This value is commonly given the symbol *c.* The speed of light in a material is $v = c/n$, where *n* is the *refractive index* of the material. The refractive index of a vacuum is exactly 1. The index of air at sea level is 1.000293. Water has a refractive index of 1.33. The indexes of most kinds of glass are around 1.5 to 1.6.

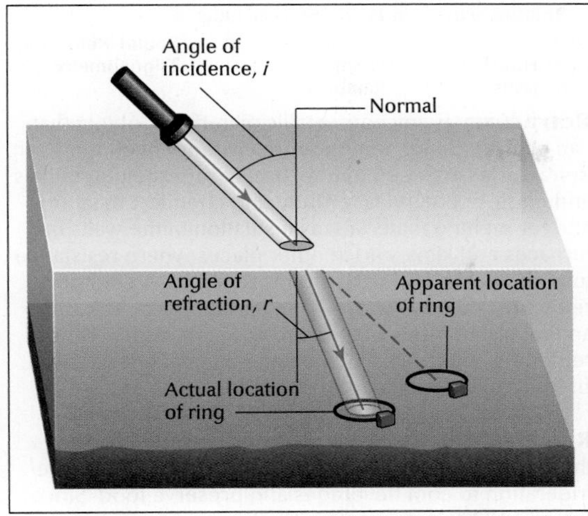

WORLD BOOK diagram by Precision Graphics

Refraction distorts the apparent location of a ring on the bottom of a pond, as viewed from above. Light entering the water bends toward the *normal,* a line perpendicular to the surface.

An equation known as *Snell's law* gives the relationship between two factors involved in refraction: (1) the amount of bending that occurs when a light ray passes from one material to another and (2) the indexes of refraction of the two materials. Snell's law is commonly given as $n_i \sin i = n_r \sin r$. The terms n_i and n_r represent the indexes of refraction of the first and second materials, respectively. The letter *i* represents the *angle of incidence.* This is the angle between the ray traveling through the first material and the *normal,* a line perpendicular to the point where the ray enters the second material. The letter *r* represents the *angle of refraction,* which is the angle between the normal and the ray traveling through the second material.

The expressions "sin *i*" and "sin *r*" are the *sines* of the two angles. A sine is a function in a branch of mathematics known as *trigonometry.* As an angle increases from 0° to 90°, its sine increases from 0 to 1.

WORLD BOOK photo by Odyssey Productions

A pencil in a glass of water appears to be broken at the water's surface as a result of light refraction.

Suppose a ray travels from air into a typical glass at a given angle and another ray travels from air into water at the same angle. Because n_r for glass is larger than n_r for water, sin *r* for glass must be smaller than sin *r* for water. Therefore *r* for glass will be smaller than *r* for water. A smaller *r* indicates a larger amount of bending toward the normal, and so the glass will bend the light more than the water will bend it. Snell's law is named for the Dutch mathematician Willebrord Snell van Roijen, who formulated it around 1621.

W. Thomas Roberts, Jr.

Related articles in *World Book* include:

Lens
Light (How light behaves)
Mirage
Prism
Rainbow
Sound (Refraction)
Trigonometry

Refractory is any nonmetallic material or object that can withstand high temperatures without becoming soft. Refractories are used to line furnaces for melting metals and glass, in crucibles for inducing chemical reactions and for melting materials, as insulation in the walls of furnaces and kilns, and in other places where resistance to temperature and corrosion is required. A common refractory called *firebrick* contains aluminum silicates and minor amounts of titanium and iron oxides. Other refractory substances include alumina, magnesia, silica, zirconia, silicon carbide, and graphite.

James S. Reed

Refrigeration is the process of removing heat. For thousands of years, people have used some kind of refrigeration to cool beverages and preserve food. Since the mid-1800's, refrigeration has been widely used to keep food from spoiling. Today, food is stored in home refrigerators and freezers. Grocery stores and supermarkets use refrigerated display cases, freezing rooms, and cold-storage warehouses. Frozen and fresh produce is carried locally in delivery vans and long distances in refrigerated trucks and containers. Industry uses refrigeration in the processing of chemicals, lubricants, rubber, and steel.

Refrigeration has many uses besides preserving food. Air conditioning depends on refrigeration to cool the interiors of all types of buildings: homes, offices, theaters, and stores. It also cools passenger transport, including automobiles, trains, and airplane cabins. Computers generate heat, so cooling at data centers is essential for the electronic communications necessary for business and social networks. Hospitals require close climate control in many areas used for storage of serums, vaccines, blood plasma, and other lifesaving medical supplies. Drug companies use refrigeration to make penicillin and other drugs. Florists refrigerate cut flowers to preserve their fresh appearance. Drinking fountains supply cold water. Ice machines provide blocks, cubes, flakes, and chips of ice. Ice plants and skating rinks use refrigerating machines to manufacture ice. Refrigeration is also used in producing frozen fruit juices, candy, ice cream, and many other products.

Additionally, refrigeration technology is now becoming widely applied in providing useful heat by means of heat pumps. Heat pumps can help conserve energy. Refrigeration, air conditioning, and heat pump equipment consumes 25 to 30 percent of the world's electricity. However, the refrigeration industry's power use goes largely unnoticed by conservationists.

Principles of refrigeration

Refrigeration removes heat from solids, liquids, and gases. Removal of heat requires the presence of a colder substance because, according to the second law of thermodynamics, heat flows only from warmer bodies to colder bodies (see **Thermodynamics**). For example, hot cocoa becomes cooler and slightly heats the surrounding air. It will never increase in temperature unless the surrounding air is hotter. Heat cannot go from a colder substance to a warmer substance on its own accord. During refrigeration, heat transfer occurs when we place the substance we wish to cool near a *refrigerant* (cooling agent).

Heat transfer. The flow of heat from warmer bodies to colder bodies is called *heat transfer.* Heat transfer will always occur at a rate that depends on the temperature difference between the bodies and on the *resistance* of the bodies to the flow of heat. Resistance is commonly called *insulation.*

A simple type of refrigeration occurs when we cool a warm bottle of water in a running stream. The stream's water acts as a refrigerant. It absorbs heat and slightly rises in temperature as it flows over the bottle, which cools.

Effects of heat transfer. Heat transfer produces several effects. It can both cool the warmer body and warm the body that absorbs the heat. Heat transfer may also change the physical state of a substance. For example, removing sufficient heat may cause a gas to change to a liquid. This process is called *condensation.* The reverse of condensation is *vaporization* or *evaporation* (the process of a liquid changing to a gas). A gas loses heat when it condenses, but it does not change in temperature. Likewise, a liquid absorbs heat when it vaporizes. The temperature at which a substance condenses or vaporizes at a given pressure is its *boiling point.* Boiling points increase as pressure rises. Removing enough heat from a liquid causes it to *freeze* (become solid). The temperature at which a substance freezes is called its *freezing point.* The reverse of freezing is *melting.* Melting is the process of changing a solid to a liquid. Liquids lose heat when they freeze. Solids gain heat when they melt. The heat gained or lost during a change of state is called *latent heat.* The heat gained or lost during temperature change is called *sensible heat.* See **Heat** (Changes in state).

Ice refrigeration

Ice is one of the oldest methods of refrigeration. The Chinese cut and stored ice as long ago as 1000 B.C. Ice makes a useful refrigerant because it always maintains the same temperature—its constant melting temperature of 32 °F (0 °C). Ice absorbs large quantities of heat as it changes into water.

Iceboxes work because warm air rises. A block of ice in the upper part of an icebox absorbs heat from the warm air. This cools the warm air and increases its density. The colder, heavier air flows downward to the food compartments. The air becomes warmer and lighter as it absorbs heat from the food. The warmer, lighter air rises and again loses heat to the ice.

Ice can be enhanced by *endothermic reactions,* in which chemical reactions absorb heat from the atmosphere. By itself, ice could never absorb enough heat to reduce the temperature of a substance below its own melting point of 32 °F (0 °C). But endothermic reactions enable ice to further reduce the temperature of a substance. Certain chemical compounds, particularly salts, produce a cooling effect when mixed with ice or snow. These chemical combinations are called *endothermic mixtures.* Such compounds as calcium chloride, sodium chloride, and ammonium nitrate form endothermic mixtures when mixed with ice or snow. These mixtures create a chemical reaction that absorbs heat. This allows

Republic Steel Corp.

Ice was the only form of home refrigeration until mechanical refrigerators became widespread during the 1920's. Blocks of ice were delivered to home iceboxes several times a week.

more heat to be transferred from the substance to the mixture, so the substance can be cooled to a lower temperature than could be reached with ice alone. Adding sodium chloride can lower the melting point of ice to about −15 °F (−9 °C). Some mixtures can produce even lower temperatures. See **Salt, Chemical.**

Homemade ice cream production is an example of the use of endothermic mixtures. Ice cream begins to freeze at about 28 °F (−2 °C). The ingredients for homemade ice cream are cooled by mixing them in a container that is surrounded by crushed ice and salt. The endothermic reaction of the ice and salt absorbs latent heat from the ingredients, causing them to freeze.

Using chemicals to reduce temperature is not new. About 1550, people in Italy found that a mixture of potassium nitrate (saltpeter) and water could be used to cool bottled liquors.

Dry ice is solid carbon dioxide. As a refrigerant, it has two important advantages over ice made from water. Like water ice, dry ice undergoes change at a constant temperature. But instead of changing to a liquid, dry ice *sublimes* (vaporizes) directly to a gas (see **Sublimation**). For this reason, boxes containing food packed in dry ice do not leak fluid as they would if they were packed in water ice. This characteristic gives dry ice its name.

Dry ice sublimes at −109.3 °F (−78.5 °C), which is much lower than the melting temperature of water ice. Food processing companies find dry ice especially valuable for maintaining a freezing temperature in foods and ice cream because it produces much lower temperatures than water ice. Dry ice must be handled carefully because it can cause frostbite and severe burnlike injuries. See **Dry ice.**

Mechanical refrigeration

The first mechanical refrigeration systems used air as a refrigerant. The air refrigeration cycle works when air is compressed and then has heat removed from it. The air is then allowed to expand, which reduces its temperature to below the temperature it had before it was compressed. With its pressure reduced, the air is ready to be compressed again, and the cycle can be repeated. Early mechanical refrigeration systems were pioneered by J & E Hall, a company in England. The effectiveness of J & E Hall's cold air machinery was demonstrated when one of the first cargoes of frozen meat was successfully shipped from the Falkland Islands to England in 1886. See **Gas** (Gas laws).

Today, air refrigeration is commonly used for cooling aircraft cabins. Heavy and costly air cycle machines, however, were replaced when more compact and cheaper *vapor compression cycle* systems became available for aircraft. The vapor compression cycle makes use of a refrigerant that exists as both liquid and gas at convenient temperatures and pressures.

The electric refrigerator. Most modern household refrigerators utilize the vapor compression cycle. Gas at a low pressure and low temperature enters the compressor, where it is compressed. The compressor is powered by an electric motor. The compression raises the temperature of the gas. The heated gas is then transferred to a *condenser* (the coils behind the refrigerator), where heat is released into the surrounding air. Vent fins help heat transfer by increasing the contact area with the surrounding air. Because the gas is now at high pressure, condensation occurs. As the gas condenses into a liquid, it goes through an expansion device where its pressure is suddenly lowered. When the liquid's pressure is reduced, its boiling point becomes much lower, and a portion of it vaporizes. This change of state from liquid to gas has a cooling effect. Cooled liquid is then fed through evaporator coils within the refrigerator itself, where it absorbs heat from the air inside. The low-pressure, low-temperature gas that exits the evaporator coils then reenters the compressor, and the cycle begins again.

Non-vapor compression methods. There are alternatives to vapor compression. The most significant are the *absorption system* and *evaporative cooling.* In the absorption system, the refrigerant is heated directly by gas, steam, or some other heat source instead of by compression. In the 1850's, Ferdinand Carré, a French engineer, developed the first absorption system.

The gas refrigerator works on the absorption system. It uses heat energy as a source of power. A gas refrigerator has no moving parts. Its five basic parts are the generator, the separator, the condenser, the evaporator, and the absorber.

In one type of gas refrigerator, ammonia serves as the refrigerant. Heat from a gas flame is applied to the *generator,* a tank containing a solution of ammonia dissolved in water. The heat causes the solution to boil. Ammonia vapor and some of the solution rise to the *separator.* The separator removes the liquid. The hot ammonia gas continues its rise to the *condenser.* In the condenser, it cools and liquefies. Because water has been separated from the ammonia, the liquid is now almost pure ammonia. The liquid ammonia flows through a tube into the *evaporator,* or freezing unit. There it vaporizes with hydrogen gas. The hydrogen equalizes the pressure between the condenser and the evaporator.

The vapor *absorbs* heat and produces refrigeration. The heavy mixture passes downward into the air-cooled *absorber*. There the ammonia is absorbed by water. The light hydrogen gas separates from the solution. The hydrogen rises through a pipe above the absorber and returns to the evaporator. The cool ammonia-water solution flows back to the generator.

Gas refrigerators in recreational vehicles (RVs), campers, and some industrial units use absorption systems. Large absorption systems are frequently used where waste heat is available from an industrial process.

Evaporative refrigeration can provide air cooling over a limited temperature range from vaporization of water at atmospheric pressure. An example is covering food containers with a damp cloth in warm weather. Evaporative coolers draw air over a wet pad and send the cooled air into a designated space. Sometimes called *adiabatic cooling,* these systems are simple and inexpensive ways to provide comfort in hot climates. However, the systems are limited in the amount of cooling they provide and dependent on the weather.

Steam-jet refrigeration systems work on the principle that water vaporizes easily when it is under low pressure. The lower the pressure on the water, the faster the evaporation and the lower the temperature that will be produced.

In such systems, water flows through a chamber with an opening. A high-speed jet of steam passes across the opening. The steam creates suction within the space above the water and lowers the pressure in the chamber. Some of the water evaporates, absorbing heat from the liquid water remaining in the chamber, which can then be circulated to cool other things.

Steam-jet refrigeration has wide use in industrial and shipboard cooling. In addition, many brewers and distillers use this type of mechanical refrigeration.

Very low temperature refrigerators are called *cryogenic refrigerators* or *cryocoolers.* They can produce temperatures as low as −459 °F (−273 °C), near absolute zero. Cryogenic refrigerators have important uses in science and industry. For example, physicians use them to freeze living parts of the body for future use. Manufacturers use them to cool miniature electronic systems. See **Cryogenics**.

A cryogenic refrigerator uses helium, nitrogen, or another gas as a refrigerant. Typically, it utilizes the *Joule-Thomson effect.* This effect is the temperature change of a gas when it is forced through a valve or other resistance, from high pressure to low pressure. Several stages may be involved. Helium is used as the refrigerant in the lowest-temperature refrigeration. Helium is the only substance that can remain liquid below −435 °F (−259 °C).

Some new cooling methods are magnetic cooling, thermoelectric cooling, and adsorption systems. They are currently the subject of investigation and research.

Refrigerants. The first vapor compression cycle applications used carbon dioxide and ammonia as refrigerants. Carl von Linde of Germany patented the first commercially successful compression refrigerator using ammonia in 1876. It suited the larger type of refrigerators in use at the time. But the properties of these refrigerants limited their use. Ammonia is *toxic* (poisonous), and carbon dioxide must be kept under high pressure. A breakthrough came in the 1930's when the American chemist Thomas Midgley, Jr., introduced the first *chlorofluorocarbon* (CFC) refrigerant, known by its trade name, Freon. This refrigerant had a high latent heat, meaning it could absorb much heat, and it could be used at moderate pressures. Freon is nonflammable and nontoxic. It is also inexpensive. As more CFC's, and similar refrigerants called *hydrochlorofluorocarbons* (HCFC's), were developed to suit various temperature ranges, more companies began to produce them.

Around the same time, compressor technology saw the introduction of the first *hermetically sealed* (gastight) compressors. Small compressors with integral motors suitable for home appliances became available and were manufactured on a large scale. Prior to this, refrigerator compressors were powered by a belt drive and motor. The airtight-sealed unit was much more compact. It also eliminated refrigerant leakage and the maintenance associated with an external drive.

These developments allowed refrigeration and air conditioning to become widespread. Refrigeration applications are typically divided among domestic, commercial, and industrial sectors. The commercial sector includes retail refrigerators, cold rooms, and small cold stores. Larger scale industrial systems are often custom designed and custom built. Up until the 1980's, chlorine-containing CFC's and HCFC's were typically used in household and commercial refrigeration. Ammonia remained desirable as an industrial refrigerant despite safety concerns, due to its low cost and superior perfor-

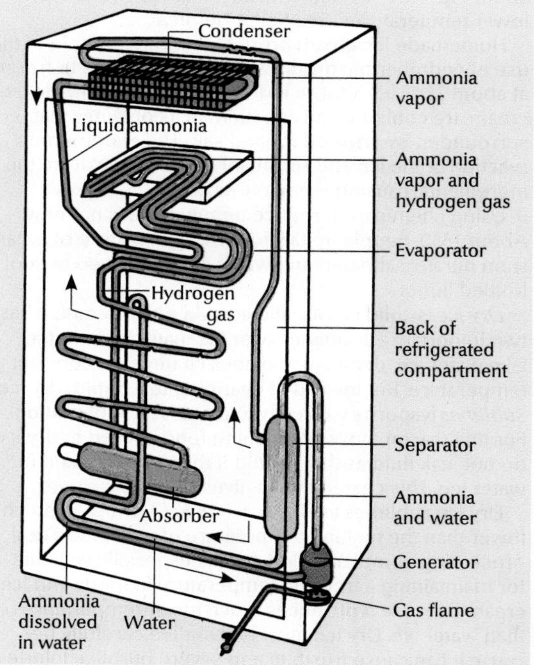

WORLD BOOK diagram

A gas refrigerator circulates an ammonia refrigerant, using heat from a gas flame, and an absorber, a generator, and a separator. The ammonia vapor loses heat in the condenser and becomes a liquid. It then picks up heat from the refrigerated compartment and becomes a vapor again in the evaporator.

mance. Carbon dioxide refrigerants were only used in applications where ammonia could not be safely used.

Refrigeration and the environment

In the mid-1980's, scientists discovered that CFC's were damaging the protective ozone layer in Earth's upper atmosphere. Although these refrigerants were typically used in sealed appliances, inevitable leaks and repairs released CFC gas into the atmosphere. In 1987, an international agreement called the Montreal Protocol went into effect. It provided a global framework to reduce the production and use of CFC's, ending the use of these chemicals in refrigeration. CFC refrigerants were largely replaced with chemicals called *hydrofluorocarbons* (HFC's). These refrigerants do not have chlorine and do not harm the ozone layer of the atmosphere.

However, in the early 1990's, HFC's were found to be powerful greenhouse gases. Such gases trap heat in the atmosphere, increasing Earth's surface temperature. The production and use of such gases are now regulated through international agreements. The agreements restrict the use of HFC's with the goal of drastically reducing their contribution to global warming.

HFC's must be replaced with refrigerants that have sufficiently low *Global Warming Potential* (GWP) to meet the regulations. Ammonia and carbon dioxide refrigerants have been mainly restricted to the industrial sector. Ammonia is considered too dangerous to use in occupied spaces due to its toxicity. Carbon dioxide, which has rarely been used as a refrigerant, is now being applied in some commercial systems. Commercial and home refrigeration systems, and most air conditioning, had previously used only nonflammable refrigerants. Some systems now use flammable propane as a refrigerant. However, safety codes in Europe and the United States now call for refrigerants that have low flammability. The use of *hydrofluoroolefins* (HFO's), a new class of refrigerants that are nonflammable and have low GWP, is becoming more widespread.

Carbon emissions. The refrigeration industry is responsible for a significant percentage of the world's electricity consumption. A portion of that electricity is generated by burning fossil fuels that contribute to global warming. Powering a refrigeration system contributes more to global warming over the system's operational lifetime than does any contribution due to the system's leakage of refrigerant. Therefore, any new refrigeration system must operate more efficiently and consume less electricity to reduce GWP. Good practices in operation and maintenance are also essential if newer refrigeration systems are to deliver the results intended by their designers. Guy F. Hundy

Related articles in *World Book* include:

Air conditioning	Dry ice	Melting point
Ammonia	Food, Frozen	Railroad (pictures: Refrigerator cars; Kinds of railroad cars)
Chlorofluorocarbon	Food preservation	
Cold storage	Freezing point	
Cryogenics	Heat	
	Ice	

Refugee is a person forced to flee from his or her country and find safety elsewhere. Many refugees seek to escape persecution based on religion, nationality, membership in a social group, or political beliefs. Some flee from war, famine, or other dangers. Many refugees give up everything—home, possessions, and family and friends—to pursue an uncertain future in a foreign land.

The term *refugee* comes from the French word *réfugié*, which was used to describe Protestant Huguenots who fled France in 1685 because of Roman Catholic persecution. The term *displaced person*, or *DP*, is sometimes used interchangeably with *refugee*.

The flow of refugees from one country to another can present major international challenges. Countries that receive refugees—often called *host countries*—may have difficulty providing shelter, food, sanitation, and medical treatment for large numbers of people in need.

The rights of refugees. Under international law, governments in host countries must respect the basic human rights of refugees. Refugees, in turn, are expected to respect the laws and regulations of host countries. The shelter and protection that host countries provide to refugees is called *asylum*. In host countries, refugees generally have freedom of movement, freedom of religion, and the ability to pursue education and work. However, some refugees have no choice but to stay in crowded refugee camps. *Refoulement*—that is, the forcible return of refugees to countries where they face persecution—is a violation of international law.

International law follows a strict definition of the term *refugee*. The definition includes only individuals who are not criminals, traitors, government officials, or members of the military. Refugees must have fled their country because of a well-founded fear of persecution and cannot, or do not want to, return. Many who have fled their homes are not technically refugees and lack the same rights as refugees. Such people include *internally displaced persons*, who have left their homes but remain in their own country, and *economic migrants*, who have fled to escape poor economic conditions.

Efforts to help refugees. National governments and international organizations have long sought to address refugee problems associated with wars and other conflicts. In 1921, the League of Nations appointed the Norwegian explorer and scientist Fridtjof Nansen as a special commissioner to help refugees uprooted by World War I (1914-1918). Following Nansen's death in 1930, the League established the Nansen International Office for Refugees. During World War II (1939-1945), the Allied nations set up the United Nations Relief and Rehabilitation Administration. After the United Nations formed in 1945, it set up a new agency, the International Refugee Organization (IRO). The IRO began operating in 1947.

In 1951, the United Nations High Commissioner for Refugees (UNHCR) replaced the IRO. The UNHCR has helped millions of refugees throughout the world. Other international efforts—including the International Organization for Migration and the European Council on Refugees and Exiles—have also provided assistance to refugees. Thomas R. Mockaitis

Related articles in *World Book* include:

Asia (picture: Palestinian refugees)	Immigration (Causes of immigration)
Asian Americans (Arrivals of the late 1900's)	Nansen, Fridtjof
Asylum	United Nations (Aid to refugees)

Regeneration, in plants and animals, is the capacity to replace lost or damaged parts by growing new ones. Regeneration is common in plants. If a tree or shrub is cut off near the ground, new shoots may spring up from the stump. Among animals, the sponges, cnidarians, and the simpler worms show remarkable power of regeneration. They can be cut in pieces, and each piece can grow into a new animal. Starfishes can grow new arms. Crayfishes can grow new claws, eyes, and legs.

Animals with a backbone—called *vertebrates*—have only limited powers of regeneration. But a reptile called the *glass lizard* escapes from its enemies by breaking off the end of its tail. The glass lizard later grows a new one. Salamanders can regenerate lost limbs. People and other mammals can regenerate only hair, nails, skin, and a few other tissues. In some cases, a different sort of tissue grows over the damaged area and forms a scar.

George B. Johnson

See also **Animal** (Regeneration); **Crustacean** (Growth and development); **Flatworm; Planarian; Sponge** (Regeneration).

Regent, *REE juhnt,* is a person who rules a country when the rightful ruler cannot, either because he or she is too young, out of the country, or ill. In some countries, a member of the royal family acts as regent. In others, a council may exercise duties of the ruler.

The British had no special arrangements providing for a regency until the Regency Act of 1937 was passed. This law provides for the appointment of a regent if the monarch is unable to rule. A council of state can act as regent for short periods of time. This council is composed of the husband or wife of the ruler and the next four people in succession to the crown.

In the United States, members of the governing body of libraries, museums, school systems, and universities and colleges are called *regents.* I. J. Sanders

Reggae, *REHG ay* or *RAY gay,* is a type of popular music that developed in Jamaica in the 1960's. At first it was primarily performed by and for poor Jamaicans. It later became popular throughout Jamaica and also in England and the United States. Reggae has influenced soul, rhythm and blues, and rock music.

The words in most reggae songs deal with the social concerns and religious beliefs of poor Jamaicans. The songs are in 4/4 time and feature strong accents off the beat. Short rhythmic patterns are repeated many times by electric guitars and drums. They are also sometimes repeated with organ or piano. The rhythms in reggae are sometimes complex, but the harmonies are simple. As with rock music, the volume of reggae is loud.

Reggae has its roots in traditional African music, Jamaican folk music, and North American popular music. It developed from two other types of Jamaican popular music—*ska* and *rocksteady.* Reggae began to gain popularity outside Jamaica in the late 1960's through the recordings of a number of reggae musicians. The most important was Bob Marley, who grew up in the slums of Kingston, Jamaica. Marley led a group called the Wailers, founded in 1964. He was the most famous reggae star internationally until his death in 1981 at the age of 36. Songs that became hits in the United States include Eric Clapton's "I Shot the Sheriff" and Johnny Nash's "Stir It Up" (both written by Marley) and Desmond Dekker's "The Israelites." Valerie Woodring Goertzen

See also **Marley, Bob.**

Regina, *rih JY nuh,* is the capital and second largest city of Saskatchewan. Only Saskatoon is larger. Regina is located on a plain in southern Saskatchewan and is about 100 miles (160 kilometers) north of the Canadian-United States border. The Latin word *regina* means *queen,* and Regina is sometimes called the *Queen City of the Plains.*

Regina is the commercial, financial, and industrial center of Saskatchewan. The city lies in the heart of Canada's richest wheat-growing region. Until the 1960's, Regina served mainly as a marketing and supply center for this region. Since then, it has become a manufacturing center as well.

Before white settlers came, the Cree Indians often camped on a site near what is now Regina. They butchered buffalo there, and the bones piled up. The Indians called the place *Oskunah-kasas-take,* which the whites translated as *Pile o' Bones,* and the stream that ran by it became known as Wascana Creek. In 1882, the Canadian government chose a small settlement on the creek as the new capital of what was then the North-West Territories. At the time, the settlement was also called Pile o' Bones. The site was only a treeless plain, but it lay near the new Canadian Pacific Railway. This railroad, which linked eastern and western Canada, attracted the first settlers to Pile o' Bones. In 1882, they renamed the settlement Regina, in honor of Queen Victoria of England.

The city. Regina covers 69 square miles (180 square kilometers). Wascana Creek winds through the city. Southeast of the downtown area, a dam widens the

Saskatchewan Economic Development

Regina is Saskatchewan's capital and commercial, financial, and industrial center. It lies on a plain in the southern part of the province. High-rise buildings of downtown Regina rise in the background of this photograph.

City of Regina

Regina, the capital of Saskatchewan, is the chief industrial and market center of the southern plains area of the province. The city map shows Regina and its major landmarks.

WORLD BOOK maps

City boundary
Expressway
Other road
Railroad
Point of interest
Park

SASKATCHEWAN
Regina

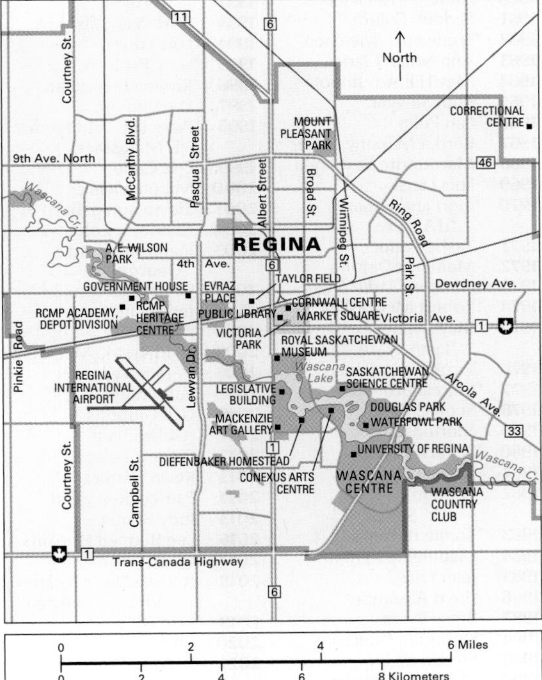

creek into an artificially created lake, Wascana Lake. Wascana Centre, a 2,300-acre (930-hectare) belt of parks and public buildings, surrounds the lake. Buildings in Wascana Centre include the Legislative Building, where the Saskatchewan legislature meets; the University of Regina; the Royal Saskatchewan Museum; and the Conexus Arts Centre. See **Saskatchewan** (picture: The Legislative Building).

About 25 percent of Regina's people have some English ancestry. Other large ethnic groups, in order of size, are people of German, Scottish, or Irish descent.

Economy. Regina has hundreds of manufacturing plants. They account for more than a third of Saskatchewan's industrial production. The city's chief manufactured products include cement, fertilizer, and steel.

The rich agricultural region around Regina makes the city a center for the distribution of farm machinery. Viterra, one of the largest grain-handling and marketing companies in the world, has its North American headquarters in the city.

The oil fields of southern Saskatchewan have helped make Regina an important oil center. The city has oil refining facilities. The petroleum pipeline that links the Alberta oil fields with ports on the Great Lakes runs through Regina.

Regina is the trade and distribution center for the surrounding region. Many of the city's workers have jobs in wholesale or retail trade. Many others work for the city, provincial, or federal government. The Royal Canadian Mounted Police has its training headquarters there.

The Canadian National Railway and the Canadian Pacific Railway connect Regina with the East and West coasts. Regina lies on the Trans-Canada Highway, and Regina International Airport is located just west of the city center.

Education and cultural life. An elected Board of Education supervises Regina's public school system. The city also has a number of private and parochial schools. The University of Regina is a coeducational school that grants bachelor's, master's, and doctor's degrees. First Nations University of Canada, which has a campus in Regina, is the only university in Canada that is controlled by the country's native peoples.

The Regina Public Library operates a main library and a number of branch libraries. The Saskatchewan Provincial Library is also in the city. Regina has a daily newspaper, the *Leader-Post*.

The Conexus Arts Centre includes two theaters and a convention hall. The Regina Symphony Orchestra performs at the center. The Globe Theatre, a professional company, stages productions in its own theater in downtown Regina.

Wascana Waterfowl Park features hundreds of water birds and animals. The Royal Saskatchewan Museum features galleries that trace the human history and geological history of Saskatchewan.

The MacKenzie Art Gallery displays paintings and sculpture. The Royal Canadian Mounted Police Heritage Centre features exhibits that show how the Mounties brought law and order to Canada's frontier. The Mounties' chapel, part of which dates from 1883, ranks as one of Regina's oldest buildings.

Queen City Ex, an annual festival held in late July and early August, celebrates Regina's frontier days. The festival includes parades, rodeos, and square dances. The Saskatchewan Roughriders play in the Canadian Football League. The Lawson Aquatic Centre features an Olympic-sized swimming pool. The 102-acre (41-hectare) Evraz Place hosts conventions, concerts, trade shows, and other events.

Government. Regina has a council-manager form of government. The voters elect a mayor and 10 council members to the City Council. The council establishes

Facts in brief

Population: 215,106. *Metropolitan area population*—236,481.
Area: 69 mi² (180 km²). *Metropolitan area*—1,670 mi² (4,324 km²).
Altitude: 1,890 ft (576 m) above sea level.
Climate: *Average temperature*—January, 5 °F (−15 °C); July, 66 °F (19 °C). *Average annual precipitation* (rainfall, melted snow, and other forms of moisture)—15 in (39 cm). For the monthly weather in Regina, see **Saskatchewan** (Climate).
Government: Council-manager. *Terms*—3 years for the mayor and 10 councillors.
Founded: 1882. Incorporated as a city in 1903.

city policies and appoints a professional administrator called a city manager to carry them out. The mayor and council members serve four-year terms. The city gets more than half its revenue from property taxes.

History. The Cree Indians hunted buffalo in what is now the Regina area before whites arrived. In 1857, the British explorer John Palliser visited the site and reported that it was unfit for farming. But in 1880, a Canadian botanist named John Macoun realized the Regina plains would make fertile wheatlands. He persuaded the Canadian Pacific Railway Company to build its transcontinental railroad across the area.

The railroad reached Regina in 1882, and the Canadian government chose the site for the new capital of the North-West Territories. Regina actually became the capital in 1883. Battleford, the former capital, lay more than 225 miles (362 kilometers) north of the railroad and was too hard to reach. Also in 1882, the North-West Mounted Police (now the Royal Canadian Mounted Police) established its headquarters in Regina. By 1903, when Regina was incorporated as a city, it had 3,000 people.

In 1905, the province of Saskatchewan was created with Regina as its capital. Settlers from eastern Canada, Europe, and the United States poured into the area's rich wheatlands. The city grew into an important trade and supply center for the surrounding farms. By 1911, Regina's population had reached 30,000.

A cyclone destroyed much of Regina in 1912, but the city was quickly rebuilt. During World War I (1914-1918), the Regina area produced huge quantities of wheat for the Allies. However, the demand for wheat dropped after the war, and falling wheat prices created a depression in Saskatchewan. The city's economy continued to slump during the Great Depression of the 1930's, and many workers were unemployed. By 1937, about a fifth of the population was receiving welfare payments.

In 1933, the Co-operative Commonwealth Federation (CCF), a socialist political party, held its first national convention in Regina. The CCF adopted a statement, the Regina Manifesto, that called for the end of capitalism. In 1944, the CCF gained control of the provincial government, which thus became the first socialist government in Canada. Regina served as CCF headquarters from 1933 until the party joined with a group of Canadian trade unions to form the New Democratic Party in 1961.

During the 1950's and 1960's, the discovery of underground resources—chiefly potash, used for fertilizer, and petroleum—strengthened the region's economy. Many new industries came to Regina, and the city's economy became less dependent on a good annual wheat crop. Regina's population nearly doubled during this period, rising from 71,000 in 1951 to 139,000 in 1971.

A construction boom changed Regina's skyline in the 1960's. Three of the city's tallest structures went up—the Avord Tower, the Canadian Imperial Bank of Commerce, and the Saskatchewan Power (now SaskPower) building.

Regina faced financial problems in the 1970's. Taxes did not provide enough money to run the government, and the public transportation system operated at a loss. Another construction boom in Regina began in the mid-1970's. A new City Hall opened in 1976. In 1980, a huge, enclosed shopping mall called the Cornwall Centre was completed. In 1983, the Bank of Montreal Building opened near the Cornwall Centre. A. D. Rosseker

Regina Medal, *rih JEE nuh,* is an award honoring a person for a lifetime contribution to children's literature. The award is sponsored by the Catholic Library Association and is given regardless of nationality or creed. The face of the medal bears a crown superimposed on an *M,* signifying *Mary,* for whom the medal is named. The words "Regina Medal, Continued Distinguished Contribution to Children's Literature," encircle the symbols. On the reverse side, names of the winner, the sponsor, and the year encircle a shield that bears a quotation from Walter de la Mare's collection of poems *Bells and Grass* (1941). The quotation reads: "... only the rarest kind of best in anything can be good enough for the young."

Winners of the Regina Medal

Year	Winner	Year	Winner
1959	*Eleanor Farjeon	**1991**	Leonard Everett Fisher
1960	Anne Carroll Moore	**1992**	Jane Yolen
1961	Padraic Colum	**1993**	*Chris Van Allsburg
1962	*Frederic G. Melcher	**1994**	*Lois Lowry
1963	Ann Nolan Clark	**1995**	*Gary Paulsen
1964	May Hill Arbuthnot	**1996**	*Russell Freedman
1965	*Ruth Sawyer	**1997**	Eve Bunting
1966	Leo Politi	**1998**	*Patricia C. and Fredrick L. McKissack
1967	Bertha Mahony Miller	**1999**	Eric Carle
1968	*Marguerite de Angeli	**2000**	Milton Meltzer
1969	Lois Lenski	**2001**	*Elaine Konigsburg
1970	Ingri and Edgar *d'Aulaire	**2002**	Charlotte Zolotow
1971	Tasha Tudor	**2003**	*Jean Craighead George
1972	Meindert DeJong	**2004**	Susan Hirschman
1973	Frances Clarke Sayers	**2005**	Jerry Pinkney
1974	*Robert McCloskey	**2006**	Paul Goble
1975	May McNeer and *Lynd Ward	**2007**	Margaret K. McElderry
1976	Virginia Haviland	**2008**	Vera B. Williams
1977	*Marcia Brown	**2009**	Lois Ehlert
1978	*Scott O'Dell	**2010**	Gail Gibbons
1979	Morton Schindel	**2011**	Ashley Bryan
1980	*Beverly Cleary	**2012**	Patricia Polacco
1981	Augusta Baker	**2013**	*Kevin Henkes
1982	Theodor Geisel (*Dr. Seuss)	**2014**	Patricia Reilly Giff
1983	*Tomie dePaola	**2015**	*Judy Blume
1984	*Madeleine L'Engle	**2016**	Lee Bennett Hopkins
1985	Jean Fritz	**2017**	David A. Adler
1986	Lloyd Alexander	**2018**	Andrea Davis Pinkney and Brian Pinkney
1987	*Betsy Byars	**2019**	*Kate DiCamillo
1988	*Katherine Paterson	**2020**	Christopher Paul Curtis
1989	Steven Kellogg	**2021**	Jan Brett
1990	*Virginia Hamilton		

*Has a separate biography in *World Book.*

Critically reviewed by the Catholic Library Association

Regression is a characteristic sign of certain mental illnesses. It comes from a Latin word meaning *to go backward.* Doctors use the word to mean a return to a way of thinking or behaving normally characteristic of an earlier period of life. If a 4-year-old child, after the birth of a baby brother or sister, began to act like a baby, doctors would call the behavior regression. Mentally healthy people also sometimes exhibit regression, as when they play games or daydream. Nancy C. Andreasen

Regulus, Marcus Atilius, *REHG yuh luhs, MAHR kuhs uh TIHL ee uhs* (? -249? B.C.), was a Roman general who became a national hero. His life story was repeated as an example of true patriotism. As *consul* (chief government official) in 256 B.C., he commanded the Roman invasion of Africa against Carthage in the First Punic War (see **Punic Wars**). He was victorious and demanded harsh peace terms. But the Carthaginians raised more troops and hired Xanthippus, a Spartan general, who defeated the Romans and captured Regulus.

Carthage sent Regulus to Rome about 249 B.C. with its own terms. He promised to return if the Romans refused to make peace. He urged the Roman Senate to reject the terms, though he knew this meant his death upon his return to Carthage. Romans later said the Carthaginians tortured him to death, but his family may have made up this story. Regulus, an aristocrat, was not rich. Before the war, he lived a simple life on his farm. Arthur M. Eckstein

Rehnquist, *REHN kwihst,* **William Hubbs** (1924-2005), served as chief justice of the United States from 1986 until his death. President Ronald Reagan nominated him to succeed Chief Justice Warren E. Burger, who retired. Rehnquist had served as an associate justice of the Supreme Court of the United States since 1972.

As chief justice, Rehnquist became the main spokesman of a group of conservative Supreme Court justices. These justices issued decisions supporting state authority and limiting the power of Congress. Under Rehnquist, the court also took a conservative approach to *criminal procedures* (methods for arresting, prosecuting, and punishing people accused of crimes). In 1999, Rehnquist presided over the Senate impeachment trial of President Bill Clinton, which ended in Clinton's acquittal.

Rehnquist was born on Oct. 1, 1924, in Milwaukee. He earned both a bachelor's and a master's degree in political science from Stanford University in 1948. He received a master's degree in government from Harvard University in 1950. Rehnquist graduated as the top student in his class from Stanford Law School in 1952. In 1952 and 1953, he served as law clerk to Supreme Court Justice Robert H. Jackson. From 1953 to 1969, Rehnquist practiced law in Phoenix. He was a United States assistant attorney general from 1969 to 1971.

In 1972, President Richard M. Nixon sparked a debate in the Senate when he nominated Rehnquist to the Supreme Court. Rehnquist's opponents called his philosophy "ultraconservative." During Senate hearings on the nomination, several civil rights groups and many liberals objected to positions Rehnquist had taken on such issues as school desegregation and police surveillance.

As an associate justice, Rehnquist reflected the conservative view on almost every issue. When Reagan named him chief justice, debate again broke out in the Senate over Rehnquist's conservatism. Rehnquist died on Sept. 3, 2005. Dennis J. Hutchinson

Reich, *ryk,* is a German word meaning *empire* or *state.* German dictator Adolf Hitler called his government the Third Reich. The first was the Holy Roman Empire. The second was the German Empire that lasted from 1871 to 1918. See also **Germany** [History]. Donald M. McKale

Reid, Harry (1939-), was a member of the United States Senate from 1987 to 2017. Reid, a Democrat, represented Nevada. He became the leader of the Senate Democrats in 2005. He served as Senate majority leader from 2007 to 2015.

As a senator, Reid supported legislation to increase funding for research on diseases affecting women. He worked for passage of the 1996 Safe Drinking Water Act. He opposed proposals for a constitutional amendment requiring a balanced federal budget. Reid supported proposals to develop renewable energy sources. He was also a strong supporter of health insurance reform legislation signed into law by President Barack Obama in 2010.

Harry Mason Reid was born on Dec. 2, 1939, in Searchlight, Nevada. He received a bachelor's degree from Utah State University in 1961 and a law degree from George Washington University in 1964.

From 1964 to 1966, Reid was city attorney for Henderson, Nevada. In 1969 and 1970, he was a member of the Nevada State Assembly. He served as lieutenant governor of Nevada from 1970 to 1974. In 1974, Reid ran for the U.S. Senate but lost. He headed the Nevada Gaming Commission from 1977 to 1981. He was elected to the U.S. House of Representatives in 1982 and reelected in 1984. In 1986, Reid ran again for the U.S. Senate and won. He was the Senate Democratic *whip* (assistant leader) from 1999 to 2005. Reid retired from the Senate when his term ended in January 2017. Jeremy D. Mayer

See also **Democratic Party** (picture: The 2006 elections).

Reid, *reed,* **Whitelaw** (1837-1912), was an American journalist and diplomat. He bought control of the New York *Tribune* in 1872. From 1905 until his death, he served as ambassador to the United Kingdom. Reid was born on Oct. 27, 1837, in Xenia, Ohio. During the American Civil War (1861-1865), he was war correspondent for the Cincinnati *Gazette.* In 1892, Reid was the Republican nominee for vice president of the United States, but he was defeated. He died on Dec. 15, 1912. See also **Harrison, Benjamin** (Bid for reelection). Joseph P. McKerns

Reign of Terror was a bloody period of the French Revolution (1789-1799). From September 1793 to July 1794, the revolutionary government killed thousands of people in a wave of executions intended to defend the revolution. The Terror began primarily in response to a series of military setbacks and civil uprisings. It ended with the execution of Robespierre, one of the leaders of the revolution.

In early 1793, peasants rebelled against the new French ruling convention in the Vendée, an area on France's west coast. To help put down this and other rebellions, the convention created the Committee of Public Safety and the revolutionary tribunal. Together, they had thousands of suspected opponents of the revolution executed. Hundreds of thousands of people were imprisoned without trial. The many victims of the Reign of Terror included Marie Antoinette, the queen of France, and the great French chemist Antoine Lavoisier.

Many people in France questioned the necessity and methods of the Terror. Revolutionary leader Georges-Jacques Danton was executed for trying to stop it. Robespierre became one of its last victims on July 28, 1794. The guillotine, a beheading machine, gained infamy for its public use during the Terror. William Doyle

See also **Danton, Georges-Jacques; French Revolution; Robespierre; Terrorism** (with picture).

Reims, *reemz* (pop. 183,113; met. area pop. 322,473), is a city of northern France. It lies on the Vesle River about 98 miles (158 kilometers) northeast of Paris (see **France** [political map]). The beauty of Reims centers on a cathedral, which was begun in the 1200's and completed in 1430. The city contains many other historic buildings.

During World War I, Reims was bombed daily for nearly four years. After the war ended in 1918, the peo-

SEF/Art Resource

The Cathedral of Notre Dame in Reims, France, is a beautiful example of Gothic architecture. It was completed in 1430.

ple rebuilt many homes and buildings. In World War II, the Germans occupied Reims from 1940 to 1944. Reims later became a major supply base for Allied troops. Germany signed its surrender at Reims on May 7, 1945.

Reims lies in the Champagne region, which produces the sparkling wine called champagne. The city is a center for champagne production and an important wool market. Other products of Reims include chemicals, machinery, paper, soap, and wine bottles and casks.

Lovers of art and architecture have long admired the Cathedral of Notre Dame at Reims, one of the most beautiful examples of Gothic architecture. Nearly all the French kings were crowned in the cathedral. Heavy bombing during World War I badly damaged the cathedral, but it was repaired by 1937. William M. Reddy

See also **Sculpture** (picture: Visitation group).

Reincarnation, *REE ihn kahr NAY shuhn,* is the belief that the soul survives after death and is reborn in the body of another person or some other living thing. The word *reincarnation* means *coming back into the flesh.* This concept is also called *transmigration of the soul.*

The ancient Greeks and some primitive peoples believed in reincarnation. The concept is an important part of Buddhism, Hinduism, Jainism, Sikhism, and other religions that originated in India. It also is a doctrine of some modern *spiritualist* movements (see **Spiritualism**).

In the religions of India, reincarnation is related to the law of *karma.* According to this law, a person's actions determine the type of body that the soul will enter during reincarnation. If a person leads a good life, his or her soul will be reborn in a higher state, such as the body of a priest. If a person leads a bad life, the soul will be reborn in a lower state, such as the body of a dog.

Other religions explain reincarnation in different ways. Some teach that the soul may be reborn in the body of a descendant of the person. Nancy E. Auer Falk

Related articles in *World Book* include:

Buddhism
Hinduism (Reincarnation and karma)
Jainism
Karma
Plato (Immortality of the soul)
Pythagoras
Religion (A doctrine of salvation)
Sikhism
Theosophy

Reindeer is a large deer that lives in the northernmost regions of Europe and Asia. Reindeer and caribou make up a single *species* (type) of deer. Scientists break up this species into *subspecies.* The subspecies that live in Europe and Asia are called reindeer, while those that live in Greenland and northern North America are called caribou. Nomadic peoples from Europe and Asia herded and tamed reindeer. See **Caribou.**

Reindeer differ from other deer in several ways. For example, reindeer have larger antlers, larger and wider hoofs, and a heavy coat that is grayish-brown to almost white. These features help reindeer survive in the cold Arctic. The large hoofs, for example, prevent the reindeer from sinking into the snow during winter. Female reindeer and caribou are the only female deer to have antlers. Reindeer often make a variety of noises. When frightened, adults snort and young reindeer bawl. When reindeer walk, their feet make a clicking sound.

In summer, reindeer may eat grasses and leaves from willows and birches. In winter, they paw through the snow to find lichens to eat. In the short Arctic summers, plants grow slowly and cannot stand much grazing. So reindeer move frequently to a new place when their food becomes scarce. They may migrate several hundred miles or kilometers in a year. They are excellent swimmers and can cross large rivers and lakes. During migration, several thousand reindeer may gather into one herd. By traveling in herds, individual reindeer are protected from enemies. Animals that prey on reindeer include grizzly bears, lynxes, wolves, and wolverines.

The male reindeer is known as a *bull.* The female is called a *cow.* In the fall, the bulls fight with one another to gather their own group of cows, called a *harem.* A bull then mates with the cows in his harem, and later the harem breaks up. In the spring, a cow usually will bear one offspring, called a *calf.* After a few days, the calf is strong enough to join the herd. Adult reindeer stand about 3 to 4 feet (90 to 120 centimeters) high and weigh

Bruce Coleman Inc.

The reindeer lives in Arctic regions of Europe and Asia. It has large antlers and a grayish-brown to almost white coat.

up to 400 pounds (180 kilograms).

Reindeer are useful to the Sami of northern Scandinavia. The Sami (formerly known, to outsiders, as Lapps) are one of the nomadic peoples known for developing much of their way of life around migrating herds of reindeer. They have trained reindeer to serve as pack animals and to pull sleds and sleighs. They use reindeer skin for boots, clothing, and tents. They also consume reindeer milk and meat. In some areas, snowmobiles, trucks, helicopters, two-way radios, and cell phones are used to herd reindeer. But nomads in northern Siberia still follow herds in the traditional way, with their possessions on a reindeer-pulled sled. Kenneth J. Raedeke

Scientific classification. The scientific name of reindeer is *Rangifer tarandus.*

See also **Deer; Tundra.**

Reindeer Lake covers 2,570 square miles (6,650 square kilometers) in central Canada. It lies on the border between northern Saskatchewan and Manitoba. For location, see **Saskatchewan** (physical map). The waters of Reindeer Lake drain south, into Reindeer River and the Churchill river system. Adrian A. Seaborne

Reindeer moss is a lichen that grows in the Arctic and sometimes farther south. It is an important food for caribou and reindeer of the Arctic. People sometimes eat reindeer moss. In Scandinavia, it has been used to make bread. See also **Lichen.** Joe F. Ammirati

Scientific classification. The scientific name of reindeer moss is *Cladonia rangiferina.*

Reinforcement, in psychology. See **Learning** (Classical conditioning; Instrumental conditioning).

Reinhardt, *RYN hahrt,* **Max** (1873-1943), was a theatrical producer and director. He became a leader of the German-speaking theater during the early 1900's.

Reinhardt was born on Sept. 9, 1873, in Baden, near Vienna. His given and family name was Max Goldmann. Beginning in 1917, he helped found and plan the famous Salzburg music and theater festival. He directed the festival's first production in 1920. Reinhardt staged such classics as *Faust* and *Everyman* as well as productions of such modern playwrights as George Bernard Shaw, August Strindberg, and Henrik Ibsen. Reinhardt became famous for his imaginative productions. He staged the Greek tragedies *Oresteia* and *Oedipus Rex* as mass spectacles. For the pageant *The Miracle,* Reinhardt rebuilt the inside of theaters to resemble a Gothic cathedral. He moved to the United States in 1934. Reinhardt died on Oct. 31, 1943. Daniel J. Watermeier

Relapsing fever is an infectious disease that occurs chiefly in the tropics, often as an epidemic. It is caused by bacteria called *spirochetes.* A person with relapsing fever develops chills, fever, headache, and muscular aches and pains. Vomiting also may occur. These symptoms may last for several days or a week. Then the patient seems to return to good health for about a week. Suddenly, however, the symptoms return, and if the patient is not treated, he or she may have as many as 10 relapses. Doctors advise bed rest and use antibiotics.

Lice and ticks transmit the bacteria to human beings. Like typhus, louse-borne relapsing fever is found in regions with poor living conditions (see **Typhus**). The two diseases often occur together. Tick-borne relapsing fever is found in the western United States as well as in other parts of the world. Thomas J. Gill III

Relativity is either of two theories of physics developed by the German-born American physicist Albert Einstein. Those theories are (1) the special theory of relativity, which was published in 1905; and (2) the general theory of relativity, announced in 1915. Einstein's theories explain the behavior of matter, energy, and even time and space. They are two of the "foundation blocks" upon which modern physics is built.

The theories of relativity describe events so strange that people find it difficult to understand how they could possibly occur. For example, one person can observe that two events happen at the same time, while another person observes that they occur at different times. A clock can appear to one observer to be running at a given rate, yet seem to another observer to run at a different rate. Two observers can measure the length of the same rod correctly but obtain different results. Matter can turn into energy, and energy can turn into matter.

Galilean relativity

In developing his theories, Einstein used ideas from a principle of relativity developed by the Italian astronomer and physicist Galileo. That principle is now known as *Galilean relativity.*

Undetectable motion. Galileo presented the main idea behind Galilean relativity in the *Dialogue Concerning the Two Chief World Systems* (1632). In this work, a character named Salvatius describes two scenarios involving a ship's cabin. In both scenarios, two friends are in the cabin, along with some small flying animals, fish swimming in a bowl, a bottle from which drops of water fall into another container, and a ball. The cabin is below decks, so neither person can see outside.

In the first scenario, the ship is at rest. The animals move about naturally, and the two friends throw the ball to each other and jump about. The friends observe that the flying animals fly with equal speed to all sides of the cabin, the fish swim in all directions, and the drops of water fall straight downward. When one friend throws the ball to the other, the effort required for the throw does not depend on the direction of the throw. When either person jumps forward, the effort required for the jump does not depend on the direction of the jump.

In the second scenario, the ship is traveling at a *constant velocity.* That is, both the speed and direction of the ship are unchanging. All the events that occurred in the first scenario happen again: The small creatures fly and swim, the water drips, and the two friends throw the ball and jump. The motion of the ship has no effect on any of these events. Salvatius explains why this is so: All the objects in the cabin, including the living things, share in the motion of the ship.

Because the ship's motion has no effect on the events in the cabin, neither friend can tell by observing those events whether the ship is at rest or moving. This is the main idea behind Galilean relativity.

Strictly speaking, an actual ship would not travel at a constant velocity. For example, the ship would travel in a curve because Earth's surface—including the surface of the water—is curved. The ship would also curve due to Earth's rotation on its axis and its revolution around the sun. During periods of a few seconds, however, the ship's velocity could be almost perfectly constant.

Inertial frames. Physicists would refer to the cabin as

an *inertial* (pronounced *ihn UR shuhl) frame.* This term comes from the fact that, in the cabin, the *principle of inertia* would apply relative to the cabin. Inertia is a body's resistance to a change in its motion. A body at rest tends to remain at rest due to inertia. A moving body tends to maintain its velocity. For example, the fishbowl would be at rest relative to the cabin. Due to inertia, the bowl would tend to remain at rest relative to the cabin.

But suppose the ship suddenly gained speed, causing the bowl to slide. The friends in the cabin would observe that the principle of inertia no longer applied relative to the cabin. The cabin would no longer be moving at a constant velocity, so it would no longer be an inertial frame. Because the cabin was *accelerating* (changing speed), it would be an *accelerating frame of reference.*

The principle of inertia is also known as *Newton's first law of motion.* It is one of three laws of motion discovered by the English scientist Isaac Newton. Those laws were published in 1687 in *Philosophiae naturalis principia mathematica (Mathematical Principles of Natural Philosophy),* a work usually called simply *Principia* or *Principia mathematica.*

Until the late 1800's, most scientists thought that all natural events could be explained by Newton's laws. So the principle of Galilean relativity could be stated as: "The laws of nature are the same in all inertial frames," where the laws of nature were understood to be Newton's laws of motion and any laws based on them.

Galilean transformations. Certain kinds of calculations involving Galilean relativity are an important part of the background of Einstein's theories. Such calculations are known as *Galilean transformations.* They show how an event occurring in one inertial frame would appear to an observer in another inertial frame.

Galilean transformations apply a principle that is based on Newton's first law: Any frame of reference that is moving at a constant velocity relative to an inertial frame is also an inertial frame.

Suppose, for example, two jet aircraft, Jet A and Jet B, are flying in the same direction. Jet A is traveling 30 kilometers per hour (kph) faster than Jet B. A flight attendant in Jet A is walking at a speed of 5 kph in Jet A's direction of flight. A Galilean transformation will give the speed of the flight attendant relative to Jet B. The transformation will be an addition: 30 kph + 5 kph = 35 kph.

Now, suppose the attendant walks at a speed of 5 kph in the opposite direction. The transformation will be a subtraction: 30 kph − 5 kph = 25 kph.

The Michelson-Morley experiment. In 1887, an experiment conducted by two American physicists showed that there was something incorrect about Galileo's principle of relativity. The physicists, Albert A. Michelson and Edward W. Morley, performed their experiment on light rays.

The Michelson-Morley experiment can be traced back to a theory produced in 1864 by the Scottish scientist James Clerk Maxwell. Part of this theory describes the relationship between electric and magnetic *fields.* An electric field is an influence that an electrically charged object creates in the region around it. Electrically charged objects can act through their electric fields to attract or repel one another. Similarly, a magnetic field is an influence that a magnet or an electric current creates in the region around it. And similarly, magnets and objects that carry current can act through their magnetic fields to attract or repel one another.

Maxwell developed equations showing that electric and magnetic fields can combine in ways that create waves. The equations also indicate that these *electromagnetic waves* travel at the speed of light. Maxwell said that light itself consists of electromagnetic waves—a statement later proved to be true. He also said that other kinds of electromagnetic waves exist. The German physicist Heinrich Hertz discovered such waves—now known as radio waves—about 1887.

Physicists reasoned that, if light consisted of waves, the waves had to travel through some substance, just as water waves travel through water. They called the substance *ether,* and they imagined that it filled all space. Although the ether could transmit waves, they said, it could not move from place to place. The ether's immovability made it a special inertial frame.

Maxwell's equations indicate that light moves at a particular speed, represented by the letter *c;* the value of *c* is now known to be 186,282 miles (299,792 kilometers) per second. Maxwell assumed that *c* was the speed of light relative to the ether. According to this assumption, light would travel faster or slower than *c* in an inertial frame moving relative to the ether.

Physicists also reasoned that Earth moved through the ether as the planet spun on its axis and circled the sun. Thus, any object on Earth's surface—including Michelson and Morley's laboratory—moved relative to the ether. The speed of light relative to the lab would therefore be different for light rays moving in different directions relative to the lab. And one could use Galilean transformations to calculate the speed of various rays relative to the lab.

For example, suppose the lab moved through the ether at a speed of 150 kilometers per second (kps). Imagine that a ray of light were emitted in the direction of the lab's movement. A Galilean transformation would show that the expected speed of the light relative to the lab would be $c - 150$ kps.

Now, imagine that a light ray were emitted in the opposite direction. The expected speed of the light relative to the lab would be $c + 150$ kps.

Michelson and Morley conducted their experiment to measure expected differences in the speed of light relative to their laboratory. Although light travels extremely rapidly, their experiment could measure tiny differences in speed. Surprisingly, Michelson and Morley found no difference at all. This result was a great puzzle.

Special relativity

Einstein noted that there was no evidence for the existence of the ether. He therefore eliminated the ether from consideration. He argued that Maxwell's equations mean that the speed of light must be the same in all inertial frames. Therefore, Galileo's principle cannot be absolutely correct.

Accordingly, Einstein introduced a new principle, the special principle of relativity. This principle has two parts: (1) There is no ether, and the speed of light is the same for all observers, whatever their relative motion. (2) The laws of nature are the same in all inertial frames, where the laws are understood to include those described by Maxwell.

Einstein based his special theory of relativity on this principle. The theory solved the puzzle of the Michelson-Morley experiment. It also made dramatic new predictions that were verified by later experiments.

Lorentz transformations. Special relativity uses equations known as *Lorentz transformations* to describe how an event occurring in one inertial frame would appear to an observer in another inertial frame. The equations are named for the Dutch physicist Hendrik A. Lorentz, who first wrote them down in 1895. Lorentz developed the equations in an attempt to understand the Michelson-Morley experiment.

In the complex mathematics of special relativity, time and space are not absolutely separate. Instead, physicists refer to a single entity, *space-time.* This entity is a combination of the dimension of time and the three dimensions of space—length, width, and height. Thus, space-time is four-dimensional.

Time dilation. The Lorentz transformations show that a number of strange effects can occur. One of these is known as *time dilation; dilation* means *widening.*

For an example of this effect, consider two spaceships, A and B. The ships are moving relative to each other at a speed close to *c.* There is a clock in each ship. Both clocks keep time accurately, and people in both ships can see both clocks. Strangely, the people in the two ships will read the clocks differently. The people in Spaceship A will observe that the clock in Spaceship B is running more slowly than the clock in Spaceship A. But the people in Spaceship B will observe that the clock in Spaceship A is running more slowly than the clock in Spaceship B.

Time dilation actually occurs at all relative velocities. But at everyday velocities, even the most sensitive instruments cannot detect it. Thus, people are not aware of time dilation as they go about their normal activities.

However, time dilation is important in the study of *cosmic rays,* high-energy particles that travel through space. Some cosmic rays that originate in outer space collide with atoms at the top of Earth's atmosphere. The collisions create a variety of particles, including *muons.* The muons travel at almost the speed of light. They are also *radioactive*—that is, they break apart as they travel.

Each muon can be considered to be its own reference frame. Physicists have measured how quickly muons break apart in terms of the passage of time in their reference frames. They break apart so rapidly that one might conclude that hardly any of them could ever reach Earth's surface. But due to time dilation, the muons break apart much more slowly relative to Earth's reference frame. As a result, many of them reach the surface.

Lorentz-Fitzgerald contraction. Another strange effect of special relativity is the *Lorentz-Fitzgerald contraction,* or simply the *Fitzgerald contraction.* Lorentz proposed that contraction occurred as an effect of the Lorentz transformations. In 1889, the Irish physicist George F. Fitzgerald had made a similar proposal.

For an example of this contraction, again consider the two spaceships. The people in Spaceship A will observe that Spaceship B and all the objects in it have become shorter in the direction of Spaceship B's motion relative to Spaceship A. But they will observe no change in the size of Spaceship B or any of the objects as measured from top to bottom or from side to side.

This effect, like time dilation, also occurs in reverse: The people in Spaceship B will observe that Spaceship A and all the objects in it have shrunk in the direction of Spaceship A's motion relative to Spaceship B. This contraction also occurs at all relative velocities.

Mass-energy relationship. One of the most famous effects of special relativity is the relation between mass and energy: $E = mc^2$. Mass can be thought of as the amount of matter in an object. The equation says that an object at rest has an energy E equal to its mass m times the speed of light c multiplied by itself, or *squared.*

The speed of light is so high that the conversion of a tiny quantity of mass releases a tremendous amount of energy. For example, the complete conversion of an object with a mass of 1 gram would release 90 trillion joules of energy. This quantity is roughly equal to the energy released in the explosion of 22,000 tons (20,000 metric tons) of TNT.

The conversion of mass creates energy in the sun and other stars. It also produces the heat energy that is converted to electric energy in nuclear power plants. In addition, mass-to-energy conversion is responsible for the tremendous destructive force of nuclear weapons.

General relativity

Einstein developed the general theory of relativity to modify Newton's law of gravitation so that it would agree with special relativity. The key disagreement lay in descriptions of how objects exert forces on one another.

In special relativity, nothing can travel between two points faster than the speed of light. This principle applies to forces as well as rays of light.

Consider, for example, an atom of the simplest form of hydrogen. This atom consists of a single electron in orbit around a single proton. The electron carries a negative electric charge, while the proton is positively charged. The position of the proton determines the motion of the electron. It does so by exerting a force of attraction on the electron—an application of the familiar principle "opposite charges attract."

The proton exerts the force by means of electromagnetic waves that can be thought of as light rays. The proton *emits* (sends out) a ray, which the electron then absorbs. Thus, the electron's motion depends on what the proton's position was when the proton emitted the ray.

In the *Principia,* Newton had given the law of gravity as $F = m_1 m_2 \div d^2$, where F is the gravitational force between two objects, m_1 and m_2 are the masses of the objects, and d^2 is the distance between them squared. This law explained the motion of the planets. According to the law, a planet's motion depends on the position of the sun and the other planets. All these objects influence one another by means of gravitational force.

However, Newton's law says that the force between two objects is transmitted instantaneously, no matter how great the distance between the objects is. That is, the law describes a gravitational *action at a distance.* This description does not agree with special relativity, which states that there is no action at a distance.

Principle of equivalence. To eliminate action at a distance from Newton's laws, Einstein began with an observation that he called the *principle of equivalence.* According to this principle, an object's *gravitational mass* equals its *inertial mass.*

Gravitational mass helps determine the force of gravity on an object. The masses m_1 and m_2 in Newton's law of gravity are gravitational masses.

Inertial mass is a measure of an object's inertia. Inertial mass is given in the equation for Newton's second law of motion: $F = ma$, where F is the force exerted on an object, m is the inertial mass of the object, and a is the acceleration of the object. This equation applies, for example, when you push an object across the floor. If your force is greater than the force of friction between the object and the floor and any other force that is working against you, the object will go faster and faster. The amount of acceleration will depend on the mass of the object and on your force minus the opposing forces.

The Hungarian physicist Loránd Eötvös had verified the principle of equivalence experimentally in 1889. Einstein saw that the principle reveals a close connection between the way an object moves through space-time and the gravitational force that acts on the object. He recognized that gravity is therefore related to the structure of space-time.

A "thought experiment." To describe how he would work to eliminate action at a distance, Einstein offered an example called a "thought experiment": First, consider an elevator that is falling freely toward Earth's surface. Suppose a person in the elevator drops a rock. The rock will fall with the person, and so it will merely hover in the air beside the person. Now, imagine that the elevator is in outer space—so far from any planet or star that almost no gravitational force is present. The person drops the rock. Again, it hovers beside the person.

Einstein said that the "thought experiment" reveals a general truth: A person in free fall cannot determine by observation within his or her reference frame that gravitation is present. Thus, gravitation must be a characteristic of the space-time in which the observer is falling.

Nowadays, the principle that underlies Einstein's example is familiar in the phenomenon of *weightlessness.* Astronauts in the space station are so close to Earth that the planet's gravity acts on them. But, like the rock in the elevator, the space station and its passengers are in free fall. Therefore, their experience is the same as it would be if there were no gravity at all.

Distortions in space-time. Einstein translated this principle into mathematical terms in his general theory of relativity. In this theory, matter and energy *distort* (change the shape of) space-time, and the distortion is experienced as gravity. A more common way of explaining the distortion is "Mass curves space."

Einstein suggested that astronomers could make certain observations to test the general theory of relativity. The most dramatic would be a bending of light rays by the sun's gravitation. In relativity, mass and energy are equivalent. Because light carries energy, it also is affected by gravity. The light-bending effect is small, but Einstein calculated that it could be observed during a solar eclipse. In 1919, the British astronomer Arthur S. Eddington observed it, thereby making Einstein world-famous.

In 2011, scientists announced that data gathered by the National Aeronautics and Space Administration's Gravity Probe B (GP-B) confirmed two predictions derived from Einstein's general theory of relativity. The experiment revealed the *geodetic effect,* the warping of space and time around a gravitational body, and *frame-dragging,* the amount a spinning object pulls space and time with it as it rotates.

Gravitational waves. General relativity indicates that *gravitational waves* transmit gravitational force, just as electromagnetic waves transmit electric and magnetic forces. Scientists have observed gravitational waves indirectly in a pair of *neutron stars* that orbit each other. Neutron stars are the smallest and densest stars known. A neutron star measures only about 12 miles (20 kilometers) across, but has more mass than the sun.

By observing the pair of stars for several years, the scientists determined that the stars' orbit is becoming smaller. Calculations involving equations of general relativity show that the orbit is shrinking because the stars are emitting gravitational waves.

Most gravitational waves produce such small distortions of space-time that they are impossible to detect directly. However, collisions between neutron stars and even more compact objects called *black holes* create tremendous distortions. Physicists have built observatories to detect the resulting waves directly.

The Laser Interferometer Gravitational-Wave Observatory (LIGO) first detected the presence of gravitational waves in late 2015. Scientists announced the findings in early 2016. LIGO has three detectors—two in Hanford, Washington, and one in Livingston, Louisiana. Each facility is designed to detect gravitational waves by sensing their effect on two metal tubes that are 2 ½ miles (4 kilometers) long. The tubes are built along the ground and connected in the shape of an L. When a gravitational wave passes through them, it changes their lengths by an amount much smaller than an atomic nucleus. A laser system detects changes in the lengths.

Michael Dine

Related articles in *World Book* include:

Dark energy
$E=mc^2$
Eddington, Sir Arthur Stanley
Einstein, Albert
Electromagnetism
Force (Gravitation)
Fourth dimension
Galileo
Gravitation
Gravitational wave
Hertz, Heinrich R.
Inertia
Mass
Maxwell, James Clerk
Michelson, Albert Abraham
Neutron star
Newton, Sir Isaac
String theory
Time (Time in relativity theory; The past, present, and future)

Relaxation. See Health (Rest and sleep).

Relief, in art, is sculpture in which the figures or designs project from their background. It differs from *sculpture in the round,* in which the figures stand alone and have three full dimensions. In relief sculpture, the figures are only partly modeled, but give an illusion of being fully modeled. They may stand out from the background surface, or may be carved into it. The sculpture is called *hollow relief* or *intaglio* if they are carved into it.

Relief sculpture may be of three types: high relief; low relief; and half relief, or semirelief. Some relief sculpture combines two or more types.

High relief. Figures modeled in high relief project from their background more than half of their implied thickness. High relief is often called by its Italian name, *alto-rilievo.*

Low relief. Figures that stand out from their background less than half of their suggested thickness are in low relief. When the work is well done, they appear to stand out more than they actually do. The frieze of the Parthenon is the most famous example of low-relief

SEF/Art Resource

A low relief shows a pharaoh offering gifts to Horus, the Egyptian god of light and heaven. Reliefs portraying gods and royalty decorated many ancient Egyptian structures.

SCALA/Art Resource

Half-relief figures appear in panels on the marble pulpit of the Baptistery of Pisa, Italy. The pulpit, completed by sculptor Nicola Pisano in 1260, also includes realistic carved figures in high relief, extending above the pillars.

Bronze panel (1425 to 1452) by Lorenzo Ghiberti from the east doors of the baptistery in Florence, Italy (SCALA/Art Resource)

High-relief figures in the foreground add drama to a scene from the Old Testament story of Joseph. Italian sculptor Lorenzo Ghiberti designed the background in low relief.

sculpture (see **Parthenon**). Sometimes low relief may be nearly flat, as in the design on a coin. Low relief is also known by its French name, *bas-relief.*

Half relief, or semirelief. Figures in half relief stand out half their thickness. Half relief is a little higher than low relief, but lower than high relief. It is often called by its Italian name, *mezzo-rilievo.*

History. Sculptors have carved figures in relief for thousands of years. Peoples of the stone ages often carved or scratched figures and designs in relief. The Assyrians, Egyptians, and Greeks used all forms of relief sculpture in their palaces and temples.

Relief sculpture is used in many ways today. It is almost the only form used in making coins and medals. As in all sculpture, the subject matter, design, and execution of relief reflect the development of civilization, the religious trends, and the art of the time in which it is made. Harold L. Enlow

See also **Cameo; Engraving; Intaglio; Sculpture** (Kinds of sculpture).

Relief. See Welfare.

Relief Corps, National Woman's. See Woman's Relief Corps, National.

© Sebastian D'Sousa, AFP/Getty Images

The Hindu festival of Kumbh Mela is a huge religious gathering. These Hindus carrying offerings walk to the Godavari River in India to bathe in its sacred waters during Kumbh Mela.

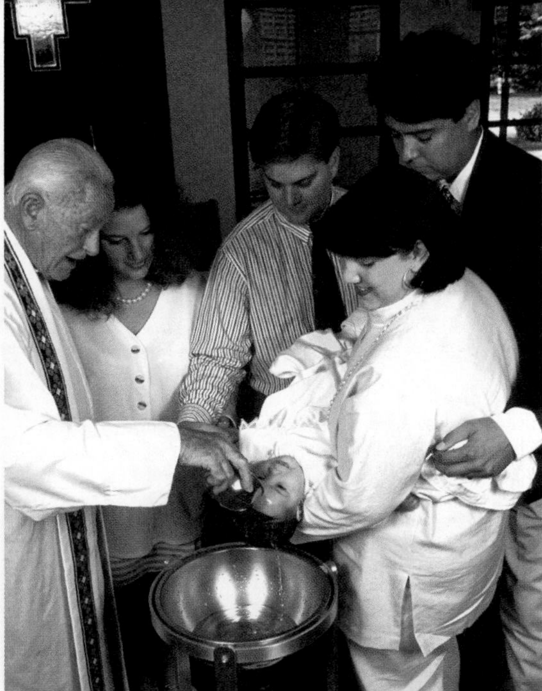

© Myrleen Ferguson Cate, PhotoEdit

The Christian sacrament of baptism indicates or transmits the cleansing of sin and the starting of a new life with God. The priest shown here baptizes a baby by pouring water on its head.

© AFP/Getty Images

Muslim pilgrims in Mecca, Saudi Arabia, wait outside the Great Mosque, Islam's holiest shrine, to break their fast on the 27th day of the sacred month of Ramadan. Muslims believe that the Qur'ān, their holy book, was revealed to the Prophet Muhammad on this night. Muslims spend the night, known as Laylāt al-Qadr, reading the book and praying.

Religion

Religion. No simple definition can describe the many religions in the world. Every society has a religion. For many people, religion is an organized system of beliefs, *rituals* (acts and ceremonies), personal practices, and worship directed toward a supreme power or *deity* (god). For others, religion involves a number of gods or deities. Some people follow religions that worship no specific god or gods. There are also people who practice their own religious beliefs in a personal way, largely independent of any organized religion.

Almost all people who participate in a religion believe that a divine power is at work in the world. Some believe that this power created the world and can influence their lives in various ways. Others believe that the goal of human life is to live in harmony with this power.

In its most basic sense, religion deals with primary concerns: What is the purpose of life? What is the final destiny of human beings and animals? What is the difference between right and wrong? What is the meaning of suffering and evil? What are a person's obligations to other people and to the world?

People practice religions for many reasons. Some an-

Carole R. Fontaine, the contributor of this article, is John Taylor Professor of Biblical History and Theology at Andover Newton Theological School in Newton, Massachusetts.

thropologists believe that the religious impulse may be one of the most fundamental traits of the human species. Throughout the world, many people follow a religious tradition simply because it is part of the heritage of their nation, culture, tribe, ethnic group, or family. One objective of religion is to give groups a sense of identity and purpose.

Religion can provide a sense of personal security in a confusing world because believers feel that a supreme power, God, watches over them. Believers may request help or protection from their god or gods through prayer or ritual. Many people follow a religion because it promises them happiness in life or in some kind of life after death, or because they believe it will save them from eternal damnation. The prospect of an afterlife also offers hope to those who suffer in this life. Religion provides individual fulfillment in this way and helps people to understand their place in the universe.

There are thousands of religions in the world. The three religions with the most followers are Christianity, Islam, and Hinduism. Other religions include Buddhism, Confucianism, Jainism, Judaism, Shinto, Sikhism, and Taoism. Hinduism, Shinto, and Taoism developed over many centuries. Many other religions base their faith on the lives or teachings of specific individuals. They include for Buddhism, Siddhartha Gautama, who became known as Gautama Buddha; for Christianity, Jesus, known as Jesus Christ; for Confucianism, Confucius; for Islam, Muhammad; for Jainism, Mahavira; for Judaism, Abraham and Moses; and for Sikhism, Nanak.

The religions that trace their history to individuals follow a general pattern of development. During the individual's lifetime or soon after his death, a distinctive system of worship and ceremonies developed, based on the individual's life and teachings. In addition to inspiring worship, the individual represented an ideal way of life that followers tried to imitate.

The teachings of religions have shaped the lives of people since prehistoric times. Judaism, Islam, and especially Christianity have been major influences in the formation of Western culture. These religions are called *Religions of the Book* because they all are at least partly inspired by the Hebrew Bible, or Old Testament. These three faiths, particularly Islam, have also played a crucial role in the development of Middle Eastern and African culture. The cultures of Asia have been shaped by Buddhism, Confucianism, Hinduism, Shinto, and Taoism.

Religion has been a supreme source of inspiration in the arts. In ancient times, almost all art was probably religious in nature. Some of the most beautiful buildings in the world are houses of worship. Much of the world's greatest music is religious. Religious stories have provided countless subjects for paintings, sculpture, literature, theater, dances, and motion pictures.

This article describes the chief characteristics of religion. It also examines the origin of religion in prehistoric times. In addition, the article describes the history and organization of many of the world's major religions. Many separate *World Book* articles provide information on topics related to religion. For a list of these articles, see the *Related articles* at the end of this article.

Chief characteristics of religion

Most leading religions share certain characteristics. The chief characteristics include (1) belief in a deity or in a power beyond the individual, (2) a *doctrine* (accepted teaching) of salvation, (3) a code of conduct, (4) the use of sacred stories, and (5) religious rituals.

The essential qualities of a religion are maintained and passed from generation to generation by sources, called *authority,* that the followers accept as sacred. To be sacred or holy, a thing must be considered set apart and different, either because it is commanded by a deity or is related to a god or gods. Sacred things have more power than ordinary things. The most important religious authorities are writings known as *scriptures.* Scriptures include the Bibles of Christians and Jews, the Qur'ān of Muslims, and the Vedas of Hindus. Most believers consider scriptures sacred because they believe the writings are *inspired*—that is, dictated by or guided by a deity. Religious authority also comes from the writings of saints and other holy people and from decisions by religious councils and leaders. Unwritten customs and laws known as *traditions* also form a basic part of authority.

Belief in a deity. There are three main philosophical views regarding the existence of a deity: (1) *Theists* believe in a deity or deities. (2) *Atheists* believe that no deity exists. (3) *Agnostics* say that the existence of a deity cannot be proved or disproved. Most major religions are theistic. They teach that deities govern or greatly influence human actions as well as events in nature. Some religions are not theistic. Examples include Confucianism and some forms of Buddhism.

Religions that acknowledge only one god are called *monotheistic.* Judaism, Christianity, and Islam are examples of monotheistic religions. A religion that has a number of deities is called *polytheistic.* The ancient Greeks and Romans had polytheistic religions. Each of their many gods and goddesses had one or more special areas of influence. For example, Aphrodite was the Greek goddess of love, and Mars was the Roman god of war. In *henotheistic* religions, the worship of a supreme deity does not deny the existence and power of other deities. For example, Hinduism teaches that a world spirit called Brahman is the supreme power. But Hindus also worship numerous other gods and goddesses. Many peoples in Africa and the Pacific Islands also worship a supreme power as well as many other deities.

The followers of some religions worship deities who are or were people or that are images of people. The ancient Egyptian people considered their pharaohs to be living gods. Before World War II (1939-1945), the Japanese honored their emperor as divine. Taoists believe in deities that look and act like human beings. They also worship some deities who were once human beings and became gods or goddesses after death. Jains worship *Tirthankaras*—that is, people who have become enlightened and broken the cycle of birth and death.

Many people worship nature gods—that is, deities who dwell in or control various aspects of nature. The Chinese, in particular, have worshiped gods of the soil and grain. Followers of Shinto worship *kami,* spirits that live in nature. Some American Indians worship a *spirit power,* a mysterious, powerful force in nature.

A doctrine of salvation. Among the major religions, Christianity, Hinduism, Buddhism, Islam, and Jainism teach a doctrine of salvation. They stress that salvation is the highest goal of the faithful and one that all followers should try to achieve. Religions differ, however, in their understanding of salvation, when and how it occurs, and how it can be gained. In many religions, the quest for salvation is aided by the work of a "savior." The savior may be a god or some other divine figure, or the individual on whose teachings the religion is based.

A doctrine of salvation is based on the belief that individuals or groups are in some danger from which they must be "saved." The danger may be the threat of physical misfortune in this world, such as disease or war, or the danger may await people in a life after death. Christianity and several other religions teach that the danger is primarily spiritual and is centered in each person's soul. The soul is thought to be that part of a person that survives after the body dies.

Christianity teaches that people are sinful by nature. They can, however, wipe out their sinfulness and past offenses toward God and humanity by believing in the sacrificial death of Jesus. If a Christian is saved, then the soul enters a state of eternal happiness, often called heaven. If a person is not saved, the soul may spend eternity in a state of punishment, often called hell.

Most Eastern religions teach that a person gains salvation by finding release from obstacles that can block human fulfillment. In most Asian religions, the obstacles take the form of worldly desires and attachments to material things. Salvation depends on whether people can free themselves from these desires and attachments, which only bring suffering.

Hinduism teaches that each person's soul, called *atman,* is identical with the supreme spirit, Brahman, that is the source of all material creation. Hindus believe they achieve a kind of immortality, as well as union with their god, through discovering the Brahman in themselves.

In Buddhism, a person must undertake the difficult task of purification by following a set of guidelines called the Noble Eightfold Path. By following this path, people rid themselves of the delusions that doom them to an endless cycle of birth, suffering, death, and rebirth.

© Nippon Television Network Corporation Tokyo 1991

The Sistine Chapel is in the Vatican Palace in Rome. From 1508 to 1512, the Italian artist Michelangelo decorated the ceiling with fresco paintings of Biblical stories. From 1536 to 1541, he painted the fresco *The Last Judgment* on the wall behind the altar. Other artists painted the side walls with stories of Moses and Jesus Christ.

Islam teaches that actions in this life bring salvation in the next. Followers must "submit" their whole selves to the will of Allah through daily prayer and other acts of worship called the Five Pillars of Islam (see **Islam** [The Five Pillars of Islam]). By following these practices, Muslims will be saved from future punishment by Allah.

A code of conduct is a set of moral teachings and values that all religions have in some form. Such a code, or *ethic,* tells believers how to conduct their lives. It instructs them how to act toward the deity and toward one another. Religious codes of conduct differ in many ways, but most agree on several major themes. For example, they stress some form of the *golden rule,* which states that believers ideally should treat others as they would like to be treated themselves. A religion's code of conduct also may determine such matters as whom believers may marry, what jobs they may hold, how they dress, and what foods they may eat.

The use of sacred stories. For thousands of years, followers of religions have believed in sacred stories, sometimes called *myths* or *legends.* Religious leaders often use these stories to dramatize their teachings.

Originally, people told stories to describe how the sacred powers influenced the world. The stories showed how the sacred powers directly or indirectly caused some feature or event in the world. Many stories described the creation of the world. Others told how human beings or a particular people began. Some of the stories tried to explain the cause of natural occurrences, such as thunderstorms or the changes in seasons.

Today, there are scientific explanations for many of the subjects dealt with in sacred stories. But some religious groups still insist that the stories are true in every detail. Other groups believe only in the message contained in the stories, not in the specific details. Still other religious groups regard sacred stories as symbolic expressions of the ideals and values of their faith.

Religious rituals include the acts and ceremonies by which believers appeal to and serve God, deities, or other sacred powers. Some rituals are performed by individuals alone, and others by groups of worshipers. Religious groups perform their important rituals according to a schedule and often repeat them regularly. The performance of a ritual is often called a *service.* Leaders of rituals often require special training and must be authorized before they are allowed to lead. This training and authorization is sometimes called *ordination.*

The most common ritual is prayer. Through prayer, a believer or someone on behalf of believers addresses words and thoughts to an object of worship. Prayer includes requests, expressions of thanksgiving, confessions of sins, and praise. Most major religions have a daily schedule of prayer.

Meditation, in some ways like prayer, is a spiritual exercise important in Asian religions. Buddhist monks try to be masters of meditation. By clearing the mind of day-to-day distractions, people who meditate attempt to gain a higher form of consciousness.

Many religions have rituals intended to purify the body. For example, Hindus consider the waters of the Ganges River in India to be sacred. Every year, millions of Hindus purify their bodies by bathing in the river, especially at the holy city of Varanasi.

In some religions, *pilgrimages* are significant rituals. Pilgrimages are journeys to the sites of holy objects or to places credited with miraculous healing powers. Believers also make pilgrimages to sacred places, such as the birthplace or tomb of the founder of their faith. All devout Muslims hope to make a pilgrimage to Mecca, the birthplace of Muhammad. Many Christians travel to the Holy Land, today the nation of Israel and a Palestinian territory called the West Bank. This land is where Jesus of Nazareth lived, worked, and died.

Shamans are holy men and women who are believed to have special powers to communicate with the gods or the spirit world. Many shamans are thought to leave their bodies while in a trance, taking "spirit" journeys to find answers or healing for their people.

Many rituals are scheduled at certain times of the day, week, or year. Various religions have services at sunrise, in the morning, at sunset, and in the evening. Special services mark the beginning of a new year. Many religions celebrate springtime, harvesttime, and the new or full moon. Religious attention to the marking of the seasons may be a survival from prehistoric and ancient religions. These early religions attempted to secure survival of the community through good harvests and hunting, which depended on a knowledge of the seasons.

© ASAP Ltd. from Index Stock Imagery

Passover is a Jewish festival that celebrates the ancient Israelites' escape from slavery in Egypt. The highlight of this annual festival is a ceremonial feast called the Seder, *shown here.* At the Seder, the story of the flight of the Israelites is read from a book called the Haggadah.

Many rituals commemorate events in the history of religions. For example, the Jewish festival of Passover recalls the meal the Israelites ate just before their departure from slavery in Egypt. Various Christian celebrations of Holy Communion are related to the last meal Jesus shared with his disciples before his death.

Rituals also mark important events in a person's life. Various ceremonies make such events as birth, marriage, and death into sacred occasions. Some rituals accept young people into the religion and into adult society. These rituals are called *rites of passage.* In Judaism, the ritual of circumcision is performed on male infants. Some Christians baptize babies soon after birth. Other Christians baptize only youths or adults.

How the major religions are organized

The organization of the world's major religions ranges from simple to complex. Many religions have spiritual leaders, often called the *clergy.* These leaders have the authority and responsibility to conduct religious services, to advise or command believers, and to govern the religious organization at various levels. In some religions, the *laity*—that is, the believers who are not members of the clergy—also have important roles.

In many countries, there is a *state* (official or favored) religion. For example, Islam is the state religion of Iran, Pakistan, Saudi Arabia, and many other nations. Lutheranism is the state religion of Denmark and Norway, and Buddhism is the state religion of the Asian nations of Bhutan, Cambodia, and Thailand. The United Kingdom has two *established* (official) churches—the Church of England, which is Anglican, and the Church of Scotland, which is Presbyterian.

Judaism has no one person as its head. Each local congregation or synagogue supervises its own affairs, usually under the leadership of a rabbi. Israel and a few other countries have chief rabbis. These rabbis are scholars who serve as the top judges of religious law.

Christian *denominations* (groups) are organized in various ways. In the Roman Catholic Church, believers are organized into districts called *parishes,* which belong to larger districts called *dioceses.* Dioceses, in turn, belong to *provinces.* The main diocese in each province is called an *archdiocese.* Pastors preside over parishes, bishops over dioceses, and archbishops over archdioceses. The pope presides over the entire Roman Catholic Church with the advice and assistance of high officials called *cardinals.* Some Protestant denominations are governed by similar patterns of *hierarchies* (levels of authority). Others are governed by boards of the clergy and laity or by local congregations. Throughout most of history, women have had fewer rights and a lower social status than men. Largely because of women's lower status, most religious hierarchies have tended to exclude women from leadership roles.

Confucianism and Islam have no ordained clergy. Leadership is provided by scholars who interpret religious teachings. In Shinto and Taoism, the basic organizational unit is the priesthood. In Buddhism, the chief unit is an order of monks called the *sangha.* The monks serve as advisers and teachers and play a vital part in everyday life. In some Buddhist countries, the head of state is also the leader of the national order of monks.

Hinduism has no consistent pattern of organization. There are no congregations or parishes. Hindus tend to worship individually or in families. Services in temples are performed by the Brahmans, members of the highest Hindu *caste* (social class).

The origin of religion

Experts think prehistoric religions arose out of fear and wonder about natural events, such as storms, earthquakes, and the birth of babies. To explain why someone died, people credited supernatural powers greater than themselves or greater than the world around them.

Prehistoric people most likely centered their religious activities on the most important elements of their existence, such as adequate rainfall or success in hunting. They often placed food, ornaments, and tools in the graves of members of the group who had died. They probably believed that these items would be useful to, or desired by, the dead. Archaeologists believe that prehistoric people drew pictures and may have performed other rituals intended to promote the fertility of women and animals and to ensure good hunting. They likely made sacrifices for the same reason.

Earlier theories. In the 1800's, the British anthropologist Edward Burnett Tylor and the German-born language scholar Friedrich Max Müller developed influential ideas about the origin of religion. Tylor proposed that ancient people thought spirits, or *animae,* existed in and controlled all things in nature. This concept was called *animism.* Many people still practice animism today, especially in Africa.

Müller agreed with Tylor that religion began as spirit worship. He also thought that early people saw human qualities in natural forces. For example, they understood thunderstorms as a god who controlled thunder. Müller thought the belief in deities originated in this way.

In the early 1900's, the German scholar Rudolf Otto and the Austrian physician Sigmund Freud proposed theories of religion that went beyond those of earlier scholars. Otto believed that religion came into existence when people encountered what they felt was holy or sacred. Such an event provoked feelings of awe and wonder, and people continued to try to recapture that encounter. Worship and an ethical code of conduct are

Religious beliefs of the world

Percentage of the world that follows each religious belief.

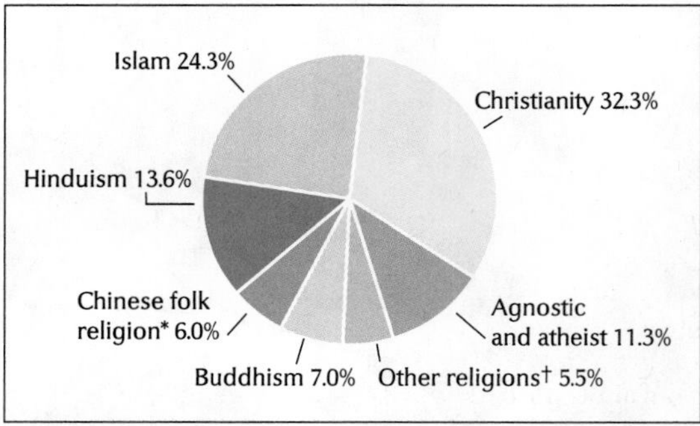

*A system of beliefs that includes Confucianism and Taoism.
†Includes Judaism, Shinto, Sikhism, and other religions. Each of these religions is followed by less than one-half of 1 percent of the world's people.
Figures are for 2020.
Source: Todd M. Johnson and Brian J. Grim, eds. World Religion Database (Leiden/Boston: Brill, accessed in June 2020).

A prehistoric religious ritual was performed to ensure a sufficient food supply. Anthropologists think this late Stone Age rock painting records a trance dance known as *simbo* among the Sandawe people of eastern Africa thousands of years ago. The masked figures may represent *shamans,* whom the Sandawe believed to have special powers to contact the spirit world.

© Werner Forman Archive, Art Resource

ways that people hope to sustain their sense of the sacred in their lives. For Freud, the father of modern psychoanalysis, religion emerged from the consciousness of the child. A child typically relies on a dominant, nearby mother figure and a distant, all-powerful father figure. The child's dependence on these parental figures eventually leads, in adults, to the concept of a supreme being strongly at work in a person's life. Religion, according to Freud, is a formal attempt to please and influence this universal parent.

In the 1920's, the Austrian-born Jewish philosopher Martin Buber wrote that the basic religious impulse arises when a person encounters someone or something as a being with whom one can have a direct, deeply personal relationship. Buber called it an "I-Thou" relationship. He located the foundation of all meaning in life in this satisfying experience of knowing or being known by another consciousness.

Later theories. By the end of the 1900's, many other scholars had added to the understanding of the rise of religions and their many features. Evelyn Underhill, a British religious scholar, studied mystical experience, in which a person seeks union with a supreme power. Mircea Eliade, a Romanian-born religious historian, studied early religions. He found that religions arose from people's need to distinguish between that which is *sacred*—that is, special and holy—and that which is *profane*—that is, ordinary and not sacred.

Newer theories seek to understand religion as a form of social control, especially of selected men over women, over nature, and over men who do not belong to their group. Still other theories draw on the findings of psychology to describe religion as a set of activities by which human beings attempt to impose order on the chaos of experience. These theories see religion helping people to resolve unbearable and unexplainable paradoxes (contradictions) in life, such as why bad things happen to good people.

History of the world's major religions

The major religions in the world today originated between about 1500 B.C. and A.D. 600. The following discussion traces the history of many of these religions.

Judaism traces its origins to the Near East, probably from about 1550 to 1200 B.C. A group of people, later known as Israelites and Judaeans, believed they were descendants of one father, Abraham. According to tradition, Abraham migrated from southern Mesopotamia (now Iraq) to the land of Canaan (roughly an area from east of the Jordan River to the Mediterranean Sea).

The Bible claims that God had promised Canaan to Abraham and his descendants. The Bible says that Abraham's grandson Jacob (later named Israel) had 12 sons who became the heads of the Twelve Tribes of Israel. Some of these tribes fled into the Nile Delta during times of famine, eventually becoming slaves in Egypt. God then sent a leader, Moses, to bring the people out of slavery and back to the Promised Land of Canaan. Archaeology has not confirmed any of these events. However, an ancient Egyptian inscription states that Pharaoh Merneptah defeated a tribe known as Israel in the late 1200's B.C.

According to the Bible, Moses led the wandering tribes after the Exodus from Egypt. During the wandering of the tribes in the Sinai Desert, Moses received from God a set of laws for conduct and worship. These laws are called the Ten Commandments. Moses wrote down the teachings he received from God and told the story of the Israelites for future generations in five books called the Pentateuch or Torah. These books, which make up the first five books of the Bible, are sometimes known as the Mosaic Law. Their interpretation forms the basis of the Jewish religion.

Judaism was the first religion to successfully develop monotheism. Pharaoh Akhenaten of Egypt had tried to introduce the worship of a single god in the 1300's B.C. But after his death, his successors ruthlessly put down his new religion, and Egypt returned to polytheism. Scholars disagree on when the Jewish religion became monotheistic. Some scholars trace that change to the time of Moses. Others place it much later, under reforms by the Hebrew prophets and kings in the 600's and 500's B.C.

Over time, the group that had fled Egypt during the Exodus developed a system of religious beliefs that became Judaism. Their common religion helped unite the people to form the kingdom of Israel under King David and David's son King Solomon. After Solomon's death about 928 B.C., the kingdom split in two to form the Kingdom of Israel in the north and the Kingdom of Judah in the south. For two centuries, the kingdoms fought with each other and with their neighbors. The Assyrians destroyed Israel in 722 or 721 B.C., annexing the land and deporting the population to the east. The people of Israel scattered and lost their identity as a nation, becoming the "Lost Tribes" of Israel.

Judah continued to exist until 587 or 586 B.C., when the Babylonians destroyed the city of Jerusalem and its

Illustration (about 1300) by an unknown German artist from a Haggadah; Collection of the Israel Museum, Jerusalem (photo © the Israel Museum)

The Ten Commandments contain the basic laws of Judaism and Christianity. In this picture, the Jewish leader Moses gives the commandments to the Jews, after getting them from God.

holy Temple. The Babylonians deported the upper-class population to Babylon during a period called the Babylonian Exile. After King Cyrus of Persia conquered Babylon in 539 B.C., he said that all the captive peoples could return to their homes. Many Jews returned to Judah and rebuilt the Temple in Jerusalem. Jews who chose not to return to Judah became part of the Diaspora, the name for the scattered communities of Jews.

Great powers continued to fight over Judah, including Greece and Rome. Many Jews fled and settled in the Middle East and later in Europe. Everywhere they were a religious minority. After the spread of Christianity, Christian authorities and worshipers often persecuted them.

After about 1800, Jews divided into three general groups—Orthodox, Conservative, and Reform. Orthodox Jews observed rituals in traditional ways. Conservative and Reform Jews modernized certain practices. Most Eastern European Jews followed Orthodox Judaism, and most Western European and North American Jews followed Conservative or Reform Judaism.

In the 1930's, the German dictator Adolf Hitler and his Nazi Party began a vicious campaign against Jews. By 1945, the Nazis had killed about 6 million of the 8 million to 9 million Jews in Europe. Many of the survivors joined Jews living in Palestine. Together, they established the state of Israel in 1948 under the sponsorship of the United Nations. It was the first homeland Jews had known since Biblical times. In a war fought in 1967, Israel occupied territory on the West Bank of the Jordan River and the Gaza Strip, a small area on the coast of the Mediterranean Sea. Many Palestinians had lived on these lands for centuries. Today, there are still questions about which group has legitimate ownership of the West Bank and Gaza, often called the *occupied territories.*

Hinduism began about 1500 B.C. At that time, a central Asian people called the Aryans invaded and conquered India. The Aryan culture gradually combined with the culture of a local people known as the Dravidians. Hinduism developed from a blend of the two.

The oldest Hindu scriptures are the Vedas. They were composed over a period of nearly 1,000 years, beginning about 1400 B.C. This stage in Hindu history is often called the Vedic period. During Vedic times, believers worshiped a number of nature deities.

By the 500's B.C., Hinduism began to split into various schools of thought. Two of these schools—Buddhism and Jainism—became new religions. The Hindu schools further split into smaller divisions. Today, Hinduism includes a great number of schools and divisions. Many of the divisions were formed by saints or spiritual teachers called *gurus.* Each school has its own philosophy and form of worship, but all accept basic Hindu doctrines.

Buddhism developed in India around 500 B.C. or a little later from the teachings of a prince named Siddhartha Gautama. He became known as *Buddha,* meaning *Enlightened One.* Buddhism was partly a rebellion against certain features of Hinduism. Buddhism opposed the Hindu worship of many deities, the Hindu emphasis on *caste* (social class) and the supernatural, and the power of the Brahmans, the highest Hindu class.

Buddha taught that people should devote themselves to finding release from the suffering of life. Through this release, people would gain *nirvana,* a state of perfect peace and happiness. To achieve nirvana, they had to free themselves from all worldly desires and attachments to material things. Buddha taught that nirvana could be gained by following the *Middle Way* between the extremes of severe self-denial and uncontrolled passion. As Buddha preached, he attracted a growing number of followers. By the time of his death, about 483 B.C., Buddhism had become firmly established in India.

Buddhism spread into central Asia. By the end of the A.D. 100's, it had reached China. Buddhism swept through much of China from the 300's to the 500's, challenging the native Chinese religions of Confucianism and Taoism in popularity. In the 500's, Chinese Buddhism spread to Korea and Japan. Buddhism became the chief Japanese religion for the next 1,000 years.

Early in its history, Buddhism divided into two forms, Theravada and Mahayana. Theravada emphasizes personal salvation through one's own efforts at purification. Mahayana stresses feeling compassion for all who suffer and working for their salvation. Today, Theravada Buddhism is strongest in Cambodia, Laos, Myanmar, Sri Lanka, and Thailand. Most Mahayana Buddhists live in Japan, Mongolia, Nepal, South Korea, Tibet, Vietnam, and parts of India and Russia.

Confucianism is a Chinese religion based on the teachings of Confucius, a philosopher who died about 479 B.C. Confucianism has no organization or clergy. It does not teach belief in a deity or an afterlife. Confucian-

Giant Buddha in the Ling Yin Temple, Hang-chou, China; Artstreet

Buddha preached that people can gain *nirvana,* or salvation, by freeing themselves from worldly attachments and desires. Buddhism began in India and spread to China and other Asian lands.

ism stresses moral and political ideas. It emphasizes respect for ancestors and for authority, and teaches that rulers must govern according to high moral standards.

Confucianism, Buddhism, and Taoism have been the major religions in China. However, Confucianism has had the greatest impact on Chinese society. Confucianism was the state religion of China from the 100's B.C. until the A.D. 1900's. Chinese rulers approved of its emphasis on respect for authority and dedication to public service. Confucian scriptures called the Five Classics and Four Books served as the foundation of the Chinese educational system for centuries. Candidates applying for government jobs had to pass examinations based on these scriptures.

Beginning in the 1000's, a more philosophical approach to Confucianism known as Neo-Confucianism became widely popular. Neo-Confucianism also influenced Japanese moral codes and philosophy from the 1600's through the 1800's.

In 1949, Chinese Communists gained control of China. The government officially condemned Confucianism, as well as other religions. As a result, most followers live outside mainland China, especially in Taiwan. In the late 1970's, however, the Communist government relaxed its policy against religion, and Confucianism has begun to revive on the mainland.

Taoism, like Confucianism, is a native Chinese religion. Its roots go back to the earliest history of China. However, Taoism did not begin to develop as an organized religion until the 100's B.C.

Taoism teaches that everyone should try to achieve two goals, happiness and immortality. The religion has many practices and ceremonies to help people achieve these goals. Taoist practices include prayer, magic, special diets, breath control, meditation, and recitation of scriptures. Taoists also believe in astrology, fortunetelling, witchcraft, and communication with the dead.

Taoists worship more deities than do the followers of almost any other religion. Some deities are ancestors, and others are the spirits of famous people.

During its early history, Taoism borrowed heavily from Buddhism. Many Taoist deities, temples, and ceremonies show the influence of Buddhism. By the A.D. 1000's, Taoism had split into many divisions. The members of some divisions withdrew from everyday life to meditate and study in monasteries. Other divisions were based in temples. The temple priests passed their positions on to their children. The members of this hereditary priesthood lived among the common people. They gained a reputation as highly skilled magicians who could tell the future and protect believers from illness, accidents, and other misfortune.

Chinese governments of the early and middle 1900's opposed Taoism, claiming it was based on superstition. Today, the Chinese government permits the practice of the religion, and its followers are gradually increasing. Taoists also remain active in Chinese societies outside China, especially in Taiwan.

Shinto is the native religion of Japan. According to Shinto beliefs, deities created Japan and its people. Until the mid-1900's, the Japanese worshiped their emperor as a direct descendant of Amaterasu-Omikami, the sun goddess and most important Shinto deity.

Shinto developed from Japanese folk beliefs. Followers worship spirits and demons that live in animals, trees, and other parts of nature. In early Japanese histo-

© Milt and Joan Mann

Confucius's birthday is a holiday in Taiwan. The men in the temple shown here help perform special birthday ceremonies. Followers of Confucius placed the food offerings before the altar.

Detail of a fresco (late 1200's or early 1300's) by an unknown Chinese artist; Royal Ontario Museum, Toronto

Taoist deities outnumber those of almost every other religion. They include the Jade Emperor, *center,* who rules the earth, and the Empress of Heaven, *left,* who rules heaven. The figure at the right is Laozi, an ancient Chinese philosopher who is considered a founder of Taoism.

ry, Shinto was devoted chiefly to this form of nature worship. Beginning in the A.D. 500's, Buddhism influenced the development of Shinto. Confucianism became influential in the A.D. 600's. Both of these religions helped shape Shinto rituals and doctrines. Buddhist and Shinto services have occasionally been held in the same temples. But unlike Buddhism, Shinto never developed strong doctrines on either salvation or life after death.

In the late 1800's, the Japanese government sponsored a form of Shinto called State Shinto. State Shinto stressed patriotic religious ceremonies and the divine origins of the emperor. In 1882, the government officially separated Shinto into State and Sectarian Shinto. The government administered State Shinto. Sectarian Shinto was popular among the common people. After Japan's defeat in World War II (1939-1945), the government abolished State Shinto and the doctrine of a divine emperor.

Christianity is based on the life and teachings of Jesus of Nazareth, a Galilean Jew. Christians believe He is the Messiah or Savior who came to fulfill God's promise to bring justice and healing to the world. Jesus was put to death by crucifixion by the Romans, who had conquered Palestine. According to the New Testament, Jesus rose from the dead after His Crucifixion and preached to His followers for a short time before returning to heaven. Christianity teaches that people can achieve salvation in this life and eternal salvation from death through believing in Jesus's miraculous return to life, known as the Resurrection.

After Jesus's Resurrection, a number of His followers spread His teachings. Although Christianity began as a reform movement within Judaism, it quickly spread to non-Jewish populations. Much of its spread can be attributed to the preaching of Paul, an early Jewish con-

AP/Wide World

A Shinto game called *kemari* developed from a sport played at Japan's royal court into a religious ritual to secure peace, happiness, and a good harvest for Japan. The participants kick a ball among them so that it never hits the ground. These kemari players are taking part in a Shinto festival at the Shimogamo shrine in Kyoto, Japan.

vert to Christianity. After Paul's death, about A.D. 67, Christianity continued to grow despite persecution by the Romans. In the early 300's, the Roman emperor Constantine the Great became a Christian. By the late 300's, Christianity was the official religion of the Roman Empire. It was widely practiced throughout the empire, which covered most of Europe, the Middle East, and northern Africa.

During the Middle Ages, from about the A.D. 400's through the 1400's, Christian missionaries converted many European peoples. As a result, the Christian church dominated European life for centuries. Differences developed between Christians in western Europe and those in eastern Europe and western Asia. The two groups of Christians split in the 1000's. The churches in Greece, Russia, and other parts of eastern Europe and western Asia became known as the Eastern Orthodox Churches. The church in western Europe became known as the Roman Catholic Church.

In the 1500's, a religious movement called the Reformation divided western Christianity into several bodies. Most southern Europeans remained Roman Catholics. Many northern Europeans formed new churches and became known as Protestants. Protestant churches emphasized the authority of Holy Scripture, rather than tradition or the solemn ceremonies called *sacraments.* The largest Protestant groups include the Baptist, Anglican, Lutheran, Methodist, and Presbyterian churches.

Beginning in the 1500's, Catholic missionaries converted many people in Africa, Asia, and the Americas to Christianity. Protestant missionaries became active in the 1600's and made converts in East Asia, Africa, and North America.

Islam is based on the life and teachings of the prophet Muhammad, who lived in Arabia during the early A.D. 600's. Before Muhammad's time, the people in the region worshiped Allah (God) as well as other deities. But Muhammad said Allah was the only God.

According to Islamic tradition, Muhammad had the first of several visions about 610. The vision occurred while Muhammad meditated in a cave on Mount Hira, a hill near his birthplace of Mecca in what is now Saudi Arabia. The vision commanded Muhammad to preach the message of Allah to the people of his country. He began preaching in Mecca. A tribe called the Quraysh controlled Mecca and opposed Muhammad. To avoid persecution by the Quraysh, Muhammad fled to the city of Medina. Muhammad's journey from Mecca to Medina is called the Hijra, also spelled *Hijrah* or *Hegira,* and is one of the central events in the founding of Islam.

In 630, Muhammad led an army to Mecca. He offered the people of the city generous peace terms. As a result, his forces took the city with little resistance. He made Mecca the sacred city and center of Islam.

After Muhammad's death in 632, his friend and disciple Abū Bakr became the first *caliph* (leader) of Islam. Abū Bakr defeated a rebellion against his rule by Arabian tribes and began a campaign of religious conquest outside Arabia. Succeeding caliphs continued Abū Bakr's conquests. Within 100 years of Muhammad's death, Islam had spread throughout the Middle East, across northern Africa, and into Spain. The religion also split into two divisions, the Sunnis and the Shī'ites. In 732, Muslim and Christian armies fought a major battle near Tours, France, called the Battle of Poitiers or the Battle of Tours. The Muslims were defeated, and western Europe remained Christian.

Muslim missionaries, mystics called Sufis, and traders carried Islam to India and other parts of Asia. From the 1000's to the 1200's, Islam spread into western Africa. The success of Islam, especially its control over the Holy Land, caused European church authorities to launch a crusade, a religious war against Islam to retake Jerusalem. Beginning in 1096, Europeans organized several crusades, causing much suffering on both sides.

Today, Islam is the major religion of nearly all countries in northern Africa and the Middle East. It is also the chief religion in Bangladesh, Indonesia, Malaysia, and Pakistan.

Religion since 1900

Numerous thinkers severely criticized religion in the West in the 1900's. They charged that many religious doctrines had become dry and uninspiring and no longer satisfied spiritual needs. For many, the rise of science cast doubt on older doctrines. Critics also claimed that traditional religions failed to deal with current social issues and that they supported outdated moral attitudes.

Some religious groups have tried to meet society's needs and problems. For example, most religions have traditionally prohibited the ordination of women as clergy and barred women from other leadership positions. For many women, these limitations left their spiritual needs unfulfilled. Many Christian denominations and groups in Judaism now allow women roles equal to those of men. In addition, many women are now scholars of Islam, Buddhism, and Hinduism.

Many people see the *ecumenical movement* in Christianity as a step toward bringing a spirit of cooperation and renewal to Western religion. The ecumenical movement seeks to unify Christians worldwide. It began in the early 1900's and was almost exclusively confined to Protestantism for many years. Many Protestant groups combined and formed new denominations. In the mid-1900's, the Roman Catholic Church began to take a more active part in the movement. A document issued by Vatican Council II (1962-1965), a meeting of Catholic leaders, endorsed the movement's goals. Leaders of the Eastern Orthodox Churches and the Roman Catholic Church also met during the mid-1900's to investigate ways to bring the denominations closer together.

Many people have turned to other religions or new movements that originated outside their own region or tradition. A large number of people in Europe and the Americas have sought fulfillment in the teachings of Asian religions. Some of these people have been attracted to Zen, a form of Buddhism that emphasizes meditation. Others follow the teachings of Hinduism. Islam has also gained many followers.

Within Christianity, a movement called *charismatic Christianity* has attracted millions of followers. The movement began with the founding of Pentecostalism in the United States in 1901. Pentecostalism is a form of religious worship that believes the presence of the Holy Spirit is revealed in physical healing, speaking in unknown languages called *tongues,* and having visions. *Christian fundamentalism* is a conservative religious movement that has had great social and political influence in the United States. Fundamentalists believe that the Bible is without factual or theological error, and that its teachings cannot be questioned. In addition, Islam and Judaism have developed strong conservative movements since the mid-1900's, both in the West and in the Middle East.

Some Westerners have turned to other kinds of beliefs or faiths. For example, some people have been attracted to the *occult*—mysterious forms of supernatural teachings, such as spiritualism, nature worship, and shamanism. Spiritualists believe that it is possible to communicate with the spirits of the dead. Nature worship reveres natural forces and objects, such as weather, stars, and animals. Many nature worshipers link their beliefs with environmental concerns. Shamanism centers on shamans, who are believed to have the ability to contact the gods or the spirit world. Shamans can go into trances and other states of consciousness beyond the body.

Carole R. Fontaine

Related articles. See the *Religion* section of the articles on various countries, such as **Canada** (Religion); **Israel** (Religion). See also the following articles and their lists of *Related articles:*

Christianity

Christianity
Eastern Catholic Churches
Eastern Orthodox Churches
Protestantism
Religious life
Roman Catholic Church
Saint

Other religions

Bahá'ís
Buddhism
Confucianism
Druses
Hinduism
Islam
Jainism
Judaism
Rastafarians
Shinto
Sikhism
Sufism
Taoism
Vodou
Zoroastrianism

Founders of religions

Bahá'u'lláh
Buddha
Confucius
Jesus Christ
Mahavira
Muhammad

Deities

For lists of articles on deities of early religions, see the Related articles with **Mythology.** See also the following articles:

Allah
Brahman
Elohim
God
Jehovah
Krishna
Mithra
Shiva
Vishnu

Beliefs and doctrines

Agnosticism
Ancestor worship
Atheism
Creationism
Deism
Devil
Ethics
Faith healing
Free will
Gnosticism
Golden rule
Heaven
Hell
Immaculate Conception
Immortality
Jihad
Liberation theology
Messiah
New Age Movement
Pantheism
Polytheism
Predestination
Purgatory
Resurrection
Spiritualism
Theism
Theology
Theosophy
Transfiguration
Transubstantiation
Trinity

Sacred writings

Bhagavad-Gita
Bible
Mahabharata
Qur'ān
Ramayana
Talmud
Vedas

Officials and organization

Abbot
Archbishop
Bishop
Cardinal
Deacon
Dervish
Fakir
Friar
High priest
Levites
Magi
Minister
Missionary
Monk
Mullah
Nun
Patriarch
Pope
Priest
Rabbi
Sanhedrin

Religious practices

Anointing of the sick
Baptism
Bar mitzvah
Bat mitzvah
Celibacy
Communion
Confirmation
Coronation
Drama (Religious plays)
Exorcism
Fast
Feasts and festivals
Funeral customs
Grace
Hajj
Hymn
Kosher
Liturgy
Marriage
Mass
Meditation
Prayer
Ramadan
Sacrament
Taboo

Ancient and traditional religions

Animal worship
Animism
Assyria (Religion)
Aztec (Religion)
Babylonia (Religion)
Devil worship
Egypt, Ancient (Religion)
Fetish
Fire worship
Greece, Ancient (Religion)
Inca (Religion)
Indian, American (Religion)
Inuit (Religion)
Maya (Religion)
Mysteries
Mythology
Pacific Islands (Religions)
Persia, Ancient (Religion)
Phoenicia (Religion)
Rome, Ancient (Religion)
Sun worship

Other related articles

Church and state
Cult
Dance (Why people dance)
Education (Religion and early Western education)
Evolution (Acceptance of evolution)
Freedom of religion
Heresy
Hermit
Idolatry
Magic
Mysticism
Occultism
Philosophy (Philosophy and religion)
Religious education
Revivalism
School prayer
Scientology
Theocracy
Witchcraft (Witchcraft as a religion)

Outline

I. Chief characteristics of religion
- A. Belief in a deity
- B. A doctrine of salvation
- C. A code of conduct
- D. The use of sacred stories
- E. Religious rituals

II. How the major religions are organized

III. The origin of religion
- A. Earlier theories
- B. Later theories

IV. History of the world's major religions
- A. Judaism
- B. Hinduism
- C. Buddhism
- D. Confucianism
- E. Taoism
- F. Shinto
- G. Christianity
- H. Islam

V. Religion since 1900

Questions

How long have people practiced some form of religion?
What is the Pentateuch? The Qur'ān? The Five Classics and Four Books?
Who founded Buddhism? Islam?
What is *charismatic Christianity?*
What are some reasons people practice religion?
How do *monotheistic, polytheistic,* and *henotheistic* religions differ?
What is the theory of *animism?*
What are some countries that have state religions?
Who is the most important Shinto deity?
What is the most common religious ritual?

Additional resources

For additional resources on specific religions, see the lists at the end of such articles as **Hinduism** and **Judaism.**

Level I

For books on religion for younger readers, see **Literature for children** (Information books/Religion).

Level II

Armstrong, Karen. *The Great Transformation: The Beginning of Our Religious Traditions.* Knopf, 2006.

Bowker, John W., ed. *The Cambridge Illustrated History of Religions.* Cambridge, 2002.

Breuilly, Elizabeth, and others. *Religions of the World.* Rev. ed. Checkmark, 2005.

Esposito, John L., and others. *World Religions Today.* 3rd ed. Oxford, 2009.

Hinnells, John R., ed. *A Handbook of Ancient Religions.* Cambridge, 2007.

Jones, Lindsay, ed. *Encyclopedia of Religion.* 15 vols. 2nd ed. Macmillan Reference USA, 2005.

Melton, J. Gordon, ed. *Melton's Encyclopedia of American Religions.* 8th ed. Gale Cengage Learning, 2009.

Momen, Moojan. *The Phenomenon of Religion.* Oneworld, 1999.

Stark, Rodney. *Discovering God: The Origins of the Great Religions and the Evolution of Belief.* HarperOne, 2007.

Wilkinson, Philip. *Religions.* DK Pub., 2008.

Religion, Freedom of. See **Freedom of religion.**

Religious education involves instruction in the beliefs of a particular religion. This type of education is the work of organized religions, through their school and religious organizations. Religious education may also be defined as general education that follows religious instructions and ideals.

Public schools in the United States have sometimes offered religious instruction to students through various arrangements. But many people feel that such instruction violates the principle of the separation of church and state.

Various court decisions have affected religious education in the public schools. In the 1948 case of *Illinois ex rel. McCollum v. Board of Education,* the Supreme Court of the United States ruled that religious instruction could not be conducted within public school buildings. In the 1962 case of *Engel v. Vitale,* the court forbade public schools to require the recitation of prayers. A year later, in *School District of Abington Township, Pennsylvania v. Schempp,* the court banned school-sponsored prayers and Bible readings even if student participation in them was voluntary (see **School prayer**).

All three of these Supreme Court decisions held that religious activities conducted in the public schools violate the First Amendment to the United States Constitution. The First Amendment guarantees freedom of religion and separation of church and state (see **Freedom of religion**).

However, the Supreme Court also stated that public schools could teach about religion as long as they did so without favoring some religious beliefs over others. As a result, many schools in the United States introduced courses in *comparative religion,* the study of various faiths. Other courses dealt with the role of religion in history or with the Bible and other religious writings as literature.

Since the late 1940's, there has been new interest in religious education provided during school hours in classes held outside of the school. Churches or religious organizations pay the cost of such instruction, known as *release-time* instruction. The school merely arranges for the time. Some communities release students from regular school hours so that they may attend such classes in the faith of their choice. These classes are taught by special teachers provided by the religious organizations. In addition, these groups provide the materials for the lessons. However, release-time instruction is declining in popularity.

There are differences of opinion as to the merits of this system. Some parents say their children are embarrassed by it. If they belong to no particular church, they may not wish to attend these classes. In that case, their classmates may point to them as "different." Other parents feel it is not the function of the school to teach the doctrines of any religion, or to provide the time for such instruction.

Private education. Many religious groups have their own educational buildings. Roman Catholic and some Protestant groups maintain grade schools, high schools, and colleges. Such schools offer both secular and religious courses. Some Jewish elementary schools, high schools, and colleges have been established. Jewish synagogues and temples offer instruction in religious subjects and Hebrew to children after school hours and on Sunday mornings. The various religious groups educate their own leaders for teaching their doctrines. See **Parochial school.**

The Roman Catholic Church conducts religion classes at least once a week for students attending non-Catholic schools. The classes present oral and written instruction in the doctrines of the Catholic faith. Many Protestant churches offer similar classes. Some of these classes, held in a series, are concluded by a ceremony called *confirmation.*

In Protestant churches, one of the chief methods for religious education is the Sunday school. The modern Sunday school uses specially prepared programs and lessons, such as the International Sunday School Lessons. These courses present graded lesson materials. Other material includes religious history and background, problems in living, and ideals as taught in the Bible and interpreted today. Some churches also sponsor *vacation Bible schools.* These Bible schools offer religious education for one or more weeks during summer vacation.

Children who do not attend church seldom receive any formal religious education. However, their parents may educate them in their own religious beliefs and teach them from the Bible.

Career opportunities. The clergy and various religious orders offer the best opportunities for religious education. Churches may give training for students interested in pursuing employment in this type of career. Most students attend college for a general background and continue specific study at a seminary. At a seminary, the students study religion and related subjects, as well as educational techniques. With this training, students can preach, instruct, and counsel, as well as perform other duties that are connected with the field of religious education.

Persons serving in religious education may teach religion classes in colleges, lead educational programs for such organizations as the YMCA, or teach in missionary schools. Some churches have a director of religious education who is responsible for planning and directing the church's overall program of religious education. These officials usually work with the pastor of the church. They direct and supervise the Sunday school and other activities, such as adult classes, teacher training classes, club programs, family life education, and home Bible-study classes. Most people holding such positions have studied religious education. Some of them have attended a seminary and have graduated as ordained ministers.

Educators in religious education may also work with young people. The director of children's work handles the religious program of children up to the age of 12. A director of youth work plans and guides the study, worship, and recreation of junior and senior high-school students. Other religious education that is directly connected with the church includes supervising or teaching in weekday church schools and instructing Sunday school classes.

Religious education also includes such work as publishing, editing, or writing religious literature. Many churches and religious organizations sponsor regular publications. Some may be magazines or newspapers on a national level. Others may be intended for local or parish work. Some groups publish books and pamphlets for general use or for educational purposes. So-called "inspirational" novels may also form part of educational programs. Many newspapers and magazines publish articles and columns written by religious educators. Kenneth O. Gangel

Religious festivals. For examples, see **Feasts and festivals** and its list of *Related articles.*

Religious freedom. See **Freedom of religion.**

Religious life is a term for a life bound by vows and may also include service to others. *Religious* is a name for monks and nuns dedicated to a life of prayer and for sisters, priests, and brothers actively engaged in teaching and nursing.

Most followers of the religious life are members of organizations called *orders.* The members follow a *rule* (program of life). The rule may require that they live cloistered lives of prayer. Such religious are known as *contemplative religious.* Some orders send members out to do pastoral, educational, missionary, medical, or social work. These people are called *active religious.* Other orders follow a "mixed life" that combines community prayer with external work.

Most members of orders live together in a community, or congregation, which provides training for them. After admission, an *aspirant* (candidate) serves as a *postulant* for several months. If members of the community give their approval, the individual is admitted as a *novice* for an additional year or more of training. *Profession,* the taking of vows, marks the entry of the new religious into full membership. Most orders have temporary profession for several years, followed by *life,* or *solemn,* final profession. After profession, some religious continue to live in a community. Others live alone or in small groups.

This article deals only with the religious life in Christianity. For information on religious life in other religions, see **Buddhism** (The sangha) and **Hinduism.**

Religious life in early Christianity. Some early Christian men and women chose to remain unmarried, or, if widowed, not to remarry, to serve God and their fellow Christians. In the late A.D. 200's, Christianity became socially acceptable in Roman society. At this time, many Christians chose to withdraw from their families to devote themselves to prayer and the recitation of Scripture. These people lived in seclusion in the deserts of Egypt, in the wilderness of Syria and Palestine, in city monasteries, or in the forests of Europe. Some lived as hermits and some lived in groups. Eventually, all came to be called monks or nuns.

In the early 300's, Saint Pachomius, a monk from Egypt, organized the first religious community in southern Egypt. He wrote a rule for monks who wished to live together under a superior. Later in the 300's, Saint Basil of Caesaria adopted the rule of Pachomius and made his monasteries in Asia Minor homes of charity. Today, Eastern Orthodox religious still look to the writings of Saint Pachomius and Saint Basil for inspiration.

In the mid-300's, Saint Athanasius introduced Eastern Christian monasticism to Western Christianity through his writings on the life of Saint Anthony of Thebes, a hermit. This model influenced the entire Christian community of Athanasius's time and today remains the classic model.

Religious life in the Middle Ages. In the 500's, Saint Benedict drew upon the writings of Saint Basil and of John Cassian, a monk, when he wrote the Benedictine rule. This document included instructions for the formation, government, and administration of a monastery and for the daily lives of its monks.

From the 300's to the 900's, the Benedictines provided missionaries to such remote areas as Germany and northern England. The Benedictine missionaries provided the liturgical and devotional standards of European Christendom. In many countries, the missionaries were the only people who could read and write, and so they became the record keepers in these societies.

In the late 1000's and early 1100's, several new orders were formed that placed more emphasis on solitude than had been customary in large Benedictine abbeys. These new orders included the Cistercians and the Carthusians. Men who followed the rule of Saint Augustine became prominent teachers at universities and cathedral schools throughout Europe.

During the 1200's, the growth of the cities produced often violent social change. Society became more divided between the poor and the wealthy. New orders of religious sprang up to take the Christian message to poor people and to heretics. Prominent orders that developed during this time included the Franciscans and the Dominicans.

The Franciscans were founded by Saint Francis of Assisi. Francis left a well-to-do merchant family to embrace a life of poverty. He attracted a group of followers, who eventually became the Franciscans. The Franciscans vowed poverty, chastity, and obedience. Their poverty originally forbade them from owning anything, either as individuals or as a group. The Dominicans were founded by Saint Dominic to preach doctrine to those who had fallen under the influence of heretical ideas. Both the Franciscan and the Dominican orders soon emphasized study in preparation for preaching. Many members of these orders became professors at universities across Europe.

Religious life in the 1500's and 1600's. During the Protestant Reformation of the 1500's, Protestant leaders did not encourage religious life under vows. Following the Reformation, several new Roman Catholic orders were founded with the goal of winning Protestants back to the church. The Jesuits, founded by Saint Ignatius Loyola, trained their men in theology and secular subjects. The Discalced Carmelites, founded in Spain by Saint Teresa of Avila, stimulated a widespread spiritual renaissance. Saint Angela Merici and her companions established a fellowship of teachers that later became the Ursuline order. In 1610, Saint Francis de Sales and Saint Jane Frances de Chantal founded the Visitation Nuns, an order of nuns devoted to visiting the sick in their homes. The Trappists, a strict branch of the Cistercians, were formed in 1664.

Religious life in the 1700's and 1800's. The Enlightenment and the French Revolution led to a period in which governments dissolved many orders (see **Enlightenment; French Revolution**). Some governments did tolerate those religious who cared for the sick or who taught. A revival of religious life began in the 1800's. The Jesuit order was restored in 1814, and both active and contemplative orders were reestablished throughout Europe.

By the mid-1800's, several Protestant denominations began to establish religious communities. Communities of deaconesses were organized in Germany to provide Lutheran and Calvinist women with support and discipline in their lives of service. In the Church of England, a group for men was founded in 1842, and another for women in 1845. These were the first such groups formed since the Church of England had closed all monasteries during the Reformation.

Religious life in the 1900's. From the early to the mid-1900's, several new Protestant communities formed throughout the world. Lutheran and Calvinist communities appeared in Germany, France, Africa, and the Scandinavian countries. In the 1940's, the Taizé community of men and the Grandchamp community for women were formed in France under Lutheran and Reformed sponsorship.

Vatican Council II (1962-1965) called on members of monastic and religious orders to rediscover the ideals of their founders. As a result, many active followers of the religious life have discontinued monastic customs that had been introduced into their societies. Monastic orders have, in turn, reexamined regulations that were not originally part of their religious tradition.

The Eastern Orthodox Churches regard monasticism as an essential feature of their tradition. All Eastern Christian religious look to Saint Basil as their spiritual guide, though they do not have a rule in the same sense as do Western monks and nuns. Several forms of monastic life have developed in Eastern Christianity. The *cenobitic* follows community life. The *idiorrhythmic* gives religious the freedom to choose their own life style. *Eremetical* religious live as hermits.

In the 1900's, a few active religious associations similar to Western orders began to appear in Eastern churches. The most famous monastic center in the Orthodox world is Mount Athos, a collection of about 20 monasteries of various nationalities located on a rocky peninsula in Greece. As Eastern Christians moved into Europe, North America, Australia, and New Zealand, they established monasteries in these areas.

E. Rozanne Elder

Related articles in *World Book* include:

Religious orders

Benedictines	Dominicans
Capuchins	Franciscans
Carmelites	Jesuits
Carthusians	Knights Hospitallers
Cistercians	Knights Templars

Some leading Christian religious orders

Popular name	Official name	Religion	Founder	Place founded	Date
Benedictines	Order of St. Benedict	Roman Catholic	St. Benedict	Italy	529?
Carmelites	Order of Our Lady of Mount Carmel	Roman Catholic	St. Berthold	Palestine	1100's
Christian Brothers	Brothers of the Christian Schools	Roman Catholic	St. Jean Baptiste de la Salle	France	1680
Cowley Fathers	Society of St. John the Evangelist	Anglican	R. M. Benson	England	1866
Dominicans	Order of Friars Preachers	Roman Catholic	St. Dominic	France	1216
Franciscans	Order of Friars Minor	Roman Catholic	St. Francis of Assisi	Italy	1209
Irish Christian Brothers	Brothers of the Christian Schools of Ireland	Roman Catholic	Edmund Ignatius Rice	Ireland	1802
Jesuits	Society of Jesus	Roman Catholic	St. Ignatius Loyola	France	1534
Monastic Brotherhood	None	Eastern Orthodox	Sts. Pachomius, Basil, Theodore, and Athanasius	Egypt, Asia Minor, and Greece	300's-1000's
Redemptorists	Congregation of the Most Holy Redeemer	Roman Catholic	St. Alphonsus Liguori	Italy	1732
Salesians	Society of St. Francis de Sales	Roman Catholic	St. John Bosco	Italy	1859
Sisters of Charity	Many branches	Roman Catholic	Sts. Vincent de Paul and Louise de Marillac	France	1633
Trappists	Order of Cistercians of the Strict Observance	Roman Catholic	St. Robert of Molesme	France	1664
Wantage Community	Community of St. Mary the Virgin	Anglican	William J. Butler	England	1848

Saint Lazarus, Order of
Trappists

Other related articles

Abbot
Anthony of Thebes, Saint
Asceticism
Benedict of Nursia, Saint
Celibacy
Convent
Friar
Hermit
Monasticism
Monk
Nun

Religious Society of Friends. See Quakers.

Religious tolerance. See Freedom of religion.

Remarque, *rih MAHRK,* **Erich Maria** (1898-1970), a German-American author, wrote realistic, suspenseful novels about the horrors and effects of war. His *All Quiet on the Western Front* (1929) is among the most famous of all war stories. This story relates the shattering experiences of a group of German soldiers in World War I (1914-1918).

Remarque followed this success with *The Road Back* (1931) and *Three Comrades* (1937), stories that depict the confusion in postwar German society and the hardships faced by combat veterans. Remarque continued to explore the theme of war in *Arch of Triumph* (1946), a novel about a German doctor who fled to Paris to escape the Nazis at the beginning of World War II (1939-1945). *Spark of Life* (1952) is a story of human suffering and courage in a Nazi concentration camp. *The Night in Lisbon* (1964) also describes human suffering during World War II.

Remarque was born on June 22, 1898, in Osnabrück, Germany. He fought in World War I and was wounded several times. In 1933, the Nazis publicly burned his books because of their antigovernment and antimilitarist themes. The Nazis took away his citizenship in 1938. Remarque lived in Switzerland from 1931 to 1939. He moved to the United States in 1939 but often returned to Switzerland. Remarque became a United States citizen in 1947. He died on Sept. 25, 1970.

Werner Hoffmeister

Rembrandt, *REHM brant* (1606-1669), was the Netherlands' greatest artist. Rembrandt's output of works of art was tremendous. Some scholars credit him with about 600 paintings, 300 etchings, and 1,400 drawings, though several of his paintings are now attributed to his students. Many other works have been lost. Unlike some other great artists, Rembrandt wrote almost nothing about his art.

The range of Rembrandt's subjects is extraordinary. His works depict stories inspired by the Bible, history, and mythology. He also painted portraits, landscapes, nudes, and scenes of everyday life. Throughout his career, Rembrandt also made about 100 known self-portraits, in which he portrayed himself in various roles and contexts.

Rembrandt's reputation rests on his power as a story-teller, his warm sympathy, and his ability to show the innermost feelings of the people he portrayed. His use of light and shadow and warm colors creates an atmosphere that enables us to share his profound understanding of the individual's inner life. Few artists match his genius for showing the human aspect of Biblical characters, which he conveys through moving facial expressions and gestures.

© Peter Willi, SuperStock

Christ at Emmaus (1648) is one of many works Rembrandt created about the life of Jesus Christ. In this painting, Rembrandt portrays the resurrected Jesus revealing himself to two disciples in the village of Emmaus three days after his Crucifixion.

Early years. Rembrandt was born in Leiden on July 15, 1606. His full name was Rembrandt Harmenszoon van Rijn. Rembrandt first studied art with an obscure Leiden painter from about 1621 to 1624. Then he studied with the Dutch artist Pieter Lastman in Amsterdam. About 1625, Rembrandt returned to Leiden to paint on his own.

Leiden years: 1625-1631. Most of Rembrandt's early works are small, precisely finished pictures of Biblical and historical subjects. The influence of Lastman can be seen in the lively gestures and expressions of his figures and in his vivid colors and glossy paint. It can also be seen in his often crowded compositions and in his frequent use of less well known Biblical or historical sub-

Mauritshaus Museum, The Hague, Netherlands; © The Frick Collection, New York City

Rembrandt's self-portraits form a vivid record of his life. The portrait at the left was completed in 1629. The portrait at the right was finished in 1658, after he declared bankruptcy.

jects. However, Rembrandt rapidly surpassed his teacher's ability to tell a story. He used light and shadow to heighten the drama of his works.

Rembrandt quickly achieved local success. He began to teach in 1628, and his strong personality continued to attract students and followers throughout his career.

Early Amsterdam years: 1632-1640. About 1632, Rembrandt moved to Amsterdam, where he painted portraits of wealthy middle-class patrons. He remained there for the rest of his life, except for a few short trips within the Netherlands. In 1634, he married Saskia van Uylenburgh. They had four children, but only one, Titus (1641-1668), survived infancy.

In 1632, Rembrandt painted the *Anatomy Lesson of Professor Tulp.* The painting was a group portrait of eight men that showed a sense of integrated activity at the same time he portrayed each person as an individual. The painting immediately established Rembrandt's reputation as the most fashionable portrait painter in Amsterdam. See **World, History of the** (picture: The study of the body). Rembrandt became wealthy and eagerly collected works of art. In 1639, he bought a large, heavily mortgaged house.

Rembrandt's paintings *Blinding of Samson, Danae,* and *Rape of Ganymede* show the exciting subjects he favored during these years. They, like most of his other works during this period, emphasize dramatic movement, emphatic gestures, sharp contrasts of light and shadow, and striking color accents.

The last years: 1640-1669. Rembrandt's most famous picture, *The Night Watch,* was painted in 1642. The painting represents a civic militia group of Amsterdam preparing to march. Such guards had only a social function in the 1600's, but Rembrandt brilliantly captured a sense of their original active and heroic role from an earlier time. Rembrandt received a high price for *The Night Watch,* and he continued to receive important public and private commissions during the last years of his life.

However, tragedy struck Rembrandt in 1642 when his beloved wife, Saskia, died. Also, the mature Rembrandt did not enjoy the wide popularity he had as a young painter. Although he still ranked as one of his country's leading artists, he ran short of money. The house he purchased in 1639 was too expensive. Rembrandt also collected works of art on a scale he could not afford. Most important, he began to paint more and more for himself. His late majestic Biblical paintings were not commissioned works. An example of these works, *Jacob Blessing the Sons of Joseph,* was painted in 1656.

During this period, Rembrandt's art gained steadily in spiritual depth and pictorial richness. His wonderful light now seemed to glow from within his works. The shadows became more intense and vibrant. Rembrandt reduced his palette to warm colors, such as browns, reds, and oranges, and applied paint thickly to create texture. In place of earlier sensational effects, his work shows solemn restraint, calmness, and tenderness. When humanity is represented, the thoughtful rather than active side of human nature is stressed. A detail of *The Return of the Prodigal Son,* an example from this period, is reproduced in the **Painting** article.

Rembrandt was forced to declare bankruptcy in 1656. His house and possessions were sold at auction in 1657

The British Museum, London, England

Rembrandt's etching *The Ratkiller* was completed in 1632, the year he established his reputation as a leading artist in the Netherlands. The etching shows Rembrandt's ability to portray common people and scenes from everyday life dramatically.

and 1658. But when he died on Oct. 4, 1669, he left his surviving relatives a fairly large inheritance.

Linda Stone-Ferrier

See also **Aristotle** (picture); **Painting** (The 1600's and 1700's).

Additional resources

Ackley, Clifford S., and others. *Rembrandt's Journey: Painter, Draftsman, Etcher.* MFA Pubns., 2003.

Mason, Antony. *Rembrandt.* World Almanac Lib., 2005. Younger readers.

Schama, Simon. *Rembrandt's Eyes.* Knopf, 1999.

White, Christopher. *Rembrandt as an Etcher.* 2nd ed. Yale, 1999.

Remembrance Day is a holiday that honors the memory of those who died in World Wars I and II and later conflicts. In Canada, Australia, and New Zealand, it is observed on November 11. The armistice that ended World War I was signed on this date in 1918. In the United Kingdom, the holiday is observed on the Sunday nearest November 11. The red poppy serves as the symbol of Remembrance Day. Carole S. Angell

Remington, Frederic (1861-1909), was an American artist best known for his action-filled paintings, drawings, and sculptures of cowboys and Indians. His works became famous for capturing the vitality and spirit of the West.

Remington was born on Oct. 4, 1861, in Canton, New York. He loved horses and outdoor life as a child and often sketched Western characters and battle scenes. He studied art at Yale University from 1878 to 1880. His first published drawing appeared in the campus paper.

In 1881, Remington traveled to Montana on the first of many Western trips. He decided in 1885 to become an artist and to devote his art to portraying the rapidly van-

Bronze sculpture (1895); Frederic Remington Art Museum, Ogdensburg, New York

Bronco Buster by Frederic Remington shows the action-filled style he used in his sculptures of life in the Old West.

ishing soldiers, cowboys, Indians, and open lands of the West. He lived in the East, but traveled throughout the West to gather material for his pictures.

Remington's early works were precisely drawn and full of detail. His illustrations for Henry Wadsworth Longfellow's poem *The Song of Hiawatha* (1891) show his technique of this period. Remington later painted with less detail, but he expressed more moods and emotions. He used broader brushstrokes and became more concerned with color and the effects of light. *Downing the Nigh Leader* (1907) illustrates his late dramatic style. He also gained praise for his quietly romantic night scenes. In his sculptures, Remington made dynamically balanced figures, as in *Bronco Buster* (two versions, 1895 and 1909).

Remington illustrated many of his own books, including *Pony Tracks* (1895) and *The Way of an Indian* (1906). He died on Dec. 26, 1909. Many of his works are in the Remington Art Memorial in Ogdensburg, New York, and the Whitney Gallery of Western Art in Cody, Wyoming. Sarah E. Boehme

For examples of Remington's paintings, see the pictures with the articles **Cavalry** and **Pony express**. An example of his sculptures appears in **Sculpture** (American sculpture).

Additional resources

Dippie, Brian W. *The Frederic Remington Art Museum Collection.* Abrams, 2001.

Samuels, Peggy and Harold. *Frederic Remington.* Doubleday, 1982. *Remington: The Complete Prints.* Crown, 1990.

Remora, *REHM uhr uh,* is a fish with a sucker at the top of its head that it uses to attach itself to larger marine animals. Remoras live in warm to tropical seas. They measure about 7 inches (17 centimeters) to 3 ½ feet (110 centimeters) long.

The remora's sucker is a modified *dorsal fin* (back fin) that resembles the sole of a rubber boot. Slatlike structures on the sucker open and close to create powerful suction. Remoras attach themselves to a variety of animals, which are called the *hosts.* These animals include sharks, rays, and other large fish; sea turtles; and whales. Certain types of remoras are found almost exclusively on specific host animals. For example, a species of remora called the *whalesucker* attaches itself only to whales. A remora receives a "free ride" from its host and also may eat scraps of food left by this animal. In turn, the remora rids its host of external parasites. Some remoras attach to the hulls of ships or other floating objects.

Samuel H. Gruber

Scientific classification. Remoras belong to the remora family, Echeneidae. The whalesucker is *Remora australis.*

See also **Fish** (picture: Three remoras).

Remote control is the control of a system from a distance. Remote controlled systems include television sets, automatic garage door openers, guided missiles, manufacturing equipment, model aircraft, robots, and spacecraft. The distance from which they can be controlled ranges from a few feet or meters to millions of miles or kilometers. Remote control improves the ease and efficiency of many operations. It also helps perform tasks that otherwise would be too difficult or dangerous.

The parts of a remote control system. All remote control systems include three basic types of mechanisms: (1) communication mechanisms, (2) actuating mechanisms, and (3) measuring mechanisms.

Communication mechanisms are used in the *encoding* (translation), transmission, reception, and decoding of the operator's commands. The command is encoded into a signal. The signal may travel through the air as radio frequency (RF) waves, infrared light waves, or ultrasound waves; through wires as an electrical signal; or through optical fibers as a pattern of light signals. A corresponding detector receives and decodes the signal.

Actuating mechanisms put commands into motion. The decoded signal may directly *actuate* (turn on) switches and motors. Alternatively, it may be stored in a *microcomputer* or *microprocessor.* These tiny electronic devices can be programmed to perform computer tasks—in this case, controlling the switches and motors.

Measuring mechanisms provide a means of determining if the remote system is performing as desired. The operator may make such determinations by direct observation or by examining data collected by an electronic device. If necessary, the operator may issue new commands to correct the performance of a remote system. In addition, a system may have an automatic control mechanism. Such a mechanism makes adjustments based on measurements of actual performance and either a set of programmed rules or an operator's commands. The system may need an automatic control mechanism if incorrect performance can have serious consequences, the environment is too dangerous for a person to be present, or a quicker response to change is needed than a human operator can provide.

Applications of remote control. A common example of a remote control system is a radio control model airplane. A human operator uses a transmitter to send

© Lester Lefkowitz, Corbis/The Stock Market

Remote control can be used to operate heavy machinery from a safe, quiet location. This operator in a copper-processing plant controls equipment that is used to crush copper ore.

RF signals to a receiver in the plane. The receiver decodes the signals and uses them to direct electric motors that control the plane's movements. The operator corrects the airplane's motion by providing different commands to the transmitter. See **Airplane, Model** (Radio control models).

RF waves also make possible the remote control of antennas and spacecraft. Infrared remote control operates such home entertainment equipment as television sets, videocassette recorders, compact disc players, and DVD players. Infrared remote control also enables personal computers to communicate with printers. Human operators in a command center send electrical signals through wires to control processing equipment in industrial plants. Fiber optics can instantaneously send a motion picture from a supplier on the Internet to a television set equipped with a remote control device.

History. The first machines operated by remote control were radio-controlled motorboats. The German Navy developed them to ram enemy ships during World War I (1914-1918). The military on both sides developed radio-controlled bombs and other remote control weapons during World War II (1939-1945). Manufacturers introduced automatic garage door openers in the late 1940's and remote control televisions in the mid-1950's.

Robots operated by remote control performed much of the cleanup of the Three Mile Island nuclear power plant near Harrisburg, Pennsylvania, after an accident in 1979 released radioactive materials. The National Aeronautics and Space Administration used a remote-controlled vehicle, the Mars Sojourner Rover, in 1997 to study the composition of rocks and soil on Mars.

Today, the Internet allows people to control various distant systems and observe their responses. Using applications on the World Wide Web, a system of interconnected files of text, illustrations, sounds, and moving pictures on the Internet, people can control such devices as robots, telescopes, and cameras. Molly H. Shor

See also **Automation; Guided missile; Hammond, John Hays, Jr.; Mars** (Observation by spacecraft); **Surgery** (picture: Robotic surgery).

Remote sensing is a technique used to gather information about an object without actually touching it. We practice remote sensing with our eyes, ears, and even our skin. These *sensors* obtain information about the size, color, location, and temperature of objects.

Television also is a form of remote sensing. A TV camera acts as a sensor when it picks up an image and transmits it to a studio. The image is then relayed by cable, broadcasting station, or satellite into viewers' homes. Sensors similar to TV cameras are flown in aircraft and satellites. They relay images of the earth to stations on the ground. Cloud maps used on TV weather forecasts are created from images relayed by satellites about 22,300 miles (35,900 kilometers) above the earth.

Some sensors detect invisible forms of energy, especially *infrared rays* (heat rays) that the earth sends out. A computer converts the data into images for study on TV screens or in photographs. The colors created by computer are called *false colors* because they do not correspond to the colors we normally see. Radar is a sensor that uses radio waves to make images of the planets (see **Radar**). Sonar uses sound waves to map the ocean floor and search for sunken ships (see **Sonar**).

Remote sensing is useful for obtaining information about the earth. Images from satellites are used for estimating crop yields and searching for mineral and petroleum deposits. Remote sensing also helps scientists understand how human activity affects the environment. For example, sensors monitor the health of forests threatened by pollution, map the destruction of tropical rain forests, and measure the warming of the earth's atmosphere known as the *greenhouse effect* (see **Greenhouse effect**). We can even learn about past environments. Imaging radar has mapped stream channels under the Sahara in southern Egypt, showing that this desert once had a wetter climate. Alexander F. H. Goetz

Remus. See **Romulus and Remus.**

NASA

Remote sensing can provide information about the earth's environment. This aerial view from a satellite reveals the extent of a flood in Australia. Water and wet land appear blue or black, vegetation is red, and dry land ranges from brown to white.

Detail of *Family and Court of Ludovico Gonzaga II* (1474), a fresco by Andrea Mantegna; Ducal Palace, Mantua (SCALA/Art Resource)

The ruling families of the Italian city-states strongly supported the Renaissance. Like the Gonzaga family of Mantua, *shown here,* they employed many leading artists and scholars at their courts.

Renaissance

Renaissance, *REHN uh sahns,* was a great cultural movement that began in Italy during the early 1300's. It spread to England, France, Germany, the Netherlands, Spain, and other countries in the late 1400's and ended about 1600. The French word *Renaissance* comes from the Latin word *renascor* and refers to the act of rebirth.

During the Renaissance, many European scholars and artists, especially in Italy, studied the learning and art of ancient Greece and Rome. They wanted to recapture the spirit of the Greek and Roman cultures in their own artistic, literary, and philosophic works. The cultures of ancient Greece and Rome are often called *classical antiquity.* The Renaissance thus represented a rebirth of these cultures and is therefore also known as the *revival of antiquity* or the *revival of learning.*

The Renaissance overlapped the end of a period in European history called the Middle Ages, which began in the 400's. The leaders of the Renaissance rejected many of the attitudes and ideas of the Middle Ages. For example, religious authorities in the Middle Ages taught that cities were dangerous, wicked places that distracted people from the important task of saving their souls. Renaissance thinkers commonly saw cities as positive

James Hankins, the contributor of this article, is Professor of History at Harvard University.

Painted terra-cotta statue (about 1485) by Andrea del Verrocchio; National Gallery of Art, Washington, D.C., Samuel H. Kress collection, 1939

Lorenzo de' Medici was the political and cultural leader of Florence when the city was the center of the Italian Renaissance in the 1400's. Lorenzo was called "the Magnificent" because of his achievements as a ruler, supporter of the arts, and author.

places where people could exercise such civic virtues as justice, devotion to the common good, courage, and self-sacrifice. Such Renaissance religious leaders as Girolamo Savonarola believed corrupt cities could be redeemed if their citizens fervently practiced Christianity.

During the Middle Ages, the most important branch of learning was *theology* (the study of God). However, many Renaissance thinkers paid greater attention to the study of humanity. They examined the great accomplishments of different cultures, particularly those of ancient Greece and Rome. These thinkers organized a new group of intellectual disciplines, called the *humanities,* that emphasized language, *oratory* (public speaking), history, poetry, and moral philosophy. These disciplines aimed to enrich Earthly life rather than an afterlife.

Medieval artists painted human figures that looked stiff and unrealistic and which often served symbolic purposes or aimed to instruct. But Renaissance artists stressed the beauty of the human body. They tried to capture the dignity and majesty of human beings in lifelike paintings and sculptures. They believed that people could relate more easily to realistic art, and thus the artwork could more strongly influence its viewers.

Renaissance culture spread gradually. At the height of the Renaissance, during the late 1400's and early 1500's, relatively few Europeans accepted Renaissance ideas. But the influence of the movement on future generations was to prove immense in many fields—from art and literature to education, political science, and history. For centuries, most scholars have agreed that the modern era of human history began with the Renaissance.

The Italian Renaissance

Political background. Italy was not a unified country until the 1860's. At the start of the Renaissance, it consisted of about 250 separate states, most of which were ruled by a city. Most cities had only 5,000 to 10,000 people. But others were among the largest cities in Europe. For example, Florence, Milan, and Venice had at least 100,000 people each in the early 1300's.

At the dawn of the Renaissance, much of Italy was supposedly controlled by the Holy Roman Empire. However, the emperors lived in Germany and had little power over their Italian lands. The popes ruled central Italy, including the city of Rome, but were unable to extend political control to the rest of Italy. No central authority was thus established in Italy to unify all the states.

During the mid-1300's and early 1400's, a number of major Italian cities came under the control of one family. For example, the Visconti family governed Milan from the early 1300's until 1447, when the last male member died. Soon after, the Sforza family took control of Milan and governed the city until the late 1400's. The Este family in Ferrara, the Gonzaga family in Mantua, and the Montefeltro family in Urbino were other ruling families.

The form of government established by the ruling families of the Italian cities was called the *signoria* (principality), and the ruling prince was known as the *signore.* All power was concentrated in the signore and his friends and relatives. An elaborate court slowly grew up around each signorial government. At the court, the area's leading artists, intellectuals, and politicians gathered under the sponsorship of the signore.

Other Italian cities had a form of government known as *republicanism.* In republican cities, a ruling class controlled the government. Members of the ruling class considered themselves superior to the other residents of the city. The most important examples of republican government were in Florence and Venice.

In the republican government of Florence, about 800 of the city's wealthiest families made up the ruling class. The members of these families intermarried and lived in large, beautiful palaces built by Renaissance architects. They paid for the construction of great religious and civic buildings and impressive monuments throughout Florence. They also supported artists and intellectuals. In addition, the ruling class encouraged the study of ancient Greek and Roman authors in the desire to have their society resemble the cultures of classical antiquity.

By the 1430's, the Medici family dominated the ruling class of Florence. The family controlled Europe's largest bank and was headed by a series of talented and ambitious men. Under Medici domination, the Florentine republic in some ways resembled a signorial government.

About 180 families controlled the republican government of Venice. All government leaders came from these families. A law passed in 1297 restricted membership in the Great Council, the principal governing body, to descendants of families that had already sat in the council. Like Florence, Venice became a leading center of Renaissance art under the support of the ruling class.

Humanism was the most significant intellectual movement of the Renaissance. It blended concern for the history and actions of human beings with religious concerns. The humanists were scholars and artists who studied subjects that they believed would help them better understand the problems of humanity. These subjects included history, literature and philosophy. The humanists shared the view that the civilizations of ancient

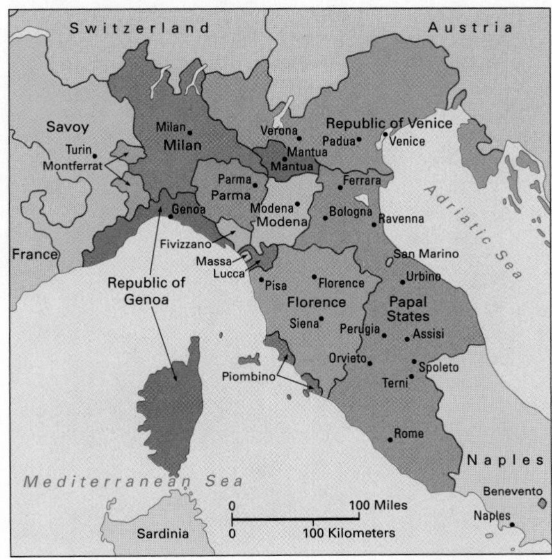

WORLD BOOK map

Renaissance Italy consisted of about 250 states, most of which were ruled by a city. The Renaissance began during the 1300's in the *city-states* of northern Italy. Early centers of the Renaissance included the cities of Florence, Milan, and Venice.

Greece and Rome had achieved greatness in the arts and sciences, government, and military affairs and thus could serve as models. They believed that modern people should understand and appreciate classical antiquity to learn how to conduct their lives.

To understand the customs, laws, and ideas of ancient Greece and Rome, the humanists had first to master the languages of classical antiquity. The Greeks had used a language foreign to Italians, and the Romans had used a form of Latin far different from that used in the 1300's and 1400's. To learn ancient Greek and Latin, the humanists studied *philology* (the science of the meaning and history of words). Philology became one of the two principal concerns of the humanists. The other was history, which the humanists saw as the study of great actions taken by brave, noble, or wise men of classical antiquity.

The interest of the humanists in ancient Greece and Rome led them to search for manuscripts, statues, coins, and other surviving examples of classical civilization. For example, they combed monastery libraries throughout Europe, locating on dusty shelves long-neglected manuscripts by classical authors. The humanists carefully studied these manuscripts, prepared critical editions of them, and often translated them.

Petrarch and Giovanni Boccaccio were the first Renaissance humanists. In the mid-1300's, the two friends recovered many important but long ignored ancient manuscripts. Petrarch discovered the most influential of these works. It was *Letters to Atticus,* a collection of letters on Roman political life by the statesman and orator Marcus Tullius Cicero. As Petrarch and Boccaccio studied the classical writings, they grew to dislike the clumsy, limited form of Latin widely used by their contemporaries. They urged people to adopt the precise and powerful writing style of classical literature.

Petrarch became known for his poetry, and Boccaccio for his collection of stories called the *Decameron* (about 1349-1353). In their works, they tried to describe human feelings and situations that people could easily understand. Petrarch and Boccaccio insisted that the duty of intellectuals was to concentrate on human problems, which they believed were more important than an understanding of the mysteries of nature or of God's will. Many of Boccaccio's works contain the idea that it is socially harmful to impose upon people severe moral standards that contradict normal human behavior.

The revival of Platonism. Petrarch urged people to study the ancient Greek philosopher Plato. He believed that reading Plato would strengthen Christian faith. During the 1400's, the study of Plato's works became popular with many humanists. In 1484, the Florentine philosopher Marsilio Ficino published the first Latin translation of Plato's writing. Platonic philosophy and Christianity share such ideas as the immortality of the individual human soul and the creation of the world by an all-powerful God. Renaissance thinkers saw in Plato's works a harmony between wisdom and Christian devotion.

Niccolò Machiavelli. Medieval political thinkers viewed politics idealistically, within a religious framework. But during the Renaissance, the statesman Nic-

Detail of *The Madonna Enthroned with Angels* (about 1285), an oil painting on wood panel by Cimabue; Uffizi Palace, Florence, Italy (SCALA/Art Resource)

Detail of *The Small Cowper Madonna* (1505), an oil painting on wood panel by Raphael; National Gallery of Art, Washington, D.C., Widener collection, 1942

Medieval and Renaissance art differed in the portrayal of the human figure. The medieval painting at the left has unlifelike figures that represent religious ideas, not flesh-and-blood people. The Renaissance painting at the right shows realistic figures in a natural setting.

colò Machiavelli developed a new, more practical philosophy of politics. His writings, contained in *The Prince* (written in 1513 and published in 1532) and other books, explain politics based on human nature and Roman history rather than on moral or religious ideals. Machiavelli determined that sometimes a leader must resort to such strong measures as cruelty, deception, or force to protect the power of the state against its rival states. Machiavelli's separation of morality from political success has led many historians to consider him the first political scientist.

The ideal courtier. Some Italian humanists spent most of their time in signorial courts. In the late 1400's, they began to develop ideas about the proper conduct of *courtiers*—the noblemen and noblewomen who lived in a royal court. In 1528, *The Book of the Courtier*, by the

Bronze statue (1430's), 5 ft 2 $\frac{1}{4}$ in (1.58 m) high; Bargello, Florence, Italy (SCALA/Art Resource)

Donatello's *David* was the first large free-standing nude since classical antiquity. The sculptor's emphasis on the subject's physical beauty greatly influenced other Renaissance artists.

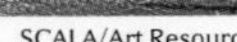

SCALA/Art Resource

SCALA/Art Resource

The Pazzi Chapel in Florence, Italy, was one of the first buildings designed in the Renaissance style. The chapel was commissioned in 1429, begun in 1442, and completed about 1465. The architect, Filippo Brunelleschi, incorporated arches, columns, and other elements of classical architecture into his design. The exterior and interior, *both shown here,* have been praised for the beauty and harmony of their proportions.

author and diplomat Baldassare Castiglione, was published. He based the work on his experiences at the court of Urbino. It was translated into several European languages and influenced the conduct of courtiers throughout Europe. This book also strongly influenced educational theory in England during the Renaissance.

Castiglione wrote that the ideal male courtier is refined in writing and speaking and skilled in the arts, sports, and the use of weapons. He willingly devotes himself to his signore, always seeking to please him. The courtier is polite and attentive to women. Whatever he does is achieved with an easy, natural style, which reflects his command of every situation. An ideal court woman knows literature and art and how to entertain the court. She exhibits the highest moral character and acts in a feminine manner. The highest form of love that a courtier can express is *platonic love*—that is, nonromantic love. The highest form of courtiership is one in which the courtier helps the prince to rule virtuously.

The fine arts. During the Middle Ages, painters and sculptors tried to give their works a spiritual quality. They wanted viewers to concentrate on the deep religious meaning of their art. They were not concerned with making their subjects appear natural or lifelike. But Renaissance painters and sculptors, like Renaissance writers, wanted to portray people and nature realistically. Medieval architects designed huge cathedrals to emphasize the grandeur of God and to humble the human spirit. Renaissance architects designed buildings whose proportions were based on those of the human body and whose ornamentation imitated ancient designs.

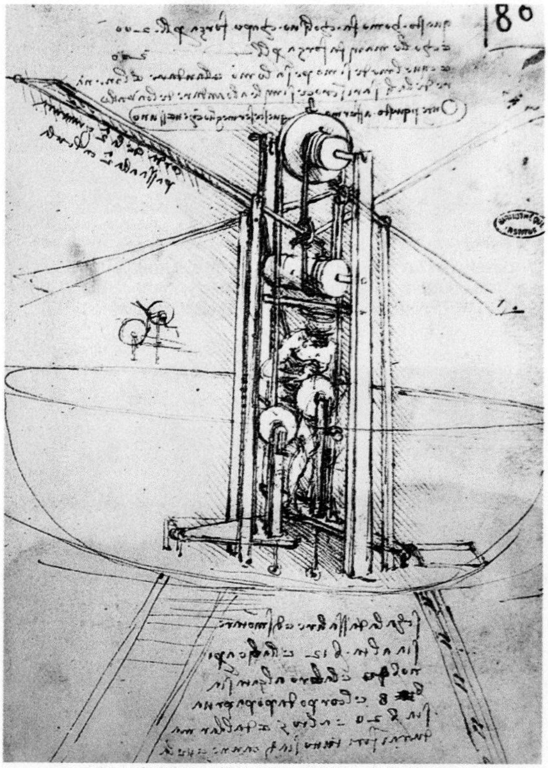

Arts of the 1300's and early 1400's. During the early 1300's, the Florentine painter Giotto became the first artist to portray nature realistically. He produced magnificent *frescoes* (paintings on damp plaster) for churches in Assisi, Florence, Padua, and Rome. Giotto attempted to create lifelike figures showing real emotions. He portrayed many of his figures in realistic settings.

A remarkable group of Florentine architects, painters, and sculptors worked during the early 1400's. They included the painter Masaccio, the sculptor Donatello, and the architect Filippo Brunelleschi.

Masaccio's finest work was a series of frescoes he painted about 1427 in the Brancacci Chapel of the Church of Santa Maria del Carmine in Florence. The frescoes realistically show Biblical scenes of emotional intensity. In these paintings, Masaccio utilized Brunelleschi's system for achieving linear perspective.

In his sculptures, Donatello tried to portray the dignity of the human body in realistic and often dramatic detail. His masterpieces include three statues of the Biblical hero David. In a version finished in the 1430's, Donatello portrayed David as a graceful, nude youth, moments after he slew the giant Goliath. The work, which is about 5 feet (1.5 meters) tall, was the first large free-standing nude created in Western art since classical antiquity.

Brunelleschi was the first Renaissance architect to revive the ancient Roman style of architecture. He used arches, columns, and other elements of classical architecture in his designs. One of his best-known buildings is the beautifully and harmoniously proportioned Pazzi Chapel in Florence. The chapel, begun in 1442 and completed about 1465, was one of the first buildings designed in the new Renaissance style. Brunelleschi also was the first Renaissance artist to master *linear perspective,* a mathematical system with which painters could show space and depth on a flat surface.

Arts of the late 1400's and early 1500's were dominated by three men. They were Michelangelo, Raphael, and Leonardo da Vinci.

Michelangelo excelled as a painter, architect, and poet. He has also been called the greatest sculptor in history. Michelangelo was a master of portraying the human figure. For example, his famous statue of the Israelite leader Moses (1516) gives an overwhelming impression of physical and spiritual power. These qualities also appear in the frescoes of Biblical and classical subjects that Michelangelo painted on the ceiling of the Vatican's Sistine Chapel. The frescoes, painted from 1508 to 1512, rank among the greatest works of Renaissance art.

Raphael's paintings are softer in outline and more poetic than those of Michelangelo. Raphael was skilled in creating perspective and in the delicate use of color. He painted a number of beautiful pictures of the Madonna (Virgin Mary) and many outstanding portraits. One of his greatest works is the fresco *School of Athens* (1511). The painting was influenced by classical Greek and Roman models. It portrays the great philosophers and scientists of ancient Greece in a setting of classical arches. Raphael was thus making a connection between the culture of classical antiquity and the Italian culture of his time.

Pen-and-ink drawing (about 1488); Bibliothèque Nationale, Paris (Art Resource)

The drawings of Leonardo da Vinci reveal the inquiring mind of perhaps the greatest intellect of the Renaissance. Leonardo was fascinated by the possibility of human flight. He designed a flying machine that used revolving paddles, *shown here.*

Detail of a fresco (1510-1511); The Vatican, Rome (SCALA/Art Resource)

Raphael's *School of Athens* portrays an imaginary gathering of ancient Greek philosophers and scientists, including the mathematician Euclid, *bending forward, foreground.* The painting shows the Renaissance respect for classical culture.

Leonardo da Vinci painted two of the most famous works of Renaissance art, the wallpainting *The Last Supper* (about 1497) and the portrait *Mona Lisa* (begun in 1503). Da Vinci had one of the most searching minds in all history. He wanted to know how everything that he saw in nature worked. In over 4,000 pages of notebooks, he drew detailed diagrams and wrote his observations. Da Vinci made careful drawings of human skeletons and muscles, trying to learn how the body worked. Due to his inquiring mind, da Vinci has become a symbol of the Renaissance spirit of learning and intellectual curiosity.

The Renaissance outside Italy

In the late 1400's, the Renaissance spread from Italy to such countries as France, Germany, England, and Spain. Such visitors to Italy as bankers, diplomats, merchants, and young scholars carried Renaissance culture home with them. The scholars acquired from the Italians the basic tools of humanistic study—history and philology.

A series of invasions of Italy played a major role in the spread of the Renaissance to other parts of Europe. From 1494 to the early 1500's, French, German, and Spanish armies invaded Italy. The invaders were dazzled by the beauty of Italian art and architecture and returned home deeply influenced by Italian culture.

In Italy, evidence of classical antiquity, especially Roman antiquity, could be seen almost everywhere. Ruins of Roman monuments and buildings stood in every Italian city. This link between the present and the classical past was much weaker elsewhere in Europe. In ancient times, Roman culture had been forced upon northern and western Europeans by conquering Roman armies. But that culture quickly disappeared after the Roman Empire in the West fell in the A.D. 400's.

The relative scarcity of classical art affected the development of European art outside Italy during the 1400's. Painters had few examples of classical antiquity to imitate, and so they tended to be more influenced by the northern Gothic style of the late Middle Ages. The first great achievements in Renaissance painting outside Italy appeared in the works of artists living in Flanders. Most of the Flanders region lies in what are now Belgium and France. Flemish painting was known for its precise details. The human figures were realistic but lacked the sculptural quality characteristic of Italian painting.

Political background. During the Renaissance, the political structure of northern and western Europe differed greatly from that of Italy. By the late 1400's, England, France, and Spain were being united into nations under monarchies. These monarchies provided political and cultural leadership for their countries. Germany, like Italy, was divided into many largely independent states. But Germany was the heart of the Holy Roman Empire, which unified the various German states to some extent.

The great royal courts supported the Renaissance in northern and western Europe much as the princes did in Italy. The French king Francis I, who ruled from 1515 to 1547, tried to surround himself with the finest representatives of the Italian Renaissance. The king brought

Oil painting on wood panel (about 1460); Uffizi Palace, Florence, Italy (SCALA/Art Resource)

Mythological subjects were popular with Italian artists. Antonio del Pollaiuolo painted the Greek hero Hercules killing a monster called the Hydra, *shown here.* His portrayal of the human body in vigorous action inspired other Renaissance artists.

The Madonna and Child with Chancellor Rolin (about 1436), an oil painting on wood panel; the Louvre, Paris (SCALA/Art Resource)

A northern Renaissance painting by the Flemish artist Jan van Eyck emphasizes lighting, perspective, and details. Van Eyck was one of the first major Renaissance artists outside Italy.

Leonardo da Vinci and many other Italian artists and scholars to France. In England, the House of Tudor became the most important patron of the Renaissance. The Tudors ruled from 1485 to 1603. Henry VII, the first Tudor monarch, invited many Italian humanists to England. These men encouraged English scholars to study ancient Greek and Roman literature and philosophy.

Christian humanism. After about 1500, humanists in northern Europe increasingly emphasized the study and revival of ancient Christianity. Humanist scholars identified and edited ancient Christian texts to remove any distortions that had been introduced into the writings over time. These texts included the Bible and the works of such Catholic thinkers and churchmen as Saint Augustine and Saint Jerome, as well as the leaders of the ancient Greek church. This attempt to purify the sources of Christian tradition implied a criticism of existing Church practices and an attempt to reform them. In addition, many *Christian humanists* believed they could reform religion through education.

Desiderius Erasmus and Saint Thomas More were the leading Christian humanists. They were close friends who courageously refused to abandon their ideals.

Erasmus was born in the Netherlands. He was educated in Paris and traveled throughout Germany, England, and Italy. He was an excellent scholar, with a thorough knowledge of Latin and Greek.

Erasmus refused to take sides in any political or religious controversy. In particular, he would not support either side during the Reformation, the religious movement of the 1500's that gave birth to Protestantism. Both Roman Catholics and Protestants sought Erasmus's support. He stubbornly kept his independence and was called a coward by both sides. However, Erasmus did attack abuses he saw in the church in a famous witty work called *The Praise of Folly* (1511). In this book, he criticized the moral quality of church leaders. Erasmus accused them of overemphasizing procedures and ceremonies while neglecting Christianity's spiritual values.

Saint Thomas More was born in England and devoted his life to serving his country. He gained the confidence of King Henry VIII and carried out a number of important missions for him. In 1529, the king appointed More lord chancellor, England's highest judicial official.

Throughout his career, More dedicated himself to the principles that had inspired Erasmus. Like Erasmus, he believed it was important to eliminate the abuses, inequalities, and evils that were accepted as normal in his day. More's best-known work is *Utopia* (1516). In this book, More described an imaginary society in which the divisions between the rich and the poor and the powerful and the weak were replaced by a common concern for the health and happiness of everyone. The abolition of private property would help to create equality between people in More's ideal society.

More's strong principles finally cost him his life. He objected to Henry VIII's decision to *annul* (cancel) his marriage to Catherine of Aragon and remarry. More then refused to acknowledge the king's authority over that of the pope. In 1535, he was beheaded for treason.

The heritage of the Renaissance

The Renaissance left an intellectual and artistic heritage that still remains important. Since the Renaissance, scholars have used Renaissance methods of humanistic inquiry, even when they did not share the ideas and spirit of the Renaissance humanists. Writers have tried for centuries to imitate and improve upon the works of such Renaissance authors as Petrarch and Boccaccio.

Detail of an oil painting on wood panel (about 1523) by Hans Holbein the Younger; the Louvre, Paris (Art Resource)

Desiderius Erasmus, a Dutch priest and scholar, became a leading Christian humanist during the Renaissance. He often attacked religious superstition and abuses he saw in the church.

The influence of Renaissance painters, sculptors, and architects has been particularly strong. The artists of Florence and Rome set lasting standards for painting in the Western world. For hundreds of years, painters have traveled to Florence to admire the frescoes of Giotto and Masaccio. They have visited Rome to study the paintings of Raphael and Michelangelo. The works of Donatello and Michelangelo have inspired sculptors for generations. The beautifully scaled buildings of Brunelleschi and other Renaissance architects still serve as models for architects. Since the Renaissance, people have also been inspired by the intellectual daring of such thinkers as Petrarch and Erasmus. Leaders of the Renaissance seemed to be breaking out of intellectual boundaries and entering unknown territories.

It is no accident that some of the greatest explorers of the late 1400's and early 1500's were Italians exposed to the traditions of the Renaissance. Christopher Columbus was a sailor from Genoa and an expert navigator. Before setting out on the voyage in which he hoped to find a western sea route to Asia, Columbus consulted the same scientist who taught mathematics to the architect Filippo Brunelleschi. Columbus—like such other Italian explorers as John Cabot, Giovanni da Verrazzano, and Amerigo Vespucci—was willing to take enormous risks to achieve results never dreamed of. In a sense, Columbus's arrival in America in 1492 was one of the greatest achievements of the Renaissance.

James Hankins

Related articles in *World Book* include:

Architects

Alberti, Leon Battista
Bramante, Donato
Brunelleschi, Filippo
Jones, Inigo
Palladio, Andrea
Pisano, Giovanni

Painters

Angelico, Fra
Bellini, Gentile
Bellini, Giovanni
Bellini, Jacopo
Botticelli, Sandro
Bruegel, Pieter, the Elder
Campin, Robert
Caravaggio, Michelangelo Merisi da
Correggio
Cranach, Lucas, the Elder
Dürer, Albrecht
Giorgione
Giotto
Greco, El
Grünewald, Matthias
Holbein, Hans, the Elder
Holbein, Hans, the Younger
Leonardo da Vinci
Lippi, Filippino
Lippi, Filippo
Mantegna, Andrea
Masaccio
Michelangelo
Piero della Francesca
Pollaiuolo, Antonio del
Raphael
Tintoretto
Titian
Uccello, Paolo
Van der Goes, Hugo
Van der Weyden, Rogier
Van Eyck, Jan
Veronese, Paolo

Political leaders

Borgia, Cesare
Borgia, Lucrezia
Francis I (of France)
Medici
Medici, Cosimo de'
Medici, Lorenzo de'

Sculptors

Cellini, Benvenuto
Della Robbia, Luca
Donatello
Ghiberti, Lorenzo
Michelangelo
Pisano, Giovanni
Pisano, Nicola
Verrocchio, Andrea del

Writers

Ariosto, Ludovico
Boccaccio, Giovanni
Bruno, Giordano
Castiglione, Baldassare
Cervantes, Miguel de
Du Bellay, Joachim
Erasmus, Desiderius
Machiavelli, Niccolò
Marlowe, Christopher
Marot, Clement
Montaigne, Michel de
More, Sir Thomas
Petrarch
Rabelais, François
Ronsard, Pierre de
Shakespeare, William
Spenser, Edmund
Surrey, Earl of
Tasso, Torquato
Vega, Lope de
Wyatt, Sir Thomas

Other related articles

See the section on the *Renaissance* in the various articles on national literatures, such as **French literature** (The Renaissance). See also the following articles:

Architecture
Ballet (The birth of ballet)
Classical music (The Renaissance)
Democracy (The Renaissance and the Reformation)
Drama (Italian Renaissance drama)
Education (The Renaissance)
Exploration (The age of European exploration)
Florence
Fresco
Furniture (The Renaissance)
Humanism
Italy (History)
Jewelry
Mural
Painting (The Renaissance)
Perspective
Philosophy (Modern philosophy)
Reformation
Science (The rebirth of science)
Sculpture (Italian Renaissance sculpture)

Outline

I. The Italian Renaissance
A. Political background
B. Humanism
C. The fine arts

II. The Renaissance outside Italy
A. Political background
B. Christian humanism
C. Desiderius Erasmus and Sir Thomas More

III. The heritage of the Renaissance

Renewable energy is energy from natural resources that can be used over and over. It includes energy from the sun, from wind, from moving water, from heat beneath the ground, and from plants. Such energy sources differ from *fossil fuels* (coal, oil, and natural gas) and nuclear fuel. These *nonrenewable* resources have limited supplies and cannot be restored once they are used. Many governments fund the research and development of renewable energy technology. They also provide incentives such as tax credits to help make such technology affordable.

People have long made use of renewable energy. Prehistoric people used the sun's energy for heat and for drying food. By about 3,000 B.C., the ancient Egyptians had made sailing ships, which are powered by wind. By 100 B.C., people in parts of the Mediterranean were using water to power grain mills. Flowing water spun wheels connected by gears to circular millstones, grinding grain into flour. The Persians, a people living in what is now Iran, probably developed windmills for grinding grain during the 600's.

The first renewable energy source used to make electric power was flowing water, in the 1880's. The water spun devices called *turbines,* which powered electric generators. Around the same time, engineers designed wind-driven turbines. Wind turbines became especially popular after the 1973 energy crisis, when Arab countries severely restricted global supplies of oil. Oil had previously been used to generate much electric power. By the early 2000's, several kinds of renewable energy had become affordable for many uses. Richard F. Hirsh

See also **Energy supply; Geothermal energy; Solar energy; Sustainability; Water power; Wind energy.**

Reno, *REE noh* (pop. 225,221; met. area pop. 425,417), is a tourist center and the third largest city in Nevada. Only Las Vegas and Henderson have more people. Reno lies in western Nevada at the foot of the Sierra Nevada. For location, see **Nevada** (political map). The Truckee River flows through the downtown area of the city.

Reno's attractions include gambling casinos; skiing, hiking, and other recreational activities; and such annual events as air races, a balloon race, and a classic car celebration. The city is the home of the University of Nevada, Reno. Reno-Tahoe International Airport serves the area.

Reno was established as a station on the Central Pacific Railroad in 1868, at what had been called Lake's Crossing. Railroad officials named it for Jesse Lee Reno, a Union general killed in the American Civil War (1861-1865). Reno was incorporated as a city in 1903. It grew rapidly after Nevada legalized gambling in 1931.

Reno has a council-manager form of government. It is the county seat of Washoe County. Lenita Powers

See also **Nevada** (picture: The Reno skyline).

Reno, Janet (1938-2016), was the first woman to serve as attorney general of the United States. Reno, who was appointed by President Bill Clinton, held the Cabinet post from 1993 to 2001.

As U.S. attorney general, Reno made several decisions that were seen as controversial. The first involved a 51-day stand-off between federal law-enforcement agents and a cult called the Branch Davidians at the cult's compound near Waco, Texas. The stand-off had begun in February 1993, when the agents attempted to arrest the cult's leader, David Koresh, because the group had a large stock of high-powered weapons. In April, Reno authorized the Federal Bureau of Investigation (FBI) to use tear gas to try to drive the cult members from their compound. A fire broke out, apparently set by cult members, and over 80 people died, including Koresh.

A major controversy erupted in late 1999 over custody of a 6-year-old Cuban shipwreck survivor named Elián González. Elián's relatives in Miami, Florida, applied for political asylum for the boy. However, Elián's father wanted the child returned to him in Cuba. In April 2000, at Reno's direction, armed federal agents seized Elián, enforcing a government order that the boy be returned to his father.

Reno also faced the problem of deciding when to order independent investigations of suspected wrongdoing by government officials rather than having her Department of Justice do the investigating. In some cases, she approved independent investigations. For example, she appointed an independent special prosecutor to look into charges about Whitewater, a business deal in which Clinton was involved before he became president. In addition, she approved an investigation into whether Clinton had lied under oath and committed other offenses related to an alleged affair with a White House intern named Monica Lewinsky. For more details, see **Clinton, Bill** (Domestic events). But Reno rejected demands by Republican leaders for an independent investigation of charges about Democratic fund-raising practices.

Reno was born on July 21, 1938, in Miami. She earned a bachelor's degree from Cornell University and a law degree from Harvard University. She practiced law in Miami. In 1972, Reno ran for a seat in the Florida Legislature, but lost. She then joined the state attorney office of Dade County (now Miami-Dade County) as a prosecutor. She was appointed state attorney in 1978 and elected to the office in November of that year. She won reelection four times.

In 2001, Reno began campaigning for the Democratic nomination for governor of Florida. She lost the primary election in 2002 in a close contest. Reno died on Nov. 7, 2016. Lee Thornton

Reno, *REE noh,* **Marcus Albert** (1834-1889), was a United States Army officer known for his role in the Battle of the Little Bighorn in Montana Territory in 1876. In this battle, often called "Custer's Last Stand," Indians killed Lieutenant Colonel George A. Custer and all the men of the Seventh Cavalry under his direct command.

News of Custer's defeat led to a bitter dispute. Supporters of Custer accused Major Reno of cowardice for failing to attack the Indian village and then rejoin Custer. Reno claimed he had tried to attack the village but that the Indians outnumbered his unit, forced it to retreat, and kept it from helping Custer. Reno asked the Army to investigate his conduct, and a military court cleared him of blame in 1879. But later that year, a court-martial convicted him of drunkenness and conduct unbecoming an officer. The Army gave him a dishonorable discharge in 1880. In 1967, Reno's case was reopened and the Army changed his record to reflect an honorable discharge.

Reno was born on Nov. 15, 1834, in Carrollton, Illinois. He graduated from the U.S. Military Academy in 1857 and served in the cavalry in the American Civil War (1861-1865). He died on March 30, 1889. Brian W. Dippie

See also **Custer, George Armstrong** (The battle); **Little Bighorn, Battle of.**

Renoir, *REHN wahr* or *ruh NWAHR,* **Jean** (1894-1979), was a French motion-picture director whose films expose human faults and ridicule social attitudes. They also show compassion for people and their failings. Renoir also acted in a number of his films.

Renoir directed 36 films, including 2 of the most acclaimed movies ever made. One of them, *Grand Illusion* (1937), attacks the futility of war. The other, *The Rules of the Game* (1939), satirizes relationships among upper-class people at a weekend house party. Renoir's first film was *A Life Without Joy* (1924). His other films include *Nana* (1926), *Boudu Saved from Drowning* (1932), *The Crime of Monsieur Lange* (1935), *Toni* (1935), and *La Bête Humaine* (1938). His last film, *The Little Theatre of Jean Renoir* (1970), was made for French television.

Renoir was born on Sept. 15, 1894, in Paris. His father was the French painter Pierre Auguste Renoir. After World War II began in 1939, Jean Renoir fled France. He settled in the United States in 1941. Renoir made several films in the United States, including *Swamp Water* (1941) and *The Southerner* (1945). He died on Feb. 12, 1979. John F. Mariani

Renoir, *REHN wahr* or *ruh NWAHR,* **Pierre Auguste,** *pyair oh GOOST* (1841-1919), a French Impressionist painter, is famous for his pictures of young girls and children, and intimate portraits of French middle-class life. He loved to show lively groups in sensuous surroundings and often used his friends as models. Renoir frequently painted his wife and children.

In the 1870's, Renoir and Claude Monet together developed the broken color technique of the Impressionists. Instead of mixing paints completely, they left small dabs of color in a sketchy manner. But Renoir was more interested in rich color effects and a sense of volume than Monet. Renoir also preferred figure painting to landscapes. During the 1870's, he painted a large number of portraits on commission. Perhaps his most famous is *Mme. Charpentier and Her Children.* While many Impressionists brought Japanese qualities into their work, Renoir revived the rococo style of such artists as François Boucher and Jean Honoré Fragonard.

Renoir visited Italy in 1881 and 1882, and his study of Renaissance painters there led him to a new appreciation of the importance of line. He returned to France, where he gave up his broad, coloristic manner and spent several years concentrating on drawing. Renoir painted a famous series, *The Bathers,* during this time.

The happy quality of Renoir's later work does not show the agony he suffered from arthritis, which finally crippled his hands. He had brushes tied to his hands and developed a final style of painting in broad brushstrokes and vivid colors.

Renoir was born on Feb. 25, 1841, in Limoges, France. He was apprenticed to learn porcelain painting after he showed an early talent for drawing. He painted window shades and fans in Paris. He studied at Charles Gleyre's studio, where he met Monet and other young painters who were to form the Impressionist group. He was influenced also by Édouard Manet and the color methods of Eugène Delacroix. Renoir died on Dec. 3, 1919.

Richard Shiff

See also **Delacroix, Eugène; Impressionism; Manet, Édouard; Monet, Claude.**

Reorganized Church of Jesus Christ of Latter Day Saints. See Community of Christ.

Reparations are efforts, usually by a nation's government, to make up for harm or wrongdoing that has occurred in the past. Reparations often include the payment of money or the return of property to individuals or groups. Other forms of reparations include formal apologies and changes in government policy.

Historically, reparations have been payments that victorious nations demanded from defeated nations after a war. However, reparations of this kind have become unpopular because they can lead to resentment and further fighting. Today, reparations more often involve a government's payments to people it has mistreated. After World War II (1939-1945), for example, West Germany paid more than $800 million to Jews and the state of Israel to make up for Nazi persecution and murder in the Holocaust. This agreement became a model for later reparations demands.

In 1988, the United States government agreed to pay $20,000 per person to Japanese Americans who had been held in U.S. detention camps during World War II. Native groups in many countries have fought, sometimes successfully, for the return of land taken through fraud and broken treaties. Some African Americans have called on the U.S. government to pay reparations to the descendants of slaves. Belinda Cooper

Repeal means wiping out a law already on the books. A legislative body has the power not only to pass new laws, but also to do away with laws that have been passed earlier. Sometimes, the legislature may pass an act which directly states that an earlier law is repealed. Such an act is known as an *express repeal.* Sometimes, a new law may simply make it quite clear that an older one no longer applies. In this case, the repeal is known as a *repeal by implication.* A new law will sometimes conflict only with a certain portion of an earlier one. The new law is understood to repeal by implication those portions of the earlier law that are inconsistent with the new law.

Oil painting on canvas (1881); the Phillips Collection, Washington, D.C.

Brown Bros.

Pierre Auguste Renoir, a master of Impressionist painting, became famous for his luminous colors and cheerful scenes of everyday life. In such works as *The Luncheon of the Boating Party, shown here,* he portrayed a carefree group of people at an informal moment. The woman holding the dog is Renoir's wife.

To avoid confusion, legislatures often enact an *express repeal* of a law which has already been repealed by implication. For example, the passage by Congress of the Kansas-Nebraska Bill had the effect of repealing the Missouri Compromise. But Congress later passed a second bill specifically declaring the Missouri Compromise "void and inoperative." Peter Woll

Repetitive strain injury is any of a group of painful medical disorders caused by performing a similar activity over and over again. Such injuries, often called RSI's, are responsible for more than half of all workplace illnesses. Other names for such disorders include *cumulative trauma disorders* (CTD's) and *repetitive stress injuries,* also shortened to RSI's.

Anyone who regularly performs a repetitive task is at risk of developing an RSI. Computer users, meat cutters, and assembly-line workers often develop such problems. The number of RSI sufferers increased greatly during the late 1900's, possibly due to increased computer use. Dentists, cashiers, and musicians also frequently complain of symptoms.

Carpal tunnel syndrome, a wrist disorder, is the most common RSI. Others include *de Quervain's disease* (inflammation of the tendon sheaths in the thumb) and *lateral epicondylitis* (tennis elbow). Workers may also suffer from numbness in the fingers; pain in the arms, neck, and back; and aching muscles.

Prevention is the best treatment. An expert in *ergonomics* (the science of designing objects and environments to meet the physical and psychological needs of people) can recommend changes to the work area. Employees should be taught proper posture and use of tools and machines. They also should be encouraged to maintain a reasonable pace and take rest breaks. Medical treatment may be necessary in some cases. Anti-inflammatory drugs or steroid injections may be prescribed. Surgery may be necessary if other treatments fail. Gordon H. Derman

See also **Backache; Carpal tunnel syndrome.**

Reporter. See **Foreign correspondent; Journalism; Newspaper** (Gathering the news); **War correspondent.**

Representative is the name for a member of the lower house of the Congress of the United States (the House of Representatives), or of the lower house of a state legislature. See also **Address, Forms of; Congressman; House of Representatives.**

Representative government. See **Democracy; Republic.**

Representatives, House of. See **House of Representatives.**

Reprieve, *rih PREEV,* is the temporary suspension of a sentence passed on a criminal. The sentence is postponed for a definite period of time. Reprieves are sometimes granted to permit consideration of new evidence, or a further investigation of the case. The chief executive of a state or country usually grants reprieves.

A reprieve is not a pardon (see **Pardon**). A reprieve makes no change in the sentence, but merely changes the date when the sentence goes into effect. A delay or reprieve granted to a prisoner by the court which passed the sentence is often called a *stay of execution.*
James O. Finckenauer

Reproduction is the process by which living things create more of their own kind. All types of living creatures reproduce, from the tiniest bacteria to the largest plants and animals. Without reproduction, all forms of life would die out.

Organisms can produce offspring like themselves because they possess *genes.* Genes are tiny segments of DNA (deoxyribonucleic acid), the substance that determines an organism's essential traits. Genes are contained in each cell of an organism and are transferred to the organism's offspring during reproduction.

There are two general types of reproduction—*sexual* and *asexual.* In sexual reproduction, a new organism is formed by the joining of a *gamete* (sex cell) from one organism with a gamete from another organism. Human beings and almost all other animals reproduce sexually. In asexual reproduction, a new organism develops from parts of, or parts produced by, one organism. Living things that reproduce asexually include bacteria and other simple organisms. Many organisms can reproduce both sexually and asexually. They include most plants and fungi and certain simple animals, such as sponges.

Scientists believe that the first living things lived in the sea and reproduced asexually. Sexual reproduction also *evolved* (developed gradually) in the sea. After organisms began to live on land, they evolved increasingly complex methods of sexual reproduction.

This article describes reproduction in living things other than human beings. For a discussion of human reproduction, see **Reproduction, Human.**

How genes are transferred

During reproduction, an organism transmits a copy of its genes to its offspring. Genes are contained in thread-like structures called *chromosomes.* Bacteria, which are one-celled organisms, have only one chromosome, consisting of a single strand of DNA. In more complex organisms, each body cell contains two copies of each chromosome, and the two copies are arranged in pairs. Cells with pairs of chromosomes are called *diploid cells.* Cells that contain only one copy of each chromosome are called *haploid cells.*

Through sexual reproduction, the offspring inherits its genes from two parents. The genes are transmitted by the two gametes that form the new individual. Sexual reproduction involves a cycle of two processes, *meiosis* and *fertilization.* In meiosis, diploid cells produce gametes, which are haploid cells. The male gamete is called a *sperm,* and the female gamete is called an *egg.* Fertilization is the union of these gametes. It produces a diploid cell, the fertilized egg. The fertilized egg develops into the new organism. Because it receives genes from each parent, the offspring has a unique genetic makeup and traits that differ from those of either parent.

Through asexual reproduction. Although many diploid organisms reproduce sexually, others reproduce asexually. For example, sponges are diploid animals that can reproduce by a process called *budding.* In this process, a small portion of the sponge breaks off and gives rise to a new individual. There is no meiosis and no fertilization. A similar process, called *vegetative propagation,* occurs in many plants (see **Plant** [The reproduction of plants]).

Another form of asexual reproduction occurs in bacteria and other one-celled organisms. Such organisms simply divide when they grow to a certain size. This process is called *binary fission.* Before dividing, the organism makes a copy of its chromosomes, which contain the genes. The cell splits between the two copies so that each of the resulting cells gets one of the copies. Thus, in asexual reproduction, every cell of the new organism has the same genes as the parent, and the offspring and the parent are identical.

How reproduction has evolved

Most scientists believe that life arose on Earth about 3 ½ billion years ago. The first living things probably were microscopic, one-celled organisms that lived in the sea and reproduced asexually. Sexual reproduction also evolved in the sea. Sea animals reproduce sexually by means of *external fertilization.* In this process, the female releases eggs into the water. Fertilization occurs after a male releases sperm into the water and the sperm unite with the eggs.

About 400 million years ago, some organisms left the sea to inhabit land. The new, dry environment presented problems for existing reproduction methods. Organisms that reproduced sexually could not simply release their gametes near one another on land since the gametes would dry up and die. Thus, organisms evolved with new reproduction methods suitable for land.

Plants evolved to produce seeds, watertight structures that enclose the plant's *embryo* (fertilized egg). The seed keeps the embryo from drying out until enough water is available for it to grow.

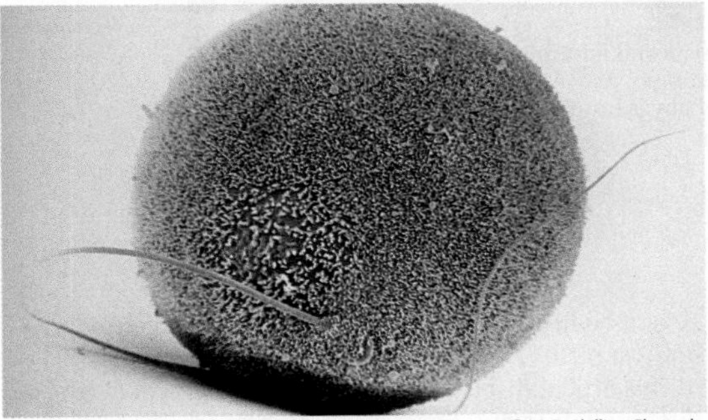

© M. D. Phillips, Phototake

In sexual reproduction, a new organism forms from the union of a sperm from the male parent and an egg from the female parent. In this photograph, the whiplike sperm of a hamster penetrates a round hamster egg.

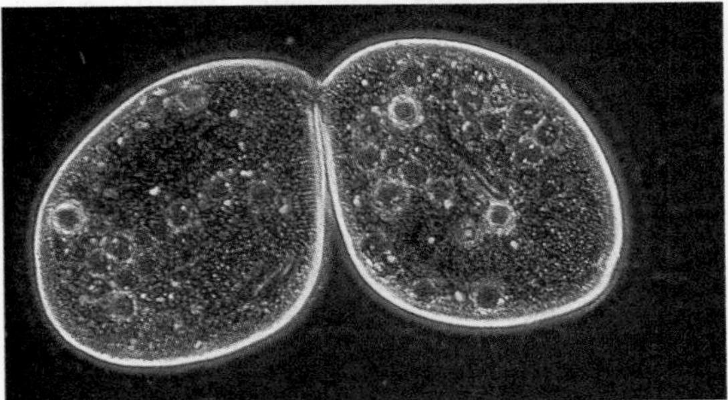

© M. I. Walker from Photo Researchers

In asexual reproduction, a new organism develops from a single parent organism. This photograph shows a paramecium splitting into two individuals, a process called *binary fission.*

Fungi evolved to produce a form of reproductive cell called the *spore.* Like the seeds of plants, the spores of fungi only begin to grow when water is available.

Amphibians, such as frogs, fertilize their eggs externally in a puddle or pond. The fertilized egg of an amphibian does not contain enough nutrients for the offspring to develop completely by the time the egg hatches. As a result, an amphibian goes through a *larval stage* after it hatches and before it becomes an adult. During the larval stage, the animal gathers and eats the food it needs to reach full maturity.

Insects evolved to make eggs with shells that retain water. The female can lay the eggs on twigs and other places exposed to air without their loss of moisture. In most insects, the eggs are fertilized as they leave the female's body by sperm stored in her abdomen.

Reptiles and birds. Reproduction in reptiles involves *internal fertilization,* a process in which the male releases sperm into an opening in the female's body. The egg is fertilized within the female's body, where it cannot dry out. Most scientists believe birds evolved from reptiles. The eggs of reptiles and birds contain a large amount of nutrients and are contained within a watertight shell, so they can be laid in dry places. The offspring grows within the egg, eventually using up all the nutrients and developing into a miniature adult before hatching.

Mammals. Reproduction in mammals involves internal fertilization. Like reptiles, the earliest mammals laid eggs. Only two such mammals, the echidna and the platypus, survive today. In all other mammals, the young are born alive.

Certain mammals, called *marsupials,* give birth to extremely underdeveloped young. The young continue their development in a pouch on the mother's body, where they feed on the mother's milk. Marsupials include kangaroos, opossums, and koalas.

The great majority of mammals, however, give birth to well-developed offspring. While in the body of the mother, the young of these mammals receive nourishment from the mother's blood through a specialized organ called the *placenta* (see **Placenta**). Such mammals are called *placentals.* George B. Johnson

Related articles in ***World Book*** include:

Alternation of generations
Animal (How animals reproduce)
Bacteria (How bacteria reproduce)
Biogenesis
Bird (Laying and hatching eggs)
Cell (Cell division)
Cloning
Dinosaur (Dinosaur life cycle)
Egg
Estrous cycle
Evolution
Fertilization
Fish (How fish reproduce)
Fungi
Genetics
Heredity
Insect (Reproduction)
Mammal (How mammals reproduce)
Plant (The reproduction of plants)
Reptile (Reproduction)
Seed
Sponge (How sponges reproduce)

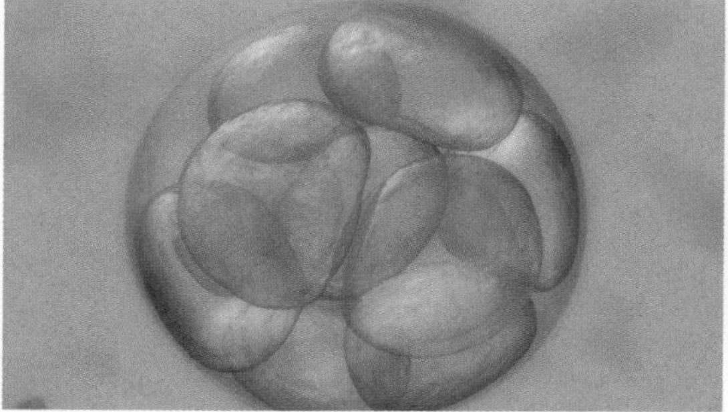
© Thinkstock

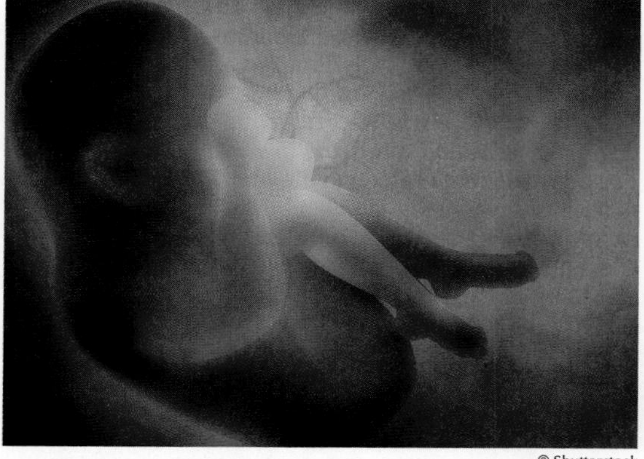
© Shutterstock

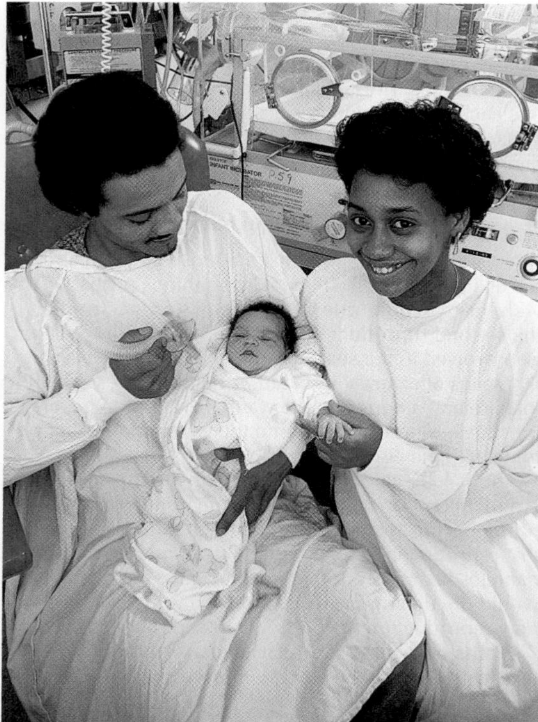
© Dan McCoy, Rainbow

Human reproduction begins when a sperm from the father unites with and fertilizes an egg from the mother. The egg divides rapidly, *top left,* and soon becomes an embryo, *above left,* that develops and grows within the mother's body. After about nine months, a baby is born, *right.*

Human reproduction

Reproduction, Human, is the process by which human beings create more of their own kind. Human beings reproduce sexually. That is, a new individual develops from the joining of two sex cells, one from a female parent and one from a male parent. The union of these cells is called *fertilization.*

Biologists refer to sex cells as *gametes.* Females produce gametes called *eggs* or *ova.* Male gametes are called *sperm.* Fertilization may occur after a male delivers sperm to the female's egg by means of sexual intercourse. Fertilization begins a remarkable period of development in which the egg develops into a fully formed baby within the body of the female. This period of development, called *pregnancy,* takes about nine months.

At the beginning of pregnancy, the fertilized egg is smaller than the period at the end of this sentence. The egg develops into a growing mass of cells called an *embryo.* Gradually, the cells rearrange themselves to form tissues. By the end of the second month of pregnancy, all the major body organs and organ systems have formed, and the embryo looks distinctly human. During the rest of pregnancy, the embryo is called a *fetus.* The fetus grows while its systems prepare for the day when they must function outside the mother's body. Pregnancy ends when the new baby passes out of the mother's body at birth.

This article discusses the biological aspects of reproduction in humans. For a discussion of some of the moral and social issues related to human reproduction, see such articles as **Abortion, Baby, Birth control,** and **Family.** For information on reproduction among other living things, see **Reproduction.**

The human reproductive system

Human beings are born with the body organs needed for reproduction. But reproduction cannot actually occur until these organs mature. This maturation process takes place during *puberty,* a period in which a boy or girl goes through dramatic physical changes. These changes are regulated by certain *hormones* (chemicals produced by the body). Puberty begins during or just before the early teenage years.

The reproductive systems of females and males differ greatly in shape and structure. But both systems are specifically designed to produce, nourish, and transport the eggs or sperm.

In females, the reproductive system consists primarily of a group of organs located within the pelvis. A woman or girl has external organs called the *vulva* between her legs. The outer parts of the vulva cover the opening to a narrow canal called the *vagina.* The vagina leads to the *uterus,* a hollow, pear-shaped, muscular organ in which a baby develops. Two small, oval organs called *ovaries* lie to the right and left of the uterus. The ovaries produce, store, and release eggs. These organs also produce two types of hormones—*progesterone* and *estrogens.* Eggs from the ovaries reach the uterus through tubes called *fallopian tubes* or *oviducts.*

Females produce eggs as part of a monthly process called the *menstrual cycle,* which begins during puberty. Each menstrual cycle, the female reproductive system undergoes a series of changes that prepares it for fertilization and pregnancy. If the egg is not fertilized, a shedding or loss of tissue in the uterus called *menstruation* occurs. Bleeding is associated with this process and lasts three to seven days. Menstruation marks the beginning of each menstrual cycle. Each cycle lasts about 28 days. See **Menstruation.**

Other changes during a menstrual cycle involve cells in the ovaries called *oocytes.* Eggs develop from these cells. At birth, each ovary has about 400,000 oocytes. These cells remain inactive until the first menstrual cycle. Thereafter, many oocytes grow and begin to mature each month. Normally, only one oocyte in either of the ovaries reaches full maturity. This fully developed cell—the mature egg—is released from the ovary in a process called *ovulation.* This process occurs at about the midpoint of the menstrual cycle. After ovulation, the egg travels toward the uterus through one of the fallopian tubes by means of wavelike contractions of muscles and the beating of *cilia* (hairlike structures) located on cells in the walls of the oviduct. Fertilization may occur in one of the tubes. An unfertilized egg lives for about 24 hours after it leaves the ovary.

Important changes also occur in the *endometrium* (lining of the uterus). During the first half of the menstrual cycle, the ovaries release relatively large amounts of estrogens, which cause the endometrium to thicken. The endometrium reaches its maximum thickness at about the time of ovulation. After ovulation, the ovaries release relatively large amounts of progesterone. This hormone maintains the thickness of the endometrium, so that a fertilized egg can attach to the uterus.

If fertilization occurs, the endometrium continues to develop. If fertilization does not occur, the egg breaks down and the production of progesterone decreases. The thickened endometrium also breaks down and passes out of the body during menstruation.

Most women produce eggs until the ages of about 45 to 55, when the menstrual cycles become increasingly infrequent and then stop. This period of a woman's life is called *menopause.* The completion of menopause marks the end of a woman's natural childbearing years.

In males, the reproductive system includes the *testicles,* a *duct system, accessory glands,* and the *penis.* The testicles, also called *testes,* are the organs that produce sperm. The duct system, which includes the *epididymis* and the *vas deferens,* transports the sperm. The accessory glands, mainly the *seminal vesicles* and the *prostate gland,* provide fluids that lubricate the duct system and nourish the sperm. The sperm leave the body through the penis, a cylindrical organ that is located between the legs.

The testicles are contained in the *scrotum,* a pouch behind the penis. The location of the scrotum keeps the testicles about 4 to 5 Fahrenheit degrees (2.2 to 2.8 Celsius degrees) cooler than the normal body temperature of 98.6 °F (37.0 °C). Unlike other cells of the body, sperm cells cannot develop properly at normal body temperature. In addition to producing sperm, the testicles also produce hormones, particularly *testosterone.*

Sperm develop in the testicles within a complex system of tubes called *seminiferous tubules.* At birth, a

The human reproductive system

The reproductive systems of males and females are specifically designed to produce, nourish, and transport the sperm or egg. After sperm are deposited in the vagina, they pass through the uterus and into the fallopian tubes, where fertilization usually occurs.

WORLD BOOK diagrams by George Suyeoka

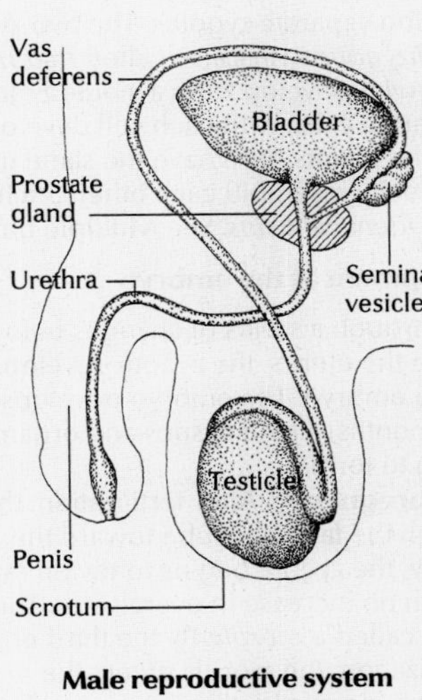

Vas deferens

Bladder

Prostate gland

Urethra

Seminal vesicle

Testicle

Penis

Scrotum

Special organs are involved in human reproduction. In the male, *left,* sperm from each testicle travel through the vas deferens, are mixed there with semen, and are released through the urethra. In the female, *right,* eggs from the ovaries pass through the fallopian tubes to the uterus.

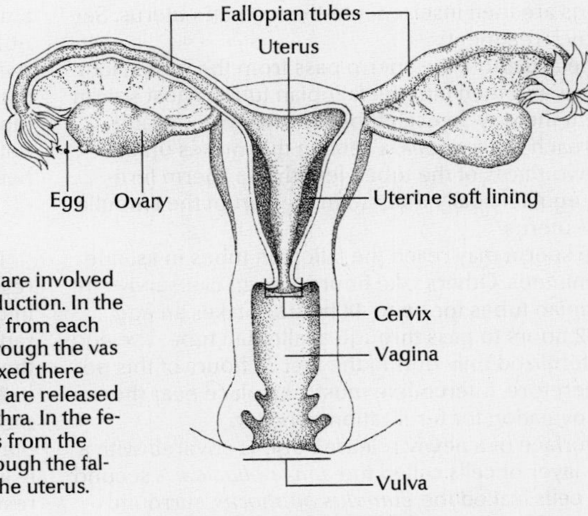

Fallopian tubes

Uterus

Egg

Ovary

Uterine soft lining

Cervix

Vagina

Vulva

Male reproductive system

Female reproductive system

male baby's tubules contain only simple round cells. But during puberty, the testicles begin to produce testosterone and other hormones that make the round cells divide, and undergo changes to become slender cells with a tail. A sperm cell uses its tail, called a *flagellum,* to propel itself forward. Sperm pass from the testicles into the epididymis, where they complete their development in about 12 days and are stored.

A healthy adult male normally produces about 200 million sperm per day. Although sperm production begins to decline gradually at about 45 years of age, it normally continues throughout life.

From the epididymis, sperm move to a long tube that is called the vas deferens. The seminal vesicles and prostate gland produce a whitish fluid called *seminal fluid.* This fluid mixes with sperm to form *semen.* The vas deferens leads to the *urethra,* a tube that runs through the penis.

Semen, which contains the sperm, is expelled from the body through the urethra. This process is called *ejaculation.* The penis usually hangs limp. But when a male becomes sexually excited, special tissues in the penis fill with blood, and the organ becomes stiff and erect. When the erect penis is stimulated, muscles around the reproductive organs contract. This contraction forces fluid from the glands and propels the semen through the duct system and the urethra. The amount of semen ejaculated varies from 2 to 6 milliliters (0.07 to 0.2 fluid ounce). Each milliliter has about 100 million sperm.

Fertilization

A pregnancy begins when a sperm fertilizes an egg. Fertilization, also called *conception,* normally occurs by means of sexual intercourse. Sexual intercourse takes place when the man's erect penis is inserted in the woman's vagina. When a man ejaculates, semen containing the millions of sperm is deposited in the vagina.

Scientists have developed techniques of achieving fertilization without sexual intercourse. In a process called *artificial insemination,* sperm are collected from a man and later injected into a woman's uterus. In another technique, called *in vitro fertilization,* collected sperm are used to fertilize eggs in a laboratory dish. The fertilized eggs are then inserted into the woman's uterus. See **Infertility** (Treatment).

After ejaculation, the sperm pass from the vagina into the uterus and then into the fallopian tubes. Most sperm die along the way. In each tube, only a few thousand sperm reach the *ampulla,* a section that makes up one-half to two-thirds of the tube's length. If a sperm fertilizes an egg, it usually does so in the part of the ampulla near the uterus.

Some sperm may reach the fallopian tubes in as little as five minutes. Others take hours. Sperm can survive in the fallopian tubes for up to 48 hours. It takes an egg about 72 hours to pass through a fallopian tube. The egg can be fertilized only during the first 24 hours of this period. Therefore, intercourse must take place near the time of ovulation for fertilization to occur.

The surface of a newly released egg is covered with a jellylike layer of cells called the *zona pellucida.* A second layer of cells, called the *cumulus oophorus,* surrounds the zona pellucida. A sperm must pass through both layers to fertilize the egg. The *acrosome* (tip) of the sperm releases special enzymes that scatter the cells of both layers. Although several sperm may begin to penetrate the zona pellucida, usually only one can fertilize the egg. After the first sperm enters, the egg releases substances that prevent other sperm from entering.

How sex is determined. Fertilization is complete when the *chromosomes* of the sperm unite with the chromosomes of the egg. Chromosomes are threadlike structures that contain *genes,* the units of heredity that determine each person's unique traits. Most body cells have 46 chromosomes that occur in 23 pairs. However, as each egg or sperm develops, it undergoes a special series of cell divisions called *meiosis.* As a result, each sperm or egg cell contains only one member of each chromosome pair, or 23 unpaired chromosomes. During fertilization, the chromosomes pair up so that the fertilized egg has the normal number of 46 chromosomes. The fertilized egg is called a *zygote.*

Special *sex chromosomes* determine whether the zygote will develop into a boy or a girl. Each body cell contains a pair of sex chromosomes. In females, the two sex chromosomes are identical. Each of the chromosomes is called an *X chromosome.* The cells of males have one X chromosome and a smaller chromosome called the *Y chromosome.*

After meiosis, each sperm or egg cell has only one sex chromosome. All egg cells carry one X chromosome. Half the sperm cells carry an X chromosome, and the other half have a Y chromosome. At fertilization, a sperm with an X chromosome uniting with an egg will develop into a girl baby because the fertilized egg will have two X chromosomes. A sperm with a Y chromosome uniting with an egg will form a boy baby because the fertilized egg will have the X and Y combination. See **Heredity** (Chromosomes and genes).

Multiple birth. In most cases, a single egg is fertilized and develops into one baby. Occasionally, however, two or more infants develop and are born at the same time. The birth of more than one baby from the same pregnancy is called *multiple birth.*

Multiple births can result from separate zygotes or from a single zygote. For example, if two eggs are released during ovulation, each may be fertilized by a separate sperm, producing separate zygotes. The two zygotes develop into *dizygotic twins,* also called *fraternal twins. Monozygotic twins* develop from a single zygote that divides into separate cells, with each cell developing independently. The infants born have the same genetic makeup and usually resemble each other. Such twins are also called *identical twins.* See **Multiple birth.**

Development of the embryo

The zygote goes through a series of changes before it reaches the uterus. In the uterus, the zygote develops into a form called the embryo. The embryo develops rapidly. Within two months, all the tissues and organs of the body have begun to form.

The first days of pregnancy. After fertilization, the zygote travels through the fallopian tube toward the uterus. Along the way, the zygote begins to divide rapidly into many cells with no increase in overall size. The resulting cell mass is called a *morula.* By the third or fourth day after fertilization, the morula enters the uterus. At that time, the morula is still surrounded by the

The development of a human embryo

During the first two months of pregnancy, an embryo develops from a single cell to a recognizably human shape about 1 $\frac{1}{4}$ inches (3 centimeters) long. After this period, the embryo is called a *fetus.*

WORLD BOOK illustrations by Barbara Cousins

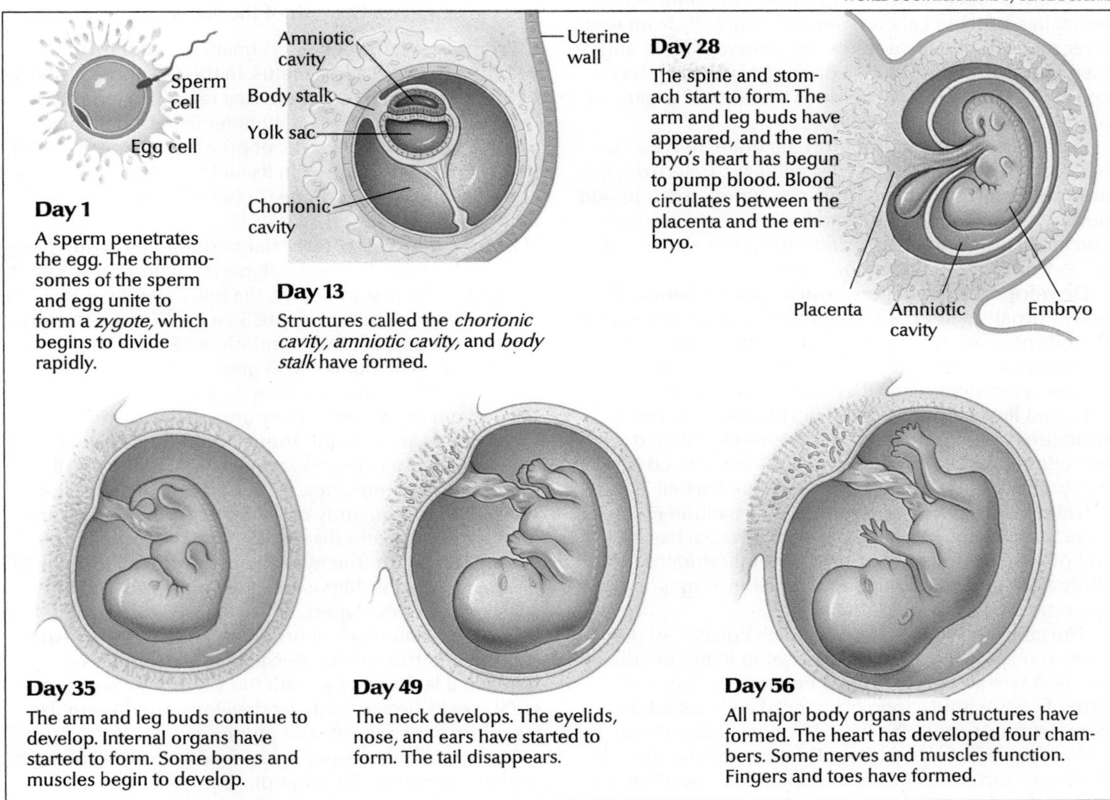

zona pellucida and consists of about 12 to 16 cells.

The embryo develops from the central cells of the morula. These cells are called the *inner cell mass.* The outer cells of the morula are called the *outer cell mass.* They develop into the *placenta,* a special organ that enables the embryo to obtain food and oxygen from the mother.

After the morula enters the uterus, it continues to divide. A fluid-filled cavity forms between the inner cell mass and the outer cell mass, and the zona pellucida begins to disintegrate. At this stage, the ball of cells is called a *blastocyst* or *blastula.* The cells of the blastocyst divide as it floats in the uterus for one or two days.

About the fifth or sixth day of pregnancy, the blastocyst becomes attached to the internal surface of the uterus. The outer cells of the blastocyst, called the *trophoblast,* secrete an enzyme that breaks down the lining of the uterus. The trophoblast begins to divide rapidly, invading the uterine tissue. The process of attachment to the uterine wall is called *implantation.* By the 11th day of the pregnancy, the blastocyst is firmly implanted in the uterus.

Nourishing the embryo. Various structures develop in the uterus to help the embryo grow. These structures include the placenta and certain membranes.

By the 13th day of pregnancy, a space called the *chorionic cavity* has formed around the embryo. Two membranes surround the chorionic cavity. The outer membrane is called the *chorion,* and the inner membrane is called the *amnion.* The chorion interacts with tissues of the uterus to form the placenta. The chorion pushes into the wall of the uterus with fingerlike projections called *chorionic villi.* The chorionic villi contain the embryo's first blood vessels. The chorion is attached to the embryo by a structure called the *body stalk.* The body stalk develops into the *umbilical cord,* which joins the embryo to the placenta.

The amnion forms a sac around the embryo and is filled with fluid. The embryo floats in this fluid, called *amniotic fluid.* The amniotic fluid protects the embryo by absorbing jolts to the uterus. It also allows the embryo to move without damaging the amnion and other tissues.

About the 21st day of pregnancy, blood begins to circulate between the placenta and the embryo. The blood vessels of the mother and those of the embryo exchange substances through a thin layer of cells called the *placental barrier.* Waste products from the embryo are carried away through the barrier. Likewise, nutrients and oxygen from the mother's blood pass through the thin walls of the barrier and enter the embryo's blood. However, such organisms as viruses and bacteria, as well as chemical substances, including drugs, also may cross the placental barrier and harm the embryo.

Origin of tissues and organs. At about the same time that the placenta begins to form, the inner cell mass flattens and develops into three layers of cells in what is called the *embryonic disc.* The three types of cell layers are the *ectoderm,* the *mesoderm,* and the *endoderm.* In a process called *differentiation,* cells from each layer move to certain areas of the embryonic disc and then fold over to form tubes or clusters. These tubes and clusters develop into various tissues and organs of the body.

Cells from the ectoderm form the brain, nerves, skin, hair, nails, and parts of the eyes and ears. Cells from the mesoderm form the heart, muscles, bones, tendons, kidneys, glands, blood vessels, and reproductive organs. The linings of the digestive and respiratory systems develop from cells of the endoderm.

Development of organs and organ systems. The body's organs and organ systems grow rapidly from the third through eighth weeks of pregnancy. The major structures include the central nervous system and the circulatory system, as well as such organs as the eyes, ears, and limbs. Defects in the development of these structures often occur during these weeks. Such defects sometimes are caused by substances introduced from the mother's body through the placental barrier. These substances are called *teratogens.* They include medications taken by the mother, as well as viruses, bacteria, and other infectious organisms. Other teratogens include nonmedicinal drugs, alcoholic beverages, and cigarette smoke.

The central nervous system, which consists of the brain and spinal cord, starts to develop in the middle of the third week of pregnancy. It begins as a flattened strip of cells within a long cylinder of cells called the *neural tube.* At about the 25th day of pregnancy, one end of the neural tube closes. The brain develops from three sacs formed in this end of the tube. The other end of the tube closes two days later. Failure of the tube to close can result in birth defects, especially *spina bifida,* a disorder of the spine.

The circulatory system also begins to develop in the third week of pregnancy. Two tubes of cells combine to form a single tube that becomes the heart. By the fourth week, a simple circulatory system is functioning and the heart has begun to pump blood. During the fourth to seventh weeks of pregnancy, the heart tube divides into four chambers. Any irregularity in the normal pattern of development during this period can produce a defect in the heart.

The eyes and ears begin to develop in the fourth week of pregnancy. Both these organs form rapidly. The external parts of the ears appear by the sixth week. Defects in the eyes or ears often stem from abnormalities that occur during the fourth to sixth weeks.

The arms and legs appear as buds of tissue during the fifth week of pregnancy. The arms develop a few days ahead of the legs. The fingers and toes become recognizable in the sixth week. They form when certain cells die and leave spaces in the remaining tissue.

The structures of the mouth, such as the lips and palate, begin to form during the fourth and fifth weeks of pregnancy. The lips and palate form during the sixth to ninth weeks. Each forms from paired structures that gradually move from the sides toward the middle of the face and *fuse* (join). If anything interferes with normal development during this period, a split in the upper lip or palate may develop. Such a defect is called *cleft lip* or *cleft palate.* See **Cleft palate.**

Growth of the fetus

From the ninth week of pregnancy until birth, the developing baby is called a fetus. In the first three months of this period, the fetus increases rapidly in length. It grows about 2 inches (5 centimeters) in each of these months. In the later months of pregnancy, the most striking change in the fetus is in its weight. Most fetuses gain about 25 ounces (700 grams) in both the eighth and ninth months of pregnancy.

Stages of growth. Physicians commonly divide pregnancy into three, three-month parts called *trimesters.* At the end of the first trimester, the fetus weighs about 1 ounce (28 grams) and is about 3 inches (7.6 centimeters) long. At the end of the second trimester, the fetus weighs about 30 ounces (850 grams) and measures about 14 inches (36 centimeters) long. At the end of the third trimester, the fetus measures about 20 inches (50 centimeters) and weighs about 7 pounds (3.2 kilograms).

The mother can feel movements of the fetus by the fifth month of pregnancy. By this time, fine hair called *lanugo* covers the body of the fetus. Hair also appears on the head. Lanugo disappears late in pregnancy or shortly after birth. The eyelids open by the 26th week of pregnancy. By the 28th week, the fingernails and toenails are well developed.

Until the 30th week of pregnancy, the fetus appears reddish and transparent because of the thinness of its skin and a lack of fat beneath the skin. In the last six to eight weeks before birth, fat develops rapidly and the fetus becomes smooth and plump.

The mother also experiences many physical changes during pregnancy. For example, a pregnant woman gains weight and her breasts increase in size. For more information on such changes, see **Pregnancy.**

Checking the fetus. Physicians can use several procedures to monitor the development of the fetus in the mother's uterus. Two of the most commonly used techniques are *ultrasonography* and *amniocentesis.*

Ultrasonography, also called *ultrasound,* involves the use of high-frequency sound waves to produce an image of the fetus on a screen. By viewing the shape and body features of the fetus, a physician can measure its growth and detect malformations. Fetal abnormalities also can be detected through amniocentesis. This technique involves the removal of a sample of the amniotic fluid, which contains cells of the fetus. The fluid and cells are then analyzed and examined. See **Amniocentesis; Ultrasound.**

Birth

The process of giving birth is called *parturition* or *labor.* By this process, the fetus and the placenta are pushed out of the uterus. Scientists believe that labor is triggered by the release of certain hormones from the adrenal glands of the fetus.

A fetus that undergoes the normal period of development before labor begins is considered to have reached *term.* Labor occurs at term if it begins during the 38th to 41st week of pregnancy. Labor that starts before the 38th week is called *preterm labor.* Labor that begins after the 41st week is called *postterm labor.* Babies born at

The birth of a baby Before birth (1), the head of the baby lies near the opening of the uterus. As muscle action forces the baby out of the uterus (2), the head turns and (3) the baby passes through the vagina.

WORLD BOOK illustrations by Joann Harling

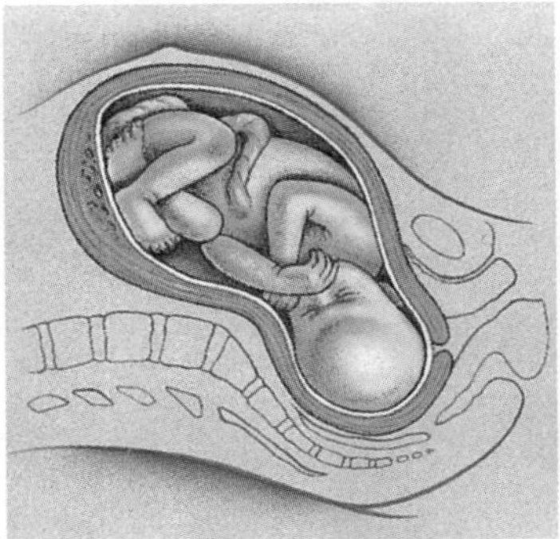

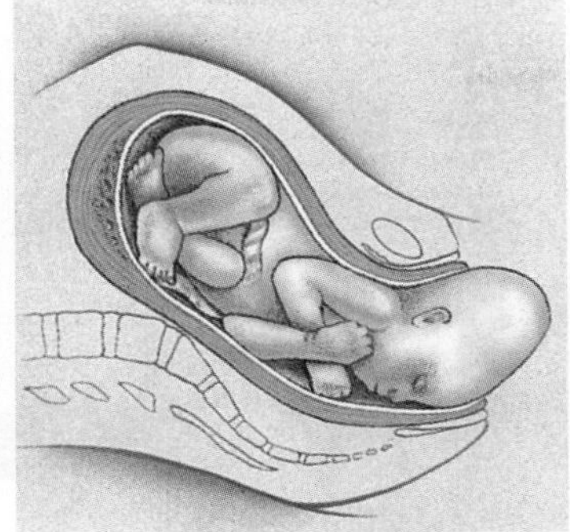

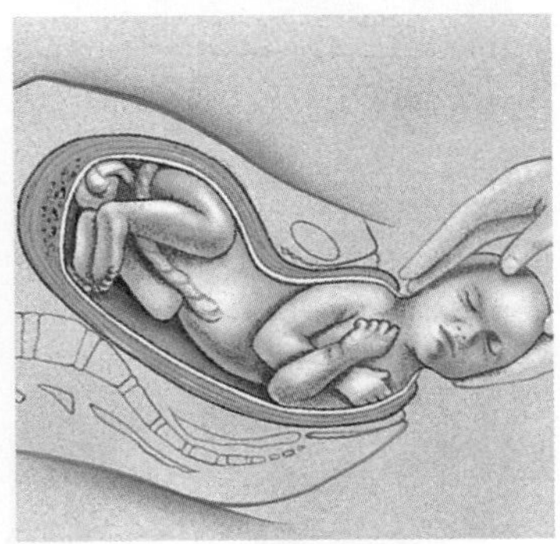

term or postterm have the best chance for survival. Most babies born from the 26th to 36th weeks of pregnancy also will live, but some of these babies may experience serious health problems because their respiratory and central nervous systems are not fully developed at birth. Babies born before the 26th week have a poor chance of surviving.

The stages of labor. Labor has three stages. The first stage begins with an alternating tensing and relaxing of muscles in the uterus. These muscle contractions are called *labor pains.* When labor begins, the fetus lies within its protective membranes and is held in place by the *cervix* (neck of the uterus). During the first stage of labor, the cervix begins to *dilate* (open). This stage ends when the cervix has fully dilated to a diameter of about 4 inches (10 centimeters). The first stage of labor is the longest, averaging about 14 hours in women giving birth for the first time. In women who have had children before, this stage normally takes 8 hours or less.

The second stage of labor begins at full dilation of the cervix and ends with the delivery of the baby. This stage may last from one to five hours. The muscle contractions of the uterus and abdomen help push the baby through the cervix and out the vagina. Most babies are born headfirst, but some are born with their shoulders or buttocks first. After the head comes out, the rest of the baby follows easily.

The third stage of labor starts after the baby's delivery and ends when the placenta, now called the *afterbirth,* is expelled from the uterus. This stage lasts about 30 minutes. A few minutes after the baby is born, the umbilical cord is clamped and cut. The placenta then detaches from the uterus and passes out the vagina.

Sometimes, the smallness of a woman's pelvis or some other condition makes it difficult to deliver a child through the vagina. In these situations, doctors may perform surgery to remove the baby through the mother's abdomen. This procedure is called a *cesarean section.* See **Childbirth.**

The newborn infant. At birth, most babies weigh about 7 pounds (3.2 kilograms) and measure about 20 inches (50 centimeters) long. The newborn infant is fed with the mother's breast milk or with a formula of milk and other nutrients. The baby can now survive outside its mother's body but needs constant care.

Lynn J. Romrell

Related articles in *World Book* include:

Abortion
Baby
Birth control
Birth defect
Cervical cancer
Childbirth
Conjoined twins
Embryo
Erectile dysfunction
Fallopian tube
Fertilization
Genetics
Heredity
Hormone (Other hormones)
Infertility
Medical ethics
Menstruation
Miscarriage
Multiple birth
Ovary
Penis
Placenta
Postpartum depression
Pregnancy
Prostate cancer
Prostate gland
Sexuality
Sexually transmitted disease
Sterility
Testicle
Uterus
Vagina
Vasectomy

Outline

I. **The human reproductive system**
   A. In females
   B. In males
II. **Fertilization**
   A. How sex is determined
   B. Multiple birth
III. **Development of the embryo**
   A. The first days of pregnancy
   B. Nourishing the embryo
   C. Origin of tissues and organs
   D. Development of organs and organ systems
IV. **Growth of the fetus**
   A. Stages of growth
   B. Checking the fetus
V. **Birth**
   A. The stages of labor
   B. The newborn infant

Questions

What are the three stages of labor?
How many chromosomes does a fertilized egg have?
What is *lanugo?*
How long does an egg survive after being released by a woman's ovary?
Where in a woman's body does fertilization usually occur?
What is *menopause?* When does it occur?
How long does pregnancy last?
What are *dizygotic twins? Monozygotic twins?*
How does a sperm propel itself?
What are *teratogens?*

Additional resources

Harris, Robie H. *It's So Amazing! A Book About Eggs, Sperm, Birth, Babies, and Families.* Candlewick Pr., 1999. Younger readers.

Parker, Steve. *The Reproductive System.* Raintree Steck-Vaughn, 1997. Younger readers.

Piñón, Ramón, Jr. *Biology of Human Reproduction.* Univ. Science Bks., 2002.

Zach, Kim K. *Reproductive Technology.* Lucent Bks., 2004.

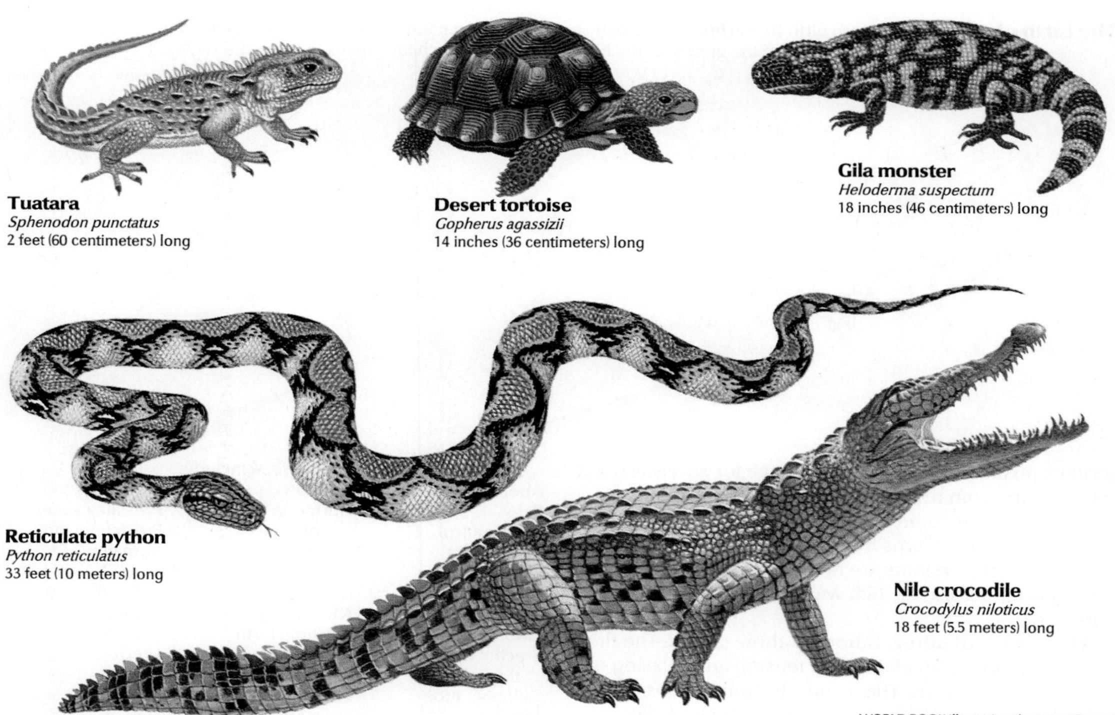

Reptiles vary greatly in size, shape, and color. However, they all have skin that consists of dry, tough scales. There are thousands of species of reptiles. Most of these animals live on land, but some make their home in the ocean and others dwell in fresh water.

Reptile is an animal that has dry, scaly skin and breathes by means of lungs. There are about 8,000 species of reptiles, and they make up one of the classes of *vertebrates* (animals that have a backbone). Reptiles include alligators, amphisbaenians, crocodiles, lizards, snakes, tuataras, and turtles.

Reptiles are cold-blooded—that is, their body temperature stays about the same as the temperature of their surroundings. To stay alive, these animals must avoid extremely high or low temperatures. Most reptiles that are active during the day keep moving from sunny places to shady spots. Many species of reptiles that live in hot climates are active mainly at night. Reptiles in regions that have harsh winters hibernate during the winter.

Reptiles vary greatly in size. For example, pythons grow more than 30 feet (9 meters) long, and leatherback turtles may weigh more than 1 ton (0.9 metric ton). On the other hand, some species of lizards measure no more than 2 inches (5 centimeters) long.

Many reptiles live a long time, and some turtles have lived in captivity for more than 100 years. For life spans of other reptiles in captivity, see **Animal** (table: Length of life of animals).

Reptiles live on every continent except Antarctica and in all the oceans except those of the polar regions. They are most abundant in the tropics. Many kinds of lizards and snakes thrive in deserts. Other reptiles, such as rat snakes and box turtles, live in forests. Still others, including marine iguanas and sea turtles, spend much of their life in the ocean. Some sea snakes live entirely in water.

Many people fear reptiles, but most species are harmless and avoid human beings if possible. The Nile crocodile and the saltwater crocodile may attack and kill people. The Gila monster, the Mexican beaded lizard, and numerous snakes, including the rattlesnake, have *venomous* (poisonous) bites.

Many people eat reptiles and reptile eggs. Some reptiles, including alligators, crocodiles, lizards, and snakes, are hunted for their skin. Manufacturers use the skin as leather for belts, shoes, and other products. The United States government prohibits the import of the hides of those reptiles classified as endangered species.

Kinds of reptiles

Zoologists divide reptiles into four main groups: (1) lizards, amphisbaenians, and snakes, (2) turtles, (3) crocodilians, and (4) tuataras.

Lizards, amphisbaenians, and snakes make up the largest group of reptiles. There are more than 4,500 species of lizards, around 150 species of amphisbaenians, and about 3,000 species of snakes. Most lizards have four legs, long tails, movable eyelids, and external ear openings. A few species, such as glass snakes and slow worms, have no legs. Lizards thrive in regions that have a hot or warm climate and are common in deserts.

Amphisbaenians resemble worms. Most species have no limbs, but a few kinds possess very small front legs. Amphisbaenians live in many warm regions, inhabiting underground tunnels that they burrow themselves.

Snakes have tails that vary in length, depending on

the species. But snakes have no legs, eyelids, or ear openings. An unmovable covering of transparent scales protects their eyes. Snakes live mostly in the tropics and in warm regions. However, the European viper lives north of the Arctic Circle, in Finland and Sweden.

Turtles are the only reptiles with a shell. They pull their head, legs, and tail into the shell for protection. There are about 300 species of turtles. They live on land, in fresh water, and in the ocean.

Crocodilians include alligators, caimans, crocodiles, and gavials. There are more than 20 species of crocodilians, all of which live in or near water. These reptiles have a long snout, strong jaws, and webbed hind feet. They use their long, powerful tail to swim. All except a few crocodilians dwell in the fresh waters and lowlands of the tropics. Alligators live in the southeastern United States and in southern China.

Tuataras inhabit several islands off the coast of New Zealand. The two species look like lizards but are more closely related to extinct dinosaurs.

The body of a reptile

Reptiles vary greatly in size, shape, and color, but all of them share certain physical characteristics. These characteristics, in addition to the animals' being cold-blooded, include various features of the skin, skeleton, internal organs, and sense organs.

Skin of a reptile consists of scales. Lizards and snakes have a single sheet of overlapping scales. The scales of turtles, crocodilians, and tuataras grow in the form of individual areas called *plates.* Crocodilians and some lizards have pieces of bone called *osteoderms* within scales. Such skin serves as protective armor.

Many reptiles shed their skin several times a year. New scales form under the old layer of scales, and chemicals called *enzymes* loosen this old layer. Among snakes, the skin on the snout is forced loose first. The snake pushes this skin backward against a rock or plant stem. The animal then crawls out of the old skin and sheds it in one piece. Most lizards shed their skin in large strips, and crocodilian skin wears away gradually.

Skeleton of reptiles provides a framework for the head, trunk, and tail. Most reptiles have hip and shoulder bones called *girdles* that support the legs. The majority of snakes do not have girdles. The hip and shoulder girdles of turtles, unlike those of any other animal, are inside the ribcage. The ribs and vertebrae make up the inner layer of the turtle's shell.

Internal organs. Reptiles breathe by means of lungs. Most species have two lungs, but some snakes have only one. The digestive system of reptiles varies among the species, according to the kind of food the animal eats. Reptiles that feed mainly on animals or on such animal products as eggs have a fairly simple stomach and a short intestine. Such reptiles include boa constrictors and Gila monsters. Species that eat plants, including iguanas and most tortoises, have a more complicated stomach and long intestines. Crocodilians have very large stomach muscles that grind flesh into tiny pieces.

Poisonous reptiles produce their venom by means of venom glands on the sides of the head. The venom affects a victim's circulatory system or nervous system.

Sense organs. Most reptiles have good vision. Species active during the day have eyes with round pupils.

Interesting facts about reptiles

Cold-blooded animals. Reptiles are cold-blooded—that is, their body temperature rarely differs much from the temperature of their surroundings. Reptiles that are active on hot, sunny days cool off by moving to shady spots.

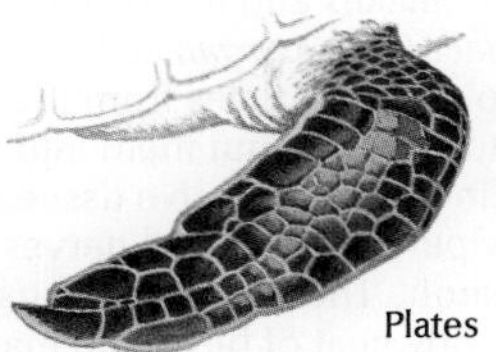

The skin of reptiles. Lizards and snakes have a single sheet of overlapping scales, *left.* Other reptiles grow *plates* (separate areas of scales), *right.* The main function of the skin is to keep water in the animal's body. Reptiles can go without water for long periods, and many species thrive in deserts.

Molting. Many kinds of reptiles *molt* (shed their skin) several times a year. The skin loosens after new scales form under it. The skin of lizards comes off in large strips, as shown at the right.

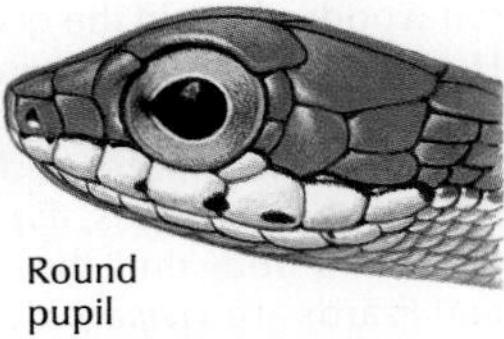

The shape of a reptile's pupil indicates whether the animal is active at night or during the day. Most reptiles active at night have slitlike pupils that can be closed almost completely in bright light. Reptiles active in daytime have round pupils. Most reptiles have good vision, and some can tell the difference among colors.

Egg-laying reptiles include most of the species. The eggs are laid in decayed wood, a nest of leaves and moist soil, or elsewhere on land. Heat from the sun causes the eggs to hatch.

WORLD BOOK illustrations by James Teason

WORLD BOOK illustration by John F. Eggert

Dinosaurs, the most spectacular reptiles, dominated land animals for millions of years. These creatures died out about 65 million years ago. The Diplodocus, *shown here,* a plant-eating dinosaur that measured about 90 feet (27 meters) long, was one of the largest animals that ever lived.

Most species active at night have slitlike eye pupils, which can be closed almost completely in bright light.

The hearing of reptiles varies among the species, but most can hear at least low-pitched sounds. The majority of reptiles have an eardrum, a middle ear, and an inner ear. However, snakes lack a middle ear and cannot hear most sounds carried through the air. They "hear" by sensing vibrations from the ground.

Snakes and lizards have two tiny cavities called the *Jacobson's organ* in the roof of the mouth. The animals pick up particles from the air and the ground with their tongue and put them into this organ. The cavities are lined with sensitive tissue that aids the sense of smell. Pit vipers have special nerves in two depressions near the snout. The nerves are sensitive to heat—including the body heat of birds and mammals—and help the snakes hunt these animals as prey.

Ways of life

Reproduction. Most reptiles reproduce sexually. The male releases *sperm* (male sex cells) into the female opening that leads to the reproductive organs. In a process called *fertilization,* the sperm unite with *eggs* (female sex cells) within the female's body. The fertilized eggs then develop into new animals. In some lizards and snakes, females can reproduce without mating. This process is called *parthenogenesis.*

Most reptiles mate in the spring, and the young are born in summer. All turtles, crocodilians, tuataras, and some lizards and snakes are *oviparous*—that is, the female lays eggs that have shells. She lays her eggs in rotten wood, a hole in the ground, or elsewhere on land. Heat from the sun—and, in some cases, from rotting plant matter—*incubates* (warms) the eggs, causing them to hatch. Some snakes and lizards are *ovoviviparous.* Among these species, the female protects the eggs within her body until they hatch. A few species of snakes and lizards are *viviparous.* The unborn young of these species receive nourishment through the *placenta,* a structure that attaches them to the female's body. Young of ovoviviparous and viviparous reptiles are born alive.

Only a few species of reptiles provide care for their eggs or young. Among pythons, mud snakes, and some skinks, the female wraps her body around the eggs and protects them. A female alligator carries her newly hatched young to water in her mouth.

Food. Most reptiles eat other animals, and they prey on almost any creature they can catch. However, some lizards and turtles eat mainly plants. Other reptiles eat only certain animals or animal products. For example, map turtles eat freshwater clams and snails, and African egg-eating snakes feed on birds' eggs.

Most reptiles simply grab their food and either chew it or swallow it whole. Crocodilians may drown prey before eating it. Venomous reptiles paralyze victims by biting them. Pythons, king snakes, and rat snakes suffocate prey by wrapping themselves tightly around it. Reptiles can go without food for long periods. After a snake eats a large meal, it might not feed again for several weeks.

Protection. The chief enemies of reptiles include birds, mammals, and other reptiles. Most of the enemies prey on small or young reptiles. Large adult reptiles generally are safe from all attackers except people.

Reptiles avoid their enemies in a variety of ways. Many reptiles have protective coloration that blends with their surroundings and makes them hard to see. Several kinds of lizards can change color to match their surroundings. Other reptiles bluff or play tricks to avoid attack. For example, if a hognose snake is approached, it rolls over on its back and lies completely motionless. The snake plays dead until the attacker goes away.

Most reptiles fight by biting and scratching, and some of the larger species inflict deep wounds. Crocodilians and large lizards strike sharp blows with their powerful tail, which they use as a whip. The bite of a venomous reptile can be fatal.

Hibernation. Reptiles that hibernate in winter do so by burrowing into the ground or slipping into a crack between two rocks. They stay there until the weather warms up. Before hibernating, a reptile eats a lot of food, which forms a layer of fat in its body. The fat serves as food during hibernation. Reptiles that live in the tropics sometimes enter an inactive state during dry periods, when food becomes scarce. This type of inactivity, called *estivation,* resembles hibernation.

The evolution of reptiles

The oldest fossils of reptiles date back to the Pennsylvanian Period—from 318 million to 299 million years ago. Reptiles *evolved* (developed slowly) from early *amniotes.* Unlike the amphibianlike animals that were the first to live on land, amniotes laid eggs with leathery shells that would not dry out on land. As a result, amniotes could live away from water.

The first animals considered reptiles evolved from amniotes called *sauropsids.* They became Earth's dominant animals during the Mesozoic Era—from about 251 million to 65 million years ago. This period is sometimes called the Age of Reptiles. Mesozoic reptiles included fishlike ichthyosaurs and birdlike pterodactyls. But the most spectacular ancient reptiles were dinosaurs. Huge plant-eating dinosaurs, such as *Seismosaurus,* were the largest land animals that ever lived. Ferocious *Tyrannosaurus* was a powerful land-dwelling meat eater. Most scientists believe modern birds evolved from small meat-eating dinosaurs.

Dinosaurs died out at the end of the Mesozoic. Most scientists believe that the impact of a giant asteroid caused the dinosaurs and other large reptiles to become extinct. The asteroid impact caused catastrophic environmental damage that made it difficult for large animals to survive. Large volcanic eruptions and other factors may also have played a role.

Today, the future of wild reptiles is threatened by the continual need of people for more farmland and living space. This need may destroy the habitats of many species of reptiles and thus wipe out the animals themselves. Other species are endangered by continued hunting and egg collecting. The survival of a number of species depends on conservation action by governments and individuals. D. Bruce Means

Related articles in *World Book* include:

Reptiles

See **Lizard** and **Snake** with their *Related articles.* See also:

Other related articles

Cold-blooded animal
Fossil
Heart (Amphibians and reptiles)
Herpetology
Hibernation

Additional resources

Level I

Behler, John L. *National Audubon Society First Field Guide: Reptiles.* Scholastic, 1999.

Crump, Marty L. *Amphibians, Reptiles, and Their Conservation.* Linnet, 2002.

Miller, Ruth. *Reptiles.* Raintree, 2005.

Level II

Adler, Kraig, and Halliday, Tim, eds. *Firefly Encyclopedia of Reptiles and Amphibians.* Firefly Bks., 2002.

Cogger, Harold G., and Zweifel, R. G., eds. *Encyclopedia of Reptiles and Amphibians.* 2nd ed. Academic Pr., 1998.

Zug, George R., and others. *Herpetology.* 2nd ed. Academic Pr., 2001.

Republic is any form of government whose leader or leaders are elected, usually for a specific term of office. The word *republic* also refers to a country that has an elective form of government.

In the United States, the idea of a republic is widely associated with the notion of a *democratic republic.* In a democratic republic, the people as a whole exercise important controls over their elected leaders through elections, lobbying, and other processes. The leaders are expected to represent the interests of the people who elected them. If the voters believe their interests have not been represented well enough, they may decide not to reelect the leaders. In this way, the voters in a democratic republic have some control over their government.

There are many other kinds of republics besides democratic republics. In some republics, the leaders are elected by a relatively small number of people and may be reelected more or less automatically. Communist nations traditionally allowed only candidates approved by the Communist Party to run for election, and there was only one candidate for each post. As a result, voters had no real choice of candidates when they went to the polls. These practices are still in effect in China and a few other Communist countries.

In some countries that are republics according to their constitutions, elections typically are not free, open, or honest. In some Latin American republics, for example, widespread charges of vote fraud accompany nearly every election.

The most important early republic was established in ancient Rome in 509 B.C. This republic lasted until 27 B.C., when the political and military leader Augustus declared himself emperor. When the United States was founded in 1776, it became the only major country at the time that had a republican form of government.

Today, many of the countries of Western Europe are republics, including Austria, Finland, France, Germany, Italy, and Switzerland. Many of the newer African and Asian nations are republics, as are all Latin American countries. The Commonwealth of Nations, an association of nations that includes the United Kingdom and many of its former possessions, has numerous members that are republics (see **Commonwealth of Nations** [table: Independent members]). Rebecca E. Zietlow

See also **Democracy; Government.**

Republican Party is one of the two principal political parties of the United States. The other is the Democratic Party. The Republican Party is often called the *G.O.P.,* which stands for *Grand Old Party,* a nickname Republicans gave their party in the 1880's. The Republican Party has greatly influenced the nation's history and politics.

The policies of the Republican Party, like those of other political parties, have changed through the years. At first, Republican candidates received most of their support from people who opposed slavery. To gain wider support, the party passed land legislation that appealed to farmers. Republicans won the backing of business leaders by endorsing sound money policies and high tariffs. By the late 1800's, the party represented a firm alliance of the agricultural West and the industrial East.

The Republican Party dominated politics in the United States in the 1920's. The economy boomed during much of the decade, and the party became known as the "party of prosperity." However, the Republicans fell out of power in the 1930's, when the Great Depression, a worldwide economic downturn, hit the nation.

The Republican Party includes members who are strongly *conservative* (favoring traditional values and ideas), as well as less-conservative members called *moderates.* During the 1950's, the party prospered under the moderate leader Dwight D. Eisenhower, who won presidential elections in 1952 and 1956. He was the first Republican to win two terms as president since William McKinley in 1896 and 1900. The conservatives of the Republican Party gained strength during the 1980's under the leadership of Ronald Reagan and during the early 2000's under George W. Bush. Both Reagan and Bush won two terms as president.

This article describes chiefly the history of the Republican Party. For information about the party's national convention and organization, see **Political convention** and **Political party.**

Origin of the Republican Party dates back to the strong opposition to the Kansas-Nebraska Bill of 1854. The bill permitted slavery in the new territories of Kansas and Nebraska if the people there voted for it.

The Republican Party grew out of a series of antislavery meetings held throughout the North to protest the Kansas-Nebraska Bill. One such meeting was held by Alvan E. Bovay, a leading Whig, on Feb. 28, 1854, in Ripon, Wisconsin. This meeting passed a resolution declaring that a new party—the Republican Party—would be organized if Congress passed the Kansas-Nebraska Bill.

Bovay held a second meeting in Ripon on March 20, after the Senate had approved the bill. The 53 men at this meeting appointed a committee to form the new party. Congress passed the Kansas-Nebraska Act on May 30. On July 6, at a party meeting in Jackson, Michigan, the delegates formally adopted the name *Republican.*

The new party had chiefly sectional appeal. Few Southern voters supported the Republicans, because almost all Southerners wanted to expand slavery, not restrict it. Many Northerners supported the party. But some feared that the extreme antislavery views of such Republican leaders as Senator Charles Sumner of Massachusetts threatened the Union.

The election of 1856. The Republicans chose John Charles Frémont, a dashing young explorer and soldier, as their first presidential candidate. During the campaign, antislavery and proslavery groups fought in Kansas. The chief campaign issue became "bleeding Kansas." Democrats predicted that the South would secede from the Union if the antislavery Frémont won.

The voting reflected the sectional appeal of the Democratic and Republican parties. Frémont won 11 Northern states. His Democratic opponent, James Buchanan, carried 19 states—including every Southern state except Maryland—and won.

Changes in party policy. After the Republican defeat in 1856, party leaders realized that they could not win the presidency on just the slavery issue. To broaden their appeal, Republicans endorsed construction of a transcontinental railroad system and federal aid to improve harbors and rivers. They also promised to open Western land for settlement, to raise U.S. tariff rates, and to permit slavery where it already existed.

In 1860, the Republicans chose Abraham Lincoln, a self-educated Illinois lawyer, as their presidential candidate. Lincoln had received national attention by expressing moderate antislavery views in his debates with Illinois Senator Stephen A. Douglas, a Democrat.

Lincoln easily won the election, even though he received less than 40 percent of the popular vote. The Democrats had split over the slavery issue. Northern Democrats nominated Douglas, and Southern Democrats chose Vice President John C. Breckinridge.

The American Civil War began in April 1861. Most Southerners believed the election of Lincoln justified secession. In 1860 and 1861—both before and after the shooting started—11 Southern states left the Union and formed the Confederate States of America.

Above all, Lincoln wanted to save the Union. But many Republicans—the so-called Radical Republicans—made the abolition of slavery their main goal. Many Northern Democrats supported Lincoln and the war and were called War Democrats.

Lincoln tried to bring all groups of both parties together, but he succeeded only partly. By 1864, Lincoln's chances of reelection looked doubtful. To stress the national character of the war—and to gain more supporters—the Republican Party used the name *Union Party* in the 1864 election. It nominated Andrew Johnson, a War Democrat, for vice president. With the help of Northern military victories just before the election, Lincoln won a second term.

On April 9, 1865, Confederate General Robert E. Lee surrendered to Union General Ulysses S. Grant. Five days later, Lincoln was assassinated.

The Radical Republicans and Reconstruction. Johnson hoped to follow Lincoln's moderate plan of Reconstruction. But the Radical Republicans in Congress favored harsh punishment for the South. The Radicals dominated Congress after the congressional elections of 1866. They divided the South into five military districts, deprived former Confederate soldiers of the vote, and gave the vote to formerly enslaved people.

The dispute over Reconstruction hardened political loyalties along sectional lines. Most Northern Republicans supported the Radical Republicans who, by 1868, felt strong enough to drop the Union Party label. Many Northern Democrats also backed Republican policies. Southerners, however, rejected Republican leadership. As a result, Reconstruction led to the birth of the Democratic "Solid South." The Democrats dominated elections at all levels in the region. See **Reconstruction.**

The Republicans nominated Grant, the great Union war hero, for president in 1868, and he won an easy victory. Grant won reelection in 1872, but by this time many voters had become alarmed over corruption in both business and government. A depression in 1873 helped the Democrats win a sweeping victory in the congressional elections of the next year.

In 1876, the Republicans nominated a cautious reformer, Rutherford B. Hayes. A group of conservative Republicans called *Stalwarts* opposed Hayes because he favored civil service reform and friendly relations with the South. Hayes and his followers became known

From *Thomas Nast* by Albert Bigelow Paine, permission of Harper & Row

The elephant as a Republican symbol first appeared in this 1874 cartoon by Thomas Nast in *Harper's Weekly.* The elephant in the cartoon represented the Republican vote. Nast used the elephant many times as a Republican symbol, and it soon came to stand for the Republican Party.

Republican presidential and vice presidential candidates

Year	President	Vice president	Year	President	Vice president
1856	John C. Frémont	William L. Dayton	1940	Wendell L. Willkie	Charles L. McNary
1860	*Abraham Lincoln*	*Hannibal Hamlin*	1944	Thomas E. Dewey	John W. Bricker
1864	*Abraham Lincoln*	*Andrew Johnson*	1948	Thomas E. Dewey	Earl Warren
1868	*Ulysses S. Grant*	*Schuyler Colfax*	1952	*Dwight D. Eisenhower*	*Richard M. Nixon*
1872	*Ulysses S. Grant*	*Henry Wilson*	1956	*Dwight D. Eisenhower*	*Richard M. Nixon*
1876	*Rutherford B. Hayes*	*William A. Wheeler*	1960	Richard M. Nixon	Henry Cabot Lodge, Jr.
1880	*James A. Garfield*	*Chester A. Arthur*	1964	Barry M. Goldwater	William E. Miller
1884	James G. Blaine	John A. Logan	1968	*Richard M. Nixon*	*Spiro T. Agnew*
1888	*Benjamin Harrison*	*Levi P. Morton*	1972	*Richard M. Nixon*	*Spiro T. Agnew*
1892	Benjamin Harrison	Whitelaw Reid	1976	Gerald R. Ford	Robert J. Dole
1896	*William McKinley*	*Garret A. Hobart*	1980	*Ronald W. Reagan*	*George H. W. Bush*
1900	*William McKinley*	*Theodore Roosevelt*	1984	*Ronald W. Reagan*	*George H. W. Bush*
1904	*Theodore Roosevelt*	*Charles W. Fairbanks*	1988	*George H. W. Bush*	*Dan Quayle*
1908	*William Howard Taft*	*James S. Sherman*	1992	George H. W. Bush	Dan Quayle
1912	William Howard Taft	James S. Sherman	1996	Robert J. Dole	Jack Kemp
1916	Charles Evans Hughes	Charles W. Fairbanks	2000	*George W. Bush*	*Richard B. Cheney*
1920	*Warren G. Harding*	*Calvin Coolidge*	2004	*George W. Bush*	*Richard B. Cheney*
1924	*Calvin Coolidge*	*Charles G. Dawes*	2008	John McCain	Sarah Palin
1928	*Herbert Hoover*	*Charles Curtis*	2012	Mitt Romney	Paul Ryan
1932	Herbert Hoover	Charles Curtis	2016	*Donald Trump*	*Mike Pence*
1936	Alfred M. Landon	Frank Knox	2020	Donald Trump	Mike Pence

Names of elected candidates are in italics. Each candidate has a separate biography in *World Book*.

as *Half-Breeds.* Samuel J. Tilden, the Democratic candidate, won more popular votes than Hayes, but the electoral vote was disputed. A special commission declared Hayes the winner by one vote. The Democrats accepted the verdict only because the Republicans had promised to end Reconstruction and withdraw federal troops from the South. Hayes kept the promise.

Political inactivity marked the 1880's and 1890's. Both major parties failed to face the problems resulting from the rapid industrialization that followed the Civil War. Many industrial monopolies set high prices for their products and services. Economic power became centered with a few wealthy business leaders, and farmers and wage earners suffered increasingly hard times.

In 1880, Republican James A. Garfield won the presidency. He was assassinated in 1881, only a few months after taking office, and Vice President Chester A. Arthur, a Stalwart, succeeded him. Arthur surprised his fellow Stalwarts by supporting civil service reform. In 1883, Congress passed the Pendleton Act, which established the merit system in the civil service.

In 1884, the Republican presidential candidate, James G. Blaine, narrowly lost to Grover Cleveland. The party made the protective tariff its chief campaign issue in 1888 and won the presidency with Benjamin Harrison. In 1890, the McKinley Tariff pushed tariffs higher than they had ever been before. Dissatisfaction with the tariff helped Cleveland defeat Harrison in 1892.

The money issue dominated the election of 1896. A third party, the Populist Party, had appeared during the early 1890's. The Populists demanded that the government increase the amount of money in circulation by permitting unlimited coinage of silver. They believed such action would help farmers and wage earners and improve the nation's economy. Many Democrats joined the Populists in their demand for silver coinage. In 1896, the Democrats nominated William Jennings Bryan, the leading silver spokesman, for president. The Republican candidate, William McKinley, supported a currency backed by gold. McKinley won the election.

Economic conditions improved rapidly during the late 1890's. The U.S. victory in the Spanish-American War also gained support for the Republicans. McKinley defeated Bryan again in 1900. Six months into his second term, however, McKinley was assassinated. Vice President Theodore Roosevelt succeeded him.

The party splits. "Teddy" Roosevelt supported much reform legislation. He brought suits against several large monopolies and crusaded for honesty in government. Roosevelt also sponsored a conservation policy, laws to protect the American public from impure food and drugs, and legislation to regulate railroad rates.

In 1908, Roosevelt chose Secretary of War William Howard Taft to succeed him and continue his policies. Taft easily beat Bryan, who ran for the third time as the Democratic nominee.

Taft brought many more suits against monopolies than Roosevelt had. But Taft, by nature quieter and more conservative than Roosevelt, lost favor with Republican progressives. He faced open hostility from the progressives after signing into law the high Payne-Aldrich Tariff in 1909. By 1912, Taft no longer led a united party, and the progressives turned to Roosevelt, who wanted to be president again. After the Republicans renominated Taft, Roosevelt left the party and formed the Progressive, or "Bull Moose," Party. The Republican split helped Woodrow Wilson, the Democratic candidate, win the election.

The Republicans began to reunite after their defeat, and in 1916, most of them supported the party candidate, Charles Evans Hughes. But some backed Wilson because he had promoted progressive legislation and had kept the nation out of World War I, which had begun in 1914. Wilson won reelection by a close margin. A month after he took office for the second time, the United States went to war against Germany.

By the congressional elections of 1918, the Republicans had reunited, and they gained control of Congress. After the war, the Republican-controlled Senate rejected American membership in the League of Nations (see **League of Nations**).

During the Roaring Twenties, the Republicans won every presidential and congressional election. In 1920,

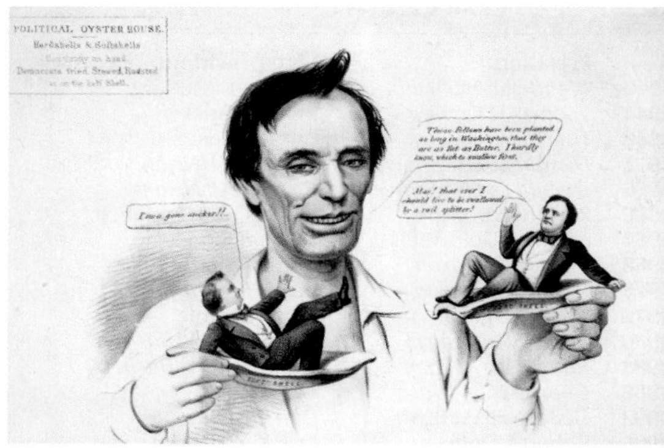

Library of Congress

Abraham Lincoln is about to devour his Democratic opponents, Stephen A. Douglas and John C. Breckinridge, in a political cartoon published during the 1860 presidential race.

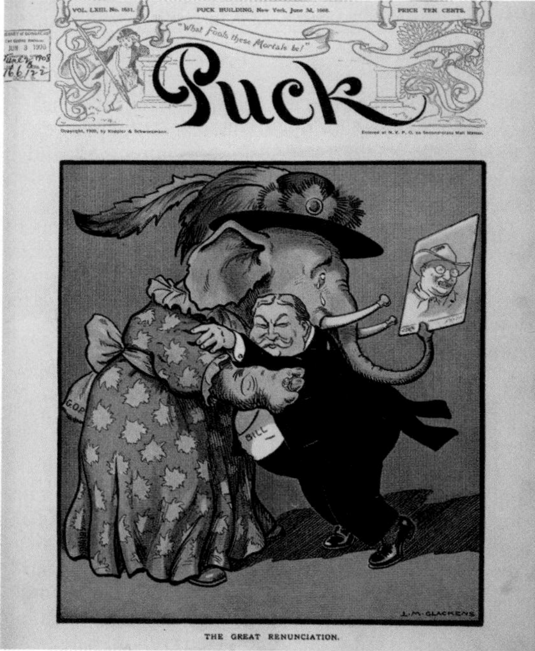

Library of Congress

A party split developed among the Republicans as Theodore Roosevelt neared the end of his presidency. Roosevelt chose Secretary of War William Howard Taft to continue his policies. This June 1908 cover of *Puck* magazine shows an elephant, representing the Republican Party, looking wistfully at a picture of the popular Roosevelt as it embraces Taft.

the party's candidate, Warren G. Harding, promised a return to "normalcy." Americans, weary of wartime controls and world problems, wanted just that—and Harding won in a landslide.

The nation's economy boomed during the 1920's as business and industry expanded. Successive Republican administrations helped big business by keeping government spending and taxes low and by raising tariffs.

After Harding's death in 1923, congressional investigations revealed corruption in several government departments during his administration. But the exposures did not prevent Harding's successor, Vice President Calvin Coolidge, from easily winning the 1924 election. Coolidge's administration seemed to reflect the largely antiforeign, anti-immigration, antilabor mood of the nation.

In 1928, the Republicans turned to Herbert Hoover, Coolidge's secretary of commerce. Hoover easily defeated his Democratic opponent, Alfred E. Smith.

Soon after Hoover took office in 1929, the worst stock-market crash in the nation's history occurred. The Great Depression followed. Hoover tried to stop the Depression but could not, and he lost badly in 1932 to the Democratic candidate, Franklin D. Roosevelt. Hoover's defeat reduced the Republicans to a hard core of business leaders, Midwestern farmers, and conservative workers.

After the Great Depression, the Republican Party remained the minority party for a generation. Roosevelt led the nation through the economic crisis with a massive federal program called the New Deal (see **New Deal**). The Republicans, far outnumbered in both houses of Congress, took little action against his policies. The 1936 Republican Party platform criticized the New Deal, but Roosevelt won reelection by a landslide over Alfred M. Landon. By the election of 1940, World War II (1939-1945) had started. The Republicans nominated Wendell L. Willkie and continued to attack the New Deal, but Roosevelt easily won a third term. The United States entered the war in 1941. Roosevelt defeated Thomas E. Dewey in 1944 and became the only candidate to be elected president four times.

In the 1930's and 1940's, many Republicans accepted the idea of federal welfare programs and of U.S. leadership in world affairs. They also accepted U.S. membership in the United Nations, formed in 1945. Vice President Harry S. Truman became president after the death of Roosevelt in 1945. The Republicans expected to win the 1948 election easily, and they nominated Dewey again. But Truman won a surprise victory.

The Eisenhower years. Dwight D. Eisenhower, a U.S. Army general and World War II hero, sought the Republican nomination for the 1952 election. He ran partly to prevent Ohio Senator Robert A. Taft, a conservative isolationist, from becoming the nominee. Eisenhower gained the nomination and easily won the general election, defeating Adlai E. Stevenson. Eisenhower carried four Southern states and broke the Democratic Solid South for the first time in over 20 years. Voters turned to Eisenhower for a variety of reasons. Many voted Republican because of dissatisfaction with the government's conduct of the Korean War (1950-1953). Others believed charges that the Democrats had harbored Communists in high government posts. Eisenhower won reelection in 1956 by a landslide, again over Stevenson.

Eisenhower, a moderate, won support from his own party and from many Southern Democrats. During his presidency, Congress extended Social Security benefits and passed the first civil rights act since Reconstruction. Despite his popularity, however, Eisenhower failed to make the Republican Party the country's majority party.

Defeat, then victory. Vice President Richard M. Nixon won the Republican presidential nomination in 1960, but he narrowly lost the election to his Democratic opponent, John F. Kennedy. Following Kennedy's assassination in 1963, Vice President Lyndon B. Johnson succeeded to the presidency. In 1964, the Republicans nominated Barry M. Goldwater, who stood for an extreme form of conservatism. Johnson defeated him overwhelmingly. At Johnson's urging, Congress passed additional civil rights legislation and other laws to help disadvantaged Americans. Conservative Republicans and conservative Southern Democrats joined forces to oppose many of Johnson's programs.

For the 1968 presidential election, the Republicans turned to Nixon again. The Democrats nominated Vice President Hubert H. Humphrey. A third party, the American Independent Party, nominated George C. Wallace, a Southern Democrat who strongly opposed civil rights legislation. Nixon won even though he received only about 43 percent of the popular vote. He triumphed partly because of his "Southern strategy," in which he appealed to conservative white Southerners. Nixon emphasized patriotism and law and order. He favored slower school integration than liberals did. In 1972, the Republicans renominated Nixon, and the Democrats nominated George S. McGovern. Nixon received over 17 ¾ million more popular votes than McGovern—the widest margin of any presidential election in U.S. history.

The Watergate scandal. In 1973, Nixon helped end U.S. involvement in the Vietnam War. But his administration suffered a loss of public confidence later that year, because of the Watergate scandal and another criminal investigation that led to the resignation of Vice President Spiro T. Agnew (see **Watergate; Agnew, Spiro T.**).

House Minority Leader Gerald R. Ford replaced Agnew as vice president. In July 1974, the House Judiciary Committee recommended that Nixon be impeached on charges related to the Watergate scandal. Nixon resigned in August, before the House voted on impeachment, and Ford became president.

The Agnew and Watergate scandals damaged the party. In 1976, the Republicans suffered a split, as Ronald Reagan, a conservative who had served as governor of California, challenged the more moderate Ford for the presidential nomination. Ford won the nomination but lost to Democrat Jimmy Carter in the general election.

Victories in the 1980's. The Republicans won every presidential election in the 1980's. The party, strengthened by social conservatives who opposed abortion and supported school prayer, solidified the gains Nixon had made in the South. The party also continued to appeal to economic conservatives by supporting tax cuts and a balanced federal budget.

AP/Wide World

Ronald Reagan and George H. W. Bush were the leading Republican politicians of the 1980's. This photo shows Reagan, *left,* and Bush at the 1984 Republican National Convention in Dallas.

In 1980, Republicans chose Ronald Reagan as their presidential candidate. The Democrats renominated Carter, and Representative John B. Anderson of Illinois ran as an independent. Reagan won by a wide margin. The Republicans also won control of the Senate.

In the 1984 presidential election, Reagan defeated his Democratic opponent, Walter F. Mondale. In the 1986 elections, the Democrats regained control of the Senate. In 1988, Vice President George H. W. Bush won the Republican presidential nomination. He went on to defeat his Democratic opponent, Michael S. Dukakis.

Control of Congress. In 1992, the Republicans renominated Bush for president. The Democrats nominated Arkansas Governor Bill Clinton, and Texas businessman Ross Perot ran as an independent. Bush and Perot lost the election to Clinton. In 1994, the Republicans won control of both houses of Congress. They had not controlled both houses since 1955. In 1996, Senator Robert Dole of Kansas, the Republican nominee, lost the presidential election to Clinton. But the Republicans kept control of both houses of Congress in 1996 and 1998.

The early 2000's. Texas Governor George W. Bush, son of former President George H. W. Bush, won the Republican presidential nomination in 2000. He defeated the Democratic candidate, Vice President Al Gore, in a close election. The Republicans kept control of the House, but the election left the Senate with 50 Republican members and 50 Democrats.

In 2001, the Republicans lost a Senate seat when James Jeffords of Vermont left the party and became an independent. As a result, the Democrats gained control of the Senate. The 2002 elections shifted control back to the Republicans, who also kept control of the House.

Bush was reelected in 2004, defeating Democratic Senator John F. Kerry of Massachusetts. During Bush's second term, however, the Republicans suffered from congressional scandals and the unpopularity of the Iraq War (2003-2011). In 2006, the Republicans lost control of both houses of Congress to the Democrats.

In the 2008 presidential election, Democratic Senator Barack Obama of Illinois defeated Senator John McCain of Arizona, the Republican nominee. An economic crisis that struck in the months before the election contributed to the Republican defeat. In 2010, voter frustration with a sluggish economy contributed to a Republican takeover of the House and a number of governorships. In 2012, Obama defeated his Republican opponent, former Massachusetts Governor Mitt Romney, to win reelection. In the 2014 elections, Republicans won a majority in the Senate, taking control of both houses of Congress.

In 2016, Republican Donald J. Trump defeated Democrat Hillary Rodham Clinton, a former U.S. secretary of state. In 2018, Democrats sought to make the elections a referendum on Trump's policies. Republicans lost the House but retained power in the Senate. In 2020, Democrat Joe Biden, a former vice president, defeated Trump. Democrats kept control of the House and gained a 50-50 tie in the Senate. Yanek Mieczkowski

Related articles in *World Book* include:

Christian Coalition of America
Free Soil Party
Liberal Republican Party
Mugwumps

Research. See **Science** (How scientists work). See also *A Guide to Research Skills* in the Research Guide/Index, Volume 22.

Reservation, called *reserve* in Canada. See **Indian reservation.**

Reserve Officers Training Corps (ROTC) trains students in schools, colleges, and universities to become officers in the United States armed services. It seeks to develop students for positions of military leadership. Qualified students take ROTC training in addition to their regular school or college work. All such training is given on campus, except for summer field training.

Students enrolled in an ROTC unit are organized along military lines. One student serves as cadet commander, and others hold staff or command positions. The commissioned officer directing the unit usually has the title of professor of military science (for Army units), naval science (for Navy units), or aerospace studies (for Air Force units). The staff includes officers and enlisted personnel who teach courses, and others who handle the administration of the unit.

Army ROTC consists of two divisions. *Junior* units provide three years of basic military training in high schools. *Senior* units enroll students for two to four years in military schools, colleges, and universities. Course work includes drills, lectures, demonstrations, and field trips. The first two years of the senior course may be required for qualified students. The last two years are voluntary. In the *Advanced ROTC Course* program, students may enter in their junior year. Instead of the regular first two-year program, they attend a qualifying basic training course in the summer before entering the advanced course. Students receive pay and allowances in their junior and senior year training. The Army grants commissions as second lieutenant in the Army Reserve, the Army National Guard, or the active Army to students who complete a two- or four-year program and a summer of field training. It designates students that demonstrate exceptional academic and leadership abilities as Distinguished Military Graduates.

Upon graduation, the new officers serve eight years in the active Army, the Reserve, or the National Guard, or a combination of two of all three of these components. The Army has ROTC units in more than 270 colleges and universities and about 800 high schools. In addition, students at many other educational institutions may enroll in ROTC units at partnership schools or at host universities. Women are admitted to ROTC units at partnership schools and host universities and colleges.

Navy ROTC has units in about 65 colleges and universities and about 230 high schools. Women are admitted to the program at host universities and colleges. The senior course level has two types of training. The *scholarship NROTC* program provides a four-year education paid for almost entirely by the government. Students in the program must take three summer cruises as part of their ROTC course work. Upon graduation, they receive commissions as ensigns in the Navy or as second lieutenants in the Marine Corps. Under the Navy's *college NROTC* program, participating students have the same course work as do those in the regular program, but they have only one summer training cruise. Students in the college NROTC program also pay their own tuition and receive a monthly allowance during their last two years in the program. They serve three years of active duty after receiving commissions in the Navy Reserve and Marine Corps Reserve. Graduates of the scholarship NROTC must serve for four years.

Air Force ROTC operates in about 150 universities and colleges and about 300 high schools. It has junior and senior programs resembling those of Army ROTC. College students who participate in Air Force ROTC take one, two, or four years of part-time military training and one summer of field training at an Air Force base. They may apply for a scholarship and allowances. Special programs are available for students seeking assignments as pilots, navigators, or missile officers, or as medical or legal personnel. The one-year program is designed to quickly fill roles in certain understaffed fields. Newly appointed second lieutenants in the Air Force Reserve must serve four years of active duty. Pilots and navigators have longer commitments. Distinguished Military Graduates are offered commissions in the regular Air Force. The Air Force admits women to ROTC programs at host universities and colleges.

History. The ROTC has its origin in the Morrill, or Land-Grant, Act of 1862. The act authorized grants of public land to state colleges. In return, the Morrill Act required those colleges to offer military training for all able-bodied male students. The first actual reserve commissions were granted to students in 1908. The National Defense Act of 1916 established the first Army ROTC units. It set up an Officers Reserve Corps to be composed of men trained in the ROTC and in training camps. By the fall of 1916, the Army had enrolled about 40,000 students. In 1926, the Navy established its ROTC program and set up units at six colleges and universities. The Air Force began its ROTC program in 1947, when it became an independent military service.

Robert Powell Smith

Reserves. See **Air Force, United States** (Air Force reserves); **Army, United States** (Organization of the Army); **Navy, United States** (The active-duty Navy and reserves).

Reservoir is a place where large quantities of water are stored to be used for irrigation, power generation, water supply, and recreation. Reservoirs may also serve as a means to control flooding. A reservoir may be either natural or artificial. Natural lakes form reservoirs from which some cities obtain their water supply.

Engineers build artificial reservoirs by constructing a dam across a narrow valley or by digging a basin in a level tract of land. Examples of reservoirs that are made by building dams are those of the Tennessee Valley Authority; Lake Mead, which is *impounded* (confined) by Hoover Dam; and Franklin D. Roosevelt Lake, which is impounded by Grand Coulee Dam. The capacity of a reservoir is measured in acre-feet or cubic meters. An acre-foot of water represents a volume of water that covers an area of one acre and has a depth of one foot. An acre-foot equals 1,233 cubic meters and contains 325,829 gallons (1,233,482 liters).

Some small cities store their water in large tanks supported on a high framework or in small *holding reser-*

Largest reservoirs in the world

Reservoir	Location	Capacity: In thousands of acre-feet*	Capacity: In millions of cubic meters	Year completed
Lake Victoria†	Kenya, Tanzania, Uganda	166,000	204,800	1954
Kariba Lake	Zambia, Zimbabwe	146,400	180,600	1959
Bratsk	Russia	137,000	169,000	1964
Lake Nasser	Egypt, Sudan	137,000	169,000	1970
Lake Volta	Ghana	121,600	150,000	1965
Manicouagan	Canada	115,000	141,900	1968
Guri	Venezuela	109,400	135,000	1986
Williston Lake	Canada	60,000	74,300	1967
Krasnoyarsk	Russia	59,400	73,300	1967
Zeya	Russia	55,500	68,400	1978

*An acre-foot equals 1 acre of water 1 foot deep.
†Enlarged natural lake.
Source: International Commission on Large Dams and other sources.

Largest reservoirs in the United States

Reservoir	Location	Normal storage: In thousands of acre-feet*	Normal storage: In millions of cubic meters	Year completed
Lake Mead	Arizona-Nevada	28,260	34,860	1935
Lake Powell	Arizona-Utah	27,000	33,300	1964
Lake Oahe	North Dakota-South Dakota	19,300	23,810	1966
Lake Sakakawea	North Dakota	18,500	22,820	1953
Fort Peck Lake	Montana	15,400	19,000	1957
Franklin D. Roosevelt Lake	Washington	9,560	11,790	1942
Lake Koocanusa	Montana	5,810	7,170	1973
Shasta Lake	California	4,550	5,610	1945
Toledo Bend Reservoir	Louisiana	4,480	5,520	1966
Lake Francis Case	South Dakota	3,800	4,690	1954

*An acre-foot equals 1 acre of water 1 foot deep.
Source: United States Society on Dams and United States Army Corps of Engineers.

voirs. The tanks or reservoirs are built at an elevation above the highest buildings to create enough pressure to force the water to the tops of the buildings. Such tanks are often called *standpipes.* Larry W. Mays

See also **Aqueduct; Dam; Irrigation** (Surface water); **Water; Water power.**

Resin, *REHZ uhn,* is a useful substance that is typically gummy, oily, sticky, or waxy. Resins are used in varnishes, medicines, soaps, paints, and many other products. There are two kinds of resins, natural resins and *synthetic* (artificial) resins.

Natural resins are mostly *viscous* (slow-flowing) liquids. They may be divided into three main groups: (1) resins that flow from plants as the result of wounds; (2) resins extracted from wood by solvents; and (3) fossil resins found with the preserved remains of animals and plants. A scale insect of the acacia tree also produces a resin, called *lac.*

Gum resins often have been used in medicines. Such resins include asafetida, aloe, and the gum of the balsam tree. However, a person should consult a doctor or pharmacist before using such medicines.

Rosin is a solid resin processed from several varieties of pine trees. It is used in paints, varnishes, and printing inks. It is also applied to the bows of stringed instruments to keep the bow from slipping across the strings.

Oleoresins are resins combined with fragrant oils from plants. They are used in turpentine and tar.

Synthetic resins have largely replaced natural resins. They are a large group of chemical compounds that includes most of our common plastics. These resins may be made as fibers or films. They can also be molded into a great variety of shapes, ranging from pocket combs to automobile bodies. Manufacturers use these compounds in paints and adhesives and as coatings for cloth, paper, metal, and flooring.

Synthetic resins consist of many simple molecules linked together to form large, complex ones. Scientists call such molecules *polymers.* The term comes from the Greek words *poly,* meaning *many,* and *meros,* meaning *part.* A polymer's nature is determined by the type of molecules it contains and by the order in which they are connected. If a substance consists of long, fibrous molecules, the substance is tough but softens when heated. If the molecules form long chains with many *cross-links* (connections between the chains), the resin is hard and brittle, and it sets when heated. If few cross-links form, the resin usually is elastic. Resins with short, chainlike molecules are gummy or waxlike.

Manufacturers make synthetic resins using coal, natural gas, petroleum, wood, salt, air, and water. Complicated processes change these common materials into a variety of chemicals. The chemicals are then combined to form the complex molecules of a resin. Manufacturers often alter a synthetic resin's original properties before making it into marketable items. They do so by combining the resin with fillers, colors, lubricants, and other materials and by treating it with heat.

Scott W. Waite

Related articles in *World Book* include:

Amber	Painting (Materials and techniques)	Polymer
Balm of Gilead	Phenolic	Rosin
Lac	Plastics	Silicone
Mastic		Urea

Resistor. See **Electronics** (Passive components).

Resorcinol, *rehz AWR suh nahl,* is a compound used in making ointments, dyes, and other useful chemical compounds. It is a colorless, crystalline phenol with the chemical formula $C_6H_4(OH)_2$ and is also known as *metadihydroxybenzene.* Resorcinol is prepared by fusing benzenedisulfonic acid with sodium hydroxide.

Resorcinol is added to ointments used to treat skin diseases such as acne and eczema. Hexylresorcinol is a general antiseptic. Chemists use resorcinol to make dyes such as *eosin,* a dye used in red ink. It is also important in the preparation of resins and adhesives.

Patrice C. Bélanger

Resources, Natural. See **Natural resources.**

Respighi, *reh SPEE gee,* **Ottorino,** *oh toh REE noh* (1879-1936), was one of the most successful Italian composers of the early 1900's. His studies with the Russian composer Nikolai Rimsky-Korsakov influenced his vividly colorful orchestrations. The symphonic poems *The Fountains of Rome* (1917) and *The Pines of Rome* (1924), his most famous compositions, also show the influence of the composers Maurice Ravel of France and Richard Strauss of Germany. Respighi's interest in older music is reflected in the use of medieval Gregorian themes. Respighi was born on July 9, 1879, in Bologna. He died on April 18, 1936. Vincent McDermott

Respiration is the process by which human beings and other living things obtain and use oxygen. Except for certain microorganisms, all living things require oxygen to live. Respiration also involves the elimination of carbon dioxide, a gas produced when cells use oxygen.

Respiration may be divided into two processes: (1) organismic respiration and (2) cellular respiration. Organismic respiration is the process by which animals take in oxygen from the environment and carry it to the cells of their tissues. Carbon dioxide is carried away from the cells and delivered to the environment. In cellular respiration, oxygen is used in chemical reactions within the cells. These reactions release energy and produce carbon dioxide and water as waste products.

Organisms carry out organismic respiration in various ways, depending on their size and environment. For example, single-celled organisms, such as diatoms and amebas, exchange oxygen and carbon dioxide directly with the environment through their cell membranes. In higher animals, however, each cell lacks direct contact with the environment. A system of specialized structures or organs is required to carry out organismic respiration in these animals.

This article deals chiefly with respiration in humans and other mammals. Respiration in other animals with lungs—such as birds, reptiles, and most adult amphibians—is carried out in similar ways. These animals all exchange gas with the environment by breathing.

Breathing

Structures of breathing. The lungs are the organs of breathing. They are elastic structures in the chest cavity. Each lung contains millions of small air chambers called *alveoli.* A network of tiny blood vessels called *capillaries* lies within the walls of each alveolus.

Other important structures are the *chest wall* and the *diaphragm.* The chest wall includes the bones that form a protective cage around the chest cavity, the muscles associated with these bones, and the abdominal muscles. The diaphragm is a dome-shaped sheet of muscle that separates the chest cavity from the abdomen.

Gas enters and leaves the body through the nose and mouth. The *pharynx* (back of the nose and mouth), the *larynx* (voice box), and the *trachea* (windpipe) are the passages that connect the nose and mouth with the lungs.

The process of breathing. Breathing consists of two acts, *inspiration* (breathing in) and *expiration* (breathing out). During inspiration, also called *inhalation,* air from the atmosphere is drawn into the lungs. During expiration, or *exhalation,* gas is expelled from the lungs.

Inspiration occurs when the diaphragm and the muscles of the chest wall contract. This action lifts the ribs and makes the chest cavity longer and wider, causing the lungs to expand. The expansion of the lungs lowers the pressure in the alveoli, drawing fresh air into the lungs. Oxygen makes up about 20 percent of the volume of this fresh air. Almost all the rest of it is nitrogen. Only about 0.03 percent is carbon dioxide.

Expiration results when the diaphragm and other muscles relax, allowing the lungs to retract. This action causes the pressure of the gas in the alveoli to become greater than the atmospheric pressure. As a result, gas flows out of the lungs. Carbon dioxide makes up about 5 percent and oxygen about 15 percent of this gas.

Oxygen and carbon dioxide are exchanged between

Breathing Breathing is the process by which the body takes in oxygen from the atmosphere and releases carbon dioxide into the atmosphere. This exchange of gases takes place in the lungs. Breathing is controlled by an area of the brain called the *respiratory center.*

WORLD BOOK diagrams by Leonard E. Morgan

Fresh air
Oxygen-poor blood
Oxygen-rich blood
Respiratory center
Windpipe
Lungs
Heart
Diaphragm

Inspiration—the act of drawing air into the lungs—occurs when the inspiratory muscles contract. Contraction of the diaphragm, the chief inspiratory muscle, makes the chest volume larger and thus expands the lungs. The expansion lowers the pressure in the lungs, and air flows in from the atmosphere.

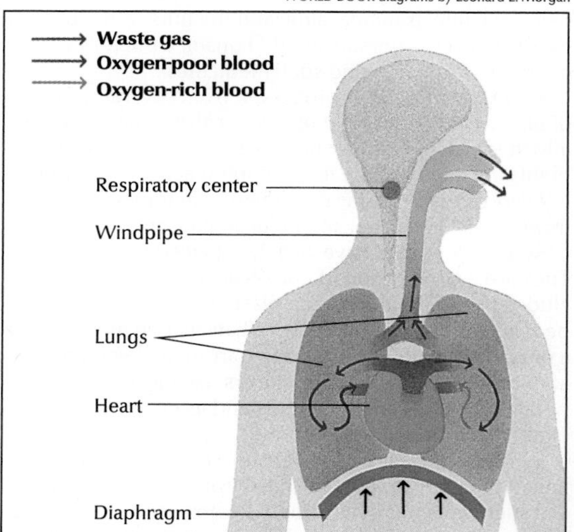

Expiration—the act of letting gas out of the lungs—takes place when the inspiratory muscles relax. The relaxation of these muscles removes the force expanding the lungs, which become smaller. Because of the smaller lung volume, gas pressure inside the lungs increases, and gas flows out into the atmosphere.

the gas and the blood in the lungs through the thin walls of capillaries in the alveoli. Blood entering these capillaries is low in oxygen and high in carbon dioxide. Oxygen that has been inhaled passes into the blood, while carbon dioxide moves from the blood into the alveoli. Between breaths, when the respiratory system is "at rest," the lungs still contain almost half the gas they are capable of holding. The exchange of oxygen and carbon dioxide continues between breaths.

Control of breathing. Breathing is regulated by the *respiratory center,* groups of nerve cells in the brain stem. Every few seconds, these cells send bursts of impulses to the muscles involved in inspiration. These signals determine the rate and depth of breathing. The average rate in adult human beings is 12 to 15 breaths per minute. Another group of special cells, called *chemoreceptors,* sense the oxygen and carbon dioxide levels in the blood and the acidity of *cerebrospinal fluid* surrounding the brain. Slight increases or decreases in carbon dioxide cause changes in the acidity of body fluids. These changes may affect various body functions. Chemoreceptors send signals to the respiratory center to adjust the rate and depth of breathing. When necessary, such as during exercise, muscles in the chest wall can be stimulated to speed up expiration. In this way, the respiratory center maintains normal levels of oxygen and acidity in the body.

Gas transport between the lungs and tissues

The circulatory system transports oxygen to body tissues and carries carbon dioxide away from them. Red blood cells play an essential role in this process. They contain *hemoglobin,* a molecule that can carry much oxygen. They also contain an enzyme called *carbonic anhydrase.* This enzyme helps change carbon dioxide into *bicarbonate ion,* a form that is easily carried in blood.

Red blood cells pick up oxygen as they pass through the lungs. The heart then pumps this oxygen-rich blood through the arteries to capillaries in the body tissues. There, oxygen is released from the hemoglobin and passes through the capillary walls to the tissue cells. At the same time, carbon dioxide produced by the tissue cells enters the blood.

Carbonic anhydrase in the red blood cells helps change most of the carbon dioxide to bicarbonate ions. Most of these bicarbonate ions move out of the red blood cells and are carried in blood plasma. The rest of the carbon dioxide entering the blood becomes associated with hemoglobin molecules or stays dissolved in plasma. When the blood reaches capillaries in the alveoli, the carbon dioxide enters the gas in the alveoli.

Cellular respiration

Respiration in cells involves a series of chemical reactions that occur in the presence of oxygen. These reactions release energy from food substances and make it available so that the cells can function.

Cells can obtain some energy without oxygen by a chemical process called *glycolysis.* Glycolysis converts molecules of *glucose* (a simple sugar) into smaller molecules of *pyruvic acid.* This action releases energy, which is captured in a compound called *adenosine triphosphate* (ATP). ATP supplies energy to all cells. However, glycolysis produces only a small amount of ATP.

Cells require oxygen to obtain large amounts of ATP. When oxygen is present in a cell, pyruvic acid enters a series of chemical reactions called the *Krebs cycle.* During the cycle, energy is captured and passed on to a series of reactions called the *electron transport chain.* As a result of these reactions, carbon dioxide and water are formed and a great deal of energy is stored as ATP.

Breathing in animals without lungs

Many animals that live in water, including fish and shellfish, have gills for exchanging oxygen and carbon dioxide with their environment. When water comes in contact with the gills, oxygen dissolved in the water moves through the thin membrane that separates the animal's blood from the water. At the same time, carbon dioxide moves from blood to water. Fish take in water through the mouth and force it out over the gills.

Other animals that lack lungs also have special ways of breathing. For example, insects have a system of tiny air tubes called *tracheae.* These tubes carry air from the environment directly to all parts of the body.

Some animals, such as amphibians, use more than one organ of respiration during their life. Frogs, for example, breathe through gills while they are tadpoles. Mature frogs breathe chiefly with lungs and also exchange gas with the environment through their skin.

Respiration in plants

In most plants, oxygen and carbon dioxide move into and out of the roots and stems through the outer layers of cells. The majority of gas exchange in plants, however, takes place through small openings in the leaves called *stomata.*

Like animal cells, plant cells obtain energy through chemical reactions that break down glucose. Green plants also produce energy through a "reverse respiration" process called *photosynthesis.* In photosynthesis, the plant uses energy from light to make glucose. During this process, the plant takes in carbon dioxide from the environment and produces oxygen as a waste product. Algae and many microbes also perform photosynthesis. Harold I. Modell and Jack Hildebrandt

Related articles in *World Book* include:

Animal (Adaptations for breathing)
Asphyxiation
Bird (The respiratory system)
Bronchodilator
Circulatory system (In respiration; diagram)
Diaphragm
Fish (Respiratory system)
Human body (The respiratory system; Anatomy of the human body)
Hyaline membrane disease
Hyperventilation
Insect (Respiratory system)
Krebs cycle
Lung
Mammal (Internal organ systems)
Nose (with diagram)
Photosynthesis
Plant (Respiration)
Sleep apnea
Spider (Respiratory system)
Spirometer
Trachea

Additional resources

Gold, Susan D. *The Respiratory System.* Enslow, 2003. Younger readers.

Kittredge, Mary. *The Respiratory System.* 1989. Reprint. Chelsea Hse., 2000.

Respirator is a machine that assists or takes over the function of breathing, or *respiration,* when a person is injured or ill and has difficulty breathing independently. The use of a respirator is called *artificial respiration* or *mechanical ventilation.* A respirator helps patients who are unable to supply enough oxygen to the body or remove waste products, such as carbon dioxide, through the lungs. There are two basic types—*positive-pressure respirators* and *negative-pressure respirators.*

Today, positive-pressure respirators are more commonly used. These devices force air through a tube into the lungs under pressure. Two main types, called *volume cycled* and *pressure cycled respirators,* precisely control the amount of air taken with each artificial breath and the pressure with which the air is forced into the lungs. After the lungs are filled, the machine cuts off, and the natural elasticity of the lungs expels the air.

Negative-pressure respirators include the *iron lung,* which encloses the entire body except for the head, and the *chest cuirass,* which covers only the chest. These machines create a vacuum that causes the patient's chest to expand, drawing air into the lungs. They then destroy the vacuum, allowing the patient's chest to contract and expel the air. Marc B. Garnick

See also **Iron lung.**

Respiratory distress syndrome is a lung condition that primarily affects premature babies. Such babies are born before the end of a normal nine-month pregnancy. The condition is related to the underdevelopment of the lungs of these infants. The air sacs of the lungs collapse, causing rapid, difficult breathing and, in many cases, death by suffocation. The condition can also occur in adults following certain illnesses, traumas, or surgery. Respiratory distress syndrome ranks as a major cause of death among premature infants.

The condition in babies is also known as *hyaline membrane disease.* The term refers to the clear, glassy membranes found in the lungs of babies that die of the disease. Many physicians believe these membranes are produced as a reaction to lung damage caused by the strain of breathing air in an immature lung.

A victim of respiratory distress syndrome has difficulty breathing within minutes after birth. Underdeveloped lungs lack a substance called *pulmonary surfactant.* This substance prevents the air sacs from collapsing. The intensive care units in many hospitals include respirators and high-humidity incubators for treating babies with respiratory distress syndrome (see **Incubator** [Incubators for babies]). Such treatment keeps many babies alive long enough for their lungs to become sufficiently developed to produce pulmonary surfactant. This development takes four to five days in most cases, but it may require several weeks. Most infants who recover have no permanent aftereffects. Scientists have developed artificial surfactants that can be given to infants soon after birth to prevent the condition.

In the early 1970's, doctors discovered a way to determine whether an unborn baby's lungs lack pulmonary surfactant. With this knowledge, a doctor may try to delay a premature birth until the lungs have developed sufficiently. If a premature birth is not delayed, a doctor can give the mother a synthetic hormone to accelerate the lung development of the fetus. Mary Ellen Avery

See also **Premature birth.**

Respiratory system. See **Respiration.**

Restaurant is a commercial establishment that serves food and beverages to the public. The first restaurants operated along roadsides, where travelers stopped to rest and to restore their energy. The word *restaurant* comes from a Latin word meaning *to restore.* Restaurants make up the largest part of the food service industry. All places that prepare food outside the home are part of this industry, including food operations in schools, hospitals, factories, and prisons.

Kinds of restaurants. People generally classify restaurants as (1) full-service or (2) fast-service.

Full-service restaurants. In most of these restaurants, customers are seated at a table and given a menu with a variety of choices. A server usually takes the customer's order and brings food to the table. The largest number of full-service restaurants are family restaurants, which offer foods at moderate prices. Full-service ethnic restaurants serve the food of a specific country, such as China, Italy, or Mexico. Fine dining restaurants offer menus that change daily or seasonally and feature somewhat unusual menu choices. Some also feature classical dishes prepared from recipes created by master chefs. Meals served in fine dining restaurants usually cost more than those served in other restaurants because of the better food quality and service provided.

Some full-service restaurants offer *home meal replacement.* Customers place their order by phone and park their cars in designated areas at the restaurant, where a server delivers their food to take home. Other full-service restaurants offer a *buffet.* Diners serve themselves various foods placed on a table. In some restaurants, the server brings the main course, and diners serve themselves from a salad bar or a dessert bar.

Fast-service restaurants provide inexpensive food and quick service. Many serve only such foods as fried chicken, hamburgers, pizza, tacos, or ice cream. Because customers have become more concerned with making healthful food choices, many fast-service restaurants also offer salads and other nutritious foods.

In addition to sit-down services, fast-service restaurants may offer *drive-through, carry-out,* and *home-delivery* services. In a drive through, customers place orders from their cars by means of a microphone outside the restaurant building and then drive to a restaurant window to pick up their food. Carry-out services enable customers to pick up prepared food and take it out of the restaurant to eat. Home-delivery service allows customers to have food delivered to their homes.

Chains and franchises. A restaurant *chain* consists of two or more restaurants owned by one person or company. Usually, all restaurants in a chain look alike and serve the same food.

In most *franchise* agreements, a restaurant owner grants another person or company the right to use the name of his or her restaurant. This right also includes use of the original owner's patented products, building designs, advertising, and trademarks. In return, the original owner receives a fee. In addition, the franchise buyer (called *franchisee)* usually pays a percentage of the restaurant's income to the original owner. The franchisee receives services from the original owner, including financial advice and training programs. In most cases, if the franchisee does not maintain standards of food quality, service, and cleanliness in the restaurant, the original owner can cancel the franchise agreement.

Career opportunities in restaurants range from part-time jobs to full-time careers. Restaurant employees include bartenders; servers; cashiers; chefs; cooks; food *prep* (preparation) workers; dishwashers; buspeople, who set and clear tables; counter workers, who serve fast food; and managers. Restaurant chains employ district and regional managers to oversee several operations. Many restaurant employees learn their jobs while working. Vocational schools and colleges prepare people for restaurant careers through food service and business courses. Cooking schools and apprentice programs provide chef's training. Restaurants also hire people trained in advertising, marketing, design, engineering, economics, and nutrition. Annette Graham

See also **McDonald's Corporation.**

Restoration (1660-1688) was the period in English history that began with the return of the royal family, the House of Stuart, to the throne. The Puritan leader Oliver Cromwell, who had ruled as Lord Protector, died in 1658. His son Richard succeeded him. Richard was a weak ruler, and civil war threatened the country. General George Monck seized control of the government and led Parliament in restoring the Stuart Prince Charles to the throne. The prince had lived in exile after the execution of his father, Charles I, in January 1649. A new Parliament, elected in 1660, restored the monarchy in the name of Charles II in May 1660.

The English welcomed Charles back to the throne. His reign was dated back to the execution of Charles I, instead of the actual year of the restoration. Parliament reestablished the Anglican Church as England's official church and returned property that had been taken from it. Parliament also passed laws against the Puritans and other religious Nonconformists. Their worship was restricted, and their political rights were limited.

During the Restoration, a reaction set in against the strict morality of the Puritans. The court of Charles II was notorious for immorality, gambling, and dueling. However, the arts, particularly poetry and drama, flourished. The theaters, which had been shut down by the Puritans, were reopened. Charles also supported the establishment of the first scientific society, the Royal Society.

The Restoration marked the return of royal power, but governmental power actually was divided between the monarch and Parliament. When King James II succeeded Charles II, James refused to maintain this division of power, and English political leaders deposed him in the Glorious Revolution of 1688. This revolution limited the king's authority and gave Parliament greater power.

Melinda S. Zook

See also **Charles II** (of England); **Cromwell, Oliver; England** (The Restoration); **English literature** (Restoration literature); **Monck, George.**

Restraining order is a court order that requires a person or group to stop a particular action defined by the court. Restraining orders can be either temporary, long-term, or permanent in nature.

The use of restraining orders is a common method for protecting victims of domestic violence. Restraining orders used in such cases are sometimes called *protection from abuse orders, protective orders,* or *orders of protection.* Such orders usually target people who are believed to have committed acts of violence or abuse. Most require that a threatening individual avoid coming into contact with the person who sought the order. Orders may also force an individual to provide financial support or to hand over to authorities any firearms the individual possesses. The violation of a restraining order may result in arrest, a fine, or imprisonment.

Courts also use restraining orders to stop other kinds of activity. For instance, a court might issue a restraining order against a company that has used a copyrighted image without permission. Courts sometimes use temporary restraining orders, also called *temporary injunctions,* to halt contested activities until a case can be heard in court. Richard J. Gelles

See also **Domestic violence.**

Résumé. See **Careers** (Getting a job; pictures).

Resurrection, *REHZ uh REHK shuhn,* is a religious belief that a dead person will return to life through the power of God. The person will be restored to life in his

The Resurrection (about 1597-1604), an oil painting on canvas; The Prado, Madrid (MAS)

The Resurrection of Jesus Christ is a central doctrine of Christianity. The artist El Greco painted a Resurrection scene of a serene Jesus rising above figures overcome by awe and fear.

or her physical body and individuality, but in perfected form. Most believers expect resurrection to occur at the end of time and be accompanied by God judging people based on the good and evil of their lives.

The belief in resurrection is important in Judaism, Christianity, and Islam. The first references in Jewish literature to the resurrection of individuals at the end of time appear in the Book of Daniel (probably composed in the 160's B.C.). Belief in final resurrection and judgment is also a major doctrine in Islam.

In Christianity, the resurrection of believers to eternal life at the Last Judgment is linked to the Resurrection of Jesus. Christians have traditionally believed that God defeated death through Jesus's Crucifixion and Resurrection. The story of Jesus's Resurrection is told in all four Gospels. Saint Paul discusses the resurrection of believers in I Corinthians 15. Resurrection is a topic of sermons in the Acts of the Apostles. During the first 300 years of Christianity, Easter Sunday gradually developed as a major celebration of Jesus's return to life.

Stanley K. Stowers

See also **Easter; Jesus Christ** (The Resurrection); **Mormons** (Church doctrines).

Resurrection plant, *REHZ uh REHK shuhn,* is the name of several different plants that can be dried but turn green again when watered. The dried stems curl into a tight ball but spread out when the plant is put into water. A common plant of this type, called the *rose of Jericho,* belongs to the mustard family. It grows from seeds and is native to northern Africa and many regions of the Middle East. The mature plant loses its leaves, curls up with its seed pods inside, and blows across the land. Another resurrection plant, also called *rose of Jericho,* is in the selaginella family. It reproduces by means of microscopic cells called *spores.* Thomas B. Croat

Scientific classification. The rose of Jericho of the mustard family, Brassicaceae or Cruciferae, is *Anastatica hierochuntica.* The rose of Jericho of the selaginella family, Selaginellaceae, is *Selaginella lepidophylla.*

Resuscitator. See Respirator.

Retailing consists of all the activities that result in the offering for sale of merchandise or services to consumers for their own use. Retailing is the final step in bringing goods to consumers. Not all retailers sell merchandise. Instead, many retailers sell services, such as automobile maintenance and repair, or the rental of tools or other items. Some retailers sell both goods and services. A clothing store, for example, may perform alterations as well as sell clothes.

Retailers sell to consumers for use, rather than to producers or other firms for resale. When an automobile manufacturer needs tires for the cars it builds, it does not buy from a retailer. But individuals who need tires for their cars do buy them from a retailer. Some retailers do not operate from a store. Instead, they sell goods by such techniques as door-to-door selling and selling through catalogs, the Internet, and the telephone.

Retailers perform several functions as part of the marketing system. They assume risk by buying merchandise without any guarantee that they will be able to sell it and by extending credit to consumers who purchase their goods. Retailers bring buyers and merchandise together by purchasing products in large lots and dividing them up for sale in smaller quantities that are more convenient for consumers. Retailers stock a variety of goods to provide customers with a wide range of choice.

Through advertising and other types of promotion, retailers help attract consumers to a producer's goods. Because of their day-to-day contact with customers, retailers are in a good position to know what consumers want. They can therefore provide producers with information on consumers' buying habits. Some retailers sell *private label merchandise*—that is, merchandise that is developed and produced specifically for their stores. Careers in retailing include such positions as salesperson, credit manager, designer, fashion coordinator, merchandise buyer, store manager, and store owner.

Retail firms can be classified in a variety of ways. Some stores are in downtown areas, but others are in shopping malls. Some firms are owned by individual proprietors, and others belong to large, national or international chains. Some retail businesses are *cooperatives* and are owned by the people who use their services (see **Cooperative**). This article discusses (1) special-

© Ugo Cei, Alamy Images

© blickwinkel, Alamy Images

A resurrection plant differs in appearance depending on whether it is dry or wet, as shown here. A dry resurrection plant has shriveled, brownish stems. After the plant receives water, the stems open and become green.

© Kenneth V. Pilon, Shutterstock

A modern supermarket is a large retail store that sells food and many other kinds of goods, such as health and beauty products, cleaning supplies, and hardware.

ty stores, (2) department stores, (3) discount stores, (4) supermarkets, (5) chain stores, (6) service retailing, and (7) nonstore retailing.

Specialty stores normally sell a single type of merchandise, such as clothing, books, or jewelry. These stores may also carry a few related lines of merchandise.

Department stores have separate departments devoted to selling a particular line of goods. Department stores usually sell perfumes, jewelry, cosmetics, and similar articles on the first floor. Such *hard goods* as furniture and appliances are sold in one section of the store, and such *soft goods* as clothes and home furnishings are sold in other areas. Many department stores also have separate areas that provide such services as gift wrapping and credit. The first department stores were established in the 1850's in Europe and in the 1860's in the United States. See **Department store.**

Discount stores operate largely on a self-service basis. They sell hard and soft goods, beauty aids, and other general merchandise at low prices. They became important after World War II ended in 1945, and they grew significantly in the late 1900's and early 2000's.

Supermarkets are large retail food stores. Supermarkets began operating in the United States during the 1930's. At first, they sold only food products. But today, many supermarkets also stock auto supplies, cleaning products, greeting cards, and other nonfood items.

Chain stores are groups of stores with a common, central management. In some chains, all the stores are owned by one company. In others, each store is owned by an individual who pays a fee for the franchise (see **Franchise**). Historians consider the Great Atlantic and Pacific Tea Company (A&P) to be the first retail chain in the United States. It began in 1859 as the Great American Tea Company. Today, many specialty stores, department stores, discount stores, and supermarkets belong to chains. See **Chain store; Walton, Sam.**

Service retailing is the selling of services. These services include hair styling, interior design, lawn care, photography, car rental, and many other activities.

Nonstore retailing is selling that does not take place in a store building. It includes such methods as selling via the internet, mail order, vending machine, telephone, door-to-door visits, and in-home events. Some retailers offer their products for sale online or in catalogs, as well as in retail shops. Other companies do not have stores but only sell their products online. Selling products online is known as *electronic commerce,* or *e-commerce.* See **Mail-order business; Telemarketing; Vending machine.**

V. Ann Paulins

See also **Sales; Sears, Roebuck and Co.; Walmart Inc.**

Retainer is a formal agreement between a lawyer and a client in which the lawyer agrees to take the client's case. This type of agreement is called a *special* retainer. There is also a *general* retainer, in which the lawyer agrees to act for the client when needed. Usually, a client retains a lawyer by paying a *retaining fee,* which may also be called a retainer. After a lawyer has entered into a retainer agreement with a client, the lawyer is legally bound to represent that client in the case. The lawyer cannot agree to represent any other party in the case. A lawyer who accepts a general retainer cannot perform services for anyone else that would be against the client's best interests. Sherman L. Cohn

Retardation. See **Intellectual disability.**

Retina. See **Eye.**

Retinol. See **Vitamin** (Vitamin A).

Retirement is the stage of life that begins when a person's working career ends. People often retire from their occupations to devote more time to hobbies, leisure, travel, and friends and family. Most people retire when they are in their 60's, though some retire earlier or later in life. Retirement age depends on a number of factors, including health, job demands, and financial situation. Many individuals who have attained great wealth retire young. Retirement practices vary in different countries.

Most retirees in industrialized nations receive money from income plans called *pensions.* The governments of many countries provide *social security* and other pension plans to provide financial security for retired workers. In addition, many retirees receive money from private pension plans offered by employers. Some people whose employers do not offer pension plans establish individual pension plans with financial institutions. In many cases, a decision to retire depends largely on the worker's eligibility for pension plans and on the amount of money the person saved while working.

During retirement, many people continue to live in the communities and homes where they lived while working. But many retirees change location, sometimes seeking warmer climates or greater recreational opportunities. Some retirees move to *retirement communities,* which are housing arrangements that provide services geared toward retirees and elderly people.

The development of retirement as a distinct life stage took place primarily in the 1900's. Before then, people usually worked until they were physically unable to work, or until they died. In 1935, the United States Congress passed the Social Security Act, which provided a retirement income to workers in commerce and industry. By 1956, the act had expanded to cover most people with work experience who retired. In Canada, the Old Age Security program began providing retirement funds in 1952, and the Canada Pension Plan did so in 1966. Also in the mid-1900's, several organizations began addressing the specific needs of retirees and elderly people. The American Association of Retired Persons (now AARP) was founded in the United States in 1958.

For many years, people viewed retirement as a period for a person to withdraw from the workplace and the community in preparation for death. Today, however, people increasingly view retirement as a time to pursue interests and activities, and as a period of intellectual growth. Most retirees maintain their preretirement levels of activity for many years. Many join church groups, senior citizens' clubs, and other organizations for social and recreational activities. Some retirees begin new careers after retiring from previous ones. Many others work part-time. Amy Mehraban Pienta

See also **AARP; Old age; Pension; Pension Benefit Guaranty Corporation; Social security.**

Retrieval system. See **Information retrieval.**

Retriever, *rih TREE vuhr,* is a hunting dog trained to *retrieve* (find and bring back) game that has been shot. The dog's coat protects it from water and cold. Retrievers are good swimmers and have a fine sense of smell. They take training easily. Dog breeders in the United States classify retrievers as sporting dogs. Recognized retriever breeds include the Chesapeake Bay retriever, the curly-coated retriever, the flat-coated retriever, the golden retriever, the Labrador retriever, and the Nova Scotia duck tolling retriever. Each breed has an article in *World Book.* Critically reviewed by the American Kennel Club

See also **Dog** (pictures; table: Sporting group).

© Tomislav Stajduhar, Shutterstock

The Labrador retriever can be trained to bring back game.

Retrovirus is a type of virus whose genetic material consists of RNA (ribonucleic acid). The genetic material of most viruses is made up of DNA (deoxyribonucleic acid), a molecule closely related to RNA. All viruses must infect a living *host* cell to reproduce.

After they enter a host cell, retroviruses use an enzyme called *reverse transcriptase* to make DNA copies of their RNA. This DNA is then inserted into the host cell's DNA. There, the DNA begins the process of producing proteins that are used to make new copies of the retrovirus.

Several different kinds of retroviruses infect many organisms. One of the most important for humans is the human immunodeficiency virus (HIV), the virus that causes AIDS. HIV is part of a larger group of retroviruses called *lentiviruses.* Following infection, such viruses can remain in the body for a long time before causing symptoms of disease.

Scientists have developed medications called *antiretroviral drugs* to treat diseases caused by retroviruses, including HIV. Many of these drugs work by *inhibiting* (blocking) enzymes, such as reverse transcriptase or protease, that retroviruses need to reproduce inside a host cell. Amanda H. Corbett

See also **AIDS; Virus.**

Rett syndrome, often abbreviated RS and also called RTT, is a serious developmental disorder that appears almost exclusively in girls and persists throughout life. Children with RS progressively lose communication skills and purposeful hand movements; develop involuntary repetitive hand movements, such as hand wringing, hand clapping, or finger rubbing; and have *cognitive* (intellectual) disabilities. Other symptoms include *apraxia* (the inability to perform certain voluntary movements), seizures, breathing difficulties, slowed growth, difficulty crawling or walking, teeth grinding, and sleep disorders. Scientists estimate that RS occurs in about 1 of every 10,000 to 23,000 girls born worldwide.

Andreas Rett, an Austrian physician, first described RS in 1966. However, medical professionals did not widely recognize the syndrome until Bengt Hagberg, a Swedish physician, published a description in 1983.

Symptoms. For most children with RS, early growth and development appear normal after birth. By 6 to 18 months of age, however, language and communication skills begin to decline. During this time, the head grows more slowly than normal, and the child eventually loses voluntary, purposeful use of the hands. Repetitive patterns of hand movements develop. Children with RS may have intellectual disabilities. However, many RS children are unable to speak or to move well, making it difficult for physicians to assess their intellectual abilities. Some girls with RS exhibit behaviors similar to those seen in the disorder autism. See **Autism.**

Cause. Medical researchers have discovered that RS is caused by a *mutation* (change) in a gene called *MECP2.* The *MECP2* gene appears on the X chromosome, one of the two chromosomes that determine a person's sex. The other is the Y chromosome. Males have one X chromosome and one Y chromosome, and females have two X chromosomes. Physicians use tests to identify mutations of the *MECP2* gene. However, a diagnosis of RS is determined by symptoms, rather than the presence of the mutation.

Scientists know the *MECP2* gene regulates the activity of other genes. A mutation in this gene causes this regulatory function to fail, enabling the other genes to function abnormally. Scientists think that the mutation damages the *MECP2* gene's ability to regulate genes involved in brain development.

RS occurs only rarely in males. Because males have only one X chromosome, the *MECP2* mutation harms them even more severely than it does females. Females have a normal copy of the gene on one X chromosome to help counteract the effects of the abnormal copy. Boys born with the mutated gene have no such protection and usually die shortly after birth.

Treatment. Physicians have yet to develop a specific treatment or cure for RS, but they may prescribe drugs to help control many of its symptoms. Physical therapy aimed at increasing mobility and reducing apraxia can also help people with RS. Most girls with RS require assistance for most activities of daily living, but they can often learn to do some things for themselves. Some RS children can use electronic devices to communicate. With assistance, some children with RS can take part in social, educational, and recreational activities. Scientists are studying the biology of RS in the hope of developing specific treatments for the disorder.

Kathy Hunter, Valerie Owen, and Alan Percy

Return, Law of. See **Citizenship** (Naturalization); **Immigration** (Asia).

Réunion, *ree YOON yuhn* or *ray oon YAWN,* is an island in the Indian Ocean, about 400 miles (640 kilometers) east of Madagascar (see **Indian Ocean** [map]). Of volcanic origin, it covers 969 square miles (2,510 square kilometers). The population of 908,000 consists largely of French Creoles, with some Indians and Chinese. Saint-Denis (pop. 147,920) is the capital. The island's main product is sugar. Farmers also grow tropical fruits and vanilla, and flowers for perfume.

The French took possession of the island in 1642 and named it Bourbon. In 1848, the name was changed to Réunion. Since 1946, it has been an overseas department of France. In 1974, it also became a region of France. French regions are administrative divisions that roughly resemble states in the United States, and each region has one or more departments. Local affairs in Réunion are handled by two elected bodies, a general council and a regional council. Larry W. Bowman

Reuter, *ROY tuhr,* **Baron de** (1816-1899), founded Reuters (now Thomson Reuters), one of the world's leading news services. Reuters was one of the first news services to furnish financial, political, and general news to European newspapers.

In 1849, Reuter began a service that used pigeons to carry stock quotations between the terminal points of the telegraph lines in Belgium and Germany. He later settled in London and established Reuters in 1851 to relay European financial news. He entered the general news business in 1858. Reuter started a cooperative effort among several news agencies that expanded the worldwide distribution of news. He directed the operations of Reuters until his retirement in 1878.

Reuter's full name was Paul Julius Reuter. He was also called Baron von Reuter. He was born in Kassel, Germany, on July 21, 1816. He died in Nice, France, on Feb. 25, 1899. See also **Thomson Reuters.** Robert K. Stewart

Reuters. See **Thomson Reuters.**

Revelation, *REHV uh LAY shuhn,* **Book of,** is the last book of the New Testament. It is also called the Apocalypse, from a Greek word translated as *revelation.* The book was written by a man named John while he was in exile on the island of Patmos in the Aegean Sea, probably about A.D. 95. Many scholars believe that this was not the apostle John, but another person of that name.

The Book of Revelation is an example of *apocalyptic literature.* Another example of this type of literature in the Bible appears in the Book of Daniel. Like other apocalyptic literature, Revelation is addressed to people undergoing persecution. It encourages them to withstand the persecution, principally by predicting the rapidly approaching end of the world, when God will rescue them by destroying the powers of evil. The author presented this prediction in symbolic language. To the original readers of the book, the meaning of these symbols was clear. To modern readers, the symbols require close study to understand their meaning. Terrance D. Callan

See also **Bible** (Revelation); **Four Horsemen of the Apocalypse.**

Revels, Hiram Rhodes (1822-1901), was the first African American to serve in the United States Senate. He was a Republican senator from Mississippi in 1870 and 1871. He completed the unfinished term of Jefferson Davis, the former president of the Confederacy. In the Senate, Revels supported civil rights for blacks.

Library of Congress
Hiram Revels

Revels was born free on Sept. 1, 1822, in Fayetteville, North Carolina. He was educated at seminaries in Indiana and Ohio and attended Knox College. In 1845, he became a minister of the African Methodist Episcopal Church. Revels helped establish black churches and schools in the Midwest and the South. During the American Civil War (1861-1865), he recruited black soldiers for the Union Army. In 1866, he settled in Natchez, Mississippi. He became an alderman and, later, a state senator. After leaving the U.S. Senate, he became president of Alcorn University (now Alcorn State University). Revels died on Jan. 16, 1901. Nancy J. Weiss

Revenue, Internal. See **Internal revenue.**

Revere, Paul (1734-1818), an American craftsman and patriot, became famous for his contributions during the American Revolution (1775-1783). In April 1775, he rode on horseback from Boston to Lexington, Massachusetts, carrying news of the approach of the British. He warned the patriot leaders Samuel Adams and John Hancock of their danger and called the citizens of the countryside to arms. His exploit inspired Henry Wadsworth Longfellow's "Paul Revere's Ride" (1861), one of the most popular

Oil painting on canvas by John Singleton Copley (about 1769); Museum of Fine Arts, Boston, gift of Joseph W. Revere, William B. Revere, and Edward H. R. Revere

Paul Revere was a noted American craftsman who won fame for his patriotic activities at the time of the American Revolution.

Templeman Tea Service; The Minneapolis Institute of Arts, Minneapolis, Minnesota, gift of Mr. and Mrs. James Ford Bell

A silver tea set made by Paul Revere in 1792 featured decorated grooves on, *left to right,* a teapot, a sugar bowl, a creamer, and a tea caddy. The set included sugar tongs and a tea scoop, *foreground.* The noted silversmith's *touchmark,* or identifying mark, is enlarged at the right.

Museum of Fine Arts, Boston

poems in American literature. Revere made other contributions during the American Revolution and aided the industrial growth of the United States.

His early life. Revere was born in Boston. No official records exist of his birth, only of his baptism. It is believed he was born in December 1734. He was baptized on Jan. 1, 1735 (Dec. 22, 1734, on the Old Style Calendar then in use; see **Calendar**).

Revere was the son of a silversmith. His family was of French Protestant, or Huguenot, descent. His father changed the family name from Rivoire "merely on account that the Bumpkins should pronounce it easier." Paul studied at North Writing School in Boston and learned the silversmith's trade. In 1756, he served briefly in the French and Indian War. Then he married Sarah Orne and took over his father's silversmith business.

The patriot. Revere soon became interested in supporting American liberty. He engraved many political cartoons that received wide attention. As the leader of the Boston craftworkers, he cooperated closely with revolutionary leaders. Revere took part in the Boston Tea Party on Dec. 16, 1773. Revere also served as a special messenger for the Boston patriots. He was so familiar to the British in this role that his name appeared in London journals before his famous ride. Two days before the ride took place, he galloped to Concord to warn patriots there to move their military supplies.

Paul Revere's ride. In 1775, King George III instructed General Thomas Gage, the British commander in chief in North America, to enforce order among the rebellious colonists. Gage sent 700 troops from Boston under Lieutenant Colonel Francis Smith to seize or destroy the supplies at Concord. Smith and his soldiers were also ordered to arrest Samuel Adams and John Hancock for treason.

Smith assembled his force on Boston Common on the evening of April 18. His orders were secret, but the patriots knew about them. Patriot leader Joseph Warren sent Revere and William Dawes by separate routes to warn Adams and Hancock in Lexington and the patriots in Concord. Revere arranged for a signal to be flashed from the steeple of Boston's Old North Church. Two lanterns would mean the British were coming by water, and one, by land. Contrary to Longfellow's account, the signal was not sent to Revere. Instead, Revere directed that the signal be sent to friends in Charlestown.

Revere left Boston at about 10 p.m. and arrived in Lexington about midnight, riding a borrowed horse. Shortly after 1 a.m., Revere, William Dawes, and Samuel Prescott left for Concord. A British patrol surprised them on their way. Prescott and Dawes escaped, but Revere was captured. Only Prescott got through to Concord. The British released Revere and let him return to Lexington without his horse. There, he joined Adams and Hancock. The men fled to safety in Burlington, but Revere returned to Lexington to rescue valuable papers in Hancock's trunk. When the British arrived in Lexington on April 19, they found the minutemen waiting.

Revolutionary soldier. From 1776 to 1779, Revere commanded a garrison at Castle William in Boston Harbor. In 1779, he commanded artillery in the disastrous Penobscot Expedition, an attempt to regain control of British-held territory in Maine. The expedition cost Massachusetts much of its trading fleet. Revere was accused of cowardice and insubordination, but a court-martial cleared him of wrongdoing in 1782.

Craftsman and industrialist. When the war started, Revere visited a gunpowder mill near Philadelphia. He then supplied plans, based on this visit, for a gunpowder mill at Canton, Massachusetts. Historians believe he probably oversaw the mill's construction. He also engraved and printed paper currency for Massachusetts, and he made the state seal still used by Massachusetts.

During and after the war, Revere continued his silversmith trade in Boston. Craftworkers still copy the graceful lines of his work. He marked his own work with the name *Revere* in a rectangle or with the initials *P.R.* He cast cannon and bells in bronze, and many of his bells are still used in New England. He made the copper fittings for the frigate U.S.S. *Constitution* ("Old Ironsides").

Revere was the first American to discover the process of rolling sheet copper, and he built the first successful copper-rolling mill in the United States. Revere died on May 10, 1818. Critically reviewed by the Paul Revere House

Related articles in *World Book* include:

Boston (illustration: Boston's Freedom Trail)
Boston Massacre (picture)
Dawes, William
Harvard University (picture)
Prescott, Samuel
Revolution, American (Lexington and Concord)

Reversing Falls of Saint John is a waterfall in the Saint John River at Saint John, New Brunswick, just before the river enters the Bay of Fundy. The name refers to the fact that the river's current sometimes runs backward up the falls.

The waterfall is formed as the river valley becomes a narrow gorge. At low tide, the river falls 14 feet (3.7 meters) in going through this gorge to the harbor below. At high tide, a *bore* (rushing tide) sweeps in from the bay and makes the level of the harbor water 14 feet (3.7 meters) higher than the level of the river. The current then flows upstream and up over the falls. T. W. Acheson

Revivalism is an approach to religion that emphasizes individual religious experience rather than church doctrines. In the United States, revivalism has been associated with frontier camp meetings, outdoor religious services, and fervent, emotional forms of preaching.

Periods of revivalism occurred in Europe among German Pietists and English Methodists in the 1700's. The first major U.S. revival movement was the Great Awakening, which began in the 1730's. This movement took place primarily within Congregational and Presbyterian denominations along the East Coast (see **Great Awakening**). A second Great Awakening occurred from about 1790 to about 1820. During the mid-1800's, the Baptists and Methodists were the chief denominations that used revivalistic methods. The leading revivalists of this period included Peter Cartwright and Charles G. Finney.

During the late 1800's and early 1900's, many preachers, including Dwight L. Moody and Billy Sunday, brought frontier revivalism to growing U.S. cities. In the late 1900's, the revivalist tradition was carried on by such preachers as Billy Graham. Charles H. Lippy

See also **Graham, Billy; Moody, Dwight L.; Sunday, Billy; Tennent, William.**

Revolution is a fundamental change in the character of a nation's government, political system, or way of life. Political revolutions can lead to the overthrow of a nation's leaders, the formation of a new kind of government, or even the establishment of a new nation. Revolutions may also occur in other areas, such as cultural, economic, and social activities. Revolutionary changes may be achieved through violent or nonviolent means. People who work to replace an old system with a new one are often called *revolutionaries* or *revolutionists.*

A revolution may dramatically change various ways of life in a country. For example, the Russian Revolution of 1917 not only deposed the czar but also began major social changes, such as the elimination of private property. The American Revolution (1775-1783) changed a political system without causing basic social changes.

Many revolutions involve citizen uprisings, but others occur after a legal transfer of power within the existing system. For example, Adolf Hitler took power as dictator of Germany after the country's president had appointed him chancellor. Some movements that appear to be revolutions only change a country's rulers, without making major changes in political systems. Political scientists call such movements *rebellions* rather than revolutions.

Features of revolution. Many revolutions involve rioting, widespread violence, and *guerrilla warfare.* Guerrilla warfare includes ambushes, assassinations, sabotage, and other terrorist methods. But revolutionary changes may also result from nonviolent acts, such as protests, demonstrations, and *civil disobedience*—that is, the deliberate and public refusal to obey certain laws. Many people in India, led by Mohandas K. Gandhi, used various nonviolent methods to free themselves from British rule. India became independent in 1947.

Political revolutions have sometimes led to wars between nations. Some countries have used military force to try to overturn another country's revolution, or to prevent the revolution from spreading to other countries. After the Russian Revolution, for example, the United States and the United Kingdom backed a war against Russia's new Communist government. Other countries have waged war to take advantage of instability caused by a revolution in another country. For instance, Iraq invaded Iran following Iran's Islamic revolution in 1979.

Some of history's most widespread revolutions did not have political beginnings. The Industrial Revolution of the 1700's and early 1800's was a period of rapid industrialization that changed the basic nature of Western society from rural to urban (see **Industrial Revolution**). Technological advances since the late 1800's—such as the telephone and the computer—have also caused revolutions in industry and everyday life.

Causes of revolution. Most political revolutions occur because of widespread dissatisfaction with a system. Poverty and injustice under cruel, corrupt, or incapable rulers may contribute. But in most cases, social problems alone do not cause revolutions. Revolutions need leaders who can use unsatisfactory conditions to unite people under a program that promises improvements.

Many revolutions occur after rulers begin to yield to demands from rivals. Such compromises, or rapidly improving social conditions, create a *revolution of rising expectations* as people begin to hope for a better life. If changes do not meet their expectations, the people lose faith in their rulers and start listening to revolutionaries. The French Revolution of 1789 and the Russian Revolution both began after the rulers agreed to the people's demands for representative assemblies. Bruce Cronin

Related articles in *World Book* include:

Coup d'état
French Revolution
Guerrilla warfare
Junta
Mexican Revolution of 1910
Radicalism
Revolution, American
Revolution of 1848
Russia (History)
Terrorism

The Battle of Lexington, 19th April 1775 (1910) oil on canvas by William Barnes Wollen; National Army Museum, London (© Bridgeman Art Library/Getty Images)

The American Revolution began in 1775 when colonial militias clashed with British redcoats at Lexington, Massachusetts. No one knows who fired the first shot. The conflict, which arose from colonial resistance to British tax laws, led to American self-government based on individual liberty.

Revolution, American

Revolution, American (1775-1783), led to the birth of a new nation—the United States. The revolution caused a military conflict called the Revolutionary War in America. The war was fought between Britain (now also called the United Kingdom) and its 13 colonies that lay along the Atlantic Ocean in North America. The war began on April 19, 1775, when British soldiers and American patriots clashed at Lexington, Massachusetts, and at nearby Concord. The war lasted eight years. On Sept. 3, 1783, Britain signed the Treaty of Paris, by which it recognized the independence of the United States. The revolution stood as an example to peoples in many lands who later fought to gain their freedom. In 1836, the American author Ralph Waldo Emerson referred to the first shot fired by the patriots at Concord as "the shot heard round the world."

Tension had been building between Britain and the American Colonies for more than 10 years before the Revolutionary War began. Starting in the mid-1760's, the British government passed a series of laws to increase its control over the colonies. Americans had grown used to a large measure of self-government. They strongly resisted the new laws, especially tax laws. Fierce debate developed over the British Parliament's right to tax the colonies without their consent.

The disobedience of the American Colonies angered the British government. In 1775, Britain's Parliament declared Massachusetts—the site of much protest—to be in rebellion. The British government ordered its troops in Boston to take swift action against the rebels. The Revolutionary War broke out soon afterward.

The American Colonies were unprepared for war. They lacked a central government, an army, and a navy. Delegates from the colonies formed the Continental Congress, which took on the duties of a national government. The Congress directed the war effort and voted to organize an army and a navy. It appointed George Washington commander in chief of the colonial army, called the Continental Army. Washington was a wealthy Virginia landowner and former militia officer. On July 4, 1776—more than a year after the beginning of the Revolutionary War in America—the Congress adopted the Declaration of Independence. In that document, the colonies declared their freedom from British rule.

Britain launched a huge land and sea effort to crush the revolution. The British had a far larger and better-trained army than did the Americans. But Britain had to transport and supply its army across the Atlantic Ocean and pacify a vast territory. Although the British won many battles, they gained little from their victories. The American patriots were able to form new forces and fight on.

In 1777, the Americans won an important victory at Saratoga, New York. The victory convinced France that the Americans could win the war. As a result, France went to war against Britain, its long-time enemy. France provided the Americans with the money and military equipment they badly needed to fight the war.

In October 1781, a large British force surrendered to Washington at Yorktown, Virginia. That defeat led the British government to begin peace talks with the Americans. The Treaty of Paris formally ended the war in 1783.

This article will trace the background and causes of the American Revolution; the beginning of the Revolutionary War; the conduct of the war, including weapons and tactics and how the war was financed; the war in the North, West, and South; the end of the war; and the results of the revolution.

Outline

Background and causes of the revolution

Britain's power in North America was at its height in 1763, only 12 years before the Revolutionary War began. Britain had just defeated France in the French and Indian War (1754-1763). The treaty that ended the war gave Britain almost all of France's territory in North America. That territory stretched from the Appalachian Mountains in the east to the Mississippi River and included much of Canada. Most American colonists took pride in being part of the British Empire, which was then the world's most powerful empire.

Yet in 1775, the American Colonies rebelled against British authority. The dramatic turnabout resulted from disagreements over the proper relationship between Britain and its colonies. Britain expected the colonists to obey the British Parliament "in all cases whatsoever." The colonists, on the other hand, believed that there were limits to Parliament's power. They believed they had certain rights that Britain should respect. Each side refused to yield, which led to a military showdown.

Life in the American Colonies during the 1700's differed in important ways from life in the most advanced European nations. Well-to-do merchants and planters formed a small upper class, or *gentry,* in the seaboard colonies, but they lacked the wealth and power of the English aristocracy. A large middle class consisted mainly of farmers who owned their land, of shopkeepers, and of craftworkers. Unskilled workers and farmers who rented their land ranked among the poor, or "lower sort." In addition, by the mid-1700's, about 20 percent of the colonists were enslaved people of African descent. Enslaved people lived in all the mainland colonies, though they were most numerous in the South.

Farming was by far the main occupation in the American Colonies. It provided a living for nearly 90 percent of the people. Only about 10 percent of the colonists lived in towns or cities. Philadelphia, with about 40,000 people, was the largest American city in 1775. The next largest cities were New York City and Boston.

The opportunity to own land had drawn many settlers to the American Colonies. Owning property gave a person a chance to get ahead. It could also give men the right to vote, though some colonies denied that right to Roman Catholics and Jews. All colonies denied it to Black people and most women. In each colony, voters elected representatives to a legislature. Colonial legislatures passed laws and could tax the people. But the governor of a colony could veto any laws passed by the legislature. The king appointed the governor in most colonies.

Britain expected the American Colonies to serve its economic interests, and it regulated colonial trade. In general, the colonists accepted British regulations. For example, they agreed not to manufacture goods that would compete with British products.

British policy changes. Britain had largely neglected the American Colonies while it fought France in a series

Important dates in the Revolutionary War

1775

April 19 Minutemen and redcoats clashed at Lexington and Concord.
June 15 The Congress named George Washington commander in chief of the Continental Army.
June 17 The British drove the Americans from Breed's Hill in the Battle of Bunker Hill.

1776

Feb. 27 The patriots defeated the Loyalists at Moore's Creek Bridge.
March 17 The British evacuated Boston.
July 4 The Declaration of Independence was adopted.
Aug. 27 The redcoats defeated the patriots on Long Island.
Sept. 15 The British occupied New York City.
Dec. 26 Washington mounted a surprise attack on Hessian troops at Trenton.

1777

Jan. 3 Washington gained a victory at Princeton.
Aug. 6 Loyalists and Native Americans forced the patriots back at Oriskany but then withdrew.
Aug. 16 The patriots crushed the Hessians near Bennington.
Sept. 11 The British won the Battle of Brandywine.
Sept. 19 Gates's forces checked Burgoyne's army in the First Battle of Freeman's Farm.
Sept. 26 The British occupied Philadelphia.
Oct. 4 Washington's forces met defeat in the Battle of Germantown.
Oct. 7 The patriots defeated the British in the Second Battle of Freeman's Farm.
Oct. 17 Burgoyne surrendered at Saratoga.
Dec. 19 Washington's army retired to winter quarters at Valley Forge.

1778

Feb. 6 The United States and France signed an alliance.
June 28 The Battle of Monmouth ended in a draw.
Dec. 29 The redcoats took Savannah.

1779

Feb. 25 British defenders of Vincennes surrendered to George Rogers Clark.
June 21 Spain declared war on Britain.
Sept. 23 John Paul Jones's ship, the *Bonhomme Richard,* captured the British ship *Serapis.*

1780

May 12 Charleston fell after a British siege.
Aug. 16 The British defeated the Americans at Camden.
Oct. 7 Americans stormed the Loyalist positions on Kings Mountain.

1781

Jan. 17 The patriots won a victory at Cowpens.
March 15 Cornwallis clashed with Greene at Guilford Courthouse.
Sept. 5 A French fleet inflicted great damage on a British naval force at Chesapeake Bay.
Oct. 19 Cornwallis's forces surrendered at Yorktown.

1782

March 20 King George's chief minister, Lord North, resigned.
Nov. 30 The Americans and British signed a preliminary peace treaty in Paris.

1783

April 15 Congress ratified the preliminary peace treaty.
Sept. 3 The United States and Britain signed the final peace treaty in Paris.

of wars during the 1700's. But after the French and Indian War ended in 1763, the British government sought to tighten its control over the colonies. The war had drained Britain's treasury and left a huge debt. Most British leaders did not expect the colonists to help pay off the debt. However, Britain planned to station troops in America to defend the colonies' western frontier. It wanted the colonists to help pay for those troops.

Relations between the colonies and the mother country steadily worsened from 1763 to 1775. During that time, Parliament passed a number of laws to increase Britain's income from the colonies. The colonists reacted angrily. They lived far from Britain and had grown increasingly self-reliant. Many Americans believed that the new British policies threatened their freedom. In late 1774, Britain's King George III declared, "The die is now cast, the colonies must either submit or triumph." A few months later, the Revolutionary War broke out.

The Proclamation of 1763. Before the French and Indian War, France had helped prevent colonists from settling on *Indigenous* (native) hunting lands west of the Appalachians. But settlers began crossing the frontier soon after Britain defeated France. In the spring of 1763, an Ottawa chief named Pontiac began an uprising in which tribes attacked many western forts the British had taken from the French. Hundreds of colonists along the western frontier were killed.

Britain feared a long and bloody war, which it could not afford. To prevent future uprisings, King George issued the Proclamation of 1763. The document reserved lands west of the Appalachians for Native Americans and forbade white settlements there. Britain sent soldiers to guard the frontier and keep settlers out.

The Proclamation of 1763 angered many colonists. Some wealthy Americans hoped to profit from the purchase of Western lands. Poorer colonists saw the lands as an opportunity to escape poverty. Colonists living on the frontier, or the "backcountry," resisted British efforts to enforce the Proclamation of 1763.

The Sugar Act. George Grenville became King George's chief Cabinet minister in 1763. Grenville was determined to increase Britain's income from the American Colonies. At his urging, Parliament passed the Revenue Act of 1764, also known as the Sugar Act. The act placed a threepenny tax on each gallon (3.8 liters) of molasses entering the colonies from ports outside the British Empire. Several Northern colonies had thriving rum industries that depended on imported molasses. Rum distillers angrily protested that the tax would eat up their profits. In 1766, Parliament reduced the tax on molasses to a penny a gallon.

The Quartering and Stamp acts were passed by Parliament in 1765, again with Grenville's support. The laws were intended to make the colonists pay part of the cost of stationing British troops in America. The Quartering Act ordered the colonies to supply the soldiers with living quarters, fuel, candles, and cider or beer. The Stamp Act required the colonists to buy tax stamps for newspapers, playing cards, diplomas, and various legal documents.

Most colonies half-heartedly obeyed the Quartering Act, often providing fewer supplies than requested. But the Stamp Act resulted in riots. Angry colonists refused to allow the tax stamps to be sold. Merchants in port cities agreed not to order British goods until Parliament abolished the act.

In October 1765, delegates from nine colonies met in New York City and prepared a statement protesting the

Stamp Act. The objections of that so-called Stamp Act Congress stemmed from the colonists' belief that the right of taxation belonged only to the people and their elected representatives. The delegates argued that Parliament had no power to tax the colonies because the colonies had no representatives in Parliament. The meeting of the Stamp Act Congress was the first united action by the colonies against an unpopular British law.

Parliament repealed the Stamp Act in 1766. But at the same time, it passed the Declaratory Act, which stated that the king and Parliament had full legislative authority over the colonies in all matters.

The Townshend Acts. Many members of the British government disliked giving in to the disobedient colonies over the Stamp Act. They included Chancellor of the Exchequer Charles Townshend, who developed a new plan for raising money from the colonies. Townshend convinced Parliament that the colonists would find a *duty* (tax on imported goods) more agreeable than the Stamp Act. Whereas the Stamp Act had taxed the colonists directly, the government would collect duties only from importers. In 1767, Parliament passed the Townshend Acts. One act placed duties on glass, lead, paint, paper, and tea imported into the colonies. Another act set up a customs agency in Boston to collect the duties efficiently.

The Townshend Acts led to renewed protests in the colonies. The colonists accepted Britain's right to regulate their trade. But they argued that the Townshend duties were taxes in disguise. To protest the duties, Americans stopped buying British goods. In 1770, Parliament withdrew all the Townshend duties except the one on tea. It kept the tea duty to demonstrate its right to tax the colonies.

Protests against what the colonists called "taxation without representation" were especially violent in Boston. In 1768, British officials sent soldiers to police Boston and to protect the city's customs collectors. Nearly 1,000 soldiers entered the city on October 1, and more soon followed. Sending the soldiers made matters worse. On March 5, 1770, soldiers and townspeople clashed in a street fight. During the fight, frightened British soldiers fired into a crowd of rioters. Five men died, including a Black patriot named Crispus Attucks. Patriots called the killing of the five colonists "the Boston Massacre" and spread news of it to turn public opinion in America against Britain.

Massachusetts Historical Society

A tax stamp placed on certain items showed that colonists had paid taxes on them.

In 1772, Boston political leaders formed the Committee of Correspondence to explain to other communities by letters and other means how British actions threatened American liberties. Other committees of correspondence soon sprang up throughout the colonies. The committees helped unite the colonies in their growing struggle with the British government.

The Tea Act. To avoid paying the Townshend duty on tea, colonial merchants smuggled in tea from the Netherlands. A British trading company called the East India Company had been the chief source of tea for the colonies. The smuggling hurt the company financially, and it asked Parliament for help. In 1773, Parliament passed the Tea Act, which enabled the East India Company to sell its tea below the price of smuggled tea. Lord North, who had become the king's chief minister in 1770, believed that the colonists would buy the cheaper British tea and thereby acknowledge Parliament's right

Detail of *The Boston Massacre, 5th March 1770* (1770) engraving by Paul Revere; Worcester Art Museum (© Bridgeman Art Library/SuperStock)

The Boston Massacre took place on March 5, 1770, when British soldiers fired into a mob, killing five Americans. Patriot propaganda like this engraving by Paul Revere called the incident a massacre to stir up feeling against the British government. Hundreds of British soldiers had come to Boston two years earlier to keep order and protect the city's customs collectors.

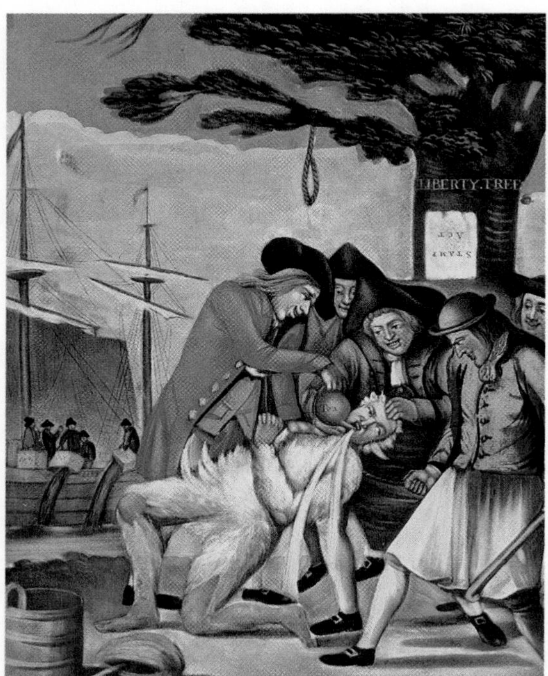

Detail of *The Bostonians Paying the Excise Man* (1774), a color engraving by an unknown artist; John Carter Brown Library at Brown University, Providence, Rhode Island

British propaganda showed unruly colonists forcing a tax collector they had tarred and feathered to drink scalding tea. The colonists in the background are dumping British tea overboard.

to tax them. In the process, the colonists would lose their argument against taxation without representation.

Samuel Adams, a Boston patriot, led the resistance to the Tea Act. On the evening of Dec. 16, 1773, Bostonians disguised as Native Americans raided British ships docked in Boston Harbor and dumped their cargoes of tea overboard. The so-called Boston Tea Party enraged King George and Lord North and the king's other ministers. They wanted the Bostonians punished as a warning to all colonists not to challenge British authority.

The Intolerable Acts. Britain responded to the Boston Tea Party in 1774 by passing several laws that became known in America as the Intolerable Acts. One law closed Boston Harbor and stated that it would reopen only after Bostonians paid for the tea and showed proper respect for British authority. Another law restricted the activities of the Massachusetts legislature and gave added powers to the governor of Massachusetts. Those powers in effect made him a dictator. King George named Lieutenant General Thomas Gage, the commander of British forces in North America, the new governor of Massachusetts. Gage was sent to Boston with troops.

Committees of correspondence throughout the colonies warned citizens that Britain could also disband their legislatures and take away their political rights. Several committees called for a convention of delegates from the colonies to organize resistance to the Intolerable Acts. The convention was later called the Continental Congress.

The First Continental Congress met in Philadelphia from Sept. 5 to Oct. 26, 1774, to protest the Intolerable Acts. Representatives attended from all the colonies except Georgia. The leaders included Samuel Adams and John Adams of Massachusetts and George Washington and Patrick Henry of Virginia. The Congress voted to cut off colonial trade with Britain unless Parliament abolished certain laws and taxes, including the Intolerable Acts. It also approved resolutions advising the colonies to begin training their citizens for war.

None of the delegates to the First Continental Congress called for independence from Britain. Instead, the delegates hoped that the colonies would regain the rights Parliament had taken away. The Congress agreed to hold another Continental Congress in May 1775 if Britain did not change its policies before that time.

The beginning of the war

Fighting broke out between American patriots and British soldiers in April 1775. The Americans were defended at first by the members of their citizen army, the *militia.* The militia came out to fight when the British neared their homes. The patriots soon established a regular military force known as the Continental Army. Britain depended chiefly on professional soldiers who had enlisted for long terms. The British soldiers were called *redcoats* because they wore bright red jackets.

The patriots won several victories in New England, the two Chesapeake colonies of Virginia and Maryland, and the Southern colonies during the early months of the Revolutionary War. As the fighting spread, many Americans became convinced of the need to cut their ties with Britain.

Lexington and Concord. In February 1775, Parliament declared that Massachusetts was in open rebellion. This declaration made it legal for British troops to treat troublesome colonists as rebels and shoot them on sight. The king and his ministers hoped to avoid a war by crushing the disorder in Boston. In April, General Gage received secret orders from the British government to take military action against the Massachusetts troublemakers and arrest their principal leaders.

Boston patriots learned about the secret orders be-

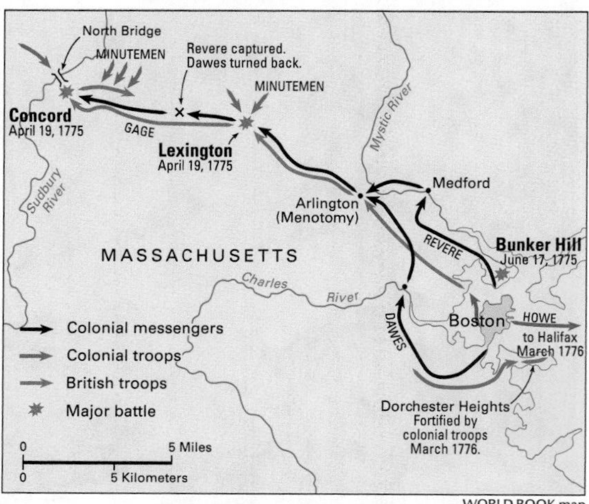

WORLD BOOK map

Clashes at Lexington and Concord opened the Revolutionary War. In March 1776, the British evacuated Boston. This map locates major battles and troop movements in and around Boston.

fore Gage did, and the leaders of the rebellion fled Boston to avoid arrest. Gage decided to capture or destroy arms and gunpowder stored by the patriots in the town of Concord, near Boston. On the night of April 18, 1775, about 700 British soldiers marched toward Concord. Joseph Warren, a Boston patriot, discovered that the British were on the march. He sent two couriers, William Dawes and Paul Revere, by separate routes to ride to Concord and warn the people about the coming redcoats. A third rider, Samuel Prescott, joined them on the road outside Lexington. Only he made it past British patrols to warn the patriots at Concord.

The redcoats reached the town of Lexington, on the way to Concord, near dawn on April 19, 1775. Revere's ride had alerted American volunteer soldiers who were called *minutemen* because they were prepared to take up arms on a minute's notice. About 70 minutemen *mustered* (gathered) on the Lexington village green to watch the redcoats pass. Suddenly, shots were fired. No one knows who fired first. But 8 minutemen fell dead, and 10 more were wounded. One British soldier had been hurt.

The British force continued to Concord, where they searched for hidden arms. One group of redcoats met minutemen at North Bridge, just outside Concord. In a brief clash, three redcoats and two minutemen were killed. The British then turned back to Boston. Along the way, militia fired at them from behind trees and stone fences. British dead and wounded for the day numbered about 250, and American losses came to about 90.

Word spread rapidly that fighting had broken out. Militias throughout New England took up arms and gathered outside Boston. The Americans prepared to pounce on Gage's troops if they marched out of Boston. Three British officers—Major Generals John Burgoyne, Henry Clinton, and William Howe—arrived in Boston with more troops in late May 1775.

Bunker Hill. The British and the Americans each hoped to gain an advantage by occupying hills overlooking Boston. The Americans moved first. They dug in on Breed's Hill, close to the city.

On June 17, 1775, British troops led by Howe attacked American positions on Breed's Hill. To save ammunition, American officers ordered the patriots: "Don't fire until you see the whites of their eyes." The Americans drove back two British charges before they ran out of ammunition. During a third charge, British bayonets forced the Americans to flee. The fighting, usually called the Battle of Bunker Hill, was the bloodiest battle of the entire war. More than 1,000 British soldiers and about 400 Americans were killed or wounded.

The Continental Army. The Second Continental Congress began meeting in Philadelphia in May 1775, soon after the battles at Lexington and Concord. Patriot leaders in Massachusetts urged the Congress to take charge of militia units outside Boston and raise an army strong enough to challenge the redcoats. On June 14, the Congress established the Continental Army. The next day, George Washington was made the Army's commander in chief. The Congress named 13 more generals soon afterward. It then had to figure out how to recruit troops, supply an army, and pay for a war.

Washington took command of the military camps near Boston on July 3, 1775. He immediately worked to establish order and discipline in the army. The militia units were poorly trained and lacked weapons and overall organization. Their camps were filthy. Most soldiers had volunteered for service to defend their families and farms. They expected to return home after a few months. Washington issued a flood of orders and dismissed junior officers who failed to enforce them. Soldiers who disobeyed were punished.

The evacuation of Boston. Soon after Washington took charge of the Continental Army, he sought to drive the British from Boston. To accomplish that task, the Americans needed artillery. In May 1775, Colonels Ethan Allen and Benedict Arnold had seized Fort Ticonderoga, a British post in the colony of New York. Shortly afterward, their troops captured another British post at nearby Crown Point. The two victories provided the Americans with much-needed artillery.

In November 1775, Colonel Henry Knox, Washington's chief of artillery, proposed a plan to move the heavy guns by sled from Ticonderoga across the snow-covered Berkshire Mountains to Boston. The guns reached Framingham, near Boston, by late January 1776.

The arrival of the artillery enabled the patriots to fortify a high ground south of Boston known as Dorchester Heights. They completed the work during the night of March 4, 1776. General Howe, who had taken command of the British army several months earlier, realized his soldiers could not hold Boston with American cannons pointed at them. By March 17, the British troops had boarded ships headed for Nova Scotia, a British colony in Canada. But the evacuation of British troops from Boston was only a temporary victory for the Americans. Howe and his troops landed at New York City in July.

The invasion of Canada. To prevent British forces from sweeping down from Canada into New York, the

The Noble Train of Artillery (1946) oil on canvas by Tom Lovell; Fort Ticonderoga Museum, NY (© SuperStock)

Colonel Henry Knox led an American expedition that moved captured cannons over snowy mountains to high ground near Boston, forcing the British to evacuate the city in March 1776.

Continental Congress ordered an invasion of Canada. Some delegates also hoped that Canada might join the colonies in their rebellion against Britain.

In the fall of 1775, two American expeditions marched northward into Canada. Benedict Arnold led one force along rivers and over rugged terrain toward the city of Quebec. Disease and hunger caused many of his troops to turn back. The other expedition, under Brigadier General Richard Montgomery, headed toward Montreal. Montgomery captured Montreal on November 13. He then joined Arnold outside Quebec.

On Dec. 31, 1775, under cover of a blizzard, the Americans stormed Quebec, but they failed to take the city. Montgomery died in the attack, and Arnold was seriously wounded. Major General Guy Carleton, governor of the colony of Quebec, commanded the British forces in Canada. The Americans retreated to New York in the spring, after British reinforcements reached Canada. The invasion of Canada had ended in failure for the patriots.

Fighting in the Chesapeake and Southern colonies. Some planters in the Chesapeake and Southern colonies feared that a rebellion against Britain in the name of liberty might inspire enslaved Black people to rise up against them. For that reason, Britain expected to restore its authority more easily in the Chesapeake and Southern colonies than in the North. However, the patriots had great success in the Chesapeake and South at the start of the Revolution. A few weeks before the

Major battles of the American Revolution

Name	Place	Date	Commander		Dead and wounded*		Results
			American	British	American	British	
Bennington	New York, near Bennington, Vermont	Aug. 16, 1777	Stark	Baum, Breymann	70	200	British defeat encouraged the patriots in their campaign against Burgoyne.
Brandywine	Pennsylvania	Sept. 11, 1777	Washington	Howe	700	600	An American retreat enabled the British to occupy Philadelphia.
Bunker Hill	Massachusetts	June 17, 1775	Prescott	Howe	400	1,000	The patriots were driven from their positions overlooking Boston.
Camden	South Carolina	Aug. 16, 1780	Gates	Cornwallis	900	325	The British crushed an American army.
Cowpens	South Carolina	Jan. 17, 1781	Morgan	Tarleton	70	330	Patriot victory encouraged Southern militias to fight.
Germantown	Pennsylvania	Oct. 4, 1777	Washington	Howe	650	550	An American attack turned into a loss and a retreat.
Guilford Courthouse	North Carolina	March 15, 1781	Greene	Cornwallis	250	650	The British decided to give up most of North Carolina.
Kings Mountain	South Carolina	Oct. 7, 1780	Campbell	Ferguson	100	300	The British advance into North Carolina was delayed.
Lexington and Concord	Massachusetts	April 19, 1775	Parker and others	Smith	90	250	The American Revolution began.
Long Island	New York	Aug. 27, 1776	Washington	Howe	300	400	The British forced the Americans from Long Island.
Monmouth	New Jersey	June 28, 1778	Washington	Clinton	250	400	A patriot attack ended in a draw.
Moores Creek Bridge	North Carolina	Feb. 27, 1776	Caswell and others	McLeod	2	70	Lopsided patriot defeat of Loyalist militia.
Princeton	New Jersey	Jan. 3, 1777	Washington	Cornwallis	45	170	The British withdrew from western New Jersey.
Quebec	Quebec	Dec. 31, 1775	Arnold, Montgomery	Carleton	100	18	The Americans failed to seize the city of Quebec.
Saratoga (Freeman's Farm), First Battle	New York	Sept. 19, 1777	Gates	Burgoyne	300	600	The British advance from Canada was halted.
Saratoga (Freeman's Farm), Second Battle	New York	Oct. 7, 1777	Gates	Burgoyne	150	600	The patriots turned back a second attack.
Trenton	New Jersey	Dec. 26, 1776	Washington	Rall	10	100	The patriots crushed the Hessians in a surprise assault.
Yorktown	Virginia	Oct. 6-19, 1781	Washington	Cornwallis	100	600	The British surrendered in the war's last major battle.

*Approximate totals. The figures listed are a compromise between several conflicting estimates.

Revolutionary War battles and campaigns

British strategy at first called for crushing the American Revolution in the North. After 1778, the fighting shifted to the South. In 1781, an American and French force defeated the British at Yorktown in the last major battle of the war. This map locates important battles and campaigns.

WORLD BOOK map

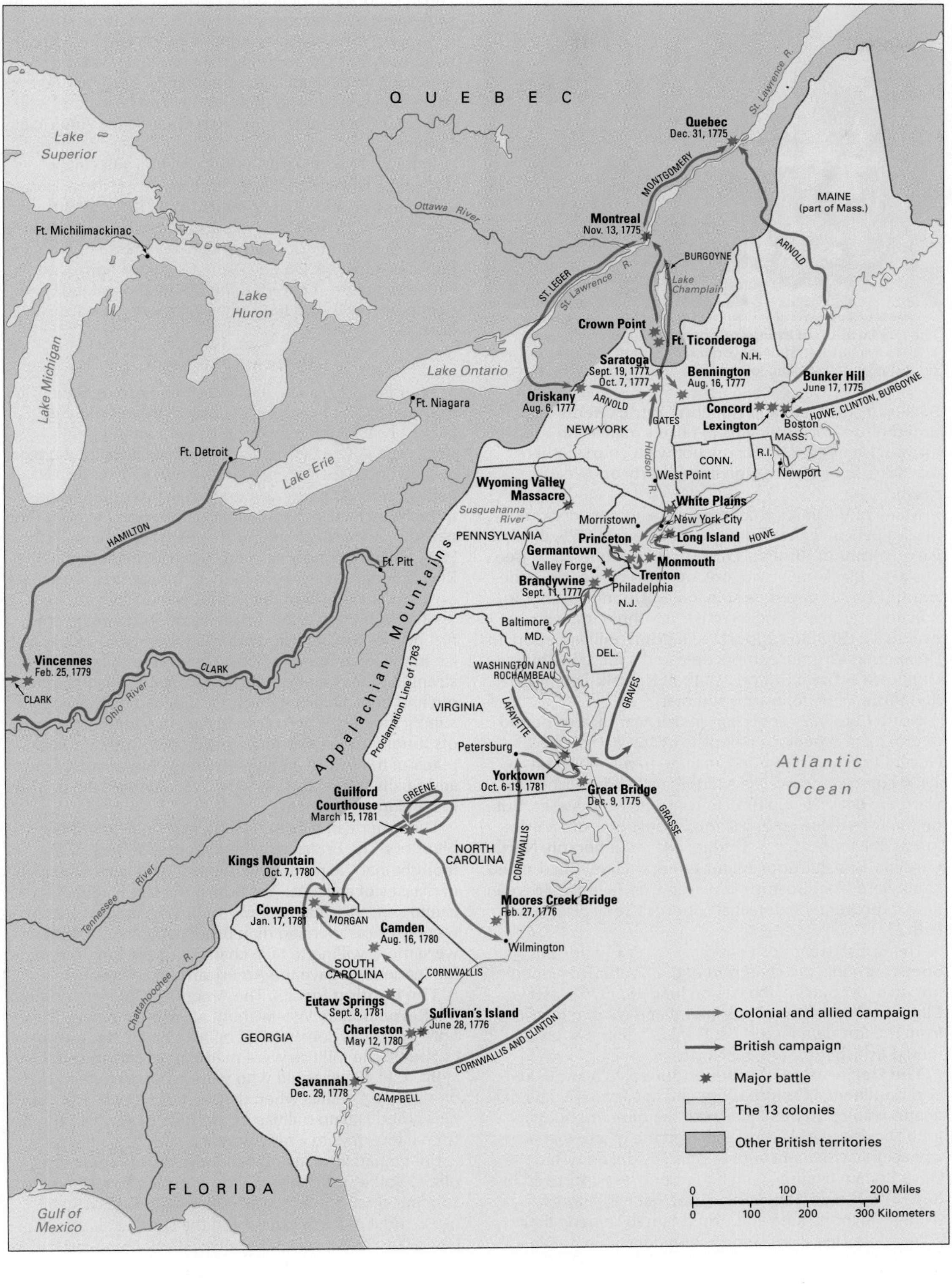

Detail of an oil painting on canvas (1921), by J. L. G. Ferris; Archives of 76, Bay Village, Ohio

The Declaration of Independence was adopted on July 4, 1776. The statesmen shown working on a draft are, *from left to right,* Benjamin Franklin, John Adams, and Thomas Jefferson.

battles of Lexington and Concord, Patrick Henry had urged his fellow Virginians to raise a militia and prepare for war. He declared, "I know not what course others may take, but as for me, give me liberty or give me death."

Many of Virginia's wealthiest slaveholders disagreed, urging patience and caution. In November 1775, the British governor of Virginia, Lord Dunmore, offered to free enslaved Black men who took up arms on Britain's side. About 1,000 enslaved people joined Dunmore. This action angered many conservative slaveholders, who eventually came to support the patriots' military effort. In December, Virginia patriots defeated a force led by Dunmore at Great Bridge, south of Norfolk. Dunmore fled Virginia the following summer.

North Carolina's governor, Josiah Martin, also hoped to crush the rebellious colonists by force. He urged North Carolinians loyal to Britain to join him. About 1,400 colonists answered Martin's call and marched toward the coast to join British troops arriving by sea. But on the way, these colonists took a beating from patriot forces at Moores Creek Bridge, near Wilmington, North Carolina. British troops under General Clinton had sailed southward from Boston. However, they failed to arrive in time to prevent the defeat at Moores Creek Bridge on Feb. 27, 1776.

The British warships continued on to Charleston, South Carolina, the chief port in the South. They opened fire on a fort outside the city on June 28, 1776. However, Clinton called off the attack later that day, after gunfire from the fort damaged several ships. Clinton soon rejoined British forces in the North.

The Declaration of Independence. When the Second Continental Congress opened in May 1775, few delegates wanted to break ties with the mother country. John Dickinson of Pennsylvania led the group that urged a peaceful settlement with Britain. Dickinson wrote the Olive Branch Petition, which the Congress approved in July 1775. The document declared that the colonists were loyal to the king and urged him to remedy their complaints. However, George III ignored the petition. On August 23, he declared all the colonies to be in rebellion. In December, Parliament passed the Prohibitory Act, which closed all American ports to overseas trade. Those actions convinced many delegates that a peaceful settlement of differences with Britain was impossible.

Support for American independence continued to build early in 1776. In January, the political writer Thomas Paine issued a pamphlet titled *Common Sense.* Paine attacked George III as unjust, and he argued brilliantly for the complete independence of the American Colonies.

In June 1776, Richard Henry Lee of Virginia introduced the resolution in the Congress "That these United Colonies are, and of right ought to be, free and independent States...." The Congress appointed a committee to draft a declaration of independence in case Lee's resolution was adopted. On July 2, the Congress approved Lee's resolution. It adopted the Declaration of Independence on July 4, and the United States of America was born.

Progress of the war

After the Americans declared their independence, they had to win it by force. The task proved difficult, partly because the people never fully united behind the war effort. A large number of colonists remained unconcerned about the outcome of the war and supported neither side. As many as a third of the people sympathized with Britain. They called themselves Loyalists. The patriots called those people Tories, after Britain's Tory Party, which strongly supported the king. Victory in the Revolutionary War depended on the patriots, who made up less than a third of the population.

Although the patriots formed a minority of the colonial population, they had many advantages over the British in the Revolutionary War. They had plenty of troop strength, if they could only persuade citizens to come out and fight. Unlike the British, they did not have to supply their army across an ocean. In addition, the patriots fought on familiar terrain and could retreat out of reach of the British. In time, Britain's chief rivals, France and Spain, joined the war. Their aid enabled the patriots to win independence.

The American patriots also benefited from British blunders. The British expected an easy victory. They thought that the patriots would turn and run at the sight of masses of redcoats. Yet British military leaders were cautious in their battle plans. American military leaders were less experienced than British officers, but they were more willing to take chances. In the long run, daring leadership gave the Americans an advantage.

The fighting forces. The American Colonies entered the Revolutionary War without an army or a navy. Their fighting forces consisted of militia units in the various colonies. The militias were made up of citizen-soldiers from 16 to 60 years old who were ready to defend their homes and families when danger threatened. The colonies could call up militias for periods of service ranging from a few days to a few months.

Britain had an army of well-trained and highly disciplined soldiers. Britain also hired professional German soldiers. Such soldiers were often called Hessians because most of them came from the German state of Hesse-Kassel. American Loyalists, Black men who had

British soldiers, commonly known as redcoats, lined up shoulder-to-shoulder in firing formation, as demonstrated in this battle reenactment. Soldiers fired in massed formations because of the musket's inaccuracy and limited range. The British fighting force was better trained and equipped than that of the Americans for much of the war.

AP Images

escaped slavery, and Native Americans also joined British fighting forces during the war. At its peak, the British military force in North America numbered about 50,000.

Washington and other patriot leaders doubted that part-time militias could defeat the British in a long war. Therefore, Washington worked to build an army of disciplined soldiers who had enlisted for several years. However, recruitment for the Continental Army remained a constant problem. Most citizens preferred to serve in local militias and support the Continental Army when a major battle threatened nearby.

Washington rarely commanded as many as 15,000 soldiers at a time, and he frequently commanded far fewer. Soldiers often went without pay, food, and proper clothing because the Continental Congress was so poor and transportation in the colonies was so bad. Yet many poor soldiers stayed in the army because they had been promised free land after the war. They fought as much for economic gain as for political liberty.

In time, most states permitted Black men to serve in the Continental Army. In all, about 5,000 African Americans fought on the patriot side in the war. Many were enslaved people who had been promised freedom in exchange for military service.

Weapons and tactics. The most important weapons of the war were the flintlock musket, the rifle, and the

The flintlock musket was the chief firearm of the Revolutionary War. Loading a musket required great care, as demonstrated by the Continental Army soldier *at left.* First, he bites open a paper cartridge to release the gunpowder. He next pours powder into the firing pan. More gunpowder and a lead ball are then rammed down the barrel. After the flintlock is cocked, the musket is ready to fire.

Artillery took part in attacks and defense. Cannons fired slowly because soldiers had to swab the barrel after each round, as these British gunners demonstrate.

A rifle fired more accurately than a musket, and many Americans on the frontier were good shots with rifles. This sharpshooter takes aim at a British officer.

WORLD BOOK illustrations by David A. Cunningham

A bayonet fastened to a musket was used in hand-to-hand combat. A German soldier hired by the British, *left,* clashes with an American infantryman, *right.*

Detail of an oil painting on canvas (1789) by William Elliott; U.S. Naval Academy Museum

A naval battle between the frigate *Bonhomme Richard,* commanded by Continental Navy Captain John Paul Jones, and the British warship *Serapis* took place off the coast of England in September 1779. The two ships were lashed together much of the time, and the crews fought in hand-to-hand combat. Jones captured the *Serapis* though his own ship was badly damaged.

cannon. The musket discharged a large lead ball and could fire three or four rounds a minute. Rifles had much greater accuracy than muskets, but they took longer to reload, which made them less efficient in battle. Colonists from the western frontier improved the rifle's value by developing their skill at rapid loading. Cannons hurled shells long distances and blasted soldiers at closer range.

On the battlefield, soldiers lined up shoulder to shoulder, two or three rows deep. Their muskets had little accuracy beyond about 60 yards (55 meters). For that reason, the attackers advanced as far as possible before shooting. After firing several rounds, the two sides closed in for hand-to-hand combat with *bayonets* (knives that fit on the barrel of a gun). The battle ended when one side broke through enemy lines or forced the other side to retreat. In the early years of the war, the Americans had few bayonets, which gave the redcoats an enormous advantage.

Maritime forces. The Congress established the Continental Navy in 1775, but it was small and poorly equipped to challenge Britain's powerful Royal Navy. The British Navy loosely blockaded American ports and supported British military operations along the Atlantic coast. However, the Continental Navy sank or captured many smaller British vessels, especially cargo ships. Privately owned American vessels known as *privateers* also captured enemy cargo ships. The privateers then sold the stolen cargoes and divided the profits among investors, the ship captains, and the crews.

Patriot governments. The Continental Congress provided leadership for the 13 former colonies during most of the war. After the Declaration of Independence, each former colony called itself a state. The Congress drew up a plan called the Articles of Confederation to unify the states under a central government. The Articles left nearly all powers to the states because many delegates distrusted a strong central government. By March 1781, all 13 states had approved the Articles.

Each state formed a government to replace its former British administration. In most states, an elected legislature drafted a written constitution that defined the powers of the government. In 1780, Massachusetts became the last of the states to introduce a new constitution.

Patriot committees in each state stirred support for the war effort. Such committees tormented citizens suspected of sympathizing with Britain. Many Loyalists left the colonies rather than submit to the demands of patriot committees. By the end of the war, as many as 100,000 Loyalists had fled to Canada, England, the Bahamas, and other British territories.

The home front. With husbands, fathers, and brothers away at war, many women assumed new roles at home. They took responsibility for the daily functioning of family farms and businesses. They policed their communities with a watchful eye and took a greater interest in community issues. On a number of occasions, for example, city women rioted to force merchants to lower the price of grain and other items. Women also contributed directly to the war effort. In 1780, Esther De Berdt Reed helped to found the Philadelphia Ladies Association, which raised over $300,000 for the Continental Army.

Financing the war. The Continental Congress had to pay for the Revolutionary War, but it had no power to tax the people. Late in 1775, the Congress began to issue paper currency known as Continental dollars, or Continentals. However, it issued so many Continentals that they became nearly worthless. The Congress received some money from the states, but never enough. Loans and gifts of cash from other nations—especially from France, the Netherlands, and Spain—saved the patriots. The Congress also obtained loans from patriot merchants and other Americans who had cash or goods to spare. Those citizens received certificates that promised full repayment of their loans with interest.

Diplomacy. Vital support for the American cause came from France, Spain, and the Netherlands. Benjamin Franklin represented the Americans in France and helped win French support for the patriots.

The Battle of Princeton, which took place on Jan. 3, 1777, resulted in a major victory for the Americans. This painting shows George Washington, on horseback in the foreground, rallying his troops shortly before they drove the redcoats from the field. The patriot victories at Princeton and at Trenton a week earlier raised American morale and allowed Washington to rebuild his army.

Detail of an oil painting on canvas (about 1790) by William Mercer; Historical Society of Pennsylvania, Philadelphia

Before the Revolutionary War began, French leaders had watched with interest the widening split between Britain and the American Colonies. France still smarted from its defeat by Britain in the French and Indian War. France's foreign minister, the Count de Vergennes, believed that a patriot victory would benefit France by weakening the mighty British Empire. France agreed to aid the patriots secretly. However, France refused to ally itself openly with the Americans before they had proved themselves in battle.

From 1776 to 1778, France gave the American government loans, gifts of money, and weapons. In 1778, treaties of alliance were signed, making France and America "good and faithful" allies. Thereafter, France also provided the patriots with troops and warships. Spain entered the war as an ally of France in 1779. The Netherlands joined the war in 1780.

The war in the North

The outcome of the battles in 1775 convinced the British that defeating the American Colonies required a major military effort and an effective strategy. As a result, Britain sent additional troops and a large naval force to America. The initial British strategy called for isolating and destroying the uprising in the North first. Once New England was knocked out, Britain expected resistance to crumble in the remaining colonies.

Britain nearly conquered the patriots several times during the fighting in the North, which lasted from 1775 to 1778. But British generals failed to carry out their strategy effectively.

The campaign in New York. After the British evacuated Boston in March 1776, General Howe began to plan his return to the American Colonies. In July, he landed on Staten Island in New York Harbor. Howe was joined by General Clinton's troops, following their defeat in South Carolina, and by Hessian soldiers from Europe. Howe commanded a total force of more than 45,000 experienced soldiers and sailors. They faced about 20,000 poorly trained and poorly equipped Americans.

Washington had shifted his forces to New York City after the redcoats withdrew from Boston. He did not expect to hold New York City, but he wanted to make the British fight for it. To defend the city, patriot troops fortified Brooklyn Heights, an area of high ground on the western tip of Long Island.

Howe saw an opportunity to trap patriot troops in Brooklyn. In August 1776, British troops landed on Long Island in front of the American lines. Howe surrounded the patriots' forward positions in the Battle of Long Island on August 27. However, the slow-moving Howe paused before attacking again, enabling the remainder

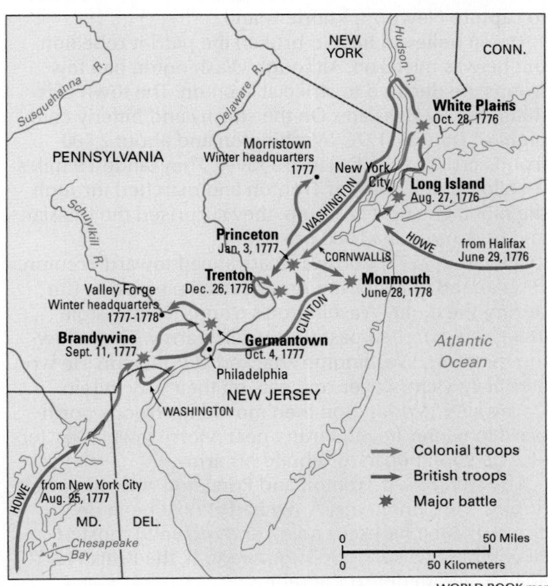

WORLD BOOK map

In the North, Washington and the redcoats fought a seesaw campaign. The patriots lost several battles but kept on fighting. British generals acted cautiously and failed to cooperate.

of the Americans to escape. In September, Washington sent Captain Nathan Hale behind British lines to obtain information about British positions on Long Island. The British caught Hale and hanged him for spying. Before being hanged, he reportedly said, "I only regret that I have but one life to lose for my country."

By mid-September 1776, Howe had driven Washington's troops from New York City. Howe slowly pursued the Americans as they retreated toward White Plains, New York, but his hesitation cost the British a chance to crush Washington's army. Another patriot force remained on Manhattan Island to defend Fort Washington. The fort fell to Howe in November, and Britain captured nearly 3,000 Americans. New York City remained in British hands until the war ended.

During the summer and fall of 1776, General Carleton led a British force southward from Canada. British strategy called for Carleton to link up with Howe in the Hudson River Valley, thereby cutting New England off from the rest of the colonies. But Carleton met heavy resistance from patriot forces under Brigadier General Benedict Arnold in a naval battle near Valcour Island on Lake Champlain. In November, Carleton turned back to Canada for the winter.

Trenton and Princeton. The patriot situation appeared dark at the end of 1776. Washington's discouraged forces had withdrawn to New Jersey. In late November, British troops led by Major General Charles Cornwallis poured into New Jersey in pursuit of Washington. The patriots barely escaped to safety by crossing the Delaware River into Pennsylvania on December 7.

Washington's forces were near collapse, and the New Jersey militias failed to come to their aid. Yet Howe again missed an opportunity to destroy the Continental Army. He decided to wait until spring to attack and ordered his troops into winter quarters in Trenton, Princeton, and other New Jersey towns. Clinton was assigned to capture Newport, Rhode Island.

Howe believed he had broken the patriot rebellion, but he was mistaken. Although Washington had few troops, he decided to strike at Trenton. The town was defended by Hessians. On the stormy and bitterly cold night of Dec. 25, 1776, Washington and about 2,400 troops crossed the Delaware River. They landed 9 miles (14 kilometers) north of Trenton and marched through the night. The next morning, they surprised the Hessians and took more than 900 prisoners.

On Jan. 2, 1777, Cornwallis advanced toward Trenton. He planned to attack the Americans the next day. But during the night, Washington's troops silently stole away and marched past Cornwallis's army. The following morning, Washington attacked at Princeton. He won a brilliant victory over redcoats on their way to join Cornwallis. Washington then moved his troops northward to winter headquarters near Morristown, New Jersey. He soon began to rebuild his army.

The victories at Trenton and Princeton revived patriot hopes. The Continental Army had almost been destroyed, but it had kept going and regained most of New Jersey. Despite superior strength, the British had again failed to defeat the rebels.

Brandywine and Germantown. Washington's successful maneuvering at Trenton and Princeton had embarrassed Howe. In the spring of 1777, Howe sought to

Detail of an oil painting on canvas (1786), by John Trumbull; Yale University Art Gallery

The British surrender at Saratoga on Oct. 17, 1777, marked a turning point in the war. In this painting, defeated General John Burgoyne, *left,* offers his sword to General Horatio Gates.

lure Washington into battle and destroy his army. After failing to draw Washington into battle in New Jersey, Howe set out to take Philadelphia, the patriot capital.

In the summer of 1777, Howe's redcoats sailed from New York City to the top of Chesapeake Bay, about 50 miles (80 kilometers) southwest of Philadelphia. Washington had rebuilt his army during the spring, and he had received weapons from France. He positioned his troops between Howe's forces and Philadelphia.

The opposing armies clashed on Sept. 11, 1777, at Brandywine Creek in southeastern Pennsylvania. One wing of the British army swung around the Americans and attacked from behind. The surprised patriots had to retreat. Howe skillfully moved his troops after the Battle of Brandywine and occupied Philadelphia on September 26. The Continental Congress had fled to York, Pennsylvania, where it continued to direct American affairs.

On Oct. 4, 1777, Washington struck back at British forces camping at Germantown, north of Philadelphia. However, his complicated battle plan created confusion. In a heavy fog, patriot forces fired on each other. The Americans again had to retreat.

Victory at Saratoga. While Howe won victories at Brandywine Creek and Germantown, another British force became stranded near Saratoga, New York. That force had advanced southward from Canada under Lieutenant General John Burgoyne.

Burgoyne had a successful start against the Americans. On July 6, 1777, he recaptured the British post of Fort Ticonderoga in New York from the Americans without a struggle. A second British expedition, led by Lieutenant Colonel Barry St. Leger, marched up the Mohawk River Valley to meet Burgoyne. In August, St. Leger ambushed militias outside Oriskany, New York. In the bloody Battle of Oriskany, the British beat back patriot forces. General Arnold stopped St. Leger soon afterward. By then, conditions favored the patriots.

As Burgoyne advanced southward, patriot forces destroyed bridges and cut down trees to block his path. American rifles fired on the British from the woods, and Burgoyne ran short of food and other supplies. In August 1777, the Congress appointed Major General Horatio Gates to command the Northern Department of the Continental Army. Gates was popular with New England patriots, and they poured out to support him and his soldiers, called Continentals. On August 16, militias overwhelmed two groups of Hessians and Loyalists looking for horses and food in New York, just west of Bennington, Vermont.

Burgoyne trudged slowly through the wilderness along the Hudson River. His slowness gave the Americans time to fortify a wooded area along the Hudson about 40 miles (64 kilometers) north of Albany. On Sept. 19, 1777, British troops attacked the fortifications, but they were met by patriot forces in a clearing on a nearby farm. Nightfall and the bravery of Hessian soldiers saved Burgoyne's troops from destruction in what became known as the First Battle of Freeman's Farm.

Although the patriot forces greatly outnumbered his army, Burgoyne chose not to retreat toward Canada. On Oct. 7, 1777, he attacked again. Arnold's daring leadership won the Second Battle of Freeman's Farm for the patriots. Burgoyne finally began to retreat, but he soon found himself encircled by the Americans at Saratoga. On October 17, Burgoyne surrendered. The Americans took nearly 6,000 prisoners and large supplies of arms.

The victory at Saratoga marked a turning point in the Revolutionary War. It revealed the failure of British strategy. More importantly, the decisive victory at Saratoga helped convince France that it could safely enter the war on the American side.

Valley Forge. Washington's army of about 10,000 soldiers spent the winter camped at Valley Forge, about 20 miles (32 kilometers) northwest of Philadelphia. Many of the troops lacked shoes and other clothing. They also suffered from a severe shortage of food. By spring 1778, nearly a fourth of the soldiers had died of malnutrition, exposure to the cold, and such diseases as smallpox and typhoid fever. Many soldiers deserted because of the miserable conditions.

In February 1778, a Prussian officer called Baron Friedrich von Steuben arrived at Valley Forge. He convinced Washington that he could train the Continental Army in European military formations and bayonet charges. By late spring, Steuben had created a disciplined fighting force. The Marquis de Lafayette, a young French soldier, also spent part of the winter at Valley Forge. Fired with enthusiasm for the revolution, Lafayette had joined Washington's staff as a major general without pay.

France's entry into the Revolutionary War in 1778 forced Britain to defend the rest of its empire. The British expected to fight the French in the West Indies and elsewhere, and so they scattered their military resources. As a result, Britain no longer had a force strong enough to battle the Americans in the North.

In May 1778, General Clinton became commander in chief of British forces in North America. He replaced Howe, who had occupied Philadelphia since September 1777. Clinton received orders to abandon Philadelphia and move his army to New York City. He was also told to send troops to the West Indies and other areas.

Monmouth. Clinton left Philadelphia on June 18, 1778, and marched across New Jersey toward New York City. The Continental Army followed him. On June 28, the patriots attacked near Monmouth Court House, New Jersey. Clinton soon counterattacked. After early confusion, the Americans held their ground, and the battle ended in a draw. During the night, Clinton's exhausted forces limped off the battleground and continued the march toward New York. The Battle of Monmouth was the last major Revolutionary War battle in the North.

Stalemate in the North. Washington hoped to drive the British from New York City in a joint operation with the French. In July 1778, a fleet under the French admiral Charles Hector, Comte d'Estaing, reached America. But a sandbar at the mouth of New York Harbor blocked the French warships. Later that summer, a combined French and American effort to take Newport, Rhode Island, also failed. In November, d'Estaing sailed south to protect the French West Indies from British attack.

The war in the West

When the Revolutionary War began, about 150,000 Native Americans lived in territory claimed by Britain.

Detail of an oil painting on canvas (1883) by William B. Trego; Valley Forge Historical Society

A ragged and hungry Continental Army was reviewed by General Washington, mounted on the white horse, as it marched toward winter quarters at Valley Forge, Pennsylvania, in December 1777. The army suffered from a severe shortage of food, shoes, and warm clothing that winter, and many soldiers died or deserted as a result.

Colonel George Rogers Clark led a force of colonists from the western frontier across flooded countryside to recapture Fort Sackville at Vincennes in 1779. Clark's successful campaign in the Illinois country disrupted the flow of British supplies to allied western Indian tribes and helped to prevent Indian war leaders from coordinating attacks along the frontier.

© North Wind Images

East of the Appalachian Mountains, native people lived mainly in separate communities surrounded by English-speaking colonists. The Indians participated in the colonial economy as whalers, agricultural laborers, and craftworkers. West of the Appalachians, they inhabited what was sometimes called "Indian country"—a patchwork of hundreds of villages belonging to a number of distinct Indian nations. Native people in this region lived by a combination of farming and hunting. They traded with American colonists for necessities they could not produce themselves, such as iron utensils, firearms, and ammunition. However, they guarded their land and welcomed British efforts to prevent the colonists from settling west of the Appalachian Mountains.

When the fighting began in 1775, Native Americans faced a difficult choice. Some native communities attempted to remain neutral in the conflict. Others, such as the Stockbridge and Mashpee Indians of Massachusetts and the Catawba Indians of South Carolina, contributed soldiers to the American war effort. In the West, however, most native communities allied with the British. They feared that an American victory would threaten their survival. American colonists had crossed the Appalachian Mountains and settled on Indian land, often in violation of British policy. During the Revolutionary War, Indians attacked and tried to disperse these settlements.

Invasion of the Iroquois country. Burgoyne's campaign in the Hudson Valley prompted four of the six Iroquois nations—the Mohawks, Senecas, Cayugas, and Onondagas—to enter the war as British allies. After Burgoyne's surrender at Saratoga in 1777, the Iroquois continued to harass American settlements on the frontiers of New York and Pennsylvania. In 1779, Washington sought to remove the Iroquois from the war through "the total destruction and devastation of their settlements." Patriot troops commanded by General John Sullivan invaded the Iroquois country in the late summer and fall of that year. They burned 40 villages and destroyed crops ready for harvest. That winter, some Iroquois died of starvation. Several thousand fled as refugees to Fort Niagara, a British post on the southwestern shore of Lake Ontario. But Iroquois warriors continued to fight.

The Illinois campaign. Soon after the war began, some Native American war leaders in the West began raiding settlements to try to push settlers out of Kentucky and the Ohio River Valley. Colonel George Rogers Clark of Virginia executed a daring campaign in the Illinois country that disrupted the flow of British supplies to the western tribes and helped to prevent Native American war leaders from coordinating attacks along the frontier. In the summer of 1778, Clark captured several settlements in what are now southern Illinois and southern Indiana. The British recaptured the settlement at Vincennes in Indiana. Clark and his troops fought their way back to Vincennes across flooded countryside and took its British and Indian defenders by surprise in February 1779.

The war in the South

Britain changed its strategy after France entered the Revolutionary War. Rather than attack in the North, the British concentrated on conquering the colonies from the South. British leaders believed that most Southerners supported the king. Although the British failed to find as much Loyalist support as they expected, they defeated the Americans in several key battles. This strategy forced the patriots onto the defensive in the South.

Savannah and Charleston. The first stage of Britain's Southern strategy called for the capture of a major Southern port, such as Charleston, South Carolina, or Savannah, Georgia. Britain would then use the port as a base for rallying Southern Loyalists and for launching further military campaigns. After Britain's army moved on, the British expected Loyalists to keep control of the conquered areas. Britain assumed it could more easily retake the North after overcoming resistance in the South.

Britain's Southern campaign opened late in 1778. On December 29, a large British force that had sailed from New York City easily captured Savannah. Within a few months, the British controlled all of Georgia.

The Continental Congress named Major General Benjamin Lincoln commander of the Southern Department of the Continental Army. In October 1779, Lincoln and Comte d'Estaing tried to drive the British from Savannah but failed. Afterward, d'Estaing returned to France, and Lincoln retreated to Charleston.

Success at Savannah led the British to invade South Carolina. In February 1780, British forces commanded by General Clinton landed near Charleston. They slowly closed in on the city, trapping its defenders. On May 12, General Lincoln surrendered his force of over 5,000 soldiers—almost the entire Southern army. Clinton placed General Cornwallis in charge of British forces in the South and returned to New York City.

The loss of Charleston and Lincoln's army badly damaged American morale. However, the British victory had an unexpected result. Soon afterward, bands of South Carolina patriots began to roam the countryside, battling Loyalists and attacking British supply lines. The rebels made it risky for Loyalists to support Cornwallis. The chief rebel leaders included Francis Marion, Andrew Pickens, and Thomas Sumter.

Camden. In July 1780, the Continental Congress ordered General Gates, the victor at Saratoga, to form a new Southern army to replace the one lost at Charleston. Gates hastily assembled a force made up largely of untrained militias. The rest of his troops consisted of disciplined Continentals. He rushed to challenge Cornwallis at a British base in Camden, South Carolina.

On Aug. 16, 1780, the armies of Gates and Cornwallis met outside Camden and went into battle. The militias quickly panicked. Most of them turned and ran without firing a shot. The Continentals fought on until heavy casualties forced them to withdraw. The British had defeated a second American army in the South.

The disaster at Camden marked a low point for the patriots. They then received a further blow. In September 1780, the patriots discovered that General Arnold, who commanded a military post at West Point, New York, had joined the British side. The Americans learned of Arnold's treason just in time to stop him from turning West Point over to the enemy.

Kings Mountain. Cornwallis's victory at Camden in August 1780 led him to act more boldly. In September, he charged into North Carolina before the Loyalists had gained firm control of South Carolina. After Cornwallis's departure, rebels in South Carolina terrorized suspected Loyalists. In addition, colonists from the western frontier turned out to fight the British.

In October 1780, the patriots surrounded and captured the left wing of Cornwallis's army, which was made up of Loyalist troops, on Kings Mountain, just inside South Carolina. After the defeat at Kings Mountain, Cornwallis temporarily halted his Southern campaign and retreated into South Carolina.

Cowpens and Guilford Courthouse. In October 1780, the Continental Congress named Major General Nathanael Greene to replace Gates as commander of the Southern army. Greene was a superb choice because he knew how to accomplish much with few resources. Greene divided his troops into two small armies. He led one army and put Brigadier General Daniel Morgan in charge of the other. Greene hoped to avoid battle with Cornwallis's far stronger force while he rebuilt the Southern army. Greene planned to let the British chase the Americans around the countryside.

Cornwallis set out to trap Morgan's army. Just before the British caught up with him, Morgan prepared for battle in a cattle-grazing area known as the Cowpens in northern South Carolina. On Jan. 17, 1781, Morgan's troops, armed with sharpshooting rifles, quickly killed or captured nearly all the attacking redcoats.

The patriot victory at Cowpens enraged Cornwallis, and he pursued Morgan with even greater determination. Greene rushed to join Morgan, hoping to crush Cornwallis's weakened force. On March 15, 1781, a bloody conflict occurred at Guilford Courthouse in North Carolina. Although Cornwallis drove Greene from the battlefield, the British took a battering. Cornwallis halted the chase after the Battle of Guilford Courthouse. He moved to Wilmington, North Carolina, where he gave his exhausted army a brief rest.

Greene challenged British posts in South Carolina during the spring of 1781. The patriots fought several small battles but failed to win clear victories. Yet the fact that a rebel army moved freely about the countryside proved that Britain did not control the Carolinas.

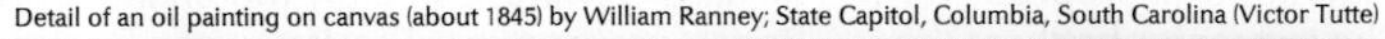
Detail of an oil painting on canvas (about 1845) by William Ranney; State Capitol, Columbia, South Carolina (Victor Tutte)

The Battle of Cowpens was fought in a cattle-grazing area of South Carolina in January 1781. It ended in victory for the patriots. In the clash shown here, a young American bugler shoots a British officer who is trying to stab an American cavalry commander. The inability of the British to secure the Southern Colonies hindered their efforts to retake positions in the North.

General Cornwallis surrendered his army to George Washington at Yorktown, the site of the war's last major battle, on Oct. 19, 1781. This painting shows French and American officers, including Washington, lined up to receive the surrender. Britain began peace talks with the Americans several months after its defeat at Yorktown. The war officially ended with the signing of the Treaty of Paris on Sept. 3, 1783.

The Surrender of Lord Cornwallis at Yorktown (1817-1824), an oil painting by John Trumbull; Yale University Art Gallery

The end of the war

The fighting in the Revolutionary War centered in Virginia during 1781. In January, Benedict Arnold began conducting raids in Virginia for the British, who had made him a brigadier general. Arnold's troops set fire to crops, military supplies, and other patriot property. In response, Washington sent Lafayette with a force of Continentals to rally Virginia's militia and to go after Arnold. But Lafayette had too few troops to stop Arnold.

Cornwallis rushed into Virginia in the spring of 1781 and made it his new base in the campaign to conquer the South. However, Cornwallis had departed from Britain's Southern strategy by failing to gain control of North and South Carolina before advancing northward. General Clinton believed that the Southern campaign was therefore doomed. He also feared an American attack on his base at New York City. Clinton ordered Cornwallis to adopt a defensive position along the Virginia coast and to prepare to send his troops north. Cornwallis moved to Yorktown, which lay along Chesapeake Bay.

Surrender at Yorktown. The last major battle of the Revolutionary War was fought at Yorktown. French and American forces cooperated to deliver a crushing defeat to British forces under Cornwallis.

About 5,500 French soldiers had reached America in July 1780. They were led by Lieutenant General Jean Rochambeau. Washington still hoped to drive the British from New York City in a combined operation with the French. In August 1781, however, Washington learned that a large French fleet under Admiral François de Grasse was headed toward Virginia. De Grasse planned to block Chesapeake Bay and prevent Cornwallis from escaping by sea. Washington and Rochambeau rushed their forces southward to trap Cornwallis on land. A British naval force sailed from New York City and battled de Grasse at the mouth of Chesapeake Bay in early September. But after several days, the British ships returned to New York for repairs.

By late September 1781, Cornwallis knew that he was in trouble. A combined French and American force of about 18,000 soldiers and sailors surrounded him at Yorktown. The soldiers slowly and steadily closed in on the trapped British troops. Cornwallis made a desperate attempt to ferry his forces across the York River to safety on the night of October 16, but a storm drove them back. Cornwallis asked for surrender terms the next day.

The surrender at Yorktown took place on Oct. 19, 1781. More than 8,000 soldiers laid down their arms as a British band reportedly played a tune called "The World Turned Upside Down." They represented about a fourth of Britain's military force in America.

Britain's defeat at Yorktown did not end the Revolutionary War. The fighting dragged on in some areas for two more years. However, British leaders feared they might lose other parts of Britain's empire if they continued the war in America. Cornwallis's defeat at Yorktown brought a new group of British ministers to power early in 1782. They began peace talks with the Americans.

The Treaty of Paris. Peace discussions between the Americans and the British opened in Paris in April 1782. Richard Oswald, a wealthy merchant, represented the British government. The statesmen Benjamin Franklin, John Adams, and John Jay negotiated for the United States.

The Congress instructed the American delegates to consult with the French before they took any action. But the Americans disregarded the instructions and concluded a preliminary peace treaty with Britain on Nov. 30, 1782. The warring nations signed the treaty on Sept. 3, 1783. The Congress *ratified* (confirmed) the treaty on Jan. 14, 1784, and the British Parliament did so on April 9.

The Treaty of Paris recognized the independence of the United States and established the new nation's borders. United States territory extended west to the Mississippi River, north to Canada, east to the Atlantic Ocean, and south to about Florida. Britain gave Florida to Spain. The treaty also granted the Americans fishing rights off Newfoundland and Nova Scotia. It also instructed the Congress to recommend that the states restore property taken from Loyalists during the war. The last British soldiers withdrew from New York City in November 1783.

Results of the revolution

As a result of the American Revolution, the Thirteen Colonies threw off royal rule. In its place, they established governments ruled by law and dedicated to the guarantee of certain basic rights, including life, liberty, and the pursuit of happiness. Admiration for the principles that guided the revolution led peoples elsewhere to demand political reforms. Thomas Paine declared that the American Revolution "contributed more to enlighten the world, and diffuse a spirit of freedom and liberality among mankind, than any human event ... that ever preceded it."

War losses. Most historians estimate that about 7,200 Americans were killed in battle during the Revolutionary War. Approximately 8,200 more were wounded. About 10,000 others died in military camps from disease or exposure. Some 8,500 died in prison after being captured by the British. American military deaths from all causes during the war thus numbered about 25,700. In addition, approximately 1,400 soldiers were missing. British military deaths during the war totaled about 10,000.

Many soldiers in the Continental Army came out of the war penniless, as they had received little or no pay while they served. Soldiers who had enlisted for the entire war received certificates for Western land. But many veterans had to sell the certificates because they needed money before Western lands became available. In 1818, Congress agreed to pay pensions to needy veterans.

Costs of the war. The 13 states and the Congress went deeply into debt to finance the Revolutionary War. A new Constitution, approved in 1788, gave Congress the power of taxation. Largely through taxes, Congress paid off much of the war debt by the early 1800's.

The borders of the United States were set by the Treaty of Paris, which ended the Revolutionary War. The new nation extended from the Atlantic Ocean west to the Mississippi River.

The Revolutionary War severely strained Britain's economy. The king and Parliament feared the war might bankrupt the country. But after the war, greatly expanded trade with the United States helped the economy recover. Taxes on trade reduced Britain's debt.

Of all the warring nations, France could least afford its expenditures on the Revolutionary War. By 1788, the country was nearly bankrupt. France's financial troubles helped bring on the French Revolution in 1789.

Historical significance. The American Revolution fundamentally changed life in America. Above all, the revolution opened the doors that shut ordinary citizens out of the political process. Previously, the right to vote had been limited to adult white males who owned property. The property requirement was based on the idea that property owners had the strongest interest in good government and so were best qualified to make decisions. During and after the revolution, requirements for property ownership were reduced. By the 1830's, they were eliminated in nearly all the states. Black men and women of all races, however, did not gain the vote for many years.

Revolutionary ideals and the practical circumstances of the war also made it possible for African Americans, with others, to mount a challenge to slavery. In the Northern states, their efforts succeeded. Between 1777 and 1804, every state north of Maryland adopted a plan to end slavery within its boundaries. Meanwhile, in the South, slaveholders worked to shore up and preserve the institution of slavery. The American Revolution thus helped create a new division between free and slave states. This division laid the foundation for the American Civil War (1861-1865) and, with it, the ultimate end of slavery in the United States. Nathaniel Sheidley

Related articles in *World Book*. See the *History* section of the articles on the states that fought in the Revolutionary War, such as **Massachusetts** (History). See also the following:

Background and causes of the war

Boston Massacre
Boston Port Act
Boston Tea Party
Committees of correspondence
Committees of safety
Continental Congress
Declaration of Independence
Intolerable Acts
Minutemen
Navigation Acts
Stamp Act
Writ of assistance

American military leaders

Allen, Ethan
Arnold, Benedict
Barry, John
Clark, George R.
Clinton, George
Dearborn, Henry
Gates, Horatio
Greene, Nathanael
Hale, Nathan
Jones, John Paul
Knox, Henry
Lee, Charles
Lee, Henry
Marion, Francis
Moultrie, William
Putnam, Israel
Putnam, Rufus
Saint Clair, Arthur
Schuyler, Philip J.
Stark, John
Warner, Seth
Washington, George
Wayne, Anthony

American civilian leaders

Adams, John
Adams, Samuel
Deane, Silas
Franklin, Benjamin
Hancock, John
Henry, Patrick
Jay, John
Jefferson, Thomas
Lee, Richard Henry
Livingston, Robert R.
Mason, George
Morris, Robert
Otis, James
Revere, Paul
Salomon, Haym
Warren, Joseph

British leaders

André, John
Burgoyne, John
Burke, Edmund
Carleton, Sir Guy
Clinton, Sir Henry
Cornwallis, Charles
Gage, Thomas
George III
Howe, Richard
Howe, William
North, Lord

Saint Leger, Barry
Simcoe, John Graves

Other biographies

Attucks, Crispus
Brant, Joseph
Corbin, Margaret Cochran
De Grasse, François Joseph Paul
Forten, James
Galloway, Joseph
Gálvez, Bernardo de
Girty, Simon
Jouett, Jack
Kalb, Johann
Kościuszko, Tadeusz
Lafayette, Marquis de
Ludington, Sybil
Mazzei, Philip
Paine, Thomas
Pitcher, Molly
Pulaski, Casimir
Rochambeau, Comte de
Ross, Betsy
Rutledge, John
Salem, Peter
Sampson, Deborah
Steuben, Baron von

Other related articles

Army, United States (History)
Brother Jonathan
Bunker Hill, Battle of
Cabal
Camden, Battle of
Cincinnati, Society of the
Constitution of the United States
Daughters of the American Revolution
Flag (Flags in U.S. history; pictures)
Fort Ticonderoga
Green Mountain Boys
Hessians
Lexington and Concord, Battles of
Marine Corps, United States (History)
Monmouth, Battle of
National Park System
Navy, United States (History)
Paris, Treaties of
Privateer
Saratoga, Battle of
Sons of Liberty
Sons of the American Revolution
Trenton, Battle of
United States, History of the
Valley Forge
Wyoming Valley Massacre
Yankee Doodle

Additional resources

Level I

Lanser, Amanda. *The American Revolution by the Numbers.* Edge Bks., 2016.
Raum, Elizabeth. *A Revolutionary War Timeline.* Capstone Pr., 2014.
Roberts, Cokie. *Founding Mothers.* HarperCollins, 2014.
Woelfle, Gretchen. *Answering the Cry for Freedom: Stories of African Americans and the American Revolution.* Calkins Creek, 2016.

Level II

Ellis, Joseph J. *Revolutionary Summer: The Birth of American Independence.* Knopf, 2013.
Ferling, John E. *Whirlwind: The American Revolution and the War that Won It.* Bloomsbury Pr., 2015.
Kennedy, Frances H., ed. *The American Revolution: A Historical Guidebook.* Oxford, 2014.
Mays, Terry M. *Historical Dictionary of the American Revolution.* 2nd ed. Scarecrow, 2010.

Revolution of 1848 involved a series of uprisings in France, Germany, and the Austrian Empire, including parts of Italy. Causes of the revolution included demands for constitutional government; growing nationalism among Germans, Italians, Hungarians, and Czechs; and peasant opposition to the manorial system in Germany and in the Austrian Empire (see **Manorialism**).

The revolution began in France in February 1848 as a protest against voting restrictions, political corruption, and poor economic conditions. Soon after, the French king, Louis Philippe, abdicated. Liberal politicians then set up a new government called the Second Republic.

The revolution quickly spread to the Austrian Empire and Germany. In the Austrian Empire, students and workers rioted in Vienna. Elsewhere, Hungarian and Czech nationalists rebelled. Italians also tried to drive their Austrian rulers from northern Italy. In Germany, liberal uprisings swept through the German Confederation, which consisted of Prussia and 38 other independent states. Workers in German cities demanded social reform. Representatives of various parts of Germany met in Frankfurt to try to unify the states into a single nation.

The Revolution of 1848 quickly failed. In France, Louis Napoleon Bonaparte, who had been elected president, declared himself emperor. Protests by French workers were brutally put down. In the Austrian Empire, troops crushed the nationalist uprisings and defeated the Italian rebels. In Germany, monarchies became more firmly established in the major German states. The assembly at Frankfurt broke up without achieving German unity. But one major goal of the revolution was achieved—the ending of the manorial system in Germany and the Austrian Empire. Also, European rulers became more sensitive to the demands of nationalists and began experimenting with more liberal forms of government. Peter N. Stearns

See also **Austria** (Metternich and revolution); **France** (The revolutions of 1830 and 1848); **Germany** (Revolution); **Italy** (Italy united).

Reye's syndrome, *ryz SIHN drohm,* is a rare childhood disease of the liver and central nervous system. Advanced cases can result in brain damage or death. The disease kills about 3 to 5 percent of its victims.

Most patients with Reye's syndrome are from 4 to 15 years old. The majority of them develop the disease while recovering from a mild viral illness, such as chickenpox or influenza. For some unknown reason, the virus apparently triggers Reye's syndrome. Studies indicate that many Reye's syndrome patients had been given aspirin during the viral illness. Based on these studies, experts and government health agencies have cautioned against using aspirin to treat chickenpox, influenza, or various other viral illnesses in children.

The first symptom of Reye's syndrome is repeated vomiting. In mild cases, the patient recovers with no aftereffects. But if the disease progresses, convulsions and alternating states of excitation and confused sleepiness may occur. In the final stages of the disease, brain cells swell and pressure builds in the skull, followed by a coma and possible brain damage or death.

The cause of Reye's syndrome has not been determined. Physicians treat the disease by giving the patient glucose and other nutrients, and by reducing the body's production of ammonia. They use drugs or surgery to lower the pressure within the skull if it reaches dangerous levels. This treatment has saved many patients. Reye's syndrome was first described by R. D. K. Reye, an Australian pathologist, in 1963. Henry L. Nadler

Reykjavík, *RAY kyuh VEEK* (pop. 118,918; met. area pop. 201,831), is the capital and largest city of Iceland. It is a seaport on the southwest coast, at the head of Faxaflói, a bay (see **Iceland** [map]). The city is Iceland's trading center and its center of government and education. It has many schools, a university, an observatory, a theater, a national museum, and a national library.

Water from nearby hot springs is used to heat buildings and homes in Reykjavík. The hot springs are also used to generate electricity for the area.

The Reykjavík area was first settled in A.D. 877, but it remained thinly populated for hundreds of years. In the 1700's, Skúli Magnússon built several workshops in Reykjavík, and more people began to settle in the village. When Iceland gained independence in 1944, Reykjavík became the country's capital. Kirsten Wolf

See also **Iceland** (picture).

Reynolds, *REHN uhldz,* **Sir Joshua** (1723-1792), was a great English portrait painter. Reynolds's portraits show his skill in capturing the likeness of his subjects, as well as his keen understanding of human nature. Among Reynolds's masterpieces are the portraits *Hon. Augustus Keppel* (1754), *William Robertsen* (1772), and *Sarah Siddons as the Tragic Muse* (1784). Reynolds wrote 15 essays on art education called *Discourses* that stressed the importance of grandeur in art and rigid academic training. His writings influenced generations of artists.

Reynolds became the most fashionable painter of his time. His close friends included James Boswell, Edmund Burke, Samuel Johnson, and other leading intellectual figures of the late 1700's. Reynolds helped found the Royal Academy of Arts in 1768 and became its first president. In 1784, he was appointed painter to the king.

Reynolds was born on July 16, 1723, in Plympton-Earl's, near Plymouth. In 1740, he was apprenticed to Thomas Hudson, a leading London portrait painter. Reynolds later studied the works of Sir Anthony Van Dyck, the most famous portrait painter of the 1600's. In 1749, Reynolds traveled to Italy. There he was influenced by the warm colors and sculptural clarity he saw in paintings of such Renaissance artists as Tintoretto, Titian, and Paolo Veronese.

Reynolds returned to England in 1753. He soon became a favorite portrait painter of the wealthy and the leaders of society. In addition, he painted charming and sensitive portraits of children. In 1781, Reynolds visited Flanders and the Netherlands, where he was influenced by the rich colors of the Flemish artist Peter Paul Rubens. Reynolds died on Feb. 23, 1792.

Douglas K. S. Hyland

Oil painting on canvas (1788); Tate Gallery, London (John Webb)

Reynolds's ***The Age of Innocence*** shows the artist's skill in painting sensitive and appealing portraits of young children.

Reza Shah Pahlavi, *rih ZAH SHAH pah lah VEE* (1878-1944), was the *shah* (king) of Iran from 1925 to 1941. Reza helped make Iran a more modern and self-reliant country. He built railroads and factories, promoted education, reformed the legal system, and increased the role of women in society. But Reza was also an authoritarian ruler who expected strict obedience.

Reza was born on March 16, 1878, in Alasht, a village northeast of Tehran, Iran's capital. His original name was Reza Khan, also spelled *Riza Khan.* Reza enlisted in the armed forces, and by 1915, he was a colonel in the Cossack Brigade, the principal military unit of Iran. In 1921, he worked to overthrow Iran's government in a British-supported military coup. Reza became prime minister in 1923. In 1925, he overthrew Ahmad Shah, the last king of the Qajar dynasty. Reza was crowned king in 1926. He changed his family name to Pahlavi, also spelled *Pahlevi.* He named his oldest son, Mohammad Reza Pahlavi, crown prince.

Soon after World War II (1939-1945) began, Reza declared Iran's neutrality in the war. However, the Allies felt Germany had too much political influence in Iran. During the war, Allied troops needed to use Iran as a supply route. When Reza refused to cooperate, British and Soviet troops invaded the country and forced him to hand power to his oldest son. Reza died in exile in South Africa on July 26, 1944. Maziar Behrooz

See also **Iran** (History).

Icelandic Photo & Press Service

Reykjavík is the capital and largest city of Iceland. More than half the people of Iceland live in or near Reykjavík. Rugged land lies beyond a residential area of the city, *shown here.*

Rh factor is a substance on the red blood cells of most people. Red blood cells that contain the Rh factor *agglutinate* (clump) if they come into contact with an antibody called *anti-Rh.* This reaction can produce serious illness or death. People who have the Rh factor are known as Rh-positive. Those lacking it are Rh-negative. Karl Landsteiner, Philip Levine, and Alexander Wiener discovered the factor in rhesus monkeys in 1940. They named it *Rh* for the monkey.

Anti-Rh does not occur naturally in the blood. But if an Rh-negative person receives a transfusion of Rh-positive blood, anti-Rh may build up in the blood plasma. If the patient receives later transfusions of Rh-positive blood, the anti-Rh will attack the Rh-positive red blood cells and cause agglutination.

The Rh factor is inherited. The child of an Rh-negative mother and an Rh-positive father may be Rh-positive. Before birth, some of the baby's blood cells may enter the mother's blood. Then the mother may build up anti-Rh. Most of the antibody does not form until after the baby is born, however, so it seldom causes any problems with the first child. But if the mother becomes pregnant with another Rh-positive baby, the flow of large amounts of her anti-Rh into the child's blood can cause clumping and destruction of the infant's red blood cells. This condition, which is called *erythroblastosis fetalis,* can result in severe anemia, brain damage, and even death. Such severe reactions take place in only about 1 of 20 cases in which the mother is Rh-negative and the father is Rh-positive. Even among these couples, physicians can usually prevent erythroblastosis fetalis by injecting the mother with a serum shortly after she gives birth to an Rh-positive child. The serum contains anti-Rh, which destroys any of the baby's cells in her blood before her body has time to produce its own anti-Rh. When erythroblastosis fetalis does occur, doctors treat the condition by replacing the baby's blood with fresh blood. In most cases, this procedure eliminates any long-term effects of the disease. Joseph V. Simone

See also **Blood transfusion; Landsteiner, Karl.**

Rhea, *REE uh,* is a large South American bird that cannot fly. It looks like a small ostrich, and it is often called the *South American ostrich.* However, it has three toes on each foot, while the ostrich has two. The rhea also has larger wings and more feathers on its neck and head than the ostrich (see **Ostrich**). The common rhea stands about 5 feet (1.5 meters) tall and weighs about 50 pounds (23 kilograms).

WORLD BOOK illustration by Trevor Boyer, Linden Artists Ltd.

The rhea, a bird that cannot fly, resembles a small ostrich. Rheas live on the grasslands of South America.

Rheas live on the plains of southern Brazil, Uruguay, Paraguay, and Argentina. They usually live in flocks of 5 to 30, generally in brush-covered land near water where they can bathe and swim. The birds eat leaves, roots, and insects.

Rheas have unusual nesting habits. The male scrapes a shallow hole in the ground, lines it with dry grass, and leads several hens to the nest. Each hen lays an egg. This process may be repeated several times, and a nest may have up to 30 eggs. The male then hatches the eggs and cares for the young. John W. Fitzpatrick

Scientific classification. Rheas make up the genus *Rhea.* The common, larger species is *Rhea americana.*

Rhea, *REE uh,* in Greek mythology, was the wife and sister of Cronus, ruler of the race of gods and goddesses called *Titans.* Her mother was Gaea, the earth, and her father was Uranus, the sky. She became queen of the gods when Cronus overthrew Uranus. In many parts of Asia, Rhea was known as Cybele.

According to myth, Rhea and Cronus had six children—the goddesses Demeter, Hera, and Hestia; and the gods Hades, Poseidon, and Zeus. Cronus swallowed five of the children when they were born to prevent them from deposing him. However, Rhea deceived Cronus by tricking him into swallowing a stone wrapped in baby clothes in place of their youngest child, Zeus. Rhea then hid Zeus in a cave on the island of Crete.

After Zeus was grown, he returned and tricked Cronus into vomiting up his other children. The five brothers and sisters helped Zeus defeat Cronus and the other Titans in a 10-year battle called the *Titanomachy.*

Nancy Felson

See also **Mythology** (Greek mythology); **Titans.**

Rhea Silvia. See **Romulus and Remus.**

Rhee, *ree,* **Syngman,** *SIHNG muhn* (1875-1965), a Korean statesman, served as the first president of the Republic of Korea from 1948 to 1960. He resigned in 1960, soon after his election to a fourth term, because of widespread riots following unfair election practices.

Rhee was born on March 26, 1875, in Hwanghae province and was educated in Seoul. Imprisoned from 1897 to 1904 for leading student demonstrations for independence, he wrote the book *Spirit of Independence* (1904). He then studied in the United States at George Washington, Harvard, and Princeton universities. Rhee lived in exile in Honolulu for 20 years. He returned to Korea after Japan surrendered in World War II (1939-1945). He died on July 19, 1965.

Bonnie Bongwan Cho Oh and John K. C. Oh

Rhenium, *REE nee uhm,* is a rare, costly, silvery-white metal. It is found in small amounts in such minerals as *gadolinite* and *molybdenite.* Rhenium has one of the highest melting points of the chemical elements. Because it withstands high temperatures, rhenium is valuable in certain *alloys* (mixtures of metals). It is sometimes mixed with tungsten or platinum to make heat-resistant electrical equipment. It is also used in making *filaments* (fine wires) for instruments called *mass spectrometers* that measure the mass of atoms and molecules.

The German scientists Walter Noddack, Ida Tacke, and Otto Berg discovered rhenium in 1925. It has the chemical symbol Re. Its *atomic number* (number of protons in its nucleus) is 75. Its *relative atomic mass* is 186.207. An element's relative atomic mass equals its *mass* (amount of matter) divided by 1/12 of the mass of carbon 12, the most abundant form of carbon. Rhenium melts at 3180 °C and boils at 5627 °C. S. C. Cummings

Rhesus monkey, *REE suhs,* also called the *rhesus macaque,* is a familiar and widespread monkey of Asia. The rhesus monkey lives across southern Asia and as far north as northern China. Among *primates* (the order of mammals that includes monkeys, apes, and human beings), only human beings have a wider range.

The rhesus monkey has brown to gray fur with yellowish markings and a pink face and rump. Adults measure from 18 to 25 inches (46 to 64 centimeters) long, not including the tail. The tail is typically about half as long. Adults weigh from 10 to 20 pounds (4.5 to 9 kilograms) or more. Males are generally larger than females.

Rhesus monkeys have adapted to life in many environments, including deserts, swamps, and mountain forests. They spend much of the day collecting food, which consists mostly of fruit, insects, and leaves.

Rhesus monkeys live in groups that can range from one dozen to several dozen individuals. The group's activities are organized around several older females. Kinship with these females strongly influences rank within the group. High-ranking individuals strictly enforce the privileges of rank, such as access to preferred foods. Upon reaching sexual maturity, young males leave to join another group. High-ranking males often father more offspring than lower-ranking males.

Rhesus monkeys are easily bred in captivity and suffer many of the same or similar diseases as do people. For these reasons, scientists use rhesus monkeys more than any other nonhuman primate in the study of human disease. Rhesus monkeys and human beings share about 93 percent of their *DNA* (deoxyribonucleic acid, the substance that determines a living thing's inherited traits). In 2007, scientists mapped out the rhesus monkey's *genome,* the complete set of its DNA. David Glenn Smith

© Kovalev Serguei, Shutterstock

Rhesus monkeys are social animals. This photograph shows two rhesus monkeys grooming a third monkey's fur. Social grooming helps maintain friendly relations among monkeys.

Scientific classification. The rhesus monkey's scientific name is *Macaca mulatta.*

See also **Macaque; Monkey** (picture); **Rh factor.**

Rhetoric. See **Oratory.**

Rheumatic fever, *roo MAT ihk,* is a disease that occurs primarily in children from 5 to 15 years old. It also strikes younger children and adults. Rheumatic fever gets its name from its most common symptoms—*rheumatism* (inflammation of the joints) and fever. The disease may last several weeks or months. Rheumatic fever can cause permanent damage to the heart valves.

Rheumatic fever is caused by bacteria called *streptococci.* People who develop the disease have had a recent streptococcal infection, such as strep throat. The streptococci subsequently trigger the immune system to attack the body's own tissues.

Before antibiotic drugs were developed in the mid-1900's, rheumatic fever with its resulting valve damage was a leading cause of heart disease throughout the world. Today, prompt treatment of streptococcal infections with penicillin and other antibiotics usually prevents rheumatic fever, and the disease has become rare in industrialized countries. However, rheumatic fever remains a problem in many developing nations.

The first symptoms of rheumatic fever usually occur a few weeks after the streptococcal infection. Common symptoms include fever; with pain and swelling in such joints as the elbows, wrists, knees, or ankles. Nodules (lumps) may develop under the skin over bony areas and a mild rash sometimes occurs. Some patients develop *chorea,* a condition marked by jerky, involuntary movements (see **Chorea**).

Mild to severe *carditis* (inflammation of the heart) occurs in many cases of rheumatic fever. Severe carditis can lead to heart failure. Both mild and severe carditis can cause permanent damage to the heart valves resulting in the condition called *rheumatic heart disease.* In rheumatic heart disease, the damaged valves no longer open and close properly, and the resulting turbulent passage of blood produces a sound called a heart murmur (see **Heart murmur**). Severe rheumatic heart disease can lead to heart failure. Surgical replacement of badly damaged valves may prevent this outcome.

Toby R. Engel

See also **Heart** (Valve disease).

Rheumatism, *ROO muh tihz uhm,* is a general term for disorders involving inflammation and pain, particularly in the muscles and joints. Physicians do not usually use this term. Major diseases that are frequently called rheumatism include *osteoarthritis, fibromyalgia,* and *rheumatoid arthritis.* Marc B. Garnick

See also **Arthritis; Fibromyalgia; Rheumatology.**

Rheumatology is the study of diseases affecting the body's joints and their associated tissues, including the bones, muscles, tendons, cartilage, and ligaments. Such diseases are called *rheumatic diseases.* Doctors who specialize in the care of patients with rheumatic diseases are called *rheumatologists.*

Diseases most commonly treated by rheumatologists include various forms of arthritis, particularly osteoarthritis, rheumatoid arthritis, gout, and disorders of the body's connective tissues, such as scleroderma and systemic lupus erythematosus. Rheumatologists also care for patients with general back pain and aching muscles, bones, and joints. In addition, other doctors often consult rheumatologists for help in treating patients with nonrheumatic diseases that involve the joints, muscles, and bones. Rheumatologists do not perform surgery, but they often work closely with orthopedic surgeons and specialists in rehabilitation medicine.

To become a certified rheumatologist in the United States, a doctor must study rheumatology for two to three years after completing medical school and residency training. The doctor must then pass a series of examinations conducted by an authorized medical board.

Research in rheumatology often involves specialists from other fields, such as biochemistry, cell biology, genetics, immunology, and molecular biology. Some researchers search for the causes and cures of rheumatic diseases, and others study how a rheumatic disease progresses. Michael D. Lockshin

Rhine River, *ryn,* is an important inland waterway in Europe. It is about 820 miles (1,320 kilometers) long and drains an area of about 86,700 square miles (224,600 square kilometers). The river rises in eastern Switzerland. It forms part of the borders of Switzerland, Liechtenstein, Austria, France, and Germany. It flows through Germany and the Netherlands into the North Sea. Many German legends relate to the Rhine (Rhein in German).

The Rhine serves as a means of transporting goods through central Europe. Many cities and industries are located near the river. During the 1900's, industrial waste and urban sewage polluted the Rhine. Countries along the river worked together to reduce the pollution.

The course of the Rhine. Two glacier-fed mountain torrents rise and flow eastward in the high Alps of eastern Switzerland, close to the Italian border. One is the *Vorder* Rhine, and the other is the *Hinter* Rhine. From their union, the Rhine flows along the western borders of Liechtenstein and Austria to Lake Constance, 1,306

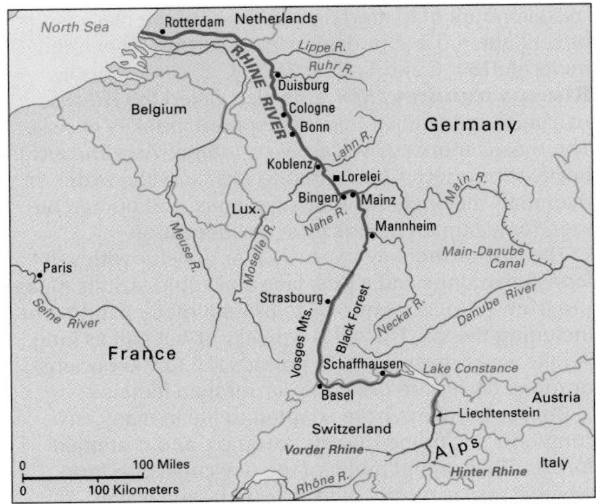

WORLD BOOK map

The Rhine River flows from the Alps to the North Sea.

feet (398 meters) above the sea. This lake sends the river westward to tumble over a fall 70 feet (21 meters) high at Schaffhausen. From there the Rhine flows between Germany and Switzerland to Basel. This city serves as landlocked Switzerland's principal port.

North of Basel, the Rhine flows between the Black Forest on the east and Vosges Mountains on the west. It runs down the middle of a plain that is about 20 miles (32 kilometers) wide and 180 miles (290 kilometers) long. In the southern part of the plain, the Rhine serves as the boundary between France and Germany.

From Basel, the river gradually widens and, at Bingen, it leaves the plain and travels through a narrow gorge in the Rhenish Slate Mountains. A cliff called the Lorelei

Shostal

The Rhine River in Germany winds past a cliff called the Lorelei, *center.* According to legend, the lure of a nymph, also called Lorelei, dooms sailors at the cliff.

stands along this section. According to legend, a siren here lures boatmen to destruction with her song (see **Lorelei**). The legends of Roland, Siegfried, and other historic and mythical figures also developed in this region. At Bonn, the river and valley widen again as the Rhine enters the North German Plain on its way to the Netherlands and its broad delta leading into the North Sea.

Along its course, the Rhine receives the waters of the Neckar, Main, Lahn, Ruhr, and Lippe rivers from the east. The Nahe and Moselle rivers flow into the Rhine from the west. Canals connect the Rhine to the Danube, Elbe, Ems, Marne, Oder, Rhône, and Weser rivers and so make the Rhine part of a great inland navigation system. North of Basel, major Rhine ports are Strasbourg, Mannheim, Cologne, Duisburg, and Rotterdam. Duisburg is the gateway to the industrial Ruhr Valley.

The Rhine in history. The Rhine has played an important role in Europe since the time of Ancient Rome. For 400 years, the Rhine was the boundary between the Romans and the Germanic tribes. On the west bank of the Rhine grew up the Roman cities of Colonia Agrippinensis (Cologne), Bonna (Bonn), Confluentes (Koblenz), Mogontiacum (Mainz), all in Germany; Argentoratum (Strasbourg), in France; and Basilia (Basel), in Switzerland. In the Middle Ages, the Rhine was under German rule from Basel to the Netherlands. But in 1648, at the close of the Thirty Years' War, France gained a foothold on the western bank of the Rhine. This started a struggle between France and Germany that lasted into the 1900's.

King Louis XIV made gains in the Rhine Valley, and Napoleon extended French control into the Rhineland. Even after Napoleon was defeated, Alsace, which borders the Rhine from Switzerland to beyond Strasbourg, remained in French hands. But Germany gained almost all of Alsace and northern Lorraine in 1871.

The same territory was battled over in World War I. The Treaty of Versailles returned Alsace and Lorraine to France, again extending that country's domain to the Rhine. Germany signed an agreement not to fortify the Rhineland. In 1936, German dictator Adolf Hitler violated this agreement and began to militarize the region. During World War II, heavy fighting occurred along the Rhine in the last part of the European struggle. After the war, the river again became one of the world's busiest waterways. Hugh D. Clout

Rhineland is a historic area in what is now western Germany. It lies along the Rhine River and extends west to the borders of Belgium, France, Luxembourg, and the Netherlands. For the location of the Rhineland, see **Germany** (map: German unification).

The Rhineland was settled during ancient times. Through the years, it was ruled by the Celts, the Romans, the Huns, and the Franks. About 800, such Rhineland cities as Cologne, Mainz, and Trier began to grow in importance. In time, they became religious and political centers of the Holy Roman Empire. The Rhineland was made part of France during the Napoleonic Wars of the late 1790's. The region became part of the German state of Prussia in 1815.

The Rhineland's rich mineral resources and location on the Rhine River led to the growth of important industrial centers there, including the Ruhr coal-mining district. After World War I (1914-1918), Germany signed treaties agreeing not to fortify the region or station troops there. But German troops occupied the Rhineland in 1936 and used it for military purposes during World War II (1939-1945). The area remains one of Germany's major industrial districts. Tourists visit the Rhineland to see its picturesque towns, historic castles, and extensive vineyards. Hugh D. Clout

Rhinitis, *ry NY tihs,* is an inflammation of the mucous membranes that line the nose. The inflammation increases the production of nasal mucus and can make breathing through the nose difficult. Rhinitis can result from infections, allergic reactions, and unknown causes. It occurs most frequently as part of the common cold, a viral infection. Many other cases result from hay fever. Certain *chronic* (long-lasting) forms of rhinitis can cause the mucous membranes to thicken or to wear away.

Neil R. Blacklow

See also **Cold, Common; Hay fever.**

Rhinoceros is a mammal known for its large size and horned nose. A mammal is an animal that feeds its young on mother's milk. The rhinoceros ranks as one of the largest land animals, with many adults weighing several tons. All *species* (kinds) of rhinoceros are threatened with *extinction* (dying out completely), and some rank among the world's most endangered animals. The rhinoceros is sometimes called the "rhino" for short.

The rhinoceros has an immense, solid body and short, stocky legs. Its thick skin appears to lie in folds but is actually just creased at the joints. Most species have little hair. Depending on the species, the rhinoceros has one or two slightly curving horns sticking up from the top of its long nose. Rhinoceros horn continues to grow throughout the life of the animal. It consists of a fiberlike material called *keratin*—the same material that makes up human hair and fingernails, among other things. The horn is not fixed to the rhinoceros's skull and can be torn out during fighting. The name *rhinoceros* comes from two Greek words and means *nose-horned.*

The rhinoceros is in a group of mammals noted for having an odd number of developed toes on each foot. Each rhinoceros foot has three developed toes. The center toe holds the majority of the animal's weight. The rhinoceros and hippopotamus may appear similar in body shape, but they are not closely related. The hippopotamus is a relative of pigs, camels, and cows. The rhinoceros is more closely related to the horse.

Some rhinoceroses are *grazers.* They eat mostly grass. Others are *browsers.* They eat leaves, twigs, and shrubs. Wild rhinoceroses live in Africa, in southeastern Asia, and on a few large islands near the Asiatic coast. In prehistoric times, they also roamed over Europe, North America, and northern Asia. *Paraceratherium,* a prehistoric relative of the modern rhinoceros, was the largest land mammal to ever live. This animal reached over 16 feet (5 meters) in height. On average, a rhinoceros lives from about 18 to 34 years. Some, however, have been known to live about 50 years.

Kinds of rhinoceroses

There are five living species of rhinoceroses. Three of them live in Asia and two in Africa.

Indian rhinoceroses include two species that have a single horn: the greater one-horned rhinoceros and the Javan rhinoceros. A third species, the Sumatran rhinoceros, has two horns.

© Shutterstock

© HPH Image Library/Shutterstock

African rhinoceroses. The white rhinoceros, *left,* is the largest kind of rhinoceros. All rhinoceroses like to rest in the water after drinking. A charging black rhinoceros, *right,* is a frightening sight. Rhinoceroses have poor vision and often attack things that they do not recognize.

The greater one-horned rhinoceros, also known as the Indian rhinoceros, is the largest of the three Asian species. It stands about 5 feet 8 inches (1.7 meters) high at the shoulder and weighs 2 tons (1.8 metric tons) or more. It has a single horn that is thick at the base and about 1 to 2 feet (30 to 60 centimeters) in length. In rare cases, the animal may stand up to 6 ½ feet (2 meters) high at the shoulder. The skin of the Indian rhinoceros is *pebbled* (covered in round knobs) and hangs in folds that make it look as though the animal were wearing plates of armor. The skin, however, though thick, provides little protection against bullets and knives used in *poaching* (illegal hunting). The animal lives in marshy jungles among reeds and tall grass, on which it feeds morning and evening. When not grazing on land, the rhinoceros may immerse itself in water and feed on aquatic plants. Ancient peoples of Asia knew this rhinoceros well, and it was even brought to Rome to be used in the circus games before the time of Christ.

The Javan rhinoceros is similar but smaller. It is now only found on Java, though it once ranged from Bangladesh into Myanmar and southward to Java, Borneo, and Sumatra. It lives in forested hills.

The Sumatran rhinoceros is smaller than any other rhinoceros and has two horns. It stands about 4 ½ feet (1.4 meters) tall and weighs about 1 ton (0.9 metric ton). It is hairy, especially on the tail and ears. The young have more body hair than the adults. This species lives in Sumatra, Borneo, and on the Malay Peninsula. Like the Javan rhinoceros, it lives in forested hills.

African rhinoceroses. The two African species are two-horned. They are known as the black rhinoceros and the white rhinoceros, though they are almost the same bluish-gray color. Their lips differ in shape because they are specialized for eating different types of food. Thus, the black rhinoceros is also called the hook-

© RSM Images/Alamy Images

The Sumatran rhinoceros is the smallest kind of rhinoceros. It is hairy, especially on the tail and ears. This rare animal lives in Sumatra, in Borneo, and on the Malay Peninsula.

lipped rhinoceros, and the white rhinoceros is known as the square-lipped rhinoceros. In both species, the horns of the female are longer but more slender than those of the male.

The black rhinoceros has a front horn that is sometimes as long as 4 ½ feet (136 centimeters). It uses this horn to defend itself and to dig. The rear horn may be the same length or shorter. The front horn is so strong that the animal can easily uproot bushes and small trees with it. The black rhinoceros feeds on leaves and twigs. Although it appears clumsy, the black rhinoceros can run quickly, up to 35 miles (56 kilometers) per hour.

The white rhinoceros is the largest of all rhinoceroses. It stands about 5 to 6 feet (1.5 to 1.8 meters) tall. In some cases, it may be over 6 feet (1.8 meters) tall and 15 feet (4.6 meters) long. It weighs up to 4 tons (3.6 metric tons).

Threats to rhinoceroses

Various threats have caused rhinoceros populations to decline. As human populations have grown and spread, people have destroyed the habitat of the rhinoceros, particularly the Javan and Sumatran species. All rhinoceroses are threatened by poaching. Poachers kill rhinoceroses and sell their horns and skin. In some Asian traditions, the powdered horn of the rhinoceros is believed to have healing qualities and may be used to treat headaches, fevers, and many diseases, including cancer. Rhinoceros skin, blood, and urine may also be used in traditional medicine.

© Shutterstock © Shutterstock

The mouth of a rhinoceros is suited for the animal's food. The white, or *square-lipped,* rhinoceros uses its flat lips, *left,* to break off grass. The black, or *hook-lipped,* rhinoceros uses its pointed upper lip, *right,* to grasp small branches. The two species have almost the same bluish-gray color.

© Shutterstock

A baby rhinoceros begins to grow horns soon after birth. This young white rhinoceros has a small horn. Rhinoceroses have three toes on each foot. Each toe has a hoof.

All rhinoceros species are faced with extinction. Only a few thousand rhinoceroses remain in Asia. The Javan rhinoceros is now nearly extinct, with the few remaining individuals living in one national park in Java. The Sumatran rhinoceros is also nearing extinction. The black rhinoceros remains threatened with extinction, and its numbers, which were once recovering due to protective measures, are in decline. Several thousand black rhinoceroses remain in the wild. In southern Africa, increased government protection and other conservation measures led the population of white rhinoceroses to rebound from fewer than 50 animals in the early 1900's to thousands of animals in the early 2000's. But these animals are once again being threatened by poachers.

Many countries have laws intended to protect the rhinoceros from poaching, and international treaties have banned the trade in rhinoceros parts. In some countries, such as India, Indonesia, Kenya, and South Africa, special teams of antipoaching rangers keep constant watch over the animals and their habitat. In such countries as Namibia, South Africa, and Zimbabwe, wildlife officials have further attempted to reduce poaching by surgically removing the horns of some rhinoceroses. This process is called *dehorning.* But many scientists believe this approach puts the animals in even greater danger. Hornless rhinoceroses are less able to protect their young against such predators as lions and hyenas. Also, poachers may kill hornless rhinoceroses for the horn root or in defiance of those who would protect rhinoceroses.

In addition to antipoaching efforts, attempts have been made to increase the populations of certain species of rhinoceros, both within and outside of their home countries. For example, black and white rhinoceroses have been sent to Australia and the United States to form breeding populations for future return to their natural habitats. Despite these efforts, the future remains bleak for wild rhinoceroses. Gina M. Ferrie

Scientific classification. The greater one-horned (or Indian) rhinoceros is *Rhinoceros unicornis;* the Javan is *R. sondaicus;* the Sumatran is *Dicerorhinus sumatrensis;* the black is *Diceros bicornis;* and the white is *Ceratotherium simum.*

See also **Animal** (pictures: Animals of the grasslands); **Poaching.**

Rhizoid. See **Moss** (The structure of mosses).

Rhizome, *RY zohm,* is a horizontal stem that grows at or just below the soil surface. Rhizomes produce leaves and flowers that rise above the soil, and small roots below. They can also produce buds that develop into branches. Some nonwoody perennial plants, such as iris, ginseng, wild ginger, and bloodroot, have rhizomes. Ginger root, which is used in Asian cooking, is a rhizome. In many plants, rhizomes can be thick and can function as an organ for the storage of food.

Joseph E. Armstrong

See also **Bulb; Orrisroot; Perennial.**

© John T. Hopf, The Preservation Society of Newport County

Cliff Walk winds past The Breakers, the beautiful estate of Cornelius Vanderbilt in Newport. Rhode Island's scenic Atlantic coast and water sports attract thousands of vacationers each year.

Rhode Island *The Ocean State*

Rhode Island is the smallest state in the United States. It covers only 1,221 square miles (3,162 square kilometers) and is a little more than half the size of Delaware, the second smallest state. In spite of its size, Rhode Island is an important industrial state. It ranks high among the states in the production of jewelry. Rhode Island's official nickname is *The Ocean State.* However, because of its size, the state has traditionally been called *Little Rhody.* Providence is the capital and largest city of the state.

Rhode Island lies on beautiful Narragansett Bay, an arm of the Atlantic Ocean. The bay makes the state a leading vacationland. Hundreds of thousands of tourists come to Rhode Island each summer to enjoy boating, fishing, and other water sports.

Narragansett Bay almost divides Rhode Island in two. The bay extends 28 miles (45 kilometers) inland from southern Rhode Island. The state has 36 islands, a majority of which are in the bay. Aquidneck, the largest island, was officially named Rhode Island in 1644. Towns on the mainland were called Providence Plantations. As a result, Rhode Island's official name became State of Rhode Island and Providence Plantations. In 2020, however, voters approved a constitutional amendment removing *and Providence Plantations* from the state's name.

About a sixth of Rhode Island's people live in the city of Providence. The Providence-Warwick metropolitan area extends into Massachusetts. All of Rhode Island's people live in this metropolitan area.

Roger Williams, a minister who founded Providence in 1636, worked for religious freedom. He made the settlement a haven for refugees from religious persecution. Under his leadership, Rhode Islanders gained fame for their love of personal liberty.

Rhode Islanders organized the Continental Navy when the American Revolution broke out in 1775. Esek Hopkins served as the first commander in chief. Today, Rhode Island is the site of Naval Station Newport, which includes the Naval Undersea Warfare Center and the Naval War College, the Navy's highest educational institution.

Rhode Island played an important role in the industrial development of the United States. Samuel Slater, an English machinist who settled in Rhode Island, helped Rhode Island merchant Moses Brown establish the American textile industry. In the late 1700's, Slater built the country's first water-powered cotton spinning machines. Also in the late 1700's, Nehemiah Dodge of Providence discovered how to cover base metals with silver and gold. He and his brother Seril started the American jewelry industry. Rhode Islanders were also prominent in boatbuilding, shipping, and other industries.

The contributors of this article are Stanford E. Demars, Professor Emeritus of Geography at Rhode Island College, and J. Stanley Lemons, Professor Emeritus of History at Rhode Island College and coauthor of Rhode Island: The Ocean State.

Interesting facts about Rhode Island

The first Quonset hut was built in 1941 at the Quonset Point Naval Air Station near Davisville. United States troops used the huts during World War II for barracks, storage rooms, medical facilities, and many other purposes. The Quonset hut is a prefabricated sheet-metal structure in the shape of a half cylinder with the flat side forming the floor. Most huts were built about 50 to 100 feet (15 to 30 meters) long and 20 to 40 feet (6 to 12 meters) high. They were designed for easy shipment, assembly, and disassembly.

First Quonset hut

WORLD BOOK illustrations by Kevin Chadwick

The Rhode Island Red is the chicken that made the raising of poultry a major industry in the United States. The breed was developed in 1854 on a farm in Little Compton. It became famous for its delicious meat and for the outstanding quality and quantity of its eggs.

Rhode Island Reds

The first international polo series was played in Newport in 1886. A team from the United States challenged a team from England to win two games out of three for a trophy called the Westchester Cup. England won the trophy.

The oldest Jewish synagogue still standing in the United States is in Newport. It was built in 1763, and the congregation dates back to 1658.

©Mira, Alamy Images

Historic Bowen's Wharf in Newport has restaurants and shops in restored buildings dating back to the 1700's. Newport was the East Coast's busiest port before the Revolutionary War.

© Stan Aggie, Picture Group

Downtown Providence includes the Kennedy Plaza, set among office buildings. Providence is the capital, largest city, and chief manufacturing center of Rhode Island.

Rhode Island in brief

Symbols of Rhode Island

On the state flag, adopted in 1897, 13 stars represent the original 13 colonies. The state motto, *Hope,* appears on a ribbon below an anchor, a symbol of hope. The state seal, adopted in 1896 and modified in 2020, has a design similar to that of the flag. The date 1636 is the year Roger Williams founded Providence, Rhode Island's first permanent European settlement.

State flag

State of Rhode Island
State seal

Rhode Island (brown) ranks as the smallest of all the states. It is one of the New England States (yellow).

The State House is in Providence, the capital since 1900. Rhode Island had five capitals from 1663 to 1854. Newport and Providence were co-capitals from 1854 to 1900.

General information

Statehood: May 29, 1790, the 13th state.
State abbreviations: R.I. (traditional); RI (postal).
State motto: *Hope.*
State song: "Rhode Island's It for Me." Words by Charlie Hall; music by Maria Day.

Land and climate

Area: 1,221 mi² (3,162 km²), including 187 mi² (484 km²) of inland water but excluding 9 mi² (23 km²) of coastal water.
Elevation: *Highest*—Jerimoth Hill, 812 ft (247 m) above sea level. *Lowest*—sea level along the Atlantic coast.
Coastline: 40 mi (64 km).
Record high temperature: 104 °F (40 °C) at Providence on Aug. 2, 1975.
Record low temperature: −28 °F (−33 °C) at Wood River Junction on Jan. 11, 1942.
Average July temperature: 71 °F (22 °C).
Average January temperature: 29 °F (−2 °C).
Average yearly precipitation: 44 in (112 cm).

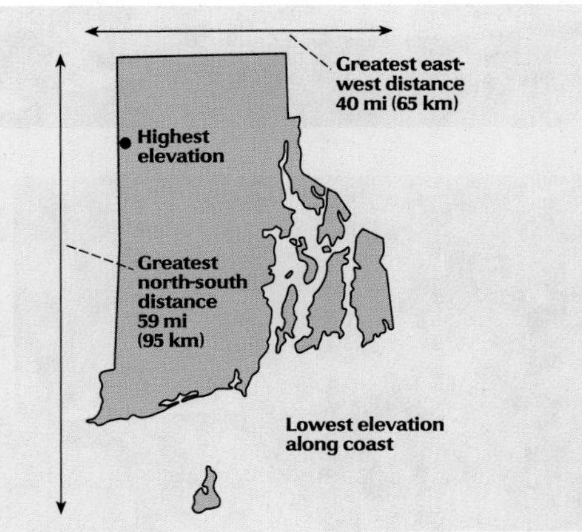

Important dates

- **1524** Giovanni da Verrazzano, an Italian navigator in service of France, sailed into Narragansett Bay.
- **1636** Roger Williams founded Providence.
- **1647** Providence, Portsmouth, Newport, and Warwick united under an English charter granted in 1644.
- **1663** England granted Rhode Island its second charter.
- **1774** Rhode Island prohibited the importation of slaves.

State bird
Rhode Island Red chicken

State flower
Common blue violet

State tree
Red maple

People

Population: 1,052,567
Rank among the states: 43rd
Density: 862 per mi^2 (333 per km^2), U.S. average 85 per mi^2 (33 per km^2)
Distribution: 91 percent urban, 9 percent rural

Largest cities in Rhode Island

City	Population
Providence	178,042
Warwick	82,672
Cranston	80,387
Pawtucket	71,148
East Providence	47,037
Woonsocket	41,186

Source: 2010 census.

Population trend

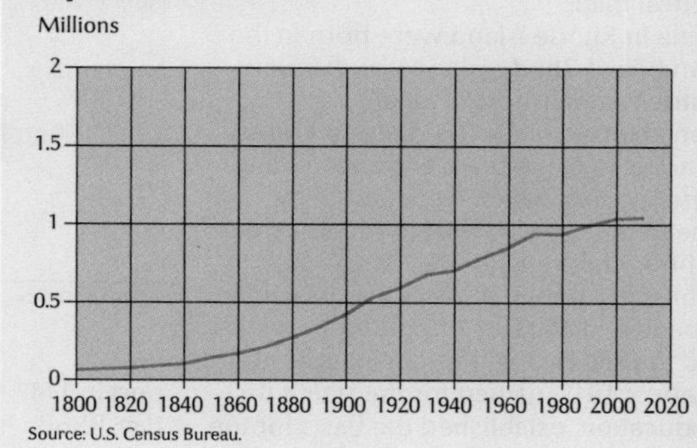

Source: U.S. Census Bureau.

Year	Population
2010	1,052,567
2000	1,048,319
1990	1,003,464
1980	947,154
1970	946,725
1960	859,488
1950	791,896
1940	713,346
1930	687,497
1920	604,397
1910	542,610
1900	428,556
1890	345,506
1880	276,531
1870	217,353
1860	174,620
1850	147,545
1840	108,830
1830	97,199
1820	83,059
1810	76,931
1800	69,122
1790	68,825

Economy

Chief products

Agriculture: apples, greenhouse and nursery products, milk, potatoes, sweet corn.
Fishing industry: clams, flounder, lobster, scallops, squid.
Manufacturing: chemicals, computer and electronic products, fabricated metal products, jewelry and silverware, medical equipment, primary metals.

Gross domestic product

Value of goods and services produced in 2016: $57,860,000,000. *Services* include community, business, and personal services; finance; government; trade; and transportation and communication. *Industry* includes construction, manufacturing, mining, and utilities. *Agriculture* includes agriculture, fishing, and forestry.

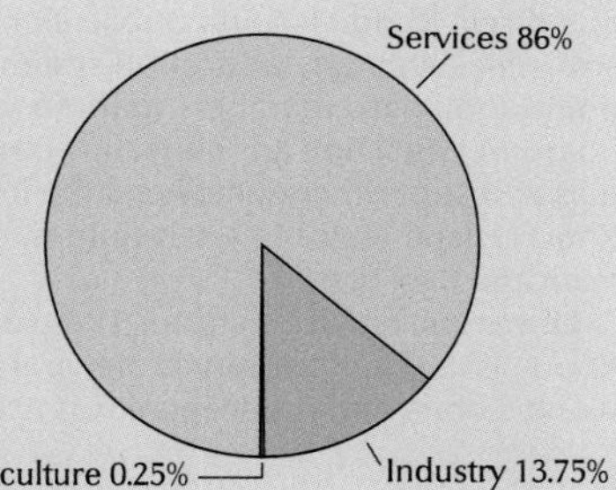

Source: U.S. Bureau of Economic Analysis.

Government

State government

Governor: 4-year term
State senators: 38; 2-year terms
State representatives: 75; 2-year terms
Cities and towns: 39 with local governments (no county governments)

Federal government

United States senators: 2
United States representatives: 2
Electoral votes: 4

Sources of information

Rhode Island's official website at http://www.ri.gov provides a gateway to much information on the state's government, history, and economy.

In addition, the website at http://www.visitrhodeisland.com provides information about tourism.

1790 Rhode Island became the 13th state on May 29.

1842 The Dorr Rebellion helped bring about a more liberal state constitution.

1969 Newport Bridge over Narragansett Bay was completed, linking Newport and Jamestown.

1990 Rhode Island marked the bicentennial of its statehood.

2003 The General Assembly was reduced in size.

People

Population. The 2010 United States census reported that Rhode Island had 1,052,567 people. The state's population had increased less than 1 percent from the 2000 census figure, 1,048,319. According to the 2010 census, Rhode Island ranks 43rd in population among the 50 states.

Rhode Island has eight cities. The state's other communities are called towns. The cities, in order of size, are Providence, Warwick, Cranston, Pawtucket, East Providence, Woonsocket, Newport, and Central Falls.

Approximately one-sixth of all Rhode Islanders live in Providence. All of the state's people live in the Providence-Warwick metropolitan area (see **Metropolitan area**). For the population of this area, see the *Index* to Rhode Island's political map.

Most of the people in Rhode Island were born in the United States. A number of Rhode Islanders who were born in other countries came from Portugal.

Schools. In colonial times, many Rhode Island ministers established schools to teach boys. Girls and young boys attended *dame schools,* which were taught by women. In 1640, the people of Newport founded a free school to educate poor children. Rhode Island's first statewide law establishing public schools was passed in 1800, but it was repealed in 1803. In 1828, Rhode Island's legislature adopted the state's first permanent school law. The Barnard Law of 1845, named for the state's first commissioner of education, established the basis for the current public education system.

A commissioner of education and a Board of Education direct Rhode Island's public elementary, secondary, and post-secondary education system. The governor appoints the board members to three-year terms. The Board of Education appoints the commissioner. Committees and superintendents head the local school districts. Rhode Island children are required to attend school from age 6 to 18.

Libraries. English minister Thomas Bray founded Rhode Island's first library in Newport in 1700. The Redwood Library and Athenaeum was established in Newport in 1747. It is the oldest library in Rhode Island. Today, Rhode Island has public libraries throughout the state and many university and college libraries and special libraries. The Providence Public Library has branches throughout the city. The library's collections include the Rhode Island Collection about the state and its people and the Nicholson Whaling Collection, one of the largest collections of whaling materials in the United States.

The libraries of Brown University have many special collections. The university's John Hay Library houses the McLellan Lincoln Collection of writings by and about Abraham Lincoln. The library also includes the famous Harris Collection of American Poetry and Plays.

The Rhode Island State Library in Providence includes

Population density

Eastern Rhode Island is more heavily populated than the western part of the state. All of the state's people live in the Providence-Warwick metropolitan area.

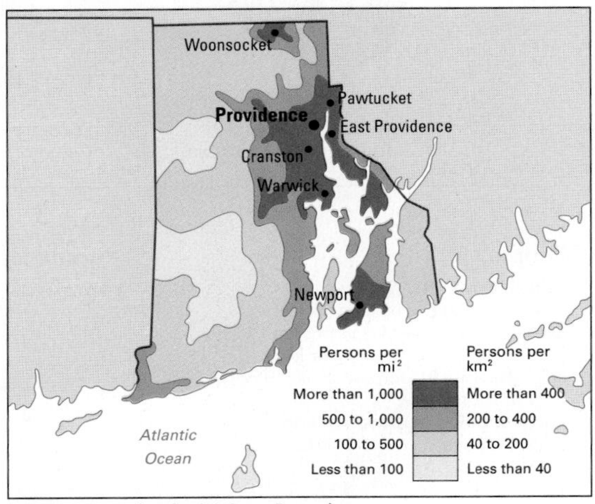

WORLD BOOK map; based on U.S. Census Bureau data.

Rhode Island Department of Economic Development

A crowded ferry takes passengers to Block Island, a popular Rhode Island resort and recreation area. The island lies about 10 miles (16 kilometers) off the mainland.

© Shutterstock

Tennis is a tradition at the Newport Casino, the site of the United States Tennis Championships from 1881 to 1915. Lawn tennis in America began at the Casino, which now houses the International Tennis Hall of Fame.

a special law collection that may be used by government officials and the public. Other special libraries in the state include those of the Newport Historical Society and the Rhode Island Historical Society in Providence.

The Office of Library and Information Services administers both state and federal funds for libraries in Rhode Island. The office also administers the Library of Rhode Island Network.

Museums. The Museum of Art at the Rhode Island School of Design in Providence has tens of thousands of works of art. The Museum of Natural History and Planetarium at Roger Williams Park, also in Providence, has science displays and exhibits of preserved animals and plants. It also owns a large collection of American Indian relics. The South County Museum in Narragansett displays tools used by American colonists. Other museums in the state include the Haffenreffer Museum of Anthropology of Brown University in Providence, the Museum of Primitive Art and Culture in Peace Dale, the Newport Art Museum, the Providence Children's Museum, and the Museum of Work and Culture in Woonsocket.

Universities and colleges

This table lists the nonprofit universities and colleges based in Rhode Island that grant bachelor's or advanced degrees and are accredited by the New England Commission of Higher Education.

Name	Mailing address
Brown University	Providence
Bryant University	Smithfield
Johnson & Wales University	Providence
Naval War College, U.S.	Newport
New England Institute of Technology	Warwick
Providence College	Providence
Rhode Island, University of	Kingston
Rhode Island College	Providence
Rhode Island School of Design	Providence
Roger Williams University	Bristol
Salve Regina University	Newport

© Thinkstock

Brown University in Providence is one of the oldest colleges in the United States. It was chartered in 1764. University Hall, *shown here,* is the university's oldest building. It was completed in 1770.

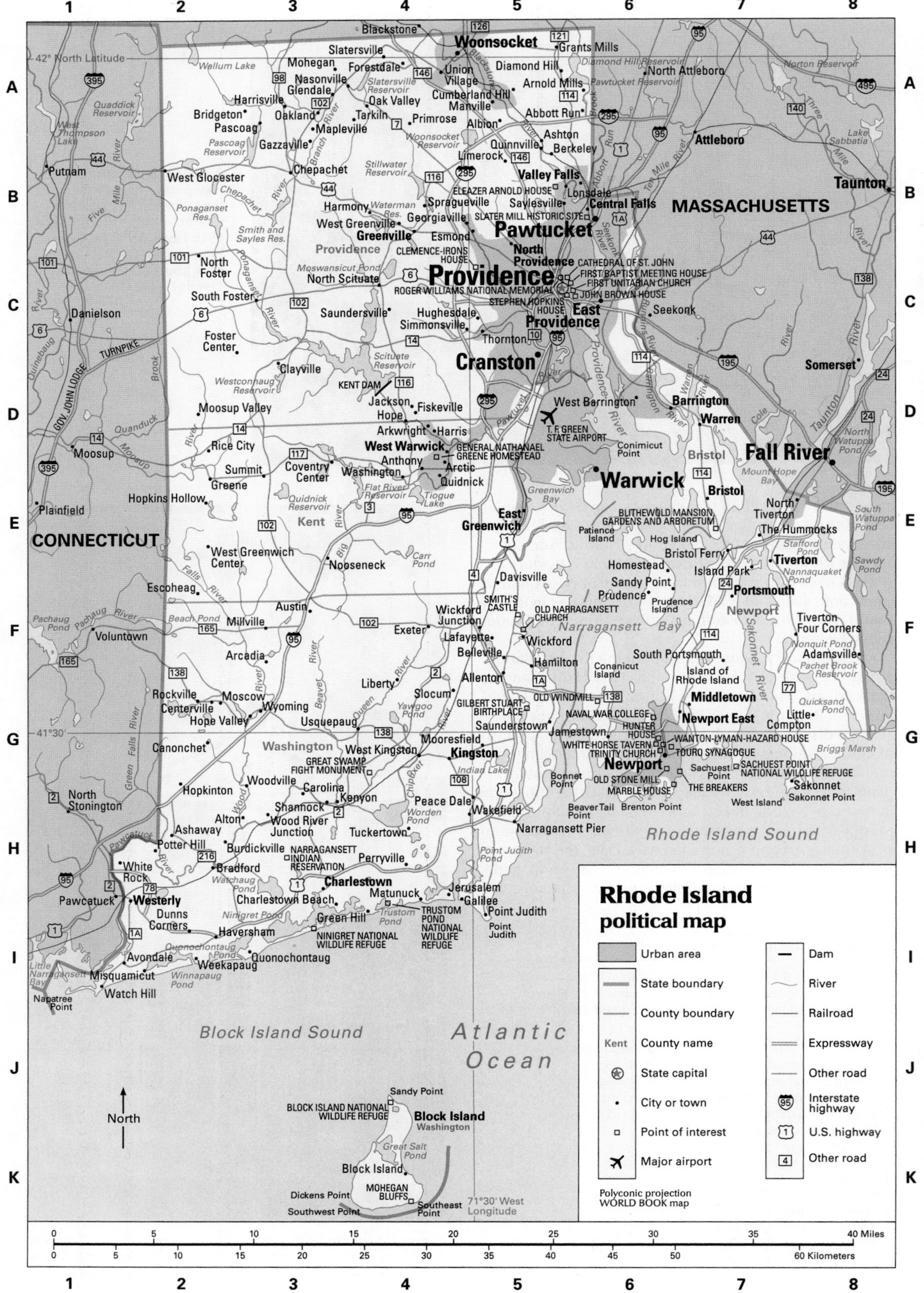

Rhode Island
political map
Urban area
State boundary
County boundary
Kent County name
State capital
City or town
Point of interest
Major airport
Dam
River
Railroad
Expressway
Other road
Interstate highway
U.S. highway
Other road
Polyconic projection
WORLD BOOK map
1 2 3 4 5 6 7 8
A B C D E F G H I J K
0 5 10 15 20 25 30 35 40 Miles
0 5 10 15 20 25 30 35 40 45 50 60 Kilometers
42° North Latitude
41°30'
71°30' West Longitude
North
MASSACHUSETTS
CONNECTICUT
Rhode Island Sound
Block Island Sound
Atlantic Ocean
Providence
Kent
Washington
Newport
Bristol
Blackstone
Woonsocket
Slatersville
Mohegan
Forestdale
Union Village
Nasonville
Glendale
Harrisville
Oakland
Oak Valley
Tarkiln
Mapleville
Bridgeton
Pascoag
Gazzaville
Chepachet
Primrose
Cumberland Hill
Manville
Albion
Diamond Hill
Arnold Mills
Grants Mills
North Attleboro
Abbott Run
Ashton
Berkeley
Quinnville
Limerock
Valley Falls
Lonsdale
Central Falls
Saylesville
ELEAZER ARNOLD HOUSE
SLATER MILL HISTORIC SITE
Attleboro
Taunton
Putnam
West Glocester
Harmony
Spragueville
Georgiaville
West Greenville
Greenville
Esmond
Pawtucket
North Providence
CLEMENCE-IRONS HOUSE
North Scituate
CATHEDRAL OF ST. JOHN
FIRST BAPTIST MEETING HOUSE
FIRST UNITARIAN CHURCH
JOHN BROWN HOUSE
ROGER WILLIAMS NATIONAL MEMORIAL
STEPHEN HOPKINS HOUSE
East Providence
Seekonk
North Foster
South Foster
Danielson
Saundersville
Hughesdale
Simmonsville
Thornton
Foster Center
Cranston
Clayville
KENT DAM
Somerset
Jackson
Hope
Fiskeville
Moosup Valley
West Barrington
Barrington
Warren
Arkwright
Harris
T. F. GREEN STATE AIRPORT
West Warwick
GENERAL NATHANAEL GREENE HOMESTEAD
Anthony
Arctic
Quidnick
Rice City
Moosup
Summit
Coventry Center
Washington
Conimicut Point
Fall River
Warwick
Greene
Hopkins Hollow
Plainfield
Bristol
North Tiverton
BLITHEWOLD MANSION, GARDENS AND ARBORETUM
East Greenwich
Patience Island
Hog Island
The Hummocks
West Greenwich Center
Nooseneck
Bristol Ferry
Tiverton
Homestead
Island Park
Sandy Point
Prudence
Prudence Island
Portsmouth
Escoheag
Davisville
SMITH'S CASTLE
OLD NARRAGANSETT CHURCH
Wickford Junction
Austin
Millville
Voluntown
Exeter
Lafayette
Wickford
Tiverton Four Corners
Arcadia
Belleville
Hamilton
South Portsmouth
Adamsville
Conanicut Island
Island of Rhode Island
Liberty
Allenton
Slocum
Rockville
Centerville
Moscow
Wyoming
Hope Valley
Usquepaug
GILBERT STUART BIRTHPLACE
OLD WINDMILL
NAVAL WAR COLLEGE
Middletown
Newport East
HUNTER HOUSE
Little Compton
Saunderstown
Jamestown
WANTON-LYMAN-HAZARD HOUSE
WHITE HORSE TAVERN
TRINITY CHURCH
TOURO SYNAGOGUE
Canonchet
West Kingston
Mooresfield
Kingston
GREAT SWAMP FIGHT MONUMENT
Newport
SACHUEST POINT NATIONAL WILDLIFE REFUGE
Sachuest Point
Bonnet Point
OLD STONE MILL
MARBLE HOUSE
THE BREAKERS
Sakonnet
West Island
Sakonnet Point
Hopkinton
Woodville
Carolina
North Stonington
Kenyon
Shannock
Peace Dale
Wakefield
Beaver Tail Point
Brenton Point
Alton
Wood River Junction
Ashaway
Tuckertown
Narragansett Pier
Potter Hill
Burdickville
NARRAGANSETT INDIAN RESERVATION
Perryville
White Rock
Bradford
Charlestown
Pawcatuck
Westerly
Charlestown Beach
Matunuck
Jerusalem
Galilee
Point Judith
Dunns Corners
Green Hill
TRUSTOM POND NATIONAL WILDLIFE REFUGE
Haversham
NINIGRET NATIONAL WILDLIFE REFUGE
Avondale
Weekapaug
Quonochontaug
Misquamicut
Watch Hill
Napatree Point
Little Narragansett Bay
Sandy Point
BLOCK ISLAND NATIONAL WILDLIFE REFUGE
Block Island
Great Salt Pond
MOHEGAN BLUFFS
Dickens Point
Southwest Point
Southeast Point
Narragansett Bay
Wallum Lake
Quaddick Reservoir
West Thompson Lake
Pascoag Reservoir
Slatersville Reservoir
Woonsocket Reservoir
Stillwater Reservoir
Waterman Res.
Ponaganset Res.
Smith and Sayles Res.
Moswansicut Pond
Scituate Reservoir
Westconnaug Reservoir
Diamond Hill Reservoir
Pawtucket Reservoir
Norton Reservoir
Lake Sabbatia
Flat River Reservoir
Tiogue Lake
Quidnick Reservoir
Greenwich Bay
Carr Pond
Mount Hope Bay
North Watuppa Pond
South Watuppa Pond
Stafford Pond
Sawdy Pond
Nannaquaket Pond
Nonquit Pond
Pachet Brook Reservoir
Quicksand Pond
Briggs Marsh
Beach Pond
Pachaug Pond
Yawgoo Pond
Indian Lake
Worden Pond
Point Judith Pond
Watchaug Pond
Ninigret Pond
Trustom Pond
Quonochontaug Pond
Winnapaug Pond
GOV. JOHN LODGE TURNPIKE

Rhode Island map index

Metropolitan area

Providence-Warwick ....1,600,852 (1,052,567 in RI, 548,285 in MA)

Counties

Bristol ....49,875 ..D 7
Kent ....166,158 ..E 4
Newport ....82,888 ..F 6
Providence ....626,667 ..C 3
Washington ...126,979 ..G 2

Cities, towns, and other populated places

Adamsville ....F 8
Albion ....A 5
Allenton ....F 5
Alton ....H 2
Anthony ....D 4
Arcadia ....F 3
Arctic ....D 4
Arkwright ....D 4
Arnold Mills ....A 5
Ashaway† ....1,485 ..H 2
Ashton ....B 5
Austin ....F 3
Avondale ....I 1
Barrington▲ ....16,310 ..D 6
Belleville ....F 5
Berkeley ....B 5
Block Island ....K 4
Bradford† ....1,406 ..H 2
Bridgeton ....A 2
Bristol▲ ....22,954 ..E 7
Bristol Ferry ....E 7
Burdickville ....H 2
Burrillville*▲ ...15,955 ..A 3
Canonchet ....G 2
Carolina† ....970 ..G 3
Centerville ....G 2
Central Falls ....19,376 ..B 6
Charlestown▲ ...7,827 ..H 3
Chepachet† ......1,675 ..B 3
Clayville† ....300 ..D 3
Coventry*▲ .....35,014 ..E 5
Coventry Center ....D 3
Cranston ....80,387 ..D 5
Cumberland*▲ ....33,506 ..A 5
Cumberland Hill† ....7,934 ..A 5
Davisville ....F 5
Diamond Hill ....A 5
Dunns Corner ....I 2
East Greenwich▲ ....13,146 ..E 5
East Providence ....47,037 ..C 6
Esmond ....B 5
Exeter▲ ....6,425 ..F 4
Fiskeville ....D 4
Forestdale ....A 4
Foster*▲ ....4,606 ..C 2
FosterCenter† .....355 ..C 2
Galilee ....H 4
Georgiaville ....B 4
Glendale ....A 3
Glocester*▲ .....9,746 ..B 3
Grants Mills ....A 5
Green Hill ....I 4
Greene† ....888 ..E 2
Greenville† ......8,658 ..B 4
Hamilton ....F 5
Harmony† ....985 ..B 4
Harris ....D 4
Harrisville† ......1,605 ..A 3
Haversham ....I 2
Homestead ....E 6
Hope ....D 4
Hope Valley† ....1,612 ..G 3
Hopkins Hollow ....E 2
Hopkinton▲ .....8,188 ..G 2
Hughesdale ....C 5
Hummocks, The ....E 7
Island Park ....F 7
Jackson ....D 4
Jamestown▲ .....5,405 ..G 6
Jerusalem ....H 4
Johnston*▲ .....28,769 ..C 5
Kenyon ....H 3
Kingston† ....6,974 ..G 4
Lafayette ....F 5
Liberty ....E 4
Limerock ....B 5
Lincoln*▲ ....21,105 ..B 5
Little Compton▲ ....3,492 ..G 8
Lonsdale ....B 5
Manville ....A 5
Mapleville ....A 3
Matunuck ....H 4
Melville*† ....1,320 ..F 6
Middletown▲ ..16,150 ..G 7
Misquamicut† .....390 ..I 2
Mohegan ....A 3
Mooresfield ....G 5
Moosup Valley ....D 2
Moscow ....G 2
Narragansett*▲ ....15,868 ..H 5
Narragansett Pier† ....3,409 ..H 5
Narragansett Indian Reservation ....I 1
Nasonville ....A 3
New Shoreham*▲ ....1,051 ..K 4
Newport ....24,672 ..G 6
Newport East† ..11,769 ..G 6
Nooseneck ....E 3
North Foster ....C 2
North Kingstown*▲ ....26,486 ..F 5
North Providence▲ ......32,078 ..C 5
North Scituate ....C 4
North Smithfield*▲ ....11,967 ..A 4
North Tiverton ....E 7
Oak Valley ....A 4
Oakland ....A 3
Pascoag† ....4,577 ..A 3
Pawtucket ......71,148 ..B 6
Peace Dale ....H 5
Perryville ....H 4
Point Judith ....I 5
Portsmouth▲ ...17,389 ..F 7
Potter Hill ....H 2
Primrose ....A 4
Providence ....178,042 ..C 5
Prudence ....F 6
Quidnick ....E 4
Quinnville ....B 5
Quonochontaug† ..333 ..I 3
Rice City ....D 2
Richmond*▲ .....7,708 ..H 2
Rockville ....G 2
Sakonnet ....G 7
Saunderstown ....G 5
Saylesville ....B 5
Scituate*▲ ......10,329 ..D 3
Shannock ....H 3
Simmonsville ....C 4
Slatersville ....A 4
Slocum ....G 4
Smithfield*▲ ....21,430 ..B 4
South Foster ....C 3
South Kingstown▲* ......30,639 ..H 4
Spragueville ....B 4
Summit ....E 3
Tarkiln ....A 4
Thornton ....C 5
Tiverton† ....7,557 ▲15,780 ..E 7
Tuckertown ....H 4
Union Village ....A 4
Usquepaug ....G 3
Valley Falls† ....11,547 ..B 5
Wakefield ....H 5
Wakefield-Peacedale*† ...8,487 ..H 5
Warren▲ ....10,611 ..D 7
Warwick ....82,672 ..E 6
Watch Hill† ....154 ..I 1
Weekapaug† ......425 ..I 2
West Barrington ....D 6
West Glocester ....B 2
West Greenville ....B 4
West Greenwich*▲ ....6,135 ..E 2
West Greenwich Center ....E 2
West Kingston ....G 4
West Warwick▲ ...29,191 ..D 4
Westerly† ....17,936 ▲22,787 ..H 2
White Rock ....H 1
Wickford ....F 5
Wickford Junction ....F 5
Woonsocket ....41,186 ..A 4
Wyoming† ....270 ..G 3

*Does not appear on map; key shows general location.
†Census designated place—unincorporated, but recognized as a significant settled community by the U.S. Census Bureau.
▲Population is for entire town (township), including rural areas.

Places without population figures are unincorporated areas.
Source: 2010 census. Metropolitan area figures are based on the 2013 Office of Management and Budget reorganization of 2010 census data.

© Shutterstock

The Newport Bridge, New England's longest suspension bridge, opened in 1969. It replaced the Jamestown ferry, providing a more direct route between Newport and western Rhode Island. The bridge was renamed the Claiborne Pell Bridge in 1992, but residents commonly refer to it by its former name.

Visitor's guide

Thousands of vacationers visit the coastal resorts of Rhode Island each year. The resorts in the state offer swimming, boating, fishing, and beautiful scenery. Rhode Island's leading resort centers include Block Island, Narragansett, Newport, and Watch Hill. In addition, tourists can visit the many historic sites, colonial buildings, and old churches in Rhode Island. Many of Rhode Island's most popular annual events include boat races, fishing contests, and tennis tournaments. The annual Newport Music Festival is held in July. This event features internationally known classical artists performing in Newport mansion settings.

© J. H. Peterson, Marine Photographic Services

A yacht race off the coast of Newport

Places to visit

Following are brief descriptions of some of Rhode Island's most interesting places to visit.

Blithewold Mansion, Gardens and Arboretum, in Bristol, is set on a large estate overlooking Narragansett Bay. The gardens feature many old and exotic plants and trees.

Block Island and Southeast Lighthouse lie about 10 miles (16 kilometers) off the Rhode Island mainland. The Mohegan Bluffs, which rise about 200 feet (60 meters) above the ocean, add to the island's spectacular scenery. The famous Southeast Lighthouse stands on Mohegan Bluffs.

Cliff Walk, in Newport, is a 3 ½-mile (5.6-kilometer) path along the rocky coast of the Atlantic Ocean. It passes several famous Newport mansions. It is a National Recreation Trail.

Colonial buildings rank among Rhode Island's most interesting landmarks. They include the Gilbert Stuart Birthplace, built in North Kingstown in 1751, and the General Nathanael Greene Homestead, built in Coventry in 1770. Stuart was the foremost painter of portraits of George Washington. Greene was a great patriot leader of the Revolutionary War in America (1775-1783). Other Rhode Island colonial buildings include White Horse Tavern (Newport, 1673); Smith's Castle (near Wickford, 1678); Clemence-Irons House (Johnston, 1691); Eleazer Arnold House (Lincoln, c. 1693); Wanton-Lyman-Hazard House (Newport, 1697); Old Narragansett Church (North Kingstown, 1707); Trinity Church (Newport, 1726); Hunter House (Newport, 1748); Touro Synagogue (Newport, 1763); First Baptist Meeting House (Providence, 1775); John Brown House (Providence, 1786); and Old Windmill (Jamestown, 1787).

Newport mansions also rank among Rhode Island's points of interest. Many of these beautiful mansions were built as summer houses for wealthy American families. The Breakers, the estate of Cornelius Vanderbilt, is among the most famous. Its 70-room mansion was built in 1895. A nearby mansion called Marble House is one of the most ornate buildings in the United States. It was built for William K. Vanderbilt in 1892. Other famous Newport mansions include Chateau-sur-Mer (1852), The Elms (1901), Kingscote (1839), and Rosecliff (1902).

Rhode Island State House, in Providence, has one of the world's few self-supporting marble domes. Construction of the State House began in 1895 and was completed in 1904.

Roger Williams Park Zoo, in Providence, was designed in 1878. The Victorian park includes waterways, walks, gardens, and a museum. The zoo features more than 100 species of animals.

Slater Mill Historic Site, in Pawtucket, includes one of the first successful textile mills in North America. This mill was built in 1793 by Samuel Slater, the founder of the American textile industry. The mill is now a museum.

State parks. Rhode Island has a number of state parks and state beaches. Visit the official website of the Rhode Island State Parks at http://www.riparks.com for more information.

© Shutterstock

Gilbert Stuart Birthplace in North Kingstown

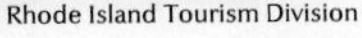

Rhode Island Tourism Division

Blithewold Mansion, Gardens and Arboretum in Bristol

Rhode Island Tourism

Slater Mill Historic Site in Pawtucket

Land regions. Rhode Island has two main land regions. These regions are, from east to west, (1) the Coastal Lowlands, and (2) the Eastern New England Upland.

The Coastal Lowlands cover more than half the Rhode Island mainland, the islands in Narragansett Bay, and the land east of the bay. The Coastal Lowlands are part of a larger land region of the same name that covers the entire New England coast.

Many sandy beaches and plains line the shores of Rhode Island's lowlands. The shore west of Point Judith has sandy beaches, lagoons, and salt ponds. Rocky cliffs are found on the islands and the shore along the bay. Inland, the land rises to form higher elevations. East of Narragansett Bay, the slopes are low, round, and have few trees. West of the bay, the slopes are rugged and forested.

The Eastern New England Upland covers the northwestern third of Rhode Island. The entire Eastern New England Upland extends from Maine to Connecticut. The portion in Rhode Island is often called the *Western Rocky Upland.* It has sloping hills and a higher elevation than the Coastal Lowlands. The land of the Western Rocky Upland rises from about 200 feet (60 meters) above sea level in the east to over 800 feet (240 meters) in the northwest.

Lakes, reservoirs, and ponds nestle among the region's many hills. These hills include 812-foot (247-meter) Jerimoth Hill, the state's highest point. The state has no mountains.

Islands. Rhode Island includes 36 islands. They range in size from Aquidneck Island (officially named Rhode Island) with an area of 45 square miles (117 square kilometers), to Despair, a clump of rocks in Narragansett Bay. Block Island (officially New Shoreham) covers about 11 square miles (28 square kilometers). It lies in the Atlantic, about 10 miles (16 kilometers) south of the Rhode Island mainland. Bridges and ferry service connect the largest islands and the mainland.

Coastline. Rhode Island has a 40-mile (64-kilometer) general coastline. If the tidal shoreline of the state's bays and islands were included, the coastline would measure 384 miles (618 kilometers). The largest bay, Narragansett Bay, extends 28 miles (45 kilometers) inland. The many arms of Narragansett Bay include Greenwich and Mount Hope bays.

Rivers and lakes. Three of Rhode Island's chief rivers—Providence, Sakonnet, and Seekonk—are really saltwater arms of Narragansett Bay. Several freshwater rivers flow into the bay. These include the Pawtuxet, Pettaquamscutt, Potowomut, and Woonasquatucket. One river, the Blackstone, becomes the Pawtucket and then the Seekonk before flowing into the bay. The Pawcatuck River flows through southwestern Rhode Island and

Rhode Island Department of Economic Development

A farm in Lincoln is part of the Coastal Lowlands region that stretches along the entire New England coast. The lowlands of Rhode Island include many plains and sandy beaches.

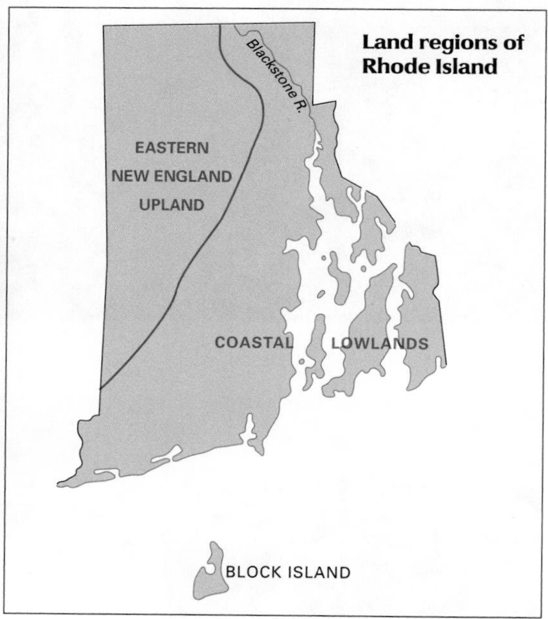

WORLD BOOK map

Map index

Bald Hill .... D 3
Barden Reservoir .... C 3
Beach Pond .... E 3
Beavertail Pt. .... F 5
Big R. .... D 4
Blackstone R. .... A 5
Block I. .... I 3
Block Island Sound .... I 2
Brenton Pt. .... F 6
Chepachet R. .... A 3
Chipuxet R. .... F 4
Coasters Harbor I. .... F 6
Conanicut I. .... E 5
Conimicut Pt. .... D 6
Coventry Reservoir .... D 3
Fishers Island Sound .... H 1
Flat River Reservoir .... D 3
Great Salt Pond .... I 4
Greenwich Bay .... D 5
Hog I. .... D 6
Jerimoth Hill (highest point in R.I.) .... B 3
Lands End .... F 6
Moosup R. .... D 2
Moswansicut Pond .... B 4
Mount Hope Bay .... D 7
Napatree Pt. .... H 2
Narragansett Bay .... E 5
Ninigret Pond .... G 3
Nonquit Pond .... E 7
North Pt. .... D 6
Pascoag Reservoir .... A 3
Pawcatuck R. .... F 3
Pawtucket R. .... B 6
Pawtuxet R. .... C 5
Pettaquamscutt R. .... F 5
Point Judith .... G 5
Point Judith Neck .... G 5
Point Judith Pond .... G 4
Ponaganset Reservoir .... B 3
Ponaganset R. .... C 3
Providence R. .... C 5
Prudence I. .... D 6
Queen R. .... E 4
Quicksand Pond .... F 7
Quonochontaug Pond .... G 3
Rhode I. (Aquidneck I.) .... E 6
Rhode Island Sound .... G 6
Sachuest Pt. .... F 7
Sakonnet Pt. .... F 7
Sakonnet R. .... F 7
Sandy Pt. .... H 4
Scituate Reservoir .... C 4
Seekonk R. .... B 5
Smith and Sayles Reservoir .... B 3
Southeast Point .... I 4
Stafford Pond .... D 7
Tenmile R. .... B 6
Tiogue Lake .... D 4
Wallum Lake .... A 2
Watchaug Pond .... G 3
Waterman Reservoir .... B 4
Weekapaug Pt. .... H 3
West I. .... F 7
Wilson Reservoir .... A 3
Wood R. .... F 3
Woonasquatucket R. .... A 4
Woonsocket Hill .... A 4
Worden Pond .... F 4

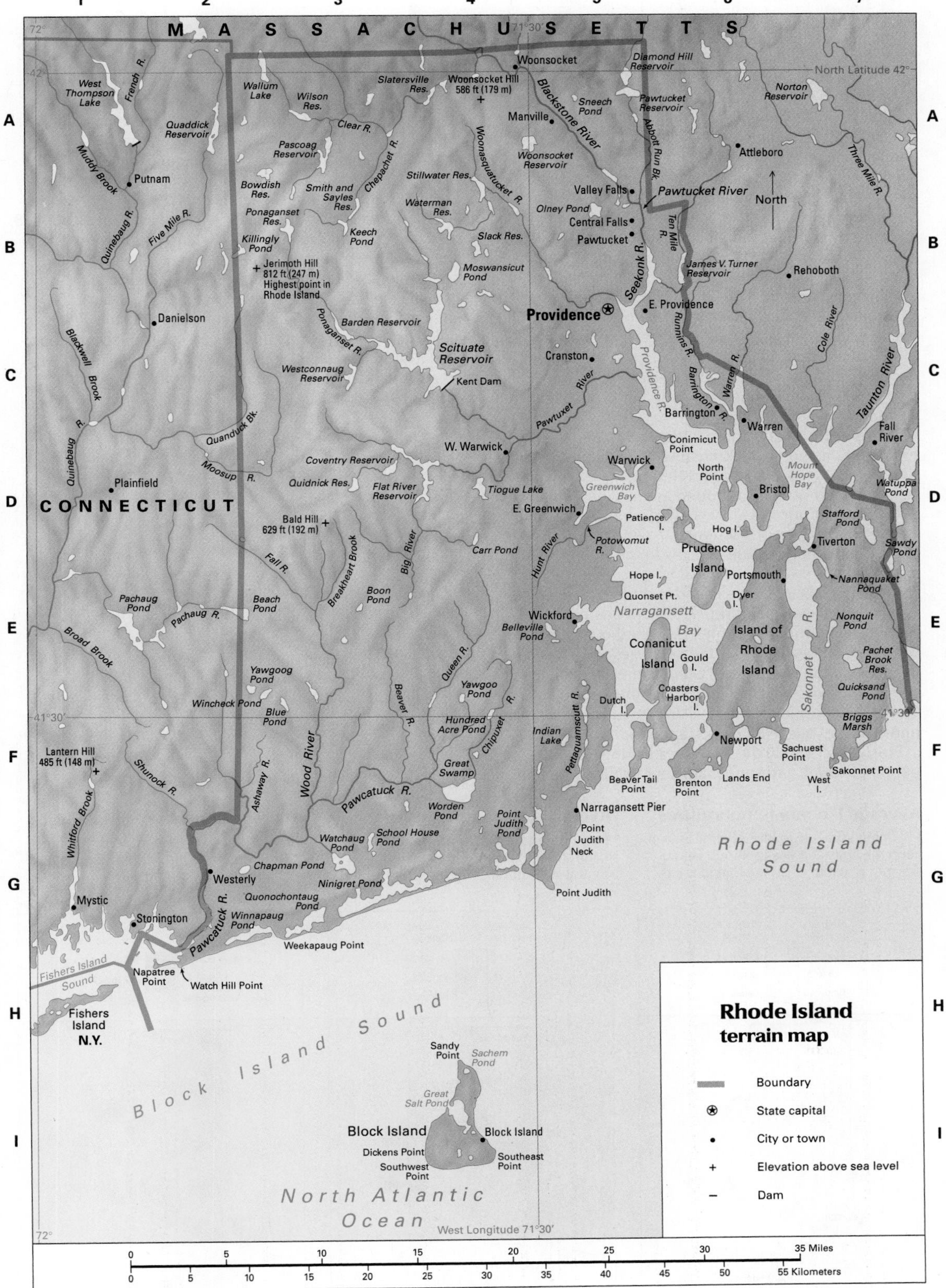

WORLD BOOK map

forms part of the Rhode Island-Connecticut border. Other important rivers include the Chepachet, Ponaganset, and Wood.

Most of the state's inland rivers are small but swift. Many of the rivers have waterfalls. Water was once the most important source of power for Rhode Island's mills and factories.

Many lakes, ponds, and reservoirs dot the Rhode Island countryside. Scituate Reservoir, the largest inland body of water in the state, supplies water for Providence and nearby communities. Other large bodies of water in Rhode Island include Watchaug Pond and Worden Pond.

Plant and animal life. Forests cover about three-fifths of Rhode Island. The state's trees include ashes, birches, black walnuts, cedars, elms, hickories, maples, oaks, pines, poplars, and willows. Pin and post oaks are found near the north shore of Wickford Harbor. Paper birches, also called canoe birches, thrive in the northern part of the state.

Asters and cattails bloom in the marshlands of Charlestown and South Kingstown. Scarlet pimpernels grow on the cliffs of Newport. Red deer grass, white daisies, and wild carrots are found in the state's meadows. Dogwoods, mountain laurels, rhododendrons, trilliums, and violets grow in the woodlands. A variety of freshwater and saltwater seaweeds grow in the waters of Rhode Island.

Wild animals in Rhode Island include beavers, coyotes, deer, foxes, minks, muskrats, opossums, otters, rabbits, raccoons, and squirrels. Barred owls, blue jays, catbirds, flickers, robins, ruffed grouse, and screech-owls live in the woodlands. Gulls, loons, ospreys, terns, and other shore birds make their homes along the coast. Game birds found in Rhode Island include partridges, pheasants, quails, wild ducks, and woodcocks.

Freshwater fish in the state's waters include bass, eels, perch, pickerel, and trout. Saltwater fish include bluefish, butterfish, flounder, mackerel, menhaden, sea bass, striped bass, swordfish, and tuna.

Climate. Warming winds from Narragansett Bay help give Rhode Island a mild climate. January temperatures average 29 °F (−2 °C), and July temperatures average 72 °F (22 °C). The state's highest temperature, 104 °F (40 °C), was recorded at Providence on Aug. 2, 1975. The lowest temperature, −28 °F (−33 °C), was recorded at Wood River Junction on Jan. 11, 1942.

Yearly precipitation in Rhode Island averages about 48 inches (122 centimeters). Block Island averages about 20 inches (51 centimeters) of snow a year. The rest of the state averages about 34 inches (86 centimeters) of snow a year. The state has a growing season of about 200 days. Hurricanes and their accompanying *storm surges,* produced when winds drive ocean waters ashore, lash the Rhode Island coast and the shores of Narragansett Bay. The most destructive hurricanes occurred in 1815, 1938, 1944, and 1954.

Average monthly weather

Providence

	Temperatures °F High	Temperatures °F Low	Temperatures °C High	Temperatures °C Low	Days of rain or snow
Jan.	37	21	3	-6	11
Feb.	40	24	4	-4	9
Mar.	48	30	9	-1	11
Apr.	59	40	15	4	11
May	68	49	20	9	11
June	78	58	26	14	10
July	83	64	28	18	9
Aug.	81	63	27	17	9
Sept.	74	55	23	13	8
Oct.	63	44	17	7	9
Nov.	53	36	12	2	10
Dec.	42	26	6	-3	11

Average January temperatures

Warming winds from the Atlantic Ocean keep the coastal areas of Rhode Island warmer in winter than the inland areas.

Degrees Fahrenheit / Degrees Celsius
Above 30 / Above -1
28 to 30 / -2 to -1
Below 28 / Below -2

Woonsocket
Providence
Warwick
Newport
Westerly
Block Island

Average July temperatures

Summer temperatures are generally even throughout the state. The southern and central sections are slightly warmer.

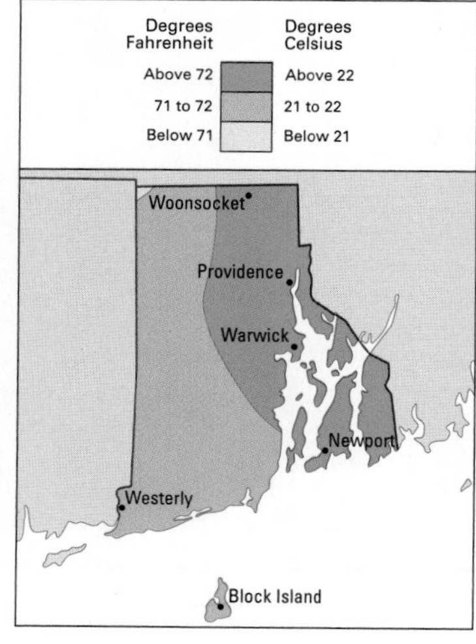

Average annual precipitation

There is little variation in precipitation throughout the state, but the west is generally the wettest section.

WORLD BOOK maps

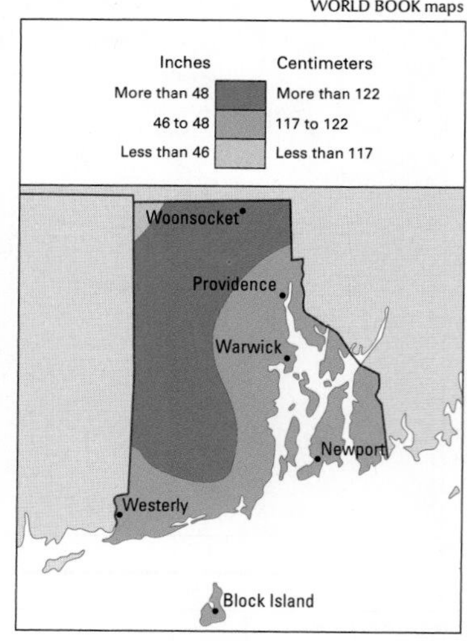

Service industries, which include such wide-ranging activities as real estate, health care, and trade, employ most of Rhode Island's work force. Manufacturing is also an important economic activity in the state.

Natural resources. Rhode Island has only a few large mineral deposits and other natural resources.

Soil. Rhode Island's richest soil is found along Narragansett Bay. Miami stony loam covers the bay's basin and tableland. This firm brown soil holds moisture for an entire growing season. Glocester stony loam is the state's least fertile soil. This light brown sand covers much of western and northern Rhode Island.

Rhode Island economy

General economy

Gross domestic product (GDP)* (2017)	$59,306,000,000
Rank among U.S. states	44th
Unemployment rate (2018)	4.1% (U.S. avg: 3.9%)

*Gross domestic product is the total value of goods and services produced in a year.
Sources: U.S. Bureau of Economic Analysis and U.S. Bureau of Labor Statistics.

Agriculture

Cash receipts	$71,553,000
Rank among U.S. states	49th
Distribution	68% crops, 32% livestock
Farms	1,100
Farm acres (hectares)	60,000 (20,000)
Rank among U.S. states	50th
Farmland	8% of Rhode Island

Leading products

Greenhouse and nursery products

Other products: apples, cattle and calves, dairy products, eggs, hay, hogs, honey, potatoes, sweet corn, turkeys.

Manufacturing

Value added by manufacture*	$5,607,462,000
Rank among U.S. states	43rd

Leading products

1. Chemicals
2. Fabricated metal products

Other products: computer and electronic products, jewelry and silverware, medical equipment, primary metals.

*Value added by manufacture is the increase in value of raw materials as they become finished products.

Fishing

Commercial catch	$93,869,000
Rank among U.S. states	15th

Leading catches

1. Squid (ranks 2nd in U.S.)
2. Lobsters

Other catches: clams, flounder, goosefish, scallops, scups.

Mining

Nonfuel mineral production*	$53,400,000
Rank among U.S. states	49th
Coal	†
Crude oil	†
Natural gas	†

*Partial total, excludes values that must be concealed to not disclose company data.
†No significant mining of this product in Rhode Island.

Leading products

Sand and gravel

Other products: gemstones, granite, limestone, traprock.

Electric power

Natural gas	94.4%
Other	5.6%

Agriculture and electric power figures are for 2017; fishing and manufacturing figures are for 2016, mining figures are for 2015.
Sources: U.S. Census Bureau, U.S. Department of Agriculture, U.S. Energy Information Administration, U.S. Geological Survey, U.S. National Marine Fisheries Service.

Production and workers by economic activities

Economic activities	Percent of GDP produced	Employed workers: Number of people	Employed workers: Percent of total
Finance, insurance, & real estate	28	79,700	13
Community, business, & personal services	25	248,200	39
Trade, restaurants, & hotels	15	126,800	20
Government	13	72,100	11
Manufacturing	9	42,900	7
Transportation & communication	5	26,200	4
Construction	4	30,700	5
Utilities	1	1,700	*
Agriculture & mining	*	4,200	1
Total	100	632,500	100

*Less than one-half of 1 percent.
Figures are for 2016; employment figures include full- and part-time workers.
Source: *World Book* estimates based on data from U.S. Bureau of Economic Analysis.

Economy of Rhode Island

This map shows the economic uses of land in Rhode Island and where the leading farm and mineral products are produced. The state's major manufacturing centers are shown in red.

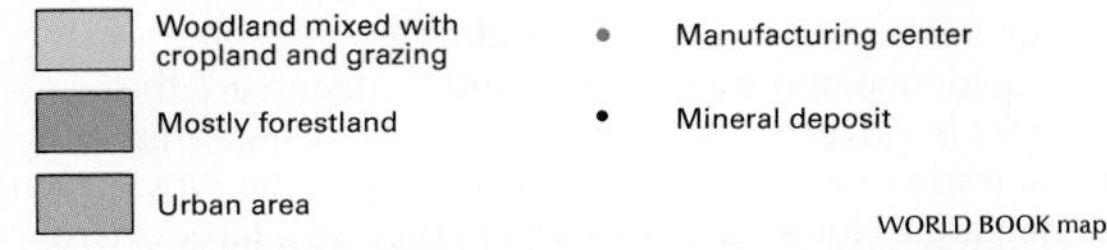

WORLD BOOK map

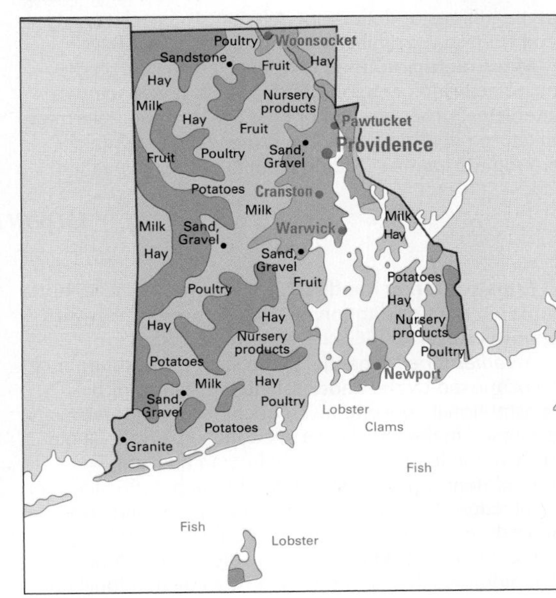

Swarovsky Jewelry U.S. Limited

Crystal stones are set by hand in beautiful jewelry by a Rhode Island jeweler. The production of jewelry and silverware ranks as one of Rhode Island's most important manufacturing activities.

Minerals. Westerly granite is Rhode Island's best-known mineral. Its hardness and fine grain make it an excellent building material. Deposits of this granite lie mainly in southwestern Rhode Island, near the town of Westerly. The Coastal Lowlands have large sand and gravel deposits. Other mined products found in Rhode Island include limestone and traprock.

Service industries account for most of both Rhode Island's employment and its *gross domestic product*—the total value of all goods and services produced in the state in a year. Finance, insurance, and real estate is the state's leading service industry group. Providence is one of New England's leading financial centers. Some of the nation's largest banking and insurance companies have major operations in Rhode Island.

Providence, the state capital, and Cranston are the centers of government activities. Hotels, restaurants, and retail trade establishments are primarily in the Providence area. Hotels and restaurants receive a large share of the billions of dollars spent by tourists each year. Several U.S. Navy facilities lie along Narragansett Bay.

Manufacturing. The Providence area is the leading manufacturing center in Rhode Island. *Pharmaceuticals* (medicinal drugs) and other chemical products are manufactured in Providence. The Providence area ranks among the nation's leading centers of the jewelry and silverware industries. The production of both costume jewelry and fine jewelry is important in Rhode Island.

Fabricated metal products are made in the mainland part of the state. Architectural and structural metals and machine shop products are among the leading fabricated metal products made in Rhode Island. The state also manufactures medical equipment and primary metals.

Agriculture. Farmland covers less than 10 percent of Rhode Island's land area. Greenhouse and nursery products are the leading source of agricultural income. They earn over half of the state's agricultural income.

Milk is another important source of agricultural income in Rhode Island. Dairy cows are primarily found in Newport and Washington counties. Hay, which is grown throughout the state, is the leading field crop. Potatoes and sweet corn are the state's leading vegetables. Apples are the leading fruit.

Fishing industry. Rhode Island's annual fish catch includes a variety of fish and shellfish. Lobster and squid are among its leading catches. The state is a leading producer of flounder, scallops, and squid.

Mining accounts for less than one-half of 1 percent of Rhode Island's gross domestic product. Sand and gravel, and stone, are the most valuable mined products.

Electric power and utilities. Plants that burn natural gas produce almost all of Rhode Island's electric power. The rest is provided by plants that burn petroleum and by plants that use renewable sources.

Transportation. Newport and Providence were international shipping centers from colonial days until the 1830's. Their importance as shipping centers declined with the development of railroads. Rhode Island's first railroad began operating between Providence and Boston in 1835. Today, the Providence and Worcester Railroad provides freight service in the state.

Rhode Island has an extensive system of roads and highways. The state's portion of Interstate Highway 95 extends between the Connecticut border, near Ashaway, and Pawtucket. Interstate 295 skirts Providence to the north and west. The biggest airport in Rhode Island is T. F. Green Airport in Warwick.

Communication. Rhode Island's first newspaper, the *Rhode Island Gazette,* began publication in 1732. Its publisher, James Franklin, was the brother of Benjamin Franklin. Today, the state's leading daily newspapers include *The Call* of Woonsocket, *The Newport Daily News, The Providence Journal,* and *The Times* of Pawtucket.

Government

Constitution of Rhode Island was adopted in 1986. It replaced the Constitution of 1842. Before that, a royal English charter of 1663 served as the constitution.

An *amendment* (change) to the state Constitution may be proposed by the Rhode Island legislature or by a constitutional convention. To become law, amendments proposed in the legislature need the approval of a majority of the legislators once before an election. The amendments are then submitted to the people in a regular election. A majority of those voting must approve the amendments. To call a constitutional convention, a majority vote by the legislators and voters is needed. Amendments that are proposed by a constitutional convention require the approval of a majority of the voters in a regular election.

Executive. The governor of Rhode Island is elected to a four-year term and may serve no more than two consecutive terms. Rhode Island has no official residence for its governor. Rhode Island voters also elect the lieutenant governor, attorney general, secretary of state, and state treasurer to four-year terms.

The governor, with the Senate's approval, appoints most other key executive officials. These executive officials include the directors of administration, business regulation, environmental management, health, human services, labor and training, and transportation.

Legislature of Rhode Island is called the General Assembly. It consists of a 38-member Senate and a 75-member House of Representatives. Senators and representatives serve two-year terms. The General Assembly meets annually, beginning on the first Tuesday of January. Regular and special legislative sessions have no time limit.

Courts. The Supreme Court of Rhode Island has a chief justice and four associate justices. The governor, with the advice and consent of the House and Senate, appoints Supreme Court justices, including a chief justice, to life terms.

Other Rhode Island courts include a district court, a family court, a superior court, and a workers' compensation court. The governor, with the consent of the Senate, appoints district, family, superior, and workers' compensation court judges to life terms.

Local government. Most of Rhode Island's cities and towns have *home rule.* That is, they can write and amend their charters without permission from the legislature. Rhode Island *towns* are similar to *townships* in other states. They are geographic districts that may include rural areas and several unincorporated villages under one government. Rhode Island and Connecticut are the only states with no county governments. But the two states do have geographical areas called counties.

Most large cities in Rhode Island have the mayor-council form of government. These cities include Central Falls, Cranston, Pawtucket, Providence, Warwick, and Woonsocket. East Providence and Newport are the cities that use the council-manager form of government. Most of Rhode Island's towns have a council-manager form of government.

Revenue. Taxation provides about 40 percent of the state government's *general revenue* (income). Other major sources of revenue are federal grants, municipal bonds, and charges for government services.

The largest source of tax revenue in Rhode Island is a personal income tax. A general sales tax is the second largest source of tax revenue. Other important sources of tax revenue include taxes on corporate income, insurance premiums, motor vehicle licenses, public utilities, and tobacco products. The state also receives revenue from a lottery.

The state governors of Rhode Island

	Party	Term
Nicholas Cooke	None	1775-1778
William Greene	None	1778-1786
John Collins	None	1786-1790
Arthur Fenner	Anti-Federalist	1790-1805
Henry Smith	Unknown	1805
Isaac Wilbur	Unknown	1806-1807
James Fenner	*Dem.-Rep.	1807-1811
William Jones	Federalist	1811-1817
Nehemiah R. Knight	*Dem.-Rep.	1817-1821
William C. Gibbs	*Dem.-Rep.	1821-1824
James Fenner	*Dem.-Rep.	1824-1831
Lemuel H. Arnold	†Nat. Rep.	1831-1833
John Brown Francis	Democratic	1833-1838
William Sprague	Democratic	1838-1839
Samuel Ward King	Rhode Island Party	1840-1843
James Fenner	Law and Order	1843-1845
Charles Jackson	Liberation	1845-1846
Byron Diman	Law and Order	1846-1847
Elisha Harris	Whig	1847-1849
Henry B. Anthony	Whig	1849-1851
Philip Allen	Democratic	1851-1853
Francis M. Dimond	Democratic	1853-1854
William W. Hoppin	Whig and Know-Nothing	1854-1857
Elisha Dyer	Republican	1857-1859
Thomas G. Turner	Republican	1859-1860
William Sprague	Democratic & Conservative	1860-1863
William C. Cozzens	Democratic	1863
James Y. Smith	Republican	1863-1866
Ambrose E. Burnside	Republican	1866-1869
Seth Padelford	Republican	1869-1873
Henry Howard	Republican	1873-1875
Henry Lippitt	Republican	1875-1877
Charles C. Van Zandt	Republican	1877-1880
Alfred H. Littlefield	Republican	1880-1883
Augustus O. Bourn	Republican	1883-1885
George P. Wetmore	Republican	1885-1887
John W. Davis	Democratic	1887-1888
Royal C. Taft	Republican	1888-1889
Herbert W. Ladd	Republican	1889-1890
John W. Davis	Democratic	1890-1891
Herbert W. Ladd	Republican	1891-1892
D. Russell Brown	Republican	1892-1895
Charles W. Lippitt	Republican	1895-1897
Elisha Dyer	Republican	1897-1900
William Gregory	Republican	1900-1901
Charles D. Kimball	Republican	1901-1903
Lucius F. C. Garvin	Democratic	1903-1905
George H. Utter	Republican	1905-1907
James H. Higgins	Democratic	1907-1909
Aram J. Pothier	Republican	1909-1915
R. Livingston Beeckman	Republican	1915-1921
Emery J. San Souci	Republican	1921-1923
William S. Flynn	Democratic	1923-1925
Aram J. Pothier	Republican	1925-1928
Norman S. Case	Republican	1928-1933
Theodore F. Green	Democratic	1933-1937
Robert E. Quinn	Democratic	1937-1939
William H. Vanderbilt	Republican	1939-1941
J. Howard McGrath	Democratic	1941-1945
John O. Pastore	Democratic	1945-1950
John S. McKiernan	Democratic	1950-1951
Dennis J. Roberts	Democratic	1951-1959
Christopher Del Sesto	Republican	1959-1961
John A. Notte, Jr.	Democratic	1961-1963
John H. Chafee	Republican	1963-1969
Frank Licht	Democratic	1969-1973
Philip W. Noel	Democratic	1973-1977
J. Joseph Garrahy	Democratic	1977-1985
Edward D. DiPrete	Republican	1985-1991
Bruce Sundlun	Democratic	1991-1995
Lincoln C. Almond	Republican	1995-2003
Donald Carcieri	Republican	2003-2011
Lincoln Chaffee	Independent	2011-2015
Gina Raimondo	Democratic	2015-2021
Daniel McKee	Democratic	2021-

*Democratic-Republican †National Republican

Rhode Island Department of Economic Development

The Rhode Island Senate meets in the State House in Providence. Voters elect the senators to two-year terms.

Politics. Rhode Island became a Republican state just before the American Civil War (1861-1865). Most voters in the state favored the antislavery and pro-Northern policies of the Republican Party. The growth of cities, usually favorable to the Democratic Party, helped Rhode Island become a two-party state during the 1920's.

Rhode Island voters supported the Republican presidential candidate in every election but one from 1856 to 1928. The exception was the election of 1912, when they voted for Woodrow Wilson, a Democrat. Since 1928, the state has voted Democratic in most presidential elections. For the state's electoral votes and voting record in presidential elections, see **Electoral College** (table).

In state and congressional elections, the people of Rhode Island usually voted for Republicans from the 1860's to the 1920's. Since the 1930's, however, they have generally favored Democratic candidates for the state legislature, the governorship, and the U.S. Congress.

History

Early days. Archaeological evidence suggests that Native Americans came to what is now the Rhode Island area about 10,000 years ago. When European settlers began arriving in the 1630's, Algonquian-speaking tribes were living in the area. They included the powerful Narragansett, who occupied about two-thirds of what is now Rhode Island, and the Niantic, Nipmuck, Pequot, and Wampanoag.

Exploration. Giovanni da Verrazzano, an Italian navigator working for France, sailed along the Rhode Island coast in 1524 and was the first known explorer to enter Narragansett Bay. Dutch navigator Adriaen Block sailed into the bay in 1614.

Historians are not sure why the state came to be called Rhode Island, but the following facts are known. Verrazzano remarked that an island off Rhode Island's southern coast reminded him of Rhodes, an island in the Mediterranean Sea. Block named Aquidneck Island, in Narragansett Bay, *Roodt Eylandt* (Red Island) because of the red earth along its shore. Roger Williams, who founded Providence, called Aquidneck Island *Rode Island,* which he said meant *Isle of Roses.* European settlers later officially changed the name of Aquidneck Island to *Rhode Island.*

Settlement. In 1636, Roger Williams established Rhode Island's first permanent white settlement, which he called *Providence Plantations,* at the head of Narragansett Bay. Williams, a Puritan minister, had fled the Massachusetts Bay Colony after being sentenced to banishment for promoting certain ideas. He said, for example, that the civil authorities did not have the power to enforce obedience to religious beliefs. In Providence, the government was restricted to civil matters, and the people had complete religious freedom.

In 1638, Anne Hutchinson, William Coddington, John Clarke, and others expelled from Massachusetts founded the settlement of Pocasset at the north end of Aquidneck Island. Coddington, Clarke, and others left Pocasset in disagreement over political and religious issues and founded Newport at the south end of the island in 1639. Hutchinson and her followers remained at Pocasset and renamed it Portsmouth.

Samuel Gorton and his followers left Pocasset and went to Providence but then founded a fourth town, Shawomet, in 1642. Gorton later secured a grant from England for the town, which he renamed Warwick.

In 1643, the Massachusetts Bay, Plymouth, Connecticut, and New Haven colonies formed a military alliance, excluding the Narragansett Bay towns. Their leaders regarded Rhode Island as a wicked, disorderly place and called it *Rogue's Island.* Williams proposed that the four Rhode Island settlements unite for protection. In 1644, he obtained a charter from England for the *Province of Providence Plantations in Narragansett in New England.* But it was not until 1647 that Portsmouth and Newport agreed to the union. The charter was voided when the monarchy was restored in England in 1660. King Charles II granted a new charter in 1663. It was called the *Charter of Rhode Island and Providence Plantations.* It remained the law of Rhode Island until 1843.

King Philip's War. Roger Williams respected the rights of the Native Americans and worked to live in peace with them. But the growing conflict between settlers and Indians in the Plymouth and Massachusetts Bay colonies developed into a war that engulfed New England, including most of Rhode Island. Fighting began in

June 1675 between Plymouth and the Wampanoag, who were led by Metacom (also known as King Philip). In December, colonial soldiers from the surrounding colonies entered Rhode Island and attacked the Narragansett in the Great Swamp Fight, near present-day West Kingston. The Indians retaliated by destroying the white settlements on the west side of Narragansett Bay, including Providence. In 1676, the Native Americans in southern New England were defeated and Metacom himself was killed near Mount Hope (now Bristol).

The growth of ocean trade. Newport escaped the destruction of King Philip's War, and its farmers and merchants led the way to a new economy for Rhode Island. The coastal regions and islands of Narragansett Bay had excellent farm and grazing land. Rhode Island began to produce a surplus of agricultural products that could be sold. A number of Quakers and Jews had been attracted to the colony because of its religious freedom. They developed trading networks through their widespread family and religious connections and helped the city to enter international trade. Newport ships began carrying products to other parts of the world.

In the 1700's, Rhode Islanders also entered the slave trade, bringing slaves from Africa to the colonies. They remained the main American slave traders through the 1700's. In the 1730's, some Newport families developed large farms on the west side of the bay and used slave labor to raise crops and care for sheep, cattle, and horses. But Rhode Island banned the importation of slaves in 1774, enacted a law in 1784 that established a process for gradually ending slavery, and outlawed the slave trade in 1787.

The Revolutionary War. In the 1760's, Britain attempted to tighten control over its American colonies through new taxes and trade restrictions. Rhode Island's many acts of rebellion included the burning of the British ship *Liberty* in Newport harbor in 1769 and the burning of the *Gaspee* near Warwick in 1772. When the Revolutionary War in America broke out in Massachusetts in 1775, hundreds of Rhode Island volunteers went to Massachusetts to fight. On July 18, 1776, the Rhode Island General Assembly ratified the colonies' Declaration of Independence.

Stephen Hopkins and other Rhode Island men were the chief organizers of the Continental Navy. Esek Hopkins was the navy's first commander in chief. Nathanael Greene, a general in the Continental Army, became recognized as a great military leader.

The British occupied Newport from December 1776 to October 1779. In August 1778, American soldiers attempted to drive out the British, but they were not successful and retreated. A group of freed slaves in the First Rhode Island Regiment won praise for their role in protecting the American forces.

On July 9, 1778, Rhode Island was one of the first of the original 13 states to ratify the Articles of Confederation (the forerunner of the United States Constitution), but it was the last one to ratify the U.S. Constitution. Rhode Island opposed the Constitution because it took power from the states and gave the federal government the right to levy taxes and regulate commerce. The Constitution also prohibited the states from issuing their own money, something Rhode Island had done frequently. Finally, on May 29, 1790, delegates to Rhode Island's constitutional convention accepted the Constitution by a vote of 34 to 32.

Industrial expansion. After the Revolutionary War, the merchants and manufacturers of Providence played an important role in turning Rhode Island into a leading industrial state.

Moses Brown, who sought to develop a successful textile industry in the United States, hired Samuel Slater to reproduce machinery that had been developed in England. England had built the first water-powered textile mill. Its textile workers were forbidden to leave the country to keep the process secret. Slater, a mill manager, had disguised himself as a farmer and escaped to the United States. He built machines to produce cotton thread and, in 1790, began operating a water-powered cotton-spinning mill in Pawtucket. By 1815, Rhode Island had 100 mills in 21 towns. From the 1820's to the 1920's, the production of cotton and woolen textiles was the state's leading industry.

In 1794, Nehemiah Dodge of Providence discovered how to cover base metals with silver and gold. He and his brother Seril began a jewelry-making industry, and Rhode Island became a major jewelry-making center.

The Dorr Rebellion. In the 1830's, about half of the men in Rhode Island were not eligible to vote because only property owners had voting rights. The state was still governed under its 1663 charter, which *apportioned* (divided) seats in the General Assembly and gave the legislature the power to set voting requirements. As more and more people moved to the industrial cities, fewer men were able to meet the property requirement. The legislature was dominated by declining rural towns, and the heavily populated urban areas had little representation. The legislature refused to change voting requirements or to consider reapportionment. Therefore, a reform movement began to grow.

Thomas Dorr, a lawyer, led the reformers in drafting a new constitution and forming a new government. In 1842, when the state government refused to step aside, the Dorrites attempted to overthrow it by force. They failed, but their action led to the adoption of a new state constitution, which took effect in 1843. The Constitution gave voting rights to native-born adult Rhode Island men who paid taxes of $1 a year or served in the militia. Also, urban areas gained more seats in the legislature. Foreign-born citizens still had to own property to vote.

The Civil War. During the American Civil War (1861-1865), more than 24,000 Rhode Islanders served in the Union Army and Navy. The state's most famous officer was Major General Ambrose E. Burnside, who commanded the Army of the Potomac for a brief period. Burnside later served as Rhode Island's governor and as a U.S. senator. Rhode Island was heavily involved in supplying Union war needs. The state made cannons, rifles, uniforms, boots, blankets, tents, and other equipment.

The Gilded Age. After the Civil War, American industry boomed. Some people amassed large fortunes. American author Mark Twain, referring to the culture of the newly rich, called this period the Gilded Age.

In Rhode Island, the textile industry and other industries expanded. By the 1890's, Providence had the world's largest textile company. It also boasted of its *Five Industrial Wonders of the World*—the world's largest factories for making files, screws, silverware, steam en-

Historic Rhode Island

Roger Williams founded Rhode Island's first European settlement at Providence in 1636. He helped establish a complete separation of church and state for the colony.

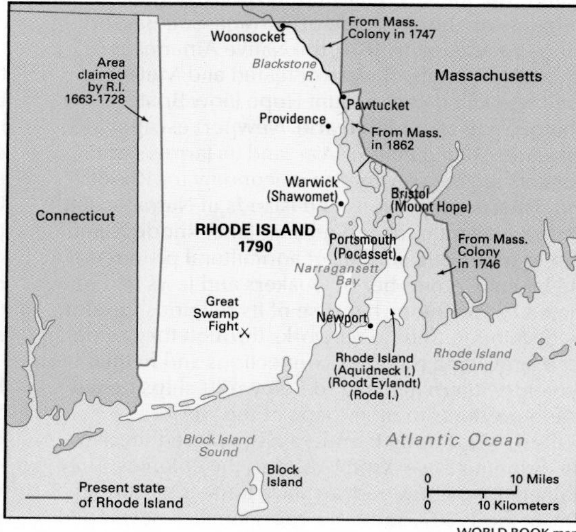

Rhode Island received its first charter from England in 1644. Rhode Island gained territory from Massachusetts in the 1740's and in 1862. Rhode Island became a U.S. state in 1790.

The Slater Mill in Pawtucket, Rhode Island, was one of the first successful textile mills in North America. Built in 1793, it was the second such mill Samuel Slater, *inset,* helped establish in Pawtucket.

WORLD BOOK illustrations by Richard Bonson, the Art Agency

Important dates in Rhode Island

1524 Giovanni da Verrazzano sailed Narragansett Bay.

1636 Roger Williams founded Providence.

1638 William Coddington, John Clarke, Anne Hutchinson, and others settled on Aquidneck Island.

1647 The settlements of Providence, Portsmouth, Newport, and Warwick were united after England granted Roger Williams a charter in 1644.

1663 England granted Rhode Island its second charter.

1774 Rhode Island prohibited the importation of slaves.

1776 Rhode Island ratified the colonies' Declaration of Independence.

1790 Rhode Island became the 13th state when it ratified the U.S. Constitution on May 29.

1842 The Dorr Rebellion helped bring about a more liberal state constitution.

1938 A disastrous hurricane struck Rhode Island.

1969 Newport Bridge over Narragansett Bay was completed, linking Newport with Jamestown.

1990 Rhode Island celebrated the bicentennial of its statehood.

2003 A reduction in size of the General Assembly, approved by voters in 1994, took effect.

2020 Voters approved a constitutional amendment changing the state's official name—State of Rhode Island and Providence Plantations—to, simply, State of Rhode Island.

gines and tools. Pawtucket was the home of the largest thread company, and Woonsocket had the largest rubber footwear factory. Many Canadian and European immigrants poured in to work in the mills and factories. The population almost doubled between 1870 and 1900.

Newport became a favorite summer resort for many wealthy families. They lived in huge mansions and enjoyed such sports as golf, polo, tennis, and yachting. The resorts, parks, and beaches dotting the shores of Narragansett Bay attracted people of all economic levels.

The state's strong naval tradition continued. In 1883, Newport became the home of the Newport Naval Training Station, where naval recruits were trained until 1952. The Naval War College, the Navy's highest educational institution, opened there in 1884.

A changing economy. At the beginning of the 1900's, Rhode Island had more than 1,500 factories, making products from locomotives to ribbons. In 1910, about half the state's workers were involved in manufacturing. During World War I (1914-1918), Rhode Island shipyards built combat and cargo ships, and the state's factories produced war materials. But by the 1920's, manufacturing was declining. Many textile plants were moving to the South, where labor costs were lower and the mills newer. The state began to experience an economic depression, which was worsened by the Great Depression of the 1930's.

In 1938, Rhode Island suffered one of its worst natural disasters. A hurricane and tidal wave struck, killing 317 people and causing $100 million in property damage.

World War II (1939-1945) brought a temporary revival of manufacturing. But after the war, defense contracts ended, and a number of Rhode Island companies closed. The decline of manufacturing continued through the rest of the 1900's.

Tourism became increasingly important in the 1960's. New roads and highways opened much of the state to tourists. In 1969, the Rhode Island section of Interstate Highway 95 opened, and the Newport Bridge was completed across Narragansett Bay between Jamestown and Newport. The bridge was named for Senator Claiborne Pell in 1992, but many residents continued to refer to it by its former name.

The Cruiser-Destroyer Force of the U.S. Atlantic Fleet, which had been headquartered at Newport in 1952, moved out of Rhode Island in 1973. The Naval Undersea Warfare Center remains in the state. The fleet's departure plunged Newport and other cities into economic crisis. The state's population declined during the 1970's as many people left the state.

Rhode Island shared in the national defense build-up in the 1980's. But U.S. defense spending decreased as the Cold War drew to a close in the late 1980's and early 1990's. Many defense-related industries in Rhode Island declined. In the 1990's, the state's jewelry industry faced much competition from international companies, and it suffered a major decline. The textile industry had left the state, except for the making of specialty textiles, lace, and narrow braid.

By the end of the 1900's, the state's economy had shifted from manufacturing to service industries. Tourism was an important contributor to the economy, and such services as government and health care were leading employers. The state's universities had become centers of research and development. The oceanographic research program of the University of Rhode Island was recognized as one of the finest in the nation.

Library of Congress

Cotton and woolen textile production was Rhode Island's top economic activity from the 1820's to the 1920's. In this image from 1912, a woman works on a weaving machine in Pawtucket.

Political reform. The Republican Party dominated Rhode Island's government from the Civil War until the 1930's. The party maintained control despite the growing popularity of the Democratic Party in the heavily populated urban areas. Rural Republican towns controlled the state Senate. Under the 1842 state Constitution, each city and town had one vote in the Senate. In 1925, for example, Providence, with 267,918 people, and West Greenwich, with 407 people, each had one vote.

Pressure for change mounted in the 1920's. In 1935, in the Great Depression, the Democratic Party gained control of the state through a government reorganization called the *Bloodless Revolution.* The party's control increased in the 1960's, when a reapportionment on the basis of population took place. In the 1970's, a Rhode Island Republican won a seat in the U.S. Congress for the first time in almost 40 years. But the Democratic Party has continued to control the General Assembly.

A number of political scandals in the 1980's and 1990's led to calls for reform. State officeholders guilty of being involved in wrongdoing included two Supreme Court chief justices, an auditor general, several city mayors, and a former governor. In 1991, the organization that insured state-chartered credit unions collapsed. Such factors as mismanagement, lack of governmental oversight, and corruption led to the financial disaster, which resulted in the closing of 45 banks and credit unions. The state restored the lost funds to depositors at a large cost to Rhode Island taxpayers.

Demands from citizens groups helped bring about the enactment of stricter ethical standards and other changes, including the reduction in size of the General Assembly, an end to a corrupt legislative pension system, and term limits for the governor and other officials. In the early 2000's, a campaign to bring about the separation of powers among the three branches of government gathered strength. Observers said that the state's legislative branch had greater power than the executive and judicial branches, leading to conflicts of interest and corruption among its members.

The early 2000's. In a nonbinding referendum in 2002, 76 percent of the state's voters approved a proposal for separation of powers. The vote led the General Assembly to consider the matter. A separation-of-powers amendment passed in both houses in 2003, and voters approved it in 2004.

In January 2003, the reduction in the size of the General Assembly, which had been approved by voters in 1994, went into effect. The Senate was reduced from 50 to 38 members. The House of Representatives went from 100 to 75 members.

In March and April 2010, heavy rains caused the Pawtuxet River and other rivers in the state to reach record high levels. Flooding damaged many homes and businesses throughout Rhode Island.

Rhode Island's economy struggled during a national economic downturn that began in 2008. The state's unemployment rate ranked among the highest of all states during the early 2010's.

In 2020, voters approved a constitutional amendment changing the state's official name—State of Rhode Island and Providence Plantations—because of the associations of the word *plantation* with slavery. The state's name became, simply, State of Rhode Island.

Stanford E. Demars and J. Stanley Lemons

Study aids

Related articles in *World Book* include:

Biographies

Burnside, Ambrose E.
Cohan, George M.
Ellery, William
Gray, Robert
Green, Theodore F.
Greene, Nathanael
Hopkins, Stephen
Hutchinson, Anne M.
Philip, King
Slater, Samuel
Williams, Roger

Cities

Newport
Pawtucket
Providence
Warwick

History

Colonial life in America
Dorr Rebellion
Flag (picture: Flags in United States history; New England flags)
Indian wars (King Philip's War)
Narragansett Indians
Revolution, American

Outline

I. People
- A. Population
- B. Schools
- C. Libraries
- D. Museums

II. Visitor's guide

III. Land and climate
- A. Land regions
- B. Islands
- C. Coastline
- D. Rivers and lakes
- E. Plant and animal life
- F. Climate

IV. Economy
- A. Natural resources
- B. Service industries
- C. Manufacturing
- D. Agriculture
- E. Fishing industry
- F. Mining
- G. Electric power and utilities
- H. Transportation
- I. Communication

V. Government
- A. Constitution
- B. Executive
- C. Legislature
- D. Courts
- E. Local government
- F. Revenue
- G. Politics

VI. History

Additional resources

Level I

Cunningham, Kevin. *The Rhode Island Colony.* Children's Pr., 2012.
Petreycik, Rick, and Herrington, L. M. *Rhode Island.* Cavendish Square, 2014.
Tieck, Sarah. *Rhode Island.* Big Buddy Bks., 2013.

Level II

Conley, Patrick T. *The Makers of Modern Rhode Island.* Hist. Pr., 2012.
Curley, Robert P. *Rhode Island: Off the Beaten Path.* 7th ed. Globe Pequot, 2010. A travel guide.
Gaustad, Edwin S. *Roger Williams.* Oxford, 2005.
Lehnert, Tim. *Rhode Island 101.* MacIntyre Purcell, 2011. Facts and stories about the state.
Méras, Phyllis, and Imbrie, Katherine. *An Explorer's Guide: Rhode Island.* 6th ed. Countryman, 2012.
Rappleye, Charles. *Sons of Providence: The Brown Brothers, the Slave Trade, and the American Revolution.* Simon & Schuster, 2006.

Rhode Island, University of, is a state-supported institution of higher education. The university's main campus is in Kingston, Rhode Island. It also has three additional campuses in Providence, Narragansett, and West Greenwich. The university grants bachelor's, master's, and doctor's degrees. Its athletic teams are called the Rams. The University of Rhode Island's website at https://www.uri.edu offers additional information.

The university was chartered in Kingston in 1888 as the state's agricultural school. It became the Rhode Island College of Agriculture and Mechanic Arts in 1892. It was renamed Rhode Island State College in 1909. The college became the University of Rhode Island in 1951.

Critically reviewed by the University of Rhode Island

Rhode Island Red is an important breed of chicken that is the state bird of Rhode Island. It is usually raised for its eggs, which have brown shells. It also is raised for its meat. A mature Rhode Island Red weighs about 7 to 9 pounds (3 to 4 kilograms). These birds remain popular in backyard flocks. Commercial chickens that lay brown eggs may descend in part from Rhode Island Reds.

The Rhode Island Red gets its name from its rust-colored feathers and from Rhode Island, where it was developed. Breeders produced it by crossing a variety of breeds, including Malay, leghorn, and Asiatic chickens. It became Rhode Island's state bird in 1954.

Carmen R. Parkhurst

Rhodes, *rohdz,* is the largest of the Dodecanese Islands in the Aegean Sea. It lies 12 miles (19 kilometers) off the southwestern coast of Turkey (see **Greece** [terrain map]). The island is part of Greece.

Rhodes (also referred to as Ródhos) has a total area of 540 square miles (1,398 square kilometers) and a population of about 90,000. One of the island's chief physical features is a mountain range that runs lengthwise across the island, rising to a height of 3,986 feet (1,215 meters) above the sea. Tourism is the chief industry. The island's manufactured goods include cigarettes, food products, machinery, and textiles. The major crops of Rhodes include citrus fruits, olives, tobacco, and vegetables.

In early days, Rhodes was a wealthy and independent state of Greece. Rhodes was the home of numerous poets, artists, and philosophers. A great statue of Helios, called the *Colossus of Rhodes,* was one of the Seven Wonders of the Ancient World (see **Seven Wonders of the Ancient World**). In 1310, the Knights Hospitallers occupied Rhodes. In 1522, the Turks captured it. Then Rhodes declined in glory and grandeur.

Italy occupied Rhodes during the Turko-Italian War of 1911-1912. Italy held Rhodes and the rest of the Dodecanese Islands until 1947. It then ceded them to Greece. The island's capital is the city of Rhodes (or Ródhos). It is a major tourist attraction. John J. Baxevanis

See also **Dodecanese Islands.**

Rhodes, *rohdz,* **Cecil John** (1853-1902), was a British businessman and statesman. He made a fortune in the diamond industry and probably did more than anyone else of his time to enlarge the British Empire in Africa. Rhodes used his wealth and his ability as a statesman to gain control of most of southern Africa. He spent his fortune freely when he thought he could advance the empire. But he was often ruthless and racist in pursuing his goals. Rhodes left much of his fortune to Oxford University for the establishment of the Rhodes Scholarship (see **Rhodes Scholarship**).

Early life. Rhodes was born on July 5, 1853, in the county of Hertfordshire in England. In 1870, he went to Natal (then a British colony in what is now South Africa), where one of his brothers was a cotton grower. In 1871, he became a supervisor in a diamond mine his brother had opened at Kimberley, also in present-day South Africa. By 1873, Rhodes had taken control of the mine. Rhodes enrolled at Oxford University in 1873 and spent half of each year there until he graduated in 1881. He also got control of more diamond mines at Kimberley.

Gains Rhodesia. In 1881, Rhodes was elected to the assembly of Britain's Cape Colony in what is now South Africa. Aided by his wealth, he set out to advance British imperial authority in southern Africa. He forced the annexation of Bechuanaland (now Botswana) to the British Empire in 1885. By 1888, when he combined all his mines into the De Beers Consolidated Mines, Rhodes had become rich and powerful. In 1889, he forced the Shona and Ndebele (often called Matabele) peoples to surrender most of their land to the United Kingdom. This huge territory later became the state of Southern Rhodesia (now Zimbabwe). He also arranged the annexation of what later became Northern Rhodesia (now Zambia). The British South Africa Company, created by Rhodes, effectively ruled both territories.

In 1890, Rhodes became prime minister of the Cape Colony. He dreamed of building a railroad from the colony to Egypt and of extending British power over much of Africa. He also sought cooperation between English-speaking white colonists and moderate *Boers* (now called Afrikaners), especially in the Cape Colony. The Boers were white settlers, mainly of Dutch descent.

Culver Pictures

Cecil Rhodes

In 1892, Rhodes approved the Franchise and Ballot Bill, which denied almost all the colony's blacks the right to vote. In 1894, he enacted the Glen Grey Act, which restricted the amount of land blacks could own.

Conflict with the Boers. Rhodes saw that British rule in southern Africa could only be expanded at the expense of the Boers, who had large possessions in the region. Rhodes interfered in the politics of the Transvaal area (in what later became South Africa). The area was settled by the Boers. Rhodes was largely responsible for the Jameson Raid of 1895, in which Rhodesian troops attacked the Transvaal. This incident was badly planned and widely criticized. After the raid, Rhodes resigned as prime minister of the Cape Colony and withdrew into Rhodesia. Rhodes was at Kimberley when the Anglo-Boer War of 1899-1902 finally broke out between the United Kingdom and the Boers (see **Anglo-Boer Wars**). He assisted in the defense of the city and helped direct the course of the war. But he had a fatal heart attack on March 26, 1902, before the war ended. Denis Judd

Rhodes Scholarship, *rohdz,* is an award that enables students from many countries to study at Oxford University in England. The scholarship pays the student's tuition and fees directly to the university. It also provides an allowance for living expenses. Scholarships are given for two years but may be extended for a third year.

The scholarships were established in the will of Cecil J. Rhodes, a British colonial statesman who died in 1902. Rhodes's aim was to strengthen ties among the English-speaking peoples. He also wanted to provide potential leaders of many nations with an opportunity to study at Oxford. The scholarship program began full operation in 1904. At first, Rhodes scholars came to Oxford from the United States, Germany, and several nations of the British Empire. Since then, the program has expanded to include several additional nations.

About 100 Rhodes Scholarships are awarded yearly. The United States receives 32 scholarships each year. Canada receives 11. Rhodes Scholarships are also given to students in Australia, New Zealand, Germany, South Africa, Nigeria, Kenya, Zambia, Zimbabwe, India, Pakistan, Hong Kong, Malaysia, Singapore, Bermuda, Jamaica, and the British Caribbean, which includes the Bahamas, Barbados, and Trinidad and Tobago.

The committees who select Rhodes scholars seek people with superior scholastic records. Candidates also must display qualities of character, leadership, and personal vigor.

Applicants from the United States must be U.S. citizens who are at least 18 years old and not older than 24. They also must have completed enough college to ensure that they will receive a bachelor's degree before arriving in Oxford. The candidates apply to state committees. The committee in each state nominates up to three candidates to the district competition. There are eight U.S. districts for this contest. Each district committee selects four Rhodes scholars from the state nominees who appear before it. Critically reviewed by the Rhodes Trust

See also **Oxford, University of; Rhodes, Cecil J.**

Rhodesia. See **Zimbabwe.**

Rhodesian ridgeback, *roh DEE zhuhn,* is a large hound that originated in southern Africa. It is also called

WORLD BOOK photo by Ken Love

The Rhodesian ridgeback is a powerful hunting dog that originated in southern Africa. It is an excellent watchdog.

the *African lion hound* because it was bred to find and hold off lions so that hunters could get a good shot at their prey. The dog has a ridge of hair on the back that grows in a direction opposite to the rest of the coat. The coat has a light to reddish-wheatlike color. The ridgeback stands 24 to 27 inches (61 to 69 centimeters) high at the shoulder. It makes an excellent watchdog and is good with children.

Critically reviewed by the Rhodesian Ridgeback Club of the United States

See also **Dog** (picture: Hounds).

Rhodium is a rare, silver-white, metallic element that serves mainly as a *catalyst,* a substance which increases the speed of a chemical reaction. Rhodium is a catalyst in the production of nitric acid and various organic compounds and medicinal drugs. It is also used in *catalytic converters,* which reduce pollutants in automobile exhausts. Rhodium *alloys* (metal mixtures) are used in aircraft turbine engines, electric connections, and reflective surfaces of mirrors and searchlights.

Rhodium's chemical symbol is Rh. Its *atomic number* (number of protons in its nucleus) is 45. Rhodium's *relative atomic mass* is 102.90550. An element's relative atomic mass equals its *mass* (amount of matter) divided by $\frac{1}{12}$ of the mass of carbon 12, the most abundant form of carbon. Rhodium melts at 1963±3 °C and boils at 3697±100 °C. The English chemist William H. Wollaston first isolated rhodium in 1803. It occurs in Brazil, Canada, Colombia, Russia, South Africa, and Sri Lanka.

Emily Jane Rose

See also **Element, Chemical** (Periodic table).

Rhododendron, *ROH duh DEHN druhn,* is a type of tree or shrub known for the beauty of its blossoms and for its evergreen leaves. The name means *rose tree.* There are many *species* (kinds) of rhododendrons. One of the best known is the *great rhododendron,* which is also called *great laurel* and *rosebay.* It grows widely in the Allegheny Mountains. There, the interlocking branches form almost impassable thickets. This rhododendron rarely grows higher than 35 feet (11 meters). Its white or rose-colored flowers grow in a large cluster.

Another species, the *mountain rosebay,* is a common shrub in Virginia. It produces brilliant, lilac-purple flowers. Other species are found in the Pacific Coast region.

© E. R. Ricciuti, Photo Researchers

© Dale Athenas, Photo Researchers

The rhododendron has large clusters of colorful flowers that make this evergreen plant a popular ornamental shrub. The showy blossoms, *right,* appear in the spring. Rhododendrons generally grow in cool, mountainous regions.

Some magnificent rhododendrons grow in the mountainous regions of India. The leaves of most rhododendrons are poisonous. James L. Luteyn

Scientific classification. Rhododendrons make up the genus *Rhododendron.* The great rhododendron is *Rhododendron maximum.* The mountain rosebay is *R. catawbiense.*

See also **West Virginia** (picture: State flower).

Rhombus, *RAHM buhs,* is a plane figure with two pairs of straight, parallel sides, all of equal length. The parallel sides of a rhombus make it a parallelogram. A square is a rhombus with sides at right angles to each other.

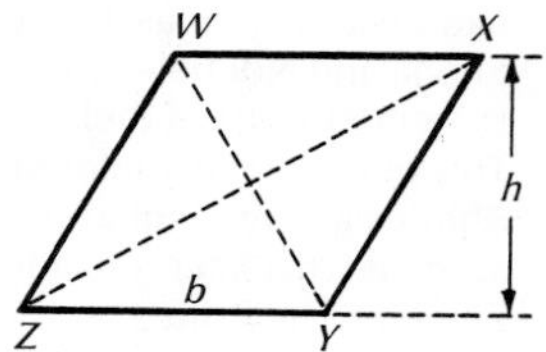

The area of a rhombus is found by multiplying base by altitude, or $A = bh$. The area of a rhombus can also be found by determining the product of its diagonals, $\overline{WY}$ and $\overline{XZ}$ in the figure, then dividing this product in half.

Mary Kay Corbitt

Rhône River, *rohn,* is an important commercial waterway of France. It is famous for the beauty of its valley.

The river rises in the Rhône glacier of Switzerland, at an altitude of over 5,000 feet (1,500 meters). Glacial clay picked up by the river in the Swiss Alps makes the water of the Rhône appear almost milky. But as the Rhône passes through Lake Geneva, most of the clay drops to the bottom of the lake. The clear blue of the river, after leaving Lake Geneva, inspired the English poet Lord By-

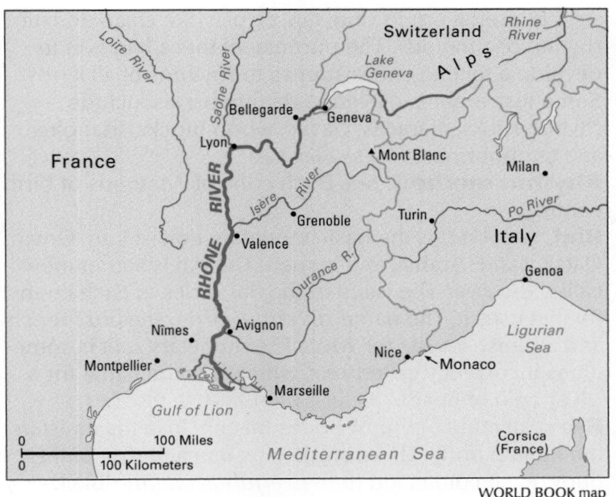

WORLD BOOK map

Location of the Rhône River

ron to describe it as "the blue rushing of the arrowy Rhône." After the Rhône leaves Switzerland and enters France, it flows southwestward to Lyon. It then winds south and empties through a large delta into the Gulf of Lion, an arm of the Mediterranean Sea.

The Rhône is over 500 miles (800 kilometers) long, and navigable for about 300 miles (480 kilometers). Chief branches are the Saône, the Isère, and the Durance. Hydroelectric power plants along the Rhône generate electricity. Canals feed irrigation projects along the lower course of the river. A canal near the mouth of the Rhône connects the river with France's largest Mediterranean port, Marseille.

Greek and Roman civilizations followed the Rhône to Lyon, and up its tributaries. Ruins of ancient settlements still stand in many towns along the river. Hugh D. Clout

See also **Lyon** (picture); **River** (picture: A melting glacier).

Rhubarb, *ROO bahrb,* also called the *pieplant,* is a plant that produces reddish, juicy stalks. People use the stalks for food, usually in desserts. Rhubarb often is used in pie fillings and sauces. The plant forms a large, yellow storage root and a mass of feeder roots underground. Its *rhizome* (underground stem) produces buds from which grow long, thick leafstalks with large leaves. A person may become ill from eating the leaves because they contain poisonous oxalic acid salts (see **Oxalic acid**). Rhubarb originally came from Mongolia. It is now grown in many areas of the world.

Stores sell rhubarb fresh, frozen, or in cans. Many people prefer to cook the fresh stalks. Rhubarb contains some vitamin C.

Rhubarb plants produce many seeds, but plants from the seeds are not always like the parent plant. Growers plant pieces of the big storage root that have several buds from which new plants can grow. Rhubarb is one of the few perennial vegetables. Each plant lasts five to eight years. Rhubarb is relatively free from insect attack and suffers from few diseases. Hugh C. Price

Scientific classification. Rhubarb's scientific name is *Rheum rhaponticum.*

Rhumb line. See **Great-circle route.**

Rhumba. See **Rumba.**

Rhyme, also spelled *rime,* means echoing or repeating sounds at the end of words. In poetry, rhyme usually occurs at the end of lines, as in this quotation from the Irish poet William Butler Yeats:

O body swayed to music, O brightening glance,
How can we know the dancer from the dance?

This is an example of *end rhyme. Glance* in the first line rhymes with *dance* in the second. *Internal rhyme* refers to the rhyming of two or more words within a line, such as *seared, bleared,* and *smeared* in this line by the English poet Gerard Manley Hopkins: "And all is seared with trade; bleared, smeared with toil."

In *single rhyme,* the final vowel and consonant sounds of the rhyming words are repeated, as in *glance* and *dance.* In *double rhyme,* the last two syllables of the rhyming words are repeated, as in *staples* and *maples.* Less frequently, rhymes involve many syllables, as in *Tennyson* and *venison.*

In *near rhyme,* also called *slant rhyme,* the words almost rhyme. The words repeat either (1) the final consonant sounds after the last stressed vowel sound, as in *have* and *grave,* or (2) the final stressed vowel sound but not the final consonant sounds, as in *wake* and *late.* In *visual rhyme,* also called *eye rhyme,* the words are connected by the eye, not by the ear, as in *tough* and *through.*

Poets often use a rhyme pattern to create an overall form for a poem, as in a sonnet. In addition, they may use individual rhymes for various effects of sound and meaning. However, rhyme is not necessary in poetry. Blank verse and much free verse do not use rhyme.

Paul B. Diehl

See also **Alliteration; Blank verse; Free verse; Poetry** (Sounds); **Sonnet.**

Rhyolite. See **Granite.**

Rhythm is the regular repetition of a beat, accent, or rise and fall in dance, music, and language. The word comes from the Greek word *rhythmos,* meaning *measured motion.* In dancing, rhythmic patterns and variations are created by physical motions of shorter or

WORLD BOOK illustration by Jill Coombs

The rhubarb plant has juicy, reddish stalks with a tangy flavor. Rhubarb, though a vegetable, is popular as a dessert.

longer duration and of greater or lesser emphasis. In music, rhythmic figures and phrases come from an arrangement of tones, organized according to their duration and stresses, or accents. Rhythm is the most primitive element of music. Unlike the other elements, it can exist independently. Any sound, even noise, can establish a rhythm. In language, rhythm is the rise and fall of sounds according to syllables, vocal inflections, physical speech accents, and pauses. Modern English and German are of the language type that has physically stressed, or accented, syllables. Greek and Latin use long and short syllables or inflections to give stress.

Stewart L. Ross

See also **Dance; Language; Meter** (Poetry); **Music** (Rhythm; Musical notation).

Rhythm and blues is a style of blues music with an aggressive, driving beat. It developed in the United States by the late 1940's. It is also called *rhythm 'n' blues* or *R&B* for short. See **Blues.**

Rhythm and blues developed among African American communities mainly in large industrial cities of the United States, many of them in the North. These cities included Chicago; Detroit; Kansas City, Missouri; Los Angeles; and New York City. Many African Americans came to these cities from the Deep South in search of better lives. They brought with them their music, including the blues. The blues had generally featured simple sung melodies with a guitar accompaniment. In the cities of the North, rhythm and blues developed into a separate sound. This new music featured stronger dance rhythms. It also included additional instruments, including drums, bass guitars, trumpets, saxophones, and keyboards.

The music magazine *Billboard* first used the term *rhythm and blues* in 1949. By then, however, it was probably already widespread in the Black community. The terms "Harlem Hit Parade" and "race records" had previously been used to refer to *charts* (lists) of Black music. These charts tracked the popularity of African American recordings played on the radio and sold in stores. Rhythm and blues was aimed primarily at a Black audience. Records were also marketed to a lesser degree to white audiences. Small, independent record labels produced most of the rhythm and blues recordings of the 1940's and 1950's. During that time, both the rise of radio stations playing Black music and the popularity of jukeboxes that played records spread the music to a widening audience.

In the mid-1950's, such rhythm and blues performers as Ruth Brown, Fats Domino, Etta James, Little Richard, Hank Ballard, and Ray Charles produced a string of hit songs, all with a strong, danceable beat. The lyrics primarily celebrated dancing, romance, and good times.

With the rise of rock and roll, white performers adopted the rhythm and blues style of such popular performers as Chuck Berry and Bo Diddley. Many of the early hits by rock's first stars, including Bill Haley and the Comets and Elvis Presley, were faster versions of rhythm and blues songs. Robert F. Darden

Rhythm band describes a group of performers playing *percussion instruments* (instruments that produce musical tones when struck). Elementary school music teachers in the United States use rhythm bands as a method of teaching children about basic rhythm in music. Children learn to sing, tap, or play the characteristic rhythm of a melody. The purpose of these bands is to develop a feeling and response to rhythms of all kinds. Some instruments played in rhythm bands include rhythm sticks, maracas, claves, wood blocks, triangles, and tambourines. Stewart L. Ross

Rhythm method. See **Birth control** (Methods of birth control).

Rial, *ree AWL,* is the basic monetary unit of Iran, Oman, Qatar, Saudi Arabia, and Yemen. The rial is sometimes called the *riyal.* The value of the rial varies in each country that uses it. The name *rial* comes from the old French and Spanish words for *royal.* The monetary unit is sometimes incorrectly called *real,* which was the name for a silver coin of Spain. Burton H. Hobson

Rib is any one of the 24 bones that enclose the chest in the human body. There are 12 ribs on each side of the body, each connected to the *vertebral column* (backbone) by small joints called *costovertebral joints.* In the front of the body, the uppermost seven ribs on each side are connected directly to the *sternum* (breastbone) by a tough, elastic material called *cartilage.* These are called the *true ribs.* The five lower ribs, called *false ribs,* are not linked directly to the breastbone. Each of the upper three false ribs is attached to the rib above by cartilage. The lowest two ribs are attached only to the backbone. They are known as *floating ribs.* The spaces between the ribs, called *intercostal spaces,* contain arteries, veins, muscles, and nerves.

Most *vertebrates* (animals with backbones) have ribs, but the number of ribs varies considerably. In mammals the number of ribs varies from 9 pairs, as in some whales, to 24 pairs, as in two-toed sloths.

The ribs perform two functions in the body. They form a cage around the chest cavity that protects the heart and lungs. They also move up and down and, together with the diaphragm, control the movement of air in and out of the lungs. When the ribs move up, the chest cavity enlarges and air is sucked into the lungs. When they move down, air is forced out of the lungs.

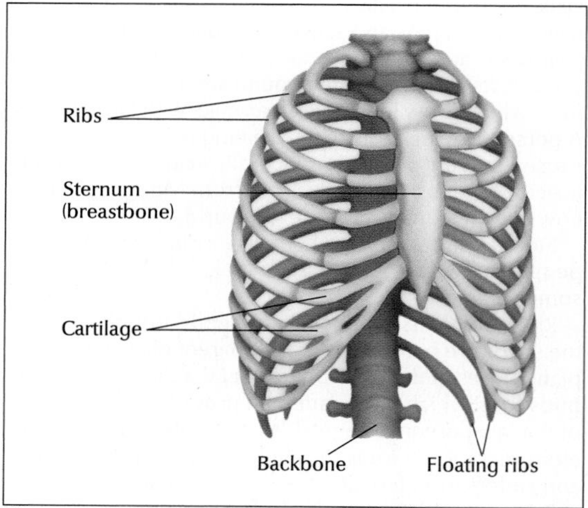

WORLD BOOK illustration by Leonard Morgan

The ribs are connected to the backbone, from which they curve downward and forward to form a protective cage around the heart and lungs. The human body has 24 ribs, 12 on each side.

A hard blow on the chest can fracture a rib. Fractured ribs cause sharp pain when the injured person breathes, and tenderness when pressure is applied to the fracture area. A person who has an injured chest should call a doctor. Bruce Reider

See also **Human body** (Anatomy of the human body).

Ribaut, *REE BOH,* **Jean** (1520?-1565), a French colonizer, took part in setting up French colonies in South Carolina and Florida. His name is also spelled *Ribault.* In 1562, Ribaut led the expedition that built Fort Charles, where Port Royal, South Carolina, now stands. He then returned to France. The 26 soldiers he left behind later deserted. In 1565, he led an expedition to the French Protestant settlement of Fort Caroline in Florida. He arrived safely, but the Spanish later destroyed the fort. Ribaut was shipwrecked and captured by the Spanish. Ribaut refused Spanish demands to convert to Catholicism, and he was executed in Florida on Oct. 12, 1565. Ribaut was born in Dieppe, France, about 1520. D. Peter MacLeod

Ribbentrop, *RIHB uhn TROHP,* **Joachim von,** *YOH ah khihm fuhn* (1893-1946), was Adolf Hitler's top diplomat. Ribbentrop served as foreign minister of Germany from 1938 to 1945. He helped engineer the seizure of Austria, the partition of Czechoslovakia, and alliances with Italy and Japan. In 1939, he made a deal with Joseph Stalin of the Soviet Union in which Germany and the Soviet Union agreed to divide Poland and much of Eastern Europe. After World War II ended in 1945, Ribbentrop was tried for war crimes and crimes against humanity and peace. He was hanged on Oct. 16, 1946. See **World War II** (picture; The Nuremberg Trials).

Ribbentrop was born on April 30, 1893, in Wesel, Germany. His familiarity with different languages helped him greatly in diplomacy. In 1935, he gained from the United Kingdom a naval treaty that gave Germany equality in submarines and the right to expand its fleet of surface ships to 35 percent the size of the British surface fleet. Donald M. McKale

Ribbon Falls is a beautiful waterfall that looks like a narrow ribbon as it drops 1,612 feet (491 meters) in the Yosemite Valley in California's Yosemite National Park. One of the world's highest waterfalls, it is fed by a creek that rises in the mountains above the Yosemite Valley. The water drops down a narrow gorge into the Merced River, which flows through the valley. Ribbon Falls goes dry in early August during the California summer. It becomes a torrent during May and June. Tom L. McKnight

See also **Waterfall** (table; picture).

Ribbon worm is any of a group of worms with a slender, often flattened body and a long *proboscis* (snout). The proboscis lies above the mouth and can be thrown out quickly and wrapped around the prey. In some ribbon worms, the proboscis has daggerlike *stylets.*

A ribbon worm has a full digestive tract, with openings at the mouth and anus. Ribbon worms feed on other worms and mollusks, living and dead. They are not harmful to people. Most ribbon worms live in the ocean, but a few live in moist earth and fresh water. They range from less than 1 inch (2.5 centimeters) to 100 feet (30 meters). Some of them are very colorful. David F. Oetinger

Scientific classification. Ribbon worms make up the phylum Nemertea, also called Nemertina or Rhynchocoela.

Ribera, *ree BAY rah,* **Jusepe de,** *hoo SAY pay day* (1588-1652), was a Spanish painter. Many of his paintings show Christian martyrdoms and saints doing penance. Until 1635, Ribera's style showed the influence of the Italian painter Michelangelo Caravaggio. Ribera then used somber colors and placed realistic figures in simple, diagonal compositions. Between 1635 and 1639, influenced by the Italian painters Correggio and Titian, he used brighter colors and more complex compositions. Elements of these styles are found in his work after 1639.

Ribera was born in Játiva, near Valencia, Spain. In 1616, he settled in Naples, Italy, then a Spanish territory. He became very successful and never returned to Spain. The Italians nicknamed him *Lo Spagnoletto* (Little Spaniard). Ribera died on Sept. 3, 1652. Marilyn Stokstad

Ribicoff, *RIHB uh KAWF,* **Abraham A.** (1910-1998), a Connecticut Democrat, served in many high government posts. He served in the United States Senate from 1963 to 1981. Ribicoff was secretary of health, education, and welfare under President John F. Kennedy in 1961 and 1962. He also served in the Connecticut House of Representatives from 1938 to 1942 and in the U.S. House of Representatives from 1949 to 1953. Ribicoff was governor of Connecticut from 1955 to 1961.

Ribicoff was born on April 9, 1910, in New Britain, Connecticut, and graduated with honors from the University of Chicago Law School in 1933. He practiced law and was a police court judge before entering politics. As governor and as a senator, he led efforts to increase car safety. Ribicoff died on Feb. 22, 1998. James I. Lengle

Riboflavin. See **Vitamin; Nutrition** (Vitamins).

Ricardo, *rih KAHR doh,* **David** (1772-1823), was the leading British economist of the early 1800's. He helped establish the field of *classical economics,* which stresses the importance of free trade and market competition for economic growth. In his book *Principles of Political Economy and Taxation* (1817), Ricardo defined the conditions that would enable a nation's economy to reach its greatest potential. He argued that private businesses should be free to seek high profits so they can accumulate capital and expand business operations.

Ricardo considered labor the most important source of wealth. He also thought that population growth would push wages down to a level that would barely support the people. As the economy expanded and the population grew, land rent would rise. This would reduce profits and limit economic growth. Ricardo recommended free international trade to remedy this problem.

Ricardo was influenced by *The Wealth of Nations* (1776), the classic book by the economist Adam Smith of Scotland. In turn, Ricardo's theories influenced other economists. His theory of *comparative advantage*—which states that each country should concentrate on making goods it can produce most efficiently—remains central to the modern theory of international trade (see **International trade**). Karl Marx was influenced by Ricardo's *labor theory of value,* which held that the value of a commodity is determined by the amount of labor needed in its production. Henry George, a land reformer, expanded on Ricardo's theory of rent. John Stuart Mill, a British philosopher and economist, used Ricardo's ideas as the basis for a philosophy of social reform.

Ricardo was born on April 19, 1772, in London. He made a fortune on the stock exchange while still in his 20's. He served in Parliament from 1819 until his death on Sept. 11, 1823. David B. Sicilia

E. R. Degginger, Bruce Coleman Inc. W. E. Ruth, Bruce Coleman Inc.

Farmers cultivate rice on many kinds of land. In hilly areas, farmers build terraces and *dikes* (dirt walls) to catch rainfall for growing rice, *left.* In lowland regions, farmers plant rice in fields that are surrounded by dikes and then flooded, *right.* Rice is one of the world's most important food crops.

Rice

Rice is one of the world's most important food crops. More than half of the people in the world eat this grain as the main part of their meals. Nearly all the people who depend on rice for food live in Asia. In some Asian languages, the same word means *eat* and *eat rice.* Most rice is eaten as boiled, white grain.

Rice is a cereal grain. Like other cereal grains, including wheat, corn, and oats, rice belongs to the grass family. But unlike other grains, rice grows best in shallow water. Rice thrives in many tropical areas because of their warm, wet climate. Farmers usually flood rice fields to supply the growing plants with moisture and to control weeds and other pests. China and India rank as the world's leading rice-producing countries. Together, China and India produce more than half of the world's yearly rice harvest.

A type of grass called *wild rice* grows in central Canada and parts of the northern United States. In spite of its name, this grain is not closely related to rice.

The rice plant

Young rice plants have a bright green color. As the grain ripens, the plants turn golden-yellow. The grain becomes fully ripe from 90 to 150 days after planting.

J. Neil Rutger, the contributor of this article, is a research geneticist and former Director of the Dale Bumpers National Rice Research Center of the United States Department of Agriculture.

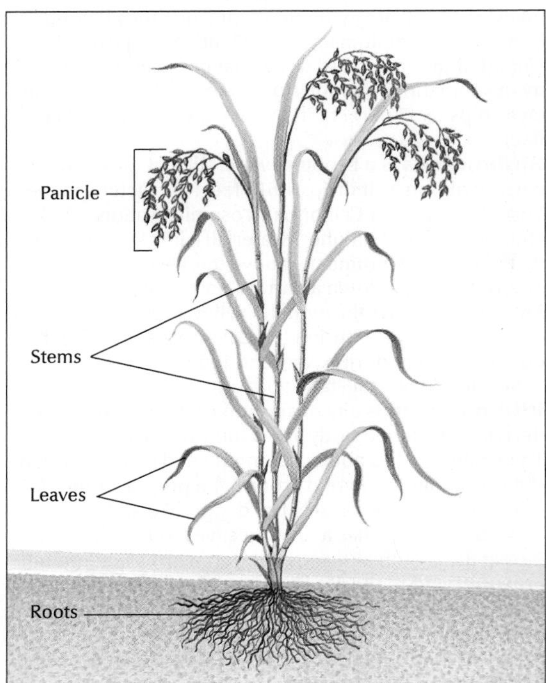

WORLD BOOK diagram by James Teason

The rice plant grows from 31 to 72 inches (80 to 180 centimeters) tall and has several stems. At the end of each stem is a *head,* or *panicle,* which holds the kernels of rice. Each panicle bears from 60 to 150 kernels.

Structure. The main parts of a mature rice plant are the roots, stems, leaves, and head. A system of slender roots supports the plant's hollow stems. Each stem may have as many as 12 to 14 *nodes* (joints). Long, narrow leaves grow from the nodes. The head, also known as the *panicle,* grows from the top of the stem. The panicle holds the kernels—that is, the seeds or grains—of the rice plant. Each panicle carries from 60 to 150 kernels.

A typical rice kernel measures from ¼ to ⅜ inch (6 to 10 millimeters) long. The kernel has a hard covering called a *hull.* Underneath the hull are the *bran layers,* the *endosperm,* and the *embryo.* Several bran layers provide the outer coat of the kernel. They contain many of the kernel's nutrients. The starchy endosperm makes up most of the kernel. It is the part of the kernel most often eaten. The tiny embryo, also called the *germ,* is the part of the kernel from which a new plant grows.

Growth and reproduction. A new rice plant develops from the embryo inside the seed. The seed begins to sprout a few days after it is exposed to warm temperatures and plentiful moisture. The first *tiller* (shoot) appears 5 to 10 days after planting. Some rice plants may send out as many as 30 tillers, but most grow far fewer. More leaves appear as the tillers grow taller. The panicle grows from the top of the tiller. Some older varieties of rice grow from 48 to 72 inches (120 to 180 centimeters) tall. But most newer varieties stand from 31 to 39 inches (80 to 100 centimeters) high.

Rice plants begin to develop flowering parts 6 to 10 weeks after planting. The panicle forms inside the *sheath*—a tubelike, leafy covering that surrounds the stem. After about 4 weeks, the panicle emerges from the sheath and bears flowers. Pollination must occur for grains of rice to develop. Rice can pollinate itself because each flower has both male and female reproductive parts (see **Pollen**). The flowers give rise to mature grains of rice 4 to 6 weeks after pollination.

Uses of rice

Food. Nearly all the rice produced in the world provides food for people. Rice supplies about half the calories in the daily diet of many people in Asia. It is an excellent source of *carbohydrates*—nourishing substances that provide the body with energy. Although low in protein, rice becomes an important source of protein if eaten in large amounts. Rice also has small amounts of the B vitamins—niacin, riboflavin, and thiamine—and the minerals iron, phosphorus, potassium, and sodium. Rice has very little fat and is easy to digest.

Most rice is eaten as *milled white rice*—rice that has had both its hull and bran layers removed during milling. *Brown rice* has had its hull removed but not its bran layers. Brown rice is more nutritious than white rice because the bran layers contain most of the kernel's vitamins and minerals. However, most people prefer white rice because it is less chewy than brown rice and takes about half as long to cook.

White rice may be treated in various ways to make it more nutritious. For example, much white rice is *enriched* with vitamins and minerals to replace the nutrients lost in removing the bran. In areas where rice is the main food, enrichment helps prevent *beriberi,* a disease caused by lack of thiamine (see **Beriberi**).

Rice may also be steamed under pressure with the hulls on before milling. This process, called *parboiling,* makes the kernels less likely to break during milling. In addition, parboiled rice keeps many of the vitamins and minerals usually lost during milling because these nutrients spread throughout the grain during parboiling. *Quick-cooking rice* is partially cooked after milling. The kernels become more absorbent in the process and need less time for final cooking.

Other uses. Rice appears in many processed foods, including certain breakfast cereals, soup, baby food, snack foods, frozen foods, and flour. Breweries use broken rice kernels to make *mash,* an important ingredient in beer (see **Brewing** [Mashing]). In Japan, rice kernels are used to make an alcoholic drink called *sake,* or rice wine.

Farmers may use rice hulls for fertilizer and may add bran layers to livestock feed. Manufacturers sometimes use hulls in such products as insulation, cement, and the liquid chemical *furfural* (see **Furfural**). A few producers extract cooking oil from the bran. Many people in Asia use the *straw* (dried stalks) from rice plants to thatch roofs and weave sandals, hats, and baskets.

Kinds of rice

Scientists have identified 20 *species* (kinds) of rice. One of these species, Asian rice, accounts for nearly all of the rice cultivated today. A species known as African rice is grown in small quantities, mostly in western Africa.

Cross section of a grain of rice

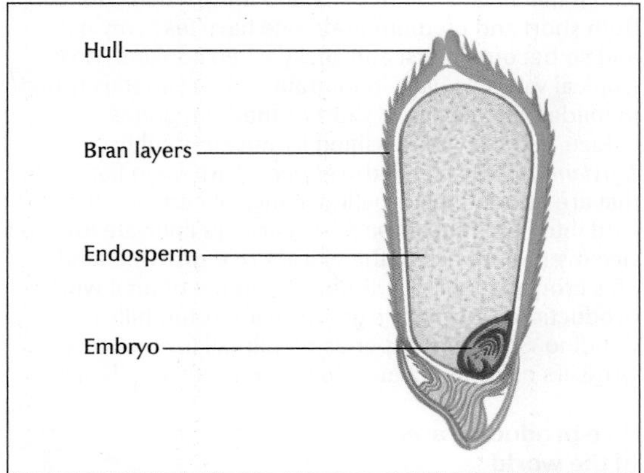

WORLD BOOK diagram by James Teason

Food value of white rice

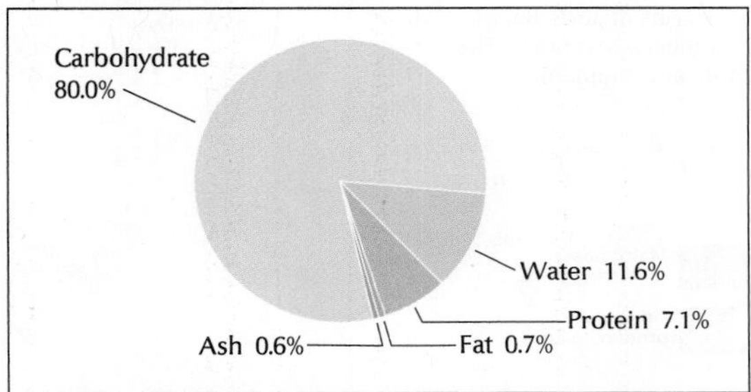

Source: U.S. Department of Agriculture, National Nutrient Database. Data are for uncooked long-grained white rice.

Leading rice-growing countries

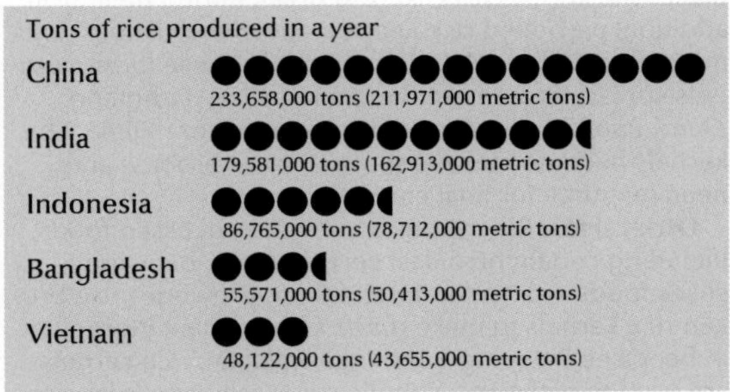

Figures are for a three-year average, 2015-2017.
Source: FAOSTAT, Statistics Division, Food and Agriculture Organization of the UN. http://www.faostat.fao.org. Data accessed in 2019.

Leading rice-growing states

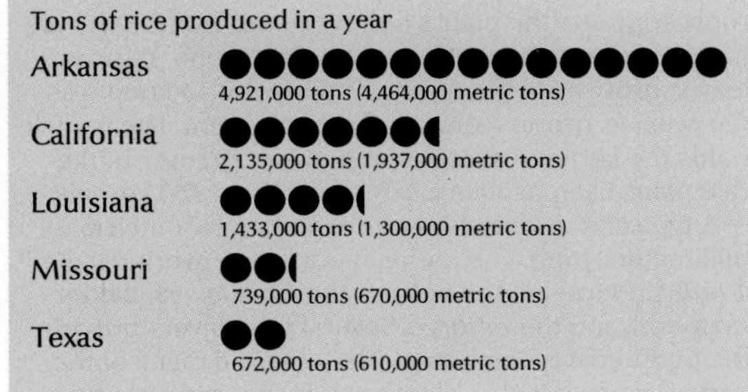

Figures are for a three-year average, 2016-2018.
Source: U.S. Department of Agriculture.

Asian rice can be divided into three main groups: Indica, Japonica, and Javanica. Indica rice is grown in India and other tropical regions. Japonica rice is grown in the cooler areas of Asia, including China, Japan, and Korea, as well as in Europe, North America, and Australia. Javanica rice is grown in Indonesia. Within these groups, agricultural researchers have identified over 70,000 varieties, but only a few hundred varieties are grown.

For marketing purposes, growers classify rice into three types by the length of its grain. Short grain rice is less than ⅕ inch (5 millimeters) long. Medium grain rice ranges in length from ⅕ to ¼ inch (5 to 6 millimeters); and long grain rice, from ¼ to 5/16 inch (6 to 8 millimeters). Long grain rice contains a large amount of *amylose,* a starch that makes the rice dry and fluffy when cooked. Both short and medium grain rice have less amylose and so become moist and sticky when cooked. Most tropical varieties have long grains. Most varieties grown in milder climates have short or medium grains.

Rice also may be classified by how it is cultivated. *Lowland rice,* also called *wet rice,* is grown in flat fields that are flooded by irrigation. Banks of earth enclose the land into fields called *paddies.* Farmers cultivate lowland rice over about half of the world's rice-growing land. This crop accounts for about 75 percent of total world production. *Upland rice* grows in areas too hilly for flooding. Such rice depends on rainfall for moisture. Growers cultivate upland rice over about a sixth of the world's rice-producing area. *Rainfed paddy rice* is grown in the remaining rice-producing lands. Its cultivation combines features of lowland and upland cultivation. This rice thrives in paddies watered by rainfall rather than by irrigation.

Researchers produce *hybrids* by *crossing* (mating) different varieties of rice. Hybrids have improved yields. China grows most of the world's hybrid rice.

Where rice is grown

Farmers grow rice in more than 110 countries. In all, they plant about 410 million acres (165 million hectares) of rice each year and harvest about 840 million tons (760 million metric tons). Rice grows best in areas with warm temperatures and with plentiful moisture from rainfall or irrigation. Such favorable growing conditions occur mainly in many tropical regions and the valleys and deltas of certain rivers. These rivers include the Yangtze in China, the Ganges in India, and the Mekong in Vietnam.

Asian farmers grow about 90 percent of the world's rice. China and India rank as the leading producers. Together, they grow about 50 percent of the world's rice. Other top producers include Bangladesh, Indonesia, Myanmar, the Philippines, Thailand, and Vietnam. The chief rice-producing areas of the United States lie along the Mississippi River in Arkansas, Mississippi, and Missouri; the Sacramento River in California; and the Gulf of Mexico in Texas and Louisiana.

WORLD BOOK map

Rice-producing areas of the world

China and India produce about half of the world's rice. Other major rice-producing countries include Bangladesh, Indonesia, Myanmar, Thailand, and Vietnam.

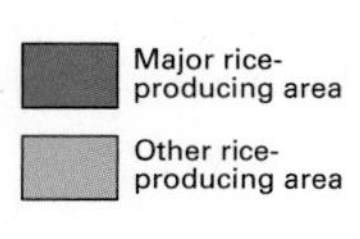

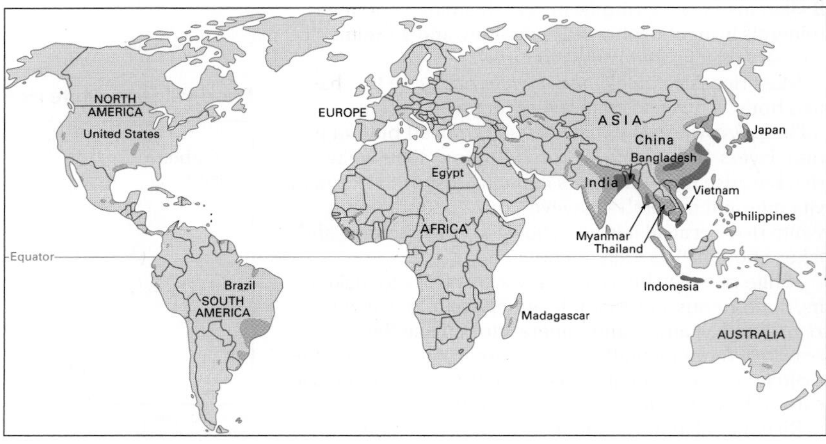

Nearly all rice is eaten in the country where it is grown. About 5 percent of the world's rice crop is traded internationally. A few countries regularly import rice. Other nations import rice if their crop fails. The chief exporters of rice include India, Pakistan, Thailand, the United States, and Vietnam.

How rice is grown

Methods of growing rice vary, depending on the labor supply and the level of *mechanization* (work done by machinery). In Southeast Asia and other developing areas, labor is plentiful, and much work is done by hand. Some farmers have oxen or water buffaloes for pulling plows. In the United States and other developed countries, farmers use machinery for most production stages.

Most rice grows in areas of the world with a yearly rainfall of at least 40 inches (100 centimeters). But farmers can cultivate rice in drier regions by irrigating the land. Rice needs an average temperature of at least 70 °F (21 °C) throughout its growing season. It grows best in heavy, slightly acid soils that contain fine particles of clay. Such soils hold water well.

Growing rice involves four main steps: They are (1) preparing the ground, (2) planting, (3) controlling diseases and pests, and (4) harvesting.

Preparing the ground. Rice grows best in a field covered with shallow water. Farmers build low dirt walls called *dikes* or *levees* to hold water in the paddies. Many Asian farmers flood their fields before leveling them. They work the soil into a soft mud to make it easier to plow and to bury weeds. The practice of working flooded land is called *puddling.*

In certain industrialized countries, rice growers level the ground with large earth movers. They make sure the land slopes slightly so it can drain quickly before the harvest. Farmers use special machines to *till* (plow) the land and build dikes. Before planting, they may add mineral fertilizers to the soil to enrich it. Commonly applied fertilizers include nitrogen, phosphorus, and potassium.

Planting. In developing countries, farmers sometimes plant rice seeds directly in the ground. But more commonly they sow seeds thickly in small seedbeds and transplant the seedlings to a flooded field after several weeks. This method reduces the length of time rice occupies the main field by about 15 to 20 days. This is important in areas where several crops are grown on the same land each year. Transplanting seedlings also permits better weed control. Fewer weeds are able to grow in the thickly sown seedbeds. In addition, farmers can remove weeds more easily in the main rice fields when the plants are larger.

© V. Rastelli, Woodfin Camp, Inc.

Planting rice seeds along dirt ridges may be done by hand, as shown here, or by machine. Many Asian farmers plant small seedbeds and later transplant the seedlings to a flooded field.

Farmers transplant clumps of 3 to 6 seedlings into the muddy soil. The clumps are spaced 4 to 8 inches (10 to 20 centimeters) apart and may be lined up in rows.

In industrialized nations, rice growers use a machine called a *drill* to place the seeds directly in the soil. After planting if the soil's moisture is low, they may flood the field briefly and then drain it so that the seeds can sprout and grow. The field may be flooded and drained a few more times before the plants reach a height of 3 to 6 inches (8 to 15 centimeters). A layer of water 2 to 8

© Shutterstock

John Launois, Black Star

Norman Myers, Bruce Coleman Inc.

Most rice farming in Asia is done by hand. Seedlings are transplanted from beds into flooded fields, *left.* At harvest, farmers cut the rice stalks with knives or sickles and tie the stalks into bundles to dry, *center.* The dried stalks are then beaten against "screens" to separate the grain, *right.*

inches (5 to 20 centimeters) deep is then left in the field until a few weeks before harvest. Rice growers in Australia and California scatter seeds onto a flooded field from small, low-flying airplanes. The seeds are allowed to sprout before they are sown in order to help speed their growth and to ensure that they will sink in the water. Fertilizers also may be sprayed on the plants from an airplane.

Controlling diseases and pests is an important part of growing a good rice crop. Fungi, bacteria, and viruses infect rice plants with diseases. Weeds compete with rice plants for nutrients in the soil. Such destructive insect pests as leaf hoppers and stem borers also attack rice. Farmers use chemicals to control many of these enemies. However, since many of these chemicals may be harmful to people and the environment, farmers must use care in applying them. Rice growers can best protect their crop from damage by planting varieties that can resist diseases and pests.

Harvesting. Farmers drain the rice fields one to two weeks before harvest. The grain is ready for harvesting when moisture makes up 18 to 25 percent of its weight. The wet rice must be dried after harvesting, before storage and milling.

In developing countries, farmers harvest the rice by hand. They usually cut the stalks with sickles or knives, tie the stalks in bundles, and dry them in the sun. The crop is then ready for *threshing,* the process of separating the grain from the rest of the plant. The farmers may thresh the grain by beating the panicles against a slatted bamboo screen and letting the grain fall between the slats. Some farmers put the bundles of rice through a gasoline-powered thresher. In some areas, farm animals walk over the bundles to thresh the grain. If the grain needs further drying after threshing, it is spread out on mats in the sun.

In industrialized countries, large self-powered machines called *combines* harvest and thresh rice in one operation. The wet grain is then dried by heated air.

How rice is processed

Harvested rice, still in its hull, is called *rough rice* or *paddy rice.* Most rough rice is processed in mills and sold as milled white rice. Millers use machines for most of the work, even in developing countries. There are three basic steps in processing harvested rice: (1) cleaning and hulling, (2) removing the bran layers, and (3) grading.

Cleaning and hulling. Cleaning removes dirt, straw, weeds, and other impurities from the rough rice. The cleaning equipment uses screens to sift out unwanted materials and fans to blow away lightweight debris.

After cleaning, the rice is placed in a machine called a *sheller* for hulling. In the sheller, the grains pass between rubber rollers or stone disks that loosen the hulls without breaking the kernels. The hulls are separated from the grain by suction. A screen then separates the hulled grain from any remaining unhulled rice. Some hulled rice may be packaged as brown rice. But most of it is processed into white rice. Rice may be treated by parboiling or other methods to improve its food value.

Removing the bran layers. After hulling, the brown rice passes through a series of machines that rub off its bran layers and embryo. The remaining endosperm becomes the white rice we eat. In some Asian countries, a single machine called a *huller mill* strips off both the hull and most of the bran. After milling, the kernels are packaged for sale. Most of the bran removed during milling is used in livestock feed.

Grading. Millers sort the processed rice into different grades for marketing. In the United States, the Department of Agriculture sets standards for grading rice. It bases these grades on such qualities as the size of the kernels, the moisture content of the kernels, and the number of chalky or damaged kernels. These grades range from U.S. No. 1, for the highest quality rice, to U.S. No. 6, which is a lower quality rice. U.S. Sample is the lowest grade of rice.

History

No one knows exactly when or where rice originated. But it probably first grew wild and was gathered and eaten by people in Southeast Asia thousands of years ago. Archaeologists have found evidence that people

© Shutterstock

Powerful machines called *combines, left,* are used to harvest rice in the United States and other developed countries. Combines also thresh the grain as they harvest it.

Charles Moore, Black Star

Hulling rice separates the shell-like hulls from the grain. The machine shown above loosens the rice hulls but does not remove the bran coats from the kernels.

cultivated rice at least 10,000 years ago in southern China and Korea. Rice then spread northward in China and to Japan; westward to India; and southward to Indonesia. Cultivation of a separate species of rice began independently in West Africa's Niger River Valley by about 1500 B.C.

Traders and explorers carried rice from Asia to other parts of the world. Rice cultivation had spread to Persia (now Iran) and Syria by 300 B.C. Europeans first learned of rice from Greek soldiers who accompanied Alexander the Great's military expedition to India in the 320's B.C. But rice was not cultivated in Europe until the Moors of northwestern Africa conquered Spain about A.D. 700 and brought rice with them. Rice was brought from Spain to Italy several hundred years later and afterward spread to southeastern Europe. Spanish explorers introduced rice to the Caribbean region and South America on voyages during the 1400's, 1500's, and 1600's.

Rice reached the American Colonies in the 1600's. Colonists first grew it commercially in South Carolina about 1685. Rice soon thrived in the Carolinas and Georgia. After the Civil War (1861-1865), rice production shifted westward. By 1900, farmers in Louisiana were growing about 70 percent of the rice in the United States. It was established as a crop in California in the early 1900's.

In 1960, government agencies and private foundations set up the International Rice Research Institute in the Philippines. The institute worked to improve rice production as part of a worldwide effort to increase food production in developing countries. This successful effort was an important part of what became known as the Green Revolution. In the 1960's, researchers at the institute developed new varieties of rice that produce more grain than older varieties, especially when fertilized. Traditional rice plants often grow so tall that they fall over and destroy their panicles. The new high-yield varieties have shorter, sturdier stalks and are less likely to topple.

In 2002, scientists finished determining the *sequence* (order) of all the *genes* (units of heredity) in rice cells. Biologists are using this information to determine ways to create varieties of rice that resist disease and provide better yields.

Today, farmers in developing countries use machines for plowing and other work once done by hand. In developed countries, computers help rice farmers plan production and control irrigation. J. Neil Rutger

Scientific classification. Rice species make up the genus *Oryza.* The scientific name for Asian rice is *Oryza sativa.* African rice is *O. glaberrima.*

See also **Grain weevil; Sushi; Wild rice.**

Outline

I. The rice plant
- A. Structure
- B. Growth and reproduction

II. Uses of rice
- A. Food
- B. Other uses

III. Kinds of rice

IV. Where rice is grown

V. How rice is grown
- A. Preparing the ground
- B. Planting
- C. Controlling diseases and pests
- D. Harvesting

VI. How rice is processed
- A. Cleaning and hulling
- B. Removing the bran layers
- C. Grading

VII. History

Questions

Which two countries produce the most rice?
Why is brown rice more nutritious than white rice?
What are the four main parts of a rice plant?
How can farmers best protect rice crops from diseases and insects?
How do rice planting methods in developing countries differ from those in developed countries?
Why do rice farmers usually flood their fields?
What are some advantages of new varieties of rice?
Which part of a rice kernel is most often eaten?
How does the cultivation of lowland rice differ from that of upland rice?

Rice, Condoleezza (1954-), served as United States secretary of state from 2005 to 2009. She was the second woman, after Madeleine K. Albright, to hold the post and the first African American woman to do so. Rice had served as President George W. Bush's national security adviser since 2001 and was the first woman to hold that post.

Rice was born in Birmingham, Alabama, on Nov. 14, 1954. She graduated from the University of Denver with a bachelor's degree at the age of 19, in 1974. She earned a master's degree from the University of Notre Dame in 1975 and a Ph.D. from the University of Denver in 1981. Rice then began teaching political science at Stanford University, where she won a teaching award in 1984.

Rice, who speaks Russian, became known for her knowledge of the Soviet Union. In 1986, she served as an adviser to the U.S. Joint Chiefs of Staff. In 1989, during George H. W. Bush's administration, she was appointed director of Soviet and East European affairs on the National Security Council. Rice left the council in 1991 and returned to Stanford to teach. From 1993 to 1999, she served as provost of the university. Rice was the first woman and the first African American named to that post. In 1999 and 2000, she acted as chief foreign policy consultant to George W. Bush during Bush's presidential

White House photo by Tina Hager

Condoleezza Rice

campaign. Rice returned to Stanford after leaving the Cabinet in 2009, becoming a senior fellow at Stanford's Hoover Institution on War, Revolution, and Peace, a center for research in social science. Lee Thornton

See also **African Americans** (picture).

Rice, Elmer (1892-1967), was an American dramatist who championed moral, social, and personal freedom. His many plays reflect his belief that it is better to love than to hate, to question than to accept, to be free than to be bound.

Rice is best known for two plays. *The Adding Machine* (1923) is an Expressionistic satire on the growing mechanization of humanity. Rice used distorted settings and nonrealistic acting to show the tortured mind of the chief character, Mr. Zero. *Street Scene* (1929), a Pulitzer Prize winner, gives a naturalistic picture of life in a crowded big-city apartment house. Rice's other plays include *On Trial* (1914), *Counsellor-at-Law* (1931), *We, the People* (1933), and *Dream Girl* (1945). Rice also wrote novels and an autobiography, *Minority Report* (1963).

Rice was born Elmer Leopold Reizenstein on Sept. 28, 1892, in New York City. He died on May 8, 1967.

Mardi Valgemae

See also **Expressionism** (Expressionist drama).

Rice, Grantland (1880-1954), was the first United States newspaperman to gain fame by writing about sports. He wrote about Bobby Jones, Jack Dempsey, Bill Tilden, Helen Wills, and other sports champions during the 1920's. Rice's autobiography, *The Tumult and the Shouting,* was published in 1954. Rice was born on Nov. 1, 1880, in Murfreesboro, Tennessee. He died on July 13, 1954. Pat Harmon

Rice, Jerry (1962-), ranks among the greatest pass receivers in football history. Rice combined speed, strength, the ability to get open for passes, and skill at making difficult catches. Rice holds many regular-season National Football League (NFL) records, including touchdowns scored (208), passes caught (1,549), and yards gained by a pass receiver (22,895).

Jerry Lee Rice was born on Oct. 13, 1962, in Starkville, Mississippi. He played for four years at Mississippi Valley State University. The NFL's San Francisco 49ers drafted Rice in 1985. In the 1987-1988 season, he scored a record 22 touchdowns on pass receptions and led the league in scoring. In 2007, Randy Moss of the New England Patriots broke Rice's record by catching 23 touchdown passes.

Rice helped the 49ers win Super Bowls in 1989, 1990, and 1995. He was the Most Valuable Player in the 1989 game. San Francisco released Rice in 2001, and he joined the Oakland (now Las Vegas) Raiders. Oakland traded Rice to the Seattle Seahawks in 2004. Rice signed to play with the Denver Broncos in 2005 but retired before the regular season began. In 2010, he was inducted into the Pro Football Hall of Fame. Bob Carroll

Rich, Adrienne (1929-2012), was one of the leading American poets of her generation and a major voice in the women's movement. Rich attacked what she saw as the male-dominated structure of society. Rich blamed this system for women's oppression and other forms of injustice and violence. She advocated replacing the male-dominated structure with a set of values derived from the experiences and insights of women. In her later work, Rich also increasingly addressed issues of race, class, and ethnic background. She wrote several poems in which she reflected on her own Jewish background.

Rich anchored her larger political concerns in individual lives, her own and those of other women. Rich's poetry reflects her willingness to admit and wrestle with contradictions—for example, her awareness that anger can be both destructive and creative. Such contradictions often give her poems a charged, dramatic quality, as though the poet were struggling to make up her mind before our eyes. She began writing in rhyme and meter in the 1950's but gradually developed a looser, more flexible style.

Adrienne Cecile Rich was born in Baltimore on May 16, 1929. The best introduction to her work is *The Fact of a Doorframe: Poems 1950-2001* (2002). Later collections include *The School Among the Ruins* (2004), *Telephone Ringing in the Labyrinth* (2007), *Tonight No Poetry Will Serve: Poems 2007-2010* (2011), and *Later Poems: Selected and New 1971-2012* (2012). Rich also wrote several important prose books, including *Of Woman Born* (1976), *Arts of the Possible* (2002), and *Essential Essays: Culture, Politics, and the Art of Poetry* (published in 2018, after her death). Rich died on March 27, 2012. Roger Gilbert

Richard I (1157-1199) was king of England from 1189 to 1199. He is known in history as Richard the Lion-Hearted, or Richard Coeur de Lion. He was a son of Henry II, the first king of the Plantagenet dynasty, and Eleanor of Aquitaine. After Richard became king, he joined Philip II of France in a crusade to the Holy Land, which was under Muslim control. Richard captured Acre (now called Akko) but saw that Jerusalem could not be recovered.

During the crusade, Richard aroused the hatred of Leopold V, Duke of Austria. In 1192, while Richard was on his journey home, Leopold seized him. Leopold kept Richard in a castle as a prisoner of the Holy Roman emperor, Henry VI. Richard was later taken to Henry, who released him in 1194 after a ransom was paid.

As a Plantagenet, Richard had inherited not only England but also most of northern and western France. While Richard was in prison, Philip II seized some of the Plantagenet lands in France. Richard spent the rest of his reign fighting to get the lands back. He left efficient ministers in charge of England while he concentrated on the war with Philip. In 1199, Richard was killed during the siege of a castle, and his brother John became king.

Richard was born in Oxford, England, but spent nearly all of his life in France. In 1183, Richard's older brother died. However, the brothers' father, Henry II, refused to recognize Richard as the heir to the throne of England. Richard rebelled against his father several times. Richard finally defeated Henry II in 1189.

John Gillingham

See also **Flag** (picture: Historical flags of the world [English and French]); **Plantagenet.**

Detail of an engraving (1743) by George Vertue; The Newberry Library, Chicago

Richard I

Richard II (1367-1400) was king of England from 1377 to 1399. He ascended the throne at the age of 10 when his grandfather King

Edward III died.

During the first four years of Richard's reign, a council ruled England on his behalf, and Richard's uncle John of Gaunt exercised much influence. However, the council could not agree on a consistent governing policy. One result was Wat Tyler's Rebellion of 1381, which the young king courageously put down. For the next few years, Richard tried to increase his control over the government with the help of favorite advisers. But many of his favorites were imprisoned or executed by the "Merciless Parliament" of 1388. In 1389, Richard began to rule on his own.

Detail of an illuminated manuscript (about 1389) by an unknown artist; St. John's College, Cambridge, England

Richard II

Richard ruled well in the early 1390's. However, through his control of the "Revenge Parliament" of 1397, he began to punish many of his enemies. Richard became increasingly tyrannical and angered the English people with such measures as forced loans and loyalty oaths.

In 1399, Richard led an expedition to Ireland. While he was there, John of Gaunt's son Henry of Bolingbroke led a revolt against Richard in England. The revolt resulted in Richard's removal from the throne. Bolingbroke became King Henry IV. Richard died in early 1400. He was probably murdered.

Richard was born in Bordeaux, France. His father was Edward, the Black Prince, a famous English warrior. Richard supported the arts and the famous English writer Geoffrey Chaucer. George B. Stow

See also **John of Gaunt; Wat Tyler's Rebellion.**

Richard III (1452-1485) was king of England from 1483 to 1485. Richard's reign brought on the revolt that ended the Wars of the Roses. These wars were fought between the two branches of the royal family—the House of Lancaster and the House of York. Richard belonged to the House of York.

National Portrait Gallery

Richard III

Richard was born in Northamptonshire, England, a son of Richard, Duke of York. In 1461, young Richard's oldest brother became King Edward IV. Richard was made Duke of Gloucester the same year.

In 1483, Edward IV died, and his elder son became King Edward V at the age of 12. The government was put in the care of Richard, who was named protector of the realm. The Woodvilles, the family of the young king's mother, attempted to seize power. In crushing their conspiracy, Richard sought to become king himself. He was crowned early in July 1483, after Parliament had declared him king. Edward V and his younger brother Richard were put in the Tower of London. Some scholars believe that King Richard had the boys killed. However, there is no proof that such a crime took place.

Richard tried to govern well, but he lacked widespread support. Powerful Yorkist and Lancastrian nobles plotted against him. With their help, Henry Tudor, Earl of Richmond, a kinsman of the House of Lancaster, invaded England from his exile in France. Henry Tudor's forces won the Battle of Bosworth Field in 1485, killing Richard. Henry Tudor became king as Henry VII.

In 2012, archaeologists discovered Richard's remains in Leicester not far from Bosworth Field. In 2015, his remains were reburied in a royal tomb at Leicester Cathedral. Ralph A. Griffiths

See also **Wars of the Roses.**

Richard, *REE shahrd,* **Maurice** (1921-2000), ranks among the leading goal scorers in National Hockey League (NHL) history. During his career, Richard scored 544 goals and 421 assists for a total of 965 points in 978 regular-season games. Richard's explosive skating speed and high-powered offensive skills earned him the nickname "Rocket."

Richard played right wing for the Montreal Canadiens from the 1942-1943 season through the 1959-1960 season, helping the Canadiens win eight Stanley Cup championships. In the 1944-1945 season, Richard became the first player in NHL history to score a total of 50 goals in one season. He won the Hart Trophy (now the Hart Memorial Trophy) in 1947 as the NHL's most valuable player.

Richard was born on Aug. 4, 1921, in Montreal. He was inducted into the Hockey Hall of Fame in 1961. Richard died on May 27, 2000. Henri Richard, Maurice's younger brother, was a hockey star who played in the NHL from 1955 to 1975. Henri Richard was inducted into the Hockey Hall of Fame in 1979. Larry Wigge

Richard the Lion-Hearted. See **Richard I.**

Richards, I. A. (1893-1979), was an influential English literary critic and poet. His criticism was mainly concerned with the differences between ordinary language and poetry. Richards argued that ordinary language is made up of statements that relate to and can be tested against matters of fact. Poetry, by contrast, consists of statements that cannot be verified, but that arouse or quiet our feelings. He discussed his theories in *Principles of Literary Criticism* (1924).

Richards became one of the founders of the New Criticism, a critical movement of the mid-1900's that shifted the direction of literary criticism from historical scholarship to interpretation (see **Criticism**). He became interested in the close reading of a text partly through his studies in psychology and semantics. His ideas on this subject appear in *The Meaning of Meaning* (1923), cowritten with English scholar Charles Kay Ogden; and in *Practical Criticism* (1929).

Ivor Armstrong Richards was born on Feb. 26, 1893, in Sandbach, near Crewe. He died on Sept. 7, 1979.

David H. Richter

See also **Semantics.**

Richards, Sir William Buell, *BOO uhl* (1815-1889), a Canadian lawyer and statesman, served as the first chief justice of the Supreme Court of Canada from 1875 to 1879. His judicial career began in 1853 when he was appointed to the Court of Common Pleas of Canada West (now Ontario). He rose to become chief justice of Ontario in 1868, and then was called to head the newly established Supreme Court of Canada. He also served as attorney general of Canada from 1851 to 1853. Richards was born on May 2, 1815, in Brockville, Ontario. He died on Jan. 26, 1889. Philip Girard

Richardson, Bill (1947-), was governor of New Mexico from 2003 to 2011. A Democrat and former congressman, he had served as United States secretary of energy. He was also the first Hispanic American to become U.S. ambassador to the United Nations (UN) and the first Hispanic American to run for U.S. president.

William Blaine Richardson was born on Nov. 15, 1947, in Pasadena, California. His mother was Mexican, and his father was a non-Hispanic banker from Boston who worked in Mexico. Bill grew up in Mexico City. He and his family moved to Concord, Massachusetts, in 1961.

Richardson earned a B.A. degree from Tufts University in 1970 and an M.A. from the Fletcher School of Law and Diplomacy at Tufts in 1971. He moved to New Mexico in 1978. In 1982, he was elected there to the U.S. House of Representatives. He served in the House until 1997. President Bill Clinton sent him on several diplomatic missions in the 1990's. Richardson negotiated the release of Americans held hostage in North Korea, Iraq, and Sudan. He was U.S. ambassador to the UN from January 1997 until Clinton appointed him energy secretary. Richardson held the Cabinet post from 1998 to 2001. He was elected governor of New Mexico in 2002 and reelected in 2006. He campaigned for the 2008 Democratic nomination for president of the United States. Richardson wrote an autobiography, *Between Worlds: The Making of an American Life* (2005). Jackie Koszczuk

Richardson, Elliot Lee (1920-1999), held four Cabinet offices, more than any other person in United States history. Richardson, a Republican, served as secretary of health, education, and welfare from 1970 until January 1973, when he became secretary of defense. From May to October 1973, he was attorney general. He served as secretary of commerce in 1976 and 1977.

Richardson resigned as attorney general in protest against President Richard M. Nixon's order to fire Archibald Cox, the chief prosecutor in the investigation of the Watergate scandal (see **Watergate**). Richardson had appointed Cox and had promised him he would have complete independence. In October 1973, a dispute over the investigation arose between Nixon and Cox. Nixon ordered Richardson to dismiss Cox. Richardson refused and resigned. Richardson served as U.S. ambassador to the United Kingdom from March 1975 to January 1976.

Richardson was born on July 20, 1920, in Boston. He graduated from Harvard Law School in 1947. From 1959 to 1961, he served as U.S. attorney in Massachusetts. He was lieutenant governor of Massachusetts from 1964 to 1967 and Massachusetts attorney general from 1967 to 1969. In 1969, Richardson became undersecretary of state in the Nixon administration. Richardson died on Dec. 31, 1999. Jeremy D. Mayer

Richardson, Henry Hobson (1838-1886), was the first American architect to achieve international fame. He introduced the Romanesque Revival style to the United States and dominated American architectural practice during the 1870's and 1880's.

In his buildings, Richardson united a highly developed sense of craftsmanship with the subdued grandeur of the Romanesque style. He used stone and wood for public buildings, and wood and wood shingles for many of his houses. His work, notably the Marshall Field Wholesale Store (1887) in Chicago, profoundly influenced Louis H. Sullivan and other architects. *Richardsonian Romanesque* is a term used loosely to describe buildings in stone or shingle with large round-arched openings. See **Architecture** (Early modern architecture in America; Romanesque architecture).

© Tom Evans

Henry H. Richardson's Glessner House was finished in 1887 in Chicago. It is noted for its massiveness and rough stone surface.

Richardson was born Sept. 29, 1838, on a plantation near New Orleans. His first major work, Trinity Church (1877) in Boston, contained the basic elements of his style. It was built of monumental cut stone with an asymmetrical plan and French Romanesque forms. Richardson designed several public libraries in the Boston area and buildings for the Harvard campus. His other commissions included the Glessner House (1887) in Chicago and the Allegheny County Courthouse and Jail (1888) in Pittsburgh. He died on April 27, 1886. Nicholas Adams

Richardson, Samuel (1689-1761), an English writer, is considered one of the founding fathers of the novel. He wrote three novels: *Pamela; or, Virtue Rewarded* (1740), *Clarissa; or, The History of a Young Lady* (1748), and *Sir Charles Grandison* (1754). These books brought various important, and in some ways new, elements to the novel. Each of his novels has a genuinely unified plot rather than disconnected episodes. The characters maintain a consistent point of view, without interference by the author. The works established the theme of courtship leading to marriage as a basic plot of the novel.

All three novels are written in the form of letters. The idea for the form of *Pamela* originated from a manual of model letters written by Richardson. *Pamela* was published anonymously and was a sensational success. All the novels have a breathless quality that sweeps the reader along from letter to letter.

It is easy to mock the somewhat dubious, often priggish morality of these novels. Indeed, *Pamela* inspired witty parodies by writers of his time. Still, Richardson set the novel firmly in what became its main direction: a detailed description of real people in common situations of domestic life. In particular, Richardson's novels treat women's concern for security, marriage, and a proper social role. This reflects how, with the rise of the new middle class, women with conscious individual identities and problems were coming to the forefront. This tendency has grown since Richardson's time, and in him, as in many later novelists, women have found a sympathetic and sensitive voice.

Richardson was born in Derbyshire. He became one of London's most successful publishers. Ian Watt

Richelieu, *RIHSH uh LOO* or *REE sheh LYU,* **Cardinal** (1585-1642), served as prime minister of France from 1624 to 1642. He and King Louis XIII worked closely to govern the country. Richelieu strengthened the king's rule and helped make France the most powerful country in Europe.

Rise to power. Richelieu was born on Sept. 9, 1585, in Paris. His given and family name was Armand Jean du Plessis. He took the title of Richelieu from the name of his family's estate. In 1607, Richelieu became the Roman Catholic bishop of Luçon, near La Rochelle in western France. In 1614, he was elected to France's Estates-General, a legislative body consisting of representatives of three *estates* (groups)—the clergy, the nobility, and the common people. Richelieu was chosen as spokesman for the clergy. In 1616, he became a member of Louis XIII's royal council. But this lasted only a short time.

Pope Gregory XV named Richelieu a cardinal in 1622. In 1624, Richelieu regained his post on the royal council and soon headed the council. As the council's head, he was known as *prime minister.* In the council, he showed a deep understanding of politics and great skill at helping to put the king's policies into effect. Richelieu soon became the dominant power in the French government.

Strengthening the monarchy. When Richelieu rose to power, Louis XIII had not yet firmly established his authority in France. The Huguenots, a Protestant group, exercised much political and religious power even though most of France was Roman Catholic. The independence of the nobility and unreliability among government officials also threatened the monarchy's rule. Richelieu wanted to ensure that the king's will would be obeyed.

In 1627, Richelieu directed a siege of the French city of La Rochelle, where the Huguenots maintained self-rule. After 14 months of fighting, La Rochelle surrendered in October 1628. The royal forces then attacked other cities controlled by the Huguenots. In 1629, the Huguenots and the French government signed the Peace of Alais. This treaty eliminated the Huguenots' right to maintain military forces in the cities they governed, a right granted by the Edict of Nantes in 1598. As a result, the Huguenots could no longer wage civil war or act as a state within the state.

To control the nobles, Richelieu severely punished people who plotted against the king. Richelieu ordered the destruction of all fortresses controlled by the nobility, except those protecting the French borders. Many nobles who rebelled were executed or exiled.

By 1631, Richelieu had replaced his enemies in the government with officials he could trust. Marie de Médicis, the king's mother, was forced into exile for plotting against Richelieu. In addition, Richelieu expanded the king's control over local governments by sending royal agents called *intendants* into the provinces.

Thirty Years' War. During Richelieu's service as prime minister, Europe fought a series of religious and political wars called the Thirty Years' War (1618-1648).

Members of the Habsburg (or Hapsburg) royal family ruled Spain and the Holy Roman Empire. Lands controlled by Spain included what are now Belgium and parts of Italy. The Holy Roman Empire included what are now Austria, the Czech Republic, Germany, the Netherlands, Switzerland, and part of Italy. To stop the growth of Habsburg power, Richelieu supported others fighting the Habsburgs. For example, he gave Sweden funds to continue fighting. But the Habsburgs grew stronger.

In 1635, France declared war on Spain. At first, the war went poorly for France. Spanish armies quickly penetrated French borders, and tax revolts and uprisings by French nobles distracted Richelieu. France regained its position against Spain in later years and eventually won the war. But Richelieu died before the war ended.

Historical reputation. Many historians have admired Richelieu for his extraordinary intelligence and energy. He promoted the growth of royal authority and helped France become Europe's leading power. Richelieu's work also led to the building of a French navy and expansion of French ports. He helped establish French colonies in Africa, Canada, and the West Indies. However, Richelieu concentrated on France's foreign affairs and, as a result, failed to resolve many domestic problems and even aggravated some of them.

Richelieu took great interest in the arts. He rebuilt the Sorbonne, the theological college of the University of Paris. He also supported promising writers and founded the French Academy, an organization of France's leading writers and other thinkers. Donald A. Bailey

Related articles in *World Book* include:

French Academy	Louis XIII	Sorbonne
Huguenots	Marie de Médicis	Thirty Years' War
La Rochelle		

Richler, *RIHCH luhr,* **Mordecai,** *MAWR duh ky* (1931-2001), was a Canadian novelist. As a boy, Richler lived in a poor Jewish district of Montreal, where he was born on Jan. 27, 1931. His experiences there provided the background for *Son of a Smaller Hero* (1955) and *The Apprenticeship of Duddy Kravitz* (1959).

From 1954 to 1972, Richler lived mainly in England. In *Cocksure* (1968) and *St. Urbain's Horseman* (1971), he wrote about Canadians living in Europe. These novels and *Joshua Then and Now* (1980) are character studies that satirize sophisticated, urban society. *Solomon Gursky Was Here* (1989) is a comic satire about four generations of a family. *Barney's Version* (1997) is set against a background of working class Jewish neighborhoods in Montreal and explores the life of a failed writer.

Richler also wrote short stories, motion-picture and television scripts, and children's books about a boy called Jacob Two-Two. The best of his essays and articles were published as *Notes on an Endangered Species and Others* (1974) and *Broadsides* (1990). He described his impressions of Canada in *Home Sweet Home* (1984) and *Oh Canada! Oh Quebec: Requiem for a Divided Country* (1992). Richler reported on a trip to Israel in *This Year in Jerusalem* (1994). His *On Snooker* (2001) is a witty examination of the game of snooker. Laurie R. Ricou

Richmond. See Staten Island.

© Dreamstime

Richmond is the capital of Virginia and a center for commerce and education. It lies on the James River, in the east-central part of the state.

Richmond, Virginia (pop. 204,214; met. area pop. 1,208,101) is the capital of Virginia and a major commercial, cultural, educational, and historical center. It also ranks as one of Virginia's largest cities. It was the capital of the Confederate States of America during most of the American Civil War (1861-1865).

Richmond lies on the James River, in east-central Virginia. For location, see **Virginia** (political map). In the mid-1600's, English colonists chose the site because of its natural advantages for trade and transportation. Richmond was named for a suburb of London, England.

The city. Richmond covers 60 square miles (155 square kilometers) on both sides of the James River. About half of the city's people are African Americans. The Richmond metropolitan area covers 4,576 square miles (11,852 square kilometers).

A government area in downtown Richmond includes the City Hall and a federal office building. The State Capitol stands in Capitol Square. Thomas Jefferson, before he became president, designed the building. Jefferson modeled it after a Roman temple in Nîmes, France. The Capitol has influenced the architecture of many public buildings in the United States.

A famous marble statue of George Washington stands under the dome of the Capitol. The statue was completed in 1791 by the French sculptor Jean Antoine Houdon. Busts of seven other presidents born in Virginia are displayed in the encircling wall. The presidents are William Henry Harrison, Jefferson, James Madison, James Monroe, Zachary Taylor, John Tyler, and Woodrow Wilson. See **Virginia** (picture: The State Capitol).

A bronze statue of Washington on horseback stands in Capitol Square. Six bronze figures of important Virginia statesmen flank its stone base. Statues of Jefferson Davis, Stonewall Jackson, Robert E. Lee, Jeb Stuart, and other Confederate leaders once stood along Richmond's Monument Avenue. The Confederate statues were taken down in 2020, however, following demonstrations protesting racial injustice and the lasting effects of slavery and white supremacy. In 1996, a statue of the tennis star Arthur Ashe, who was born in Richmond, was added to Monument Avenue.

Education and cultural life. A nine-member elected School Board supervises Richmond's public school system. The Richmond area also has a number of private and parochial schools. Richmond is the home of the University of Richmond, Virginia Commonwealth University, and Virginia Union University. Virginia Commonwealth University includes the Medical College of Virginia. Also in the city is Union Presbyterian Seminary.

The Virginia Museum of Fine Arts owns a valuable collection of paintings, and Russian imperial jewels and jeweled Easter eggs designed by the Russian jeweler Peter Carl Fabergé. The Science Museum of Virginia has science education exhibits and a planetarium theater. The Valentine history museum features exhibits that illustrate the history of Richmond. Exhibits at the Virginia Museum of History & Culture, displayed in a building known as Battle Abbey, explore themes from throughout Virginia's history. The Black History Museum and Cultural Center of Virginia, in the Leigh Street Armory, details centuries of African American life in Virginia. The Library of Virginia houses materials on the early history of Virginia.

The Richmond Symphony presents concerts at Richmond CenterStage, a performing arts center. Many popular music concerts and Broadway plays are held in the Altria Theater.

Other interesting places to visit include:

St. John's Church, built in 1741. It is one of the oldest wooden buildings in the state. There, in 1775, the Virginia orator and statesman Patrick Henry delivered his famous speech that, according to tradition, ended with the words, "Give me liberty or give me death!"

American Civil War Museum, which has exhibits that explain the perspectives of the Union, the Confederacy, and African American enslaved people and freedmen. It includes Historic Tredegar, a former ironworks; and the White House of the Confederacy.

John Marshall House, occupied by the fourth chief justice of the United States from about 1790 until his death in 1835.

Edgar Allan Poe Museum, a group of buildings that form a shrine to the famous American author. Poe lived in Richmond as a child and later as editor of the *Southern Literary Messenger,* a magazine. One of the buildings, the Old Stone House, is believed to date from about 1737 and is probably Richmond's oldest house.

Hollywood Cemetery, the burial place of Confederate President Jefferson Davis and U.S. Presidents James Monroe and John Tyler.

Economy. Many of Richmond's people are employed by the local, state, and federal governments. Financial services are the largest private employers. These employers include banking, credit card, brokerage, and insurance companies. Manufacturing and trade and other service industries are also important to the economy. Richmond is the headquarters for a number of large companies. The city's chief products include cigarettes, machinery for manufacturing and packaging tobacco products, chemicals, food products, and paper. Industrial research concerning tobacco and other products takes place in Richmond.

Airlines use nearby Richmond International Airport.

Railroads provide freight and passenger service to Richmond. Bus and truck lines connect Richmond with other cities. Oceangoing freighters use Richmond's port on the James River. The *Richmond Times-Dispatch,* the city's daily newspaper, ranks among the most influential newspapers in the South.

Government. A mayor and a nine-member City Council govern Richmond. The mayor and the council members serve four-year terms. The mayor, with council approval, hires a city administrator, who oversees the government's day-to-day operations. Richmond gets most of its revenue from real estate taxes and from state and federal sources.

History. Before European settlers arrived, Native American tribes of the Powhatan Confederacy lived in what is now the Richmond area. The city's history began in 1607, when Captain Christopher Newport led an exploring party of English settlers to the site of what became Richmond. Two early attempts to establish a settlement there failed. The construction of Fort Charles at the site in 1644 attracted new settlers, and their community grew into a trading post for furs, hides, and tobacco.

In 1742, when Richmond was established as a town, it had a population of 250. In 1780, Virginia moved its capital from Williamsburg to Richmond, which had a more central location. Richmond had only 684 people at that time. It was incorporated as a city in 1782.

In 1781, during the American Revolution, British troops led by Benedict Arnold raided Richmond. Arnold was an American general who turned traitor and joined the British. His soldiers looted Richmond and burned several important buildings.

After the war ended in 1783, Richmond entered a period of growth. Its population increased to 3,761 by 1790 and reached 5,737 by 1800. The city developed around the tobacco trade, the slave trade, and trade to the west over the James River Canal. With the coming of the railroads in the mid-1800's, Richmond grew rapidly as a commercial and industrial center. By 1860, it had about 38,000 people. From the 1830's until the start of the Civil War in 1861, Richmond was one of the largest slave markets in the United States. Traders in the city bought and sold thousands of enslaved people each year.

In May 1861, a month after the outbreak of the Civil War, Richmond replaced Montgomery, Alabama, as the capital of the Confederacy. The capture of Richmond became a prime goal of the Union forces, especially during the campaigns of 1862 and 1864. In April 1865, the Confederate government moved from Richmond to Danville, Virginia. Richmond's people burned part of their city so it would not fall undamaged to the Union. The task of rebuilding the city began immediately after the end of the Civil War.

In the early 1900's, the city attracted many industries. By 1950, it had 230,310 people. In 1970, it annexed 23 square miles (60 square kilometers) from neighboring Chesterfield County. A civil rights leader sued the city. He charged that the primarily white population of the annexed area would injure the rights of Richmond's Black voters. A federal court approved the annexation in 1976. The city was divided into nine districts, each of which elects one member to the City Council.

In 1977, African Americans won races for five of the nine seats on the City Council. The council then elected Richmond's first African American mayor, Henry L. Marsh III. Marsh served as mayor until 1982.

Several major construction projects were completed in the late 1900's. The projects included a downtown canal walk, three major hotels, and a floodwall along the James River. In 2003, a new convention center opened.

Also in 2003, Richmond voters approved a plan to have the mayor directly elected by the voters instead of by the City Council. The change became effective in 2004, and L. Douglas Wilder was elected mayor. He served as mayor from 2005 to 2009. Wilder had served as Virginia's governor from 1990 to 1994 and was the first African American to be elected governor of a U.S. state. Andrew C. Taylor III

Metropolitan Richmond Chamber of Commerce

The White House of the Confederacy in Richmond was the home of Jefferson Davis, president of the Confederate States of America during the American Civil War (1861-1865).

Richmond Town is a historic area of Staten Island in New York City. The first settlement of Europeans in what is now Richmond Town dates from the 1690's. Richmond Town became the county seat of Richmond County in 1729. The county became one of the five boroughs of New York City in 1898, and the city took over the administration of the Richmond County government.

In 1939, the Staten Island Historical Society began a project called the Richmond Town Restoration. The project included moving, rebuilding, and restoring 27 buildings constructed in the 1600's, 1700's, or 1800's. One building, the Voorlezer's House, was built about 1695 and is the oldest elementary school building in the United States. New York City and private individuals and organizations are financing the project. Brian J. Laline

Richter, *RIHK tuhr,* **Conrad** (1890-1968), was an American author known for his novels about pioneer life. His work celebrates such pioneer virtues as endurance, independence, and self-discipline. He also wrote about the close relationship between individuals and nature. Richter's historical novels display his knowledge and appreciation of the traditional tales of the American West.

Richter wrote 14 novels, 3 books of essays, and 5 collections of essays. He is best known for *The Awakening Land,* a *trilogy* (three related novels) about a pioneer family in Ohio. It consists of *The Trees* (1940), *The Fields* (1946), and *The Town* (1950). Richter won the 1951 Pulitzer Prize for fiction for *The Town.* He also wrote three novels about Southwest pioneer life. They are *The Sea of Grass* (1937), his first novel; *Tacey Cromwell* (1942); and *The Lady* (1957). He won the National Book Award for fiction in 1961 for *The Waters of Kronos* (1960), an autobiographical novel. Richter's short stories were collected in *The Rawhide Knot and Other Stories* (1978).

Richter was born on Oct. 13, 1890, in Pine Grove, Pennsylvania. He died on Oct. 30, 1968.

Samuel Chase Coale

Richter magnitude, *RIHK tuhr,* is a number that indicates the strength of an earthquake. It is based on data obtained by a *seismograph,* an instrument that records ground movements. Charles F. Richter, an American *seismologist* (scientist who studies earthquakes), developed the magnitude numbering system in 1935. The system is sometimes called the *Richter scale.*

Each number on the scale represents a tenfold increase in the *amplitude* of waves of ground motion recorded on a seismograph. The seismograph measures the back-and-forth movement of the ground beneath it. Amplitude is the distance this ground moves from its original position during the passage of a wave. Thus, each number represents ground motion 10 times greater than that represented by the next lower number. In an earthquake of magnitude 7, the ground moves 10 times as much as it moves in a quake of magnitude 6.

Calculations based on the Richter scale can show the amount of energy released by an earthquake. Each number represents a release of about 32 times the energy represented by the next lower number. Thus, an earthquake of magnitude 7 releases about 32 times the energy released by a quake of magnitude 6.

To measure the largest earthquakes, seismologists now use another system, the *moment magnitude scale.* Moment magnitude is based on data recorded by instruments that are more sensitive than those of Richter's time. Moment magnitude and Richter magnitude are about the same for earthquakes up to magnitude 7. The highest recorded moment magnitude was 9.5, for an earthquake in the Pacific Ocean near Chile in 1960. The Richter magnitude of this quake registered at 8.3.

Over 1,000 earthquakes with a Richter magnitude of at least 2 occur daily. But few earthquakes of magnitude 5 or less cause serious damage. An earthquake of magnitude 7 or more can cause much damage and kill many people. Sean C. Solomon

See also **Earthquake; Moment magnitude; Seismograph; Seismology.**

Richthofen, *RIHKT hoh fuhn,* **Baron Manfred von** (1892-1918), was the leading German fighter pilot of World War I (1914-1918). He shot down 80 enemy planes. He also trained and led his own fighter squadron. Richthofen became known as the *Red Baron* because he flew planes painted red.

Manfred Albrecht von Richthofen was born on May 2, 1892, in Breslau, Germany (now Wrocław, Poland). He was educated at military schools and became a cavalry officer in the German army. In 1915, Richthofen transferred to the air service. He began flying as an observer, gathering intelligence while a pilot flew the plane, but he soon took flying lessons and became a pilot himself.

In 1916, Richthofen joined the squadron of Oswald Boelcke, an accomplished fighter pilot who had developed successful air battle strategies. In January 1917, Richthofen was given command of his own squadron. That April, he shot down 21 planes. In July, he received a bullet wound to the head but managed to land his plane. He returned to combat the next month.

On April 21, 1918, Richthofen was killed as he pursued an enemy plane far into hostile territory. He was shot through the chest, and his plane crashed. It is unclear whether Richthofen was brought down by Australian troops on the ground or by a Canadian pilot coming to the aid of the other plane. Edward Bristow

Rickenbacker, Eddie (1890-1973), was the leading United States air ace in World War I (1914-1918). He shot down 22 enemy planes and 4 balloons.

Rickenbacker was born Edward Rickenbacher on Oct. 8, 1890, in Columbus, Ohio. In 1918, he changed the spelling of his name to *Rickenbacker.* Before World War I, he became a professional automobile racer and won an international reputation as a racing-car driver. Rickenbacker enlisted in the Army in 1917, after the United States had entered the war. He served as a staff driver and as an engineering officer before becoming a pilot.

After the war, Rickenbacker worked with several automobile firms and was co-owner of the Indianapolis Speedway from 1927 to 1945. He served as president of Eastern Airlines from 1938 to 1959 and chairman of its board of directors from 1954 to 1963.

During World War II (1939-1945), Rickenbacker was a civilian inspector of American air bases abroad. On an inspection trip in 1942, his plane was forced down in the Pacific Ocean. Rickenbacker and six others survived on rubber rafts for 24 days before being rescued. He told of his wartime experiences in *Fighting the Flying Circus* (1919) and *Seven Came Through: Rickenbacker's Full Story* (1943). He died on July 23, 1973. Christopher R. Gabel

Rickets is a bone disease that occurs mostly in children. It may be caused by a lack of calcium, phosphate, or vitamin D. Rickets also may be caused by the body's inability to use those substances properly. In rickets, bones are so soft they bend into abnormal shapes and may develop bumps called *knobs.* Rickets results in conditions called rosary ribs, knobbed forehead, and funnel chest. As the child grows, bones harden, but the abnormal shape usually remains. In severe rickets, bones may be so deformed a child's height is greatly reduced. Symptoms of rickets are sweating, weakness, pain in the bones, general body tenderness, and misshapen bones.

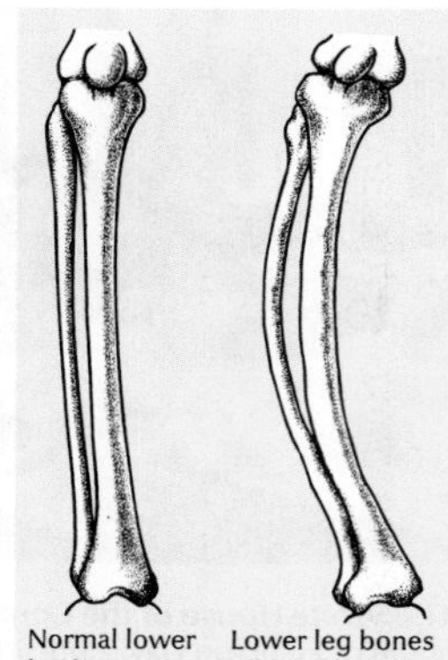
Normal lower leg bones — Lower leg bones affected by rickets

Eating foods rich in calcium and vitamin D usually prevents rickets. Milk and green vegetables are good sources of calcium. The best sources of vitamin D include vitamin-D enriched milk, sunlight, and fish oils. Rickets in children usually can be halted by giving them vitamin D and calcium. *Osteomalacia* is a disease similar to rickets that occurs in adults. Madison B. Cole, Jr.

See also **Vitamin** (Vitamin D).

Rickettsia, *rih KEHT see uh,* is any of a group of microorganisms that cause certain infectious diseases in human beings. Rickettsias are usually regarded as a special kind of bacteria. They are smaller than most bacteria and, unlike bacteria, cannot reproduce outside of living cells.

Rickettsias live primarily in the cells of certain insects and other arthropods, such as mites and ticks. A few species can infect human cells and cause such diseases as epidemic typhus, Rocky Mountain spotted fever, scrub typhus, and Q fever.

Epidemic typhus is spread among people by the bite of infected body lice. This disease occurs in colder regions, particularly those with poor sanitary facilities. The rickettsia that causes Rocky Mountain spotted fever lives in ticks and wild rodents and is spread to people by tick bites. This disease occurs most frequently in the southeastern United States. Scrub typhus is common in southern and southeast Asia, northern Australia, and Japan. Rodents and chigger mites carry the rickettsia that causes this disease, and it is spread to people by mites.

Unlike other rickettsias, the Q-fever organism infects people by being inhaled. Q fever is common in many livestock-raising regions. Cattle and sheep bitten by infected ticks pass Q-fever rickettsias in their urine and in the fluids lost while giving birth. The rickettsias may infect people who inhale dust from livestock pens.

Symptoms of rickettsial diseases include chills, fever, headaches, and rashes. Untreated rickettsial diseases—particularly epidemic typhus and Rocky Mountain spotted fever—are often fatal. But they can be treated effectively with antibiotics. Rickettsias were named for Howard Taylor Ricketts, an American pathologist who first identified the organisms in 1909. Thomas P. Monath

Rickey, Branch (1881-1965), was one of the greatest executives in major league baseball history. Rickey, nicknamed "the Mahatma," pioneered in creating the farm system, in which major league teams developed players in the minor leagues. He was an early advocate of batting helmets, batting cages, and pitching machines. He also broadened the role of spring training in the baseball season. Perhaps Rickey's most important achievement was hiring Jackie Robinson, who became the first African American in major league baseball in 1947.

Wesley Branch Rickey was born on Dec. 20, 1881, in Stockdale, Ohio. He played briefly in the major leagues from 1905 to 1907 and then for two games in 1914. Rickey managed the St. Louis Browns from 1913 to 1915 and the St. Louis Cardinals from 1919 to 1925. He was also the Cardinals' team president from 1917 to 1919. In 1925, Rickey became the Cardinals' general manager. At the time, the Cardinals were one of the weakest teams in the National League. Under his leadership, the team became a National League powerhouse.

Rickey left St. Louis in 1942 and was general manager of the Brooklyn Dodgers from 1943 to 1950. He ended his career with the Pittsburgh Pirates, as general manager from 1950 to 1955 and board chairman from 1955 to 1959. Rickey died on Dec. 9, 1965. He was elected to the National Baseball Hall of Fame in 1967. Dave Nightingale

See also **Robinson, Jackie.**

Rickover, Hyman George (1900-1986), an American naval officer, pioneered in developing the USS *Nautilus,* the first nuclear-powered submarine. In 1965, he received the Enrico Fermi Medal, the highest United States atomic science award. Rickover stated his views on education in *Education and Freedom* (1959).

In 1947, Rickover became head of the Naval Reactors Branch of the U.S. Atomic Energy Commission. He also headed the Nuclear Power Division of the U.S. Navy. He was promoted to vice admiral in 1959. Rickover reached compulsory retirement age in 1964, but his active duty was extended. In 1973, he was promoted to admiral. He served in the Navy's nuclear propulsion program until 1982. Rickover was born on Jan. 27, 1900, in Maków, a town about 50 miles (80 kilometers) north of Warsaw in an area of Poland that was then part of the Russian Empire. He came to the United States with his family when he was 6 years old. He and his family soon became citizens. Rickover died on July 8, 1986. Kenneth J. Hagan

Riddle is a question or statement that contains a deliberately hidden meaning. Riddles today are usually meant to be amusing. They often take the form of a *conundrum,* a kind of riddle that depends on puns. A typical riddle of this type is: "What has four wheels and flies?" The answer, "A garbage truck," makes sense when we realize that the word *flies* has two meanings.

Another popular type of riddle depends on possible but unexpected assumptions in a given question. The answer to the riddle, "Where does an elephant go when he wants to lie down?" is "Anywhere he pleases." That answer is both humorous and surprising because the question seems to concern the habits of elephants, but it is really about the intimidating size of elephants.

For many centuries, the riddle was often regarded as a kind of coded message that came from divine inspiration. People believed the message could be understood only by individuals with special knowledge. In ancient Greece, priests and priestesses called *oracles* often expressed their messages in riddles (see **Oracle**).

During the Middle Ages, from about the A.D. 400's through the 1400's, poets in Europe seem to have particularly enjoyed composing riddles. The so-called *Exeter Book* contains nearly 100 examples of riddles. They were written in an early form of English called Old English, probably in the early 700's. The answers to some of these riddles are obvious, but other riddles are extremely difficult to understand. However, they are valuable for the insights they provide into the way people of that period regarded events of nature and everyday life.

Collections of riddles were among the first books ever printed for popular entertainment. A book of riddles called *Amusing Questions* was published in England in 1511 by a printer called Wynkyn de Worde. Many nursery rhymes, such as "Humpty Dumpty," are actually riddles invented centuries ago. Marcus Klein

See also **Nursery rhyme** (Rhyming riddles); **Rebus; Sphinx** (The Greek sphinx).

Ride, Sally Kristen (1951-2012), was a United States astronaut who became the first American woman to travel in space. In 1983, she and astronauts Robert L. Crippen, John M. Fabian, Frederick H. Hauck, and Norman E. Thagard made a six-day flight on the space shuttle Challenger. During the mission, Ride and Fabian launched communications satellites for the Canadian and Indonesian governments and conducted experiments involving the production of pharmaceuticals. They also tested the shuttle's *remote manipulator arm.* They used the arm to release a satellite, then retrieve and place it in the shuttle's cargo area. Ride made a second shuttle flight in 1984. On this mission, she used the remote manipulator arm to launch a satellite designed to measure the sun's effect on Earth's weather.

NASA
Sally Ride

Ride was born on May 26, 1951, in Los Angeles. In 1978, she received a Ph.D. degree in physics from Stanford University and became an astronaut candidate. On Jan. 28, 1986, Challenger broke apart shortly after takeoff, killing all seven crew members. In February, Ride was appointed to the presidential commission established to investigate the accident. Ride resigned from the astronaut program in 1987 to accept a fellowship at the Stanford University Center for International Security and Arms Control. In 1989, she became a professor of physics at the University of California at San Diego and the director of the California Space Institute. On Feb. 1, 2003, the shuttle Columbia broke apart over Texas as it reentered Earth's atmosphere. Ride served on a federal board that investigated the accident. Ride died on July 23, 2012, in La Jolla, California, after a months-long battle with pancreatic cancer. James E. Hannigan

Rideau Canal, *rih DOH,* is a Canadian waterway connecting the Ottawa River at Ottawa with Lake Ontario at Kingston. It consists of the Rideau and Cataraqui rivers, several lakes, and some short canals. It is 123 miles (198 kilometers) long and has 47 locks, each 134 feet (41 meters) long, 33 feet (10 meters) wide, and 5 feet (1.5 meters) deep. One branch of the canal, known as the Tay branch, extends to the town of Perth and has two locks. The Rideau Canal was finished in 1832. It was designed to offer a safe route for gunboats and military supplies between Montreal and the Great Lakes. It is a national historic site of Canada. See also **Ottawa.** Roger Nadeau

Ridge, Tom (1945-), was the first secretary of the United States Department of Homeland Security. He took office in 2003, when the department began operations, and held the post until 2005. Ridge, a former governor of Pennsylvania, served as director of the smaller Office of Homeland Security from 2001 until 2003. As the nation's security director, Ridge was responsible for overseeing and coordinating national efforts to protect against and respond to attacks of terrorism.

President George W. Bush created the Office of Homeland Security after Sept. 11, 2001, when the nation experienced the worst terrorist attacks in its history. In November 2002, Congress passed legislation to replace the agency with a Cabinet-level department.

Thomas Joseph Ridge was born on Aug. 26, 1945, in Munhall, Pennsylvania. He graduated from Harvard University in 1967 with a bachelor's degree in government. He served in the Army in Vietnam from 1968 to 1970. He received a law degree in 1972 from Dickinson School of Law. Ridge was elected to the U.S. House of Representatives in 1982 and reelected five times. In 1994, he won election to his first term as governor of Pennsylvania and was reelected in 1998. Jeremy D. Mayer

See also **Bush, George Walker** (picture: A new Cabinet department); **Homeland Security, Department of; September 11 terrorist attacks.**

Ridgway, Matthew Bunker (1895-1993), was one of the greatest combat commanders in the history of the United States Army. He gained fame for leading U.S. forces in some of the most important battles of World War II (1939-1945) and the Korean War (1950-1953).

Ridgway was born in Fort Monroe, Virginia, on March 3, 1895. He graduated from the U.S. Military Academy in 1917. He served in China, Nicaragua, the Panama Canal Zone, and the Philippines.

In World War II, Ridgway commanded the Army's famed 82nd Airborne Division during the 1943 invasion of Sicily and the 1944 Normandy invasion. The Normandy invasion was the largest *amphibious assault*—that is, an attack combining land, sea, and air forces—in history. Ridgway also commanded the XVIII (18th) Airborne Corps during the Battle of the Bulge, in which Allied forces stopped a German advance. The Battle of the Bulge took place in December 1944 in the Ardennes Forest in Belgium and Luxembourg.

In December 1950, Ridgway took command of the U.S. Eighth Army in Korea. Chinese Communist forces had recently entered the war on the side of North Korea, and the U.S. Army was in retreat. Ridgway reversed the situation and fought back to the 38th Parallel, thus saving South Korea. In 1951, President Harry S. Truman selected Ridgway to replace General Douglas MacArthur as commander of U.S., United Nations, and South Korean forces. In 1952, Ridgway was promoted to full general and supreme commander of Allied forces in Europe.

From 1953 to 1955, Ridgway served as Army chief of staff under President Dwight D. Eisenhower. Ridgway's belief in maintaining a large number of troops to limit the size of potential conflicts put him at odds with Eisenhower, who cut troop numbers and believed in relying more on the threat of using nuclear weapons to prevent a major Communist attack. Ridgway's memoir, *Soldier* (1956), details his position. He died on July 26, 1993.
Adrian R. Lewis

Ridley, Nicholas (1500?-1555), an English bishop, was a martyr of the Protestant Reformation. Many regarded him as the master spirit among the English reformers. He helped compile the first Book of Common Prayer of 1549 and the Forty-Two Articles of Religion in 1553. The Forty-Two Articles later served as the basis for the Thirty-Nine Articles (see **Thirty-Nine Articles**). Ridley supported Lady Jane Grey's unsuccessful claim to the throne, and in 1553 Queen Mary imprisoned him. In 1554, he was condemned for heresy, and he was burned at the stake at Oxford on Oct. 16, 1555. Ridley was born in Northumberland and graduated from Cambridge University. In 1547, he became bishop of Rochester, and in 1550, bishop of London. Peter W. Williams

Riel, *ree EHL,* **Louis** (1844-1885), led uprisings against the Canadian government from 1869 to 1870 and in 1885. He led protesting *Métis* (people of mixed white and Indian ancestry), who feared the land they had settled would be taken over by new settlers.

Glenbow Museum, Calgary
Louis Riel

The first uprising began after the Canadian government decided to buy some land from the Hudson's Bay Company in what is now Manitoba and open the land to new settlers. The Métis in the Red River Valley feared they would lose their land to the settlers. Riel protested in vain. In 1869, Métis led by Riel captured Fort Garry (present-day Winnipeg). Government troops put an end to the revolt of the Métis in 1870. Riel fled and was classed as an outlaw. But the government set aside land for the Métis and established the Province of Manitoba.

Riel was elected to the Canadian House of Commons in 1873 and 1874, but was denied his seat. He was given a pardon in 1875 on the condition that he leave Canada for five years. But Riel suffered a mental breakdown in 1875 and was in insane asylums from 1876 until 1878. Then he moved to Montana. He became a United States citizen in 1883.

By 1884, hundreds of Métis had moved from the Red River Valley in Manitoba to what is now Saskatchewan. They feared that whites would take over their new settlements. At their request, Riel returned to Canada to lead the fight for Métis land claims. Fighting broke out in 1885. Government troops defeated the Métis and their aboriginal supporters. Riel surrendered, was convicted of treason, and was hanged on Nov. 16, 1885. His death caused racial tension between French and English Canadians and weakened Canadian unity. Riel was born on Oct. 22, 1844, in what is now St. Boniface, Manitoba. In 1992, the Canadian Parliament recognized Riel's role in the creation of Manitoba. José António Brandão

See also **Dumont, Gabriel; Manitoba** (The Red River Rebellion); **Métis; North West Rebellion; Red River Rebellion.**

Riemann, *REE mahn,* **Georg Friedrich Bernhard,** *gay AWRK FREE drihkh BEHRN hart* (1826-1866), a German mathematician, developed a branch of advanced geometry. Riemann also did important work in other areas of advanced mathematics, including calculus, mathematical analysis, and mathematical physics.

Riemann's 1854 lecture "On the Hypotheses Which Lie at the Foundation of Geometry" became one of the most famous presentations in the history of mathematics. It dealt with a type of *non-Euclidian geometry,* which replaces a famous *postulate* (basic statement) developed by the ancient Greek mathematician Euclid. The postulate, often called the *parallel postulate,* can be stated: *Through a point not on a given line, only one line can be drawn parallel to the given line.* Riemann's system of geometry replaced Euclid's parallel postulate with an alternate statement that can be written: *Through a point not on a given line, no lines can be drawn that are parallel to the given line.* This system has become known as *elliptic geometry* or *Riemannian geometry.* See **Geometry** (Non-Euclidean geometry).

Riemann pioneered the view of geometry as the general study of "curved spaces." His work later enabled the German-born physicist Albert Einstein to develop his theory of general relativity, which holds that gravity results from the *curvature* (bending) of space and time.

Riemann was born on Sept. 17, 1826, in Breselenz, Hanover (now part of Germany). He studied at the universities of Berlin and Göttingen, earning a doctor's degree in 1851. Riemann became a professor at Göttingen in 1859. He died on July 20, 1866. Blake E. Peterson

See also **Geometry** (Rise of non-Euclidean geometry).

Riemenschneider, *REE muhn SHNY dur,* **Tilman** (1460?-1531), was one of the best-known sculptors of his day in Germany. Riemenschneider carved in both stone and wood. He was the first German woodcarver to leave the surfaces of his works unpainted. Riemenschneider worked in a late Gothic style, with elaborate drapery and weightless figures. Most of his sculpture is concerned with religious subjects. Riemenschneider's work is noted for its quiet religious feeling.

Riemenschneider was born in Thuringia. He studied his trade in several German cities before settling in Würzburg. He spent most of his life there, becoming a prominent citizen and a member of the Würzburg city council. He died on July 7, 1531. Alison McNeil Kettering

Herrgottskirche, Creglingen, Germany (Erick Lessing from Art Resource)

A Riemenschneider altarpiece was completed about 1505 for a German church. The central panel shows the Assumption of the Virgin Mary into heaven. The wings portray scenes from Mary's life. The altarpiece stands 32 feet (9.75 meters) high.

Rifle is a gun with spiral grooves in its long barrel that spin the bullet as it is shot. Rifles are usually held against the shoulder when firing. Soldiers use rifles in battle. People also use rifles to hunt game and to compete in shooting matches.

Military rifles and sporting rifles differ greatly. Military rifles are ruggedly built and are designed to work under the harshest conditions. Most military rifles are *automatic* or *semiautomatic.* An automatic rifle can fire bullets rapidly one after another with one squeeze of the trigger. A semiautomatic rifle fires and reloads one bullet with each squeeze of the trigger. Most hunting and target rifles are operated by hand after each firing and are designed for beauty as well as accuracy.

The parts of a rifle

All rifles have four basic parts: (1) the barrel, (2) the stock, (3) the action, and (4) the sights.

The *barrel* is a strong steel tube with spiral grooves called *rifling* cut along the inside. The front end of the barrel is called the *muzzle,* and the rear end is the *breech.*

The *stock* of a rifle helps keep the rifle steady when firing. The butt of the stock is placed against the shoulder when firing. The front end extends under the barrel. Stocks of military rifles are made of wood, plastic, metal, or fiberglass. Many sporting rifles have stocks made of expensive wood with decorative or grip-aiding carving called *checkering.*

The *action* is the basic machinery of the rifle. The action includes the parts that feed a *cartridge* into the *firing chamber.* A cartridge is a metal case that holds an explosive charge and a bullet. The firing chamber, which holds the cartridge, is a widened hole at the breech. The action also includes the parts that fire the bullet and *eject* (force out) the used cartridge.

The *sights* are used to aim the rifle. When aimed properly, the rear sight, the front sight, and the target should be in a straight line. Some rifles have *telescopic sights* that make distant targets appear closer.

How a rifle works

A rifle is ready to be fired when a cartridge has been fed into the firing chamber. Then the rifle is aimed and the trigger squeezed. The rifle's *hammer* or *firing pin* strikes the rear end of the cartridge and ignites the *primer.* The primer in turn ignites the propellant powder in the cartridge. The powder burns rapidly, creating pressure that drives the bullet down the barrel.

The rifling in the barrel makes the bullet spin. Without spin, a bullet would not stay pointed forward in flight, but would tumble over and over. The spinning motion increases the accuracy of a bullet.

Kinds of rifles

Rifles are classified by type of action (manually operated, automatic, or semiautomatic); by the name of the designer or manufacturer (for example, Remington or Winchester); or by *caliber.* Caliber may refer to the inside diameter of the barrel or the diameter of the bullet. The caliber is measured in *millimeters* or in decimal fractions of an inch.

There are three kinds of repeating rifles with hand-operated actions—*bolt-action, lever-action,* and *slide-action.* These rifles have *magazines* (cartridge holders) that feed cartridges into the firing chamber. The action on two other kinds of rifles—automatic and semiautomatic—is operated by forces caused by the burning of the propellant powder in the firing chamber.

Bolt-action rifles have an action that resembles a bolt used to lock a door. When the bolt on the rifle is pulled back, the used cartridge is thrown out and the hammer is cocked. When the bolt is moved forward, it pushes a new cartridge into the firing chamber.

Lever-action rifles are loaded by moving a lever under the breech down and back up. The down move-

WORLD BOOK diagram by Oxford Illustrators Limited

Parts of a rifle

A bolt-action rifle is generally used for hunting or target shooting. The weapon is fired by first pulling the bolt back to throw out the used cartridge and to cock the firing pin. Moving the bolt forward pushes a new cartridge into the firing chamber. When the trigger is squeezed, the firing pin strikes and ignites the cartridge's primer.

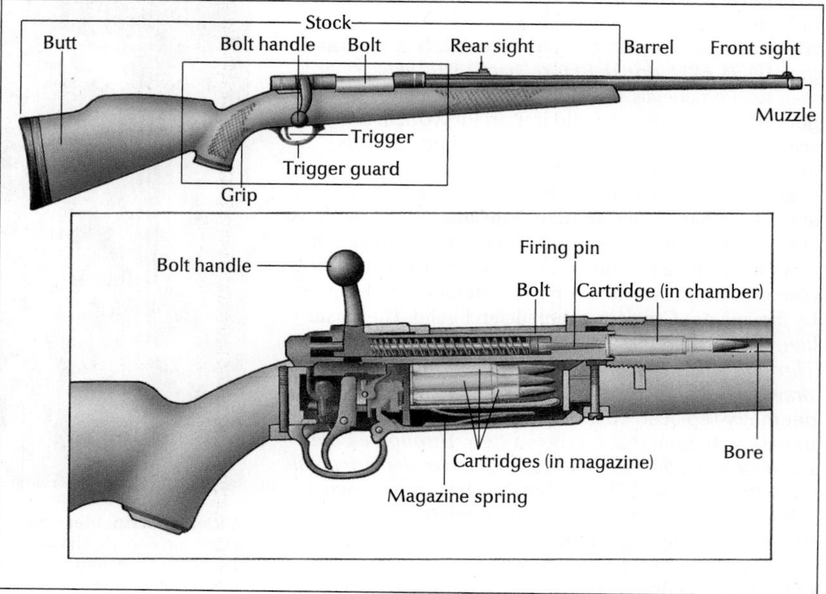

ment throws out the used cartridge and cocks the hammer. The up movement inserts a new cartridge into the firing chamber.

Slide-action rifles, also called *pump-action rifles,* are loaded with a back-and-forth movement of a rod and handle beneath the front part of the barrel. When the handle is pulled back, the breech opens and the used cartridge is thrown out. A live cartridge is inserted when the handle is pushed forward.

Automatic and semiautomatic rifles are used mainly by soldiers and police officers. When a rifle is fired, gas is formed by the burning powder in the firing chamber. The expanding gas drives the bullet out of the barrel. In most modern automatic and semiautomatic rifles, some of this gas operates the action. When a cartridge is fired, a fresh cartridge is moved out of the magazine into the firing chamber, and the firing mechanism is cocked.

The M16A2 is the automatic rifle used by the U.S. armed forces. It weighs 8.9 pounds (4 kilograms) when loaded with a 30-cartridge magazine. The M16A2 can fire one shot at a time, or three shots in a single burst. It uses a 5.56-millimeter cartridge.

Rifle cartridges

Rifle cartridges are enclosed in a *casing* (metal covering) made of brass or steel. Cartridges vary in size according to the caliber of the rifle. The names of some cartridges include the year the cartridge was put into use. The .30-06 is a .30-caliber cartridge chosen for use by the U.S. Army in 1906. The classification of some cartridges includes the caliber and *velocity* (speed) of the bullet. The bullet from a .250-3000 cartridge has a velocity of 3,000 feet (910 meters) per second.

History

Modern rifles developed from the crude, muzzle-loading firearms of the 1400's. Rifling of barrels was invented in Europe about 1500. *Smooth-bore* firearms (weapons without rifling) could not be depended on to hit targets more than 100 steps away.

The jaeger rifle of central and northern Europe was

Famous rifles Early rifles were used for hunting, target shooting, and warfare. The same type of rifle was used for all three purposes. Today's automatic and semiautomatic rifles are used mainly by the military, and repeating rifles with hand-operated actions are used for hunting and target shooting.

Garry James Collection (Roger Roland Fuhr, *ROLAND*esign)

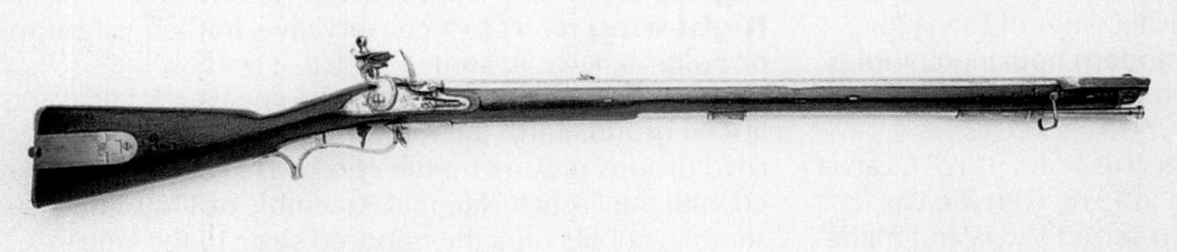

The flintlock rifle had to be reloaded through the muzzle after each firing. This British military rifle—the Baker—was used during the first half of the 1800's.

Phil Spangenberger Collection (Roger Roland Fuhr, *ROLAND*esign)

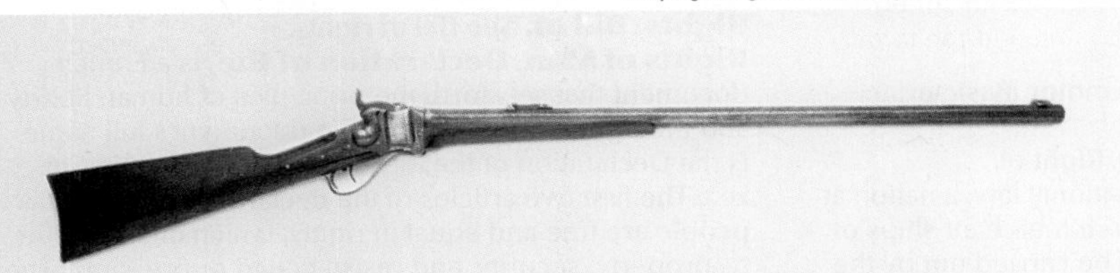

The Sharps buffalo rifle was a long-range hunting rifle popular during the 1870's and 1880's. It could be fired by lightly touching one trigger after pulling the other.

Sherwood International Inc. (Roger Roland Fuhr, *ROLAND*esign)

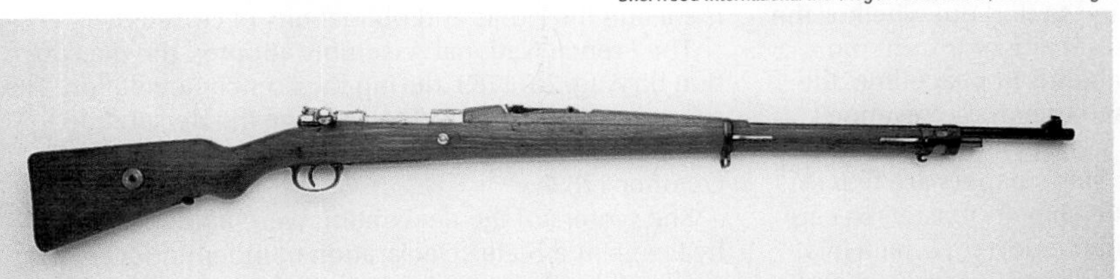

The Mauser 1898 was a bolt-action military rifle. It was the model for the American Springfield rifle used during World War I and many other military and sporting rifles.

Sherwood International Inc. (Roger Roland Fuhr, *ROLAND*esign)

The M16A2 rifle is capable of firing one shot at a time, or three bullets in less than a second. The M16A2 is the official rifle of the United States armed forces.

the first accurate rifle. It was developed about 1665. German immigrants brought jaegers to Pennsylvania in the early 1700's and gave them new features, including longer barrels. The Pennsylvania-made Kentucky rifle developed from the jaeger. Some Kentucky rifles were used in the American Revolution (1775-1783).

Rifles used round bullets until the 1850's, when more accurate Minié bullets became popular. Minié bullets had hollow bases and pointed tips and were used in the American Civil War (1861-1865). Improvements of the late 1800's included repeating rifles, smokeless explosive powder, and *jacketed* bullets, which have a tough metal cover over a lead or steel core. Frances M. Lussier

Related articles in *World Book* include:

Ammunition	Firearm	Night vision systems
Bullet	Garand rifle	Shotgun
Carbine	Gunpowder	
Cartridge	Musket	

Rift Valley. See **Great Rift Valley.**

Riga, *REE guh* (pop. 920,000), is the capital and largest city of Latvia. The city lies at the south end of the Gulf of Riga, at the mouth of the Western Dvina (Daugava) River. Riga's population is made up of nearly equal numbers of Latvians and Russians. For location, see **Latvia** (map).

Riga is a shipping center, and it accounts for about half of Latvia's industrial output. Its products include chemicals, electronics, and industrial machinery. It also has been the cultural and political center of Latvia for hundreds of years. In the city, modern housing complexes rise near lovely churches and merchant houses that date from the Middle Ages.

Riga was founded by German crusaders in 1201. Latvia became an independent nation in 1918, with Riga as its capital. In 1940, the Soviet Union seized Latvia and made it part of the Soviet Union. In 1991, Latvia broke away from the Soviet Union and became an independent nation again. Jaroslaw Bilocerkowycz

Rigging. See **Sailing** (Rigging).

Right-hand rule. See **Electric motor** (Basic principles).

Right of privacy. See **Privacy, Right of.**

Right of search. Under international law, a nation at war has the right to visit and search merchant ships of neutral nations. The search must be carried out by the officers of a warship. The purposes are to determine the true nationality of the vessel, and to find out whether the vessel is engaged in unneutral service or in carrying contraband of war (see **Contraband**). In peacetime, the right of search may be exercised to enforce revenue laws or prevent piracy.

When a search is made, the ship's papers are first examined. These papers name the ship; its master, or captain; the port it sailed from; and the port for which it is bound. The papers should describe the cargo and certify that the officers have met the customs regulations of the country from which the ship has sailed.

If the papers are correct, the search usually ends. But if suspicion is aroused, the cargo may be examined. Officers who refuse to stop their ship and allow it to be searched run the risk of having both ship and cargo confiscated. The Hague Peace Conference of 1907 and the London Conference of 1909 tried to set limits to the right of search. Conference members agreed that the mail of neutral nations should be free from search. However, all sides disregarded these agreements in wartime.

During Prohibition in the United States, some countries agreed to extend their territorial limits to the number of nautical miles that could be covered in one hour's sailing from their coasts. These agreements made it easier to search for smuggled articles, and they remain in force. For other purposes, the limits are 3 to 12 nautical miles, depending on the kind of search. For revenue purposes, the president may authorize a search up to 62 nautical miles from the U.S. coast. Robert J. Pranger

Right-to-work law provides that a person need not belong to a labor union to get or keep a job. It also provides that a person may not be denied a job because of union membership. More than half the states in the United States have such laws. Unions, which strongly oppose right-to-work laws, generally have little power in states with these laws.

Right-to-work laws have the effect of barring closed shop, union shop, and maintenance-of-membership agreements between employers and unions. In the *closed shop*, the employer can hire only members of the union. In the *union shop*, all employees must join the union after they have worked there for a certain period. *Maintenance-of-membership clauses* require that employees who are union members retain membership until the union contract expires. Paul L. Burgess

Right whale. See **Whale** (Conservation; Right whales).

Right wing refers to a conservative, traditional group or political party. In some legislative bodies, the conservatives sit to the right of the speaker. Radical and liberal groups form the *left wing*, with middle-of-the-road groups making up the *center*. This custom originated with the French National Assembly of 1789. In that assembly, nobles took the honored seats to the king's right. Carl L. Davis

See also **Conservatism.**

Rights, Bill of. See **Bill of rights.**

Rights of Man, Declaration of the, is a French document that sets forth the principles of human liberty and the rights of individuals. The document's full name is the Declaration of the Rights of Man and of the Citizen. The first two articles of the declaration state that all people are free and equal in rights, which include "liberty, property, security, and resistance to oppression." The other 15 articles concern both the limitations of government and the rights and obligations of citizens.

The French National Assembly adopted the declaration on Aug. 26, 1789, during the French Revolution. The refusal of King Louis XVI to approve the declaration helped bring about increased revolutionary activity in October 1789.

The writers of the declaration were influenced partly by the United States Declaration of Independence, but above all by the circumstances of the revolution. The document was intended to be the statement of principle for the new regime. Isser Woloch

Riis, *rees,* **Jacob August** (1849-1914), was an American journalist, photographer, and social reformer. During the late 1800's and early 1900's, he helped improve living conditions in New York City slums by exposing them to the public through his writings and photographs. Photographs taken by Riis were among the first photos to appear in newspapers. Riis was born in Ribe, Denmark, on May 3, 1849. He immigrated to the

United States in 1870. In 1877, Riis became a reporter for the *New York Tribune.* He moved to the *New York Evening Sun* in 1890. As a reporter, Riis worked for improvements in education, housing, and law enforcement and for child labor laws and playground construction. In 1888, he helped bring about the elimination of a New York City slum district called Mulberry Bend.

Besides writing for newspapers, Riis wrote 12 books. They include *How the Other Half Lives* (1890), *The Children of the Poor* (1892), and *The Battle with the Slum* (1902). An autobiographical work, *The Making of an American* (1901), tells the story of his immigration to the United States. Michael Emery

See also **Playground** (with picture); **United States, History of the** (picture: The lives of the poor and the rich).

Riley, James Whitcomb (1849-1916), won fame as the *Hoosier Poet.* He wrote much verse in pure English, but his most popular poems were those he wrote in the dialect of his home state of Indiana. They include "When the Frost Is on the Punkin'," "Out to Aunt Mary's," and "Little Orphant Annie." These works are characterized by light humor, pathos, and sentiment. Riley's poems were published in a number of collections, including *The Old Swimmin'-Hole and 'Leven More Poems* (1883), *Rhymes of Childhood* (1890), *Poems Here at Home* (1893), and *Book of Joyous Children* (1902).

Riley, the son of a lawyer, was born on Oct. 7, 1849, in Greenfield, Indiana. He left home after receiving a grammar school education and worked for a time as a sign painter. For a short period, he traveled with a medicine show. Riley had heard the dialect and learned the manners of the country folk of Indiana from his childhood, and he began to write poems about them.

Riley joined the *Indianapolis Journal* in 1877. He made his home in Indianapolis. He began to contribute poems to several papers under the name "Benj. F. Johnson of Boone." He became a celebrated platform reader and appeared throughout the United States, often with the humorist Bill Nye. Marcus Klein

See also **Indiana** (Places to visit).

Rilke, *RIHL kuh,* **Rainer Maria,** *RY nuhr mah REE ah* (1875-1926), was an important lyric poet in German literature and a major representative of the symbolism movement. His poems are characterized by richness of imagery and melody and fine shades of meaning. They have a tone of self-examination and prophecy.

Rilke's cycle of poems *The Book of Hours* (1905) expresses a longing for a mystic union with God. *New Poems* (1907, 1908) contains works that try to express the essence, or "idea," of an object or experience. Rilke's novel *The Notebooks of Malte Laurids Brigge* (1910) is a highly innovative "modernist" work in style and structure. It portrays the loneliness and confusion of a young poet searching for identity in turbulent Paris. The *Duino Elegies* (1923) and *Sonnets to Orpheus* (1923) are poems that praise human existence.

Rilke was born on Dec. 4, 1875, in Prague. He spent much of his life wandering through Europe.

Werner Hoffmeister

Rillieux, *RIHL ee yoo,* **Norbert** (1806-1894), an American engineer, revolutionized the sugar industry by making the first practical multiple-effect vacuum evaporator. This machine used an improved process to remove water from sugar cane.

In one chamber of Rillieux's machine, the sugar cane juice was boiled until it became syrup. Then, in a connected chamber, the hot vapor from the first chamber boiled the syrup until it became grains of sugar. This double use of the same heat greatly reduced the cost and improved the quality of the final product. Other products, including soap, gelatin, some glues, and condensed milk, are now manufactured through a process based on Rillieux's invention.

Rillieux was born on March 17, 1806, in New Orleans, the son of a French engineer and a free black woman. He studied in Paris and became an engineering teacher there in 1830. In the 1840's, he installed his invention on many sugar plantations in the United States. He returned to Paris permanently in the 1850's. Douglas E. Bowers

Rimbaud, *ram BOH,* **Arthur,** *ar TEWR* (1854-1891), was a French poet of extraordinary originality. Rimbaud wrote his major verse between the ages of 15 and 20. He then abandoned his literary career and became a trader in what is now Ethiopia.

Rimbaud was born in Charleville, France, on Oct. 20, 1854. His first poems satirize the people of his hometown and celebrate the joys of youth, often in violent, colloquial language. In 1871, he went to Paris to deliver his visionary poem, "Le Bateau ivre" ("The Drunken Boat") to the French poet Paul Verlaine. Rimbaud quickly built a reputation as a wild poet of genius. He also became involved in a homosexual relationship with Verlaine.

Rimbaud's major work, *Une Saison en enfer (A Season in Hell,* 1873), is an autobiographical narrative that evokes his painful relationship with Verlaine. The poem describes Rimbaud's struggles with Christianity and French imperialism, and his experiments with hallucinatory poetry, the "verbal alchemy" which almost drove him insane. Verlaine published Rimbaud's prose poems, *Illuminations* (1886), after Rimbaud left France. These innovative works create a verbal universe almost entirely separate from the outside world.

Rimbaud's "Lettre du voyant" ("Visionary Letter," 1871) describes the "long, immense and calculated derangement of all the senses" required to reach truth. His statement in this letter that "The Self is other than myself" became a philosophical statement by the Surrealist movement of the 1920's. Edward K. Kaplan

See also **Symbolism; Verlaine, Paul.**

Rimsky-Korsakov, *RIHM skih KAWR suh kawf,* **Nikolai** (1844-1908), was a celebrated Russian composer and teacher. He is especially known for his imaginative and colorful orchestral compositions, including *Spanish Capriccio* (1887), *Scheherazade* (1888), and the *Russian Easter Overture* (1888). Russian folk songs can be heard in his music, as can choral music and bell ringing of the Russian Orthodox Church.

In spite of his orchestral successes, Rimsky-Korsakov's main emphasis was on opera. He based many of his 15 operas on Russian history and folklore. Only two of them, however, have gained success outside Russia. They are *Sadko* (1898) and *The Golden Cockerel* (1909). But still popular today in Russia are *The Snow Maiden* (completed in 1881, revised about 1895), *The Tsar's Bride* (1899), and *The Tale of Tsar Saltan* (1900). His masterpiece, *The Legend of the Invisible City of Kitezh and the Maiden Fevroniia* (1907), is virtually unknown in the West. Two of his best-known pieces come from his operas—"Song of India" from *Sadko* and "The Flight of the Bumblebee" from *Tsar Saltan.*

Rimsky-Korsakov was born on March 18, 1844, in Tikhvin, near Velikiy Novgorod. In 1861, he met the composer Mily Balakirev and joined a group of his students who later became known as The Five. Balakirev encouraged them to draw upon their Russian heritage in their music.

In 1871, Rimsky-Korsakov joined the faculty of the St. Petersburg Conservatory. Realizing he knew almost no music theory, he began to teach himself counterpoint, harmony, and musical form. As a musical theorist and teacher, Rimsky-Korsakov had a decisive influence on the course of Russian music in the early 1900's. Several of his students became important composers, including Sergei Prokofiev and Igor Stravinsky. Rimsky-Korsakov's book *Principles of Orchestration* (published in 1913, after his death) has become a standard work. He also wrote an autobiography published in 1909, after his death. The book was translated into English as *My Musical Life.*

Rimsky-Korsakov edited and revised compositions that his friends Alexander Borodin and Modest Mussorgsky had left unfinished at their deaths. Today, his version of Mussorgsky's opera *Boris Godunov* (1874) is usually performed. Borodin's opera *Prince Igor* (1890) is usually performed in the version completed by Rimsky-Korsakov and the Russian composer Alexander Glazunov. Edward V. Williams

Rinderpest, *RIHN duhr PEHST,* also called *cattle plague,* is a highly contagious, usually fatal disease of cattle and other members of the ox family. The disease is caused by a virus. Symptoms include sudden loss of milk in cows, fever, diarrhea, and ulcers in the mouth. The death rate is as high as 98 percent. Rinderpest hindered the development of Western civilization for many hundreds of years. It swept over Europe from the East with every war. The last European outbreak occurred in Belgium following World War I (1914-1918). The disease never reached the United States and was chiefly confined to Asian countries. In 2010, the United Nations announced that a program of *eradication* (elimination) had completely wiped out rinderpest. Monitoring of the disease stopped throughout the world. Lawrence D. McGill

Ring is a circular band made of metal or other material worn as jewelry. Some rings are decorated with gems Each pope gets a ring engraved with a picture of Saint Peter in a fishing boat. After the pope dies, the ring is destroyed and a new one is made for the next pope.

A ring is often used to symbolize an engagement or or engraving. Rings are commonly worn on the fingers, but they may also be worn on the ears, nose, or toes.

Rings also serve functional or symbolic purposes. For example, rings have long been a symbol of authority. marriage. Engagement and wedding rings were likely first worn by the ancient Romans. Some early wedding rings may have been made of gold. The custom of decorating engagement and wedding rings with gems began about 1200. In the 1600's, many people exchanged *posey rings* as a sign of love or friendship. This ring was a simple band engraved with a short love poem.

Rings often indicate membership or rank in an organization, such as a fraternity or sorority. Many people wear class rings to represent the year they graduated

Kinds of rings

Ancient Egyptian ring
Mycenaean gold ring
Grecian gold ring
Roman bronze ring
Key ring
Anglo-Saxon engagement ring
Papal ring, 1400's
Brahman signet ring
Jewish wedding ring

from high school or college. Another popular type of ring has a gem that is associated with the month of a person's birth (see **Birthstone**).

In the past, people used *signets,* which were small seals attached to rings, to authenticate official documents. Rings were once used to indicate social status. In ancient Egypt, the wealthy wore heavy gold and silver rings. The poorer Egyptians wore rings made from bronze, glass, and glazed pottery. John S. Lizzadro

See also **Jewelry**.

Ring of Fire is a zone along the edge of the Pacific Ocean that has many volcanoes and earthquakes. This horseshoe-shaped belt stretches about 25,000 miles (40,000 kilometers) from New Zealand northwest to the Philippines, northeast to Japan, east to Alaska, and south to Oregon, California, Mexico, and the Andes Mountains of South America.

Scientists believe that the motion of *tectonic plates* (pieces that make up the strong outer shell of Earth) cause the Ring of Fire's earthquakes and volcanic eruptions. Tectonic plates move slowly on an underlying layer of weak rock that is so hot it flows, even though it remains solid. The edge of one plate sinks beneath the edge of a neighboring plate in a process called *subduction.* The movements of subduction generate many earthquakes and usually a line of volcanoes along the upper plate's boundary. A volcano erupts where melted rock, hot gases, and fragments of solid rock burst through to Earth's surface.

The Ring of Fire is the site of thousands of earthquakes each year. The largest earthquake ever recorded occurred there, along the coast of Chile in 1960.

Although the Ring of Fire covers only about 1 percent of Earth's surface, it has more than half of the world's active volcanoes. There are about 350 historically active volcanoes in the zone. Eruptions occurred in the late

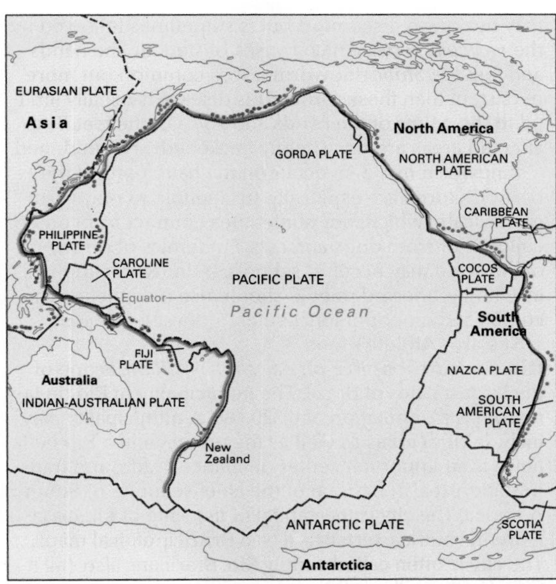

WORLD BOOK map

The Ring of Fire is a zone of volcanic and earthquake activity mostly along the rim of the Pacific Ocean. It has more than half the world's active volcanoes, many of which are shown here.

1900's at Mount St. Helens in the United States and Mount Pinatubo in the Philippines. The hot gases of volcanic activity carry dissolved metals toward the surface, where they settle out. Geologists have found copper, gold, molybdenum, silver, tin, and tungsten where ancient volcanic activity occurred within the Ring of Fire.

Mark Cloos

See also **Earthquake; Plate tectonics; Volcano.**

Ringette, *rihng EHT,* is a team sport primarily played by girls and young women that is similar to ice hockey. The game was invented in Ontario, Canada, in 1963. It is now played in the northern United States and in several European countries as well as in Canada.

As in ice hockey, ringette teams have six players, all of whom wear ice skates. The game is played on a rink divided into three sections by blue lines. The object of the game is to score goals by shooting a hollow rubber ring into a net guarded by a goaltender. The ring has an outer diameter of 16.5 centimeters (6.5 inches), an inner diameter of 11.5 centimeters (4.5 inches), and a thickness of 2.7 centimeters (1.06 inches). Players use a straight stick that resembles a bladeless hockey stick to shoot and pass the ring. Most sticks are made of wood, but aluminum and plastic sticks are also used. Players must wear knee and elbow pads and helmets with face masks. Players commonly wear a track suit as a uniform, sometimes combined with a hockey sweater.

A ringette team consists of a goaltender, a center, two forwards, and two defensive players. The center is the only player who can skate anywhere on the ice. Forwards may not skate closer to the net their team is defending than the blue line nearest the net. Defensive players may not come closer to the net their opponents are defending than the blue line nearest the net. Centers play with white sticks, forwards with blue sticks, and defensive players with red sticks. Ringette games consist of two 15-minute halves. Violations are similar to those of ice hockey. But unlike hockey, ringette prohibits body contact and requires passing over each blue line.

Organized ringette in Canada features five major age groups: petites (age 11 and under), tweens (13 and under), juniors (15 and under), belles (18 and under), and open (19 and over). Teams compete for provincial and national championships in Canada each year.

Critically reviewed by Ringette Canada

Ringling brothers were five brothers who founded the most famous circus in American entertainment history. The brothers were Albert (1852-1916), Otto (1858-1911), Alfred (1861-1919), Charles (1864-1926), and John (1866-1936). Their dedication and organizational skills helped build a small group of performers into one of the greatest circuses in the world.

The Ringlings were the sons of a harness maker from Germany. Albert was born in Chicago, Illinois; Otto in Baraboo, Wisconsin; and Alfred, Charles, and John in McGregor, Iowa. In 1884, the brothers started a traveling circus. At the time, there were a number of circuses touring the United States, including the huge Barnum show that traveled on 60 railroad cars. The Ringlings had little money for equipment or performers, so they did most of the work themselves. They held their first performance on May 19, 1884, in Baraboo. The brothers and 17 other employees sewed and pitched the tent, sold tickets, played in the band, and performed the acts.

Two other brothers, Henry and August, joined the Ringling circus later in the 1880's. Each of the seven brothers was responsible for one aspect of the circus

Library of Congress

The five Ringling brothers built up the world's largest, most famous, and most spectacular circus in the early 1900's.

management. The brothers invested almost all the profits back into the circus, which grew rapidly. At first, they took their show from town to town in wagons pulled by horses. By 1890, the circus traveled by railroad. The Ringlings soon became strong competitors of the Barnum & Bailey circus, the largest of the time. In 1907, the Ringlings purchased the Barnum & Bailey circus, but the two shows toured separately until 1919. That year, they merged to form the Ringling Brothers and Barnum & Bailey Circus. The Ringling family sold the circus in 1967, but the new owners kept the name. In January 2017, after years of declining attendance, rising costs, and criticism by animal rights activists, the owners announced the circus would close. The Ringling Brothers and Barnum & Bailey Circus gave its final performance on May 21, 2017.

Robert L. Parkinson

See also **Barnum, P. T.; Circus.**

Ringtail is a small North American mammal of the raccoon family. It is also called ring-tailed cat. The ringtail has a slender, grayish-tan body and a long, bushy tail with white and black bands. The animal measures 25 to 32 inches (64 to 81 centimeters) long, including the tail, which is 12 to 17 inches (30 to 43 centimeters) long. Ringtails have large eyes ringed with black; whitish facial fur; large, pointed ears; and catlike feet.

Ringtails inhabit woodlands, *chaparrals* (regions of shrubs and undersized trees), and deserts from southern Oregon and southwestern Wyoming south to central Mexico and east to Louisiana. A closely related species called the *cacomistle* lives in forests of southern Mexico and Central America. Ringtails make nests of leaves and grass in caves, hollow tree trunks, tangled roots, cracks in rocks, abandoned burrows, and buildings. They feed on mice and other small mammals, insects, fruits, acorns, and birds. Ringtails are hunted by great horned owls and bobcats.

Ringtails mate in late winter or early spring. The female gives birth to two to four babies about eight weeks later. The parents bring food to the young until late summer, when the young begin to hunt. Ringtails can live up to 10 years. They can be tamed as pets. Charles A. Long

Scientific classification. The ringtail's scientific name is *Bassariscus astutus.* The cacomistle is *B. sumichrasti.*

Ringworm is a general name for several kinds of skin diseases that are caused by tiny fungi. Itching may or may not be a symptom. Common ringworm of the skin is often seen on children. It begins as a small red area the size of a split pea. This grows larger and sometimes reaches the size of a silver dollar. The inside of the area clears, and the eruption appears as a red, scaly ring. There may be one or several patches. This form of ringworm occurs on the nonhairy parts of the body.

Ringworm is highly infectious, but it can usually be easily cured if treated with local applications of fungicidal compounds as advised by a physician. The spots of this type of ringworm may disappear without treatment after a few weeks, or they may persist for months. Body ringworm may attack people of any age. Flat yellowish or brownish patches may appear on the patient's neck, back, chest, or abdomen.

Ringworm of the hands and feet is another common ailment and has three types. A soft, white area between the toes, especially the part next to the little toe, may be *interdigital* ringworm, commonly called *athlete's foot.* It may not cause discomfort but is sometimes followed by the *vesicular* form, which causes blisters on the hands and feet. *Keratotic* ringworm is less common but more persistent than these forms. This disease is usually limited to the palms of the hands and soles of the feet. The affected areas are dry, slightly thickened, and reddened.

Ringworm may also occur on the hairy parts of the body. Children are especially susceptible to ringworm of the scalp, which they sometimes contract from other children or from dogs and cats. Epidemics of ringworm of the scalp may occur in schools. If ringworm appears in a family, affected people should use only their own combs and other personal items. Paul R. Bergstresser

See also **Athlete's foot.**

Rio de Janeiro, *REE oh day zhuh NAIR oh,* is one of the largest cities of Brazil. The municipality of Rio de Janeiro has a population of 6,320,466. A municipality may include rural areas as well as the urban center. Rio de Janeiro is an important center of finance, trade, and transportation. It also has one of the chief seaports of South America. The city is the capital of the state of Rio de Janeiro in southeastern Brazil (see **Brazil** [political map]). The city is often called simply Rio. Brazilians also call it Cidade Maravilhosa (Marvelous City).

Rio de Janeiro's exciting scenery makes it one of the world's most beautiful cities. Rio lies between forested mountains and the sparkling blue waters of the Atlantic Ocean and Guanabara Bay. Gleaming white beaches and graceful palm trees rim the shore. Sugar Loaf Mountain rises 1,325 feet (404 meters) from a peninsula in the bay.

Rio developed from a fort established by Portuguese soldiers in 1565 on what is now Guanabara Bay. The Portuguese named their settlement for the bay, at that time called Rio de Janeiro (River of January). Historians think the Portuguese explorer Gonçalo Coelho had named the bay for the month in 1502 when he arrived there. Coelho thought the bay was the outlet of a great river.

Victor Englebert, Black Star

Rio de Janeiro lies on Guanabara Bay, on the Atlantic Ocean. Sugar Loaf Mountain, a landmark of Rio, rises above the bay.

Rio de Janeiro

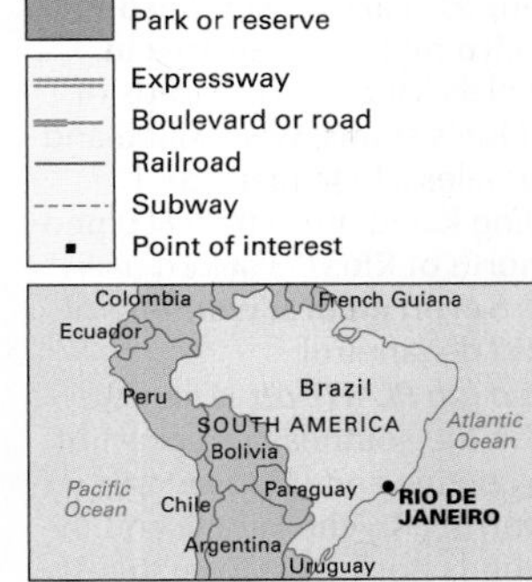

Location of Rio de Janeiro

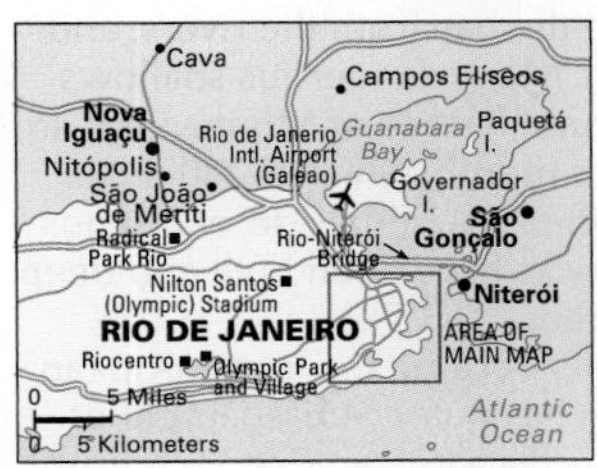

Rio de Janeiro metro area

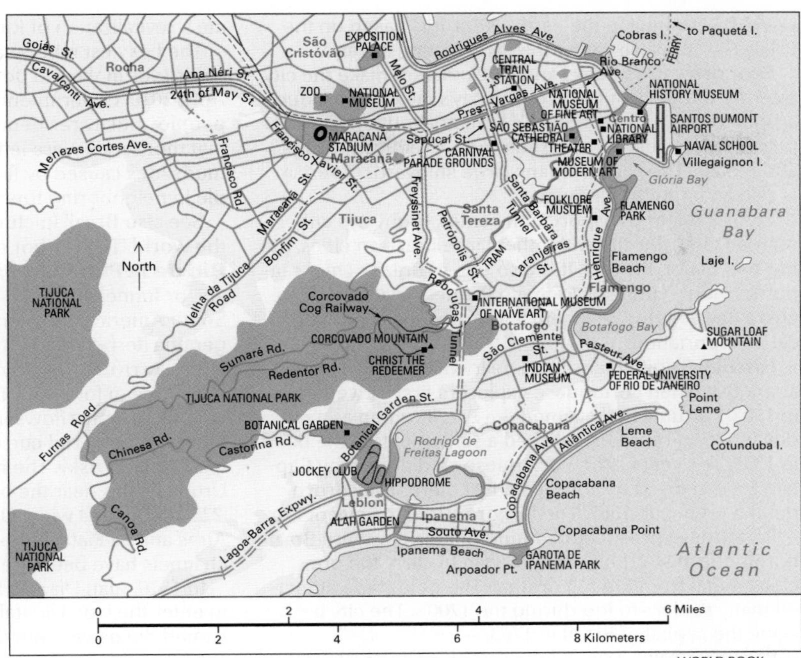

WORLD BOOK maps

The city covers about 487 square miles (1,261 square kilometers). The ocean shore forms Rio's southern boundary. Guanabara Bay borders the city on the east. Mountains rise to the north and west. The city itself includes many steep hills. A huge statue called *Christ the Redeemer* (1931) overlooks the city from atop Corcovado Mountain, the highest of these hills.

Rio has three main sections called the north, center, and south zones. The north zone is the largest zone. It has many docks and factories and large, poor residential areas. The Rio-Niterói Bridge, which stretches about 8 ¾ miles (14 kilometers), connects the north zone with Niterói, a city east of Guanabara Bay. The water in parts of the bay is polluted by sewage and industrial waste.

The small center zone includes the main business district. In downtown Rio, large modern office buildings stand near pastel churches built during the city's colonial period (the 1500's to the 1800's). Automobiles crowd such broad boulevards as President Vargas and Rio Branco avenues. Other downtown streets are narrow and limited to pedestrians. Most of Rio's chief libraries, museums, and theaters are in the central zone.

The long, narrow south zone includes a lake, Rodrigo de Freitas Lagoon. The nearby Botanical Garden features tropical plants. Hundreds of tall apartment buildings overlook the many beaches of the area. Copacabana Beach is famous for its elegant hotels and patterned sidewalks made of colored stone.

Slums called *favelas* form a sharp contrast to the luxury of Copacabana. Thousands of people live in shabby shacks on the steep hillsides and swampy shorelands of the bay. Suburban communities lie in valleys near Rio. Many low-income workers live in these towns.

People of Rio de Janeiro have long been called *Cariocas*. The Portuguese settlers may have taken this nickname from a South American Indian expression meaning *white man's house*. Today, Cariocas include people of American Indian, European, and African descent. Many have ancestors from two or three of these groups. Cariocas, like other Brazilians, speak Portuguese.

Most of the city's people belong to the Roman Catholic Church. Many Catholics also participate in Macumba religious ceremonies. Followers of Macumba pray to divine beings identified both with Christian saints and with the gods and goddesses of certain African religions. On New Year's Eve, hundreds of thousands of Cariocas crowd the beaches for candlelit Macumba ceremonies that honor the sea goddess Iemanjá.

Many Cariocas go to the beach to sunbathe, swim, or play volleyball. Huge crowds cheer soccer teams at Maracanã Stadium, one of the world's largest sports arenas. In the evening, many people go to one of Rio's many nightclubs or chat with friends at a sidewalk cafe.

Rio has won fame for an annual festival called Carnival. Carnival takes place just before Lent, the religious season that comes before Easter. Carnival features four days and nights of parades and dancing in the streets.

Education and cultural life. Rio's schools, libraries, and museums make the city the leading cultural center of Brazil. The Federal University of Rio de Janeiro is the largest of Rio's several institutions of higher learning. The city's libraries include the National Library. The National Archives of Brazil also are in Rio. Many visitors view the exhibits at such museums as the National Museum of Fine Arts, the Edison Carneiro Folklore Museum, and the Indian Museum. The Museum of Tomorrow, designed by the famous Spanish architect Santiago Calatrava, focuses on science and the environment. The Municipal Theater and other auditoriums host concerts and plays. The Municipal Theater is an opera house built in the early 1900's. It is based on the Palais Garnier, also called the Paris Opera, in Paris.

Economy. Rio's banks and stock market make the city a center of Brazilian finance. The city's factories produce a significant portion of Brazil's industrial output. Products of Rio include processed foods, chemicals, drugs, and metals. The city has many large shipyards. Tourism is also an important industry.

Rio is a major transportation center. Highways and railroads link the city with other large Brazilian cities. Rio has two major airports. It is also one of Brazil's chief seaports. A ferry connects Rio with Paquetá Island in Guanabara Bay. A subway system and many buses provide local transportation.

History. Tupi Indians lived near what is now Guanabara Bay when Portuguese explorers first arrived there in 1502. Portugal had claimed the Brazil region as a colony in 1494. France established a settlement on the bay in 1555. Ten years later, Portuguese soldiers led by Captain Estácio de Sá established a fort there. They drove out the French in 1567. The fort grew into the city of Rio.

Portuguese prospectors found gold in southern Brazil during the 1690's. Ships then began to carry the precious metal from Rio to Portugal. The gold trade attracted many settlers to Rio during the 1700's. The city became the capital of Brazil in 1763.

Portugal's ruler, Prince John (later King John VI), came to Rio in 1808 to escape a French invasion of Lisbon, the Portuguese capital. He made Rio the capital of the Portuguese Empire. Thousands of other wealthy Portuguese also fled to Rio. They established medical and military schools and a large city library. Lisbon again became the empire's capital in 1821, when John returned there. In 1822, Brazil became independent with Rio as its capital. Trade expanded with Europe and North America in the mid-1800's. Coffee became an important export. Rio had more than half a million people in 1890.

Rio was modernized in the early 1900's. The port was redesigned. Broad boulevards were constructed. Millions of people moved to the city from rural Brazil during the early and mid-1900's. Apartment buildings were erected to provide housing for the growing population. However, many of the newcomers could not afford to rent apartments. They had to live in the favelas. Since the mid-1900's, the federal government has built a number of housing projects in Rio for low-income residents. It has also granted financial aid to manufacturers in an effort to attract new industrial employers to Rio de Janeiro.

Brasília replaced Rio as the national capital in 1960. The federal government moved there during the 1960's and 1970's. Since 1975, Rio has absorbed some of its suburbs and outlying areas. As a result, the city's area has increased from 60 square miles (155 square kilometers) to 487 square miles (1,261 square kilometers). The population has also increased greatly. In the early 2000's, housing for the poor and pollution were among the problems facing the government of Rio.

In 2009, the International Olympic Committee chose Rio to host the 2016 Olympic Games. It was the first time a South American city had been chosen as the site for the Olympics. In 2014, Rio was one of 12 Brazilian cities that hosted the World Cup soccer competition, held every four years. Rio had hosted World Cup games once before, in 1950. Such sporting events helped initiate a revitalization of Rio's port area in the early 2000's.

The heaviest rains in about 50 years caused deadly landslides in the Rio de Janeiro metropolitan area in April 2010. Government officials said that hundreds of people, mostly residents of Rio's slums, were killed and that thousands were left homeless. In January 2011, mudslides caused by flooding killed more than 800 people in neighboring towns north of Rio. Anne G. Hanley

See also **Brazil** (pictures); **Seven natural wonders of the world** (The Harbor of Rio de Janeiro).

Río de la Plata, *REE oh duh luh PLAHT uh,* is an estuary, or funnel-shaped bay, on the southeastern coast of South America between Argentina and Uruguay (see **Argentina** [terrain map]). It is formed by the Paraná and the Uruguay rivers. The bay extends northwest from the Atlantic Ocean for about 170 miles (270 kilometers). A great volume of water flows into the bay from the rivers, and there is a powerful current. Many dangerous shallows make sailing risky. The natural harbor of Montevideo, in Uruguay, lies near the bay's mouth, which is 140 miles (225 kilometers) wide. On the Argentine side, at Buenos Aires and La Plata, huge docks have been built and deep channels have been dredged.

In 1516, Juan Díaz de Solís became the first European to enter the bay. The Italian navigator Sebastian Cabot named the estuary Río de la Plata (Silver River). He probably chose this name because the local American Indians wore silver ornaments. Richard W. Wilkie

Rio Grande, *REE oh GRAND,* one of the longest rivers in North America, flows for 1,900 miles (3,058 kilometers) through the southwestern United States. It forms the international boundary between the United States and Mexico for about 1,240 miles (1,996 kilometers), or almost two-thirds of the common border. Early Spanish explorers gave the river its name. *Rio Grande* means

Rio Grande

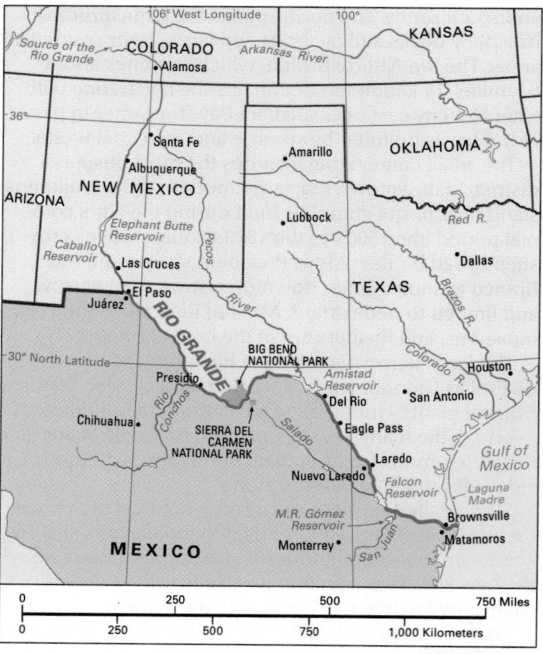

WORLD BOOK map

large river. Mexicans call the river Río Bravo *(bold river)* or Río Bravo del Norte *(bold river of the north).*

Upper course. The Rio Grande rises on the Continental Divide in the southern Rocky Mountains in southwestern Colorado. It flows southeast through the San Luis Valley Reclamation Project. At Alamosa, the river turns south. It crosses into New Mexico, and flows from north to south through the center of the state. In northern New Mexico, the Rio Grande, fed by mountain streams, passes through a series of basins separated by narrow valleys. The Rio Grande's valley widens near Albuquerque, and the river flows out upon a dry plateau to the south. On the plateau, Elephant Butte Dam blocks the Rio Grande and forms the Elephant Butte Reservoir. Farther downstream is the Caballo Reservoir. Both of these reservoirs store water for the Rio Grande Reclamation Project at Las Cruces. The American Dam controls the waters of the Rio Grande north of El Paso at the Texas, New Mexico, and Mexico borders.

Middle course. From El Paso to the Gulf of Mexico, the Rio Grande forms the international boundary. The river flows southeast from El Paso. At Presidio, it is joined by the Rio Conchos, a tributary from Mexico. At Big Bend National Park, the river turns north to pass around the mountainous Big Bend country. It then flows east until the Pecos River joins it. The Rio Grande turns southeast for the rest of its course. Amistad Dam spans the river about 12 miles (19 kilometers) northwest of Del Rio, Texas. The dam forms Amistad Reservoir, which extends upstream 86 miles (138 kilometers). During its middle course, the Rio Grande flows through very dry country. The river may be dry in late summer, because of little rainfall and the amount of water used for irrigation. Railroads cross the border at El Paso and Presidio.

Lower course. The Rio Grande widens between Eagle Pass and Laredo, both important railroad crossings. About 50 miles (80 kilometers) below Laredo, the Salado River, a major tributary from Mexico, joins the Rio Grande. Falcon Dam, about 20 miles (32 kilometers) below the mouth of the Salado River, forms Falcon Reservoir, which extends upstream more than 35 miles (56 kilometers). El Azúcar Reservoir lies across the Rio Grande at Camargo in Mexico. These reservoirs hold back floodwaters for the lower valley's irrigation projects. Between Rio Grande City and Brownsville, farmers grow citrus fruits, vegetables, and cotton in the irrigated valley. In 1936, a 17-mile (27-kilometer) canal was built from Brownsville to Laguna Madre, which leads to the Gulf of Mexico. Most of the river is too shallow for boats. Daniel D. Arreola

See also **Pecos River; Rio Grande Project; Texas** (picture: Big Bend National Park).

Rio Grande Project, *REE oh GRAND,* is a United States federal flood-control, power, and irrigation project that extends along the Rio Grande from Elephant Butte Reservoir in southern New Mexico into western Texas. The U.S. Congress authorized the project in 1905. Elephant Butte Dam was completed in New Mexico in 1916. The project also includes the Caballo Dam and Reservoir, six diversion dams, and more than 1,000 miles (1,600 kilometers) of canals and ditches. It irrigates 178,000 acres (72,000 hectares) in New Mexico and Texas. Under a 1906 treaty, the project also irrigates 20,000 acres (8,100 hectares) In Mexico. Gary L. Esslinger

Riordan, *REER duhn,* **Rick** (1964-), is an American author of fantasy novels for young readers and detective stories for adults. He is best known for his "Percy Jackson and the Olympians" series for children. Critics have praised the series for its colorful characters, exciting action, and humor.

Percy Jackson is a boy with a learning disability. He discovers his father is Poseidon, the Greek god of the sea. Throughout the series, Percy finds himself involved in the rivalries and plotting among the Greek gods, who are active in the modern world. Percy shares his adventures with young people who are either mythological characters or have a Greek god or goddess as a parent.

In *The Lightning Thief* (2005), the first book in the series, Percy must find the lightning bolt of Zeus, king of the gods. The other books in the series are *The Sea of Monsters* (2006), *The Titan's Curse* (2007), *The Battle of the Labyrinth* (2008), and *The Last Olympian* (2009). The series was followed by the sequel series "The Heroes of Olympus." The books in that series are *The Lost Hero* (2010), *The Son of Neptune* (2011), *The Mark of Athena* (2012), *The House of Hades* (2013), and *Blood of Olympus* (2014). Riordan also wrote the anthologies *Percy Jackson's Greek Gods* (2014) and *Percy Jackson's Greek Heroes* (2015). A related series, "The Trials of Apollo," began with *The Hidden Oracle* (2016), *The Dark Prophecy* (2017), and *The Burning Maze* (2018). A musical called *The Lightning Thief,* based on the first book in the "Percy Jackson and the Olympians" series, opened in New York City in 2014. It re-opened as a longer musical in 2017.

Riordan created a fantasy series called "The Kane Chronicles" based on Egyptian mythology. The first three books are *The Red Pyramid* (2010), *The Throne of Fire* (2011), and *The Serpent's Shadow* (2012). Riordan also wrote *The Kane Chronicles Survival Guide* (2012), a readers' handbook on the series. He created a series called "Magnus Chase and the Gods of Asgard," based on Norse legend. The first three books in the series are *The Sword of Summer* (2015), *The Hammer of Thor* (2016), and *The Ship of the Dead* (2017). Riordan first gained recognition for his "Tres Navarre" adult detective series. The series began with *Big Red Tequila* (1997).

Richard Russell Riordan, Jr., was born on June 5, 1964, in San Antonio. He received a B.A. degree from the University of Texas in 1986. Beginning in 1990, he taught at middle schools in California and Texas for several years before becoming a full-time writer. John Cech

Riot is a noisy, violent outbreak of disorder by a group of people. Rioters often harm others and damage property. Rioting or urging people to riot is a crime in most countries, including the United States. But the precise legal definition of a riot differs from place to place.

Rioting cannot always be easily distinguished from vandalism, disorderly conduct, or other similar offenses. But most riots involve hundreds or thousands of people, and follow an aggravation of already severe economic, social, or political grievances. A riot may occur spontaneously, or it may be planned through conspiracy. Few riots—unlike revolts or rebellions—aim at overthrowing a government or removing specific leaders. But a riot may set forces in motion that bring about such a result.

A riot may break out during a demonstration. In a demonstration, many people gather merely to protest publicly against some policy of the government, an industry, a university, or some other institution. But when passions run high, the massing together of thousands of persons and the efforts of police to keep order can lead to violence. In the United States, the Constitution guarantees everyone the rights to assemble in peace, to petition the government for grievances, and to *dissent* (disagree) as an individual or in a group (see **Freedom of speech**). But when dissent changes into disruption of order and is accompanied by violence that injures others or causes physical damage, it is a riot.

Causes of riots

Riots have occurred throughout the world since the beginning of history. In most societies, at one time or another, the poor have rioted to press their demands for food. But poverty and need are not the only reasons. For example, in Britain during the early 1800's, workers called Luddites staged riots in which they destroyed labor-saving machines, which they feared would replace them. In Mexico City in 1968, rioting students fought with police over various issues, including alleged police brutality during student demonstrations.

The specific issues that trigger riots vary. However, the underlying causes of many riots are similar. Many riots occur because some groups believe they do not have an equal chance for economic, political, or social advancement. Members of most minority groups live in this situation (see **Minority group**). Many people in such groups may feel they are mistreated by individuals or by government agencies or other organizations that influence their lives. They may become depressed because they feel they cannot help make decisions that affect themselves and their community. People who believe their grievances are being ignored often become defiant, and their feelings can erupt.

Members of a majority group may also become rioters if they fear a minority. They may attack members of the minority to keep them in an inferior social or economic position. Most lynch mobs in the western and southern United States were composed of members of dominant, majority groups (see **Lynching**).

Many social scientists classify riots into two groups: (1) *instrumental riots* and (2) *expressive riots.*

Instrumental riots occur when groups resort to violence because of discontent over specific issues. Most riots have been of this type. The violence results from attempts to change certain policies or to improve certain conditions. Most labor riots, especially those in the past, fall into this category. During the 1800's and early 1900's, for example, U.S. laborers fought to improve working conditions in mines, on railroads, and in factories. Union disputes with management often resulted in violence. Other instrumental riots include prison, antidraft, antiwar, and student riots.

Instrumental riots frequently indicate that the organizations being attacked have not listened effectively to or acted upon grievances previously voiced through orderly channels. But most people condemn the use of violence to achieve even the most desirable goals when peaceful means of change are available.

Expressive riots occur when many people in a minority group use violence to express dissatisfaction with their living conditions. Studies of urban riots of the 1960's show that African Americans in the riot areas had many grievances, including few job opportunities, bad housing, and inferior schools, and the use of what they felt was excessive force by the police. Several riots were triggered by arrests or other routine police actions that people of the black ghettos considered police provocation or brutality. These police actions brought crowds into the streets in protest. The small number of police at the scene could not control them.

The resulting riots became chiefly symbolic gestures of widespread discontent. For some rioters, however, they became opportunities to loot stores for personal gain. For others, the riots were little more than destructive play. In trying to restrain the rioters and promote a return to order, the police sometimes used more force than many people thought necessary. Such action caused many rioters to become even more violent. See **African Americans** (Unrest in the cities).

Major riots in the United States

During the 1700's, most riots in the United States were instrumental riots. High and unfair taxation was a leading cause of such riots. During the 1760's and 1770's, American colonists rioted against tax collectors and other British-appointed officials (see **Boston Tea Party; Revolution, American** [Background and causes of the revolution]). For information on other riots resulting from taxation, see **Shays's Rebellion; Whiskey Rebellion.**

During the 1800's, anti-Catholic, anti-immigrant, and antiblack riots were common. Many native-born Americans strongly disliked immigrants, especially Irish

United Press Int.

Labor riots broke out frequently in the United States during the late 1800's and early 1900's. In 1916, rioting during a steel strike in Youngstown, Ohio, *shown here,* caused extensive property damage.

Roman Catholics and Asians. In the mid-1850's, members of the Know-Nothing, or American, Party opposed the Catholic Church. The Know-Nothings feared rising Irish Catholic political power. They attacked Irish Catholics in several cities, including Baltimore, Louisville, New Orleans, and St. Louis. The uprisings took several lives. See **Know-Nothings.**

In 1863, during the Civil War, antidraft riots broke out in New York City. Armed mobs swarmed through downtown to protest the drafting of men into the Union Army. Rioters looted, set buildings on fire, and shot Black people, policemen, and federal troops. Over 100 people were killed and hundreds more were wounded.

Race riots in the United States have been especially destructive. Violence aimed at Black people and abolitionists broke out in several Northern cities before the Civil War. After the war, in 1866, white Southerners attacked Black Southerners in New Orleans and Memphis.

Many Chinese immigrants were victims of mob violence during a depression in the 1870's. Many native-born Americans believed the immigrants were taking their jobs and forcing down wages. Anti-Chinese riots in California and other states resulted in several deaths and the passage of laws prohibiting Asians from entering the United States. See **Oriental Exclusion Acts.**

Labor riots of the late 1800's caused great bloodshed. Dozens of people were killed in riots in several cities during the great railroad strikes of 1877 (see **Labor movement** [Opposition to unions]). The Haymarket Riot of 1886 in Chicago erupted when someone threw a bomb during a meeting of anarchists who were protesting police tactics against strikers at an industrial plant (see **Haymarket riot**).

During the 1900's, labor and race riots continued to cause destruction. In 1919, efforts to unionize the steel industry led to riots at plants in Indiana, Ohio, and Pennsylvania. In 1934, a dispute between unions and management in the cotton-textile industry led to riots in Georgia, South Carolina, Alabama, Rhode Island, and other states. These riots took about 20 lives.

In the early 1900's, attempts to segregate Black Southerners and keep them from voting led to lynchings and riots. During World War I (1914-1918), many Black people moved to the North to work in defense plants. White people feared they would take their jobs and move into their neighborhoods. Black people claimed white law officers treated them unfairly. These grievances led to clashes between white and Black people. In 1917 in East St. Louis, Illinois, 39 Black people and 9 white people died in a riot. A riot in Chicago in 1919 caused 38 deaths. Racial violence also broke out during World War II (1939-1945). The most destructive riot occurred in 1943 in Detroit, where 34 people died.

Many riots erupted in U.S. cities in the 1960's, largely because of the economic deprivation and social injustices suffered by Black people in poverty-stricken areas. They included riots in the Watts section of Los Angeles in 1965, in Detroit and Newark in 1967, and in Cleveland in 1968. The Detroit riot was the most violent. It led to 43 deaths. About 2,500 stores were burned or looted.

After the Detroit riot, President Lyndon B. Johnson established the National Advisory Commission on Civil Disorders—also known as the Kerner Commission—to study the causes of urban riots. The commission put much of the blame on the racial prejudice and discrimination of white people against Black people. In 1968, Johnson established the National Commission on the Causes and Prevention of Violence. It recommended such measures as better housing and increased economic opportunities for Black and poor people.

In 1968, riots broke out during the Democratic National Convention in Chicago. Thousands of young people assembled downtown. Many were protesting the nation's part in the Vietnam War (1957-1975). Many supported the presidential nomination of Senator Eugene J. McCarthy of Minnesota, a critic of the war. Several bloody clashes took place between demonstrators and the police, but no one was killed. U.S. involvement in the war led to an increasing number of small riots and demonstrations across the country.

During the late 1960's and early 1970's, student riots occurred in many U.S. cities. Most of the rioters were middle-class students who demanded a greater voice in the administration of their schools. Militant Black students also used violence in efforts to enforce their demands, which included the addition of African American history and culture courses.

In 1971, one of the worst prison riots in U.S. history occurred at the state prison in Attica, New York. The inmates, mostly Black, charged that the white prison guards mistreated them. Rioters seized the prison and held it for four days. Finally, state troopers stormed the prison to regain control. The uprising resulted in the deaths of 11 prison employees and 32 prisoners.

In 1992, riots triggered by a court decision broke out in Los Angeles and other U.S. cities. The riots erupted after a California jury decided not to convict four white Los Angeles police officers of assault and other charges that resulted from their beating of Rodney G. King, a Black motorist, in 1991. No Black people served on the jury. King had been stopped after a pursuit, and a local resident videotaped the beating. The videotape was then broadcast by television stations throughout the nation. The court decision set off several days of rioting, mainly in Black areas of South-Central Los Angeles (now called South Los Angeles). The rioting in Los Angeles resulted in 53 deaths, over 4,000 injuries, and about $1 billion in property damage. Later in 1992, the federal government indicted the four police officers on charges that they had violated King's civil rights. In 1993, a federal jury convicted two of the officers on these charges.

In 1997, the Oklahoma Legislature created a commission to investigate a major riot that occurred in Tulsa in 1921. During the riot, more than 300 people were killed, mostly Black, and 1,200 buildings were destroyed. In early 2000, the commission recommended that survivors of the riot and their descendants be paid to compensate for their losses during the riot. See **Tulsa race massacre of 1921.**

M. Cherif Bassiouni

Rip Van Winkle is one of the most famous short stories in American literature. The author, Washington Irving, published the story in his collection *The Sketch Book of Geoffrey Crayon, Gent.* (1819-1820). His story, based on a German folk tale, "Peter Klaus," is set in the Catskill Mountains of New York. Irving's picturesque descriptions of the Hudson River Valley help create the story's dreamy mood.

Rip, a cheerful but lazy man, is married to a nagging

wife in American colonial times. One day he takes his dog and gun into the mountains to hunt. He meets an odd little man in old-fashioned Dutch clothing who gets Rip to help him carry a keg of liquor up the mountain. Other little men are there playing a game of *ninepins* (a bowling game). Rip samples the liquor and falls asleep.

Rip awakens 20 years later and returns to his village. There he finds that his wife has died and his children have grown. The American Colonies have become an independent nation. The villagers smile at Rip's account, though few believe him. Rip goes to live with his daughter, and he repeatedly tells his story in the village until it becomes a piece of local tradition. The reader must decide how much of Rip's story should be believed.

The tale is an outstanding piece of comic literature. It also deals with such themes as change, aging, independence, and the importance of the imagination. It is considered a *foundational text* of American literature. Such texts help form a nation's literature. John Hay

See also **Irving, Washington; Jefferson, Joseph.**

Ripken, Cal, Jr. (1960-), holds the record for the most consecutive games played by a major league baseball player. On Sept. 6, 1995, Ripken broke the previous record of 2,130 consecutive games held by Lou Gehrig. Ripken's consecutive game streak began on May 30, 1982. Ripken chose not to play in the game of Sept. 20, 1998, ending his streak of consecutive games at 2,632.

In addition to his record for durability, Ripken established himself as one of the finest shortstops in baseball. Ripken played his entire major league career with the Baltimore Orioles of the American League, beginning late in the 1981 season.

Calvin Edwin Ripken, Jr., was born on Aug. 24, 1960, in Havre de Grace, Maryland. His father, Cal Ripken, Sr., was a major league manager and coach. Ripken holds or shares several major league and American League records for shortstops. He was named American League Rookie of the Year in 1982 and American League Most Valuable Player in 1983 and 1991. In 2000, Ripken became the 7th player in major league history to get 3,000 hits and 400 home runs during his career. He retired after the 2001 season. Ripken was elected to the National Baseball Hall of Fame in 2007. He wrote a children's book about his 1988 season with Baltimore called *The Longest Season* (2007). Dave Nightingale

Ripley, Robert LeRoy (1893-1949), was an American cartoonist who became internationally famous for his cartoon panel "Believe It or Not." The panel describes oddities and strange facts and occurrences from around the world. At its peak of popularity, "Believe It or Not" had an estimated daily newspaper readership of 80 million. The feature also provided material for lectures and personal appearances by Ripley, and for radio and television shows, books, motion pictures, and museums.

Ripley was born on Dec. 26, 1893, in Santa Rosa, California. His given and family name was LeRoy Ripley, and he later added Robert. He began his career as a sports cartoonist for the *Bulletin* and the *Chronicle* in San Francisco and the *Globe* in New York City. "Believe It or Not" first appeared in the *Globe* on Dec. 19, 1918. Ripley died on May 27, 1949. Charles P. Green

Ritalin, *RIHT uh lihn,* is the trade name for the drug *methylphenidate (MEHTH uhl FEHN uh dayt).* It is the drug most often prescribed to treat attention-deficit/hyperactivity disorder (ADHD). ADHD is a behavior problem in which people have unusual difficulty paying attention, sitting still, or controlling their impulses. Because the disorder is common, millions of people worldwide take Ritalin. For most ADHD patients, the drug improves concentration and reduces restlessness.

Some medical experts worry that doctors may sometimes prescribe Ritalin for people who do not really need it. Although most doctors consider the drug safe, they caution that the benefits and risks of taking it for long periods are not yet fully known.

Ritalin improves attention by stimulating the brain. It provides stimulation by lengthening the time during which two brain chemicals called *dopamine (DOH puh meen)* and *norepinephrine (NAWR ehp uh NEHF rihn)* remain active. These chemicals are *neurotransmitters* that carry messages among nerve cells. Prolonging activity of these chemicals helps nerve cells in some parts of the brain function more efficiently.

By itself, Ritalin cannot usually overcome all the symptoms of ADHD. Most patients also require treatment involving behavioral or psychological techniques. The most common side effects of Ritalin are decreased appetite and difficulty falling asleep. F. Xavier Castellanos

See also **Attention deficit disorder.**

Rite of passage is a form of ritual ceremony found in all societies to mark and recognize a person's entry into a new stage of life. Rites of passage note such occasions as birth, the achievement of adult status, graduation, marriage, and even death. People may pass through rites of passage individually or in groups. A rite of passage celebrates and acknowledges the new status and position of a person within the society.

Rites of passage usually have three stages—*separation, transition,* and *incorporation.* First, a participant in the rite is temporarily separated from the rest of society and from his or her former role. In many rites, participants wear special costumes to emphasize their temporary separation from society and to symbolize the change they experience. Such costumes include wedding dresses and graduation gowns. During the transitional stage, also called the *liminal period,* the participant may learn the behavior appropriate to their new role in society. In some African societies, boys who will soon become men are separated for days or months while they learn legends and technical skills. A public ritual then announces that the participant is incorporated, or admitted, into a new social role within the society.

The term *rites of passage* was coined by French anthropologist Arnold van Gennep. He used it to describe such ceremonies as baptisms, weddings, and funerals in his book *Les Rites de Passage* (1909). John W. Burton

See also **Bar mitzvah; Bat mitzvah; Confirmation; Quinceañera.**

Ritter, Tex (1905-1974), was an American country music singer and songwriter. Ritter also gained popularity as a radio actor and as a singing cowboy in motion-picture Westerns. His most popular recording was the theme song from the movie *High Noon* (1952).

Maurice Woodward Ritter was born on Jan. 12, 1905, on a farm in Panola County, Texas. He became a radio actor in New York City in 1929. He performed on such Western shows as "The Lone Ranger" and "Death Valley Days." He also appeared in several stage plays. Ritter moved to Hollywood in the mid-1930's. He made his first movie in 1936 and appeared in about 80 Western films. Ritter spent his final years in Nashville, where he often appeared on the "Grand Ole Opry" radio program. He was elected to the Country Music Hall of Fame in 1964. He died on Jan. 2, 1974. John Ritter, Tex's son, became a popular television and motion-picture actor. Lee Rector

Ritty, James (1836-1918), an American restaurant owner, invented the cash register. While traveling to Europe in 1878, he saw a device for counting the revolutions of the ship's propellers. When he came home, he devised a similar machine to record business transactions. In 1879, he and his brother John built and patented a gear-operated adding machine. They sold the business in 1881. James Ritty was born on Oct. 29, 1836, in Dayton, Ohio. He died on March 29, 1918. George H. Daniels

Ritual. See **Religion** (Religious rituals).

River is a large, natural stream of water that flows overland within a channel. Most rivers begin in mountains or hills. A river ends where it flows into another river, desert basin, ocean, or lake. A river is the main part of a *river system,* which also includes all the smaller streams that supply water to the river. A region of land that is drained by a river system is known as a *drainage basin.*

The world's longest river is the Nile River in Africa, which flows for 4,160 miles (6,695 kilometers). The next longest is the Amazon River in South America, which is about 4,000 miles (6,437 kilometers) long. The Amazon carries more water than any other river—and more water than the Nile, the Mississippi River in the United States, and the Yangtze River in China combined.

Uses of rivers

For centuries, people have used rivers for transportation and trade. In North and South America, for example, early explorers, traders, and pioneers traveled on rivers. Later, they built towns along major rivers. Several of these towns grew into large cities. On the Mississippi River, for instance, Minneapolis, St. Louis, Memphis, and New Orleans became large cities.

Rivers are also valuable to agriculture. Farmers grow crops in the fertile land of river plains and the terraced surfaces above those plains. In dry regions, farmers use river water to irrigate their land. They dig irrigation ditches to carry water from rivers to farmland.

In addition, rivers serve as a source of power. The energy of flowing water at waterfalls and other steep places along a river can drive machines and generate electric power.

Sources of river water

Almost all river water comes from rain or melted snow. Most of the water reaches rivers indirectly. In some cases, water called *surface runoff* flows over the land to the river. In other cases, the water soaks into soil and rocks and becomes *ground water* (water beneath the surface of the earth). The ground water then moves slowly through the soil or underground rocks to the rivers. This subsurface supply of water can keep a river flowing between periods of rain. Other sources of river water include glaciers, springs, and overflowing lakes.

Where rainfall is seasonal, a river may be dry for part of the year. This kind of river is known as an *intermittent river.* A river that flows across a desert may also be intermittent. Such a river does not receive ground water. Rather, it gives up water to the ground beneath it. This loss, together with evaporation, may cause the river to dry up for part of the year.

Exotic rivers are large rivers that begin in a rainy area, then flow across a desert without drying up. The Nile River and the Colorado River, which is in the United States, are exotic rivers in parts of their channels.

River systems

A river system consists of the river itself and all the smaller streams that supply water to the river. A river is highest at its *headwaters,* where it begins. It is lowest at its *mouth,* where it ends.

A river *erodes* (wears away) a great deal of material from the land over which it flows. This material is called the river's *load* while it is flowing and *sediment* when it is deposited. In many rivers, most of the material is dissolved in the water and cannot be seen. This *invisible load* mixes with lake or ocean water at the mouth. A river also carries a *visible load* that consists of material ranging from tiny particles of clay to large boulders. The finer particles may determine the color of the water, which may range from red to brown or yellow.

Some rivers flow gradually from headwaters to mouth. Other rivers have irregular features, such as waterfalls, rapids, and canyons. Many rivers that empty into oceans have deep, broad mouths called *estuaries.*

Tributaries. Runoff collects in tiny, temporary channels called *rills.* Rills often flow into streams that eventually join to form rivers. Smaller streams that flow into larger ones are called *tributaries.*

Scientists often classify streams by *stream order.* For example, a stream with no permanent tributaries is a first order stream. Two first order streams meet to form a second order stream. Two second order streams join

© Thinkstock

A melting glacier near Furka Pass in the Swiss Alps is the source of the Rhône River. The Rhône flows from Switzerland through southern France. It empties into the Mediterranean Sea.

to form a third order stream, and so on. Low order streams are commonly called *brooks* or *creeks,* while higher order streams are commonly called rivers. One river may be a tributary of another river. For example, the Missouri River is a tributary of the Mississippi.

Channels are passages in which river water flows. A river's channel extends from the headwaters to the mouth. The channel bottom is the river's *bed,* and the edges of the channel are the *banks.*

The slope of a channel tends to be steep near the source of a river and almost flat near the mouth. Channel width and depth typically increase downstream due to the increasing flow of water.

Waterfalls and rapids occur in the upper *courses* (segments) of many rivers. A waterfall occurs where a river crosses a layer of hard rock that resists erosion. The water erodes softer rock downstream, creating a steep drop in the channel. *Rapids* occur where water tumbles over large boulders or rock ledges.

Canyons. In the upper course of a river, the channel may occupy the full width of the valley floor. The river may undercut the sides of the valley from place to place, and it also deepens the valley. Valley sides are typically V-shaped above the valley floor. Rapid cutting can produce a canyon, a deep valley with cliffs above the floor.

Estuaries contain a mixture of salt water from the ocean and fresh water from the river. The Amazon River is an estuary for several hundred miles or kilometers upstream from its mouth.

Estuaries formed as a result of ancient changes in sea level. During the Pleistocene Epoch, which lasted from about 2.6 million to 11,500 years ago, sea level moved down and up several times. This movement occurred because vast ice sheets accumulated on the land and then melted away several times. At the end of the epoch, the sea level was low, and rivers near the ocean had cut their valleys down to the low level. Since then, many of the ice sheets have melted. As a result, sea level has

Famous rivers of the world

Name	Length* In miles	Length* In kilometers	Location	Interesting facts
Amazon	4,000	6,437	South America	Carries more water than any other river; world's second longest river; only the Nile is longer.
Colorado	1,450	2,334	United States	River's current, combined with other agents of erosion, created the Grand Canyon.
Congo	2,900	4,667	Africa	Second longest river in Africa and second in the amount of water carried in the world.
Danube	1,770	2,850	Europe	Its beauty inspired Austrian composer Johann Strauss, Jr., to write the famous waltz "On the Beautiful Blue Danube."
Euphrates	1,700	2,736	Turkey-Syria-Iraq	Longest river in southwestern Asia; part of the Tigris-Euphrates river system, in which the world's first civilization developed.
Ganges	1,560	2,510	India-Bangladesh	Considered sacred by members of the Hindu faith.
Huang He	3,395	5,464	China	Name means *yellow river;* large amounts of yellow silt are deposited along its course; world's fourth longest river.
Indus	1,900	3,058	Tibet-Pakistan	Source of one of the largest irrigation systems in the world.
Jordan	200	320	Israel-Jordan	River mentioned most often in the Bible.
Lena	2,734	4,400	Russia	Russia's longest river.
Mackenzie	1,100	1,770	Canada	Canada's longest river.
Mekong	2,700	4,345	Asia	Largest river on the Indochinese Peninsula.
Mississippi	2,340	3,766	United States	Second longest river in the United States.
Missouri	2,540	4,090	United States	Longest river in the United States.
Murray	1,609	2,589	Australia	Longest permanently flowing river in Australia.
Niagara	35	56	United States-Canada	Famous for its spectacular Niagara Falls.
Niger	2,600	4,180	Africa	Its delta is the largest in Africa.
Nile	4,160	6,695	Northeast Africa	World's longest river.
Rhine	820	1,320	Europe	Most important inland waterway in Europe; one of the world's busiest rivers.
Rio Grande	1,900	3,058	United States-Mexico	Spanish name for *large river;* forms part of international boundary between United States and Mexico.
St. Lawrence	800	1,300	Canada-United States	Links the Great Lakes and the Atlantic Ocean.
Seine	480	770	France	Flows through the heart of Paris, where more than 30 bridges span it.
Thames	210	340	United Kingdom	Longest and most important waterway entirely within England; flows through the center of London.
Volga	2,300	3,700	Russia	Longest river in Europe.
Yangtze	3,900	6,275	China	China's longest river; third longest river in the world; only the Nile and the Amazon are longer.
Zambezi	1,700	2,736	Africa	Its Victoria Falls is considered one of the natural wonders of the world.

*Refers only to the length of the river itself and not the length of the river system.

Parts of a river system

A river may drain water from a huge area. The source of the river in this diagram is a melting glacier high in the mountains. But all the water that flows into the river—and the river itself—make up the parts of the river system.

WORLD BOOK diagram by Laura Lee Lizak

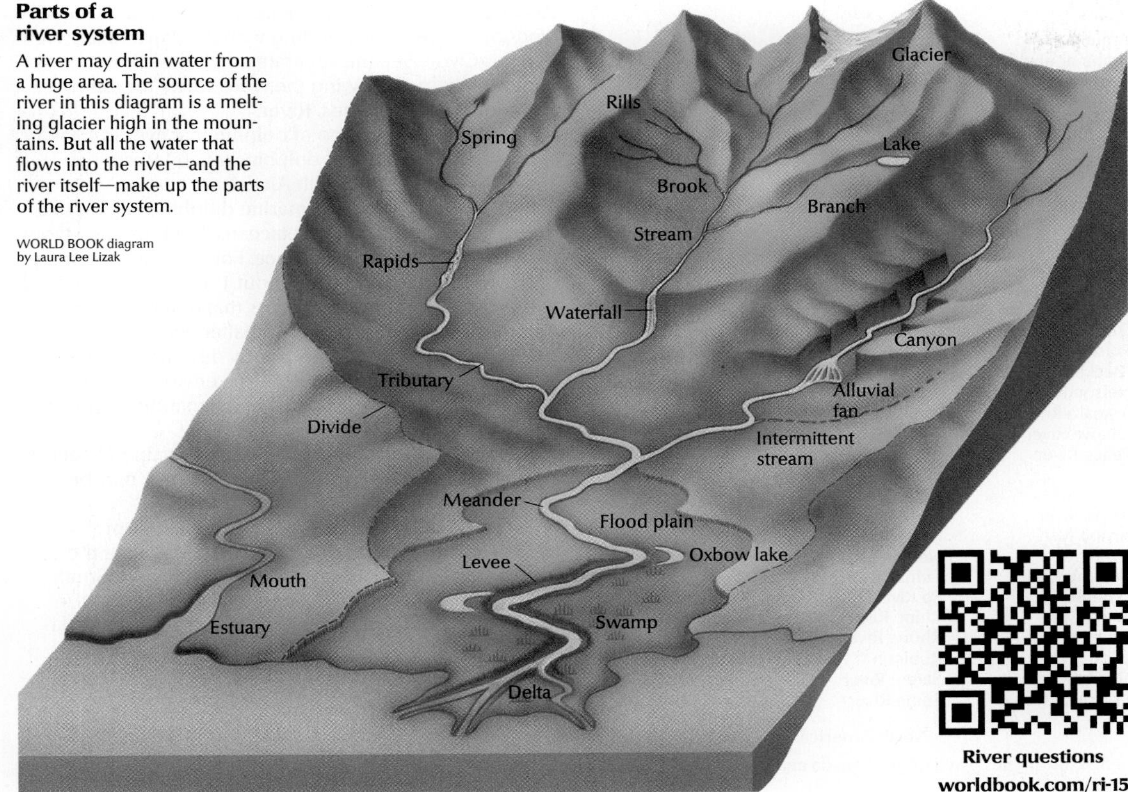

River questions
worldbook.com/ri-15

risen. Ocean water has flowed into the valleys that had been cut, forming the estuaries.

Drainage basins

A drainage basin consists of the region drained by a river system. The Amazon River has a drainage basin of about 2,700,000 square miles (7,000,000 square kilometers). The Mississippi River drains about 1,244,000 square miles (3,220,000 square kilometers) of land in North America. This land includes about 40 percent of the United States, except Alaska and Hawaii. A basin's waters make up a *drainage net.*

Divides. The rim of a drainage basin is called a *drainage divide.* One major drainage divide follows the crest of the Rocky Mountains. This divide splits the continent of North America into two large drainage regions. It is therefore known as the Continental Divide. Basins to the west of the divide carry water to the Pacific Ocean. To the east is the Mississippi River basin, which carries water to the Gulf of Mexico. Other eastern basins carry water to the Atlantic Ocean and the Arctic Ocean.

Flood plains are flat areas on one or both sides of the middle or lower course of a river. When the river overflows its banks, it floods these areas. A flood plain can be hundreds of miles or kilometers wide.

Floodwaters deposit sediment on the flood plain, particularly on the parts of the plain next to the channel. The deposits create banks called *natural levees.* Marshy areas called *back swamps* occupy the parts of flood plains beyond the natural levees.

A channel in a wide flood plain tends to curve from one side of the plain to the other. The snakelike bends in the channel are known as *meanders.* Meanders can form almost complete loops, with only a narrow neck of land separating the beginning and end of each loop. Eventually, floodwater flows across this neck, cutting off the loop and creating a new, straight channel for the river. The separated loop then fills with rain water or ground water. The loop may continue to exist for many years as a crescent-shaped *oxbow lake.*

Alluvial fans and deltas are land masses that build up where a flow of river water decreases quickly. The decrease in the flow causes the river to deposit its visible load rapidly, forming the land mass. An alluvial fan is a fan-shaped land mass that forms where a river flows from a steep mountain slope to a flatter plain next to the slope. The decrease in elevation slows the river down, causing some of the river's load to be deposited. River flow also slows down where a river reaches a lake or ocean, so most of the remaining load is deposited there.

A delta is a low plain that may form at a river's mouth. The Mississippi River and the Nile River have large deltas. David S. McArthur

Related articles in *World Book.* See the *Rivers and lakes* section in the various country, state, and province articles, such as **Alabama** (Rivers and lakes). See also:

Africa

Congo River
Limpopo River
Niger River
Nile River
Orange River
Ubangi River
Zambezi River

Asia

Amur River
Brahmaputra River
Euphrates River
Ganges River
Hooghly River
Huang He
Indus River
Irrawaddy River
Jordan River
Lena River
Mekong River
Ob River
Tigris River
Ural River
Xi Jiang
Yalu River
Yangtze River

Australia

Murray River
Torrens River

Canada

Athabasca River
Churchill River
Columbia River
Detroit River
Fraser River
Mackenzie River
Nelson River
Niagara River
Ottawa River
Peace River
Red River of the North
Saguenay River
Saint John River
Saint Lawrence River
Saint Marys River
Saskatchewan River
Skeena River
Winnipeg River
Yukon River

Europe

Aisne River
Arno River
Avon, River
Danube River
Dnieper River
Don River
Elbe River
Loire River
Marne River
Mersey, River
Meuse River
Moselle River
Neman River
Oder River
Po River
Rhine River
Rhône River
Rubicon
Saône River
Seine River
Severn, River
Shannon, River
Tagus River
Thames, River
Tiber River
Torne River
Ural River
Vistula River
Volga River
Weser River

North America

See the articles listed under Canada and United States in this section.

South America

Amazon River
Madeira River
Orinoco River
Paraguay River
Paraná River
São Francisco River
Uruguay River

United States

Allegheny River
Arkansas River
Colorado River
Columbia River
Connecticut River
Cumberland River
Delaware River
Detroit River
Housatonic River
Hudson River
Illinois River
James River
Kanawha River
Merrimack River
Minnesota River
Mississippi River
Missouri River
Mobile River
Mohawk River
Monongahela River
Niagara River
Ohio River
Pecos River
Penobscot River
Platte River
Potomac River
Rappahannock River
Red River
Red River of the North
Rio Grande
Sacramento River
Saint Marys River
Salt River
San Joaquin River
Savannah River
Schuylkill River
Shenandoah River
Snake River
Susquehanna River
Suwannee River
Tennessee River
Tombigbee River
Wabash River
Willamette River
Wisconsin River
Yellowstone River
Yukon River

Other related articles

Basin
Bayou
Canyon
Dam
Delta
Divide
Erosion
Estuary
Flood
Lagoon
Levee
Oxbow lake
Reservoir
Silt
Valley
Water power
Water wheel
Waterfall
World (graph: Longest river on each continent)

River . . . Some rivers, particularly those in the United Kingdom, have names starting with the word *River,* such as River Clyde. See the separate articles for these rivers under the name following the word *River,* for example, **Shannon, River; Thames, River.**

River dolphin is a type of dolphin that lives in fresh or slightly salty water. River dolphins inhabit warm rivers and lakes of Asia and South America.

Both river dolphins and marine dolphins belong to a group of mammals called cetaceans. But these two types of dolphins differ in appearance. For example, the snout of a river dolphin measures about 1 foot (30 centimeters) long, about four times as long as that of most marine dolphins. River dolphins have smaller eyes than marine dolphins, and their vision is poorly developed because they live in dark, muddy water. This environment also makes river dolphins less active than marine dolphins. River dolphins feed primarily on fish.

The largest river dolphins usually grow up to 8 feet (2.4 meters) long, but most are smaller. They may be white, pink, yellow, brown, gray, or black.

There are at least four living *species* (kinds) of river dolphins. The *Amazon River dolphin,* also called the *boto* or *pink dolphin,* lives in rivers of northern South America. The nearly blind *Ganges dolphin* and *Indus River dolphin* inhabit rivers of northern India and Pakistan. The *La Plata dolphin,* also known as *Franciscana,* lives in rivers and coastal waters of eastern South America. The *baiji,* also called the *Yangtze River dolphin,* historically was found in Dongting Lake in China. However, scientists think the species likely went extinct in the first decade of the 2000's. All species of river dolphins are threatened by human activities that kill the animals or destroy their habitat. Daniel K. Odell

La Plata dolphin
Pontoporia blainvillei

WORLD BOOK illustration by James Teason

River dolphins live in warm rivers and lakes of Asia and South America. They have a long snout and feed mainly on fish. One of the five kinds of river dolphins is shown here.

Scientific classification. River dolphins belong to the order Cetacea. The scientific name for the bouta is *Inia geoffrensis.* The white fin dolphin is *Lipotes vexillifer;* the Ganges dolphin, *Platanista gangetica;* the Indus River dolphin, *Platanista minor;* and the La Plata dolphin, *Pontoporia blainvillei.*

See also **Cetacean; Dolphin; Mammal** (pictures).

River horse. See **Hippopotamus.**

Rivera, Diego (1886-1957), was a Mexican artist. He became famous for murals about Mexican life and history. Rivera was controversial because of his radical political beliefs and his attacks on the church and clergy.

Rivera was born on Dec. 8, 1886, in Guanajuato. In the 1920's, he became involved in the new Mexican mural movement. With such Mexican artists as José Clemente

Paintings by Diego Rivera portray the culture and history of Mexico. The mural at the left shows the Zapotec Indians of southern Mexico making gold jewelry before Spain conquered Mexico in the 1500's. The mural is one of a series by Rivera in the National Palace in Mexico City.

Fresco (1942) by Diego Rivera; Giraudon

Orozco and David Siqueiros, he began to experiment with fresco painting on large walls (see **Fresco**). Rivera soon developed his own style of large, simplified figures and bold colors. Many of his murals deal with Mexican society and thought. Some of his best murals are in the National Palace in Mexico City and at the National Agricultural School in Chapingo, near Mexico City.

Rivera painted several significant works in the United States, which he visited in the early 1930's and again in 1940. Perhaps his finest surviving U.S. work is a mural at the Detroit Institute of Arts. Rivera died on Nov. 25, 1957. Frida Kahlo, Rivera's wife, was also a noted Mexican painter. Judith Berg Sobré

See also **Aztec** (picture); **Kahlo, Frida.**

Rivers, Larry (1923-2002), was an American painter. Beginning in the early 1950's, Rivers chose American symbols as his subjects. They were either historical themes or images of commercial products, such as cigarette packages. Rivers's deliberately unidealistic works have an amusing, ironical nature. With his introduction

Oil, graphite, and charcoal painting on linen (1953) © Estate of Larry Rivers/Licensed by VAGA, New York City; The Museum of Modern Art (digital image © The Museum of Modern Art, New York City)

Rivers's *Washington Crossing the Delaware* (1953) was one of the earliest paintings in his series on American historical themes. Rivers based the painting on a familiar work by Emanuel Leutze that is reproduced in the *World Book* article on **Leutze, Emanuel G.** Rivers's picture shows George Washington in several poses. Because of such adaptations of popular images, Rivers is often considered a forerunner of the Pop Art movement.

of popular imagery as subjects, he is often considered a forerunner of the Pop Art movement (see **Pop Art**).

Rivers's subjects emerge from loosely painted backgrounds with visible brushstrokes or sometimes bare canvas. Many of his paintings have an appearance of rapid execution and fragmentation, almost as if they were unfinished. Some works show parts of the same figure from several points of view. Rivers was born on Aug. 17, 1923, in New York City. His real name was Yitzroch Loiza Grossberg. He died on Aug. 14, 2002.

Deborah Leveton

Riveting is a method of joining two metal plates with aluminum, brass, copper, or steel bolts, called *rivets*. Rivets also hold scissors and blue jean pockets together. A rivet has a rounded or flat head at one end. A rivet's shaft is a smooth cylinder. Unlike the shaft of a screw, it lacks threads.

To join two plates, a rivet is inserted through holes that have been drilled or punched through the plates. The rivet's head is placed on an anvil or other support. A hammer or *pneumatic tool* is used to pound the rivet's tail, or *open* end. A pneumatic tool is a tool powered by compressed air. The rivet's tail expands to become a second head. The rivet is then said to be *closed*. It holds the two plates firmly together.

People use a wide variety of rivets and shaping tools. There are two main processes in riveting. One is called *cold heading*. In cold heading, soft metal rivets are shaped and closed without being heated. The cold forming of soft metal increases the rivet's strength. The second process, using heat, is often used to rivet together thick metal plates. In this process, large metal rivets are first heated to high temperatures. They are quickly placed through holes in the plates. Then the hot rivets are formed with a press or hammer. The heat makes the rivet soft, so that less force is required to close the tail.

Welding has replaced riveting for many uses. In welding, metal parts are fused together, without the use of a fastener. Parts of boilers, bridges, and ships—once commonly riveted together—are now joined by welding. But riveting is still often used to join together thin sheets of metal parts—for example, the aluminum in aircraft wings and body panels. Rose M. Torielli and Robert C. Voigt

Riviera, *RIHV ee AIR uh,* is a narrow strip of land on the Mediterranean Sea. The region runs from Hyères in southern France to La Spezia in northwestern Italy. The Alps rise back of the Riviera. Each year, travelers from many parts of the world bask in the warm sunshine of the Riviera for both health and pleasure. Balmy southern breezes drift in from the Mediterranean Sea throughout the year. The Alps shut off the cold north and east winds.

A chain of French and Italian towns lies on the Riviera. They are connected by an excellent road that follows an ancient Roman highway. A railroad also links the towns together. The towns are colorful with brightly painted houses and green, fragrant gardens. The people of the Riviera cultivate bananas, dates, flowers, pomegranates, and prickly pears.

The towns along the Riviera include Antibes, Cannes, Hyères, Menton, Nice, and St. Tropez in France; Monte Carlo in Monaco; and Albenga, Genoa, La Spezia, Rapallo, San Remo, Savona, and Ventimiglia in Italy.

William M. Reddy

See also **Cannes; France** (picture); **Monaco; Nice.**

© Marc Riboud, Magnum

Riyadh is the capital and largest city of Saudi Arabia. Oil income has made it one of the world's fastest-growing cities. Riyadh features modern skyscrapers and wide, busy streets.

Riyadh, *ree YAHD* (pop. 5,188,286), is the capital and largest city of Saudi Arabia. Riyadh lies among oases on a dry, rocky plateau near the center of the country (see **Saudi Arabia** [political map]). Riyadh is a business center and serves as the administrative headquarters of Saudi Arabia's vast oil industry. The city is also the center of Wahhabism, a conservative form of Sunni Islam.

Since the mid-1970's, when Saudi Arabia's oil income increased dramatically, Riyadh has been one of the fastest-growing cities in the world. Hundreds of thousands of people have moved from rural areas of Saudi Arabia and from other countries to Riyadh in search of employment.

High-rise office buildings and large homes of concrete, steel, and marble have replaced nearly all of Riyadh's old mud-brick buildings. Wide avenues and highways have taken the place of most narrow, unpaved streets. Many schools and hospitals have also been built in Riyadh. The Saudi government has laid a pipeline to help supply the city's residents with water. The pipeline extends 290 miles (467 kilometers) between Riyadh and Al Jubayl on the Persian Gulf coast. It delivers *desalinated* seawater—that is, seawater from which the salt has been removed. In the 1980's, a huge embassy complex,

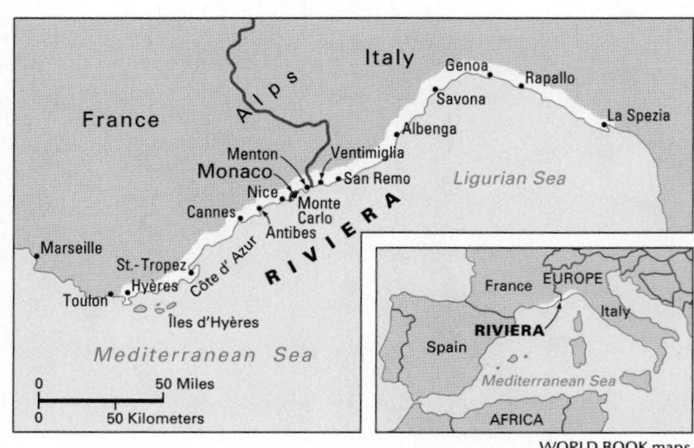

WORLD BOOK maps

The Riviera lies on Europe's Mediterranean coast.

called the Diplomatic Quarter, was built in Riyadh to accommodate diplomatic missions to Saudi Arabia. Previously, such missions had their embassies in Jiddah.

Riyadh has numerous public gardens, parks, children's playgrounds, and a zoo. A covered stadium in the city hosts international sports events. The Riyadh Museum displays objects from the country's past. King Saud University Museum in Riyadh exhibits items from the university's archaeological excavations. The university itself is the largest one in Saudi Arabia.

The Saudi government, which controls the country's oil industry, is Riyadh's largest employer. Factories there produce aluminum, chemicals, china, paper, plastics, prefabricated houses, and many other products. A railroad links Riyadh to Ad Dammam on the Persian Gulf. King Khalid International Airport serves the city.

Riyadh became the center of Wahhabism after Egyptian forces destroyed the nearby town of Dariyah, capital of the Wahhabi empire, in 1818. The Saud family controlled Riyadh from 1824 to 1891, when they were expelled by a rival group. They retook the town in 1902. Riyadh then became the capital of the growing Saudi territory, which was recognized as the Kingdom of Saudi Arabia in 1932. Eleanor Abdella Doumato

See also **Saudi Arabia** (History).

Rizal, *ree ZAHL,* **José,** *hoh SAY* (1861-1896), a Filipino doctor and novelist, became a national hero of the Philippines. He was an early leader of the Filipino movement for political and social freedom from Spain. The Spaniards, who ruled the Philippines at the time, executed Rizal for his activities.

José Mercado y Alonso Rizal was born on June 19, 1861, in Calamba, the Philippines. After obtaining his qualifications in medicine in Madrid, Spain, Rizal traveled to Germany, England, and France, where he continued to study medicine. He wrote for *La Solidaridad,* a magazine published in Barcelona, Spain, that campaigned for reforms in the Philippines.

While living in Europe, Rizal gained worldwide attention with two novels. *Noli Me Tangere* (Latin for *Touch Me Not*) was published in Berlin in 1887. Rizal's second book, *El Filibusterismo (The Subversive),* was published in Belgium in 1891. Both novels exposed the ills of the Spanish colonial government and Filipino society. Spanish colonial authorities considered the books dangerously radical and had them banned.

While conducting research at the British Museum in London, Rizal came across a history of the Philippines written by Antonio de Morga in 1609. Morga's book described an attractive civilization in the Philippines before Spanish colonization. In 1890, Rizal printed a new edition of the history with his own notes added to the text.

In 1892, Rizal returned to Manila, where he founded *La Liga Filipina* (the Philippine League) on July 3. The League was a partly secret association devoted to promoting unity and reforming the colony. On July 6, Rizal was arrested and exiled to the Philippine island of Mindanao.

In 1896, the Katipunan, a secret Filipino revolutionary society, tried to overthrow the Spanish government. Though Rizal had no connection with the Katipunan or the uprising, a Spanish military court found him guilty of promoting the rebellion. On the morning of Dec. 30, 1896, Rizal was executed by firing squad.

Rizal, a gifted linguist, was said to have understood 22 languages. He also was a novelist, poet, essayist, historian, musician, painter, and sculptor. James Putzel

RNA, also known as *ribonucleic acid,* is a complex molecule that plays a major role in all living cells. RNA molecules help produce substances called *proteins.* Proteins are chains of smaller organic molecules known as *amino acids.* The body uses proteins to build cells and to carry out the cells' work.

RNA is similar in structure to *DNA (deoxyribonucleic acid),* another important molecule found in cells. Like DNA, all RNA molecules contain hundreds of smaller chemical units called *nucleotides.* These nucleotides are bonded together chemically to form thin, chainlike molecules called *polynucleotides.* Unlike DNA, each RNA molecule consists of a single polynucleotide chain. A DNA molecule has two chains. In addition, RNA occurs throughout the cell, while DNA is found mainly in the cell's nucleus.

RNA nucleotides contain a compound called a *phosphate,* a sugar called *ribose,* and a compound called a *base.* The phosphate and sugar are the same in all RNA nucleotides, but the bases vary. There are four RNA bases: (1) *adenine,* (2) *guanine,* (3) *cytosine,* and (4) *uracil.*

Different types of RNA perform different jobs. One type, known as *messenger RNA* or *mRNA,* copies chemical instructions from DNA for making proteins. The mRNA then leaves the nucleus and carries the instructions to protein-making cell structures called *ribosomes.* These instructions tell the cell how to put amino acids together in the right order to make a specific protein. Some RNA molecules act as enzymes to speed up certain chemical reactions.

Another type of RNA is called *transfer RNA* or *tRNA.* A tRNA molecule collects amino acids and brings them to the ribosome. A third type of RNA, *ribosomal RNA* or *rRNA,* is an important physical component of ribosomes.

Irwin Rubenstein

See also **Cell; DNA; Heredity.**

Roach. See **Cockroach.**

Roach is a fish of the carp and minnow family that lives in slightly salty lowland rivers and lakes in Europe. It is caught for sport and for food. The fish usually grows 6 to 8 inches (15 to 20 centimeters) in length, but may reach a length of 14 inches (36 centimeters). The roach is silvery, with a greenish back. The iris of the eye is bright red. The name *roach* is also given to a large American minnow called the *golden shiner.* David W. Greenfield

Scientific classification. The scientific name for the roach is *Rutilus rutilus.*

Road is a strip of land that provides routes for travel by automobiles and other wheeled vehicles. Roads within towns and cities are often called *streets.*

Roads and highways are vital lifelines. Farmers use them to ship their products to market. Trucks can transport manufactured products from one area to another. Roads carry automobiles, buses, bicycles, and other vehicles on business and pleasure trips.

Kinds of roads and highways

Local and secondary roads. *Local roads* carry traffic within a local area. *Secondary roads* link small communities and connect local roads to main highways leading to more distant places.

Primary highways. The most important roads generally are those that carry the greatest number of automobiles, trucks, and buses. These main roads, called *primary highways,* connect the larger communities.

Major types of primary highways include *divided highways* and *controlled access highways.* Divided highways are roads with four or more traffic lanes divided in the center with a strip of land, called a *median strip.* This strip separates vehicles going in opposite directions and helps prevent collisions.

Controlled access highways are designed to achieve safety and smooth traffic flow through the principle of *controlled access.* On fully controlled access highways, a vehicle can enter or leave a main highway only at certain locations called *interchanges.* Most of these interchanges are at main crossroads. *Grade separations* are often used to separate crossing streams of traffic. In a grade separation, one of the intersecting highways crosses over the other on a bridge. The two are connected by sloping, curved roadways called *ramps.*

With controlled access, no driveways from homes or commercial establishments connect directly with the main highway. Minor roads and streets pass over or under the road without connecting to it. Minor roads may also dead-end at the highway or connect with a service road that runs parallel to the highway.

Freeways or *superhighways,* called *motorways* in some countries, are main highways with full access control and grade-separated interchanges. Those with four or more lanes are divided by a median strip. Freeways in congested parts of large cities are often *elevated* (built above surface streets) or *depressed* (built below surface streets). The term *freeway* refers only to the free flow of traffic. Motorists may have to pay a toll to travel on these roads. Roads that require a toll are called *tollways* or *toll roads.*

Expressways are similar to freeways but sometimes have only partial access control. *Parkways* are roads resembling freeways. But they are built in parklike surroundings with attractive landscaping and scenery. Most parkways are limited to passenger vehicles.

Freeways and other roads are numbered to help travelers. In some countries, roads are designated by a combination of numbers and letters. In the United Kingdom, for example, freeways are designated by the letter M and a number, while minor roads begin with the letter B. The letters and numbers that represent the roads appear on road signs and on maps.

Signs on freeways and expressways alert drivers to exits and indicate the distance to the next rest area or service area with fuel and restaurant facilities. Emergency warning signs may be posted to tell drivers to slow down when approaching road construction or some type of hazard.

How roads and highways are built

Planning. Highway planners study everything from the long-range needs of a region or an entire country to a particular section of a single route. This planning determines what the highway needs of the region are and how these needs can best be fulfilled and paid for.

Much road work involves improving existing roads. This may mean paving over a dirt road that is experiencing increasing traffic. New roads may be needed to cope with increasing traffic or to connect with a new town or development area.

In planning a system or a route, planners must learn: (1) where people live, (2) where they want to go, (3) by what means and route they get there, (4) where goods are produced, (5) what markets the goods are sent to, and (6) how the goods reach their final users. Traffic counts tell how many and what kinds of vehicles travel on a road, and when traffic is heaviest. From these and other facts about the past and present, planners try to predict future growth in population and industry, changes in land use, and how such growth and change will affect highway needs.

Public participation in road planning is essential. In many countries, planners hold public hearings on most major highway projects. These meetings enable citizens to present their views before a project begins.

Engineers have set standards for various kinds of roads, highways, and bridges. These standards govern the thickness and kind of foundation and surfacing for different kinds of traffic; the number of lanes needed; the sharpness of curves; and the steepness of hills.

Engineers run tests where a new road is to be built to find out how the soil's properties differ when it is wet or dry. Such tests help determine the weight of traffic the road can support.

In planning a new road or rebuilding an existing one, maps must be drawn if they are not already available. These maps show the location of other roads, railroads, towns, farms, houses, and other buildings. They also show such natural features as rivers, lakes, forests, hills, and the slope of the land. Soil types may be identified.

Using these maps, engineers locate new highways and make drawings called *plans,* which show the boundaries of the *right of way.* The right of way is land needed for road pavement, shoulders, ditches, and side slopes. The plans also show the location, grades, and curves of the pavement, and the location of bridges and culverts.

In the United States, highway planners must also prepare an *environmental impact statement* before beginning construction. The purpose of such a statement is to discover in advance all the possible good and bad effects that a new highway may have on the public and on the environment.

Bypasses are built to take motorists around cities. Motorists traveling some distance often do not want to drive through small towns or the centers of large cities that lie on their routes. Those traveling from one part of a city to another also usually prefer to avoid downtown traffic. The bypass helps these motorists avoid city traffic, and reduces traffic congestion for those who want to drive into town.

Bypasses are usually built as freeways, sometimes with service roads on one or both sides to serve local traffic. In large cities, a bypass may be called a *circumferential* or a *beltway.*

Intersections, called *junctions* in some countries, are crossings of one road by another. Most intersections are at the same level, so that vehicles going east and west have to take turns crossing with vehicles going north and south. Sometimes roads intersect at odd angles, and it is especially difficult to make a safe crossing. At such places, the traffic engineer may put *islands* in the paved

A typical design for a paved road

WORLD BOOK illustration by Oxford Illustrators Limited

Subgrade is the natural soil that forms the roadbed. The soil is either naturally firm, or is leveled off and packed by heavy machines.

Base provides support for the surface and prevents moisture from forming under it. Materials include sand, stone, and bitumen or portland cement.

Surface, or wearing course, is smooth, firm, and water-shedding. This pavement has a concrete surface. Many pavements have bituminous surfaces.

Shoulders are wide for safe emergency stopping, and sloped for proper drainage. They often have an asphalt surface and a gravel or soil-cement base.

area to keep traffic in the proper paths. The best and safest kind of intersection is the grade-separated interchange. One common type of interchange is called a *cloverleaf,* because its curved inner ramps form the pattern of a four-leaf clover. A simpler kind is called a *diamond* because its ramps form that shape. Diamonds often connect a major highway and a secondary road. When two freeways intersect, more complex interchanges are sometimes needed. These may require a number of bridges and many ramps.

Grading. The first job in building a new highway is to clear the right of way. There may be trees to cut down and stumps to pull up. Sometimes buildings must be torn down or moved. The right of way then is ready for rough grading. At this stage, huge machines called earth movers, which can dig up a roomful of dirt in one scoop, are used. They cut into the hills, carry the earth along, and drop it into the valleys to make a road with gentle grades. This method is known as *cut-and-fill construction.*

Sometimes, the right kind of earth to be used for the foundation of the road must be hauled in, perhaps from some distance away. While the grading is going on, *culverts* (pipes to carry away rain water) are put in place under the road or under driveway entrances. Ditches are cut at the roadsides to carry rain water to the culverts. After the right-of-way is shaped roughly for traffic lanes, shoulders, and ditches, it is smoothed and packed down to the required level and shape.

Paving begins after grading is completed. The pavement is of definite thickness and is of stronger materials than the earth underneath. The kind and thickness of pavements depend largely on the weight and amount of traffic expected to use them.

In some places, different kinds of earth or soil are mixed together to form a pavement. Certain chemicals, lime, cement, or *bitumens* (asphalts and tars) may also be mixed with soil to act as a binder and to make it harder and more durable. On most of the low-traffic surfaced roads, however, the pavements are of gravel, crushed rock, or other mined materials. These types of pavements may be given a thin surfacing of bitumens known as *seal coat.*

Roads that carry heavy traffic must have a durable surface. An intermediate type of surfacing is called *bituminous macadam.* This is made by placing crushed stone or gravel on the roadbed, packing it down firmly, and filling the spaces with a bitumen. Better types of bituminous surfacing are made with sand, gravel, or crushed stone premixed with bitumens. These types of surfacing are laid with a paving machine, and then rolled hard and smooth. Bituminous pavement is sometimes referred to as *blacktop.*

Another hard surfacing material is portland cement concrete. It is made with sand, portland cement, water, and gravel or crushed stone. In both kinds of surfacing—bituminous and portland cement concrete—the *aggregate* (stone and sand) forms the body of the material and the bitumen or portland cement serves as a binder.

As roads are built, they are inspected continually, and tests are also made on the construction materials. After a road is finished, drilling machines take core samples of the paving and the base. Engineers use these samples to be sure that the finished paving is as thick and as strong as was planned.

Storm-water drainage. Storm-water runoff from paved highways and parking lots may contain oil, exhaust emissions, and other dangerous chemicals from vehicles. These chemicals once mixed with other storm water and entered rivers and streams. Many areas now require that highway projects include ditches or channels that direct storm water into temporary storage ponds. The water eventually evaporates or is absorbed into the ground. Storm-water storage facilities are also built near large parking areas.

Lighting. Good lighting helps reduce the number of accidents for both vehicles and pedestrians. On most roads and highways, nearly all the light comes from the headlights of the trucks and cars. But on busy streets and at dangerous rural locations, overhead lights are used. Reflectors for the lamps are designed specifically to shine most of the light down on the roadway without glaring into the eyes of drivers.

Noise control. The increased use of highways causes loud traffic noise, creating a problem for people who live nearby. For this reason, engineers have designed noise barriers made of concrete, wood, metal, plastic, and other materials that block sound. In some areas, trees, vegetation, or mounds of earth provide protection from traffic noise. Noise barriers are costly, but they successfully reduce highway noise in many areas.

Roadside improvement. Roadsides are often planted with special grasses or vines to keep the earth from washing into the ditches. In addition, many roadsides are beautified with trees and bushes. Such planting and landscaping help break the monotony of travel and make the countryside more attractive. Many areas have laws that prohibit putting billboards and other commercial signs close to the road. Many highways have turnouts of various types where travelers can stop to picnic, to refuel, or to admire a scenic view.

How roads and highways are maintained

Repairing damage and resurfacing. Roads and highways gradually wear out. The work of repairing and resurfacing is called *maintenance.* Maintenance also includes removing ice and snow, painting stripes on pavement, cutting grass, putting up signs, and caring for roadside shoulders, roadsides, and bridges.

Gravel and other similar type roads have to be smoothed quite often. Surfaces and edges of bituminous materials are repaired by patching with new material where worn spots develop from travel or because of weak spots in the ground underneath. Every 10 or 15 years, many roads with bituminous surfaces are resurfaced completely.

Workers repair concrete pavements by digging out broken sections and putting in new concrete. They often repair cracks by filling them with asphalt. Many older concrete pavements must be resurfaced completely.

Clearing ice and snow. Most roads and highways must serve the year around. So roads in cold regions must be kept free from snow and ice in the winter. In some places, *snow fences* are put up. These are thin pickets wired together and placed parallel to the road, on the side from which the storm winds usually blow, and about 50 to 100 feet (15 to 30 meters) from the road. Snowdrifts then form between the fence and the road instead of piling up in the road.

Trucks with V-shaped or straight-blade plows attached to the front clear the roads when it snows. In deep drifts, special snowplows are needed. Some of the most powerful snowplows are called *rotary plows.* Rotary plows have a big screw at the front that chews into the snowdrifts and pulls the snow back into a large fan. The fan shoots the snow to one side of the road. Often roads and highways that are slippery from ice and snow must have salt, chemicals, sand, or cinders spread on them to keep them passable.

How roads and highways are paid for

Roads and highways are built and maintained by local and national governments.

In the United States, local governments build and maintain most local and secondary roads, while state governments construct and care for primary highways. The federal government helps the states pay the cost of building and improving primary and secondary roads and streets. The routes are selected by the states.

State and local communities pay for roadbuilding and maintenance with tax receipts. Much of this money comes from taxes levied on highway and road users. Every state levies taxes on motor fuel and charges fees for registering motor vehicles. In some states, trucks and buses pay special fees. Some states levy a *weight-distance* or a *ton-mile* tax. This tax requires trucks to pay a set amount, based on the weight of the load and the distance it is carried.

Most highway-user taxes are spent only for roads and streets. Using this money for other purposes is called *diversion.* For example, some states set aside part of their motor fuel tax money for education. Constitutional amendments in many states prohibit such diversion.

Most states give part of the taxes they collect from highway users to local governments, to be spent on local roads. The local governments provide whatever additional money they need for roads, usually from general funds raised by property taxes.

State and local governments often borrow money to build roads. These loans, which are made by selling *bonds,* are repaid with tax money. Some state governments set aside part of their motor fuel tax money to repay these loans.

The cost of building many bridges and *turnpikes* (toll roads) is paid by the travelers who use them. Motorists pay a flat fee for crossing toll bridges. Fees for using turnpikes usually depend on how far the motorist travels. Large vehicles, such as trucks and trailers, usually pay more than passenger cars.

Since 1916, the federal government has aided states in building and improving the nation's highways. This aid reflects the federal government's interest in adequate roads for mail delivery, interstate commerce, national defense, and the general welfare of the country.

The federal-aid program was greatly expanded by legislation passed by Congress in 1956 and later years. Federal aid for primary and secondary roads and streets totals several billion dollars a year. The federal interstate highway system cost a total of about $100 billion over a period of about 40 years. The federal government paid 90 percent of the cost and the states 10 percent. To finance the interstate program, Congress established a highway trust fund. This fund receives money from taxes on motor fuel; tires; new trucks, trailers, and buses; and an annual tax on heavy vehicles. Construction or improvement of the roads is done by the states, with federal aid. The roads belong to the state or local governments, which must maintain them.

In other countries. Road and highway construction and maintenance in industrialized countries are financed in ways like those in the United States. In the United Kingdom, the national and local governments work together on issues concerning road improvement. In Australia, a part of a national gasoline tax, fees collected by the states for drivers' licenses, and local property taxes contribute to the funding for road construction and development.

Artstreet

Blacktopping a highway involves laying an asphalt mixture with a paving truck, *right.* The paver spreads the mixture to the desired thickness. A compacting machine, *left,* rolls the pavement hard and smooth. Workers heat and mix asphalt cement and crushed stone to make the paving material.

In less developed countries, funds for road construction may come from a development budget that is part of a country's total annual budget. The total budget is supported by customs duties, sales taxes, taxes on mined resources, and other revenues. Foreign investors often pay for the construction of roads in areas in which they operate businesses.

History of roads and highways

The first roads. Because roads are so old, experts are uncertain of the origin of the word *road.* Most think that it came from the Middle English word *rode,* meaning *a mounted journey.* This may have come from the Old English *rad,* from the word *ridan,* meaning *to ride.*

In England, hundreds of years ago, certain main roads were higher than the surrounding ground. This was because earth was thrown from the side ditches toward the center. Because they were higher, they were called *highways.* These roads were under protection of the king's men and were open to all travelers. Private roads were known as *byways.*

The first roads in the world probably followed trails and paths made by animals. These trails and paths led from feeding grounds to watering places. People followed these trails to hunt for animals. People also made their own trails and paths in searching for water, food, and fuel. Explorers followed these trails as they investigated new lands.

Early roads were built in the Near East about 3000 B.C., soon after the wheel was invented. As trade developed between villages, towns, and cities, other paths, or trade routes, were made. One such early system of roads was the Silk Road, which ran about 5,000 miles (8,050 kilometers), connecting China with Europe. Merchants used this ancient route to carry Chinese silk across Turkestan, India, and Persia.

The first road markers were piles of stones at intervals. Trails through forests were marked by *blazing* trees, or cutting a piece from the bark of the tree.

The Egyptians, Carthaginians, and Etruscans all built roads. But the first really great road builders were the Romans. They laid a solid base and gave the road a pavement of flat stones. The Romans knew that the road must slope slightly from the center toward both sides to drain off water. This gave the road a *crown.* The Roman road builders knew also that there must be ditches along the sides of the road to carry water away. Roman roads were built to assist in the movement of soldiers and for communication and trade throughout the Roman Empire. These roads ran in almost straight lines and passed over hills instead of cutting around them. The Romans built more than 50,000 miles (80,000 kilometers) of roads in their empire and some of them still are in use. See **Appian Way** (picture).

From the 500's to the 1800's, most roads in Europe were just clearings in the forests. Cobblestone paving was used in some urban areas. There was not much reason to build good roads, because most of the travel was on horseback. The cleared way was sometimes quite wide, so that robbers hiding in the woods could not leap out suddenly upon unsuspecting travelers.

In South America, from the 1200's to the 1500's, the Inca Indians built a network of 10,000 miles (16,000 kilometers) of roads. The roads connected their cities.

The first highway department was established in France in 1716. This department built Europe's finest gravel and stone roads of the 1700's using methods developed by Pierre M. J. Tresaguet, an engineer.

In the early 1800's, the person who did more for European roadbuilding than anyone else up to that time was John Loudon McAdam, a Scottish engineer. McAdam is remembered for the surface he developed for roads. This kind of surface, called *macadam,* is still used today. McAdam also stressed the importance of proper drainage to keep roads on a solid foundation.

Early American roads. The first settlers in North America found a wilderness. They located their homes along the rivers and bays and used the water for transportation. As new settlers went inland, they usually built crude roads to the nearest wharf. Until after the War of 1812, people traveled mainly on foot or on horseback.

The first extensive hard-surfaced road was completed in 1794. This road was called the Lancaster (Pennsylvania) Turnpike. It measured 62 miles (100 kilometers) long and was surfaced with hand-broken stone and gravel. In the next 40 years, many turnpikes were built. Most surfaces were of earth, gravel, or broken stone. Some roads were covered with logs or planks. Where logs were used, the roads were called *corduroy roads.* Both corduroy roads and plank roads were very bumpy.

In 1830, the steam locomotive was successfully operated, and rapid development of railroads began. Many people became convinced the railroad was the best way to travel long distances. From 1830 to 1900, there was little change in road and highway surfacing materials.

Modern roads. By 1900, there was a growing demand for good roads. Roads that extended a short distance were built in the United States to give farmers access to the railroads, which hauled farm products. The first freeway was completed in 1921 in the Grunewald, a forest area in Berlin, Germany. This road, which was 6 miles (10 kilometers) long, served as a route for suburban commuters and as a race track. Italy soon began building freeways. In 1925, the United States adopted its system of numbering highways, which was suggested by the Wisconsin highway engineer A. R. Hirst in 1917.

In 1934, Germany began building its Autobahn (expressway) system. This extensive system featured divided highways, grade-separated interchanges, and well-designed service areas. A section of the Pennsylvania Turnpike, the first U.S. freeway, opened in 1940. It ran between Middlesex (near Carlisle) and Irwin. In California, the Arroyo Seco Parkway opened in 1940 between Pasadena and Los Angeles. This and similar roads opened new suburban areas to development, and population often grew quickly where freeways were built. Few other highways were built from the Great Depression of the 1930's to the end of World War II in 1945. After the war, road construction in industrialized countries increased, as more and more families bought cars.

In the 1950's, many U.S. industry and civic groups supported highway improvement programs. The major work on the U.S. federal interstate highway system began in 1956. That system became part of the National Highway System in 1995.

The governments of many of the developing nations of Africa and Asia have begun modernization and industrialization programs that include the building of new roads. Industrialized nations continue to improve and expand their road systems. Engineers continue to seek ways of increasing highway safety through better construction. They also seek to improve traffic flow by using computers to help plan road systems. David Boyce

Related articles. See the *Transportation* section in the various state, province, and country articles. See also:

Some roads and highways

Alaska Highway
Appian Way
Boston Post Road
Burma Road
El Camino Real
Interstate Highway System
Lincoln Highway
National Road
Oregon Trail
Pan American Highway
Pennsylvania Turnpike
Route 66
San Francisco (picture: The Crookedest Street)
Trans-Canada Highway
United States (map: The U.S. interstate highway system)

Construction and maintenance

Asphalt
Bridge
Bulldozer
Cement and concrete
Electric light
Eminent domain
Gravel
Lighting
Traffic
Tunnel
Viaduct

Other related articles

Automobile
Bus
Gasoline tax
Interstate commerce
McAdam, John Loudon
Rome, Ancient (Transportation and communication)
Safety (Safety in transportation)
Telford, Thomas
Transportation
Truck
Turnpike

Roadrunner is the name for two swift, ground-dwelling birds found in brushy deserts and woodlands of the southwestern United States, Mexico, and Central America. Roadrunners can fly, but they are most at home on the ground. They can run faster than 15 miles (24 kilometers) per hour. The name *roadrunner* comes from the birds' habit of racing down roads in front of moving vehicles and then darting to safety in the brush. Other names for the birds include *chaparral cock, ground cuckoo, paisano,* and *snake killer.*

The two types of roadrunners differ chiefly in size and where they live. The *greater roadrunner* measures nearly 2 feet (61 centimeters) in length and lives in Mexico and the United States. The *lesser roadrunner* grows about 18 inches (46 centimeters) long and is found in Mexico and Central America. Both species have slim bodies with long tails comprising nearly half of their length. They have long, sturdy legs and a slender, pointed bill. The mostly brown upper body has black streaks and white spots. The neck and upper breast are white or pale brown with dark brown streaks. The belly is white. A shaggy crest of brown feathers sticks up on the head. A bare patch of red-and-blue skin lies behind each eye.

Roadrunners eat chiefly baby birds, gophers, insects, lizards, mice, and snakes. The birds kill their larger prey by beating it against a hard object and then swallowing it whole. Roadrunners build a cup-shaped nest of sticks in a low tree or a clump of cactuses. They line the nest with leaves, grass, and other soft materials. The female roadrunner lays from two to eight white or yellowish eggs. Both the male and female incubate the eggs and feed the young. Sandra L. Vehrencamp

Scientific classification. Roadrunners belong to the genus *Geococcyx.* The scientific name of the greater roadrunner is *Geococcyx californianus.* The lesser roadrunner is *G. velox.*

See also **Bird** (picture: Birds of the desert).

Roanoke, *ROH uh* NOHK (pop. 97,032; met. area pop. 308,707), is a city on the Roanoke River in Virginia. It lies between the Blue Ridge and Allegheny mountains (see **Virginia** [political map]). Roanoke is a railroad center and the major retail, financial, and health care center for western Virginia. It also serves as a convention center.

Manufacturers in the Roanoke Valley produce electronic equipment, fiber optics, furniture, night vision goggles, and robots. Schools in the Roanoke area include Hollins University, Radford University, Roanoke College, and Virginia Polytechnic Institute and State University. The city has a symphony orchestra. The Virginia Museum of Transportation is in Roanoke.

Roanoke was originally the small pioneer settlement of Big Lick, named after a large salt marsh where deer fed. In 1882, the Norfolk and Western and the Shenandoah railroads made a junction at Big Lick. The town was renamed Roanoke the same year and became a city in 1884. The name *Roanoke* comes from the Indian word *Rawenoke,* meaning *shell money.*

Roanoke has a council-manager form of government. For the monthly weather, see **Virginia** (Climate).

Susan L. Woodward

Roanoke Island. See **Lost Colony.**

Roaring Twenties was the period of the 1920's in the United States. The Roaring Twenties were years of rapid economic growth, rising prosperity for many people, and far-reaching social changes for the nation. The period is sometimes called the *Jazz Age,* because of the new style of music and the pleasure-seeking people who made it popular. It is also called the *Tribal Twenties,* because of the rise of *nativism* (hostility toward foreigners). This nativism led to immigration restrictions and the growth of the Ku Klux Klan, a white secret society.

More than 116,000 American soldiers had died in World War I (1914-1918), answering President Woodrow Wilson's call to "make the world safe for democracy." After the war ended, large numbers of Americans wanted to forget about the troubles of Europeans and return to a normal life. But the war had brought many changes that set the stage for social and cultural clashes during the 1920's. Spurred on by new prosperity and a desire to be "modern," large numbers of Americans adopted new attitudes and lifestyles. They listened to jazz, drank bootleg liquor, and enjoyed other new thrills. Many other Americans, however, strongly disapproved of what they saw as immoral behavior and tried to enforce a national prohibition of alcoholic beverages.

Rising prosperity. During the economic expansion of the Roaring Twenties, business profits boomed and the living standard rose for most Americans. From 1922 to 1929, the national income increased more than 40 percent, from $60.7 billion annually to $87.2 billion. The increased use of labor-saving machinery in factories and on farms enabled workers to produce more goods faster and less expensively.

Several new major industries expanded in the 1920's. More and more people could afford to buy the Model T, the inexpensive automobile that Henry Ford had developed in 1908. The number of passenger cars in the United States jumped from fewer than 7 million in 1919 to about 23 million in 1929. Traffic jammed the nation's highways and created a need for gas stations, roadside restaurants, tire manufacturers, and other businesses.

Radio also helped the economy. The value of radio sales in the United States jumped from $60 million in 1922 to almost $850 million in 1929. Popular network programs, such as "Amos 'n' Andy" and "The Philco Hour," provided an effective method of advertising products to a nationwide audience. Radio commercials persuaded listeners to spend a larger share of their rising income. Stores developed installment payment plans and urged customers to "Buy now, pay later." Higher wages and the use of credit enabled millions of Americans to purchase their first automobile, refrigerator, and washing machine.

During the 1920's, most Americans came to regard big business as the foundation of society. They agreed with President Calvin Coolidge that "the business of America is business." Coolidge's comment symbolized the spirit of the era. Republican candidates—Warren G. Harding, Coolidge, and Herbert Hoover—won all three presidential elections of the 1920's. Their policies reflected the belief that the economy can best regulate itself without government controls. Americans bought millions of copies of *The Man Nobody Knows* by Bruce Barton, the best-selling nonfiction book of 1925 and 1926. It called Jesus Christ the founder of modern business because he "picked twelve humble men and created an organization that won the world."

John J. Raskob, vice president of the DuPont Company and the General Motors Corporation, declared that anyone who invested $15 a month in the stock market could make $80,000 in 20 years. Such promises of wealth persuaded many Americans to buy stocks. Stock prices had risen gradually since the early 1920's, but they skyrocketed in 1927 and 1928. The average price of stocks on the New York Stock Exchange nearly tripled from 1925 to 1929. The high profits seemed to confirm President Hoover's pledge of a new era of abundance, in which "poverty will be banished from this nation."

Changing attitudes toward foreign relations, society, and leisure revolutionized American life in the 1920's. After World War I, many Americans demanded that the United States stay out of European political affairs. The Senate refused to approve the Treaty of Versailles, which officially ended the war with Germany and provided for the establishment of the League of Nations, a forerunner of the United Nations. Some senators argued that League membership could involve the United States in future European wars.

Industrial unrest and a fear of *radicalism* (desire for extreme changes or reforms) set off a nationwide panic called the Red Scare. Many Americans blamed what they regarded as an international Communist conspiracy for various protest movements and union activities in 1919 and 1920. They believed that immigrants from southern and eastern Europe were promoting radical ideas, and they called for restrictions on immigration. The Immigration Act of 1924 limited the number of immigrants from outside the Western Hemisphere.

Millions of white Americans joined a secret organization called the Ku Klux Klan. The Klan targeted blacks, Jews, Roman Catholics, and foreigners as threats to what it called "100 percent Americanism." The Klan attracted men and women from throughout the Midwest, West, and South.

Bettmann Archive

This fashionable couple wore raccoon coats for a drive in their 1928 Chrysler. The woman is sitting in an open compartment called a *rumble seat.*

Political corruption made front-page headlines during the Roaring Twenties. Albert B. Fall, secretary of the interior under President Harding, was convicted of accepting a $400,000 bribe from two oil companies. Fall had arranged to secretly lease these companies three government oil reserves, including one at Teapot Dome, Wyoming (see **Teapot Dome**).

Breaking the law became fashionable after the 18th Amendment to the Constitution went into effect in 1920. This amendment prohibited the manufacture and sale of alcoholic beverages. After prohibition began, thousands of Americans began to make their own liquor at home or bought liquor provided by underworld gangs. Gangsters bootlegged liquor from Canada, supplied it to illegal bars called *speakeasies,* and bribed the police not to interfere. More than 500 gangland murders occurred as underworld mobs fought for control of the liquor traffic.

Many people feared that morality had completely deteriorated. Before World War I, women had worn long hair, ankle-length dresses, and long cotton stockings. But in the 1920's, many wore short, tight dresses and rolled their silk stockings down to their knees. They cut their hair in a boyish style called the *bob* and wore bright lipstick and other cosmetics. Couples danced cheek-to-cheek to blaring jazz music.

Most Americans kept busy having a good time. Radio was a major source of family entertainment. Families gathered in their living rooms in the evening to listen to comedies, dramas, and other programs. Charlie Chaplin, Mary Pickford, Rudolph Valentino, and other motion-picture stars attracted crowds to theaters. Sports fans jammed stadiums to watch such top athletes as home run slugger Babe Ruth and boxing champion Jack Dempsey. Charles A. Lindbergh, the "Lone Eagle," received a hero's welcome after making the first solo nonstop airplane flight across the Atlantic Ocean. Alvin (Shipwreck) Kelly won nationwide fame by sitting on top of a flagpole for 23 days and 7 hours.

Cultural trends. The literature, art, and music of the 1920's reflected the nation's changing values. In his novel *Main Street* (1920), Sinclair Lewis attacked what he considered the dull lives and narrow-minded attitudes of people in a small town. Many American authors, including F. Scott Fitzgerald and Ernest Hemingway, lived in Paris during the period. Some of their finest works present the attitudes and experiences of the era's so-called Lost Generation. H. L. Mencken, in his witty magazine *The American Mercury,* ridiculed the antics of dim-witted politicians, prohibitionists, and others.

Artists and composers were inspired by both the traditions and changes in American life. Joseph Stella painted soaring lines and precise geometric patterns to represent skyscrapers, his favorite theme. The paintings of Edward Hopper show the loneliness experienced by some people—even among familiar surroundings. George Gershwin became the most popular composer of the 1920's. His best-known orchestral works, *Rhapsody in Blue* (1924) and *An American in Paris* (1928), feature many elements of jazz.

The end of an era. By 1929, the U.S. economy was in serious trouble despite the soaring profits in the stock market. Since the end of World War I in 1918, farm prices had dropped about 40 percent below their prewar level. Farm profits fell so low that many farmers could not pay their debts to banks. Partly as a result, about 550 banks went out of business between July 1928 and June 1929. In addition, industrial production rose about four times as fast as wages. People could not afford to buy goods as fast as industry manufactured them.

The illusion of unending prosperity was shattered on Oct. 24, 1929, when stock values plunged. Worried investors who had bought stock on credit began to sell it. A panic developed, and on October 29, stockholders sold a record 16,410,030 shares. By mid-November, stock prices had dropped about 40 percent. The stock market crash led to the Great Depression and brought an end to the Roaring Twenties. Lisa Maria McGirr

Related articles in ***World Book*** include:

Chicago (The Roaring Twenties)
Fitzgerald, F. Scott
Great Depression
Held, John, Jr.
Jazz (The 1920's)
Ness, Eliot
Prohibition
United States, History of the (The Roaring Twenties)

Rob Roy (1671-1734) was a famous Scottish outlaw whose real name was Robert MacGregor. *Roy* is a Gaelic word meaning *red.* MacGregor became known as Rob Roy because of his red hair and ruddy skin.

Rob Roy was born on Feb. 1, 1671, at Glengyle, near Loch Lomond. He inherited land from his father and was a nephew of a chieftain of the MacGregor clan. Rob Roy probably combined cattle trading with stealing cattle and with threatening to steal his neighbors' cattle if they did not pay him "protection" money. But charges that, in 1711, he fled with money that various people had given him to purchase cattle for them were never supported.

Rob Roy participated in the Jacobite rebellion of 1715. The rebellion sought to restore the Scottish House of Stuart to the British throne after George I of the House of Hanover had gained the throne in 1714. The rebellion was easily crushed. In 1722, British authorities captured Rob Roy. He was imprisoned for participating in the rebellion and sentenced to exile. But he was later pardoned. Rob Roy died on Dec. 28, 1734. The Scottish writer Sir Walter Scott gave a romantic, fictionalized account of Rob Roy's adventures in his novel *Rob Roy* (1817).

James Anthony Sharpe

Robbery means stealing money or goods from a person by violence or threats of immediate physical harm. This crime is a *felony* punishable by imprisonment. The value of the property taken has little influence in determining the legal penalty, so long as the property is of value to its owner. Robbery with a gun is usually considered more serious than simple robbery. *Carjacking* is a type of robbery in which the thief steals an automobile. Robbery occurs only when a thief uses force or threats to obtain something from a person. Stealing without using force or threats is called *larceny. Burglary* is the act of entering a home or business without permission for the purpose of committing a crime. Charles F. Wellford

See also **Bandit; Burglary; Felony; Larceny; Pirate.**

Robbins, Jerome (1918-1998), was an American dancer and *choreographer* (dance creator). He became well known to dance audiences in 1944, when he created his first ballet, *Fancy Free.* He achieved more widespread fame as the director and choreographer of many Broadway musicals, including *The King and I* (1951), *West Side*

Story (1957), and *Fiddler on the Roof* (1964). In these musicals, he blended the acting, singing, and dancing into a unified work of art. Robbins and Robert Wise shared the 1961 Academy Award as best director for *West Side Story.* Robbins again began to focus primarily on the ballet with his creation of *Les Noces* in 1965. Many of his ballets are based on American subjects. Others are abstract in nature and modern in style. They often include jazz rhythms.

Robbins was born on Oct. 11, 1918, in New York City. His real name was Jerome Wilson Rabinowitz. He was a member of Ballet Theatre from 1940 to 1948 and associate artistic director of the New York City Ballet from 1949 until 1959. He became ballet master of the New York City Ballet in 1969 and was ballet master in chief with Peter Martins from 1983 until Robbins's resignation in 1990. Robbins died on July 29, 1998. Selma Landen Odom

Roberts, Charles G. D. (1860-1943), was a Canadian author. His finest works are romantic poems of nature and country life that display his sensitive feeling for the landscape and wildlife of his native New Brunswick.

Roberts's first book of verse was *Orion and Other Poems* (1880). His successful use of traditional poetic forms and themes in this book influenced many other young Canadian poets. Roberts's sonnet sequence *Songs of the Common Day* (1893) contains some of his finest poems of rural life. Roberts also wrote much prose, including A *History of Canada* (1897) and a number of historical novels. Several of these historical novels were romances set in colonial North America. He won international fame for animal stories, many of which were collected in *The Last Barrier and Other Stories* (published in 1958).

Roberts was born on Jan. 10, 1860, in Douglas, near Fredericton, New Brunswick. In 1935, King George V knighted him. He became Sir Charles Roberts. He died on Nov. 26, 1943. Rosemary Sullivan

Roberts, John Glover, Jr. (1955-), became chief justice of the United States in 2005. The post is the highest on the Supreme Court of the United States. President George W. Bush named Roberts to fill the vacancy created by the death of Chief Justice William H. Rehnquist.

Roberts had served as a judge on the U.S. Court of Appeals for the District of Columbia Circuit. He had previously held positions in two Republican presidential administrations. He was known as a conservative.

Roberts was born Jan. 27, 1955, in Buffalo, New York. He grew up in Indiana, where his family moved when he was a boy. Roberts graduated from Harvard College in 1976 and from Harvard Law School in 1979. In 1980, he became a law clerk for Rehnquist, who was then a Supreme Court associate justice. Roberts served as associate counsel on President Ronald Reagan's staff from 1982 to 1986. From 1989 to 1993, Roberts was principal deputy solicitor general under President George H. W. Bush. Roberts practiced law for a private firm from 1986 to 1989 and from 1993 to 2003. As deputy solicitor general and as a lawyer in private practice, he argued 39 cases before the Supreme Court. He was appointed a federal appeals court judge in 2003. Dennis J. Hutchinson

Roberts, Owen Josephus (1875-1955), served as a justice of the Supreme Court of the United States from 1930 to 1945. President Calvin Coolidge appointed Roberts to prosecute the "oil scandal" cases arising from the leasing of public lands to the oil industry in 1924 (see **Teapot Dome**). In 1930, President Herbert Hoover appointed him to the Supreme Court. Roberts was born on May 2, 1875, in Philadelphia. He graduated from the University of Pennsylvania in 1898. He died on May 15, 1955. Bruce Allen Murphy

Robertson, Oscar (1938-), became one of the greatest scorers and passers in basketball history. He played for the Cincinnati Royals of the National Basketball Association (NBA) from the 1960-1961 season through the 1969-1970 season and for the Milwaukee Bucks from the 1970-1971 season through the 1973-1974 season, after which he retired. During his professional career, Robertson had 9,887 *assists*—passes to teammates that resulted in field goals. This total was an NBA record until 1991, when Magic Johnson broke it. John Stockton is the current career assists leader. Robertson also became the second NBA player to score over 25,000 points. Wilt Chamberlain was the first. Robertson was the NBA's Most Valuable Player in 1964.

Robertson was born on Nov. 24, 1938, in Charlotte, Tennessee. He is 6 feet 5 inches (196 centimeters) tall and was nicknamed the "Big O." He was an all-America guard for three seasons at the University of Cincinnati. Robertson's autobiography was published in 2003 as *The Big O: My Life, My Times, My Game.* Bob Logan

See also **Basketball** (picture).

Roberval, *raw behr val,* **Jean François de La Roque,** *zhahn frahn swah duh luh rohk,* **Sieur de,** *syur duh* (1500?-1560), was a French nobleman and soldier and an explorer and colonizer in Canada. He made the first French effort to establish a permanent colony in America, but failed.

King Francis I appointed Roberval lieutenant general of Canada in 1541. The next year, Roberval sailed to Canada with about 200 colonists. In waters near Newfoundland, he met the French navigator Jacques Cartier. Cartier had spent the winter near what is now Quebec City and was returning to France. Roberval and the colonists reoccupied Cartier's settlement. They explored the St. Lawrence River from what is now the Montreal area to the mouth of the Saguenay River, in search of a fabled kingdom of gold. But the winter of 1543 was marked by famine, disease, and mutiny, and so later that year, Roberval returned to France with the few surviving colonists. S. Dale Standen

Robeson, *ROHB suhn,* **Paul** (1898-1976), was a black American singer, actor, and political activist. He had a significant impact on the United States and the world.

Robeson was born on April 9, 1898, in Princeton, New Jersey. He attended Rutgers University, where he starred in four sports and twice was named an all-America end in football. He was class valedictorian and a member of Phi Beta Kappa, the national college honor society.

Culver
Paul Robeson

In 1923, Robeson earned a degree from the Columbia University Law School. He then began a long and successful career as an actor and singer. He performed on the stage and on radio and made many motion pictures and phonograph records. Robeson gained international acclaim for his performances in such plays as *Othello* and *The Emperor Jones.* In addition, in 1928, he appeared as Joe in the London premiere of the musical *Show Boat,* gaining praise for his performance of the song "Ol' Man River." He also won praise for his moving interpretations of black spirituals and the folk music of many countries.

In the late 1930's, Robeson became involved with national and international movements for peace, racial justice, and better labor conditions. He also supported independence for African colonies from their European rulers. This involvement, his friendship with the Soviet Union, and his association with Communists brought strong opposition from conservative groups in the United States. In 1950, the U.S. government canceled Robeson's passport. Although his musical and theatrical career declined sharply as a result of the opposition, he continued his political work.

In 1945, Robeson won the Spingarn Medal, the highest honor given by the National Association for the Advancement of Colored People. In 1958, Robeson regained his passport and moved to London, where he resumed his acting and singing career. He returned to the United States in 1963 because of ill health and lived there in retirement until his death on Jan. 23, 1976. Robeson described his political beliefs in a book called *Here I Stand* (1958). Eloise Greenfield

See also **Shakespeare, William** (picture: *Othello*).

Robespierre, *ROHBZ peer* or *ROHBZ pee air* (1758-1794), was the most famous and controversial leader of the French Revolution (1789-1799). In the name of democracy, he helped bring about the Reign of Terror, a period in which thousands of suspected opponents of the revolution were executed. In time, Robespierre met the same fate.

Maximilien Robespierre was born on May 6, 1758, in Arras. He studied at the College of Louis-le-Grand in Paris and became a successful lawyer. Robespierre was greatly influenced by the philosopher Jean-Jacques Rousseau, who argued that the right to govern came from the people.

In 1789, Robespierre was elected to the Estates-General, an assembly the king called to deal with a financial crisis in France. There, Robespierre distinguished himself as a spokesman for equality and the rights of common people. He wanted voting rights extended to all the people, including Protestants, Jews, and free blacks of the French colonies. Robespierre became a leader of the Jacobin Club of Paris, a radical political group. By 1792, most Jacobins wanted a democratic republic instead of a constitutional monarchy.

Revolutionary leader. In August 1792, the people of Paris took custody of King Louis XVI and his family and imprisoned them. Soon afterward, Robespierre was elected to the National Convention, a national assembly established to take over the government of France. The Convention declared that France was a republic, placed King Louis XVI on trial, and sentenced him to death as a traitor. Robespierre then led an attack in the Convention against moderate deputies known as the Girondists. He and his followers expelled the Girondists in June 1793 and took control of the Convention.

In July 1793, Robespierre was elected to the Committee of Public Safety, the Convention's governing body. He stressed the republic's need for a center of opinion and viewed disagreement with the committee's policies as treachery. His speeches justified the Reign of Terror to defend and "purify" the revolution. By the end of July 1794, thousands of rebels and suspected "enemies of the republic" had been executed, including Robespierre's one-time friend and fellow deputy, Georges Danton.

His death and role. As a result of his policies, many members of the Convention became Robespierre's enemies. They feared for their lives and organized a plot against him. On July 26, 1794, Robespierre seemed to call for an end to the use of terror, but he also threatened unnamed deputies. The next day, a group of his opponents persuaded the Convention to order his arrest. The Convention sentenced him to die on the guillotine. He was executed on July 28, 1794.

Historians still argue over Robespierre's role. Some scholars regard him as cold-blooded, fanatical, and self-righteous. Others view him as "The Incorruptible," a totally dedicated patriot and democrat. Isser Woloch

Related articles in *World Book* include:

Danton, Georges-Jacques
Estates-General
French Revolution
Girondists
Guillotine
Jacobins
Louis XVI

Robin is the name for two common birds with reddish breasts. The American robin lives throughout North America. The European robin inhabits most of Europe and parts of northern Africa and western Asia. The name *robin* also refers to several other, less common birds.

An American robin grows 9 to 11 inches (23 to 28 centimeters) long. The male has a brick-red breast, a brownish-gray back, and a black head and tail. Its white throat is streaked with black, and its outer tail feathers are tipped with white. Its bill is yellow. The female robin grows slightly smaller than the male and has paler coloring. The American robin is the state bird of Connecticut, Michigan, and Wisconsin.

American robins breed from northern Canada and Alaska to central Mexico. They are among the last birds to migrate south from northern regions in autumn. They also are among the first birds to return north in spring. The first robin of spring remains a popular sign that winter will soon be over.

© John Shaw, Bruce Coleman Inc.

An American robin feeds its newly hatched young.

From April to July, male American robins sing together for long periods at dawn and dusk and for shorter periods during the day. Their cheerful song consists of repeated short notes that alternately rise and fall. The song sounds as if the robins were singing "cheerily cheery."

American robins frequently return to the same place each year to build nests. They prefer to nest in trees, but they will also nest on a shelf or ledge on a barn or house. The female robin forms a cup-shaped nest from such materials as grass stems, roots, twigs, rags, string, and paper. The male often accompanies the female on trips to and from the nest, and he may help bring nest-building materials. A female typically lays 3 to 5 blue eggs that hatch after about 13 days. Both parents feed the newly hatched birds. The young leave the nest about 13 days after they hatch. The male robin then cares for the young for another 10 to 15 days. American robins may raise two or three broods in spring and summer.

During the warmer months, American robins typically consume beetles, cutworms, earthworms, and wireworms. In the fall and winter, they eat chiefly fruit.

The European robin breeds in Europe, northern Africa, and western Asia. Robins from the northern parts of this range migrate south during winter. A European robin grows about 5 inches (13 centimeters) long. It has an orange-red forehead, throat, and breast. Its back, wings, and tail are olive-brown, and its belly is grayish-white. Males and females look alike.

European robins eat insects, snails, and worms. The birds often nest in and around buildings. Females typically lay 4 to 6 white or light-bluish eggs, which hatch after about 15 days. The European robin's song varies depending on the individual. A typical song begins with a few long, high notes followed by a series of short, rapid, lower notes. Edward H. Burtt, Jr.

Scientific classification. The American robin is *Turdus migratorius.* The European robin is *Erithacus rubecula.*

Robin Hood was a legendary English outlaw who stole from the rich and gave to the poor. He is the subject of many ballads and stories, some dating as far back as the 1300's. He treated poor people kindly and fought the sheriff of Nottingham, a corrupt official who persecuted the poor. Robin Hood thus became a hero of the common people and a symbol of "right against might."

Robin Hood lived with his merry band of followers in Sherwood Forest in Nottinghamshire. His best-known companions included Friar Tuck, Little John, and Maid Marian. Friar Tuck was a fat, jolly priest. Little John stood more than 7 feet (210 centimeters) tall and was known for his great skill with a bow and arrow. Maid Marian was Robin Hood's sweetheart.

No one knows whether the character of Robin Hood was based on a real person. According to one scholar, Robin Hood was actually the Earl of Huntingdon, and his real name was Robert Fitzooth. However, many other scholars believe that Robin Hood is a fictitious character.

The oldest written reference to Robin Hood appears in the *Vision of Piers Plowman,* a long poem written about 1378. But the earliest surviving stories of Robin Hood were ballads written a century later. The first detailed description of his activities was the *Lytell Geste of Robin Hood* (about 1500). Robin Hood also appears as the character Locksley in *Ivanhoe* (1819), by the Scottish novelist Sir Walter Scott. Carl Lindahl

Robinson, Bill (1878-1949), was a popular black American tap-dancer. He was affectionately known as "Bojangles." Robinson became especially famous for a routine in which he tap-danced up and down a staircase.

Robinson performed in nightclubs, vaudeville, motion pictures, and on Broadway. He is probably best remembered for his scenes with child star Shirley Temple in four movie musicals—*The Little Colonel* (1935), *The Littlest Rebel* (1935), *Rebecca of Sunnybrook Farm* (1938), and *Just Around the Corner* (1938). Robinson also starred in the Broadway musicals *Blackbirds of 1928* (1928), *Blackbirds of 1933* (1933), and *The Hot Mikado* (1939).

Robinson was born on May 25, 1878, in Richmond, Virginia. His given name was Luther, but he changed it to Bill. He died on Nov. 25, 1949. Gerald Bordman

See also **Temple, Shirley** (picture).

Robinson, Edwin Arlington (1869-1935), an American poet, became best known for short poems in which he presents character studies. Three of his 13 volumes of poetry won Pulitzer Prizes—*Collected Poems* in 1922, *The Man Who Died Twice* in 1925, and *Tristram* in 1928.

Robinson's characters are citizens of the imaginary community of Tilbury Town. Among the most familiar characterizations are those in "Richard Corey," "Miniver Cheevy," "Flammonde," and "Mr. Flood's Party." In these poems, the characters seem doomed to failure and suffering. Yet Robinson was not a pessimistic writer. He indicated clearly that his characters suffer because they ask too much from life and themselves.

Robinson's continuing theme of the need for humility and complete self-honesty also appears in his philosophical poem "The Man Against the Sky" (1916). Robinson also wrote long narrative poems. *Merlin* (1917) and *Lancelot* (1920), along with *Tristram,* form a connected series telling the legends of King Arthur.

Robinson was born on Dec. 22, 1869, in Head Tide, Maine. With the help of President Theodore Roosevelt, Robinson became a clerk in the New York Custom

Detail of an oil painting on canvas (1917) by N. C. Wyeth (Brandywine River Museum, Chadds Ford, Pennsylvania)

Robin Hood and his men were legendary English outlaws who lived in Sherwood Forest. Stories claim that he and several of his followers were expert marksmen with a bow and arrow.

House in 1905. He resigned in 1909 to devote himself to writing. Robinson died on April 6, 1935. Bonnie Costello

Robinson, Frank (1935-2019), became the first black manager of a major league baseball team when he managed the Cleveland Indians from 1975 to 1977. He later managed the San Francisco Giants from 1981 to 1984, the Baltimore Orioles from 1988 to 1991, and the Montreal Expos (the Washington Nationals since 2005) from 2002 to 2006. He was named American League Manager of the Year in 1989.

Robinson also had been a star outfielder. He was the first man named Most Valuable Player in both the National and American leagues. In his 21-year playing career, he hit 586 home runs.

Robinson won the Rookie of the Year award in 1956 with the Cincinnati Reds. In 1961, he was voted the National League's Most Valuable Player. After the 1965 season, Cincinnati traded him to the Baltimore Orioles. Robinson won the triple crown of batting in 1966. That year, he led the American League in batting average (.316), home runs (49), and runs batted in (122). He also won the American League's Most Valuable Player award in 1966. Robinson played for the Los Angeles Dodgers in 1972 and the California Angels (now Los Angeles Angels of Anaheim) in 1973 before being sold to Cleveland in 1974. He retired as a player after the 1976 season. Robinson was elected to the National Baseball Hall of Fame in 1982. He was vice president for on-field operations for major league baseball from 2000 to 2002. He was born on Aug. 31, 1935, in Beaumont, Texas. He died on Feb. 7, 2019. Dave Nightingale

Robinson, Jackie (1919-1972), was the first African American to play modern major league baseball. The modern era of major league baseball dates from 1900. Robinson joined the Brooklyn Dodgers in 1947 and played all 10 years of his major league career with them. He finished with a .311 lifetime batting average.

Besides being an excellent hitter, Robinson was an outstanding second baseman and base stealer. In 1947, he was named Rookie of the Year. In 1949, he won the National League's Most Valuable Player award and led the league in batting with a .342 average.

Jack Roosevelt Robinson was born on Jan. 31, 1919, in Cairo, Georgia. He grew up in California. From 1939 to 1941, he attended the University of California at Los Angeles (UCLA). There, he starred in football, basketball, baseball, and track.

National Baseball Hall of Fame (UPI)

Jackie Robinson was the first black player in modern major league baseball. He gained fame with the Brooklyn Dodgers for his fielding at second base and for his hitting and base running.

From 1942 to 1944, during World War II, Robinson served in the United States Army. He started his professional baseball career in 1945 with the Kansas City Monarchs of the Negro American League. At the time, professional baseball was *racially segregated*—that is, African American players were not allowed to play in the major or minor leagues. In 1946, Robinson broke through the racial segregation barrier by playing for the Brooklyn Dodgers' minor league team in Montreal. In December 1956, the Dodgers traded Robinson to the New York Giants, but he retired to go into business.

In 1956, Robinson received the Spingarn Medal, an award given annually to an outstanding African American. He was elected to the National Baseball Hall of Fame in 1962. He died on Oct. 24, 1972. Neil Milbert

See also **Baseball** (picture).

Robinson, Joseph Taylor (1872-1937), was the Democratic candidate for vice president of the United States in 1928. He and presidential candidate Alfred E. Smith lost to Republicans Herbert C. Hoover and Charles Curtis. Robinson was elected to the U.S. House of Representatives in 1902. He was elected governor of Arkansas in 1912. Just after he took office, the state legislature elected him to the U.S. Senate. He served as Senate majority leader from 1933 until his death. Robinson was born on Aug. 26, 1872, in Lonoke County, Arkansas. He died on July 14, 1937. James S. Olson

Robinson, Sugar Ray (1921-1989), won fame as one of the greatest boxers in history. He got his nickname, "Sugar Ray," after a sportswriter described him as "a sweet fighter ... sweet as sugar." Robinson held the welterweight title from 1946 to 1951 and then won the middleweight championship five times.

Robinson defeated Jake LaMotta in 1951 to win the middleweight title for the first time. That same year, he lost it to Randy Turpin and then won it back. He retired as champion in 1952 but returned to the ring in 1954. In 1955, he regained the title by defeating Bobo Olson. Gene Fullmer won the title in 1957. Robinson won it back and lost it to Carmen Basilio that same year. In 1958, he again regained the title. In 1959, the National Boxing Association stripped Robinson of the title because he failed to defend it within a year. But he retained the New York State Athletic Commission version of the championship, losing that title to Paul Pender in 1960. Robinson retired from boxing in 1965. He had won 174 of his 201 professional fights, 109 by knockouts.

Wide World

Sugar Ray Robinson

Robinson was born on May 3, 1921, in Ailey, Georgia. He grew up in New York City. Robinson's given and family name was Walker Smith, Jr. He died on April 12, 1989.

Bert Randolph Sugar

Robinson Crusoe is an imaginary story about a merchant-adventurer shipwrecked on a desert island off the northern coast of South America. Daniel Defoe wrote this novel in 1719. He based the story partly on the experiences of a Scottish sailor, Alexander Selkirk. Defoe's realistic account of Crusoe's life has become one of the most popular books in English. The book explains how Crusoe cleverly manages to make himself at home while he lives on the island. After living alone for 26 years, Crusoe rescues a man from cannibals. He calls the man Friday because he met him on that day. Friday becomes Crusoe's trusted friend and servant. Two years later, they board a passing ship and are taken to England. See also **Defoe, Daniel.** Michael Seidel

Robot is an intelligent machine that can physically execute an action or a series of actions automatically. Robots are typically *goal-directed,* meaning that they have been programmed to accomplish a particular goal. A robot can sense the external world and its position in it, determine what action needs to be taken to bring about a goal, and perform that action. This cycle of sensation, decision, and action is frequently referred to as *sense-plan-act.*

Robots are common in factories, where they perform repetitive tasks such as welding and drilling. Robots are also used in environments that are too dangerous or impossible for humans to reach. Scientists use robots to explore the sea floor on Earth and the surface of Mars. Doctors use robots in medical diagnosis and surgery, and to assist with therapy and human mobility. Robots help pilots fly aircraft and help some cars avoid collisions and drive or park themselves. Robotics technology also can be found in many homes. Some households have robotic vacuum cleaners or robotic toys, and in the future people will have even more robots in homes doing many different types of tasks.

Robotics is the field of designing, building, programming, and studying robots. An expert in the field of robotics is called a *roboticist.*

Robot design. Robots vary greatly in shape and size, depending on their functions. They can look like humans, animals, vehicles, or other machines. Robots can be made to roll, walk, fly, swim, or stay in place. Despite vast differences in size and shape, all robots share certain features that allow them to sense and interact with their environments.

A robot requires sensors to obtain information about itself and its surroundings. A machine without sensors acts blindly and cannot be considered a robot. All robots must also measure their environment, called *exteroceptive sensing.* For example, a robot might need to locate and identify objects that it needs to interact with or avoid. This information is often obtained through cameras, laser rangefinders, infrared sensors, or sonar.

A robot requires one or more *actuators* to take action. The most common actuators are motors. An actuator moves a part of the robot's body called an *effector.* An effector is a piece of a robot that interacts with the environment to perform an action. Wheels, propellers, arms, hands, and grippers are all effectors. Robots require a power source for actuators and other components to function. Robots that remain in place may be connected directly to an electrical supply. Mobile robots typically use batteries.

Arnold Zann, Black Star

Robots efficiently perform a wide variety of tasks that are boring, hard, or dangerous for people, including welding automobile body parts, *shown here,* and assembling electronic circuits.

A robot is equipped with computer hardware that controls its actions. Computer software instructs robots on what goals they are to achieve and how they should operate to achieve them. Almost all robots can be reprogrammed to work to achieve different goals.

Autonomy is the degree to which a robot is able to make decisions without input from a human operator. Robots must sense the external world in order to exhibit autonomy. The level of autonomy in a robot is related to how much its environment has been adapted to it.

In a structured environment, such as a factory assembly line, the robot's workspace has been carefully configured to promote repeatability and to reduce unexpected events. Such robots require less autonomy. In an unstructured environment, a robot must have more autonomy to react to unexpected events. An autonomous robot makes higher-level decisions on its own.

History. For thousands of years, people imagined creating beings to ease the drudgery of work. By the 1500's, European artisans created clockwork *automata* (singular, *automaton).* These figures, often shaped like people, contained clockwork that drove lifelike movements. Automata could be designed to write, draw, drink, and play musical instruments. Because inventors were severely limited in the use of power and programmability, these automata served mostly as entertaining curiosities.

The word *robot* appeared first in the science fiction play *R.U.R.* (1921), written by the Czech author Karel Čapek. In 1927, Westinghouse Electric Corporation introduced Televox, a simple robot that could answer a telephone. That same year, the German film *Metropolis* became the first major motion picture to feature a humanlike robot. In 1954, American inventor George Devol built the first industrial robot, called Unimate. In 1961, Unimate was incorporated into the assembly line of a General Motors plant in New Jersey. Others quickly saw the value of such robots' skills in performing precise and repeatable movements. Robots quickly made their way into many kinds of factories. Today, more robots still operate in factories than in any other environment.

Historically, jobs that were "dirty, dull, or dangerous" were considered good jobs for robots. By the 2000's, however, robots began moving out of factories and research laboratories and into other areas of society.

Future of robotics. Robotics offers immense opportunities to transform society in unexpected ways. Many roboticists believe an explosive expansion of robotics technology is imminent. They predict that robotics technology will become seamlessly embedded into people's homes, workplaces, and multiple aspects of everyday life in the near future.

Machine learning will play an important role in the future of robotics. Such learning offers the possibility of robots being taught by, instead of programmed by, human instructors.

As robots are increasingly used in less structured environments, they will increasingly interact with humans. Traditional robotics design considerations must be revised when the robot is to work in close proximity with people. The unpredictability of human behavior and the inherent danger robots can pose to people remain the greatest challenges in robotics.

Ethical concerns about human-robot interactions will increase as robotics technology becomes more advanced. For instance, roboticists, philosophers, lawyers, and politicians are debating whether autonomous robots should be used in war. Other ethical concerns relate to legal responsibility when something goes wrong with an autonomous robot. For example, if a robotic car is involved in a crash, it may be difficult to determine who is responsible. Responsible parties may include the software programmer, the car manufacturer, or the car owner. Roboticists and others must determine such standards for robots. Brenna D. Argall

See also **Artificial intelligence; Automation; Čapek, Karel; Computer; Remote control.**

Robusti, Jacopo. See **Tintoretto.**

Rochambeau, *row shahn BOH,* **Comte de,** *kawnt duh* (1725-1807), a French general, came to America in 1780 with French troops to serve under General George Washington in the American Revolution (1775-1783). In 1781, Rochambeau helped plan the Battle of Yorktown and the defeat of Lord Cornwallis.

Rochambeau was born on July 1, 1725, in Vendôme, the younger son of a French noble. His full name was Jean Baptiste Donatien de Vimeur. In 1742, he began a long and distinguished career as a soldier. Rochambeau's bravery and skill in the War of the Austrian Succession (1740-1748) and the Seven Years' War (1756-1763) won him steady advancement. As inspector general of the army, he made important military reforms later used successfully in the French Revolution and by Napoleon.

On his return from America in 1783, Rochambeau was appointed governor of Picardy and Artois. He served in the French Revolution and was promoted to marshal of France in 1791. He resigned after suffering defeats early in a war that France had begun fighting against Austria and Prussia in 1792. Imprisoned during the Reign of Terror, Rochambeau narrowly escaped being executed. Napoleon later restored his rank. Rochambeau died on May 10, 1807. Isser Woloch

Roche, Mazo De la. See **De la Roche, Mazo.**

Rochester, *RAHCH ehs tuhr,* New York (pop. 210,565; met. area pop. 1,079,671), is a major manufacturing center of the United States. The city is also a leading cultural and commercial center of New York. Rochester ranks as one of the largest cities in the state. It lies in western New York along the Genesee River, near the outlet of the river into Lake Ontario. For Rochester's location, see **New York** (political map).

Nathaniel Rochester, a businessman from Hagerstown, Maryland, founded Rochester in 1812. He and two associates had purchased 100 acres (40 hectares) of land on the Genesee River in 1803. The abundance of water power and rich soil attracted settlers to the area.

Description. Rochester, the county seat of Monroe County, covers 36 square miles (93 square kilometers). Its metropolitan area covers 3,266 square miles (8,459 square kilometers). The Genesee River divides the city into two parts of almost equal size. Downtown buildings include the 30-story Innovation Square (formerly Xerox Tower), the 27-story marble and bronze Metropolitan (formerly Chase Tower), and a 20-story building that was once the headquarters of Bausch & Lomb.

An elected Board of Education supervises Rochester's public school system. The city is the home of the University of Rochester and its famous Eastman School of Music. Other institutions of higher learning in the city include Nazareth College, Roberts Wesleyan College, Rochester Institute of Technology, and St. John Fisher College. The Rochester Public Library has a main library and several branches.

The Rochester Philharmonic Orchestra performs in the Eastman Theatre, part of the Eastman School of Music. Other city attractions include the George Eastman Museum and the Memorial Art Gallery. The Rochester Museum & Science Center includes the Strasenburgh Planetarium. The Strong, a children's museum, is the home of the National Museum of Play and the National Toy Hall of Fame. The Monroe County Parks System includes the Seneca Park Zoo.

Economy. Hospitals and medical research facilities employ many people in the Rochester area. The Eastman Kodak Company, a manufacturer of cameras, printers, and related equipment, has long ranked as one of the city's chief employers. The city has many manufacturing facilities. Chief products include printers and photocopiers, lenses and other eye care products, industrial machinery, chemicals, plastics, food and food products, automobile parts, clothing, computer and electronic equipment, and tool and die equipment.

Rochester is linked to the Governor Thomas E. Dewey Thruway, the nation's longest toll superhighway. Passenger and freight trains serve the city. The Greater Rochester International Airport is in southwestern Rochester.

Government and history. Rochester has a strong-mayor form of government, in which the mayor appoints most department heads and has direct control over them. The voters elect the mayor and the nine members of the city council.

Ebenezer Allen, the first European settler in what is now Rochester, arrived in 1789. He built a flour mill on the Genesee River shore for the local Seneca people. The first permanent settlers came in 1812, and the village was incorporated as Rochesterville in 1817. Its name was changed to Rochester in 1822.

Trade flourished after construction of the Erie Canal through Rochester in the mid-1820's. The canal reduced transportation costs and opened Eastern and Western markets to Rochester farmers and manufacturers. Flour mills multiplied along the Genesee, and Rochester became known as the *Flour City.*

Rochester received a city charter in 1834. By 1856, the population had grown to about 50,000, and Rochester was called the *Flower City* as well. One of the city's many plant nurseries covered 440 acres (178 hectares) and ranked among the largest in the world.

In 1880, George Eastman established a photographic plate-making business in Rochester. His company began to sell Kodak cameras and film in 1888. The company's success gave Rochester a third nickname, *Film City.*

During the early 1900's, the city's harbor was deepened, and piers and a terminal were expanded. Rochester became an ocean port in 1959 when the St. Lawrence Seaway opened. The seaway lets ships sail inland from the Atlantic Ocean to ports on the Great Lakes.

Redevelopment projects gave downtown Rochester a new look in the 1960's and 1970's. Projects included new shopping malls, offices, hotels, and parks. In 1985, the Rochester Riverside Convention Center opened. A new baseball stadium opened near downtown in 1996.

The city's population declined from more than 330,000 in 1950 to about 210,000 in 2010. Since the late 1900's, the decline in jobs provided by such companies as Eastman Kodak and Xerox has presented many challenges to the area's economy. Rochester's skilled workforce, however, has attracted many smaller businesses to the area. Thomas P. Flynn

Rock is the hard mineral substance that forms the solid part of Earth's crust. Mountains and canyons expose many different types of rock on their surfaces. Great cliffs of rock line the seashore in such places as Maine, California, and southern England. In many desert regions, rock formations rise above sandy plains. In most fairly flat areas, a layer of soil covers the underlying rock. Soil consists of tiny fragments of rock and grains of minerals mixed with decaying remains of plants and animals. Stones and pebbles are pieces of rock, and gravel consists of loose, rounded rock fragments.

Most rocks are *aggregates.* Aggregates contain crystals or grains of two or more minerals. Much granite, for example, contains grains of clear quartz, pinkish potassium feldspar, white plagioclase, and black biotite or hornblende. Some rocks have grains so small that they can be seen only under a microscope. A few kinds of rock consist almost entirely of only one mineral. *Quartzite,* for example, is composed of the mineral quartz, and *limestone* is made up of the mineral calcite.

People use rocks in many ways. Builders use granite, marble, and other rocks as construction materials. Cement is made from finely crushed and heated limestone. Sand and gravel or crushed stone mixed with wet cement makes strong, durable concrete, an artificial rock, for use in buildings, highways, and dams.

Such metals as aluminum, copper, iron, lead, tin, and zinc come from rocks called *ores.* Ores also supply radioactive metals, such as uranium, and nonmetallic minerals, such as borax, graphite, and trona. In Minnesota and western Australia, deposits of iron ore make up entire mountains. In tropical climates, *weathering* (the breaking down of rock) creates thick soils rich in the aluminum-bearing ore *bauxite.*

Some rocks hold valuable crystals. In Africa and Australia, workers mine diamonds from a rock called *kimberlite.* Beautiful green emeralds come from rocks in Colombia, India, Russia, and South Africa. Most blue aquamarine comes from Brazil and Madagascar. Emerald and aquamarine are gem forms of the mineral beryl.

Geologists study rocks to trace Earth's history. Petroleum geologists analyze the age, structure, and composition of rock layers to find petroleum deposits. *Paleontologists* study fossils found in rock to learn about living things that existed millions of years ago.

Many young people and adults collect rocks and minerals as a hobby. There are thousands of rock and mineral clubs throughout the world. These clubs hold regular meetings, sponsor study groups and museum exhibits, and organize field trips to collecting areas.

Geologists classify rock according to how it formed. The three classes of rock are: (1) *igneous* rock, (2) *sedimentary* rock, and (3) *metamorphic* rock.

Igneous rock

Igneous rock forms from *magma* (molten rock). Magma is extremely hot, with temperatures ranging from 1400 to 2300 °F (760 to 1300 °C). Most magma lies deep below Earth's surface. Sometimes, magma rises to the surface through *fissures* (deep cracks) in Earth's crust. Other times, magma travels up *conduits* (pipelike channels in the rock) and erupts at the surface, forming a volcano. Magma cools and hardens into igneous rock. Geologists divide igneous rock into two types: *extrusive* rock and *intrusive* rock.

Extrusive rock, also known as *volcanic rock,* forms from magma that reaches Earth's surface. The magma emerges as streams of hot lava or as fine cinders and ash. Volcanoes are piles of lava, cinder, and ash that have accumulated over tens, hundreds, or even millions of years.

Magma hardens quickly when exposed to the cooler temperatures on the surface, leaving little time for minerals to *crystallize* (develop crystals). As a result, most extrusive rocks have small grains. In some cases, magma cools so quickly that it forms *obsidian,* a smooth, shiny volcanic glass with few crystals.

Often, gas dissolved in the magma bubbles out as the magma cools. The gas bubbles leave cavities in the rock. Geologists call volcanic rock with many round or oval-shaped cavities *cinder.* Magmas rich in dissolved gases can form *pumice,* a rock filled with so many tiny cavities that some pieces can float on water. Lava that hardens more slowly forms rocks composed entirely of crystals.

Dark-colored igneous rocks called *basalts* result from magmas that contain little dissolved gas and erupt rather slowly. Light-colored igneous rocks called *andesites* commonly come from magmas that contain much dissolved gas and erupt with explosive violence. Explosive eruptions produce rock fragments ranging from tiny particles of volcanic dust to lumps called *volcanic bombs* that measure 3 feet (1 meter) or more in diameter. Rocks called *volcanic breccias* consist of fragments of cooling magma that become welded together.

Intrusive rocks, also known as *plutonic rocks,* form from magma that does not rise all the way to Earth's surface. Instead, it pushes into older rock formations and hardens into structures called *intrusions.* Intrusions that cut across older rock layers are called *dikes. Sills* are intrusions that spread out between older rock layers, forming a parallel layer. Some sills, called *laccoliths,* push the rock layers above them into a domelike formation. Magma can melt older rocks and pass through them, creating huge intrusions called *batholiths* and smaller intrusions called *stocks.*

Beneath the surface, magma cools and hardens slowly. As a result, most intrusive rocks have crystal grains large enough to be seen with the unaided eye. Intrusive rocks include dark-colored *gabbros* and light-colored *diorites* and granites. In some places, the last pockets of slowly crystallizing magma are rich in rare elements and form giant crystal grains. These rocks, known as *pegmatites,* may contain beautiful crystals of tourmaline, beryl, spodumene, and other unusual minerals.

Sedimentary rock

Sedimentary rock forms from loose pieces of rock and minerals called *sediments.* Sediments accumulate in layers called *strata.* Strata can trap plant and animal remains within them. As more strata are deposited, the sediments harden into solid rock. Most sedimentary rock forms on the ocean floor, but some develops on land and in fresh water. Geologists classify sedimentary rocks by the type of sediments that formed them.

Clastic sediments are rock fragments that range in size from large boulders and stones, through pebbles and gravel, to grains of sand and particles of *silt* (fine dirt) and clay. Air, water, and frost create these sediments by weathering rock, breaking it into fragments.

Clastic sediments can be carried about and deposited by running water, wind, or glaciers. As the sediments accumulate, the weight of the upper strata compacts the sediments below, squeezing the water from them. These lower sediments turn to rock through a process called *lithification.* In lithification, natural chemical substances left behind by groundwater cement the grains together. Deposits of silt lithify to form the rock *siltstone,* and layers of clay lithify to form *shale.* Sandstones form from layers of sand. *Conglomerates* form where layers of water-worn boulders, stones, and pebbles become cemented together. *Sedimentary breccias* form from angular pieces of rock that have not been moved far and that have been rounded by flowing water.

Chemical sediments are minerals that dissolve in water. When the water evaporates, the minerals crystallize, leaving deposits of such minerals as *rock salt* (sodium chloride), *phosphate rock* (calcium phosphate), and *gypsum* (calcium sulfate). Many limestone deposits formed from crystals of *calcite* (calcium carbonate), and most large iron ore deposits crystallized from iron oxide once dissolved in ancient oceans.

Organic sediments are the shells, skeletons, and other parts of once-living things. Shellfish take calcite from water and use it to build their shells. Corals use the same mineral to build coral reefs. Deposits of coral and shells can lithify to form *fossiliferous limestone.*

Rock can also form from the accumulation of skeletons of single-celled sea creatures, such as *foraminifera,*

Common rocks

Rocks are classified into three major groups. *Igneous rock* forms from hardened magma. Hardening of various plant, animal, and mineral materials results in *sedimentary rock. Metamorphic rock* generally forms when any kind of rock undergoes changes as a result of heat or pressure or both.

Igneous

A. W. Ambler, NAS/Photo Researchers
Basalt

Lee Boltin
Gabbro

WORLD BOOK photo
Granite

Lee Boltin
Obsidian

Sedimentary

L. S. Stepanowicz, Panographics
Bituminous coal

Lee Boltin
Breccia

L. S. Stepanowicz, Panographics
Flint

WORLD BOOK photo
Limestone

Metamorphic

L. S. Stepanowicz, Panographics
Amphibolite

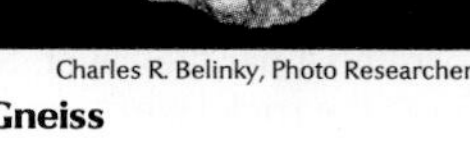
Charles R. Belinky, Photo Researchers
Gneiss

L. S. Stepanowicz, Panographics
Pink marble

A. W. Ambler, NAS/Photo Researchers
Quartzite

diatoms, and *radiolaria.* The calcite shells of foraminifera form chalky limestone, such as that which makes up the famous white cliffs of Dover, England. Diatom shells, made of the mineral silica, form *diatomite.* The silica skeletons of *radiolaria* form beds of a rock called *radiolarian chert* in the deep ocean.

Coal develops from accumulations of dead plant matter in tropical swamps. These deposits compact into a decayed plant material called *peat.* As the peat becomes buried, pressure and heat turn it into coal.

Metamorphic rock

Metamorphic rock forms when a rock's appearance—and, in most cases, its mineral composition—changes. Geologists call this process of change *metamorphism.*

Metamorphism often takes place when heat and pressure increase as rock becomes more deeply buried. The intrusion of magma can heat nearby rock, causing *contact metamorphism.* The forces that create mountains not only produce heat and pressure but also deform the rocks. Metamorphism and deformation turn granite into *gneiss,* a metamorphic rock with wavy bands of feldspar, quartz, and mica crystals. Metamorphism can cause the calcite in limestone to recrystallize, forming marble. The grains in quartz-rich sandstone can grow together to form quartzite. Shales harden to form *slate,* a rock that splits into smooth slabs. At higher temperatures, shales and siltstones turn into *schists* that glisten with mica and other minerals, such as hornblende and chlorite. Some minerals, such as andalusite, kyanite, sillimanite, and staurolite, only form during metamorphism.

The rock cycle

Each type of rock develops from other types of rock. To help explain how rocks form, geologists sometimes refer to a series of transformations called the *rock cycle.* The rock cycle begins with igneous rock created by magma flowing to Earth's surface. Weathering alters the rock chemically and breaks it into particles. The particles accumulate and harden to form sedimentary rock. As the sedimentary rock becomes buried, heat and pressure transform it into metamorphic rock. With enough heating, metamorphic rocks melt into magma that can form igneous rock, completing the cycle.

Rock rarely proceeds through the entire rock cycle. The cycle may be halted, or steps can be skipped, repeated, or reversed. For example, some igneous rocks transform directly into metamorphic rock, and sedimentary rock can weather and then lithify to form other kinds of sedimentary rock.

Rocks as a hobby

You can find interesting rocks in many places near your home. Good "hunting grounds" include mines, quarries, building excavations, ocean cliffs and beaches, and the rocky sides of road cuts and riverbanks. Be care-

Lee Boltin

Peridotite

L. S. Stepanowicz, Panographics

Pumice

Igneous rocks

Rock	Color	Structure
Basalt	Dark greenish-gray to black.	Dense, microscopic crystals, often form columns.
Gabbro	Greenish-gray to black.	Coarse crystals.
Granite	White to gray, pink to red.	Tightly arranged medium-to-coarse crystals.
Obsidian	Black, sometimes with brown streaks.	Glassy, no crystals, breaks with a shell-like fracture.
Peridotite	Greenish-gray.	Coarse crystals.
Pumice	Grayish-white.	Light, glassy, frothy, fine pores, floats on water.

A. W. Ambler, NAS/Photo Researchers

Sandstone

A. W. Ambler, NAS/Photo Researchers

Shale

Sedimentary rocks

Rock	Color	Structure
Breccia	Gray to black, tan to red.	Angular pieces of rock, held together by natural cement.
Coal	Shiny to dull black.	Brittle, in seams or layers.
Flint	Dark gray, black, brown.	Hard, glassy, breaks with a sharp edge.
Limestone	White, gray, and buff to black and red.	Dense, forms thick beds and cliffs. May contain fossils.
Sandstone	White, gray, yellow, red.	Fine or coarse grains cemented together in beds.
Shale	Yellow, red, gray, green, black.	Dense, fine particles, soft, splits easily, smells like clay.

Lee Boltin

Schist

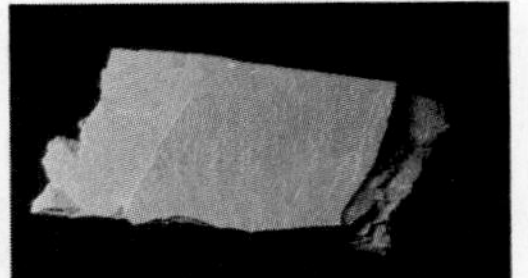
George Whitely, Photo Researchers

Slate

Metamorphic rocks

Rock	Color	Structure
Amphibolite	Light green to black.	Fine-to-coarse grains, hard, often sparkles.
Gneiss	Gray and pink to black and red.	Medium to coarse crystals arranged in bands.
Marble	Many colors, often mixed.	Medium to coarse crystals, may be banded.
Quartzite	White, gray, pink, buff.	Massive, hard, often glassy.
Schist	White, gray, red, green, black.	Flaky particles, finely banded, feels slippery, often sparkles with mica.
Slate	Black, red, green, purple.	Fine grains, dense, splits into thin, smooth slabs.

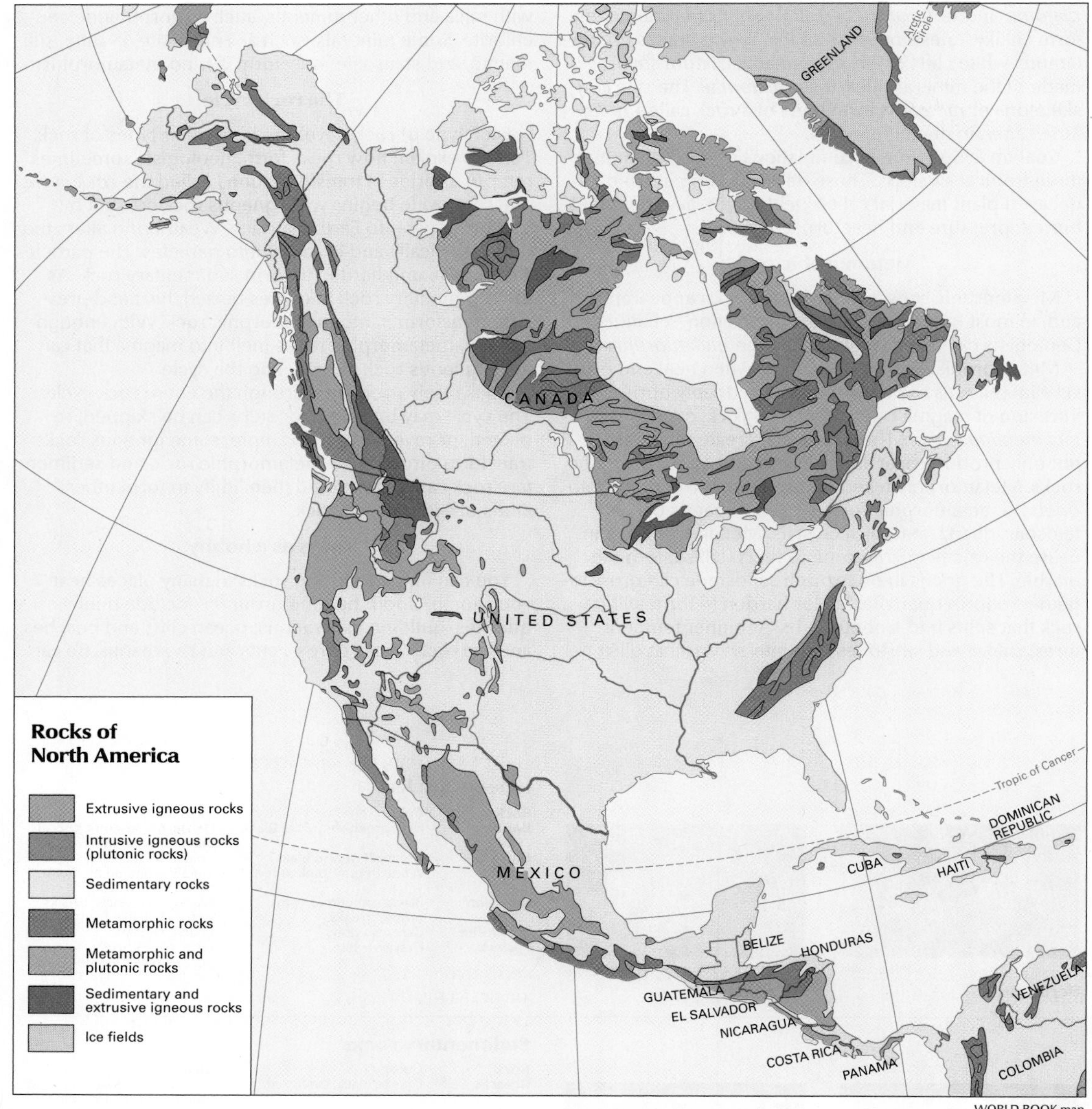

WORLD BOOK map

Interesting facts about rocks

Balanced Rock, in the Garden of the Gods near Colorado Springs, Colorado, is an enormous block of sandstone delicately balanced on a small base.

Bendable rock. Most rocks cannot be bent or squeezed out of shape. But thin slabs of itacolumite, a rare kind of sandstone found in India and North Carolina, can be bent by hand because of their crystalline structure.

Eight elements make up more than 98 percent of all the rocks in the world. These elements are found in about the following percentages: oxygen (46.5), silicon (27.6), aluminum (8.0), iron (5.0), calcium (3.6), sodium (2.8), potassium (2.6), and magnesium (2.0).

Floating rock. Pumice is a rock that floats on water. It was once volcanic lava filled with gases. When the gases escaped, they left millions of tiny holes that filled with air.

Rock of Gibraltar is a huge block of limestone near the southern tip of the mainland of Europe.

ful when working near steep rock walls, roadways, deep holes, and other dangerous areas. Always obtain permission to visit private property.

Tools. You can start a collection by gathering loose rocks, but a few simple tools will help in obtaining good specimens. A rock hammer, the most important tool, has a square head and a pointed end for breaking specimens from the surrounding rock. A chisel helps loosen crystals. Some rock hunters use a magnifying glass in choosing desirable specimens. Scratching a specimen across a piece of unglazed porcelain called a *streak plate* can help rock collectors recognize minerals. A pocketknife makes a handy tool for testing mineral hardness. You can buy all these tools inexpensively from a hardware store or mineral dealer and carry them in a small backpack. You can wrap specimens in newspaper or tissue paper to protect them.

As you collect, label each specimen with the location and date of collection and the kind of rock or mineral it may be. Later, you can transfer this information to a permanent record book or computer file.

Identifying rocks. You can identify a specimen by comparing it to pictures in a reference book or rock samples from a reference collection. A useful reference book for identifying rocks should feature good color photographs. You can purchase small reference collections of rocks and mineral specimens inexpensively from a rock or mineral dealer.

All minerals have special characteristics that can help you identify them. Experienced collectors also study the formations in which rocks are found.

Chemical composition may be determined by certain chemical tests for the mineral elements. For example, a simple chemical test for calcite in limestone is to pour a warm soft drink over the rock. The soft drink, a weak acid, fizzes vigorously on limestone.

Hardness is a measure of how easy it is to scratch a mineral. You can scratch soft minerals with your fingernail and harder minerals using a steel knife blade or pin. The hardest minerals resist scratching by all materials except diamond—the hardest mineral known.

Streak color is the color of the powder obtained by rubbing a mineral across a streak plate. The powder color often differs from the color of the mineral mass. For example, the mineral *pyrite* (ferrous sulfide) looks yellow in rocks. But its streak color is black.

Formations. You can often identify rocks by knowing where they are found and how they look. For example, you usually can recognize sedimentary rocks because they lie in *stratified* (layered) formations. Also, they often contain fossils, and many have markings, such as old mud cracks or ripple marks caused by waves.

Displaying rocks. The size of the rocks in your collection will depend on the available storage space. Some people collect *micromounts,* tiny samples that can be kept in small boxes and viewed under a low-power microscope. Others prefer larger specimens of the size found in museum collections. Probably the best size for storage ranges from 2 by 3 inches (5 by 8 centimeters) to about 3 by 4 inches (8 by 10 centimeters). You can trim rocks to the desired size with a hammer, but be careful not to damage choice crystals. You can clean specimens by washing them with soap and water and brushing them with a stiff brush. Specimens that contain rock salt cannot be washed because the salt dissolves in water. You can brush or blow dirt from most such specimens.

After cleaning your specimens, you can catalog them by painting a small white spot on each rock and writing a number on the spot with waterproof ink. You can then refer to the corresponding number in your record book or computer file for information about the specimen.

A chest of drawers or a set of bookshelves makes an ideal storage unit. Place your rocks in shallow cardboard trays. You might keep small specimens and crystals in cardboard boxes or trays that have partitions. Small exhibits of choice specimens make attractive displays on mantels or shelves or in glass-front cases.

Rock collections. Many museums throughout the world exhibit excellent collections of rocks and minerals. Museums connected with local and regional geological surveys often have exhibits of fossils, minerals, and rocks found in the surrounding area. Mark Cloos

Related articles in *World Book* include:

Famous rock formations

Garden of the Gods
Giant's Causeway
Gibraltar
Stone Mountain

Igneous rocks

Basalt
Granite
Lava
Obsidian
Pumice

Sedimentary rocks

Chalk
Clay
Coal
Coral
Coral reef
Flint
Limestone
Sandstone
Shale
Travertine

Metamorphic rocks

Gneiss
Marble
Quartzite
Schist
Slate
Soapstone

Other related articles

Building stone
Cliff
Corrosion
Crystal
Earth
Emery
Erosion
Fall line
Fossil
Gem
Geology
Gravel
Hardness
Landslide
Lodestone
Loess
Mantle
Meteor
Mining
Moon (Surface features of the moon; The interior of the moon)
Mountain
Ore
Petrology
Pyroxene
Quarrying
Sand
Silt
Soil
Taconite
Tektite
Volcano

Rock and Roll Hall of Fame and Museum in Cleveland, Ohio, is an institution that celebrates rock and roll. It is dedicated to the history and impact of rock music worldwide. Several individual performers, groups, and contributors to rock and roll are *inducted* (admitted) into the Hall of Fame each year. The museum building, designed by the Chinese-born American architect I. M. Pei, is on the shore of Lake Erie.

The museum displays a variety of exhibits, including stage costumes, sheet music, instruments, and other items that portray the historical progression of rock music. Many exhibits trace related styles of music, such as the blues, rhythm and blues, folk, country, and soul music. One section explores regional music from cities that contributed to rock and roll history, such as Detroit, Michigan; London, England; New York City; Seattle, Washington; and San Francisco, California.

The Hall of Fame is housed in the Hall of Fame wing of the museum. Each inductee's signature is engraved in glass, and each inductee is featured in a multimedia presentation.

The idea of the museum originated with the Rock and Roll Hall of Fame Foundation, established in 1983 by some music-industry professionals. The foundation, based in New York City, honored its first group of inductees in 1986. The museum building opened in 1995. It immediately became one of the most popular tourist attractions in the United States. The museum's website at https://www.rockhall.com offers a complete list of inductees and other information about the museum.

Critically reviewed by the Rock and Roll Hall of Fame and Museum

See also **Pei, I. M.; Rock music.**

Rock climbing. See Climbing.

© Kevin Winter, Getty Images

Rock music originated in the United States during the 1950's and rapidly gained worldwide popularity. The Irish rock band U2, *shown here,* achieved success internationally beginning in the 1980's.

Rock music

Rock music is the leading type of popular music in much of the world. Rock music exploded on the music scene in the United States during the mid-1950's. During its early history, it was called *rock 'n' roll* (also spelled *rock and roll).*

Much early rock was a rebellious style of music that particularly attracted young people who wanted an alternative to the musical tastes of the adult world. The creators of rock music were pioneers who turned away from the conventions of the music business, searching for a new sound. By the mid-1960's, however, rock dominated the music industry, and it remains one of the most important divisions of popular music.

Beginnings of rock music

Musical roots. Rock music originated primarily as a blend of two American musical styles—(1) country and western music and (2) blues. There were also some elements of gospel music, particularly in the style that became known as "soul music" in the 1960's.

Much of the musical vocabulary of rock 'n' roll appears in recordings made during the 1930's by African American blues singers, such as Son House, Robert Johnson, and Charley Patton. At the same time, the Carter family and Jimmie Rodgers were making the first country music recordings, which provided another vital influence on rock.

By the late 1940's, a fast-paced blues style with an aggressive, driving beat emerged through recordings released by independent American record companies. This music, which was aimed primarily at a black audience, was known as *rhythm and blues.* Roy Brown recorded "Good Rockin' Tonight" (1947), and Wynonie Harris recorded "All She Wants to Do Is Rock" (1949), two rhythm and blues standards that helped shape rock 'n' roll. Big Joe Turner introduced the song "Shake, Rattle and Roll" (1954), which became a standard among rock music performers.

The Cleveland disc jockey Alan Freed is often credited with introducing the term *rock 'n' roll* as part of his radio show in the early 1950's. In black slang, the phrase had a sexual meaning, but Freed used it to describe the high-energy rhythm and blues he played on his program. The term soon became the name for the new music.

Early rock 'n' roll caused considerable controversy. Many people objected to the loud volume of the music and its often rebellious or sexually suggestive lyrics and performing style. Some opponents of rock claimed that the music was corrupting young people.

Major record labels, such as Columbia and RCA Victor, ignored rock 'n' roll and focused on mainstream popular music during the early 1950's. Most of the musical developments that led to rock emerged from independent record companies, such as Atlantic, Chess, King, Specialty, and Sun.

Sun Records. In 1950, a radio announcer named Sam Phillips opened a recording studio in Memphis. The next year, his studio produced a song that many rock historians consider the first rock 'n' roll record. It was a song about an Oldsmobile, "Rocket '88" (1951) by Jackie Brenston with Ike Turner's band. Phillips sold the recording to Chess Records in Chicago.

After "Rocket '88" became a success for Chess, Phillips established his own label, Sun Records, to market his recordings. He recorded African American performers at first but sought a white singer with the sound and feeling of a black artist. With such a performer, Phillips believed, he could appeal to a large white audience and make a fortune.

Elvis Presley. In 1954 and 1955, Phillips recorded Elvis Presley, a teenager living in Memphis. Presley's first singles on the Sun label had a rhythm and blues song on one side and a country song on the other. The songs were only modest regional hits but became crucial to the development of rock 'n' roll.

Presley spent 18 months making innovative recordings for Sam Phillips at Sun. Then RCA bought Presley's contract in 1955 for $35,000, a remarkable sum at the time. Phillips needed the money to record his other discoveries—Johnny Cash, Jerry Lee Lewis, Roy Orbison, Carl Perkins, and Charlie Rich. They all went on to distinguished careers in rock or country music. With "Blue Suede Shoes," Perkins became the first artist to simultaneously have a top hit on the country and western, rhythm and blues, and pop charts.

Presley went on to earn mass success with his first RCA recordings, "Heartbreak Hotel" and "Don't Be Cruel" (both 1956), which led the music business to demand more songs in this new style. By the end of 1956, Presley had become a national phenomenon and established himself as rock music's greatest star.

Rock 'n' roll gains popularity

Rock 'n' roll gained in popularity during the middle and late 1950's. The first generation of rock 'n' roll artists emerged, and several different styles developed. Independent record producers played an important role in spreading the music and creating new sounds.

The first generation of rock 'n' roll artists were led by Presley and five other male performers—Chuck Berry, Little Richard, Bo Diddley, Fats Domino, and Jerry Lee Lewis. These artists appealed to black and white audiences alike, but only Presley and Lewis were white.

Chuck Berry was one of rock's first great songwriters. His songs, aimed at teenagers, combined his lyrics with a squawking guitar and pounding rhythm. Such songs as "Maybellene" (1955); "School Day (Ring! Ring! Goes the Bell)" (also known as "School Days," 1957); and "Sweet Little Sixteen" (1958) dealt with themes that included cars, young love, and the frustrations of adolescence. Berry often said that his goal was to bridge the gap between races by focusing his songs on topics important to young people regardless of their race.

Little Richard was steeped in the rich tradition of black gospel music. But he had also played piano in striptease clubs, learning a sexier style of music. Little

© Corbis/Bettmann

Elvis Presley, *center,* became rock's first superstar. His tough, rebellious manner and suggestive movements are apparent in this scene from the movie *Jailhouse Rock* (1957).

© Corbis/Bettmann

Chuck Berry helped define the rebellious spirit of rock 'n' roll in the 1950's. His rocking guitar rhythms and vivid lyrics effectively expressed the feelings and problems of youth.

William McKeen, the contributor of this article, is Professor and Chair of the Department of Journalism at the University of Florida and the editor of Rock and Roll Is Here to Stay.

© Popperfoto/Getty Images

Bill Haley, *playing the guitar,* was the first international star of rock music. In 1954, Haley recorded "Rock Around the Clock" with his band, the Comets. The song became a worldwide sensation in 1955 when it was re-released as part of the sound track of the motion picture *The Blackboard Jungle.*

Early rock music
worldbook.com/rm-15

Richard's recordings in New Orleans for Specialty Records remain some of the most energetic records in rock history. They include "Tutti Frutti" (1955), "Long Tall Sally" (1956), "Rip It Up" (1958), and "Good Golly, Miss Molly" (1958).

Bo Diddley recorded for Chess Records beginning in 1955, issuing such hits as "Bo Diddley" (1955) and "Say Man" (1959). He used a guitar as a percussion instrument, and his characteristic pounding beat would influence rock bands for decades.

Fats Domino played piano with a driving rhythm and sang vocals in a rich voice that had mass appeal for white teenagers. Domino began his career in rhythm and blues. He sold more records in the 1950's than any recording artist except Elvis Presley, beginning with his first pop music hit, "Ain't That a Shame" (1955).

Jerry Lee Lewis performed with great energy and excitement both as singer and pianist. Lewis recorded a pair of rock classics for Sun Records in 1957, "Whole Lotta Shakin' Goin' On" and "Great Balls of Fire." Lewis created controversy in 1958 when he married his 13-year-old cousin, damaging his career for several years.

A variety of styles of rock 'n' roll emerged in the 1950's. One was the blend of country music (often called *hillbilly music*) and rhythm and blues popularized by Presley. It became known as *rockabilly.* Some rockabilly artists, such as Bill Haley and Buddy Holly, were former country music singers who altered their style slightly to succeed in the rock 'n' roll market. Haley had formed a band called Bill Haley and the Saddlemen that played Western swing, which combined country music with big-band jazz music. But after hearing Joe Turner and other rhythm and blues artists, he recorded rock music's first huge hit, "Rock Around the Clock" (1954).

An African American vocal style known as *doo-wop* emerged from the streets of New York City and Philadelphia. Doo-wop, with its smooth harmonies, was the closest rock style to mainstream pop in the mid-1950's. The Orioles helped develop the doo-wop sound with their hits "It's Too Soon to Know" (1948) and "Crying in the Chapel" (1953). Other important African American doo-wop groups included the Coasters, the Drifters, the Moonglows, and the Platters. The style spread to white singing groups, such as the Capris, Dion and the Belmonts, the Earls, and the Tokens. These were all-male groups, but some "girl groups"—that is, vocal groups of young women—succeeded in the doo-wop style, notably the Chantels, the Chiffons, and the Shirelles.

Many early rock 'n' roll songs were about certain dances, some being created by the song's composer.

© Frank Driggs Collection/Getty Images

The Platters were a popular singing group that recorded many hits from the mid-1950's through the mid-1960's in the smooth rock music style known as *doo-wop.*

Hank Ballard's "The Twist," later recorded with greater success by Chubby Checker, was perhaps the most successful of these songs. Other songs of the late 1950's and the early 1960's were composed to create or perpetuate such dances as the Dog, the Funky Chicken, the Limbo Rock, the Stroll, and the Walk.

The major record companies, which had ignored rock 'n' roll at first, recognized the music's potential. The mainstream music industry rushed to create teenage idols. These young recording artists, all white, included Paul Anka, Frankie Avalon, Fabian, Connie Francis, Brenda Lee, and Ricky Nelson. Music publishing houses recruited young songwriters just out of high school, such as Neil Diamond, Carole King, and Neil Sedaka, to write songs for the youth audience.

The practice of white singers "covering"—that is, performing their own versions of—records by black artists was widespread throughout the early years of rock 'n' roll. For example, white mainstream singer Pat Boone rerecorded Little Richard's "Tutti Frutti" and "Long Tall Sally," Joe Turner's "Chains of Love," and Fats Domino's "Ain't That a Shame." Boone's "cover" versions cut into sales of the originals, costing the original artists money.

Setbacks. A number of setbacks hit rock music in the late 1950's and early 1960's. Little Richard left music and went into the ministry. Elvis Presley was drafted and served two years in the United States Army. Three important performers, Buddy Holly, Ritchie Valens, and J. P. Richardson (the Big Bopper), were killed in a 1959 airplane crash. The next year, the singer Eddie Cochran died in an automobile accident that crippled singer Gene Vincent. Chuck Berry went to prison in 1962, convicted of violating the Mann Act (transporting a minor across state lines for immoral purposes).

In 1960, Alan Freed was charged with taking money from record executives to play their recordings on his show. The press called the scandal "payola." In 1962, Freed pleaded guilty to two counts of commercial bribery. The scandal and legal battle effectively ended Freed's career.

Independent producers brought strong creative drives to rock 'n' roll during its early years. Perhaps the first superstar record producer was Phil Spector. He founded the record label Philles Records with the producer Lester Sill in 1961. Spector specialized in girl groups, such as the Crystals and the Ronettes. He backed up their singing with what he called his "wall of sound," which consisted of blended recordings of multiple guitars, drums, and other instruments. Spector also recorded the Righteous Brothers, a popular singing duo consisting of Bill Medley and Bobby Hatfield.

In 1959, Berry Gordy, Jr., founded Motown Records in Detroit, which developed into the Motown Record Corporation in 1961. Gordy built Motown into a musical empire, recording such stars as Marvin Gaye, the Jackson Five, the Temptations, Smokey Robinson, Diana Ross and the Supremes, Mary Wells, and Stevie Wonder.

Brian Wilson was another record producer. Unlike Spector and Gordy, he had a major performing career in addition to producing records. Wilson was a member of the Beach Boys, one of the most popular white singing groups of the 1960's. Most of Wilson's material depicted an ideal teenage world centered in California. This world was filled with youthful romance, surfing, and fast cars. He created a complex harmonic blend in such songs as "Surfer Girl" (1963) and "I Get Around" (1964).

© Corbis/Bettmann

The Supremes were the most successful female vocal group in rock music history. The trio recorded with Motown Records, a company that popularized many black performers in the 1960's.

Wilson produced the Beach Boys' album *Pet Sounds* (1966), which set a new standard for experimentation and sophistication in the recording studio. He gave the album layer upon layer of instruments and vocals to create a rich, symphonic sound.

The British invasion

In 1964, the arrival in the United States of the Beatles from England brought a rebirth to rock 'n' roll, now often called simply *rock*. The Beatles' appearance in the United States launched the visits of dozens of British rock bands that became known as the "British invasion." British acts dominated the American charts of best-selling records.

The Beatles were a quartet consisting of George Harrison, John Lennon, Paul McCartney, and Ringo Starr. They came from Liverpool, an English port city where American music had a big influence. British sailors brought American rock 'n' roll records home through Liverpool, and the city's nightclubs and concert halls featured groups that accented a strong beat in the American style.

By the early 1960's, the Beatles had perfected their version of rock 'n' roll through appearances in British and German bars. Under the guidance of Brian Epstein, their manager, and the record producer George Martin, the group became hugely successful in the United Kingdom in 1963. When the Beatles brought their act to the United States the next year, they caused a sensation.

The Beatles were actually reinterpreting American rock 'n' roll from the 1950's. Their performances and recordings included songs by Chuck Berry, Buddy Holly, Carl Perkins, Little Richard, and other early stars. Lennon and McCartney soon began writing songs, and many of their compositions paid tribute to these early influences. Lennon and McCartney became one of the most successful songwriting teams in music history.

The Rolling Stones, the longest lasting of the British rock groups, were even more steeped in American music than the Beatles. The Stones particularly liked the American blues singers Slim Harpo, Muddy Waters, and Howlin' Wolf.

The Rolling Stones formed in London in 1962. The quintet was led by the singer Mick Jagger. Jagger and the guitarist Keith Richards formed a songwriting partnership. Their aggressive, rebellious style can be heard in such rock classics as "(I Can't Get No) Satisfaction" (1965), "Sympathy for the Devil" (1968), and "Honky Tonk Women" (1969). The Stones rank among the most enduring rock groups. The band, still led by Jagger and Richards, continued to perform into the 2000's.

The Who ranked with the Rolling Stones among the top British rock bands expressing the dissatisfaction of young people. The quartet featured the songwriting of the guitarist Pete Townshend. His song "My Generation" (1965) is a classic rock expression of youthful alienation. Townshend and The Who created the first successful rock opera, the 90-minute *Tommy* (1969). The work began as an album and has been performed many times live. It was also made into a motion picture in 1975 and was produced on Broadway in 1993.

Other British groups followed the Beatles and the Rolling Stones and filled American music charts with their songs. They included the Animals, the Dave Clark Five, Gerry and the Pacemakers, Herman's Hermits, the Hollies (named for Buddy Holly), the Kinks, Manfred Mann, and the Moody Blues.

The British groups were rooted in American music, which led listeners to rediscover such American originals as Chuck Berry, Little Richard, and Carl Perkins. But the sheer force of the British invasion ended a number of American music careers.

New styles and sounds

The 1960's became a time of peak creativity for rock music, which earned wide respect as a legitimate art form. Rock blossomed into many new styles and sounds. By the mid-1960's, rock music had become the dominant form of popular music.

Bob Dylan was a singer-songwriter who had emerged as part of a folk music boom in the United States during the early 1960's. At first, Dylan played his music on *acoustic* (nonelectric) instruments and wrote ballads calling for social change, such as "Blowin' in the Wind" (1963) and "The Times They Are A-Changin' " (1964). Then Dylan began playing his material on electric guitar with the classic rock 'n' roll accompaniment of amplified instruments. Many of his original fans rejected the new style, which he introduced at the Newport Folk Festival in 1965. But radio listeners were attracted to his new music.

Dylan's poetic lyrics set to a rock beat produced a style known as *folk rock,* which developed in the mid-1960's. Soon other rock groups were recording Dylan songs, such as "Mr. Tambourine Man" (1965) by the Byrds. Other American artists who played folk rock included the Turtles, the Mamas and the Papas, the Lovin' Spoonful, and the team of Paul Simon and Art Garfunkel.

Fresh directions. Many prominent musicians of the 1960's returned to rock 'n' roll's early years for inspiration. The muted guitar, bass, and drum music on Bob Dylan's album *John Wesley Harding* (1968) reflected the instrumentation of the early Elvis Presley recordings. The Byrds produced a country rock album called *Sweetheart of the Rodeo* (1968), exploring rock's roots in country music. Country rock remained popular during the 1970's. Such artists as the Eagles and Linda Ronstadt combined elements of rock and country music in their recordings.

The Beach Boys recorded a tribute to rhythm and blues in the album *Wild Honey* (1967). The British musicians John Mayall and Eric Clapton schooled themselves in the blues of Robert Johnson. Mayall's Bluesbreakers and Clapton's group Cream played heavily improvised blues rock. The American group the Doors established a dark, brooding blues rock style with their first album, *The Doors* (1967), and its hit single "Light My Fire."

Many rock artists brought diversity and experimentation to their music. The Beatles left behind the simple love songs of their early days and recorded the more personal album *Rubber Soul* (1965). The Beatles' famous album *Sgt. Pepper's Lonely Hearts Club Band* (1967) was a song cycle with sound effects that were elaborate for the time. The Byrds' album *The Notorious Byrd Brothers* (1968) featured electronic instruments called *synthesizers* to combine, modify, and distort sounds. The Rolling Stones answered the *Sgt. Pepper* album with startling new music in *Their Satanic Majesties Request* (1967).

In 1968, the rock musical *Hair* opened on Broadway.

© Corbis/Bettmann

The Beatles, shown here at a 1965 press conference, earned a huge international following with their witty, sophisticated songs and whimsical humor. The Beatles were, *left to right,* Ringo Starr, John Lennon, Paul McCartney, and George Harrison. Their sensational popularity—called Beatlemania—resulted in mobbing fans, Beatle fashions, and tremendous media coverage of the band.

© David Gahr Photography

Bob Dylan became one of the most influential artists in the history of rock music. Dylan introduced an important new style known as *folk rock,* setting the poetic lyrics of his songs to a rock beat. Dylan, *in the print shirt,* performed at the 1965 Newport Folk Festival in Rhode Island, where he departed from folk music tradition by switching from an *acoustic* (nonelectric) guitar to an electric one.

Influence of rock music
worldbook.com/rr-15

Created by Galt MacDermot, James Rado, and Gerome Ragni, the show generated controversy with its use of profanity and nudity, its sympathetic view of sex and drugs, and its antiwar attitude during the Vietnam War. But *Hair* gained international popularity and established rock music as a legitimate sound for the musical theater.

Psychedelic rock, also called *acid rock,* attempted to re-create the mind-altering effects of LSD and other drugs through music. Many psychedelic rock performances featured light shows and other special effects and deliberate use of *feedback.* Feedback is the sound distortion created when a microphone or electric guitar picks up sound from an amplifier and sends it back through that amplifier.

Garage rock was another style that emerged in the 1960's. Garage rock emphasized crude or raw compositions with an unfinished and improvised sound rather than the polished sound of studio recordings. The name comes from some bands' practice of rehearsing in garages. The roots of garage rock can be heard in such songs as "Louie Louie" (1963) by the Kingsmen. Later examples include "96 Tears" (1966) by Question Mark and the Mysterians, "Pushin' Too Hard" (1966) by the Seeds, and "Dirty Water" (1966) by the Standells.

Bubblegum music was at the other end of the musical spectrum from garage rock in the 1960's. Bubblegum music focused on up-tempo, cheery songs. Many bubblegum artists recorded for the independent Buddah label, producing such hits as "Simon Says" and "1, 2, 3 Red Light" (both 1968) by the 1910 Fruitgum Company and "Yummy Yummy Yummy" (1968) by the Ohio Express. Elements of bubblegum music remained popular for decades and fed the careers of such artists as the Osmond Family, the Jackson Five, Bobby Sherman, David Cassidy, and the Partridge Family.

The San Francisco scene. San Francisco became the new center of more serious rock music in the mid-1960's. Many psychedelic rock groups originated in San Francisco, including the Grateful Dead, Jefferson Airplane, and Big Brother and the Holding Company, which briefly featured Janis Joplin as its lead singer. The devoted fans of the Grateful Dead, called Deadheads, filled stadiums and concert halls wherever the group appeared. The Grateful Dead disbanded with the death of its leader, the guitarist Jerry Garcia, in 1995.

The heavy metal sound combined screaming guitars and crashing drums with dramatic vocals. The American guitarist Jimi Hendrix was a strong influence on the heavy metal sound. Hendrix became a celebrated rock guitarist with his flashy performing style, but he was also respected for his technical skill. Early in his career, Hendrix played and toured with many famous performers, including Little Richard. Hendrix gained fame after he moved to London and issued his first major recording, *Are You Experienced?* (1967). His band, the Jimi Hendrix Experience, exploited heavily amplified guitar and bass to produce an avalanche of sound.

One of the most successful heavy metal bands was the British group Led Zeppelin, which released four best-selling albums from 1969 to 1971. Other important heavy metal artists in the late 1960's and the 1970's included the American guitarist Ted Nugent, the British groups Black Sabbath and Deep Purple, and the American groups Grand Funk (also known as Grand Funk Railroad), Aerosmith, and Van Halen.

Soul music. Perhaps the most significant development of the late 1960's was the success of soul music, which was recorded primarily by black artists. Soul music developed from gospel music and the blues, but it had a smoother sound. The singer Sam Cooke launched the style, but he was shot to death in 1964 and did not live to see the success of the music he pioneered.

James Brown was the first major soul singer to cross over to a mass audience, with "Papa's Got a Brand New Bag" (1965). Brown concentrated purely on rhythm, discarding melody altogether. Like Brown, such soul artists as Aretha Franklin, Wilson Pickett, and Otis Redding gained a following among both blacks and whites.

Atlantic Records had long been the home to some of the country's greatest rhythm and blues and soul music.

AP/Wide World

Janis Joplin was probably the first female superstar in rock music. Joplin began her career in the San Francisco rock music scene of the mid-1960's and gained national fame for her shouting, emotional blues style. Joplin had a great influence on later female rock singers.

Women in rock music
worldbook.com/rw-15

Its executives, Ahmet Ertegun and Jerry Wexler, made an alliance with the Stax label, an independent company in Memphis. Atlantic gave wide distribution to Stax recordings. The studio band at Stax, known as Booker T. and the MG's, performed on classic songs by such Memphis soul artists as Wilson Pickett, Otis Redding, Carla Thomas, Eddie Floyd, and Sam and Dave.

The small town of Muscle Shoals, Alabama, also became a recording center. In the tiny Fame Studios, Wexler produced Aretha Franklin's first recordings for Atlantic. Pickett, Percy Sledge, and the Staples Singers also recorded in Muscle Shoals.

By the 1970's, soul music achieved a slicker sound, driven by recordings produced by Kenny Gamble and Leon Huff in Philadelphia. They recorded hits by such artists as Harold Melvin & the Bluenotes, the Spinners, and the O'Jays.

Outdoor rock festivals began drawing huge audiences during the 1960's. The first major rock festival was the Monterey International Pop Festival in Monterey, California, in 1967. The most famous festival, however, was the 1969 Woodstock Music and Arts Festival in upstate New York. The event drew more than 300,000 fans and featured three days of top rock talent. It included such performers as the Grateful Dead, Jimi Hendrix, Jefferson Airplane, Janis Joplin, and The Who.

In the autumn of 1969, an attempt to create a "Woodstock West" festival was staged at Altamont, California, headlined by the Rolling Stones. The Hell's Angels motorcycle gang provided concert security. After one fan was stabbed to death in front of the stage, Altamont came to symbolize the dark side of rock music. Outdoor festivals continued to be popular into the early 2000's, though some were marked by violence.

The 1970's

During the 1970's, the popularity of rock music spread among older as well as younger listeners, extending from preteens to middle-aged adults. As the audience for rock grew, a variety of new musical styles emerged.

The early 1970's were turbulent years in rock music. The Beatles broke up in 1970. A number of drug-related deaths shook the music world, including the deaths of Hendrix and Joplin in 1970; and Jim Morrison, the lead singer and lyricist of the Doors, in 1971.

By the early 1970's, rock performers achieved a level of fame rarely gained by previous musicians. The British singer David Bowie described the ascent and decline of a rock star from outer space in his album *The Rise and Fall of Ziggy Stardust and the Spiders from Mars* (1972).

The success of *Hair* and The Who's rock opera *Tommy* opened the way for extended works for the stage by other rock composers. They included *Godspell* (1971) by Stephen Schwartz; *Jesus Christ Superstar* (1971) by Andrew Lloyd Webber and Tim Rice; and *Grease* (1972) by Warren Casey and Jim Jacobs.

The popularity of *Grease,* with its songs based on music of the 1950's, showed rock beginning to embrace its history. There was a revival of interest in early rock 'n' roll, restarting the careers of Chuck Berry, Little Richard, and Jerry Lee Lewis, among others. Many artists of the 1970's, including John Lennon and Paul McCartney, recorded their interpretations of rock "oldies."

Progressive rock, also called *art rock,* was an attempt to combine rock with elements of classical music, jazz, and other forms of music. One of the most influential progressive rock bands was the British group Pink Floyd. The group's 1973 album *The Dark Side of the Moon* became one of the most popular recordings in rock history. Other progressive rock groups—all from the United Kingdom—included Genesis, Jethro Tull, Yes, and the trio Emerson, Lake and Palmer.

Punk rock was simpler, faster, louder, and more energetic than mainstream rock. It developed primarily in two cities, New York City and London. The movement was led in New York City by such bands as the Ramones, Television, and the Patti Smith Group, and in London by the Sex Pistols, the Clash, and many other bands. The punk rockers brought an angry, rebellious attitude unseen since the early days of rock 'n' roll. The punk bands were emotional, and some of them—particularly the Sex Pistols—deliberately attempted to offend audiences with their use of profanity and their rejection of mainstream values and lifestyles.

New wave. By the end of the 1970's, the influence of the punks had led to a more commercial brand of rock called *new wave.* The anger of the punks was present, but somewhat softened, in the new wave. Important new wave artists included the English singer-songwriter Elvis Costello, the British band the Cure, and the New York City band Talking Heads, led by the singer and guitarist David Byrne. The new wave group the Cars achieved quick success with their first two albums, *The Cars* (1978) and *Candy-O* (1979).

Disco was a rhythmic style that arrived in the late 1970's. In disco music, a steady dance beat was primary, and lyrics were of secondary importance. The motion picture *Saturday Night Fever* (1977), with its best-selling sound track by the Bee Gees, popularized disco. The Bee Gees were a trio of English brothers—Barry, Maurice, and Robin Gibb—who began their music careers in Australia. Other disco stars included the American singer Donna Summer and the Swedish quartet ABBA.

Disco was partly a product of the smooth soul music from Philadelphia produced by Kenny Gamble and Leon Huff. But several of the first disco hits rose from independent studios, some of them in Miami, with such songs as "Rock the Boat" (1973) by the Hues Corporation and "Rock Your Baby" (1974) by George McCrae. As with the music of the doo-wop groups, disco was intended for dancing. Several rock artists tried to revive their careers with disco-influenced songs. The most notable was Rod Stewart with "Da Ya Think I'm Sexy?" (1978). However, traditional rock fans strongly rejected disco.

© Corbis

Bruce Springsteen has been one of the most dynamic and popular performers in rock music since the mid-1970's. He achieved success composing and singing songs that celebrate the dreams, relationships, and struggles of ordinary people.

The 1980's

A new element was introduced into rock music in the 1980's—the video. New wave music still dominated the rock music charts as the 1980's began. Rock drew strength from international musical influences, and rap music found wide acceptance.

Rock videos and MTV. A cable television channel called MTV (short for Music Television) debuted in 1981, running 24 hours a day. Its initial programming consisted of short promotional films for songs and albums, called *videos.* Such films had been a part of popular music for many years. The Beatles and Bob Dylan had made memorable promotional clips for songs in the 1960's. However, with the advent of MTV, videos became a requirement for success. Many early stars of MTV, such as the British group Duran Duran and the American group Huey Lewis and the News, succeeded largely because of the style and creativity of their videos.

Many established artists, including the American bands Van Halen and ZZ Top, reached new levels of stardom through their videos. Bruce Springsteen solidified his position as one of rock's greatest stars with his best-selling album *Born in the U.S.A.* (1984). Springsteen made his first videos for this album's singles, including the hit "Dancing in the Dark." Another artist who made compelling videos was Prince. MTV's airing of Prince's video "Little Red Corvette" helped make the song and its album, *1999* (1982), a major hit. Prince became one of the top stars of the 1980's with his album and motion picture *Purple Rain* (1984).

Madonna and Michael Jackson. Perhaps the first MTV-created rock superstar was Madonna, a dancer and singer whose sexuality dominated her cable TV appearances. Her album *Like a Virgin* (1984), with several hit singles, including "Material Girl," helped make her a star.

Michael Jackson spent his childhood performing with his family band, the Jackson Five. Jackson found stardom as an adult with his best-selling albums *Off the Wall* (1979) and *Thriller* (1982). *Thriller* was the world's best-selling album for decades, until *Their Greatest Hits 1971-1975* (1976) by the American rock band the Eagles surpassed it in 2018. The music video of the song "Thriller" combines singing and dancing with spectacular visual and sound effects. Jackson also had hits with his dance-heavy videos "Billie Jean" and "Beat It" (both 1983).

New wave and mainstream rock remained influential. The American group the B-52's and the British group New Order blended new wave elements with dance music. The Police, a new wave group with British and American members, recorded the best-selling albums *Ghost in the Machine* (1981) and *Synchronicity* (1983). *Synchronicity* included the hit "Every Breath You Take" by the group's lead singer, Sting, who later had a successful solo career. Talking Heads starred in the successful film *Stop Making Sense* (1984), a documentary based on their 1983 concert tour.

U2, a mainstream rock group from Ireland, gained international popularity in the 1980's. Their 1987 album *The Joshua Tree* sold millions of copies worldwide.

The American rock group R.E.M. also gained widespread popularity. R.E.M. incorporated influences ranging from folk rock to punk and new wave music. Many heavy metal bands became popular during the 1980's,

© Dave Bennett, Getty Images

The Rolling Stones became one of the most popular English rock bands. The group's energetic style is captured by Mick Jagger, *left,* and Ron Wood, *right.* The group was formed in 1962.

including the American groups Bon Jovi, Guns n' Roses, and Mötley Crüe, and the British band Def Leppard. Bon Jovi's *Slippery When Wet* (1986) became one of the best-selling albums of the 1980's.

World music, a combination of rock and music from other cultures, gained popularity with a large part of the rock audience. Rock artists looked outside American and European culture for other musical influences.

The English rocker Peter Gabriel, a former lead singer of Genesis, and David Byrne, the Scottish-born vocalist of Talking Heads, grafted African, Latin American, and Middle Eastern elements onto traditional rock. Reggae, a simple, pulsing form of rock that originated in the Caribbean, spread internationally. The passionate reggae music of Bob Marley of Jamaica became especially popular, even after Marley's death in 1981. The South African vocal group Ladysmith Black Mambazo participated in Paul Simon's 1986 *Graceland* album, a celebration of world music and its influence on rock 'n' roll.

Rap is an African American form of rock that is spoken or chanted, rather than sung. Early rock artists such as Bo Diddley had used elements of rap in music of the 1950's, but modern rap traces its origins to the streets of New York City in the 1970's. Rap's roots could also be heard in Jamaican music, where nightclub disc jockeys talked over the records they played. The talk was called *toasting.*

The Sugar Hill Gang scored the first major rap hit with "Rapper's Delight" (1979). Recordings by Kurtis Blow in the 1980's also found wide acceptance. Perhaps the first rap super group was Run-D.M.C. Its 1984 album *Run-D.M.C.* was the first rap gold record. The group collaborated with two members of the rock band Aerosmith on a remake of Aerosmith's hit "Walk This Way" (1986).

Public Enemy became one of the most influential and controversial rap groups of the 1980's. Many of its raps dealt with racism and other social problems.

Early rap albums were issued by independent labels. By the end of the 1980's, such major labels as Columbia and Warner Bros. were recording rap music.

Rap remained a vigorous offshoot of rock music in the 1990's and early 2000's. With his band, Body Count, the rap star Ice-T recorded the album *Body Count* (1992), a blend of rap and heavy metal rock. The album featured a track called "Cop Killer" and dealt with murdering police officers. Outraged parents and public officials boycotted the album and put pressure on the record company, Warner Bros. In response, Warner eventually cut "Cop Killer" from the album.

The 1990's

A style called *teen pop* dominated rock music during much of the 1990's. Artists on the fringes of mainstream rock music also brought new life to rock.

Teen pop, a pop music style aimed at preteen and teenage fans, achieved great commercial success during the 1990's and the early 2000's. The music industry created dozens of teenage acts. Keeping in mind the demands of video, record producers and music-industry managers sought artists who had high visual appeal. Groups of wholesome-looking boy singers gained popularity, beginning with the New Kids on the Block in the mid-1980's and continuing with the Backstreet Boys and 'N Sync, formed in the mid-1990's. Sexually appealing

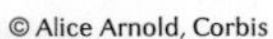

© Alice Arnold, Corbis

Rap music consists of spoken words over a rhythm accompaniment. It emerged from black inner-city culture in the 1980's and quickly became popular among young people. Arrested Development, *shown here,* became one of rap's most successful groups in the 1990's.

© Kevin Kane, WireImage/Getty Images

Modern rock stars include, *from left to right,* Britney Spears, Madonna, and Christina Aguilera. All three gained fame for their exciting live concerts as well as their recordings and high-energy videos.

teenage girl performers, such as Britney Spears and Christina Aguilera, also gained success, as much for their appeal on high-energy videos as for their music.

Alternative rock. The term *alternative rock* referred to a variety of styles, usually aimed at teenage and young adult listeners. Much alternative rock was harsher and more experimental than mainstream rock. Many alternative rock groups were heavily influenced by the punk and new wave sounds of the 1970's and 1980's.

Alternative rock found a wide audience through such bands as Nirvana, Pearl Jam, and Soundgarden, all originating in Seattle. They played a forceful style of rock with an angry, rebellious message. The press called it *grunge rock.* Nirvana, the first grunge group to reach a wide audience, exploded onto the music scene with their second album, *Nevermind* (1991). A hit video for the album's single "Smells Like Teen Spirit" helped Nirvana gain a huge following. The group broke up in 1994 after its lead vocalist, Kurt Cobain, committed suicide.

Nine Inch Nails, an American alternative rock group, mixed angry rock songs with heavy metal and synthesized electronic music. Other alternative rock groups that originated in the 1990's included the American bands Green Day, who were influenced by the punk rockers of the late 1970's; and No Doubt, who incorporated Jamaican popular music called *ska* into their sound. The Prodigy, a British group, combined aggressive messages with a hard-driving dance beat. Oasis, another British group, showed the influence of the Beatles in their melodies and harmonizing vocals.

Rock music today

Today, rock music takes many forms. Rock is so dominant that it can be defined as whatever music is played on popular radio stations. Some stations play *soft rock,* which is rock music that is slow and quiet. Others concentrate on older rock of the 1960's, 1970's, and 1980's, often called *classic rock.* Still other stations focus on rap, or on alternative rock.

Rap music remains popular. Most leading rap artists, such as Kanye West, Jay-Z, and Nelly, are black, but a few white rappers have emerged, notably Eminem.

Traditional rock maintains a foothold in the marketplace. The Rolling Stones and U2 remain huge concert draws decades after they first appeared on the rock scene. Such artists as Eric Clapton, Bob Dylan, Tom Petty and the Heartbreakers, Paul McCartney, and Bruce Springsteen also continue to tour.

Alternative rock artists continue to provide some of the most creative and stimulating rock music today. The American electronic artist Moby combines, mixes, and distorts recordings of rock and other music. Another American, Beck, mixes influences from folk, soul, rap, and other types of music. Significant alternative rock groups include the British band Radiohead, who create futuristic electronic rhythms while retaining elements of traditional rock; and the American band Wilco, who blend folk and country songwriting styles with modern rock and electronic sounds. William McKeen

Related articles in *World Book* include:

Beach Boys
Beatles
Berry, Chuck
Blues
Bono
Brown, James
Cooke, Sam
Dance (introduction; picture)
Dylan, Bob
Electronic music
Franklin, Aretha
Gaye, Marvin
Gordy, Berry, Jr.
Grateful Dead
Hendrix, Jimi
Holly, Buddy
Jackson, Michael
Jay-Z
John, Elton
Lennon, John
Madonna
Marley, Bob
MTV
Popular music
Presley, Elvis
Rap music

Rockefeller, John Davison (1839-1937), was a famous American businessman. He made a fortune in the petroleum industry and later became famous for his *philanthropy* (charity). Rockefeller was one of the wealthiest individuals of his time and a symbol of big business in the United States. Many people have criticized the business methods Rockefeller used in developing his vast industrial empire. But his contributions to the welfare of humanity also form an important part of his record.

Early life. Rockefeller, the son of a peddler, was born in Richford, New York, near Ithaca, on July 8, 1839. When he was 14 years old, his family moved to Cleveland, Ohio. After attending high school and taking several business classes, Rockefeller became a clerk and bookkeeper at a *commission house,* a firm that sells goods for others on commission. He soon formed a partnership to establish his own commission house. With two partners, he entered the oil-refining business in 1863.

The Standard Oil Company, established in 1870, grew out of Rockefeller, Andrews & Flagler, a partnership owned by Rockefeller, his younger brother William, and some associates. With Rockefeller as its president and largest stockholder, Standard Oil developed the world's largest oil refineries and drove down the cost of refining oil. Standard Oil soon owned the chief refineries in Cleveland; New York City, New York; and Philadelphia and Pittsburgh, Pennsylvania. Rockefeller and his associates also bought oil-producing lands, built tank cars and pipelines, and created an organization to market their products. Rockefeller's dealings with railroads involved rebates and other privileged treatment (see **Rebate**).

By 1879, Standard Oil controlled 90 percent of U.S. oil refining and much of the nation's oil shipping. In 1882, Rockefeller and his associates transferred the stock of all their companies to the newly formed Standard Oil Trust. This transfer of control helped unify the management of the operations and reduce administrative difficulties. However, the vastness of Rockefeller's holdings caused the Ohio Supreme Court to dissolve the Standard Oil Trust in 1892. In 1899, the Standard Oil Company (New Jersey), a holding company, replaced the trust. In 1911, the Supreme Court of the United States ordered the firm to dissolve. See **Antitrust laws; Holding company; Standard Oil Company.**

Reputation and philanthropy. As Rockefeller's wealth and power grew, he attracted heated public criticism. Former rivals accused him of selling below cost and of using ruthless negotiating tactics. Many criticized his efforts to eliminate his competition.

Rockefeller gradually retired from 1895 to 1897, and he devoted the final years of his life to philanthropy. He gave away about $540 million during his lifetime. He gave most of this money to the public through foundations he established himself and through other organizations. Institutions receiving money from Rockefeller included the Rockefeller Foundation, the Rockefeller Institute for Medical Research (later renamed Rockefeller University), the University of Chicago, the General Education Board, and the Laura Spelman Rockefeller Memorial (see **Chicago, University of** [History]; **Rockefeller Foundation**). Rockefeller died on May 23, 1937.

Rockefeller's descendants. Several of Rockefeller's descendants became well-known figures in business, finance, philanthropy, and politics. His only son, John D. Rockefeller, Jr., continued his father's philanthropic work. John D., Jr., had five sons—John D. III, Nelson, Laurance, Winthrop, and David. John D. III served as chairman of the Rockefeller Foundation from 1952 to 1971. Nelson was governor of New York from late 1958 to 1973 and vice president of the United States from 1974 to 1977. Laurance was a noted conservationist. Winthrop served as governor of Arkansas from 1967 to 1971. David was chief executive officer of Chase Manhattan Bank from 1969 to 1980. John D. Rockefeller IV, the son of John D. III, served as governor of West Virginia from 1977 to 1985 and represented that state as a member of the U.S. Senate from 1985 to 2015. David B. Sicilia

See also **Rockefeller, John D., Jr.; Rockefeller, John D., III; Rockefeller, John D., IV; Rockefeller, Nelson A.**

Rockefeller, John Davison, Jr. (1874-1960), was the son of the wealthy American businessman John D. Rockefeller. He joined his father's business after graduating

AP/Wide World

John D. Rockefeller, shown here with a young boy, became famous for his philanthropies. In his later years, Rockefeller often gave shiny new dimes as mementos to strangers he met. At his death, his heirs included, *left to right,* his son, John D., Jr., and his grandsons David, Nelson, Winthrop, Laurance, and John D. III.

from Brown University in 1897. He spent most of his life extending the *philanthropic* (charitable) work his father had started. John D. Rockefeller, Jr., ultimately gave away more than $537 million for medical research, international education, social reform, conservation efforts, and other charitable projects. He donated $8 ½ million to buy land for the United Nations Headquarters in New York City. His other major projects included Rockefeller Center in New York City, New York, and the restoration of historic Williamsburg, Virginia. He was born on Jan. 29, 1874, in Cleveland, Ohio, and died on May 11, 1960.

David B. Sicilia

See also **New York City** (Manhattan; A visitor's guide); **Rockefeller, John D.; Williamsburg.**

Rockefeller, John Davison, III (1906-1978), served as chairman of the board of trustees of the Rockefeller Foundation from 1952 to 1971. He founded the Population Council, a group that conducts research on population problems throughout the world. He also helped found the Lincoln Center for the Performing Arts in New York City, New York, and later became its chairman.

Rockefeller was born in New York City on March 21, 1906, and died on July 10, 1978. He was the oldest son of John D. Rockefeller, Jr. (see **Rockefeller, John D., Jr.**).

David B. Sicilia

Rockefeller, John Davison, IV (1937-), was a member of the United States Senate from 1985 to 2015. Rockefeller, a Democrat, represented West Virginia. He served as West Virginia's governor from 1977 to 1985.

Rockefeller was born in New York City on June 18, 1937. He is the son of John D. Rockefeller III (see **Rockefeller, John D., III**). The younger Rockefeller graduated from Harvard University in 1961 and then worked for the Peace Corps and Volunteers in Service to America (VISTA). He was a member of the West Virginia House of Delegates from 1967 to 1969 and West Virginia secretary of state from 1969 to 1973. He served as president of West Virginia Wesleyan College from 1973 until 1976, when he was elected governor of West Virginia. He took office as governor in 1977.

As a senator, Rockefeller supported efforts to expand access to education and affordable health care. He also became known for his work to support industries important to West Virginians. He served as the chairman of the Senate Committee on Commerce, Science, and Transportation. He also chaired the Health Care Subcommittee on Finance and served on the Committee on Veterans' Affairs. Rockefeller did not seek reelection in 2014. He retired from the Senate in 2015.

David B. Sicilia

Rockefeller, Nelson Aldrich (1908-1979), served as vice president of the United States from 1974 to 1977. He filled a vacancy that was created when Vice President Gerald R. Ford succeeded Richard M. Nixon, who had resigned as president. Ford nominated Rockefeller for the vice presidency.

Rockefeller's nomination required the approval of both houses of Congress under the procedures that were established in 1967 by the 25th Amendment to the United States Constitution. Rockefeller was the second person to become vice president under terms of the 25th Amendment. Ford became the first in 1973. Before adoption of the amendment, vacancies in the vice presidency stayed unfilled until the next presidential election.

Rockefeller, a Republican, had been governor of New York from 1959 to 1973. Before becoming governor, he had held a number of posts in the federal government.

Wide World

Nelson A. Rockefeller

Early life. Rockefeller was born on July 8, 1908, in Bar Harbor, Maine. His grandfather, John D. Rockefeller, and father, John D. Rockefeller, Jr., became famous for their many contributions to U.S. business and human welfare. Nelson graduated from Dartmouth College in 1930. During the 1930's, he took part in his family's business and philanthropic activities.

In 1930, Rockefeller married Mary Todhunter Clark. They had five children: Rodman, Anne, Steven, and the twins Mary and Michael. The Rockefellers divorced in 1962. In 1963, Rockefeller married Margaretta (Happy) Fitler Murphy. The couple had two children: Nelson, Jr., and Mark.

Career in government. In 1940, President Franklin D. Roosevelt appointed Rockefeller coordinator of inter-American affairs. In 1944 and 1945, Rockefeller served as assistant secretary of state. He was undersecretary of health, education, and welfare in 1953 and 1954 and special assistant to President Dwight D. Eisenhower in 1954 and 1955. Rockefeller was elected governor of New York in 1958 and won reelection in 1962, 1966, and 1970. He sought the Republican presidential nomination in 1964 and 1968. In 1973, he resigned as governor of New York.

On Aug. 9, 1974, Nixon resigned the presidency while facing almost certain impeachment because of his role in the Watergate political scandal. Ford became president and nominated Rockefeller for vice president. Rockefeller took office on Dec. 19, 1974. As vice president, he helped develop U.S. domestic policies and headed a federal commission that investigated the Central Intelligence Agency. He died on Jan. 26, 1979.

J. F. terHorst

See also **Ford, Gerald R.; Vice president of the United States; Watergate.**

Rockefeller Foundation is a philanthropic organization chartered in 1913. It sponsors programs to fight hunger, to improve health, to provide education and jobs, and to deal with problems of overpopulation and environmental degradation. It works to ensure that poor people share in the benefits of new technology and global changes. It also seeks to preserve and support the world's many forms of culture and creative arts.

In the United States, for example, some of the foundation's programs work to provide equal opportunities for minority groups, to improve public education, and to encourage international and intercultural understanding through the arts and the humanities. Aid is given through grants and fellowships.

John D. Rockefeller originally provided an endowment of $100 million for the foundation. Later, he increased it to more than $183 million. The foundation's offices are in New York City, New York. For the foundation's assets, see **Foundation** (table).

Critically reviewed by the Rockefeller Foundation

© Agence France Presse/Getty Images

A Chinese Long March rocket rises from its launch pad carrying an astronaut on the spacecraft Shenzhou 5. Most rockets use chemical reactions to expel gas, producing thrust.

Rocket

Rocket is a type of engine that pushes itself forward or upward by producing thrust. Unlike a jet engine, which draws in outside air, a rocket engine uses only the substances carried within it. As a result, a rocket can operate in outer space, where there is no air. A rocket can produce more power for its size than any other kind of engine. For example, the main rocket engine of the space shuttle weighed only a fraction as much as a train engine, but it would take 39 train engines to produce the same amount of power. The word *rocket* can also mean a vehicle or object driven by a rocket engine.

Rockets come in a variety of sizes. Some rockets that shoot fireworks into the sky measure less than 2 feet (60 centimeters) long. Rockets 50 to 100 feet (15 to 30 meters) long serve as long-range missiles that can be used to bomb distant targets during wartime. Larger and more powerful rockets lift spacecraft, artificial satellites, and scientific probes into space. For example, the Saturn V rocket that carried astronauts to the moon stood about 363 feet (111 meters) tall.

Rockets generate thrust by expelling gas. Most produce thrust by burning a mixture of fuel and an *oxidizer,* a substance that enables fuel to burn without drawing in outside air. This kind of rocket is called a *chemical rocket* because the burning of fuel is a chemical reaction. The fuel and oxidizer are called the *propellants.*

A chemical rocket can produce great power, but it burns propellants rapidly. As a result, it needs a large amount of propellants to work for even a short time. The Saturn V rocket burned more than 560,000 gallons (2,120,000 liters) of propellants during the first 2 ¾ minutes of flight. Chemical rocket engines become extremely hot as the propellants burn. The temperature in some engines reaches 6000 °F (3300 °C), much higher than the temperature at which steel melts.

Jet engines also burn fuel to generate thrust. Unlike rocket engines, however, jet engines work by drawing in oxygen from the surrounding air. For more information on jet engines, see **Jet propulsion**.

Researchers have also developed rockets that do not burn propellants. *Nuclear rockets* use heat generated by a nuclear fuel to produce thrust. *Ion rockets* expel *ions* (electrically charged particles) to produce thrust.

Military forces have used rockets in war for centuries. In the 1200's, Chinese soldiers fired rockets against attacking armies. British troops used rockets to attack Fort McHenry in Maryland during the War of 1812 (1812-1815). After watching the battle, the American lawyer Francis Scott Key described "the rocket's red glare" in the song "The Star-Spangled Banner." During World War I (1914-1918), the French used rockets to shoot down enemy observation balloons. Germany attacked London with V-2 rockets during World War II (1939-1945). In the Persian Gulf War of 1991 and the Iraq War (2003-2011), United States troops launched rocket-powered Patriot missiles to destroy Iraqi missiles.

Rockets are the only vehicles powerful enough to carry people and equipment into space. Since 1957, rockets have lifted hundreds of artificial satellites into orbit around Earth. These satellites take pictures of Earth's weather, gather information for scientific study, and transmit communications around the world. Rockets also carry scientific instruments far into space to explore and study other planets. Since 1961, rockets have launched spacecraft carrying astronauts and cosmonauts into orbit around Earth. In 1969, rockets carried astronauts to the first landing on the moon. In 1981, rockets lifted the first space shuttle into Earth orbit.

How rockets work

Rocket engines generate thrust by putting a gas under pressure. The pressure forces the gas out the end of the rocket. The gas escaping the rocket is called exhaust. As it escapes, the exhaust produces thrust according to the laws of motion developed by the English scientist Isaac Newton. Newton's third law of motion states that for every action, there is an equal and opposite reaction. Thus, as the rocket pushes the exhaust backward, the exhaust pushes the rocket forward.

The amount of thrust produced by a rocket depends on the *momentum* of the exhaust—that is, its total amount of motion.The exhaust's momentum equals its *mass* (amount of matter) multiplied by the speed at which it exits the rocket. The more momentum the exhaust has, the more thrust the rocket produces. Engineers can therefore increase a rocket's thrust by increasing the mass of exhaust it produces. Alternately, they can increase the thrust by increasing the speed at which the exhaust leaves the rocket.

Parts of a rocket include the rocket engine and the equipment and cargo the rocket carries. The four major parts of a rocket are (1) the payload, (2) propellants, (3) the chamber, and (4) the nozzle.

The payload of a rocket includes the cargo, passengers, and equipment the rocket carries. The payload may consist of a spacecraft, scientific instruments, or even explosives. The space shuttle's payload, for example, consisted of the shuttle orbiter and the mission astronauts and any satellites, scientific experiments, or supplies the orbiter carries. The payload of a missile may include explosives or other weapons. This kind of payload is called a *warhead.*

Propellants generally make up most of the weight of a rocket. For example, the fuel and oxidizer used by the space shuttle accounted for nearly 90 percent of its weight at liftoff. The shuttle needed such a large amount of propellant to overcome Earth's gravity and the resistance of the atmosphere.

Many chemical rockets use liquid hydrogen as fuel. Hydrogen becomes a liquid only at extremely low temperatures, requiring powerful cooling systems. Kerosene, another liquid fuel, is easier to store because it remains liquid at room temperature.

Many rockets use liquid oxygen, or *lox,* as their oxidizer. Like hydrogen, oxygen must be cooled to low temperatures to become a liquid. Other commonly used oxidizers include nitrogen tetroxide and hydrogen peroxide. These oxidizers remain liquid at room temperature and do not require cooling.

An electric or nuclear rocket uses a single propellant. These rockets store the propellant as a gas or liquid.

The chamber is the area of the rocket where propellants are put under pressure. Pressurizing the propellants enables the rocket to expel them at high speeds.

In a chemical rocket, the fuel and oxidizer combine and burn in an area called the *combustion chamber.* As they burn, the propellants expand rapidly, creating intense pressure.

Burning propellants create extreme heat and pressure in the combustion chamber. Temperatures in the chamber become hot enough to melt the steel, nickel, copper, and other materials used in its construction. Combustion chambers need insulation or cooling to survive the heat. The walls of the chamber must also be strong enough to withstand intense pressure. The pressure inside a rocket engine can exceed 3,000 pounds per square inch (200 kilograms per square centimeter), nearly 100 times the pressure in the tires of a car or truck.

In a nuclear rocket, the chamber is the area where nuclear fuel heats the propellant, producing pressure. In an ion rocket, the chamber contains the electric devices used to force the propellant out of the nozzle.

The nozzle is the opening at the end of the chamber that allows the pressurized gases to escape. It converts the high pressure of the gases into thrust by forcing the

How a multistage rocket works

A two-stage rocket consists of two units called *stages.* Each stage has its own propellant tanks and one or more engines. When the first stage runs out of propellant, it drops away. The second stage ignites, carrying the payload farther. Additional rockets called boosters can be attached to increase the rocket's power.

WORLD BOOK diagram by Oxford Designers and Illustrators

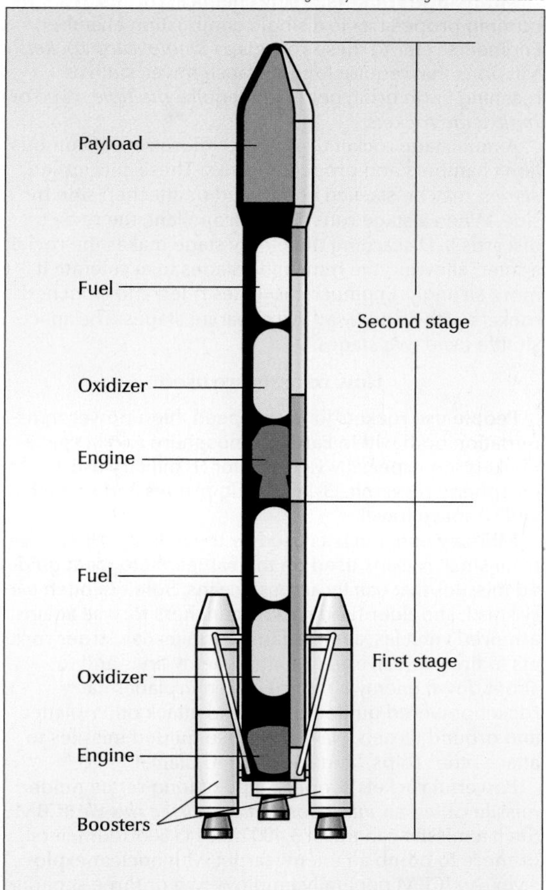

Raytheon Company

A Patriot missile takes off from its launcher in a blast of heat and smoke. Military rockets, such as the Patriot, use sophisticated guidance systems to reach distant targets. The Patriot can destroy enemy missiles in midair.

exhaust through a narrow opening, which accelerates the exhaust to high speeds. The exhaust from the nozzle can travel more than 1 mile (1.6 kilometers) per second. Like the chamber, the nozzle requires cooling or insulation to withstand the heat of the exhaust.

Multistage rockets. Many chemical rockets work by burning propellants in a single combustion chamber. Engineers refer to these rockets as *single-stage rockets.* Missions that require long-distance travel, such as reaching Earth orbit, generally require *multiple-stage* or *multistage rockets.*

A multistage rocket uses two or more sets of combustion chambers and propellant tanks. These sets, called *stages,* may be stacked end to end or attached side by side. When a stage runs out of propellant, the rocket discards it. Discarding the empty stage makes the rocket lighter, allowing the remaining stages to accelerate it more strongly. Engineers have designed and launched rockets with as many as five separate stages. The space shuttle used two stages.

How rockets are used

People use rockets for high-speed, high-power transportation both within Earth's atmosphere and in space. Rockets are especially valuable for (1) military use, (2) atmospheric research, (3) launching probes and satellites, and (4) space travel.

Military use. Rockets used by the military vary in size from small rockets used on the battlefield to giant guided missiles that can fly across oceans. Soldiers often carry small, shoulder-fired rocket launchers for use against armored vehicles, such as tanks. Armies use larger rockets to fire explosives far behind enemy lines and to shoot down enemy aircraft. Fighter airplanes carry rocket-powered guided missiles to attack other planes and ground targets. Navy ships use guided missiles to attack other ships, land targets, and planes.

Powerful rockets propel a type of long-range guided missile called an *intercontinental ballistic missile* (ICBM). Such a missile can travel 3,400 miles (5,500 kilometers) or more to bomb an enemy target with nuclear explosives. An ICBM generally employs two or three separate stages to propel it during the early part of its flight. The ICBM coasts the rest of the way to its target.

Atmospheric research. Scientists use rockets to explore Earth's atmosphere. *Sounding rockets,* also called *meteorological rockets,* carry such equipment as barometers, cameras, and thermometers high into the atmosphere. These instruments collect information about the atmosphere and send it by radio to receiving equipment on the ground.

Rockets also provide the power for experimental research airplanes. Engineers use these planes in the development of spacecraft. By studying the flights of such planes as the rocket-powered X-1 and X-15, engineers learned how to control vehicles flying many times as fast as the speed of sound.

Launching probes and satellites. Rockets carry crewless spacecraft called *space probes* on long voyages to explore the solar system. Probes have explored the sun, the moon, and all the planets in the solar system. They carry scientific instruments that gather information about the planets and transmit data back to Earth. Probes have landed on the surface of the moon, Venus, Mars, and Saturn's moon Titan.

Rockets lift artificial satellites into orbit around Earth. Some orbiting satellites gather information for scientific research. Others relay telephone conversations and radio and television broadcasts across the oceans. Weather satellites track climate patterns and help scientists predict the weather. Navigation satellites, such as those that make up the Global Positioning System (GPS), enable receivers anywhere on Earth to determine their locations with great accuracy. Armed forces use satellites to observe enemy facilities and movements. They also use satellites to communicate, monitor weather, and watch for missile attacks. Not only are satellites launched by rockets, but many satellites use small rocket engines to maintain their proper orbits.

Rockets that launch satellites and probes are called *launch vehicles.* Most of these rockets have from two to four stages. The stages lift the satellite to its proper altitude and give it enough speed—about 17,000 miles (27,400 kilometers) per hour—to stay in orbit. A space probe's speed must reach about 25,000 miles (40,000 kilometers) per hour to escape Earth's gravity and continue on its voyage.

Engineers created the first launch vehicles by altering military rockets or sounding rockets to carry spacecraft. For example, they added stages to some of these rockets to increase their speed.

Today, engineers sometimes attach smaller rockets to a launch vehicle. These rockets, called *boosters,* provide additional thrust to launch heavier spacecraft.

International Launch Systems

An Atlas 5 rocket blasts off to lift a satellite into orbit. The Atlas 5 and other powerful rockets that carry their cargo into space are called *launch vehicles.*

Space travel. Rockets launch spacecraft carrying astronauts that orbit Earth and travel into space. These rockets, like the ones used to launch probes and satellites, are called *launch vehicles.*

The Saturn V rocket, which carried astronauts to the moon, was the most powerful launch vehicle ever built by the United States. Before launch, it weighed more than 6 million pounds (2.7 million kilograms). It could send a spacecraft weighing more than 100,000 pounds (45,000 kilograms) to the moon. The Saturn V used 11 rocket engines to propel three stages.

Space shuttles were reusable rocket-powered spacecraft that could fly into space and return to Earth repeatedly. The United States ended its space shuttle program in 2011.

Engineers have also worked to develop *space tugs,* smaller rocket-powered vehicles that could tow satellites, boost space probes, and carry astronauts over short distances in orbit. For more information on rockets used in space travel, see **Space exploration.**

Other uses. People have fired rockets as distress signals from ships and airplanes and from the ground. Rockets also shoot rescue lines to ships in distress. Small rockets called JATO (jet-assisted take-off) units help heavily loaded airplanes take off. Rockets have long been used in fireworks displays.

Kinds of rocket engines

The vast majority of rockets are chemical rockets. The two most common types of chemical rockets are *solid-propellant rockets* and *liquid-propellant rockets.* In addition, engineers have tested a third type of chemical rocket, called a *hybrid rocket,* that combines liquid and solid propellants. Ion rockets have propelled space probes and maneuvered orbiting satellites. Researchers have designed experimental nuclear-powered rockets.

Solid-propellant rockets burn a rubbery or plastic-like material called the *grain.* The grain consists of a fuel and an oxidizer in solid form. It is shaped like a cylinder with one or more channels or *ports* that run through it. The ports increase the surface area of the grain that the rocket burns. Unlike some liquid propellants, the fuel and oxidizer of a solid-propellant rocket do not burn upon contact with each other. Instead, an electric charge ignites a smaller grain. Hot exhaust gases from this grain ignite the main propellant surface.

The temperature in the combustion chamber of a solid-propellant rocket ranges from 3000 to 6000 °F (1600 to 3300 °C). In most of these rockets, engineers build the chamber walls from high-strength steel or titanium to withstand the pressure and heat of combustion. They also may use composite materials consisting of high-strength fibers embedded in rubber or plastic. Composite chambers made from high-strength graphite fibers in a strong adhesive called *epoxy* weigh less than steel or titanium chambers, enabling the rocket to accelerate its payload more efficiently. Solid propellants burn at a rate of about 0.6 inch (1.5 centimeters) per second.

Solid propellants can remain effective after long storage and present little danger of combusting or exploding until ignited. Furthermore, they do not need the pumping and injecting equipment required by liquid propellants. On the other hand, rocket controllers cannot easily stop or restart the burning of solid propellant. This can make a solid-propellant rocket difficult to control. One method used to stop the burning of solid propellant involves blasting the entire nozzle section from the rocket. This method, however, prevents restarting.

Rocket designers often choose solid propellants for rockets that must be easy to store, transport, and launch. Military planners prefer solid-propellant rockets for many uses because they can be stored for a long time and fired with little preparation. Solid-propellant rockets power ICBM's, including the American Minuteman III

U.S. Air Force

A shoulder-fired rocket launcher, light enough for one person to carry, fires small, explosive rockets that can destroy tanks, other armored vehicles, and many types of buildings.

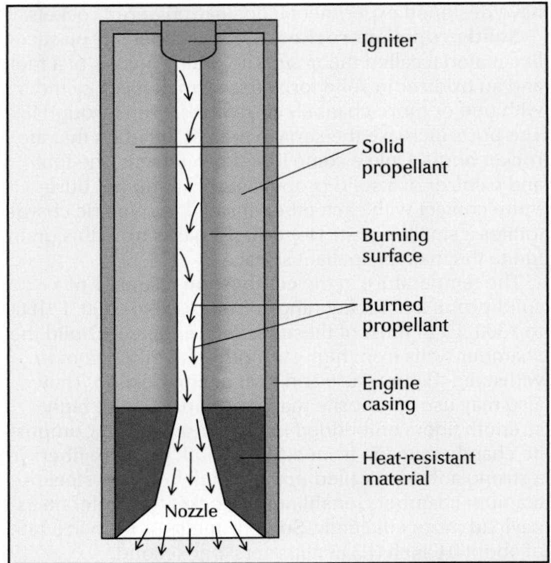

WORLD BOOK diagram by Precision Graphics

A solid-propellant rocket burns a solid material called the *grain.* Engineers design most grains with a hollow core. The propellant burns from the core outward. Unburned propellant shields the engine casing from the heat of combustion.

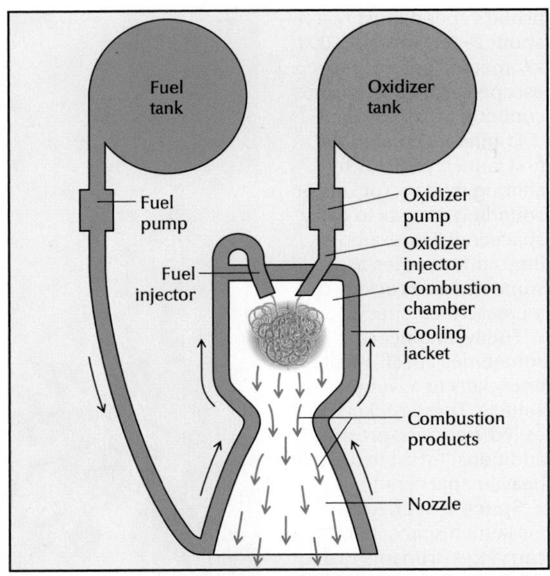

WORLD BOOK diagram by Precision Graphics

A liquid-propellant rocket carries fuel and an oxidizer in separate tanks. The fuel circulates through the engine's cooling jacket before entering the combustion chamber. This circulation preheats the fuel for combustion and helps cool the rocket.

and the Russian SS-27, or Topol-M. They also propel such smaller missiles as the American Hellfire, Patriot, Sparrow, and Sidewinder, and the British Rapier. Solid-propellant rockets often serve as sounding rockets and as boosters for launch vehicles and cruise missiles. They are also used in fireworks.

Liquid-propellant rockets burn a mixture of fuel and oxidizer in liquid form. These rockets carry the fuel and the oxidizer in separate tanks. A system of pipes and valves feeds the propellants into the combustion chamber. In larger engines, either the fuel or the oxidizer flows around the outside of the chamber before entering it. This flow cools the chamber and preheats the propellant for combustion.

A liquid-propellant rocket feeds the fuel and oxidizer into the combustion chamber using either pumps or high-pressure gas. The most common method uses pumps to force the fuel and oxidizer into the combustion chamber. Burning a small portion of the propellants provides the energy to drive the pumps. In the other method, high-pressure gas forces the fuel and oxidizer into the chamber. The gas may be nitrogen or some other gas stored under high pressure or may come from the burning of a small amount of propellants.

Some liquid propellants, called *hypergols,* ignite when the fuel and the oxidizer mix. However, most liquid propellants require an ignition system. An electric spark may ignite the propellant, or the burning of a small amount of solid propellant in the combustion chamber may do so. Liquid propellants continue to burn as long as fuel and oxidizer flow into the combustion chamber.

Engineers use thin, high-strength steel or aluminum to construct most tanks that hold liquid propellants. They may also reinforce tanks with composite materials like those used in solid-propellant rocket chambers. Most combustion chambers in liquid-propellant rockets are made of steel or nickel.

Liquid propellants usually produce greater thrust than do equal amounts of solid propellants burned in the same amount of time. Controllers can easily adjust or stop burning in a liquid-propellant rocket by increasing or decreasing the flow of propellants into the chamber. Liquid propellants, however, are difficult to handle. If the fuel and oxidizer blend without igniting, the resulting mixture often will explode easily. Liquid propellants also require complicated pumping machinery.

Scientists use liquid-propellant rockets for most space launch vehicles. Liquid-propellant rockets serve as the main engines of Europe's Ariane rocket, Russia's Soyuz rocket, and China's Long March rocket.

Hybrid rockets combine some of the advantages of both solid-propellant and liquid-propellant rockets. A hybrid rocket uses a liquid oxidizer, such as liquid oxygen, and a solid-fuel grain made of plastic or rubber. The solid-fuel grain lines the inside of the combustion chamber. A pumping system sprays the oxidizer onto the surface of the grain, which is ignited by a smaller grain or torch.

Hybrid rockets are safer than solid-propellant rockets because the propellants are not premixed and so will not ignite accidentally. Also, unlike solid-propellant rockets, hybrid rockets can vary thrust or even stop combustion by adjusting the flow of oxidizer. Hybrid engines require only half the pumping gear of liquid-propellant rockets, making them simpler to build.

A key disadvantage of hybrid rockets is that their fuel burns slowly, limiting the amount of thrust they can produce. A hybrid rocket burns grain at a rate of about 0.04 inch (1 millimeter) per second. For a given amount of

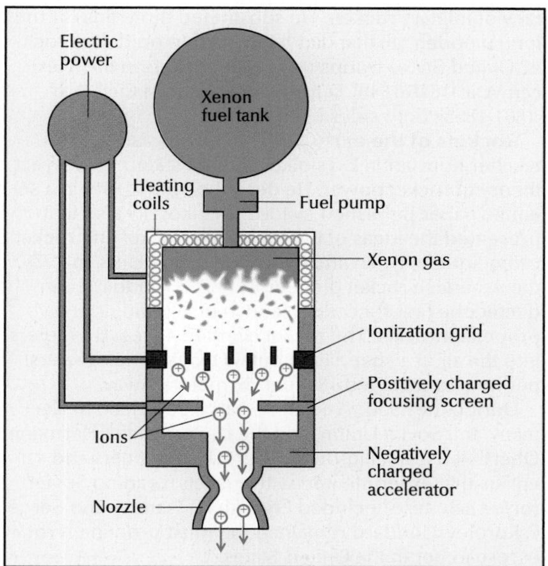

WORLD BOOK diagram by Precision Graphics

An ion rocket uses electric power to expel *ions* (charged particles). One device uses an *ionization grid* to change a gas into ions. A positively charged screen focuses the ions into a beam. A negatively charged accelerator shoots the ions out of the nozzle.

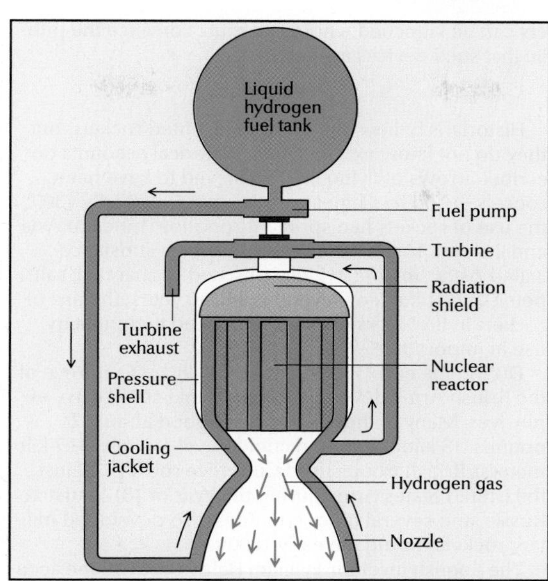

WORLD BOOK diagram by Precision Graphics

A nuclear rocket uses the heat from a nuclear reactor to change a liquid fuel into a gas. Most of the fuel flows through the reactor. Some of the fuel, heated by the nozzle of the rocket, flows through the turbine. The turbine drives the fuel pump.

propellant, hybrid rockets typically produce more thrust than solid rockets and less than liquid engines. To generate more thrust, engineers must manufacture complex fuel grains with many separate ports through which oxidizer can flow. This exposes more grain to the oxidizer.

The safety of hybrid rockets has led engineers to develop them for use in human flight. The Scaled Composites company of Mojave, California, developed a hybrid rocket called SpaceShipOne that launched from an airplane. On June 21, 2004, SpaceShipOne became the first privately funded craft to carry a person into space. It carried the American test pilot Michael Melvill more than 62 miles (100 kilometers) above Earth's surface during a brief test flight.

Researchers have also used hybrid rockets to propel targets used in missile testing and to accelerate experimental motorcycles and cars attempting land speed records. In addition, they have worked to develop hybrid rockets to boost planetary probes, maneuver satellites in orbit, and power crew escape mechanisms for launch vehicles.

Ion rockets use electric energy to expel ions from the nozzle. Engineers also call this process *ion propulsion.* Solar panels or a nuclear reactor can provide the energy.

In one design, xenon gas passes through an electrified metal grid. The grid strips electrons from the xenon atoms, turning them into positively charged ions. A positively charged screen repels the ions, focusing them into a beam. The beam then enters a negatively charged device called an *accelerator.* The accelerator speeds up the ions and shoots them out through a nozzle.

The exhaust from such rockets travels extremely fast. However, the stream of xenon ions has a relatively low mass. As a result, an ion rocket cannot produce enough thrust to overcome Earth's gravity. Ion rockets used in space must therefore be launched by chemical rockets. Once in space, though, the low rate of mass flow becomes an advantage. It enables an ion rocket to operate for a long time without running out of propellant. The xenon rocket that powered the U.S. space probe Deep Space 1, launched in 1998, fired for a total of more than 670 days using only 160 pounds (72 kilograms) of propellant. In addition, small ion rockets using xenon propellant have provided the thrust to keep communications satellites in position above Earth's surface.

Another type of ion rocket uses electromagnets rather than charged screens to accelerate xenon ions. This type of rocket carried the European Space Agency's SMART-1 lunar probe to the moon in the early 2000's.

Nuclear rockets use the heat energy of a *nuclear reactor,* a device that releases energy by splitting atoms. Some proposed designs would use hydrogen as propellant. The rocket would store the hydrogen as a liquid. Heat from the reactor would boil the liquid, creating hydrogen gas. The gas would expand rapidly and push out from the nozzle.

The exhaust speed of a nuclear rocket might reach four times that of a chemical rocket. By expelling a large quantity of hydrogen, a nuclear rocket could therefore achieve high thrust. However, a nuclear rocket would require heavy shielding because a nuclear reactor uses radioactive materials. The shielding would weigh so much that the rocket could not be practically used to boost a launch vehicle. More practical applications would use small nuclear engines with low, continuous thrust to decrease flight times to Mars or other planets.

Nuclear rocket developers must also overcome public fears that accidents involving such devices could release harmful radioactive materials. Before nuclear rockets can be launched, engineers must convince the public that such devices are safe.

History

Historians believe the Chinese invented rockets, but they do not know exactly when. Historical accounts describe "arrows of flying fire"—believed to have been rockets—used by Chinese armies in A.D. 1232. By 1300, the use of rockets had spread throughout much of Asia and Europe. These first rockets burned a substance called *black powder,* which consisted of charcoal, saltpeter, and sulfur. For several hundred years, the use of rockets in fireworks displays outranked their military use in importance.

During the early 1800's, Colonel William Congreve of the British Army developed rockets that could carry explosives. Many of these rockets weighed about 32 pounds (15 kilograms) and could travel $1\frac{3}{4}$ miles (2.7 kilometers). British troops used Congreve rockets against the United States Army during the War of 1812. Austria, Russia, and several other countries also developed military rockets during the early 1800's.

The English inventor William Hale improved the accuracy of military rockets. He substituted three fins for the long wooden tail that had been used to guide the rocket. United States troops used Hale rockets in the Mexican War (1846-1848). During the American Civil War (1861-1865), both sides used rockets.

From *Rocketry and Space Exploration* by Andrew G. Haley
© 1958 by Litton Education Publishing, Inc.

Chinese warriors fired rockets in battle during the A.D. 1200's. The use of rockets as weapons and fireworks spread from China throughout much of Asia and Europe during the next century.

Rockets of the early 1900's. The Russian school teacher Konstantin E. Tsiolkovsky first stated the correct theory of rocket power. He described his theory in a scientific paper published in 1903. Tsiolkovsky also first presented the ideas of the multistage rocket and rockets using liquid oxygen and hydrogen propellants. In 1926, the American rocket pioneer Robert H. Goddard conducted the first successful launch of a liquid-propellant rocket. The rocket climbed 41 feet (13 meters) into the air at a speed of about 60 miles (97 kilometers) per hour and landed 184 feet (56 meters) away.

During the 1930's, rocket research advanced in Germany, the Soviet Union, and the United States. Hermann Oberth led a small group of German engineers and scientists that experimented with rockets. Leading Soviet rocket scientists included Fridrikh A. Tsander and Sergei P. Korolev. Goddard remained the most prominent rocket researcher in the United States.

During World War II, German engineers under the direction of Wernher von Braun developed the powerful V-2 guided missile. Germany bombarded London and Antwerp, Belgium, with hundreds of V-2's during the last months of the war. American forces captured many V-2 missiles and sent them to the United States for use in research. After the war, von Braun and about 150 other German scientists moved to the United States to continue their work with rockets. Some other German rocket experts went to the Soviet Union.

High-altitude rockets. For several years after World War II, U.S. scientists benefited greatly by conducting experiments with captured German V-2's. These V-2's became the first rockets used for high-altitude research.

The first high-altitude rockets designed and built in the United States included the WAC Corporal, the Aerobee, and the Viking. The 16-foot (4.9-meter) WAC Corporal reached altitudes of about 45 miles (72 kilometers) during test flights in 1945. Early models of the Aerobee climbed about 70 miles (110 kilometers). In 1949, the U.S. Navy launched the Viking, an improved liquid-propellant rocket based chiefly on the V-2. The Viking measured more than 45 feet (14 meters) long, much longer than the Aerobee. But the first models of the

© National Geographic Society courtesy Esther C. Goddard

Robert H. Goddard, *left,* a pioneer American rocket scientist, inspects a gasoline- and oxygen-powered rocket as his assistants look on. This rocket was built under Goddard's supervision in 1940.

Viking rose only about 50 miles (80 kilometers).

Rockets developed by the U.S. armed forces during the 1950's included the Jupiter and the Pershing. The Jupiter could travel about 1,600 miles (2,600 kilometers), and the Pershing about 450 miles (720 kilometers).

The U.S. Navy conducted the first successful launch of a Polaris underwater missile in 1960. United States space scientists later used many military rockets developed in the 1950's as the basis for launch vehicles.

Rocket-powered airplanes. On Oct. 14, 1947, Captain Chuck Yeager of the U.S. Air Force made the first *supersonic* (faster than sound) flight. He flew a rocket-powered airplane called the X-1.

A rocket engine also powered the X-15, which set an unofficial airplane altitude record of 354,200 feet (107,960 meters) in 1963. In one flight, the X-15 reached a peak speed of 4,520 miles (7,274 kilometers) per hour—more than six times the speed of sound. A privately owned and developed rocket-powered plane called the EZ-Rocket began piloted test flights in 2001.

The space age began on Oct. 4, 1957, when the Soviet Union launched the first artificial satellite, Sputnik 1, aboard a two-stage rocket. On Jan. 31, 1958, the U.S. Army launched the first American satellite, Explorer 1, into orbit with a Jupiter-C rocket.

On April 12, 1961, a Soviet rocket put a cosmonaut, Major Yuri A. Gagarin, into orbit around Earth for the first time. On May 5, 1961, a Redstone rocket launched Commander Alan B. Shepard, Jr., the first American to travel in space. On April 12, 1981, the United States launched the rocket-powered Columbia, the first space shuttle to orbit Earth. A private company called SpaceX launched the first commercial orbiting spacecraft in 2010 and launched a spacecraft that reached the International Space Station in 2012. For more information on the history of rockets in space travel, see **Space exploration.**

Rocket research. In the early 2000's, engineers and scientists worked to develop lightweight rocket engines that used safer propellants. They also searched for more efficient propellants that did not require refrigeration. Engineers began designing and testing smaller rocket engines for use in smaller vehicles, such as tiny satellites that may weigh only a few pounds or kilograms when fully loaded. Stephen D. Heister

Related articles in *World Book* include:

Airplane (Rocket engines)
American Institute of Aeronautics and Astronautics
Army, United States (Missiles)
Bazooka
Congreve, Sir William
Fireworks
Goddard, Robert H.
Guided missile
Jet propulsion
Korolev, Sergei Pavlovich
Rocket, Model
Space exploration
Telemetry
Torpedo
Von Braun, Wernher
Yeager, Chuck

Outline

I. How rockets work
A. Parts of a rocket
B. Multistage rockets
II. How rockets are used
A. Military use
B. Atmospheric research
C. Launching probes and satellites
D. Space travel
E. Other uses
III. Kinds of rocket engines
A. Solid-propellant rockets
B. Liquid-propellant rockets
C. Hybrid rockets
D. Electric rockets
E. Nuclear rockets
IV. History

Questions

What makes a rocket move?
How do jet engines differ from rockets?
What is an intercontinental ballistic missile (ICBM)?
What is a sounding rocket? A space probe?
What nation probably invented rockets?
What are some problems with developing nuclear rockets?

Rocket was a steam locomotive that served as the model for nearly all steam locomotives built after it. The *Rocket's* boiler passed heated air through multiple tubes surrounded by water, making steam faster than boilers with only a single pipe. The *Rocket* also had driving rods connecting the pistons directly to the wheels. Many earlier locomotives used gears to drive the wheels.

In 1829, the *Rocket* won the Rainhill Trials, a competition held by the Liverpool and Manchester Railway to find the best locomotive to use on the railroad. In the competition, the *Rocket* reached a speed of 29 miles (46 kilometers) per hour. Robert Stephenson, an English engineer, designed the *Rocket* and built it with the help of his father, George. John H. White, Jr.

See also **Stephenson, Robert.**

Rocket, Model, is a miniature rocket patterned after military or space rockets. Model rockets fly the same way as do military or space rockets. But models weigh less than 3 ½ pounds (1.5 kilograms), and they usually measure only 8 to 24 inches (20 to 61 centimeters) long. Model rockets are also known as *space models.*

The engine of a model rocket produces its power by burning a specially manufactured solid fuel. Model rockets can rise as high as 2,000 feet (610 meters) in a few seconds, traveling as fast as 300 miles (480 kilometers) an hour. Some kinds of model rockets carry a *pay-*

Vinson B. Huegele

Many kinds of model rockets can be built by hobbyists. They can be realistic, futuristic, sporty, or simple. These model rockets are mounted on a club multipad launcher. The model at left ascends like a rocket and then glides back to Earth.

load. A payload is any small cargo, such as a miniature camera or a radio transmitter. A few model rockets have two or more sections called *stages* assembled on top of one another. Each stage has an engine that starts to operate when the previous stage's engine burns out.

Large numbers of young people and adults build and fly model rockets as a hobby. Most rocketeers build their first rockets with kits sold by hobby stores. Model rocketry is educational, because it teaches principles of science and mathematics.

Model rocketry is a safe hobby, but certain rules must be followed at all times: (1) Rockets must be powered by factory-made engines. (2) Rockets must be built of such lightweight materials as cardboard, plastics, and balsa wood, with no metal structural parts. (3) Rockets must be launched with electrical equipment from a distance of at least 15 feet (4.6 meters) and not in winds over 20 miles (32 kilometers) per hour. (4) The launching device must be pointed within 30 degrees of vertical. (5) Rockets must have a recovery system to provide a safe landing. In addition, payloads should never include a live animal or a flammable or explosive substance.

Parts of a model rocket

Every model rocket has seven basic parts: (1) the body tube, (2) the launch lug, (3) fins, (4) the engine holder, (5) the engine, (6) the nose cone, and (7) the recovery device. In addition, a rocket has a launch system to get it into the air.

The body tube is the main airframe. It is made of cardboard.

The launch lug is a narrow paper or plastic tube fastened to the side of the body tube. It fits loosely over the *launch rod,* a long, vertical metal rod that is part of the launch system. During liftoff, the launch lug guides the rocket and keeps it vertical.

Fins help the rocket travel straight during flight. The fins are made of cardboard, plastics, or wood.

The engine holder, or *engine mount,* securely retains the engine in the body during the flight.

The engine of most rockets consists of a thick cardboard tube that contains the solid fuel. Such an engine can be used only once. The amount of energy contained in the engine is indicated by a letter in an alphabetical label code. The power levels of model rocket engines range from "A" to "G," with the energy level increasing by twice the power of the previous letter. For example, a "C" engine has twice the power of a "B" engine and can send a rocket twice as high.

The nose cone is a rounded wood or plastic point that reduces air resistance.

The recovery device returns the rocket slowly to the ground. One such device is a small parachute or streamer made of paper, cloth, or plastic film. It is carried inside the body tube behind the nose cone. At the height of the flight, an ejection charge in the engine forces the nose cone forward and separates it from the body tube. This forward movement also releases the parachute.

The parachute is attached to the nose cone and the body tube by a strong *shock cord* made of rubber or other elastic. This cord prevents the parachute from tearing away from the rocket after the ejection. A wad of flame-resistant material is inserted into the body tube between the parachute and the engine. It protects the parachute from the heat of the ejection charge.

The launch system consists of a launch pad and an engine ignition system with a battery. A typical launch pad is made up of a three-legged base, the launch rod, and a deflector. The deflector keeps the engine's hot exhaust gases from coming into contact with the launch pad or the ground.

The ignition system includes a switching device called the *launch controller* and a battery. Wires connect the launch controller to the *igniter,* a special wire inserted into the engine. When the operator presses the launch button of the controller, an electric current from the battery makes the igniter become hot. Heat produced by the igniter starts the engine.

Building and flying model rockets

The kits used by many model rocketeers include all parts except the engine and the launch system, which must be purchased separately. Other necessary materials include an adhesive, sandpaper for smoothing the rocket's surfaces, and a sharp knife for cutting out the fins or other parts. Many enthusiasts paint their completed models to make them look more realistic.

Before flying a model, a rocketeer should find out if model rocketry is regulated by any laws in his or her area. Next, the rocketeer selects a safe launch site. The site should be a large, open area away from power lines, tall buildings, and trees. It also should be free of anything that could burn easily, such as dead grass or dry weeds. The length of the shortest side of the site should measure at least a fourth of the highest altitude

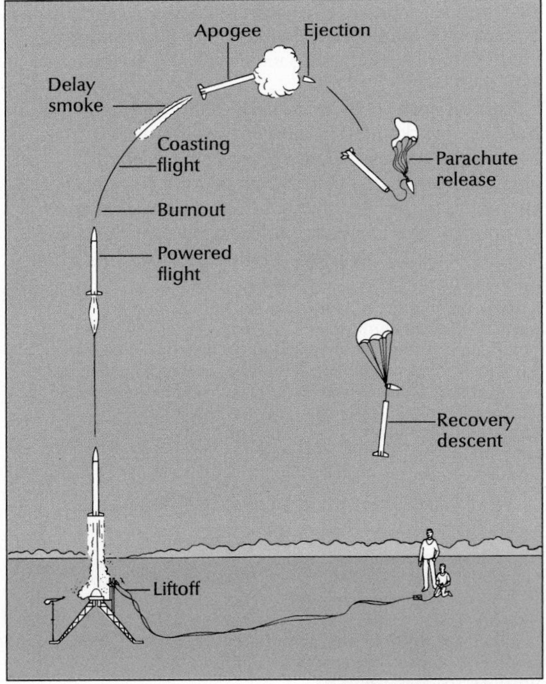

WORLD BOOK drawing by Art Grebetz

The flight pattern of a model rocket consists of several phases. The rocket's *apogee* (maximum altitude) can be varied by using engines of different sizes.

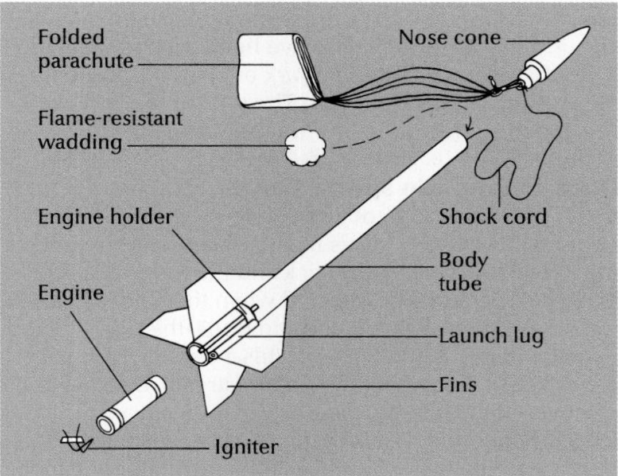

The basic parts of a model rocket are sold in kits by many hobby stores. The stores sell rocket engines separately, and a rocketeer can select from a variety of power levels.

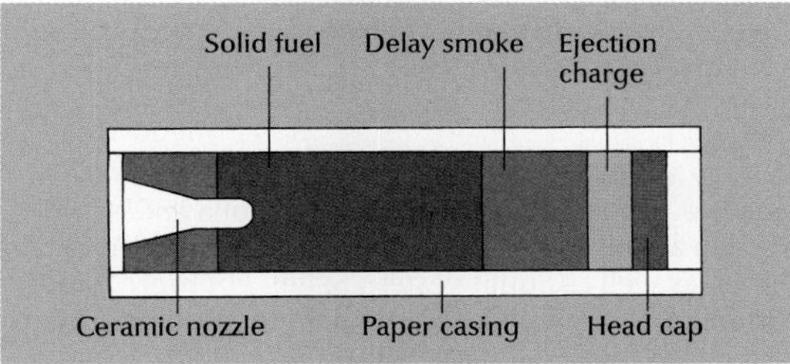

WORLD BOOK diagrams by Art Grebetz

A model rocket engine includes the solid fuel, which propels the rocket. The delay smoke allows it to slow down, and the ejection charge releases the parachute.

that the rocket will reach.

At the launch site, the rocketeer installs the engine and mounts the rocket on the launch pad. After making sure that all spectators are a safe distance from the rocket, the rocketeer calls out a five-second countdown and presses the launch button. The rocket lifts off and soars into the air. At its maximum altitude, the rocket releases its recovery device and floats to the ground.

Model rocket clubs and competition

Local model rocket clubs may be formed among almost any organization, such as a school or youth group. The groups also may have their own launch systems and other equipment. Many clubs hold contests. One contest is *egg-lofting,* which involves launching a rocket that carries an egg. Each contestant sends a rocket as high as possible and tries to recover the egg unbroken. The Team America Rocketry Challenge (TARC) is the world's largest model rocket egg-lofting contest. Hundreds of student teams compete annually in the TARC.

Several countries have national model rocket organizations. They set up safety rules, certify model rocket engines, issue publications, and charter local clubs. The national organization in the United States is the National Association of Rocketry (NAR) in Marion, Iowa. Model rocket clubs can become chartered sections of the NAR. The Canadian Association of Rocketry (Association Canadienne de Fuséologie) is in Lethbridge, Alberta. Through associations, rocketeers can set flight records and become national or world champions. The world championships are held every two years. Vinson B. Huegele

Rockford (pop. 152,871; met. area pop. 349,431) is a manufacturing center and one of the largest cities in Illinois. Rockford lies on the Rock River, 17 miles (27 kilometers) south of the Wisconsin border. The city is about halfway between Chicago and Dubuque, Iowa (see **Illinois** [political map]).

Rockford was once the nation's leading center for *screw products* (fasteners, nuts, and bolts), and the city remains an important producer of metal products and machinery. Today, the area's economy is driven by small businesses and the aerospace and service industries. Truck lines and freight railroads serve the area.

Rockford is known for its treelined streets, golf courses, extensive walking paths, and fine parks and public gardens. The city is home to Rockford University. The Burpee Museum of Natural History collection includes skeletons of a juvenile *Tyrannosaurus rex* and *Triceratops.*

Rockford was founded in 1834 and became a city in 1852. Its original settlers were chiefly New Englanders, but large numbers of Swedes, Irish, Germans, and Italians arrived after 1850. Rockford has a mayor-council government and is the seat of Winnebago County.

Catherine Forslund and Suzanne Crandall

Rockne, *RAHK nee,* **Knute,** *noot* (1888-1931), was an American college coach. From 1918 until his death on March 31, 1931, in an airplane crash in Kansas, he served as head coach at the University of Notre Dame. His teams' colorful style, emphasizing speed and deception, helped popularize football. An outstanding strategist, he was famous for his inspirational talks to his players. His "Win one for the Gipper" speech propelled Notre Dame to victory over Army in 1928. It was featured in the biographical film *Knute Rockne, All American* (1940), which starred Ronald Reagan as Notre Dame star George Gipp. Rockne's teams won 105 games, lost 12, and tied 5. His winning percentage of .881 is the highest in college football.

University of Notre Dame

Knute Rockne

Knute Kenneth Rockne was born in Voss, Norway, on March 4, 1888. His family moved to the United States in 1893 and settled in Chicago. Rockne studied chemistry at Notre Dame, graduating in 1914 with highest honors. As a player, his pass receiving was important in Notre Dame's 1913 upset of Army, a game that first brought national attention to Notre Dame and to the forward pass. Bob Carroll

Rockwell, Norman (1894-1978), was an American illustrator. His paintings of everyday, usually small-town people almost always tell stories, often humorous ones. They show careful observation and technical skill. Rockwell was a meticulous craftsman, whose works por-

Oil painting on canvas (1950); Mr. and Mrs. Ken Stuart Collection

Rockwell's painting *Saying Grace* shows his detailed, realistic style. It is also an example of the artist's sentimental treatment of scenes from middle-class American life.

tray homely incidents, well-defined character, and a wealth of supporting detail. He gained great popularity as a cover illustrator for *The Saturday Evening Post* and other magazines. He also did art work for many advertisers. He illustrated the "Four Freedoms" of the Atlantic Charter in a well-known series of paintings in 1943.

Rockwell was born on Feb. 3, 1894, in New York City. From 1908 to 1910, he studied at the Chase School of Art (later the New York School of Art), and then at the National Academy of Design and the Art Students League. As a teenager, he became the art director of *Boys' Life*, the official magazine of the Boy Scouts of America. He created his first cover for the *Saturday Evening Post* in 1916, and during the next 47 years he created another 312 covers for the magazine. In 1969, the Norman Rockwell Museum was founded in Stockbridge, Massachusetts. Rockwell died on Nov. 8, 1978. Sarah Burns

Rocky Mountain National Park, a mountain playground in northern Colorado, is one of the most magnificent sections of the Rocky Mountains. The federal government made it a national park in 1915. Some of the highest and most rugged mountain country in the United States is in the park. It has more than 60 peaks over 12,000 feet (3,660 meters) high. The highest, Longs Peak, rises 14,255 feet (4,345 meters). Rocky Mountain National Park has two main entrances, Estes Park on the east, and Grand Lake on the west. For the park's area, see **National Park System** (table: National parks).

Naturalist Enos Mills has been called "the father of Rocky Mountain National Park." It was through his efforts that the park was established. He built his log cabin in a valley that looked up to Longs Peak.

About 150 lakes lie within Rocky Mountain National Park. They reflect the snowy mountain peaks in summer and freeze in winter. The park is noted for its wildlife, including Rocky Mountain sheep (bighorn), elk, deer, and coyotes. More than 280 varieties of birds and over 1,000 species of flowering plants have been seen in the park.

Rocky Mountain National Park once was a home for the Ute and Arapaho Indians. The area of the park was also a rich source of furs for trappers.

Critically reviewed by the National Park Service

Rocky Mountain spotted fever is a serious disease that is often fatal. One of the *rickettsias,* germs slightly larger than viruses, causes the disease. The germ infects the Rocky Mountain wood tick and the American dog tick. The ticks become infected when they bite small mammals, such as field mice and dogs, that are infected with the germ. When the tick bites a person, it transfers the rickettsia to that person's bloodstream. Doctors first discovered the fever in the Rocky Mountain area of the United States, but it occurs throughout the country. It is most common in the Southeastern and Middle Atlantic States. About 600 cases are reported every year, usually in late spring or early summer. It begins with chills and fever, and severe pains in the leg muscles and the joints. Then a rash develops. Rocky Mountain spotted fever resembles many of the typhus diseases (see **Typhus**).

Tetracyclines, chloramphenicol, and other antibiotics are effective in treatment. Vaccines against the disease have proved relatively ineffective. Recovery from the fever gives complete immunity. Thomas P. Monath

See also Rickettsia.

Rocky Mountain States are Colorado, Idaho, Montana, Nevada, Utah, and Wyoming. Arizona and New Mexico are also sometimes considered Rocky Mountain States, as well as Southwestern States. For more information on the region, see **United States** (Regions). See also the articles on the states that make up the region.

Rocky Mountains are the largest mountain system in North America. The Rocky Mountain Chain extends over 3,000 miles (4,800 kilometers) through the United States and Canada. It is about 350 miles (563 kilometers) wide in some places. The U.S. Rockies stretch through New Mexico, Colorado, Utah, Wyoming, Idaho, Montana, Washington, and Alaska. The Canadian Rockies spread through the provinces of Alberta and British Columbia, and the Northwest Territories and Yukon territory. Visitors to the Rockies enjoy snow-capped peaks, sparkling lakes, and other magnificent scenery. Several U.S. and Canadian national parks are in the Rocky Mountains. The region is also famous for its ski resorts and wild game.

The Rockies form the Continental Divide, which separates rivers that flow west to the Pacific Ocean from those going east to the Atlantic Ocean (see **Divide**). The Canadian Rockies also separate rivers flowing north to the Arctic Ocean from those that empty into the Pacific Ocean to the southwest. A number of rivers, including the Arkansas, the Colorado, the Columbia, the Missouri, and the Rio Grande, begin in the Rockies.

Chief ranges of the Rockies include (1) the Southern Rockies, (2) the Middle Rockies, (3) the Northern Rockies, (4) the Canadian Rockies, (5) the Selwyn and Mackenzie mountains, and (6) the Brooks Range.

The Southern Rockies extend from the Sangre de Cristo Range in New Mexico to central Wyoming. They include the highest peaks in the Rocky Mountain System. Wheeler Peak, the highest peak in New Mexico, is 13,161 feet (4,011 meters) high. Colorado's tallest peak, Mount Elbert, rises 14,433 feet (4,399 meters). Colorado has about 55 peaks over 14,000 feet (4,270 meters) high.

The Middle Rockies, which include the Grand Tetons, run from northwestern Colorado and northern Utah to the upper Yellowstone River in Montana. The highest peaks in this range include King's Peak, 13,528 feet (4,123 meters) high, in Utah; Gannett Peak, 13,804 feet (4,207 meters) high, in Wyoming; and Granite Peak, 12,799 feet (3,901 meters) high, in Montana. Yellowstone National Park is in the Middle Rockies.

The Northern Rockies stretch from southern Idaho to the border between the United States and Canada. Borah Peak, the tallest mountain in Idaho, rises 12,662 feet (3,859 meters) in the Northern Rockies. Glacier National Park lies in this region.

The Canadian Rockies extend from the border north through British Columbia and Alberta. Some of the finest scenic areas of the Rockies lie in Alberta, including Banff and Jasper national parks.

The Selwyn Mountains extend beyond the Liard River in northern Canada. The Mackenzie Range lies east of the Selwyns. The Brooks Range crosses northern Alaska. Part of the range lies north of the Arctic Circle.

Plant and animal life. Forests of piñon pines and junipers cover the lower slopes of the Southern Rockies. Firs, pines, and spruces are abundant in the higher areas of the Rockies. Sagebrush dominates the Wyoming Basin and other valley regions of the Middle Rockies and the Southern Rockies.

Rocky Mountain goats and bighorn sheep live above the *timber line,* the elevation beyond which trees cannot grow. Bears, deer, hares, elk, minks, mountain lions, porcupines, squirrels, and other animals occupy the higher forested slopes. Chipmunks, coyotes, moose, and muskrats make their homes in the grassy valleys between the mountains. Rainbow trout, grayling, cutthroat trout, and other fishes swim in Rocky Mountain streams.

Agriculture and industry. Livestock raising is the main agricultural activity in the Rockies. Cattle and sheep are driven to mountain pastures for the summer and back to warmer valleys in winter. Farmers raise chili peppers and pinto beans in the Southern Rockies. Grains, potatoes, sugar beets, and truck vegetables are raised in Colorado, Idaho, Montana, and Utah.

The chief industrial activities of the Rocky Mountains are mining and lumbering. The Southern Rockies, especially the Leadville District of Colorado, produce gold, lead, molybdenum, silver, uranium, and zinc. The Wyoming Basin, in southwestern Wyoming, is a coal, petroleum, and natural gas producing area. Lumbering and the mining of coal, copper, lead, silver, and zinc are important in the Northern and Canadian Rockies. Much of the coking coal used in Japan's iron and steel industry is exported from the Fernie, British Columbia, area.

Tourism contributes greatly to the economy of the Rocky Mountain states and provinces. Every year, millions of visitors enjoy the region's national parks, ski resorts, and many other attractions.

History. Most peaks of the Rockies were formed millions of years ago during a great upheaval of Earth's crust. The sides of the mountains contain fossils of animals that once lived in the sea, and rocks that were formed in the hot interior of Earth. The southern half of the Rockies includes mountains that were once volcanic plateaus. Through the centuries, the peaks of the

Rocky Mountains

The Rocky Mountains extend more than 3,000 miles (4,800 kilometers) across the western part of North America, from northern Alaska to northern New Mexico. The Rockies are famous for their scenic beauty.

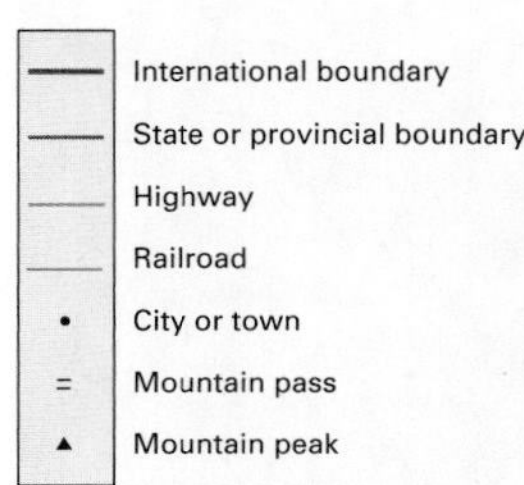

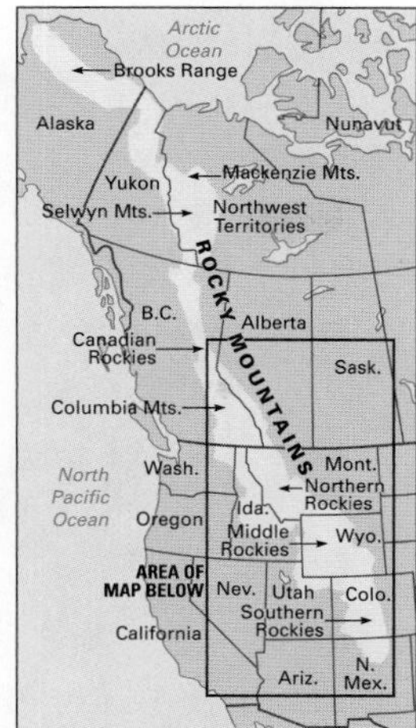

WORLD BOOK maps

Glenn Tooke, Image Finders

The Rocky Mountains are famous for their majestic peaks and other beautiful scenery. The Canadian Rockies tower over the resort town of Banff in southwestern Alberta, *shown here.*

Rockies have been cut into various formations by the forces of wind, rain, and glaciers.

Many Indian tribes lived along the flanks of the Rockies when Europeans first arrived in North America. They included the Coeur d'Alene, Flathead, Kalispel, Kutenai, Shoshone, and Ute. The first Europeans to reach the Rockies were Spanish explorers. They established a colony near what is now Santa Fe, New Mexico, in 1598.

The American explorers Meriwether Lewis and William Clark traveled through the Northern Rockies in 1805 and 1806. Another American, Zebulon M. Pike, explored the Southern Rockies during this period. Pikes Peak, in central Colorado, was named for him. In the early 1800's, the Rockies became the center of the American fur trade (see **Fur trade** [The 1800's]).

The Rockies hampered transportation during the westward movement of the 1800's. However, the Oregon Trail, the longest overland route used by explorers and pioneers, wound through the Rockies (see **Oregon Trail**). The first railroad route through the Rockies was built in the Wyoming Basin in 1868. Today, Interstate Highway 80 runs through the Wyoming Basin. Major railroad routes also go through the Rockies.

The Eisenhower Memorial Tunnel, west of Denver, is the highest motor-traffic tunnel in the world. The tunnel has an altitude of about 11,000 feet (3,400 meters). Moffat Tunnel, one of the longest railroad tunnels in the United States, cuts through James Peak, also west of Denver.

John Edwin Coffman

Related articles in *World Book* include:

Banff National Park
Bighorn
Glacier National Park
Grand Teton National Park
Jasper National Park
Pikes Peak
Rocky Mountain National Park
Teton Range
Wasatch Range
Yellowstone National Park

Rococo, *roh KOH koh,* is a style of art that flourished in western Europe from approximately 1700 to 1780. The term comes from a French word for a fanciful rock or shell design. Rococo implies a refined, elegant feeling and style.

Rococo found its fullest expression in France, where the leading representatives were the painters François Boucher, Jean Honoré Fragonard, and Antoine Watteau. They worked primarily for royal and aristocratic clients. Their paintings differed greatly in style and subject matter from those of the preceding Baroque period. A typical Baroque painting was created on a heroic and grand scale, and usually presented Christian religious subjects. Rococo paintings were intimate in scale and delicate in manner. They often portrayed scenes from classical mythology. Rococo artists also created a new category of painting called the *fête galante.* Their paintings showed gatherings of elegantly dressed figures in parks and gardens.

Outside France, there were other artists during this period who worked in a bright, lively style characteristic of Rococo. They included Giovanni Battista Tiepolo in Italy and Thomas Gainsborough in England.

The ornate and decorative style of Rococo was also applied to architecture, furniture, porcelain, tapestries, and opera and theater scenery. In architecture, Rococo reached its greatest splendor in the palaces, monasteries, and churches of southern Germany and Austria.

Eric M. Zafran

Related articles in *World Book* include:

Architecture (The 1700's)
Baroque
Boucher, François
Fragonard, Jean Honoré
Furniture (French styles; Historical revivals)
Painting (The 1600's and 1700's)
Watteau, Antoine

Rod. See **Eye** (The retina; diagram).

Roddick, Andy (1982-), an American tennis star, won the men's title at the US Open in 2003. The same year, he reached the semifinals of the Australian Open and Wimbledon championships. Roddick finished the 2003 season ranked first in the world in men's tennis. Roddick became known for his strong all-around game, especially his powerful serve, which reached a speed of more than 150 miles (241 kilometers) per hour.

Andrew Stephen Roddick was born on Aug. 30, 1982, in Omaha, Nebraska. He was a dominant player in junior tennis, finishing number one in the world as a junior in 2000. He won six junior singles titles and seven junior doubles titles before turning professional in 2000 at the age of 17. Roddick announced his retirement as a player in 2012. Tony Lance

Rodent, *ROH duhnt,* is an animal with front teeth especially suited to gnawing hard objects. Squirrels, beavers, and rats are rodents. Squirrels can break the shells of nuts with their front teeth. Beavers can gnaw through tree trunks, and rats can gnaw through some wood and plaster walls. The many kinds of rodents include gophers, hamsters, mice, and porcupines.

All rodents have two top and two bottom front teeth called *incisors.* They wear away at the tips but do not wear out until late in the animal's lifetime because they keep growing until the animal is old. The incisors wear

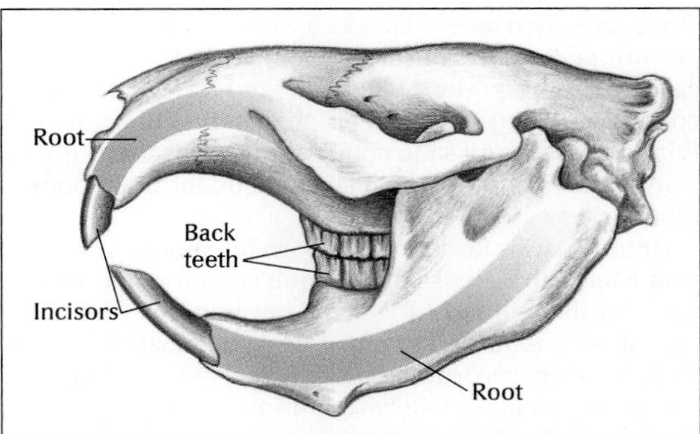

WORLD BOOK illustration by Sarah Woodward

All rodents have chisellike upper and lower front teeth called *incisors.* They can be seen in the beaver skull shown here.

faster in the back than in front. As a result, they have a chisellike edge, well-suited to gnawing. Rodents also have back teeth consisting of molars and premolars that they use for chewing. The space between the incisors and back teeth is called the *diastema.*

Rodents are *mammals* (animals that feed their young milk). There are more individual rodents than there are individuals of all other kinds of mammals combined. Rodents live in almost all parts of the world.

Mice are the smallest rodents, and capybaras of South America are the largest. Some capybaras are as much as 4 feet (1.2 meters) long. Most rodents are *herbivorous* (plant eaters). However, rats and other rodents eat almost any food.

Rodents are both helpful and harmful to people. Some rodents eat harmful insects and weeds, and some have valuable fur. Scientists use mice and rats in research. But some rodents damage crops and other property. Many rodents also carry serious diseases, such as plague and typhus. Clyde Jones

Scientific classification. Rodents make up the order Rodentia.

Related articles. See the following articles on rodents:

Agouti	Dormouse	Lemming	Porcupine
Animal (A table of animal intelligence)	Flying squirrel	Marmot	Prairie dog
Beaver	Gerbil	Mole-rat	Rat
Capybara	Gopher	Mountain beaver	Springhare
Cavy	Guinea pig	Mouse	Squirrel
Chinchilla	Hamster	Muskrat	Viscacha
Chipmunk	Jerboa	Nutria	Vole
	Jumping mouse	Paca	Woodchuck
	Kangaroo rat		Woodrat

Rodeo, *ROH dee oh* or *roh DAY oh,* is a sport that combines the riding and roping skills of cowboys and cowgirls with the color and the spirit of the Old West. In addition, the word *rodeo* refers to a rodeo contest. Rodeo contests are held in a number of regions of the United States, Canada, and Australia.

There are two main groups of rodeo events: (1) rough stock events and (2) timed events. Rough stock events feature cowboys or cowgirls trying to ride bucking horses or bulls for a specified number of seconds. The judges award points to the contestants, chiefly for their form and how well they spur the animals. Timed events are judged according to how quickly the contestants complete the required task.

Most rodeos have three rough stock events and three to five timed events. The rough stock events are bareback bronc riding, saddle bronc riding, and bull riding. The timed events are calf roping, steer wrestling, team roping, steer roping, and barrel racing. In most rodeos, only women compete in barrel racing, and only men compete in the other events. But all-women's rodeos include some events that only men enter in other rodeos. The treatment of rodeo animals in the United States follows rules established in consultation with the American Humane Association.

Bareback bronc riding is an event in which the rider must remain mounted for 8 seconds while spurring the horse as it bucks. With one hand, the rider holds onto the *bareback rigging,* a device made of leather that is cinched to the horse like a saddle.

Saddle bronc riding is an event that resembles bareback bronc riding, except that the rider uses a saddle, a halter, and a single rein. The rider must hold the rein in one hand and keep the other hand in the air without touching himself or the horse.

Bull riding does not require contestants to spur the animal. The riders try to remain seated for 8 seconds by holding onto an unknotted rope looped around the bull's belly. They hold the rope with one hand, and the free hand must not touch themselves or the bull.

Calf roping calls for teamwork between contestants and their horses. A contestant chases the calf on horseback, ropes it, and dismounts. The horse backs up so that the rope is held tight and the calf cannot break free. The contestant throws the calf to the ground and ties three of its legs together.

Steer wrestling, also called *bulldogging,* is one of two events in which the contestant may have a helper, called a *hazer.* The hazer keeps the steer running in a straight line so the cowboy can slide off his horse and grab the steer's horns. Then the cowboy wrestles the steer to the ground.

Team roping is the only event in which two contestants work together. One contestant ropes a steer's horns, and the other ropes its hind legs. The team finishes when both members have pulled their ropes tight at a 90-degree angle from the steer.

Steer roping is held at a small number of rodeos. The event displays a way to bring a running steer to the ground before the contestant dismounts from his horse. A contestant on horseback ropes a running steer around its horns from one side. Next, the rider races the horse behind the steer to the other side, causing the steer to trip over the rope. The contestant then dismounts and ties the animal's hind legs together.

Barrel racing is a regular women's event in most rodeos. Each contestant runs her horse in a cloverleaf pattern of three turns around three barrels. Judges add 5 seconds to a rider's time for each barrel she knocks over. Horses have dominant feet, just as people have a dominant hand. Contestants can choose whether to go to the right barrel or left barrel first and determine whether to make two of the three turns to the right or the left.

Cowgirl barrel racing is a fan favorite because it is easy to understand, much like a horse race. The event has become one of the most popular for contestants and commonly has the most entries in many rodeos.

© Thinkstock

Barrel racing is a women's rodeo event in which a contestant rides her horse as fast as she can in a cloverleaf pattern around three barrels. She is penalized for each barrel she knocks over.

All-women's rodeos have some events designed only for women and some that resemble men's events at other rodeos. In all-women's rodeos, cowgirls compete in bareback bronc riding and bull riding. The cowgirls must remain mounted for 6 seconds and can hold on with two hands. A steer may be substituted for a bull.

Women also compete in barrel racing, team roping, calf roping, and *break-away* roping. In all-women's rodeos, calf roping is called *tie-down* roping. In break-away roping, a rope is tied to the saddle horn with ribbon or string. After the rider ropes the calf, she stops her horse. The running calf breaks the tie, pulling the rope from the saddle horn.

Cowgirls also compete in *goat tying* and *steer undecorating*. In goat tying, a cowgirl rides up to a goat that is tied to a stake with a long rope. The cowgirl must trip the goat to the ground and tie three of its legs together. In steer undecorating, a cowgirl on horseback chases a steer that has a ribbon taped to its back. The cowgirl must get the ribbon while the steer is running in a straight line.

History. Rodeo developed from various ranching activities of the late 1800's. For example, after working on a trail drive or roundup, cowboys gathered and competed in such skills as bronc riding and steer roping. The first rodeo to charge an admission fee to spectators and offer prizes was held in Prescott, Arizona, in 1888.

Cowboys formed the first professional rodeo organization in 1936. Today, professional rodeos are sponsored by the Professional Rodeo Cowboys Association, by the Women's Professional Rodeo Association, by the International Professional Rodeo Association, and by numerous regional associations. Rodeos for young people are supervised by the National Little Britches Rodeo Association, the National High School Rodeo Association, and the National Intercollegiate Rodeo Association.

Critically reviewed by the International Professional Rodeo Association

See also **Bronco**; and the *Annual events* section of **Alberta; Colorado; Montana; Nevada; North Dakota; Oregon; South Dakota; Texas**; and **Wyoming.**

Rodgers, Jimmie (1897-1933), was a country music performer. Rodgers developed a unique style of music called the "blue yodel," which blended Negro blues and country yodeling. Often called "the Singing Brakeman," Rodgers wrote and sang songs about trains that were among the first to call national attention to rural Southern music.

James Charles Rodgers was born on Sept. 8, 1897, near Meridian, Mississippi. He quit school at age 13 to work for the railroad. In 1924, he became sick with tuberculosis and turned to music as an occupation. In 1927, Rodgers recorded for Ralph Peer, a recording company executive, who was touring the South recording folk music. Rodgers recorded two songs, "Sleep Baby Sleep" and "The Soldier's Sweetheart." Under Peer's supervision, Rodgers recorded more than 100 songs during the next six years, until he died of tuberculosis on May 26, 1933. The songs included "T. for Texas," "TB Blues," "Mule Skinner Blues," and "Waitin' for a Train." He was elected to the Country Music Hall of Fame in 1961. Lee Rector

Rodgers, Richard (1902-1979), became famous as a composer for the American musical theater. He worked chiefly with two great lyric writers, Lorenz Hart and Oscar Hammerstein II. Rodgers's songs include "The Lady Is a Tramp" and "Falling in Love with Love," written with Hart, and "People Will Say We're in Love" and "Some Enchanted Evening," written with Hammerstein.

Rodgers was born on June 28, 1902, in New York City and attended Columbia University. He began to work with Hart on amateur shows in 1919. They achieved their first professional success with *The Garrick Gaieties* (1925). During the 1920's and 1930's, Rodgers and Hart helped make musical comedy into a well-developed art form. Two of their outstanding productions were *On Your Toes* (1936), which contained Rodgers's ballet "Slaughter on Tenth Avenue," and *Pal Joey* (1940).

Shortly before Hart's death in 1943, Rodgers joined with Hammerstein to write *Oklahoma!,* one of the top musicals in history. Rodgers and Hammerstein also created several other shows that rank among the greatest musicals. These works include *Carousel* (1945), *South Pacific* (1949), *The King and I* (1951), and *The Sound of Music* (1959). They won a 1945 Academy Award for their song "It Might As Well Be Spring" from *State Fair.*

Rodgers won a Pulitzer Prize in drama for *South Pacific* and a special Pulitzer citation for *Oklahoma!* In 1952, he composed the music for *Victory at Sea,* a documentary TV series. He also wrote the music and lyrics for *No Strings* (1962) and the music for *Do I Hear a Waltz?* (1965) and *Rex* (1976). Rodgers died on Dec. 30, 1979.

Ken Bloom

See also **Hammerstein, Oscar, II; Hart, Lorenz.**

Rodin, *roh DAN,* **Auguste,** *oh GOOST* (1840-1917), a French sculptor, is often considered the greatest sculptor of the 1800's. Rodin created an enormous number of sculptures of the human figure. Many have a great deal of emotional intensity and explore a wide range of human passions. The inner feelings of his figures are expressed through a vigorous sense of movement and by gestures that emphasize different parts of the body. Many of his figures are incomplete or fragmentary. These works consist of just a torso, a head, or hands.

Rodin was primarily a modeler, preferring to work

with clay and wax rather than carve in stone. After he created an original model, his assistants translated it into marble or bronze. Inspired by the Italian Renaissance sculptor Michelangelo, many of Rodin's marble figures are smooth and finished, emerging from rough parts of the marble. The surfaces of his bronze works combine a thorough understanding of anatomy with a rough texture that allows light and shadow to enliven the work.

Rodin was born on Nov. 12, 1840, in Paris. He earned his living designing popular sculpture and ornament for commercial firms. Indifference and misunderstanding greeted his first exhibits, but appreciation for his work gradually spread. By the 1900's, he was world famous.

In 1880, Rodin was commissioned by the French government to create a large sculptural door for the Museum of Decorative Art in Paris. The subject was the "Inferno" from Dante's *Divine Comedy.* The door was never finished, but Rodin did many figures for it. Later he developed many of them as independent sculptures. The best known include *The Thinker* and *The Kiss.* Rodin's most important later works include the monumental group *The Burghers of Calais* and a monument to the French writer Honoré de Balzac. *The Thinker* appears in the **France** (Arts) article. *Orpheus* appears in the **Sculpture** article. Rodin died on Nov. 17, 1917. Joseph F. Lamb

Rodney, Caesar, *SEE zuhr* (1728-1784), an American statesman, was a Delaware signer of the Declaration of Independence and one of the leaders most responsible for Delaware's part in the American Revolution (1775-1783). He served in the Delaware legislature almost continuously from 1761 to 1776. As a Continental Congress delegate in 1776, he voted for independence after riding 80 miles (130 kilometers) on horseback to cast his vote.

Rodney was born on Oct. 7, 1728, in Dover, Delaware. He led opposition to British taxes before the revolution and was elected to the Continental Congress of 1774 and 1775. In 1777, Rodney led the Delaware militia. In 1778, he was elected president (governor) of the state. Rodney died on June 26, 1784. A statue of him represents Delaware in the United States Capitol.

Robert A. Becker

Rodó, *roh DOH,* **José Enrique,** *hoh ZAY ayn REE kay* (1872?-1917), was a Uruguayan thinker and essayist. He believed in the human spirit's infinite capacity to renew itself, but he feared that humanity was pursuing material goals at the expense of the spirit. Rodó was a leader of the Modernist movement in Spanish literature (see **Latin American literature** [Modernism]). In his landmark essay *Ariel* (1900), Rodó urged young Latin Americans to maintain their ideals in their intellectual and spiritual development, avoiding the materialism he claimed was damaging the potential of United States culture. In his philosophical work *Motives of Proteus* (1909), Rodó continued his recommendations for the direction of the mind and spirit. He discouraged the pursuit of technical knowledge in favor of the total cultivation of wisdom.

Rodó was born in Montevideo, Uruguay, probably in July 1872. He died on May 1, 1917. Naomi Lindstrom

Rodriguez, Alex (1975-), is a former professional baseball player. An athletic and powerful right-handed infielder, Rodriguez starred for three different teams over 22 Major League Baseball (MLB) seasons from 1994 to 2016. He finished his career with 696 home runs and 2,086 runs batted in—good for fourth most and third most, respectively, in MLB history. He also amassed 3,115 hits and scored 2,021 runs. Rodriguez, a 14-time All-Star, won Most Valuable Player awards as the best player in his league in 2003, 2005, and 2007. Known as "A-Rod," Rodriguez's outstanding career was tainted by his admitted use of performance-enhancing drugs.

Alexander Emmanuel Rodriguez was born on July 27, 1975, to Dominican parents in New York City. He grew up mostly in Miami, Florida. The Seattle Mariners of the American League (AL) chose him as the first selection in the free-agent MLB draft in 1993. He made his MLB debut with Seattle in 1994. He played for Seattle until the Texas Rangers signed him as a free agent in 2000. A career-long shortstop, Rodriguez moved to third base after he was traded to the New York Yankees in 2004. He finished his career with the Yankees, retiring in 2016.

Rodriguez led the AL in home runs and runs scored five times. He hit .300 or better 9 times, including a league-best .358 in 1996. He also won Gold Glove awards as the league's best shortstop in 2002 and 2003. From 1998 through 2010, Rodriguez averaged 42 home runs and 123 runs batted in per season. He retired with a lifetime .295 batting average, 329 career stolen bases, and 25 grand slams—the most grand slams in MLB history. In 2009, Rodriguez admitted using performance-enhancing drugs earlier in his career. He was suspended for the full 2014 season for his part in a performance-enhancing drug scandal. In 2021, Rodriguez became part owner of the Minnesota Timberwolves of the National Basketball Association and the Minnesota Lynx of the Women's National Basketball Association. Neil Milbert

Roe v. Wade was a 1973 landmark case in which the Supreme Court of the United States ruled that state laws could not forbid a woman to have an abortion during the first three months of pregnancy. The court also ruled that during the second three months, a state could regulate abortions only to protect women's health. Before Roe v. Wade, many U.S. states prohibited abortions in almost all circumstances.

The court based its decision in part on the principle that the Bill of Rights of the U.S. Constitution created a "zone of privacy" into which a state could not intrude. Seven of the court's nine justices supported the decision, which was written by Justice Harry A. Blackmun.

Roe v. Wade arose after Norma McCorvey, an unmarried carnival worker, was denied an abortion in Texas in 1969. Texas law permitted abortions only when the woman's life was in danger. McCorvey sued Henry Wade, the Dallas County district attorney, in an attempt to prove that the law was unconstitutional. McCorvey was called Jane Roe in the case to conceal her identity.

In *Roe v. Wade,* the Supreme Court divided the nine months of pregnancy into three stages called *trimesters.* It ruled that a state cannot regulate abortions in the first trimester, except for requiring that the doctor be licensed by the state. The court ruled that in the second trimester, the state may prevent a woman from having an abortion, but only to protect her health. It ruled that in the third trimester, the state may ban abortions entirely, except when one is needed to save a woman's life. The Supreme Court based this last decision on two considerations: (1) in the third trimester, the fetus is more likely to survive outside the mother; and (2) abortion is a serious medical procedure during the third trimester.

Roe v. Wade soon became the subject of a great national controversy. Some people considered it an important advance toward equality for women because it gave women the right to choose when and whether to have a child. But people who opposed abortion—particularly those who feel that life begins at conception—strongly disagreed with the court's decision.

After *Roe v. Wade,* the number of legal abortions performed in the United States rose. Many states enacted laws designed to restrict abortions. The Supreme Court had to decide if some of these laws conflicted with the principles of *Roe v. Wade.* In some cases, the court allowed restrictions to stand. But it also upheld the basic principles of *Roe v. Wade.* For more information about Supreme Court decisions after *Roe v. Wade,* see **Abortion** (Abortion in the United States). Susan Gluck Mezey

Roentgen, *REHNT guhn,* **Wilhelm Conrad** (1845-1923), a German physicist, in 1901 received the first Nobel Prize in physics for his discovery of X rays. Roentgen studied the passing of electric current through gases at extremely low pressure. During an experiment in 1895, he covered a *Crookes tube*—an evacuated glass tube through which an electric current was passed—with black paper. He noticed that a dark image appeared on a photographic plate substance near the tube when he turned on the electric current.

Roentgen assumed that unknown, invisible rays, which he called *X rays,* were coming from the tube. These rays passed easily through some substances, such as flesh, but were largely stopped by others, such as metal or bone. Because of this, Roentgen found he could photograph the bone structure of his wife's hand with the rays. The use of X rays revolutionized medicine and eventually gave scientists new insights into the nature of radiation as well as the structure of the atom. In Germany, X rays were called *Roentgen rays* in his honor.

Roentgen was born on March 27, 1845, in Lennep (now Remscheid), Germany. He was a professor at the University of Würzburg when he made his famous discovery. He died on Feb. 10, 1923. Roger H. Stuewer

See also **Physics** (picture: Wilhelm Roentgen); **X rays.**

Roentgenium, *REHNT gehn ee uhm,* is an artificially produced radioactive element. Its chemical symbol is Rg. Its *atomic number* (the number of protons in its nucleus) is 111. It was named in honor of the German physicist Wilhelm Conrad Roentgen, who discovered X rays.

Scientists have reported a few *isotopes* of roentgenium. Isotopes are forms of an element that have the same number of protons but different numbers of neutrons. The best-known isotope of roentgenium has an *atomic mass number* (total number of protons and neutrons) of 272. The isotope's *half-life* is 0.0015 second—that is, due to radioactive decay, only half the atoms in a sample of isotope 272 would still be atoms of that isotope after 0.0015 second.

An international group of scientists at the Heavy Ion Research Center in Darmstadt, Germany, discovered roentgenium in 1994. They bombarded atoms of bismuth, which has an atomic number of 83, with atoms of nickel, which has an atomic number of 28. The bombardment produced three atoms of the new element. It was known by the temporary name *unununium* (chemical symbol, Uuu) until late 2004, when it was given the permanent name roentgenium. Paul J. Karol

Roethke, *REHT kee,* **Theodore** (1908-1963), an American poet, received the Pulitzer Prize for poetry in 1954 for *The Waking: Poems 1933-1953. Words for the Wind* (1958) won seven awards, including the Bollingen Prize in 1958 and the National Book Award in 1959. Roethke shifted his style often between his first published work, *Open House* (1941), and his last collection, *The Far Field* (1964). His early poems have the concentrated quality of the verse of the American poet Emily Dickinson. His next works exhibit the meditative mysticism of the American-born poet T. S. Eliot. Roethke's later poems show the influence of the Irish poet William Butler Yeats.

Roethke's concerns, though, stayed constant. He studied the inner life rather than the political or social life. He sought a sense of self in childhood memories and a sense of life in growing things. His father's greenhouse revealed nature (rooting, blossoming, dying) and art (grafting, forcing bloom). Roethke also wrote poems for children. He was born on May 25, 1908, in Saginaw, Michigan. He died on Aug. 1, 1963.

Bonnie Costello

Rogers, Carl Ransom (1902-1987), was an American psychologist. He is known for developing a form of psychotherapy called *client-centered therapy.*

Client-centered therapy is based on the belief that individuals are controlled by their own values and choices rather than by such other factors as the environment or unconscious drives. Its goal is to help people fulfill their unique potential, which is called *self-actualization.* In developing client-centered therapy, Rogers emphasized the need for a close relationship between the patient (client) and the therapist (counselor). Rogers stressed the importance of the client's personal understanding of his or her experiences instead of the counselor's interpretation of them. In client-centered therapy, clients gain insights into their problems through the examination of their experiences. The counselor does not explain the meaning of experiences or tell the clients what to do.

Rogers was born on Jan. 8, 1902, in Oak Park, Illinois. He wrote several books, including *On Becoming a Person* (1961), which is probably his best-known work. Rogers died on Feb. 4, 1987.

Robert G. Weyant

Rogers, Fred (1928-2003), was one of the most popular personalities in the history of American children's television. From 1968 to 2001, Rogers was the host of "Mister Rogers' Neighborhood" on national public television. The program won praise for its optimistic messages to young people to feel good about themselves and love others.

"Mister Rogers' Neighborhood" mixed live performers with puppets, many created by Rogers himself. Rogers also composed music for the show. The program was filmed on a set that resembled a comfortable middle-class living room. Rogers began each program by changing into sneakers and a cardigan sweater. He sang the song "Won't You Be My

© Mister Rogers' Neighborhood/PBS
Fred Rogers

Neighbor?" with its familiar first line, "It's a beautiful day in this neighborhood."

Fred McFeely Rogers was born on March 20, 1928, in Latrobe, Pennsylvania. He first appeared on television in 1954 as a puppeteer in a program called "The Children's Corner." The program ran for seven years. It originated at station WQED in Pittsburgh, which became the home for "Mister Rogers' Neighborhood." In 1963, Rogers was ordained a Presbyterian minister. Rogers also wrote many books and made numerous recordings for children. He died on Feb. 27, 2003.

Collections of Rogers's writing published after his death include *The World According to Mister Rogers: Important Things to Remember* (2003) and *A Beautiful Day in the Neighborhood: The Poetry of Mister Rogers* (2019). Rogers is the subject of the motion pictures *Won't You Be My Neighbor?* (2018) and *A Beautiful Day in the Neighborhood* (2019). Dan Zeff

Rogers, Ginger (1911-1995), was an American actress perhaps best known as Fred Astaire's dancing partner in musical comedies of the 1930's. She was also a skilled dramatic performer. Rogers received the 1940 Academy Award as best actress for her performance in *Kitty Foyle*.

Rogers was born on July 16, 1911, in Independence, Missouri. Her real name was Virginia Katherine McMath. She got her first big break in show business in a leading role in the Broadway musical *Top Speed* (1929). Rogers also appeared in the musical *Girl Crazy* (1930) before moving to Hollywood in 1931 to start her motion-picture career.

Rogers played wisecracking young women in such movies as *42nd Street* (1933) and *Gold Diggers of 1933* (1933) before making *Flying Down to Rio* (1933), her first film with Astaire. Their graceful dancing and the chemistry between them led to nine more musicals. These films were *The Gay Divorcee* (1934), *Roberta* and *Top Hat* (both 1935), *Follow the Fleet* and *Swing Time* (both 1936), *Shall We Dance?* (1937), *Carefree* (1938), *The Story of Vernon and Irene Castle* (1939), and *The Barkleys of Broadway* (1949). Rogers retired from movies in 1965 after making about 70 films. She wrote an autobiography, *Ginger: My Story* (1991). Rogers died on April 25, 1995. Dan Zeff

See also **Astaire, Fred** (with picture).

Rogers, Roy (1911-1998), a popular star of Western motion pictures, was known as the "King of the Cowboys." His greatest fame extended from the late 1930's to the mid-1950's. Rogers sang in most of his films. Comedy was provided by his sidekick, George "Gabby" Hayes. The movies also featured Rogers's palomino horse, Trigger, and heroine Dale Evans, who married Rogers in 1947. Rogers and Evans starred in "The Roy Rogers Show" on television from 1951 to 1956.

Rogers was born on Nov. 5, 1911, in Cincinnati, Ohio. His real name was Leonard Franklin Slye. He began his career as a Western singer on radio and helped found the Sons of the Pioneers vocal group in the early 1930's. Rogers's first starring film role was in the Western *Under Western Skies* (1938). Soon, he was making several low-budget Westerns a year for Republic Pictures. He appeared in about 90 films before retiring from movies in the early 1950's. Rogers also became a successful businessman, establishing a chain of restaurants. He was elected to the Country Music Hall of Fame in 1988. Rogers died on July 6, 1998. Louis Giannetti

Rogers, Will (1879-1935), was an American humorist and social critic. He began his career as a cowboy and rose to international fame as an author; lecturer; and star of vaudeville, motion pictures, and radio. Rogers was known for his homespun humor, his down-to-earth philosophy, and his generosity.

Rogers gained popularity as an easygoing lecturer on current events. During his lectures, he chewed gum and performed rope tricks while kidding about business, government, people, and politics. Rogers also wrote a column that appeared in more than 350 daily newspapers. He began most of his lectures and columns by saying, "All I know is what I read in the papers." This expression became a byword during the 1920's.

Bettmann Archive

Will Rogers

Rogers also appeared in 50 silent movies and 21 talking films, and he became popular on radio. In addition, he wrote six books.

William Penn Adair Rogers was born on Nov. 4, 1879, on a ranch near Oologah in the Indian Territory (now Oklahoma). He was partly of Cherokee ancestry, of which he often expressed pride. "My ancestors may not have come over on the *Mayflower,* but they met 'em at the boat," he drawled. Rogers disliked school, and he went to work in 1898 as a cattle driver in Texas. Rogers soon returned home and tried ranching, but he disliked it as well.

In 1902, Rogers left home to seek adventure in Argentina. That same year, he went to South Africa and joined Texas Jack's Wild West Show as a trick roper. He later toured Australia and New Zealand with the Wirth Brothers' Circus. Rogers returned to the United States in 1904 and began his vaudeville career in 1905 as a trick roper and humorist. He gained fame while appearing on Broadway in the *Ziegfeld Follies of 1916*.

Rogers died in a plane crash near Point Barrow, Alaska, on Aug. 15, 1935. He was killed while flying with Wiley Post, a pioneer American aviator. A statue of Rogers stands in the United States Capitol in Washington, D.C. Another statue, at the Will Rogers Memorial Museum in Claremore, Oklahoma, bears the statement for which he was best known: "I never met a man I didn't like."

Critically reviewed by the Will Rogers Memorial Museum

See also **Oklahoma** (Places to visit [with picture]).

Rogers's Rangers were frontier scouts who served with the British Army in North America during the French and Indian War (1754-1763). Led by Captain Robert Rogers, they scouted and conducted raids on enemy positions.

The Rangers were formally commissioned by Major General William Shirley in 1756 to help the British Army fight in the American wilderness. At first, they consisted of a group of about 60 men under Rogers's command. By mid-1758, Rogers had been promoted to major and given command of nine companies that included about 600 men. Most Rangers were New England frontier farmers. Rogers taught them to move quietly through the woods and to fight under a variety of conditions.

The Rangers made many long-distance patrols and raids. The most notorious was a surprise attack on a Canadian Indian village in October 1759. Rogers and his Rangers burned the village and killed many villagers, including women and children.

Fred W. Anderson

Roget, *roh ZHAY* or *RAHZH ay,* **Peter Mark** (1779-1869), was a British physician and scholar. He is known as the compiler of *Roget's Thesaurus of English Words and Phrases* (1852). This book lists synonyms under many headings. It has been revised several times.

Roget was born on Jan. 18, 1779, near London. He received a medical degree from the University of Edinburgh and lectured on anatomy and physiology. Roget died on Sept. 12, 1869.

Patricia A. Moody

Roland was the greatest of the legendary knights who served the medieval king Charlemagne. Stories of Roland circulated during the 1000's, but the oldest surviving version is *The Song of Roland,* an epic poem written about 1100 by an unknown French author. The work may have been based on an actual event in A.D. 778, but it describes the hero as though he lived in the author's time. In the epic, Roland shows his courage and devotion by accepting the dangerous assignment of protecting Charlemagne's army from the Muslims as it crossed the Pyrenees, a mountain chain between France and Spain. A traitor betrays Roland and his men. They die in battle against the Muslims, but Roland's bravery reflects the knightly ideal of service to one's lord. Later German and Italian authors also wrote about Roland. Most of their works are longer than *The Song of Roland* and tell a more complicated story. Carl Lindahl

See also **French literature** (Early French literature).

Rolfe, *rahlf,* **John** (1585-1622), was an early English settler in Jamestown, Virginia. In 1614, he married Pocahontas, daughter of the Indian chief Powhatan. This marriage marked the beginning of a period of peace between Indians and the Jamestown colonists.

Rolfe arrived in Jamestown in 1610. In 1612, he succeeded in cultivating a type of tobacco from the Caribbean. This tobacco became the foundation of Virginia's economy. Rolfe served as the colony's secretary from 1614 to 1619. Rolfe, Pocahontas, and their infant son, Thomas, traveled to England in 1616. Pocahontas died there in 1617. Rolfe then returned to America and later remarried. He became a member of the governor's council in 1619 and joined the Council of State in 1621. Rolfe was probably born in Heacham, England, in the county of Norfolk. Karen Ordahl Kupperman

See also **Pocahontas; Powhatan.**

Rolland, *raw LAHN,* **Romain,** *raw MAN* (1866-1944), a French author, won the 1915 Nobel Prize in literature. His reputation is based on his 10-volume novel *Jean-Christophe* (1904-1912), the story of a young German-born musician somewhat resembling Ludwig van Beethoven. Rolland called the work a *roman-fleuve,* by which he meant that its form corresponded to the unpredictable whims of life, rather than to any preconceived design or plot. In *Jean-Christophe,* Rolland criticized modern civilization and commented on the artist's place in society. The novel expresses Rolland's idealism, his opposition to egotism and hypocrisy, and his love of courage, sincerity, and enthusiasm. Rolland was born on Jan. 29, 1866, in Clamecy in Burgundy. He died on Dec. 30, 1944. Elaine D. Cancalon

Roller is the name of 12 species of brightly colored birds that live in Africa, Europe, and Asia. Most rollers are striking shades of blue, pink, and cinnamon. The roller gets its name from the acrobatic flight the male performs when trying to attract a female. The male flies sharply upward over the treetops, then dives downward, calling loudly, twisting and rolling as it tumbles toward the ground.

The *European roller* has a blue head and breast, a chestnut back, and a greenish-blue and brown tail. It measures about 12 inches (30 centimeters) long. It nests in holes in trees or among rocks, where the female lays four to five white eggs. This bird breeds in Europe and winters in Africa. Peter G. Connors

Scientific classification. Rollers belong to the roller family, Coraciidae. The European roller is *Coracias garrulus.*

See also **Bird** (picture: Birds of Europe).

Roller coaster is a thrill ride found in amusement and theme parks. It consists of small open cars that run on inclined railway tracks, driven by gravity and momentum. Their path often includes twists, loops, and drops. Roller coasters are designed to seem dangerous, but the rides are safe as long as riders follow prescribed precautions.

The earliest known devices resembling roller coasters were ice-covered wooden slides constructed in Russia in the 1400's. The first American roller coaster was built at Coney Island in New York City in 1884. Today, there are thousands of large, permanent roller coasters throughout the world, some with reported speeds of about 125 miles (200 kilometers) per hour.

Don B. Wilmeth

See also **Amusement park** (picture).

Roller skating is a form of recreation and a sport in which people glide on wheeled boots called *roller skates.* Some people skate for recreation on sidewalks and in parks, and others skate to music at indoor skating centers. Many take part in competitive roller skating. Joseph Merlin of Belgium invented the roller skate about 1760.

Roller skates. Most roller skates have two major parts, the *boot* and the *skate assembly.* The boots are usually made of leather. Boots worn for recreational and artistic skating have high tops and are laced up the front to a point above the ankle. Speed skaters wear boots with low-cut tops.

The skate assembly is a metal or plastic structure attached to the sole of the boot. There are two main assembly styles, the *quad* and the *in-line* (often referred to by the brand name *Rollerblade).* In a quad skate, a piece of metal called a *plate* is fastened to the boot. Two *truck assembles* are attached to the front and back of the skate. They have movable parts that allow skaters to control the direction of their skating. A pair of wheels are attached to an axle on each truck assembly. A *toe stop,* found on most skates, allows skaters to stop quickly and to perform maneuvers.

Some people wear c*lamp-on skates,* which attach to shoes. In the mid-1980's, skates with in-line wheels gained popularity. They remain popular today. In-line wheels are arranged one behind the other, like an ice-

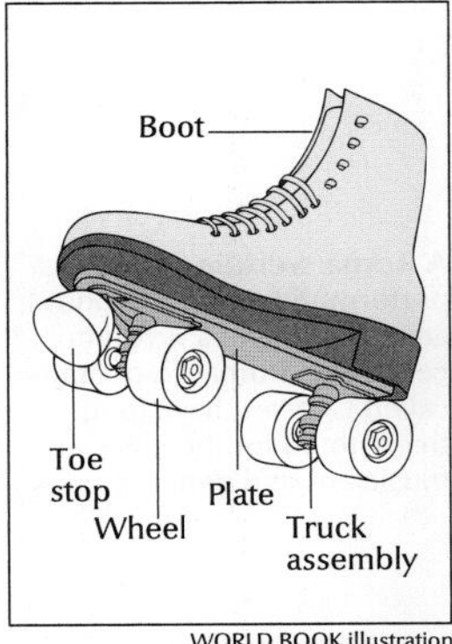

WORLD BOOK illustration by Zorica Dabich

Parts of a quad skate

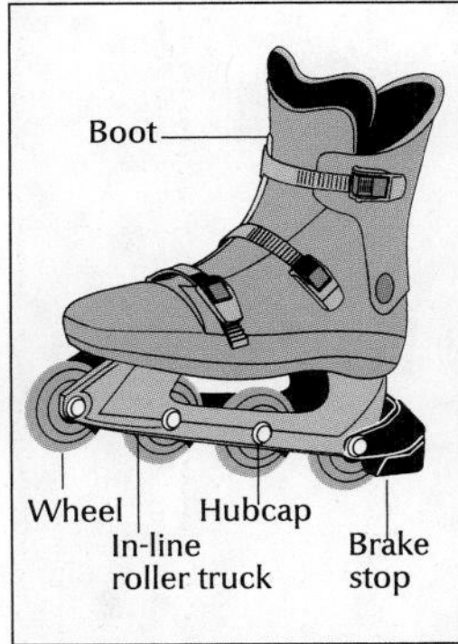

WORLD BOOK illustration by Bensen Studios

Parts of an in-line skate

skate blade. The brake is on the back of the boot.

Competitive roller skating includes three types of events. *Artistic skating* and *speed skating* are similar to competitive ice skating (see **Ice skating**). *Roller hockey* resembles ice hockey. Artistic skaters use quad skates. Speed skating and roller hockey use both quad and in-line skates.

Artistic skating competitors perform graceful movements, often to music. Artistic skating consists of *figure skating, free skating,* and *dance skating.* In figure skating, athletes retrace circular patterns marked on the floor. They are judged on accuracy and control.

Free skating can be performed alone or as a team. There are separate events for men and women. Individual free skaters, called *singles,* combine jumps, spins, and dance footwork with music. They are judged on the speed, accuracy, and difficulty of their jumps, the speed and form of their spins, the originality of their footwork, and their musical expression. Free skating teams, called *pairs,* consist of a man and a woman. They combine the moves of singles with lifts and other movements. They are judged like singles. But the judges also consider the pair's ability to precisely mirror each other's movements.

Dance skating is performed by two skaters, known as a team, or by a solo skater. Both team and solo skaters perform compulsory dances to music.

Speed skating has separate events for indoor and outdoor competition. Athletes are divided into nine age groups, with separate races for men and women. Indoor events are held on a flat, 100-meter oval track. Distances for indoor races range from 100 to 5,000 meters. Outdoor competitions take place on a road course or on a banked, oval track. Outdoor events vary in distance from 300 to 20,000 meters. There are also indoor and outdoor relay events for teams of two, three, or four skaters.

Roller hockey is a noncontact team sport played by both males and females. A team consists of five players—two forwards, two defense players, and a goalie. There are three versions of roller hockey: (1) hardball, (2) North American ball, and (3) puck. Hardball and North American ball use balls. Puck hockey uses a puck similar to the one used in ice hockey.

Critically reviewed by the Roller Skating Association International

Rolling Stones became one of the most popular English rock bands. Much of the band's music is aggressive, rebellious, and sexual. The group became known for the excitement of its live performances.

The Rolling Stones were formed in 1962 and took their name from a song by the American blues singer Muddy Waters. The original members of the group were lead singer Mick Jagger (1943-), guitarists Keith Richards (1943-) and Brian Jones (1942-1969), bassist Bill Wyman (1936-), and drummer Charlie Watts (1941-2021). Jones left the band in 1969, shortly before his death. He was replaced by guitarist Mick Taylor, who quit the group in 1974. Ron Wood has been the Stones' second guitarist since then.

At first, the Rolling Stones played the music of earlier blues and rock artists. But Jagger and Richards soon began writing most of the band's material. Their hit songs include "(I Can't Get No) Satisfaction" (1965), "Get Off of My Cloud" (1965), "As Tears Go By" (1965), "19th Nervous Breakdown" (1966), "Paint It Black" (1966), "Ruby Tuesday" (1967), "Jumpin' Jack Flash" (1968), "Honky Tonk Women" (1969), "Brown Sugar" (1971), "Tumbling Dice" (1972), "Angie" (1973), "Miss You" (1978), "Emotional Rescue" (1980), "Start Me Up" (1981), and "Mixed Emotions" (1989).

In the 1980's, the individual members of the Rolling Stones began involving themselves in solo projects, but they continued to enjoy success with the band. Wyman retired in 1993, and no permanent replacement was named. The Rolling Stones appeared in several filmed versions of their concerts. Jagger also appeared in several movies, including *Ned Kelly* (1970), *Performance* (1970), and *Freejack* (1992). Jagger, Richards, and Watts discussed the group's music and history in the book *According to the Rolling Stones* (2003). Watts died on Aug. 24, 2021. Don McLeese

See also **Rock music** (The Rolling Stones; picture).

Rollins, Sonny (1930-), an American tenor saxophone player, ranks among the most creative soloists in jazz history. He is known for his muscular sound and for his skill at improvising solos on jazz harmonies. Rollins has also composed several popular jazz numbers, including "St. Thomas," "Don't Stop the Carnival," "Airegin," "Valse Hot," "Blue 7," "Doxy," and "Oleo." The first two compositions reflect Rollins's ongoing interest in Caribbean music. "Valse Hot" introduced the now common practice in jazz of improvising in waltz time. Rollins also composed the music for the film *Alfie* (1966).

Theodore Walter Rollins was born on Sept. 7, 1930, in New York City. He first recorded at the age of 18. Rollins made his first recordings under his own name in 1951. Some of Rollins's best early work came from 1955 to 1957 as a member of a quintet led by trumpeter Clifford Brown and drummer Max Roach.

Rollins experimented with free jazz during the early 1960's with trumpeter Don Cherry, but he soon returned to his earlier style. Rollins withdrew from music from 1968 to 1971, as he had on earlier occasions, this time to study in Japan and India. Since then, he has performed regularly, sometimes leading a quartet and also touring with a group of all-star jazz musicians. Frank Tirro

Roma are a traditionally wandering people whose ancestors lived in India. They are sometimes called Gypsies, Romanies, or Travellers (also spelled Travelers). The Roma live in almost every part of the world, but most live in central and eastern Europe. The Roma have faced mistrust and discrimination for centuries.

Filip Horvat, Picture Group

A Roma wedding dance is performed by friends and relatives following a wedding ceremony. Roma, sometimes called Gypsies, have long been noted for their skill as musicians and dancers.

The name *Roma* refers to the people as a whole and to the largest group of them. Most groups prefer the name *Roma* for the people in general rather than *Gypsy,* because *Gypsy* has sometimes been used as an insult. In addition to the specific group called the Roma, whose members live throughout the world, other groups include the Calé of Spain, the Manouches of France, and the Sinti (or Sinte) of Germany.

No one knows how many Roma there are because many live in small groups on the outskirts of society. Estimates suggest about 12 million Roma live throughout the world. The largest numbers of Roma live in central and eastern Europe. Bulgaria, Hungary, Romania, Russia, Slovakia, Spain, and Turkey have large Romani populations.

Language and culture. Many Roma speak their own language, called Romani. Romani belongs to the Indo-Iranian group of languages, and it varies from place to place. Most Roma also speak the language of the people among whom they live. However, many Roma cannot read or write any language.

Most Romani families consist of a husband and wife, their unmarried children, their married sons, and the sons' wives and children. In many cases, a group of related families forms a band that lives and works together. The highest authority is the *kris,* a tribunal of leaders who pass judgments based on Romani religious and philosophical beliefs.

Roma have long been noted as musicians and dancers. They have borrowed from and added to the music and dance of many other cultures. Some Roma follow traditional Romani occupations, such as fortunetelling, metalworking, horse trading, and animal training and doctoring. Because their traditional crafts are not often needed in modern society, many Roma are unemployed. They often live in extremely poor conditions. Many Roma have settled down, but some are still nomads. Many of the cultures they live among mistrust the Roma because of their poverty and different way of life.

History. The Roma left India about A.D. 1000 and began to move westward through the Middle East. They arrived in Europe by the 1300's. Some Roma claimed to have come from a country called Little Egypt. The word *Gypsy* is probably a shortened form of *Egyptian.*

At first, Europeans welcomed the Roma. But they soon turned against the Roma as the newcomers wandered through Europe, telling fortunes and begging. Many countries passed laws that banned the Roma unless they abandoned their traditional culture, settled in one place, and became employed. When Europeans began to colonize the Americas, some Roma settled there.

European prejudice against the Roma led to their mistreatment. In Moldavia and Walachia, which later became Romania, Roma were used as slaves until the mid-1800's. During World War II (1939-1945), the Nazis murdered hundreds of thousands of European Roma. In the mid-1900's, Communist governments in Europe forced many Roma to leave their traditional way of life and to settle in cities and towns.

In the late 1900's and early 2000's, violence against Roma increased. The European Union and other international bodies have frequently criticized central and eastern European governments for their lack of action to improve conditions for the Roma.

Romani leaders have formed organizations to try to improve their situation and to pressure political leaders to address their problems. The first World Romani Conference was held in London in 1971, and others have been held since. In 2001, the International Romani Union Parliament held its founding meeting in Bratislava, Slovakia. Sharon L. Wolchik

Roman alphabet. See Alphabet (The Roman alphabet).

Roman Catholic Church is the largest body of Christians in the world. It has about 1 ½ billion members. Roman Catholics are concentrated most heavily in Europe, North America, and South America. However, the percentage of the Catholic population in both Africa and Asia is growing.

The Roman Catholic Church traces its beginnings to about A.D. 30, when Jesus Christ instructed the apostles, his followers, to spread his teaching about the Kingdom of God. Roman Catholics believe that Jesus rose from the dead after being crucified and sent the Holy Spirit to guide the apostles.

Roman Catholics believe that Jesus Christ founded the

church to carry to all people the salvation he brought to the world. They also believe that, with God's assistance, the church has faithfully preserved the teachings of Jesus. According to Catholic teaching, the Holy Spirit continues to guide the church.

The pope, who is the bishop of Rome, serves as the head of the Roman Catholic Church. He governs the church from Vatican City, a tiny independent country within the city of Rome. Throughout the world, other bishops lead local churches.

The Roman Catholic Church has been an important force in world history. During much of the Middle Ages (about the 400's through the 1400's), the church had great political power in Western Europe. Its universities and monasteries were centers of learning, and they preserved much of the heritage of the Greek and Roman cultures. During the 1500's and 1600's, Catholic missionaries traveled to Africa, Asia, and the Americas, preaching the gospel and spreading European culture.

Throughout its history, the Catholic faith has inspired many great works of architecture, art, literature, and music. These works include French medieval Gothic cathedrals, the Italian artist Michelangelo's frescoes in the Vatican, the Italian writer Dante's epic poem *The Divine Comedy,* and the Austrian composer Wolfgang Amadeus Mozart's *Requiem.*

This article describes the beliefs and worship of Roman Catholics. It also discusses the organization and history of the Roman Catholic Church.

Roman Catholic beliefs

For Catholics, religious faith means belief in God's *revelation.* This revelation is the knowledge of God, revealed to humanity through nature and historical figures, particularly Jesus Christ. A Catholic's faith in God is expressed in certain teachings. These teachings, based on the Bible, are found in declarations of church councils and popes and in short statements of faith called *creeds.* The oldest and most authoritative of these creeds are the Apostles' Creed and the Nicene Creed. Catholics recite the Nicene Creed at their central act of worship, called the Eucharist or Mass.

The creeds summarize Catholic beliefs concerning (1) the Trinity and creation; (2) sin, the Incarnation, and salvation; (3) the nature of the church; and (4) life after death. These core doctrines, in turn, form the basis of Catholic *morality*—that is, guidelines for how Catholics should live their lives.

The Trinity and creation. Catholics believe there is only one God. But this one God exists as a union of three Persons—the Father; the Son, who is Christ; and the Holy Spirit. These three Persons form the *Trinity.* Each Person is distinct and is truly God. Yet there is only one God, who has no beginning or end, is beyond time and space, and is perfect and unchanging. Catholics believe that the universe owes its beginning to God, who created everything freely, from love. They believe that the world and humanity could not survive without God's continuing care.

Sin, the Incarnation, and salvation. The Catholic Church teaches that humanity was created not only *by* God but also *for* God. Its destiny is to share God's life forever, in union with God and one another. God intended humanity to achieve this destiny by lovingly obeying his will. But *original sin* interfered with God's plan for humanity. The Book of Genesis in the Bible describes Adam, the first human being, as sinning by an act of disobedience to God. The church teaches that Adam's sin affects every person born in the world.

Catholics believe that God sent his Son, the second Person of the Trinity, to save humanity from all sin—the original sin people inherit as well as the sins they themselves commit during their lifetime by deliberately turning from God. Without ceasing to be God, the Son of God became man. He was born to the Virgin Mary. Catholics especially commemorate this *Incarnation* of God in Jesus Christ at Christmas.

Catholics believe that Jesus saved humanity through his life and death and by rising from the dead and entering heaven. While on Earth, Jesus taught that salvation would be given to all who truly turn to God and live justly in God's sight.

The nature of the church. Salvation was not complete when Jesus left Earth. Salvation must be brought to each new generation. Jesus therefore commissioned his apostles to gather all human beings into a church. Catholics describe this church as the people of God, united with God and one another through Jesus Christ. They believe that the Holy Spirit guides and strengthens the church on the way to salvation. They also consider the church to be a missionary people with the function of drawing everyone into a communion of love.

Life after death. According to Catholic doctrine, life does not end with the death of the body. Instead, the soul leaves the body and enters heaven, purgatory, or hell. On the final Judgment Day, when this world has ended, all souls will be reunited with their bodies.

Heaven is the eternal communion of those who have reached their destiny. They see God as he is and love him and one another with complete joy. Purgatory is a temporary state for souls who die in God's love but must be purified of all unholiness. The Roman Catholic Church defines hell as the absence of God, which results in complete despair. It is the punishment people bring on themselves who have abandoned God and refused communion with him.

Catholic morality—how Catholics should behave—can be largely summarized as follows: The church teaches Catholics to love God with their whole heart and to love their fellow human beings as they love themselves. The church asks Catholics to do this in imitation of Jesus, who offered himself for the world's salvation. The Roman Catholic Church believes all people must follow their conscience. But a Catholic's conscience is formed not only by personal opinion of what is right and wrong. It is especially formed by the Bible, church teaching, and the faith and worship of the Christian community.

Worship

The acts of worship that Catholics perform together are called the *liturgy.* The central act of liturgy is the Eucharist or Mass. The Eucharist and certain other important liturgical acts make up the seven *sacraments* of the Roman Catholic Church. The sacraments are (1) baptism, (2) confirmation, (3) Eucharist, (4) penance, (5) holy orders, (6) marriage, and (7) anointing of the sick.

Baptism is the liturgical celebration in which a child or adult is cleansed of sin and begins a new life with

God. Water poured in the name of the Trinity over the head of the person being baptized is a sign of the person's cleansing from sin. Because water is necessary to life, the baptismal water also is a sign of new spiritual life. Thus, baptism marks the beginning of a Catholic's oneness with Jesus Christ and entry into the church.

Confirmation enables baptized people to grow to spiritual adulthood. A bishop, and in some cases, a priest, puts holy oil, called *chrism,* on the forehead of the people being confirmed. The chrism signifies that these people have been strengthened by the Holy Spirit so that they may live up to their faith.

The Eucharist or Mass is the celebration of the Lord's Supper. Catholics believe the Mass makes present Christ's sacrifice of himself. The Mass has two main parts. The first part, the *liturgy of the word,* consists of prayers, hymns, readings from the Bible, a *homily* (sermon), and the recitation of the Nicene Creed. The second part is the *liturgy of the Eucharist.* During this part, according to Catholic teaching, the priest, in Jesus's name and by the power of the Holy Spirit, transforms bread and wine into Christ's body and blood. The congregation is then invited to receive Christ himself in Holy Communion.

Catholics believe that during the Mass, Jesus is truly present, sins are forgiven, and God's Spirit is given. The members of the congregation are closely united with one another, the whole church, and their fellow human beings. Church law requires that Catholics participate in the Mass on Saturday evenings or Sundays and on *holy days of obligation,* such as Christmas. They must receive Holy Communion at least once a year, at Easter time.

Penance, also called *reconciliation* or *confession,* is the sacrament in which Catholics confess their sins to a priest, express their sincere sorrow for having sinned, and promise to avoid sin in the future. The priest forgives the sinner in God's name. The effect of penance is to bring the Roman Catholic back to God and the Christian community. Catholics must confess their sins at least once a year if the sins are serious. However, the church urges believers to receive penance as well as the Eucharist more often.

Holy orders is the sacrament in which men are made deacons, priests, or bishops. These men become ministers of God's word and sacraments, and spiritual leaders of the community.

Marriage is the sacrament in which a man and woman promise themselves to each other for life. This sacrament helps them be faithful to the duties of marriage and family life.

Anointing of the sick is the sacrament given to people who are dangerously ill or very old. The priest anoints these people with oil, a sign of healing. The priest prays that they will receive the grace of the Holy Spirit, so they may be freed from sin, comforted and strengthened in soul and body, and restored to health.

Church organization

Roman Catholics are members of a local *parish,* led by a priest called a *pastor.* The parishes in an area form a *diocese,* a territorial district headed by a bishop. The pope appoints bishops, and they are responsible to him. Bishops in turn appoint and oversee pastors.

The pope is the head of the Roman Catholic Church. He is the highest member of its *clergy* (ordained ministers). There are three *orders* (ranks) within the clergy—deacons, priests, and bishops. The organization of the clergy by rank is the church's *hierarchy.* Each order—from deacons up through the pope, who is the bishop of Rome—has more responsibilities and wider powers of ministry and governance than the one below it.

Catholics believe the pope is Jesus Christ's representative on Earth and a successor of Saint Peter, who is regarded as the first pope. They believe that the pope is *infallible* (free from error) when he formally defines matters of faith and morals. The pope is aided in governing the church by *cardinals* and the *Roman Curia.*

Cardinals are bishops chosen by the pope to be his main advisers. As a group, they form the College of Cardinals. They hold the highest rank below the pope, and they have the responsibility of electing a new pope after a reigning pope dies or resigns.

The Roman Curia is the pope's administrative arm. It consists of the Secretariat of State and a number of other departments called congregations, tribunals, councils, and offices. Cardinals and *archbishops* (highest-ranking bishops) head the departments of the Curia.

The Secretariat of State assists the pope most directly in governing the church and in communicating with the rest of the Curia. The congregations do most of the Curia's administrative work. Tribunals have judicial powers. For example, the tribunal called the Roman Rota serves as a court to settle disputes about the validity of marriages. The councils deal with matters of Christian unity and handle relations with non-Christians. The offices are responsible for such functions as drafting papal documents and gathering church statistics.

Bishop and diocese. Bishops are considered successors to Jesus's apostles. A bishop appoints the pastors of the parishes in his diocese, and the pastors are responsible to him. He also supervises the many church-supported agencies that serve local needs in the diocese, including schools, hospitals, and newspapers.

The bishops of the church, together with the pope as their head, form the *college of bishops* and share authority over the church. They are responsible for teaching and guiding the church as a whole. For example, when the bishops met at Vatican Council II (1962-1965), they issued statements that had great impact on Catholic life and practice.

Pastor and parish. A *territorial parish* includes all Catholic residents in a given area. A *national parish* primarily serves an ethnic group whose members may live in several territorial parishes. The pastor of a parish is its spiritual leader. Pastors of large parishes are assisted by other priests, by deacons, and, increasingly, by the *laity* or *lay people*—people who are not ordained.

The role of lay people is to live according to the principles of their faith. They are united with the clergy in worship and prayer, and they are called to exemplify the vision and values of the gospel at all times. Lay people participate in such church governing bodies as parish councils and parish school boards. At Mass, they act as readers, reading aloud designated passages from the Bible, and they help distribute Holy Communion.

Religious institutes are societies of Catholic men or women who live according to a set of regulations called a *rule.* Members of the institute are called *religious.*

They take vows of poverty, chastity, and obedience. Some of the men are also ordained. Well-known Catholic institutes for men include the Jesuits, the Franciscans, and the Dominicans. Institutes for women include the Sisters of Charity, the Ursulines, and the Benedictines. These institutes are governed directly by their own appointed or elected leaders.

The early church

The first 300 years. Catholics trace the beginnings of their church to Palestine, where Jesus preached, healed others, and was crucified. There, according to the Bible, after Jesus rose from the dead, he told the apostles to preach the gospel to all peoples. In Jerusalem, the Holy Spirit came upon the apostles on what Catholics call the feast of Pentecost.

The first Christians were Jews who believed Jesus was the *Messiah,* the savior expected by the Jews. The early church gradually separated itself from Judaism, the religion of the Jews, and achieved its own identity. But the church accepted the Jewish Scriptures as the record of God's dealings with his chosen people.

Saint Paul became the most important person to carry the gospel to the *gentiles* (non-Jews). He regarded himself as a divinely appointed apostle to the gentiles. Paul founded many churches and exercised authority over them through visits and letters. He also represented their interests with the mother church in Jerusalem. After Paul's death, about A.D. 67, the number of gentile churches continued to expand rapidly. By the 100's, the center of Christianity had passed from Jerusalem to Christian communities in the cities of Antioch in Syria, Alexandria in Egypt, and especially Rome.

In its early years, the church grew steadily in spite of persecution by the Romans, whose empire covered most of Europe, the Middle East, and northern Africa. The Romans believed loyalty to the emperor involved honoring the gods of the state and often the emperor himself. They regarded Christians who refused to give such honor as traitors and atheists. The Christian ideal became the *martyr*—a person who suffered persecution and even death rather than abandon Christianity. Although the church suffered widespread persecution, many of these attacks were local and brief. The church thus had time to grow and develop a distinct structure.

While the church faced persecution from outside, many movements threatened to divide it from within. Some of these movements taught what the church declared to be *heresies*—that is, teachings opposed to basic Christian beliefs. The most serious heresy during the church's first 200 years was Gnosticism. This religious philosophy had many followers throughout the Roman Empire. It held that Jesus was a spiritual being who only appeared to be human. Thus, he did not actually suffer and die. The struggle against Gnosticism was a difficult and important battle in church history.

The earliest Christians relied on the apostles, led by Saint Peter, as their authority in settling questions of doctrine and government. After the death of the apostles, the church faced the problem of where to turn for authority in such matters. In the 100's, two developments helped solve the problem. First, the church gradually recognized the books of the New Testament as sources of authority in doctrine. Second, the basic orders of Christian ministry—bishops, *presbyters* (later called priests), and deacons—became more clearly defined.

© Shutterstock

The Eucharist or Mass is the central act of Roman Catholic worship. According to Catholic teaching, the priest transforms bread and wine into the body and blood of Jesus Christ.

The recognition of Christianity. Constantine the Great was the first Roman emperor to become a Christian. In 313, Constantine and Licinius, the emperor of Rome's eastern provinces, granted freedom of worship and equal rights to all religious groups in the empire. By the late 300's, Christianity had become the favored religion of the empire.

The recognition of Christianity had some unfortunate effects on the church. For the first time, the church attracted many people who lacked the dedication of the early Christians. Emperors intruded into the internal affairs of the church. In the mid-300's, for example, the Roman Emperor Constantius II tried to force the Eastern heresy known as Arianism on the West. Arianism is named for Arius, a priest in Egypt who claimed that Jesus was not truly God.

But on the whole, the empire's recognition of Christianity benefited the church. The church was able to influence civil laws. It also expanded its work among the poor and began missionary work outside the empire.

Bishops from throughout the Christian world met several times to resolve major theological disputes in the early church. These meetings are called *general* or *ecumenical councils.* The first council, Nicaea I, met in 325 and condemned the teachings of Arius. The creed of the council, which Catholics pray at Mass, affirms that Jesus Christ is truly God, "one in being with the Father." In 451, the Council of Chalcedon denounced Monophysitism, which denied Christ's human nature. The council completed the teaching of Nicaea by declaring that Jesus is truly man.

Some of the most distinguished literature in church history was produced between 325 and 451. The most notable writers of this period included the historian Eusebius; the bishops and theologians Saint Ambrose, Saint Athanasius, and Saint Augustine; the preacher Saint John Chrysostom; the poet Prudentius; and the Biblical scholar Saint Jerome. Their writings had a great influence on church thought in later centuries.

Monasticism began to develop in the 300's. This way of life, in which a person withdraws from worldly affairs to be completely devoted to prayer and the service of God, played an important part in church history. As persecution ceased and Christianity prospered, the monk replaced the martyr as the Christian ideal. The two basic models for monastic life were the Egyptians Saint Anthony and Saint Pachomius. Anthony lived the solitary life of a hermit. Pachomius organized monastic communities governed by a rule.

Pope Saint Leo I, who reigned from 440 to 461, was perhaps the greatest early pope. Leo persuaded the Huns and the Vandals, two Germanic tribes, to halt their attacks on Italy. By the time Leo began his reign, the huge Roman Empire had been split into Eastern and Western empires. Leo emphasized that popes were successors to Saint Peter and so had *primacy* (supreme authority) as head of the universal church.

Scene from *Stories of the Life of St. Francis* (1452), a fresco by Benozzo Gozzoli, San Francesco, Montefalco, Italy (SCALA/Art Resource)

Innocent III was a powerful medieval pope. In this painting, Innocent, shown enthroned at the right, raises his right hand to grant approval of the Franciscan religious order in 1209 to the kneeling Saint Francis of Assisi.

Conflict with the East. Before the 400's, a single Christian church existed. But it consisted of several nationalities. Each nationality expressed the Christian faith in its own language and liturgy and, at times, its own theology. Gradually, cultural, geographic, political, and religious differences led to the development of several separate churches in the East Roman Empire. Beginning in the 400's, the Eastern churches began to drift away from the authority of Rome and the church in the West.

Several events helped widen the gulf between Western and Eastern Christianity. One event was the condemnation by the Council of Ephesus in 431 of the teachings of Nestorius, the *patriarch* (bishop) of Constantinople. Nestorius asserted that Mary was the mother of Jesus but not the mother of God. In reaction to the council's condemnation, the East Syrian Church separated itself from the Western Church. The gulf widened after the Council of Chalcedon condemned Monophysitism. After this condemnation, the Armenian Church, the Coptic Church of Egypt, the Ethiopian Church, and the Syrian Jacobite Church all broke away from those churches that accepted the teaching of the Council of Chalcedon.

Growth of the church in Europe

The Early Middle Ages. In A.D. 476, Germanic forces led by the general Odoacer deposed the last emperor of the West Roman Empire. Many historians use this date to mark the end of the Roman Empire in the West and the start of the Middle Ages. The influence and power of the church reached their peak in the Middle Ages.

The collapse of the West Roman Empire meant that no one power had political control in the West. Instead, all of Western Europe except Ireland came to be ruled by kings who were either Arians or non-Christians. Beginning with the reign of Pope Gregory the Great in 590, the church set out to create a Christian world in the West. Its most important instruments were the papacy and monasticism.

The papacy gradually replaced the empire as the center of authority in Western Europe. Ireland had been converted to Christianity in the 400's, mainly through the efforts of Saint Patrick. Sometime between 496 and 508, the king of the Franks, Clovis I, was converted. His conversion brought Gaul into the church and checked the spread of the Arian heresy there. Gaul was a huge region now occupied by Belgium, France, and part of western Germany. From the 500's to the 700's, the papacy directed the conversion of other peoples of the West. These peoples included the Visigoths in Spain, the Anglo-Saxons in England, and the Croats in central Europe.

Meanwhile, the growth of monasticism played a large part in the church's increasing influence. Monasticism created centers of Christian society, renewed the spiritual life of religious communities, and helped transform Western culture into a Christian civilization. In the early 500's, Saint Benedict of Nursia founded Benedictine monasticism. The Benedictine rule was moderate and humane in setting forth how its followers should live. These qualities influenced the rule of many later orders.

In the early 700's, Muslims, who followed the religion of Islam, conquered Spain. Also in the 700's, Viking raiders from northern Europe began to attack England and other Christian countries. The conquest of Spain and the Viking attacks greatly disrupted Western European economic, political, and social life. In the midst of these disruptions, the church stood out as the major force for unifying and civilizing the West.

Charlemagne, the greatest king of the Franks, became one of the most important people in European as well as church history. During his reign, he laid a foundation for the organized, civilized society that was later built in Western Europe. This foundation resulted from the ideals that Charlemagne pursued—orderly government, religious reform, and the expansion of the Christian world through conquest and missionary activity.

Charlemagne involved himself deeply in church affairs and became protector of the popes. In 800, Pope Leo III crowned him emperor of the Romans, restoring the idea of empire in the West. Charlemagne's empire formed the basis of what became the Holy Roman Empire in 962. The Holy Roman Empire lasted until 1806. It consisted largely of German and Italian states ruled by German emperors.

Cluniac reform was the name given to a vast reform movement within the church. It began in the 900's and lasted about 200 years. It was centered in the Benedictine abbey of Cluny, France. The movement introduced significant changes in the way monasteries were governed and monks lived. It also helped correct abuses within the church, such as *simony* (buying or selling sacred things or church offices). The Cistercian order—founded in 1098 in Cîteaux, France—also became a leading force for church renewal, particularly under the leadership of Saint Bernard of Clairvaux.

Split with the East. Since the 400's, the Eastern churches had continued to drift away from the church in the West. Then, in the 800's, Photius, patriarch of Constantinople, had a serious dispute with the papacy. A major issue was the pope's claim to authority over Eastern Christians. In the 1000's, a conflict also developed between Rome and the patriarch of Constantinople, Michael Cerularius. Part of this conflict arose from claims by each church that the other was interfering in its affairs. Serious *schisms* (splits) emerged from these disagreements. The disagreements led to a formal division in 1054 between the Eastern churches that used the Byzantine rite and the Western church that followed the Latin rite and acknowledged the primacy of the bishop of Rome. However, some Eastern churches eventually reunited with the Roman Catholic Church, forming what are now called the Eastern Catholic Churches.

Innocent III, elected pope in 1198, became one of the most powerful popes of the Middle Ages. He influenced the political affairs of much of Europe. He called one of the most important church councils of the period, the Fourth Lateran Council, which met in 1215. It enacted 70 *decrees* (official decisions) regulating church affairs. Innocent also encouraged the founding of the Dominican and Franciscan religious orders. Saint Dominic and Saint Francis of Assisi established these *mendicant* (begging) orders. The members sought to live a life of poverty in community as they preached the gospel.

Innocent's reign led to the establishment of the religious court known as the Inquisition. The Inquisition was set up in 1231 to investigate and combat heresy. But the inquisitors often misused their power, and they had some suspects tortured or even put to death.

Scholasticism. In the 1100's, the system of thought called *medieval scholasticism* began to develop. It reached its peak in the 1200's. Its scholars, called *scholastics,* tried to better understand Christian doctrine by the use of reason. The writings on logic by the ancient Greek philosopher Aristotle had an early influence on scholasticism. The scholastics put various doctrines and their explanations into systematic order. They also tried to resolve conflicting views in Christian theology.

The leading scholastics included Saint Albertus Magnus of Germany, Roger Bacon of England, Saint Bonaventure of Italy, and especially Saint Thomas Aquinas of Italy. The center of scholasticism was the University of Paris, where Bonaventure and Thomas Aquinas taught.

Boniface VIII became pope in 1294. He tried to unify the Christian world more closely under the papacy. Boniface insisted that kings of individual nations were subject to the Holy Roman emperor and that the emperor's power, in turn, came from the pope. In 1302, Boniface issued a *bull* (papal decree) called *Unam sanctam.* The bull declared that, for salvation, every human being must be subject to the pope. The bull angered the French king, Philip IV, who said that Boniface was trying to claim authority over the French king and the French people.

The Avignon papacy. In 1309, Pope Clement V moved from Rome to Avignon, in what is now France. The popes did not return to Rome until 1377. One reason that the popes lived in Avignon was that they wished to avoid the civil wars that were disrupting Italy in the 1300's. Also, the popes came to be increasingly influenced by the powerful French kings. During the Avignon period, papal reform efforts continued, and the church sent missionaries to Asia and encouraged the expansion of universities. But hostility against a French-dominated papacy began to grow outside of France.

The Great Schism. From 1378 to 1417, a controversy called the Great Schism deeply divided the church. During this time, candidates from Avignon and Rome both claimed to be the rightful pope. In 1409, the Council of Pisa tried to resolve the dispute but instead created a third claim to the office. Each of the three men demanded obedience from the Christian faithful, which caused much confusion and doubt.

In 1417, bishops and other high-ranking clergymen meeting at the Council of Constance finally ended the Great Schism by electing a fourth man, Martin V, as the single rightful pope. But the controversy had caused damage within the church. For example, reform efforts had been slowed. A conflict also had developed over the idea that a general council of bishops had greater authority than the pope.

The close of the Middle Ages. From the 1300's through the 1500's, medieval Europe gradually gave way to modern Europe. During these 300 years, the Middle Ages overlapped a period called the Renaissance. This was a time of great cultural and intellectual activity, when ideas and customs that had been accepted for hundreds of years were questioned or swept away. The Renaissance began in Italy in the 1300's and spread throughout Western Europe in the 1400's and 1500's.

The Renaissance emphasized the great dignity of humanity and the beauty of life on Earth and had both good and bad effects on Catholicism. Popes supported Renaissance artists and scholars, but the papacy also suffered a moral decline. The church sponsored important historical scholarship, but the popes often became involved in Italian politics. Reform efforts within the church diminished.

Meanwhile, during the 1400's, a revival of deep religious feeling occurred among clergy and the laity. Many Catholics expressed this feeling in emotional *devotions* (pious practices) to the sufferings and death of Jesus. But during this time, piety was being divorced from its roots in theology, and theology was hardening into conflicting schools of thought and losing much of its vitality.

The Council of Florence, which began in 1438, reunited the Western church with some Eastern churches. However, the reunification lasted only a few years. In 1453, Muslims captured Constantinople and ruled over most Eastern Christians until the 1800's.

The Reformation. Medieval Christian civilization ended with the Reformation, a religious revolution that gave birth to Protestantism in the 1500's. As a result of the Reformation, Europe became divided between Roman Catholic and Protestant countries and communities.

By the early 1500's, the conditions in the church that led to the Reformation were apparent. The papacy was dominated by temporal concerns. The Roman Curia often was corrupt. Many bishops lived like princes and neglected the faithful. A great number of clergymen were uneducated and ignored their pastoral duties. Members of religious orders had become worldly. Fear and superstition were common among the laity. The liturgy no longer held much meaning or inspiration for the people, and theology had generally become dry and unrelated to real life.

Some councils, popes, saints, scholars, and movements among the people had indeed attempted to reform the church during the late Middle Ages. However, the church remained largely unreformed.

In 1517, Martin Luther, a member of the Augustinian order, issued his famous Ninety-Five Theses in Wittenberg, Germany. The theses were statements attacking the church's doctrine of *indulgences* and the abuses that arose in granting indulgences. An indulgence is a release from part or all of temporal punishment due for sin, provided that the sin has already been forgiven. The church's doctrine on indulgences was neither understood nor practiced properly. Many preachers sold indulgences. Many people bought them from the church, hoping the indulgences would hasten the release of a dead person's soul from purgatory. Luther's attack on indulgences began the Reformation.

By the late 1500's, the Reformation had divided Western Europe into Protestant and Roman Catholic lands. Catholicism was reduced primarily to the Mediterranean countries, as well as to Hungary, Poland, and small areas within the Holy Roman Empire. But while the Catholic Church lost much ground in Europe to Protestantism, it achieved great success in other parts of the world. Starting in the 1500's, Catholic missionaries converted many people in Africa, Asia, and the Americas.

The Counter Reformation, also known as the Catholic Reformation, was a reform movement within Catholicism that increased in intensity as the church reacted to the Protestant Reformation. It took place during the 1500's and 1600's.

Beginning in the 1520's, such reform popes as Adrian VI, Paul III, and especially Paul IV concentrated on correcting abuses in the Roman Curia and hierarchy. By the end of the reign of Saint Pius V in 1572, the papacy had clearly committed itself to church reform.

A leading force in the Counter Reformation was the Society of Jesus, commonly called the Jesuits. Saint Ignatius Loyola founded the Jesuits in 1534, and Paul III confirmed the order in 1540. Loyola did not found the Jesuits specifically to counteract Protestantism. But the order proved well equipped for the task. The Jesuits were flexible, practical, and completely at the pope's service. They revived Catholicism both intellectually and spiritually. To a large extent, the Jesuits helped halt the advance of Protestantism, even regaining vast areas that had come under Protestant influence in Belgium, Luxembourg, the Netherlands, France, and eastern and central Europe.

Perhaps the greatest single force in renewing Catholic life and worship was the Council of Trent (1545-1563). The council issued decrees on the Mass and other areas of doctrine and discipline that eliminated much confusion within the church. Its decrees on such topics as the training of priests and the granting of indulgences reformed church life wherever they were put into effect.

The Counter Reformation drew strength from the spiritual renewal led by Saint Teresa of Avila and Saint John of the Cross. It found artistic expression in the *baroque* churches and monasteries built during this period and in the *polyphonic* music composed for religious services by the Italian composer Giovanni Palestrina and the English composer William Byrd. Baroque architecture is characterized by curved forms and lavish ornamentation. Polyphonic music has two or more voice parts with independent melodies that harmonize.

A number of religious and political wars broke out during the Counter Reformation. Between 1562 and 1598, the Catholic majority in France and French Protestants called Huguenots fought eight civil wars called the Wars of Religion. The Thirty Years' War destroyed much of Germany. It began as a civil war between Protestants and Catholics in the German states but eventually involved most European countries. The Peace of Westphalia, which ended the war in 1648, declared that the people of each state must follow the religion of their ruler. This principle greatly weakened the Holy Roman Empire. It also ended the medieval idea of a Christian commonwealth of nations harmoniously directed by the supreme authority of pope and emperor.

Catholic revival in France. Perhaps the most outstanding example of church renewal in the 1600's occurred in France. Several people especially helped create this renewal. Saint Francis de Sales, bishop of Geneva, inspired many Christians by his uniting of humanism and piety. Saint Vincent de Paul devoted his life to serving the poor. He founded the Vincentians, an order of missionary priests to country districts in France. Saint Louise de Marillac worked with Vincent de Paul in assisting the needy. She was one of many women who helped restore a sense of charity and deep religious feeling to both convent and Catholic family life.

During the 1600's, several French clergymen founded religious institutes that helped inspire a new emphasis on spirituality in the priesthood. Cardinal Pierre de Berulle established the French Oratory in 1611. Jean Jacques Olier founded the Company of Saint Sulpice in 1642, and Saint John Eudes established the Congregation of Jesus and Mary in 1643.

Gallicanism. The period from the end of the Thirty

The Council of Trent (mid-1500's), an oil painting on canvas by an unknown Italian painter; Louvre, Paris (© Jean Schormans, Réunion des Musées Nationaux/Art Resource)

The Council of Trent was a powerful force for renewing the church during the Counter Reformation. The council met for 25 sessions from 1545 to 1563 in the sanctuary of the cathedral at Trent, Italy. The council issued decrees that reformed many areas of church doctrine and discipline. The view in this painting is toward the apse of the cathedral, showing a large group of seated participants facing the leaders of the council session.

Years' War in 1648 to the outbreak of the French Revolution (1789-1799) has been called the Revolt of the Catholic Kings. The period was marked by quarrels between church and state, especially over Gallicanism—the view that the authority of national churches should be increased at the expense of papal authority.

Gallicanism developed in France, and the dispute over it became most critical there. King Louis XIV and Pope Innocent XI quarreled over Louis's attempts to increase his influence in French religious affairs. The quarrel led many French clergymen to adopt doctrines that the papacy would not accept. For example, some French clergymen believed that a general church council was superior to the pope. Although the controversy died down in the 1690's, the French clergy remained anti-Roman for many years.

Gallicanism, with its emphasis on nationalism, became popular in every European country ruled by a Catholic monarch. During the late 1700's, the Holy Roman emperor, Joseph II, tried to separate the Catholic Church in Austria from Rome. Joseph considered the church a department of state whose task was to promote morality. He controlled all levels of the clergy and even interfered with the liturgy. Rulers in Naples, Sardinia, Spain, and Venice followed Joseph's example.

Jansenism. While the church faced challenges from Catholic rulers, it also was disrupted from within by theological disputes. The most serious dispute was over a movement known as Jansenism. Jansenism arose in France in the mid-1600's. It was based on the writings of Cornelius Jansen, bishop of Ypres, Belgium. Jansen developed doctrines on divine grace that played down human freedom and denied that Jesus Christ died for all humanity. The church attacked some Jansenist doctrines as heresy.

The movement tore Catholic France apart. It divided many French bishops from Rome and even attracted the attention of Kings Louis XIV and Louis XV. The Catholic philosopher and mathematician Blaise Pascal became a leading spokesman for Jansenism and a fierce critic of the Jesuits, who spoke against it. Three popes condemned Jansenism—Innocent X in 1653, Alexander VII in 1656, and Clement XI in 1713. But their condemnation only fueled the controversy.

Jansenism finally began to lose influence in the 1730's. But its harsh theology and its understanding of human nature as thoroughly corrupted by sin and subject to divine punishment still influence some Catholics today.

The Enlightenment was a period during which philosophers emphasized the use of reason as the one sure method of learning truth. The Enlightenment lasted from the late 1600's to the late 1700's. During this time, many people attacked organized religion in general and the Catholic Church in particular. They claimed that the church favored obedience to authority over individual freedom and that it sacrificed reason to tradition. They also believed that the Catholic clergy's obedience to Rome violated national sovereignty. The leaders of the period included such French intellectuals as Denis Diderot, Jean-Jacques Rousseau, and Voltaire.

Suppression of the Jesuits. During the middle and late 1700's, several nations banned the Jesuit Order from their country and colonies. Portugal banned the Jesuits in 1759, France in 1764, and Spain in 1767. In 1773, pressure from Catholic rulers helped force Pope Clement XIV to suppress the Jesuits in all countries.

The Jesuits were banned for several reasons. Some Catholic rulers and churchmen were jealous of the order's influence. Some accused the Jesuits of accumulating too much power and wealth. Gallicans opposed the order's total obedience to the pope, and Jansenists objected to the order's emphasis on human freedom.

The suppression of the Jesuits was never completely effective. For example, the order survived in Russia through the friendship of Empress Catherine the Great. Pope Pius VII lifted the ban in 1814. But the suppression caused a severe setback in Catholic education and missionary activity.

The decline of church influence. The forces of democracy and nationalism swept across Europe from the start of the French Revolution through the 1800's. These forces often were accompanied by fierce opposition to the Roman Catholic Church because the church was viewed as a supporter of the traditional order.

The church suffered enormous losses as a result of the French Revolution. For example, many of the great abbeys of Europe disappeared, and with them the influence of the monastic orders as centers of scholarship and spiritual renewal. Catholic influence over public life was severely lessened, often by civil laws. Catholic universities yielded to state-sponsored education. Theology came to be studied mostly in seminaries rather than in universities, and it became increasingly separated from modern thought and problems.

In many countries, the church suffered from a shortage of priests. This was especially true in France. During the French Revolution, the church lost half its clergy. Many priests were executed or died in prison. Others left the church.

The papacy had governed certain territories called the Papal States, which were gradually absorbed by Italy. By 1870, the papacy had lost the last of the land that once made up the Papal States. The pope's territory was reduced to Vatican City. Although that seemed at the time to be a loss, it freed the papacy from political pressures and concerns.

Although the church suffered setbacks and hostility during the 1800's, Catholic life itself experienced renewal. The restoration of the Jesuit Order in 1814 enabled it to play a large role in that renewal. New religious orders of women became active in education in Belgium, France, and Germany. In Germany, the Congress of Mainz founded the Catholic Union in 1848. The union was an association of Catholics dedicated to promoting the ideals of their religion in social life.

Vatican Council I. In 1846, Pius IX became pope. He ruled until 1878—the longest reign in papal history. Pius's reign reached a high point when he summoned Vatican Council I (1869-1870). The council defined as Catholic doctrine the pope's primacy over the whole church. It also declared him to be *infallible*—that is, incapable of error when, as supreme pastor of the church, he formally defines matters of faith and morals. This power rarely is called upon.

Leo XIII. A new age of church history began after Leo XIII became pope in 1878. Leo tried to convince the governments of his time that they and the church could live in harmony. He faced especially strong antichurch feeling in Germany, France, and Italy. He succeeded in easing the German government's restrictions against the church, but he failed in France and Italy. In fact, the French government passed new antichurch laws in 1880, including laws that expelled religious orders from France and banned religious education in the schools.

Leo sought to make the church more active in confronting issues and problems of the modern world. He began a new policy of maintaining contact between the papacy and everyday Catholic life. He established this contact through letters to the Catholic world, called *encyclicals.* The encyclicals dealt with such subjects as philosophy and Bible studies, theology and church law, and the relations between the state and the working class. Leo's most important statement on social questions was the 1891 encyclical called *Rerum Novarum (Of New Things),* which upheld the rights of labor.

Pius X. The papacy of Saint Pius X, which lasted from 1903 to 1914, featured the most impressive reform activity since the Council of Trent in the 1500's. Reforms were made in such areas as liturgy, the reception of Holy Communion, seminary education, and church law.

However, Pius vigorously opposed Modernism, a movement that began in the late 1800's among Catholic intellectuals in several European countries. Modernists desired to bring Catholic thought into what they felt was a closer relation to the knowledge and outlook of the time. A number of church leaders believed that Modernism challenged important Catholic teachings. Some other Catholics believed that the Modernists raised valid issues. Pius formally condemned Modernism, but such Modernist issues as Biblical scholarship continued to be discussed as late as the 1960's at Vatican Council II.

During the 1920's and 1930's, the church made *concordats* (agreements) with many nations to guarantee its freedom and its spiritual authority over Catholics in the countries involved. During this period, the church also updated its worldwide missionary activities. Meanwhile, many clergy and laity made significant contributions to learning and scholarship, especially in the areas of Bible and church history.

Facing opposition. Throughout most of the 1900's, the church faced hostility from European dictatorships. During the 1920's and 1930's, dictatorships in Germany, Italy, and the Soviet Union often opposed the church. After World War II (1939-1945), the church faced persecution in the Communist countries of Eastern Europe. In the 1940's and 1950's, Pope Pius XII worked to preserve the religious freedom of Catholics living under dictatorships. Pius's encyclicals on the liturgy and other topics prepared the way for the reforms of Vatican Council II.

Vatican Council II. Pope John XXIII succeeded Pius in 1958. John called Vatican Council II, which met from 1962 to 1965. The council marked a turning point in the history of the Roman Catholic Church. The council issued 16 documents that tried to give a deeper understanding of the church and its doctrines and help the church serve the needs of the modern world. These documents led to a number of reforms. These reforms included celebration of the liturgy in the language of the people rather than in Latin, a renewed emphasis on the importance of Bible reading and study, and an encouragement of active participation of the laity in the life of the church. The council also involved the church more

Fotocronache Olympia

Vatican Council II marked a turning point in the history of the Roman Catholic Church. Church leaders met in Rome from 1962 to 1965. The meeting led to a number of reforms, including worship services in the language of the people instead of in Latin.

fully in the *ecumenical movement* to unite all Christians.

Paul VI, who succeeded John XXIII in 1963, guided the council to its completion. He led the church through the turmoil of the late 1960's, when much in society as well as the church was undergoing radical change.

Paul disheartened liberals by reaffirming the church's traditional teaching on sexual morality in his 1968 encyclical *Humanae Vitae (On Human Life).* But he also promoted the council's liturgical reforms and spoke out strongly on behalf of social justice, especially for developing nations. He directed a reform of the Roman Curia, made the College of Cardinals a more international body, and increased the number of bishops from developing countries. Paul also traveled widely. He visited the United States as well as countries in Latin America, Africa, and Asia.

John Paul II was elected pope in 1978. A native of Poland, he became the first non-Italian pope since the Renaissance. Many people believe that he played an important part in bringing about the collapse of Communism in Eastern Europe and the Soviet Union in the late 1980's and early 1990's.

In 1983, John Paul issued a new code of church law that incorporated the reforms of Vatican Council II into the institutional life of the church. For example, the code called for an active role for lay people in parish and diocesan advisory bodies. In 1992, John Paul announced the publication of a new *Catechism of the Catholic Church,* a comprehensive statement of Catholic doctrine, liturgical practice, and morality. It is intended primarily for bishops for use in religious education.

John Paul traveled throughout the world, and he wrote extensively. He addressed issues of social justice in his 1991 encyclical *Centesimus Annus (Hundredth Year),* written on the hundredth anniversary of Leo XIII's *Rerum Novarum.* He discussed principles of Catholic morality in *Veritatis Splendor (The Splendor of Truth,* 1993) and *Evangelium Vitae (The Gospel of Life,* 1995). John Paul wished to prepare the church for the task of a *new evangelization*—preaching the gospel to a world he considered to be often aimless and adrift. He encouraged ecumenical dialogue with the Eastern Orthodox Churches and furthered understanding and respect between Catholics and Jews. John Paul died in 2005, ending the longest papal reign in more than 100 years.

Growth of the church outside Europe

Before the 1500's, the Roman Catholic Church had spread to only a few areas outside Europe. But during the 1500's, due to the activities of Catholic missionaries, the church began to take root throughout the world.

In Africa in the 1500's, the most successful Catholic missions were those in the Portuguese colonies of Angola, the Congo, and Mozambique. Missionaries had begun accompanying Portuguese explorers to Africa by the late 1400's. The missions in Africa eventually declined, however, particularly because of a lack of priests. By the beginning of the 1800's, Christianity had almost completely died out on the continent. In the mid-1800's, many European countries started colonizing Africa, and missionary activity began again. The church eventually spread throughout the continent. Today, Africa has the fastest growing Catholic population in the world.

In Asia, Catholic missionaries were sent to every country that European colonial interests discovered in the 1500's. They were most successful where Spanish control was strong. In the Philippines, missionaries first arrived in 1564. By the 1800's, the majority of the Philippine population had become Catholic.

Missionaries who reached Japan in 1549 established a Roman Catholic community in Kyushu. Japanese rulers later turned away from Western influence, and in 1614 Japanese Catholics were persecuted and killed for their faith. It was not until 1873 that religious freedom was granted once more. A small group of secret Christians survived in spite of the persecution, and the church has many members in southern Japan.

In India, Catholic missionaries, especially the Jesuit Saint Francis Xavier, established churches in Goa and surrounding areas during the early 1500's. Goa was then a Portuguese colony. Today, the largest Indian Roman Catholic communities are in the southwestern states of Goa and Kerala.

In Latin America. Soon after Christopher Columbus arrived in the Western Hemisphere in 1492, Spain and Portugal claimed nearly all of Latin America. Catholic missionaries accompanied Spanish and Portuguese explorers and colonists and converted most Latin American Indians.

Many natives of Latin America accepted Christianity

only under pressure from colonial rulers and, in fact, still retained their old religious beliefs. As a result, the church tried to strengthen the faith of the converts. For example, it helped establish universities in Lima, Peru; Mexico City; and elsewhere. The church also recruited clergy from among Latin Americans. But the number of native-born priests proved inadequate for church needs. Catholicism in Latin America thus remained almost totally dependent on the church in Europe.

In the 1800's, the church in Latin America declined after many colonies gained their independence from Spain and Portugal. The church had had close ties with the colonial powers, and many clergymen had opposed the independence movements. As a result, many Latin Americans became hostile toward the church, and it lost much influence in Latin American life.

In Latin America today, there is a renewal of Catholicism, mainly because bishops and priests have become involved in social problems. Following a movement called *liberation theology,* they have established local Christian groups, called *base communities,* for prayer, reflection, and social action. However, Protestantism has won many people away from Catholicism, and anticlerical feeling remains strong in many countries.

In Canada. Canada became a flourishing territory for Catholic missionaries beginning with French colonial rule in 1534. In 1763, Canada became a British colony. Until 1774, Britain (now also called the United Kingdom) restricted the religious freedom of French Canadians, who were Catholics. In 1774, the British Parliament passed the Quebec Act, which restored religious liberties to French Canadians. Today, the Roman Catholic Church is the country's largest single body of Christians. The church has much influence in the province of Quebec, where most of the people are Catholics.

In the United States. Spanish missions covered a huge territory from Florida to California. The missions of New France extended from the Great Lakes in the north, through the Mississippi Valley, and south to Louisiana. In the 13 English colonies, along the Atlantic coast, Maryland had the largest concentration of Catholics.

The mainstream of Catholic life emerged from the minority Catholics of the English colonies rather than from the state-favored Catholics of the French and Spanish colonies. Occasionally, the governments of the English colonies passed anti-Catholic legislation. But generally they followed a policy of religious freedom. This freedom and the growing separation of church and state helped make the Catholic Church acceptable to non-Catholics. In 1789, Catholic priests in the United States elected John Carroll as the country's first bishop. Carroll established the diocese of Baltimore and the first Catholic college in the United States—Georgetown College (now Georgetown University).

During the 1800's, waves of immigration shaped the nature of the church in America. From 1790 to the mid-1860's, over 2 million Catholics arrived, mainly from Germany and Ireland. From 1870 to 1900, over 3 million more came, mostly from Italy, Austria-Hungary, and Poland. By 1900, Irish Americans had become the most powerful force in the church in the United States.

Some native-born Americans subjected Catholic immigrants to a form of prejudice called *nativism.* They questioned the immigrants' patriotism, morals, and religion. At times, this led to violence, such as the burning of the Ursuline convent in Charlestown, Massachusetts, in 1834. During the American Civil War (1861-1865), Catholics on both sides showed such loyalty and courage that they won more acceptance in the North and South.

From 1865 to 1900, several conflicts developed within the church in the United States. Many Catholics believed that Catholic children should be educated in state-supported public schools. But other Catholics believed Catholic children should attend schools operated by the church. Some Catholics supported the Knights of Labor, an early labor organization. Others attacked the organization, partly because they claimed its social programs were too extreme. Conflicts sometimes arose among the various nationalities of Catholic immigrants, especially between German Catholics and Irish Catholics.

In 1887, bishops of the United States established the Catholic University of America in Washington, D.C. They founded the school as the official national Roman Catholic university in the United States.

During the late 1800's, some European Catholic leaders accused American Catholics of a tendency toward nationalism. The Europeans labeled this tendency *Americanism* and saw in it an attempt to dilute the church's doctrines to make them fit modern culture. American Catholics denied the charges. In 1899, Pope Leo XIII condemned the views of Americanism without naming anyone as holding its principles.

During the 1900's, the church in the United States grew strong. American bishops coordinated their various activities through national meetings and, after Vatican II, established the National Conference of Catholic Bishops (now part of the United States Conference of Catholic Bishops). An increasing number of American missionaries went to other lands. Catholic education, from the elementary to the university level, spread throughout the country. The study of liturgy and theology made great strides. Catholics became a powerful political factor, especially in such large cities as Boston, Chicago, and New York City. The election in 1960 of John F. Kennedy, a Catholic, as president symbolized the final assimilation of the church into American society.

Today, concerns of the church in the United States include financial problems and a growing shortage of priests. As membership in the church has declined and donations have decreased, parishes and parish schools have been forced to close or merge. Due to the shortage of men entering the priesthood, some Catholics argue that priests should be allowed to marry and that women should be eligible to become priests. Others insist such changes would be contrary to church tradition.

Recent church history

Benedict XVI succeeded John Paul II as pope in 2005. Benedict, a theologian, maintained many of John Paul's practices and held firmly to tradition.

In 2009, the Catholic Church issued a decree making it easier for Anglicans to convert to Catholicism while keeping many Anglican traditions. At the time, Anglicans were experiencing serious conflicts about same-sex unions and the ordination of women and homosexuals.

Benedict XVI resigned as pope in 2013, citing his advanced age. He was the first pope to resign in nearly 600 years. Cardinal Jorge Mario Bergoglio, the archbishop of

UPI/Bettmann

Pope Paul VI addressed the United Nations General Assembly in New York City in 1965 to plead for world peace. Paul was the first pope to travel widely outside of Europe. In addition to the United States, he visited countries in Latin America, Africa, and Asia.

Buenos Aires, Argentina, succeeded Benedict as Pope Francis. He became the first Latin American pope. As pope, Francis continued to support traditional church doctrine. However, he promoted the idea of a warmer, more welcoming church. In 2015, for example, he simplified the process of *annulling* a marriage—that is, declaring it invalid. In 2016, Francis became the first pope to meet with a leader of the Russian Orthodox Church. The Christian church had split in 1054 over differences and developed into the Roman Catholic and Eastern Orthodox churches.

In the early 2000's, charges and convictions of sexual misconduct by clergy rocked the church. Some senior church officials had failed to discipline or remove the offenders or helped hide abuse. Catholic authorities took steps to address past wrongs and prevent further abuses. For example, in 2015, Pope Francis set up a Vatican tribunal to judge church leaders accused of overlooking or hiding sexual abuse. In 2019, he issued new laws requiring Vatican and church officials, clerics, and *religious* (monks and nuns) to report accusations and cover-ups of abuse by the clergy. Chester Gillis

Related articles in *World Book* include:

Biographies

See the separate articles **Pope,** with its table: The popes; **Cardinal,** with its tables: Canadian cardinals and American cardinals; and **Saint,** and its list of *Related articles.* See also:

Abelard, Peter
Damien, Father
Day, Dorothy
De Smet, Pierre Jean
Duns Scotus, John
Erasmus, Desiderius
Flanagan, Edward Joseph
Jansen, Cornelius
Lanfranc
Las Casas, Bartolomé de
Lombard, Peter
Maritain, Jacques
Merton, Thomas
Newman, John Henry
Nicholas of Cusa
Peter the Hermit
Savonarola, Girolamo
Sheen, Fulton J.
Teilhard de Chardin, Pierre
Teresa, Mother
Tetzel, Johann
Thomas à Kempis
Torquemada, Tomás de
William of Ockham

Doctrines, beliefs, and ceremonies

Advent
Annunciation
Anointing of the sick
Apostles' Creed
Baptism
Bible
Canonization
Communion
Confirmation
Excommunication
Feasts and festivals
Immaculate Conception
Indulgence
Lent
Liberation theology
Liturgy
Mass
Meditation
Pentecost
Purgatory
Rosary
Sacrament
Transubstantiation
Trinity

Hierarchy

Abbot
Archbishop
Bishop
Cardinal
Deacon
Friar
Monk
Nun
Patriarch
Pope
Priest

History

Arianism
Canada, History of (The Quebec Act)
Counter Reformation
Crusades
Freedom of religion
Gnosticism
Holy Roman Empire
Inquisition
Middle Ages
Mission life in America
Missionary
Nicene Councils
Papal States
Reformation
Renaissance
Scholasticism
Trent, Council of
Vatican City
Vatican Council I
Vatican Council II

Organizations

Conference of Catholic Bishops, United States
Catholic Library Association
Catholic Youth Organization
Knights of Columbus
Knights of Peter Claver

Religious institutes

For a list of articles on religious institutes, see the *Related articles* at the end of the **Religious life** article.

Other related articles

Abortion
Birth control
Bull
Christianity
Divorce
Eastern Catholic Churches
Eastern Orthodox Churches
Family (Development of the Western family)
Fátima, Our Lady of
Index of Forbidden Books
Jesus Christ
Lourdes
Old Catholic churches
Parochial school
Regina Medal
Sainte-Anne-de-Beaupré
World Council of Churches

Outline

I. **Roman Catholic beliefs**
II. **Worship**
III. **Church organization**
IV. **The early church**
V. **Growth of the church in Europe**
VI. **Growth of the church outside Europe**
VII. **The church today**

Roman Empire. See Rome, Ancient.

Roman Forum. See Forum, Roman.

Roman gods. See Mythology.

Roman law. See Law (Ancient Roman law); **Justinian I;** Rome, Ancient (The law).

Roman mythology. See Mythology.

Roman numerals are a set of symbols that stand for numbers. The ancient Romans invented Roman numerals. Today, the Roman system is used to number the faces of clocks, to list topics in outlines, and to record

Roman numerals from 1 to 1,000,000

Number	Numeral	Number	Numeral
1	I	70	LXX
2	II	80	LXXX
3	III	90	LXXXX or XC
4	IIII or IV	100	C
5	V	200	CC
6	VI	300	CCC
7	VII	400	CCCC or CD
8	VIII	500	D
9	VIIII or IX	600	DC
10	X	700	DCC
11	XI	800	DCCC
12	XII	900	DCCCC or CM
13	XIII	1,000	M
14	XIIII or XIV	2,000	MM
15	XV	3,000	MMM
16	XVI	4,000	MMMM or $M\overline{V}$
17	XVII	5,000	$\overline{V}$
18	XVIII	10,000	$\overline{X}$
19	XVIIII or XIX or IXX	25,000	$\overline{XXV}$
20	XX	50,000	$\overline{L}$
30	XXX	100,000	$\overline{C}$
40	XXXX or XL	500,000	$\overline{D}$
50	L	1,000,000	$\overline{M}$
60	LX		

© Thinkstock

Emperor Hadrian's wall, built across northern England in the A.D. 120's, consisted of fortified sites joined together by a great wall. The ruins in some places are still 5 to 6 feet (1.5 to 1.8 meters) high and wide enough to walk on.

dates on monuments and public buildings.

All Roman numerals are written using seven basic symbols, either alone or in combination. These symbols are I (1), V (5), X (10), L (50), C (100), D (500), and M (1,000). A bar is sometimes placed over a Roman numeral to multiply it by 1,000. For example, 5,000 appears as $\overline{V}$. Roman numerals are written from left to right, using the principle of addition in most cases. A person first writes the thousands, then the hundreds, then the tens, and finally the units. To write 2,763, first write MM (2,000), then DCC (500+200=700), next LX (50+10=60), then III (3). The number 2,763 appears as MMDCCLXIII.

In Roman numerals, a smaller numeral appearing before a larger numeral indicates that the smaller numeral is subtracted from the larger one. This principle is generally used for 4's and 9's. Thus, 4 usually appears as IV (5 minus 1), and 9 usually appears as IX (10 minus 1). The principle is usually applied to any number beginning with 4 or 9, such as 40 (XL) and 90 (XC). But the principle of addition can also be used in writing such numbers. For example, 400 can be written as CCCC instead of CD.

The early Roman system of about 500 B.C. differed from the system people commonly use today. For example, the Romans always wrote 4 as IIII and 9 as VIIII. In addition, they had different symbols for numbers that can be divided by 1,000. People throughout Europe used Roman numerals until the A.D. 1500's. They found it easy to add and subtract using Roman numerals but difficult to perform other calculations. In the late 1500's, Arabic numerals began replacing Roman numerals for most uses. Beatriz S. D'Ambrosio

See also **Arabic numerals.**

Roman Republic. See **Rome, Ancient** (Government; History).

Roman walls were barriers that the Romans built where no natural territorial boundaries existed. By A.D. 100, they had built a line of walls in what is now Romania and Germany. They later built Hadrian's Wall and the Antonine Wall along the northern edge of the province of Britain. These walls were named for two Roman emperors, Hadrian and Antoninus Pius, and are the most famous Roman walls. The walls discouraged raids and revolts and reminded the tribes on both sides that the Romans were masters. The walls also made it easier for the Romans to control trade and to collect taxes.

Hadrian's Wall was built in the A.D. 120's. It extended 73 miles (117 kilometers), from the mouth of the River Tyne to the Solway Firth. Parts still stand. The wall was about 10 feet (3 meters) wide at its base and 20 feet (6 meters) high. For half its length, it was all stone. The rest was stone and turf. Small forts, called *milecastles,* stood about 1 Roman mile (about 0.9 mile or 1.5 kilometers) apart along the wall, with small watch towers between the forts about every ⅓ Roman mile (0.3 mile or 0.5 kilometer). A ditch lay in front of the wall, with a wider ditch 10 feet (3 meters) deep behind it.

The Antonine Wall was built in the A.D. 140's, north of Hadrian's Wall. It was a simpler wall, made of turf, and it stretched for 37 miles (60 kilometers).

The Romans allowed Hadrian's Wall to decay until 211, when they could no longer defend the Antonine Wall. Then they rebuilt Hadrian's Wall carefully. They rebuilt it twice more in the 300's and defended it until nearly 400. Arthur M. Eckstein

Romance is a long work of fiction that is less realistic than a novel. Most novelists try to present life realistically. Romance writers try to tell an entertaining story, often using fantastic and supernatural plots and characters.

The meaning of the term *romance* has changed many times since the first romances appeared in Greece almost 2,000 years ago. In ancient Greek literature, most fiction dealt with either love or war. War stories were called epics, and love stories were called romances. The word *romance* is still used for a love story.

By about the 1200's, most Western Europeans spoke a *Romance language* (language based on Latin), such as French, Italian, or Spanish. All fiction written in Romance languages was called romance. In most Romance languages today, the word for *romance* refers to long prose fiction. The word for *novel* means short prose fiction. English is the only language in which the words *novel* and *romance* distinguish between realistic and unrealistic fiction.

The first important romance was *Daphnis and Chloë,* (A.D. 100's or 200's) by a Greek named Longus. The greatest romances were written by medieval authors from the 1100's to the 1400's. Often written in verse, these romances mingle knightly combat, adventure, and courtship. Many describe the adventures of King Arthur and his knights of the Round Table. Others tell about the ancient conqueror Alexander the Great; the Spanish hero The Cid; and the emperor Charlemagne and his devoted knight, Roland.

The romance flourished again during the late 1700's and 1800's. In England, Horace Walpole's *The Castle of Otranto* (1764) began a trend for romances that emphasized mystery, terror, and the supernatural. These romances became known as *Gothic novels.* In the United States, the famous author Nathaniel Hawthorne insisted that he wrote romances, not novels. Elements of romance continue to appear in popular novels about courtship as well as in novels about the American frontier, in Western films, and in science fiction.

Paul Strohm

Related articles in *World Book* include:

Amadís of Gaul	Hawthorne, Nathaniel
French literature (Romances)	Novel (The European novel)
Gawain, Sir	Round Table
Gothic novel	

Romance languages are a group of languages that developed from Latin and are spoken in places that were once part of the Roman Empire. They include French, Italian, Portuguese, Romanian, and Spanish. Other Romance languages are Catalan of northeastern Spain and Provençal of southeastern France. The group also includes the Sardinian dialect and Rhaeto-Romanic dialects from certain parts of Switzerland and the Tyrol region of western Austria and northern Italy.

Latin was the official language of the Roman Empire. The word *romance* comes from a Latin adverb that referred to speakers of Latin who were said to "fabulare romanice," which means "to speak in the Roman way." These people spoke one of two forms—*classical* Latin or *vernacular* Latin. The educated classes spoke classical Latin. The common people spoke vernacular Latin. Romance languages developed from vernacular Latin spoken in certain conquered European countries that became Roman provinces. This vernacular Latin adopted words and features of pronunciation from the languages of the conquered countries. For example, the vernacular Latin word *caballus* (horse) became *cheval* in French, *cavallo* in Italian, and *caballo* in Spanish.

The Romance languages developed from the many dialects of vernacular Latin over several centuries. The earliest evidence of Romance languages appeared in the 800's. By the late 1200's, much literature was written in the Romance languages. So many literary works centered on the topic of love that they became known as *romances.* The word *romance* meaning *an affair of the heart* comes from this usage. Richard P. Kinkade

Related articles in *World Book* include:

French language	Portuguese language
Italian language	Romance
Latin language	Spanish language

Giraudon/Art Resource

A typical Romanesque church had thick walls and heavy curved arches. Notre-Dame-la-Grande (1130-1145) in Poitiers, France, is noted for its richly decorated west front.

Romanesque architecture was the prevailing architectural movement in western Europe from about A.D. 800 to the 1100's. Romanesque architecture developed into a number of regional styles, including Aquitaine, Brittany, Burgundy, Île-de-France, Norman, and Provence. Romanesque buildings were frequently isolated from the few developed cities of the period. The massive character of these buildings was a response to the demands for security and defense that such locations required.

The Romanesque style was especially well developed in churches and monastic structures. A typical Romanesque church was shaped like a *Latin cross*—that is, a cross with a vertical arm and a shorter horizontal crosspiece above the center. The roof over the *nave* (main gathering area) consisted of vaults of stone constructed on the principle of the arch. Side aisles flanked the nave. Large columns called *piers* supported the roof vaults. Round arches were built in openings in the walls and between the piers. The openings and piers were decorated with stone sculpture and carvings depicting Biblical scenes and people. Walls of the church were painted in fresco and also portrayed religious subjects.

By the mid-1100's, the Romanesque style had evolved into Gothic architecture. The chief reasons for the evolution included less need for defensive buildings and a desire to celebrate Christianity in lighter and higher churches. J. William Rudd

See also **Architecture** (Romanesque architecture; pictures); **Leaning Tower of Pisa; Norman architecture.**

Additional resources

Conant, Kenneth J. *Carolingian and Romanesque Architecture: 800-1200.* 4th ed. 1959. Reprint. Yale, 1992.

Minne-Sève, Viviane, and Kergall, Herve. *Romanesque and Gothic France.* Abrams, 2000.

Strafford, Peter. *Romanesque Churches of France: A Traveller's Guide.* Giles de la Mare, 2005.

Toman, Rolf, ed. *Romanesque: Architecture, Sculpture, Painting.* 1998. Reprint. Könemann, 2004.

© Jon Arnold, Alamy

Farming villages are scattered throughout the Romanian countryside. Rich farmland covers much of Romania, and agriculture employs many of the nation's people.

Romania

Romania is a country in eastern Europe. Alternate spellings for the country's name have included *Rumania* and *Roumania.* Romania was part of the Roman Empire in ancient times, and its name means *land of the Romans.* The Romanians are the only Eastern European people who trace their ancestry and language back to the ancient Romans. Bucharest is Romania's capital and largest city.

Romania lies west of the Black Sea and north of the Balkan Peninsula, Europe's southeastern tip. A long string of mountains curves through the northern and central parts of Romania. Breathtaking scenery, hiking trails, and ski and vacation resorts make the mountains a favorite recreation area. Picturesque farm villages dot fertile flatlands around the mountains. Romania's warm, sunny east coast—which borders the Black Sea—has a number of sandy beaches and an enormous wildlife preserve.

The colorful folk culture of Romania's rural people adds to the beauty and charm of the country. These people hold annual festivals at which they dance to the lively sounds of Romanian folk music. This music was influenced by the melodies played by the Roma (sometimes called Gypsies), a nomadic people who once wandered through Romania by the thousands.

Romania has a wealth of natural resources, including fertile soil, mineral deposits, and vast forests. Even so, it has always been one of Europe's least developed nations. Foreign nations controlled the country through much of its history and did little to develop its economy. Romania also suffered from an overdependence on one economic activity, agriculture.

Communists took over Romania's government in the 1940's. At first, they ran the country according to the wishes of the Soviet Union, which was Europe's strongest Communist nation.

Beginning in the 1960's, Romania's Communists succeeded in reducing Soviet control of the country. In addition, they adopted their own domestic policies. Chief among these policies was a program to expand the country's industry. As industry grew, many people left rural areas to find jobs in cities. The industrial program changed Romania from an agricultural country to an industrial country. However, Romania still remains poor by European standards.

In the late 1980's, the Soviet Union made reforms aimed toward giving its people more freedom. As a result, reform movements increased in Romania and other European Communist countries. In late 1989, Romanians

Facts in brief

Capital: Bucharest.
Official language: Romanian.
Official name: Republica România (Republic of Romania).
Area: 92,043 mi² (238,391 km²). *Greatest distances*—east-west, about 450 mi (724 km); north-south, about 320 mi (515 km). *Coastline*—130 mi (209 km).
Elevation: *Highest*—Mount Moldoveanu, 8,343 ft (2,543 m) above sea level. *Lowest*—sea level.
Population: *Estimated 2022 population*—19,195,000; density, 209 per mi² (81 per km²); distribution, 54 percent urban, 46 percent rural. *2019 official government estimate*—19,410,000.
Chief products: *Agriculture*—beef and dairy cattle, chickens, corn, grapes, hogs, potatoes, wheat. *Manufacturing*—cement, machinery, petroleum products, pharmaceuticals, processed foods, steel, tractors. *Mining*—coal, natural gas, petroleum.
National anthem: "Deşteapta-te, Române" ("Romanian, Arise").
Money: *Basic unit*—new Romanian leu. One hundred new bani equal one new leu.

revolted against the dictatorship of Nicolae Ceauşescu, Romania's president and Communist Party leader. Ceauşescu was executed, and a temporary government was set up. Free multiparty elections have been held since 1990.

Government

The Communist Party became Romania's ruling political party in the 1940's. This party exerted its power over the country's entire governmental structure. Only a small percentage of Romania's people belonged to the Communist Party. However, Communist leaders held important positions at all levels of government and in major nongovernmental organizations. The general secretary, who headed the Communist Party, had the authority of a dictator.

The Communist Party leaders made the country's laws and planned every detail of its economy. Communist leaders also controlled Romania's police and armed forces, and therefore had power over the lives of the people.

Romania's Constitution guaranteed such rights as freedom of speech, freedom of the press, and freedom of religion. However, the Communists interpreted the Constitution to mean that they could limit these rights to maintain power.

In December 1989, Romanians revolted and overthrew the Communist government. Free multiparty elections to select a president and members of a national legislature were held in mid-1990. Romania adopted a new Constitution in late 1991.

National government. Romania's top government official is the president, who is elected by the people to a five-year term. The president appoints a prime minister, who selects a Cabinet to help carry out the day-to-day operations of government.

Romania's parliament consists of the Senate and the Chamber of Deputies. The people elect the members of parliament to four-year terms.

Local government. Romania is divided into 41 counties and 1 special district, the city of Bucharest. Each unit has its own local government, as do cities, towns, and *communes* (rural areas) within the counties.

Courts. The High Court of Cassation and Justice is Romania's highest court. It hears appeals from the country's lower courts. The city of Bucharest and each of Romania's counties have a county court and a variety of lower courts.

Armed forces. Romania has an army, navy, air force, and special armed forces. Romanians serve in the armed forces on a volunteer basis.

People

Ancestry. Approximately 85 percent of Romania's people are Romanians by ancestry. The Romanians are descended from the Dacians, the Romans, and such tribes as the Goths, Huns, and Slavs. The Dacians lived in what is now Romania as early as the 300's B.C. The Romans occupied the country in the A.D. 100's and 200's. The Goths, Huns, and Slavs began living there after the Romans left.

Hungarians form the largest minority group in Romania, making up about 6 percent of the population. Roma (sometimes called Gypsies) make up about 3 percent.

© Loveshop/Shutterstock

Symbols of Romania. Romania's flag has stripes of blue, yellow, and red. The three stripes represent Romania's national colors. The eagle on Romania's coat of arms is a symbol of the region of Walachia. The other symbols on the coat of arms represent each of Romania's five other regions.

Smaller groups include Germans, Jews, Turks, and Ukrainians.

Language. Romanian is the nation's official language and is spoken by almost all the people. Many of Romania's Germans and Hungarians prefer to speak their own ethnic languages among themselves.

Romanian developed from Latin, the language of the Romans who ruled the country in ancient times. Romanian is the only Eastern European language that comes from Latin. As a result, it is much different from all the other languages that are spoken in the region, which probably developed from an ancient Slavic language. Romanian most closely resembles French, Italian, Portuguese, and Spanish. These Western European languages also developed from Latin.

Way of life. The Romanian people have one of the lowest living standards in Europe. Almost all the workers in Romania earn enough to pay for their families' food, clothing, and shelter, and they have a little left over for recreation. But few Romanians can afford many luxury items.

Most rural Romanians live in two- or three-room wooden cottages. The houses are plain and simple, but many people beautify them with a variety of art objects that they make themselves. These objects include wall

WORLD BOOK map

Romania, in eastern Europe, is bordered by Ukraine, Moldova, the Black Sea, Bulgaria, Serbia, and Hungary.

rugs with skillfully woven patterns, colorfully decorated plates, and woodcarvings on furniture, building frames, and fences.

Festivals held to celebrate such things as weddings, christenings, and holidays are the most important part of social life in rural Romania. At the festivals, the people wear colorful costumes, and they play and dance to Romanian folk music.

Romania's cities present a striking contrast between the old and the new. Many city buildings are hundreds of years old. Others are modern structures built since industrialization began in the 1960's. Population growth has caused a housing shortage in the cities. Most city people live in crowded apartments.

Both old Romanian traditions and modern, Western culture are part of city life. Many people enjoy going to restaurants and to concert halls where orchestras play Romanian folk music. They also visit exhibits of rural Romanian folk art that the government sets up in cities. But many people—especially the young—like rock music and Western movies, plays, and books.

Before the 1989 revolt, the lives of the Romanian people were affected by the Communist government in many ways. The government decided what kind of jobs students should prepare for in school. It owned or managed most of the country's businesses and farms, and so almost all the people worked for the government. Romanians could not change their jobs or leave the country without the government's permission. After the revolution, the non-Communist government lifted most of these restrictions.

Recreation. Romanians have two favorite vacation spots—the mountains and the Black Sea coast. The mountains offer skiing, hiking, mountain climbing, and beautiful scenery. Romanians go to the Black Sea coast to swim and to relax in the sun. Soccer is the most popular spectator sport in Romania.

Food and drink. Romanians enjoy grilled meats, including *mititei* (meat balls shaped like cylinders) and *patricieni* (sausages). Another favorite food in Romania is *mamaliga,* a bread or mush made from corn meal, which can be cooked and served in many ways. Wine and a plum brandy called *tzuica* are popular drinks in Romania.

James Theologos, Keystone

Colorful festivals are held by rural Romanians to celebrate holidays, weddings, and other occasions. Bright costumes and lively folk dances are traditional features of such celebrations.

Education. Romanian law requires children from 6 to 16 to attend school. Elementary school lasts eight years. Students then take tests that are prepared by the government to determine what kind of course they will study in secondary school. About half the students are assigned to vocational courses. These students learn the basic skills that are needed for work on farms or in fac-

Kurt Scholz, © ZEFA from Publix

Crowds of vacationers enjoy the sandy beaches and sunny weather along Romania's Black Sea coast. Fashionable resort hotels line the streets in this popular recreation area.

tories. Most of the other students take courses that train them in advanced technical skills, in the arts, or in teaching. The top elementary school graduates—about 5 percent of the total—are assigned to courses that prepare them for college.

Romania has many universities. The largest ones are in Bucharest, Cluj-Napoca, Craiova, Iaşi, and Oradea.

Religion. About 80 percent of all Romanians belong to the Romanian Orthodox Church, an Eastern Orthodox Church. About 5 percent of the people—chiefly Hungarians—are Roman Catholics. Other faiths that are practiced in Romania include Islam, Judaism, and various forms of Protestantism.

To avoid popular protests, the prerevolution Communists allowed churches to operate as long as the churches avoided political activities. After the 1989 revolution, the churches were granted complete religious freedom.

The arts. Romania's rural culture has had a strong influence on the country's professional art. The lives and customs of rural Romanians have long been favorite topics of Romanian writers. The works of many composers show the influence of Romanian folk music. The best-known Romanian paintings are medieval works that appear on the outside walls of churches. These works were done outside, rather than inside, to remind peasants passing by of their faith.

In the 1950's, the government forced Romanian artists to use their works to promote Communism. Romanian art grew dull from a lack of self-expression. However, since the 1960's, the government has allowed artists more freedom, and art has flourished in Romania. Old Romanian themes and styles are still popular. But many artists have turned to modern styles, and deal with such themes as humanity's relation to the universe.

James Theologos, Keystone

Religious paintings decorate the outside walls of many Romanian churches. This form of art developed in Romania during the 1500's to remind passers-by of their religious faith.

The composer Georges Enesco, the sculptor Constantin Brancusi, and the playwright Eugène Ionesco probably rank as the best-known Romanian-born artists. But each man did most of his work in France. Enesco's masterpieces, called *Romanian Rhapsodies,* are based on Romanian folk music. Some of Brancusi's sculptures contain elements of Romanian folk art. Ionesco's plays show some influence of his youth in Romania before the outbreak of World War II in 1939.

Land and climate

Romania is bordered on the north and northeast by Moldova, on the east by Ukraine, on the west by Hungary and Serbia, and on the south by Bulgaria. The country has only 130 miles (209 kilometers) of coastline, where it borders the Black Sea in the southeast.

Surface features. A series of mountain ranges curves through the northern and central parts of Romania, forming a circular pattern. The mountains surround a vast flatland called the Transylvanian Plateau. The mountains are, in turn, surrounded by plains on the east, south, and west.

Romania's mountains are all part of the Carpathian Mountain System. The eastern part of the Carpathian range stretches from the northern border to the center of the country. The Southern Carpathians, or Transylvanian Alps, stretch westward across the center of the country. The Bihor Mountains and other ranges make up the Western Carpathians, which run through western Romania.

Romania's mountains are neither extremely high nor steep, and several passes cut through them. As a result, they are not major barriers to transportation. Most of the mountains are from 3,000 to 6,000 feet (910 to 1,800 meters) high. Mount Moldoveanu, in the Southern Carpathians, is Romania's highest mountain. It rises 8,343 feet (2,543 meters).

The Transylvanian Plateau lies approximately 1,200 feet (366 meters) above sea level, and Romania's plains lie at or near sea level. These flatlands have the country's best farmland and most of its cities and towns. Vast forests cover parts of the Transylvanian Plateau and the mountains.

Romania has many rivers. The longest and most important one by far is the Danube River. It flows about 900 miles (1,400 kilometers) through Romania. Most of the way, it flows west to east along the southern border. The Danube turns northward near the Black Sea, then eastward again, and empties into the sea. Most of Romania's other major rivers flow into the Danube from the north. They include, from west to east, the Jiu, Oltul, Argeş, Ialomiţa, Siretul, and Prut.

Romania has about 2,500 lakes. Most of them are small. The biggest lakes lie near the Danube. Numerous tiny lakes scattered throughout the region add beauty to Romania's mountains.

Land regions. Romania can be divided into six land regions. They are Transylvania, Bukovina, Moldavia, Walachia, Banat, and Dobruja.

Transylvania is the country's largest and most varied region. It extends throughout central and northwestern Romania, and includes most of the country's mountains, the Transylvanian Plateau, and the northwestern plain. The plateau and plain have good soil for farming. The plateau and the mountains yield valuable forest products and minerals. The beauty of the mountains and their ski slopes and other recreation facilities make them a favorite vacation area. Several cities have grown up in Transylvania because of its rich resources.

Bukovina, northeast of Transylvania, is a thickly forested region in the northern Carpathian range. It has ski slopes and lovely scenery. The people of Bukovina live in small villages in the valleys.

Moldavia, Walachia, and Banat. Moldavia, in northeastern Romania, extends from Transylvania to the Prut River along the border with Moldova. Walachia, in the south, stretches from the southernmost mountains to the Danube. Banat, in the west, extends from the western mountains to Serbia and Hungary. These regions have a similar physical makeup. The land descends from mountains near Transylvania, to hills, and then to plains. These plains are Romania's best farmland. Walachia has more people than any other Romanian region, chiefly because Bucharest is there. Banat has several cities, but Moldavia has few.

Dobruja is a small plain between the northern course of the Danube River and the Black Sea. The Danube Delta covers northeastern Dobruja. This marshy area has an amazing variety of wildlife. Sturgeon, the source of caviar, and numerous other kinds of fish live in its waters. About 300 species of birds, including the pelican, also live in the delta. Farmland covers most of southern Dobruja. The Danube-Black Sea Canal flows through this area. Completed in 1984, it provides a shortcut from the Danube to the Black Sea. Sandy beaches and beautiful

Land regions of Romania

The map below shows the six land regions of Romania: Transylvania, Bukovina, Moldavia, Dobruja, Walachia, and Banat.

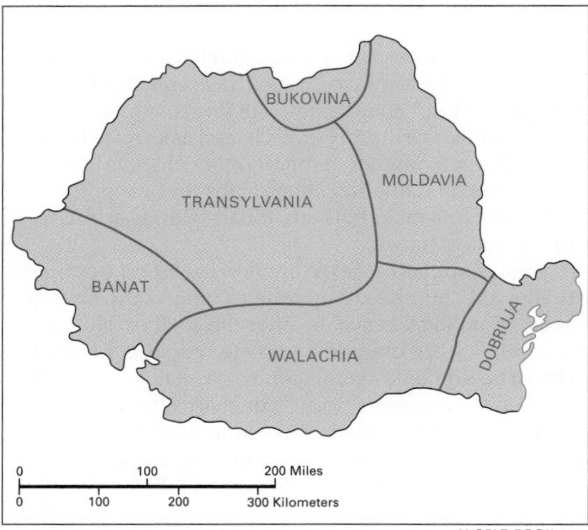

WORLD BOOK map

seaside resorts line Dobruja's Black Sea coast. Constanţa, Romania's major port city, is on the coast.

Climate. Romania has hot, sunny summers and cold, cloudy winters. The average July temperature is 70 °F (21 °C), and the average January temperature is 30 °F (−1 °C). Romania's plains are warmer than its mountain areas. *Precipitation* (rain, melted snow, and other forms

© Shutterstock

The land region of Walachia in southern Romania includes mountains, rolling hills, and some of the country's best farmland. The village of Bran, *shown here,* is near Brasov, in the Southern Carpathian Mountains.

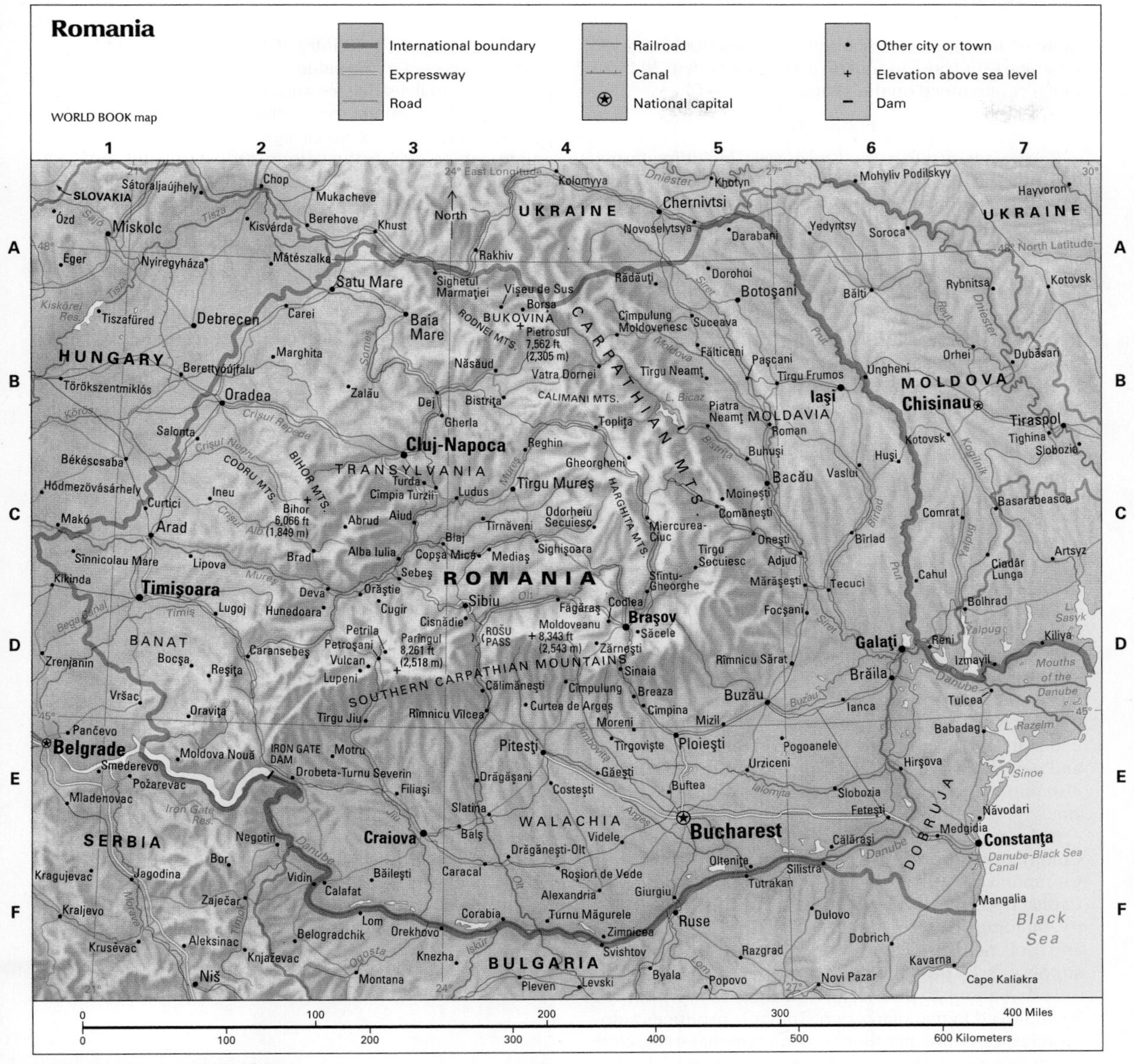

Romania map index

Cities and towns

Aiud ....22,876 ..C 3
Alba Iulia ....63,536 ..C 3
Alexandria ......45,434 ..F 4
Arad ....159,074 ..C 1
Bacău ....144,307 ..C 5
Baia Mare .....123,738 ..B 3
Băileşti ....17,437 ..F 3
Balş ....18,164 ..E 3
Bîrlad ....55,837 ..C 6
Bistriţa ....75,076 ..B 4
Blaj ....20,630 ..C 3
Bocşa ....15,842 ..D 1
Botoşani ....106,847 ..A 5
Brad ....14,495 ..C 2
Brăila ....180,302 ..D 6
Braşov ....253,200 ..D 4
Breaza ....15,928 ..D 5
Bucharest ....1,883,425 ..E 5
Buftea ....22,178 ..E 5
Buhuşi ....14,562 ..C 5
Buzău ....115,494 ..D 5
Calafat ....17,336 ..F 2
Călăraşi ....65,181 ..E 6
Caracal ....30,954 ..F 3
Caransebeş ......24,689 ..D 2
Carei ....21,112 ..A 2
Cîmpia Turzii ...22,223 ..C 3
Cîmpina ....32,935 ..D 5
Cîmpulung ......31,767 ..D 4
Cîmpulung Moldo-venesc ....16,722 ..B 4
Cisnădie ....14,282 ..D 3
Cluj-Napoca ...324,576 ..B 3
Comăneşti ......19,568 ..C 5
Constanţa ......283,872 ..E 7
Corabia ....16,441 ..F 4
Craiova ....269,506 ..E 3
Curtea de Argeş .....27,359 ..D 4
Dej ....33,497 ..B 3
Deva ....61,123 ..D 2
Dorohoi ....24,309 ..A 5
Drăgăşani ....17,871 ..E 4
Drobeta-Turnu Severin ....92,617 ..E 2
Făgăraş ....30,714 ..D 4
Fălticeni ....25,723 ..B 5
Feteşti ....30,217 ..E 6
Focşani ....79,315 ..D 6
Galaţi ....249,432 ..D 6
Gheorgheni .....18,377 ..C 4
Gherla ....20,982 ..B 3
Giurgiu ....61,353 ..F 5
Hunedoara ......60,525 ..D 2
Huşi ....26,266 ..C 6
Iaşi ....290,422 ..B 6
Lipova ....10,313 ..C 2
Luduş ....15,328 ..C 3
Lugoj ....40,361 ..D 2
Lupeni ....23,390 ..D 3
Mangalia ....36,364 ..F 7
Marghita ....15,770 ..B 2
Medgidia ....39,780 ..E 7
Mediaş ....47,204 ..C 4
Miercurea-Ciuc ....38,966 ..C 5
Moineşti ....21,787 ..C 5
Moldova Nouă ..12,350 ..E 2
Navodari ....32,981 ..E 7
Odorheiu Secuiesc ......34,257 ..C 4
Olteniţa ....24,822 ..F 5
Oneşti ....39,172 ..C 5
Oradea ....196,367 ..B 2
Orăştie ....18,227 ..D 3
Paşcani ....33,745 ..B 5
Petrila ....22,692 ..D 3
Petroşani ....37,160 ..D 3
Piatra Neamţ ....85,055 ..B 5
Piteşti ....155,383 ..E 4
Ploieşti ....209,945 ..E 5
Rădăuţi ....23,822 ..A 5
Reghin ....33,281 ..B 4
Reşiţa ....73,282 ..D 2
Rîmnicu Sărat ..33,843 ..D 5
Rîmnicu Vîlcea ....98,776 ..D 3
Roman ....50,713 ..B 5
Roşiori de Vede ....27,416 ..F 4
Săcele ....30,798 ..D 5
Salonta ....17,735 ..B 2
Satu Mare .....102,411 ..A 3
Sebeş ....27,019 ..C 3
Sibiu ....147,245 ..D 3
Sighetul Marmaţiei ....37,640 ..A 3
Şighişoara ......28,102 ..C 4
Slatina ....70,293 ..E 3
Slobozia ....45,891 ..E 6
Suceava ....92,121 ..B 5
Tecuci ....34,871 ..D 6
Timişoara ......319,279 ..D 1
Tîrgovişte ......79,610 ..E 4
Tîrgu Jiu ....82,504 ..D 3
Tîrgu Mureş ...134,290 ..C 4
Tîrgu Neamţ ....18,695 ..B 5
Tîrnăveni ....22,075 ..C 4
Topliţa ....13,929 ..B 4
Tulcea ....73,707 ..D 7
Turda ....47,744 ..C 3
Turnu Măgurele .....24,772 ..F 4
Urziceni ....15,308 ..E 5
Vaslui ....55,407 ..C 6
Vatra Dornei ....14,429 ..B 4
Vişeu de Sus ....15,037 ..A 4
Vulcan ....24,160 ..D 3
Zalău ....56,202 ..B 3
Zărneşti ....23,476 ..D 4
Zimnicea ....14,058 ..F 4

Physical features

Argeş River ....E 4
Bega Canal ....D 1
Bihor Mountains ....C 2
Bîrlad River ....C 6
Bistriţa River ....B 5
Black Sea ....F 7
Buzău River ....D 6
Calimani Mountains .....B 4
Carpathian Mountains ....B 4
Codru Mountains ....C 2
Crişul Alb River ....C 2
Crişul Repede River .....B 2
Danube River ....E 6
Dîmboviţa River ....E 4
Harghita Mountains .....C 4
Ialomiţa River ....E 5
Jiu River ....E 3
Lake Razelm ....E 7
Lake Sinoe ....E 7
Moldova River ....B 5
Moldoveanu (mtn.) ......D 4
Mureş River ....C 4
Olt River ....F 4
Prut River ....B 6
Rodnei Mountains ......B 3
Siret River ....A 5
Someş River ....B 3
Southern Carpathian Mountains ....D 3

Source: 2011 census.

of moisture) ranges from about 40 inches (100 centimeters) yearly in some mountain areas to less than 20 inches (50 centimeters) on the plains.

Economy

Romania is rich in natural resources, including fertile soil, mineral deposits, and vast forests. Even so, it has always been one of Europe's least developed nations. Before the 1960's, Romania's economy was based on agriculture. But since then, the government has built new factories and power plants and taken other steps to increase industry. Under the Communist government, industry—including manufacturing, mining, and construction—passed agriculture as the leading producer of income in Romania. Industry also passed agriculture as the leading employer. Today, service industries are both Romania's leading producer of income and its leading employer.

Under the Communists, the national government controlled Romania's economy. After the 1989 revolution, the non-Communist government loosened government control of the economy and allowed some private enterprise.

In 1992, the country began to sell shares in state-owned companies. However, the shift to a market-based economy has been slow moving. In 2007, the country joined the European Union, an organization of European countries that cooperate in economics and politics.

Natural resources. About 60 percent of Romania's land is fertile cropland and rich pastureland. Another 30 percent has forests that provide timber. The mountains and plateau have valuable mineral deposits. Natural gas and petroleum are important mineral products. Romania also mines coal, copper, gold, iron ore, lead, silver, and zinc.

Industry. Romania had very little industry when the Communists took over. To get industry started, the Communists stressed the production of *capital goods.* Capital goods include raw materials needed for industry, buildings in which industrial work is done, machines and tools needed to do the work, and power plants that supply energy for the work.

Today, about 20 percent of Romania's total workforce is employed in manufacturing. Romania produces automobiles, cement and other construction materials, clothing, furniture, machinery, petroleum products, *pharmaceuticals* (medicinal drugs), processed foods, steel, textiles, tractors, and wood products. Bucharest is the chief industrial center. Other industrial centers include Brasov, Cluj-Napoca, Ploiesti, and Timişoara.

Services. Service industries account for about half of both Romania's total employment and its *gross domestic product* (GDP). The GDP is the total value of all goods and services produced within a country in a year. Trade and transportation are the leading employers among service industries in Romania. These industries are responsible for getting the country's agricultural and industrial products from producers to buyers. Hotels, restaurants, and shops especially benefit from the millions of tourists who visit Romania each year. Many of these tourists visit from Bulgaria, Hungary, Moldova, and Ukraine.

Agriculture. Agriculture employs about 30 percent of Romania's work force. However, it accounts for less than 5 percent of the country's GDP. Crops account for about 70 percent of the value of Romania's agricultural products, and livestock for about 30 percent. Corn and wheat are the leading crops. Other crops include apples, grapes, potatoes, sugar beets, sunflower seeds, and tomatoes. Milk is the country's most valuable agricultural product. Farmers also raise beef cattle, chickens, hogs, and sheep.

In pre-Communist days, almost all of Romania's farmland was privately owned. But the Communist government gradually took control of almost all the land. It created collective farms and state farms. After the 1989 revolution, the government passed land-reform laws that allowed some collective farms to be broken up and their land redistributed to farmworkers. At first, the land-reform laws did not break up state farms. But in the late 1990's, the government began to break up some state farms. Today, the majority of agricultural land is privately owned.

Trade. Chemicals, machinery, and petroleum products are important both as exports and as imports to Romania. Other exports include clothing, iron and steel, and transportation equipment. Crude petroleum, electrical equipment, motor vehicles, and processed foods are other major imports.

Until the 1960's, Romania carried on about 80 percent of its trade with the Soviet Union and other Communist nations. But in the 1960's—as part of its policy to free itself from Soviet control—the country began expanding its trade with Western European nations and the United States. The Soviet Union broke up in 1991. Today, Romania's major trading partners include France, Germany, Hungary, Italy, Russia, Turkey, Ukraine, and the United States.

Transportation and communication. Trains are Romania's chief means of long-distance travel. The roads outside urban areas are generally unpaved and in poor condition. Bucharest, Cluj-Napoca, and Timişoara have international airports. The government owns a large share of TAROM, Romania's national airline. Constanţa

© Bob Gibbons, Alamy Images

Farmers in Romania harvest corn near the village of Saschiz in Transylvania. The manufacture of farm machinery is also an important economic activity in the country.

has a port on the Black Sea. Brăila, Galaţi, Giurgiu, and Tulcea have ports on the Danube River.

Dozens of newspapers are published in Romania. Leading daily papers include *Adevarul, Evenimentul Zilei, Jurnalul National,* and *Libertatea.* Radio and television stations operate under both private and state ownership.

History

Romanians trace their history back to the 300's B.C. But Romania did not become an independent, unified country until the mid-1800's. During most of the time in between, various foreign peoples ruled all or part of it.

Early days. Historians do not know when Romania was first settled. But a people called the Dacians were known to be living there by the 300's B.C. The Dacians farmed, mined gold and iron ore, and traded with neighboring peoples. Romania was called *Dacia* during this period.

The Romans, under Emperor Trajan, conquered Dacia in A.D. 106 and made it a province of the Roman Empire. Roman soldiers occupied Dacia, and Roman colonists settled there. The Romans intermarried with the Dacians, who adopted Roman customs and the Latin language. Dacia became known as *Romania* because of the Roman occupation and influence.

Non-Roman peoples from the east and north began invading Romania during the A.D. 200's. They forced the Romans to abandon the province in the late 200's. The invasions were to continue off and on until the 1100's. The invaders included Bulgars, Goths, Huns, Magyars, Slavs, and Tatars. These groups, especially the Slavs, intermarried with the Romanians.

Unification movement. The period of invasions slowed the development of Romania into a unified nation. For hundreds of years, various groups fought for control of the region, and no one group gained full control. The first steps toward unification took place between 1250 and 1350.

The people of Walachia, a region in southern Romania, gradually united and formed an independent state under a single ruler. The people of Moldavia, in eastern Romania, did the same. A prince ruled each state, and so they were called *principalities.*

Earlier, during the 1000's, Hungary had taken over most of what is now northern Romania. This area, called *Transylvania,* had many Romanian people. But it did not become part of Romania until the 1900's.

Ottoman rule. The independence of the principalities was short-lived. The Ottomans of Asia Minor (now part of Turkey) swept into Europe in the mid-1400's. They conquered Walachia in 1476 and Moldavia in 1504. The Ottoman Empire ruled these lands almost continuously for over 300 years.

The peasants in the principalities—who made up most of the population—led hard lives even before the Ottoman takeover. They were farmers living in poverty who had to pay high taxes to the ruling nobles. Conditions worsened under the Ottomans, who let Romanian nobles rule in their name, but demanded increased taxes from the peasants for themselves.

The Romanian nobles made several attempts to gain freedom from the Ottoman Empire. As a result, in the early 1700's, the empire sent wealthy Greeks to govern the principalities. These Greeks were called *Phanariots* because they came from the Phanar district of Constantinople (now Istanbul, Turkey). They taxed the peasants far more than ever before and treated them harshly.

Phanariot rule lasted until 1821, when a revolt by Romanians forced the Ottomans to remove the Greeks from power. Many scholars believe Romania's peasants never suffered more than they did during the Phanariot period.

Russian control. During the late 1700's, the Ottoman Empire suffered a series of military defeats at the hands of Russia. Little by little, the Ottomans lost parts of their empire. Officially, Ottoman rule of the principalities lasted until 1878. But, in effect, it ended in 1829, when Russian troops occupied the principalities.

Russia drew up a constitution for the principalities in the early 1830's. The constitution, called *Organic Statutes,* gave governing power in each principality to an assembly of nobles. This marked the beginning of representative government in Romania. Russia's troops withdrew from the principalities in 1834.

The origins of modern Romania. The idea of uniting Moldavia and Walachia existed almost from the time the principalities were founded. The unification movement grew rapidly during the mid-1800's. In 1859, the assemblies of the two principalities elected Prince Alexander John Cuza as their common ruler. In 1861, Moldavia and Walachia, unified under the name *Romania,* received international recognition.

Many leaders of the unification movement were young Romanians who had studied in Paris. There, they learned about a revolutionary spirit that was sweeping through Europe. Many Europeans were demanding an end to undemocratic government and calling for improvements in living conditions for the lower classes. The young Romanians demanded reforms after they returned home.

Prince Cuza responded. His government bought much land from wealthy Romanians and gave it to peasants. It also increased the number of free schools for the poor. Many of the wealthy Romanians opposed Cuza. They forced the prince to resign in 1866.

The wealthy Romanians selected Karl of Hohenzollern to replace Cuza. Karl was a German prince who knew little about Romania. According to one story, he even had to consult a map to learn where the country was. But he was to rule Romania for nearly 50 years.

Karl took the name Prince Carol. In 1878, the major nations of Europe officially recognized Romania's full independence from the Ottoman Empire. In 1881, Romania became a kingdom, and Carol became King Carol I.

At the start of Carol's reign, Romania's first political parties were established, and the people were given the right to elect their government representatives. But a complex election system kept the peasants from having many representatives.

Romania's economy improved under Carol. Wealthy Romanians benefited from the economic growth, but the peasants gained little from it. In 1907, Romania's peasants revolted. They burned the houses and destroyed the crops of many wealthy landowners. The Romanian Army put down the revolt, killing at least 10,000 peasants. Carol died in 1914, and his nephew Ferdinand became king.

Important dates in Romania

300's B.C. Dacians lived in what is now Romania.

A.D. 100's Romania became a province of the Roman Empire.

200's to 1100's Non-Roman peoples from the north and east invaded Romania.

1250 to 1350 Moldavia and Walachia gradually became independent principalities.

c. 1500 The principalities fell under Ottoman rule.

1861 The union of Moldavia and Walachia as Romania received international recognition.

1919 Romania about doubled in size when Transylvania and other surrounding lands became part of it.

1940-1945 Romania fought in World War II—first on the German side and then on the side of the Allies.

1947 Romania officially became a Communist country.

1950's The Soviet Union had nearly complete control over Romania.

1965 A new Romanian Constitution stressed the nation's control over its own affairs.

1977 An earthquake caused about 1,500 deaths and about $1 billion in property damage in Romania.

1989 Communist Party leader Nicolae Ceauşescu was overthrown and executed following widespread protest over his policies and corruption in his government.

1990 Romania held its first free multiparty elections since the end of World War II.

World War I was fought from 1914 to 1918. Romania remained neutral at first. But in 1916, it joined France, the United Kingdom, and the other Allies in their fight against the Central Powers (chiefly Austria-Hungary and Germany). Romania wanted to gain Banat, Bukovina, and Transylvania—three provinces of Austria-Hungary that had large Romanian populations. The Allies won the war, and Romania received the territories it wanted as part of the peace settlement. As a result, Romania about doubled in size and population. For the first time, Romania's territory included almost all the land where large numbers of Romanians lived.

Depression and fascism. Liberal political parties headed Romania's government after World War I. They divided the estates of many of the wealthy landowners into small farms and sold the farms to peasants. The liberals wanted to continue helping the peasants, but a worldwide depression that began in 1929 destroyed Romania's economy. Millions of Romanians lost their jobs, and poverty became severe throughout the country.

Romania's economic problems caused many people to seek new leadership in the early 1930's. The Iron Guard soon became a strong authoritarian movement. Its followers were fascists who sought to destroy Romania's government and establish a dictatorship. The group used terror against its political opponents and blamed Communists, Jews, and liberals for Romania's problems.

King Ferdinand died in 1927, and his son Carol became King Carol II three years later. The popularity and power of the Iron Guard grew during the early years of Carol's reign. Fearing a loss of his own authority, Carol made himself dictator of Romania. He outlawed the Iron Guard and all political parties.

World War II began in Europe in September 1939, as a struggle between Germany and the Allies—a group of nations led by France and the United Kingdom. Romania remained neutral at first. By June of 1940, Germany had gained a great military advantage over the Allies. Germany allowed Hungary to take northern Transylvania from Romania. The Soviet Union took part of northeastern Romania. Bulgaria took territory in the southeast.

The territorial losses turned the people against King Carol, and he gave up his throne on Sept. 6, 1940. Carol's son Michael became king, but Premier Ion Antonescu ruled. Antonescu cooperated with Germany, and German troops occupied Romania in October. Romania then joined the war on the side of Germany.

By August 1944, the tide of the war had turned against Germany. King Michael then overthrew Antonescu, and Romania joined the Allies. The war ended in 1945, and the Allies took northern Transylvania from Hungary and returned it to Romania. The Soviet Union and Bulgaria kept the Romanian territory they had taken.

Communist control. The Soviet Union had been formed as a Communist nation under Russia's leadership in 1922, and it existed until 1991. During World War II, the Soviet Union fought on the side of the Allies. Soviet troops occupied Romania in 1944 and stayed there until the late 1950's.

Romania's Communist Party had never been strong

Romania—History The first map shows the principalities of Moldavia and Walachia in 1350, before they fell under Ottoman control. The second map shows Romania in 1861, when the union of the principalities was internationally recognized. The third map shows Romania before the outbreak of World War II, in 1939. The boundaries of present-day Romania are shown in red.

1350

1861

1939

WORLD BOOK maps

before World War II. But under the protection of the Soviet troops, Romanian Communists took over the government after the war. They killed or imprisoned their political opponents and forced King Michael to give up his throne on Dec. 30, 1947.

The Communists declared Romania an "independent people's democracy." But Romania was a *Soviet satellite* (country controlled by the Soviet Union). In 1948 and 1952, Romania adopted constitutions that praised the Soviet Union. Romania's government, educational system, and other institutions were modeled on those of the Soviet Union. Soviet leaders directed Romania's economy and forced the country to emphasize agriculture and neglect industry. They also set foreign policy.

Opposition to the Soviet Union. Resentment of Soviet interference in Romania's affairs grew during the 1950's. In the early 1960's, Romania's Communists—led by Communist Party head Gheorghe Gheorghiu-Dej—began to oppose this interference openly. Gheorghiu-Dej died in 1965. Nicolae Ceauşescu, who succeeded him as party head, continued the opposition.

In 1962, Romania insisted that each Communist country should be free to develop its own economic system, trade freely with all nations, and make its own foreign policy. Romania's leaders then began expanding industry and increasing trade with Western nations. In 1964, Romania exchanged ambassadors with the United States. Romania's leaders hosted a visit by U.S. President Richard M. Nixon in 1969. They also declared Romania neutral in a dispute between the Soviet Union and China. In 1965, Romania adopted a Constitution that called for the nation's complete independence. In 1977, Romania began strengthening its ties with the nations of the *nonaligned movement.* These nations, primarily in Asia and Africa, had refused to support either the Communist or non-Communist bloc.

Also in 1977, an earthquake struck Bucharest and other parts of Romania. It caused about 1,500 deaths and over $1 billion in damage.

The government's industrialization policy increased the size of Romania's urban communities. Each year, thousands of young people moved from rural areas to cities to work in industry and government.

In the 1980's, new jobs were created, but Romania's living standard remained low and consumer goods were scarce. Reasons for the struggling economy included corruption in the Communist Party and overreliance on central government economic planning. In addition, Romania had to borrow heavily from Western European banks to finance its industrial build-up. Paying off this debt took funds away from further development and slowed economic growth.

Protests and political change. Ceauşescu's government maintained an extensive system of restrictions on the lives of the people. In mid-December 1989, thousands of people in the city of Timişoara staged demonstrations, calling for greater freedom from the Communist government and for an improved standard of living. Government security forces responded to the protests by firing on the people and killing hundreds. Antigovernment protests then spread across Romania. In Bucharest, tens of thousands gathered in the streets and called for increased freedoms and for Ceauşescu's resignation. Security forces fired on the crowds, bringing the death toll of demonstrators into the thousands. Army units joined the revolt, and fierce fighting between the army and Ceauşescu's security forces followed.

On December 22, Ceauşescu and his wife, Elena, fled Bucharest during a massive antigovernment demonstration. However, they were soon captured by the army. A secret trial took place and Ceauşescu and his wife were charged with murder and embezzlement of government funds. They were found guilty and were executed on December 25. The National Salvation Front, a group made up chiefly of former Communists, took control of the government. Ion Iliescu, leader of the Front, became the acting president. The Front canceled a number of Ceauşescu's restrictions on freedom. Free multiparty elections took place in May 1990. Iliescu won the presidency. The Front also won a wide majority in the legislature. Iliescu then stepped down as the Front's leader in accordance with a law established in early 1990. The law

© Reuters/Getty Images

A massive revolt in 1989 overthrew Nicolae Ceauşescu, Romania's harsh and corrupt ruler. Here, demonstrators ride a Romanian army tank through the streets of Bucharest. Army units helped defeat Ceauşescu and his security forces.

states that the head of state cannot be the leader of a political party.

Opposition parties complained of abuse and intimidation by members of the ruling party during the election. In mid-1990, progovernment and antigovernment demonstrators clashed on the streets of Bucharest. Large antigovernment demonstrations continued in the early 1990's, often in protest of economic conditions. In late 1991, following strikes and riots staged by miners, the government of the National Salvation Front resigned. It was replaced by a coalition government dominated by the Front. Iliescu remained president. New national elections were held in 1992. Iliescu was reelected, but in this election he represented a political party called the Democratic National Salvation Front. This party broke away from the National Salvation Front in 1992. In 1993, it was renamed the Social Democratic Party of Romania.

Recent developments. Ion Iliescu's government was dominated by former Communists who favored only limited political and economic reform. In 1996, Emil Constantinescu, who supported more rapid reform, was elected president. His party, the Democratic Convention of Romania, also won the most seats in the legislature. However, the progress of economic reform in Romania remained slow. In 2000, Iliescu again won the presidency.

In 2004, Romania joined the North Atlantic Treaty Organization (NATO). NATO is a military alliance that includes the United States and many European nations. Later that same year, Romanians elected opposition leader Traian Băsescu as president. In 2007, Romania joined the European Union (EU). The EU is an organization of European countries that promotes economic and political cooperation among its members.

In April 2007, Romania's parliament voted to suspend President Băsescu on charges of abuse of power. Some members of parliament accused him of violating constitutional laws and manipulating the country's Supreme Court. Băsescu denied the charges and refused to resign. Nicolae Văcăroiu, Romania's Senate leader, was appointed interim president during Băsescu's suspension. In May 2007, Romanian voters rejected his suspension, and Băsescu was reinstated as president. In 2009, Băsescu was narrowly reelected to a second term as president.

In 2014, Romanians chose Klaus Iohannis to serve as the nation's next president. Iohannis won reelection in 2019. Vladimir Tismaneanu

Related articles in *World Book* include:

Biographies

Brancusi, Constantin
Ceauşescu, Nicolae
Comaneci, Nadia
Ionesco, Eugène
Maurer, Ion Gheorghe
Steinberg, Saul

Other related articles

Balkans
Bessarabia
Black Sea
Bucharest
Carpathian Mountains
Danube River
Europe (picture: European stores)
Moldova
Radio Free Europe/Radio Liberty
Russo-Turkish Wars
Transylvania
Warsaw Pact
World War I

Outline

I. **Government**
   A. National government
   B. Local government
   C. Courts
   D. Armed forces

II. **People**
   A. Ancestry
   B. Language
   C. Way of life
   D. Recreation
   E. Food and drink
   F. Education
   G. Religion
   H. The arts

III. **Land and climate**
   A. Surface features
   B. Land regions
   C. Climate

IV. **Economy**
   A. Natural resources
   B. Industry
   C. Services
   D. Agriculture
   E. Trade
   F. Transportation and communication

V. **History**

Romanov, *ROH muh NAWF,* was the name of the family that ruled Russia from 1613 to 1917. The first Romanov ruler was Czar Michael. Michael was the grandnephew of Ivan IV's first wife, Anastasia Romanov. Michael was elected czar in 1613. His son, Czar Alexis, acquired Ukraine and sponsored the introduction of Western education, technology, and military methods in Russia.

Sixteen more Romanov rulers followed. One of the most famous was Alexis's son Peter the Great. Russian rulers after 1762 either were foreigners or had little Russian ancestry, but they kept the Romanov name. Czar Nicholas II, the last Romanov ruler, gave up his throne in March 1917. Bolshevik revolutionaries killed him and his immediate family in July 1918. Other Romanov family members survived and escaped from Russia.

Joseph T. Fuhrmann

Related articles in *World Book* include:

Alexander I (czar)
Alexander II (czar)
Alexander III (czar)
Catherine the Great
Nicholas I (czar)
Nicholas II (czar)
Peter I, the Great
Russia (History)

Romans, Epistle to the, the sixth book of the New Testament, is a letter from the apostle Paul to the Christians in Rome. Paul wrote the Epistle, probably from Corinth, Greece, about A.D. 56. The Epistle was a letter of introduction, preparing for a visit Paul intended to make on his way to do missionary work in Spain.

The Epistle to the Romans is Paul's longest and most systematic letter. The main theme of the first 11 chapters is that Jews and Gentiles are equally in need of salvation, and that both have access to salvation through faith in Jesus Christ. In the five remaining chapters, Paul discusses problems in Christian living. Some scholars doubt that Chapter 16 was originally part of the letter, mainly because Paul, who had never been to Rome, greets many people by name in this chapter. These scholars believe that the chapter is a letter Paul wrote to another place, which a later editor attached to the letter to the Romans. Terrance D. Callan

See also **Bible** (The Letters); **Paul, Saint** (Paul's letters and ideas).

Romanticism is a style in the fine arts and literature. It emphasizes passion rather than reason, and imagination and intuition rather than logic. Romanticism favors full expression of the emotions, and free, spontaneous action rather than restraint and order. In all these ways, Romanticism contrasts with another style called *Classi-*

cism (see **Classicism**). Periods of Romanticism often develop as a revolt against Classicism. Artists and writers throughout history have shown Romantic tendencies. But the term *Romantic movement* usually refers to the period from the late 1700's to the mid-1800's.

The qualities of Romanticism

Romantics yearn for the infinite. The English Romantic poet William Blake thought he could "see a World in a Grain of Sand/And a Heaven in a Wild Flower." Romantics view nature as a living spirit, attuned to human feelings of love and compassion.

Romanticism stresses freedom for the individual. It rejects restricting social conventions and unjust political rule. In literature, the Romantic hero, such as Lord Byron's "Manfred," is often a rebel or outlaw.

Just as the Romantic hero is in revolt against social conventions, the Romantic artist is in revolt against artificial ideas of good form. In drama, for example, Romantic writers reject the Classical unities of time, place, and action. They allow the events in their plays to range widely in time and space. Jean Racine's play *Phaedra* is rigidly Classical in form. Johann Wolfgang von Goethe's play *Faust* is Romantic.

Romanticism in the arts

Romanticism in literature. During the Romantic movement, most writers were discontented with their world. It seemed commercial, inhuman, and standardized. To escape from modern life, the Romantics turned their interest to remote and faraway places, the medieval past, folklore and legends, and nature and the common people. The Romantics were also drawn to the supernatural.

Many Romantic characteristics were united in the *Gothic novel.* This was a type of horror story, filled with violence and supernatural effects, and set against a background of gloomy medieval Gothic castles. The Gothic novel influenced the American writers Nathaniel Hawthorne and Edgar Allan Poe. The novels of Sir Walter Scott of Scotland and James Fenimore Cooper of the United States reveal the typically Romantic interest in the past. *Grimm's Fairy Tales,* collected by Jakob and Wilhelm Grimm, are famous examples of the Romantic interest in legends and folklore.

Many typically Romantic characteristics appear in the poetry of William Wordsworth of England. Wordsworth preferred a reflective "vacant and pensive mood" to a restless search for scientific knowledge. He believed we learn more by communing with nature or talking to country people than by reading books. He also believed that harmony with nature is the source of all goodness and truth.

Romanticism in painting. Romantic painters often used bold lighting effects and deep shadow to cast a visionary gleam over their subjects. Classical forms and themes were abandoned for faraway exotic subjects such as the Asian scenes painted by Frenchman Eugène Delacroix.

Romanticism in music. Romantic composers modified the formalism of classical music, and aimed at lyric expression and organic unity. Many Romantic composers gave their works a nationalistic character by using folk songs as themes. Romantic composers include Franz Schubert of Austria; Felix Mendelssohn, Robert Schumann, and Carl Maria von Weber of Germany; and Frédéric Chopin of Poland.

Romanticism and society. The French philosopher Jean-Jacques Rousseau taught that people are naturally good but have been corrupted by the institutions of civilization. He idealized the *noble savage,* an individual unspoiled by luxury and sophistication, and he argued that in a virtuous society children would grow up honest and free. Influenced by these ideas, many Romantics opposed political tyranny and took part in liberal and revolutionary activities. The revolutions in America and France during the late 1700's were influenced by Romantic ideals.

Many of Rousseau's theories influenced educational theory and practice. Romanticism also became associated with economic and social reform, especially in the United States. Lawrence Lipking

Related articles. There is a separate biography in ***World Book*** for each person discussed in this article. For the historical development of Romanticism, see:

Ballet (Romantic ballet)
Classical music (The Romantic era)
Drama (Romanticism)
English literature (Romantic literature)
French literature (Romanticism)
German literature (The second golden age [1750-1830])
Gothic novel
Latin American literature (Romanticism)
Painting (The 1800's)
Russian literature (The age of Romanticism)
Sculpture (Sculpture from 1600 to 1900)
Spanish literature (Neoclassicism, Romanticism, and Realism)

Additional resources

Brown, Marshall, ed. *The Cambridge History of Literary Criticism, Vol. 5: Romanticism.* Cambridge, 2000.
Murray, Christopher J., ed. *Encyclopedia of the Romantic Era, 1760-1850.* 2 vols. Fitzroy Dearborn, 2004.

Romberg, Sigmund (1887-1951), was a famous composer of operettas. He wrote the music for such famous operettas as *Maytime* (1917), *The Student Prince* (1924), *The Desert Song* (1926), *My Maryland* (1927), *The New Moon* (1928), and *Up in Central Park* (1945). He adapted the music of the Austrian composer Franz Schubert for another popular operetta, *Blossom Time* (1921). Romberg's many popular songs include "Deep in My Heart, Dear," "The Desert Song," "Stouthearted Men," and "When I Grow Too Old to Dream." He also wrote music for motion pictures and gained praise as a conductor of light classical music.

Romberg was born on July 29, 1887, in Nagykanizsa, Hungary. Although he studied the violin as a child, Romberg planned to become an engineer. To help finance his engineering studies in a Vienna technical school, he worked as assistant manager at the Theater-an-der-Wien, Vienna's leading theater for operettas. The productions Romberg saw there persuaded him to pursue a career in music.

Romberg moved to New York City in 1909. He eventually formed a small orchestra. Romberg was soon hired to write songs for musicals presented by J. J. and Lee Shubert, two brothers who operated theaters throughout the United States. Romberg composed music in the American ragtime fashion for several years before he began writing his famous European-style operettas. He died on Nov. 9, 1951. Gerald Bordman

© Michael Yamashita, Corbis

Central Rome, seen here looking northeast from Trastevere, displays its long history in the varied styles of its buildings. The white Victor Emmanuel Monument rises dramatically in the upper right part of the picture. The Tiber River, marked by the trees, winds through Rome.

Rome

Rome is the capital of Italy and one of the world's great historic cities. It has been an important center of civilization for more than 2,000 years. Because of its long history, Rome is called the *Eternal City.* It is also one of the world's most beautiful cities. Its ancient monuments and magnificent churches and palaces stand as reminders of Rome's past glory. Gleaming new buildings are a sign of its modern-day importance.

Rome ruled the ancient Western world as the capital of the mighty Roman Empire. For hundreds of years, Rome was the supreme power of Europe, northern Africa, and western Asia. Ancient Rome's influence can still be seen today in such fields as architecture, government, language, and law.

As the home of the popes, Rome also became the center of the Roman Catholic Church. During the 1500's and 1600's, the popes brought a new splendor to Rome. They employed great artists who created beautiful buildings and priceless works of art for the city. Today, millions of visitors come every year from all parts of the world to enjoy these masterpieces, as well as to see the various ruins of ancient Rome.

Visitors also enjoy the colorful life of sunny Rome. They stroll through the city's fashionable shops and open-air markets and ride in horse-drawn carriages. Like the Romans, visitors enjoy relaxing at sidewalk cafes or in the many beautiful squares. The people of Rome are friendly and proud of their city. They are happy to help strangers find their way, to select the most delicious foods in restaurants, or just to chat.

Facts in brief

Population: 2,617,175.
Area: 496 mi^2 (1,285 km^2).
Climate: *Average temperature*—January, 45 °F (7 °C); July, 78 °F (26 °C). *Average annual precipitation* (rainfall, melted snow, and other forms of moisture)—38 in (97 cm). For the monthly weather in Rome, see **Italy** (Climate).
Government: *Chief executive*—mayor (4-year term). *Legislature*—80-member City Council (4-year terms).
Founded: 753 B.C. (according to legend).

The city today

Rome lies on both banks of the Tiber River in central Italy, 10 miles (16 kilometers) east of the Tyrrhenian Sea. The city stretches over about 20 hills, but its outskirts have some wide expanses of flat ground. These hills include the famous seven hills on which ancient Rome was built—the Aventine, Caelian, Capitoline, Esquiline, Palatine, Quirinal, and Viminal hills.

Today, the ruins of ancient buildings cover most of the Aventine, Caelian, and Palatine hills. The Palatine also has a modern public park. Crowded commercial districts spread over the Esquiline and Viminal hills. The Italian presidential palace and some of Rome's government buildings stand on the Quirinal, the tallest of the seven hills. The streets of ancient Rome extended from the Capitoline, a center of Roman life. Today, this hill has famous art museums, the City Council building, and a square designed by Michelangelo, the great Renaissance artist.

Throughout the city are many beautiful squares connected by busy streets. In the heart of Rome is the *Piazza Colonna* (Colonna Square). Banks, hotels, luxury shops, office buildings, restaurants, and theaters make it the busiest place in the city. Rome's main street, the *Via del Corso* (Way of the Course), runs 1 mile (1.6 kilometers) through the Piazza Colonna and links two other squares to the north and south. The street received its name because it was used as a horse-racing course in the Middle Ages.

Vatican City, the administrative and spiritual center of the Roman Catholic Church, lies in northwestern Rome. The Vatican, as it is sometimes called, is the smallest independent country in the world. It covers only 109 acres (44 hectares), or about ⅙ square mile (0.4 square kilometer). See **Vatican City**.

Rome is also one of the world's most important art centers. Actors, musicians, painters, sculptors, and writers take part in the city's busy cultural life.

Parks and gardens. Romans enjoy the city's many public parks and gardens on the grounds of magnificent old *villas* (large estates). The villas were once owned by wealthy families. The great Villa Borghese, which was opened to the public in 1902, is the finest of these parks. Its hills, meadows, and woods seem like natural countryside. It also has a large biopark.

Many campers visit the Villa Ada, the former residence of the kings of Italy. The Villa Glori, a park honoring Italy's war dead, is covered with pine trees. The Villa Sciarra has famous fountains and rare plants. Gardens on top of the Janiculum Hill are especially popular with children.

Music and theater. The National Academy of St. Cecilia has one of Rome's leading symphony orchestras. Rome's orchestras also include the Rome Philharmonic and the Radiotelevisione Italiana. The world's oldest academies of music are in Rome.

Romans, like most Italians, enjoy opera. The Opera House offers performances from December to June. In July and August, operas are presented in an outdoor setting. Rome's many theaters offer plays and musical comedies, including productions from other countries.

Museums and art galleries. Countless visitors come to see Rome's priceless art collections. Many of the finest paintings and statues are displayed in the Vatican Palace. They include masterpieces by such famous artists as Leonardo da Vinci, Michelangelo, and Raphael. Some of Michelangelo's greatest paintings decorate the ceiling and front wall of the Vatican's Sistine Chapel.

The oldest art collection in Rome, begun in 1471, is in the Capitoline Museum. It includes many fine sculptures of ancient Rome. The National Museum of the Villa Giulia has a collection of art from central Italy dating from pre-Roman times. Greek and Roman sculptures and other items from ancient civilizations are exhibited in the National Roman Museum. The Borghese Collection in the Villa Borghese includes works of art by almost every master of the Renaissance. The National Gallery of Modern Art contains masterpieces that are chiefly of the 1800's and 1900's.

Churches, palaces, and fountains. Saint Peter's Basilica in Vatican City is Europe's largest Christian church. It is an outstanding example of Renaissance architecture. Michelangelo helped design the church during the 1500's. Many famous art masterpieces can be seen inside it (see **Saint Peter's Basilica**). Other well-known churches of Rome also date from the Renaissance, as well as from earlier and later periods.

The most famous of Rome's many palaces is the Venezia Palace, built during the mid-1400's. The Italian dictator Benito Mussolini established his office there in the Fascist period of the 1920's and 1930's. The palace now houses an art museum. The Madama Palace, once owned by the powerful Medici family, has been the seat of the Italian Senate since 1871. The Quirinal Palace is

Rome

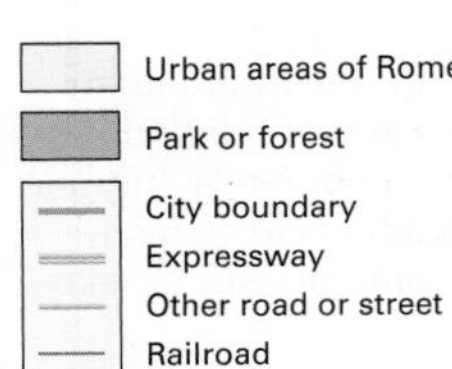

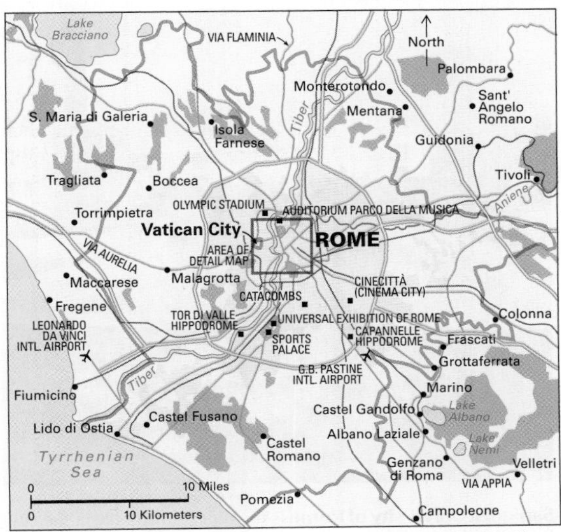

WORLD BOOK maps

E. Streichan, Shostal

The Fountain of Neptune is in Rome's Piazza Navona, a historic square surrounded by beautiful churches and palaces.

Luiz Claudio Marigo, Bruce Coleman Ltd.

The Baths of Caracalla were public baths dating from the A.D. 200's. Visitors to the site enjoy its splendid architecture.

the Italian president's official residence. It was the home of popes until 1870 and of kings of Italy from 1871 until 1946.

Rome has many magnificent fountains that are considered great works of art. The Trevi Fountain, which was completed in 1762, is the most popular with visitors from other countries. A legend says that visitors who throw coins into this fountain will someday return to the city.

Schools. Sapienza University of Rome, founded in 1303, is the city's oldest university. Various religious societies of the Roman Catholic Church operate a number of schools in Vatican City. There, students from many countries attend seminaries to become priests, or take university graduate studies. Some seminaries have been established for students from one country only. For example, the Pontifical North American College has graduated thousands of priests from the United States since it was founded in 1859.

Roman children are required to attend school between the ages of 6 and 14, which takes them through junior high school. They may also attend public schools at the next level of education. Schools at this level include senior high schools and schools of fine arts, teacher training, and technical job training. Students pay small fees to attend all these higher-level schools. A number of private schools are operated by religious groups.

© Francesco Garufi, Contrasto from Grazia Neri

Sapienza University of Rome is the oldest university in the city. Pope Boniface VIII founded the institution in 1303.

SCALA/Art Resource

The Sports Palace was built for the 1960 Summer Olympic Games. It lies on the southwestern outskirts of the city.

The Vatican Library, established in the 1400's, is one of the most important libraries in the world. The library owns many old Latin manuscripts. Other libraries in the city are operated by Roman Catholic orders.

Sports. Soccer is the most popular sport in Rome, as it is throughout Italy. Huge crowds attend club and international soccer matches held in the Olympic Stadium. Horse shows are performed in the Piazza di Siena (Siena Square) and the Capannelle and Tor di Valle Hippodromes. Other popular sports include basketball, boxing, and tennis.

Economy. Rome is not a heavily industrialized city. Most Romans earn their living through jobs related to commerce and government. Many Romans work in restaurants and in the building trades. Services related to tourism also provide a large part of the city's income. Only about a fifth of the workers in Rome are employed in industry. The city's factories produce clothing and textiles, processed foods, and other products. Most of the factories in Rome are in the northwestern part of the city.

Motion-picture production is an important part of Rome's economy. The city is one of the film capitals of the world. Motion-picture companies of Italy and other countries have produced many famous films in Rome's studios and streets.

Rome is a major transportation center of Italy. Railways and roads connect Rome with cities in most parts of the country. Airlines link the city with the rest of Italy and other parts of the world. Rome's central railroad station is one of the largest and most beautiful stations in the world. The Metropolitana, Rome's subway system, connects the railroad station to other parts of the city. Buses, streetcars, taxis, and trolleys also serve Rome. Beginning in 1973, all private vehicles were banned from part of the ancient section of the city to reduce traffic jams and air and noise pollution.

Rome has a number of daily newspapers, of which the most important are *Il Messaggero* (The Messenger), *Il Tempo* (The Time), and *La Repubblica* (The Republic). The Vatican publishes the semiofficial newspaper of the Roman Catholic Church, *L'Osservatore Romano* (The Roman Observer). Many other specialized newspapers are published in Rome, including *Corriere dello Sport* (Sport Courier). Some papers are official dailies of political parties, such as *Avanti!* (Forward!) of the Socialist Party. Still other papers support a political view without having ties to a particular party, such as the left-wing *Il Manifesto* (The Manifest). Italy's radio and television system, Radiotelevisione Italiana, has its headquarters in Rome.

Government. Rome is governed by an elected mayor and an elected city council. The city is divided into about 20 districts called *municipi.*

Central Rome

This map shows the central area of Rome and locates many of its famous landmarks. The Tiber River flows through the area. Vatican City, the world's smallest independent country and the headquarters of the Roman Catholic Church, is surrounded by Rome.

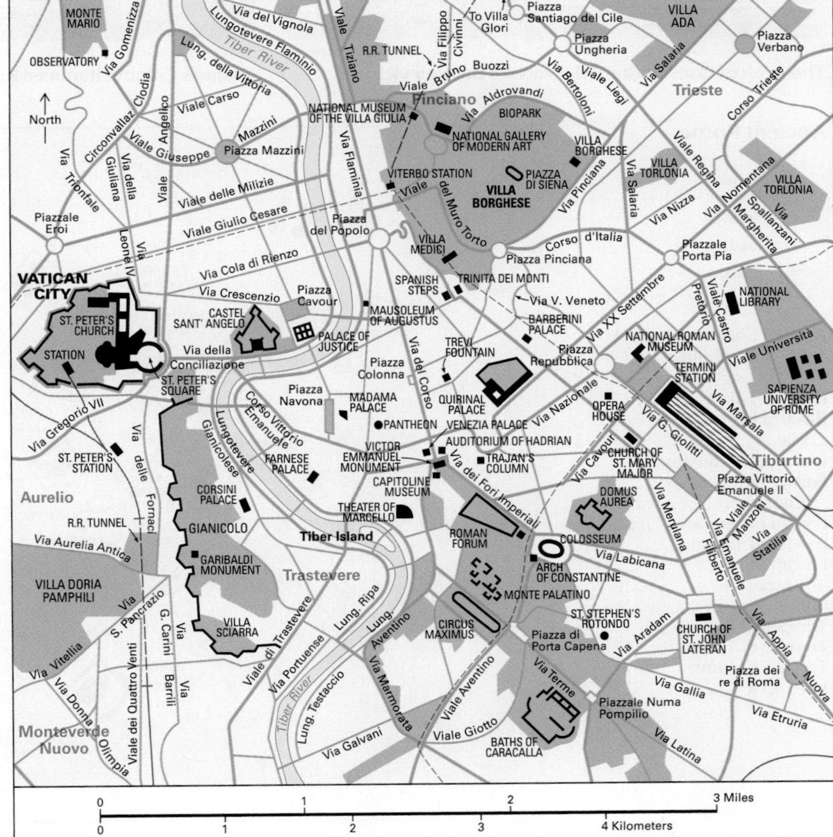

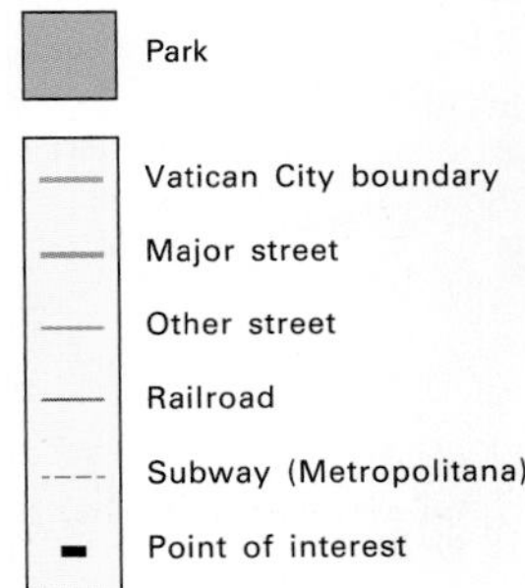

WORLD BOOK map

FPG
The Roman Forum was the center of Roman government.

SCALA/Art Resource
The Pantheon was a temple dedicated to Roman gods.

© Thinkstock
The Arch of Constantine celebrated a military victory.

The Photo Source from Shostal
Trajan's Column honored Rome's first non-Italian emperor.

Ancient Rome

Rome
City wall
Road
Aqueduct

Arch of Constantine 1
Arch of Septimius Severus 2
Basilica Julia 3
Basilica Ulpia 4
Curia 5
Forum of Augustus 6
Forum of Julius Caesar 7
Forum of Nerva 8
Forum of Trajan........9
Forum of Vespasian 10
Roman Forum 11
Temple of Saturn 12
Temple of Trajan 13
Trajan's Column 14
Via Sacra 15

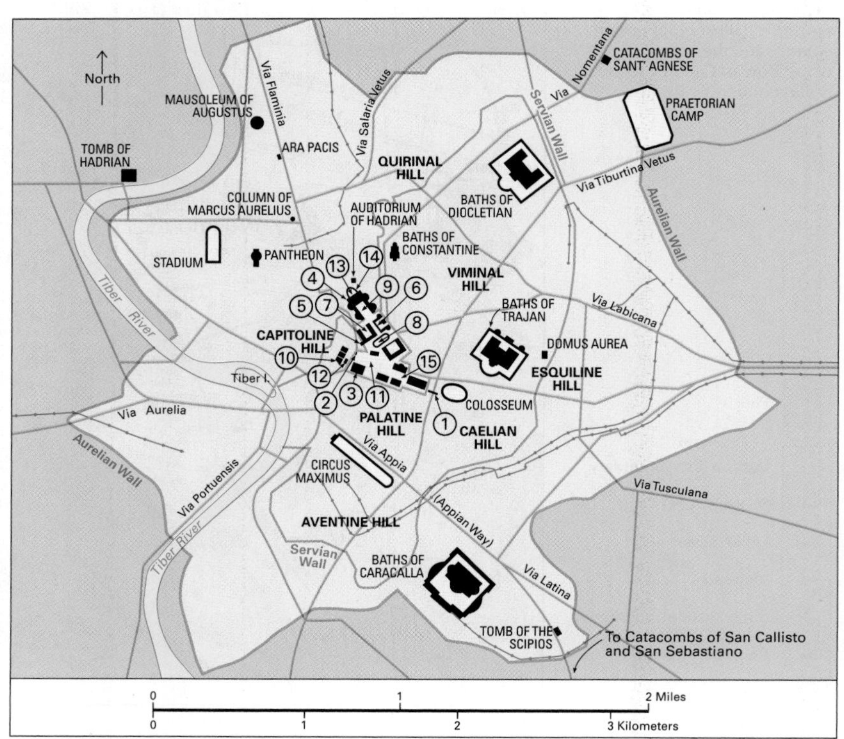

WORLD BOOK map

Remains of the splendors of ancient Rome may be seen throughout the city, especially in an area east of the Tiber River. Since the 1800's, the Italian government has cleared the main sites of the ruins and surrounded them with trees and gardens. Thousands of tourists visit these attractions yearly.

Forums. The centers of ancient Roman life were open marketplaces called *forums,* where public meetings were held. The Roman Forum, the most important one, was the center of Roman government. Many important buildings and monuments stood there. Ruins in the Roman Forum include the *Curia* (Senate House), the triumphal Arch of Septimius Severus, the Temple of Saturn, and the Basilica Julia, an assembly hall.

Most streets of ancient Rome were narrow and crooked, but a few were wide and beautiful, with high arches and white marble buildings. The chief street, the *Via Sacra* (Sacred Way), crossed the Roman Forum. Victorious emperors and generals returning from war paraded over its lava pavement. See **Forum, Roman; Rome, Ancient** (picture: A triumphal procession).

Many Roman rulers built forums of their own. The ruins of five of these forums still stand—those of Augustus, Julius Caesar, Nerva, Trajan, and Vespasian. Trajan's Forum is the finest. Most of its buildings, including the Basilica Ulpia and the Temple of Trajan, are in ruins. But Trajan's Column, 100 feet (30 meters) tall, is almost whole. It has carvings of scenes from Trajan's wars. Nearby stand the Markets of Trajan, a large semicircle of three-storied shops. One of the shops has been rebuilt to show how it looked in ancient times. See **Trajan.**

The Colosseum, dedicated in A.D. 80, is one of the chief landmarks of Rome. In this huge amphitheater, now half-ruined, Romans watched trained fighters called *gladiators* battle each other or fight wild animals. The audiences also saw persecuted Christians killed by lions. See **Colosseum.**

Baths. Only wealthy Romans could afford to own private baths, but the city had many public ones. During the time of the emperors, the public baths became luxurious meeting places. They looked like great square-shaped swimming pools and were surrounded by gardens, columned marble porches, and libraries. The bath buildings had facilities for warm and cold baths, steam baths, and massages.

The most splendid remains of baths are those of Caracalla and of Diocletian. The Baths of Caracalla, which date from the early A.D. 200's, are especially impressive. They were decorated with precious marble, statues, and *mosaics* (pictures formed of bits of colored glass, stone, or wood). Few of these decorations remain. But many tourists continue to visit the ruins each year for their history and architecture. The Baths of Diocletian, completed in the early A.D. 300's, were the largest of all Roman baths. They could serve 3,000 people at a time. Most of the site has been built over, but some rooms can still be seen.

The catacombs were systems of underground passages and rooms used as Christian burial places and chapels. The early Christians dug them from the A.D. 100's to the early 400's and hid there during periods of persecution. The catacombs are decorated with paintings on walls and ceilings and with Christian symbols. The most famous catacombs include those of San Callisto, San Sebastiano, and Sant' Agnese. See **Catacombs.**

Other remains. The Pantheon is the best preserved of all the remains of ancient Rome. The Romans built it as a temple in honor of all their gods (see **Pantheon**). The triple Arch of Constantine, built about A.D. 315, also is well preserved. It includes three connected arches, side by side, richly decorated with sculpture.

The ruins of the *Domus Aurea* (Golden House) are in a popular public park. This building was the palace of Emperor Nero. The ruins, which lie mainly underground, occupy a large area. Paintings cover some of the walls. The well-preserved Column of Marcus Aurelius, built during the A.D. 100's, honors Roman victories in battle. It has carvings of war scenes. Stairs inside the hollow marble column lead to the top, where a statue of Saint Paul has stood since 1589.

The Mausoleum of Augustus, begun about 28 B.C., is the tomb of Augustus and members of his family. Augustus, the first Roman emperor, built the nearby *Ara Pacis* (Altar of Peace) after establishing the *Pax Romana* (Roman Peace), which lasted 200 years. These buildings stood on the *Campus Martius* (Field of Mars), which had been used for military training. During the A.D. 200's, invaders from the north and the east attacked the empire, and Rome built the Aurelian Wall and other walls for defense. Many parts of these walls are still standing.

Gerald Clyde, FPG

The Colosseum was a huge amphitheater.

SCALA/Art Resource

The catacombs were used for Christian burial places.

History

Early days. A legend says that Rome was founded by twin brothers in 753 B.C. For an account of this story, see **Romulus and Remus**. Rome expanded and became the supreme power of the Western world. For the history of Rome through the fall of the West Roman Empire in A.D. 476, see **Rome, Ancient** (History).

After Rome fell to Germanic tribes, most of the once-splendid city became an unhealthful area of marshes. In the mid-500's, Emperor Justinian I of the Byzantine Empire drove the Ostrogoths from Rome. He reestablished Roman rule of the city as a Byzantine territory, but the decay of Rome continued. See **Byzantine Empire**.

The Middle Ages and the Renaissance. Rome had far-reaching importance as the official center of the Christian Church. During the 700's, the popes greatly increased their political power. When invading Lombards threatened Rome, Pope Stephen II asked for help from Pepin the Short, king of the Franks. Pepin saved Rome twice and gave the city and nearby lands to the pope in 756. Pepin's son Charlemagne later expanded these *Papal States,* as they were called. See **Papal States; Pepin the Short**.

For hundreds of years after the 800's, Rome was torn by struggles among kings and princes. Various European rulers tried to control the powerful popes, especially by influencing papal elections. In 1305, through the efforts of King Philip IV of France, a French archbishop was elected pope. The new pope, Clement V, moved his court to Avignon, France. It was returned to Rome in 1377. See **Pope** (The troubles of the papacy).

During this period, Cola di Rienzo, an Italian patriot, rebelled against the nobles. He established a popular republic in 1347. But Cola soon became cruel and greedy for power and was later killed in a riot.

Rome became one of the most splendid cities of the Renaissance. In 1527, raiding German and Spanish troops destroyed or stole many of the city's treasures and killed thousands of Romans. Soon afterward, the job of rebuilding Rome began. During the rest of the 1500's and the 1600's, the popes built hundreds of magnificent structures. They appointed the finest painters and sculptors, including Michelangelo, to design and decorate the buildings.

Under Napoleon. In 1798, after Napoleon conquered the Italian Peninsula, the victorious French troops entered Rome. Napoleon ended the pope's political power in 1809. He made the Papal States a part of his empire. He also declared Rome to be the second city of his em-

SCALA/Art Resource

A map of Rome shows the city's layout during the 1500's. Some of the 20 hills of Rome rise in the background. The Tiber River flows through the city. St. Peter's Basilica stands on what was then the city's southwestern edge.

pire, after Paris. Pope Pius VII fought these changes, and Napoleon jailed him. After Napoleon's defeat, most of the Papal States were returned to the pope in 1815.

Republic of Rome. During the early 1800's, movements for unity and freedom from foreign rule swept the Italian peninsula. But the popes opposed these movements. In 1848, revolutionists made Rome a republic, and Pope Pius IX fled. French troops captured Rome in 1849 and restored the pope to power the next year.

Italy's capital. In 1861, when Victor Emmanuel II became king of a united Italy, Rome was not yet a part of the new kingdom. Italian volunteers tried to take Rome in 1867, but French defenders stopped them. In 1870, after the French had left, Victor Emmanuel entered Rome almost without bloodshed. He ended the pope's political power and made Rome his capital in 1871. In protest, Pius IX shut himself up in the Vatican and refused to deal with the government. Succeeding popes followed the same policy until 1929. That year, by treaty, Vatican City became an independent state, and Roman Catholic Church officials recognized Rome as Italy's capital.

Period of construction. The 1900's were a period of widespread construction in Rome. New buildings and roads were built, and the city restored many ancient buildings and monuments. During the 1920's and 1930's, the Fascist dictator Benito Mussolini promoted much poorly planned construction. It later led to severe traffic jams and other city problems. Mussolini completed a new University of Rome campus in 1935 and began work on a huge central railroad station in 1938. But construction was halted by World War II (1939-1945). Rome suffered little damage during the war. Neither side wanted to endanger the life of Pope Pius XII, who was in Vatican City. The central railroad station was completed in 1950 according to improved new plans.

In 1938, Mussolini began building the Esposizione Universale di Roma (Universal Exhibition of Rome, or EUR). This world's fair was to have opened in 1942, and plans called for its buildings to form a government center later. The construction was interrupted by the war and was resumed in 1951. In 1955, Rome's subway linked the 1,075-acre (435-hectare) EUR with the new railroad station. Some of the 1960 Summer Olympic Games were held near the EUR in the city's new Sports Palace. The EUR was completed in 1976. Many large companies and government agencies operate there.

Shostal

A huge complex called the Esposizione Universale di Roma (Universal Exhibition of Rome, or EUR) includes numerous modern buildings. Many large companies and government agencies have their offices in the EUR.

During the early 1980's, Rome's city government adopted a plan to restore many of Rome's ruins. Several monuments, including Trajan's Column, the Arch of Constantine, and the Trevi Fountain, were restored.

Recent developments. In the mid-1990's, Rome began another ambitious program of restoration and construction. New projects included the Auditorium Parco della Musica, designed by Italian architect Renzo Piano. Some projects undertaken in the late 1990's to accommodate millennial celebrations stirred controversy because they threatened historic sites. Anthony James Joes

Related articles in *World Book* include:

Catacombs	Michelangelo	Romulus and Remus
City (picture)	Pantheon	Saint Peter's Basilica
Colosseum	Papal States	Sistine Chapel
Forum, Roman	Pope	Tiber River
Garibaldi, Giuseppe	Quirinal Hill	Vatican City
Mazzini, Giuseppe	Rome, Ancient	

Outline

I. **The city today**
   A. Parks and gardens
   B. Music and theater
   C. Museums and art galleries
   D. Churches, palaces, and fountains
   E. Schools
   F. Sports
   G. Economy
   H. Government

II. **The ancient city**
   A. Forums
   B. The Colosseum
   C. Baths
   D. The catacombs
   E. Other remains

III. **History**

Questions

Why is Rome called the *Eternal City?*
Where were public meetings held in ancient Rome?
What is Rome's most popular sport?
What great painter decorated the Sistine Chapel?
How did the Via del Corso get its name?
What were the catacombs? What were they used for?
What is the legend of the Fountain of Trevi?

Additional resources

Bosworth, R. J. B. *Whispering City: Modern Rome and Its Histories.* Yale, 2011.
Claridge, Amanda. *Rome.* 2nd ed. Oxford, 2010.
Nickerson, Angela K. *A Journey into Michelangelo's Rome.* Roaring Forties Pr., 2008.
Porter, Darwin, and Prince, Danforth. *Frommer's Rome.* Wiley, frequently updated.

Rome, New York (pop. 33,725), is a historic city in the central part of the state. For location, see **New York** (political map). With Utica, Rome forms part of a metropolitan area of 299,397 people. Rome's chief products are copper wire and other copper products. A United States Air Force research facility is in the city. Rome stands on the site of Fort Stanwix and is the home of the Fort Stanwix National Monument. The city was originally named Lynchville. But it was renamed Rome in 1819. Some people believe that the Stars and Stripes flew there for the first time in battle in 1777, during the Battle of Oriskany in the American Revolution. Groundbreaking for the construction of the Erie Canal took place in Rome on July 4, 1817. Today, the Erie Canal Village stands on the site of the groundbreaking. The village is a reconstruction of the area in the 1800's. Rome was incorporated in 1870. It has a mayor-council form of government.

John Kenneth White

WORLD BOOK illustration by Richard Bonson, Wildlife Art Ltd.

A triumphal procession paraded through the Roman Forum, the chief public square of ancient Rome, to celebrate a military victory. The emperor rode in a chariot drawn by white horses. Before him marched enemy prisoners, trumpeters, and sacrificial animals.

Rome, Ancient

Rome, Ancient. The story of ancient Rome is a tale of how a small farming community on the bank of the Tiber River in central Italy grew to become one of the greatest empires in history, and then collapsed. According to Roman legend, the city of Rome was founded in 753 B.C. By 272 B.C., the Roman Republic controlled most of the Italian Peninsula. At its peak, in the A.D. 100's and 200's, the Roman Empire governed about half of Europe, much of the Middle East, and the north coast of Africa. The empire then began to crumble, partly because it was too big for Rome to govern.

The Roman Empire split into two parts in A.D. 395, the West Roman Empire and the East Roman, or Byzantine, Empire. The West Roman Empire fell in A.D. 476 and was replaced by small Germanic kingdoms. The Byzantine Empire continued for centuries.

Ancient Rome had enormous influence on the development of Western civilization. Latin, the language of the ancient Romans, became the basis of French, Italian, Spanish, and the other Romance languages. Roman law provided the foundation for the legal systems of most of the countries in Western Europe and Latin America. Roman roads, bridges, and aqueducts—some of which are still used—served as models for engineers in later ages.

This article provides a broad overview of the land, people, government, way of life, arts and sciences, economy, and history of ancient Rome. Many separate *World Book* articles have more detailed information. A list of these is given at the end under *Related articles.*

The world of ancient Rome

The land. The city of Rome was founded on seven wooded hills next to the Tiber River in central Italy. The hills were steep and easily defended against enemy attacks. The valleys had fertile soil, as well as materials necessary for building.

As Rome grew, much of the city was built upon the swampy lowlands beneath the seven hills. These parts of Rome often suffered damaging floods from the Tiber. But the Tiber also provided a convenient route to the sea, which lay about 15 miles (24 kilometers) to the west. The harbor at Ostia, a town at the mouth of the Tiber, allowed for extensive trade with other communities.

The Italian Peninsula, which Rome controlled for much of its history, juts far into the Mediterranean Sea and occupies a central position among the Mediterranean lands. To the north, the Alps provided a natural defense against invaders from central Europe. But passes through the mountains allowed settlers, attracted by the mild climate and fertile soil, to travel into Italy.

Roman rule eventually spread over all the lands bordering the Mediterranean Sea. The Romans called the Mediterranean Mare Nostrum (Our Sea) or Mare Internum (Inland Sea). At the Roman Empire's greatest size, in the A.D. 100's and 200's, the empire extended as far north as Scotland and as far east as the Persian Gulf.

The people. When Rome was founded, a number of different tribes lived on the Italian Peninsula, each with its own language and culture. The Romans were Latins. Other major tribes included the Etruscans, Sabines, and Samnites.

The Roman Empire, at its height, had over 50 million people. In the east, Rome controlled Mesopotamia, Palestine, Egypt, and Greece. In the west, Rome conquered Britain and Gaul (now mainly France, Belgium, and part of Germany). Almost 1 million people lived in the city of Rome. Alexandria in Egypt, the empire's second largest city, had over 500,000 inhabitants.

Latin and Greek were the official languages of the empire. Government officials and members of the upper classes spoke those two languages. But most people in the empire continued to use their native languages. Celtic was spoken in Gaul and Britain, Berber in northern Africa, and Aramaic in Syria and Palestine.

People belonged to one of three groups in ancient Rome: (1) citizens, (2) noncitizens, and (3) slaves. Roman law recognized citizens and noncitizens as free. Slaves were treated as property. Citizenship gave protection under Roman law, and only a citizen could become a senator or government official.

The citizens of Rome were further divided into different social classes. At the top were members of the Senate, many of whom were wealthy landowners. Next were the *equites* (pronounced *EHK wuh teez*), prosperous businessmen and merchants. Under the Roman emperors, equites held important government positions and assisted in the running of the empire. The majority of Roman citizens belonged to the lower classes. They were farmers, city workers, and soldiers.

At first, only those born in Rome could become citizens, so the majority of people were noncitizens. As Rome expanded, it granted citizenship to more people in the empire. The privilege of citizenship promoted loyalty to the empire and gave all classes and all regions a greater stake in its success. Women and children could become citizens, but they could not vote.

Slaves were regarded as property by Roman law, but they were essential to the Roman way of life. They performed tasks ranging from heavy labor to teaching the young nobles of Rome. Most slaves were captured in war. A wealthy Roman family might have hundreds of slaves working on its farmland and in its home. Slaves could buy their freedom from their masters, or be given it. Freed slaves, known as freedmen, owed allegiance to their former masters, who relied on them for continued service.

Government

A series of kings ruled ancient Rome at the beginning of its history. Each king was advised by a Senate made up of the heads of Rome's leading families. Ordinary citizens had little say in the running of the state.

The Roman Republic was established in 509 B.C., after Roman nobles overthrew the king. Under this new government, the Senate became the most powerful body. It decided foreign and financial policy and passed *decrees* (official orders). The senators were former *magistrates* (government officials) who held office for life.

To succeed politically, magistrates had to follow the *cursus honorum* (ladder of offices). The first step was serving as a military officer. Next, they would try to be elected as a *quaestor* (financial official), then as an *aedile* (public works official), then as a *praetor* (judicial official). After serving as praetor, magistrates automatically entered the Senate. The highest position was *consul.* Two consuls, elected annually, headed the government and took command of the army in times of war. Each Roman year was named after the consuls who ruled that year.

All magistrates held office for one year. After serving in one position, they had to return to private life for a year before holding another office. As Rome expanded, praetors and consuls left the city after their year in office to govern the provinces as *propraetors* or *proconsuls.*

During the B.C. 400's and 300's, the landowning upper classes—the *patricians*—struggled for power with the other classes—the *plebeians.* The dispute became known as the Conflict of the Orders. Originally, only patricians could hold public office, become priests, or interpret the law. But the importance of the plebeians in fighting wars helped them gain a greater voice. The plebeians formed their own assembly, the *concilium plebis,* and elected leaders known as *tribunes* who championed their causes. By 287 B.C., plebeians had won the right to hold any public or religious office and had gained equality under the law. However, the richest families continued to control the assemblies and the Senate.

In the later republic, two political groups arose from the senatorial classes—the *optimates* and *populares.* The optimates used the Senate to increase their power and get laws passed. The populares used the people's tribunes and popular support to advance their agenda.

The Roman Empire was established in 27 B.C., after the republican government collapsed. The republican institutions of government continued, but emperors held supreme authority. They nominated the consuls and appointed new senators. The citizen assemblies had little power. Emperors headed the army and directed the making of laws. They relied more on their own advisers than on the Senate. A vast civil service handled the empire's day-to-day business.

The law. The Romans published their first known law code in 451 B.C. This code, called the Laws of the Twelve Tables, was basic. As Rome grew, its legal system developed and became more complex. Rome became the first society with experts whose job was to interpret the law on behalf of clients—experts now called lawyers.

A general set of legal principles developed, known as the *jus gentium* (law of nations). It was based on common-sense notions of fairness and took into account local customs and practices. Much of what we know of Roman law comes from the Theodosian Code of A.D. 438 and the *Digest,* law cases and interpretations compiled by the Emperor Justinian in the A.D 500's.

The army was composed of three groups: (1) the legions, (2) the auxiliaries, and (3) the Praetorian Guard. Only Roman citizens could join the legions. Each legion consisted of about 5,000 men. Besides soldiers, legions also had doctors, surveyors, and engineers. Although the chief purpose of the legions was military, legions also built roads, aqueducts, walls, and tunnels.

Noncitizens joined the auxiliaries, which fought alongside the legions. Auxiliaries were made up of specialized troops, such as archers or cavalry.

The Praetorian Guard was an elite group of soldiers who served as the emperor's personal bodyguard. It was the only army group stationed in the city of Rome.

The normal length of military service was 25 years. Most soldiers were professionals, whose training and discipline helped to make the army successful. After their term of service, many veterans and their families settled in *colonies* (towns made up of former soldiers). The colonies acted as models of Roman life for people in the provinces, and the former soldiers provided a ready peacekeeping or police force if trouble arose.

Way of life

City life. Rome was the capital and largest city of the empire. Other important cities included Alexandria in Egypt, Athens in Greece, Antioch in Syria, and Byzantium (later Constantinople, now Istanbul) in Turkey.

Cities in the Roman Empire served as centers of trade and culture. Roman engineers planned cities carefully. They set public buildings in central locations and provided efficient sewerage and water-supply systems. Emperors and other wealthy individuals paid for the construction of public buildings, such as baths, arenas, and theaters. At the heart of the Roman city was the *forum,* a large open space surrounded by markets, government buildings, and temples. It was the center for business and religious life and offered a place where everyone could mingle, rich and poor alike.

Most people in Roman cities lived in cramped apartment buildings that were three to five stories high. Many of these buildings had unsanitary conditions, and some burned to the ground. Wealthy Romans lived in houses built around two courtyards known as the *atrium* and the *peristyle.* Windowless rooms surrounded the atrium, but a roof opening let in light and air. A dining hall and other rooms circled the larger peristyle, which was also open to the sky and had a garden.

Rural life. The first Romans were shepherds and farmers. In early Rome, landowners planted their crops in the spring and harvested them in the fall. During the summer, they would fight in the army. As Rome expanded, small farmers spent longer periods away fighting. Many were forced to sell their land to wealthier landowners. This led to the development of large estates known as *latifundia,* which were worked by massive teams of slaves. For these slaves and most small landholders, rural life involved hard physical labor. The Roman calendar featured regular agricultural festivals. The games and entertainments at these festivals offered a break from the hardships of working the land.

Most rural people lived in simple dwellings made of

Reconstructed model (1900's) of a large house and apartments (A.D. 100's) in Ostia, Italy; Museo della Civita Romana, Rome, Italy (SCALA/Art Resource)

Roman apartment buildings were several stories tall, often with shops facing the street. Wealthier residents usually lived on the ground floor. The majority of city dwellers in ancient Rome lived in apartments.

An upper-class house in a Roman city, as shown in this drawing, featured two courtyards. The *atrium* was a courtyard that served as a reception area. Its roof let in air and light for the rooms built around the atrium. A second courtyard, called a *peristyle,* was planted with trees, flowers, and shrubs. It might also have had a fishpond and a fountain. A walled garden at the rear of the house provided room for raising fruits and vegetables. In some houses, small shops faced the street.

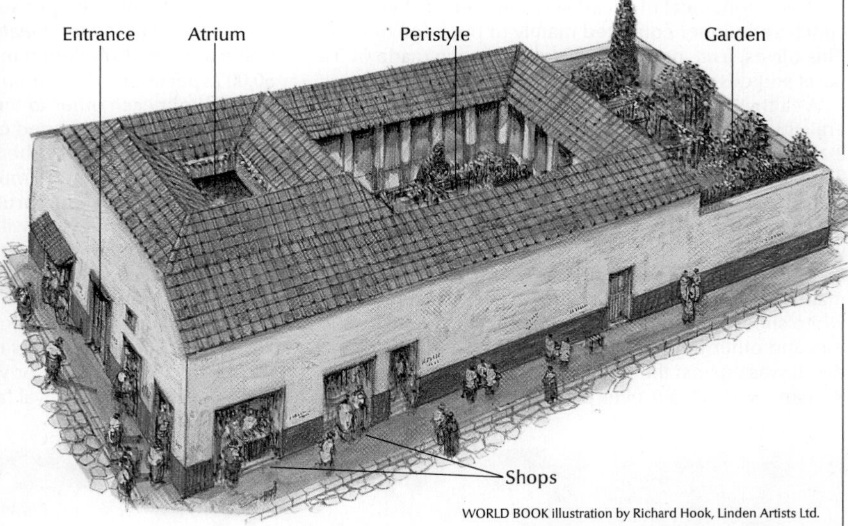

WORLD BOOK illustration by Richard Hook, Linden Artists Ltd.

Cubiculum (bedroom) from the Villa of P. Fannius Sunistor (about 40 to 30 B.C.); Metropolitan Museum of Art, Rogers Fund, 1903

Colorful wallpaintings decorated the rooms of the wealthy, such as this bedroom. The floor is covered by a *mosaic*—pictures and designs created with small colored tiles. This room was part of a country house near Mount Vesuvius. When the volcano erupted in A.D. 79, volcanic ash buried and preserved the house.

sun-dried bricks. Wealthy landowners lived in luxurious villas, which were larger than houses in the city.

Family life. The head of the Roman family was the *paterfamilias* (father of the family). Legally, he had power over his entire household, which included his wife, children (even if adults), slaves, and freedmen. As long as his father lived, a son could not own property or have legal authority over his own children. However, in practice, adult sons ruled their own families.

Girls could legally marry when they were 12 years old, and boys when they were 14. However, a man might not marry until he was in his 20's and had already begun his career. Among the upper classes, parents arranged most marriages for the economic or political benefits that the unions would bring the families. During the republic, marriage made a woman and everything she owned her husband's property. During the empire, the woman kept her legal rights and her own property.

Food. Most Romans ate simple meals. Breakfast was usually a light meal of bread and sometimes cheese. Lunch and dinner consisted mainly of porridge or bread plus olives, fruit, or cheese. *Garum,* a sauce made of fish parts and olive oil, was a popular addition.

Wealthy Romans sometimes served dinners with several courses. The first course might include eggs, vegetables, and shellfish. The main courses featured meat, fish, or chicken. For dessert, the diners often ate honey-sweetened cakes and fruit.

Clothing. The Romans wore simple clothes made of wool or linen. The main garment was the *tunic,* a gown that hung to the knees or below. On formal occasions, male citizens of Rome wore a *toga,* which resembled a white sheet draped around the body. The togas of senators and other high-ranking citizens had a purple border. It was against the law for noncitizens to wear togas. Romans wore cloaks over their tunics or togas when the weather was cold or wet.

Women often wore a *stola,* a long dress with many folds. Wealthy women wore a *palla,* which was similar to a toga, as well as jewelry, makeup, and styled hair. Most women's clothing was dyed in bright colors.

Recreation. Bathhouses served as centers for daily exercise and bathing, as well as for socializing. Normally, there were separate baths for men and women. Bathhouses had a grand exercise area, the *palaestra,* for wrestling, boxing, or running. After exercising, the bather would be massaged by a slave, then move through rooms with warm, hot, and cold pools to cleanse and energize the body.

Much of the Roman year was devoted to religious holidays in honor of gods and goddesses. During the republic, there were almost 60 of these special days. By the A.D. 100's, there were 135 each year.

Many religious holidays were celebrated with free public entertainment. Occasionally, the emperor or wealthy state officials sponsored productions in circular arenas known as *amphitheaters.* The most famous amphitheater, the Colosseum in Rome, could seat about 50,000 spectators. Here, trained fighters known as *gladiators* fought each other to the death. Most gladiators were slaves or condemned criminals, but some citizens gave up their freedom to become gladiators. Successful gladiators were admired, much as modern athletes are, but most gladiators died brutal deaths. In other events, armed men fought exotic wild animals, or beasts attacked condemned criminals or Christians.

Chariot racing was a popular spectator sport. In Rome, charioteers raced in a long, oval arena known as the Circus Maximus, which could seat more than 250,000 people. Charioteers raced for one of four teams—red, green, blue, or white. Like modern sports teams, each team had loyal fans. Success as a charioteer

WORLD BOOK illustration by Richard Hook, Linden Artists Ltd.

Crowded shops occupied the ground story of many buildings in ancient Rome. In the various shops, women marketed, men drank wine with friends, and workers sold goods they had crafted. Public fountains in the narrow streets provided water for Roman homes.

Circus Maximus (relief sculpture, 200's A.D.); Museo Archeologico, Foligno, Italy (SCALA/Art Resource)

Chariot racing was a popular spectator sport in ancient Rome. Charioteers raced in the Circus Maximus, a long, oval arena that could seat over 250,000 people. Four teams—red, white, blue, and green—competed in the races. Each team had loyal fans, much as modern sports teams do.

brought fame and fortune.

Theaters in Rome staged comedies and tragedies by Greek and Roman authors. More popular, however, were *mimes* (short plays about everyday life) or *pantomimes* (stories told through music and dancing).

Religion. The Romans adopted most of their gods from the Greeks, giving them Roman names. For example, Jupiter, the supreme god, was the Roman name for the Greek god Zeus. The Romans erected temples and shrines to honor their gods. The centerpiece of every Roman city was a temple to the three divine beings called the Capitoline triad: Jupiter, Juno, and Minerva.

Rulers of Rome were sometimes designated as gods. Romulus became the god Quirinus, and some emperors, including Augustus, Claudius, and Vespasian, were *deified* (made gods) after their death. Late in the empire, people began worshiping emperors as gods while they were still alive.

The Roman state controlled religion. Priests were government officials, elected or appointed to office. They performed sacrifices and other ceremonies to win the favor of the gods for the state. The most important priests were the *pontiffs.* The chief priest was known as the *pontifex maximus.* During the empire, this position was always held by the emperor.

An important feature of Roman religion was *divination*—telling the future and examining the will of the gods to ward off their anger. Priests known as *augurs* looked for signs in the flight of birds. The Sibylline Books, a set of religious texts, offered remedies to deal

Gladiator fighting scenes (Roman mosaic, A.D 200's); Galleria Borghese, Rome, Italy (SCALA/Art Resource)

Trained fighters called *gladiators* fought bloody battles to entertain the ancient Romans. Many gladiators were slaves or condemned criminals, but some free citizens chose to become gladiators. Successful gladiators were admired, much as modern athletes are, but most died brutal deaths.

with *portents* (natural occurrences interpreted as signs), such as earthquakes or sudden storms. Individuals used other types of divination, such as astrology.

As Roman religion became more political, people turned to other kinds of religious worship. Many practiced religions that promised salvation and happiness after death. Christianity became a popular alternative to Roman religion. The Roman government saw Christianity as a threat and persecuted its followers. But by the A.D. 300's, Christianity had become the main religion of the empire.

Education. Most children received their earliest education at home under the supervision of their parents. In wealthy homes, slaves taught the children. These slaves were often well-educated men from Greece. From the age of 6 or 7 until 10 or 11, most boys and some girls attended a private school or studied at home. They learned reading, writing, and mathematics. Most Roman children who received further education came from wealthy families. From the age of 11 until about 14, they studied mainly Latin and Greek grammar and literature, as well as mathematics, music, and astronomy.

Higher education focused on the study of *rhetoric*—the art of public speaking. Upper-class Romans prized the ability to argue persuasively before the law courts or to debate effectively in the Senate. To improve their abilities as public speakers, students also read philosophy and history. Few women received higher education.

Arts and sciences

Architecture and engineering. The ancient Romans adopted the basic forms of Greek architecture. For example, Roman temples were surrounded by columns with a covered *portico* (walkway), just like those in Greece. But the Romans generally built grander and more extravagant buildings than the Greeks.

Two achievements of Roman engineering made larger buildings possible: the arch and concrete. Arches supported such structures as bridges and the aqueducts that carried water to Roman cities. Arched roofs known as *vaults* spanned the interior of buildings. Vaults eliminated the need for columns to hold up the roof and so created more open floor space. Although the Romans did not invent the arch, they made better use of arches than previous cultures.

The Romans developed concrete, which served as a strong building material for walls, vaults, and domed buildings. The most famous Roman building made with concrete is the Pantheon in Rome, which has a concrete dome about 142 feet (43 meters) in diameter.

Sculpture, painting, and mosaics. Roman sculptors and painters borrowed styles from native Italian traditions and from Greek art. Many early Roman sculptors worked in bronze or terra cotta, materials often used in Etruscan sculpture. After the Romans conquered Greece during the 140's B.C., they adopted some of the styles of Greek art. Roman sculptors created realistic portraits that revealed individual personalities.

Roman sculptors also illustrated historical events through carvings on large public monuments. For example, the richly decorated Ara Pacis (Altar of Peace) celebrated the peace brought to the empire by the Emperor Augustus. Carvings on columns and triumphal arches celebrated the emperor and Rome.

Wallpaintings decorated the houses of the wealthy. Paintings often showed garden landscapes, events from

WORLD BOOK illustration by Richard Hook, Linden Artists Ltd.

Aqueduct construction, *shown here,* was one of the peacetime activities of the Roman army. Roman aqueducts carried water long distances from rivers and mountain springs. The water ran in a channel along the top of an aqueduct. Roman soldiers also built roads, bridges, tunnels, and walls.

Greek and Roman mythology, historical scenes, or scenes of everyday life. Romans decorated floors with *mosaics*—pictures or designs created with small colored tiles. The richly colored paintings and mosaics helped to make rooms in Roman houses seem larger and brighter and showed off the wealth of the owner.

Literature. Early Roman literature was heavily influenced by Greek poetry and drama. The first history of Rome was written in Greek. The earliest Roman poets, such as Naevius, and comic playwrights, such as Plautus and Terence, adapted or translated Greek originals for Roman audiences. Rome's greatest poets—Catullus, Lucretius, Ovid, and Virgil—produced powerful, original works, but even these works show the Greek influence.

The annual change of leadership in republican government gave rise to Rome's own particular form of history, the *annals* (year-by-year narratives). Livy wrote the annals of the history of the Roman people, and Tacitus adapted the form in his account of the first emperors of Rome. Other important literary works include the letters, speeches, and philosophical writings of Cicero; the *satires* (mocking poetry) of Horace and Juvenal; and the letters of Pliny the Younger.

Science. The ancient Romans made few scientific discoveries. Yet the work of Greek scientists flourished under Roman rule. The Greek geographer Strabo traveled widely and wrote careful descriptions of what he saw. Alexandria in Egypt became an important center for scientific study. There, Ptolemy developed a system of astronomy that was accepted for nearly 1,400 years. Galen, a Greek physician, proposed important medical theories based on scientific experiments. The Romans themselves gathered important collections of scientific information. For example, Pliny the Elder gathered the scientific knowledge of his day in a 37-volume encyclopedia.

Economy

Rome profited from the economic resources of the regions and nations it conquered. Its vast wealth funded the magnificent buildings and art that decorated Rome and other imperial cities. Roman riches also financed roads, aqueducts, and other public works projects.

Agriculture. Most of the people in the Roman world lived by farming. Roman farmers understood the need to rotate crops to maintain the fertility of the soil for future seasons. Farmers who could afford to would leave half of every field unplanted.

In fertile valleys north and south of Rome, farmers grew wheat, rye, and barley. Olives and grape vines flourished on rockier hillsides. Shepherds grazed sheep and goats, and other farmers raised hogs, cattle, and poultry. As the empire expanded, farms in Gaul, Spain, and northern Africa supplied Rome with many agricultural products. In Africa, local farmers grew rich from their export of olive oil, which was used both for cooking and as a lamp fuel.

Mining. After agriculture, mining was Rome's most important industry. The great building projects in Rome and in other cities throughout the empire required huge quantities of marble and other materials. Greece and northern Italy provided much of the marble. Italy also had rich deposits of copper and iron ore. Gold and silver were mined in Spain and Britain. Britain also produced iron for weapons and armor, lead for water pipes, and tin, much of which was used to produce bronze. Slaves, condemned criminals, and prisoners of war worked in the mines. The miners labored in cramped and unsanitary conditions, chained together.

Manufacturing industries were small compared to agriculture and mining. The city of Rome imported most of its manufactured goods from other Italian communities. They supplied Rome with such products as pottery, glassware, weapons, tools, and textiles.

Trade thrived as the empire expanded. Trade routes crossed land and sea, both within the empire and beyond its borders. Ships moved goods faster than the slow-moving carts used to carry merchandise over Roman roads. But both ships and carts had to guard against foul weather, pirates or highway robbers, and spoilage.

Rome imported foods, raw materials, and manufactured goods from within the empire. Rome also imported silk from China, spices and precious gems from India, and ivory and wild animals from Africa. Italy's leading exports were wine and olive oil.

The government issued coins of gold, silver, copper, and bronze from Rome. Local government centers, such as London in Britain (which the Romans called Londinium) or Lyon in Gaul (called Lugdunum), also issued coins. The central regulation of weights and measures for coinage made trade throughout the empire easier.

Transportation and communication. The Roman Empire's road system covered about 50,000 miles (80,000 kilometers). Roman roads were remarkably straight compared to modern highways. The Romans designed straight roads to speed up troop movements. After the

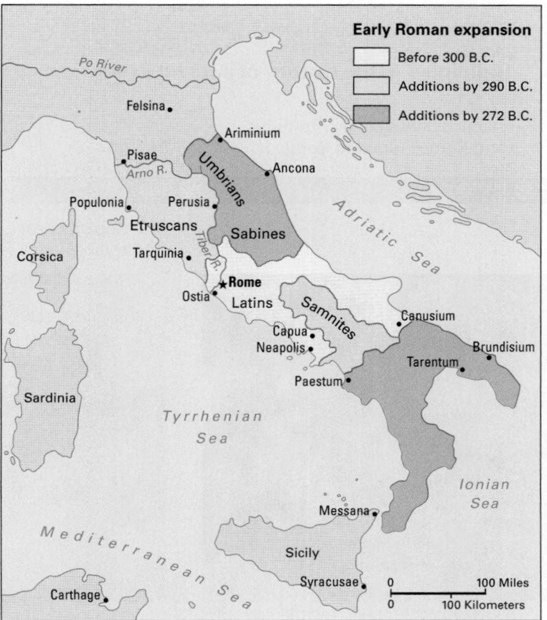

WORLD BOOK map

Rome gained control of the Italian Peninsula through a series of military victories. By 290 B.C., Rome had defeated the Etruscans and the Samnites. After a victory over the Greek colony of Tarentum in 272 B.C., Rome ruled most of the peninsula.

army had pacified a region, Roman administrators then used the roads to promote trade and communication.

Rome had a highly developed postal system that could bring a letter from the most distant outpost of the empire to Rome. Postal stations stood on main roads throughout the empire. The emperor maintained regular contact by letter with governors in the provinces.

The Romans had a huge fleet of cargo ships, which traveled to ports on the Mediterranean Sea and carried goods up and down the Rhine, Danube, and Nile rivers. Permanent navies in the Mediterranean Sea and the English Channel protected trade ships from pirates.

In Rome, a government newsletter called *Acta Diurna (Daily Events)* was posted throughout the city. The paper recorded important social and political news. Officials inscribed important decrees and notices on stone or bronze and posted them prominently in major cities.

History

The regal period. Little is known about the early days of ancient Rome. Archaeologists have found the remains of houses that were built around 900 B.C. on the Palatine Hill. The earliest settlers were a people called the Latins. They inhabited many neighboring towns in Latium, the region around Rome.

According to legend, Rome was founded in 753 B.C. by twin brothers, Romulus and Remus. A dispute between the brothers led to the death of Remus, and Romulus named the city for himself. After Romulus, six more kings governed Rome. Each contributed to the development of the new state in a unique way. For example, the second king, Numa, introduced religious ceremonies to Rome. The heads of leading noble families made up the Senate, which advised the king.

About 600 B.C., Rome and other towns in Latium came under the control of the Etruscans, who lived in northern Italy. The Etruscans, the most advanced civilization in Italy, built roads, temples, and other public buildings in Rome. Trade increased during this period, as did Rome's prosperity. The last king was an Etruscan named Tarquin the Proud. He ruled so harshly that the Roman nobles expelled him and created a new form of government called a republic, without a single, all-powerful ruler.

The republican period. The Roman Republic was established in 509 B.C. It was intended to be a partnership between the Senate and the people of Rome, as indicated by the motto *Senatus Populusque Romanus* (Senate and People of Rome). The initials SPQR appeared on the flags of the Roman legions and in official documents.

In 493 B.C., Rome entered into an alliance with the Latin League, a union of the cities of Latium. By 396 B.C., Rome was the largest city in the region and used the league's resources to fight its neighbors. When Rome conquered a city, it offered protection and certain privileges, such as special trading rights. In return, the conquered cities supplied the Roman army with soldiers.

From the 300's to mid-200's B.C., Rome won victories over the Etruscans. In 338 B.C., Rome overpowered and disbanded the Latin League. In 290 B.C., the Romans conquered the Samnites, a mountain people who lived south of Rome. In the 200's and 100's B.C., Rome defeated the Gauls, who had invaded Italy from the north and burned Rome in 390 B.C. After a victory over the Greek colony of Tarentum in southern Italy in 272 B.C., Rome ruled most of the Italian Peninsula.

Rome's conquest of Italy brought it into conflict with Carthage, a sea power and trading center on the coast

Highlights in the history of ancient Rome

- **753 B.C.** — According to legend, Romulus and Remus founded Rome.
- **509 B.C.** — The Romans drove out the Etruscans and established a republic.
- **264-146 B.C.** — Rome began its expansion overseas by defeating Carthage in three Punic Wars.
- **27 B.C.** — Augustus became the first Roman emperor.

Bronze sculpture; Museo del Palazzo dei Conservatori, Rome (SCALA/Art Resource)

The legendary founders of Rome were twin brothers named Romulus and Remus. According to Roman mythology, a wolf nursed them as babies.

Tomb painting (500's B.C.) in Tarquinia, Italy (SCALA/Art Resource)

The Etruscan culture of central Italy influenced Rome during the 500's B.C. Under Etruscan rule, Rome grew from a village into a prosperous city.

Marble sculpture by an unknown artist; Uffizi Gallery, Florence, Italy (SCALA/Art Resource)

Cicero, the great Roman statesman and orator, supported Rome's republican government. But the Roman Republic ended soon after he died in 43 B.C.

of north Africa (in what is now Tunisia). The two nations fought three wars known as the Punic Wars. In the First Punic War (264-241 B.C.), Rome conquered Sicily and made it the first Roman province. In the Second Punic War (218-201 B.C.), the Carthaginian general Hannibal led his army over the Alps into Italy. He won several key battles, but Roman manpower and endurance wore him down. Roman forces, led by the general Publius Cornelius Scipio, defeated Hannibal in 202 B.C. In the Third Punic War (149-146 B.C.), Rome destroyed the city of Carthage. These victories brought Spain and northern Africa under Roman control.

After the Second Punic War, Rome began to expand in the east toward Greece and Macedonia. In 146 B.C., the same year as the destruction of Carthage, Rome burned Corinth to the ground and took control of Greece. Soon after, King Attalus III of Pergamum died and left his kingdom to Rome, which became a wealthy province the Romans called Asia (now part of Turkey).

The later years of the republic. Acquiring territories abroad led to discontent at home. Military campaigns took longer and longer, and poverty-stricken farmers often returned to find their lands ruined. But the wealthy profited from the slaves and goods captured in the fighting and from business opportunities in the new lands. The gap between rich and poor widened, but Rome's wealthiest citizens opposed attempts to narrow it. In the 100's B.C., the tribune Tiberius Sempronius Gracchus and his brother, Gaius Sempronius Gracchus, attempted a program of reform, including giving public land to the poor. But opponents killed them and halted their reforms.

The Roman general Gaius Marius then came to power. Marius served as consul seven times from 107 to 86 B.C. He used tribunes to win popular support and to gain political power. He also reformed the army, offering rewards to his men for successful campaigns. From 91 to 89 B.C., Rome fought with its Latin allies, who wanted to be awarded citizenship in return for assisting Rome abroad.

Civil war broke out in the 80's B.C. between Marius and another general, Lucius Cornelius Sulla. Marius died in 86 B.C., and Sulla eventually triumphed over Marius's followers. Sulla declared himself dictator in 82 B.C. and reorganized the state. He enlarged the Senate, reduced the powers of the tribunes, and took measures to prevent corruption in the provinces. In 79 B.C., Sulla stepped down as dictator and retired from politics.

Pompey the Great and Marcus Licinius Crassus, allies of Sulla, became the next leading generals. In 67 B.C., Pompey rid the Mediterranean of the pirates who had plagued Roman trade. He then conquered eastern Asia Minor (now Turkey), Syria, and Judea (now mostly Israel). Crassus put down the slave rebellion led by Spartacus. But the Senate blocked the rewards that Pompey and Crassus sought for their achievements. In 60 B.C., Pompey and Crassus joined Gaius Julius Caesar to form an unofficial political alliance known as the First Triumvirate. They arranged Caesar's election as consul in 59 B.C.

From 58 to 51 B.C., Julius Caesar conquered Gaul. Pompey stayed in Rome and gained political power. Crassus took an eastern command but was killed fighting the Parthian Empire, based in what is now Iran. Caesar and Pompey then saw each other as rivals for control of the empire. In 49 B.C., Caesar returned to Italy, and another civil war began. Over the next few years, Caesar defeated Pompey and his supporters. By 45 B.C., Caesar had become sole ruler of the Roman world. But many

A.D. 96-180 — The Roman Empire reached its height of power and prosperity.

A.D. 395 — The Roman Empire split into two parts—the West Roman Empire and the East Roman Empire.

A.D. 476 — The last emperor of the West Roman Empire, Romulus Augustulus, was overthrown by a Germanic leader.

Mosaic (A.D. 200's); Bardo Museum, Tunis, Tunisia (Giraudon/Art Resource)

Latin literature flourished in the Age of Augustus, from 27 B.C. to A.D. 14. The poet Virgil, *seated*, wrote of Rome's creation in his great epic, the *Aeneid*.

Relief sculpture (A.D. 100's); The Louvre, Paris (André Martin, Arthaud)

The Praetorian Guard was an elite group of soldiers who served as the emperor's bodyguard. In time, the emperors grew removed from the people.

Head of Jesus Christ (mosaic, A.D. 300's) from a Roman villa; Hinton St. Mary, Dorset, Dorset County Museum, U.K. (Bridgeman Art Library)

Christianity spread rapidly in the Roman Empire, though Christians were often persecuted. Christians were granted freedom of worship in A.D. 313.

powerful Romans distrusted him, and in 44 B.C. a group of aristocrats assassinated him.

More civil war followed Caesar's death. In 43 B.C., Caesar's adopted son and heir, Octavian, formed the Second Triumvirate with Mark Antony and Marcus Aemilius Lepidus, the *pontifex maximus* (chief priest). They took revenge on Caesar's assassins and dealt violently with any opposition. Mark Antony and Octavian eventually pushed aside Lepidus and fought each other for control of the empire. Antony sought the support of Cleopatra, queen of Egypt. The two became lovers and had children together. In 31 B.C., Octavian defeated them in the Battle of Actium off the west coast of Greece. The next year, Egypt became a Roman province.

Imperial Rome. After the defeat of Antony, Octavian was the unchallenged leader of the Roman world. In 27 B.C., he became the first Roman emperor and took the name Augustus (Revered One), a word that held religious meaning. More than a century of internal upheavals and civil war, caused by the ambitions of powerful individuals, had destroyed the republic. Only a strong individual who had the support of the army, the Senate, and the people would be able to govern the Roman world.

The reign of Augustus marked the beginning of a period of stability known as the Pax Romana (Roman Peace), which lasted until about A.D. 180. Augustus reestablished an orderly government in which the traditional republican forms of government—Senate, consuls, tribunes—still functioned. But Augustus had supreme power. He commanded the army and controlled the most important provinces. He nominated the consuls and appointed new senators. Citizen assemblies had little power, but he kept the masses happy through entertainment and handouts of free grain and money.

The emperor relied heavily on loyal advisers and established a personal bodyguard, the Praetorian Guard, which was stationed in Rome. Augustus established strong defenses along the frontiers of the Roman Empire and kept the provinces under control. He began to develop a civil service staffed by skilled administrators to govern the empire more effectively. During what came to be known as the Age of Augustus, Roman trade, art, and literature flourished.

Augustus died in A.D. 14 and was succeeded by his stepson Tiberius. Tiberius and the other relatives of Augustus who ruled after him were known as the Julio-Claudians. They ruled Rome until 68. In the Year of the Four Emperors in 69, four generals stationed around the empire made claims to the throne. The governor of Judea, Vespasian, emerged victorious. He and his two sons, Titus and Domitian, were known as the Flavians. They ruled until 96. Domitian ruled with excessive cruelty, but a kindly emperor named Nerva succeeded him

Growth of the Roman Empire By 133 B.C., Rome had expanded from the Italian Peninsula to control much of the northern Mediterranean coast and Carthage in northern Africa. Augustus, Rome's first emperor, added Egypt and other territories before his death in A.D. 14. By A.D. 117, the Roman Empire extended over half of Europe, much of the Middle East, and the north coast of Africa.

WORLD BOOK map

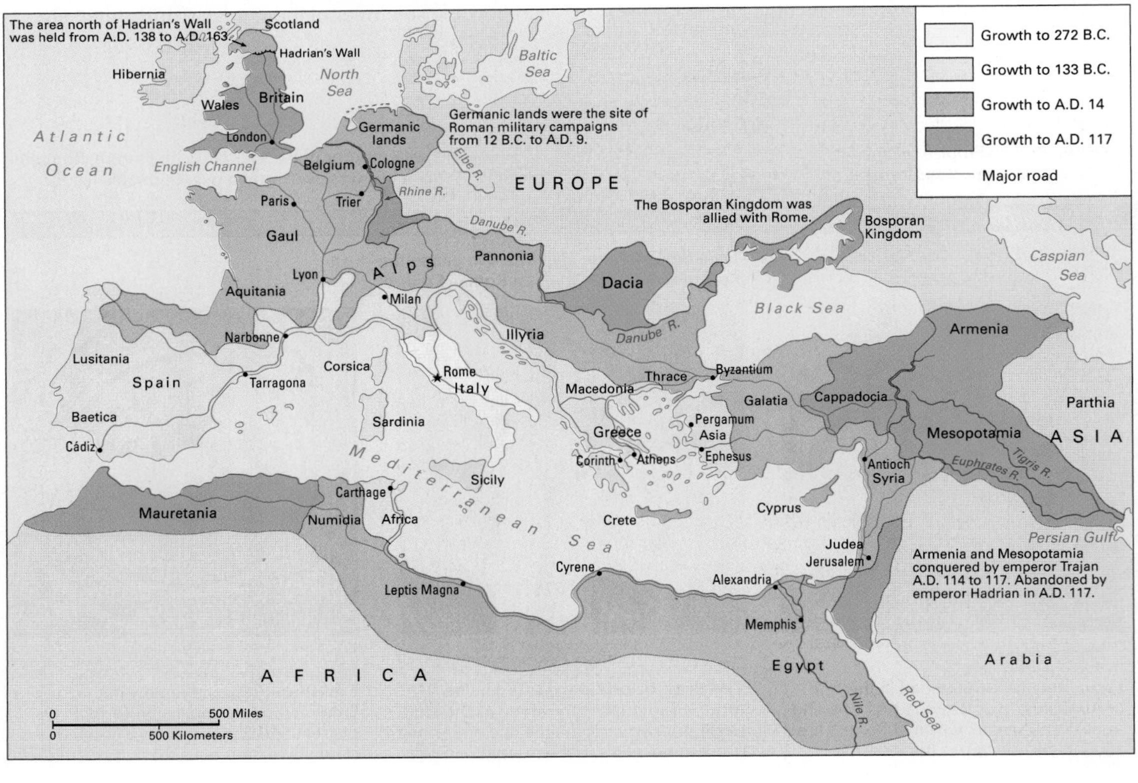

Division of the Roman Empire

In 395, the Roman Empire split into the West Roman Empire and the East Roman Empire. Each empire was subdivided into two parts called *prefectures.* The West Roman Empire soon fell to Germanic tribes. But the East Roman Empire survived as the Byzantine Empire until 1453.

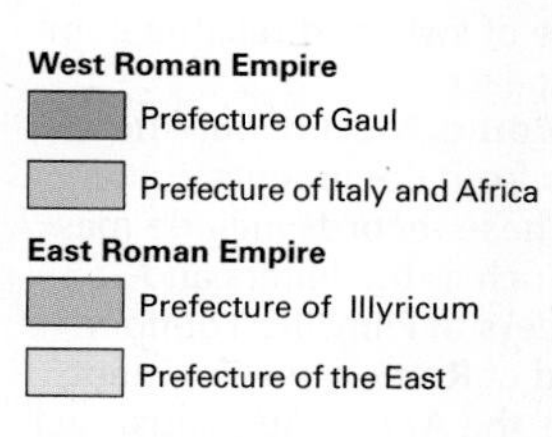

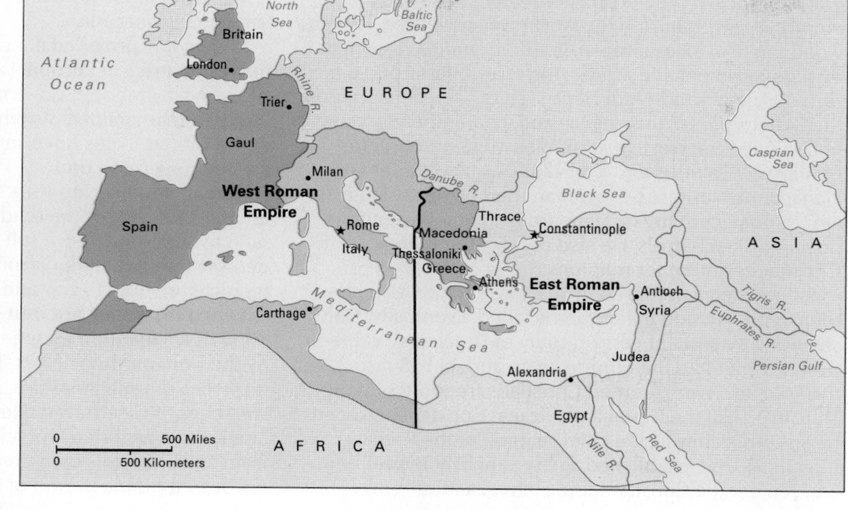

WORLD BOOK map

and brought an age of peace and prosperity. The Antonine rulers—from Nerva to Marcus Aurelius—were noted for their wisdom and ability.

Augustus had left strict instructions to his successors not to expand the empire. However, Claudius invaded Britain in 43. In northwestern Africa, Claudius added a region called Mauretania (now northern Morocco and western Algeria) to the empire. Trajan seized Dacia in eastern Europe in 106. Hadrian returned to the policy of Augustus. He marked the limits of Rome's empire with artificial frontiers on the Danube River, in northern Africa, and elsewhere. In northern Britain, he constructed Hadrian's Wall, parts of which still stand.

The expansion of the empire gave wealthy Romans new opportunities for investment. Both small farms and large estates thrived. Roman roads, built initially to speed troop movements, made trade and communication easier. The Romans erected imposing towns and cities, even in such remote areas as northern and western Britain and Mauretania. The equites controlled the civil service, which became increasingly skilled at running the day-to-day business of the empire.

The decline of the empire. As time went on, the power of the emperors increased and the people became less politically active. The Roman Empire's enormous size hastened its decline. One man in Rome could no longer hold the empire together. The far-flung armies on Rome's borders were often more loyal to their commanders than to the emperor. Enemies of Rome, such as the Goths in central Europe and the Parthians in southwest Asia, mounted serious attacks.

In 161, Marcus Aurelius became emperor and defended the Roman Empire against attacks by Germanic tribes from the north and Parthians from the east. His son Commodus succeeded him in 180 but was killed in 192. Many rivals tried to claim the empire, and several emperors seized power by force. From 235 to 284, there were 19 different emperors, many of them army commanders whose troops named them emperor.

Diocletian, a Roman military officer, was proclaimed

Emperors of Rome

Name	Reign†	Name	Reign†	Name	Reign†	Name	Reign†
*Augustus	27 B.C.-A.D. 14	Didius Julianus	193	Tacitus	275-276	*Valentinian I (W)	364-375
*Tiberius	14-37	Septimius Severus	193-211	Florian	276	*Valens (E)	364-378
*Caligula	37-41	Caracalla	211-217	Probus	276-282	Gratian (W)	367-383
*Claudius	41-54	Macrinus	217-218	Carus	282-283	Valentinian II (W)	375-392
*Nero	54-68	Elagabalus	218-222	Carinus	283-285	Eugenius	392-394
Galba	68-69	Severus Alexander	222-235	Numerianus	283-284	*Theodosius I	379-395
Otho	69	Maximinus Thrax	235-238	*Diocletian (E)	284-305		
Vitellius	69	Gordian I and Gordian II	238	Maximian (W)	286-305	**Emperors of the West**	
*Vespasian	69-79	Pupienus	238	Constantius I (W)	305-306	Honorius	395-423
*Titus	79-81	Balbinus	238	Galerius	305-311	*Valentinian III	425-455
*Domitian	81-96	Gordian III	238-244	Severus	306-307	Petronius Maximus	455
Nerva	96-98	Philippus	244-249	*Constantine I	306-337	Avitus	455-456
*Trajan	98-117	Decius	249-251	Licinius	308-324	Majorian	457-461
*Hadrian	117-138	Gallus	251-253	Maximinus	310-313	Libius Severus	461-465
*Antoninus Pius	138-161	Aemilianus	253	Constantius II	337-361	Anthemius	467-472
*Marcus Aurelius	161-180	Valerian	253-260	Constantine II	337-340	Olybrius	472
Lucius Verus	161-169	*Gallienus	253-268	Constans	337-350	Glycerius	473-474
Commodus	180-192	Claudius II	268-270	*Julian	361-363	Julius Nepos	474-475
Pertinax	193	*Aurelian	270-275	Jovian	363-364	Romulus Augustulus	475-476

*Has a separate article in *World Book.*
†Rome was ruled by two emperors from 161 to 169 and by two or more emperors much of the time from 283 to 395. Sometimes, the empire's eastern (E) and western (W) parts were ruled by separate emperors. At other times, as many as four emperors ruled.

emperor in 284. Diocletian attempted to stabilize the empire by reorganizing the way it was governed. He divided the provinces into smaller units and gave each its own government and army. Diocletian established a *tetrarchy* (rule of four). Under this system, Diocletian ruled the eastern part of the empire and a co-emperor, Maximian, ruled the west. In addition, two *caesars* (junior emperors), Galerius and Constantius, ruled under Diocletian and Maximian. Diocletian tried unsuccessfully to aid Rome's economy by standardizing coinage and imposing price controls. He also persecuted followers of Christianity and other religions.

After Diocletian retired in 305, several men struggled to gain power, and the tetrarchy failed. Eventually, Constantine I, who had been a deputy of Diocletian, came to power. He united the empire again and, in 313 through the Edict of Milan, granted Christians freedom of worship. In 325, at the Council of Nicaea, Constantine recognized Christianity as the chief religion of the Roman Empire. In 330, he established a new capital at Byzantium and renamed it Constantinople (now Istanbul, Turkey).

After Constantine died in 337, his three sons and two of his nephews battled for control of the empire. In 361, Julian gained control. He became known as the Apostate —that is, the Forsaker of Beliefs—because he tried to curb the spread of Christianity and to restore traditional Roman religious practices. Later emperors, such as Theodosius, outlawed Roman and other non-Christian religious practices. After the death of Theodosius in 395, the empire was permanently split into the West Roman Empire, with its capital in Rome, and the East Roman Empire, with its capital in Constantinople.

The West Roman Empire steadily weakened. A Germanic people called the Vandals invaded Spain and later occupied northern Africa. The Visigoths, another Germanic group, invaded and looted the city of Rome under their leader Alaric in 410. In Britain, local peoples known as the Picts, Scots, and Saxons attacked the Roman troops. The emperor Honorius finally gave up Britain so he could use the troops elsewhere in the empire. A Vandal leader named Gaiseric (or Genseric) plundered the city of Rome again in 455. The empire's final collapse came in 476, when the German leader Odoacer overthrew the last Roman emperor. Ironically, Rome's last emperor was named Romulus Augustulus, after the founder of Rome and its first emperor.

The East Roman Empire survived and thrived as the Byzantine Empire. Its people continued to call themselves Romans. The Byzantine Empire lasted until 1453, when the Ottomans captured Constantinople and made it the capital of the Ottoman Empire.

The legacy of ancient Rome

The Roman heritage. Ancient Rome had a tremendous impact on the modern world. During the Middle Ages, which lasted from about the A.D. 400's through the 1400's, the Roman Catholic Church replaced the Roman Empire as the unifying force in Europe. The church used the Latin language and preserved the classics of Latin literature.

Latin remained the language of learned Europeans for over a thousand years after the fall of the West Roman Empire. The French, Spanish, Italian, and Portuguese languages developed from forms of Latin spoken in different parts of the Roman Empire. Many words in English come from Latin.

Roman law provided a model for the legal systems of many countries in Europe, Latin America, and South Africa. Many modern governments reflect the influence of the Roman political system. For example, the Senate of the United States government gets its name from Rome's governing body.

Roman engineering feats served as models for later engineers. Some of the roads, bridges, and aqueducts built by the Romans are still used today. The Romans demonstrated the importance of swift and reliable communication, both in war and peace.

Learning about ancient Rome. Most of our knowledge of ancient Rome comes from documents written by the Romans themselves. These records include masterpieces of Latin literature, such as the letters and speeches of Cicero or the letters of Pliny the Younger. The Roman historian Livy told of Rome's development from 753 B.C. to his own time, the Age of Augustus. Tacitus described the period of Roman history from the reign of Tiberius to that of Domitian. Suetonius Tranquillus wrote biographies of Roman rulers from Julius Caesar to Domitian. Leading generals wrote autobiographies that detailed their achievements. For example, Julius Caesar described his conquest of Gaul in his *Commentaries on the Gallic War.* Other types of written records include *epigraphic records* (documents engraved in stone), such as law codes, treaties, and decrees of the Roman Senate and the emperors.

Scholars also derive information from scenes carved on monuments in Roman times. Generals and emperors erected these monuments to celebrate victories and other important events. For example, Trajan's Column and the Column of Marcus Aurelius in Rome tell us much about the military campaigns of these leaders.

The remains of Roman towns and cities and other archaeological evidence also provide valuable information. In particular, the excavations at the towns of Pompeii and Herculaneum, buried when Mount Vesuvius erupted in A.D. 79, have revealed enormous amounts of detail regarding everyday life in Roman times.

Interest in the study of ancient Rome reawakened during the Renaissance, the great cultural movement that swept across Europe from the early 1300's to about 1600. The Renaissance began in Italy when scholars rediscovered the works of ancient Greek and Roman authors. The first major history of Rome in modern times was the British scholar Edward Gibbon's *The History of the Decline and Fall of the Roman Empire* (1776-1788). By the 1800's, the study of Rome and its language was considered an essential element of a young person's education. The German historian Theodor Mommsen, one of the great modern scholars of ancient Rome, wrote the influential *History of Rome* (1854-1856). Scholars of the 1900's and 2000's have benefited from new archaeological discoveries and modern approaches to the study of language and literature. They continue to produce many books annually on the history, politics, culture, and language of ancient Rome. Alex T. Nice

Related articles in *World Book* include:

Biographies

See the table *Emperors of Rome* with this article. For biographies of Roman authors, see the *Related articles* at the end of **Latin literature.** See also:

Agrippa, Marcus
Agrippina the Younger
Antony, Mark
Brutus, Marcus Junius
Caesar, Julius
Cassius Longinus, Gaius
Catiline
Cato, Marcus Porcius, the Elder
Cato, Marcus Porcius, the Younger
Cincinnatus, Lucius Quinctius
Coriolanus, Gaius Marcius
Crassus, Marcus Licinius
Fabius Maximus, Quintus
Galen
Gracchus brothers
Marius, Gaius
Octavia
Pilate, Pontius
Plotinus
Regulus, Marcus Atilius
Scipio Africanus, Publius Cornelius
Spartacus
Sulla, Lucius Cornelius

Buildings and works

Appian Way
Aqueduct
Archaeology (pictures)
Atrium
Basilica
Catacombs
Colosseum
Column
Forum, Roman
Pantheon
Road
Roman walls

Cities and regions

Galatia
Gaul
Herculaneum
Istanbul
Latium
Numidia
Pompeii
Rome (Ancient city: pictures)

Contributions to civilization

Architecture (Roman architecture)
Drama (Roman drama)
Exploration (The Romans)
Geology (The Romans)
History (The ancient Greeks and Romans)
Julian calendar
Justinian Code
Latin language
Latin literature
Law (Ancient Roman law)
Library (History)
Mythology
Oratory (Classical orators)
Painting
Postal services (Ancient times)
Roman numerals
Romance languages
Sculpture
Twelve Tables, Laws of the

Daily life

Augur
Bath (History)
Clothing (Rome)
Education (History)
Food (Civilization)
Furniture (In ancient Rome)
Gladiator
Lares and penates
Saturnalia
Sibyl
Toga

Government

Consul
Dictatorship
Equestrian order
Fasces
Legion
Patricians
Plebeians
Praetor
Praetorian Guard
Tribune
Triumvirate

History

See the *History* section of articles on countries that Rome ruled, such as **England** (History). See also:

Actium, Battle of
Barbarian
Byzantine Empire
Etruscans
Flag (pictures: Historical flags of the world)
Gallic Wars
Middle Ages (The fall of Rome)
Punic Wars
Romulus and Remus
Rubicon
Sabines
Ship (Roman ships; pictures)
World, History of the (The Romans)

Outline

I. The world of ancient Rome
A. The land
B. The people
II. Government
A. The Roman Republic
B. The Roman Empire
C. The law
D. The army
III. Way of life
A. City life
B. Rural life
C. Family life
D. Food
E. Clothing
F. Recreation
G. Religion
H. Education
IV. Arts and sciences
A. Architecture and engineering
B. Sculpture, painting, and mosaics
C. Literature
D. Science
V. Economy
A. Agriculture
B. Mining
C. Manufacturing
D. Trade
E. Transportation and communication
VI. History
VII. The legacy of ancient Rome
A. The Roman heritage
B. Learning about ancient Rome

Additional resources

Bunson, Matthew. *Encyclopedia of Ancient Rome.* 3rd ed. Facts on File, 2012.
Ermatinger, James W. *The World of Ancient Rome: A Daily Life Encyclopedia.* 2 vols. Greenwood, 2015.
Hamen, Susan E. *Ancient Rome.* Essential Lib., 2015.
Woolf, Alex. *Meet the Ancient Romans.* Gareth Stevens, 2015. Younger readers.

Rome, University of, is the largest university in Italy. Its official name is the Sapienza University of Rome. The university was founded in 1303 by Pope Boniface VIII. In the 1500's, the University of Rome became famous as a center for the study of medicine and other sciences. The Italian government has controlled the university since 1870. The website of the University of Rome at https://www.uniroma1.it/ offers additional information.

P. A. McGinley

See also **Rome** (picture: The University of Rome).

Romeo and Juliet is a famous tragedy written by the English playwright William Shakespeare. The play was probably first performed in 1596 and was first published in 1597.

Romeo and Juliet portrays two young lovers in Verona, Italy. They are caught in a bitter feud between their families, the Montagues and the Capulets. Romeo, a Montague, and his friends come uninvited to a masked ball given by the Capulets. At the ball, Romeo meets Juliet, a Capulet. They fall in love. The next day, the couple are secretly married by Friar Laurence. Returning from the wedding, Romeo meets Juliet's cousin Tybalt, who tries to pick a fight with him. But Romeo refuses to fight his new relative. To defend the Montague honor, Romeo's friend Mercutio accepts Tybalt's challenge. As Romeo attempts to part the young men, Tybalt stabs and kills Mercutio. In revenge, Romeo kills Tybalt. The Prince of Verona is furious at the violence and exiles Romeo from the city.

Juliet's father, unaware that Juliet is already married, tries to force her to marry a kinsman named Paris. To allow Juliet to escape from her father's demand, Friar Laurence gives her a drug that puts her into a deathlike sleep. The friar sends a messenger to the exiled Romeo to tell him of the drug. But the messenger is delayed. Romeo hears that Juliet is dead and hurries to the tomb where she has been placed. There, he takes poison and dies by Juliet's side. Juliet awakens to find her husband dead and stabs herself. The discovery of the dead lovers convinces the two families that they must end their feud.

The popularity of *Romeo and Juliet* owes much to Shakespeare's sympathy for the young lovers in the play. Shakespeare does not present Romeo and Juliet as responsible for their fate. Instead, the play draws attention to the violence and aggressiveness that shape the adult world of the feuding aristocratic families. The success of the play also comes from the clearly drawn characters and liveliness and beauty of its language.

The story of *Romeo and Juliet* has inspired a number of other artistic works. They include a symphonic poem by the French composer Hector Berlioz and an opera by another French composer, Charles Gounod. The play inspired an overture by the Russian composer Peter Tchaikovsky and a ballet by another Russian composer, Sergei Prokofiev. *West Side Story,* a popular stage musical that opened on Broadway in 1957, is also based on Shakespeare's tragedy. The American composer Leonard Bernstein wrote the music for *West Side Story.* Stephen Sondheim, another American composer, wrote the words. *Romeo and Juliet* has also been filmed several times. Michael Seidel

Romero, Saint Óscar Arnulfo (1917-1980), served as archbishop of San Salvador, the capital of El Salvador, from 1977 until his death. As archbishop, he was the highest official of the Roman Catholic Church in the country.

Romero at first avoided becoming involved in political affairs. But in time he came to believe that the Roman Catholic Church should take an active role in bringing social justice to the people. Romero became an outspoken critic of the violence and human rights abuses that the military government of El Salvador committed against its citizens and opponents. On March 24, 1980, he was assassinated by an unknown gunman while celebrating Mass. Romero's death became a symbol for those who sought peace and change in the country.

Óscar Arnulfo Romero y Galdámez was born on Aug. 15, 1917, in Ciudad Barrios, El Salvador, near the city of San Miguel. He was ordained as a priest in 1942. From 1968 to 1972, Romero served as executive secretary to the Central American Bishop's Secretariat. In 1974, he became bishop of Santiago de María. Romero was *canonized* (declared a saint) by Pope Francis in 2018.

Morris J. Blachman

Rommel, *RAW muhl,* **Erwin** (1891-1944), a German field marshal, was one of the most brilliant generals of World War II (1939-1945). He led the Afrikakorps, and his clever tactics earned him the nickname "the Desert Fox." But in 1942, British forces stopped him in Egypt. In 1944, Rommel led some of the troops that opposed the Allied invasion of Normandy in France. After he recognized the significance of the superiority of the Allied air forces, he reported to German dictator Adolf Hitler that it was futile for Germany to continue the war.

Rommel was implicated in the plot to kill Hitler in July 1944. Rommel was given his choice of trial or poison. He chose death by poison. He took the poison and died on Oct. 14, 1944. Rommel was born on Nov. 15, 1891, in Heidenheim, Germany. Donald M. McKale

Romney, Mitt (1947-), an American politician, was the Republican nominee for president of the United States in the 2012 election. He lost the election to President Barack Obama. He served as governor of Massachusetts from 2003 to 2007. He also had a successful career in business. By securing the Republican nomination in 2012, Romney became the first member of the Mormon Church to become a major party's presidential nominee. In 2018, Romney won an election to represent Utah in the U.S. Senate.

Abby Brack, Romney for President, Inc.

Mitt Romney

Early life and family. Willard Mitt Romney was born in Detroit on March 12, 1947. His father, George W. Romney, served as governor of Michigan from 1963 to 1969 and as U.S. secretary of housing and urban development from 1969 to 1973. His mother, Lenore LaFount Romney, ran unsuccessfully for a Michigan seat in the U.S. Senate in 1970.

Romney enrolled at Stanford University in 1965 but left after his freshman year. In 1966, he went to France to do missionary work for the Mormon Church. He returned from France in 1968.

Mitt Romney met Ann Davies while the two were in elementary school. Mitt proposed to Ann in 1965, at his high school senior prom. The couple married in 1969. They have five sons: Tagg, Matt, Josh, Ben, and Craig.

Mitt Romney graduated from Brigham Young University in 1971. He earned a master's degree from Harvard Business School and a law degree from Harvard Law School in 1975.

Business career. In 1977, Romney joined the management consulting firm Bain & Company. He soon became a vice president of the firm. In 1984, Romney and partners of Bain & Company cofounded Bain Capital, a private investment firm. Romney earned great wealth in business.

From 1999 to 2002, Romney was president of the Salt Lake Organizing Committee for the 2002 Winter Olympic Games in Salt Lake City, Utah. Before Romney took over, the project was troubled by scandal and financial problems. Romney gained national attention for helping make the games a financial and critical success. Romney wrote a book, *Turnaround: Crisis, Leadership, and the Olympic Games* (2004), describing his efforts.

Political career. In 1994, Romney won the Republican nomination for a Massachusetts seat in the U.S. Senate. That November, he lost the election to long-time incumbent Senator Edward "Ted" Kennedy.

Romney won election as governor of Massachusetts in 2002. As governor, he worked to eliminate large budget deficits and to improve the state's education system. He proposed and signed into law a measure to provide health care for uninsured Massachusetts residents.

Romney did not seek reelection as governor in 2006. In 2007, he began campaigning for the 2008 Republican presidential nomination. He dropped out of the race in February 2008, however, after losing most nominating contests to Arizona Senator John McCain.

In 2011, Romney declared his candidacy for the 2012 Republican nomination for president. Romney clinched the nomination in May 2012. He outlasted his main opponents, former Pennsylvania Senator Rick Santorum, former Speaker of the House Newt Gingrich of Georgia, and U.S. Representative Ron Paul of Texas.

At the Republican National Convention, delegates nominated Romney for president and U.S. Representative Paul Ryan for vice president. Romney and Ryan then ran against the Democratic nominees, President Obama and Vice President Joe Biden, in the general election.

During the campaign, Romney and Obama fiercely debated a variety of issues. Chief topics included tax policy, the role of government, health care reform, and foreign affairs. In the November election, Obama defeated Romney to retain the presidency.

In June 2018, Romney won the Republican nomination for a U.S. Senate seat. Romney had begun his campaign after Orrin Hatch, a longtime Utah senator, had stated he would not seek reelection. In November, Romney easily won election to the Senate. Jeremy D. Mayer

See also **Obama, Barack; President of the United States; Republican Party.**

Romulus and Remus, *RAHM yuh luhs, REE muhs,* in Roman mythology, were twin brothers who founded the city of Rome. The Romans considered Romulus their first king.

According to tradition, Romulus and Remus were born in the ancient Italian city of Alba Longa. King Numitor ruled it until Amulius, his younger brother, deposed him. Amulius killed Numitor's sons and forced Rhea Silvia, Numitor's daughter, to become a Vestal Virgin. Vestal Virgins were priestesses who were required by law to remain virgins. Amulius hoped that Rhea Silvia's being a Vestal Virgin would prevent her from bearing children who might threaten his rule. But the god Mars seduced Rhea Silvia, and she gave birth to Romulus and Remus. Amulius had her executed and ordered the babies placed in a basket and thrown into the Tiber River.

After floating downstream, the twins washed ashore. A female wolf found the infants and nursed them.

A shepherd named Faustulus discovered Romulus and Remus. Faustulus and his wife raised the boys as their own children. After the twins became young men, they learned their true identity. They overthrew Amulius, killed him, and restored Numitor to the throne.

Soon, Romulus and Remus set out to found their own city. But the brothers quarreled over the site where the city should be built. To settle the argument, they agreed that the one who saw the largest number of vultures in flight should choose the site. Romulus claimed he saw 12 vultures, which he declared was a sign from the gods that his location was the right one. Remus, who saw only 6 vultures, thought his brother had cheated. After Romulus began to build a wall around his chosen site, Remus leaped over the ditch that was to hold the foundation of the wall. As he did so, he mocked Romulus. For this act of disloyalty, Remus was killed, either by Romulus or by one of Romulus's followers. Romulus then became the sole ruler of the city, which he named *Rome* for himself.

Rome prospered, but only men lived there. To provide wives for his subjects, Romulus had women kidnapped from the neighboring Sabine people (see **Sabines**). Romulus was a wise and popular ruler and a fine military leader. He made Rome into the most powerful city in its region. After a long reign, Romulus disappeared mysteriously during a storm. According to a later myth, he became the god Quirinus.

Romulus, Remus, and the wolf became popular subjects for Roman artists. Several ancient statues show the babies with their animal protector. Daniel P. Harmon

See also **Mythology** (Roman mythology); **Rome, Ancient** (picture: The legendary founders of Rome).

Romulus Augustulus, *ROM yuh luhs aw GUHS chuh luhs* (A.D. 460?-500?), was the last emperor of the West Roman Empire. He reigned from A.D. 475 to 476, when the empire collapsed. Although his name actually was Romulus Augustus, he became known as Romulus *Augustulus. Augustus* means *the revered. Augustulus,* a scornful term, means *little Augustus.*

Historians do not know exactly when or where Romulus Augustulus was born. His father, a Roman military official named Orestes, overthrew Julius Nepos, the West Roman emperor, in 475 and replaced him with Romulus Augustulus. By that time, the position of West Roman emperor was extremely weak. Based in Ravenna, in northeastern Italy, the emperor controlled only Italy and a small area of southern Gaul (now mostly France).

In the summer of 476, when *barbarian* (non-Roman) troops who had served Rome demanded land in Italy as their payment, Orestes influenced his son to refuse them. The troops' leader, Odoacer, then killed Orestes and deposed Romulus, but he spared Romulus's life because of his youth. In September 476, Odoacer sent Romulus to live with relatives in the Campania region of southern Italy. Historians do not know how much longer Romulus lived. His death is unrecorded.

Odoacer made the Roman Senate tell Zeno, the East Roman emperor, of Romulus's removal. The Senate also told Zeno a West Roman emperor was no longer needed. Odoacer then took over Italy. Richard J. A. Talbert

See also **Odoacer; Rome, Ancient** (The decline of the empire).

Ronaldinho, *hoh nahl JEEN yoo* or *rah nahl DEEN yoh* (1980-), a Brazilian-born soccer star, became one of the greatest players of the early 2000's. Soccer is called *football* in much of the world. In 2004 and 2005, Ronaldinho was named World Player of the Year by the Fédération Internationale de Football Association (FIFA), the governing body of international soccer.

Ronaldinho, a left wing and attacking midfielder, starred for FC Barcelona in Spain's La Liga from 2003 to 2008. La Liga is the top league in Spanish soccer. The *FC* in the name of the team stands for *football club.* Ronaldinho helped Barcelona win the La Liga title in 2005 and 2006 and the European Champions League title in 2006.

Ronaldo de Assis Moreira was born on March 21, 1980, in Pôrto Alegre, Brazil. He acquired the nickname *Ronaldinho,* Portuguese for "Little Ronaldo," because he was often the smallest player in youth club competition.

Ronaldinho began playing organized soccer in 1987 and showed skill as a scorer by age 13. He began his career in professional soccer with the Grêmio youth squad in Pôrto Alegre in 1998 and played there for three seasons. Ronaldinho joined Paris Saint-Germain in France in 2001. In 2003, he moved to FC Barcelona in Spain. In 2008, he joined AC Milan in Italy's top-rated Serie A league. *AC* stands for *Associazione Calcio,* meaning *football association.* From 2011 through 2015, Ronaldinho played for professional clubs in Brazil and Mexico.

In addition to excelling in league play, Ronaldinho starred in international competition. He was a member of the Brazilian national team in the 2000 and 2008 Summer Olympic Games and played on the 2002 Brazilian team that won the FIFA World Cup. He was captain of the Brazilian team that won the Confederations Cup international tournament in 2005. Neil Milbert

Ronaldo (1976-), a Brazilian soccer star, was one of the sport's greatest and most exciting players. Soccer is called *football* in Brazil and many other countries. A forward, Ronaldo became internationally famous for his speed and his brilliance as a goal scorer. He was named World Player of the Year in 1996, 1997, and 2002. Ronaldo led Brazil to the World Cup championship in 2002, scoring both goals in his country's 2-0 victory over Germany in the final game. He set a FIFA World Cup record in 2006 when he scored his 15th career goal in the tournament. The record stood until Miroslav Klose scored his 16th career World Cup goal for Germany in 2014. FIFA (Fédération Internationale de Football Association) is the governing body of the sport. Ronaldo played in 98 international matches for Brazil and scored 63 goals.

Ronaldo Luiz Nazario de Lima was born in Bento Ribeiro, Brazil, a poor suburb of Rio de Janeiro, on Sept. 22, 1976. He grew up in Bento Ribeiro and began playing soccer as a child. Ronaldo became a full-time player at the age of about 14. His reputation grew rapidly, and in 1993 he joined Cruzeiro, a first-division club in Belo Horizonte. Ronaldo went on to play with PSV Eindhoven in the Netherlands from 1994 to 1996, FC Barcelona in Spain in 1996 and 1997, and Inter Milan in Italy from 1997 to 2002. He played with Real Madrid in Spain from 2002 to 2007, when he moved to AC Milan in Italy to end the 2006-2007 season. After an injury shortened his 2007-2008 season, Ronaldo returned to his native Brazil to play for Corinthians in the Brazilian A league for the remainder of his career. Citing recurring injuries, Ronaldo retired as a player in 2011. Neil Milbert

© Denis Doyle, Getty Images

Ronaldo, a Brazilian soccer star, became one of the sport's greatest players. A forward, Ronaldo was famous for his speed and for his brilliance as a goal scorer.

Ronaldo, *roo NAHL doh,* **Cristiano,** *kree stee AH noh* (1985-), a Portuguese soccer star, is one of the greatest players in the world. Soccer is called *football* in much of the world. Ronaldo, a forward and midfielder, gained international fame for his speed, his accuracy shooting with either foot, and his exciting playing style. In 2008, Ronaldo was named World Player of the Year by the Fédération Internationale de Football Association (FIFA), the governing body of international soccer. Also in 2008, he received the *Ballon d'Or* (Golden Ball) award as the world's outstanding player. He won the award again in 2013, 2014, 2016, and 2017. In 2021, Ronaldo set the men's record for most career international goals.

Cristiano Ronaldo dos Santos Aveiro was born on the island of Madeira on Feb. 5, 1985. Madeira is one of the Madeira Islands, which lie off the northwest coast of Africa and belong to Portugal. He began playing amateur soccer at the age of 8. In 2002-2003, he played for the Sporting Club of Portugal, a major Portuguese team.

From 2003 to 2009, Ronaldo played for Manchester United in England's Premier League. In 2008, he helped the team win the Premier League title, the Union of European Football Associations (UEFA) Champions League title, and the FIFA Club World Cup. In 2009, he left Manchester United to play for Real Madrid in La Liga, the top league in Spanish soccer. During the 2010-2011 season, Ronaldo set a team scoring record of 53 goals and a La Liga record of 40 goals. With Ronaldo, Real Madrid won La Liga in 2012 and 2017, the Club World Cup in 2014, and the Champions League in 2014 and 2016.

Ronaldo has served as captain of the Portuguese national team since 2008. In 2016, he helped Portugal win its first UEFA European Championship. In 2018, Ronaldo joined Juventus FC in Turin, Italy. Ronaldo returned to Manchester United in 2021. Neil Milbert

Ronsard, *rawn SAR,* **Pierre de,** *pyair duh* (1524-1585), often called the Prince of Poets, led an influential group of French poets called the *Pléiade.* The *Sonnets for Hélène* (1578), perhaps his best-known work, explored the joys and sorrows of love in masterful and descriptive verse. Ronsard's *Odes* (1550-1556) were inspired by Greek and Latin poetry. Ronsard wrote many volumes of love poetry in addition to the *Sonnets for Hélène,* and he wrote the moral and philosophical *Hymnes* (1555-1556). In *Discours* (1560-1563), he wrote stirring attacks against the Protestant movement during the religious wars that shook France in the 1560's.

Ronsard was born on Sept. 11, 1524, near Vendôme, France. He trained to be a diplomat. He turned to literature after he became partially deaf. Ronsard died on Dec. 27, 1585. Robert B. Griffin

See also **French literature** (The Pléiade).

Roof is the cover of any building. The term also includes the materials that support the roof. Climate often determines the design of roofs. Ancient Syrians and Egyptians used flat roofs because of the hot sun and the lack of rain. Steep, sloping roofs covered the homes of central Europe to help drain off heavy rains.

There are many variations of flat and sloping roofs. A *gable* roof has two sides sloping up to a center ridge. The *hip* roof has four sides sloping up from all four walls. The *lean-to* is a single slope over a small building, usually set against a larger building. A *gambrel* roof has two added ridges parallel to the center gable ridge,

Types of roofs

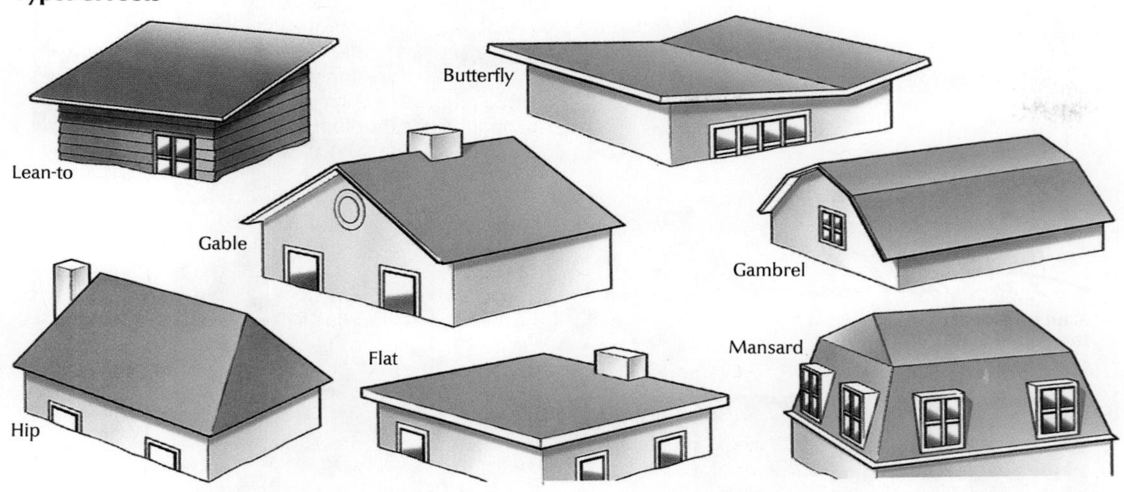

WORLD BOOK illustrations by Oxford Illustrators Limited

making steep slopes below each side of the upper, flatter slopes. *Mansard* roofs also have ridges below the center one, but on four sides, like the hip roof. Water is drained beyond the walls of a building by the *eaves* (overhang) of the roof. Jack M. Landers

See also **Architecture** (pictures); **House; Shelter.**

Rook, also called the Eurasian rook, is a bird found in Europe and Asia. It is a kind of crow. But unlike other crows, the rook has a purple gloss on its black plumage. It feeds mostly on insects and grain. When rooks reach adulthood, about 1 year old, they shed the feathers of their face, which then becomes a grayish-white color. Rooks measure about 18 inches (46 centimeters) long.

Rooks nest in communities of many hundreds, known as *rookeries.* Rooks that nest in central Europe remain in the same region all year. Those that nest farther north migrate southward for the winter. Tame rooks sometimes learn to imitate human speech. Martha Hatch Balph

See also **Crow.**

Scientific classification. The rook is *Corvus frugilegus.*

Rooney, Wayne (1985-), is an English soccer star. Soccer is called *football* in many countries. A forward, Rooney created a sensation in English soccer while he was only 16 years old. On Oct. 19, 2002, he became the youngest goal scorer in Football Association Premier League history. In 2003, Rooney became the youngest player ever to compete on an English national team. His reputation grew in 2004 when he scored four goals at the Euro 2004 international tournament. He was selected Player of the Year in England in 2008 and 2009.

Wayne Mark Rooney was born on Oct. 24, 1985, in Liverpool, England. He made his professional debut in 2002 with Everton. He signed with Manchester United in 2004, a widely publicized deal that made him one of the highest-paid players in world soccer. In 2020, Rooney began playing for Derby County FC of the English Football League Championship, the second tier of professional soccer in the United Kingdom. Neil Milbert

Roosevelt, *ROH zuh vehlt,* **Eleanor** (1884-1962), the wife of President Franklin D. Roosevelt, became a distinguished public figure in her own right. She was one of the most active first ladies in United States history. Roosevelt, a niece of President Theodore Roosevelt, won fame for her humanitarian work and became a role model for women in politics and public affairs.

Eleanor Roosevelt was born on Oct. 11, 1884, in New York City. She was named Anna Eleanor Roosevelt. But her family called her Eleanor, and she rarely used her real first name. In 1905, she married Franklin D. Roosevelt, a distant cousin. She began to work politically on his behalf after polio disabled him in 1921. During Franklin Roosevelt's terms as governor of New York and, later, as president, she frequently made fact-finding trips for him. While first lady, she traveled nationwide on lecture tours, held 350 press conferences for women reporters only, and wrote a daily newspaper column and many articles for magazines. She also worked with young people and the poor and fought for equal rights for minority groups and women.

Karsh, Ottawa

Eleanor Roosevelt

After her husband died in 1945, Roosevelt became a delegate to the United Nations (UN) General Assembly. In 1946, she was elected chairman of the UN's Human Rights Commission. She helped draft the Universal Declaration of Human Rights (see **Human Rights, Universal Declaration of**). She returned to the General Assembly in 1961. Later that year, President John F. Kennedy appointed her head of the Commission on the Status of Women.

Eleanor Roosevelt wrote several books. They include *This Is My Story* (1937), *This I Remember* (1950), *On My Own* (1958), and *Tomorrow Is Now* (published in 1963, after her death). She died on Nov. 7, 1962. Patrick J. Maney

See also **First ladies of the United States** (picture); **Roosevelt, Franklin Delano.**

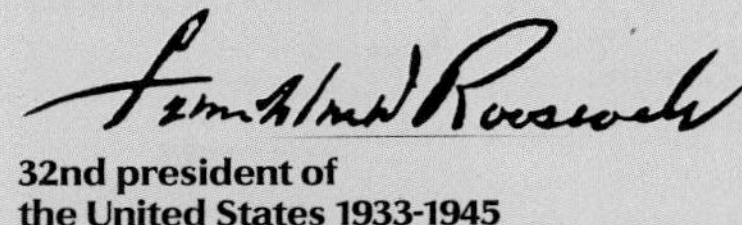

32nd president of the United States 1933-1945

Hoover
31st president
1929-1933
Republican

F. D. Roosevelt
32nd president
1933-1945
Democrat

Truman
33rd president
1945-1953
Democrat

John N. Garner
Vice president
1933-1941

Henry A. Wallace
Vice president
1941-1945

Harry S. Truman
Vice president
1945

United Press Int.

Roosevelt, *ROH zuh vehlt,* **Franklin Delano,** *FRANK lihn DEHL uh noh* (1882-1945), was the 32nd president of the United States. Roosevelt, a Democrat, held the office from 1933 to 1945. He was elected president four times and occupied the White House for over 12 years—longer than any other president in American history. Roosevelt led the United States through two of the greatest crises in the country's history: the Great Depression of the 1930's and World War II (1939-1945).

During the Depression, the United States and countries throughout the world struggled with high unemployment and declining business activity. Roosevelt led an ambitious government program—known as the New Deal—to help relieve economic distress (see **Great Depression; New Deal**). During World War II, he led the nation in a successful military operation that had farther-reaching consequences than any other war effort in history (see **World War II**). Roosevelt died in 1945, three months after the start of his fourth term. Since that time, historians have often ranked him, along with George Washington and Abraham Lincoln, as one of the nation's greatest presidents.

Roosevelt was born into a wealthy and socially prominent New York family. He was a distant cousin of Theodore Roosevelt, president of the United States from 1901 to 1909. Franklin's admiration of his cousin inspired his own entry into politics. Before becoming president, Franklin served in the New York State Senate, as assistant secretary of the U.S. Navy, and as governor of New York.

A new era in American history began under Roosevelt. For the first time, the federal government took strong action in an attempt to restore a troubled economy. Roosevelt said he wanted to help the average American, whom he called the "forgotten man." He promised relief for unemployed workers and struggling farmers.

Under Roosevelt's leadership, the government put stronger controls on business and finance than ever before. The government spent billions of dollars on relief and public works, and it set up dozens of new agencies. Many of the agencies became known mainly by their initials. They included the WPA (Works Progress Administration), CCC (Civilian Conservation Corps), TVA (Tennessee Valley Authority), and NRA (National Recovery Administration). Roosevelt himself became widely known as FDR.

President Roosevelt was both bitterly hated and deeply loved. Critics charged that his policies gave the federal government too much power. They accused Roosevelt of taking over many rights that should have belonged to the states. Many Americans thought his government controls over business threatened the country's *free enterprise* system—a system that traditionally allows people to carry out economic activities free from government control. However, millions of Roosevelt's supporters considered him a friend and protector of the "common man."

Roosevelt's cheerful personality and optimistic outlook helped give hope to a troubled nation. He had two famous "trademarks." They were the glasses that he

The Great Depression created widespread unemployment throughout the United States.

The attack on Pearl Harbor led the United States into World War II.

The world of President Franklin D. Roosevelt

Nazi leader Adolf Hitler ruled Germany from 1933 until his death in 1945. His expansionist policies led to World War II, and his anti-Semitism resulted in the killing of about 6 million Jews in Germany and German-controlled countries.
Dust storms in the Great Plains in the 1930's blew away precious topsoil and led to the ruin of many farm families. Some migrated to California. Their plight was told in John Steinbeck's novel *The Grapes of Wrath,* published in 1939.
Labor leader John L. Lewis formed the Committee for Industrial Organization (CIO) in 1935 to organize workers in the steel, rubber, automobile, and other industries.
Italian dictator Benito Mussolini conquered Ethiopia in 1936 and joined with Germany and Japan in World War II.
Edward VIII gave up the British throne in 1936 to marry Wallis Warfield Simpson, an American divorcee.
American track star Jesse Owens became a hero when he won four gold medals at the 1936 Olympics in Berlin.
The Spanish Civil War raged from 1936 to 1939 and ended in a victory for the rebel forces of Francisco Franco.
American aviator Amelia Earhart crashed into the Pacific and died in 1937 during an attempted around-the-world flight.
The "big band" era of popular music featured groups led by Glenn Miller, Count Basie, Tommy and Jimmy Dorsey, and Duke Ellington. Clarinetist Benny Goodman became known as the "King of Swing," and Americans enjoyed such dance crazes as the big apple and the jitterbug.
Research on the atomic bomb advanced after Dec. 2, 1942, when workers at the University of Chicago produced the first artificially created nuclear chain reaction.
Women joined the American work force in unprecedented numbers during World War II. "Rosie the Riveter" was a nickname that symbolized the millions of women working in wartime industries.

Library of Congress; Wide World

wore clipped to the bridge of his nose and the cigarette holder that jutted upward from his mouth.

People in all parts of the world admired Roosevelt for his personal courage. At the age of 39, polio almost completely paralyzed the main muscles below his waist. Still, he refused to give up his career of public service. During his presidency, most people knew he had developed polio. The extent of his disability, however, was largely hidden from the public.

Early life and family

Boyhood. Franklin Delano Roosevelt was born on Jan. 30, 1882, in the village of Hyde Park, New York. The family estate, called Springwood, was on the east bank of the Hudson River. Franklin was the only child of James Roosevelt and Sara Delano, both descendants of prominent families that had arrived in America before the American Revolution (1775-1783).

James was 53 years old when Franklin was born. He dabbled in business but devoted most of his time to running the family estate. James was in poor health during Franklin's youth, but he remained active in local affairs. He served as an official at the nearby St. James' Episcopal Church. Sara was 26 when she gave birth to Franklin. She was strong, intelligent, and confident of her values and way of life. Franklin had a half-brother, James Roosevelt Roosevelt, the son of James and his first wife, Rebecca Brien Howland, who had died in 1876.

Important dates in Roosevelt's life

1882	(Jan. 30) Born in Hyde Park, New York.
1905	(March 17) Married Eleanor Roosevelt.
1913	Appointed assistant secretary of the Navy.
1920	Ran unsuccessfully for vice president of the United States.
1921	Stricken with polio.
1928	Elected governor of New York.
1932	Elected president of the United States.
1936	Reelected president.
1940	Reelected president.
1944	Reelected president.
1945	(April 12) Died in Warm Springs, Georgia.

Springwood, oil painting on canvas by I. V. Lounsbery; Franklin D. Roosevelt Library, Hyde Park, New York

Franklin D. Roosevelt's birthplace was this house at Springwood, the family estate on the Hudson River in Hyde Park, New York. This painting shows the house as it looked before 1900.

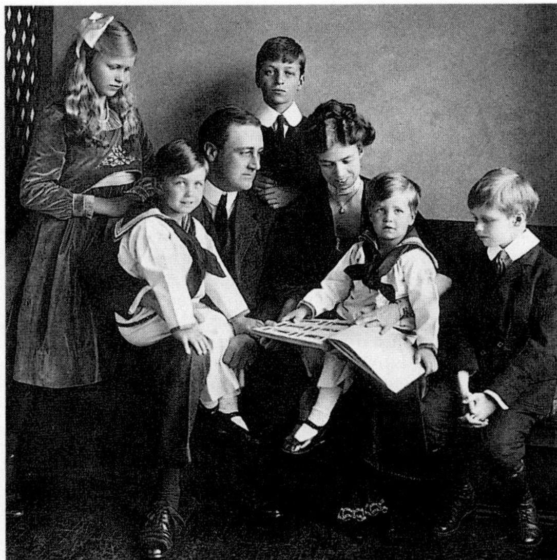

Bachrach

The Roosevelt family posed for this photograph in 1919. Franklin and Eleanor Roosevelt are surrounded by, *left to right,* Anna, Franklin Delano, Jr., Elliott, John, and James.

Outline

Franklin grew up with all the advantages that wealth and social standing could bring. By the age of 10, he had met the American writer Mark Twain, President Grover Cleveland, and members of European royalty. By the age of 15, he had traveled to Europe eight times.

Franklin's parents raised him with loving firmness. They taught him that a gentleman cares for the poor, does not flaunt his wealth, and does not burden others with his problems.

Education. As a boy, Franklin was schooled by tutors and had few friends his own age. In 1896, at the age of 14, Roosevelt entered Groton School, an exclusive boarding academy near Boston. Groton sought to prepare its students for positions of leadership in society. Roosevelt made good grades but remained something of an outsider among his fellow students.

In 1900, Roosevelt enrolled at Harvard University. He majored in history, but his real interests lay outside the classroom. He joined a number of social clubs and earned some campus fame as editor of the school newspaper, *The Crimson.*

After graduating from Harvard, Roosevelt entered Columbia Law School, but he withdrew before completing his degree. He had learned enough, however, to pass the state bar examination. He took a position as managing clerk with a New York City law firm before pursuing a career in politics.

Roosevelt's family. Roosevelt and his distant cousin Eleanor Roosevelt (1884-1962) had known each other slightly since childhood. He began to court her seriously while at Harvard, and in 1903, they became engaged. Franklin and Eleanor married on March 17, 1905. President Theodore Roosevelt, Eleanor's uncle, gave the bride away. See **Roosevelt, Eleanor.**

The Roosevelts had six children: Anna Eleanor (1906-1975); James (1907-1991); Franklin Delano, Jr. (who died in infancy in 1909); Elliott (1910-1990); Franklin Delano, Jr. (1914-1988); and John (1916-1981). James and Franklin, Jr., both served in the U.S. House of Representatives.

Entry into politics

State senator. Since his teens, Roosevelt had idolized his cousin Theodore. So when an opportunity presented itself, Franklin launched his own career in politics. Theodore was a Republican, but Franklin followed his father by joining the Democratic Party.

In 1910, Roosevelt accepted an invitation from state Democratic leaders to run for a seat in the New York State Senate. Republicans had dominated the district for over 50 years, and it seemed unlikely that an inexperienced Democrat could win. But Roosevelt appealed to voters with his earnestness and energy. He spoke out against corruption in government and "big-city bosses." The Republicans, meanwhile, suffered from divisions within the party. Roosevelt surprised veteran politicians by winning the election.

Roosevelt took his seat in the State Senate in January 1911. Early in his term, Roosevelt led an effort to defeat a U.S. Senate candidate favored by Tammany Hall, the powerful Democratic group in New York City. At that time, the state legislatures elected U.S. senators. Roosevelt's action brought him great publicity, yet some of his colleagues found him arrogant. Louis McHenry Howe, a reporter, saw promise in Roosevelt and quickly became his most valuable adviser.

Assistant secretary of the Navy. In 1912, Roosevelt endorsed Democrat Woodrow Wilson for the presiden-

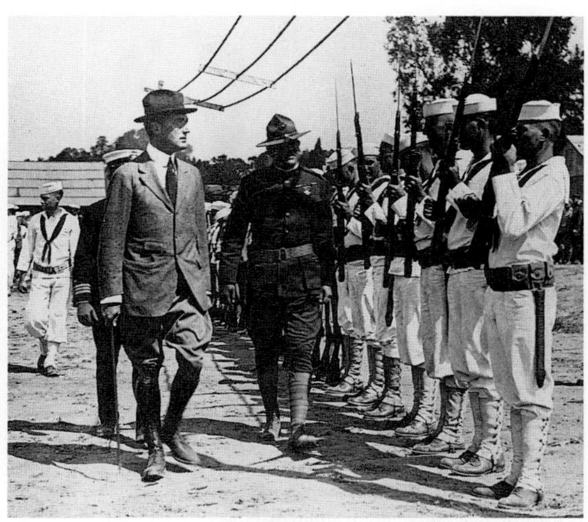

Franklin D. Roosevelt Library

As assistant secretary of the Navy, Roosevelt reviewed the troops at a U.S. naval air station in France in 1918. President Woodrow Wilson had appointed Roosevelt in 1913.

cy. After Wilson was elected, he appointed Roosevelt assistant secretary of the Navy. Roosevelt was an outspoken supporter of naval expansion and called for a larger role for the United States in world affairs. He sometimes said things that set him at odds with his boss, Secretary of the Navy Josephus Daniels. But Daniels recognized Roosevelt's talent and taught him much about national politics.

In 1914, Roosevelt sought the Democratic nomination for a U.S. Senate seat from New York. However, Tammany Hall strongly opposed him, and Roosevelt lost by a wide margin.

The United States entered World War I (1914-1918) in April 1917. Roosevelt wanted to serve in the military, but Daniels persuaded him to stay at his desk. In 1918, Roosevelt toured European battlefields and met with military leaders overseas.

Family crisis. From the beginning of their marriage, Franklin and Eleanor had slowly drifted apart. Franklin was confident and outgoing, but Eleanor often felt overwhelmed by the demands of being a political spouse. Probably in 1916, Franklin fell in love with Eleanor's social secretary, Lucy Mercer. When Eleanor learned about the relationship in 1918, she insisted that Franklin either stop seeing Lucy or agree to a divorce. Some family insiders believed the crisis matured Franklin and made Eleanor more determined to be her own person.

Candidate for vice president. In 1920, Democratic leaders selected Roosevelt as the party's candidate for vice president. Roosevelt was handsome and energetic, and he had built a strong record as assistant secretary of the Navy. Party leaders also felt that he, as a New Yorker, would provide regional balance with the party's presidential candidate, James M. Cox of Ohio.

Cox and Roosevelt lost in a landslide to the Republican team of Warren G. Harding and Calvin Coolidge. But Democratic leaders did not blame Roosevelt for the outcome. Roosevelt used the experience to build relationships with party leaders and to assemble a staff that would stay with him long after the campaign.

Battle with polio

Polio strikes. In August 1921, Roosevelt and his family vacationed at their summer home on Campobello Island, off the coast of Maine. An avid outdoorsman, Franklin loved to sail and swim. But one afternoon, he returned home feeling chilled and weary. Too tired to dress for dinner, he went to bed early. The next morning, as he climbed out of bed, he found that his left leg was numb. Before long, he ran a high fever and suffered terrible pain. Doctors diagnosed the illness as *poliomyelitis,* also called *pronounced infantile paralysis,* or polio.

At age 39, Franklin Roosevelt was almost completely paralyzed below his waist. Never again would he walk without heavy leg braces. From then on, such routine tasks as getting into and out of bed, bathing, and dressing all required great effort.

Treatment. Despite his disability, Roosevelt resolved to lead a normal life. He refused to accept that his paralysis was permanent, and he was determined to restore health to his muscles. Roosevelt tried all the cures and therapies known at the time. When one failed to work, he tried another. Eventually, he placed his hopes for recovery with the mineral-rich waters of Warm Springs, Georgia. In 1926, Roosevelt bought the springs and the surrounding land. The next year, he and a group of friends established the Georgia Warm Springs Foundation. For many years, the foundation provided low-cost treatment for polio patients.

Roosevelt never regained full use of his legs, but he managed to live with his disability. Through strenuous exercise, he learned to lift himself into and out of a wheelchair. With the help of heavy steel leg braces, he managed to stand on his feet for long periods. He even had an automobile outfitted with hand controls so that he could drive.

Roosevelt feared that the public would be unwilling to elect a "cripple" to high office, so he worked to hide the severity of his disability. He prohibited news photographers from taking pictures of him in a wheelchair, being lifted into or out of automobiles, or being carried up flights of stairs. As a result, few people during his lifetime knew the extent of his disability.

Still, Roosevelt played a major role in the efforts that ultimately led to the virtual elimination of polio in the United States. He helped establish the National Foundation for Infantile Paralysis, which eventually financed the research that led to a vaccine for polio.

Return to politics

Even as he was learning to adapt to his disability, Roosevelt was planning his political comeback. Aided by Louis Howe, he began corresponding with Democratic leaders throughout the country. In 1924, Roosevelt returned to the national scene at the Democratic National Convention, where he nominated Governor Alfred E. Smith of New York for president. Thundering cheers met Roosevelt as he moved slowly to the podium, aided by his son James. Smith did not get the nomination, but Roosevelt gained attention as a Democratic leader.

In 1928, Roosevelt again nominated Smith, and this time, Smith won the Democratic nomination for the presidency. Smith promptly asked Roosevelt to run for governor of New York. At first, Roosevelt refused, want-

Franklin D. Roosevelt Library

Swimming was one of Roosevelt's favorite forms of exercise after he contracted polio in 1921. He is shown at Warm Springs, Georgia, where he set up a foundation to treat polio victims.

International Newsreel photo from Franklin D. Roosevelt Library

Roosevelt helped Alfred E. Smith, *left,* win the 1928 Democratic presidential nomination. Smith lost the 1928 election, but Roosevelt ran for governor of New York and won.

ing instead to continue his polio treatments at Warm Springs. But Smith believed that Roosevelt's candidacy would strengthen his own chances of carrying the state, and he finally persuaded Roosevelt to run. In the election for governor, Roosevelt won a narrow victory. Smith, however, lost both New York state and the presidential election to Herbert Hoover.

Governor of New York. As governor, Roosevelt became a spokesman for a number of liberal causes. He supported old age insurance, regulation of utilities, conservation of natural resources, and abolition of the death penalty. Following the onset of the Great Depression, he set up a statewide system of relief for the unemployed—the first such system in the nation. Roosevelt used the new medium of radio to explain to the public why unemployment relief and other reforms were needed.

Roosevelt won reelection in 1930 by 725,000 votes—at that time the largest margin of victory in New York's history. The election proved his popularity and established him as the leading contender for the Democratic presidential nomination in 1932.

Election of 1932. Despite his front-runner status, Roosevelt faced obstacles on his way to the nomination. Some critics doubted his personal fitness for the presidency. Even Roosevelt's bubbling optimism struck some as oddly inappropriate in the midst of the worst economic crisis in the nation's history. Still, with the help of Louis Howe and James A. Farley, the Democratic Party chairman in New York, Roosevelt secured the nomination on the fourth ballot. For his running mate, he chose one of his rivals for the nomination, John Nance Garner of Texas, the speaker of the House of Representatives.

Roosevelt flew to Chicago for the Democratic National Convention, thus becoming the first candidate of a major party to accept the nomination in person. "I pledge you, I pledge myself, to a new deal of the American people," he told cheering delegates.

The Republicans, meanwhile, renominated President Herbert Hoover and Vice President Charles Curtis. Almost all political experts predicted a Democratic sweep in the November elections, and Roosevelt waged a cautious campaign. He offered few specifics and pledged to cut government spending and waste. As expected, Roosevelt swept to victory. He received 57 percent of the popular vote, compared with 40 percent for Hoover. He carried 42 states to only 6 for his opponent.

An uneasy transition. The economy—and the nation's spirits—hit bottom in the months between Roosevelt's election in November and the March inauguration. One of every four workers was jobless, and the nation's banking system teetered near collapse. Two meetings between Roosevelt and President Hoover to discuss emergency measures during the transition period accomplished nothing.

On Feb. 15, 1933, Giuseppe Zangara, a bricklayer suffering from mental illness, tried to assassinate Roosevelt in Miami. Roosevelt escaped injury, but the shots fired by Zangara killed Mayor Anton J. Cermak of Chicago. In the aftermath of the shooting, Roosevelt showed courage and poise. Over the objections of Secret Service agents, he remained at the scene until emergency help arrived.

Roosevelt's first administration (1933-1937)

On March 4, 1933, Roosevelt took charge of a nation on the edge of economic collapse. His first inaugural address is famous for Roosevelt's assurance that "the only thing we have to fear is fear itself." But many who heard the speech at the time found another passage even more stirring. The new president said that if Congress failed to act immediately, he would ask Congress for the power to take action himself. He would seek "broad Executive power to wage a war against the emergency, as great as the power that would be given to me if we were in fact invaded by a foreign foe."

The banking crisis was Roosevelt's first and most urgent concern. For several weeks, anxious depositors, worried about the stability of their banks, had been withdrawing large amounts of cash and gold. The "runs" on banks ruined many institutions. Since the start of the Depression, bank failures had wiped out the life savings of millions of depositors.

To prevent a collapse of the nation's financial system, Roosevelt declared a "bank holiday." This action closed

Roosevelt's first election

Place of nominating convention	Chicago
Ballot on which nominated	4th
Republican opponent	Herbert Hoover
Electoral vote*	472 (Roosevelt) to 59 (Hoover)
Popular vote	22,825,016 (Roosevelt) to 15,758,397 (Hoover)
Age at inauguration	51

*For votes by states, see **Electoral College** (table).

every bank in the United States until the Department of the Treasury could examine every bank's books. Institutions in good financial condition were allowed to reopen. Those in doubtful condition remained closed until they could regain a firm footing. See **Bank holiday.**

On March 12, 1933, Roosevelt gave the first, and perhaps most important, of his famous "fireside chats," in which he spoke to the nation over radio. In plain language, he explained the causes of the bank crisis and the steps the government was taking to resolve it. The bank holiday, coupled with the reassuring fireside address, calmed public fears and ended the bank panic.

The Hundred Days. On March 9, 1933, Roosevelt had called Congress into special session. Thus began the period of busy legislative activity that became known as the "Hundred Days." From March 9 to June 16, Congress passed—and Roosevelt signed—some 15 major recovery and relief measures. The measures eventually became known as the "First New Deal."

The laws sought to address the economic crisis in a variety of ways. The Agricultural Adjustment Act (AAA) regulated farm production and offered farmers the promise of higher prices for their products. The National Industrial Recovery Act (NIRA) allowed the president to set up codes of fair competition for businesses and industries. The Federal Emergency Relief Administration (FERA) cooperated with the states in relieving hardships caused by unemployment and drought. The Public Works Administration (PWA) and the Civilian Conservation Corps (CCC) put thousands of jobless Americans to work. Other programs came to the rescue of homeowners, bank customers, and stock market investors. See **New Deal** (table: Leading New Deal agencies).

Roosevelt and his group of advisers became known as the "Brain Trust," and many people considered them the masterminds of the entire New Deal. However, Roosevelt was more interested in providing leadership and educating the public than in crafting legislation. Of the

Franklin D. Roosevelt Library

Roosevelt ran for president in 1932 with John Nance Garner of Texas as his running mate. He promised to end Prohibition, as well as enact programs to lead the nation out of the Depression.

United Press Int.

"Fireside chats" became a regular feature of Roosevelt's presidency. These informal radio reports to the American people enabled Roosevelt to gain widespread support for his programs.

15 major bills of the Hundred Days, most originated in Congress. Many, such as unemployment relief and the Tennessee Valley Authority (TVA), had legislative histories long predating Roosevelt's time in office.

Another legislative development came in December 1933. That month, the 21st Amendment to the Constitution ended Prohibition, the ban on making, selling, or transporting alcoholic beverages. See **Prohibition.**

Opposition to the New Deal. Roosevelt remained popular, but by 1934, his administration faced increasing criticism. Millions of Americans were dissatisfied with the slow pace of recovery. Leaders of business and finance complained that Roosevelt had abandoned his campaign promise to cut spending. Critics also said that New Deal regulatory agencies, such as the Securities and Exchange Commission (SEC), were destroying the free enterprise system. Clashes between labor and management often erupted into violence. Even some of Roosevelt's admirers began to worry that he had lost his reassuring touch.

Second New Deal. In 1935, Roosevelt moved to quiet the political unrest. He demanded action on an ambitious legislative agenda, much of which was already under consideration in Congress. What followed was an outpouring of legislation comparable in importance, if not in volume, to that of the Hundred Days. The period became known as the "Second Hundred Days," or the "Second New Deal."

During 1935, the National Labor Relations Act, known as the Wagner Act, enforced the New Deal's earlier promise to protect labor's right to form unions. The Social Security Act set up a national system of unemployment compensation and old-age and survivor's insurance. Roosevelt also supported the creation of the Works Progress Administration (WPA). Under the direction of Roosevelt adviser Harry Hopkins, the WPA built thousands of bridges, hospitals, roads, and schools. It hired out-of-work actors to put on plays, artists to create paintings at post offices and train stations, and authors to write state and city guidebooks.

Keystone

The Works Progress Administration (WPA) provided jobs for workers in construction and other fields. It was one of the relief programs that Roosevelt began during the Great Depression.

Vice presidents and Cabinet

Vice president	* John N. Garner
	* Henry A. Wallace (1941)
	* Harry S. Truman (1945)
Secretary of state	* Cordell Hull
	* Edward R. Stettinius, Jr. (1944)
Secretary of the treasury	William H. Woodin
	Henry Morgenthau, Jr. (1934)
Secretary of war	George H. Dern
	Harry H. Woodring (1937)
	Henry L. Stimson (1940)
Attorney general	Homer S. Cummings
	Frank Murphy (1939)
	* Robert H. Jackson (1940)
	Francis Biddle (1941)
Postmaster general	* James A. Farley
	Frank C. Walker (1940)
Secretary of the Navy	Claude A. Swanson
	Charles Edison (1940)
	* Frank Knox (1940)
	* James Forrestal (1944)
Secretary of the interior	Harold L. Ickes
Secretary of agriculture	* Henry A. Wallace
	Claude R. Wickard (1940)
Secretary of commerce	Daniel C. Roper
	* Harry L. Hopkins (1938)
	Jesse H. Jones (1940)
	* Henry A. Wallace (1945)
Secretary of labor	* Frances Perkins

*Has a separate biography in *World Book.*

Foreign policy. Roosevelt described his foreign policy as that of a "good neighbor." This phrase came to be used to describe the U.S. attitude toward the countries of Latin America. Under Roosevelt's Good Neighbor Policy, the United States took a stronger lead in promoting good will among these nations.

In 1934, Roosevelt's government canceled the Platt Amendment, which had given the United States broad powers to become involved in Cuban affairs. The government also withdrew American occupation forces from some Caribbean republics, and it settled long-standing oil disputes with Mexico. The United States signed trade agreements with a number of Latin American countries between 1934 and 1937. These countries included Brazil, Colombia, Costa Rica, Cuba, El Salvador, Guatemala, Haiti, Honduras, and Nicaragua. In 1935, the United States signed treaties of nonaggression and conciliation with six Latin American countries. The United States also signed several trade pacts with Canada.

Roosevelt also used personal diplomacy. In July 1934, he took a trip to Cartagena, Colombia, and thus became the first president to visit South America. In 1936, he attended the Inter-American Conference for the Maintenance of Peace, in Buenos Aires, Argentina. On the way home, he visited Montevideo, Uruguay.

Roosevelt hoped that trade could resume between the United States and the Soviet Union. Partly for this reason, the Roosevelt administration recognized the Soviet government in November 1933. The United States and the Soviet Union had broken off diplomatic relations after the Russian Revolution of 1917. In 1933, for the first time in 16 years, the two countries exchanged diplomatic representatives.

Praise and criticism. As Roosevelt neared the end of his first term, millions of Americans viewed him as a friend and savior. They hung his pictures in their homes, named their children after him, and flooded the White House with personal letters, poems, and even song compositions. Roosevelt's opponents were similarly passionate. Some critics spoke of him as a dangerous radical who threatened to destroy the American way.

Eleanor Roosevelt, meanwhile, emerged as a major public figure in her own right. She wrote books and articles, held press conferences, gave speeches, traveled widely, and championed civil rights and other causes.

Election of 1936. The Democrats nominated Roosevelt for a second term in 1936. The Republicans, meanwhile, nominated Governor Alf Landon of Kansas. During the campaign, Roosevelt urged voters to ask themselves, "Am I better off now than I was four years ago?" Although the Depression was far from over, voters responded with a resounding "yes." Roosevelt swept every state except Maine and Vermont and received nearly 61 percent of the popular vote.

The 1936 election signified the emergence of the New Deal *coalition* (partnership)—a combination of voting groups that would shape national politics for decades to come. Most farmers, intellectuals, unemployed workers, wage earners, and members of minority groups supported the New Deal and voted Democratic. Most southerners and residents of big cities also backed the party.

Roosevelt's second administration (1937-1941)

In 1933, the 20th Amendment to the Constitution of the United States had established that presidential terms begin on January 20. Roosevelt's second inauguration, in 1937, was the first to take place on that date.

Roosevelt faced a variety of challenges in his second term. Chief among them were struggles with the Supreme Court of the United States, an economic downturn, and the beginning of World War II.

The Supreme Court. During Roosevelt's first term, he faced several challenges to the New Deal from the Supreme Court. In 1935 and 1936, the court had struck down a host of measures, including the National Indus-

Roosevelt's second election

Place of nominating convention	Philadelphia
Ballot on which nominated	1st
Republican opponent	Alfred M. Landon
Electoral vote*	523 (Roosevelt) to 8 (Landon)
Popular vote	27,747,636 (Roosevelt) to 16,679,543 (Landon)
Age at inauguration	54

*For votes by states, see **Electoral College** (table).

trial Recovery Act (NIRA) and the Agricultural Adjustment Act (AAA). It also had overturned important state laws, creating a legal "no man's land" where neither the federal nor state governments could act. If the court continued on its course, it might strike down the Social Security Act, the National Labor Relations Act, and other New Deal proposals.

Shortly after the inauguration, Roosevelt proposed a reorganization of the Supreme Court. One of his proposed changes would have given Roosevelt the power to appoint up to six additional justices to the court. Roosevelt described the plan as a way to improve the court's efficiency. Critics, however, charged that the proposal was an attempt by Roosevelt to "pack" the court with justices who agreed with his own views. In addition, Roosevelt offended lawmakers by springing the plan on them with no warning. Roosevelt's plan never made it to a formal vote in either house of Congress.

Roosevelt's struggle with the court injured his political reputation, encouraged his foes, and damaged Democratic Party unity. It also spurred the growth of a conservative coalition of Republicans and southern Democrats in Congress. This group, though small in number, blocked many New Deal measures.

Still, soon after Roosevelt presented his plan, the Supreme Court appeared to reverse itself. The court voted in favor of New Deal measures, such as the Social Security Act and the National Labor Relations Act. In addition, a series of retirements and deaths among the justices eventually allowed Roosevelt to appoint eight new members to the court.

Recession of 1937. The United States suffered a serious setback in 1937, when the country experienced an economic *recession.* A recession is an economic downturn that is shorter and less extreme than a depression.

Between 1933 and 1937, the economy had improved. Prices, profits, and national income had risen, and unemployment fell from about 25 to 14 percent. At long last, the country seemed to be recovering from the Great Depression. In fact, Roosevelt and his advisers now began to worry that the pace of economic recovery threatened uncontrolled *inflation,* or sharp rises in prices. To prevent an inflationary surge, Roosevelt slashed federal spending for relief and public works. He also encouraged the Federal Reserve Board to tighten credit requirements, or lending rules. Soon after these actions went into effect, however, the recession of 1937 struck. The downturn was so severe that it threatened to wipe out all the gains made since Roosevelt took office. Critics labeled the downturn "the Roosevelt Recession."

Members of the administration debated the causes of the recession and the ways to bring about recovery. Roosevelt was not convinced that spending was the best way to stimulate the economy, but he nonetheless canceled his spending cuts.

Despite the recession and other setbacks, Roosevelt had a number of legislative successes in his second term. From 1937 to 1939, Congress passed major farm legislation, created a public housing program, expanded the Social Security system, enacted a landmark child labor measure, and established a national system of minimum wages and maximum hours.

The road to war. Foreign policy surged to the forefront during Roosevelt's second term, when a series of international crises demanded the president's attention. During the 1920's and 1930's, political unrest and poor economic conditions had enabled radical dictatorships to come to power in the Soviet Union, Italy, Germany, and Japan. Adolf Hitler, the leader of Nazi Germany, began a brutal campaign of hatred and violence against Jews and others. Aggressive actions by Germany, Japan, and Italy threatened the uneasy peace that had existed since the end of World War I.

Most Americans viewed these developments with alarm. At the same time, they questioned whether the United States, with so many troubles of its own, should take an active role in addressing these global issues. By the 1930's, the majority of Americans had come to believe that the United States had made a mistake by entering World War I. Most people did not want the country to become involved in another worldwide conflict.

On Sept. 1, 1939, Germany attacked Poland, and World War II began. Two days later, the United Kingdom and France declared war on Germany. Roosevelt immediately pressed Congress to aid the Allies—the United Kingdom, France, and later the Soviet Union—in the war with Germany.

Roosevelt's request brought heated debate. On one side were the *interventionists,* who supported aid to the Allies short of an American declaration of war. On the other side were the *isolationists,* who feared being dragged into an unnecessary war. Isolationists accused Roosevelt of *warmongering*—that is, of trying to get the United States into the war. The president and his supporters argued that the isolationists were ignoring the dangers of Nazi Germany.

In most cases, Congress gave Roosevelt what he wanted. For instance, it changed the nation's neutrality law that had prohibited the United States from furnishing weapons or other war supplies to nations at war. At Roosevelt's request, Congress also approved a huge increase in defense spending. Roosevelt directed some of these funds to the Manhattan Project, a top-secret drive to develop the atomic bomb. See **Manhattan Project.**

Roosevelt took some bold steps without congressional authorization. Following a major German offensive in the spring of 1940, which ended in the fall of France, Roosevelt negotiated a deal to help the British. The United States gave the United Kingdom 50 *destroyers* (warships) in exchange for 99-year leases on British naval bases in the Western Hemisphere.

Roosevelt brought into his Cabinet two prominent Republicans: Henry L. Stimson as secretary of war and Frank Knox as secretary of the Navy. These moves served as a nod to *bipartisanship* (agreement between political parties) and strengthened the voice of interventionists within his administration. Both men favored all-out aid to the United Kingdom. The United States adopted its first peacetime *selective service,* or military draft, law in September 1940.

Election of 1940. During Roosevelt's time, the Constitution did not limit the number of terms a president could serve. However, no previous chief executive had ever served longer than eight years. As the international situation worsened, Roosevelt's supporters encouraged him to seek a third term. Roosevelt waited until the last moment to make his intentions clear. In one of the most suspenseful political conventions in history, the Democrats nominated Roosevelt for the third time.

Roosevelt would have a new running mate in the 1940 election, however. Democratic delegates chose Secretary of Agriculture Henry A. Wallace to replace Garner as the vice presidential candidate. Meanwhile, the Republicans nominated Wendell L. Willkie of Indiana, a corporation president who was new to politics. Willkie supported Roosevelt's foreign policy and favored many New Deal programs.

The Republicans based their campaign on the tradition that no president had ever sought three consecutive terms. Roosevelt defended his administration's programs and promised to try to keep the nation out of war. Roosevelt carried 38 of the 48 states to win his third term as president.

Roosevelt's third administration (1941-1945)

In the months following Roosevelt's third inauguration, the nation edged closer to war. On March 11, 1941, Congress passed the Lend-Lease Act. The law authorized the U.S. government to provide war supplies to any nation that the president deemed vital to the nation's security. See **Lend-Lease.**

Roosevelt's third election

Place of nominating convention	Chicago
Ballot on which nominated	1st
Republican opponent	Wendell L. Willkie
Electoral vote*	449 (Roosevelt) to 82 (Willkie)
Popular vote	27,263,448 (Roosevelt) to 22,336,260 (Willkie)
Age at inauguration	58

*For votes by states, see **Electoral College** (table).

In August 1941, Roosevelt met British Prime Minister Winston Churchill on a cruiser anchored off Newfoundland, Canada. The two men adopted a declaration that became known as the Atlantic Charter. They pledged not to seek gains, "territorial or otherwise"; to respect the right of every nation to choose its own form of government; to guarantee freedom of the seas; and to conduct peaceful world trade. See **Atlantic Charter.**

Pearl Harbor. Relations between the United States and Japan had become increasingly tense. Roosevelt was concerned that continued Japanese aggression would force the British to shift resources away from the European war to the defense of its colonies in Southeast Asia. Roosevelt imposed on Japan a number of tough economic and trade restrictions. The United States cut off vital exports to Japan and barred the withdrawal of Japanese funds from American banks.

On Dec. 7, 1941, U.S. Secretary of State Cordell Hull met with two Japanese diplomats. While they talked, Japanese planes launched a surprise attack on the U.S. Pacific Fleet, which lay at anchor in Pearl Harbor, Hawaii. Japanese leaders hoped to knock out the Pacific Fleet so that it could not block Japan's expansion in Asia. The at-

Library of Congress

Roosevelt signed a declaration of war against Japan on Dec. 8, 1941, the day after Japan attacked Pearl Harbor. He said that December 7 was "a date which will live in infamy."

Franklin D. Roosevelt Library

During the war, Roosevelt traveled overseas several times to confer with Allied leaders. Here he is shown riding in a jeep in Sicily with Allied Commander Dwight D. Eisenhower.

Quotations from Franklin Roosevelt

Some of Franklin Roosevelt's most famous speeches are quoted or paraphrased in the text of this article. The following are additional quotations from some of his speeches and writings.

It is common sense to take a method and try it. If it fails, admit it frankly and try another. But above all, try something.
Speech in Atlanta, May 22, 1932

The fate of America cannot depend on any one man. The greatness of America is grounded in principles and not on any single personality.
Speech in New York City, Nov. 5, 1932

Democracy is not a static thing. It is an everlasting march.
Speech in Los Angeles, Oct. 1, 1935

Nationwide thinking, nationwide planning, and nationwide action are the three great essentials to prevent nationwide crises for future generations to struggle through.
Speech in New York City, April 25, 1936

I should like to have it said of my first administration that in it the forces of selfishness and lust for power met their match. I should like to have it said of my second administration that in it these forces met their master.
Speech in New York City, Oct. 31, 1936

The test of our progress is not whether we add more to the abundance of those who have much; it is whether we provide enough for those who have too little.
Second Inaugural Address, Jan. 20, 1937

Our security is not a matter of weapons alone. The arm that wields them must be strong, the eye that guides them clear, the will that directs them indomitable.
Message to Congress, May 16, 1940

True individual freedom cannot exist without economic security and independence. People who are hungry and out of a job are the stuff of which dictatorships are made.
Message to Congress, Jan. 11, 1944

tack destroyed or damaged many U.S. ships and aircraft and killed nearly 2,400 Americans. See **Pearl Harbor**.

President Roosevelt addressed Congress the next day. He said that December 7 was "a date which will live in infamy." The United States declared war against Japan on December 8. Three days later, on December 11, Germany and Italy declared war on the United States. The United States then declared war on those countries.

The United States goes to war. Roosevelt suggested the name *United Nations* for the alliance that fought the Axis nations of Germany, Italy, and Japan. Although the group came to be known as the Allies, it formed the basis for the peacetime United Nations organization that was established in 1945.

After Pearl Harbor, the United States faced a situation as dire as that of the Great Depression. Abroad, the Axis powers had put the United States and its allies on the defensive, with Germany and Japan dangerously close to winning the war. At home, the situation was equally bleak. Production snags, labor shortages, ethnic and racial tensions, and general confusion hampered preparations for war.

Early on, Roosevelt made a key strategic decision. Even though it was Japan that had attacked the United States, he made the defeat of Germany his first priority. He reasoned that Germany posed the greater threat to the security and strategic interests of the United States.

Roosevelt's top commanders, including Army Chief of Staff George C. Marshall, argued for an American and British invasion across the English Channel into Nazi-controlled France. The Soviet Union, which had suffered huge casualties during German offensives, also favored this strategy. Winston Churchill and his advisers, however, argued for a different course of action. They favored postponing the invasion of France and instead launching a joint offensive to drive the Axis forces from North Africa. Roosevelt wavered on this question for six months. Then, to the frustration of his top commanders and the Soviet Union, he sided with Churchill.

On Nov. 8, 1942, Allied troops commanded by Lieutenant General Dwight D. Eisenhower of the U.S. Army landed in Algeria and Morocco, in North Africa. After the landings began, Roosevelt spoke by radio to the French people in their own language. He explained the need for the Allies to drive the Axis forces out of French territory in North Africa. The last Axis forces in North Africa surrendered in May 1943. Later that summer, the Allies invaded southern Italy and began pushing north.

It would not be until June 1944 that the United States, the United Kingdom, and other Allied troops launched the cross-Channel invasion into France. June 6—the date of the Allied invasion of Normandy, in northwestern France—became known as D-Day. The fighting in Normandy continued late into August and ended with an Allied victory. See **D-day; Normandy, Battle of.**

The Big Three. During the war, Roosevelt traveled outside the United States a number of times for conferences with Allied leaders. He became the first U.S. president to leave the country during wartime. Early in 1943, he met with Churchill in Casablanca, Morocco. The two leaders announced that they would accept only unconditional surrender by the Axis nations. In other conferences, Roosevelt discussed problems of war and peace with both Churchill and Premier Joseph Stalin of the Soviet Union. Roosevelt, Churchill, and Stalin came to be known as the "Big Three." Roosevelt also conferred with Generalissimo Chiang Kai-shek of China in 1943.

In November 1943, the Big Three met at Tehran, Iran. During and after this conference, Roosevelt worked to get Churchill and Stalin to agree on major war aims. At Tehran, he refused to have lunch with Churchill before meeting with Stalin. The president did not want Stalin to think he and Churchill had made a separate agreement. Still, Stalin distrusted his allies' intentions and rarely consulted them. See **Tehran Conference.**

The home front. Roosevelt's domestic leadership was critical to the war effort. His fireside chats helped reassure the nation and drive both the military and civilians to meet ambitious wartime goals. After a sluggish start, American war industries achieved astonishing feats, producing many of the guns, tanks, planes, and ships used by the Allied armies. In the end, this productivity was perhaps the single most important contribution to victory made by the United States.

The most dramatic development on the home front was the economic recovery, which was driven by the huge increase in government spending for war purposes. The production of war materials provided so many jobs that the U.S. unemployment rate fell to about 1 percent in 1944.

Congress granted Roosevelt broad authority to manage the military aspects of the war. But on matters not directly related to war conduct, Roosevelt was frequently at odds with lawmakers, including members of his own party. The conservative coalition of Republicans and southern Democrats in Congress chipped away at the remaining programs of the New Deal.

In 1944, lawmakers from both parties came together to pass, by unanimous votes, the first GI Bill, the Servicemen's Readjustment Act, for veterans of World War II. The measure guaranteed education assistance, medical benefits, unemployment insurance, and low-interest home loans to veterans of the war. Of the many laws enacted during the Roosevelt presidency, the GI Bill probably ranked second only to the Social Security Act in its long-term impact on the economy.

Roosevelt generally supported civil rights. In February 1942, however, he approved measures against Japanese Americans that many people now consider unnecessary and discriminatory. The president yielded to political pressure and ordered the *internment* (confinement) of more than 110,000 people of Japanese ancestry in the United States. At that time, many Americans viewed people of Japanese descent as potentially dangerous and disloyal. With little warning, the U.S. government forced people to leave their homes and live in camps. A government commission later concluded that the internment was the result of racism, war hysteria, and poor leadership. See **Japanese American internment.**

Roosevelt created a Fair Employment Practices Commission (FEPC) to prevent defense industries and the federal government from treating workers unfairly because of their race. But fearing a white backlash that might endanger the war effort, he declined to end *segregation* (separation of the races) in the armed services.

Roosevelt's fourth election

Place of nominating convention	Chicago
Ballot on which nominated	1st
Republican opponent	Thomas E. Dewey
Electoral vote*	432 (Roosevelt) to 99 (Dewey)
Popular vote	25,611,936 (Roosevelt) to 22,013,372 (Dewey)
Age at inauguration	62

*For votes by states, see **Electoral College** (table)

Highlights of Roosevelt's administrations

1933	Congress enacted New Deal recovery measures during the "Hundred Days." Prohibition was repealed.
1935	The Social Security Act and the first Neutrality Act were passed.
1937	Roosevelt's "court-packing" recommendations started the Supreme Court controversy.
1939	The United States began selling arms to friendly countries on a "cash-and-carry" basis.
1940	Congress passed the Selective Service Act.
1941	The Atlantic Charter was issued. (Dec. 7) Japan attacked Pearl Harbor.
1942	Twenty-six nations signed the Declaration of the United Nations.
1943	Roosevelt and Churchill announced the goal of unconditional surrender by the Axis powers. Roosevelt, Churchill, and Stalin conferred in Tehran, Iran.
1944	(June 6) The Allies invaded Normandy, France.
1945	Roosevelt, Churchill, and Stalin met at Yalta, in the Crimea.

Election of 1944. The Democrats nominated Roosevelt for the fourth time in July 1944. Delegates replaced Vice President Wallace, who was unpopular with many in the party, with Senator Harry S. Truman of Missouri. The Republicans, meanwhile, nominated Governor Thomas E. Dewey of New York for president and Governor John W. Bricker of Ohio for vice president.

Roosevelt's biggest obstacle to reelection was his health. Earlier in the year, Roosevelt's doctors had diagnosed him with heart disease at an advanced stage, but Roosevelt rallied. A grueling campaign swing through New York City, Philadelphia, and Chicago convinced his supporters that he was back in top form. Roosevelt won an easy election victory, carrying 36 of the 48 states.

Roosevelt's fourth administration (1945)

Roosevelt often claimed that he yearned to retire to his home in Hyde Park, New York. He struggled with his health, and he looked tired and pale. But with the war still in progress, he continued his presidency into a fourth term.

Yalta Conference. Just days after his fourth inauguration, Roosevelt met Churchill and Stalin at Yalta, a resort on the Black Sea in the southern Soviet Union. On Feb.

UPI/Bettmann Newsphotos

The "Big Three"—British Prime Minister Winston Churchill, President Roosevelt, and Soviet Premier Joseph Stalin—met at the Yalta Conference in February 1945.

U.S. Army

Mourners lined the streets of Washington as Franklin Roosevelt's funeral procession headed toward the White House. Millions of people around the world mourned his death.

11, 1945, the three leaders issued the Declaration on Liberated Europe, which repeated the principles of the Atlantic Charter and the Casablanca conferences.

The leaders mapped the final assault against the Germans and set out a plan for the postwar occupation of Germany. They also planned a meeting in San Francisco to lay the foundations for the United Nations (UN). In a secret agreement, the Soviet Union promised to enter the war against Japan within three months after the surrender of Germany. In return, the Soviet Union was to receive the Kuril Islands and other areas. Critics later charged that Roosevelt had been cheated by Stalin. See **Yalta Conference**.

On March 1, while reporting to Congress on the Yalta meeting, Roosevelt made one of his rare public references to his disability. "I hope that you will pardon me for this unusual posture of sitting down," he said, but "it makes it a lot easier for me not to have to carry about 10 pounds of steel around at the bottom of my legs."

Death. By the spring of 1945, the war in Europe was nearing an end, and the war in the Pacific was going well. In March, Roosevelt visited "the Little White House," his long-time retreat in Warm Springs. Eleanor, who maintained a demanding schedule, did not accompany him on the trip. Joining him instead were several staff members and cousins Laura Delano and Margaret (also known as Daisy) Suckley. Lucy Mercer Rutherfurd, the woman whom he had loved years earlier, arrived on April 9. The two had seen each other from time to time during the 1940's, especially since the death of her husband the year before.

By Thursday, April 12, Roosevelt seemed to have regained some of his strength. He spent the morning reading and chatting with his cousins and Lucy Rutherfurd. At noon, Elizabeth Shoumatoff, a portrait artist, arrived to work on a water-color painting of the president. Shortly after 1 p.m., Roosevelt passed his hand over his forehead several times. "I have a terrific headache," he said softly. He then slumped forward in his chair. By the time his doctor arrived, Roosevelt was unconscious and breathing heavily. Soon thereafter, his breathing stopped.

At 3:35 p.m., the doctor pronounced Roosevelt dead of a *cerebral hemorrhage* (bleeding from a broken blood vessel in the brain). As news of his death spread, a crowd, silent with grief, gathered in front of the White House. Millions of people in all parts of the world mourned the dead president.

Roosevelt was buried at Hyde Park. His home and library there have been set aside as the Franklin D. Roosevelt National Historic Site. In 1997, the Franklin Delano Roosevelt Memorial was dedicated on the National Mall in Washington, D.C. Patrick J. Maney

Related articles in ***World Book*** include:

Atlantic Charter
Bank holiday
Churchill, Sir Winston Leonard Spencer
Democratic Party (The New Deal)
Dewey, Thomas Edmund
Franklin Delano Roosevelt Memorial
Garner, John Nance
Great Depression
Hull, Cordell
Landon, Alfred Mossman
National Recovery Administration
New Deal
New York (Places to visit)
President of the United States
Radio (The Golden Age of Broadcasting)
Roosevelt, Eleanor
Roosevelt Campobello International Park
Tehran Conference
Truman, Harry S.
Wallace, Henry Agard
Willkie, Wendell Lewis
Works Progress Administration
World War II
Yalta Conference

Additional resources

Bardhan-Quallen, Sudipta. *Franklin Delano Roosevelt.* Sterling Pub., 2007. Younger readers.
Brinkley, Alan. *Franklin Delano Roosevelt.* Oxford, 2010.
Gillon, Steven M. *Pearl Harbor: FDR Leads the Nation into War.* Basic Bks., 2011.
Hamilton, Nigel. *The Mantle of Command: FDR at War, 1941-1942.* Houghton, 2014.
Krull, Kathleen. *A Boy Named FDR.* Knopf, 2011. Younger readers.
Marrin, Albert. *FDR and the American Crisis.* Knopf Bks. for Young Readers, 2015.
Tobin, James. *The Man He Became: How FDR Defied Polio to Win the Presidency.* Simon & Schuster, 2013.
Ward, Geoffrey C., and Burns, Ken. *The Roosevelts: An Intimate History.* Knopf, 2014.
Weintraub, Stanley. *Young Mr. Roosevelt.* Da Capo, 2013.

Roosevelt, *ROH zuh* *VEHLT,* **Nicholas J.** (1767-1854), was an American inventor and engineer. He helped pioneer the development of steamboats.

Roosevelt was born on Dec. 27, 1767, in New York City. He became interested in mechanics as a youth and, at about the age of 15, he designed a paddle wheel to drive a model boat. He later opened a metal shop in New Jersey.

In 1809, Roosevelt and the inventor Robert Fulton joined in a venture to introduce steamboats on Western rivers. In 1812, Roosevelt completed a voyage from Pittsburgh to New Orleans in their boat, the *New Orleans.* The trip was the first steamboat voyage on the Ohio and Mississippi rivers. The *New Orleans* was a success and continued to travel for about two years. Roosevelt patented the use of vertical paddle wheels in 1814. They became the chief method of propelling steamboats. Roosevelt died on July 30, 1854. David F. Channell

26th president of the United States 1901-1909

McKinley
25th president
1897-1901
Republican

T. Roosevelt
26th president
1901-1909
Republican

Taft
27th president
1909-1913
Republican

Charles W. Fairbanks
Vice president
1905-1909

Oil painting on canvas (1903) by John Singer Sargent; © White House Historical Association (National Geographic Society)

Roosevelt, *ROH zuh vehlt,* **Theodore** (1858-1919), was the youngest man ever to become president of the United States. He took office at the age of 42. Roosevelt had been vice president for only six months when President William McKinley was assassinated in September 1901. Roosevelt won wide popularity, and millions of Americans affectionately called him "Teddy" or "T.R." In 1904, the voters elected him to a full term as president. He ran for president again in 1912, as the "Bull Moose" party candidate, but lost to Woodrow Wilson.

Roosevelt was a man of great energy and practiced what he called the "strenuous life." He enjoyed horseback riding, swimming, hunting, hiking, and boxing. He often expressed enthusiasm for something by describing it as "bully." Cartoonists liked to draw Roosevelt with his rimless glasses, bushy mustache, prominent teeth, and jutting jaw. One cartoon showed him with a bear cub. Soon, toymakers were producing stuffed animals that are still known as "teddy bears."

As commander of the fearless Rough Riders, Roosevelt became a national hero during the Spanish-American War in 1898. He led this famous cavalry regiment against the Spaniards in Cuba. Roosevelt came home and won election as governor of New York. Two years later, he was elected vice president.

As president, Roosevelt used his power of leadership to help the United States meet challenges at home and abroad. "I did not usurp power," Roosevelt said, "but I did greatly broaden the use of executive power."

Roosevelt fought for reforms that would benefit the American people. He became known as a "trust buster" because he tried to limit the power of great business corporations. During his Administration, Congress passed laws to regulate the railroads, to protect the public from harmful foods and drugs, and to conserve the nation's forests and other natural resources.

In foreign relations, Roosevelt worked to make the United States a world leader. He felt that this leadership must be supported by strong armed forces. He expressed his foreign policy as: "Speak softly and carry a big stick." Roosevelt strengthened the U.S. Navy, began the construction of the Panama Canal, and kept European nations from interfering in Latin America. He helped end the Russo-Japanese War, and became the first American to receive the Nobel Peace Prize.

While Roosevelt was president, millions of Americans traveled by bicycle—even women in their sweeping, ankle-length skirts. But automobiles, along with electric lights and telephones, started to come into widespread use. Guglielmo Marconi and his staff sent and received the first radio message across the Atlantic Ocean, and a telegraph cable was laid across the Pacific to the Philippines. The air age was born when the Wright brothers flew the first successful airplane. Roosevelt enjoyed taking a ride in one of the early models.

Roosevelt regarded public life as a great stage. As president, he joyfully held the center of that stage. When Roosevelt left office, he wrote: "I do not believe that anyone else has ever enjoyed the White House as much as I have." He was probably right.

Early life

Boyhood and education. Theodore Roosevelt was born in New York City on Oct. 27, 1858. He was the second of the four children of Theodore and Martha Bulloch Roosevelt. "Teedie," as the family called him, was younger than his sister Anna, and older than his brother Elliott and his sister Corinne.

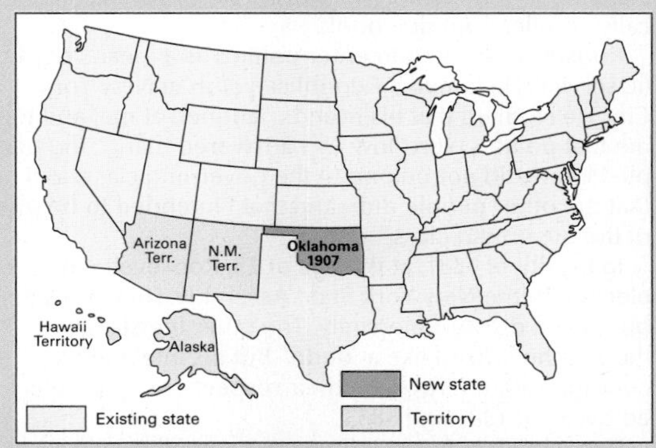

Oklahoma became a state in 1907, bringing the number of states in the Union to 46. The United States had four territories during President Roosevelt's administration.

There were 46 stars on the United States flag when Roosevelt left office. A star was added for Oklahoma on July 4, 1908.

The world of President Theodore Roosevelt

Architect Frank Lloyd Wright began designing homes in his famous "prairie style" in 1902. He eventually became one of the nation's most influential architects.
The world's first successful airplane flights were made by Orville and Wilbur Wright at Kitty Hawk, North Carolina, on Dec. 17, 1903.
The first movie to tell a story, *The Great Train Robbery,* was produced in 1903. Its tremendous popularity led to the development of nickelodeons, the first movie theaters.
Russia's Revolution of 1905 began when soldiers fired on unarmed workers who came to the czar's palace in St. Petersburg to ask for reforms.
Albert Einstein revolutionized scientific thought with his theory of relativity, which he proposed in 1905.
The San Francisco earthquake and fire of 1906 left most of the city in ruins and killed at least 3,000 people.
"Muckrakers" was a term first used by President Roosevelt in 1906 to describe writers who used a realistic style to portray social evils. The works of such writers as Upton Sinclair, Ida Tarbell, and Lincoln Steffens helped bring about much-needed reforms.
Musical theater delighted audiences of the early 1900's. George M. Cohan wrote musicals that featured such patriotic tunes as "I'm a Yankee Doodle Dandy." Victor Herbert became popular for his operettas, and Florenz Ziegfeld began to produce the *Ziegfeld Follies.*
The Model T Ford was introduced in 1908. It became the most popular car in the United States.

WORLD BOOK map

Roosevelt's ancestors, the Van Roosevelts, had come to America from Holland in the 1640's. One of these ancestors, Klaes Martensen Van Roosevelt, settled in New York, which was then called New Amsterdam. Klaes was also an ancestor of Franklin D. Roosevelt, the 32nd president of the United States. Most of the Van Roosevelts were wealthy landowners and business leaders.

Theodore Roosevelt's mother came from a prominent Georgia family. One of her brothers was an admiral in the Confederate Navy. She sympathized with the South during the Civil War. Her husband, an importer of plate glass, supported the North. But the Roosevelts did not let their differences keep them from providing a happy home life for their family.

Like his father, Teedie had great energy, curiosity, and determination. He enjoyed an active childhood although he was puny and frequently ill. He suffered greatly from asthma. While playing with friends one day, he discovered that he also was nearsighted. The other children easily read an advertisement on a billboard some distance away. "Not only was I unable to read the sign, but I could not even see the letters," Roosevelt wrote later.

Important dates in Roosevelt's life

1858	(Oct. 27) Born in New York City.
1880	(Oct. 27) Married Alice Hathaway Lee.
1882-1884	Served in the New York State Assembly.
1884	(Feb. 14) Mrs. Alice Roosevelt died.
1886	(Dec. 2) Married Edith Kermit Carow.
1889	Appointed to the U.S. Civil Service Commission.
1897	Named assistant secretary of the Navy.
1898	Led the Rough Riders in the Spanish-American War.
1898	Elected governor of New York.
1900	Elected vice president of the United States.
1901	(Sept. 14) Became president of the United States.
1904	Elected to full term as president.
1912	Defeated for president on the "Bull Moose" ticket.
1919	(Jan. 6) Died at his home in Oyster Bay, New York.

Woman's Roosevelt Memorial Association

Roosevelt's birthplace in New York City is now a national historic site. His father built a gymnasium in the house, where "Teedie," a weak and sickly child, exercised regularly.

Theodore Roosevelt Collection, Harvard College Library

Alice Hathaway Lee married Theodore Roosevelt in 1880, on his 22nd birthday. She died in 1884, two days after giving birth to a daughter, also named Alice.

From then on Theodore wore glasses.

Theodore loved both books and the outdoors. He combined these interests in nature study. His bureau drawers smelled of dead mice and birds, and so, often, did Theodore. When he was 10, and again when he was 14, Theodore went with his family on year-long trips abroad. He visited Europe and the Middle East.

When Theodore was about 12, his father told him that he would need a strong body to give his mind a chance to develop fully. The next year, while alone on a trip to Maine, Theodore was tormented by two mischievous boys. He felt ashamed because he was not strong enough to fight back. Roosevelt's father built a gymnasium in the family home, and Theodore exercised there regularly. He overcame his asthma and built up unusual physical strength.

Roosevelt studied under tutors until he entered Harvard University in 1876 at the age of 18. He earned good grades in college. Once he asked so many questions during a lecture that the professor exclaimed: "Now look here, Roosevelt, let me talk. I'm running this course!" Roosevelt graduated from Harvard in 1880.

First marriage. In October 1879, Roosevelt met Alice Hathaway Lee (1861-1884). She was the daughter of a wealthy official of a Boston investment firm. Roosevelt courted Alice during his senior year at Harvard. They were married on his 22nd birthday.

A double tragedy struck on Feb. 14, 1884. Alice Roosevelt died two days after the birth of a daughter, also named Alice (1884-1980). On the same day, Roosevelt's mother died of typhoid fever.

Political and public activities

State legislator. After graduation from Harvard in 1880, Roosevelt did not know what to do for a living. His father, who had died in 1878, had left him some money. But Theodore needed to earn more in order to live comfortably. He enrolled in the Columbia University Law School, but the courses did not interest him. While studying law, he wrote *The Naval War of 1812,* a technically excellent but dull book.

Roosevelt decided to enter politics as a means of public service. He joined a Republican club in New York City. He recalled that his friends "laughed at me, and told me that politics were 'low ...' I answered that ... the people I knew did not belong to the governing class, and that the other people did—and that I intended to be one of the governing class."

In the fall of 1881, at the age of 23, Roosevelt won election to the New York State Assembly. He wore sideburns and dressed elegantly. The other legislators thought he looked like a "dude." But his intelligence, courage, and energy won their respect. He was reelected twice, in 1882 and 1883.

Party leader. In 1882, Roosevelt served briefly as leader of the Republican minority in the Assembly. State party bosses expected him to follow orders, but he refused to obey blindly. The bosses removed him as minority leader. However, Roosevelt remained the most influential man in the Assembly. He worked closely with Governor Grover Cleveland, a Democrat, and became interested in civil service reform.

Rancher and writer. After the death of his wife and mother in 1884, Roosevelt left politics. He ran two cattle ranches on the Little Missouri River in the Dakota Territory. The hard life and endless activity of a rancher helped him recover from his sorrow. Wearing cowboy clothes, Roosevelt often spent 14 to 16 hours a day in the saddle. He hunted buffalo and other wild animals, tended cattle, and even helped law officers capture a band of outlaws.

Roosevelt wrote steadily. In one period of less than three months, he completed a biography of Senator Thomas Hart Benton of Missouri. Roosevelt also wrote a four-volume series called *The Winning of the West.*

Severe snowstorms in the winter of 1885-1886 de-

White House Historical Association

Edith Kermit Carow had known Roosevelt since childhood. They were married in 1886 and had five children. She was a devoted mother, as well as a gracious White House hostess.

stroyed most of Roosevelt's cattle. He returned to New York City in 1886 and at the request of Republican leaders, ran for mayor. He was badly defeated.

Second marriage. During several trips home from his ranches, Roosevelt had visited a childhood friend, Edith Kermit Carow (1861-1948). They were married on Dec. 2, 1886, and lived in Sagamore Hill, Roosevelt's home in Oyster Bay, Long Island, New York. Edith Roosevelt had a strong influence on her husband. He came to depend on her advice. "Whenever I go against her judgment, I regret it," he said.

The Roosevelts had five children: Theodore, Jr. (1887-1944); Kermit (1889-1943); Ethel Carow (1891-1977); Archibald Bulloch (1894-1979); and Quentin (1897-1918). Mrs. Roosevelt reared Alice Roosevelt, Theodore's daughter by his first wife, as her own child. Roosevelt loved to play with his children.

Civil Service commissioner. Benjamin Harrison won the Republican nomination for president in 1888. Roosevelt went on a speaking tour for Harrison, who was elected in November. Partly as a reward for Roosevelt's service, Harrison appointed him to the Civil Service Commission. Roosevelt brought publicity to the commission, which previously had attracted little attention. He improved the merit system by establishing examinations for some Civil Service jobs. He opposed the awarding of government jobs to political friends. Many Republicans resented his attitude. But President Grover Cleveland reappointed him in 1893.

Police commissioner. In 1895, Roosevelt gladly accepted the post of president of the Board of Police Commissioners in New York City. For the next two years, he fought to stamp out dishonesty on the police force. Sometimes he patrolled the streets at night to check on police officers suspected of illegal activities.

A national figure

Assistant secretary of the Navy. In 1895, some friends asked Roosevelt if he might be a candidate for president. "Don't you dare ask me that!" Roosevelt exclaimed. "Don't you put such ideas into my head .... I must be wanting to be president. Every young man does. But I won't let myself think of it ... because if I do, I will begin to work for it, I'll be careful, calculating, cautious... and so—I'll beat myself. See?"

Roosevelt campaigned vigorously for William McKinley, the Republican candidate for president in 1896. McKinley won, and Roosevelt asked him for a government appointment. McKinley did not want this brash young man in Washington, but Roosevelt had powerful support. The president finally made him an assistant secretary of the Navy.

Roosevelt believed that sea power was the decisive factor in world history. He worked to strengthen the Navy. He also believed that war for a righteous cause brought out the finest virtues in people and nations. "No triumph of peace is quite so great as the supreme triumphs of war," he said soon after taking office. "The diplomat is the servant, not the master, of the soldier."

The Rough Riders. Since 1895, Cuban rebels had been revolting against their Spanish rulers. Many Americans demanded that the United States help the Cubans. On Feb. 15, 1898, the U.S. battleship *Maine* blew up in Havana harbor. Roosevelt tried to rush preparations for war against Spain. He became impatient with McKinley's attempts to avoid war. In private, Roosevelt complained that the president had "no more backbone than a chocolate éclair."

Library of Congress

As assistant secretary of the Navy, which he became in 1897, Roosevelt worked to strengthen U.S. naval forces. He resigned in 1898 to fight in the Spanish-American War.

On April 25, 1898, the United States declared war on Spain. Roosevelt immediately resigned as assistant secretary of the Navy so he could fight. Even before resigning, he had started to recruit men for a cavalry regiment. This unit became the First Volunteer Cavalry Regiment. Under Roosevelt's command, it won fame as the Rough Riders. Most of the men were former college athletes and Western cowboys.

On July 1, 1898, American troops attacked a ring of fortified hills surrounding Santiago, Cuba. Colonel Roosevelt led his men in a charge up Kettle Hill, which flanked the Spanish blockhouse on San Juan Hill. He and the Rough Riders became nationally famous. Twenty years later he declared: "San Juan was the great day of my life." See **Spanish-American War.**

Governor of New York. The Republicans faced defeat in New York in 1898 because of a scandal over state canal contracts. The state party leader, Senator Thomas C. Platt, did not like Roosevelt. But Platt knew that Roosevelt's reputation might save the Republicans. Roosevelt agreed to run for governor. He won, largely because of his war record.

As governor, Roosevelt did not break with Platt. Neither did he follow Platt's wishes. He described this policy to a friend: "I have always been fond of the West African proverb: 'Speak softly and carry a big stick, you will go far.' " Roosevelt became an efficient, independent administrator. He supported mild reform legislation, including a law affecting civil service in the state. He angered large business interests by approving a bill for the taxation of corporation franchises.

Vice president. McKinley's renomination in 1900 seemed certain. Roosevelt had no wish to oppose the president, who he knew had nationwide support. But

Library of Congress

The Rough Riders, a regiment led by Roosevelt, became nationally famous for their role in helping to win the Battle of San Juan in the Spanish-American War.

Roosevelt wondered whether he himself might get the nomination in 1904. As the Republican National Convention drew near, a movement began to nominate him for vice president.

Roosevelt felt that being vice president would take him out of active politics. In this way, his chances for the presidential nomination in 1904 would be weakened. Roosevelt also knew that Senator Platt wanted to get rid of him as governor of New York. Roosevelt felt he might not win a second term as governor in opposition to Platt. He finally consented to be McKinley's running mate. The Republicans nominated both men by acclamation. In the election, McKinley and Roosevelt defeated their Democratic opponents, William Jennings Bryan and former Vice President Adlai E. Stevenson.

On Sept. 6, 1901, only six months after his second inauguration, President McKinley was shot by an assassin. The tragedy occurred while McKinley was at the Pan American Exposition in Buffalo, New York. Doctors told Roosevelt that McKinley would probably recover. But, while vacationing in the Adirondack Mountains, Roosevelt learned McKinley was near death. He hurried to Buffalo, but McKinley died before Roosevelt arrived. That day, Sept. 14, 1901, Roosevelt took the oath of office as president. See **McKinley, William** (Assassination).

Roosevelt's first administration (1901-1905)

Roosevelt became president just six weeks before his 43rd birthday. He kept all the members of McKinley's Cabinet. He said he would continue McKinley's policies "absolutely unbroken." But Roosevelt had too much originality to follow another person's plans.

Most business leaders feared Roosevelt because of some reforms he had introduced as governor of New York. Several of these reforms had brought about stricter government control over industry. Early in his administration, Roosevelt tried to convince business people that he would not interfere with them. He also tried to persuade conservative Republican leaders that he was not dangerous. But he never won them over completely. They considered much of his legislation dangerously progressive, even socialistic. The Republicans controlled Congress throughout Roosevelt's presidency. But because of conservative opposition, Roosevelt had increasing difficulty getting Congress to act on his recommendations.

"Trust buster." Many Americans had become worried about the *trusts,* or large business monopolies. These trusts were increasing rapidly in both number and power. The trusts had increased productivity and had raised the standard of living. But prices had also risen, and the people blamed the trusts. In his first message to Congress, in December 1901, Roosevelt expressed this feeling. "Captains of industry ... have on the whole done great good to our people," he said. But he also pointed to "real and grave evils." Roosevelt recommended that "combination and concentration should be, not prohibited, but supervised and, within reasonable limits, controlled."

In 1902, the government sued the Northern Securities Company on charges of trying to reduce competition. This firm had been formed by J. P. Morgan and other financiers to control key railroads in the West. Roosevelt said he did not want to use the power of the government to ruin Morgan. Rather, he wanted to keep order among all the great economic forces in the nation. The Supreme Court upheld the government's view in 1904. It dissolved the Northern Securities Company.

During Roosevelt's presidency, the government filed suits against 43 other corporations. In major cases, the government ended John D. Rockefeller's oil trust and James B. Duke's tobacco trust. Many people called Roosevelt a "trust buster." But the president declared that he wanted the government to regulate, not "bust," trusts.

Friend of labor. Roosevelt wanted the government to act justly toward labor unions as well as toward business. Government intervention in labor disputes was not new. But it had usually favored management.

In May 1902, about 140,000 members of the United Mine Workers went on strike in the hard-coal fields of

Pennsylvania. Public opinion favored the strikers, who demanded more pay and better working conditions. As the strike continued, coal supplies began to run low in Eastern cities. Many hospitals and schools had no fuel. Winter was approaching.

Roosevelt had no legal authority to intervene in the strike. But he called a conference of leaders of both sides. He proposed that the strike be settled by arbitration. The miners agreed, but the mine owners refused. Roosevelt threatened to have the army seize and operate the mines. At Roosevelt's request, J. P. Morgan helped reach a compromise with the mine owners. The miners got a pay raise the next March. Roosevelt said later that he had tried to give the miners a "square deal." He often used this phrase to refer to his policy of social reform. In 1903, Congress established the Department of Commerce and Labor (see **Labor, Department of**).

Foreign policy. Roosevelt believed that the government needed a "big stick," or threat of force, to carry out its foreign policies. He used this policy in relations with Europe and Latin America.

The Venezuela Affair. The Monroe Doctrine held that the United States should keep European powers out of the Western Hemisphere. Roosevelt upheld this doctrine in what was known as the Venezuela Affair.

Venezuela had borrowed large sums of money in Europe. In December 1902, British, German, and Italian ships blockaded Venezuelan ports to force payment of the debts. Roosevelt feared that Germany planned to seize Venezuelan territory. He warned the Germans that he might have to use force if they took any part of Venezuela. The Germans withdrew their warships. Later, Roosevelt helped settle the dispute peacefully.

The "Roosevelt Corollary." In 1904, the Dominican Republic found it could not pay its debts to several European countries. Again, Roosevelt feared European intervention. He announced that the United States might be forced "in flagrant cases of ... wrongdoing or impotence, to the exercise of an international police power." This policy was called the "Roosevelt Corollary" of the Monroe Doctrine.

Theodore Roosevelt Collection, Harvard College Library

Roosevelt spoke out against trusts on various occasions. Although he denied being a "trust buster," Roosevelt believed government should regulate large business monopolies.

Roosevelt ordered American officials to take over the customs system of the Dominican Republic in 1904. American control, which began the next year, brought order to the Dominican Republic's finances.

The Panama Canal. Between 1902 and 1905, Roosevelt persuaded Congress to approve building 10 battleships and 4 armored cruisers for the United States Navy. He believed the larger fleet would give the nation greater influence in international affairs. But the fleet would need to shift rapidly between the Atlantic and Pacific oceans. A canal across Central America seemed necessary.

In 1902, Roosevelt began negotiating with Colombia for the right to build a canal across Panama, a province of Colombia. The negotiators signed a treaty, but the Colombian Senate rejected it. Roosevelt then supported a revolutionary government that took control of Panama, and the United States recognized the Republic of Panama. Less than two weeks later, the United States and Panama signed a treaty granting to the United States the use and control of a strip of land on which to dig a canal. Roosevelt said he was prouder of the canal than of any other accomplishment of his administration. He visited Panama in 1906—the first president to travel in a foreign country while in office. See **Panama Canal** (picture: President Theodore Roosevelt).

The Alaskan boundary dispute. No one cared about the exact boundary between Canada and Alaska until gold was discovered in the Klondike in 1896. Then Canada claimed a line that gave it control of important routes to the gold fields. The United States disputed the claim. Early in 1902, the United Kingdom asked that the matter be settled by arbitration. At first, Roosevelt refused. But then he agreed that the dispute should be settled by a tribunal of six "impartial jurists" appointed by both countries. In 1903, the tribunal ruled in favor of the United States.

Conservation. Roosevelt made notable achievements in conservation. He added about 150 million acres (61 million hectares) to the national forests and in 1905 established the United States Forest Service. He also set up five new national parks. Congress passed the Reclamation Act of 1902, which provided for the reclamation and irrigation of dry Western lands. Roosevelt then started 25 irrigation or reclamation projects (see **Roosevelt Dam**). He also set aside 18 sites as national monuments and worked to preserve wildlife. By executive order, he created the first 51 federal bird reservations and established the first four national game preserves.

Life in the White House was never dull during Roosevelt's presidency. The Roosevelt children and their friends became known as the "White House Gang." The president sometimes joined in the children's games. One day, he heard that the gang was preparing an "attack" on the White House. He sent a message to the children through the War Department, ordering them to call off the "attack." Once Roosevelt scolded his sons for decorating a portrait of President Andrew Jackson with spitballs. But he allowed the boys to bring their pets, including a pony and snakes, into the White House.

The president often played tennis on the White House

Culver

Roosevelt went to Panama in 1906 to inspect progress on the construction of the Panama Canal. He considered the canal the greatest achievement of his presidency.

lawn with friends. These friends came to be known as the "tennis cabinet." The group also went horseback riding and hiking. More than once, on winter hikes, Roosevelt and his friends swam across the Potomac River through chunks of floating ice.

In 1902, the White House was remodeled and enlarged. The east and west wings were built. Workers installed new plumbing, heating, and electrical systems.

Edith Roosevelt was an efficient and gracious White House hostess. She carefully kept out of politics. The president's daughter by his first marriage was called "Princess Alice" by newspaper reporters. In 1906, Alice married Representative Nicholas Longworth of Ohio, who later served as speaker of the House of Representatives. Their wedding took place in the White House.

Election of 1904. The Republicans unanimously nominated Roosevelt for president at their 1904 national convention. They chose Senator Charles W. Fairbanks of Indiana for vice president. The Democrats nominated Judge Alton B. Parker of the New York Supreme Court for president, and Henry G. Davis of West Virginia for vice president.

During the election campaign, Roosevelt called on the voters to support his "square deal" policies. Parker appealed for an end to what he called "rule of individual caprice" and "usurpation of authority" by the president. Roosevelt won the election by more than 2 ½ million popular votes. No earlier president had won by so large a margin.

Roosevelt's second administration (1905-1909)

Domestic problems. Roosevelt believed that laws were badly needed to control the nation's railroads. The Elkins Act of 1903 had prohibited railroads from making *rebates,* or returning sums of money, to favored shippers. But the act had not stopped such practices, which often put rival shippers out of business. Roosevelt demanded legislation to curb the abuses. In 1906, Congress passed the Hepburn Railway Rate Act despite conservative opposition. The act did not end the rebates, but it was a step in that direction.

The food and drug industries were also affected by reforms. In 1906, Roosevelt read Upton Sinclair's new novel *The Jungle.* It described unsanitary conditions in the meat-packing industry. Roosevelt ordered an investigation and received what he called a "sickening report." He threatened to publish the report if Congress did not

Vice president and Cabinet

Vice president	* Charles W. Fairbanks
Secretary of state	* John Hay
	* Elihu Root (1905)
	Robert Bacon (1909)
Secretary of the treasury	Lyman J. Gage
	Leslie M. Shaw (1902)
	George B. Cortelyou (1907)
Secretary of war	* Elihu Root
	* William Howard Taft (1904)
	Luke E. Wright (1908)
Attorney general	Philander C. Knox
	William H. Moody (1904)
	Charles J. Bonaparte (1906)
Postmaster general	Charles E. Smith
	Henry C. Payne (1902)
	Robert J. Wynne (1904)
	George B. Cortelyou (1905)
	George von L. Meyer (1907)
Secretary of the Navy	John D. Long
	William H. Moody (1902)
	Paul Morton (1904)
	Charles J. Bonaparte (1905)
	Victor H. Metcalf (1906)
	Truman H. Newberry (1908)
Secretary of the interior	Ethan A. Hitchcock
	James R. Garfield (1907)
Secretary of agriculture	James Wilson
Secretary of commerce and labor	George B. Cortelyou
	Victor H. Metcalf (1904)
	Oscar S. Straus (1906)

*Has a separate biography in *World Book.*

John Todaro

Sagamore Hill, Roosevelt's home on Long Island, New York, provided a spacious setting for his large, active family. It served as a summer White House during his presidency.

Roosevelt's election

Place of nominating convention	Chicago
Ballot on which nominated	1st
Democratic opponent	Alton B. Parker
Electoral vote*	336 (Roosevelt) to 140 (Parker)
Popular vote	7,626,593 (Roosevelt) to 5,082,898 (Parker)
Age at inauguration	46

*For votes by states, see **Electoral College** (table).

correct the situation. That same year, Congress passed the Meat Inspection Act and the Food and Drugs Act. See **Pure food and drug laws**.

In 1907, the stock market slumped. A financial panic spread throughout the country. The business community blamed Roosevelt and his progressive legislation. But most historians believe that speculation and inefficient business management actually caused the panic. Prosperity returned by 1909.

Friction with Japan. In 1905, Roosevelt helped end the Russo-Japanese War. He brought representatives of Russia and Japan together in Portsmouth, New Hampshire. Then the president served as mediator in the peace talks that led to the Treaty of Portsmouth. In 1906, Roosevelt received the Nobel Peace Prize. He was the first American to win a Nobel Prize.

As the victors in the war, the Japanese demanded compensation payments from Russia. During the peace talks, Roosevelt had opposed this demand. His attitude angered the Japanese and also Japanese Americans in the United States. Their anger grew in 1906, when the San Francisco school board decided to segregate children of Japanese descent.

Relations between the United States and Japan became more strained. Roosevelt feared a Japanese attack on the Philippines. Many Americans thought war with Japan was near. But the president persuaded the San Francisco school board to end its segregation policy. He also negotiated a *gentlemen's agreement* with Japan to keep Japanese laborers out of the United States (see **Gentlemen's agreement**). In 1908, Japan and the United States signed the Root-Takahira Agreement. In this pact, the two nations promised not to seek territorial gains in the Pacific, and to honor the Open-Door Policy in China (see **Open-Door Policy**).

In 1907, Roosevelt decided to display American naval power. He sent 16 new battleships on a good-will tour of the world. These ships became known as the *Great White Fleet* because they were painted white. The fleet received enthusiastic welcomes in Japan and other countries. Roosevelt viewed the tour as a part of "big stick" diplomacy.

European power balance was maintained with Roosevelt's help. In 1905, Germany demanded a share in the control of Morocco, which was dominated by France. Two alliances of nations—one headed by Germany, the other by Britain and France—came close to war. Roosevelt persuaded Germany to attend an international conference in Spain in 1906. At the conference, the United States sided with France and Britain. Germany backed down on its demand.

A party split developed among the Republicans as Roosevelt neared the end of his presidency. Conservative Republicans put up increased resistance to Roosevelt's progressive policies. Roosevelt fought harder for "political, social, and industrial reform." But during his last year in office, he got little congressional action. His Republican opponents dared to resist him because they believed he would leave office in 1909.

Roosevelt had declared after his election in 1904 that he would "under no circumstances" run for president again. He decided to keep this pledge. He selected William Howard Taft, his secretary of war, to succeed him. At the Republican National Convention of 1908, he persuaded most of the delegates to support Taft for president. In this way, he assured Taft's nomination. Taft won an easy election victory over the Democratic candidate, William Jennings Bryan.

Later years

After leaving the presidency in March 1909, Roosevelt sailed for Africa to hunt big game. Some conservative congressmen wished "health to the lions." But Roosevelt and his party brought down 296 big-game animals, including 9 lions. When Roosevelt arrived home in June 1910, he found himself the center of national attention.

Progressive Republicans felt that Taft had betrayed them. They turned to Roosevelt.

"Bull Moose" candidate. Roosevelt tried to bring together the progressive and conservative wings of the Republican Party. But he failed. He had become identified too closely with the progressives.

In 1910, on a speaking tour of the West, Roosevelt proclaimed a policy of "New Nationalism." It became the policy of the progressive Republicans. Roosevelt declared that the president needed to be the "steward of public welfare." He frightened conservatives with his views on private property. Roosevelt said that property was "subject to the general right of the community to regulate its use to whatever degree the public welfare may require it."

In 1912, Roosevelt gave in to pleas that he run for a third term as president. He said that his statement in 1904 had meant not running for a third *consecutive* term. He won many victories in primary elections. These victories indicated he was the popular choice of the party. But President Taft controlled the party machinery and was renominated by the Republican National Convention. Roosevelt and his followers formed the Progressive Party, or *Bull Moose* party. The name came from Roosevelt's reply when a reporter asked how he felt. "I feel as strong as a bull moose," he said.

On Oct. 14, 1912, a saloonkeeper named John N. Schrank tried to assassinate Roosevelt. Schrank shot Roosevelt just before he made a speech in Milwaukee. A glasses case in Roosevelt's pocket deflected the bullet and probably saved his life. Even with the bullet in his chest, Roosevelt insisted on making the speech. He recovered from the wound in about two weeks. Schrank was committed to a mental hospital.

Roosevelt's candidacy split the Republican vote. The Democratic candidate, Governor Woodrow Wilson of New Jersey, easily won the election. See **Wilson, Woodrow** (Presidential candidate).

World War I began in 1914. Roosevelt called for American preparedness against a "strong, ruthless, ambitious, militaristic ... Germany." He developed an intense dislike of Wilson, mostly because the president did not lead the nation into war immediately. After the United States entered the war in 1917, Roosevelt asked Wilson for permission to raise a division of troops to fight in France. Wilson refused the request.

Roosevelt's sons served in France. Quentin, an aviator, was killed in an air battle with a German pilot.

Death. In 1914, Roosevelt had explored the River of Doubt in the Brazilian jungle. He contracted a form of jungle fever and returned weak and prematurely aged. Early in 1918, Roosevelt underwent operations to remove abscesses on his thigh and in his ears. The abscesses resulted from the jungle fever. He lost the hearing in his left ear. At about this time, Roosevelt revealed that he had been blind in his left eye since 1908. He lost the sight in the eye as a result of an injury he received boxing with a military aide in the White House.

Roosevelt opposed American membership in the League of Nations, which he felt would limit the United States in foreign relations. He might have won the Republican presidential nomination in 1920. But Roosevelt died unexpectedly of a blood clot in the heart on Jan. 6, 1919. He was buried in Youngs Memorial Cemetery,

© Shutterstock

Theodore Roosevelt Island lies in the Potomac River in Washington, D.C. The island, maintained by the National Park Service, features a large statue of the former president, *shown here.*

near Sagamore Hill in Oyster Bay, New York. His second wife died in 1948 and was buried beside him.

Roosevelt's birthplace in New York City and Sagamore Hill are national historic sites, as is the Wilcox Mansion in Buffalo, New York, where Roosevelt took the oath of office in 1901. Theodore Roosevelt National Park, in western North Dakota, includes one of the ranches Roosevelt operated in the 1880's. Roosevelt's other ranch is nearby. Theodore Roosevelt Island, in the Potomac River in Washington, D.C., has a large statue of the former president. Roosevelt is also one of the four presidents whose faces are carved on Mount Rushmore in South Dakota. John A. Gable

Related articles in *World Book* include:

Antitrust laws
Conservation (The rise of the conservation movement)
Fairbanks, Charles Warren
McKinley, William
Mount Rushmore National Memorial
Panama Canal (picture)
Parker, Alton Brooks
President of the United States
Progressive Party
Pure food and drug laws
Roosevelt, Theodore, Jr.
Roosevelt Dam
Rough Riders
Spanish-American War
Taft, William Howard
White House (History)

Outline

I. Early life
A. Boyhood and education
B. First marriage
II. Political and public activities
A. State legislator

B. Party leader
C. Rancher and writer
D. Second marriage
E. Civil Service commissioner
F. Police commissioner

III. A national figure
A. Assistant secretary of the Navy
B. The Rough Riders
C. Governor of New York
D. Vice president

IV. Roosevelt's first administration (1901-1905)
A. "Trust buster"
B. Friend of labor
C. Foreign policy
D. Conservation
E. Life in the White House
F. Election of 1904

V. Roosevelt's second administration (1905-1909)
A. Domestic problems
B. Friction with Japan
C. European power balance
D. A party split

VI. Later years
A. "Bull Moose" candidate
B. World War I
C. Death

Questions

As a boy, how did Roosevelt build up his strength?
What was the "White House gang"?
What phrase did Roosevelt use to describe his foreign policy?
Why did Roosevelt become known as a "trust buster"?
How did the "Bull Moose" party get its name?
What were some of Roosevelt's achievements in conservation?
How did Roosevelt first win national fame?
What did the "Roosevelt Corollary" proclaim?
What was the *Great White Fleet?*
What did Roosevelt call "the great day of my life"?

Additional resources

Adler, David A. *Colonel Theodore Roosevelt.* Holiday Hse., 2014. Younger readers.
Di Silvestro, Roger L. *Theodore Roosevelt in the Badlands.* Walker, 2011.
Gould, Lewis L. *Edith Kermit Roosevelt.* Univ. Pr. of Kans., 2013. *Theodore Roosevelt.* Oxford, 2012.
Hollihan, Kerrie L. *Theodore Roosevelt for Kids.* Chicago Review Pr., 2010. Includes activities related to Roosevelt's life. Younger readers.
Morris, Edmund. *The Rise of Theodore Roosevelt.* 1979. Reprint. Random Hse., 2010. *Theodore Rex.* 2001. *Colonel Roosevelt.* 2010. These books make up a three-part biography of Roosevelt.
Roosevelt, Theodore. *Selected Speeches and Writings of Theodore Roosevelt.* Ed. by Gordon Hutner. Vintage, 2014.
Thompson, J. Lee. *Never Call Retreat: Theodore Roosevelt and the Great War.* Palgrave Macmillan, 2013.
Ward, Geoffrey C., and Burns, Ken. *The Roosevelts: An Intimate History.* Knopf, 2014.

Roosevelt, *ROH zuh vehlt,* **Theodore, Jr.** (1887-1944), was the oldest son of President Theodore Roosevelt. Like his father, he was a soldier, statesman, and author.

Roosevelt was born on Sept. 13, 1887, in Oyster Bay, New York. He commanded an infantry battalion in 1917 and 1918 and an infantry regiment in late 1918 during World War I (1914-1918). He received the Silver Star and the Distinguished Service Cross. In 1919, Roosevelt helped organize the American Legion. A Republican, he served in the New York State Assembly in 1920 and 1921 and as assistant secretary of the Navy from 1921 to 1924. Roosevelt served as governor of Puerto Rico from 1929 to 1932 and governor general of the Philippines in 1932 and 1933, both appointed posts. Roosevelt was a brigadier general during World War II (1939-1945). He received the Medal of Honor for his actions on D-Day (June 6, 1944), when he led troops ashore at Utah Beach, in France. He died of a heart attack in France on July 12, 1944. Roosevelt wrote many books and articles on hunting, adventure, and public policy.

John A. Gable

Roosevelt Campobello International Park, *ROH zuh vehlt* KAM *puh BEHL* OH, covers about 2,800 acres (1,100 hectares) on Campobello Island in New Brunswick, Canada. For the location of the park, see **New Brunswick** (physical map). The summer home of United States President Franklin D. Roosevelt is in the park. Roosevelt's family often spent vacations there. He was stricken with poliomyelitis on the island in 1921. The United States and Canada dedicated the park in 1964. A joint U.S.-Canadian commission administers it. The Franklin D. Roosevelt Memorial Bridge connects the island and Lubec, Maine.

Critically reviewed by Roosevelt Campobello International Park

Roosevelt Dam, *ROH zuh vehlt,* is part of the Salt River irrigation project in south-central Arizona. It was originally built by the United States Bureau of Reclamation as a rubble-masonry arch-gravity dam. Construction was completed in 1911. It was officially named the Theodore Roosevelt Dam in 1959. An extensive renovation project was completed on the dam in 1996. The dam is 357 feet (109 meters) high and has a crest length of 1,210 feet (369 meters). Its reservoir covers about 21,500 acres (8,700 hectares) and stores about 1.6 million acre-feet (2 billion cubic meters) of water. The dam is used for flood control, water storage, and power production.

Critically reviewed by the Bureau of Reclamation

Roosevelt Memorial. See **Franklin Delano Roosevelt Memorial.**

Rooster. See **Chicken.**

Root, in arithmetic, is a quantity that yields a given quantity when it is taken as a factor a specified number of times (see **Factor**). The number of times the root is taken as a factor is called its *index.* Roots are named from their indexes. Thus, 3 is a *fourth* root of 81, because $3 \times 3 \times 3 \times 3 = 81$. Roots with indexes of 2 and 3 are also called *square roots* and *cube roots,* respectively. The positive *n* th root of a positive number *p* is indicated by $\sqrt[n]{p}$. Thus, $\sqrt[4]{81} = 3$. The symbol $\sqrt{\ }$ is a *radical sign.* When no index is shown, the index 2 is understood.

A root in algebra is a solution of an equation—that is, it is a quantity which, when substituted for the variable in an equation, satisfies the equation. For example, 3 is a root of $x + 2 = 5$, because if 3 is substituted for the variable *x*, the equation correctly reads $3 + 2 = 5$.

Robert M. Vancko

See also **Algebra; Cube root; Square root.**

Root is one of the three main organs of a plant. The others are the stem and the leaf. Most roots are long and round and grow underground. They anchor the plant in the soil. They also absorb water and minerals that the plant needs to grow. In addition, many roots store food for later use by the plant.

Plants with roots include all seed-producing plants and most spore-producing plants, such as ferns and horsetails. Liverworts, hornworts, and mosses do not have true roots.

Kinds of roots

The first root to develop from a seed is the *primary* root. It produces many branches called *secondary* roots. The secondary roots produce branches of their own.

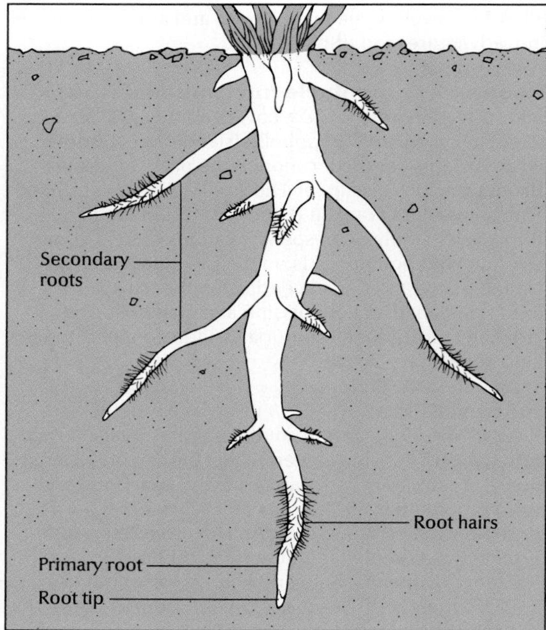

WORLD BOOK diagram by Robert Keys

The main parts of a root system appear in this illustration. The *primary root* develops first and produces branches called *secondary roots. Root hairs* grow just above the tip of each root.

There are two main kinds of root systems, *taproot* or *fibrous.* In a taproot system, the primary root grows straight down and is called the *taproot.* The taproot remains larger than any of the secondary roots throughout the life of the plant. In some plants, including beets and carrots, the taproot becomes *fleshy* (swollen).

Grass is an example of a plant with a fibrous root system. In such a system, the primary root does not remain larger than the others. Many slender secondary roots grow out in all directions. A fibrous root system may become very extensive. For example, the roots of a rye plant may have a combined length of about 380 miles (612 kilometers).

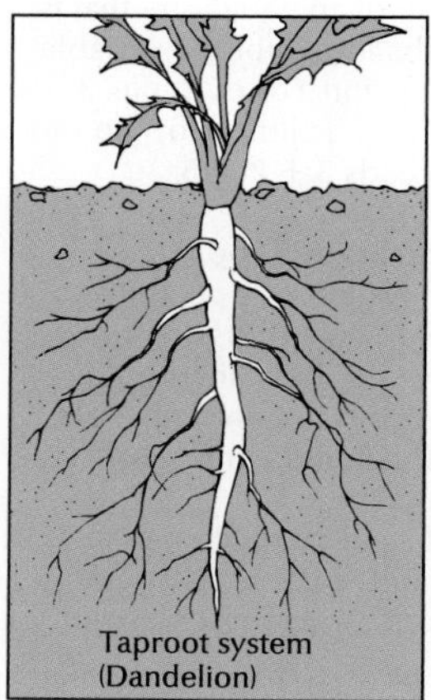

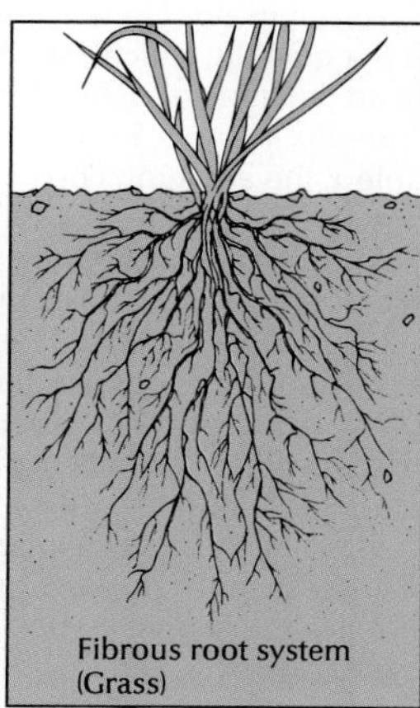

WORLD BOOK diagrams by Robert Keys

The two chief kinds of root systems. In a *taproot system,* the primary root grows straight down and remains larger than secondary roots. In a *fibrous root system,* secondary roots grow in all directions and may be as long as the primary root.

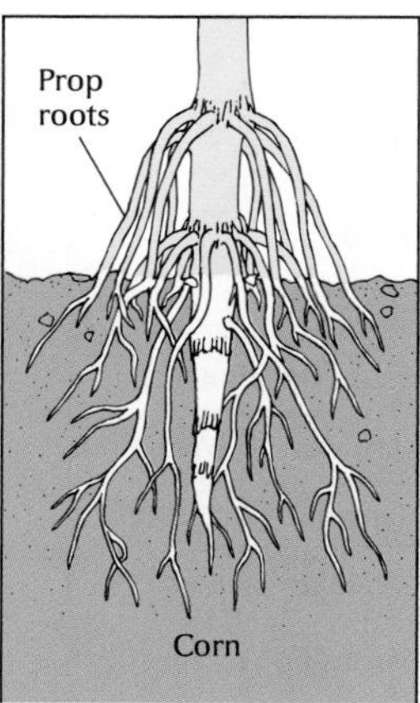

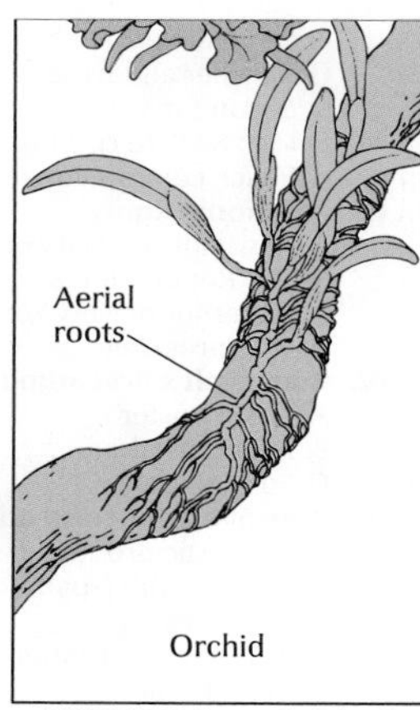

WORLD BOOK diagrams by Robert Keys

Specialized roots. *Prop roots* grow from a stem and help brace a plant against the wind. *Aerial roots* cling to tree branches and absorb water and minerals from the tree and the air.

Some plants have modified roots that perform special functions. Roots that grow from the primary root or its branches are called *adventitious roots.* They include the *prop roots* of corn and certain other plants. Prop roots grow down into the soil from the lower part of the stem and help brace the plant against the wind. Some species of orchids and other plants that live on tree branches send out *aerial roots,* which cling to the branches. Aerial roots absorb water and minerals from the surface of the tree and from the air. Mistletoe is one of the few plants with roots that penetrate the limbs of a tree. These roots, called *sinkers,* absorb food, water, and minerals directly from the tree.

Parts of a root

The root tip. A root grows in length from an area at its *apex* (tip). This growth area is called the *apical meristem.* A meristem is any part of a plant where the cells divide rapidly, forming new cells continually. The apical meristem produces the *root cap,* a thimble-shaped group of cells. The root cap protects the delicate root tip from damage as the root grows in length and the tip pushes through the soil.

The cells produced by the apical meristem are all small and nearly identical. In the *region of elongation,* just behind the apical meristem, the cells rapidly grow longer. Farther back lies the *region of maturation.* There, the cells *differentiate*—that is, they take on a different structure and appearance according to their functions in the mature root. The distance from the root cap to the region of maturation is only a few tenths of an inch or a few millimeters.

The outer tissues. The outer layer of cells of a root is called the *epidermis.* It serves as a sort of skin and protects the tissues beneath. Tiny, hairlike extensions called *root hairs* grow from the epidermis. The root hairs absorb most of the water and minerals that a plant takes in from the soil. In most kinds of plants, the root hairs live only a few days. They occupy the *root hair zone,* an area just above the root tip. This area is only a few tenths of an inch or a few millimeters long.

A thick layer of rounded cells called the *cortex* lies just inside the epidermis. These cells contain stored food and water. The inner layer of cells of the cortex makes up the *endodermis.*

The core, or *stele,* is the central portion of the root. Its outer layer of cells is called the *pericycle.* Branch roots grow from the pericycle. Inside the pericycle are two kinds of tissues, *xylem* and *phloem.* Xylem includes rows of dead, tubular cells called *vessels,* which conduct water and minerals up to the stem and leaves. Phloem consists largely of rows of long, living cells called *sieve tubes.* These cells transport food down from the leaves for use or storage by the root. In most roots, the xylem forms a pattern shaped like a star or the spokes of a wheel. The phloem lies between the points of the star or between the spokes.

Secondary tissues. All the tissues described so far have been *primary tissues.* Such tissues differentiate from cells created in the apical meristem. Many plants that live just one year have only primary tissues in their roots. But other plants, especially those that live more than one year, have *secondary tissues* in their roots in addition to primary tissues. The growth of primary tissue adds to the length of a root. Secondary tissues add to the root's thickness. Secondary-tissue growth produces the large, brown, woody roots in trees, shrubs, and other plants that live for many years.

Secondary tissues develop from two meristems. One, called the *cork cambium,* originates beneath the epidermis, generally in the pericycle. It produces cork cells

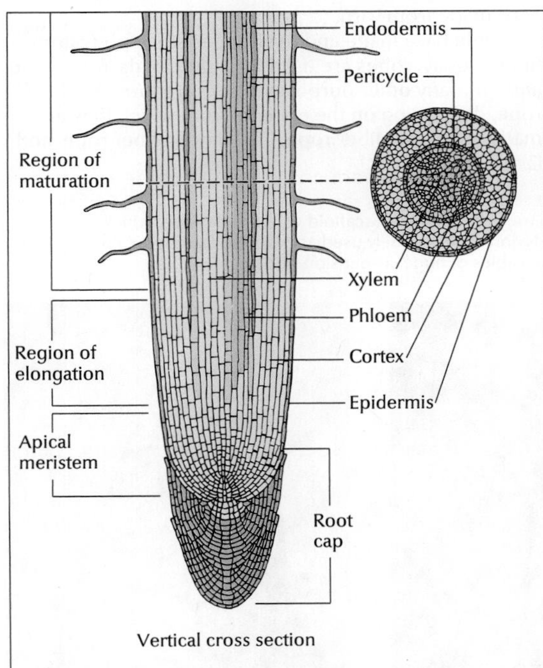

WORLD BOOK diagram by Robert Keys

The root tip comprises the regions in which cells divide *(apical meristem),* grow longer *(region of elongation),* and become specialized *(region of maturation).* The *root cap* protects the tip.

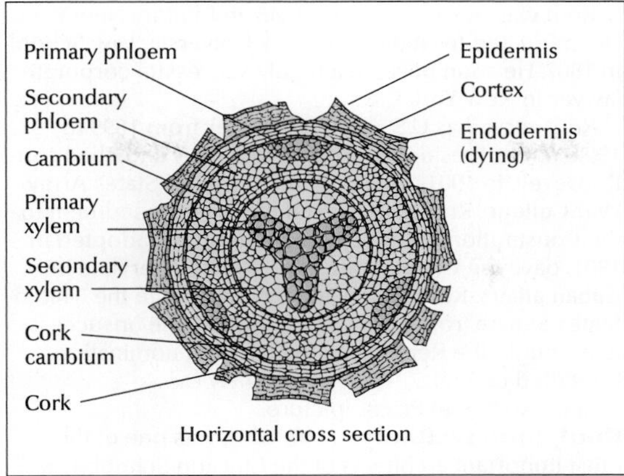

WORLD BOOK diagram by Robert Keys

Secondary tissues develop in some kinds of roots. The *cambium* produces secondary xylem and phloem. The *cork cambium* produces cork. As the cork expands, the outer tissues die.

and pushes them toward the outside of the root. As the cork expands outward, the endodermis, cortex, and epidermis die and peel off. The cork replaces them and becomes the outer covering of the root. The other secondary meristem, the *cambium,* lies between the primary xylem and the primary phloem. It produces secondary xylem cells toward the center of the root, and secondary phloem cells toward the outside.

The importance of roots

Fleshy taproots rank among the most important vegetables. Fleshy taproots include beets, carrots, radishes, rutabagas, and turnips. Sweet potatoes are a root used not only as food but also in making alcohol, starch, and syrup. Roots of the cassava plant are a popular food in the tropics. The roots of tropical yams are used in producing cortisone and related drugs.

Roots help prevent erosion of soil by wind and water. Soil is held in place by the dense network of roots of grasses, trees, and other plants. Plants called *legumes,* which include clover, peas, and soybeans, help enrich the soil. Swellings on their roots contain bacteria that convert nitrogen from the air into compounds. These compounds are useful to the plant. After the plant dies, the compounds become part of the soil.

Richard C. Keating

See also **Alfalfa** (picture); **Carrot; Mangrove; Plant** (The growth of plants; pictures).

Root, Elihu (1845-1937), an American statesman, is best remembered for his efforts to assure international peace. From 1905 to 1909, he served as secretary of state under President Theodore Roosevelt. As secretary of state, Root worked to improve United States relations with Latin American countries and Japan. He also negotiated many treaties to end disputes between the United States and other countries. In 1912, he received the Nobel Peace Prize for his contributions to world peace.

Root served as president of the Carnegie Endowment for International Peace from 1910 to 1925. In 1920 and 1921, he helped organize the Permanent Court of International Justice. For the next 10 years, he battled unsuccessfully to get the United States to join the court.

Root was born on Feb. 15, 1845, in Clinton, New York. He graduated from the New York University Law School in 1867. He soon became a highly successful corporate lawyer in New York City.

Root served as U.S. secretary of war from 1899 to 1904, under Presidents William McKinley and Theodore Roosevelt. In 1901, he founded the United States Army War College. Root also drafted the Platt Amendment to the Constitution of Cuba. This amendment, adopted in 1901, gave the United States the right to intervene in Cuban affairs. Root represented New York in the United States Senate from 1909 to 1915. In 1916, he unsuccessfully sought the Republican presidential nomination. Root died on Feb. 7, 1937. Robert W. Cherny

See also **Nobel Prizes** (picture).

Root, John Wellborn (1850-1891), was one of the most important architects of the Chicago School. The school was an influential group of architects trained in Chicago during the late 1800's. Root became a leader in the aesthetic and technical development of modern office skyscrapers.

Root gained acclaim for the skyscrapers he designed in Chicago with Daniel Hudson Burnham. The two formed a famous partnership in 1873. Their first important project was the 10-story Montauk Block office building (1881-1882). One of their most influential designs was the Rookery office building (1885-1888). Root designed the structure to resemble a hollow square. Masonry walls supported the exterior while the walls around an interior court were supported by a light iron frame. Root's Rand McNally building (1889-1890) was the first to have an all-steel frame, a structural element that became basic to modern design. Root also designed the 22-story Masonic Temple (1890-1892), the world's tallest building for a time. Before his death on Jan. 15, 1891, Root helped design the Reliance Building in Chicago, one of the great skyscrapers of the period. Root was born on Jan. 10, 1850, in Lumpkin, Georgia. Leland M. Roth

See also **Architecture** (Early modern architecture in America); **Burnham, Daniel Hudson**.

Roots is a best-selling autobiographical book by the African American author Alex Haley that traces Haley's ancestry back to 1750. Parts of the book first appeared in the periodical *Reader's Digest* in 1974. The full novel, called *Roots: The Saga of an American Family,* was published in 1976. The book was adapted into an eight-part television series in 1977 that became one of the most-watched programs in television history. A TV sequel, called *Roots: The Next Generation,* was broadcast in 1979. The success of the book and the TV series inspired a new interest in family history among African Americans who had felt distanced from their African origins. *Roots* was remade into another TV miniseries in 2016.

The idea for *Roots* began with stories Haley heard as a boy from his grandmother and aunts in Henning, Tennessee. He spent 12 years researching *Roots,* tracing his ancestry back to the Mandinka ethnic group in Juffure, a village in the Gambia region of western Africa. Haley followed several generations of his family, starting with Kunta Kinte, who was brought to the American Colonies as a slave in 1767 at the age of 17. Haley then portrayed his family's history to the mid-1900's, highlighting events that reflect the racial conflicts of various time periods.

Some critics questioned whether *Roots* should be considered a novel or history. The events are based on fact, but the dialogue and the characters' thoughts are fiction. Andreá N. Williams

See also **Haley, Alex.**

Rope consists of strands of yarn or wire that have been twisted together. It ranges in size from 3⁄16 inch (4.8 millimeters) to more than 6 inches (152 millimeters) in diameter. Rope that is less than 3⁄16 inch thick is called *twine* or *cord. Cordage* is the general term for rope, twine, or cord made from yarn.

People have made and used ropes since prehistoric times. Today, ropes are used for lifting loads, for towing, and for many other purposes. There are three kinds of rope, depending on the material from which they are made: (1) natural-fiber rope, (2) synthetic-fiber rope, and (3) wire rope.

Some uses of rope

Rope has a wide variety of uses. Window washers hang their scaffold with manila rope, which comes from the fibers of the abacá plant. Nylon rope is widely used as *mooring line* to tie ships and boats to docks. Wire ropes secure the cables of huge suspension bridges.

Artstreet

Manila rope

© Shutterstock

Nylon rope

© Shutterstock

Wire rope

Natural-fiber rope is made from fibers that come from plants. The natural fiber most widely used in rope is *manila,* a hard fiber taken from the leaf stems of the abacá plant. Abacá grows mainly in the Philippines, and most manila rope is manufactured there. Manila rope has great strength and good resistance to wind, rain, and sun. See **Abacá.**

Other natural fibers used in rope include *sisal* and *henequen.* Sisal comes from the leaves of the sisal plant, which grows mainly in Brazil and eastern Africa. It is a hard fiber that has about 80 percent of the strength of manila. Henequen is taken from the henequen plant, which grows chiefly in Mexico. Henequen is not as strong as sisal and is used primarily in twine and lower grades of rope. See **Sisal.**

In the past, much rope was also made from soft natural fibers, such as *hemp* and *jute.* Today, soft fibers are used mostly in twine and in the art of *macramé.* See **Hemp; Jute; Macramé.**

Synthetic-fiber rope is stronger, lighter, and, in most cases, more flexible than natural-fiber rope. Synthetic fibers have greater resistance to chemical damage and do not rot, as do natural fibers.

The first synthetic-fiber rope was made from *nylon* during World War II (1939-1945). It was used for parachute cords and glider towropes. Nylon rope is almost three times as strong as manila rope. The great elasticity of nylon rope makes it the best rope for towing and anchor lines.

Rope made from *polyester* fibers is expensive, but it is the best rope for general use. It has almost the same strength as nylon rope but does not have as much stretch. Polyester rope resists damage from *abrasion* (scraping) and the sun's ultraviolet rays better than any other synthetic-fiber rope. *Polypropylene* rope is about 50 percent stronger than manila rope. Special chemical compounds must be added to polypropylene to give it ultraviolet resistance.

Manufacturers make extremely strong rope from synthetic fibers called *aramids.* Rope made from aramid fibers can be used under hotter conditions than other synthetic fibers because it has a high melting point. It also resists stretching.

Manufacturers also produce ropes that combine the desirable features of two or more synthetic fibers. A common combination—polyester and polypropylene—provides a cheaper substitute for polyester.

Wire rope consists of steel wires twisted together. It is stronger and wears better than most fiber rope, but it is much heavier and not as flexible as rope made from fibers. Wire rope, often called *cable,* is used in operating such equipment as elevators, oil well derricks, and shovels used in construction work.

How rope is made. Ropes must be carefully designed to meet such usage requirements as abrasion resistance, chemical and ultraviolet resistance, strength, stretch, and weight. Rope manufacturers buy bales of natural fibers from fiber brokers. A machine called a *card* combs the fibers and lays them parallel, forming a continuous ribbon. The ribbon is drawn out until it is thin enough for spinning. A machine spins the ribbon into yarn, and strands are made by twisting together two or more yarns. Three or more strands are *laid* (twisted) together to form rope.

Parts of a three-strand rope

Rope consists of many fibers that have been spun into yarns. The yarns are then twisted into thick strands. The most common type of rope has three strands *laid* (twisted) together.

WORLD BOOK diagram by Richard Fickle

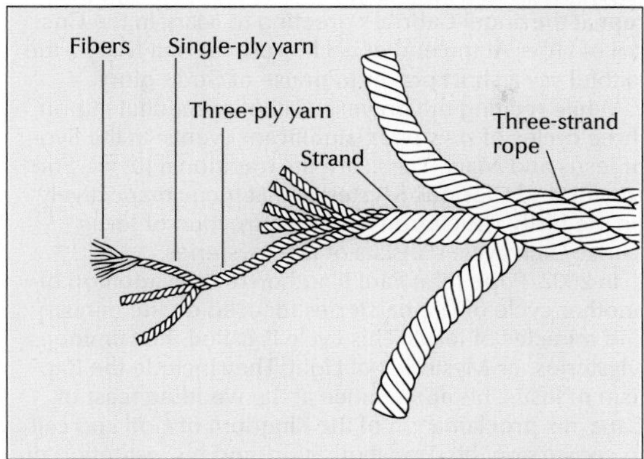

Manufacturers buy most synthetic fibers in *filament* form. A machine called a *twister* twists the long filament yarns into *plied yarns,* which are then made into rope in the same way as natural fiber yarn.

Most rope has three strands, but four- and eight-strand ropes are also popular. Another common type, called *cable-laid rope,* consists of three three-strand ropes *closed* (wrapped) together.

Manufacturers make wire rope by twisting a number of wires together to form strands and then closing the strands around a core. The strongest wire ropes have wire cores. Christine W. Cole

See also **Aramid; Century plant; Cowboy** (His rope); **Fiber; Knots, hitches, and splices; Polypropylene.**

Rorqual. See **Whale** (Rorquals).

Rosario, *roh ZAH ree OH* (pop. 948,312), is one of the largest cities in Argentina and the largest city that is not a provincial capital. It lies on the Paraná River, in the east-central part of the country. For the location of Rosario, see **Argentina** (political map). The city is a major inland seaport and an important industrial center.

Rosario was founded in 1793, but it was not declared a city until 1852. Its location on the eastern edge of the Pampas, a huge fertile plain, led to its significant growth in the late 1800's. At that time, farmers on the Pampas began producing large amounts of agricultural products. Rosario's nearness to the Paraná River made it an ideal point from which to ship the products to places outside the region. Today, five railway lines and five major highways link various parts of northern and central Argentina to Rosario's excellent port facilities. Many factories in Rosario produce processed foods from farm products. The city's other industries include petroleum refining and the manufacture of chemicals, metal products, and textiles. Rosario is modern in appearance and has many boulevards and attractive parks.

David J. Keeling

Rosary is a string of beads used as an aid to memory and concentration while praying. The rosary commonly used by Roman Catholics consists of 50 small beads divided into equal sections by 4 large beads. A pendant, composed of two large beads, three small ones, and a crucifix, hangs from the rosary.

Catholics recite the Lord's Prayer on the large beads. On the small beads, they address prayers called "Hail Marys" to the Virgin Mary. The first words of this prayer repeat the angel Gabriel's greeting to Mary in the Gospel of Luke. At the end of each group of Hail Marys, the faithful say a short prayer in praise of God's glory.

While reciting the prayers, Catholics meditate upon three cycles of *mysteries* (significant events) in the lives of Jesus and Mary. These are the traditional Joyful, Sorrowful, and Glorious Mysteries that focus respectively on the birth, Crucifixion, and Resurrection of Jesus Christ. Each cycle consists of five mysteries.

In 2002, Pope John Paul II authorized the addition of another cycle of five mysteries focused on the ministry and miracles of Jesus. This cycle is called the Luminous Mysteries, or Mysteries of Light. They include the Baptism of Jesus, his appearance at the wedding feast of Cana, his proclamation of the Kingdom of God and call to conversion, his Transfiguration, and his institution of the Eucharist at the Last Supper.

Prayer beads are of ancient origin and were probably first used by Buddhists in an attempt to combine vocal prayer with mental prayer. Buddhists, Hindus, and Muslims use them in certain forms of their prayer. Using the rosary for prayer became widespread in the Catholic Church in the 1400's, and it remains one of the most popular devotional practices. Robert P. Imbelli

Roscius, *RAHSH ee uhs,* **Quintus,** *KWIHN tuhs* (126?-62? B.C.), a Roman actor, was so famous in his day that his name came to stand for "great actor." He excelled in both tragic and comic parts. He founded a school for actors and wrote a book on acting and speaking. One of his admirers was the orator Cicero, who defended him in a famous speech. Quintus Roscius Gallus was born near Rome and became rich through his acting.

Don B. Wilmeth

Rose is any of a large group of flowers that rank among the most popular in the world. People value roses for their beauty and for the sweet fragrance of many varieties. Wild roses commonly grow in gardens and parks. Rose breeders have developed thousands of cultivated rose varieties. Many states and nations—including England, Iran, and the United States—honor the rose as their official flower.

Roses come in many colors, including shades of pink, red, yellow, white, and even lavender. Some types, such as the teas and hybrid teas, smell like tea or fruit. Others have a fragrant "rose" scent, while still others possess little odor.

Attar, an oil from rose petals, can serve as an ingredient in toilet water and perfumes. The fruits of some rose plants, called *hips,* are used in jellies and other preserves and in tea. Rose hips can also add attractive fall and winter color to the landscape.

Roses grow in numerous habitats and soils, but they prefer mild climates or *temperate* climates, which have warm summers and cold winters. Countries that export the most roses as cut flowers include Colombia, Ecuador, Israel, Kenya, and the Netherlands.

Types of roses. *Horticulturists* (experts on flowers and other plants) divide roses into three basic groups. They are (1) *species roses* (wild roses), (2) *old garden roses* (cultivated roses developed before 1867), and (3) *modern roses* (cultivated roses developed after 1867).

Wild roses grow as erect or climbing shrubs. Eglantine, or sweetbrier, is a well-known wild rose. Wild varieties bear thorns, and their flowers have one layer of five petals. Such one-layered blossoms are called *singles.* Most cultivated roses have double blossoms, each of which has many petals arranged in several layers. Some cultivated types lack thorns. Horticulturists breed most cultivated roses as *hybrids,* or as crosses between two different varieties.

Many old garden roses bloom once a year, usually in early summer. They include yellow briers, damask roses, moss roses, noisettes, tea roses, and many climbers. Other old garden roses bloom in early summer and again in fall. The best-known members of this class—called *perpetual roses* or *summer-and-autumn roses*—are the hybrid perpetuals, including the China roses.

Modern roses feature the *everblooming hybrids,* which flower almost constantly during the growing season. One popular group, the hybrid teas, typically have large blooms with many petals. They generally produce each bloom on a single long stem. Floribundas, another group, typically produce smaller blooms that grow in clusters on each stem. *Grandifloras,* developed by crossing hybrid teas and floribundas, often feature clusters of large blooms as well as single blooms. Other modern roses include miniature roses and shrub roses.

Climbing and rambler roses can grow on trellises and fences. Ramblers have more flexible canes than do climbers, and ramblers may be trained to grow into the branches of trees. Some climbers have large flowers,

Some popular varieties of roses

Kind	Description and color
Hybrid teas	Double Delight, red-and-white blend Fragrant Cloud, orange-red Gemini, white with pink edges Mister Lincoln, dark red Pascali, pure white Peace, yellow with pink edges Touch of class, orange-pink
Climbers	Altissimo, medium red Fourth of July, red-and-white blend Golden Showers, yellow New Dawn, soft pink
Floribundas	Betty Boop, red, white, and yellow blend Betty Prior, medium pink Bridal White, white Dicky, orange-pink Iceberg, pure white Nicole, white-and-pink blend Sunsprite, deep yellow
Grandifloras	Gold Medal, medium yellow Queen Elizabeth, medium pink Tournament of Roses, medium pink
Miniatures	Cupcake, medium pink Magic Carrousel, white with red edges Rainbow's end, yellow with red edges Rise 'n' Shine, medium yellow
Shrub roses	Bonica, medium pink Carefree Beauty, medium pink Knock Out, red Sally Holmes, white

© Michael Boys, Corbis

© Shutterstock

© Howard Rice, Alamy

Roses rank among the most popular flowers. In the English rose garden shown here, floribunda and hybrid tea roses grow near arches of climber roses. The deep pink damask roses shown in close-up also come from England. The light orange-pink hybrid tea rose is from New Zealand.

but true ramblers develop clusters of small flowers. Small-flowered climbers are usually the hardiest.

Shrub roses include a wide variety of plants. Horticulturists often divide them into *classic,* or *old, shrubs* and *modern shrubs.* Many shrubs, especially the classic types, may grow very large and spread widely. Modern shrubs often have more compact growth. Popular classic shrubs include hybrid musks and hybrid rugosas, while modern shrubs include ground cover roses and English roses.

Miniature roses, another popular group, range in height from 4 to 18 inches (10 to 46 centimeters). Some have flowers no larger than a small coin.

Cabbage roses bloom with flowers of many petals. These petals overlap in a way similar to the leaves of a head of cabbage. Moss roses, a type of cabbage rose, have stems that resemble moss and rough *sepals* (leaflike structures at the base of the flower).

Of the many rose varieties, some remain popular year after year. Others disappear because plant breeders produce better ones. Today, however, numerous old garden roses have become popular again, partly because people find them easier to maintain than many modern types.

Reproducing and growing roses. Almost all new rose varieties start as seedlings. Yet cultivated roses with double blossoms seldom bear seeds. In such varieties, the parts of the flower that produce seeds have changed to extra petals. Thus horticulturists usually reproduce hybrid roses using one of two systems: *grafting* and *own-rooting.* Grafting, the most common method, involves taking the shoot of one rose and joining it to the *rootstock* of another. A rootstock is a root plus a stem. Growers often use own-rooting for miniatures, old garden roses, and shrub roses. This method simply involves reproducing the plants from cuttings, without the use of grafting. By the early 2000's, some roses normally grown by grafting became available as own-root roses.

Many growers sell roses as bare-root plants, with their roots packed in moist material to prevent drying. Others sell roses in the containers in which they are grown. Gardeners should plant bare-root roses in early to mid-spring, before new shoots begin to grow, making sure to soak the roots in water before planting. Roses purchased in their containers can be planted from spring to early fall.

The location for a rose garden should get many hours of sunlight and should be sheltered from cold wind. A deep, rich, sandy loam that is slightly acidic usually provides the best soil for roses. But hybrid roses will also grow in less fertile sandy or gravelly soil. Rose beds must be well drained because the plants do not thrive in wet ground. Most soils benefit from adding fertilizer. Gardeners also should add such organic matter as compost or potting bark to improve drainage and aeration.

To plant a rose, dig a hole and mix organic matter and fertilizer into the soil. The hole should go deep enough to let the roots point downward and slant outward. Rose roots must not lie flat. Arrange the plants so the beds are easy to water and weed. Try to keep the beds 5 feet

(1.5 meters) wide or less, and space the plants 1 ½ to 2 ½ feet (46 to 76 centimeters) apart. The exact distance depends on their spreading habits. Use a sharp steel rake or similar tool to keep the soil loose and the weeds out. Do not cultivate so deeply that you injure the roots.

The rose family makes up an important group of flowering plants. The family also includes trees that produce such fruits as apples, pears, peaches, apricots, plums, and cherries. The rose family's many ornamental trees and shrubs include the meadowsweet, mountain ash, rowan tree, and hawthorn.

Plants of the rose family produce *regular flowers*, flowers with all the same parts alike in shape and size. In most species, each flower has five petals atop a five-lobed part called the *calyx*. Fred T. Davies, Jr.

Scientific classification. Roses belong to the rose family, Rosaceae. They make up the genus *Rosa*.

See also **Attar; Eglantine; Flower** (picture: Garden perennials [Flowering shrubs]); **Rose water.**

Rose, Derrick (1988-), is a star player in the National Basketball Association (NBA). Rose stands 6 feet 3 inches (191 centimeters) tall and plays guard. He became noted for his playmaking and for his acrobatic moves and slam dunks. As a member of the Chicago Bulls, Rose was named the NBA's Most Valuable Player for the 2010-2011 season. He was the youngest player in NBA history to receive the award.

Derrick Martell Rose was born on Oct. 4, 1988, in Chicago. In high school, he led Chicago's Simeon Career Academy to two Illinois state championships. Rose attended the University of Memphis for the 2007-2008 season, helping the school reach the finals of the National Collegiate Athletic Association tournament.

Rose left college after a year to join the NBA. The Bulls made him the first selection in the 2008 draft. He was the NBA Rookie of the Year for the 2008-2009 season. He missed the 2012-2013 season and most of the 2013-2014 season because of knee injuries.

Rose played for a series of teams later in his career. The Bulls traded Rose to the New York Knicks in 2016. Rose joined the Cleveland Cavaliers in 2017, and he signed with the Minnesota Timberwolves in 2018. He played for the Detroit Pistons beginning in 2019. Rose rejoined the Knicks in a 2021 trade. Sam Smith

Rose, Ernestine Potowski (1810-1892), was a leading reformer in the United States during the mid-1800's. She became especially known as an early supporter of efforts to obtain equal rights for women.

In the 1840's, Rose led a campaign in New York for legislation permitting women to keep control of property they had owned before marriage. Laws of the day gave their husbands control of such possessions. The state legislature passed the bill in 1848. Rose then became active in the new women's rights movement, which started at Seneca Falls, New York, in 1848 (see **Woman suffrage**).

Rose addressed women's rights conventions and state legislatures. She also worked to abolish slavery and to end the manufacture of alcoholic beverages. In 1869, she joined Susan B. Anthony and Elizabeth Cady Stanton in founding the National Woman Suffrage Association, which campaigned for women's right to vote.

Ernestine Potowski was born on Jan. 13, 1810, in Piotrków (now Piotrków Trybunalski), Poland. She and her husband, William E. Rose, a British silversmith, settled in the United States in 1836. The Roses moved to England about 1870. She died on Aug. 4, 1892. Nancy Woloch

Rose, Sir John (1820-1888), was Canadian minister of finance from 1867 to 1869, during the first term of Prime Minister John A. Macdonald. As minister of finance, Rose proposed procedures that helped establish the national banking system of Canada.

In 1869, Rose moved to London, where he became a partner in the banking firm of Morton, Rose and Company. Rose served at various times as an agent of the Canadian government in the United Kingdom. Rose achieved great success in handling a number of diplomatic and financial matters for Canada. In 1869 and 1870, he helped the Canadian government acquire land in western Canada previously held by the Hudson's Bay Company, a British fur-trading firm. Rose was knighted in 1870. During the 1880's, he sold bonds and other securities in the United Kingdom to provide financial aid for construction of the Canadian Pacific Railway across Canada. Rose was born on Aug. 2, 1820, in Turriff, Scotland. He died on Aug. 24, 1888. D. M. L. Farr

Rose, Pete (1941-), was one of baseball's all-time leading hitters and most exciting players. He made 4,256 hits in his career—the highest total in major-league history. Rose broke the record of 4,191 hits set by Ty Cobb, whose career ended in 1928. Rose hit safely in 44 straight games in 1978, tying a National League single-season record set in 1897 by Wee Willie Keeler. Rose was the National League's Most Valuable Player in 1973 and its batting champion in 1968, 1969, and 1973.

Peter Edward Rose was born on April 14, 1941, in Cincinnati. He played for the Cincinnati Reds from 1963 to 1978 and for the Philadelphia Phillies from 1979 to 1983. Rose played for the Montreal Expos for part of the 1984 season before returning to Cincinnati as player-manager. He ended his playing career after the 1986 season. Rose began his career as a second baseman, but later played the outfield, third base, and first base. Rose was noted for his batting skills and aggressive style of play.

In 1989, Baseball Commissioner A. Bartlett Giamatti banned Rose from baseball for life based on evidence

© Bettmann/Corbis/AP Images

Pete Rose broke Ty Cobb's record of major league career hits in 1985 with his 4,192nd base hit. He also tied a record set in 1897 by hitting safely in 44 consecutive games.

from an investigation conducted by Giamatti's office into charges that Rose violated baseball rules by betting on baseball games. Rose denied betting on games but did not challenge Giamatti's ruling. In 1990, Rose pleaded guilty to two counts of filing false federal income tax returns. His penalty included a fine and a prison sentence of five months. In his autobiography, *My Prison Without Bars* (2004), Rose finally admitted that he bet on baseball games during his baseball career. Rose's lifetime ban from baseball also removed him from consideration for election to the National Baseball Hall of Fame.

Donald Honig

Rose, Uriah Milton (1834-1913), was an American lawyer who became known both nationally and in his home state of Arkansas as an influential law scholar. A statue of Rose represents Arkansas in the United States Capitol in Washington, D.C.

Rose was born in Bradfordsville, Kentucky, on March 5, 1834. He earned a law degree from Transylvania University in Lexington, Kentucky, in 1853. That year, Rose and a brother-in-law moved to Batesville, Arkansas, where they formed a law partnership.

Rose became chancellor of the Court of Chancery of Pulaski County in 1860. He worked in the position until 1863, when Union troops captured Little Rock, the state capital, in the American Civil War (1861-1865). After the war, Rose moved to Little Rock and formed a law partnership with George Watkins, a former chief justice of Arkansas. The partnership became the leading law firm in the state.

Rose was one of the founders of the American Bar Association, a private, nationwide organization of lawyers, in 1878. He served as the group's president in 1901 and 1902. He helped to form the Arkansas State Bar Association in 1882 and to reorganize it in 1898 and 1899. After the reorganization, Rose served as the association's president until January 1900. President Theodore Roosevelt made Rose a delegate to the second Hague Peace Conference, held in the Netherlands in 1907. The conference helped establish international rules of warfare.

Rose's written works include the *Digest of Arkansas Reports* (1867) and *The Constitution of the State of Arkansas* (1891), which he published with notes. Rose died in Little Rock on Aug. 12, 1913. Kenneth J. Shenkman

Rose chafer, often called the rose bug, is a beetle about ⅓ inch (8 millimeters) long. It is light brown and has long, spiny legs. It feeds on many plants and is often found on roses, ornamental plants, grapes, and various fruit trees. The beetles eat the blossoms of grapes and roses, and often apples. They also attack many fruits. The rose chafer is particularly destructive in localities where there are large areas of grassland. It lives throughout the eastern and central regions of the United States.

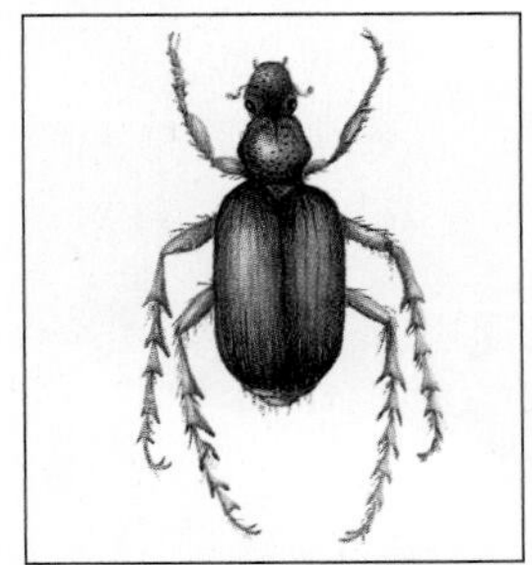

WORLD BOOK illustration by Shirley Hooper, Oxford Illustrators Limited

Rose chafer

After feeding for three or four weeks, the beetles disappear. The females deposit their eggs in the soil. These eggs hatch, and the larvae feed upon the roots of grass. Nearly full grown by fall, they go below the frost line for the winter. The larva, which looks like a white grub, comes near the surface in the spring and becomes a pupa. There is only one generation each year.

When the beetles are numerous, the best means of preventing injury is to cover small plants with cloth, or to pick the beetles off by hand. Large numbers can be collected in a pan containing water and kerosene. Commercial plantings of grapes, apples, and other fruit may be protected by cultivating all nearby areas during May and June to destroy any eggs that may have been laid. Insecticides may also be used on the plants.

Ellis W. Huddleston

Scientific classification. The rose chafer belongs to the family Scarabaeidae. It is *Macrodactylus subspinosus.*

Rose of Jericho. See **Resurrection plant.**

Rose of Lima, Saint (1586-1617), was the first person born in the Western Hemisphere to be *canonized* (declared a saint) by the Roman Catholic Church. She was canonized in 1671. Rose was born on April 20, 1586, in Lima, Peru. She modeled her life upon that of Saint Catherine of Siena. In 1606, Rose joined the Dominican religious community. She ran an infirmary for poor children and elderly people in the garden of her home. People from all of Lima's social classes loved her. Rose practiced extreme *mortification* and penance and had remarkable mystical experiences and visions. Mortification means overcoming bodily desires by causing oneself pain or going without things. Rose died on Aug. 24, 1617. She is the Patroness of South America. August 23 is her feast day. Anne E. Carr

Rose of Sharon, also called Althaea, is a large hibiscus shrub with lovely rose, purple, white, or blue flowers about 3 inches (8 centimeters) wide. The flowers bloom from midsummer to early fall. The rose of Sharon grows about 12 feet (3.7 meters) high and has large, three-lobed leaves. It is hardy and does well under unfavorable conditions, either in the city or in the country. It is native to Eastern Asia and grows in many North American gardens. Gardeners have developed several forms

WORLD BOOK illustration by Robert Hynes

The rose of Sharon, a popular ornamental shrub, has large and attractively colored flowers.

of the shrub. The rose of Sharon may be grown in pots and later transplanted outdoors. See also **Flower** (Garden perennials; picture); **Hibiscus.** Walter S. Judd

Scientific classification. The rose of Sharon is in the mallow family, Malvaceae. Its scientific name is *Hibiscus syriacus.*

Rose water is a clear, colorless solution made from fresh rose flowers and used in making perfumes and certain medicines. Rose water has a fragrant odor much like that of fresh rose blossoms. It is made by distilling with water the fragrant parts of the flowers, such as the petals and the *sepals* (leaflike divisions of the outer covering of the flowers). This is done by placing the flowers in water, boiling the water, and separating the vapor into a vessel. The vapor is then condensed back into a liquid, which is rose water. Patricia Ann Mullen

Roseau, *roh ZOH,* is the capital and largest city of Dominica, an island country in the Caribbean Sea. Roseau has a population of about 15,000. The city lies on the southwestern coast of the island, at the mouth of the Roseau River. For location, see **Dominica** (map).

Roseau has a busy port whose import and export activities are the basis of the city's economy. The city includes modern commercial buildings as well as stone structures dating from the 1700's. Many of Roseau's people live in small wooden or cement-block houses.

Roseau was founded in the mid-1700's by French settlers. They named the site Roseau, which means *reed* in French, because reeds grew there. From the 1600's to 1759, France and Britain struggled for control of Dominica. Britain ruled the country from 1759 to 1978, when Dominica gained independence. Hurricanes have sometimes struck Roseau, causing deaths and damage to the city. Lennox Honychurch

Rosecrans, William Starke (1819-1898), was a Union general in the American Civil War (1861-1865). He commanded forces in western Virginia in 1861, and at Corinth and Luka, Mississippi, in 1862. Rosecrans became commander of the Army of the Cumberland in 1862. He fought in the Battle of Stones River (Murfreesboro), and later forced the Confederates out of Chattanooga. But he was defeated at Chickamauga in 1863. He was then assigned command of the Department of the Missouri.

Rosecrans was born on Sept. 6, 1819, in Delaware County, Ohio. He graduated from the United States Military Academy in 1842. He was minister to Mexico in 1868 and represented California in Congress from 1881 to 1885. Rosecrans died on March 11, 1898.

John F. Marszalek

Rosemary is an evergreen shrub noted for the fragrance of its leaves. Rosemary grows wild in the Mediterranean region and measures from 2 to 6 feet (60 to 180 centimeters) high. It bears shiny, dark-green leaves and small, pale blue flowers. In masses, blossoming rosemary looks like blue-gray mist blown inland from the sea. Its name comes from the Latin word *rosmarinus,* meaning *sea dew.*

© Shutterstock

Rosemary is a plant often used as an herb for seasoning. It is native to the Mediterranean region and has shiny, dark-green leaves and small, pale blue flowers.

Rosemary is used fresh or dried as an herb for seasoning. The plant yields an oil for perfumes. The dried leaves have been used in *sachets* (small bags of perfumed powder), as a moth repellent, and to brew tea for stomachaches and headaches. Rosemary has long been a symbol of remembrance. Europeans carried rosemary

© George H. H. Huey, Alamy Images

Roseau is the capital and largest city of Dominica. It lies on the southwestern coast of the island. The city has both modern buildings and stone structures from the 1700's. A sea wall, *shown here,* protects Roseau from ocean waves.

at weddings and funerals because they believed it would aid their memories. Donna M. Eggers Ware

Scientific classification. Rosemary's scientific name is *Rosmarinus officinalis.*

Rosenberg, *ROH zuhn behrk,* **Alfred** (1893-1946), was the philosopher of the German Nazi movement. His *Myth of the Twentieth Century* (1930) stressed "Aryan" racial superiority and depicted Judaism and Christianity as deadly enemies of the Germanic spirit. He wanted to replace Christianity with a Germanic pagan religion. During World War II (1939-1945), Rosenberg looted the art treasures of France and other Nazi-occupied countries and shipped them to Germany.

Rosenberg was born of German parents in Estonia on Jan. 12, 1893. He became minister for Germany's eastern occupied territories during the war. Rosenberg pressed for extermination of the Jews. On Oct. 16, 1946, he was executed for war crimes. Donald M. McKale

Rosenberg, *ROH zuhn burg,* **Julius and Ethel,** were American citizens, husband and wife, who were executed for spying for the Soviet Union during World War II (1939-1945). They became the first United States civilians ever put to death for wartime spying.

Julius Rosenberg (1918-1953) and Ethel Greenglass Rosenberg (1915-1953) were born and raised on the Lower East Side of New York City. Julius was born on Sept. 28, 1918, and Ethel was born on May 12, 1915. They married in 1939. By then, both had been involved in radical political activities. In 1940, Julius began working for the U.S. Army Signal Corps as a civilian junior engineer. Early in 1945, the Army fired him for being a Communist. Between 1946 and late 1949, Julius worked with Ethel's brother David Greenglass in a small machine shop they owned in New York City. In 1944 and 1945, Greenglass had worked as a machinist at Los Alamos, New Mexico, on the U.S. project to make an atomic bomb.

In 1950, Greenglass was arrested for spying for the Soviet Union while working at Los Alamos. The U.S. government charged that the information he supplied was used to build the first Soviet atomic bomb. Greenglass claimed that Julius had recruited him to collect the information. As a result, the Rosenbergs were arrested and accused of passing secret atomic-bomb information to the Soviet Union. The Rosenbergs pleaded innocent.

In 1951, a jury found the Rosenbergs guilty of conspiracy to commit espionage. Judge Irving Kaufman sentenced them to die in the electric chair. Protests against the conviction and sentence were organized in the United States and Europe. Numerous people believed that the Rosenbergs did not get a fair trial or that their sentence was too harsh. Many respected people, including the scientist Albert Einstein and Pope Pius XII, urged clemency. The case was appealed to the Supreme Court of the United States, but the court denied all appeals. President Dwight D. Eisenhower twice rejected pleas for clemency. The Rosenbergs were executed on June 19, 1953, at Sing Sing prison in Ossining, New York. Greenglass was sentenced to 15 years in prison. He was released in 1960. Thomas C. Reeves

Rosenquist, James Albert (1933-2017), was an American painter who came to prominence as a member of the Pop Art movement in the 1960's. His works combine realistically painted, magnified fragments of everyday objects and images. He used extremely large canvases, bright colors, and a painting style that resembles billboard and outdoor sign art. He often attached actual objects to his canvases. Rosenquist's placement and recombination of seemingly unrelated items make his works seem somewhat surrealistic, but the title of each painting helps bring the message into focus.

Rosenquist's most famous painting, *The F-111* (1965), is 86 feet (26.2 meters) long. It includes images of a fighter plane, a little girl under a hairdryer, a light bulb, a mass of spaghetti, an umbrella, and an atomic explosion. The title refers to a United States fighter used in the Vietnam War (1957-1975). It is an indictment of U.S. society of the time, attacking particularly consumer habits and war.

Rosenquist was born on Nov. 29, 1933, in Grand Forks, North Dakota. He supported himself painting billboards before and after moving to New York City in 1955. Rosenquist wrote an autobiography, *Painting Below Zero: Notes on a Life in Art* (2009). Rosenquist died on March 31, 2017. Deborah Leveton

Roses, Wars of the. See Wars of the Roses.

Rosetta stone, *roh ZEHT uh,* gave the world the key to the long-forgotten language of ancient Egypt. A French officer of Napoleon's engineering corps discovered it in 1799. He found the stone half buried in the mud near Rosetta, a city near Alexandria, Egypt. The Rosetta stone was later taken to England, where it is still preserved in the British Museum.

On the stone is carved a decree by Egyptian priests to commemorate the crowning of Ptolemy V Epiphanes, king of Egypt from 205 to 180 B.C. The first inscription is in ancient Egyptian hieroglyphics. The second is in *de-*

British Museum, London (Art Resource)

The Rosetta stone is a piece of a tablet of pinkish-gray granite-like rock covered with ancient Egyptian hieroglyphics. It provided the key to translating the language of the ancient Egyptians.

motic, the popular language of Egypt at that time. At the bottom of the stone, the same message is written again in Greek. See **Hieroglyphics.**

The stone is made of a dark gray granitelike rock with a pinkish tone and a pink streak at the top. It is about 11 inches (28 centimeters) thick, 3 feet 9 inches (114 centimeters) high, and 2 feet 4 ½ inches (72 centimeters) across. Parts of the top and the right side are missing.

The language of ancient Egypt had been a riddle to scholars for hundreds of years. A French scholar named Jean François Champollion used the Rosetta stone to solve the riddle. Using the Greek text as a guide, he studied the position and repetition of proper names in the Greek text and was able to pick out the same names in the Egyptian text. This enabled him to learn the sounds of many of the Egyptian hieroglyphic characters.

Champollion had a thorough knowledge of Coptic, the last stage of the Egyptian language that was written mainly with Greek letters. This knowledge enabled him to recognize the meanings of many Egyptian words in the upper part of the inscription. After much work, Champollion could read the entire text. In 1822, he published a pamphlet, *Lettre à M. Dacier,* containing the results of his work. This pamphlet enabled scholars to read the literature of ancient Egypt. Leonard H. Lesko

Rosewood is the name of several kinds of wood used to make knife handles, brush handles, and ornamental furniture. Rosewood is valued for its ability to take a high polish and for its rich color, which ranges from dark reddish-brown to purplish-brown. Its name comes from the roselike odor of the wood when it is sawed. The wood is sometimes called *blackwood.*

Rosewood comes from trees in the genus *Dalbergia.* These trees grow in Brazil, Central America, Southern Asia, and Madagascar. Jim L. Bowyer

Rosh Ha-Shanah, *rohsh hah SHAH nah* or *rohsh hah shah NAH,* is the Jewish New Year celebration. The Hebrew words *Rosh Ha-Shanah* (which are also written *Rosh Hashanah)* mean *Beginning of the Year.* During this solemn religious festival, Jews pray for God's forgiveness, for a good year, and for long life. Rosh Ha-Shanah usually begins in September, on the first day of the Hebrew month of Tishri, and lasts two days. Some Reform Jews celebrate it for one day. Rosh Ha-Shanah begins the Ten Days of Penitence, which end on Yom Kippur, the Day of Atonement (see **Yom Kippur**). Jews believe Rosh Ha-Shanah is the start of God's annual judgment of humanity. At that time, God decides who will continue to live and who will die during the coming year.

© Howard Sandler, Shutterstock

The shofar is a ram's horn used during services for Rosh-Ha-Shanah, the Jewish New Year. It is blown to call people to repentance and awaken them to the service of God.

Jews attend synagogue services on Rosh Ha-Shanah. These services emphasize the themes of judgment, penitence, and forgiveness. A ram's horn, called a *shofar,* is blown to call the people to repentance and to awaken the Jews to the service of God. Three special groups of prayers are recited during the holiday. The first group reminds the people that God rules the world. The second group tells them that God responds to the sound of the shofar, and the third group that he remembers people's deeds. Lawrence H. Schiffman

See also **Judaism** (The High Holidays).

Rosicrucian Order, *ROH zuh KROO shuhn,* is an international nonsectarian fraternity that studies the higher principles of life as expressed in humanity and nature. Members learn about philosophy and the arts and sciences. The order originated in ancient Egypt.

The Rosicrucian Order first came to America in 1694. Many of its members made important studies in music, art, and painting. Today, Rosicrucians study the trends of history and attempt to apply their philosophy to meeting life's problems. Members believe people must understand and live in harmony with nature. The order is not a religion. The order's full name is the *Ancient Mystical Order Rosae Crucis.* Its emblem is a gold cross with a red rose in the center. Headquarters are in San Jose.

Critically reviewed by the Rosicrucian Order

Rosin, *RAHZ uhn,* is resin derived from several varieties of North American and European pine trees. It ranges in color from pale yellow to dark brown and dark red. There are three main types of rosin. *Gum rosin* is produced by distilling resin collected from living trees. The crude resin is obtained from the trees by making lengthwise cuts in them. The resin then flows from the cuts. *Wood rosin* is extracted from tree stumps with the use of solvents. *Sulfate rosin,* also called *tall oil rosin,* is a by-product of the manufacture of wood pulp.

Rosin has many industrial uses. For example, it is used with other substances to *size* (coat) paper. The sizing helps keep the paper from absorbing moisture. Rosin is also used in the preparation of paints, varnishes, adhesives, sealants, and printing inks.

Rosin is sometimes used to make smooth surfaces less slippery. Such athletes as baseball pitchers, bowlers, golfers, and tennis players sometimes squeeze a *rosin bag,* a small cloth bag filled with powdered rosin, to improve their grip. Musicians rub rosin on the ribbon of hair that is attached to the bows they use to play stringed instruments. Lewis T. Hendricks

See also **Resin.**

Ross, Alexander (1783-1856), was a Scottish-born explorer, fur trader, and author. He explored much of the Oregon region, which then extended from present-day Alaska to California.

Ross was born on May 9, 1783, in Morayshire, Scotland. He moved to Canada in 1804 and became a schoolteacher. In 1810, he went to work for John Jacob Astor's

Pacific Fur Company. The next year, he helped build Fort Astoria, which was the first white settlement in the Oregon region. From 1811 to 1813, Ross was at Fort Okanagan. There, he took an Okanagan Indian woman as his wife. Ross helped found Fort Nez Perce, also called Fort Walla Walla. He was in charge of it for five years. Beginning in 1824, Ross explored much of what is now Idaho.

In 1825, Ross moved to the Red River area, near present-day Winnipeg. He received a grant of land there. He served as sheriff of Assiniboia (now southern Manitoba) in 1835 and as justice of the peace from 1839 to 1851. He died at the Red River colony on Oct. 23, 1856.

Ross wrote extensively. He was one of western Canada's early historians. His works include *Adventures of the First Settlers on the Oregon or Columbia River* (1849), *The Fur Hunters of the Far West* (1855), and *The Red River Settlement* (1856). Barry M. Gough

Ross, Barnaby. See **Queen, Ellery.**

Ross, Betsy (1752-1836), was an upholsterer who made flags in Philadelphia at the time of the American Revolution (1775-1783). Some people believe she made the first American flag that had stars and stripes.

Betsy Ross was born on Jan. 1, 1752, in Philadelphia, the daughter of Samuel Griscom, a Quaker carpenter. She is believed to have attended the Friends School. In 1773, she eloped with John Ross, an upholsterer. Soon afterward, Ross was killed. Mrs. Ross took over his shop and became an expert seamstress. She remarried twice and had seven daughters. She died on Jan. 30, 1836.

William J. Canby, a grandson of Betsy Ross, wrote a paper about her in 1870. Canby said that when he was 11, his 84-year-old grandmother told him the story of how she made the first official United States flag. As the story goes, a committee headed by General George Washington visited Mrs. Ross in June 1776. George Ross, a signer of the Declaration of Independence and an uncle of Betsy Ross's first husband, was a member of the committee. These men asked Mrs. Ross to make a flag according to the rough design they gave her. Washington wanted six-pointed stars in the flag, but Mrs. Ross persuaded him to make the stars five-pointed. No proof has been found that this incident actually happened. But it is known that Betsy Ross was an official flagmaker for the Pennsylvania Navy. The stars-and-stripes design she may have sewed was adopted by Congress on June 14, 1777. Gregory J. W. Urwin

See also **Flag** (First United States flags); **Philadelphia** (Downtown Philadelphia); **United States flag.**

Ross, Diana (1944-), gained fame as the glamorous lead singer of the Supremes, one of the most successful singing groups in the history of American rock music. In the 1960's, the Supremes became one of the first African American groups to gain popularity with both black and white audiences. Ross sang with the Supremes from 1961 until she left the group in 1970 to start a solo career as a singer and motion-picture actress.

Diane Ernestine Earle Ross was born in Detroit on March 26, 1944. While in high school, Ross began singing with three other girls in a group called the Primettes. They changed their name to the Supremes in 1961 when they signed a record contract with the Tamla label owned by Berry Gordy, Jr. (see **Gordy, Berry, Jr.**). Later that year, the Supremes became a trio consisting of Ross, Mary Wilson, and Florence Ballard. They moved to Gordy's Motown label where the trio's first release was "Your Heart Belongs to Me" (1962). From 1964 to 1967, the Supremes had more than 10 hit songs, including "Where Did Our Love Go?," "Baby Love," and "Come See About Me" (all 1964); "Stop! In the Name of Love" (1965); and "You Keep Me Hangin' On" (1966). In 1967, the group changed its name to Diana Ross and the Supremes.

Ross began her solo career in early 1970. Later that year, she had her first hit with "Ain't No Mountain High Enough." Ross made her motion-picture debut in *Lady*

© SuperStock

Betsy Ross was a seamstress who made flags at the time of the American Revolution. Some people believe she made the first American flag, as illustrated in the patriotic postcard shown here.

© ZUMA Wire Service/Alamy Images

Diana Ross became famous as the lead singer of the Supremes, one of the most successful singing groups in American rock history. Ross then developed a career as a solo artist.

Sings the Blues (1972), receiving an Academy Award nomination for her performance as jazz singer Billie Holiday. Ross also starred in *Mahogany* (1975) and *The Wiz* (1978). Her recording of the theme from *Mahogany,* "Do You Know Where You're Going To," became a hit. Ross's other hit recordings include "Touch Me in the Morning" (1973), "Love Hangover" (1976), "Upside Down" and "I'm Coming Out" (both 1980), and a duet with Lionel Richie called "Endless Love" (1981). In 2000, Ross appeared with the Supremes on the group's "Return to Love" tour. Ross was the only original member of the trio to appear, however. The other two singers were members of the Supremes who had joined the group after Ross left. Ross wrote an autobiography, *Secrets of a Sparrow* (1993). Shawn Brennan

Ross, Edmund Gibson (1826-1907), was an American statesman. Though he opposed President Andrew Johnson, he voted in the United States Senate against convicting Johnson during the impeachment trial in 1868. This vote earned him the hatred of his fellow Republicans, but won him a reputation for political courage.

Ross was born on Dec. 7, 1826, in Ashland, Ohio. In 1856, he led settlers to Kansas to oppose slavery in the territory. He served in the U.S. Senate from 1866 to 1871 and then became a newspaper editor. He was governor of the New Mexico Territory from 1885 to 1889. Ross died on May 8, 1907. James E. Sefton

Ross, George (1730-1779), a Pennsylvania lawyer, signed the Declaration of Independence. From 1768 to 1776, he served in the Pennsylvania assembly, where he opposed the governor. He helped draft Pennsylvania's first constitution in 1776. Ross also served as a delegate to the Continental Congress from 1774 to 1777. In 1779, he was commissioned an admiralty judge of the state of Pennsylvania. He served in the position until his death. Ross was born on May 10, 1730, in New Castle, Delaware, and died on July 14, 1779. Jack N. Rakove

Ross, Harold Wallace (1892-1951), founded *The New Yorker* magazine and edited it for 26 years, until his death on Dec. 6, 1951. Ross began *The New Yorker* in 1925 as a publication for and about New York City. It became a national magazine famous for excellent writing, clever cartoons, and penetrating observations.

Ross was born on Nov. 6, 1892, in Aspen, Colorado. He left school at 14 to work for newspapers. In World War I, which the United States entered in 1917, he was editor of *The Stars and Stripes,* a newspaper for U.S. soldiers. Daniel W. Pfaff

Ross, Sir James Clark (1800-1862), was a British polar explorer. He led an expedition to the Antarctic aboard the ships *Erebus* and *Terror* from 1839 to 1843 and discovered the Ross Ice Shelf, Victoria Land, and Mount Erebus, an active volcano. He reached 78° 10′ south latitude, the southernmost point reached by any person until 1900. His uncle, Sir John Ross, and Sir William Edward Parry trained him during six Arctic voyages in search of the Northwest Passage between 1818 and 1834. Ross discovered the north magnetic pole in 1831 while serving under his uncle. Ross was born on April 15, 1800, in London and died on April 3, 1862. William Barr

Ross, John (1790-1866), was the principal chief of the Cherokee Indians from 1828 to 1866. His father was Scottish, and his mother was Scottish and Cherokee. But he won the support of the tribe and led it through one of its most difficult periods. As chief, Ross resisted pressure from federal and state governments to move the Cherokee from their homelands in the southeastern United States to Indian Territory, in what is now Oklahoma. In the 1830's, non-Indians began taking Cherokee lands, particularly in Georgia. Ross appealed to the courts, Congress, and President Andrew Jackson, but he could not stop the flow of illegal settlers. In the winter of 1838-1839, Ross unwillingly led his people to the Indian Territory. Thousands of Cherokee died on the way. Ross was born on Oct. 3, 1790, near Lookout Mountain, Tennessee. He died on Aug. 1, 1866. See also **Cherokee Indians.** Gary E. Moulton

Ross, Nellie Tayloe (1876-1977), an American politician and public official, was the first woman governor in the United States. She was elected to succeed her husband, William B. Ross, as governor of Wyoming after his death in 1924. She served as governor from 1925 to 1927. In 1933, President Franklin D. Roosevelt named her director of the United States Mint, a position she held until 1953. She was the first woman to hold that post. For several years, she served as a vice chairman of the Democratic National Committee in charge of the activities for women of the Democratic Party. Ross was born on Nov. 29, 1876, in St. Joseph, Missouri, and died on Dec. 19, 1977. James S. Olson

Ross Dam was built in a narrow gorge of the Skagit River north of Seattle. The arch-type dam was one of the highest in the United States when it was built in 1949. It is part of the Seattle power system and produces 360,000 kilowatts of power. Ross Dam is 540 feet (165 meters) high and 1,300 feet (396 meters) long. It forms a lake nearly 25 miles (40 kilometers) long, which stores about 1 ½ million acre-feet (1.9 billion cubic meters) of water. Edward C. Pritchett

Ross Dependency is a wedge-shaped section of Antarctica that includes the Ross Sea, the Ross Ice Shelf, and McMurdo Sound. It covers about 160,000 square miles (414,400 square kilometers) of land, and about 130,000 square miles (337,000 square kilometers) of permanent ice shelf. The Ross Dependency is uninhabited except for personnel from various nations working at scientific bases. New Zealand has administered the area since 1923 and owns Scott Base, constructed on Ross Island in 1957. The United States established McMurdo Base on Ross Island in 1955. Wendy Lawson

Rossetti, *roh SEHT ee,* **Christina Georgina** (1830-1894), was a gifted English poet. Many of her poems are melancholy and treat symbolic religious themes. One of her best works is "Goblin Market" (1862), a fantasy about a girl's love for her sister. She wrote "Goblin Market" in an exciting, fast-paced style that makes the poem particularly effective when read aloud. Rossetti's other works include *Sing-Song* (1872), a nursery rhyme collection; and two volumes of religious prose—*Annus Domini* (1874) and *Seek and Find* (1879).

Rossetti was born on Dec. 5, 1830, in London. She lived a quiet, religious life and died on Dec. 29, 1894. Her brother Dante Rossetti was a famous English poet and painter. K. K. Collins

Rossetti, *roh SEHT ee,* **Dante Gabriel,** *DAN tee* (1828-1882), was one of the most famous English poets and painters of the 1800's. Rossetti was a central figure in the Pre-Raphaelite Brotherhood, an art movement he

The Wedding of St. George and Princess Sabra (about 1857), a water color; Tate Gallery, London

A Rossetti painting is typical of the artist's style in its bright colors and many details. The subject reflects Rossetti's interest in religious and historical themes.

helped found in 1848 (see **Pre-Raphaelite Brotherhood**).

Rossetti's poetry uses unconventional and sensuous language, vivid descriptions, and fantastic and symbolic themes. As a painter, Rossetti produced works that are noted for their rich colors and attention to detail.

Many of Rossetti's poems and paintings were inspired by Elizabeth Siddal, whom he married in 1860. She died less than two years later, and the grief-stricken Rossetti buried the only copy of his poems with her.

Rossetti agreed in 1869 to get the manuscript from his wife's grave. The collection was published in 1870 as *Poems* and made Rossetti known as a major poet. In 1881, he published *Ballads and Sonnets.* Rossetti's best-known poems include "The Blessed Damozel," "Sister Helen," and a series of love sonnets, *The House of Life.* He also translated many European works into English.

Rossetti was born on May 12, 1828, in London and died on April 9, 1882. His sister Christina also was a famous poet. K. K. Collins

Rossi, Aldo (1931-1997), was an influential Italian architect, teacher, and theorist. Rossi's designs are a distinctive blend of Modernist architecture and primary architectural elements often based on historical forms, such as repeated rows of windows or columns. Rossi considered the city as an organism rooted in history, represented by monuments that provide structure to an urban area. In 1990, Rossi was awarded the Pritzker Architecture Prize, the most prestigious international award in architecture.

Rossi first gained attention with his designs for the San Cataldo Cemetery in Modena, Italy, in 1971 and 1980. He then designed a wide variety of projects in Europe and the United States, including theaters, apartments, commercial structures, schools, and museums. His most acclaimed designs in Italy include the temporary floating Theater of the World (completed in 1980) in Venice, the civic center (1988) in Perugia, the Carlo Felice Theatre (1990) in Genoa, and the town hall (1990) in Borgoricco.

Rossi executed many commissions outside Italy. They include the Lighthouse Theatre (1989) in Toronto; the Hotel Il Palazzo (1989) with Morris Adjmi in Fukuoka, Japan; the Cirque de Soleil-Haus (1990) in Berlin; the Canary Wharf office complex (1993) in London; the School of Architecture (1993) at the University of Miami in Florida; and the Scholastic Buildings (completed in 2000, af-

© travelstock 44/Alamy Images

Aldo Rossi's Quartier Schuetzenstrasse is a housing project in Berlin, Germany. Rossi merged 12 individual buildings that stand out against the surrounding environment through the bright use of color.

ter his death) in New York City.

Rossi was born on May 3, 1931, in Milan. He received a degree in architecture from Milan Polytechnic in 1959. Rossi explored his theories of urban architecture in *The Architecture of the City* (1966) and *A Scientific Autobiography* (1981). Witty and playful, Rossi's drawings are considered works of art in themselves. In his drawings, Rossi attempted to represent elements of urban life lost during modernization. Rossi also designed furniture and other commercial products. He died on Sept. 4, 1997.

Nicholas Adams

Rossini, *roh SEE nee,* **Gioachino Antonio,** *JOH ahk KEE noh ahn TAW nyoh* (1792-1868), was perhaps the most popular and important Italian opera composer during the first half of the 1800's. *The Barber of Seville* (1816) is probably the greatest comic opera ever written.

Rossini was born on Feb. 29, 1792, in Pesaro and received advanced musical training in Bologna. His second opera, *La Cambiale di matrimonio* (1810), made him an important force in Italian music and was the first of his operas to be performed. For the next 13 years, Rossini wrote *opera buffa* (comic opera) and *opera seria* (serious opera), sometimes three or four per year. The most popular include *The Italian in Algiers* (1813), *The Turk in Italy* (1814), *Otello* (1816), *Cinderella* (1817), *Moses in Egypt* (1818), *The Lady of the Lake* (1819), and *Semiramide* (1823). They are noted for their rich and catchy melodies, surging vitality, and expert vocal writing.

© AF Archive/Alamy Images

Gioachino Rossini

In 1824, Rossini moved to Paris, then the opera capital of the world. In 1826 and 1827, he revised two of his Italian operas for French words. He then composed—to French texts—the masterly comic *Le Comte Ory* (1828) and his serious masterpiece *William Tell* (1829), which represented a high point in Rossini's operatic style.

Rossini composed no operas after 1829, partly because he was often in poor health, and partly because he did not like the new operatic styles. His compositions after that year include the religious work *Stabat Mater* (1842) and many small instrumental and vocal pieces that he called *Péchés de vieillesse (Sins of Old Age).* Rossini had intelligence, wit, and humor, and became a famous host in Paris. He died on Nov. 13, 1868. Charles H. Webb

See also **Opera** *(Barber of Seville, The).*

Rostand, *raw STAHN,* **Edmond,** *ehd MAWN* (1868-1918), was a French playwright best known for his fourth play, *Cyrano de Bergerac* (1897). It is set in the 1600's and tells the touching story of Cyrano, a poet who has a long, ugly nose. Because of his nose, he is ashamed to woo the woman he loves. Instead, he writes letters to her signed by a handsome young friend who also loves her. She falls in love with the young man through the letters, not knowing that Cyrano is the true author.

Rostand wrote romantic plays in verse during a period when most dramatists preferred a style known as Naturalism. A typical Naturalistic play is extremely realistic, pessimistic, and written in prose. Rostand's first play, *Les Romanesques* (1894), is a charming story of young love. It became the basis for the American musical *The Fantasticks* (1960). Edmond Eugene Alexis Rostand was born on April 1, 1868, in Marseille and died on Dec. 2, 1918. Malcolm Goldstein

See also **Cyrano de Bergerac, Savinien de.**

Rostock, *RAHS tahk* (pop. 200,265), is a German seaport and industrial center on the Baltic Sea. For location, see **Germany** (political map).

The city lies at the mouth of the Warnow River and has been a key shipping point for centuries. It is the port of entry for much of Germany's petroleum supplies. Rostock's industries produce machinery, motors, container ships, and cargo ships. Warnemünde, a suburb north of the city, is a seaside resort with white sand beaches.

Rostock was chartered in 1218. The city joined the Hanseatic League, a loose grouping of German cities, in the A.D. 1200's (see **Hanseatic League**). The University of Rostock was founded in 1419. John W. Boyer

Rostov-on-Don, also called Rostov, *ruh STAWF* (pop. 1,089,851), is a manufacturing and trading center in southwest Russia. Called Rostov-na-Donu in Russian, the city lies on the Don River, 25 miles (40 kilometers) from the Sea of Azov (see **Russia** [political map]). Rostov is sometimes called the *Gateway to the Caucasus* because of its position on the main trade route between Europe and the Caucasus (see **Caucasus**). Rostov's products include farm machinery and military equipment.

Rostov was founded in 1749. It developed into a trading center in the 1800's. Germany captured and occupied Rostov during World War II (1939-1945), and the fighting damaged much of the city. Donald J. Raleigh

Rostropovich, *rahs truh POH vihch,* **Mstislav,** *MIHS tuh slahv* (1927-2007), was one of the world's great cello players. He was also a distinguished conductor. As a cellist, Rostropovich expressed emotion and imagination through a range of tone variety. Many composers wrote works for him, notably Sergei Prokofiev, Dimitri Shostakovich, and Aram Khachaturian of the Soviet Union and Benjamin Britten of the United Kingdom. In 1977, Rostropovich became music director of the National Symphony Orchestra in Washington, D.C.

Rostropovich was born on March 27, 1927, in Baku, Azerbaijan, then part of the Soviet Union. In 1953, he was appointed to the cello faculty at the Moscow Conservatory. That same year, he played cello recitals in London and New York City that established his international reputation. In the 1970's, he protested Soviet oppression, especially of Russian writer Alexander Solzhenitsyn. Rostropovich left the Soviet Union in 1974. In 1994, after the collapse of the Soviet Union, he resigned from the National Symphony and announced his intention to return to Russian musical life. Rostropovich died on April 27, 2007. Stephen Clapp

Roswell (pop. 48,366) is a city in southeastern New Mexico best known for the mysterious 1947 crash of what many people called an *unidentified flying object* (UFO). A rancher named William W. (Mac) Brazel claimed that he discovered debris from the crash on land north of the city. He reported it to the United States Army Air Forces, which had a base in Roswell. On July 8, 1947, an officer from the base reported that the debris was a crashed "flying saucer," a spaceship from another planet. The military reversed its report the next day and stated that the wreckage was in fact a weather balloon.

The UFO incident has attracted hundreds of thousands of tourists, UFO researchers, and enthusiasts to Roswell. The city is the home of the International UFO Museum and Research Center and hosts an annual UFO festival in July. Apart from UFO-related businesses, Roswell's economy is largely agricultural. It produces chili peppers and dairy products, especially cheese. The city also has many oil and natural gas businesses.

Ranchers and farmers settled the area in the mid-1800's. In the early 1870's, the town was named Roswell for an early settler's father. Roswell was incorporated as a city in 1891. It is the seat of Chaves County and has a council-manager government. Andrew Poertner

Roszak, *RAW shahk,* **Theodore** (1907-1981), was an American sculptor known for welded metal forms that appear violent and expressionistic. His works in this style often deal with menacing, fossilized savage birds and animals. Roszak described these works as "blunt reminders of primordial strife and struggle."

Roszak was born on May 1, 1907, in Poznań, Poland, and moved to Chicago with his family in 1909. He studied at the Art Institute of Chicago, the National Academy of Design, and Columbia University. His earliest works were paintings. From 1935 to 1945, he produced sculptured abstract works, severely geometrical and impersonal in style. He died on Sept. 7, 1981. George Gurney

Steel brazed with copper sculpture (1951); Cleveland Museum of Art, Gift of the Cleveland Society for Contemporary Art

Theodore Roszak's *Mandrake* is typical of the fierce, menacing, birdlike forms that appear in many of the sculptor's works.

Rot is a symptom of many plant diseases in which the plant decays. The decaying part of the plant may be soft and watery, or it may be firm and dry. Rot diseases are caused by bacteria or fungi that infect the plant and kill its cells. Rot destroys fruits and vegetables. Plant growers help prevent rot by spraying plants with pesticides.

Common rot diseases include *bitter rot, black rot, brown rot, dry rot, heart rot, potato late blight,* and *soft rot.* Bitter rot occurs chiefly in apples but also attacks quinces, pears, and other plants. It is caused by a fungus that destroys the fruit, twigs, and limbs of the trees. The fungus produces a brown spot in the fruit that grows and may give the fruit a bitter taste. Black rot attacks cultivated plants, including apples, grapes, pears, quinces, and sweet potatoes. The disease causes dark brown spots in the infected parts. Brown rot destroys peaches and other stone fruits, such as cherries and plums. Small brown spots appear on the fruit. Dry rot and heart rot affect chiefly timber. Potato late blight produces rot in potatoes. It caused the potato crop of Ireland to fail from 1845 to 1848. Soft rot is a common disease of vegetables that occurs during storage and transit. It may result in serious crop losses. Joseph G. Hancock

Rotary engine is a type of internal-combustion engine that uses a *rotor* (rotating part) instead of a piston. A West German engineer, Felix Wankel, developed the first practical rotary engine, called the *Wankel engine,* during the 1950's. It has a triangular rotor design.

A rotary engine differs from a piston engine in several ways. For example, a rotary engine has fewer parts than a piston engine of the same power. A rotary engine also uses lower-octane gasoline. However, lower-octane gasoline burns less efficiently, and thus rotary engines use more fuel and emit more exhaust pollutants. The noise and vibration produced by a rotary engine tend to be opposite to those of a piston engine. At high speed, a rotary engine operates more quietly and smoothly than

How a rotary engine works A rotary engine uses triangular rotors instead of pistons in its specially shaped combustion chambers. As a rotor turns, each of its three sides goes through a four-step cycle that produces power. These steps are (1) intake, (2) compression, (3) expansion or power, and (4) exhaust.

WORLD BOOK diagrams

Intake opening
Combustion chamber
Fuel and air mixture
Spark plug
Rotor
Output shaft
Burning gases
Exhaust port
Exhaust gases

Intake

Fresh air mixed with fuel is drawn into the engine as a tip of the rotor, shown by a dot, passes the intake opening.

Compression

The rotor begins to compress the fuel and air mixture when the following tip of the rotor passes the intake opening.

Expansion or power

The spark plug ignites the mixture. The burning gases expand and move the rotor around the output shaft.

Exhaust

The burned gases leave through the exhaust port after the rotor tip uncovers it. The cycle then begins again.

a piston engine. But at low speed, a rotary engine makes more noise and vibrates more.

How a rotary engine works. The most important parts of a rotary engine are its triangular rotor and specially shaped chamber. The rotor moves so that its tips always touch the walls of the chamber and divide the chamber into three areas. A different part of the combustion process takes place in each of the three areas of the chamber. A rotary engine may have several rotors, each with its own chamber.

In a piston engine, each piston must move back and forth twice and stop four times to complete the cycle (see **Gasoline engine** [diagram: How a four-stroke cycle gasoline engine works]). A rotary engine operates continuously. It completes three combustion cycles with each full rotation of its rotor. Each revolution of the rotor produces three power strokes. The output shaft connected to the rotor makes three revolutions each time the rotor turns once. As a result, a single-rotor engine produces one power stroke per turn of its output shaft. A piston engine produces one power stroke every other time a piston moves down its cylinder. A dual-rotor engine therefore generates the same number of power strokes as a four-cylinder piston engine.

History. Felix Wankel developed the rotary engine's basic principles in the early 1950's. By 1958, Wankel and researchers at a West German engine plant had worked out the engine's design. Automobile manufacturers rejected the engine at first because of its short operating life, poor fuel economy, and dirty exhaust. But after engineers began to solve some of these problems, the engine's simplicity and low cost drew interest. Several automakers in Japan, West Germany, and the United States sought to develop efficient rotary engines. But many of the engine's original problems proved difficult to overcome. Today, few manufacturers produce automobiles with rotary engines. David E. Foster

Rotary International is the worldwide association of all Rotary clubs. A Rotary club is a group of community leaders, each in a different profession or business. The association supervises member clubs and works for the advancement of Rotary. Members provide humanitarian services, encourage high ethical standards, and help build good will and peace in the world.

Rotary International has a cogwheel for an emblem.

The Rotary Foundation of Rotary International sponsors scholarships for study abroad and the exchange of young business and professional people between countries. The foundation also sponsors projects to improve worldwide health. For example, it funds immunization projects in developing countries to protect children against infectious diseases, especially polio.

Paul P. Harris, a lawyer in Chicago, founded Rotary in 1905. It got its name from an early practice of members meeting in rotation at their places of business. Rotary headquarters are in Evanston, Illinois.

Critically reviewed by Rotary International

Rotator cuff is a group of four muscles and their tendons that connect the *scapula* (shoulder blade) to the *humerus* (upper arm bone). The four muscles are the *subscapularis, supraspinatus, infraspinatus,* and *teres minor.* These muscles act to move the shoulder and to keep the shoulder joint in its socket. Each one originates near the scapula and ends in a *tendon* that attaches the muscle to the humerus.

Injuries to the rotator cuff can occur among people who make repetitive overhead or throwing motions. Such *overuse injuries* are common among professional baseball pitchers and other athletes. Symptoms of rotator cuff injury include pain and weakness in the shoulder. Pain is often worse while making overhead motions, such as throwing or reaching behind one's back.

Injuries to the rotator cuff can be mild and reversible or can be severe and permanent. *Rotator cuff tendinitis* occurs when the tendons of the rotator cuff become inflamed. It is common in athletes who use overhead motions. It is also becoming more common in youngsters as their organized sports activity increases. Physicians prescribe rest, medications, and often physical therapy to treat rotator cuff tendinitis. Older people may suffer tears of the rotator cuff, particularly after a fall. Surgery may be required to repair a tear. James M. Nieman

See also **Shoulder.**

Rotavirus is a microscopic organism that causes diarrhea and other symptoms in human beings, especially children. Rotaviruses usually pass from person to person through contact with objects or people contaminated with the *feces* (solid waste matter) of infected individuals. The virus can also be passed through contaminated food or drinking water. Rotavirus is a common infection and can occur year-round, especially in tropical areas. In the United States and other countries with a *temperate* (mild) climate, outbreaks generally peak from late fall to early spring.

Rotaviruses rank as the most common cause of childhood diarrhea. Individuals usually become ill within one to three days after exposure. Symptoms include watery diarrhea lasting three to eight days. In addition, the illness may cause vomiting, fever, and abdominal pains. People can become dehydrated if unable to drink enough to replace liquids lost through vomiting and diarrhea. In severe cases, the illness requires hospitalization. But most people recover in a few days without treatment.

In regions that lack adequate health care, rotavirus infection causes many thousands of deaths each year, particularly among children. In 2006, the United States Food and Drug Administration (FDA) approved an oral vaccine for rotavirus. The vaccine can help prevent the illness but cannot be used as a treatment once illness has occurred. Joanna L. Shisler

Rotblat, Joseph (1908-2005), a Polish-born British physicist, became known for his strong opposition to nuclear weapons. He was a founder of the Pugwash Conferences on Science and World Affairs. He dedicated himself to informing his fellow scientists and the general public about the dangers of nuclear war. Rotblat and the Pugwash Conferences shared the 1995 Nobel Prize for peace for their efforts to eliminate nuclear weapons.

Rotblat was born on Nov. 4, 1908, in Warsaw, Poland.

He received a doctorate in physics from the University of Warsaw in 1938. In 1939, he traveled to the United Kingdom, where he accepted a research fellowship at the University of Liverpool. At Liverpool, he worked with Sir James Chadwick on the *fission* (splitting) of uranium-235 atoms (see **Chadwick, Sir James**).

Rotblat became an expert in atomic radiation physics, and in January 1944, he went with Chadwick to Los Alamos, New Mexico, to join the British group of scientists involved in the Manhattan Project (see **Manhattan Project**). The aim of the project was at first to develop an atomic bomb for the Allies before Nazi Germany could make its own atomic weapon. But by late 1944, the research work was being used instead in a nuclear arms race between the United States and the Soviet Union. In December 1944, risking a charge of military desertion, Rotblat resigned from the Manhattan team and returned to England. He became the only scientist to quit the project based on his moral beliefs.

Rotblat continued to work at the University of Liverpool, serving as director of research in nuclear physics from 1945 to 1949. In 1950, he became professor of physics and chief physicist at St. Bartholomew's Hospital in London. He retired from his professorship in 1976. From 1957 to 1973, Rotblat served as the first secretary-general of the Pugwash Conferences, which became a forum for advocating the abolition of nuclear arms. He was president of the conferences from 1988 to 1997. He was knighted in 1998 and became known as Sir Joseph Rotblat. He died on Aug. 31, 2005. Janis F. Kearney

ROTC. See **Reserve Officers Training Corps.**

Roth, Henry (1906-1995), was an American author known for his novel *Call It Sleep* (1934). The book is considered perhaps the greatest novel about working-class Jewish immigrants in New York City in the early 1900's.

The novel covers two years in the life of young David Schearl. Early reviewers praised Roth for his realistic treatment of Jewish slum life and his intense, poetic style. But some critics disapproved of the book's frank language, violence, preoccupation with sex, and unsparing look at a troubled Jewish family. Both the book and Roth dropped from public view for almost 25 years. The novel was reissued to unexpected acclaim in 1960. Critics in the 1960's, especially Jewish critics, recognized the artistic merit of Roth's account of an important time in America's multiethnic urban experience.

Roth was born on Feb. 8, 1906, in Ukraine. His family immigrated to New York City when he was 18 months old. Roth worked for many years on a projected six-volume autobiographical series of novels called *Mercy of a Rude Stream*. The first two volumes were published during his lifetime, *A Star Shines Over Mt. Morris Park* and *A Diving Rock on the Hudson* (both 1994). Roth died on Oct. 13, 1995. Two more volumes were published after his death, *From Bondage* (1996) and *Requiem for Harlem* (1998). James M. Mellard

Roth, Mark (1951-), is one of the greatest professional bowlers in the history of the sport. In 1987, he broke the career money-winning record set by Earl Anthony. Roth's record was later broken by Marshall Holman. Walter Ray Williams, Jr., is the current recordholder. Roth had the highest average among professional bowlers five times—in 1976, 1977, 1978, 1979, and 1981. In 1979, he set a then-record average of 221.662. In 1978, he won a record eight Professional Bowlers Association (PBA) titles.

Roth has been named PBA Player of the Year four times—in 1977, 1978, 1979, and 1984. He won the U.S. Open and the Touring Players Championship in 1984. He was elected to the PBA Hall of Fame in 1987. Roth was born on April 10, 1951, in the Brooklyn section of New York City. He became a member of the PBA in 1970. Roth left the PBA tour in 2002 but came out of retirement in 2006 to join the new Generations Bowling Tour for bowlers at least 50 years old. Nelson Burton, Jr.

Roth, Philip (1933-2018), was an American writer known for his frank, comic, and often satirical portraits of modern Jewish society and family life in the United States. He gained fame for *Goodbye, Columbus* (1959), a collection of five short stories and a short novel. In the title novel, Roth explored the material attractions and spiritual costs he saw in suburban upper-class Jewish life.

Roth's most famous novel is *Portnoy's Complaint* (1969). Critics have praised it as a funny, intimate, and accurate study of the guilt feelings of a typical American Jewish son. The book generated controversy because of its explicit sexual descriptions, which Roth would return to in his novel *Sabbath's Theater* (1995).

Roth featured the artistic and psychological struggles of a Jewish American author named Nathan Zuckerman in several works. Zuckerman is the central character in the novels *The Ghost Writer* (1979), *Zuckerman Unbound* (1981), and *The Anatomy Lesson* (1983). The three novels were issued along with the story "The Prague Orgy" as *Zuckerman Bound* (1985). A fourth Zuckerman novel, *The Counterlife*, was published in 1986. Zuckerman also narrates *The Human Stain* (2000), in which racial, sexual, and academic politics collide. The novel makes up a trilogy, along with *American Pastoral* (1997) and *I Married a Communist* (1998), that investigates political and social conflicts after the end of World War II in 1945. Zuckerman is also the central character in *Exit Ghost* (2007).

In the novels *The Facts* (1988), *Deception* (1990), and *Patrimony* (1991), Roth explored the uncertain territory between autobiography and fiction. The narrator of *The Plot Against America* (2004) is the author, Roth, as a young man. The novel considers an alternative history in which the famed aviator Charles Lindbergh defeats Franklin D. Roosevelt for the presidency of the United States in 1940. Roth's other novels include *Letting Go* (1962), *When She Was Good* (1967), *Our Gang* (1971), *The Great American Novel* (1973), *My Life As a Man* (1974), *The Professor of Desire* (1977), *Operation Shylock* (1993), *The Dying Animal* (2001), *Everyman* (2006), *Indignation* (2008), *The Humbling* (2009), and *Nemesis* (2010).

Philip Milton Roth was born on March 19, 1933, in Newark, New Jersey. He graduated from Bucknell University in 1954 and received a master's degree in English literature from the University of Chicago in 1955. In 2011, Roth received the Man Booker International Prize. He received the prize, now called the International Booker Prize, for lifetime achievement for fiction in English. Roth died on May 22, 2018. Arthur M. Saltzman

Rothko, *RAHTH koh,* **Mark** (1903-1970), an American painter, was a leader of the Abstract Expressionist movement. His best-known paintings are large, boldly simplified abstract compositions. He relied chiefly on color and ambiguous boundaries on rectangular forms to cre-

Oil painting on canvas (1952); collection of Mr. and Mrs. Burton Tremaine, Meriden, CT (WORLD BOOK photo by Lee Boltin)

A typical painting by Mark Rothko emphasizes rectangles of color. Rothko used this type of composition in this painting, called *Number 8,* and in hundreds of other large works. Different combinations of color vary the mood of his paintings.

ate a range of moods. See **Abstract Expressionism.**

Marcus Rothkovitz was born on Sept. 25, 1903, in Russia. His family settled in Portland, Oregon, in 1913. Until the early 1940's, Rothko mainly painted recognizable subjects, including city scenes, plants, and animals. Gradually, he began to adapt themes from ancient myths to a poetic, semiabstract style. From there, he moved into a highly personal reduction of forms to the moody surfaces of glimmering color of his mature style. Shortly before his death on Feb. 25, 1970, Rothko completed a group of murals for the interdenominational Rothko Chapel in Houston. He worked with dark, low-keyed colors to induce a meditative atmosphere. Dore Ashton

Rothschild, *RAHTH chyld,* is the name of a German family that founded a famous banking firm in the late 1700's. The family opened banks in several European countries in the 1800's, and the company became known as the House of Rothschild. Today, the family operates banks, investment firms, and offices in France, the United Kingdom, the United States, and other countries. The family has also been prominent in politics.

Mayer Amschel Rothschild (1743-1812), who founded the banking dynasty, was the son of a German merchant. Mayer opened a bank in Frankfurt, where he made profitable investments for royal families of several European nations. He trained his five sons in conservative money management. He made investments that produced reasonable profits rather than excessive earnings. These methods helped him make a spectacular fortune.

After Rothschild's death, his sons expanded the family business. The oldest son, Amschel Mayer Rothschild (1773-1855), took control of the Frankfurt bank. Branches of the House of Rothschild were opened in Vienna, Austria, by Salomon Mayer Rothschild (1774-1855); in Naples, Italy, by Carl Mayer Rothschild (1788-1855); and in Paris, France, by James Mayer Rothschild (1792-1868).

Nathan Mayer Rothschild (1777-1836), the third son of Mayer Rothschild, founded the London branch of the House of Rothschild. He later became a financial agent of the English government. Rothschild helped Britain defeat France in the Napoleonic Wars (1796-1815) by providing funds for the British Army.

Lionel Rothschild (1808-1879), Nathan Rothschild's oldest son, won election to the British Parliament six times between 1847 and 1857. But each time he was denied admission because, as a Jew, he refused to take an oath supporting Christianity. Rothschild worked to change the law that required the oath and, in 1858, he became the first Jewish member of the House of Commons. In 1885, his son Nathan Mayer Rothschild (1840-1915) became the first Jew in the House of Lords.

Guy de Rothschild (1909-2007), Mayer Rothschild's great-great-grandson, was president of the family's Paris bank from 1949 to 1981. In 1981, the French government took over all privately owned banks in France. The Rothschild bank in Paris had controlled many of the family's industrial holdings, which the government also nationalized. The Paris branch had been the family's main bank since its bank in Austria closed in 1938, just before World War II. In 1981, Rothschild and his cousin Evelyn de Rothschild, the London bank's chairman, became co-chairmen of the family's American investment company.

David de Rothschild (1942-), son of Guy de Rothschild, rebuilt the French branch of the family's bank in the mid-1980's. In 2003, the British and French branches merged under his leadership. William R. Summerhill

Rotifer, *ROH tuh fuhr,* is a type of tiny multicellular animal that lives in water. The largest rotifers are about 1/26 inch (1 millimeter) long. Rotifers have cylinder- or vase-shaped bodies. Most species live in lakes, rivers, or streams. Some live in the ocean.

The name *rotifer* means *wheel bearer.* It refers to the circles of hairlike projections called *cilia* on the animal's

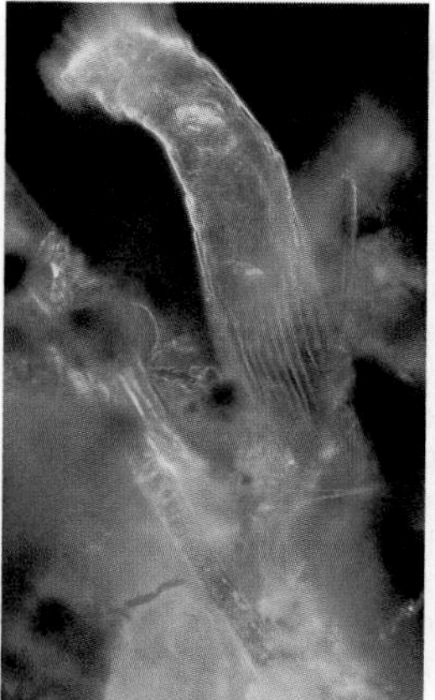

John Walsh, Science Photo Library

Rotifers are microscopic animals that live in fresh water. The common rotifer, *left,* uses its hairlike cilia to swim. The tube-building rotifer, *right,* can be seen atop a brown tube that it has formed from its own body secretions.

head (see **Cilia**). The cilia create a circular water current that draws food to the rotifer. This current also enables most species of rotifers to "swim." Other species spend their lives attached to such objects as stones and leaves.

Some rotifer species consist only of females that produce young by themselves in a reproductive process called *parthenogenesis.* In other species, the female produces eggs by herself. The eggs hatch into females or into undeveloped males that cannot feed themselves but can fertilize eggs. Still other species have fully developed males and females. P. A. McLaughlin

Scientific classification. Rotifers make up the phylum Rotifera.

Rotterdam, *RAHT uhr DAM* (pop. 618,357), is the second largest city in the Netherlands. Only Amsterdam is larger. Rotterdam has one of the world's busiest seaports. The city lies on both banks of the Nieuwe Maas River about 19 miles (31 kilometers) east of the North Sea (see **Netherlands** [map]). In 1872, engineers completed a channel called the Nieuwe Waterweg, which links Rotterdam with the sea. More than 150 nationalities are represented in the city, where half of the residents are foreign born.

Almost all the buildings in the heart of Rotterdam have been constructed since World War II ended in 1945. The city center was destroyed in the Rotterdam Blitz, the German attack on the city in 1940. One of the few surviving buildings there, the medieval St. Laurens (or St. Lawrence) Church, is a landmark. It was badly damaged by the bombing but was repaired after the war. Rotterdam's old harbor district, Delfshaven, escaped destruction. It has many buildings that date from the 1600's. Some of the Pilgrims who sailed to America in 1620 began their journey from Delfshaven.

In 1968, the first subway system in the Netherlands opened in Rotterdam. The Erasmus Bridge, opened in 1996, has become a symbol of the city. In the 1990's and 2000's, the city gained several new skyscrapers. The Maastoren building is the tallest structure in the country.

The Boymans-Van Beuningen Museum houses a large collection of Dutch art. A music center, the Doelen, includes several concert halls. Erasmus University Rotterdam was founded in 1973.

Rotterdam's economy depends largely on its huge shipping industry. Europoort, the city's vast harbor, serves the Netherlands, major industrial regions of Germany, and parts of France, Switzerland, and the United Kingdom. Other important industries include oil refining, shipbuilding and repair, insurance, and banking.

Rotterdam became a city in 1328, when it received a municipal charter. Rotterdam was a small fishing community until the 1600's, when merchants increased their trade with England and France. Rotterdam became a thriving port in the late 1800's after the Nieuwe Waterweg enabled large ships to travel between the city and the North Sea. Inez Hollander

See also **Europe** (picture); **Netherlands** (pictures).

Rottweiler, *RAHT WY luhr,* is a muscular dog with short, coarse black hair. This breed has tan or mahogany markings on the head, chest, and legs. When full-grown, rottweilers stand from 22 to 27 inches (56 to 69 centimeters) high. Most males are larger than the females. Rottweilers were developed in southern Germany, near the village of Rottweil. They are descended from the camp dogs that followed Roman armies in their conquest of

WORLD BOOK photo by E. F. Hoppe

Powerful rottweilers once guarded Roman herds.

southern Europe about 1,900 years ago. The Romans used them to herd the cattle and sheep that provided meat for the armies. Today, rottweilers make excellent pets and guard dogs, but owners must train them carefully. Critically reviewed by the American Rottweiler Club

Rouault, *roo OH,* **Georges,** *zhawrzh* (1871-1958), was a deeply religious French artist. His works show his ha-

Oil painting on canvas (1938); Museum of Art, Carnegie Institute, Pittsburgh, PA (WORLD BOOK photo by Elton Schnellbacher)

Rouault's *The Old King* resembles a stained-glass window with its thick black lines enclosing areas of bright color.

tred of hypocrisy, poverty, sin, and war.

Rouault was born on May 27, 1871, in Paris. From 1885 to 1890, he worked for a stained-glass window maker. His paintings, with their thick black outlines and intense, glowing color, show the influence of stained-glass design. About 1905, Rouault was briefly associated with a group of painters called the Fauves (see **Fauves**). The Fauves' bold brushstrokes and dramatic color contrasts became important parts of his style. From about 1903 to 1916, he painted religious subjects and sad clowns, and satirical pictures of prostitutes and corrupt judges. These works reflect misery and pain as expressed by the crude, rugged forms with their hacked-out edges.

From 1916 to 1927, Rouault worked on a series of 58 aquatints and etchings. This series, *Miserere,* was published in 1948 and ranks among the great achievements in modern printmaking. From 1927 until his death on Feb. 13, 1958, he painted clowns and religious pictures, but chose fewer satirical subjects. Alison McNeil Kettering

Rouen, *roo AHN* (pop. 110,117; met. area pop. 665,249), is a city in France. It is a major industrial center and has many artistic masterpieces. It lies in northern France on the Seine River. For location, see **France** (political map).

Rouen's many industries include food processing, petroleum refining, shipping, and the production of chemicals, medicines, metals, paper, and textiles. A magnificent Gothic cathedral built between the 1200's and 1500's stands near the center of Rouen. The city has several other beautiful old churches, art museums that house outstanding collections, and a university. The *Gros-Horloge,* a huge clock dating from the 1300's, is another landmark. Rouen serves as the capital of the Seine-Maritime *department* (administrative district) and the Normandie (Normandy) region.

A settlement existed at what is now Rouen in ancient times. In 1431, the English—who then controlled the city—burned Joan of Arc at the stake there (see **Joan of Arc, Saint**). Rouen suffered heavy damage in World War II (1939-1945), but was later rebuilt. Mark Kesselman

Rough Riders is the nickname for a famous American regiment that fought in Cuba under Theodore Roosevelt's leadership during the Spanish-American War of 1898. The official name of the regiment was the First United States Volunteer Cavalry. About 1,000 men enlisted in the unit—all, Roosevelt said, "born adventurers." The press named them the "Rough Riders" during their training in San Antonio. Leonard Wood commanded the Rough Riders when the regiment was first formed. Later, Roosevelt became colonel in command.

The Rough Riders fought at the Battle of Las Guasimas on June 24, 1898. In the Battle of San Juan Hill on July 1, Roosevelt led a victorious charge up Kettle Hill, near San Juan Hill. In the charge, 15 of the regiment's men were killed and 76 were wounded. The daring of the Rough Riders helped make Roosevelt a national hero and, later, president of the United States. Lewis L. Gould

See also **Spanish-American War** (picture).

Roughy, *RUHF ee,* is the name of a group of fish that live in temperate oceans throughout the world. Roughies range from 3 to 20 inches (8 to 51 centimeters) long. The *orange roughy* is the most common and one of the largest species. It is important commercially, especially around New Zealand. It is sold fresh or frozen for use as food. A freshly caught adult orange roughy is actually red. It turns orangish after several hours out of water.

WORLD BOOK illustration by John F. Eggert

Orange roughy is a popular food fish.

Unlike most fish, orange roughies have a *swim bladder* (baglike organ) that is filled with oil and wax. Most fish have a gas-filled swim bladder. Oil from the swim bladder of orange roughies is similar to the oil in sperm whales and in *jojoba,* a desert shrub. It is used in such products as lubricants and cosmetics.

Studies indicate that the orange roughy takes 18 to 20 years to mature. Some research indicates that the fish may live 100 years or more. Dan Robertson

Scientific classification. Roughies belong to the family Trachichthyidae. The orange roughy is *Hoplostethus atlanticus.*

Roulette, *roo LEHT,* is a popular game in gambling casinos. A roulette table consists of a wheel at one end

© Jean Guamy, Magnum

The Cathedral of Rouen stands near the center of the city. It was built from the 1200's to the 1500's and ranks as a masterpiece of French Gothic architecture.

and a betting layout extending across the rest of the table surface. There are 38 symbols around the circumference of the wheel, numbered 1 through 36 plus a 0 and 00. Many wheels in Europe do not have 00. Each symbol has an identical small slot on the wheel. The numbers are marked on a background alternately of red and black, with the 0 and 00 on a green background.

Players bet by placing chips on the betting layout. Players are given their own color chips to avoid confusion. Then the dealer, often called the *croupier,* rotates the wheel while spinning a small white ball on the rim of the wheel in the direction opposite that of the turning wheel. The ball finally drops into a slot, whose symbol and color become the winner for that spin. Players can bet on the red or black colors, a single symbol, or combinations of symbols. Stanley R. Sludikoff

Roumania, a variant of Romania. See **Romania.**

Round. See **Canon.**

Round Table was the table at which King Arthur, the legendary British ruler, sat with his knights. The term *Round Table* also refers to Arthur's entire royal court. The Round Table inspired some of the greatest literature of the Middle Ages. The fullest English account of Arthur and his knights appears in *Le Morte Darthur* (about 1470), a group of *romances* collected and rewritten by Sir Thomas Malory. A romance, in medieval literature, was a long work of fiction that described the remarkable adventures of a hero. See also **Merlin.**

Origin. The first mention of the Round Table occurs in *Le Roman de Brut* (1155), a verse history by the Norman poet Wace. This book tells how Arthur decided to seat his knights around a circular table to avoid quarrels over who should occupy the seats of honor.

About 1205, the English priest Layamon adapted Wace's book into an English version called *The Brut.* In *The Brut,* bloody fighting broke out among Arthur's knights over the choicest seats at a Christmas feast. To avoid such conflicts, Arthur had a Welsh carpenter build a wondrous round table. The table would seat 1,600 men and yet fold up so it could be carried on horseback. According to still another source, Merlin the magician had the table built for Uther, Arthur's father. Uther apparently gave the table to King Leodegan. Later, Leodegan gave the table to Arthur after Arthur married Guenevere, Leodegan's daughter.

Another tradition describes the Round Table as seating 12 and resembling the table at the Last Supper, with an empty place representing Judas's seat. This seat was called the *Siege Perilous* and was reserved for the knight so pure that he would someday find the Holy Grail, the cup or dish used by Jesus at the Last Supper. Any other knight who sat in the seat would die. One day, Sir Galahad's name appeared on the seat. From then on, he occupied the Siege Perilous. He later was one of three knights who found the Holy Grail.

The knights of the Round Table. In medieval literature, knights considered membership at the Round Table a great honor. Brave men came to Arthur's court from many countries hoping to be chosen a member.

Many romances describe the career of various knights of the Round Table. Several tell of the adventures of Sir Tristram. These stories describe his skill as a hunter and harp player and his bravery in killing a dragon and a giant. The best-known tale concerns his love affair with Isolt, the wife of his uncle, King Mark.

Sir Gawain was another famous knight of the Round Table. The great English romance *Sir Gawain and the Green Knight* describes Gawain's bravery and sense of honor as he faces possible death from the gigantic Green Knight. Gawain also shows his moral purity by refusing to be seduced by the Green Knight's beautiful but deceitful wife. Other Round Table heroes included Ban, Bedevere, Ector, Gareth, Kay, Lancelot, Launfal, Palomides, Sagramore, and Ywain.

The decline of the Round Table. For several reasons, the fellowship of the Round Table declined and in time was destroyed. The Round Table's greatest adventure was the search for the Holy Grail. But only three knights—Bors, Galahad, and Perceval—were morally perfect and thus able to find the Grail. The fact that so many of Arthur's knights proved to be morally imperfect damaged the Round Table's reputation. A scandal also developed over the love affair between Queen Guenevere and Sir Lancelot, perhaps the greatest of the Round Table knights. The scandal destroyed the bonds of respect and friendship that had united all the knights.

The villainous actions of Sir Modred, a knight who was either Arthur's nephew or his son, led to the final destruction of the fellowship of the Round Table. Modred seized Arthur's throne while Arthur was in France. Arthur quickly returned to Britain after learning of Modred's treachery, and war broke out between the two men's forces. Arthur killed Modred in battle but received fatal wounds. The brotherhood of the Round Table dissolved following Arthur's death. Edmund Reise

Related articles in *World Book* include:

Arthur, King	Holy Grail
Chrétien de Troyes	Knights and knighthood
Galahad, Sir	Lancelot, Sir
Gawain, Sir	Launfal, Sir
Geoffrey of Monmouth	Malory, Sir Thomas

Roundheads. See **England** (The Civil War).

Roundworm, also called *nematode* or *eelworm,* is any of more than 12,000 species of worms. Most kinds of roundworms live freely in soil, water, dead plants, or dead animals. Other roundworms are parasites. They live and feed on living plants and animals, which serve as hosts. Some parasitic species cause serious diseases in people, livestock, and crop plants. One species of roundworm, *Caenorhabditis elegans,* has proved especially valuable in biological research.

Roundworms range in size from microscopic to more than 3 feet (90 centimeters) long. They have slender, round bodies with tapered ends. Roundworms have remarkable powers of reproduction and are extremely numerous. Researchers have found more than 90,000 roundworms in a single rotting apple.

Nearly all species of roundworms reproduce by laying eggs. Some produce great quantities of eggs. For example, females of the species *Ascaris lumbricoides* each lay about 200,000 eggs per day for at least 10 months. In many roundworms, the eggs hatch into tiny young that look like adults. Eggs of other species hatch into young called *larvae,* which gradually transform into adults. Roundworms that do not lay eggs give birth to larvae.

Parasitic roundworms may infect a host in a number of ways. Some species enter the host when the host swallows food that contains the roundworm, its eggs, or its larvae. Among other species, the larva burrows into the host's skin. In still other roundworms, the larva is taken up by an insect, such as a fly or a mosquito, and transmitted through the bite of that insect to the host.

At least 14 species of roundworms cause infection in human beings. *A. lumbricoides,* which inhabits the small intestine, infects millions of people around the world. It causes a disease called *ascariasis.* Symptoms of this disease include pneumonia and intestinal pain. The roundworm *Trichuris trichiura* infects the large intestine and occurs in millions more people worldwide. It causes *trichuriasis,* a disease characterized by diarrhea. Other roundworms that cause disease in humans include *filariae, hookworms, pinworms,* and *trichinae* (see **Filaria; Hookworm; Pinworm; Trichina**). David F. Oetinger

Scientific classification. Roundworms make up the roundworm phylum, Nematoda.

See also **Vinegar eel; Worm** (picture).

Rous, *rows,* **Francis Peyton,** *FRAN sihs PAY tuhn,* (1879-1970), an American medical researcher, proved that viruses cause some types of cancer. In 1910, Rous ground up a cancerous tumor from a chicken and filtered out everything larger than a virus. The resulting liquid produced cancer when injected into other chickens. For many years, scientists scoffed at Rous's discovery. These scientists believed cancer could not be caused by a virus because the disease is not contagious. In 1966, Rous shared the Nobel Prize in physiology or medicine for his work.

Rous was born on Oct. 5, 1879, in Baltimore and earned an M.D. from Johns Hopkins University in 1905. He joined the Rockefeller Institute for Medical Research (now Rockefeller University) in 1909 and worked there for more than 60 years. In 1915 and 1916, during World War I, Rous helped develop a method of storing blood for transfusions. This technique made possible the establishment of blood banks. Rous died on Feb. 16, 1970.

Eric Howard Christianson

Rousseau, *roo SOH,* **Henri,** *ahn REE* (1844-1910), was a French artist who painted some of the most unusual pictures in early modern art. He is called a *primitive* painter because he had no professional training.

The bold colors and decorative patterns of Rousseau's paintings indicate his debt to works by artists called Impressionists and *Nabis.* But unlike such artists, Rousseau portrayed each detail precisely and polished the surfaces of his canvases to a high gloss. He took many of his subjects—such as a wedding party or a patriotic celebration—from French middle-class life. But he also painted realistic figures and objects in fantastic or mysterious relationships and exotic environments. Such pictures strongly influenced the Surrealism movement of the 1920's (see **Surrealism**).

Rousseau was born May 21, 1844, in Laval. He worked as a minor customs official until about 1885, when he retired to devote his life to painting. Rousseau died on Sept. 2, 1910. Nancy J. Troy

Rousseau, *roo SOH,* **Jean-Jacques,** *jhahn zhahk* (1712-1778), was a French philosopher. He was the most important writer of the Enlightenment, a period of European history that extended from the late 1600's to the late 1700's. Rousseau's philosophy helped shape the political events that led to the French Revolution. His works have influenced education, literature, and politics.

Early life. Rousseau was born on June 28, 1712, in Geneva, in what is now Switzerland. His family was of French Protestant origin and had been living in Geneva for nearly 200 years. Rousseau's mother died as a result of giving birth to him, leaving the infant to be raised by his quarrelsome father. As the result of a fight in 1722, Rousseau's father was forced to flee Geneva. The boy's uncle then took responsibility for his upbringing.

In 1728, Rousseau ran away from Geneva and began a life of wandering, trying and failing at many jobs. He was continually attracted to music. For years, Rousseau was undecided between careers in literature or music.

Shortly after leaving Geneva, at the age of 15, Rousseau met Louise de Warens, a well-to-do widow. Under her influence, Rousseau joined the Roman Catholic Church. Although he was 12 or 13 years younger than Madame de Warens, Rousseau settled down with her near Chambery in the Duchy of Savoy. He described the happiness of their relationship in his famous autobiography, *Confessions* (written 1765 or 1766-1770, published in 1782, 1788). However, the relationship did not last and Rousseau eventually left in 1740.

In 1741 or 1742, Rousseau was in Paris seeking fame and fortune and hoping to establish himself in a musical career. His hope lay in a new system of musical notation that he had invented. He presented the project to the Academy of Sciences, but it aroused little interest.

In Paris, Rousseau befriended the *philosophes,* a group of famous writers and philosophers of the time. He gained the patronage of well-known financiers. Through their sponsorship, he served in Venice as secretary to the French ambassador in 1743 and 1744.

The turning point in Rousseau's life came in 1749, when he read about a contest sponsored by the Academy of Dijon. The academy was offering a prize for the best essay on the question: Whether the revival of activity in the sciences and arts was contributing to moral purification. As he read about the contest, Rousseau realized the course his life would take. He would oppose the existing social structure, spending the rest of his life indicating new directions for social development. Rousseau submitted an essay to the academy. His "Discourse on the Sciences and the Arts" (1750 or 1751) attacked the arts and sciences for corrupting humanity. He won the prize and the fame he had so long desired.

Later life. When Rousseau converted to Catholicism, he lost his citizenship in Geneva. To regain his citizenship, he reconverted to Protestantism in 1754. In 1757, he quarreled with the philosophes, feeling they were persecuting him. Rousseau's last works are marked by emotional distress and guilt. They reflect his attempt to overcome a deep sense of inadequacy and to find an identity in a world that seemed to have rejected him.

In three *Dialogues,* also called *Rousseau, Judge of Jean-Jacques* (written 1772-1776, published 1782), Rousseau tried to answer charges by his critics and those he believed were persecuting him. His final work was the beautiful and serene *Reveries of the Solitary Stroller* (written 1776-1778, published 1782). Rousseau also wrote poetry and plays in both verse and prose. His musical works include many essays on music, an influential opera called *The Village Soothsayer* (1752), a highly respected *Dictionary of Music* (1767), and a collection of folk songs entitled *The Consolation of My Life's Mis-*

eries (1781). In addition, he wrote on botany, an interest he cherished, especially during the last years of his life. Rousseau died on July 2, 1778.

His ideas. Rousseau criticized society in several essays. For example, in "Discourse on the Origin and Foundations of Inequality" (1755), he attacked society and private property as causes of inequality and oppression. *Julie, or The New Heloise* (1761), is both a romantic novel and a work that strongly criticizes the false codes of morality Rousseau saw in society. In *The Social Contract* (1762), a landmark in the history of political science, Rousseau gave his views concerning government and the rights of citizens. In the novel *Emile* (1762), Rousseau stated that children should be taught with patience and understanding. Rousseau recommended that the teacher appeal to the child's interests, and he discouraged strict discipline and tiresome lessons. But he also felt children's thoughts and behavior should be controlled.

Rousseau believed that people are not social beings by nature. He stated that people, living in a natural condition, isolated and without language, are kind and without motive or impulse to hurt one another. However, once they live together in society, people become evil. Society corrupts individuals by bringing out their inclination toward aggression and selfishness.

Rousseau did not advise people to return to a natural condition. Instead, he recommended a simple agricultural society in which desires could be limited, sexual and egotistical drives controlled, and energies directed toward community life. In his writings, he outlined institutions he believed were necessary to establish a democracy in which all citizens would participate.

Rousseau believed that laws should express the general will of the people. Any kind of government could be considered legitimate, provided that it ruled by common consent. According to Rousseau, all forms of government would eventually tend to decline. The degeneration could be restrained only through the control of moral standards and the elimination of special interest groups. Robespierre and other leaders of the French Revolution were influenced by Rousseau's ideas on the state, as were many Socialists and some Communists.

His literary influence. Rousseau foreshadowed Romanticism, a movement that dominated the arts from the late 1700's to the mid-1800's. In both his writings and his personal life, Rousseau exemplified the spirit of Romanticism by valuing feeling more than reason, impulse and spontaneity more than self-discipline. Rousseau introduced true and passionate love to the French novel, popularized descriptions of nature, and created a lyrical and eloquent prose style. His *Confessions* created a fashion for intimate autobiographies. Jean Terrasse

See also **Enlightenment; Philosophes; Romanticism.**

Route 66 is perhaps the most famous highway in the United States. Officially named U.S. Highway 66 in 1926, this nearly 2,500-mile (4,000-kilometer) road between Chicago and Los Angeles was one of the first paved highways. It crossed parts of Illinois, Missouri, Kansas, Oklahoma, Texas, New Mexico, Arizona, and California.

Route 66 linked small towns to larger cities and gave rise to a network of roadside motels, diners, and gas stations. The popularity of these enterprises helped cement the relationship between Americans and their cars.

In the 1930's, hundreds of thousands of farmers traveled west on Route 66 to California to escape the "Dust Bowl," a region of the southern Great Plains devastated by severe dust storms. John Steinbeck nicknamed Route 66 the "Mother Road" in his 1939 novel, *The Grapes of Wrath.* The novel vividly portrayed a Dust Bowl family's hardships. After World War II (1939-1945), Route 66 came to symbolize postwar optimism and freedom, as thousands of returning soldiers and their families traveled west to forge new lives.

In the 1950's, Route 66 began to be replaced by interstate highways, which had faster speed limits. The last part of the original road was replaced by an interstate highway in 1984. Sections of the road are still maintained and designated "Historic Route 66." Bruce E. Seely

Rowan, *ROH uhn,* **Carl Thomas** (1925-2000), an American journalist, was director of the United States Information Agency (USIA) in 1964 and 1965. He was the first African American to serve on the National Security Council. He also served as deputy assistant secretary of state for public affairs from 1961 to 1963 and as ambassador to Finland in 1963 and 1964. He was a columnist for the *Chicago Daily News* from 1965 to 1978, when he became a columnist for the *Chicago Sun-Times.*

Rowan was an outstanding reporter for the *Minneapolis Tribune* from 1948 to 1961. His books include *South of Freedom* (1952), *Go South in Sorrow* (1957), and *Dream Makers, Dream Breakers* (1993). In 1997, Rowan won the Spingarn Medal for his achievements. He was born on Aug. 11, 1925, in Ravenscroft, Tennessee. He attended Oberlin College and received a master's degree from the University of Minnesota. Rowan died on Sept. 23, 2000. Rich Gordon

Rowing is the act of propelling a boat with oars. Many people find rowing on lakes, rivers, and lagoons to be a pleasant form of exercise. Rowing races have also developed into well-organized amateur sporting events.

Types of rowing. In racing, there are two main kinds of rowing: (1) sculling and (2) sweep oar rowing.

In *sculling,* each rower, or *sculler,* uses two oars. Both the boat and the oars are called *sculls.* Sculling crafts include *single* sculls, for one person; *double* sculls, for two people; and *quadruple* sculls, for four. A few eight-place sculls, known as *octuples,* have also been built.

In *sweep oar rowing,* each person uses one oar. Sweep oars are larger and longer than sculling oars. The boats used hold two, four, or eight people and are

© ImageState/Alamy Images

Rowing in a race, the rowers respond to the commands of the coxswain, who faces them. The coxswain also steers the shell.

called *pairs, fours,* and *eights.* Eights, some fours, and pairs are designed to hold an additional crew member called the *coxswain.* The coxswain steers the boat. The coxswain may also direct the timing of the oar strokes for the *stroke,* the rower who sits closest to the coxswain and sets the pace for the other rowers.

Racing boats are lighter and more fragile than ordinary rowboats. For this reason, they are called *shells.* There are no rules limiting the length, width, or shape of a shell. A single scull may weigh a minimum of 30 pounds (14 kilograms). An eight shell may be 60 feet (18 meters) long and 2 feet (60 centimeters) wide and weigh a minimum of 205 pounds (93 kilograms).

Competition. The Olympic Games offer 14 rowing events in open weight classes for both men and women. World championships are held each year for junior and lightweight classes. World championships for open weight classes are held each non-Olympic year. The events are held by the Fédération Internationale des Sociétés d'Aviron (FISA), the ruling body for rowing.

Racing meets called *regattas* are held annually all over the world. A number are open to contestants from all nations. The Henley Royal Regatta, an English event that began in 1839, is held each year at Henley-on-Thames. Other important regattas include the Royal Canadian Henley Regatta at St. Catharines, Ontario, and the USRowing National Championships.

History. Thomas Doggett, an English comedian, helped originate boat racing in the 1700's. He offered a trophy known as the "Doggett Coat and Badge" to the winner of a race on the River Thames. Later, regattas became important sporting events at many universities. The first race, between Oxford University and Cambridge University, took place in 1829. In the United States, the oldest collegiate regatta is held annually by Harvard University and Yale University. It started in 1852.

Critically reviewed by the United States Rowing Association

See also **Olympic Games** (table: Rowing).

Rowling, *ROH lihng,* **J. K.** (1965-), a British children's author, became an international sensation with her fantasy novels about schoolboy Harry Potter. The series starts as Harry, an orphan, turns 11 years old and learns he is a wizard. The stories center on his adventures at Hogwarts School of Witchcraft and Wizardry.

The novels in the series follow Harry through seven years. He ages a year in each book. The first novel was published in the United Kingdom in 1997 as *Harry Potter and the Philosopher's Stone.* It appeared in a slightly revised version in the United States in 1998 as *Harry Potter and the Sorcerer's Stone.* The other novels are *Harry Potter and the Chamber of Secrets* (1998), *Harry Potter and the Prisoner of Azkaban* (1999), *Harry Potter and the Goblet of Fire* (2000), *Harry Potter and the Order of the Phoenix* (2003), *Harry Potter and the Half-Blood Prince* (2005), and *Harry Potter and the Deathly Hallows* (2007). Popular movies were made from the series.

Rowling published two short books in 2001 as Harry's schoolbooks and not as continuations of the series. They are *Fantastic Beasts and Where to Find Them* and *Quidditch Through the Ages. Fantastic Beasts* was made into a movie that was released in 2016. A sequel, *Fantastic Beasts: The Crimes of Grindelwald,* and a book version of its original screenplay followed in 2018. In 2016, Rowling released *Harry Potter and the Cursed Child Parts I & II,* a play and a script book of the play. The story is set 19 years after the events of *Harry Potter and the Deathly Hallows* and follows Harry, now a Ministry of Magic employee, and his younger son, Albus Severus Potter.

In 2016, Rowling also released the "Pottermore Presents" trio of e-books set in the world of Harry Potter. They began with *Short Stories from Hogwarts of Power, Politics and Pesky Poltergeists.* In 2019, a new four-book series of e-books called "Harry Potter: A Journey Through..." began with *Harry Potter: A Journey Through Charms and Defence Against the Dark Arts.*

Rowling wrote and illustrated *The Tales of Beedle the Bard* (2008), a book of fairy tales. In 2020, she released *The Ickabog,* a fairy tale novel. She has also written works for adults. She wrote the novel *The Casual Vacancy* (2012). In 2013, she began the "Cormoran Strike" series of detective stories, published under the name Robert Galbraith. The series began with *The Cuckoo's Calling.*

Joanne Kathleen Rowling was born on July 31, 1965, in Chipping Sodbury, northeast of Bristol, England. She studied French at Exeter University. She taught English in Portugal before settling in Edinburgh, Scotland. She said she conceived the idea for the *Harry Potter* characters on a train in London in 1990 and finished the first novel while unemployed in Edinburgh. Ann D. Carlson

See also **Potter, Harry; Publishing** (picture).

Roxas y Acuña, *RAW hahs ee ah KOO nyah,* **Manuel,** *mah NWEHL* (1892-1948), served as the first president of the Philippine Republic, after it received its independence from the United States on July 4, 1946. He fought the Japanese in World War II (1939-1945), first as a colonel and then as a guerrilla on the island of Mindanao. The Japanese captured him and forced him to serve as a minor official under the puppet government of José P. Laurel. Roxas used his position to shield a spy ring he formed to aid the United States. Roxas was born on Jan. 1, 1892, in Capiz (now Roxas), on Panay Island. He studied law at the University of the Philippines and became governor of his home province. As speaker of the House of Representatives, he became a strong supporter of independence. Roxas died on April 15, 1948. See also **Philippines** (History) Socorro L. Reyes

Roy, Gabrielle (1909-1983), was a French-Canadian novelist. Roy wrote with sympathy and understanding about the sufferings of ordinary, often underprivileged people. Her writing has been praised for its psychological subtlety and vivid descriptions. Roy gained fame for her first novel, *Bonheur d'occasion* (1945), translated into English as *The Tin Flute* (1947). The novel describes the poverty-stricken lives of a working-class family in the slums of Montreal during the 1930's and early 1940's. Other novels include *Street of Riches* (1955), *The Road Past Altamont* (1966), and *Garden in the Wind* (1975).

Roy was born on March 22, 1909, in St.-Boniface (now part of Winnipeg), Manitoba. Many of her novels take place there. She died on July 13, 1983. Rosemary Sullivan

Roy, *WAH,* **Patrick** (1965-), a Canadian hockey player, ranks among the greatest goaltenders in the history of the National Hockey League (NHL). Roy holds the league record for most regular-season games played by a goaltender, with 1,029. He held the record for most regular-season wins, with 551, until Martin Brodeur broke it in 2009. Roy also holds many playoff records, including most wins, with 151. Roy starred on four Stanley Cup winners, with the Montreal Canadiens in 1986 and 1993 and the Colorado Avalanche in 1996 and 2001. He won the Conn Smythe Award three times as Most Valuable Player in the playoffs. He won the Vezina Trophy three times as the league's outstanding goaltender.

Patrick Jacques Roy was born on Oct. 5, 1965, in Quebec City, Quebec. He played in the Quebec Major Junior Hockey League (QMJHL) from 1982 to 1985. Montreal drafted him in the third round in 1984. He joined Montreal during the 1984-1985 season. Roy was traded to Colorado during the 1995-1996 season. He retired after the 2002-2003 season. From 2006 to 2013, Roy was variously the head coach, general manager, and co-owner of the Quebec Ramparts of the QMJHL. He was head coach and vice president of hockey operations for Colorado from 2013 to 2016. Roy was awarded the Jack Adams Trophy as the NHL's coach of the year for the 2013-2014 season. In 2006, Roy was elected to the Hockey Hall of Fame. Hayne Ellis IV

Royal Air Force. See **Air force** (The British Air Force; World War II); **World War II** (The Battle of Britain).

Royal Canadian Legion is Canada's largest organization of veterans. Its membership consists of former and active members of the Canadian Armed Forces and the Royal Canadian Mounted Police, their children, and others who support the legion's aims. Wives of members may join the Ladies Auxiliary, which supports legion programs and activities.

The legion encourages patriotism and national unity, assists needy veterans and former service members and their families, and promotes government programs for veterans. It sponsors memorial services on Remembrance Day, November 11, a national holiday that honors Canadians who died in war. The legion also performs community service. It supports housing projects for veterans and senior citizens and awards grants and scholarships to students. Each November, legion members distribute poppies. The donations received are used to fund legion activities.

The legion was formed in 1925 when a number of veterans' groups merged. It has branches in Canada, the United States, and Germany. Headquarters are in Ottawa, Canada. Critically reviewed by the Royal Canadian Legion

Royal Canadian Mounted Police (RCMP) is the federal police force of Canada. It also serves as a provincial and municipal police force on a contract basis in all provinces and territories except Ontario and Quebec. Members of the Royal Canadian Mounted Police commonly are called "Mounties," though they now ride horses only in special ceremonies.

Duties. As a federal police force, the RCMP's scope of operations includes fighting organized crime, terrorism, crimes related to the illegal drug trade, crimes of an economic nature, and offenses that threaten the integrity of Canada's national borders. The RCMP also protects high-level individuals, such as the prime minister of Canada and important foreign dignitaries. In addition, it provides the government of Canada with a full range of physical and computerized security services.

The RCMP also manages the National Police Services, a group that offers valuable resources to members of all

Royal Canadian Mounted Police

The RCMP badge has a motto in French that means *Maintain the Right.* Maple leaves, a symbol of Canada, frame the badge.

© Dreamstime

Royal Canadian Mounted Police perform the Musical Ride, a series of complex movements including the Dome, *shown here.* They wear the ceremonial uniform of the RCMP.

Royal Canadian Mounted Police badges of rank

Officers

Commissioner

Deputy commissioner

Assistant commissioner

Chief superintendent

Superintendent

Inspector

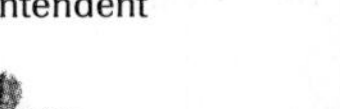

Enlisted personnel

Corps sergeant major

Sergeant major

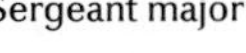

Staff sergeant major

Staff sergeant

Sergeant

Corporal

© (2003) Her Majesty the Queen in Right of Canada as represented by the Royal Canadian Mounted Police

Royal Canadian Mounted Police

An RCMP constable does police work in the Canadian territory of Nunavut. Applicants to the Royal Canadian Mounted Police must have Canadian citizenship, be at least 19 years old, and have a high school education.

Canada's law enforcement and criminal justice agencies. These resources include national criminal databases and specialized services, such as police education and scientific analyses of criminal evidence.

Contract policing—that is, police work governed by contracts between the RCMP and various municipalities and provinces or territories—is a major function of the force. Such contracts are in effect in about three-fourths of Canada. Contract policing is the way most RCMP members get started and acquire the hands-on skills that will serve them throughout their careers.

Organization and training. The Royal Canadian Mounted Police is organized under the authority of the RCMP Act. In accordance with the act, a commissioner who reports to Canada's minister of public safety heads the force. The RCMP employs thousands of police officers, civilians, and public service workers. Employees are arranged into more than a dozen organizational units called *divisions* and several hundred *detachments* across the country.

All policemen and policewomen undergo a 24-week period of rigorous training at the RCMP Academy in Regina, Saskatchewan. Among other requirements, applicants to the RCMP must have Canadian citizenship, be at least 19 years old, and have a high school education.

Uniform. The original Canadian Mounties wore uniforms modeled upon British military standards. The uniforms included gray or beige riding breeches, loose-fitting red tunics, black riding boots, spurs, and pith helmets or pillbox-shaped caps. These uniforms soon evolved to fit the demands of the Canadian landscape and weather.

Today, the ceremonial uniform of the RCMP includes a fitted red jacket, dark blue riding breeches, tall brown riding boots, and a wide-brimmed hat. The everyday uniform consists of a gray shirt and dark blue trousers, a police cap, a bulletproof vest, and police equipment. RCMP members who follow the Sikh religion may wear turbans as part of their uniform.

History. In May 1873, the Parliament of Canada established a police force to bring law, order, and federal authority to the nation's western plains. By the spring of 1874, the federal government in Ottawa, Ontario, had sent about 300 recruits to Manitoba for training. That summer, the recruits set out for southern Alberta, where whisky traders were operating illegally among the First Nations (Native American) people. The new police force was named the North-West Mounted Police (NWMP).

By 1885, the NWMP had grown to include 1,000 members. That year, the North West Rebellion, an uprising against the Canadian government, broke out in what is now central Saskatchewan (see **North West Rebellion**). The NWMP helped the Canadian militia stop the uprising. During the Klondike Gold Rush of the 1890's and the Anglo-Boer War of 1899-1902 (also known as the South African War), the NWMP gained respect for its police work. As a result, King Edward VII of the United Kingdom, who also served as Canada's monarch, bestowed the title *Royal* on the force. Its name thus became the Royal North-West Mounted Police (RNWMP).

In 1917, the western provinces of Alberta, Manitoba, and Saskatchewan created their own provincial police organizations. The RNWMP was then free to shift its attention back to policing the Canadian frontier. However, changes came in 1919, when Parliament decided to merge the RNWMP with the Dominion Police, a federal police force with authority in eastern Canada. When the merger took effect on Feb. 1, 1920, the new organization was renamed the Royal Canadian Mounted Police. Its headquarters were moved to Ottawa from Regina.

The RCMP returned to provincial policing under a new contract with Saskatchewan in 1928. From 1932 to 1938, the size of the RCMP rose to about 2,350 members. The force took over provincial policing in Alberta, Manitoba, New Brunswick, Nova Scotia, and Prince Edward Island. The years following World War II (1939-1945) saw a continuous expansion of the role of the RCMP as a provincial force. In 1950, it assumed responsibility for provincial policing in Newfoundland (now Newfoundland and Labrador) and absorbed the British Columbia Provincial Police.

During the 1900's, the RCMP participated in some major military conflicts. During World War I (1914-1918), RNWMP squadrons served in France, Belgium, and Siberia. In World War II, a Provost Corps consisting of RCMP volunteers went overseas to provide military police support for Canadian troops. Its aviation and marine sections became part of the Royal Canadian Air Force and the Royal Canadian Navy. The RCMP also took over many responsibilities related to home-front defense, in-

Canadian Pacific

The Royal Canadian Mounted Police were first called the North-West Mounted Police. The force was established in 1873 to eliminate illegal trade in whiskey, collect customs duties, calm unrest among Canadian Indians, and fight lawlessness in western Canada.

cluding domestic security and *intelligence* (gathering secret information).

During the second half of the 1900's, the RCMP began to modernize. It actively recruited women and minority groups and increased its use of new technologies. After two commissions of inquiry into the organization and operations of the RCMP, the force was reorganized. In 1984, the Canadian government created a separate agency for domestic intelligence, known as the Canadian Security Intelligence Service (CSIS).

Critically reviewed by the Royal Canadian Mounted Police Historical Section

See also **Police** (In Canada; picture).

Royal Dutch Shell plc (public limited company) is a global energy company that operates in many countries. The company, known informally as Shell, grew out of an alliance made in 1907 between a Dutch company, the Royal Dutch Petroleum Company, and the British oil company Shell Transport and Trading Company (formerly the Tank Syndicate). Shell has its headquarters in The Hague, the Netherlands.

Shell's major activities involve oil and gas exploration and production, power generation, and the manufacture, marketing, and shipping of oil products and chemicals. Shell is also involved in developing renewable energy sources.

Since the late 1900's, the company has been involved in a series of oil spills in the Niger Delta region in Nigeria. Shell is Nigeria's biggest oil producer. In 2011, the company accepted responsibility for much of the damage caused by those spills. In 2015, Shell agreed to pay nearly $84 million (55 million British pounds) for two oil spills that occurred in the community of Bodo in the Ogoniland region in 2008 and 2009. Shell faces additional lawsuits for environmental damage caused by multiple oil spills beginning in 1989 in two other communities in the Niger Delta region. Janis F. Kearney

Royal Geographical Society is a British organization composed of people interested in geographical education and discoveries. It has one of the world's largest private map collections, which is open to the public, and a large library. The society organizes geographical research projects and sponsors scientific expeditions. It produces *Geographical* magazine, a variety of academic journals, and other publications.

The society was founded in 1830. It now has members in many countries. Headquarters are in London.

Critically reviewed by the Royal Geographical Society

Royal Gorge is a canyon of the Arkansas River, extending about 10 miles (16 kilometers) from Canon City, Colorado. The gorge is more than 1,000 feet (300 meters) deep. A railroad passes through this remarkable chasm. The canyon is only 30 feet (9 meters) wide at some points. Many bridgelike structures had to be built along the walls of the gorge for the railroad tracks. This roadway provides a water-level route through a mountainous section of the Rockies. One of the highest suspension bridges in the world, 1,053 feet (321 meters) above the water, spans the gorge at the top. John L. Dietz

See also **Arkansas River.**

Royal Household of the United Kingdom includes officials who conduct the private business of the monarch and supervise court life. They have few powers of government. The *lord chamberlain* supervises the household. The *lord steward* controls household finances and supervises the treasurer and the comptroller of the household. The *master of the horse* cares for the royal stables. The queen's chief attendant is the *mistress of the robes.* She attends the queen on state occasions. The *ladies of the bedchamber* are the queen's personal attendants.

The original household offices, such as marshal, steward, and chamberlain, are hereditary in some families. These officials act only on ceremonial occasions.

Richard W. Davis

Royal Institution is a scientific society founded in England in 1799. King George III granted the society a charter in 1800. Its purpose is to encourage scientific study and to spread technical knowledge.

Headquarters of the Royal Institution are in London. Many scientists have made important discoveries there. These scientists include Sir Humphry Davy, who invented the safety lamp for use in mines, and Michael Faraday, who did important work in the field of electrical research. A museum in the building houses Faraday's research equipment and manuscripts. Scientific research continues today in the building's Davy Faraday Research Laboratory. Critically reviewed by the Royal Institution

Royal Military College of Canada is a university in Kingston, Ontario, that trains young men and women to become officers in the Canadian Armed Forces. It provides a broad program of academic, military, and physical training. Graduates receive a bachelor's degree in arts, engineering, or science, and a commission as an officer in the Canadian Armed Forces. The college also has a program of graduate studies.

The Royal Military College is one of two Canadian military colleges. The other is the Collège militaire royal de Saint-Jean, in Saint-Jean, Quebec. Students may begin their studies at either college. But all engineering students and most science students will spend their last two years of study at the Royal Military College.

The college was founded in 1874 and opened in 1876. The school's website at http://www.rmcc-cmrc.ca offers more information.

Critically reviewed by the Royal Military College of Canada

Royal palm is a tall, graceful tree common in tropical America. The tree's trunk resembles a pillar, and a cluster of featherlike leaves crowns its top. The tree grows in southern Florida, the Caribbean, and Central America.

Scientific classification. Royal palms make up the genus *Roystonea.*

Royal Society is the oldest continuously existing scientific organization in the world. Its full title is the Royal Society of London for Improving Natural Knowledge. The organization was founded in 1660 to promote the natural sciences. Its fellowship consists largely of leading British and Commonwealth scientists in such fields as chemistry, engineering, mathematics, and physics.

The society encourages scientific advancement by supporting scientific research and its applications throughout the world. It maintains international contacts with scientists and scientific academies; provides advice on scientific matters to many groups, including the government of the United Kingdom; and promotes science education.

The Royal Society has a library of books and manuscripts. It publishes several journals, including *Philo-*

sophical Transactions and *Proceedings.* Its offices are in London. Critically reviewed by the Royal Society

Royal Society of Canada (RSC) is a national organization that promotes learning and research in the arts and sciences. The organization elects as its members people who have made important contributions in the humanities, sciences, or literature. Fellows and specially elected fellows must be Canadian or have at least three years' status as Canadian permanent residents. Foreign fellows are neither residents nor citizens of Canada. The RSC also elects honorary fellows from time to time. The society awards medals for achievement and administers scholarships to aid research. It publishes newsletters and annual reports. RSC also publishes annual or semiannual volumes called *Transactions and Proceedings* containing the proceedings of its conferences and studies on matters of public interest.

The Royal Society of Canada was founded in 1882. Its headquarters are in Ottawa.

Critically reviewed by the Royal Society of Canada

Royall, Anne Newport (1769-1854), was an early American newspaperwoman. She wrote for two Washington, D.C., newspapers that she founded when in her 60's. She published a weekly newspaper, *Paul Pry,* from 1831 to 1836. In 1836, she founded another newspaper, *The Huntress,* which appeared until shortly before her death.

Anne Newport was born on June 11, 1769, near Baltimore. She moved to the frontier of Pennsylvania with her parents when she was 3 years old. In 1797, she married Captain William Royall, an officer in the American Revolution (1775-1783). Before Anne Newport Royall became a newspaperwoman, she traveled through the United States and wrote a number of books about her experiences. Royall became an author in her 50's in order to earn a living. Her husband's family had cheated her out of the money he left her upon his death in 1812. Social historians still value Royall's descriptions of the 1800's. She died on Oct. 1, 1854. Robert K. Stewart

Royalty, a commission. See **Writing.**

Royalty. See **King** and its *Related articles.*

Royce, Josiah, *joh SY uh* (1855-1916), an American philosopher, was the leading representative of a movement that was called *Idealism.* He emphasized the religious aspect of philosophy and the need for a philosophical interpretation of religion. He also developed a philosophy of loyalty that included an ethics system, a self-knowledge theory, and a human society theory.

According to Royce, a person gains self-knowledge through interaction with other people, not in isolated contemplation. Royce urged people to be "loyal to loyalty." He believed that humanity's deepest problems can be solved by harmonizing conflicting interests through a commitment to a higher loyalty. For example, Royce regarded Christianity as the religion of loyalty that binds its followers together in a "beloved community."

Royce was born in Grass Valley, California. His best-known works include *The Spirit of Modern Philosophy* (1892), *The World and the Individual* (two volumes, 1900-1901), *The Philosophy of Loyalty* (1908), and *The Problem of Christianity* (1913). John E. Smith

Ruanda-Urundi, *roo AHN dah oo ROON dee,* was a European-controlled territory in east-central Africa that consisted of two kingdoms, Rwanda and Burundi. European control of the region began in the 1890's. The European colonial powers used the spellings *Ruanda* and *Urundi.* Both of these kingdoms became independent nations in 1962.

The Germans first set up a military post in the region in 1896. Soon, they made the area part of German East Africa. Belgium gained control of the territory in 1916, during World War I. In 1923, Ruanda-Urundi became a mandated territory, administered by Belgium under the League of Nations (see **Mandated territory**). In 1946, it became a United Nations trust territory under Belgian control.

The peoples of Ruanda-Urundi spoke nearly identical Bantu languages. One group, the Tutsi (sometimes called the Batusi, or Watusi), formed a small minority that dominated a larger group, the Hutu, politically and economically. The Europeans strengthened Tutsi dominance by giving them privileged access to education at missions and to administrative training.

During the 1950's, tension created by Tutsi domination led to social unrest. In 1962, after much fighting, the Hutu gained control of the newly independent Rwanda government. In Burundi, the Tutsi continued to dominate a large Hutu majority, even after the kingdom had gained its independence in 1962. David Lee Schoenbrun

See also **Burundi; Hutu; Rwanda; Tutsi.**

Rubaiyat, *ROO by yaht* or *ROO bee yaht,* is the shortened form of *The Rubaiyat of Omar Khayyam.* This title was given by English writer Edward FitzGerald to his translation of a group of short poems attributed to the Persian poet, astronomer, and mathematician Omar Khayyam. FitzGerald published four editions of the *Rubaiyat*—in 1859, 1868, 1872, and 1879. He changed the work considerably each time.

The title of the collection comes from the plural of the Arabic word *rubai,* which the Persians used to refer to a form of poetry. A rubai is a *quatrain* (four-line stanza) in which usually the first, second, and fourth lines rhyme with each other. Occasionally all four lines rhyme. In theory, the name *rubaiyat* can be used to refer to any group of such quatrains by any poet. But in English it is almost always used to refer to FitzGerald's version of Khayyam.

In the original Persian, each quatrain is a separate poem. FitzGerald made a selection from the many hundreds of these poems attributed to Khayyam and arranged them into one long poem forming a continuous narrative. The narrative describes a day in the life of a disillusioned would-be philosopher. Finding no meaning in the world and its hardships, he looks for comfort in friendship, wine, and love. Many of FitzGerald's quatrains are frequently quoted in English. They include:

> The Moving Finger writes; and, having writ,
> Moves on: nor all thy Piety nor Wit
> Shall lure it back to cancel half a Line,
> Nor all thy Tears wash out a Word of it.
>
> A book of Verses underneath the Bough,
> A Jug of wine, a Loaf of Bread—and Thou
> Beside me singing in the Wilderness—
> Oh Wilderness were Paradise enow!

A few of FitzGerald's quatrains are translated from passages written by other Persian poets. One or two quatrains are entirely his own creation. Dick Davis

See also **FitzGerald, Edward; Omar Khayyam.**

© Susan McCartney, Photo Researchers

Natural rubber comes chiefly from rubber trees grown on plantations in hot, moist regions. Workers remove a white juice called latex by cutting grooves in the bark, *shown here.* Latex is about one-third rubber. It is refined to produce crude rubber.

Goodyear Tire & Rubber Co.

Synthetic rubber is made by mixing chemicals to produce latex that looks like natural latex from rubber trees. Manufacturers make some synthetic rubber in crumb form, *shown here.* Synthetic rubber performs better than natural rubber in many ways.

Rubber is one of our most interesting and most important raw materials. *Natural rubber* comes from the juice of a tree. *Synthetic rubber* is manufactured from chemicals.

Rubber is especially useful for several reasons. It holds air, keeps out moisture, and does not readily conduct electricity. But its chief importance to us is that it is *elastic.* When you stretch a rubber band and let it go, its elasticity makes it quickly spring back to its original shape. A rubber ball bounces because of this same springiness. Your rubber heels absorb shock when you walk because they have elasticity.

We depend so much on rubber that it would be almost impossible to get along without it. This is not the case with most other materials. If we lack one material, we can usually substitute another. A house can be built using such materials as wood, brick, stone, concrete, glass, or metal. Clothes can be made of cotton, silk, wool, or other fibers.

But what about the tires of an automobile, truck, or bus? It is hard to imagine making them of anything but rubber. Only rubber is elastic, airtight, water-resistant, shock-absorbing, and long-wearing.

Manufacturers make between 40,000 and 50,000 rubber products. A typical automobile has about 600 rubber parts. Some cars, of course, use less rubber than this, and some use more. Many trucks and buses even have springs made of rubber instead of steel.

Uses of rubber

About three-fifths of the rubber used in the United States goes into tires and tubes. These are used on automobiles, airplanes, buses, trucks, tractors, and construction machinery. About one-tenth is used for mechanical products such as gaskets, sealing devices, belting, and printing rollers.

Manufacturers use rubber to make waterproof aprons, boots, raincoats, gloves, and hats, and to give elasticity to other types of clothing and household fabrics. Hard-rubber goods include hair combs and automobile storage-battery cases. Doctors use rubber hot-water bottles, ice bags, syringes, elastic tapes, and surgeon's gloves. Hearing aids, oxygen tents, and many other pieces of equipment have rubber parts.

Swimmers wear rubber bathing suits and caps, goggles, and ear stoppers, and sunbathe on rubber rafts. Many sports are played with rubber balls that range in size from small golfballs to large beach balls. Other rubber products include thread, bottle stoppers, toys, jar rings, elastic bands, and rubber-based paints.

Air pockets in sponge and foam rubbers make them springy. Manufacturers use such kinds of rubber for cushions, mattresses, pillows, and upholstery padding. They are also used as an insulating material. For example, some shoes have a layer of foam rubber next to the leather to keep out the cold.

Rubber cement can be used to hold pieces of paper together, but the pieces can be pulled apart easily. This cement is made of a solution of raw natural rubber in a chemical solvent. The solvent evaporates, and the sticky rubber holds the pieces of paper together.

The development of rubber

First uses. When the early European explorers came to Central and South America, they saw the Indians playing with bouncing balls made of rubber. The explorers learned that the Indians made "waterproof" shoes from *latex,* the milky white juice of the rubber tree. They spread the latex on their feet and let it dry. The Indians also made waterproof bottles by smoothing latex on a bottle-shaped clay mold. They dried the latex over a fire and then washed out the clay.

The South American Indians called the rubber tree *cahuchu,* which means *weeping wood.* The drops of latex oozing from the bark made them think of big white tears. A French explorer, Charles Marie de La Condamine, gathered samples of hardened latex in Peru in 1735, and took them back to France. The French called this new material *caoutchouc,* the French pronunciation of the Indian name *cahuchu.* Variations of the French spelling are used as the word for rubber in most European countries. In 1770, the English chemist Joseph Priestley discovered that the material could be used as an eraser to *rub* out pencil marks. From this use, we get the name *rubber.*

The rubber industry begins. By the late 1700's, scientists had found that hardened latex dissolved in turpentine made a waterproofing liquid for cloth. In the early 1820's, the English inventor Thomas Hancock built a machine to knead scraps of rubber into a solid mass. His inventions and experiments led to the development of present-day rubber processing.

In 1823, Charles Macintosh, a Scottish chemist, began manufacturing the "mackintosh" raincoats that became famous. Macintosh made them with a layer of rubber between two layers of cloth. Manufacturers in Europe and the United States began to make rubber products, including elastic bands, raincoats, hoses, tubes, and shoes.

Discovery of vulcanization. Early rubber products became sticky in hot weather and stiff and brittle in cold weather. In 1839, Charles Goodyear, a Connecticut inventor, discovered a way to make rubber stronger and give it resistance to heat and cold. Goodyear accidentally spilled a sulfur-rubber mixture containing other ingredients on a hot stove while conducting an experiment. The rubber compound was "cured" by the heat and stayed tough and firm in heat and cold. The process of heating sulfur-rubber mixtures became known as *vulcanization,* after Vulcan, the Roman god of fire. With vulcanized rubber, manufacturers could make dependable products, and the rubber industry grew rapidly. Vulcanized rubber was elastic, airtight, and watertight. It could be used to make tight seals between the moving parts of machinery.

The first plantations. At first, manufacturers used only wild rubber. Most of it came from the Amazon Valley of Brazil, although some was from latex-bearing vines in Africa. In 1876, a botanist brought rubber tree seeds to England. Some of the seeds sprouted and were taken to Ceylon (now Sri Lanka) and Malaya (now part of Malaysia) for replanting on plantations. Almost all the plantation trees in the Far East come from these seedlings. The British, Dutch, and French developed plantations in Indonesia, Thailand, Indochina, and other countries of the Far East.

The invention of the automobile in the late 1800's created a tremendous demand for rubber. By 1914, the yearly production of plantation rubber exceeded the yearly production of wild rubber. Later, plantations were established in Africa, South and Central America, and the Philippines.

Development of synthetic rubbers. The importance of rubber in wartime became obvious during World War I (1914-1918). Armies needed vehicles with rubber tires to carry troops and supplies. The Germans were cut off from their natural-rubber supplies by the Allied blockade. They began to make synthetic rubber, but it did not work well. Experiments in producing synthetic rubber continued in the 1920's, chiefly by scientists in Germany and the United States.

When World War II began in 1939, Germany was manufacturing two chief types of synthetic rubber: (1) *Buna S,* made from *butadiene* (a gas) and *styrene* (a liquid made from coal tar and petroleum); and (2) *Buna N,* made from butadiene and acrylonitrile (a liquid obtained from acetylene and hydrocyanic acid). Before 1939, experimenters in the United States made small amounts of several types of synthetic rubber. However, the estimated cost of making these synthetic rubbers was much higher than that of natural rubber.

In 1942, the Japanese captured the rubber-growing lands of the Far East. This capture cut off nine-tenths of the natural-rubber supply to the United States. Almost overnight, the United States developed a synthetic-rubber industry.

The world now uses more synthetic rubber than natural rubber. Synthetic rubber has a greater variety of uses and can be produced cheaply enough to compete with the cost of natural rubber. But the rising cost of petroleum, used in making synthetic rubber, has slowed the growth of synthetic rubber production. Synthetic rubber production has also been affected by the increasing popularity of long-lasting radial tires. These tires require more natural rubber than does another kind of tire called a *bias tire* (see **Tire**).

The chemistry of rubber

In 1826, the English chemist and physicist Michael Faraday discovered that rubber is a hydrocarbon—that is, it consists of the chemical elements hydrogen and carbon. In 1860, another English scientist, Greville Williams, heated some rubber and obtained a liquid he called *isoprene.* Each isoprene molecule contains five carbon atoms and eight hydrogen atoms. In natural rubber, thousands of tiny isoprene molecules link up into a chain to form large molecules of rubber. Chemists call these molecular chains *polymers.* They call the single molecules, such as isoprene, *monomers.*

The particular chainlike structure of the rubber polymer explains why rubber is elastic. Polymer molecules of unstretched rubber fold back on themselves somewhat like irregular coils. Vulcanization attaches the polymer coils to each other. Stretching the rubber straightens the chain of folded molecules. Releasing the rubber lets the chain return to its coiled position.

For years, scientists tried to duplicate the true rubber polymer with molecules of the isoprene monomer. They finally built the first successful synthetic rubbers from the monomers of other hydrocarbons, including butadiene, styrene, and isobutylene.

The rubber industry

Production and uses. More than 80 percent of the world's natural rubber grows on plantations in the Far East, chiefly in Thailand, Indonesia, and Vietnam. Other

Far Eastern countries that produce natural rubber include Cambodia, China, Malaysia, Myanmar, and the Philippines. India and Sri Lanka grow about 10 percent of the world's supply of natural rubber, and Africa grows about 5 percent. Most of the rest comes from Latin America. The world's annual production of natural rubber is about 15 million tons (13.7 million metric tons). Asian countries, especially China, use most of the world's natural rubber.

The world's synthetic rubber production is about 16 million tons (14.5 million metric tons) a year. China is the world's leading synthetic rubber producer and consumer. Other important synthetic rubber producers include France, Germany, Japan, Russia, South Korea, Taiwan, and the United States.

Leading rubber manufacturers usually grow part of their natural rubber on their own plantations, and produce synthetic rubber in their own plants. These rubber companies make varied products such as tires, mechanical goods, industrial products, shoe materials and footwear, aircraft parts, and rubberized textiles. Some companies also produce, for their own use and for sale to other firms, raw materials used to make synthetic rubber. More rubber is used in the manufacture of tires than for any other purpose. The number of tire manufacturers decreased during the 1980's as large companies bought smaller companies. Today, the largest tire manufacturers are the Bridgestone Corporation of Japan, the Goodyear Tire & Rubber Company of the United States, and the Michelin Company of France.

Research in rubber is directed mainly toward making better synthetic rubbers to provide improved rubber products for home, automotive, and industrial use. In addition, many unusual types of rubber are required in the age of nuclear energy and space travel. As new planes and missiles fly higher and faster, they require rubber parts that can withstand temperatures from −120 to 700 °F (−84 to 370 °C). Chemists hope to develop rubbers that will increase protection against harmful radiation in nuclear power plants.

Scientists are studying the possible use of the guayule plant as an inexpensive source of natural rubber. This plant could reduce the nation's dependence on foreign sources of natural rubber and on synthetic rubbers made from petroleum.

Leading natural rubber producing countries

Tons of rubber produced in a year

Country	Tons of rubber produced in a year
Thailand	4,981,000 tons (4,519,000 metric tons)
Indonesia	3,705,000 tons (3,361,000 metric tons)
Vietnam	1,155,000 tons (1,048,000 metric tons)
India	1,055,000 tons (957,000 metric tons)
China	900,000 tons (816,000 metric tons)
Malaysia	785,000 tons (712,000 metric tons)
Côte d'Ivoire	508,000 tons (461,000 metric tons)
Philippines	429,000 tons (389,000 metric tons)
Guatemala	371,000 tons (337,000 metric tons)
Myanmar	245,000 tons (222,000 metric tons)

Figures are for a three-year average, 2015-2017.
Source: FAOSTAT, Statistics Division, Food and Agriculture Organization of the UN. http://www.fao.org. Data accessed in 2019.

Natural rubber

Latex is found in a wide variety of trees and other types of plants. You can see latex oozing from the broken stem of a dandelion or from a cut branch of goldenrod. Scientists are not sure of its use to the plant. Some scientists believe that latex acts as a kind of protective substance when a plant has been wounded.

Chemical analysis shows that about 30 to 35 percent of latex consists of pure rubber. Water makes up another 60 to 65 percent. Latex holds little *globules* (particles) of rubber in the same way that milk holds butterfat. Latex spoils easily and must be processed into *crude rubber* as soon as possible after tapping. This is done by separating the natural rubber in the latex from water and other materials. About 99 percent of all natural rubber comes from the latex of the *Hevea brasiliensis*. This is the tree that we call the *rubber tree*.

The rubber tree. The hevea tree grows best in hot, moist climates in acid, well-drained soils. The finest rubber-growing regions lie within a *rubber belt* that extends about 700 miles (1,100 kilometers) on each side of the equator. Almost all natural rubber comes from huge plantations of rubber trees in the Far East.

The rubber tree cultivated on plantations grows straight and slender, about 60 to 70 feet (18 to 21 meters) tall. It has smooth, light-colored bark and shiny, dark leaves. When its pale yellow blossoms fade, seed pods grow in their place. Each pod contains three brownish, speckled seeds about 1 inch (2.5 centimeters) long. The latex containing the rubber flows through a series of tubes in the tree's *cambium layer*, the layer between the wood and bark. When this layer is pierced, the milky white latex oozes out. By grafting and breeding, botanists have developed trees that produce over 10 times as much natural rubber as the wild hevea.

Rubber has also been collected from *landolphia* vines that grow in Africa. In Mexico, *guayule* bushes have been cultivated for their rubber, but they produce only a small amount. In Brazil, a small amount of rubber comes from wild hevea trees. Other rubber-bearing trees include the *manihot* tree, also found in Brazil, and the trees of the genus *Castilloa* found in Central America, Colombia, and Ecuador.

Tapping the tree. Rubber plantations employ workers known as *tappers* who collect latex from the trees. A tapper cuts a narrow groove in the bark of a tree approximately 4 feet (1.2 meters) above the ground. The groove slants diagonally downward about halfway around the trunk. At the bottom of the cut, the tapper attaches a U-shaped metal spout, and below the spout, a small cup. Latex oozes from the cut and flows down the groove through the spout into the cup. Tappers collect about a teacupful of latex at each tree. The latex is then

Rubber comes from two main sources. Natural rubber is provided chiefly by rubber trees grown on plantations in hot, humid areas. Synthetic rubber is manufactured in many industrialized nations. The map shows the leading countries for each type of rubber production.

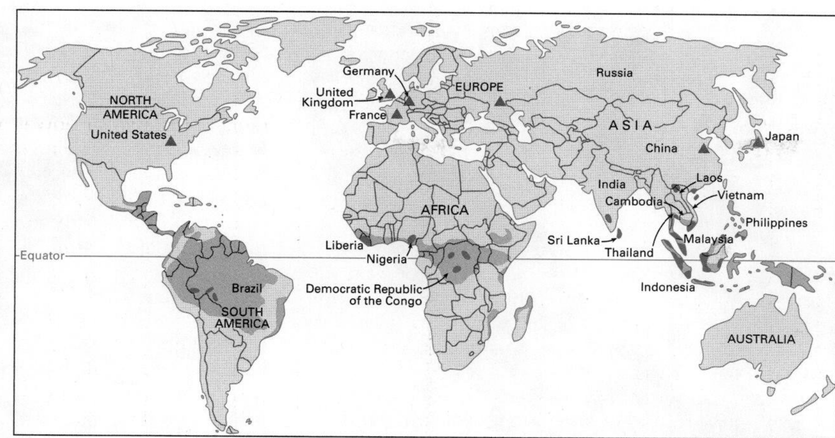

WORLD BOOK map

transported to the factory for processing into liquid latex or dry rubber.

Some plantations tap the trees every other day. Other plantations tap every day for 15 days, and then allow the trees to "rest" for 15 days. On each tapping, the worker slices off a thin shaving of bark from the bottom edge of the groove near the cambium layer. The tapper does not cut into the cambium layer of the tree, because deep cuts that penetrate the wood harm the tree. After three or four years, the groove reaches the ground, and the tapper cuts the bark on the opposite side of the trunk. By the time the second groove reaches the ground, the bark has grown back on the first groove, and it can be tapped again.

Workers begin to tap rubber trees about five to seven years after planting. But younger trees do not give as much rubber as they do about the 10th year, when they are fully grown. Rubber trees yield their full capacity of latex for about 25 to 30 years. About 100 trees grow on 1 acre (0.4 hectare), and each full-grown tree produces from 1 to 4 gallons (4 to 15 liters) of latex a year. One acre of trees on a large, well-developed plantation may yield about 1,800 pounds (816 kilograms) of dry crude rubber a year.

Separating the latex. Most plantations make crude rubber from latex by *coagulation.* Tappers pour latex from their collecting pails into tanks and add an equal amount of water. They strain the diluted latex through sieves to remove dirt, bark, and twigs. Formic acid is then added to the strained latex to make it *coagulate,* or form solid particles. The rubber particles rise to the surface and form a curdlike mass of crude rubber.

Processing crude rubber. Workers feed the crude rubber through rollers that squeeze out the water and form it into a sheet. *Crumb rubber* is produced by special machines that chop or shred the sheets into fine, wet crumbs. The crumb rubber is dried in hot air tunnels and then compressed into 75-pound (34-kilogram) bales for shipment to market.

Ribbed smoke sheet is made by putting crude rubber through rollers that give the sheets a ribbed appearance. The sheets are hung to dry for several days in a hot smokehouse. The smoke turns the rubber sheets brown and kills mold and bacteria that would damage them. The dried rubber sheets are pressed into bales for shipment.

Crepe rubber is formed by passing the curdlike mass through rollers that roughen and crinkle the sheets so that they look like thick crepe paper. The rubber is constantly washed while being rolled. The sheets hang in heating rooms to dry. Workers bale the pale, crinkled sheets for shipment.

Processing latex. Sometimes, all the latex collected on plantations is not coagulated. Workers place part of the fresh latex in machines called *separators* that remove part of the water from the latex. Ammonia or another preservative keeps the latex from coagulating and prevents spoiling. The preserved liquid latex is sent to market in drums or tanks. Rubber manufacturers use

How a rubber tree is tapped

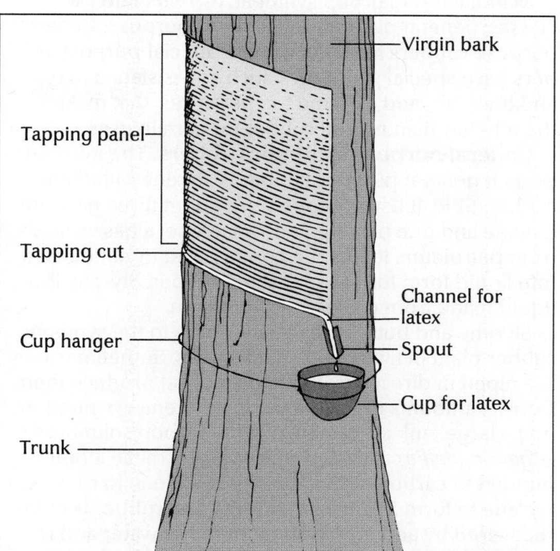

WORLD BOOK illustration by David Cunningham

This diagram shows how latex is obtained from a rubber tree. The liquid oozes down to the spout through the channel produced by the tapping cut. It flows down the spout into the cup.

Firestone Tire & Rubber Company

Freshly tapped latex flows from a tank truck into vats at a processing plant, *shown here.* The plant uses a process called *coagulation* to remove impurities from latex and form crude rubber.

Firestone Tire & Rubber Company

Sheets of crepe rubber, *shown here,* are formed by rollers that roughen and crinkle doughy masses of crude rubber passing through them. The rubber is constantly washed as it is rolled.

latex to make articles such as surgeon's gloves, foam-backed carpeting, tubing, and elastic thread.

Synthetic rubber

Rubberlike materials made from chemicals were called synthetic rubbers because they were intended as substitutes for natural rubber. Chemists use the word *elastomer* for any substance, including rubber, that stretches easily to several times its length, and returns to its original shape.

Manufacturers group synthetic rubbers into two classes: general-purpose and special-purpose. General-purpose rubbers have many uses. Special-purpose rubbers have special properties such as resistance to oils and fuels, air, and extreme temperatures, that make them better than natural rubber for certain uses.

General-purpose synthetic rubbers. The most important general-purpose rubber is styrene-butadiene rubber (SBR). It usually consists of about three parts butadiene and one part styrene. Butadiene, a gas, is made from petroleum. It must be compressed or condensed into liquid form for use in making rubber. Styrene is a liquid made from coal tar or petroleum.

Styrene and butadiene usually come to the synthetic-rubber plant in tank cars or tank trucks. Sometimes they are piped in directly from the plants that produce them. Correct amounts of styrene and butadiene are pumped into a large tank containing a hydrocarbon solution. An *organometallic* catalyst, which contains metal atoms bonded to carbon atoms, causes butadiene to react with styrene to form SBR (see **Catalysis**). The rubber is then recovered by adding the solution to hot water and removing the solvent with steam. The crumbs of rubber are then filtered from the water. After drying, the rubber is usually pressed into large bales.

SBR can also be prepared using styrene and butadiene in a mixture of soap and water. The mixture is heated or cooled depending on the type of SBR being made. A catalyst causes the styrene and butadiene to combine with each other. Gradually, with stirring, the ingredients change to a milky white fluid, also called *latex.*

Workers pump the latex into another tank where *antioxidants* are added to prevent the rubber from decaying. The latex is sent to a third tank containing acids and salts. The salts and acids coagulate the latex. The rubber forms into lumps that float on top of the liquid. Washing the rubber lumps removes extra chemicals. The rubber may then be packed as loose crumbs or pressed into bales of dry rubber.

Special-purpose rubbers. Contact with gasoline, oils, sunlight, and air harms natural rubber. Special-purpose synthetic rubbers resist these "enemies" better than natural rubber or SBR do. Also, some of these special-purpose rubbers have greater resistance to heat and cold. They cost more than natural rubber or SBR, but their special properties make them worth the difference. Special-purpose rubbers include butyl rubber, neoprene rubber, and polyurethane rubbers.

Manufacturing rubber products

Manufacturers obtain bales of dry rubber from plantations and from synthetic-rubber manufacturing plants. Latex comes to them in big tanks on ships and in tank cars. Manufacturers usually process natural and synthetic rubber in much the same way, although latex requires different steps.

Plasticization involves only dry rubber. It is a series of processes that makes dry rubber softer and easier to mold. Workers first slice the bales into small pieces of rubber that they can handle easily. The lower grades of natural rubber receive a thorough washing in a wringer-like machine called a *wash mill.* Then the rubber slices

Firestone Tire & Rubber Company

Washed and shredded rubber is dried by an *extrusion-dryer,* such as the one shown here. The dried rubber is baked and pressed into bales for shipment to rubber manufacturers.

are fed into mixing mills and other machines that *plasticize,* or soften, them into a doughlike mass. Manufacturers plasticize the rubber faster by heating it and adding materials called *plasticizers* and *softeners.*

Compounding and mixing. Compounding means adding carefully measured amounts of various ingredients to plasticized rubber and to latex. The compounding "recipe" helps control the elasticity, strength, and other properties of the final product. Sulfur is commonly added to bring about vulcanization, a process that takes place later in rubber manufacturing. Other ingredients used include accelerators, which speed vulcanization; fillers, which increase the volume and strength of the rubber; and antioxidants, which slow down the rate at which the rubber wears out.

Shaping. Manufacturers use several methods to shape rubber into final products. These include (1) calendering, (2) extrusion, (3) molding, and (4) dipping.

Calendering means rolling rubber into sheets. It is done on a machine that has two to five rolls. The rubber passes between the rolls to form sheets. Workers cut the sheets into various sizes and patterns, or stack the sheets in layers to make many products. These products include rubber flooring, toys, bedsheets, baby pants, and mechanical goods, such as wrapping tapes, washers, rings, and disks.

Extrusion is the final step in the processing of some rubber products. The word *extrude* means to push out. *Tube machines* push soft rubber through a hole, much as toothpaste is squeezed from a tube. Extruded products include hoses, inner tubes, and rubber strips used on refrigerators and automobile windshields.

Molding produces shoe soles and heels, rubber tires, hot-water bottles, mattresses, hard-rubber articles, and industrial products, such as gaskets and fittings. Workers prepare pieces of rubber in the approximate size and shape of the finished product. They put the pieces in molds shaped to form the product. Many products are molded and vulcanized at the same time.

Dipping is used only to make products from liquid latex. Products made by dipping include rubber gloves and toy balloons. Workers dip molds, usually made of metal, glass, or ceramic materials, into tanks of latex. They drain the excess latex and dry the mold at low temperatures. By repeating this process, they build up several layers on the mold.

Vulcanization is usually the last step in preparing a final product. It gives strength, hardness, and elasticity to rubber by treating it with heat and vulcanizing agents, such as sulfur. During vulcanization, the heat causes the sulfur to combine with the rubber and cure it. This makes the rubber stronger and more durable. Generally, the more sulfur that is added, the firmer the vulcanized compound will be. Vulcanization may take from a few minutes to several hours.

Manufacturers vulcanize and shape molded products at the same time by heating the molds under pressure. They vulcanize extruded and sheet products on pans in hot-air or steam chambers. Dipped products are vulcanized in hot water, hot air, or open steam while still on the molds. Foam products in their molds are vulcanized in steam chambers or in boiling water.

Sponge rubber may be made from either latex or dry rubber. *Blowing* produces one type of sponge rubber from dry rubber. During vulcanization, the chemicals that have been added turn to gas and "blow" tiny bubbles of air in the rubber compound. When the rubber *gels,* or sets, in the mold, the bubbles are trapped in the rubber. Blown sponge rubber may be hard or soft.

Foam rubber is a type of sponge rubber made by whipping air into latex, much as a cook whips air into egg whites. Vulcanization takes place after the foam gels in a mold. Foam rubber has millions of tiny cells filled with air. Some types may be nine-tenths air and only one-tenth rubber. Foam rubber is used for upholstery and foam strips for surgical use.

Howard A. Colvin

Related articles in *World Book* include:

Elasticity	Guayule
Faraday, Michael	Latex
Firestone, Harvey S.	Plastics
Goodrich, Benjamin F.	Tire
Goodyear, Charles	

Outline

I. Uses of rubber

II. The development of rubber

III. The chemistry of rubber

IV. The rubber industry

A. Production and uses
B. Leading rubber manufacturers
C. Research

V. Natural rubber

A. The rubber tree
B. Tapping the tree
C. Separating the latex
D. Processing crude rubber
E. Processing latex

VI. Synthetic rubber

A. General-purpose synthetic rubbers
B. Special-purpose synthetic rubbers

VII. Manufacturing rubber products

A. Plasticization
B. Compounding and mixing
C. Shaping
D. Vulcanization
E. Sponge rubber

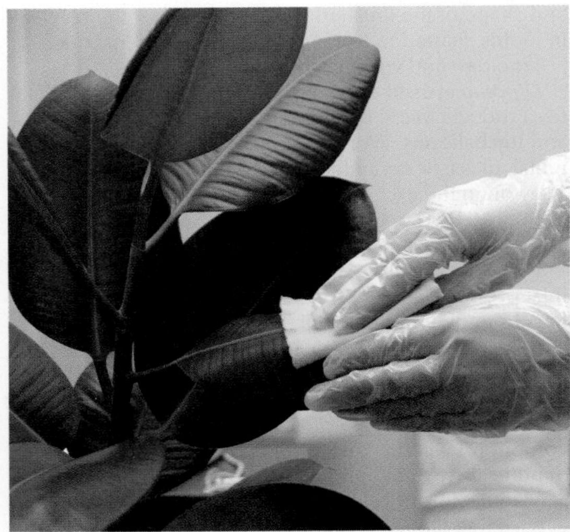

© Shutterstock

The attractive rubber plant is frequently grown in pots in the home. It has thick, rubberlike leaves.

Rubber plant is the common name for a house plant that is a kind of fig. The rubber plant can grow well in the heat and low humidity of houses. It grows tall rapidly and lives a long time. The plant's leaves are large and broad and may grow from 2 to 12 inches (5 to 30 centimeters) long. The upper surface of the leaf is a shiny, dark green, and the underside is dull and lighter green.

The rubber plant requires little care. It will grow well if the soil in the pot is rich in minerals and the plant is given enough sunlight, water, and room. The plant should be placed outdoors during the summer so that it will get enough sunlight to last the winter. A rubber plant may grow so tall that it may be necessary to cut it back to make it branch. Sometimes a new plant can be grown from the tip of the stem that is cut off.

Rubber plants are often attacked by scale insects. These pests can be destroyed by spraying the plants with nicotine. Commercial rubber does not come from these rubber plants, but from a tropical tree that belongs to the castor-bean family. Alwyn H. Gentry

Scientific classification. Rubber plants are in the mulberry family, Moraceae. The common rubber plant is *Ficus elastica.* The more decorative rubber plant is the fiddle fig, *F. lyrata.*

Rubella is a common contagious disease that most often affects children. It is also called *German measles.* Most cases of rubella are not serious. But if a woman develops the disease during early pregnancy, it may result in her baby having one or more birth defects. Such birth defects may include mental retardation, impaired vision and hearing, and malformations of the heart.

Rubella is caused by a virus, which is spread chiefly in droplets expelled when an infected person coughs or sneezes. Two to three weeks after contact with the disease, a person may develop a runny nose or mild fever. Pink, slightly raised spots appear on the face and spread to the trunk and limbs. Lymph nodes on the back of the scalp, behind the ears, and on the side of the neck may become tender. These symptoms usually disappear in a few days. In adolescents and adults, the symptoms often are more severe than in children and may include painful, swollen joints. In some cases of rubella, no symptoms appear. Infected people can spread the virus to others from about seven days before the rash develops until about five days after its appearance.

There is no specific treatment for rubella. A case of rubella results in *immunity* (resistance) to the disease afterward. In 1969, a vaccine became available that also provides immunity to rubella. Doctors recommend that children 15 months of age or older be given this vaccine and that a second dose be given from 4 to 12 years of age. It is generally combined with vaccines for measles and mumps. Widespread vaccination has eliminated the disease from the United States, but rubella still occurs in other regions of the world. Neil R. Blacklow

See also Measles.

Rubens, Peter Paul (1577-1640), was the greatest Flemish painter of the 1600's. In addition to his paintings, Rubens made designs for book illustrations and tapestries and occasionally for architecture and sculpture. He was also a scholar and a respected diplomat.

His life. Rubens was born on June 28, 1577, in Siegen, Germany, of Flemish parents. After his father died in 1587, his mother returned with her children to her native city of Antwerp, in what is now Belgium. There, Rubens studied under local painters. He went to Italy in 1600 to study art. In Italy, he was employed as a painter by Vincenzo Gonzaga, Duke of Mantua. In 1603, the duke sent Rubens to Spain as a member of a diplomatic mission. Rubens also spent time in Genoa and Rome.

Rubens went back to Antwerp in 1608 to visit his sick mother, but she died before he arrived. In Antwerp, Rubens was offered several important commissions for paintings, and he decided to remain in the city. In 1609, he married Isabella Brant, a member of a prominent Antwerp family. They had four children.

Also in 1609, Rubens became court painter to the governors of the Netherlands, Archduke Albert and the Infanta Isabella, at Brussels. Rubens's fame as a painter spread, and nobility and royalty throughout Europe sought his services. He also received many commissions from the Roman Catholic Church.

To carry out commissions for large-scale works, Rubens formed a large workshop with assistants. Rubens never claimed any of their pictures as his unless he had retouched them thoroughly. His most famous assistant was the Flemish artist Sir Anthony Van Dyck.

After his wife died in 1626, Rubens accepted several diplomatic assignments involving peace negotiations between England and Spain. His assignments took him to Madrid in 1628 and to London in 1629. King Charles I of England knighted Rubens for his skill in diplomacy.

Rubens married again in 1630 and gradually withdrew from political life. His second wife was a beautiful 16-year-old girl, Hélène Fourment. Hélène, like Rubens's first wife, was a member of a prominent Antwerp family. Rubens painted her many times. They had five children. After 1635, Rubens spent much time at his country estate near Brussels. The beautiful landscape there became the setting for many of his late works. Rubens died on May 30, 1640, in Antwerp.

His art. The most important influence on Rubens's style was the ancient Roman sculpture he studied in

Hélène Fourment and Her Children (1637), an oil painting on canvas; The Louvre, Paris (SCALA/Art Resource)

An affectionate Rubens portrait of his second wife and two of their children reflects the intimacy and serenity of the works the artist painted during the final 10 years of his life.

Italy. He was also influenced by the paintings and sculptures of such Italian Renaissance artists as Michelangelo, Raphael, Tintoretto, Titian, and Veronese. Among the artists of his own time, Rubens especially admired Caravaggio and Carracci.

Rubens was the most important Baroque artist of northern Europe. His paintings are known for their vast scale, brilliant colors, and emotional intensity. In one commission during the 1620's, he painted 21 large pictures on the life of Marie de Médicis, the widow of King Henry IV of France. From 1630 to 1635, he painted nine huge canvases for the Banqueting House at Whitehall in London. In the mid-1630's, he organized the artists of Antwerp to decorate structures in the city according to his designs to celebrate the visit of a new Spanish governor of the Netherlands. His last major commission was for a series of paintings to decorate the hunting lodge of King Philip IV of Spain.

Rubens's subjects include hunting scenes, Biblical episodes, stories from classical mythology, portraits and self-portraits, and landscapes. *Battle of the Amazons* is an example of his Baroque style. It is reproduced in the **Painting** article. Eric M. Zafran

See also **Baroque; Daniel, Book of** (picture); **Drawing** (picture: A chalk drawing); **Jesus Christ** (picture: Jesus was crucified).

Rubeola. See Measles.

Rubicon, *ROO buh kahn,* is a stream near Rimini, Italy, that Julius Caesar made famous when he was governor of Gaul. The Rubicon was part of the boundary between Roman Italy and the Roman province of Cisalpine Gaul (the Po Valley). Caesar and other Roman governors were forbidden to cross the boundary with troops. Caesar was commanding troops in Gaul when the Roman Senate, fearing his power, ordered him to give up his command. Caesar refused and led his men across the Rubicon on Jan. 10, 49 B.C. This action symbolized the start of Caesar's successful drive for the leadership of Rome. The expression *to cross the Rubicon* means to make a decision that cannot be changed.

The name Rubicon comes from the Latin word *rubeus* meaning *red.* The stream got its name because its waters are colored red by mud deposits. It may be the same as the present-day Fiumicino River. Arther Ferrill

See also **Caesar, Julius.**

Rubidium, *roo BIHD ee uhm,* (chemical symbol, Rb) is a soft, silvery-white metallic element. It is used in the making of photoelectric cells and vacuum tubes and as a *catalyst* (substance that stimulates a chemical reaction). Pure rubidium does not occur in nature because it is extremely reactive. It burns on exposure to air and reacts violently with water and acids. Rubidium compounds occur widely in Earth's crust. Rubidium's *atomic number* (number of protons in its nucleus) is 37. Its *relative atomic mass* is 85.4678. An element's relative atomic mass equals its *mass* (amount of matter) divided by $\frac{1}{12}$ of the mass of carbon 12, the most abundant form of carbon. Rubidium melts at 39.31 °C and boils at 688 °C. The German scientists Gustav Kirchhoff and Robert Bunsen discovered the element in 1861. Kenton H. Whitmire

Rubin, Robert Edward (1938-), was United States secretary of the treasury under President Bill Clinton from 1995 to 1999. Before Rubin became secretary, he had been director of the National Economic Council since 1993. As the council's director, Rubin helped shape the Clinton administration's economic policies. He also helped win congressional approval of the North American Free Trade Agreement (NAFTA) between the United States, Canada, and Mexico. Before he became director of the National Economic Council, Rubin had been a major political fund-raiser for Clinton and other Democratic presidential nominees.

Rubin was born on Aug. 29, 1938, in New York City. He earned a bachelor's degree from Harvard University in 1960 and studied at the London School of Economics in 1960 and 1961. He graduated from Yale Law School in 1964. That same year, Rubin began working as a corporate lawyer in New York City. In 1966, he joined Goldman, Sachs & Co., a New York investment-banking firm. He was cochairman of the firm from 1990 to 1992. After stepping down as secretary of the treasury in 1999, Rubin joined Citigroup, a large U.S. financial services company, becoming a cochairman. He was a coauthor of *In an Uncertain World: Tough Choices from Wall Street to Washington* (2003). Alan Greenblatt

Rubinstein, *ROO bihn styn,* **Anton Gregor,** *ahn TAWN gray GAWR* (1829-1894), was a Russian pianist and composer. He was one of the greatest pianists of the 1800's, and his tours through Europe and America made him the most famous pianist of his time. Rubinstein composed many works, but few are performed today. He was born on Nov. 28, 1829, near Balta, Ukraine. At 10, he made his first public appearance in Moscow.

When Rubinstein was 16, he began to teach in Vienna, Austria. Two years later, he went to St. Petersburg, Russia. There, the Grand Duchess Helen became his patroness and gave him many opportunities to be heard in public. In 1858, he became court pianist and concert conductor. The next year, he became director of the Royal Russian Musical Society. Four years later, he founded the St. Petersburg Conservatory. He served as its director until 1867, and again from 1887 to 1890. Rubinstein toured the United States in 1872 and 1873. He died on Nov. 20, 1894. Lydia Hailparn Ledeen

Rubinstein, *ROO bihn styn,* **Arthur** (1887-1982), was a Polish-born concert pianist. He became famous throughout the world for his warmly expressive interpretations of music by Romantic composers of the 1800's, especially the Polish composer Frédéric Chopin.

Rubinstein also gained praise for his performances of works by the composers Franz Liszt of Hungary, Robert Schumann of Germany, Peter Ilich Tchaikovsky of Russia, Manuel de Falla of Spain, and Heitor Villa-Lobos of Brazil. Besides his solo concerts, Rubinstein performed chamber music with other prominent musicians.

Rubinstein was born in Łódź, Poland, on Jan. 28, 1887. He studied in Berlin and Warsaw with the German composer Max Bruch and the Polish pianist Ignace Paderewski, among others. Rubinstein made his concert debut at the age of 11. He moved to the United States in 1939 and became a U.S. citizen in 1946. Rubinstein wrote two autobiographies, *My Young Years* (1973) and *My Many Years* (1980). He died on Dec. 20, 1982. F. E. Kirby

Ruble, *ROO buhl,* also spelled *rouble,* is the monetary unit of Russia and Belarus. Russia and Belarus decide the value of the ruble in their countries independently of each other. The Russian and the Belarusian ruble are each divided into 100 *kopecks* (also spelled *copecks).* Currency in circulation in Russia includes paper treasury notes and coins. Coins are issued in several denominations of rubles and kopecks. Burton H. Hobson

Ruby is the red gem variety of the mineral corundum. Varieties of corundum are called *sapphires* if they are any color other than red. Chemically, a ruby is an aluminum oxide. Rubies get their color from traces of chromium in the aluminum oxide. The red of most rubies has a brownish or yellowish tint. The rarest, most highly prized rubies are pure red.

Rubies and sapphires are second only to diamonds in hardness, and fine-quality rubies are among the costliest of all gems. The finest rubies come from Myanmar. Other primary producers of rubies are Kenya, Tanzania, and Madagascar.

A *star ruby cabochon* shows a six-rayed star within it when seen in a bright light. A cabochon is a rounded, polished stone.

Millions of carats of inexpensive synthetic rubies are made each year. But a demand for real gems has allowed the natural stones to maintain their high value. It can be hard to distinguish between natural and synthetic rubies, even for experts. Experts are also challenged when determining if the color of a natural ruby has been improved by heating. Ruby is the birthstone for July.

Art Resource
Red ruby

Mark A. Helper

See also **Corundum; Gem** (Imitation and synthetic gems); **Sapphire.**

Rudd, Kevin Michael (1957-), was prime minister of Australia from 2007 to 2010 and again briefly in 2013. He led the Australian Labor Party (ALP).

© Commonwealth of Australia
Kevin Rudd

Rudd was born on Sept. 21, 1957, in Nambour, Queensland. In 1981, he earned a bachelor's degree in Asian studies from the Australian National University in Canberra. From 1981 to 1988, he served the Department of Foreign Affairs as a diplomat in Stockholm, Sweden, and in Beijing. In 1988, he became chief of staff to Queensland's state opposition leader, Wayne Goss. Rudd continued as chief of staff after Goss became premier of Queensland in 1989. In 1991, Rudd was named director-general of Queensland's Cabinet Office. He joined KPMG Australia, an accounting firm, as a consultant in 1996.

Rudd was elected to the House of Representatives in 1998 and reelected in 2001 and 2004. In 2006, he became head of the ALP and leader of the opposition in Parliament. In 2007, he led the ALP to victory in a general election and became prime minister. In 2010, he lost the party leadership and the office of prime minister. He regained those offices in 2013. Later that year, a coalition of the Liberal and National parties defeated the ALP in a general election, and Rudd lost the prime ministership. In November, he announced his retirement from politics. Rudd was named a Companion of the Order of Australia in 2019. Critically reviewed by Clement Macintyre

Rudolf, Lake. See **Lake Turkana.**

Rudolph, Paul (1918-1997), was an American architect. He became best known for his dramatic and complex designs, especially buildings for urban and academic environments. His imaginative use of concrete and the

© ESTO
A building by Paul Rudolph is home to Yale University's school of architecture. It features an exterior of glass and rough concrete. The absence of ornament is typical of Rudolph's designs.

absence of ornamentation in his exteriors show the influence of the French architect Le Corbusier (see **Le Corbusier**).

Rudolph served as chairman of the architecture department at Yale University in New Haven, Connecticut, from 1958 to 1965. Several of his important buildings are located in New Haven. Rudolph's most controversial work is the Art and Architecture Building (1963) at Yale, a complicated, 9-story building with 36 interior levels. The Temple Street parking garage (1963) is an example of his skill in integrating structures into urban settings. The garage is also an attempt to turn a simple, functional building into an object of beauty. During the 1960's, Rudolph began to design low-cost, prefabricated residential buildings, such as Crawford Manor (1966) in New Haven.

Rudolph was born on Oct. 28, 1918, in Elkton, Kentucky. He studied with architect Walter Gropius at Harvard University from 1941 to 1943 and in 1947. Rudolph died on Aug. 8, 1997. Nicholas Adams

Rudolph, Wilma (1940-1994), was an American athlete. In the 1960 Olympic Games in Rome, she became the first American woman to win three gold medals in track and field competition. She won the 100-meter and 200-meter individual races, and she was a member of the winning American 400-meter relay team. During her career, Rudolph set world records in the 100-meter and 200-meter races.

UPI/Bettmann Newsphotos

Wilma Rudolph

Wilma Glodean Rudolph was born on June 23, 1940, in St. Bethlehem, Tennessee. At the age of 4, she suffered an attack of double pneumonia and scarlet fever, followed by polio, which left her unable to walk properly until she was 11 years old. She competed in her first Olympics at the age of 16 in the 1956 games. She won a bronze medal as a member of the American Olympic 400-meter relay team. After retiring from competition, Rudolph worked with young people, in both sports and educational programs. She died on Nov. 12, 1994. Michael Takaha

Ruff is a sandpiper native to the Eastern Hemisphere. Ruffs range in color from black and chestnut to buff and whitish. During the mating season, the male develops a tuft of feathers on its neck that it can erect into a ruff. The female, called a reeve, has more modest plumage than the male. Ruffs are occasionally seen on the East Coast of North America. Fritz L. Knopf

Scientific classification. The scientific name for the ruff is *Philomachus pugnax.*

Ruffe, *ruhf,* is a small freshwater fish that is a major pest in North America. Ruffe are native to Europe and Asia. But they appeared in the Great Lakes of North America in the 1980's and quickly became plentiful. Their explosive growth threatened the food supply of many fish native to the Great Lakes. Ruffe further endangered these native fish by eating the fishes' eggs and *larvae* (young).

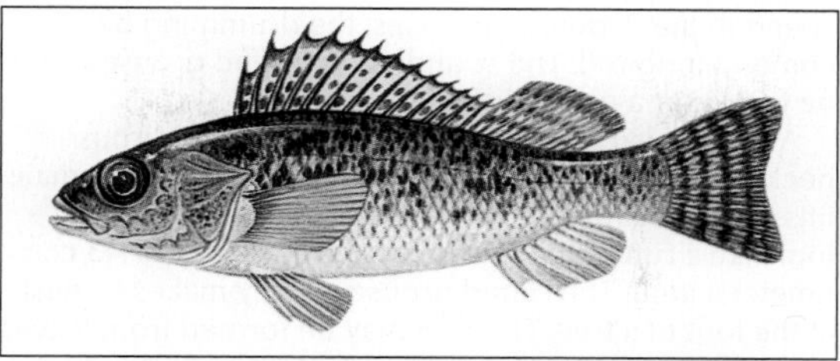

WORLD BOOK illustration by Colin Newman, Bernard Thornton Artists

The ruffe has a greenish back and a yellowish belly. Sharp spikes stick out of both the *dorsal* (back) fin and the bones that cover the gills. Ruffe are major pests in North America.

Ruffe grow up to 10 inches (25 centimeters) in length and have a drooping, scaleless head. Their bodies are brownish-green in color on the back and yellowish on the belly. Sharp spikes stick out of both the *dorsal* (back) fin and the bones that cover the gills. Ruffe live in lakes and slow-moving rivers. In addition to eggs and larvae of other fish, the ruffe's diet includes a variety of insects and shellfish.

Ruffe were first discovered in Lake Superior in 1987. Ships probably transported ruffe larvae from Europe to North America. The larvae may have been trapped in the ships' *ballast* (water kept in the hold of a ship to stabilize the vessel). Once the ships reached Lake Superior, they unintentionally released the young fish with the ballast.
John E. McCosker

Scientific classification. The scientific name of the ruffe is *Gymnocephalus cernuus.*

Ruffed grouse is a thickly feathered grouse of North America. It is famous for the drumming sounds that the male bird makes with his wings during the spring. He chooses a log for his drumming and perches on it daily early in the morning. For many years, naturalists thought that the bird drummed by beating his wings against the log, against his breast, or against each other. High-speed photographs have shown that the ruffed grouse actually beats the air with his wings, creating a sonic boom. At first the sounds are dull and well spaced, but as the

© Harry Engels, Animals Animals

A male ruffed grouse beats the air with its wings, *shown here,* making a drumming sound that can be heard far away.

speed of the flapping increases, the drumming becomes a long roll. The sound of the ruffed grouse can be heard for a great distance.

A thick collar of feathers around the ruffed grouse's neck gives the bird its name. During courtship, the male lifts these gleaming black feathers outward until they look like a ruff. Adult males are about 17 inches (43 centimeters) long. The ruffed grouse usually makes its nest at the foot of a tree. The nest may be formed from leaves and may contain from 9 to 14 eggs. The birds do not fly south in the autumn. In winter, the leg feathers of the ruffed grouse grow longer for warmth, and a weblike structure grows between its toes, enabling the bird to walk on top of snow. The ruffed grouse is the state bird of Pennsylvania. Bertin W. Anderson

Scientific classification. The scientific name of the ruffed grouse is *Bonasa umbellus.*

See also **Grouse; Partridge.**

Ruffin, Edmund (1794-1865), was a noted Virginia agriculturist and a strong supporter of slavery. Ruffin favored *secession* (withdrawal) from the Union, and he was given the honor of firing the first shot on Fort Sumter, South Carolina, where the American Civil War was started in 1861.

Ruffin was born on Jan. 5, 1794, in Prince George County, Virginia. He experimented in crop rotation and with improved plowing, drainage, and fertilizing methods. He wrote about his theories and experiments, and helped bring about important changes in farming methods in the South. Ruffin founded the *Farmer's Register,* an agricultural journal, in 1833, and headed the Virginia State Agricultural Society from 1852 to 1854. Ruffin was so disturbed when the South lost the Civil War that he committed suicide on June 18, 1865. James M. McPherson

Rugby football, also called *rugger,* is a fast contact sport played by two teams. Players on each team try to score by kicking, passing, or carrying the ball until they can kick it over the opponent's goal or touch it down behind the opponent's goal line. The team that scores the most points wins the match.

There are two versions of rugby football—Rugby Union and Rugby League. Rugby Union is the older of the two. Both versions are played by amateurs at the lower levels and by professionals at the top level. Both types of rugby football originated in the United Kingdom in the 1800's, and both are now played worldwide.

Both forms of rugby feature almost continuous play. Stoppages occur only if a player is injured, after points are scored, or if the ball crosses the boundaries of the field. Play also stops if there is a restart of play resulting from a rules violation. A match is divided into two 40-minute halves separated by a half-time rest period of no more than 15 minutes.

Both Rugby Union and Rugby League matches involve tackling and other physical play, but the players wear little protective equipment. A typical uniform consists of a shirt, shorts, knee-length stockings, and cleated boots. Some players wear shin guards and mouth guards.

Rugby Union

The field and equipment. The field is a maximum of 69 meters (75 yards) wide and 144 meters (157 yards) long. The goal lines are 100 meters (109 yards) apart. An area called the *in-goal* extends up to 22 meters (24 yards) beyond each goal line. A *halfway line* parallel to the goal line divides the field in half. The field is further divided by two *22-meter lines,* which lie 22 meters from each goal line, and two *10-meter lines,* which are 10 meters (11 yards) from the halfway line.

Two goal posts stand on each goal line. The posts are 5.6 meters (6.1 yards) apart. They are connected by a crossbar that is 3 meters (3.4 yards) above the ground.

The Rugby Union ball is an inflated oval rubber bladder encased in leather. It measures from 28 to 29 centimeters (11 to 11 ½ inches) in length and weighs from 400 to 450 grams (14 to 16 ounces).

The officials. A referee and two touch judges officiate a match. The referee controls the game. The referee's judgment is final. The touch judges signal when and where the ball goes *into touch* (out of bounds), and they indicate whether a kick at goal is successful. They also inform the referee of any foul play.

The team consists of 15 players—8 forwards and 7 backs. The forwards attempt to win possession of the ball. The backs then advance the ball toward the goal by running, passing, or kicking. Forwards may also participate in the running, passing, and kicking.

Scoring. A team can score a *try,* a *conversion,* and a *goal.* A try is scored when any player touches the ball down on the ground in the opponent's in-goal area. A try counts 5 points. After a try is scored, a player on the scoring team attempts to *convert* the try. To convert a try, the player place-kicks the ball over the crossbar from a point opposite the spot where the player's team scored the try. A player makes a place kick by placing the ball upright on a plastic tee or in a small hole in the turf dug with the heel of a boot. Defensive players stand behind their goal line during the conversion attempt. A successful conversion scores 2 points.

There are two kinds of goals, a *penalty goal* and a *dropped goal.* Each counts 3 points. A player scores a goal by *drop-kicking*—dropping the ball and kicking it on the first bounce—or by place-kicking the ball over the crossbar on a *penalty kick.* A penalty kick is awarded if the opposing team breaks certain rules. A player scores a dropped goal by drop-kicking the ball over the crossbar while the ball is in play.

How to play Rugby Union. A kickoff starts a Rugby Union match and also starts play in the second half. A player restarts play after either team has scored by place-kicking or drop-kicking from the center spot. The receiving team takes positions behind its 10-meter line.

Moving the ball. The team with the ball tries to move it toward the opponent's goal line by running, passing, or kicking the ball. Players are not allowed to pass the ball *forward* (toward the opponent's goal). The ball can only be passed *laterally* (sideways) or backward. Players also cannot *knock on* (hit the ball toward the opponent's goal line with their hand or arm).

Players can tackle any opponent who is carrying the ball. The ball carrier avoids a tackle by dodging opponents or by passing the ball to a teammate. The ball carrier also may avoid a tackle by *handing off* the opponent with an action called a *fend.* That is, the player may push the opponent away with the palm of the hand. However, no player is allowed to strike or punch any opponent. If a player is tackled, the player must release the ball. Any player may pick up the ball and run with it or kick it.

A player can advance the ball by kicking it over the *touch line* (sideline) in certain circumstances. A player may kick the ball directly over the touch line only from behind the 22-meter line of the player's team. A player can kick the ball over the touch line from in front of the 22-meter line only if the ball bounces before going over the touch line. In such cases, the opposing team takes a *throw-in* from the point the ball went into touch—that is, a player flings the ball with both hands overhead back onto the field.

The scrum. A contest called a *scrum* restarts play after one of the teams has made a minor violation, such as a forward pass. In a scrum, the two opposing sets of forwards link themselves together, bending forward from the waist to form a tunnellike formation. The halfback from the team not responsible for the violation "feeds" the ball into the tunnel. The two sets of forwards push from opposite sides as soon as the ball enters the scrum. Each side attempts to move the scrum into a position that allows a central forward called a *hooker* to heel the ball back through the hooker's own scrum to gain possession. The hooker takes a position in the front and center of the front row of the forwards in the scrum.

The line out. A play called a *line out* restarts the game after the ball has gone into touch. A player from the team not responsible for putting the ball in touch throws the ball in bounds between two opposing lines of forwards. Each set of forwards tries to outjump the other and secure possession of the ball for its backs.

The forwards also gather in formations called a *ruck* and a *maul.* Both formations continue play without interruption after a tackle. In a ruck, the forwards close in around the ball after the ball carrier has been tackled and the ball has gone to ground. The forwards attempt to heel, or "ruck," the ball back for their backs to continue play. A maul occurs when several forwards surround the ball carrier during a tackle and the tackled player remains standing. The opposition players in the maul attempt to wrestle the ball from the ball carrier.

Replacements and substitutes. In international matches, a *union* (governing body) may allow up to seven replacements or substitutes. A *replacement* is a player who takes the place of an injured teammate. A *substitute* is a player who replaces a teammate for tactical reasons. For other matches, individual unions decide the number of substitutions and replacements.

Organization. Separate unions govern the sport in England, Ireland, Scotland, and Wales. Australia and

Rugby Union field

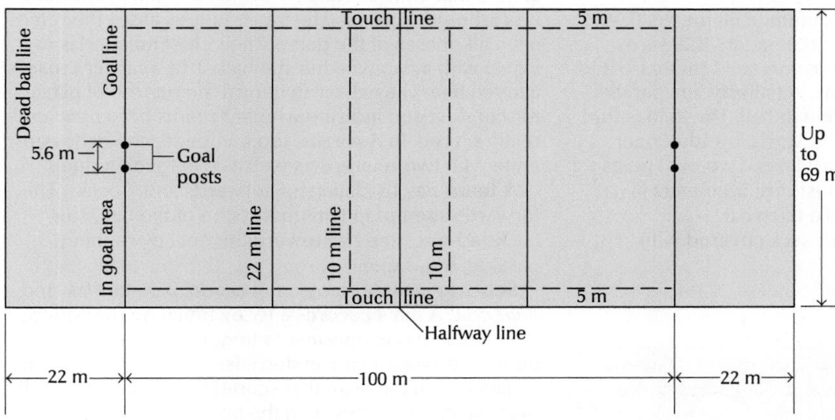

Rugby League field

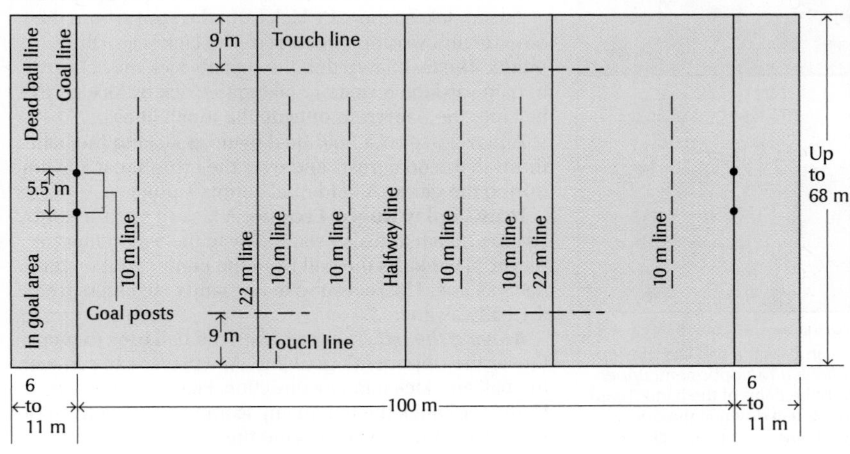

A rugby football field consists of the field of play and the in-goal areas. The field of play is a rectangle bordered by the touch lines and the goal lines. The in-goal areas are behind each goal line and are enclosed by the goal lines and dead-ball lines. Rugby League and Rugby Union fields are about the same size, but they have some different markings. The diagram at the upper left shows a Rugby Union field. The diagram at the lower left shows a Rugby League field.

WORLD BOOK diagrams

© Shutterstock

A line out restarts play in Rugby Union after the ball has gone out-of-bounds. A player tosses the ball in between two lines of forwards, and each group tries to pass the ball to its backs.

Focus on Sports

A scrum puts the ball in play in Rugby League. The ball is tossed into a tunnellike formation made by the forwards from each team. Players in the center try to kick it to a teammate.

New Zealand both field national teams. Australia's team is called the Wallabies. New Zealand's team is known as the All Blacks because of their black clothing.

Rugby League

The field. The field is a maximum of 68 meters (74 yards) wide. The goal lines are 100 meters (109 yards) apart. An in-goal area extends from 6 to 11 meters (6 ½ to 12 yards) beyond each goal line. A halfway line parallel to the goal lines divides the field in half. The field is further divided every 10 meters (11 yards) by additional lines that are parallel to the goal lines. Two goal posts stand on each goal line. The posts are 5.5 meters (6 yards) apart and connected by a crossbar.

The ball is an inflated rubber sack covered with leather or synthetic material. It is oval-shaped and averages about 28 centimeters (11 inches) long and weighs about 410 grams (14 ½ ounces).

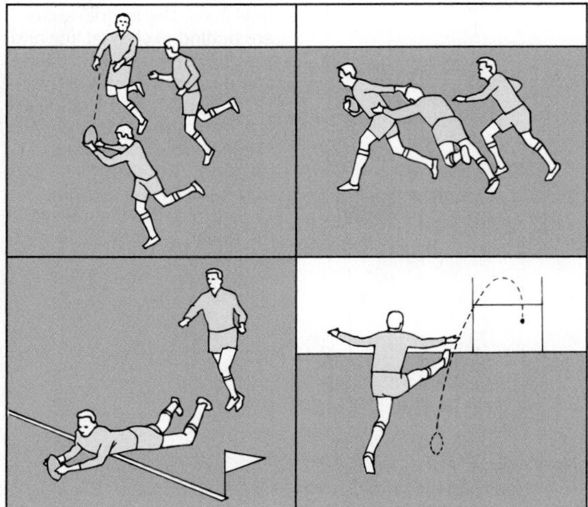

WORLD BOOK illustrations by David Cunningham

Plays in rugby football. A player can pass the ball laterally, *upper left.* A player with the ball can *hand off* an opponent, *upper right,* by pushing the opponent with the palm of the hand. Teams score a try, *lower left,* by touching the ball down in the opponent's in-goal area. They score a goal, *lower right,* by kicking.

The officials. A referee and two touch judges officiate the match. The referee controls the game. The referee's judgment is final. The touch judges assist the referee in all phases of the game. Their chief function is to signal with a flag whether the ball or ball carrier crosses a touch line. They also can inform the referee of player misconduct and indicate whether points have been correctly scored. In Australia, top competitive matches operate with two referees as well as two touch judges.

A team has 13 players—6 forwards and 7 backs. The forwards attempt to win possession of the ball. The backs advance the ball toward the goal by running, passing, or kicking.

Scoring includes a *try, conversion, penalty kick,* and *field goal.* A player scores a try by touching the ball to the ground in the opponent's in-goal area. A try counts 4 points. To score a conversion (also called a *kick at goal),* a player from the team that scored the try kicks the ball over the crossbar between the goal posts. The player place-kicks the ball from a point opposite the spot where the try was scored. A conversion counts 2 points.

A team takes a penalty kick from the spot where the other team's violation occurred. The kick is worth 2 points. The team awarded the penalty kick may choose to gain yardage instead of taking the kick by kicking the ball into the field from outside the touch lines.

A player scores a field goal by drop-kicking the ball through the goal posts and over the crossbar at any time during the game. A field goal counts 1 point.

How to play Rugby League. A kickoff starts a Rugby League match and also starts play in the second half. A player place-kicks the ball from the center spot on the halfway line. The receiving team stands 10 meters from the halfway line.

Moving the ball. The team with the ball tries to move it over the opponent's goal line. Any player can run with the ball and kick it in any direction. Players may pass, throw, or knock the ball to any teammate not in front of them. Only the player carrying the ball can be tackled.

Playing the ball. A team in possession is allowed six tackles, or *downs,* to score points. If the team does not score, a hand-over occurs to allow the opposing team six tackles. After each tackle, the ball carrier places the ball on the ground and plays it back with a foot to a teammate. That player can then pick up the ball to continue play. All players from both teams must be 5 meters (5 ½ yards) away from where the ball is played. They cannot move until the ball is played.

The scrum. A scrum restarts play after one of the teams has committed a minor violation or a ball carrier goes over the sideline. A player from the team not responsible for the violation tosses the ball into the scrum. Each side attempts to move the scrum into a position that allows its hooker to kick the ball out of the scrum to a teammate.

Replacements. Each team has four replacements who can interchange with players on the field. The number of permitted interchanges varies according to the competition but generally ranges from 10 to unlimited.

Organization. Until the 1980's, Rugby League was played chiefly in northern England. It expanded with the formation of teams in Wales and southern England. Most professionals in Rugby League are part-time players. Several hundred clubs play in various age groups.

History

According to tradition, rugby football originated from a soccer game at Rugby School in Rugby, England, in 1823. During the game, a student named William Webb Ellis broke the rules of soccer by picking up the ball and running with it. Players of the new game adopted use of an oval-shaped ball to make passing and carrying easier.

Rugby football quickly became popular throughout the United Kingdom. In 1871, a conference of Rugby clubs formed the English Rugby Union, made up of 17 amateur clubs. The conference set the number of players on a team at 15 and established other general rules. Scotland formed its Rugby Union in 1873, and Ireland organized a Rugby Union in 1874. The Welsh Rugby Union formed in 1881.

In 1895, 21 teams from northern England broke away from the Rugby Union to form the Northern Rugby Union. It changed its name to the Rugby Football League in 1922. Brian Kennedy

See also **Australia** (Recreation); **Football** (Beginnings); **New Zealand** (Recreation); **Rugby School.**

Rugby School is a famous English public school founded in 1567 at Rugby, England. England's "public" schools are not free schools. They are privately supported institutions for secondary education. Rugby's playground was one of the founding places of rugby football. The school became one of the leading public schools in England under Thomas Arnold, who served as headmaster from 1828 to 1842. Arnold is the popular headmaster who appears in the novel *Tom Brown's School Days* (1857), by Thomas Hughes. Rugby's average enrollment is more than 750. P. A. McGinley

Rugs and carpets are fabrics used as floor coverings. They add beauty, comfort, and warmth to a room, and they help absorb sound. Rugs and carpets also protect floors and provide a less slippery surface than a waxed or tiled floor. Most rugs and carpets are used in homes and other buildings, but some cover outdoor surfaces. Some rugs are used as decorative wallhangings.

The words *rug* and *carpet* are sometimes used interchangeably, but they refer to different types of floor coverings. A rug covers only part of the floor of a room and is not fastened down. A carpet covers an entire floor and is nailed, tacked, or glued down.

Most rugs and carpets are mass-produced and are made in a variety of textures and an almost unlimited number of colors and patterns. Some rugs are manufactured in standard sizes, such as 4 feet by 6 feet (1.2 meters by 1.8 meters) or 9 feet by 15 feet (2.7 meters by 5 meters). Other rugs are cut from large rolls of carpeting. Most carpeting is produced in 12-foot (3.7-meter) widths, but some is 15 feet (5 meters) wide. Other carpeting is cut into 9-, 12-, or 18-inch (23-, 30-, or 46-centimeter) squares called *carpet tiles.* Carpeting made on a loom or other machine more than 6 feet (1.8 meters) wide is called *broadloom carpeting.*

Rugs may also be made by hand. Handmade Oriental rugs are valued for their rareness and beauty.

The United States produces about 1 ⅕ billion square yards (1 billion square meters) of rugs and carpets annually. Georgia is the leading state in the production of rugs and carpets, making more than 70 percent of these floor coverings. California ranks second in the production of rugs and carpets.

© Mason Morfit, FPG

Modern carpeting is mass-produced by machines in a variety of textures, colors, and patterns. Rugs and carpets help protect floors and provide beauty and warmth to a room.

Materials used in rugs and carpets

Rugs and carpets have two main parts, the *pile,* or *face,* and the *backing.* The pile is the top surface, and the backing is the undersurface. Various manufactured or natural fibers are used in making both the pile and the backing. A few manufacturers produce pile with a blend of both manufactured and natural fibers.

The chief manufactured materials in pile fibers are nylon, olefin, and polyester. All these materials resist soiling and staining well. About 75 percent of the rugs and carpets manufactured in the United States have nylon pile. Nylon fibers are durable and easy to dye. Olefin fibers make up the pile in about 14 percent of the rugs and carpets produced in the United States. People use olefin floor coverings widely both indoors and outdoors because olefin resists moisture and fading. About 10 percent of the rugs and carpets have polyester pile. Polyester fibers can absorb and hold brighter colors of dye than other manufactured fibers can. A small number of rugs and carpets have acrylic pile. Acrylic floor coverings are bulky but light in weight, and they resist fading. Tough nylon fibers make up the pile in *artificial turf,* a type of carpet used both indoors and outdoors for landscaping and playing surfaces.

Wool is the main natural fiber used in making pile. Until the 1940's, nearly all rugs and carpets manufactured in the United States were made of wool. Today, wool is used for only about 1 percent of the rugs and carpets made in the United States. Wool floor coverings are attractive, soft, and durable. Many people consider them the finest made. But most wool floor coverings cost more than those made from manufactured fibers.

The backing of most rugs and carpets is made of olefin or of jute, a natural fiber. Linen, polyester, and cotton are also used.

Kinds of rugs and carpets

Rugs and carpets are classified according to their pile textures. There are six main kinds of rugs and carpets: (1) level loop, (2) multilevel loop, (3) plush, (4) saxony, (5) frieze, and (6) cut and loop.

Level loop and multilevel loop floor coverings have a *loop pile,* which consists of loops of yarn. Plush, saxony,

Kinds of rugs and carpets Rugs and carpets are classified according to the texture of their top surface, called the *pile.* Examples of the six main types of rugs and carpets are shown here.

Bigelow-Sanford, Inc. (WORLD BOOK photos); WORLD BOOK illustrations by Koralik Associates

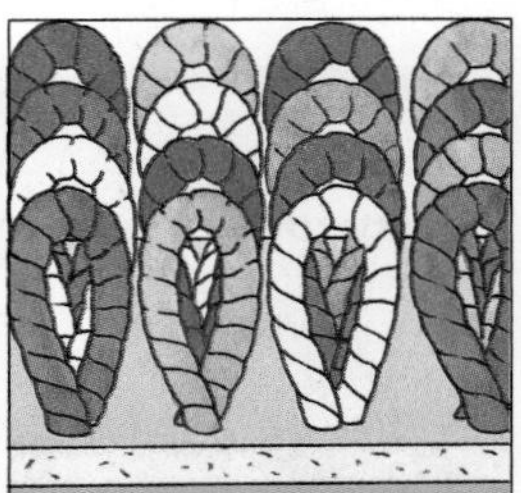
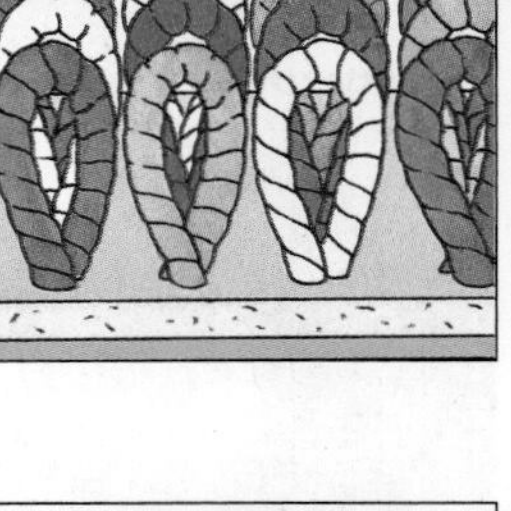

Level loop

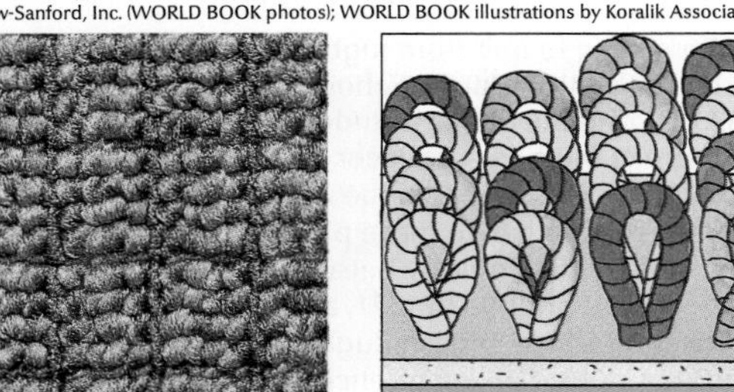

Multilevel loop

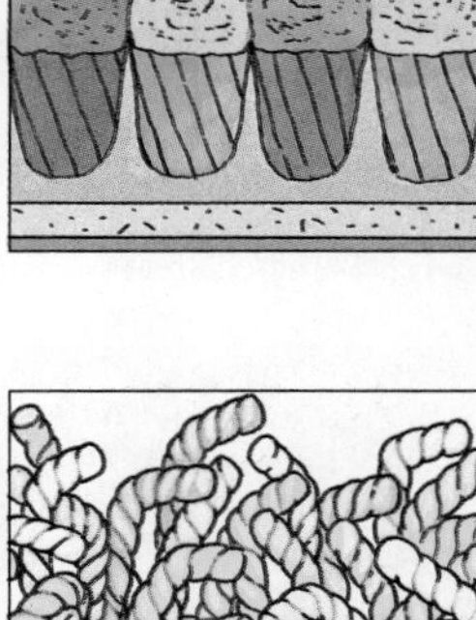

Plush

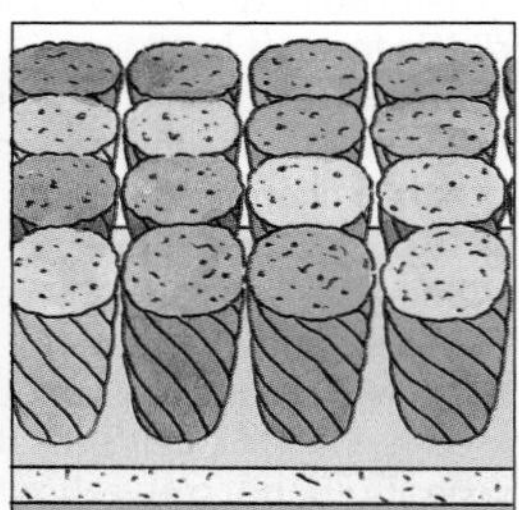

Saxony

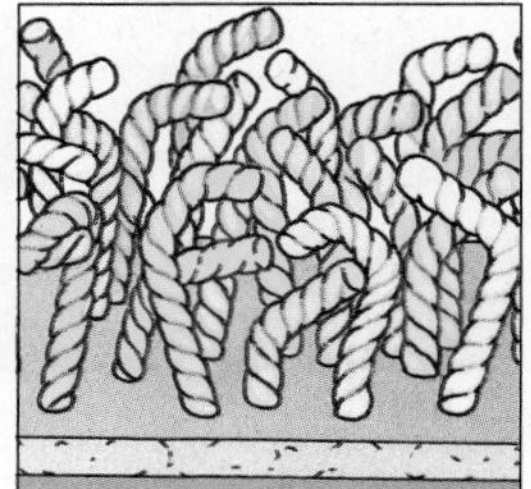

Frieze

Cut and loop

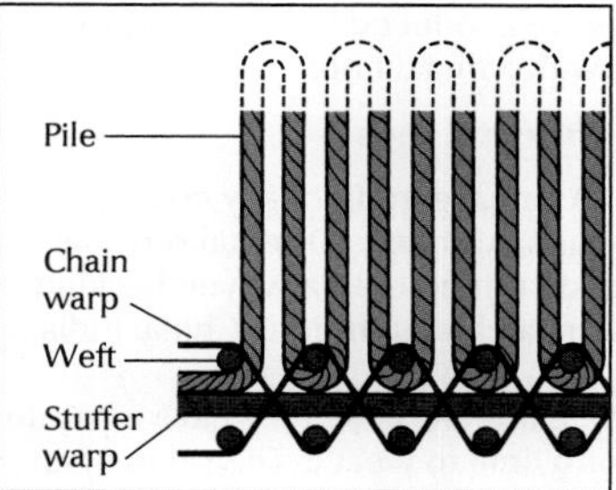

A velvet weave is the simplest type. Almost all the pile yarn appears on the surface of the floor covering.

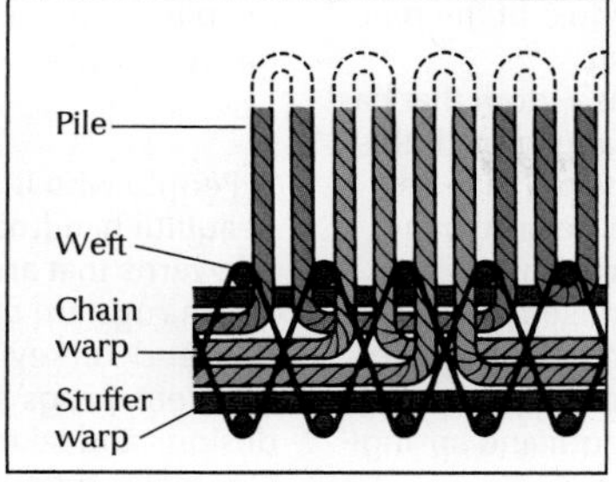

A Wilton weave has all its yarns running in rows along the backing, but only one color is raised to the surface at a time.

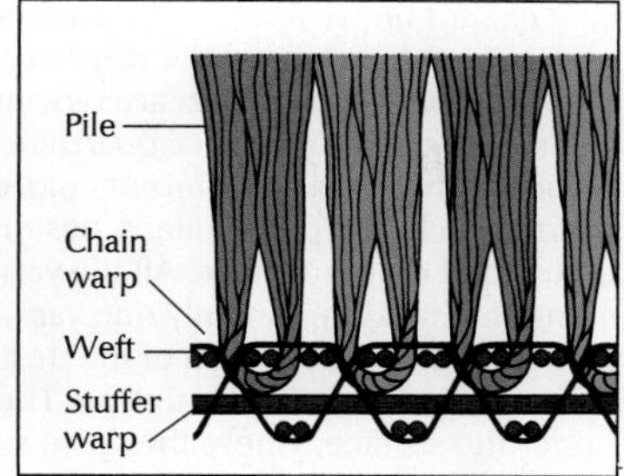

WORLD BOOK diagrams by Zorica Dabich

An Axminster weave has each pile yarn inserted independently. Most of the pile yarn appears on the surface.

and frieze rugs and carpets have a *cut pile.* They are made with loops of yarn, but each loop is then cut in two, producing a surface of cut ends. The cut and loop type has a combination pile.

Level loop rugs and carpets have a smooth, tight texture. All the loops of yarn that make up the pile have the same height.

Multilevel loop rugs and carpets have an uneven texture. The loops of their pile vary in height, giving the surface a patterned effect.

Plush rugs and carpets are soft and have a luxurious appearance. The yarns of plush pile are short and loosely twisted. Plush pile provides a thick, level floor covering that is often desired in formal settings.

Saxony rugs and carpets resemble the plush type. However, each yarn of a saxony floor covering stands erect and is clearly distinguishable. The ends of the yarn in plush pile tend to blend together.

Frieze rugs and carpets have a rougher texture than the other members of the cut pile group. The yarns of a frieze pile are tightly twisted, and they curl when inserted into the surface.

Cut and loop rugs and carpets have yarns that vary in height. The longer yarns provide a cut pile. The shorter yarns are looped and may be hidden by the longer ones.

How rugs and carpets are made

More than 95 percent of the rugs and carpets produced in the United States are made by a process called *tufting.* The rest are made by weaving or by other methods.

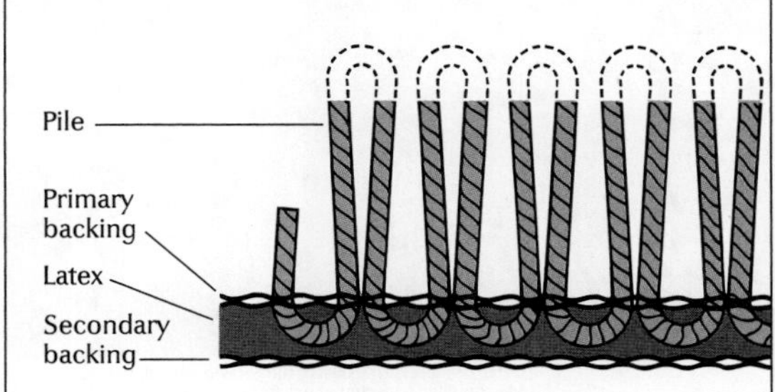

WORLD BOOK diagram by Steven Liska

A tufted floor covering consists of pile yarns called *tufts,* which are forced through a backing by needles.

Tufting is the fastest and cheapest method of making rugs and carpets. Tufted floor coverings consist of clusters of pile yarns called *tufts.* Eyed needles insert the tufts into the backing.

A tufting machine has hundreds of needles set in a row on a device called a *needle bar.* When the needle bar is lowered, each needle forces a loop of yarn through a layer of backing called *primary backing.* The loops form a row of tufts. As the needle bar is lifted, devices called *loopers* hold the tufts in place to form a looped pile. A cut pile can be made by attaching a knife blade to each looper.

A synthetic latex compound is applied to the primary backing to secure the tufts. A layer of backing called *secondary backing* may be added over the latex to provide extra durability. The secondary backing is made of jute or synthetic materials. Some tufted floor coverings have a layer of plastic foam instead of a secondary backing.

Weaving was the chief method of manufacturing rugs and carpets in the United States until the development of tufting in the 1950's. Woven floor coverings are made on looms by interlacing the pile yarns with backing yarns. Weaving the two kinds of yarns together holds the pile yarns securely in the backing.

The pile of a woven rug or carpet is formed from one set of yarns. The backing is made from two sets. The pile yarns are woven into the backing in rows. During the weaving process, these yarns form loops over long, flat pieces of metal called *wires* that lie across the loom. This action creates a looped pile. A cut pile is produced by wires that have a knife blade at one end. In the backing, one set of yarns, called the *weft,* runs crosswise on the loom. Another set, called the *warp,* runs lengthwise. There are two kinds of warp yarns, *chains* and *stuffers.* Chain warps cross over and under the weft yarns to form the weave. Stuffer warps are extra yarns that run through the backing in order to give it greater bulk and strength.

There are three chief types of woven rugs and carpets: (1) velvet, (2) Wilton, and (3) Axminster. They differ in the way their pile yarns are woven into the backing, and each type is made on a different kind of loom. The backing for all three is made in basically the same way.

Velvet rugs and carpets are made with the simplest type of weave. They are woven on looms similar to those used in making regular cloth. The majority of velvet floor coverings have a pile of one color, and a design cannot be woven into the surface. Most of the pile yarn is on the surface of the rug or carpet.

Wilton rugs and carpets are woven on a loom that has a special device called a *Jacquard mechanism.* With this device, as many as six different colored yarns may be used in each row of the pile. A design, if desired, may be created on the surface. All the yarns run in rows along the backing, but only one yarn is raised to the surface at a time. Thus, a yarn of the desired color appears in the proper place in the design. The other yarns run under the surface, where they give strength and springiness to the backing.

Axminster rugs and carpets may be produced in an unlimited number of colors and patterns. Most of the pile yarns of an Axminster floor covering appear on the surface. Each pile yarn is inserted into the carpet independently. As each yarn is inserted, it is interwoven with the backing yarns.

Other methods include *knitting, needlepunching, braiding, embroidering,* and *hooking.*

Knitted rugs and carpets are produced on knitting machines by a process that is similar to hand knitting. The pile yarns and the backing yarns are knitted together. Needlepunched floor coverings are made from fibers that have been tangled together by means of barbed needles. This tangled mass is then compressed into thick, feltlike material that can be used both indoors and outdoors.

Braided floor coverings are manufactured from individual braids of yarn or fabric. The braids are sewn together and coiled into a circle, an oval, or some other shape. Embroidered floor coverings are created by stitching designs onto the backing. The designs form the pile. Hooked rugs are produced by punching yarns through the backing with a metal hook.

Oriental rugs

People who live in Asia have traditionally created beautiful handmade rugs. Authentic Oriental rugs have pile yarns that are hand-knotted onto a woven backing. These rugs are made in such countries as China, India, Iran, and Turkey.

Oriental rugs are valuable because they have intricate designs and take a long time to weave. The value of an Oriental rug depends in part on the type of material used to create the rug and on the size and closeness of the rug's weave. Tightly woven Oriental rugs are more expensive because they require the most time to make and are the most durable. Age, condition, and color also contribute to a rug's value.

An Oriental rug is not as perfect as a mass-produced rug. The size and shape of an Oriental rug may not be exact, and the color in various areas of the rug may differ slightly.

Oriental rugs are woven on simple looms. A small rug may be woven by one person, but most large Oriental rugs are made by several weavers. First, the rug makers knot a row of pile yarns to the warp yarns. Next, they weave one or more weft yarns through the warp. The knots and weft yarns are then packed down tightly on the previously woven rows with a comblike device. The knotting process is then repeated. Trimming the ends of the knotted pile yarns creates the rug's even surface.

Almost every Oriental rug is made with one of two types of knots. A *Persian,* or *Sehna, knot* twists the pile and warp yarns together. A *Turkish,* or *Ghiordes, knot*

©dbimages/Alamy Images

Detail of a silk rug (1500's) of the Safavid period; the Metropolitan Museum of Art, Bequest of Benjamin Altman, 1913

Persian rugs are prized for their soft colors and graceful patterns. They are made by hand in Iran (formerly Persia). At *left,* a weaver ties colorful yarn to two vertical strands of a Persian rug. Patterns woven into such rugs include pictures of leaves, flowers, and animals, *right.*

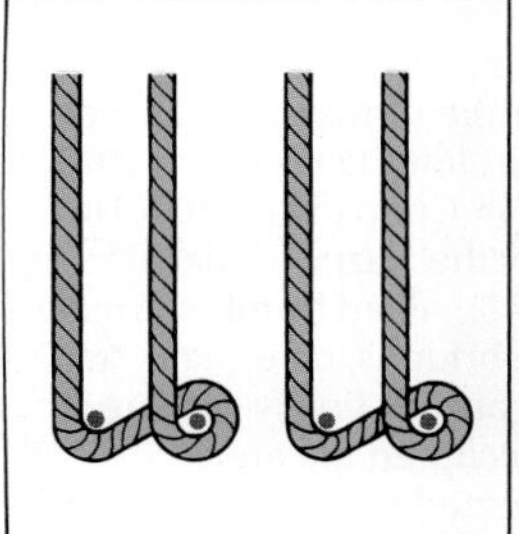
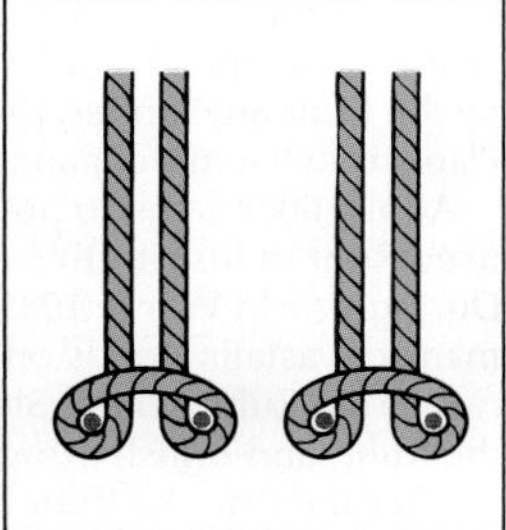

WORLD BOOK diagrams by Zorica Dabich

Knots for most Oriental rugs are made in one of two ways. A *Persian,* or *Sehna, knot, left,* twists the pile and warp yarns together. A *Turkish,* or *Ghiordes, knot, right,* ties them together.

ties the yarns. The majority of Oriental rugs have from 50 to 500 knots per square inch (8 to 78 knots per square centimeter).

Most Oriental rugs have wool pile yarns, but some have pile yarns of silk. The warp and weft yarns of most Oriental rugs are made of cotton or wool. Hemp, jute, and silk are less commonly used.

The chief colors in most Oriental rugs are blue, brown, red, and white. Most yarns are treated with chemical dyes to obtain various shades of these colors. Before these chemical dyes were developed, the yarns were colored with natural dyes made from plants and minerals. Today, a few rug makers still use natural dyes.

Oriental rugs called *prayer rugs* are made in Islamic regions of Asia. The design of a prayer rug includes a pointed or arch-shaped pattern representing the prayer niche of the mosque. Muslims face Mecca, their holy city, as they kneel in prayer, and the rug is placed with the design pointed toward it.

There are six chief types of Oriental rugs. They are (1) Caucasian rugs, (2) Chinese rugs, (3) Indian rugs, (4) Persian rugs, (5) Turkish rugs, and (6) Turkoman rugs. The rugs are named for regions where they are made.

Genesis by Helen Webber; Edward Fields, Inc. (WORLD BOOK photo)

A handmade rug used as a wallhanging adds a modern decorative touch to a home or office.

Caucasian rugs come from the Caucasus Mountains between Europe and Asia. They have geometric designs woven in bold reds, blues, yellows, and other colors.

Chinese rugs have designs that feature philosophical and religious symbols of China. The designs are woven into backgrounds originally of blue, red, and yellow. Time may have changed the reds in some older rugs to lighter colors.

Indian rugs resemble Persian rugs in color and pattern. Many of the designs feature plants and animals.

Persian rugs are made in Iran (formerly Persia). Their graceful patterns feature flowers, leaves, and birds. Some Persian rugs feature animal combat scenes. Persian rugs have soft, blended colors.

Turkish rugs are known for their rectangular patterns and their floral designs arranged in rows. Most of these rugs have large areas of solid colors.

Turkoman rugs come from Turkestan, a region of central Asia. They are woven primarily in reddish tones and have simple geometric designs.

History

Some prehistoric people may have used animal skins as floor coverings in their caves or huts. After people learned to weave, they made floor mats from grasses and other plant material. No one knows when rug making began. The earliest known fabric made with pile is called the *Pazyryk rug.* It was made around the 400's B.C. and was discovered in a tomb in southern Siberia.

Crusaders who traveled to the Middle East during the A.D. 1100's and 1200's probably brought rugs back to Europe. In the 1200's, Spain became the first European country to produce rugs. England started making pile rugs in the 1500's.

During the 1600's, France began to make a style of rug called the *Savonnerie,* which had a deep pile. In the 1700's, England was the center of the European rug and carpet industry. An English inventor named Edmund Cartwright developed the power loom in the 1780's.

In North America, the most common rugs during colonial times were braided rugs, hooked rugs, and *rag rugs,* which were made from scraps of cloth. The first U.S. carpet mill was set up in 1791 in Philadelphia.

Joseph M. Jacquard, a French weaver, invented the Jacquard mechanism about 1800. Erastus B. Bigelow, a Massachusetts inventor, perfected a power loom for making carpets in the early 1840's. A power loom for producing Axminster carpets was patented in 1856.

The tufting machine for carpeting was introduced in the early 1950's. By the mid-1950's, more tufted rugs and carpets than woven ones were being produced in the United States. R. Carroll Turner

Related articles in *World Book* include:

Artificial turf
Asia (picture: Skilled craft workers)
Carpet beetle
Cartwright, Edmund
Indian, American (picture: The Navajo)
Industry (pictures)
Interior design (Floor coverings)
Islamic art (picture)
Jacquard, Joseph M.
Tapestry
Turkey (picture: A Turkish weaver)
Weaving

Ruhr, *roor,* is a historic industrial region within the modern Rhein-Ruhr metropolitan area in western Germany. Several tributaries of the Rhine River run through the region, including the Ruhr River, from which the region takes its name. The area known as the Ruhr includes Dortmund, Duisburg, and Essen. The Ruhr covers about 1,000 square miles (2,500 square kilometers). The Rhine-Ruhr area includes such cities as Bonn, Cologne, Düsseldorf, Hamm, Wesel, and Wuppertal.

The people and their work. The Ruhr is one of the most crowded areas of Europe. The Ruhr has a population of about 5 million people, excluding the Cologne and Bonn areas. Dortmund, Duisburg, and Essen are large industrial cities in the Ruhr.

The Ruhr has one of the largest concentrations of industry in the world. The region's industries produce chemicals, electronics, iron and steel, and textiles. Service industries, tourism, and cultural and educational institutions are valuable to the Ruhr's economy. The region also has a dense transportation network that includes canals, highways, railroads, and rivers.

WORLD BOOK maps

The Ruhr is a region in western Germany.

History. The Ruhr became important to German industry in the mid-1800's. Its huge coal fields and fine transportation facilities helped it grow as a coal-mining area. In 1871, Germany won control of almost all of Alsace and part of Lorraine after the Franco-Prussian War. The German take-over made iron ore from Lorraine available to German industries without customs duties. Industrialists in the Ruhr began to bring in ore from Lorraine, and the region grew into an industrial center.

Germany lost Lorraine after World War I (1914-1918). For a time, it seemed the Ruhr would again be only a mining district. But the German government paid huge sums to iron manufacturers for the loss of Lorraine. With this money, the industrialists built smelting works that could process iron ore from Sweden.

By 1922, Germany had fallen behind in paying France and Belgium for damages caused during World War I. French and Belgian troops occupied the Ruhr in January 1923 to force Germany to make its payments. But the German government encouraged Ruhr workers to follow a policy of passive resistance and to produce as little as possible during the occupation.

The French took harsh steps to increase German production, but all their measures failed. The decrease in production of the Ruhr soon affected the economic life of France and Germany disastrously. Both countries headed toward national bankruptcy. On Sept. 26, 1923, Germany finally ended its passive resistance in the Ruhr. At the same time, France saw that it was useless to occupy the Ruhr any longer. Under the terms of the Dawes Plan, French and Belgian troops left the region in 1925.

Adolf Hitler came to power in Germany in 1933. He used Ruhr industries to supply the Nazi war machine. During World War II (1939-1945), Allied bombers made many devastating raids on the bridges, cities, and factories of the Ruhr. United States armies finally captured the Ruhr, and British troops occupied the area.

After the war, the Ruhr benefited from the creation of the European Economic Community, a forerunner of the European Union that worked to improve economic relations among its members. In the late 1900's, a number of mines and factories in the Ruhr closed. However, new tourist attractions and increased jobs in service industries and technology helped stabilize the Ruhr's economy. William H. Berentsen

Ruhr River, *roor,* rises in Westphalia, Germany, and flows 144 miles (232 kilometers) through the famous industrial region of the Ruhr Valley. It joins the Rhine River near Duisburg. See **Ruhr.**

Another Ruhr (Roer) River rises on the Belgian frontier and flows north through Germany for 67 miles (108 kilometers). It enters the Maas (Meuse) River at Roermond, the Netherlands. Hugh D. Clout

Ruisdael, *ROYS dahl,* **Jacob van,** *YAH kawp vahn* (1628?-1682), was the greatest Dutch landscape painter of his time. His name is also spelled *Ruysdael.* Other artists of Ruisdael's time stressed the placid character of the Dutch countryside, but Ruisdael depicted nature as filled with drama and mood. He painted stormy seas, rushing waterfalls, melancholy ruins, dark forests, and clouded skies pierced by rays of light. Romantic painters of the 1800's admired Ruisdael's poetic approach to nature and often imitated his style and subject matter.

© World History Archive/Alamy Images

Ruisdael's *A Waterfall in a Rocky Landscape* combines a rushing waterfall, a dark forest, and a cloudy sky to create a dramatic and moody scene of nature.

Ruisdael was born in Haarlem and in 1648 became a member of the painters' guild there. In 1656, Ruisdael moved to Amsterdam, where he produced his finest paintings. In Amsterdam, he expanded his range of subjects to include urban scenes. Ruisdael died in Haarlem on March 14, 1682. Linda Stone-Ferrier

Ruiz, *roo EES,* **Juan** (1283?-1350?), ranks among Spain's important poets on the strength of a single known work. His *Book of Good Love* (*Libro de buen amor,* 1330, revised and enlarged 1343), a collection of stories in verse and song, is the most entertaining and human book in medieval Spanish literature. "Good love" in the title stands for love of God and the Virgin Mary, a popular topic in medieval Spain. However, the work is more a praise of human love than spiritual love. See **Spanish literature** (Early medieval literature).

Ruiz was born in Alcala de Henares and was archpriest of Hita, a town in Castile. He probably suffered a long prison term by order of the Archbishop of Toledo. Ruiz's *Book of Good Love* mingles mock allegories, tales from medieval French literature, and references to classical authors with realistic episodes. Harry Sieber

Ruiz Cortines, *roo EES kawr TEE nays,* **Adolfo** (1890-1973), served as president of Mexico from 1952 to 1958. A civil servant for 30 years, he was governor of Veracruz from 1944 to 1948 and secretary of the interior under President Miguel Alemán.

As president, Ruiz Cortines fought dishonesty and corruption in reforming the civil service. He also consolidated gains made by Aleman's administration in developing agriculture and industry. In addition, Ruiz Cortines took measures that led to a decrease in Mexico's high inflation rate. He directed reform of Mexico City's government and effectively met the crisis caused by an earthquake in 1957. Ruiz Cortines was born on Dec. 30, 1890, in Veracruz, Mexico. He died on Dec. 3, 1973. W. Dirk Raat

Rum. See **Alcoholic beverage** (Rum).

Rumania. See **Romania.**

Rumba, also spelled *rhumba,* is a Latin ballroom dance that originated in Africa and achieved its modern form in Cuba. Couples perform the rumba in 4/4 time with a quick-quick-slow rhythm. The rumba emphasizes a swaying hip motion that is achieved by taking small steps with the knees relaxed. Steps are typically performed in a square pattern. The rumba is most often accompanied by music with a repeated beat played on percussion instruments.

A version of the rumba was first introduced into the United States from Cuba about 1914. However, the dance's exaggerated hip movements were considered too sexually suggestive, and the dance did not gain acceptance. A more refined version was introduced about 1930. The dance kept its popularity in the 1930's and 1940's, especially in England, where ballroom dance teachers standardized the figures and step rhythms. Rumbas also appear in music not intended for ballroom dancing, as in French-born composer Darius Milhaud's ballet *La creation du monde* (1923). Patricia W. Rader

Rumford, Count. See **Thompson, Benjamin.**

Ruminant is the name given to a grazing animal that has a highly specialized digestive system and split hoofs. Such mammals as sheep, cows, oxen, deer, antelope, camels, llamas, and giraffes are ruminants. Most kinds of ruminants have a stomach with four *cavities* (compartments). Each cavity helps digest food with the aid of numerous microorganisms, such as bacteria and yeasts,

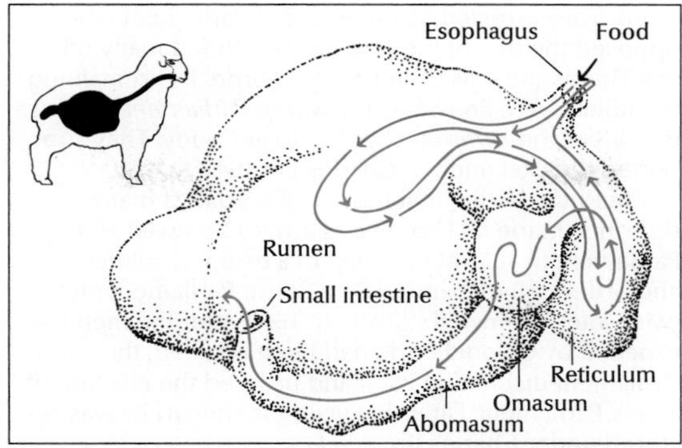

WORLD BOOK illustration by Marion Pahl

Most ruminants have a stomach with four compartments: the *rumen, reticulum, omasum,* and *abomasum.* These drawings show a sheep's stomach. Food enters the rumen and reticulum, *red arrows,* and is then rechewed as cud. Cud eventually passes into the omasum and abomasum, *blue arrows.*

that live in the stomach. The microorganisms break down *cellulose,* a substance found in the cell walls of plants, into important nutrients. These nutrients provide the main source of energy for many ruminants.

A ruminant chews its food with its molars. It has no *incisors* (biting teeth) in the upper jaw. When a ruminant eats, it swallows its food, which is usually grass, after chewing it only slightly. The food goes down the *esophagus* (food pipe) into the first cavity of the stomach. This cavity is called the *rumen* or *paunch.* Most of the food collects in the rumen, but some passes directly into the second cavity, called the *reticulum.* The reticulum has tiny pockets in its walls, which look like a honeycomb.

Food stored in the rumen eventually passes into the reticulum, where it is softened and formed into soft masses called *cuds.* As the animal rests, the muscles of the reticulum send the food back to the mouth to be chewed and mixed with saliva. The animal chews with a roundish motion of the jaw and swallows again. The cud then passes through the rumen and reticulum to the third cavity, called the *omasum.* The rumen, reticulum, and omasum all serve as "vats" for storing the stomach's microorganisms.

Finally, the food enters the fourth cavity, the *abomasum.* This cavity is the "true stomach." It functions the same way as the stomach in human beings and other mammals that are not ruminants. There, the food mixes with stomach juice and passes into the intestine, where digestion is completed. The digested food is absorbed through the lining of the intestine and passes to all parts of the body through the bloodstream. C. Richard Taylor

Scientific classification. Ruminants are in the order Artiodactyla.

Rump Parliament was a name given the English Parliament during the civil war in the mid-1600's. That Parliament had less than a fourth of the usual number of members. The other members had been excluded by troops of the Puritan leader Oliver Cromwell.

Civil war broke out in 1642 between the forces of King Charles I and those of the *Long Parliament* (see **Long Parliament**). Later, members of Parliament disagreed on the conduct of the war. On Dec. 6, 1648, soldiers led by Colonel Thomas Pride surrounded the House of Commons. They arrested 47 members of Parliament who opposed the trial of the king, and excluded many others. This action was called *Pride's Purge.* The remaining members were known as the *Rump Parliament,* because they were the *rump* (end) of the larger body. They supported the execution of Charles I in 1649.

The Rump Parliament fought later against many demands made by Cromwell's army. Cromwell entered Parliament in 1653 at the head of a troop of soldiers and ordered it disbanded. The Rump Parliament met twice after Cromwell's death. In 1660, after the members expelled by Colonel Pride had been recalled, the Long Parliament disbanded itself and ordered the election of a new Parliament. Later that year, the monarchy was restored under Charles II. Charles Carlton

See also **Charles I** (of England); **Cromwell, Oliver.**

Rumsfeld, Donald Henry (1932-2021), a Republican, served twice as United States secretary of defense. He held the Cabinet post from 1975 to 1977 under President Gerald R. Ford and from 2001 to 2006 under President George W. Bush. As defense secretary under Bush, Rumsfeld helped lead the country's military response to the terrorist attacks of Sept. 11, 2001 (see **September 11 terrorist attacks**). He also helped direct U.S. military operations in the Iraq War (2003-2011). See **Iraq War.**

During his career, Rumsfeld held many government and business posts. He represented Illinois in the U.S. House of Representatives from 1963 to 1969. He then headed the Office of Economic Opportunity under President Richard M. Nixon. In 1971 and 1972, Rumsfeld directed the government's Cost of Living Council. In 1973 and 1974, he was U.S. ambassador to the North Atlantic Treaty Organization (NATO). Rumsfeld served as Ford's White House chief of staff in 1974 and 1975.

In 1977, Rumsfeld became president and chief executive officer of G. D. Searle & Company, a manufacturer of health products. In 1983 and 1984, he served under President Ronald Reagan as special U.S. negotiator for problems in the Middle East. From 1990 to 1993, he was chief executive officer and chairman of General Instrument Corp. (now part of Motorola, Inc.). He was national chairman of Senator Robert J. Dole's presidential campaign in 1996. Dole lost the election to President Bill Clinton.

Rumsfeld was born in Chicago on July 9, 1932. He graduated from Princeton University in 1954. Rumsfeld wrote an autobiography, *Known and Unknown* (2011). He died on June 29, 2021. Lee Thornton

Rune, *roon,* is any one of the characters of the earliest written alphabet used by the Germanic peoples of Europe. The oldest runic writings date back to the A.D. 200's. Most runic inscriptions known today were written before the 1000's. Many runes were carved in wood, but most surviving runes were written in stone.

The word *rune* comes from a Gothic word meaning *secret.* Members of early Germanic tribes associated runes with secrecy or mystery because few people understood the inscriptions. Runic characters were probably first used by Germanic priests in making charms and magic spells. The characters were also scratched on coins, jewelry, monuments, and slabs of stone or wood. The earliest runes consisted almost entirely of straight lines, arranged singly or in combinations of two or more. Later runes had more complex forms.

Archaeologists have discovered thousands of runic inscriptions. Over 3,000 of these writings were found in Sweden, and many dated from the 800's to the 1000's, the period of the Vikings. Other runic writings were discovered in Denmark, Germany, Norway, and the United Kingdom. By the 1000's, missionaries had converted the Germanic peoples to Christianity. Their conversion led to the introduction of the Roman alphabet, which eventually replaced runic characters. James E. Cathey

See also **Kensington rune stone.**

Running is a vigorous form of exercise and a popular sport. Millions of people run because they enjoy the activity or want to be physically fit. Some runners compete in long-distance races that do not form part of organized track meets. Most of these races are run on city streets and roads. This article includes information on such long-distance races. For information about other kinds of running events, see **Track and field.**

Some people use the terms *running* and *jogging* interchangeably. However, running is usually considered faster than jogging. In addition, people jog only to exercise, not to compete against others.

Running requires no special skills or facilities. The only equipment needed is well-cushioned, flexible shoes and comfortable clothing. People considering a running program should have a complete medical examination before starting.

A daily running program improves a person's physical condition. Running is an *aerobic exercise*—that is, it promotes the circulation of oxygen through the bloodstream to the organs and tissues. It also builds up the heart and increases endurance. Running strengthens the leg muscles and makes the body more limber. It helps control weight because runners burn up more than 100 calories per mile (62 calories per kilometer). Running

Letters of the runic alphabet were used for writing ancient Anglo-Saxon inscriptions.

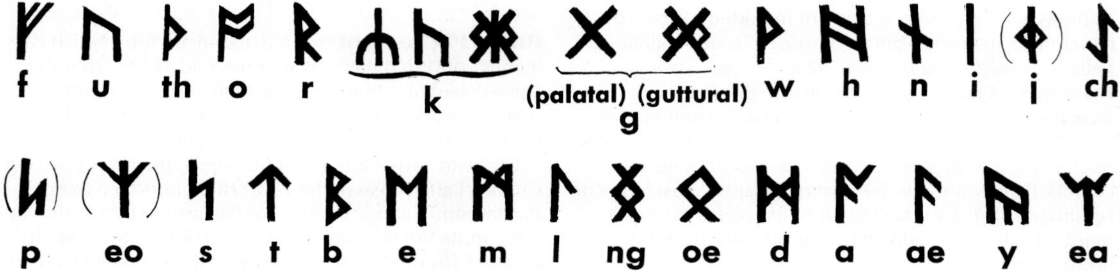

also helps relieve emotional stress.

Running competitions have been held since ancient times. The Olympic Games feature several running events, including the *marathon.* Officially, a marathon is a race that covers 26 miles 385 yards (42.2 kilometers).

Many cities in the United States hold annual marathons. Over 45,000 runners compete in the New York City Marathon, more than in any other marathon in the world. However, races covering 10 kilometers (6.2 miles) are more popular than official marathons.

Running became extremely popular throughout the United States during the 1960's and 1970's. In the book *Aerobics* (1968), Kenneth Cooper, an American physician, brought attention to the advantages of running. A large number of newspaper and magazine articles described the benefits of running, and many more books about running were published. Michael Takaha

See also **Cross-country; Jogging; Marathon; Physical fitness.**

Runnymede, *RUHN ih* MEED, is a meadow in England on the south bank of the River Thames, about 36 miles (58 kilometers) southwest of London. At this site in June 1215, the barons of England forced King John to approve Magna Carta, a document that limited the king's powers. A monument to Magna Carta was built at Runnymede in 1957. In 1965, a memorial to United States President John F. Kennedy was dedicated there. Emily Zack Tabuteau

See also **Magna Carta.**

Runyon, Damon (1884-1946), was an American short-story writer and journalist. His best-known stories deal with colorful gamblers, chorus girls, and various characters who live on the fringes of the criminal world in the Broadway district of New York City. Runyon wrote these stories in a distinctive style noted for its use of wise-cracks and slang. The popular musical comedy *Guys and Dolls* (1950) is based on the Runyon tale "The Idyll of Sarah Brown" and on characters from other Runyon stories.

Runyon's full name was Alfred Damon Runyon. He was born on Oct. 4, 1884, in Manhattan, Kansas. In 1911, he became a sports reporter for the *New York American.* Runyon soon became the highest paid sportswriter of his time. He based many stories on his experiences in the sports world. Throughout his newspaper career, Runyon wrote short stories for magazines. These stories were published in collections, beginning with *Guys and Dolls* (1931). He died on Dec. 10, 1946. Arthur M. Saltzman

Rupee, *roo PEE,* is the chief monetary unit of India and the basic unit in India's decimal currency system. It is divided into 100 smaller units called *paise.* Paise circulate as nickel, copper-nickel, or bronze coins. Ten million rupees, or 100 *lacs,* are called a *crore.* The monetary systems of Mauritius, Nepal, Pakistan, and Sri Lanka are also based on rupees. But all of these rupees have different monetary values. Burton H. Hobson

WORLD BOOK photo by James Simek

A rupee coin of India pictures Jawaharlal Nehru, India's first prime minister. The image of three lions on the other side is India's national emblem.

Rupp, Adolph (1901-1977), was one of the top college basketball coaches in the United States. Rupp coached the University of Kentucky basketball team to 876 victories, a college record until Dean Smith broke it in 1997. Mike Krzyzewski is the current men's Division 1 leader with over 1,000 victories. Under Rupp, Kentucky won the National Collegiate Athletic Association (NCAA) championship in 1948, 1949, 1951, and 1958. His Kentucky teams also won 27 Southeastern Conference championships. Rupp became coach at Kentucky in 1930 and retired in 1972. That same year, he became president of the Memphis Tams of the American Basketball Association.

Adolph Frederick Rupp was born in Halstead, Kansas, on Sept. 2, 1901. He played guard on the University of Kansas basketball team from 1921 to 1923. Rupp's coach at Kansas was Forrest C. (Phog) Allen. Allen ranked as the college coach with the most victories until Rupp broke his record. Rupp died on Dec. 10, 1977. Bob Logan

Rupture. See **Hernia.**

Rural delivery is a service that provides mail delivery to rural and suburban communities throughout the United States. Rural carriers place letters and packages into boxes, most of which stand along curbs. Each carrier has an assigned delivery route. The carriers use their own automobiles or U.S. Postal Service vehicles to deliver mail. In the early 2020's, rural letter carriers served about 45 million homes and businesses.

Before 1896, there was no rural delivery system in the country. Farmers' organizations, especially the National Grange, were active in getting the U.S. Congress to provide money for free delivery of mail to rural areas. In 1896, the first rural deliveries were made in West Virginia. The system was called Rural Free Delivery (R.F.D.). The number of delivery routes grew in the early 1900's. In 1917, the service was extended to most rural areas.

The development of the rural delivery system was important to the development of farm areas. For the first time, the farmer could receive the newspaper daily by mail. The system led to parcel-post service and the development of large mail-order firms.

Critically reviewed by the United States Postal Service

Rural Electrification Administration (REA) was an agency of the United States Department of Agriculture from 1935 to 1994. It made insured loans and loan guarantees to rural electric and telephone cooperatives and companies in 47 states and many U.S. territories. The loans financed the construction, operation, and improvement of electric and telephone service. The REA also provided engineering and management assistance. The agency also lent money to its borrowers for them to invest in economic development projects in their communities. An administrator appointed by the president with the approval of the U.S. Senate headed the REA.

Electric program. When the REA was established in 1935, about 10 percent of the farms in the United States had electricity. By the early 1990's, 99 percent of all U.S. farms had electric service, and REA-financed systems served about half of them. About 95 percent of the REA's electric loans were made to *cooperatives* (independent, private, nonprofit organizations). Other borrowers included public power districts and other public bodies.

Telephone program. When the telephone program began in 1949, about 35 percent of United States farms had telephone service. By the early 1990's, over 95 percent of the nation's farms had telephones. About 75 percent of the borrowers in the telephone program were commercial telephone companies. Almost all the rest were cooperatives. Borrowers received insured loans and loan guarantees as well as supplemental loans from the Rural Telephone Bank, which was set up in 1971.

Rural development program. Beginning in 1989, the REA was authorized by Congress to make rural development loans. In most cases, the rural electric and telephone utilities receiving the loans made these funds available to businesses or other organizations to promote economic development and create jobs. The loans were interest-free, and most of them ran for 10 years.

History. President Franklin D. Roosevelt founded the REA in 1935 as an emergency relief program. The Rural Electrification Act of 1936 made the REA a provider of loans for rural electrification. In 1949, the REA was able to make loans to improve and extend telephone service in rural areas. It was authorized to guarantee the loans of other organizations in 1973. In 1994, the agency was replaced by the Rural Utilities Service. The new service became responsible for providing funds for the development of rural water and waste-disposal systems.

Critically reviewed by the United States Department of Agriculture

Rural life. See **Farm and farming**.

Rush is the common name for a group of grasslike plants that generally grow in marshes and meadows and sometimes in standing water. True rushes belong to one family. They have round stems with three rows of leaves, and tiny greenish or brown flowers. The small seed pod contains many dustlike brown seeds. The *slender rush* is a wiry, dark green plant that often grows on damp paths and lawns. Most other species grow in marshes or damp meadows. Rushes are used to weave baskets, mats, and chair seats. The pith of the stems was once used for wicks in candles called *rushlights.* Some plants called rushes are not true rushes. *Scouring rushes,* also called *horsetails,* are related to ferns (see **Horsetail**). *Bulrushes* are sedges (see **Bulrush**).

David A. Francko

Scientific classification. Rushes belong to the rush family, Juncaceae. The slender rush is *Juncus tenuis.*

Rush, Benjamin (1745-1813), was an American physician and a prominent figure in public life. He was the most influential physician in the United States, but his ideas were controversial. His beliefs in bloodletting and in purging with *calomel* (mercurous chloride) were extreme even for his day. But his efforts to improve treatment of mental illnesses were advanced and humane.

Rush was born on Dec. 24, 1745, in Byberry, Pennsylvania, near Philadelphia. He graduated from the College of New Jersey (now Princeton University) at age 15. In 1768, he received his medicine degree from the University of Edinburgh. In 1783, Rush joined the Pennsylvania Hospital. He became interested in social reform. In 1786, he opened the first free clinic in the United States.

Rush believed in the republican form of government. He helped found the first American antislavery society, served as a member of the Continental Congress, and signed the Declaration of Independence. In the American Revolution (1775-1783), Rush was surgeon general in the Continental Army. With James Wilson, he led Pennsylvania to *ratify* (approve) the federal Constitution. He also helped frame the Pennsylvania state constitution. He served as treasurer of the U.S. Mint from 1797 to 1813. Rush died on April 19, 1813. Matthew Ramsey

Rushdie, *RUHSH dee* or *ROOSH dee,* **Salman,** *SAHL man* (1947-), is a noted Indian-born novelist. Rushdie has gained praise for his skill as a storyteller and for his imaginative style, which often features fantasy and high-spirited humor. His major themes include homelessness, exile, and the redefinition of identity.

Rushdie became the center of an international controversy with the publication in 1988 of *The Satanic Verses.* The novel plays upon the legend that Satan inserted certain verses into the revelation of the Qur'ān, the sacred book of Islam. The prophet Muhammad later rejected the verses after an angel revealed they were fake. Many Islamic leaders denounced the novel as blasphemy. In 1989, Iran's spiritual leader, Ayatollah Ruhollah Khomeini, pronounced a *fatwa* (death sentence) on Rushdie. Fearing assassination, the writer went into hiding during the 1990's. The British government awarded Rushdie a knighthood in 2008, angering several Muslim countries.

Rushdie first won literary recognition with *Midnight's Children* (1981), a panoramic story of the history of India since its independence from the United Kingdom in 1947. In the novel, actual historical figures mingle with deities and bizarre fictional human characters. This narrative style, called *magic realism,* combines detailed realism with grotesque and fantastic elements to achieve a dreamlike quality. The novel won the 1981 Booker Prize, the United Kingdom's highest literary award. *Shame* (1983), set in an imaginary country resembling Pakistan, shuttles between past and future to show how forces of history and culture can distort human relationships.

In the 1990's, Rushdie wrote most of his books in hiding. They included the short-story collection *East, West* (1994) and the novels *Haroun and the Sea of Stories* (1990) and *The Moor's Last Sigh* (1995). Rushdie came out of hiding and settled in the United States in 2000. He wrote *Fury* (2001), a satirical comic novel set in New York City. *Shalimar the Clown* (2005) explores the roots of terrorism. In *The Enchantress of Florence* (2008), a traveler from Italy visits the great Mughal emperor Akbar in India in the late 1500's. *Two Years Eight Months and Twenty-Eight Nights* (2015) is a satirical fantasy inspired by the Arabic collection of tales called *The Arabian Nights.* In *Quichotte* (2019), he reimagined the Spanish story of Don Quixote in a modern American setting with magical overtones. *Step Across This Line: Collected Nonfiction 1992-2002* was published in 2002. *Languages of Truth: Essays 2003-2020* was published in 2021.

Ahmed Salman Rushdie was born on June 19, 1947, in Bombay (now Mumbai), India. He wrote a memoir of his life in hiding, *Joseph Anton* (2012). Ranjit Hoskote

Rushmore, Mount. See **Mount Rushmore National Memorial.**

Rusk, Dean (1909-1994), served as United States secretary of state from 1961 to 1969 under Presidents John F. Kennedy and Lyndon B. Johnson. As secretary of state, Rusk became a leading spokesman for the Johnson administration's Vietnam War policy.

Rusk was born David Dean Rusk on Feb. 9, 1909, in Cherokee County, Georgia. He graduated from Davidson College in North Carolina in 1931 and studied at Oxford University as a Rhodes scholar in 1933 and 1934. In 1934, he became a political science professor at Mills College in California. He was made dean of the faculty at Mills in 1938.

Rusk joined the Department of State in 1946 and served as director of its office of United Nations affairs from 1947 to 1949. During these years, he helped bring the Marshall Plan and the North Atlantic Treaty Organization (NATO) into being. From 1950 to 1952, during the Korean War, Rusk served as assistant secretary of state for far eastern affairs. From 1952 to 1960, he was president of the Rockefeller Foundation. Rusk was made a "distinguished fellow" by the foundation in 1969. In 1970, he became a law professor at the University of Georgia. Rusk died on Dec. 20, 1994. James I. Lengle

Ruskin, John (1819-1900), was probably the most influential English critic of the 1800's. His many writings on art, literature, and social issues helped form the tastes of Victorian England.

Ruskin was born on Feb. 8, 1819, in London. He attended Oxford University. While a student there, Ruskin became a strong supporter of the British artist J. M. W. Turner, whose paintings had aroused much controversy. Ruskin's first book, *Modern Painters I* (1843), defended Turner's style (see **Turner, J. M. W.**). Ruskin's other works on art and architecture include four more volumes of *Modern Painters* (1846-1860), *The Seven Lamps of Architecture* (1849), and *The Stones of Venice* (three volumes, 1851-1853).

Ruskin believed that education, morality, and healthy social conditions were needed to produce good art. As a result, he concerned himself with social and economic issues. In lectures, essays, and books, Ruskin questioned the operations and motives of the free enterprise system. He attacked the quality of mass-produced products and encouraged workers to express their individuality. Ruskin had little political effect on his own time, but his ideas later influenced many British socialists, such writers as D. H. Lawrence and Leo Tolstoy, and the Hindu spiritual leader Mohandas Gandhi.

Ruskin's writings on social issues include four essays, published as *Unto This Last* (1862), and *Fors Clavigera,* a series of letters to British workers published from 1871 to 1884. Ruskin's last important work was an unfinished autobiography, *Praeterita,* written from 1885 to 1889. Ruskin died on Jan. 20, 1900. K. K. Collins

See also **Whistler, James Abbott McNeill.**

Russell, Bertrand (1872-1970), was a British philosopher and mathematician. Russell ranks among the greatest philosophers of the 1900's. He has also been called the most important *logician* (expert in logic) since the ancient Greek philosopher Aristotle.

Russell made his most important contributions in formal logic and the theory of knowledge. However, his influence extends far beyond these fields. Russell developed a prose style of extraordinary clarity, wit, and passion. He received the 1950 Nobel Prize for literature.

Russell became an influential and controversial figure on social, political, and educational issues. He was an outspoken pacifist and advocated extremely liberal attitudes toward sex, marriage, and methods of education. Russell was a critic of World War I (1914-1918). He was imprisoned in 1918 for statements considered harmful to British-American relations, and again in 1961 for "incitement to civil disobedience" in a campaign for nuclear disarmament.

Russell made his major contributions to philosophy and mathematics in the early 1900's. He wanted to derive all of mathematics from logic, thus putting it on a sure foundation. Russell collaborated with the English mathematician and philosopher Alfred North Whitehead on the monumental three-volume *Principia Mathematica* (1910-1913). This work attempts to show that all pure mathematics follows from premises that are strictly logical and uses only those concepts that can be defined in purely logical terms. Although Russell's ideas have been refined and corrected by later mathematicians, all modern work in logic and the foundations of mathematics begins with his ideas.

Russell made important contributions to the history of philosophy in such books as *A Critical Exposition of the Philosophy of Leibniz* (1900) and *A History of Western Philosophy* (1945). He expressed his social and political ideas in a number of works, including *German Social Democracy* (1896), *Roads to Freedom* (1918), *Power* (1938), and *Authority and the Individual* (1949).

Russell also influenced morality and education in essays and such books as *Why I Am Not a Christian* (1927), *Marriage and Morals* (1929), and *The Conquest of Happiness* (1930). Russell wrote numerous accounts of his life, including a three-volume autobiography (1967 to 1969).

Russell was born on May 18, 1872, near Trellek, Wales, north of Chepstow. His full name was Bertrand Arthur William Russell. He was a member of an old and noble family. In 1931, he inherited the family title and became Earl Russell. Russell died on Feb. 2, 1970. See **Russell family.** W. W. Bartley III

Russell, Bill (1934-), became one of the finest defensive players in basketball history. A 6-foot 10-inch (208-centimeter) center for the Boston Celtics, Russell became a master at blocking shots and rebounding. He ranks second only to Wilt Chamberlain among the leading rebounders in the history of the National Basketball Association (NBA).

William Felton Russell was born on Feb. 12, 1934, in Monroe, Louisiana. He helped lead the University of San Francisco to win 57 of 58 games during the 1954-1955 and 1955-1956 seasons. Russell joined the Celtics in the 1956-1957 season and helped lead the team to 11 NBA championships in the 13 years he played.

Russell served as player-coach of the Celtics from 1966 to 1969. He was the first African American head coach in major league professional sports. Russell retired as a player in 1969. He served as general manager and coach of the Seattle SuperSonics of the NBA from 1973 to 1977. He coached the Sacramento Kings of the NBA from 1987 to 1988, and served as a vice president for the team in 1988 and 1989.

Russell was a TV sports commentator between coaching assignments. He discussed his life and his views on basketball in *Go Up for Glory* (1970), *Second Wind* (1979), and *Red and Me* (2009). Bob Logan

See also **Basketball** (picture).

Russell, Charles Marion (1864-1926), was an American painter and sculptor famous for his scenes of cowboys and life in the West. Russell's work shows action and great detail, with authentic backgrounds and settings. Russell taught himself art. He worked almost equally well with pen-and-ink, oil paint or water color, and clay. He also wrote stories about the West, which were published with his illustrations.

Russell was born in St. Louis, Missouri, on March 19, 1864. As a child, he loved to sketch and model animals, cowboys, and Indians. Because of his interest in the West, his parents let him visit the Montana Territory when he was 16 years old. He quickly made Montana his permanent home. Russell earned his living as a hunter for 2 years and then worked as a cowboy for about 10 years. He lived with the Blood Indians in Canada one winter. His experiences provided dramatic, often humorous, material for his paintings and sculptures.

In 1893, Russell gave up cowboy living so that he could paint and sculpt full-time. Three years later, he married Nancy Cooper, who encouraged his artistic career. Russell died on Oct. 24, 1926. His statue represents Montana in Statuary Hall in the United States Capitol.

Sarah E. Boehme

See also **Cowboy** (picture); **Dodge City** (picture).

Russell, George William (1867-1935), an Irish poet, painter, and journalist, was a leader of the Irish Literary Revival that began in the late 1800's. This movement encouraged the creation of works based on Irish culture.

Russell's mystical poetry and paintings reflect his deep love of nature. He developed a personal religion that sought spiritual truths in nature. Russell was born on April 10, 1867, in Lurgan, in what is now Northern Ireland. He spent most of his adult life as a journalist in Dublin. He wrote under the pen name "AE," which he took from a printer's error on one of his essays. Russell was an authority on farming and devoted much time to improving Irish agriculture. He died on July 17, 1935.

James MacKillop

Russell, Henry Norris (1877-1957), an American astronomer, influenced the growth of theoretical astrophysics in the United States. Around 1910, he and the Danish astronomer Ejnar Hertzsprung independently developed a diagram that relates the brightness of a star to its surface temperature. Research based on this diagram has helped scientists interpret the physical nature and evolution of stars. In 1929, Russell presented strong evidence that hydrogen is by far the most abundant chemical element in the atmosphere of stars.

Russell was born on Oct. 25, 1877, in Oyster Bay, New York. From 1912 to 1947, he was director of the observatory at Princeton University. Russell died on Feb. 18, 1957. Karl Hufbauer

See also **Star** (The Hertzsprung-Russell diagram [diagram]).

Russell, Lord John (1792-1878), served as prime minister of the United Kingdom from 1846 to 1852 and in 1865 and 1866. But he is probably more famous for his earlier leadership of the British reform movement.

Russell was born on Aug. 18, 1792, in London, a son of the sixth Duke of Bedford. His family had been active in the Whig Party and was known for its support of civil rights. Russell was elected to the British House of Commons in 1813. In 1828, he made a motion that led to the repeal of the Test acts and the Corporation Act. As a result, Protestants who did not belong to the Church of England were allowed to participate fully in English politics. Russell also helped write and pass the Reform Act of 1832, which gave more middle-class men the right to vote. He became Earl Russell in 1861. Lord Russell died on May 28, 1878. Richard W. Davis

See also **United Kingdom** (The era of reform).

Russell, Lillian (1861-1922), an American actress and singer, was the ideal of feminine beauty in the late 1800's. She made her debut in 1879 in the chorus in *H.M.S. Pinafore.* She became famous in the 1880's when she was billed at Tony Pastor's Theatre in New York City as "the beautiful English ballad singer." Her costumes, especially her hats, became the talk of the town. Beginning in 1899, she performed for five seasons with the musical comedy troupe of Weber and Fields. Helen Louise Leonard was born on Dec. 4, 1861, in Clinton, Iowa. She died on June 6, 1922. Don B. Wilmeth

Brown Bros.

Lillian Russell

Russell, Richard Brevard (1897-1971), a Georgia Democrat, was one of the most influential people ever to serve in the United States Senate. He served as chairman of the Senate Armed Services Committee in 1951 and 1952 and again from 1955 until 1969, when he became chairman of the Senate Appropriations Committee. In 1969, he also was elected president *pro tempore* of the Senate. As chairman of the appropriations group, Russell had great influence on the nation's spending, especially in gaining Senate approval of military budgets.

Russell was born on Nov. 2, 1897, in Winder, Georgia, and graduated from the University of Georgia School of Law. He was elected to the Georgia House of Representatives in 1920 and became its speaker in 1927. In 1930, he was elected governor of Georgia. In 1932, he was elected to complete the term of U.S. Senator William J. Harris, who had died. Russell served in the Senate from 1933 until his death on Jan. 21, 1971. His firm defense of segregation and his opposition to civil rights legislation undercut his presidential ambitions. James C. Cobb

Russell family became one of England's most famous families. Its best-known members included Bertrand Russell, a mathematician and philosopher, and Lord John Russell, a prime minister (see **Russell, Bertrand; Russell, Lord John**). Others were prominent in politics.

John Russell (1486?-1555) distinguished himself as a soldier and diplomat during the reign of King Henry VIII. In 1549, he was made the first Earl of Bedford. Francis Russell (1593-1641) played an important part in Parliament's struggle to limit the power of King Charles I. William Russell (1613-1700) switched his support from Parliament to Charles I and then back to Parliament during the English Civil War in the 1640's.

Hastings William Sackville Russell (1888-1953) was a pacifist. He defended some Nazi policies during World War II (1939-1945). John Robert Russell (1917-2002) was a journalist and farmer in South Africa. He made his land at Woburn a public park in 1955. Richard W. Davis

Superstock

Red Square in Moscow, Russia's capital and largest city, is the site of such famous landmarks as St. Basil's Cathedral, *left,* the Lenin Mausoleum, *center,* and the Kremlin, *right.* The large plaza took its name in Russian from an old word meaning both *beautiful* and *red.*

Russia

Russia is the world's largest country in area. It is almost twice as big as Canada, the second largest country. From 1922 until 1991, Russia was the most important republic in the Soviet Union, which was the most powerful Communist country in the world. The Soviet Union broke apart in 1991. After the breakup, Russia set up new political, legal, and economic systems.

Russia extends from the Arctic Ocean south to the Black Sea and from the Baltic Sea east to the Pacific Ocean. It covers much of the continents of Europe and Asia. Moscow is the capital and largest city of Russia. St. Petersburg, on the coast of the Baltic Sea, is Russia's chief seaport.

Most of Russia's people are ethnic Russians—that is, descendants of an early Slavic people called the Russians. More than 100 minority nationalities also live in Russia. Approximately three-fourths of the people make their homes in urban areas. Russian cities have better schools and health-care facilities than the rural areas do. However, the cities suffer from such urban problems as overcrowding, crime, and environmental pollution.

Russia has abundant natural resources, including vast deposits of petroleum, natural gas, coal, and iron ore. Many of these reserves, however, lie far from settled areas. Russia's harsh, cold climate makes it difficult to take advantage of many of the country's valuable resources.

Russia traces its history back to a state that emerged in Europe among the East Slavs during the 800's. Over time, large amounts of territory and many different peoples came under Russian rule. For hundreds of years, *czars* (emperors) and empresses ruled Russia. They had almost complete control over most aspects of Russian life. Under these rulers, the country's economic development lagged behind the rapid industrial progress that began in Western Europe in the 1700's. Most of the people were poor, uneducated peasants.

Russia made many great contributions to the arts dur-

Donald J. Raleigh, the contributor of this article, is Jay Richard Judson Distinguished Professor of History at the University of North Carolina at Chapel Hill.

ITAR-Tass from Sovfoto

Fields of wheat spread over vast areas of Russian farmland. Russia ranks as one of the world's major producers of wheat and other grains.

Scene from a Kirov Ballet production of *Don Quixote* (ITAR-Tass from Sovfoto)

Russian ballet troupes perform throughout the world. They are famous for their skill and beauty.

© Ken Proctor, Superstock

Snow covers more than half of Russia for six months of the year. This village is near the city of Irkutsk in Siberia.

ing the 1800's. Such authors as Anton Chekhov, Fyodor Dostoevsky, and Leo Tolstoy wrote masterpieces of literature. Russian composers, including Modest Mussorgsky, Nikolai Rimsky-Korsakov, and Peter Ilich Tchaikovsky, created music of lasting greatness. Russians also made valuable artistic contributions in the fields of architecture, ballet, and painting.

Opposition to the czars' absolute power increased during the late 1800's and the early 1900's. Revolutionaries overthrew the Russian government in 1917. The next year, Russia became the Russian Soviet Federative Socialist Republic (R.S.F.S.R.).

In 1922, the R.S.F.S.R. and three other republics established a new nation called the Union of Soviet Socialist Republics (U.S.S.R.), also known as the Soviet Union. The R.S.F.S.R. became the largest and most influential republic of the Soviet Union, which included 15 republics by 1956. In 1991, Communist rule in the Soviet Union collapsed, and the country broke apart. Russia and most of the other republics formed a new, loose federation called the Commonwealth of Independent States.

After the breakup of the Soviet Union, Russia entered a transitional period. The Communist leaders of the Soviet Union had controlled all aspects of the country's economy and government. Russia's new national government worked to move the country from a state-controlled economy to one based on private enterprise. The government also began to establish new political and legal systems in Russia.

This article deals with Russia from its early history to the present. For more detailed information about the history of Russia between 1922 and 1991—when it was part of the Soviet Union—see **Union of Soviet Socialist Republics.**

Russia in brief

General information

Capital: Moscow.
Official language: Russian.
Official names: Rossiya (Russia) or Rossiyskaya Federatsiya (Russian Federation).
Largest cities (2010 census)

Moscow	11,514,330
St. Petersburg	4,848,742

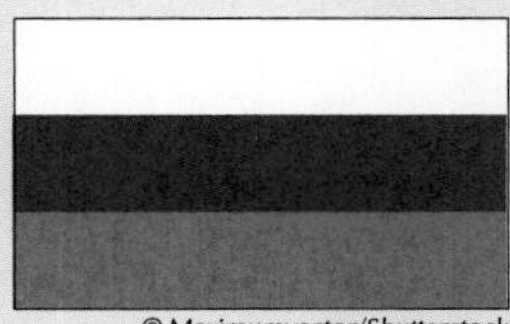
© Maximumvector/Shutterstock

The Russian flag has stripes of white, blue, and red. It was adopted in 1991. The Russian Empire used the flag from 1699 to 1918.

The state seal was adopted in 1993. It includes symbols of the Russian Empire.

Land and climate

Land: Russia is the world's largest country in area. It covers a large part of both Europe and Asia. It has coastlines on the Arctic Ocean, Baltic Sea, Black Sea, Caspian Sea, and Pacific Ocean. Russia borders eight European countries, three Asian countries, and three countries with lands in both Europe and Asia. Much of the west is a large plain. The Ural Mountains separate Europe and Asia. Siberia, east of the Urals, has low western plains, a central plateau, and a mountainous wilderness in the east. Major Russian rivers include the Lena in Asia and the Volga in Europe. Lake Baikal in Siberia is the world's deepest lake.
Area: 6,601,670 mi² (17,098,246 km²). *Greatest distances*—east-west, 6,000 mi (9,650 km); north-south, 2,800 mi (4,500 km). *Coastline*—23,396 mi (37,653 km).
Elevation: *Highest*—Mount Elbrus, 18,510 ft (5,642 m). *Lowest*—coast of Caspian Sea, 92 ft (28 m) below sea level.
Climate: Most of Russia has long, bitterly cold winters and mild to warm—but short—summers. In northeastern Siberia, the country's coldest area, January temperatures average below -50 °F (-46 °C). Rainfall is moderate in most of Russia. Snow covers more than half of the country during six months of the year.

WORLD BOOK map

Government

Form of government: Republic.
Head of state: President.
Head of government: Prime minister.
Legislature: Russia's parliament is called the Federal Assembly. It consists of two houses—the State Duma and the Federation Council.
Executive: The president is the chief executive and most powerful official.
Judiciary: Highest court is the Constitutional Court.
Political subdivisions: Russia has dozens of federal administrative units. They include *oblasts* (regions), republics, autonomous *okrugs* (areas), *krais* (territories), autonomous oblasts, and federal cities. Some of these divisions may contain smaller units called *raions* (districts).

People

Population: *Estimated 2022 population*—146,279,000; *2020 official government estimate*—146,748,600.
Population density: 22 per mi² (9 per km²).
Distribution: 75 percent urban, 25 percent rural.
Major ethnic/national groups: About 80 percent Russian. Smaller groups include Tatars (or Tartars), Ukrainians, Chuvash, Bashkirs, Belarusians, Mordvins, Chechens, Germans, Udmurts, Mari, Kazakhs, Avars, Jews, and Armenians.
Major religions: The Russian Orthodox Church is the largest religious group. Other religious groups include Muslims, Protestants, Roman Catholics, Buddhists, Hindus, and Jews.

Population trend

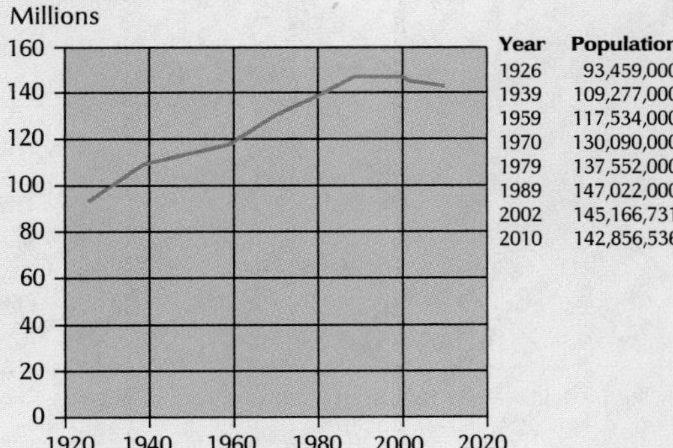

Year	Population
1926	93,459,000
1939	109,277,000
1959	117,534,000
1970	130,090,000
1979	137,552,000
1989	147,022,000
2002	145,166,731
2010	142,856,536

Economy

Chief products: *Agriculture*—barley, beef and dairy cattle, chickens, fruits, hogs, potatoes, rye, sugar beets, sunflower seeds, vegetables, wheat. *Fishing*—cod, haddock, herring, salmon. *Manufacturing*—chemicals, electronics, machinery, processed foods, refined oil, transportation equipment. *Mining*—coal, copper, gold, iron ore, natural gas, nickel, petroleum, platinum, tin, tungsten.
Money: *Basic unit*—Russian ruble. One hundred kopecks equal one ruble.
International trade: *Major exports*—chemicals, machinery, metals, natural gas, paper products, petroleum, wood products. *Major imports*—consumer goods, foods and beverages, industrial equipment, machinery. *Major trading partners*—other former Soviet republics, China, Germany, Italy, Japan, Poland, United Kingdom, United States.

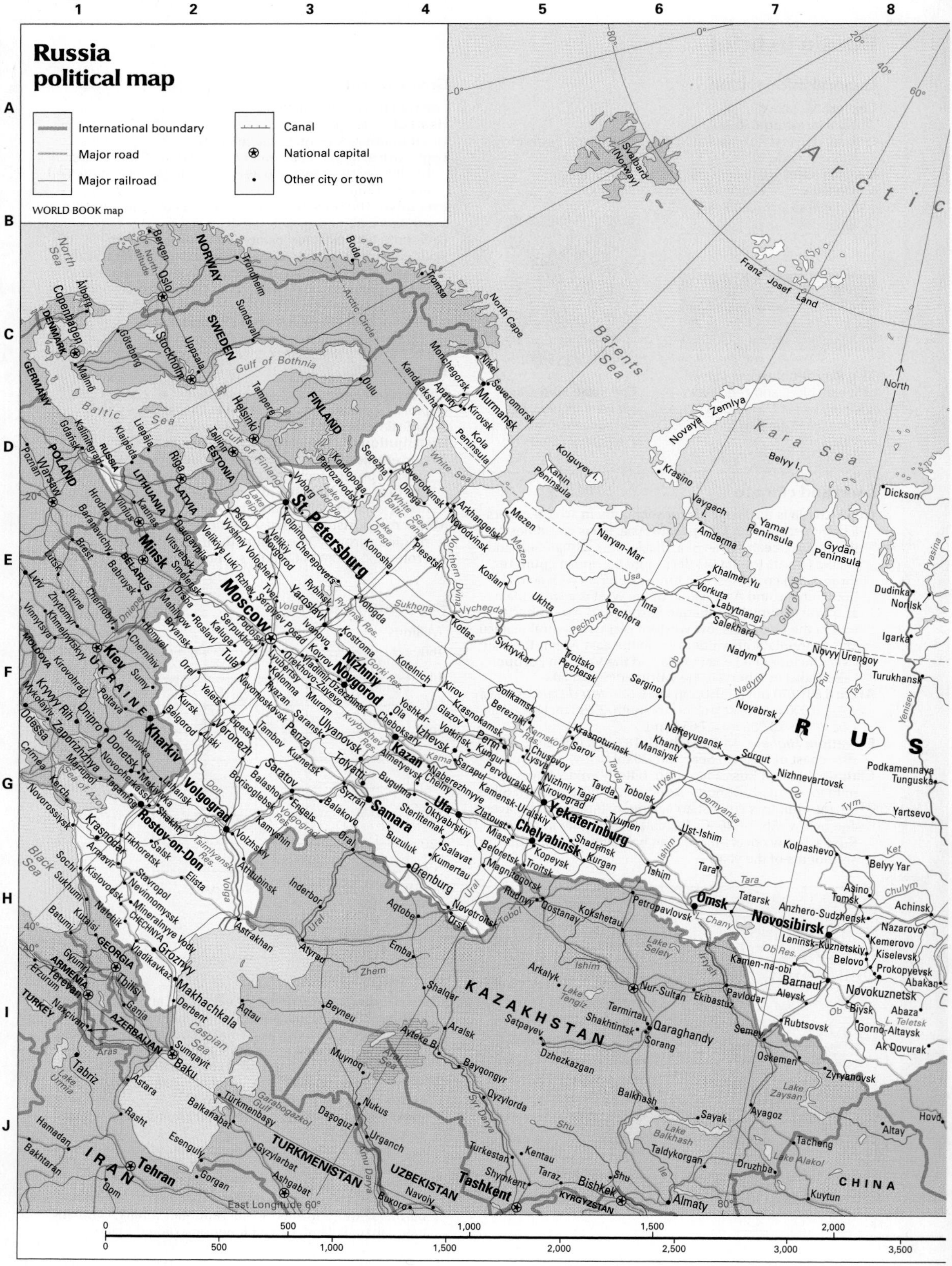

Russia political map

- International boundary
- Major road
- Major railroad
- Canal
- National capital
- Other city or town

WORLD BOOK map

East Longitude 60°

0 500 1,000 1,500 2,000

0 500 1,000 1,500 2,000 2,500 3,000 3,500

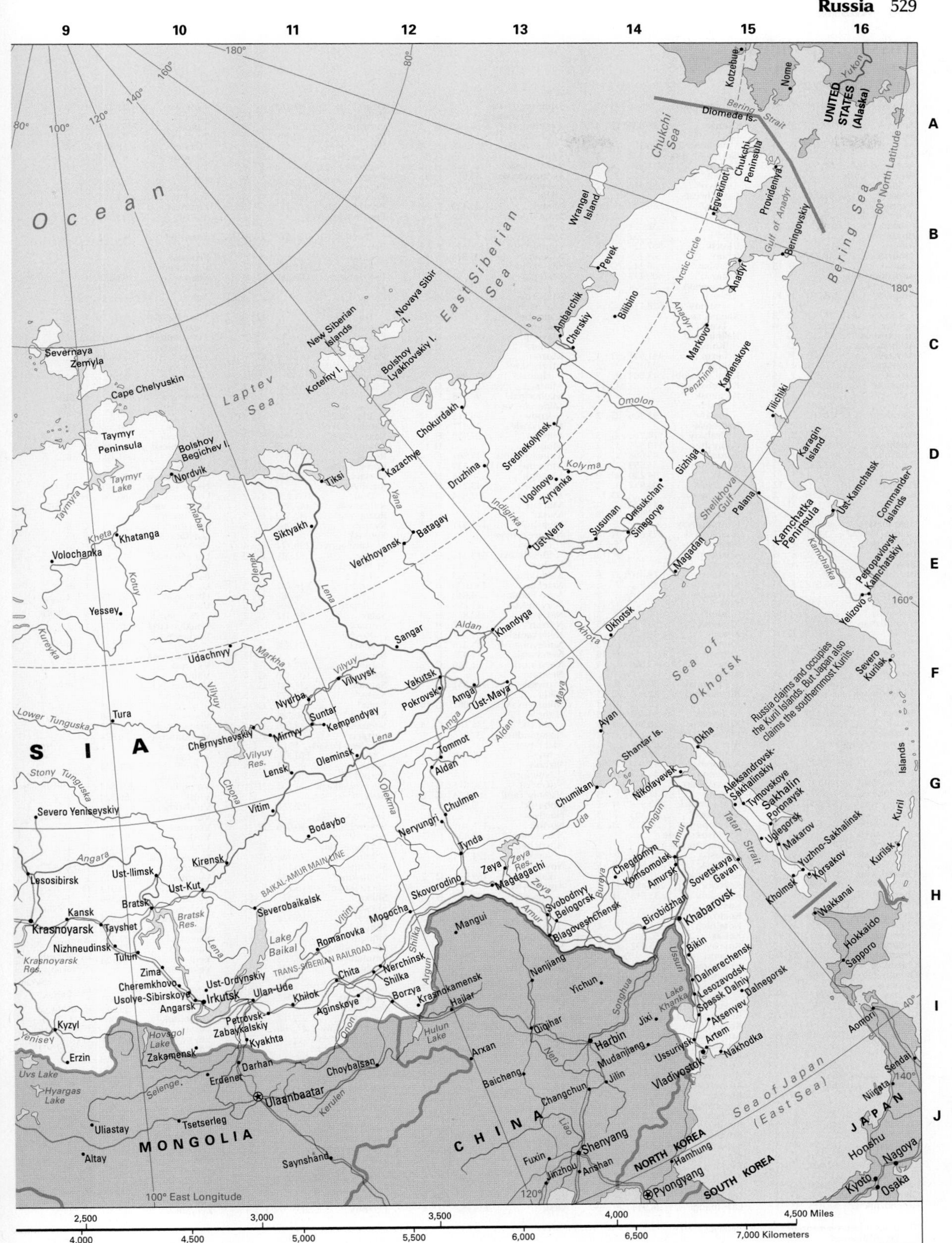

Ocean
S I A
Severnaya Zemlya
Cape Chelyuskin
Taymyr Peninsula
Laptev Sea
New Siberian Islands
Novaya Sibir I.
Kotelny I.
Bolshoy Lyakhovskiy I.
East Siberian Sea
Wrangel Island
Chukchi Sea
Bering Strait
Diomede Is.
Chukchi Peninsula
Gulf of Anadyr
Bering Sea
UNITED STATES (Alaska)
Kotzebue
Nome
Yukon
Arctic Circle
Sea of Okhotsk
Kamchatka Peninsula
Karagin Island
Commander Islands
Kuril Islands
Shelikhova Gulf
Shantar Is.
Tatar Strait
Sakhalin
Russia claims and occupies the Kuril Islands. But Japan also claims the southernmost Kurils.
Lake Baikal
Bratsk Res.
Vilyuy Res.
Zeya Res.
Krasnoyarsk Res.
BAIKAL-AMUR MAIN LINE
TRANS-SIBERIAN RAILROAD
Lena
Yana
Indigirka
Kolyma
Omolon
Anadyr
Penzhina
Aldan
Vilyuy
Markha
Lower Tunguska
Stony Tunguska
Angara
Yenisey
Amur
Zeya
Bureya
Amgun
Uda
Maya
Okhota
Olekma
Vitim
Chona
Shilka
Argun
Onon
Kerulen
Selenge
Songhua
Nen
Liao
Ussuri
Lake Khanka
Hulun Lake
Hovsgol Lake
Uvs Lake
Hyargas Lake
Kheta
Taymyra
Taymyr Lake
Anabar
Olenek
Kotuy
Kureyka
Kamchatka
Nordvik
Bolshoy Begichev I.
Khatanga
Volochanka
Yessey
Tiksi
Siktyakh
Kazachye
Verkhoyansk
Batagay
Chokurdakh
Druzhina
Srednekolymsk
Ugolnoye
Zyryanka
Ust-Nera
Susuman
Omsukchan
Sinegorye
Magadan
Gizhiga
Ambarchik
Cherskiy
Pevek
Bilibino
Markovo
Kamenskoye
Egvekinot
Providenlya
Anadyr
Beringovskiy
Tilichiki
Palana
Ust-Kamchatsk
Petropavlovsk Kamchatskiy
Yelizovo
Severo Kurilsk
Kurilsk
Okhotsk
Ayan
Chumikan
Nikolayevsk
Okha
Aleksandrovsk-Sakhalinskiy
Tymovskoye
Poronaysk
Uglegorsk
Makarov
Yuzhno-Sakhalinsk
Kholmsk
Korsakov
Wakkanai
Hokkaido
Sapporo
Aomori
Sendai
Niigata
Honshu
JAPAN
Nagoya
Kyoto
Osaka
Sea of Japan (East Sea)
Udachnyy
Sangar
Khandyga
Yakutsk
Pokrovsk
Vilyuysk
Nyurba
Suntar
Kempendyay
Amga
Ust-Maya
Mirnyy
Chernyshevskiy
Tura
Lensk
Olekminsk
Tommot
Aldan
Neryungri
Chulmen
Tynda
Vitim
Bodaybo
Severo Yeniseyskiy
Kirensk
Lesosibirsk
Ust-Ilimsk
Ust-Kut
Bratsk
Kansk
Krasnoyarsk
Tayshet
Nizhneudinsk
Tulun
Zima
Cheremkhovo
Usolye-Sibirskoye
Angarsk
Irkutsk
Ust-Ordynskiy
Ulan-Ude
Severobaikalsk
Romanovka
Mogocha
Skovorodino
Zeya
Magdagachi
Svobodnyy
Belogorsk
Blagoveshchensk
Chegdomyn
Komsomolsk
Amursk
Sovetskaya Gavan
Birobidzhan
Khabarovsk
Bikin
Dalnerechensk
Lesozavodsk
Spassk Dalniy
Dalnegorsk
Arsenyev
Artem
Nakhodka
Ussuriysk
Vladivostok
Chita
Nerchinsk
Shilka
Borzya
Krasnokamensk
Aginskoye
Khilok
Petrovsk-Zabaykalskiy
Kyakhta
Zakamensk
Kyzyl
Erzin
Mangui
Hailar
Nenjiang
Yichun
Qiqihar
Harbin
Jixi
Mudanjiang
Jilin
Changchun
Baicheng
Arxan
Choybalsan
Darhan
Erdenet
Ulaanbaatar
Uliastay
Tsetserleg
Altay
Saynshand
MONGOLIA
CHINA
Shenyang
Fuxin
Jinzhou
Anshan
NORTH KOREA
Hamhung
Pyongyang
SOUTH KOREA
100° East Longitude
60° North Latitude
80°
100°
120°
140°
160°
180°
40°
2,500
3,000
3,500
4,000
4,500 Miles
4,000
4,500
5,000
5,500
6,000
6,500
7,000 Kilometers
9
10
11
12
13
14
15
16
A
B
C
D
E
F
G
H
I
J

Russia map index

Cities and towns

Abakan ....165,183 ..I 8
Abaza ....17,111 ..I 8
Achinsk ....109,156 ..H 8
Aginskoye ....I 11
Ak Dovurak ....13,469 ..I 8
Aldan ....21,277 ..G 12
Aleksandrov* ...61,544 ..F 4
Aleksandrovsk Sakhalinskiy ....G 15
Aleksin* ....61,738 ..F 2
Aleysk ....29,512 ..I 7
Almetyevsk ....146,309 ..G 4
Ambarchik ....C 13
Amderma ....E 6
Amga ....F 13
Amursk ....42,977 ..H 15
Anadyr ....13,053 ..B 15
Andropov, see Rybinsk
Angarsk ....233,765 ..I 10
Anzhero-Sudzhensk ...76,669 ..H 8
Apatity ....59,690 ..D 4
Apsheronsk* ....40,229 ..G 1
Arkhangelsk ...348,716 ..D 4
Armavir ....188,897 ..H 1
Arsenyev ....56,742 ..I 15
Artem ....102,636 ..I 15
Arzamas* ....106,367 ..F 3
Asbest* ....68,914 ..G 5
Asino ....25,614 ..H 8
Astrakhan ....520,662 ..H 2
Ayan ....F 14
Azov* ....82,882 ..G 1
Balakovo ......199,573 ..G 3
Balashikha* ...215,353 ..F 3
Balashov ....82,222 ..G 3
Barnaul ....612,091 ..I 7
Batagay ....E 12
Bataysk* ....111,856 ..G 2
Belebey* ....60,183 ..G 4
Belgorod ......356,426 ..F 2
Belogorsk ....68,220 ..H 13
Belorechensk* ...53,891 ..G 1
Beloretsk ....68,804 ..G 5
Belovo ....76,752 ..I 8
Belyy Yar ....H 8
Berdsk* ....97,288 ..H 7
Berezniki ......156,512 ..F 5
Beringovskiy ....B 15
Bikin ....17,156 ..I 15
Bilibino ....C 14
Birobidzhan ....75,419 ..H 14
Birsk* ....41,637 ..G 4
Biysk ....210,055 ..I 8
Blagoveshchensk ....214,397 ..H 13
Bodaybo ....15,331 ..G 11
Bor* ....78,079 ..F 3
Borisoglebsk ...65,585 ..G 2
Borovichi* ......53,699 ..E 3
Borzya ....31,376 ..I 12
Bratsk ....246,348 ..H 10
Brezhnev, see Naberezhnyye Chelny
Bryansk ....415,640 ..F 2
Bugulma ....89,144 ..G 4
Buguruslan* ....49,737 ..G 4
Buzuluk ....82,655 ..G 4
Chapayevsk* ....72,689 ..G 4
Chaykovskiy* ...82,933 ..G 4
Cheboksary ...453,645 ..F 4
Chegdomyn ....H 14
Chekhov* ....60,677 ..F 2
Chelyabinsk ..1,130,273 ..G 5
Cheremkhovo ..52,650 ..I 10
Cherepovets ...312,311 ..E 3
Cherkessk* ....121,439 ..H 1
Chernogorsk* ...72,177 ..I 9
Cherskiy ....C 13
Chistopol* ......60,703 ..G 4
Chita ....323,964 ..I 11
Chokurdakh ....D 12
Chulmen ....G 12
Chumikan ....G 14
Chusovoy ......46,740 ..G 5
Dalnegorsk .....37,503 ..I 15
Dalnerechensk ....27,601 ..I 15
Derbent ....119,961 ..I 2
Dickson ....D 8
Dimitrovgrad* ....122,549 ..G 4
Dmitrov* ....61,454 ..F 3
Dolgoprudnyy* .....90,976 ..F 3
Domodedovo* ..96,123 ..F 3
Donskoy* ......64,561 ..F 2
Druzhina ....D 13
Dubna* ....70,569 ..F 3
Dudinka ....22,207 ..E 8
Dzerzhinsk ....240,762 ..F 3
Egvekinot ....B 15
Elektrostal* ....155,324 ..F 3
Elista ....103,728 ..H 2
Engels ....202,401 ..G 3
Erzin ....I 9
Frolovo* ....39,489 ..G 3
Gatchina* ....92,566 ..D 3
Gelendzhik* .....54,813 ..G 1
Georgievsk* ....72,126 ..H 1
Gizhiga ....D 15
Glazov ....95,835 ..F 4
Gorki, see Nizhniy Novgorod
Gorno-Altaysk ..56,928 ..I 8
Groznyy ....271,596 ..H 2
Gubkin* ....88,562 ..F 2
Gukovo* ....67,268 ..G 2
Gus-Khrustalnyy* ....60,773 ..F 3
Igarka ....F 8
Inta ....32,021 ..E 6
Irbit* ....38,352 ..G 5
Irkutsk ....587,225 ..I 10
Ishim ....65,229 ..H 6
Ishimbay* ......66,242 ..G 4
Ivanovo ....409,277 ..F 3
Ivantyeyevka* ...58,594 ..F 3
Izhevsk (Ustinov) .....628,116 ..G 4
Kalinin, see Tver
Kaliningrad (Konigsberg) ....431,941 ..D 1
Kaluga ....325,185 ..F 2
Kamen-na-obi ...43,880 ..I 7
Kamenskoye ....C 15
Kamensk Shakhtinskiy* ......95,306 ..G 2
Kamensk-Uralskiy .....174,710 ..G 5
Kamyshin ......119,924 ..G 3
Kanash* ....45,608 ..G 4
Kandalaksha ....35,659 ..D 4
Kansk ....94,230 ..H 9
Kaspiysk* ......103,914 ..I 2
Kazachye ....D 12
Kazan ....1,143,546 ..G 4
Kemerovo .....532,884 ..H 8
Kempendyay ....F 11
Khabarovsk ....577,668 ..H 14
Khalmer-Yu ....E 6
Khandyga ....F 13
Khanty-Mansiysk .....79,410 ..G 6
Khasavyurt* ....133,929 ..I 2
Khatanga ....E 9
Khilok ....I 11
Khimki* ....207,125 ..F 3
Kholmsk ....30,936 ..H 15
Kimry* ....49,623 ..F 3
Kineshma* ......88,113 ..F 3
Kirensk ....H 10
Kirov (Vyatka) ..473,668 ..F 4
Kirovo-Chepetsk* ....80,920 ..F 4
Kirovograd .....21,006 ..G 5
Kirovsk ....28,639 ..D 4
Kiselevsk ......98,382 ..H 8
Kislovodsk ....128,502 ..H 1
Klimovsk* ......56,133 ..F 2
Klin* ....80,584 ..E 3
Klintsy* ....62,510 ..F 2
Kolcugino* ......45,804 ..F 3
Kolomna ......144,642 ..F 3
Kolpashevo .....24,126 ..H 8
Kolpino ....138,013 ..E 3
Komsomolsk ..263,906 ..H 14
Konakovo* ......41,303 ..E 3
Kondopoga .....32,978 ..D 3
Konigsberg, see Kaliningrad
Konosha ....E 4
Kopeysk ......137,604 ..G 5
Korenovsk* .....41,179 ..H 1
Korolëv* ......183,452 ..F 3
Korsakov ....33,518 ..H 15
Koslan ....E 5
Kostroma ......268,617 ..F 3
Kotelnich ....24,979 ..F 4
Kotlas ....60,562 ..F 4
Kovrov ....145,492 ..F 3
Krasino ....D 6
Krasnodar ......744,933 ..G 1
Krasnogorsk* ..116,738 ..H 15
Krasnokamensk .....55,668 ..I 12
Krasnokamsk ...51,929 ..F 5
Krasnoturinsk ..59,701 ..F 5
Krasnoyarsk ..973,891 ..H 9
Kropotkin* ......80,743 ..G 2
Krymsk* ....57,370 ..G 1
Kstovo* ....66,641 ..F 3
Kujbysev* ......45,298 ..H 7
Kulebaki* ......35,762 ..F 3
Kumertau ......62,854 ..H 4
Kungur ....66,110 ..G 5
Kurchatov* ......42,691 ..F 2
Kurgan ....333,640 ..H 5
Kursk ....414,595 ..F 2
Kuybyshev, see Samara
Kuznetsk ....88,883 ..G 3
Kyakhta ....20,041 ..I 10
Kyshtym* ....38,950 ..G 5
Kyzyl ....109,906 ..I 9
Labinsk* ....62,822 ..H 1
Labytnangi ......26,948 ..E 6
Leningrad, see St. Petersburg
Leninogorsk* ...64,145 ..G 4
Leninsk-Kuznetskiy ..101,666 ..H 8
Lensk ....24,955 ..G 11
Lesosibirsk .....61,146 ..H 9
Lesozavodsk ....36,975 ..I 15
Lipetsk ....508,124 ..F 2
Liski ....G 2
Livny* ....50,430 ..F 2
Luga* ....36,409 ..D 3
Lysva ....65,931 ..G 5
Lytkarino* ......55,147 ..F 3
Lyubertsy ......171,978 ..F 3
Magadan ......95,925 ..E 14
Magdagachi ....H 13
Magnitogorsk ....408,401 ..H 5
Makarov ....H 15
Makhachkala ..577,990 ..I 2
Malgobek* ......31,076 ..H 2
Markovo ....C 15
Maykop* ....144,246 ..G 1
Meleuz* ....61,408 ..G 4
Mezen ....E 5
Mezhdurechensk* .....101,995 ..F 5
Miass ....151,812 ..G 5
Michurinsk* .....98,758 ..F 3
Mineralnyye Vody ....76,715 ..H 2
Minusinsk* ......71,171 ..I 9
Mirnyy ....37,179 ..F 11
Mogocha ....H 12
Monchegorsk ..45,381 ..C 4
Moscow ....11,514,330 ..F 3
Mozdok* ....38,748 ..H 2
Mtsensk* ....43,216 ..F 2
Murmansk .....307,664 ..D 4
Murom ....116,078 ..F 3
Myski* ....43,029 ..I 8
Mytishchi* .....173,341 ..F 3
Naberezhnyye Chelny (Brezhnev) ..513,242 ..G 4
Nadym ....46,550 ..F 7
Nakhodka ......159,695 ..I 15
Nalchik ....240,095 ..H 1
Naro-Fominsk* ..64,640 ..F 3
Naryan-Mar .....21,296 ..E 5
Nazarovo ....52,829 ..H 8
Nazran* ....93,357 ..H 2
Neftekamsk* ...121,757 ..G 4
Nefteyugansk ..123,276 ..G 7
Nerchinsk ....14,976 ..I 12
Neryungri ......61,746 ..G 12
Nevinnomyssk ....118,351 ..H 1
Nikel ....C 4
Nikolayevsk .....15,081 ..G 14
Nizhnekamsk* ......234,108 ..G 4
Nizhneudinsk ...37,056 ..H 9
Nizhnevartovsk ....251,860 ..G 7
Nizhniy Novgorod (Gorki) .....1,250,615 ..F 3
Nizhniy Tagil ..361,883 ..G 5
Noginsk* ....99,762 ..F 3
Nordvik ....D 10
Norilsk ....175,301 ..E 8
Novoaltaysk* ....70,438 ..I 7
Novocheboksarsk* ....124,113 ..G 3
Novocherkassk ....169,039 ..G 2
Novokuybyshevsk* ......108,449 ..G 3
Novokuznetsk ....547,885 ..I 8
Novomoskovsk ...131,277 ..F 2
Novorossiysk .....241,788 ..G 1
Novoshakhtinsk* ....111,087 ..G 1
Novosibirsk ..1,473,737 ..H 7
Novotroitsk .....98,184 ..H 4
Novozybkov* ...40,552 ..F 2
Novyy Urengoy ....104,144 ..F 7
Noyabrsk ......110,572 ..F 7
Nyurba ....F 11
Obinsk* ....104,798 ..F 3
Odintsovo* ....139,021 ..F 2
Okha ....23,007 ..G 15
Okhotsk ....F 14
Oktyabrskiy ...109,379 ..G 4
Oleminsk ....G 12
Omsk ....1,153,971 ..H 6
Omsukchan ....D 14
Onega ....21,359 ..D 4
Ordzhonikidze, see Vladikavkaz
Orekhovo-Zuevo ....120,620 ..F 3
Orel ....317,854 ..F 2
Orenburg ......546,987 ..H 4
Orsk ....239,752 ..H 4
Ozersk* ....82,268 ..G 5
Palana ....D 15
Partizansk* ......38,648 ..I 15
Pavlovo* ....60,699 ..F 3
Pavlovskiy Posad* ....63,771 ..F 3
Pechora ....43,458 ..E 6
Penza ....517,137 ..G 3
Perm ....991,530 ..G 5
Pervouralsk ...124,555 ..G 5
Petrodvorets* ...73,154 ..D 3
Petropavlovsk-Kamchatskiy .....179,526 ..E 16
Petrovsk Zabaykalskiy ....18,555 ..I 11
Petrozavodsk ..263,540 ..D 3
Pevek ....B 14
Plesetsk ....E 4
Podkamennaya Tunguska ....G 8
Podolsk ....187,956 ..F 3
Pokrovsk ....F 12
Polevskoy* ......64,191 ..G 5
Poronaysk ......16,099 ..G 15
Prokopyevsk ..210,150 ..I 8
Provideniya ....A 15
Pskov ....203,281 ..E 2
Pushkin* ....92,721 ..D 3
Pushkino* ......102,840 ..F 3
Pyatigorsk* ....142,397 ..H 1
Ramenskoye* ...96,355 ..F 3
Rasskazovo* ....45,484 ..F 3
Reutov* ....87,195 ..F 3
Revda* ....61,890 ..G 5
Romanovka ....H 11
Roslavl ....54,898 ..E 2
Rostov-on-Don ....1,089,851 ..G 2
Rubtsovsk .....147,008 ..I 7
Ruzajevka* ......47,529 ..F 3
Ryazan ....525,062 ..F 3
Rybinsk (Andropov) ..200,771 ..E 4
Rzhev ....62,026 ..E 2
St. Petersburg (Leningrad) ......4,848,742 ..D 3
Salavat ....156,085 ..H 4
Salekhard ......42,494 ..E 6
Salsk ....61,312 ..G 2
Samara (Kuybyshev) ......1,164,896 ..G 4
Sangar ....F 12
Saransk ....297,425 ..F 3
Sarapul ....101,390 ..G 4
Saratov ....837,831 ..G 3
Sarov* ....92,073 ..F 3
Satka* ....45,184 ..G 5
Sayansk* ....40,786 ..I 10
Segezha ....29,660 ..D 4
Sergino ....F 6
Sergiyev Posad (Zagorsk) ....110,878 ..E 3
Serov ....99,381 ..G 5
Serpukhov ....126,496 ..F 3
Severobaikask ..24,935 ..H 11
Severodvinsk ....192,265 ..D 4
Severo Kurilsk ....F 16
Severomorsk ...50,076 ..D 4
Severo Yeniseyskiy ....G 9
Shadrinsk ....77,744 ..G 5
Shakhty ....240,152 ..G 2
Shchekino* .....58,154 ..F 2
Shchelkovo* ...110,380 ..F 3
Shilka ....13,947 ..I 12
Shostka* ....E 2
Shuya* ....58,528 ..D 4
Siktyakh ....E 11
Sinegorye ....E 14
Skovarodino ....H 11
Smolensk ......326,863 ..E 2
Sochi ....343,285 ..H 1
Solikamsk ......97,239 ..F 5
Solnechnegorsk* .....52,996 ..F 3
Sovetskaya Gavan ....27,712 ..H 15
Spassk Dalniy ..44,166 ..I 15
Srednekolymsk ....D 13
Stalingrad, see Volgograd
Staryy Oskol* ..221,163 ..F 2
Stavropol ......398,266 ..H 1
Sterlitamak ....273,432 ..G 4
Stupino* ....66,942 ..F 3
Suntar ....F 11
Surgut ....306,703 ..G 7
Susuman ....E 14
Sverdlovsk, see Yekaterinburg
Svetlograd* .....38,520 ..H 1
Svobodnyy .....58,594 ..H 13
Syktyvkar ......235,006 ..F 5
Syzran ....178,773 ..G 3
Taganrog ......257,692 ..G 1
Tambov ......280,457 ..F 3
Tara ....27,322 ..H 7
Tatarsk ....24,217 ..H 7
Tavda ....35,415 ..G 6
Tayshet ....35,481 ..H 9
Tikhvin* ....58,843 ..E 3
Tikhoretsk ......61,825 ..G 1
Tiksi ....D 11
Tilichiki ....D 15
Tobolsk ....99,698 ..G 6
Tolyatti ....719,514 ..G 3
Tommot ....G 12
Tomsk ....522,940 ..H 8
Torey* ....I 10
Torzhok* ....47,702 ..E 3
Troitsk ....78,637 ..H 5
Troitsko Pechorsk ....F 5
Tuapse* ....63,233 ..G 1
Tula ....501,129 ..F 2
Tulun ....44,603 ..H 10
Tura ....F 9
Turukhansk ....F 8
Tutayev* ....41,001 ..E 3
Tver (Kalinin) ..403,726 ..E 2
Tymoskoye ....G 15
Tynda ....35,574 ..H 12
Tyumen ......581,758 ..G 6
Udachnyy ......12,611 ..F 10
Ufa ....1,062,300 ..G 4
Uglegorsk ....G 15
Ugolnoye ....D 13
Ukhta ....99,642 ..E 5
Ulan-Ude ......404,357 ..I 11
Ulyanovsk (Simbirsk) ...613,793 ..G 3
Usinsk* ....41,100 ..E 6
Usolye-Sibirskoye ....83,364 ..I 10
Ussuriysk ......157,946 ..I 14
Ust-Ilimsk ....86,591 ..H 10
Ustinov, see Izhevsk
Ust-Ishim ....G 6
Ust-Kamchatsk ....E 16
Ust-Kut ....45,061 ..H 10
Ust-Labinsk* ....43,268 ..H 1
Ust-Maya ....F 13
Ust-Nera ....E 13
Ust-Ordynskiy ....I 10
Uzlovaya* ......55,282 ..F 2
Velikiy Novgorod ...218,724 ..E 3
Velikiye Luki ....98,778 ..E 2
Verknyaya Salda* ....46,240 ..G 5
Verkhoyansk ....E 12
Vilyuysk ....F 11
Vitim ....G 11
Vladikavkaz (Ordzhonikidze) .....311,635 ..H 2
Vladimir ......345,598 ..F 3
Vladivostok ....592,069 ..J 15
Volgodonsk* ...170,621 ..G 2
Volgograd (Stalingrad) ......1,021,244 ..G 2
Volochanka ....E 9
Vologda ......301,642 ..E 3
Volsk* ....66,520 ..I 9
Volzhskiy ......314,436 ..G 2
Vorkuta ....70,551 ..E 7
Voronezh ......889,989 ..F 2
Voskresensk* ...91,301 ..F 3
Votkinsk ......100,034 ..G 4
Vsevolozhsk* ...59,689 ..D 3
Vyazniki* ....41,252 ..F 3
Vyazma* ....57,103 ..E 3
Vyborg ....80,013 ..D 3
Vyksa* ....56,196 ..F 3
Vyshniy Volochek ....52,326 ..E 3
Yakutsk ....269,486 ..F 12
Yaroslavl ......591,486 ..E 3
Yartsevo ....47,853 ..G 8
Yegoryevsk* ....70,133 ..F 3
Yekaterinburg (Sverdlovsk) ......1,350,136 ..G 5
Yelets ....108,404 ..F 2
Yelizovo ....39,548 ..E 16
Yessentuki* .....100,969 ..H 1
Yessey ....E 9
Yeysk* ....87,771 ..G 1
Yoshkar-Ola ..248,688 ..F 4
Yurga* ....81,536 ..H 7
Yuzhno-Sakhalinsk ..181,727 ..H 15
Zagorsk, see Sergiyev Posad
Zakamansk ....I 10
Zelenodolsk* ...97,651 ..G 4
Zeya ....25,042 ..H 13
Zheleznodorozhnyy* ....131,729 ..F 3
Zheleznogorsk* ....95,057 ..F 2
Zhukovskiy* ...102,729 ..F 3
Zima ....32,522 ..I 10
Zlatoust ....174,985 ..G 5
Zyryanka ....D 13

*Does not appear on map; key shows general location.
Source: 2010 census.

Government

National government. In 1992—shortly after the Soviet Union broke up—Russia established a *transitional* (temporary) government that was headed by Boris N. Yeltsin. Yeltsin had been elected president of the R.S.F.S.R. in 1991. After the breakup of the Soviet Union, Yeltsin continued to serve as president of Russia until he resigned in 1999. In December 1993, Russia adopted a new constitution that established a permanent government.

The president of Russia is the government's chief executive, head of state, and most powerful official. The president is elected by the people to a six-year term.

The president, with the approval of the lower house of parliament, appoints a prime minister to serve as head of government. The prime minister is the top-ranking official of a Council of Ministers (cabinet). The Council of Ministers carries out the operations of the government.

Russia's parliament, called the Federal Assembly, consists of a lower house known as the State Duma and an upper house called the Federation Council. The State Duma makes the country's laws. The Federation Council and the president must approve legislation proposed by the Duma before the legislation can become law. But the State Duma can override a veto by the Federation Council and send legislation directly to the president. The Federation Council approves government appointments and such presidential actions as the declaration of martial law and the use of armed forces outside of Russia.

Members of the State Duma are elected to five-year terms. Half of the members are directly elected by the people. The other half are elected by *proportional representation.* Under this method, each political party that receives at least 5 percent of the popular vote gets a number of seats determined by the percentage of the vote it receives. Members of the Federation Council are local government officials. They are not elected directly by the people. Half of the members are appointed by local governors. The other half are elected by local legislatures. All Russian citizens 18 years of age and older may vote in the country's elections.

Local government. Russia consists of dozens of federal administrative units. These include *oblasts* (regions), republics, autonomous *okrugs* (areas), *krais* (territories), autonomous oblasts, and federal cities. Some of these divisions may contain smaller units called *raions* (districts). Councils called *soviets* manage local affairs in both urban and rural areas.

Many of the administrative units have taken more control over their own affairs since the breakup of the Soviet Union. Some administrative units have pressed for independence from Russia. In 2000, however, the president and the State Duma began passing measures designed to reassert federal control over local governments.

Politics. The Communist Party was the only legal political party in the Soviet Union until March 1990. At that time, the Soviet Constitution—which gave the Communist Party its broad powers—was amended. A coalition of political parties with a democratic platform, known as the Democratic Russia Movement, began to play a key role in the reform movement. The collapse of the Soviet Union in 1991 led to the end of the Democratic Russia Movement. Its component groups developed into separate political parties.

In the 1999 parliamentary elections, the Communist Party won the largest number of seats in the State Duma. A new political group called Unity won the second highest number. Unity favored continuing the reforms begun by Yeltsin's administration. In a move that surprised many political observers, Unity formed a coalition government with the Communists, who opposed Yeltsin's reforms. Vladimir V. Putin, who was named Russia's acting president in 1999 and was elected president in 2000, put together the coalition.

AP/Wide World

The State Duma makes Russia's laws. Russia's parliament consists of the State Duma and the Federation Council. This photo shows Duma members standing for the national anthem in their Moscow meeting chambers.

Elections in 2003 gave a vast majority of seats to the new United Russia party, which was formed from Unity and several other parties. United Russia supported Putin's government. United Russia again won a vast majority of seats in Duma elections held in 2007, 2011, and 2016. Other political parties represented in the Duma include the Communist Party, which supports more government control of land and industries; the nationalist Liberal Democratic Party; and the left-leaning A Just Russia party.

Courts. The former Soviet government had a political police system called the Committee on State Security, which was also known as the KGB. The KGB could interfere with and influence the legal system, and major violations of human rights took place. The KGB no longer exists in Russia.

Today, Russia has two security agencies. The Federal Security Service handles internal security, and the Foreign Intelligence Service collects information from other countries. Russia's 1993 Constitution protects the civil rights of all Russian citizens. The president of Russia nominates and the Federation Council approves the *prosecutor-general,* who serves as Russia's chief legal officer.

Russia's highest court is called the Constitutional Court. This court, which was established in 1992, rules on the constitutionality of the country's laws. Russia's local courts are called *people's courts.*

Armed forces. The Soviet Union had the largest armed forces in the world. Approximately 4 million people served in its army, navy, and air force combined. Following the collapse of the Soviet Union, the command of its armed forces passed to the Commonwealth of Independent States. Several former republics, including Russia, said that they would also create their own armed forces. In 1992, Russia began to form its own armed forces and absorbed some of the former Soviet forces. Russian men must serve for one year in the military. In addition, Russian women may volunteer to serve in the military.

People

The people of Russia are distributed unevenly throughout the country. The vast majority live in the western—or European—part of Russia. The more rugged and remote areas to the east are sparsely inhabited.

Ancestry. Approximately 80 percent of Russia's people are of Russian ancestry. They make up the largest group of Slavic peoples. Members of over 100 other nationality groups also live in Russia. The largest groups include Tatars (or Tartars), Ukrainians, Chuvash, Bashkirs, Belarusians, Mordvins, Chechens, Germans, Udmurts, Mari, Kazakhs, Avars, Armenians, and Jews, who are considered a nationality group in Russia. Many members of these groups live in Russia's autonomous territories. Remote parts of the Far North are sparsely inhabited by small Siberian groups, including Aleuts, Chukchi, Inuit, and Koryaks. These northern peoples differ from one another in ancestry and language. However, they share a common way of life shaped by the harsh, cold climate.

The Soviet Union's government had granted special political and economic privileges to Russians who were loyal to the Communist Party. It repressed the distinctive cultures of other nationalities and did not always uphold their rights. This policy sharpened resentment among some peoples. Today, pride in their culture and the desire for greater independence are growing among the members of many nationalities, including Russians.

Ethnic Russians are descended from Slavs who lived in eastern Europe several thousand years ago. Over time, migration split the Slavs into three subgroups—the East Slavs, the West Slavs, and the South Slavs. The Russians trace their heritage to the first East Slav state, Kievan Rus, which emerged in the 800's.

Kievan Rus suffered repeated invasions by Asian tribes, including the Pechenegs, Polovtsians, and Mongols. The Mongol invasions forced some people to migrate to safer, forested regions near present-day Moscow. Moscow became an important Russian state in

Population density

The map at the right shows the population density throughout Russia. Most of Russia's people live in the western part of the country. Central and eastern Russia are sparsely inhabited.

Major cities

- More than 2 million inhabitants
- Less than 2 million inhabitants

Persons per mi^2	Persons per km^2
More than 125	More than 50
60 to 125	25 to 50
25 to 60	10 to 25
5 to 25	2 to 10
Less than 5	Less than 2

WORLD BOOK map

the 1300's. This area has remained at the heart of Russia ever since. But people of many ethnic groups have lived in Russia, especially since the 1500's, when extensive expansion and colonization began.

Language. Russian is the official language of Russia. Spoken Russian sounds fairly uniform from one end of the country to the other. Nevertheless, the Russian language has three major regional accents—northern, southern, and central. The small differences rarely interfere with communication among Russian speakers. Russian is written in the Cyrillic alphabet (see **Alphabet** [Other alphabets]). Many minority nationality groups in Russia have their own language and speak Russian as a second language.

Way of life

The government of the Soviet Union controlled many aspects of life in the country. It exerted great influence over religion, education, and the arts. The independence of Russia following the breakup of the Soviet Union brought greater freedom and triggered many other changes in the lives of the people.

City life. About three-fourths of Russia's people live in urban areas. Approximately 35 cities in Russia have populations larger than 500,000. Two of Russia's cities—Moscow and St. Petersburg—each have more than 4 million inhabitants.

Some Russian cities remain crowded. Beginning in the 1930's, large numbers of people migrated from the countryside to urban areas. During World War II (1939-1945), bombs destroyed many houses and other buildings. These circumstances combined to create a severe housing shortage in Russian cities. Many families had to share kitchen and bathroom facilities. Although the situation has greatly improved, millions of city dwellers live in small apartments in high-rise buildings. Single-family houses are more common in small towns and in the older neighborhoods of many cities. Some of these dwellings lack indoor plumbing and other modern conveniences. At the same time, Russia's newly wealthy inhabit luxury apartments and large homes.

Shortages of food, services, and manufactured goods have been common features of city life in Russia. The shift toward capitalism that began in the 1990's has not yet cured the shortages. Even when goods become available, they are often too expensive for many people to afford. Russian cities also face such urban problems as crime and environmental pollution.

Rural life. About one-fourth of the Russian population lives in rural areas. Single-family housing is common in these areas, but the Soviet government built many city-style apartment buildings. In the most remote areas of Russia, some homes lack gas, plumbing, running water, and electric power. In addition, the quality of education, health care, and cultural life is lower than in the cities. Rural life is changing, however. Rural stores, for example, have a wider selection of goods available than they once offered.

When Russia was part of the Soviet Union, most rural people worked on huge farms run by the government. After the Soviet Union collapsed, Russia began to break up these farms. New laws allow people to withdraw from the government farms and set up private farms.

Clothing. Most people in the Soviet Union wore plain clothing. Stores offered little variety in styles, and most people had a limited number of outfits. In the 1970's, consumers began to demand greater variety. They preferred to buy imported clothing whenever it was available. As a result, Soviet clothing manufacturers began to pay more attention to style and quality.

Now that Russia has opened its markets, stylish clothing made in Russia and in other parts of the world has become more widely available. Many young people dress fashionably. Russia's harsh winters affect styles.

© Sergey Kompaniychenko, Gamma Presse

St. Petersburg is Russia's second largest city—behind Moscow—and the nation's leading port. The city is also an important cultural center. Vasilyevskiy Island, *shown here,* sits on the delta of the Neva River in St. Petersburg. Many beautiful and historic buildings stand on the island.

© Shutterstock

High-rise apartment buildings, such as this one in Novosibirsk, house millions of people in Russia's cities. Nevertheless, a housing shortage persists in some urban areas.

Traditional Russian clothing consists of colorfully embroidered shirts and blouses, embroidered headwear, and shoes woven from *bast,* a tough fiber from the bark of certain trees. Rural dwellers wore these costumes on special occasions, such as weddings and holidays. The traditional costumes are rarely worn today, however.

Food and drink. The traditional Russian diet is hearty. Eating habits are changing, however, as more people turn to convenience and fast foods. Beef, chicken, pork, and fish are popular main dishes. The most commonly eaten vegetables include beets, cabbage, carrots, cucumbers, onions, potatoes, radishes, and tomatoes. Russians are fond of soups, breads, and dairy products, and they consume large quantities of sugar. Frying remains a widespread method of preparing food.

Many Russian dishes are popular around the world. They include *blinis* (thin pancakes served with smoked salmon or other fillings and sour cream) and *beef Stroganoff* (sautéed beef strips with onions, mushrooms, and a sour cream sauce). Other favorite dishes include *borscht* (beet soup) and *piroshki* (baked or fried dumplings filled with meat and cabbage).

Typical breakfast foods in Russia include eggs, porridge, sausages, cheese, bread, butter, and jam. Most of the people eat their main meal at midday. It consists of a salad or appetizer; soup; meat or fish with potatoes or *kasha* (cooked buckwheat); and dessert, such as stewed fruit or pastries. In the evening, most Russians eat a light supper.

Russians drink large quantities of tea, but coffee has become popular, especially among urban Russians. *Kvass,* a beerlike beverage made from fermented black bread, is especially popular in summer. Russians also enjoy soft drinks, juices, and mineral water.

Vodka is Russia's trademark alcoholic beverage. Russians also drink wine, champagne, cognac, beer, and other alcoholic beverages. Alcohol abuse has been and remains a major social problem in Russia.

Health care in the Soviet Union was free. The Russian government remains committed to meeting the basic health-care needs of its people. An insurance program to finance health care was introduced in 1993. A private health-care sector has begun to grow. Russia has many doctors, nurses, and health-care facilities. However,

© TNT Magazine/Alamy Images

At indoor markets, Russian farmers sell produce to city dwellers. The fruits and vegetables are often fresher than those found in urban stores but also often more expensive. This market is in Irkutsk, a city in southern Siberia.

Tennis is an increasingly popular sport in Russia. Several Russian tennis players have become world-famous athletes. In the photo shown here, an instructor at a private tennis school demonstrates a stance for a young student.

© Maxim Marmur, AFP/Getty Images

tight government budgets for health care, shortages of medicines and equipment, low wages for health-care providers, and bureaucracy continue to create problems. Conditions in rural areas are worse than in the cities.

Recreation. Russians enjoy watching television, reading, playing chess, seeing motion pictures and plays, visiting museums, walking, and taking part in sports. The government actively promotes athletic activities, especially team sports. Soccer is the most popular participant and spectator sport in Russia. Other popular sports include gymnastics, basketball, and such winter sports as hockey, ice skating, and skiing. Tennis is growing in popularity.

Russia has many athletic clubs, stadiums, recreational centers, and other sporting facilities. Schools provide physical education at all levels. There are also special sports camps and clubs for children and adults.

The people of Russia are avid nature lovers, and they enjoy spending time in the countryside. Many Russians have country cottages called *dachas.* There, they garden, hike, bicycle, swim, fish, gather mushrooms, and take part in other outdoor activities.

The majority of Russia's people vacation in the summer. Price increases, an end to government support, and ethnic unrest have made vacationing away from home more difficult for many Russians. However, resort areas along the Black Sea, the Baltic Sea, and the Volga River—and in Siberia—remain popular destinations.

Religion. The Russian Orthodox Church is the largest religious denomination in the country. January 7, the Russian Orthodox Christmas, is a national holiday. In addition to Russian Orthodoxy, religions that have full freedom in Russia include Buddhism, Islam, Judaism, and certain Christian denominations. These religions enjoy full freedom because they were recognized by the state prior to the fall of the Soviet Union.

Religions that were not registered in Russia prior to the fall of the Soviet Union face certain restrictions. Many of these religions conduct intense recruiting efforts in Russia. Restricted religions include Baptists, Mormons, Pentecostalists, Roman Catholics, and Seventh-day Adventists. These groups must register annually for 15 years before they are allowed to participate in such activities as publishing religious literature and operating religious schools. However, the Russian government has not strictly enforced the law.

Education. The Soviet government controlled education and considered it a major vehicle of social advancement. As a result, almost all Russians can read and write. Today, public education in Russia remains free for all citizens. New private schools are also opening. The Soviet government had banned such schools. Russian educators are changing the school curriculum to better prepare students for the new economy. They are also trying to satisfy the needs of Russia's many nationality groups.

All children attend school for 11 years, from age 6 to 17. Elementary education includes nine primary and intermediate grades. When pupils finish ninth grade, they may choose to complete their schooling by enrolling in a secondary school or vocational school. The secondary schools emphasize science and mathematics. They also teach language, literature, history, social sciences, and physical education. English is the most widely taught foreign language. The vocational schools prepare young people for careers as technicians or in various branches of industry and agriculture.

Starting with the intermediate grades, pupils must pass annual exams to advance to the next grade. Students who pass a national examination upon the completion of secondary school receive a certificate, and those who score well also get a gold or silver medal. Schools use a number grading scale of 1 to 5, with 5 being the highest.

Many gifted children attend special schools. These schools stress individual subjects, such as mathematics or physics, languages, or the arts. Russia also has schools for children with physical disabilities or learning differences.

Students must pass an entrance exam to be admitted to a university or other institution of higher education. Russia has hundreds of institutions of higher education equivalent to colleges and universities. Important universities include Lomonosov Moscow State University and St. Petersburg State University.

Museums and libraries. The people of Russia spend more time in museums than do the people of the United States or most European countries. Russia has hundreds of museums. The State Historical Museum in Moscow is the country's chief historical museum. Several museums deal with the Russian Revolution. They include Moscow's State Central Museum of Contemporary History of Russia, commonly called the Revolution Museum. The Hermitage Museum in St. Petersburg has one of the largest art collections in the world.

Russia has thousands of libraries. Most towns and large villages have a public library. There are also libraries that specialize in particular subjects and libraries run by factories, schools, labor unions, and professional and civic organizations. The Russian State Library in Moscow is the largest library in Russia. Other major libraries in Moscow include the All-Russian State Library of Foreign Literature, the Institute of Scientific Information for Social Sciences of the Russian Academy of Sciences, the State Historical Public Library, and the library at Lomonosov Moscow State University. St. Petersburg is home to the National Library of Russia and the Library of the Russian Academy of Sciences.

The arts

The arts in Russia date back to the earliest days of the country. But Russian artists did not produce internationally recognized works in many fields until the early 1800's. Throughout much of the 1800's and the early 1900's, Russia became an international leader in classical music, ballet, drama, and literature. Several Russian painters and sculptors also gained worldwide fame.

This section discusses Russian architecture, music, ballet, painting, and sculpture. For information on Russian drama and literature, see **Russian literature** with its list of *Related articles.*

Architecture in Russia has been shaped by religious and Western influences combined with local traditions. About 988, Grand Prince Vladimir I, ruler of the state of Kievan Rus, was converted to the Byzantine (Eastern Orthodox Christian) faith. For hundreds of years, Russian architecture reflected the influence of the Byzantine style. The most important structures were churches, which had distinctive onion-shaped domes. The best-known Byzantine church is St. Basil's Cathedral in Moscow, built by Czar Ivan IV (also called Ivan the Terrible), from 1555 to 1560. See **Byzantine art.**

In 1682, Peter I, also known as Peter the Great, became czar. Peter introduced Western European artistic styles into Russia. He founded the city of St. Petersburg in 1703 and brought Western European architects and artists to help design it. Many of the buildings dating from his reign and through the mid-1700's were designed in the Western European Baroque style by Italian and French architects. A famous example is the Great Palace, which was begun in the early 1700's at Peterhof (now Petrodvorets), near St. Petersburg.

Among the most widely recognized architectural works in Russia are the buildings within the enclosed fortress in Moscow called the Kremlin. The Kremlin includes churches, palaces, and other buildings erected from the late 1400's to the mid-1900's. Some Kremlin buildings house Russia's government, and others serve as museums.

Music. Until the mid-1700's, Russian music consisted almost entirely of vocal music sung in church worship services and of folk music, which was also mainly vocal. Nonreligious music began to flower during the reign of Elizabeth, the empress of Russia from 1741 to 1762. She established the Academy of Arts in 1757, which taught music. Italian opera became popular during her reign. The popularity of music in Russia expanded further during the reign of Catherine II, known as Catherine the Great, who ruled from 1762 to 1796. The earliest written collection of Russian folk songs appeared in four vol-

Steve Raymer, Black Star

The Hermitage Museum in St. Petersburg is Russia's largest art museum. Its outstanding collection includes numerous masterpieces of ancient Greek and Roman art, Islamic art, Baroque and Renaissance paintings and sculpture, and French Impressionist paintings.

Kurt Scholz, Shostal

St. Basil's Cathedral in Moscow has colorful onion-shaped domes that have made it one of the most widely recognized buildings in Russia. The Byzantine-style cathedral was built from 1555 to 1560 by Czar Ivan IV (also called Ivan the Terrible).

umes published between 1776 and 1795.

Mikhail Glinka is credited with founding a distinctively Russian school of classical music in the early and middle 1800's. He blended folk songs and religious music into his works and also introduced subjects from Russian history. His most influential work is probably his second opera, *Ruslan and Lyudmila* (1842), based on a fairy tale written by the Russian poet Alexander Pushkin.

By the late 1800's, Russian music flourished. Such composers as Modest Mussorgsky, Nikolai Rimsky-Korsakov, Peter Ilich Tchaikovsky, and Alexander Borodin wrote operas and instrumental music. Much of their work was based on Russian history and folklore. In the early 1900's, Sergei Rachmaninoff and Igor Stravinsky gained international fame for their musical compositions. Stravinsky wrote several influential ballet scores, including *The Firebird* (1910), *Petrouchka* (1911), and *The Rite of Spring* (1913). See the list of Russian composers in the *Related articles* section of **Classical music.**

Ballet. Russian ballet became internationally famous starting in the mid-1800's. The leading ballet companies that continue to perform today are the Mariinsky Ballet (once known as the Russian Imperial Ballet, and then as the Kirov Ballet) of St. Petersburg and the Bolshoi Ballet of Moscow. See **Ballet** (History); **Ballets Russes; Bolshoi Ballet.**

Painting and sculpture. Until the early 1900's, the most important Russian paintings were created for religious purposes. Russian artists decorated the interiors of churches with wallpaintings and mosaics. Stylized paintings called *icons* were produced for many centuries. An icon is a religious painting considered sacred in Eastern Orthodox Christianity. Icons were produced according to strict rules established by the church, and their style changed little over the years. See **Icon.**

By the mid-1800's, Moscow and St. Petersburg had busy art schools. Russian artists also began to create paintings and sculptures on more varied subjects.

A burst of creativity in Russian art exploded during the years before the start of World War I in 1914. Russian artists were strongly influenced by the modern art movements emerging in Western Europe. The painters Marc Chagall, Alexei von Jawlensky, and Wassily Kandinsky eventually settled in Western Europe.

Artists who remained in Russia developed two major art movements, *suprematism* and *constructivism.* Both movements produced paintings that were *abstract*—that is, they had no recognizable subject matter. The leading suprematist was Kasimir Malevich. The major constructivists included Naum Gabo, Antoine Pevsner, and Vladimir Tatlin. See **Malevich, Kasimir; Chagall, Marc; Gabo, Naum; Kandinsky, Wassily; Pevsner, Antoine.**

The Trinity by Andrei Rublev; Tretyakov Gallery, Moscow

Religious paintings called *icons* dominated Russian art from the late 900's to the late 1600's. Icons were created for Russian Orthodox worship services and were considered sacred.

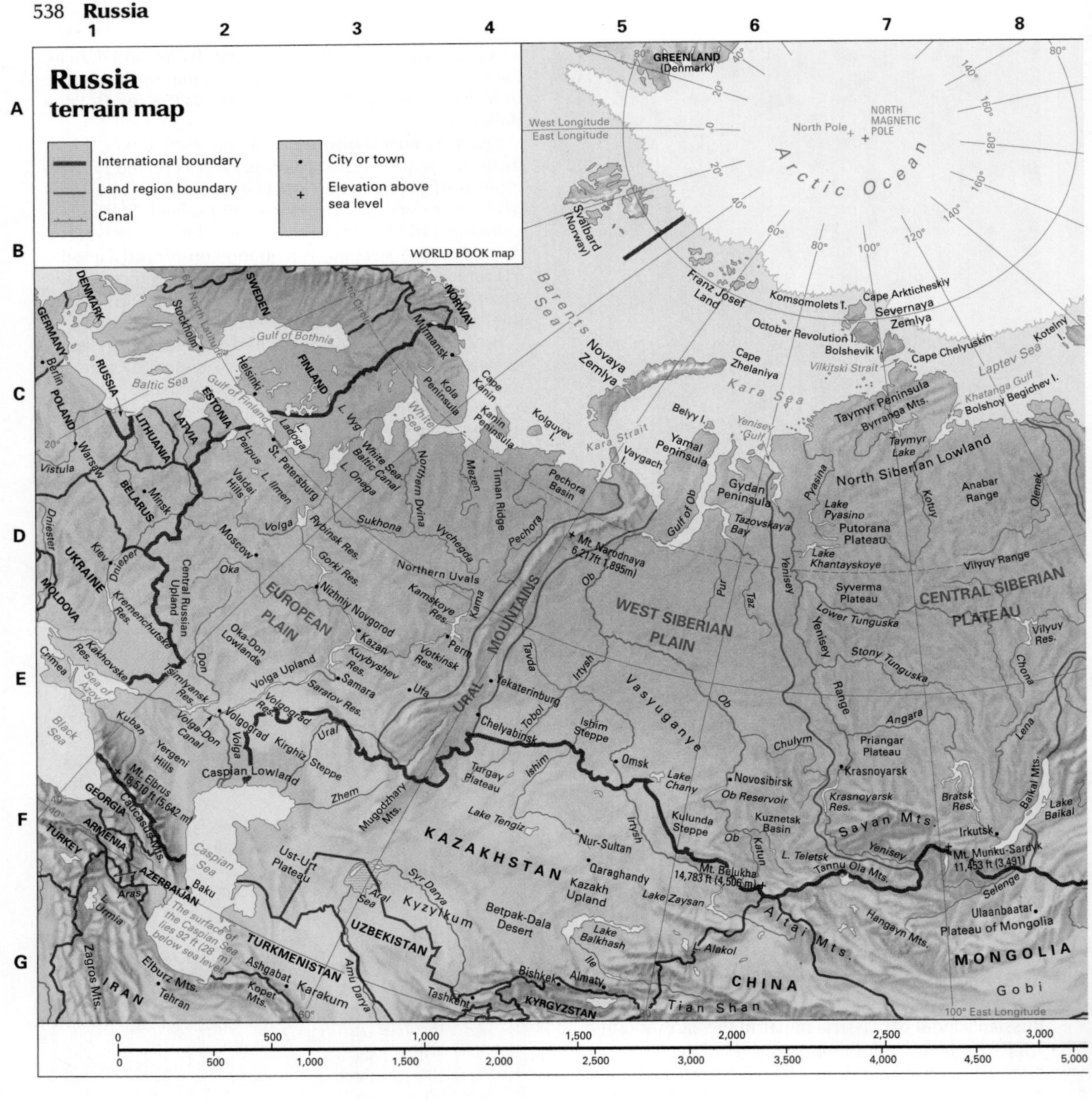

Physical features

Aldan Mountains........E 10
Aldan River..............E 10
Amga River..............E 9
Amgun River.............E 11
Amur River..............F 10
Anabar Range (mountains)............D 8
Anadyr Range (mountains)............B 10
Anadyr River.............B 11
Angara River.............E 7
Argun River..............F 9
Ayon Island..............B 10
Baikal Mountains........F 8
Barents Sea..............B 4
Bear Island...............B 10
Belyy Island..............C 6
Bering Strait.............A 11
Black Sea................E 1
Bolshoy Begichev Island..................C 8
Bratsk Reservoir.........F 7
Bureya River.............F 10
Byrranga Mountains.....C 7
Caspian Lowland.........F 2
Caspian Sea..............F 2
Caucasus Mountains.....F 1
Central Russian Upland.................D 2
Cherskiy Range (mountains)............D 10
Chona River..............E 8
Chukchi Sea..............A 10
Chukotsk Mountains.....B 10
Chulym River............F 6
Commander Islands.....C 12
Don River................E 2
Dzugdzhur Range (mountains)............E 10
East Siberian Sea........B 10
Franz Josef Land (islands)...............B 6
Gorki Reservoir..........D 3
Gulf of Anadyr...........B 11
Gulf of Ob................D 5
Gydan Peninsula.........D 6
Indigirka River...........C 10
Irtysh River..............E 5
Ishim River...............F 4
Ishim Steppe.............E 5
Kama River..............E 4
Kamchatka Peninsula....D 12
Kamskoye Reservoir.....D 4
Kanin Peninsula..........C 4
Kara Sea.................G 6
Kara Strait...............C 5
Khatanga Gulf............C 8
Klyuchevskaya (volcano)...............C 12
Kola Peninsula...........C 4
Kolguyev Island..........C 4
Kolyma Lowland.........C 10
Kolyma Mountains.......C 11
Kolyma River............C 10
Komsomolets Island.....B 7
Koryak Mountains.......B 11
Kotelny Island............C 8
Kotuy River..............D 7
Krasnoyarsk Reservoir..F 7
Kulunda Steppe..........F 5
Kuril Islands..............E 12
Kuybyshev Reservoir....E 3
Kuznetsk Basin...........F 6
Lake Baikal...............F 8
Lake Chany..............F 5
Lake Ilmen...............D 2
Lake Ladoga.............C 3
Lake Onega..............D 3
Lake Peipus..............C 2
Lake Teletsk.............F 6
Laptev Sea...............C 8
Laptev Strait.............C 9
Lena Plateau.............E 9
Lena River...............E 9
Longa Strait..............B 10
Lower Tunguska River...E 7
Maya River...............D 10
Mezen River.............D 4
Mount Elbrus............F 1
Mount Munku-Sardyk...F 7
Mount Narodnaya.......D 5
Mount Pobeda...........C 10
New Siberian Islands....C 9
North Siberian Lowland...............D 7
Northern Dvina River....D 3
Northern Uvals (hills).....D 4
Novaya Sibir Island......B 9
Novaya Zemlya (island)..C 5
Ob Reservoir............F 6
Ob River.................E 6
October Revolution Island..................B 6
Oka River................D 2
Oka-Don Lowlands......E 2
Okhota River.............D 10
Olenek River.............D 8
Oloyskiy Mountains......C 11
Omolon River............C 10
Onon River..............F 9
Pechora Basin...........D 5
Pechora River............D 4
Prianger Plateau.........F 7
Putorana Plateau.........D 7
Pyasina River............D 6
Sakhalin Island...........E 11
Sayan Mountains........F 7
Sea of Azov..............E 1
Sea of Japan (East Sea)...G 12
Sea of Okhotsk...........D 11
Severnaya Zemlya (islands)................B 7
Shantar Island...........E 11
Shelikhova Gulf..........C 11
Shilka River..............F 9

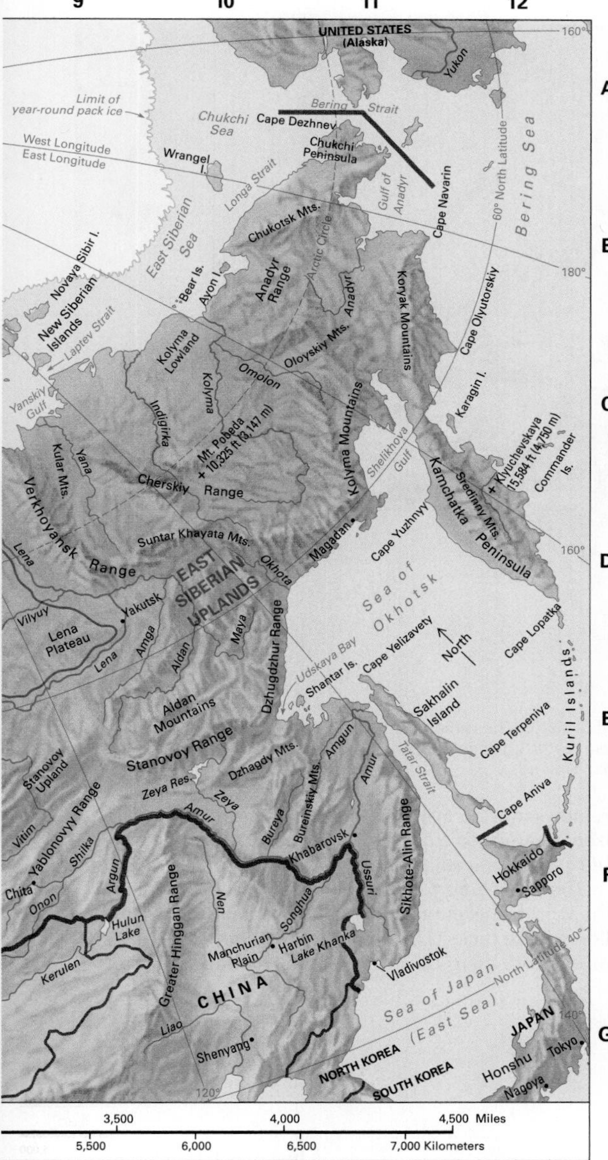

Land and climate

Russia is the largest country in the world. It has an area of 6,601,670 square miles (17,098,246 square kilometers), almost twice that of Canada, the second largest country. A train trip between Moscow in the west and Vladivostok in the east takes seven days and passes through eight time zones, including that of Moscow.

Land regions. Many scientists divide Russia into four zones according to soil conditions and plant life, which are based mainly on climate. The zones form broad belts across Russia, and no sharp transitions separate them. From north to south, the zones are (1) the tundra, (2) the forest zone, (3) the steppes, and (4) the semidesert and mountainous zone.

The tundra lies in the northernmost part of Russia. It is largely a treeless plain. The tundra has short summers and long, severe winters. About half the region has permanently frozen soil called *permafrost*. Few people live in this bleak area. Plant life consists chiefly of low shrubs, dwarf trees, and moss. Animals of the tundra include reindeer, Arctic foxes, ermines, hares, and lemmings. Waterfowl live near the Arctic Ocean in summer.

The forest belt lies south of the tundra. The northern part of this belt is called the *taiga*. It consists of *coniferous* (cone-bearing) trees, such as cedar, fir, pine, and spruce. This area has poor, ashy soil, known as *podzol*, that makes it largely unfit for agriculture. Farther south, the coniferous forests give way to mixed forests of conifers, aspen, birch, elm, maple, oak, and other species. The soils in this zone support agriculture in some areas, and the area has a mild, moist climate. Brown bears, deer, elk, lynx, reindeer, and smaller animals, such as beavers, rabbits, and squirrels, roam the forests.

The steppes are grassy plains that stretch across Russia south of the forests. The northern part of the steppe zone consists of wooded plains and meadows. The massive southern part is largely a treeless prairie. The best soils in Russia—brown soil and black, rich soil called *chernozem*—are found there. Most of the steppe zone is farmland. Birds, squirrels, and mouselike mammals called *jerboas* live in the steppes. Antelope inhabit the eastern steppes.

The semidesert and mountainous zone, the southernmost zone in Russia, has diverse soils and climate due to variations in elevation. It includes the dry, semidesert lowlands near the Caspian Sea, as well as the lush vegetation and mild climate of the Caucasus Mountains.

Geologists also divide Russia into five land regions that differ from the soil and vegetation zones. From west to east, the regions are (1) the European Plain, (2) the Ural Mountains, (3) the West Siberian Plain, (4) the Central Siberian Plateau, and (5) the East Siberian Uplands.

The European Plain makes up most of the European part of Russia. It is the most densely populated region in the country. The European Plain is predominantly flat, averaging about 600 feet (180 meters) above sea level. Most of the nation's industries are there, but the region is poor in natural resources. Forests cover much of the northern European Plain. The southern part is largely cropland. The plain is home to a variety of animal life. The Caucasus Mountains rise at the southern edge of the plain, between the Black and the Caspian seas. The mountains include 18,510-foot (5,642-meter) Mount El-

Sikhote-Alin Range (mountains)............F 11
Stanovoy Range (mountains)............E 10
Stanovoy Upland.........E 9
Stony Tunguska River ...E 7
Sukhona River...........D 3
Suntar Khayata Mountains.............D 10
Syverma Plateau.........D 7
Tatar Strait...............E 11
Tavda River..............E 4
Taymyr Lake.............C 7
Taymyr Peninsula........C 7
Taz River.................D 6
Tazovskaya Bay..........D 6
Tobol River..............E 4
Tsimlyansk Reservoir....E 2
Udskaya Bay.............E 10
Ural River.................E 3
Ussuri River..............F 11
Valdai Hills...............D 2
Vasyuganye (marshes)...E 5
Verkhoyansk Range (mountains)............D 9
Vilkitski Strait............C 7
Vilyuy Range (mountains)............D 8
Vilyuy Reservoir.........E 8
Vilyuy River..............D 9
Vitim River...............F 9
Volga River ....E 2
Volga Upland ....E 2
Volga-Don Canal.........E 2
Volgograd Reservoir ....E 2
White Sea................C 3
White Sea-Baltic Canal..................C 3
Wrangel Island ....A 10
Yablonovyy Range (mountains)............F 9
Yamal Peninsula ....C 6
Yana River ....C 9
Yanskiy Gulf ....C 9
Yenisey Gulf ....C 6
Yenisey Range (mountains)............E 6
Yenisey River............D 6
Zeya Reservoir ....E 10
Zeya River ....F 10

© Patrick David, Sipa Press

The East Siberian Uplands are mainly a wilderness of mountains and plateaus. The region has valuable mineral resources, but its harsh climate makes it difficult to use them. Small towns, such as the one shown here, are sparsely scattered throughout the East Siberian Uplands.

brus, the highest point in Europe.

The Ural Mountains form the traditional boundary between the European and Asian parts of Russia. These mountains, worn down by streams, reach an average height of only about 2,000 feet (610 meters). The middle and southern Ural Mountains are rich in deposits of iron, copper, and other metals. The middle section is the region's most heavily populated and highly industrialized area. Major cities in the region include Yekaterinburg and Chelyabinsk.

The West Siberian Plain is the largest level region in the world. This enormous plain covers more than 1 million square miles (2.6 million square kilometers) and rises no more than 500 feet (150 meters) above sea level.

© Bill Swersey, Liaison Agency

A belt of rich farmland stretches across Russia from east to west. In this photograph, farmworkers harvest potatoes on the European Plain. This mainly flat landform makes up most of the European part of Russia.

It is drained by the Ob River system, which flows northward into the Arctic Ocean. But drainage is poor, and the plain is marshy. The West Siberian Plain is rich in oil and natural gas deposits, and it is being developed rapidly. Cropland covers the southern-most part of the plain. The cities of Novosibirsk and Omsk are in this region.

The Central Siberian Plateau slopes upward toward the south from coastal plains along the Arctic Ocean. It has an average height of about 2,000 feet (610 meters). Streams cut deeply through the region. The Sayan and Baikal mountains rise more than 11,000 feet (3,350 meters) along the plateau's southern edge. Thick pine forests cover much of the Central Siberian Plateau, and its climate reaches extremes of heat and cold. The region has a wide variety of rich mineral deposits. Krasnoyarsk and Irkutsk are its largest cities.

The East Siberian Uplands are mainly a wilderness of mountains and plateaus. The mountains rise to 10,000 feet (3,000 meters) and form part of a series of ranges along the eastern coast of Asia and some offshore islands. About 25 active volcanoes are found on the Kamchatka Peninsula. The tallest volcano, snow-capped Klyuchevskaya, rises 15,584 feet (4,750 meters). The region has valuable mineral resources, but its harsh climate makes it difficult to tap them. Vladivostok on the Pacific Ocean and Khabarovsk on the Amur River are the region's most important cities.

Rivers and lakes. Russia's many large rivers have served as important means of communication and commerce. The construction of canals further improved these activities.

The Lena River in Siberia, 2,734 miles (4,400 kilometers) long, is Russia's longest river. It empties into the Arctic Ocean. Other major rivers in Siberia include the Amur, Ob, and Yenisey rivers, all frozen seven to nine months a year. The Volga River is the longest river in European Russia. It originates in the Valdai Hills northwest of Moscow and flows 2,300 miles (3,700 kilometers) to the Caspian Sea. The Volga freezes for about three months each year. Other important rivers in European Russia include the Don and the Northern Dvina.

Russia has about 200,000 lakes. The Caspian Sea, a saltwater lake 92 feet (28 meters) below sea level, is the world's largest inland body of water. It touches the southern part of European Russia. Lake Ladoga, near St. Petersburg, covers 6,835 square miles (17,703 square kilometers). It is the largest lake entirely in Europe. Lake Baikal, near the Baikal Mountains, is the deepest lake in the world. It plunges 5,315 feet (1,620 meters) deep.

A thick forest blankets the northern part of Russia from Europe to the Pacific Ocean. It covers much of Siberia. Few people live in this vast area.

ITAR-Tass from Sovfoto

© Paolo Koch, Photo Researchers

Lake Baikal, the deepest lake in the world, lies in Siberia. It has a depth of 5,315 feet (1,620 meters). A small community, *right,* is nestled between Lake Baikal and the surrounding mountains.

Climate. Russia is known for its long and bitter winters. The country's harsh climate helped stop various invaders during its history, including the large armies of Napoleon in 1812 and of Adolf Hitler in 1941 and 1942. In the Moscow region, snow covers the ground for about five months each year. In the northernmost part of Russia, snow abounds for eight to nine months a year. Half the land has permafrost beneath the surface. Russia's main cropland, in the southwest part of the country, has a short growing season and insufficient rainfall. Most of the coastal waters, lakes, and rivers freeze for much of the year.

Russia's weather varies from extremely cold to extremely hot. Northeastern Siberia is one of the coldest regions in the world. January temperatures there average below −50 °F (−46 °C). Temperatures as low as −90 °F (−68 °C) have been recorded. The average July temperature in this region is 60 °F (16 °C), but it can climb to nearly 100 °F (38 °C). No other part of the world registers such a wide range of temperatures.

Precipitation (rain, melted snow, and other forms of moisture) is light to moderate. The European Plain and parts of the East Siberian Uplands receive the most rain. Vast inland areas get little rain. The heaviest snowfalls—up to 4 feet (120 centimeters) of snow a year—occur in western and central Siberia.

ITAR-Tass from Sovfoto

Winters are long and cold in most parts of Russia. Snow covers the ground in the Moscow region for about five months each year. This photograph shows a Moscow street in winter.

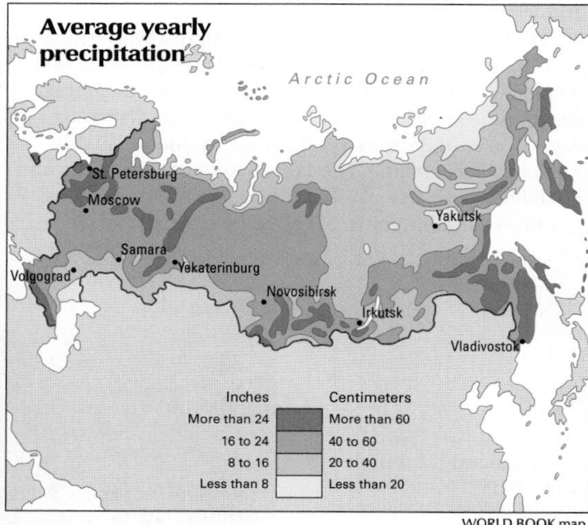

WORLD BOOK map

Rainfall in Russia is heaviest on the European Plain, in parts of the East Siberian Uplands, and in mountainous regions along the southern border. Vast areas of the interior get little rain.

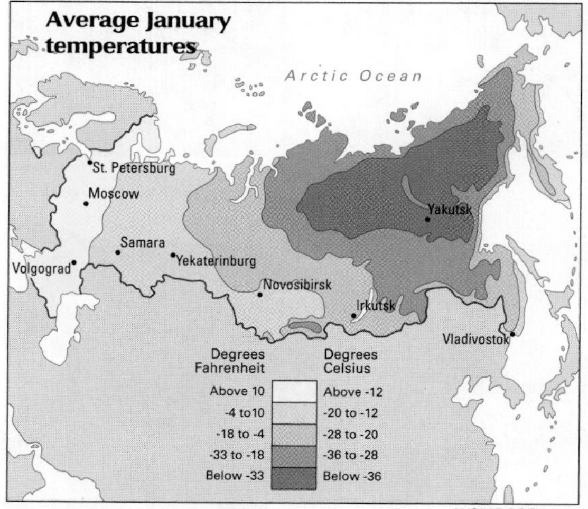

WORLD BOOK map

January temperatures in eastern Siberia are among the coldest in the world, dropping as low as −90 °F (−68 °C). January temperatures in Russia average above 10 °F (−12 °C) only in the westernmost part of the country.

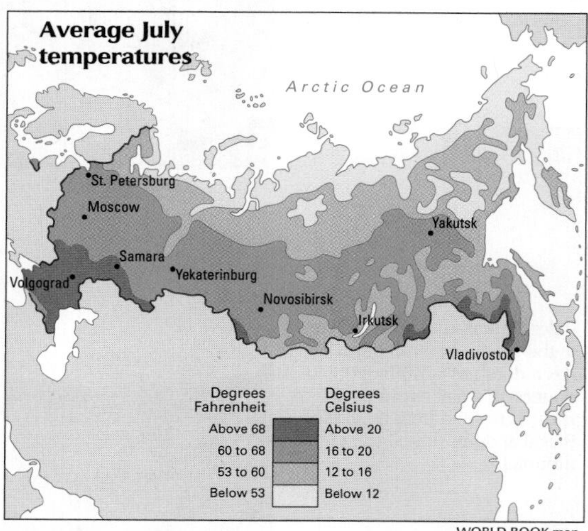

WORLD BOOK map

July temperatures in Russia vary widely. Most of the country has an average July temperature above 60 °F (16 °C), but temperatures can hit almost 100 °F (38 °C) in northeastern Siberia and drop below 32 °F (0 °C) on islands in the Arctic Ocean.

Economy

Since the fall of the Soviet Union in 1991, Russia has worked to reform its economic system. The country has shifted from a state-controlled economy to a market-driven economy.

In the Soviet Union, central government agencies planned almost all aspects of economic life. The government owned and controlled all factories and farms, and private businesses were illegal. Soviet leaders transformed Russia from a farming country into an industrial giant. Heavy industry—such as chemicals, construction, machine tools, and steel—developed rapidly. Government ministries set production quotas and told managers what to produce and to whom to sell their goods. This planning led to rapid industrial development and impressive economic gains. But central control also suppressed new ideas and discouraged quality.

When the Soviet Union collapsed in 1991, so did Russia's economy. The most immediate problem was shortages of many goods. To overcome this situation, the new Russian government removed Soviet-era controls from the economy. The government let businesses set prices for nearly all goods and services and dropped restrictions on imports and exports. It allowed the ruble to be exchanged for other currencies at international rates.

Russia's government also *privatized* (sold to companies or individuals) many state-owned enterprises. By 1997, privately owned businesses contributed more than half of the country's *gross domestic product* (GDP)—the total value of all goods and services produced yearly. However, privatization left a small number of wealthy Russians in control of many of Russia's largest firms.

The reforms brought goods back to the shops, but prices skyrocketed. The Russian government struggled to get inflation and the country's budget deficit under control. In 1998, the country experienced a major financial crisis. The government could not pay its debts, and the value of the ruble plunged. In response, Russia's government began pursuing a more cautious economic policy. It managed the budget better, reduced public debt, and controlled inflation. As a result, the country's economy quickly recovered.

Russia's gross domestic product

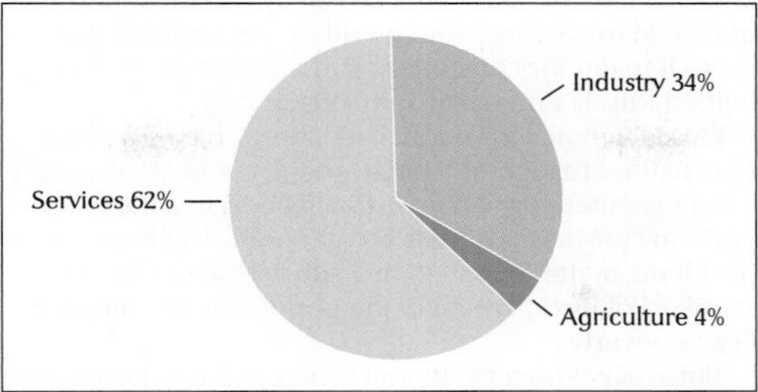

Russia's gross domestic product (GDP) was $1,578,420,000,000 in 2017. The GDP is the total value of goods and services produced within a country in a year. *Services* include community, government, and personal services; finance, insurance, real estate, and business services; trade, restaurants, and hotels; and transportation and communication. *Industry* includes construction, manufacturing, mining, and utilities. *Agriculture* includes agriculture, forestry, and fishing.

Production and workers by economic activities

Economic activities	Percent of GDP produced	Employed workers: Number of people	Employed workers: Percent of total
Community, government, & personal services	23	16,297,000	23
Trade, restaurants, & hotels	15	15,597,000	22
Manufacturing	14	10,259,000	14
Finance, insurance, real estate, & business services	14	7,986,000	11
Mining	11	1,119,000	2
Transportation & communication	10	6,689,000	9
Construction	6	6,414,000	9
Agriculture, forestry, & fishing	4	5,059,000	7
Utilities	3	2,258,000	3
Total	100	71,678,000	100

Figures are for 2017.
Sources: International Monetary Fund; Russia's Federal Service of State Statistics.

Sovfoto/Eastfoto

Mining is an important industry in Russia. The country is rich in minerals and has abundant deposits of coal, natural gas, and petroleum. A coal miner, *shown here,* operates equipment that twists coal out of the side of a coal pit in the northern Ural Mountains.

Russia's GDP grew at a steady pace through most of the 2000's. This growth was driven by increasing exports of oil and metals and high world prices for these products. Demand for consumer products also grew, which helped Russia's domestic industries.

Russia benefits from a skilled labor force and abundant natural resources. However, the country has attracted only limited foreign investments because the prospects for business success remain poor. The economic problems of the 1990's led to a substantial decline in standard of living. Much of the population continues to live in poverty.

Natural resources. Russia is one of the richest countries in terms of natural resources. It has the world's largest forest reserves, enormous energy supplies, vast stretches of farmland, extensive mineral deposits, and many potential sources of hydroelectric power. Many of its resources, however, are far from the factories where they are put to use. Russia also has a wide variety of plant and animal life.

Manufacturing accounts for about 15 percent of both Russia's GDP and its employment. Much of Russia's manufacturing takes place in the Moscow area. Heavy industry remains the most highly developed sector of the Russian economy. The machine-building industry makes a variety of heavy machinery and electrical equipment. Russia is one of the world's leading automobile manufacturers. The country also manufactures aircraft, ships, spacecraft, tractors, and trains. The chemical industry produces chemical fibers, mineral fertilizers, petrochemicals, and soda ash. Most oil refining takes place in western Siberia and in the Volga-Urals region. The construction materials industry is also important. Russia also manufactures electronics, processed foods, and textiles.

Agriculture. Russia has a large amount of farmland. But a short growing season, insufficient rainfall, and a lack of fertile soil make farming difficult. The Soviet Union's wasteful and inefficient system of state-run farms added to Russia's agricultural problems.

When the Soviet Union collapsed, Russia had about 15,000 large state-controlled farms. About half were state farms operated like government factories, called *sovkhozy.* Workers on sovkhozy received wages. The rest were collective farms called *kolkhozy,* which were government-controlled but managed in part by farmers.

The Russian government introduced a program to break up the state-controlled farms. The farms set up committees to decide how to divide the farms into producer cooperatives or joint-stock companies. Many farms were reorganized. As agricultural land was privatized, some companies created large industrial farms.

Economy of Russia

This map shows the major uses of land in Russia. The map also shows where the leading farm, fishing, mineral, and forest products are produced, and it locates the chief manufacturing centers.

ITAR-Tass from Sovfoto

Long pipelines, such as the one shown here, transport oil and gas from fields in Siberia to western Russia. The country is one of the world's leading producers of oil and gas.

Russian farmers grow many different crops. One of the main agricultural regions is the Black Earth Belt, which is a portion of the *steppes* (grassy plains) that stretches from the Ukrainian border to southwestern Siberia. This belt is famous for its dark, rich soil, known as *chernozem* (black earth). Other important farming regions include the Volga area, the northern Caucasus Mountains, and western Siberia.

Russia is one of the world's major grain producers. After years of needing to import grain during Soviet times, Russia has now become a grain exporter. Russia is one of the world's leading producers of barley, oats, potatoes, rye, sugar beets, sunflower seeds, and wheat. Russian farmers also grow many *fodder crops* (food crops for animals), fruits and vegetables, and rice. Grasses and corn are the primary fodder crops.

Livestock breeding is another important part of Russian agriculture. Cattle, chickens, hogs, and sheep are the livestock most commonly raised in the country.

Mining. Russia has vast amounts of most of the minerals used in modern industrial production. The country has abundant coal deposits and huge reserves of petroleum and natural gas. Other resources include calcium phosphate minerals and phosphorites, which are used in fertilizers, and diamonds.

Russia is a major producer of iron ore, which is mined primarily in the western and southern parts of the country. Russia is also a leading producer of nickel. Nickel is mined in the Kola Peninsula, southern Urals, and the Taymyr Peninsula. The country is also an important producer of cobalt, copper, gold, silver, tin, and

© Oleg Nikishin, Getty Images

Shoppers fill their carts at a warehouse store in Moscow. Economic reforms and a strong demand for consumer goods helped stimulate Russia's economy in 1999 and the early 2000's.

ITAR-Tass from Sovfoto

Railroads transport freight and passengers between Russia's major cities, many of which are separated by vast distances. This photograph shows a train on the Trans-Siberian Railroad, which runs between Vladivostok in the southeast and Moscow in the west.

tungsten. Other materials mined in Russia include lead, platinum, salt, and zinc. Bauxite, a material used in making aluminum, is mined in western Siberia.

Fishing industry. In the northern Barents Sea and the White Sea, Russian fishing crews catch blue whiting, cod, haddock, herring, and other fishes. Herring, pollock, and salmon are caught in the Pacific Ocean. Crews also fish in inland waterways, the Atlantic Ocean, and the Baltic and Black seas.

Caviar, the salted eggs of sturgeon, is a famous Russian delicacy. Many gourmets consider the caviar from sturgeon caught in the Caspian Sea to be the best in the world. However, overfishing has reduced the number of sturgeon in the Caspian to dangerously low levels.

Service industries are industries that provide services rather than produce goods. Service industries account for about three-fifths of both Russia's GDP and its employment. In the former Soviet Union, these industries were underdeveloped. Most service-industry workers were poorly trained and underpaid. They had little incentive to provide good service because their customers had few or no alternatives.

Today, private economic activity in the service sector flourishes. Hotels, restaurants, and retail shops benefit from the tens of millions of tourists who visit Russia each year. Many Russians work in the government, hospitals, real estate, or schools.

Energy sources. Russia has enormous natural energy reserves, especially petroleum and natural gas. The country is one of the world's largest producers of petroleum, natural gas, and coal. Much of Russia's petroleum is found in western Siberia and the Volga-Ural Oil-Gas Region. Pipelines carry oil and natural gas from western Siberia to European Russia. Much of the coal is mined from the Kuznetsk Basin.

About two-thirds of Russia's electric power is generated from coal, natural gas, and oil. Hydroelectric plants also generate electric power. In addition, Russia uses nuclear energy to generate electric power.

Trade. The Soviet Union traded mainly with Eastern European Communist countries, such as Bulgaria, Hungary, and Poland. Since the overthrow of the Communist regimes of Eastern Europe and the breakup of the Soviet Union, Russia's trade with most of those countries has become less important. Today, Russia's main trading partners are the other former Soviet republics as well as China, Finland, Germany, Italy, Japan, the Netherlands, Poland, and the United States. In 2012, after many years of negotiations, Russia joined the World Trade Organization (WTO), a group that promotes international trade.

Russia exports more than it imports. The country exports chemicals, machinery, metals, natural gas, petroleum, and wood and paper products. Major imports include chemicals, foods and beverages, machinery, and motor vehicles.

Transportation and communication. Because of Russia's vast size and harsh climate, transportation facilities and communications systems are unevenly distributed throughout the country. They are less developed than the transportation and communications networks of Western Europe, the United States, and Japan.

Truck transport has grown rapidly since the introduction of private enterprise. However, Russia's poorly developed highway network, along with the country's vast size, make truck transport difficult and costly. Railroads still handle a large amount of freight and passenger transportation in Russia, but much of the system needs modernization. A high-speed passenger rail line connects Moscow and St. Petersburg. River transportation carries only a small percentage of Russia's freight traffic, because most rivers are frozen for much of the year.

Russia inherited its national airline, Aeroflot, from the Soviet Union. Aeroflot must now compete with new, privately owned companies. Russia has international airports in Moscow, Rostov-on-Don, St. Petersburg, Vladivostok, and other cities.

Russia's most important seaports—Arkhangelsk, Kaliningrad, Murmansk, Nakhodka, Novorossiysk, St. Petersburg, and Vladivostok—handle a large portion of the country's foreign trade. However, the water at many Russian ports is frozen for many months of the year.

Public transportation is modern and inexpensive, but crowded. Several large cities, including Moscow, have clean, efficient subway systems. Buses, trams, and trolleys also operate in the cities. Bicycles are seen in large cities, but they are more common in rural and vacation areas. Horses and buggies can also be found in rural parts of Russia.

Most Russians have access to at least basic telephone service. Cellular telephone service has become popular, especially in urban areas. Internet usage is expanding as more Russians gain access to computers.

Russia's government owns or controls most of the national television and radio networks and newspapers. Hundreds of daily newspapers and thousands of other periodicals are published in Russia. The government often attempts to control or silence broadcasters and publishers that criticize it.

History

Russia's unique geographic location astride both Europe and Asia has influenced its history and shaped its destiny. Russia never has been entirely an Eastern or a Western country. As a result, Russian intellectuals have long debated the country's development and contribution to world history.

This section traces the major developments of Russian history. In 1917, revolutionaries overthrew the Russian czarist government. They changed Russia's name to the Russian Soviet Federative Socialist Republic (R.S.F.S.R.). In 1922, the R.S.F.S.R. and three other republics formed a new nation called the Union of Soviet Socialist Republics (U.S.S.R.), also known as the Soviet Union. The U.S.S.R. broke apart in 1991, and Belarus, Russia, and Ukraine invited the other republics to join a federation called the Commonwealth of Independent States. For more detailed information about this period, see **Union of Soviet Socialist Republics** (History).

Early days. Beginning about 1200 B.C., the Cimmerians, a Balkan people, lived north of the Black Sea in what is now southern Ukraine. Around 700 B.C., the Scythians, a nomadic people from central Asia, defeated the Cimmerians and drove them south. The Scythians controlled the region until about 200 B.C. They fell to the Sarmatians, an Iranian people. The Scythians and Sarmatians lived in close contact with Greek colonies—later controlled by the Romans—along the northern coast of the Black Sea. They absorbed many Greek and Roman ways of life through trade, marriage, and other contacts. See **Cimmerians**.

Germanic tribes from the west, called the Goths, conquered the region about A.D. 200. The Goths ruled the region until about 370, when they were defeated by the Huns, a warlike Asian people. The Hun empire broke up after their leader, Attila, died in 453. The Avars, a tribe related to the Huns, began to rule the region in the mid-500's. The Khazars, another Asian people, won the southern Volga and northern Caucasus regions in the mid-600's. King Bulan led the conversion of Khazars to Judaism. The Khazars established a busy trade with other peoples. See **Goths; Huns.**

By the 800's, Slavic groups had built many towns in eastern Europe, including what became the European part of Russia. They had also developed an active trade. No one knows where the Slavs came from. Some historians believe they came in the 400's from what is now Poland. Others think the Slavs were farmers in the Black Sea region under Scythian rule or earlier. Slavs of what are now Belarus, Russia, and Ukraine became known as East Slavs. See **Slavs.**

The earliest written Russian history of the 800's is the *Primary Chronicle,* written in Kiev, probably in 1111. It says that quarreling Slavic groups in the town of Novgorod (now Velikiy Novgorod) asked a Viking tribe to rule them and bring order to the land. The Vikings were called the *Varangian Russes.* Historians who accept the *Primary Chronicle* as true believe that Russia took its name from this tribe. According to the *Primary Chronicle,* a group of related Varangian families led by a prince named Rurik arrived in 862. Rurik settled in Novgorod, and the area became known as the "land of the Rus."

Many historians doubt that the Slavs of Novgorod invited the Vikings to rule them. They believe the Vikings invaded the region. Some historians claim the word *Rus,* from which Russia took its name, was the name of an early Slavic tribe in the Black Sea region. It is known, however, that the first state founded by East Slavs—called Kievan Rus—was established at present-day Kiev in the 800's. Kiev, now the capital of Ukraine, was an important trading center on the Dnieper River. Whether it had been developed by the Vikings is unclear.

The state of Kievan Rus. The *Primary Chronicle* states that Oleg, a Varangian, captured Kiev in 882 and

Important dates in Russia

A.D. 800's East Slavs established the state of Kievan Rus.
1237-1240 The Mongols conquered Russia.
c. 1318 The Mongols appointed Prince Yuri of Moscow as the Russian grand prince.
1480 Ivan III broke Mongol control over Russia.
1547 Ivan IV became the first Russian ruler to be crowned czar.
1604-1613 Russia was torn by civil war, invasion, and political confusion during the Time of Troubles.
1613 Michael Romanov became czar. He started the Romanov line of czars, which ruled until 1917.
1703 Peter I founded St. Petersburg and began building his capital there.
1812 Napoleon invaded Russia but was forced to retreat.
1861 Alexander II freed the serfs.
1905 Japan defeated Russia in the Russo-Japanese War. A revolution forced Czar Nicholas II to form a parliament.
1914-1917 Russia fought Germany and Austria-Hungary in World War I.
1917 The February Revolution overthrew Czar Nicholas II. The Bolsheviks (who were later called Communists) seized power in the October Revolution. V. I. Lenin became head of the government. Russia withdrew from World War I.
1918-1920 The Communists defeated their anti-Communist opponents in a civil war.
1922 The U.S.S.R. was established.
1941-1945 The U.S.S.R. fought Germany in World War II.
1957 The U.S.S.R. launched Sputnik 1, the first artificial satellite.
1991 Communist rule ended, and the Soviet Union was dissolved. Russia and the other Soviet republics became independent nations.

ruled as its prince. During the 900's, the other *principalities* (regions ruled by a prince) of Kievan Rus recognized Kiev's major importance. Kiev lay on the main trade route connecting the Baltic Sea with the Black Sea and the Byzantine Empire. In addition, Kiev's forces defended Kievan Rus against invading tribes from the south and east. The ruler of Kiev came to be called *grand prince* and ranked above the other princes of Kievan Rus.

About 988, Grand Prince Vladimir I *(Volodymyr* in Ukrainian) became a Christian. At that time, the East Slavs worshiped the forces of nature. Vladimir made Christianity the state religion, and most people under his rule turned Christian. Vladimir later became a saint of the Russian Orthodox Church.

Several grand princes were strong rulers, but Kiev's power began to decrease after the mid-1000's. The rulers of other Kievan Rus principalities grew in power, and they fought many destructive wars. In Novgorod and a few other towns with strong local governments, the princes were driven out. Badly weakened by civil wars and without strong central control, Kievan Rus fell to huge armies of Mongols called Tatars, or Tartars, who swept across Russia from the east during the 1200's (see **Tatars**).

Mongol rule. In 1237, Batu, a grandson of the conqueror Genghis Khan, led between 150,000 and 200,000 Mongol troops into Russia. The Mongols destroyed one Russian town after another. In 1240, they destroyed Kiev, and Russia became part of the Mongol Empire. It was included in a section called the Golden Horde. The capital of the Golden Horde was at Sarai, near what is now Volgograd.

Batu forced the surviving Russian princes to pledge allegiance to the Golden Horde and to pay heavy taxes. From time to time, the Mongols left their capital and wiped out the people of various areas because of their disloyalty. The Mongols also appointed the Russian grand prince and forced many Russians to serve in their armies. But they interfered little with Russian life in general. The Mongols were chiefly interested in maintaining their power and collecting taxes.

Illustration from a Russian manuscript of the 1500's; Russian State Library, Moscow (Historical Pictures Service)

The Battle of Kulikovo in 1380 was the first Russian victory over the Mongol forces. It took place near the Don River.

During the period of Mongol rule, which ended in the late 1400's, the new ideas and reforming spirit of the Renaissance were dramatically changing many aspects of life in Western Europe. But under Mongol control, Russia was to a great extent cut off from these important Western influences.

The rise of Moscow. In the early 1300's, Prince Yuri of Moscow married the sister of the Golden Horde's *khan* (ruler). Yuri was appointed the Russian grand prince about 1318. Mongol troops helped him put down threats to his leadership from other principalities. The Mongols also began letting the grand prince of Moscow collect taxes for them. This practice started with Ivan I (called the Moneybag) about 1330. Ivan kept some of the tax money. He bought much land and expanded his territory greatly. Other princes and *boyars* (high-ranking landowners) began to serve in Moscow's army and government. In addition, Ivan persuaded the chief bishop of the Russian Orthodox Church to remain in Moscow. Until then, Kiev had been the spiritual center of Russia.

Moscow grew stronger and richer as the Golden Horde grew weaker, chiefly because of struggles for leadership. In 1380, Grand Prince Dmitriy defeated a Mongol force in the Battle of Kulikovo, near the Don River. The victory briefly freed Moscow of Mongol control. The Mongols recaptured Moscow in 1382, but they no longer believed they could not be beaten.

During the late 1400's, Moscow became the most powerful Russian city. Ivan III (called Ivan the Great) won control of Moscow's main rival cities, Velikiy Novgorod and Tver, and great numbers of boyars entered his service. In 1480, Ivan made the final break from Mongol control by refusing to pay taxes to the Golden Horde. Mongol troops moved toward Moscow but turned back to defend their capital from Russian attack.

Ivan the Terrible. After the rise of Moscow, its grand prince came to be called *czar.* In 1547, Ivan IV, also known as Ivan the Terrible, became the first ruler to be crowned czar. Ivan made the power of the czar over all Russia complete.

Ivan was brutal, extremely suspicious, and perhaps, at times, insane. He formed a special police force and began a reign of terror in which he ordered the arrest and murder of hundreds of aristocrats. Ivan gave his victims' estates as payment to the *service gentry* (landowners serving in the army and government). He also established strict rules concerning the number of warriors and horses each landowner had to supply to the army. Ivan burned many towns and villages, and he killed church leaders who opposed him. In a fit of rage, Ivan even struck and killed his oldest son.

The number of service gentry increased rapidly. But their estates had no value unless the peasants remained on the land and farmed it. Ivan and later czars passed a series of laws that bound the peasants to the land as *serfs.* Serfdom became the economic basis of Russian power. The development of Russian serfdom differed sharply from changes occurring in Western Europe at the time. There, during the Renaissance, the growth of trade led to the use of money as royal payment. It also led to the disappearance of serfdom in Western Europe. See **Serf**.

Ivan fought Tatars at Astrakhan and Kazan to the southeast, and he won their lands. Russian forces then crossed the Ural Mountains and conquered western Siberia. Ivan also tried to win lands northwest to the Baltic Sea, but he was defeated by Lithuanian, Polish, and Swedish armies.

The Time of Troubles developed because of a breakdown of the czar's power after Ivan's death. Fedor I, Ivan's second son, was a weak czar. His wife's brother, Boris Godunov, became the real ruler of Russia. Fedor's younger brother, Dmitriy, was found dead in 1591, and Fedor died in 1598 without leaving a male heir.

The *zemskii sobor* (land council), a kind of parliament with little power, elected Boris czar. But a man believed to be Gregory Otrepiev, a former monk, posed as Dmitriy. This *False Dmitriy* claimed Dmitriy had not died, and he fled to Lithuania to avoid arrest. In 1604, False Dmitriy invaded Russia with Polish troops. The invaders were joined by many discontented Russians. This invasion marked the beginning of the Time of Troubles. Russia was torn by civil war, invasion, and political confusion until 1613.

False Dmitriy became czar in 1605, but a group of boyars killed him the next year. Prince Basil Shuisky then became czar. In 1610, Polish invaders occupied Moscow. They ruled through a powerless council of boyars until 1612. Meanwhile, a new False Dmitriy and a number of other pretenders to the throne won many followers. Peasant revolts swept through Russia. Landowners and frontier people called Cossacks fought each other, and sometimes joined together to fight powerful aristocrats (see **Cossacks**). The Polish control of Moscow led the Russians to unite their forces and drive out the invaders. They recaptured the capital in 1612.

Czars and empresses of Russia

Ruler	Reign	Ruler	Reign
* **Ivan IV**	1547-1584	**Peter II**	1727-1730
Fedor I	1584-1598	**Anne**	1730-1740
Boris Godunov	1598-1605	**Ivan VI**	1740-1741
Fedor II	1605	**Elizabeth**	1741-1762
False Dmitriy	1605-1606	**Peter III**	1762
Basil Shuisky	1606-1610	* **Catherine II**	1762-1796
Michael Romanov	1613-1645	**Paul**	1796-1801
Alexis	1645-1676	* **Alexander I**	1801-1825
Fedor III	1676-1682	* **Nicholas I**	1825-1855
Ivan V	1682-1696	* **Alexander II**	1855-1881
* **Peter I**	1682-1725	* **Alexander III**	1881-1894
Catherine I	1725-1727	* **Nicholas II**	1894-1917

*Has a separate article in *World Book*.

The early Romanovs. After the Poles were defeated, there was no one of royal birth to take the throne. In 1613, the zemskii sobor elected Michael Romanov czar. The Romanov czars ruled Russia for the next 300 years, until the February Revolution of 1917 ended czarist rule.

During the 1600's, Russia annexed much of Ukraine and extended its control of Siberia eastward to the Pacific Ocean. During this same period, the Russian Orthodox Church made changes in religious texts and ceremonies. People called *Old Believers* objected to these changes and broke away from the church. This group still follows the old practices today.

Peter the Great. In 1682, a struggle for power resulted in the crowning of two half brothers—Peter I (later known as Peter the Great) and Ivan V—as co-czars. Both were children, and Ivan's sister Sophia ruled as *regent* (temporary ruler) until Peter's followers forced her to retire in 1689. Peter made close contact with the many Western Europeans living in Moscow and absorbed

Oil painting (1885) by I. Repin; Tretyakov Gallery, Moscow (ITAR-Tass from Sovfoto)

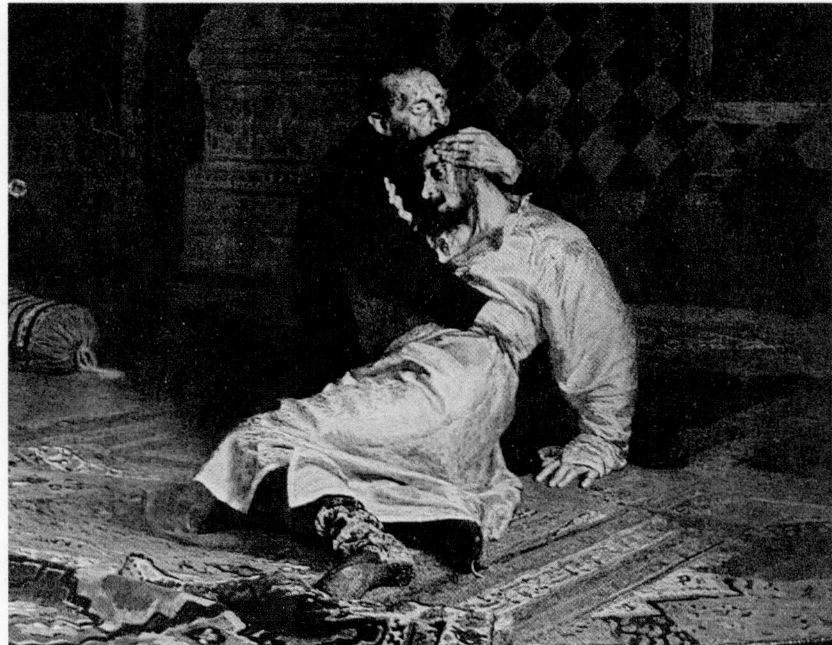

Ivan the Terrible became the first Russian ruler to be crowned czar, in 1547. He expanded Russia's territory and made Moscow his capital. This painting shows Ivan holding his son after he killed him in a fit of rage.

RIA-Novosti from Sovfoto

Peter the Great ruled Russia from 1682 until his death in 1725. Peter was a powerful ruler whose many conquests expanded Russia's empire. He also reorganized the government.

much new information from them. He came into full power in 1696, when Ivan died.

Peter was greatly influenced by ideas of commerce and government then popular in Western Europe. A powerful ruler, he improved Russia's military and made many important conquests. During Peter's reign, Russia expanded its territory to the Baltic Sea in the Great Northern War with Sweden. In 1703, Peter founded St. Petersburg on the Baltic, and he moved the capital there in 1712. After traveling throughout Europe, he introduced Western-type clothing, factories, and schools in Russia, and reorganized Russia's government to make it run more efficiently.

Peter forced Russia's nobility to adopt many Western customs. He also increased the czar's power over the aristocrats, church officials, and serfs. He dealt harshly with those who opposed these changes. Under Peter, the legal status of serfs further deteriorated.

Catherine the Great. After Peter's death in 1725, a series of struggles for the throne took place. The service gentry and the leading nobles were on opposite sides. Candidates for the throne who were supported by the service gentry won most of these struggles and rewarded their followers. The rulers increased the gentry's power over the serfs and local affairs. The gentry's enforced service to the state was gradually reduced. It was ended altogether in 1762. Later that year, Empress Catherine II, known as Catherine the Great, came to power.

Magnificent royal parties and other festivities, all in the latest Western fashion, took place during the 1700's. The arts were promoted, and many new schools were started, mainly for the upper classes. The Russian Imperial School of Ballet was founded, and Italian opera and chamber music were brought to Russia. It also became fashionable in Russia to repeat the newest Western ideas on freedom and social reform, especially during the rule of Catherine the Great. In 1767, Catherine called a large legislative assembly to reform Russian laws. However, the assembly achieved nothing.

The great majority of Russians remained in extreme poverty and ignorance during this period. In 1773 and 1774, the peasants' discontent boiled over in a revolt led by Emelian Pugachev, a Cossack. The revolt swept through Russia from the Ural Mountains to the Volga River. It spread almost to Moscow before being crushed by government troops. In 1775, Catherine further tightened the landowners' control over the serfs.

Under Catherine the Great, Russia rose to new importance as a major world power. In the late 1700's, Austria, Prussia, and Russia gradually divided Poland among themselves. Russia gained nearly all of Belarus, Lithuania, and Ukraine from Poland. In wars against the Ottoman Empire (based in present-day Turkey), Russia gained the Crimea and other Ottoman lands. Catherine died in 1796. She was succeeded by her son, Paul.

Alexander I. Paul's five-year rule ended with his murder in 1801. Alexander I, Paul's son, became czar and talked about freeing the serfs, building schools for all young Russians, and even giving up the throne and making Russia a republic. He introduced several reforms, such as freeing many political prisoners and spreading Western ways and ideas. But he did nothing to lessen the czar's total power or to end serfdom. Alexander knew that Russia's military strength and its position as a major world power depended on income that was provided by serfdom. Under Alexander's rule, Russia continued to win territory from Persia, Sweden, and the Ottoman Empire.

In June 1812, Napoleon led the Grand Army of France into Russia. He wanted to stop Russian trade with the United Kingdom, France's chief enemy, and to halt Russian expansion in the Balkan region. The French swept forward and reached Moscow in September 1812. Most people had left the city, and Napoleon and his army entered easily.

Soon afterward, fire destroyed most of Moscow. Historians believe the Russians themselves set the fire. After 35 days, the French left the city because they feared they might not survive the approaching bitter Russian winter. They began a disastrous retreat with little food and under continual attack by the Russians. Of the estimated 600,000 French troops in Russia, about 500,000 died, deserted, or were captured. Russia then became a major force in the campaign by several European countries that defeated Napoleon. See **Napoleon I** (Disaster in Russia).

Although Alexander had begun some reforms, harsh rule continued in Russia. Beginning in 1816, many young aristocrats became revolutionaries. They formed secret groups, wrote constitutions for Russia, and prepared to revolt. Alexander died in 1825, and Nicholas I became czar. In December of 1825, a group of revolutionaries, later called the *Decembrists,* took action. At the urging of the Decembrists, about 3,000 soldiers and officers gathered in Senate Square in St. Petersburg, and government troops arrived to face them. After several hours, the Decembrists fired a few shots. Government

RIA-Novosti from Sovfoto

Catherine the Great became empress of Russia in 1762. She expanded the country's territory and encouraged the development of the arts. But she preserved and extended serfdom.

cannons ended the revolt by the Decembrists.

Nicholas I. The Decembrist revolt deeply impressed and frightened Nicholas. He removed aristocrats, whom he now distrusted, from government office and replaced them with professional military officers. He tightened his control over the press and education, reduced travel outside Russia, and prohibited organizations that might have political influence. He established six special government departments. These departments, which included a secret police system, handled important economic and political matters. Through the special departments, Nicholas avoided the regular processes of Russian government and increased his control over Russian life.

In spite of Nicholas's harsh rule, the period was one of outstanding achievement in Russian literature. Nikolai Gogol, Mikhail Lermontov, Alexander Pushkin, and others wrote their finest works. Fyodor Dostoevsky, Leo Tolstoy, and Ivan Turgenev launched their careers. Many educated Russians began to debate the values of Westernized Russian life against those of old Russian life. The pro-Western group argued that Russia must learn from the West and catch up with it economically and politically. The other group argued for the old Russian ways, including the czarist system, a strong church, and the quiet life of the Russian countryside.

Nicholas became known as the "policeman of Europe" because he sent troops to put down revolutions in Poland and Hungary. Nicholas also declared himself the defender of the Eastern Orthodox Churches and fought two wars with the Muslim Ottoman Empire. In the war of 1828 and 1829, Russia gained much territory around the Black Sea. Russia also won the right to move merchant ships through the straits connecting the Black Sea with the Mediterranean Sea. The Ottoman Empire controlled these straits.

In 1853, the Crimean War broke out between Russia and the Ottoman Empire. The United Kingdom and France, which objected to Russian expansion in the Black Sea region, aided the Ottomans. Russia was defeated and signed the Treaty of Paris in 1856. This treaty forced Russia to give up some of the territory it had taken earlier from the Ottomans, and the pact forbade warships on and fortifications around the Black Sea.

Expansion in Asia. After its defeat in the Crimean War, Russia began to expand in Asia. In the Far East, Russia won disputed territories from China. In 1858 and 1860, the Chinese signed treaties giving Russia lands north of the Amur River and east of the Ussuri River. By 1864, Russian forces defeated Muslim rebels in the Caucasus. Central Asia was won during a series of military campaigns from 1865 to 1876. In 1867, Russia sold its Alaskan territory to the United States for $7,200,000.

Alexander II. Nicholas I died in 1855, during the Crimean War. His son, Alexander II, became czar. Russia's defeat in the Crimean War taught Alexander a lesson. He realized that Russia had to catch up with the West to remain a major power. Alexander began a series of reforms to strengthen the economy and Russian life in general. In 1861, he freed the serfs and distributed land among them. He began developing railroads and organizing a banking system. Alexander promoted reforms in education, reduced controls on the press, and introduced a jury system and other reforms in the courts. He also established forms of self-government in towns and villages and modernized the armed forces.

But many young Russians believed that Alexander's reforms did not go far enough. Some revolutionary groups wanted to establish socialism in Russia. Others wanted a constitution and a republic. These groups formed a number of public and secret organizations. After a revolutionary tried to kill Alexander in 1866, the czar began to weaken many of his reforms. The revolutionaries then argued that Alexander had never been a sincere reformer at all. During the mid-1870's, a group of revolutionaries tried to get the peasants to revolt. They wanted to achieve either socialism or *anarchism* (absence of government) for Russia (see **Anarchism**). After this effort failed, a terrorist group called the People's Will tried several times to kill the czar. Alexander then decided to set up a new reform program. But in 1881, he was killed by a terrorist's bomb in St. Petersburg.

Alexander III, Alexander's son, became czar and soon began a program of harsh rule. Alexander III limited the freedom of the press and of the universities, and he sharply reduced the powers of Russia's local self-governments. He set up a special bank to help the aristocrats increase their property. He also appointed officials called *land captains* from among the aristocrats and gave them much political power over the peasants. Alexander started some programs to help the peasants and industrial workers. But their living and working conditions improved little during his reign.

Nicholas II became Russia's next, and last, czar in 1894. The revolutionary movement had been kept in check until the 1890's, when a series of bad harvests caused starvation among the peasants. In addition, as industrialization increased, discontent grew among the rising middle class and workers in the cities. Discontented Russians were attracted to three political movements. (1) The *liberal constitutionalists* wanted to replace czarist rule with a Western type of parliamentary government. (2) The *populists,* who later formed the Socialist Revolutionary Party, sought to promote a revolution among rural peasants and workers in the cities. (3) The *Marxists* wanted to promote revolution among the city workers. The Marxists followed the socialist teachings of Karl Marx, a German social philosopher (see **Marx, Karl**). In 1898, the Marxists established the Russian Social Democratic Labor Party.

Between 1899 and 1904, the discontent of the Russian people increased. Worker strikes and other forms of protest took place. In 1903, the Russian Social Democratic Labor Party split into two groups—the *Bolsheviks* (members of the majority) and the *Mensheviks* (members of the minority). V. I. Lenin was the leader of the Bolsheviks, later called Communists.

The Revolution of 1905. On Jan. 22, 1905, thousands of unarmed workers marched to the czar's Winter Palace in St. Petersburg. The workers were on strike, and they planned to ask Nicholas II for reforms. Government troops fired on the crowd and killed or wounded hundreds of marchers. After this *Bloody Sunday* slaughter, the revolutionary movement, led mainly by the liberal constitutionalists, gained much strength. In February, Nicholas agreed to establish an elected lawmaking body, called the Duma, to advise him. More strikes broke out during the summer, however, and peasant and military groups revolted. In part, the growing unrest was linked to the increasingly unpopular Russo-Japanese War. This war had broken out in February 1904 after a Japanese attack on Russian ships. The war ended with Russia's defeat in September 1905.

In October 1905, a general strike paralyzed the country. Revolutionaries in St. Petersburg formed a *soviet* (council) called the Soviet of Workers' Deputies. Nicholas then granted the Duma the power to pass or reject all proposed laws. Many Russians were satisfied with this action, but others were not. The revolution continued, especially in Moscow, where the army crushed a serious uprising in December.

Each of the first two Dumas, which met in 1906 and 1907, was dissolved after a few months. The Dumas could not work with Nicholas and his high-ranking officials, who refused to give up much power. Nicholas illegally changed the election law and made the selection of Duma candidates less democratic. The peasants and workers were allowed far fewer representatives in the Duma than the upper classes. The third Duma served from 1907 to 1912, and the fourth Duma met from 1912 to 1917. During this period, Russia made important advances in the arts, education, farming, and industry.

World War I. By the time World War I began in 1914, Europe was divided into two tense armed camps. On one side was the Triple Entente (Triple Agreement), consisting of Russia, France, and the United Kingdom. Russia and France had agreed in 1894 to defend each other against attack. France and the United Kingdom had signed the Entente Cordiale (Friendly Understanding) in 1904, and Russia had signed a similar agreement with the United Kingdom in 1907. The Triple Entente developed from these treaties. Fighting against the Triple Entente was the Triple Alliance, which was an alliance formed in 1882 by Austria-Hungary, Germany, and Italy.

On Aug. 1, 1914, Germany declared war on Russia. Soon afterward, Russia changed the German-sounding name of St. Petersburg to Petrograd. German troops crushed the Russian army at Tannenberg, in East Prussia. However, the Russians defeated an Austrian army in the Battles of Lemberg in the Galicia region of Austria-Hungary, near present-day Lviv, Ukraine.

In 1915, Austrian and German forces drove back the Russians. The next year, the Russians attacked along a 70-mile (113-kilometer) front in Galicia. They advanced about 50 miles (80 kilometers). Russian troops moved into the Carpathian Mountains in 1917, but the Germans

Expansion of Russia

This map shows the increase in territory that took place in Russia between 1462 and 1914. Russia gained these lands through wars, conquests, and annexations. The boundary of present-day Russia appears as a solid red line on the map.

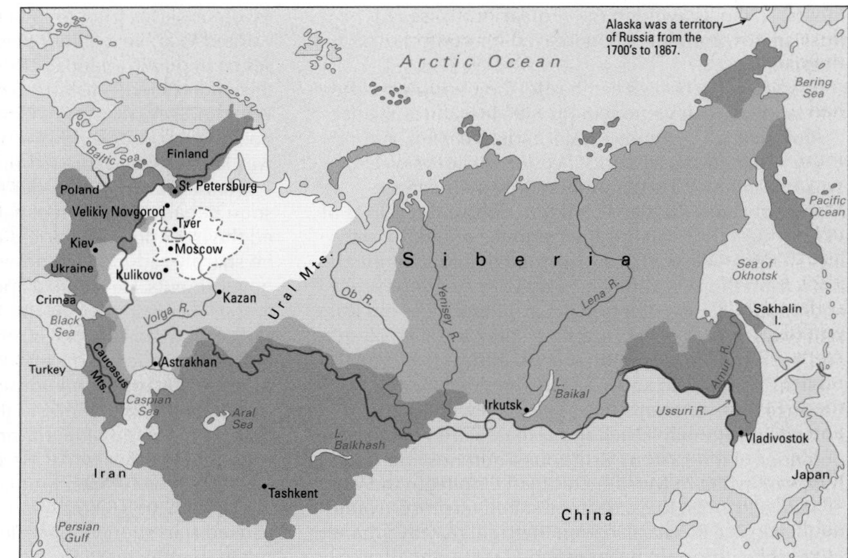

WORLD BOOK map

Sovfoto

V. I. Lenin, *with raised arm,* led the Bolshevik take-over of the Russian government in the October Revolution of 1917. He became the first leader of the Soviet Union.

pushed them back. For more information on Russia's role in the war, see **World War I.**

The February Revolution. During World War I, the Russian economy could not meet the needs of both the soldiers and the people at home. The railroads carried military supplies and could not serve the cities. The people suffered severe shortages of food, fuel, and housing. Russian troops at the front were loyal, but the untrained soldiers behind the fighting lines began to question the war. They knew they would probably be sent to the front and be killed. The soldiers and civilians behind the lines grew increasingly dissatisfied.

By the end of 1916, almost all educated Russians opposed the czar. Nicholas had removed many capable executives from high government offices and replaced them with weak, unpopular officials. He was accused of crippling the war effort by such acts. Many Russians blamed his action on the influence of Grigori Rasputin, adviser to the czar and the czarina. The royal couple believed that Rasputin was a holy man who was saving their sick son's life. In December 1916, a group of nobles murdered Rasputin. But the officials who supposedly had been appointed through his influence remained.

In March 1917, the people of Russia revolted. (The month was February in the old Russian calendar, which was replaced in 1918.) Violent riots and strikes over shortages of bread and coal accompanied the uprising in Petrograd, the capital of Russia. (Petrograd was known as St. Petersburg until 1914, was renamed Leningrad in 1924, and again became St. Petersburg in 1991.) Nicholas ordered the Duma to dissolve itself, but it ignored his command and set up a *provisional* (temporary) government. Nicholas had lost all political support, and he gave up the throne on March 15. Nicholas and his family were then imprisoned. Bolshevik revolutionaries shot the czar and his family to death in July 1918.

Many soviets were established in Russia at the same time as the provisional government was formed. The soviets rivaled the provisional government. Workers and soldiers tried to seize power in Petrograd in July, but the attempt failed.

The October Revolution. In August 1917, General Lavr Kornilov tried to curb the growing power of the soviets. But the attempt failed, and the Russian masses became increasingly radical. On November 7 (October 25 in the old Russian calendar), workers, soldiers, and sailors led by the Bolsheviks took over the Winter Palace, a former royal residence that had become the headquarters of the provisional government. They overthrew the provisional government and formed a new government headed by Lenin. Lenin immediately withdrew Russia from World War I. The new government soon took over Russia's industries and also seized most of the peasants' farm products.

In 1918, the Bolsheviks made Moscow the capital of Russia. They also changed the name of the Russian Social Democratic Labor Party to the Russian Communist Party. This name was later changed to the Communist Party of the Soviet Union. See **Communism.**

Civil war and the formation of the U.S.S.R. From 1918 to 1920, civil war raged between the Communists and the anti-Communists over control of Russia. The anti-Communists received support from several other countries, including France, Japan, the United Kingdom, and the United States. Nevertheless, the Communists defeated their opponents. They also established Communist rule in Georgia, Ukraine, eastern Armenia, Belarus, and central Asia. The civil war contributed to the increasing discontent among the Russian people.

In 1921, peasant uprisings and workers' strikes broke out in opposition to Bolshevik policies. That same year, Lenin established a New Economic Policy to strengthen Russia. Under this policy, the government controlled the most important aspects of the economy, including banking, foreign trade, heavy industry, and transportation. But small businesses could control their own operations, and peasants could keep their farm products.

In December 1922, the Communist government created a new nation called the Union of Soviet Socialist Republics (U.S.S.R.). It consisted of four republics—the Russian Soviet Federative Socialist Republic, Byelorussia (formerly Belarus and now again known by that name), Transcaucasia, and Ukraine. By late 1940, Transcaucasia had been divided into Azerbaijan, Armenia, and Georgia, and 10 other republics had been established. The new republics included what are now Estonia, Kazakhstan, Kyrgyzstan, Latvia, Lithuania, Moldova (then Moldavia), Tajikistan, Turkmenistan, and Uzbekistan.

Stalin. Lenin died in 1924. Joseph Stalin, who had been general secretary of the Communist Party since 1922, rapidly gained power. He defeated his rivals one by one. By 1929, Stalin had become dictator of the Soviet Union.

In the late 1920's, Stalin began a socialist economic program. It emphasized the development of heavy industry and the combining of privately owned farms into large, government-run farms. Many citizens of the Soviet Union opposed Stalin's policies.

In the mid-1930's, Stalin started a program of terror called the Great Purge. His secret police arrested millions of people. Most of the prisoners were shot or sent to prison labor camps. Many of those arrested had helped Stalin rise to power. Stalin thus eliminated all possible threats to his power and tightened his hold over the Soviet Union.

World War II. By the late 1930's, German dictator Adolf Hitler was ready to conquer Europe. In August 1939, the U.S.S.R. and Germany signed a *nonaggression pact,* a treaty agreeing that neither nation would attack the other. In September, German forces invaded Poland from the west. The Soviet Union's forces quickly occupied the eastern part of Poland.

In June 1941, Germany invaded the Soviet Union and began a rapid advance into the country. The turning point of the war in the Soviet Union was the Soviet defeat of the Germans in the Battle of Stalingrad (now Volgograd) in 1943. Soviet troops then drove the Germans back out of the country and across eastern Europe. They attacked Berlin in April 1945. Berlin fell to the Soviets on May 2, and German troops surrendered to the Allies five days later.

The Soviet Union suffered more military casualties than all the other Allied countries combined. Russians call the Soviet Union's fight against the Germans the Great Patriotic War. For more information on Russia's role in the war, see **World War II.**

The Cold War. After World War II ended, the Soviet Union extended the influence of Communism into Eastern Europe. By early 1948, several Eastern European countries had become *Soviet satellites* (countries controlled by the Soviet Union). The satellites were Bulgaria, Czechoslovakia, Hungary, Poland, Romania, and—later—East Germany. The U.S.S.R. also influenced Communist regimes in Albania and Yugoslavia. It cut off nearly all contact between its satellites and the West. Mutual distrust and suspicion between East and West developed into a rivalry that became known as the Cold War. The Cold War shaped the foreign policy of the Soviet Union and of many Western countries until the late 1980's.

Stalin died on March 5, 1953. In September of that year, Nikita S. Khrushchev became the head of the Communist Party. In 1958, he also became premier of the Soviet Union.

Khrushchev eased the terror that had characterized Stalin's dictatorship and relaxed some of the restrictions on communication, trade, and travel between East and West. He also improved the Soviet people's standard of living. However, the U.S.S.R. continued working to expand its influence in non-Communist countries. Khrushchev improved Soviet relations with the West, but many of his other policies failed.

ITAR-Tass from Sovfoto

Leonid I. Brezhnev pursued a policy of friendly relations with the West called *détente.* In the 1970's, Brezhnev, *left,* and U.S. President Richard M. Nixon signed an agreement limiting production of nuclear weapons as a result of a series of meetings called the Strategic Arms Limitation Talks (SALT).

In 1964, the highest-ranking Communists overthrew Khrushchev. Leonid I. Brezhnev became Communist Party head, and Aleksei N. Kosygin became premier. Brezhnev and Kosygin increased the production of consumer goods and the construction of housing, and they expanded Soviet influence in Africa.

By the mid-1970's, Brezhnev was the most powerful Soviet leader. He sought to ease tensions between East and West, a policy that became known as *détente.* However, détente began to collapse in the late 1970's. Relations between the Soviet Union and the United States worsened over such issues as Soviet violations of human rights, the Soviet invasion of Afghanistan, and an increase in the number of nuclear weapons held by both the Soviet Union and the United States.

The rise of Gorbachev. In 1985, Mikhail S. Gorbachev became head of the Communist Party. Gorbachev instituted many changes in the U.S.S.R., including increased freedom of expression in politics, literature, and the arts. He worked to improve relations between the Soviet Union and the West and to reduce government control over the Soviet economy.

In 1989, the U.S.S.R. held its first contested elections for the newly created Congress of People's Deputies. The following year, the government voted to allow non-Communist political parties. Many Communist Party members and other Soviet officials opposed Gorbachev's reforms. But in March 1990, Gorbachev was elected by the Congress of People's Deputies to the newly created office of president of the Soviet Union.

The breakup of the U.S.S.R. During the late 1980's, people in many parts of the Soviet Union increased their demands for greater freedom from the central government. In June 1990, the Russian republic declared that laws passed by its legislature took precedence over laws passed by the central government. By the end of the year, each of the other 14 Soviet republics had made similar declarations.

In July 1991, Gorbachev and the leaders of 10 republics agreed to sign a treaty giving the republics a large amount of self-government. Five of the republics were scheduled to sign the treaty on August 20. But on August 19, conservative Communist Party leaders staged a coup against Gorbachev's government. They imprisoned Gorbachev and his family in their vacation home. The president of the Russian republic, Boris N. Yeltsin, led popular opposition to the coup. The coup collapsed on August 21. Gorbachev then regained his office as president but resigned as head of the Communist Party.

With the coup's collapse, the republics renewed their demands for more self-government. In September 1991, an interim government was established to rule until a new union treaty and constitution could be written and approved. This government included a State Council, made up of Gorbachev and the leaders of the republics.

On Dec. 8, 1991, Yeltsin and the presidents of Belarus and Ukraine announced the formation of the Commonwealth of Independent States (C.I.S.). They declared that the Soviet Union had ceased to exist and invited the remaining republics to join the commonwealth. The mem-

AP/Wide World

Boris N. Yeltsin, *center, holding papers,* led opposition to the coup against Soviet leader Mikhail S. Gorbachev in 1991. The coup failed, and the Soviet Union rapidly dissolved. Yeltsin continued leading Russia through a difficult transition period.

bers would be independent countries tied by economic and defense links. Most of the republics joined the C.I.S.

Yeltsin took control of what remained of the central government of the Soviet Union, including the Kremlin. On Dec. 25, 1991, Gorbachev resigned as Soviet president, and the Soviet Union ceased to exist. The breakup of the Soviet Union helped ease remaining tensions between East and West.

The new nation. In 1992, the Russian government slashed military spending and reduced the number of people employed in the armed forces. That same year, the other former Soviet republics with nuclear weapons—Ukraine, Belarus, and Kazakhstan—agreed to eliminate all nuclear weapons on their territories within seven years. By the end of 1996, the three countries had turned over their nuclear weapons to Russia.

Russia faced many challenges in setting up new economic and governmental systems. The government ended price controls, which caused prices to soar and resulted in a lower standard of living for the Russian people. President Yeltsin and his government took steps to increase private ownership of businesses. However, the process left a small number of wealthy Russians in control of many of the country's largest companies.

Opposition to Yeltsin's economic policies grew in parliament, which included many Communist Party members and former Soviet leaders. In a referendum held in April 1993, a majority of the voters supported Yeltsin and his economic policies. But opposition to Yeltsin in parliament continued. In September, Yeltsin suspended Vice President Alexander V. Rutskoi, who had become a leader of the opposition. Yeltsin also dissolved parliament and called for new parliamentary elections in December. Parliament, in turn, voted to remove Yeltsin from office and to make Rutskoi acting president.

Rutskoi and many other foes of Yeltsin barricaded themselves in the parliament building. At Yeltsin's order, police and forces of the internal affairs ministry blockaded the building, known as the White House. In October 1993, anti-Yeltsin crowds rioted and tried to break up the blockade. The next day, Yeltsin ordered the military to take control of the White House. Rutskoi and other leaders of the movement against Yeltsin were arrested.

In December 1993, Russians elected a new parliament and approved a new constitution. In 1994, the new State Duma granted amnesty to those who revolted against Yeltsin in 1993 and to those who led the failed coup in 1991. Yeltsin won a second presidential term in 1996.

In 1991, the government of Chechnya, a republic in southwestern Russia, demanded independence. In 1992, the Chechen government clashed with citizens who wanted the region to remain part of Russia. In 1994, Russian troops launched attacks against Chechen separatist forces. A cease-fire ended the fighting in 1996.

In 1998, Russia faced severe economic problems. In March, Yeltsin dismissed his cabinet, including Prime Minister Viktor S. Chernomyrdin. He forced parliament to accept young, reform-minded Sergei Kiriyenko as prime minister. In August, he dismissed Kiriyenko. In September, parliament approved Yevgeny M. Primakov, the minister of foreign affairs, as the new prime minister. In October, Yeltsin, in poor health, gave most of his duties to Primakov. Russia's economic crisis continued.

Conflict in Chechnya. In May 1999, Yeltsin abruptly dismissed Primakov and the rest of the cabinet members. Yeltsin appointed the minister of internal affairs, Sergei V. Stepashin, as prime minister. In August, Yeltsin replaced Stepashin with Vladimir V. Putin, former head of Russia's domestic intelligence service.

Also in August, Islamic militants who wanted to unite Chechnya and the neighboring republic of Dagestan seized several Dagestan towns. Russia invaded Chechnya to oppose the rebellion. Russian attacks damaged Chechnya's cities and killed many civilians. Russian forces gained control of Chechnya's main cities by mid-2000, but the rebellion continued. Rebels launched surprise attacks on Russian forces. Chechen terrorists conducted bomb attacks in Moscow and southwest Russia, killing and injuring hundreds of civilians.

In parliamentary elections in December 1999, the Communist Party again won the largest number of seats in the State Duma. Unity, a political group supported by Prime Minister Putin, won the second highest number of seats. On Dec. 31, 1999, Yeltsin resigned and appointed Putin as acting president. In presidential elections in March 2000, Russians formally elected Putin.

Putin's first two terms. In October 2002, Chechen terrorists seized a theater in Moscow and took about 700 hostages. They demanded a withdrawal of Russian troops from Chechnya. Russian security forces stormed the theater and killed or captured the terrorists. However, more than 100 hostages were killed in the raid.

Putin strengthened the central government. He restricted political expression and increased state control over the media. His government clashed with Russia's *oligarchs,* wealthy individuals who controlled major Russian businesses. In 2003, for example, the government arrested businessman Mikhail Khodorkovsky, a potential political rival, on financial crime charges. It then charged his Yukos Oil Company with billions of dollars in unpaid taxes. Khodorkovsky was convicted on several charges in 2005 and served eight years in prison.

Putin was reelected as president in March 2004. That September, Chechen terrorists seized a school in southwest Russia and held over 1,000 hostages. On the third day of the crisis, a bomb in the school exploded, and Russian security forces stormed the school. More than 300 hostages died and hundreds more were injured.

Recent developments. Dmitry Medvedev succeeded Putin as president in 2008. He chose Putin to be his prime minister. Many international observers believed Putin was unofficially still in control. Later in 2008, Russia and Georgia clashed over control of South Ossetia, a region in north-central Georgia. In 2009, Russia ended its antiterrorist operations in Chechnya, claiming to have stabilized the situation there.

Putin was again elected president in 2012. He chose Medvedev as his prime minister. In March 2014, Russian armed forces seized the Crimean Peninsula, which had been part of Ukraine since 1954. Later that month, the Crimean parliament voted to withdraw from Ukraine. Putin signed legislation annexing Crimea. Ukraine's government, and many of its allies, considered these moves illegal. In April 2014, pro-Russian separatists seized several regions of eastern Ukraine. Putin denied allegations of sending troops to Ukraine and of arming the rebels. As tensions rose, several Western governments imposed sanctions on Russia, targeting its oil and gas industries. Russia soon entered into a recession. In 2015, Russia and Ukraine agreed to withdraw heavy weapons from eastern Ukraine, but fighting continued.

Later in 2015, Russia began launching air strikes in Syria during that country's civil war. Targets included Islamic militants and rebel opponents of Syrian President Bashar al-Assad. Russia supported Assad in the following years as the war continued. In 2018, Putin was elected to a fourth term as Russia's president. Mikhail Mishustin succeeded Medvedev as prime minister in early 2020. In the following months, the legislature passed, and voters approved, a constitutional change potentially allowing Putin to seek reelection in 2024 and 2030.

In 2020 and 2021, Russia became one of the nations hardest hit by the COVID-19 pandemic. The government began distributing a vaccine developed in Russia in December 2020. Donald J. Raleigh

Related articles in *World Book.* For more information about Russia between 1917 and 1991, see **Union of Soviet Socialist Republics** and its list of *Related articles.* See also:

Biographies

See the *Related articles* of **Classical music; Drama;** and **Russian literature.** See also:

Alexander I (czar)
Alexander II (czar)
Alexander III (czar)
Catherine the Great
Fabergé, Peter Carl
Ivan III, the Great
Ivan IV, the Terrible
Kerensky, Alexander F.
Krupskaya, Nadezhda Konstantinovna
Lenin, V. I.
Mayakovsky, Vladimir
Nicholas I (czar)
Nicholas II (czar)
Peter I, the Great
Putin, Vladimir V.
Rasputin, Grigori E.

Cities

Arkhangelsk
Irkutsk
Kaliningrad
Kazan
Moscow
Murmansk
Nizhniy Novgorod
Novosibirsk
Omsk
Rostov-on-Don
Saint Petersburg
Samara
Sochi
Velikiy Novgorod
Vladivostok
Volgograd
Yekaterinburg

History

Berlin, Congress of
Bloody Sunday
Bolsheviks
Crimean War
Duma
Hungary (History)
Mensheviks
Mongol Empire
Poland (History)
Russian Revolution of 1917
Russo-Japanese War
Russo-Turkish wars
Scythians
World War I
World War II

Physical features

Amur River
Azov, Sea of
Barents Sea
Black Sea
Caspian Sea
Caucasus Mountains
Don River
Franz Josef Land
Kamchatka Peninsula
Kara Sea
Kuril Islands
Lake Baikal
Lake Ilmen
Lake Ladoga
Lake Onega
Lake Peipus
Lena River
Mount Elbrus
Ob River
Sakhalin
Taiga
Ural Mountains
Ural River
Volga River
White Sea
Yablonovyy Mountains

Other related articles

Air force (The Russian Air Force)
Army (The world's major armies)
Balalaika
Ballet (Ballet in Russia)
Chechnya
Clothing (picture: Traditional costumes)
Commonwealth of Independent States
Doll (Traditional dolls; picture)
Drama (Russian drama and Chekhov)
Kremlin
Mir
Nihilism
Novel (Russia)
Ruble
Russian language
Russian literature
Siberia
Strategic Arms Reduction Treaty
Tatars
Theater (Russia)

Outline

I. Government
A. National government
B. Local government
C. Politics
D. Courts
E. Armed forces

II. People
A. Ancestry
B. Language

III. Way of life
A. City life
B. Rural life
C. Clothing
D. Food and drink
E. Health care
F. Recreation
G. Religion
H. Education
I. Museums and libraries

IV. The arts
A. Architecture
B. Music
C. Ballet
D. Painting and sculpture

V. Land and climate
A. Land regions
B. Rivers and lakes
C. Climate

VI. Economy
A. Natural resources
B. Manufacturing
C. Agriculture
D. Mining
E. Fishing industry
F. Service industries
G. Energy sources
H. Trade
I. Transportation and communication

VII. History

Additional resources

Level I

Nickles, Greg. *Russia: The Culture.* Crabtree Pub. Co., 2008. *Russia: The Land.* 2008. *Russia: The People.* 2008. All revised editions.

Schemenauer, Elma. *Welcome to Russia.* Child's World, 2008.

Torchinsky, Oleg, and others. *Russia.* 3rd ed. Cavendish Square, 2016.

Yomtov, Nelson. *Russia.* Children's Pr., 2012.

Level II

Allen, John. *The Russian Federation: Then and Now.* ReferencePoint, 2015.

Fleming, Candace. *The Family Romanov.* Schwartz & Wade, 2014.

Plokhy, Serhii. *The Last Empire: The Final Days of the Soviet Union.* Basic Bks., 2014.

Saunders, Robert A., and Strukov, Vlad. *Historical Dictionary of the Russian Federation.* Scarecrow, 2010.

Russian language is one of the world's most important and widely spoken languages. It is one of the six official languages of the United Nations, along with Arabic, Chinese, English, French, and Spanish. Many scientific publications are written in Russian.

Russian is the official language of Russia and is an official second language of many countries of the former Soviet Union, which existed from 1922 to 1991. The language still serves those countries as the common means of communication among most ethnic groups. Russian is also an important second language in countries with large Russian immigrant populations, such as Israel.

Russian belongs to the eastern branch of the Slavic linguistic family. Ukrainian and Belarusian also belong to this branch. Russian is closely related to other Slavic languages, such as Bulgarian, Croatian, Czech, Macedonian, Polish, Serbian, Slovak, and Slovenian.

The Russian language used across the vast distances of the country of Russia is remarkably uniform. Its three main dialects—northern, central, and southern—do not differ radically from each other. Modern standard Russian is based on the central dialect, spoken in Moscow and surrounding areas. The language became fairly stabilized by the end of the 1700's.

Alphabet. The Russian alphabet has 33 letters. The alphabet is also called Cyrillic and is based on the Greek alphabet. The letters and their approximate sounds in English are shown on the table on this page.

Russian		English translation	Approximate sound in English
А	а	a	far
Б	б	b	bog
В	в	v	vault
Г	г	g	go
Д	д	d	dog
Е	е	ye	yet
Ё	ё	yo	yolk
Ж	ж	zh	azure
З	з	z	zone
И	и	i	feet
Й	й	y	boy
К	к	k	calm
Л	л	l	law
М	m	m	moose
Н	н	n	not
О	о	o	bowl
П	п	p	pot
Р	р	r	thrifty
С	с	s	soot
Т	т	t	toe
Y	у	u	fool
Ф	ф	f	for
Х	х	kh	Ba*ch*
Ц	ц	ts	i*ts*
Ч	ч	ch	cheeks
Ш	ш	sh	shucks
Щ	щ	shch	fre*sh sh*eets
Ъ	ъ	—	indicates a break for syllable and *ye*-sound before next vowel
Ы	ы	y	rhythm
Ь	ь	—	usually softens preceding consonant, adding a *ye*-sound, as *n* in canyon
Э	э	e	effort
Ю	ю	yu	use
Я	я	ya	yard

Pronunciation. Most Russian consonants have two distinct pronunciations—an ordinary *hard* sound and a *soft* sound. Soft consonants are pronounced with the tongue raised toward the *palate* (roof of the mouth). The vowels е, ё, и, ю, and я (as well as ь) normally indicate that any preceding consonant is soft, or *palatalized.* This palatalization is a distinctive feature of Russian speech. In most Russian words, one syllable is heavily stressed. In questions, the stressed syllable of the main word is pronounced a tone higher than the rest of the sentence. Russian spelling reflects actual pronunciation much more regularly than English spelling does.

Grammar. Russian belongs to the Indo-European family of languages. Like German, Latin, and Greek, its words can have many different endings. Nouns have six cases and three genders. Adjectives change their forms to agree with the words they modify. Russian verbs have only three tense forms—present, past, and future. Completed, continued, and repetitive actions are expressed by *aspect,* an essential feature of all Russian verb forms. Word order in a Russian sentence is flexible, with important new information tending to appear near the end of the sentence.

Vocabulary. Russian is a rich, expressive, and flexible language. Many Russian and English words have a common ancestor. Examples include the Russian word *sestra* and the English word *sister,* both derived from the Indo-European word *swesor;* and the Russian word *moloko* and the English word *milk,* both derived from the Indo-European *melg.* Since the 1700's, standard Russian has adopted many foreign terms. After the fall of the Soviet Union in 1991, the language borrowed hundreds of new words from English, such as *Internet, displei* (display), and *videoklip* (video clip). A few Russian words have been adopted into English, such as *czar, vodka,* and *sputnik.*

History. All Slavic languages probably developed from an ancient Common Slavic language. The language of the Russian Orthodox Church, Old Church Slavonic, resembles Common Slavic more closely than does any other existing language. Church Slavonic is a modified form of Old Church Slavonic, which played a role in the history of the Russian language similar to that played by Latin in the history of French, Italian, Portuguese, and Spanish.

Russian has many word pairs in which a native Russian word is used for a concrete, everyday meaning and an Old Church Slavonic term is used to express a more technical or abstract aspect. This feature of the language resembles word pairs in English, which often consist of a common word from Anglo-Saxon *(house)* and a more formal word from Latin through French *(residence).*

The earliest formal literature was written chiefly in Old Church Slavonic, with some native Russian words and forms. By the 1000's, a distinct Russian language existed and was used for legal and business documents. By the 1700's, authors were writing works of literature in Russian, which gradually replaced Old Church Slavonic except for religious use. Donald K. Jarvis

See also **Alphabet** (Other alphabets); **Language** (Language families [Indo-European]); **Russian literature; Ukraine** (Language).

© Geraint Lewis, Alamy Images

Russian literature includes many famous works, including *The Cherry Orchard,* a drama by Anton Chekhov about sensitive characters trapped in unhappy lives. A scene from a production of the play by the Royal National Theatre in London is shown here.

Russian literature

Russian literature includes some of the greatest masterpieces ever written. Russian authors have written in all literary *genres* (forms), but they are best known outside Russia for their novels and poetry. Style, content, and keen character analysis are central to Russian writing. The most famous Russian works show a deep concern for moral, religious, and philosophical problems.

History has had an important influence on Russian literature. The East Slavic lands known as Kievan Rus—from which many historians believe Russia took its name—accepted Christianity during the late 900's. Kievan Rus was a state made up of a number of *principalities* (regions ruled by a prince). Its main city was present-day Kiev (now the capital of Ukraine). Christianity brought with it literacy that led to a literature consisting mostly of religious works.

The Tatar (Mongol) invasion and conquest dominated Russian literature from the 1200's to the late 1400's. But by the end of the 1600's, translations and imitations of Western European works were appearing in Russia. By the late 1700's, literature included expressions of social protest against the *czars* (emperors), serfdom, and moral and political corruption.

Much great Russian poetry, prose, and drama was written during the 1800's. The mid-1800's were the age of Realism in Russian literature. Beginning in the 1890's, an artistic and cultural revival known as the Silver Age took shape. It developed from a combination of Russian religious philosophy, the ideas of German philosophers such as Friedrich Nietzsche, and artistic doctrines and poetry from France and elsewhere. The first 20 years of the 1900's were dominated by poetry.

After the Russian Revolution of 1917, literary activity was controlled by the Communist government. In 1922, the Soviet Union was formed, and it lasted until 1991. Socialist Realism, enforced by government censors and literary bureaucrats, required that literature portray Soviet society as full of optimism and joy. Writers who strayed from this script faced the threat of severe punishment. Under dictator Joseph Stalin, many writers were arrested and killed. However, the constant struggle of Soviet writers against censorship also led to periods of creative freedom and experimentation. Since 1991, Russian literature has developed in many new directions, reflecting new patterns of post-socialist society.

Early literature

Religious literature. The first documents written in Kievan Rus appeared around the time of the Slavic state's conversion to Christianity about A.D. 988. This literature, like the new religion, came from the Byzantine Empire and the Slavic kingdoms in the Balkans (an area that covers a peninsula in the southeast corner of what is now Europe). These writings were largely religious, in the form of sermons, hymns, and biographies of saints. Many of these works display imagination and vivid details of everyday life. Some works were original, but many more were based on Greek writings. Greek was the common language of the Byzantine Empire. Some saints' lives continued to influence later literary works in Russia.

Early Russian literature was written in a mixture of Old Russian (also called Old East Slavic), from which modern Russian developed, and Old Church Slavonic, a related language. Old Church Slavonic came from the Slavic peoples of the Balkans after they accepted Christianity. The East Slavs could understand the new written language without much difficulty. Old Church Slavonic became the official language of the Russian Orthodox

Church. This language contributed stylistic elements that are still used even in nonreligious literature to give it a more dignified tone.

Most of the literary works were both written and read by monks and clergymen. Until 1564, when the first books were printed in Russia, monks or government scribes copied all manuscripts by hand.

Nonreligious literature. The *chronicles,* which were records of outstanding events, were probably the most important early nonreligious Russian writings. The capital of each principality had its own chronicle. In the 1100's, the Grand Prince of Kiev had some of these chronicles combined into what is now known as *The Primary Chronicle.* Later chronicles, particularly those of Moscow, claimed that their principalities had the right to reunite and rule all Russia. Along with dry narrative, some accounts were vivid descriptions of military or political battles. Others were fantastic stories based on legend rather than fact.

The greatest work of Old Russian literature was "The Lay of Igor's Campaign," written by an anonymous author of the late 1100's. This epic prose poem, famous for its vivid imagery and nature symbolism, describes the defeat of the Kievan Rus Prince Igor by the Polovtsians, a Turkic tribe, in 1185. The work pleads for cooperation among the princes to prevent a foreign invasion. It warns that squabbles among the princes will lead to destruction. The poem proved to be a prophecy. The Tatars invaded the East Slavic lands in 1223 and 1237. By 1240, they controlled most of Kievan Rus.

Literature from the Tatar period showed less original thought than the literature of any other period in Russian history. Tatar rule, which lasted until 1480, was the dominant theme of the small amount of writing that was preserved. The "Zadonshchina" ("The Battle Beyond the Don"), an important work of the 1400's, describes a major Russian victory over the Tatars. It has much Christian imagery and echoes of the language and imagery of "The Lay of Igor's Campaign."

Muscovite literature developed as the principality of Moscow rose to power after 1480. All Russian-speaking territories were gradually united into a single state under the Grand Prince of Moscow. Eventually, the Prince of Moscow became known as the *czar* (from *Caesar,* as pronounced in Byzantine Greek). Muscovite literature stressed Moscow's right to rule the Russian lands and the czar's absolute authority. The most remarkable stylistic development of the Muscovite period is elaborate word-weaving, which emphasizes style rather than content. This style was introduced by Orthodox monks who fled to Moscow after the fall of Constantinople, the capital of the Byzantine Empire, in 1453.

Beginnings of modern literature

Western influences. The 1600's saw a significant reshaping of Russian literature. Western Europe, from which Russia had been isolated since the early 1200's, began to influence Russian writing. Western works, such as anecdotes, fables, moral tales, poetry, and stories of knights, were translated and imitated. For the first time, rhymed verse appeared in Russia. Russian folklore was translated into written fairy tales, *satires* (writings that ridiculed persons or their actions), and other works. Some authors discarded Old Church Slavonic, the old literary language, and wrote in a language that was already recognizably Russian.

The most outstanding writer of the new literature was Avvakum, a conservative clergyman who belonged to the Old Believers. This group opposed changes made in the ritual of the Russian Orthodox Church in the 1650's, which led to a split in the church. Avvakum's autobiography reveals his colorful personality and strong religious convictions. His expressive language and striking descriptions of daily life make his writings some of the most revealing works of this period, surprisingly fresh in their style even today.

Simeon Polotsky, a monk who received a Western education in Kiev, was a prominent author of the 1600's. His most important contribution to literature was the introduction of a rigid syllabic system, drawn from Polish poetry, to Russian verse. Each line has a fixed number of syllables with regularly placed pauses. Polotsky wrote quaint but serious verse. Many of his works praise the czar and the ruling family. He also wrote several plays on Biblical subjects.

Czar Peter I (the Great), whose rule began in 1682, Westernized Russia and officially declared himself emperor. His adoption of Western culture and institutions led to great changes in Russian literature. Peter encouraged the translation of many European works and sent people abroad to study Western life. He also invited large numbers of Europeans to Russia. European historians, architects, musicians, dancers, and writers came to Russia during and after Peter's rule. Many settled down to raise families in Russia.

Russian literature was completely Westernized during the 1700's, with French, German, and English works influencing Russian authors. Antioch Kantemir, a leading poet and diplomat, wrote nine satires in syllabic verse supporting Peter the Great's reforms and the spread of Western culture. Kantemir used everyday speech in his

Outline

works, and the informal language helped his characters appear lively and typical. He also wrote in Romanian.

Mikhail Lomonosov has been called the founder of modern Russian literature and the forerunner of Russian Classicism. His dignified *odes* (lyric poems) praise the czar and the greatness of God. Lomonosov introduced a new and more suitable type of poetry to Russia. Called *syllabo-tonic* verse, it features a regular pattern of stressed and unstressed syllables. He also established a system of three literary styles. These styles varied among (1) the highest, or most dignified, language, full of Old Church Slavonic elements; (2) the middle language, based on spoken Russian, but without conversational expressions; and (3) the lowest, or most popular, speech. According to Lomonosov, the highest style was most suited for tragedies and odes; the middle style, for drama and satire; and the lowest, for fables or comedies. Lomonosov was also a scientist, and some of his poems are on scientific topics.

The Classical movement, sparked by Lomonosov's literary reforms, emerged fully in Russia by the 1740's. Classicism came to Russia as part of the continual cultural flow from Western Europe. It provided strict rules for composition, style, and subject matter. These guidelines were inspired by models of ancient Greek and Roman literature and influenced by the literary criticism in *The Art of Poetry* (1674) by the French literary critic Nicolas Boileau-Despréaux.

The most typical Russian Classicist was Alexander Sumarokov. His works included fables, plays, satires, and songs. Sumarokov drew on episodes from Russian history, found in old chronicles, for some of his plays.

Vasili Ivanovich Maykov, one of Sumarokov's followers, wrote the mock epic poem *Elisey*, or *Bacchus Infuriated* (1771). This more realistic work describes the adventures of a drunken coachman. Another important Classicist, Denis Fonvizin, became famous for his satirical comedies. *The Adolescent* (1782) is considered his finest work and is still widely read today. The play attacks the ignorance and cruelty of country landowners. Fonvizin was forced out of literature in the 1780's after Empress Catherine the Great prohibited him from publishing.

The outstanding poet of the 1700's was Gavriil Derzhavin who, like Lomonosov, was famous for his odes. In "Ode to Felitsa" (1783) and other poems, Derzhavin praised Catherine and ridiculed the vices of her courtiers. In his hands, the ode became a fresh expression of life and feeling. His work marked the turning point in Russian literature from Classical to Romantic writing.

During the late 1700's and early 1800's, fables were a very popular form of literature. Russia's greatest writer of fables was Ivan Krylov. His works, which used everyday Russian language and humorous characterizations, ridiculed ignorance and vanity. Some of his fables were translations of French writer Jean de La Fontaine, though Krylov wrote original fables, too.

The age of Romanticism

Romanticism, which spread to Russia from Germany and England, stressed the full expression of emotions in literature. The movement developed as a revolt against the logic and formality of Classical writers. Romantic characteristics began to appear in Russian literature during the late 1700's. But Romanticism did not become a significant influence until the early 1800's.

© Pictorial Press Ltd/Alamy Images

Alexander Pushkin

Sentimentalism, a strong early Romantic trend, came to Russia from Europe in the 1790's. Followers of this movement emphasized the importance of feelings and imagination but continued to use Classical forms in poetry. The leading Russian sentimentalist was Nikolai Karamzin. His *Letters of a Russian Traveler* (written in 1789 and 1790) is filled with the excitement of a young man's trip to the West and his meetings with famous writers. "Poor Liza" (1792) is a popular tale about a peasant girl abandoned by her upper-class lover. Karamzin's writing style shifted from the strict division of style into three levels toward a single conversational "middle style," influenced by French. His *History of the Russian State* (1816-1829) was a fundamental work of Russian historical scholarship that is still important.

Preromanticism. Another group of writers of the early 1800's could be described as Preromantics. They showed a greater interest in nature than previous writers did and paid more attention to mood. Leading Preromantic writers included Vasili Zhukovsky and Konstantin Batyushkov. Zhukovsky, a gifted poet, translated works by several German and English Romantics. Batyushkov was famous primarily for his *elegies* (sad poems on love and death). He also wrote passionate *lyrics* (short poems).

Early Romanticism. A new generation of poets appeared during the 1820's, as the Golden Age of Russian poetry began. These poets also combined Classical forms with Romantic sentiments. However, the early Romantics showed a greater concern for individual freedom and were interested in a broader range of subjects. The poets of the Golden Age were strongly influenced by two English authors, William Shakespeare and Lord Byron.

Russia's best-loved poet was (and still is) Alexander Pushkin, the leading writer of early Romanticism. His poems are distinguished by their economical but very expressive language. Pushkin's concise style makes his works difficult to translate, or to appreciate in any language except Russian. Pushkin's narrative poems deal with the place of human beings in society. Many of his main characters, such as the title hero of *Eugene Onegin* (1825-1832), are unable to find a purpose in life. They end up bored and indifferent to love.

In 1825, Pushkin wrote *Boris Godunov*, a historical drama in blank verse. He hoped to introduce Shakespeare's type of historical play into Russian drama. "The Bronze Horseman" (written in 1833), one of Pushkin's greatest narrative poems, centers on Peter the Great's Westernization of Russia and its effect on ordinary Russians. The work tells of both the glorious and tragic consequences of his grand design for Russia.

Pushkin's novel *The Captain's Daughter* (1836) resembles the historical novels of Sir Walter Scott, a Scottish Romantic. One of Pushkin's best stories, "The Queen of Spades" (1834), is about a gambler who goes mad after failing to win a fortune at cards.

Other poets of the Golden Age included Yevgeny Baratynsky, Baron Anton Delvig, and Wilhelm Kuchelbecker. Baratynsky became famous for his precise, original style. His narrative poems include *Eda* (1825), *The Ball* (1828), and *The Gypsy Girl* (1842).

Another important writer of the 1820's was Alexander Griboyedov. His most famous work, *Woe from Wit* (1825), is a satirical comedy in rhymed verse. The hero, Chatsky, like Pushkin's Eugene Onegin, is unable to fit in with the society of his time. Onegin and Chatsky became known as *superfluous* (unnecessary) men whose weak natures prevented them from pursuing constructive goals. Later writers used this character type to describe Russian nobles who could not provide strong leadership in support of political and social reforms. The superfluous man often appeared in Russian literature during the 1800's and early 1900's.

Late Romanticism featured a new freedom of form and style and a focus on human feelings and passions. In the 1830's, this movement also stressed the deep significance of dreams, visions, and fantasies. Some Late Romantic Russian literature addressed political and moral corruption. However, censorship had become severe under Czar Nicholas I, whose rule began in 1825. There was strict censorship of all literary works that criticized Russian society, especially the institution of serfdom.

Mikhail Lermontov was an outstanding poet and novelist. His lyrics expressed intense frustration and boredom with life in Russia. In several of his poems, Lermontov's speakers dream of an unattainable paradise. Pride and unrestrained desire cause the hero of *The Demon* (written about 1839) to lose this ideal state. Lermontov's *A Hero of Our Times* (1840) was the first psychological novel in Russian literature. Its hero, Pechorin, is another superfluous man. He wastes his life in senseless adventures because the strictness of Russian social and political life keeps him from any useful activities except his military duties.

Fyodor Tyutchev, a brilliant Romantic poet, wrote on such philosophical themes as the place of human beings in the universe, the limits of their understanding of nature, and the difficulty of communicating through language. His poems include "Silentium" (1830), "A Dream at Sea" (1833), and "Nature Is Not What You Think" (1836). The Late Romantic poet Karolina Pavlova wrote both verse and incisive prose that analyzed the habits of Russian society. Her short novel *The Double Life* (1846) uses an innovative combination of prose and poetry.

Nikolai Gogol was one of Russia's greatest writers. His early works give colorful and often folkloric descriptions of life in Ukraine, where he was born. *Taras Bulba* (1835), a historical novel, praises the past glory of Ukrainian *Cossacks* (elite cavalry warriors). Literary critics regarded many of Gogol's later works as political satires, but his main objective was to make fun of humanity's spiritual weaknesses. The characters in his play *The Inspector-General* (1836) represent common vices. "The Overcoat" (1842), the story of a pathetic copy clerk, protests the spiritual poverty of human beings. The novel *Dead Souls* (1842), though never completed, is one of Gogol's most brilliant satires. The hero, Chichikov, travels around Russia buying up *titles* (deeds of ownership) to dead serfs whose names are still in the census lists, planning to use the titles in a swindle.

The age of Realism

In the 1840's, Realism began to emerge as an important literary trend in Russia. Its followers were influenced by the teachings of Vissarion Belinsky, a leading *left-wing* (liberal) literary critic. Belinsky believed that literature should give an honest picture of life and, at the same time, preach social reform. His view that literature should serve the needs of society became an established principle in Russian criticism during the later 1800's. This view continued to influence the choice and treatment of themes in Russian prose well into the 1900's.

Early Realism. Russian literature of the 1840's and the 1850's had both Romantic and Realist traits. Early Realists combined Romantic sentiments with more realistic portrayals of social and political problems.

Ivan Turgenev, an outstanding novelist and playwright, displayed a deep understanding of Russian society and people. *A Sportsman's Sketches* (1852) helped stir public sympathy for Russia's serfs, depicting them as kind and dignified, and portrayed landowners as crude and insensitive. In *Rudin* (1856), Turgenev shows the traditional superfluous man as a frustrated liberal. The novel *Fathers and Sons* (1862) is superior to Turgenev's other works in dramatic content and in character analysis. It shows the *nihilists* (radical Russian youths of the early 1860's) as strong-willed and disrespectful of authority and tradition. They want to change Russian society, but the country is not yet ready for great change. The hero, Bazarov, dies inactive and frustrated. One of Turgenev's favorite themes was young love, the subject of *Asya* (1858) and *First Love* (1860). In *First Love,* a boy experiences his first crush, only to learn that the girl has become his father's mistress. Turgenev's most successful play, *A Month in the Country* (completed in 1850), tells a similar story. A girl and her guardian compete for the love of a young tutor.

The novelist Ivan Goncharov tried to convince Russian liberals that only practical action, not lofty sentiment, could lead to social reform. In his novel *Oblomov* (1859), the superfluous man is Oblomov, a well-bred landowner and a charming and intelligent man whose almost total failure to act keeps him from achieving the dreams of his youth. After this novel, Russians began to refer to inactivity within the privileged class as "Oblomovism."

Alexander N. Ostrovsky, one of the most popular and productive Russian dramatists, wrote plays that critically depicted the middle classes. His use of everyday Russian speech gives his work strong national appeal. Ostrovsky's villains, products of the merchant world, are greedy, dishonest, and dominating. Ostrovsky's greatest play, *The Storm* (1860), tells the tragic story of a merchant's wife who is driven to suicide by her domineering mother-in-law.

Sergey Aksakov, another leading writer of the 1850's, based his vivid descriptions of nature and people on childhood experiences. Unlike other Russian Realists, Aksakov neither attacked nor defended Russian society in his writings. His works include *Family Chronicle* (1856) and *The Childhood of Grandson Bagrov* (1858).

The 1860's and 1870's brought an end to Romanticism in Russian literature. Russian Realists emphasized social conditions in their works. A simpler prose replaced the elegant style of Romanticism. The novel became the principal literary form. Many novels had vivid characters but little plot structure. As in the rest of Europe, many were first published serially in journals. Prose fiction and literary criticism served as means of discussing important issues in society, such as the position of the newly liberated serfs or the role of women.

Count Leo Tolstoy, considered by many to be Russia's greatest writer of Realistic fiction, produced his major novels in the 1860's and 1870's. He discarded Romantic values of heroism and spiritual love. Instead, he showed deep concern for the natural stages of human development: birth, marriage, and death. Tolstoy's magnificent novel *War and Peace* (1869) captures the color and fire of Russia in 1812, during the invasion of the French Emperor Napoleon I's army. But the novel also opposes war and reveals Tolstoy's desire for a quiet life in close harmony with nature. In *Anna Karenina* (1875-1877), Tolstoy attacked romantic love as self-indulgence and encouraged a sense of moral duty and love of family instead.

Fyodor Dostoevsky was another great Russian novelist. His works are famous for their dramatic portrayals of inner conflicts and their psychological depth. His characters experience violent spiritual struggles between their belief in God and their strong sense of pride and self-centeredness. *Crime and Punishment* (1866), Dostoevsky's most exciting novel, describes the drama of a murderer who is tortured by his conscience. The hero, Raskolnikov, is spiritually redeemed when he finally confesses his crime and accepts punishment. *The Brothers Karamazov* (1879-1880), Dostoevsky's last and greatest novel, tells about the murder of an evil man by one of his four sons. The symbolic redemption of the other sons represents the author's faith in the saving power of God.

Russian Realism was a large and varied movement. Other important novelists include Nadezhda Khvoshchinskaya, Nikolai Leskov, and the satirist Mikhail Saltykov-Shchedrin. The foremost poet of the Realist era was Nikolai Nekrasov, whose verse often addressed the same social concerns as prose of the time.

Late Realism. Alexander III, who became czar in 1881, opposed many of the reforms made by his father, Alexander II. Themes of despair and bitterness under the czar's harsh rule appeared in Russian writings of the 1880's and 1890's. Stories and plays became the major literary forms of late Realism.

Anton Chekhov was a leading writer of short stories, short novels, and plays. Many of his works deal with the boredom and frustration of life. "Ionych" (1898) tells the story of a sensitive, idealistic doctor who becomes lazy and conceited as he grows older. The play *The Three Sisters* (1901) describes a family whose members are too weak-willed to change their dull lives. *Sakhalin Island* (1893-1894) describes the notorious prison colony in the Russian Far East, which Chekhov visited in 1890.

Maxim Gorki, the last great Russian Realist, wrote novels, plays, and stories. His early works describe the terrible poverty of the lower classes. His most famous play, *The Lower Depths* (1902), dramatizes the miserable lives of the inhabitants of a cheap hotel. A frequent theme of Gorki's later works was the decline of the upper middle class, shown in the novel *The Artamanovs' Business* (1925). He also wrote a multivolume autobiography and published reminiscences of his meetings and friendships with such leading Russian authors as Tolstoy.

Literary revival

A spirit of revolution spread throughout Russia from the 1890's until the 1920's. This period is now often described as the Silver Age. It was a time of social upheaval and transition in Russia and also of tremendous vitality and renewal in the arts, especially literature.

Symbolism in Russian poetry and fiction began in the mid-1890's. The Symbolists rejected the Realist portrayals of everyday life and its problems and disapproved of the artistic standards of many Realist writers. Symbolists drew inspiration from earlier Russian authors, particularly Tyutchev, Lermontov, and Dostoevsky, as well as from other European writers. Followers of the movement returned to the dreams and fantasies of the Romantics. Some concentrated on religious and philosophical theories, while others considered music the highest art form.

Leading Symbolists included Andrei Bely, Alexander Blok, and Zinaida Gippius. Bely was an outstanding novelist and also a poet. His novel *Petersburg* (1913-1914) pictures the Russian capital as a place where Eastern and Western philosophies meet and conflict with almost explosive violence.

© Fine Art Images/SuperStock

Maxim Gorki and Leo Tolstoy were two of the most important figures in Russian literature. Gorki, *left*, was known for his short stories and plays and Tolstoy, *right*, for his novels.

Blok, a poet and playwright, expressed his religious ideals in his early works. His later poetry describes what he saw as the ugliness of the world. Blok's famous long poem, *The Twelve* (1918), interprets the Russian Revolution of 1917 as a troubling but effective spiritual purification of Russia.

Gippius wrote poetry, plays, and stories, as well as literary criticism under the name Anton the Extreme. Her writing often expressed despair at the conditions of human life.

Leonid Andreyev combined elements of Realism and Symbolism in his works. He wrote sensational stories with themes of sex, madness, and terror. Examples of this style include the short story "The Red Laugh" (1904) and the play *He Who Gets Slapped* (1915).

Another leading writer of the early 1900's was Ivan Bunin. Although he was not a Symbolist, his work, dominated by themes of love and death, resembles the works of the Symbolists. Bunin's masterpiece, "The Gentleman from San Francisco" (1915), is a story about an American who works too hard and is unable to enjoy life later. In 1933, Bunin became the first Russian to receive the Nobel Prize in literature.

Post-Symbolism grew out of Symbolism around 1910 and rejected the vague, philosophical works of the Symbolists. The Acmeists, one of the most important Post-Symbolist groups, wrote poetry that focused on the present world with clear-cut images and more concrete language. Nikolai Gumilyov became known for his poetry about seafarers and safaris as well as his literary criticism. Osip Mandelshtam was absorbed with philosophy, religion, and *aesthetics* (a branch of philosophy that tries to establish basic rules for interpreting and judging the arts). Anna Akhmatova wrote lyric poems that suggested the psychological depths of Realist novels.

The Futurists formed several competing radical Post-Symbolist groups, all departing from traditional poetic themes and *diction* (word usage). Vladimir Mayakovsky, the most famous Futurist and an outspoken Communist, shocked readers with his strong language, innovative rhyming, and unusual imagery. Velimir Khlebnikov wrote poetry that drew from Slavic antiquity, folklore, and nature more than from the urban topics that fascinated most Futurists.

Boris Pasternak, one of the greatest poets of the 1900's, created highly original poetry about nature and life. His early prose was strikingly experimental. Marina Tsvetaeva, another great poet, experimented with sounds and words. Her works include lyric poems, plays, and long poems, some based on classical Greek myths or the plots of Russian folktales. She strongly influenced later generations of Russian poets.

Silver Age poets experimented with verse forms and developed a new kind of long poem with varied *meters* and strong psychological interest. Meter is the pattern of rhythm in a poem. However, most Russian poetry in the early 1900's still followed traditional patterns of rhyme and meter.

Soviet literature

The Russian Revolution of 1917 marked the beginning of a new era in Russian literature. For a few years, many writers engaged in creative experimentation. Then, the new Communist government tightened censorship, which had also existed under the czars. Many writers who opposed the Communist government left the country or were imprisoned or executed. Those who remained had to serve the interests of the state or stop writing. They were not allowed to criticize the government. Writers were told to describe Soviet life as happy and prosperous.

From 1917 to 1928. Following the revolution, publishing houses closed and book production and sales dropped as a civil war devastated the economy. Newspapers and magazines became political tools of the Communist Party. Printing presses were taken over by the state. The government encouraged the development of a *proletarian* literature to express the interests of Russian workers and peasants. However, few works of value were written during this period.

Russian literature rebounded during the 1920's. The government restored some literary freedom, reopened publishing houses, and permitted literary criticism to resume. Many new young poets and novelists in the Soviet Union at this time became known as *fellow travelers* (people willing to cooperate with the Soviet regime though they did not actively support it). Isaak Babel's series of stories, *Red Cavalry* (1926), described the often horrifying events of the civil war that followed the Russian Revolution. Leonid Leonov, inspired by Dostoevsky, also explored the psychological effects of the revolution on the Russian people. His greatest novels are *The Badgers* (1924) and *The Thief* (1927). Yevgeni Zamyatin's novel *We* (1921) described a dismal, distant future. It was not published in the Soviet Union until decades later. However, after it appeared in English translation in 1924, *We* influenced such works of Western science fiction as Aldous Huxley's *Brave New World* (1932) and George Orwell's *1984* (1949).

The period of industrial literature began in 1928 with the Soviet Union's first five-year plan. This program aimed, in part, to build up Soviet industry. Writers were expected to produce works dealing with economic problems. Factory and production novels began to appear in the Soviet Union, describing the building of a factory or the organization of collective farms. Most of this literature is considered inferior, but a few works, such as *Cement* (1925) by Fyodor Gladkov or *Time, Forward!* (1932) by Valentin Kataev, are interesting and skillfully written.

The period of Socialist Realism started in the early 1930's. The government, headed by Joseph Stalin, clearly believed that literature was extremely important. It banned private literary associations and established a Union of Soviet Writers. All professional writers were required to join the union, which endorsed the new doctrine of Socialist Realism. According to this doctrine, the main purpose of literature is to portray the building of a *socialist* society. A socialist society is one that emphasizes public or community ownership of all property that produces goods and services. The union ordered Soviet authors to produce optimistic works that were easy to understand and similar to the style of Tolstoy and Gorki. Censorship eliminated undesirable material from manuscripts, and writers soon learned to censor themselves. Writers who ignored the doctrine were expelled from the union. This meant the end of their careers, and some writers were imprisoned or even killed.

Historical literature became more common during the 1930's and early 1940's. The scholar Yuri Tynyanov wrote novels set in the 1800's based on his research on literary history. One of the finest works about the revolution and the civil war was *The Quiet Don* (1928-1940) by Mikhail Sholokhov. This long epic novel tells the story of a young Cossack whose happiness is destroyed by the tragedy of war. Sholokhov received the Nobel Prize for literature in 1965.

World War II (1939-1945). During the war against Germany from 1941 to 1945, the Soviet government gave writers greater freedom, hoping to build the nation's morale. Themes of individual suffering and death dominated this period. *Days and Nights* (1943-1944) by Konstantin Simonov was one of many patriotic war novels. Not long after the war ended, the government reestablished strict controls over literature. It also forced several leading authors out of the Union of Soviet Writers. These writers included Akhmatova and Mikhail Zoshchenko, a noted humorist and satirist.

For most of the time from 1930 to 1953, writers did their best work "for the desk drawer" and only published it after Stalin's death in 1953. Lidia Chukovskaya's short novel *Sofia Petrovna,* written in 1939, tells how a good Soviet worker and mother watches as friends and coworkers are fired and arrested. She finally goes mad when her son, too, disappears into prison and then a labor camp. Playwright and prose writer Mikhail Bulgakov died in 1940, but his brilliant novel *The Master and Margarita* was not published until the 1960's. In the early 1950's, some of the most prominent Jewish writers in the Soviet Union were arrested and many of them were killed, especially those who wrote and published in Yiddish.

Post-Stalin Soviet literature. Stalin's death was followed by a period of relaxed restrictions in Soviet life and literature. This change became known as *The Thaw,* from the title of a short novel written by Ilya Ehrenburg in 1954. In contrast to the policy of describing Soviet life as happy and optimistic, Ehrenburg wrote about frustrated, lonely people. The height of freedom during The Thaw was marked in literature by the publication in 1962 of *One Day in the Life of Ivan Denisovich* by Alexander Solzhenitsyn. This short novel describes Soviet labor camps in Stalin's time. Solzhenitsyn had spent years in a labor camp, and one of his life's goals was to record the history of people's suffering under Stalin's tyranny.

A number of young liberal writers appeared in the Soviet Union during the 1960's. Three popular young poets were Yevgeny Yevtushenko, Andrey Voznesensky, and Bella Akhmadulina. They all spoke up for freedom and creativity in Soviet life. In "Babi Yar" (1961), Yevtushenko attacks the prejudice against Jews in the Soviet Union (see **Babi Yar**). The main theme of Voznesensky's work is self-analysis through personal experience. Akhmadulina wrote about the creative personality's conflict with the expectations of polite society.

Several talented young prose writers, including Vasily Aksyonov, wrote about the shortcomings of Soviet life. Vasily Shukshin and other writers described the hardships suffered by farmers and other non-elite members of Soviet society. Science fiction became popular, reflecting excitement at new discoveries and the successes of the Soviet space program. The brothers Arkady and Boris Strugatsky were the most prominent authors of Soviet science fiction, writing many stories and novels together.

© ITAR-TASS/Alamy Images

Alexander Solzhenitsyn

Censorship in the Soviet Union prevented many works from being published, though typewritten or *mimeographed* copies of some of the manuscripts circulated secretly. Mimeograph machines made duplicate copies from a stencil. This type of self-publishing became known as *samizdat.* Some Soviet writers published works abroad that had not been officially published in their own country. In 1957, Boris Pasternak's novel *Doctor Zhivago* appeared in Italy. Pasternak was awarded the 1958 Nobel Prize for his works, including this novel. He refused the prize under pressure from the Soviet government.

Andrey Sinyavsky, writing under the name of Abram Tertz, wrote several short stories that were published abroad beginning in 1959. Sinyavsky's works, including *The Trial Begins,* describe the terrors of life in a police state. Sinyavsky was arrested in 1966 and imprisoned in a labor camp until 1971. In 1973, he was allowed to emigrate to France. *The First Circle* by Solzhenitsyn was published in the West in 1968. The novel tells about the life of political prisoners in a research institute during the Stalin era. Solzhenitsyn won the Nobel Prize for literature in 1970. He was exiled from the Soviet Union in 1974 but returned to live in Russia in 1994, after the Soviet Union had broken up.

Joseph Brodsky was forced to leave the Soviet Union in 1972, though his poetry and his translations from English and Polish had no clear connections with politics. Brodsky won the Nobel Prize for literature in 1987. He was named poet laureate of the United States for 1991 and 1992, the first foreign-born poet so honored.

Modern Russian literature

From 1970 to 1991, political restrictions made publishing difficult in the Soviet Union. But many writers continued to resist or stretch the rules of Socialist Realism. Valentin Rasputin wrote about the decay of morals and standards and the loss of cultural traditions in rural areas due to neglect by the centralized Soviet government. Vladimir Voinovich wrote a humorous satire of Soviet life in *The Life and Extraordinary Adventures of Private Ivan Chonkin* (1975). Yuri Trifonov dealt with moral dilemmas faced by Soviet intellectuals in such works as *Another Life* (1975) and *Old Man* (1978).

Venedikt Erofeev's short novel, translated as *Moscow to the End of the Line* (1970), was first published abroad in samizdat and became a cult favorite. The book conveys the reflections of a thoughtful alcoholic on a short train ride and suggests the voyage of Russia in search of herself. Chingiz Aitmatov and Fazil Iskander became important Soviet authors, writing in Russian about characters, events, and concerns in Abkhazia, Kazakhstan, or Kyrgyzstan. Such experimental underground poets as Gennadi Aigi, Dmitri Prigov, Lev Rubinshtein, and

Vsevolod Nekrasov employed styles of writing very different from officially published poetry.

In the mid-1980's, Soviet leader Mikhail Gorbachev introduced a policy of *glasnost* (openness) that greatly relaxed censorship and led to freer public expression of information and opinion. The Soviet Union began publishing uncensored works of such important Soviet writers as Akhmatova, Bulgakov, and Pasternak. Pasternak's *Doctor Zhivago* and Zamyatin's *We* were published in the Soviet Union for the first time in 1988.

The Gorbachev period and the following years of political transition in Russia saw the massive publication of translations from foreign languages and also of works by formerly suppressed writers. They included works by Tsvetaeva, Mandelshtam, and Solzhenitsyn and by such religious thinkers as Nicolas Berdyaev, Vasily Rozanov, and Lev Shestov. Several talented women writers gained popularity, including Liudmila Petrushevskaia and Tatiana Tolstaya, a distant cousin of Leo Tolstoy. Such prominent poets as Olga Sedakova, Boris Slutsky, and David Samoilov were read more widely than ever. The era of Soviet literature ended in 1991, when the Soviet Union broke up into many independent countries.

Russian literature today is marked by dynamism and diversity, though no clear trends have emerged since the breakup of the Soviet Union. Many new writers have gained prominence. In general, poets and fiction writers no longer enjoy the high cultural status they had in the imperial and Soviet periods, and it is generally harder now for a professional writer to make a living.

Vladimir Makanin has written novels that treat the guilt of Russian intellectuals during the Soviet period. Viktor Erofeyev and Vladimir Sorokin write fiction dealing with sex, violence, horror, absurdity, and power used for evil, often using obscene language that was banned from print during the Soviet period.

Viktor Pelevin's fictional topics range from the everyday deceptions of the Soviet era to the negative impact of economic changes in post-Soviet Russia. Pelevin's works contain a strong element of mythology and great philosophical sophistication. Liudmila Ulitskaya is one of the most popular Russian prose authors of the early 2000's. Her works often trace the history of fictional families whose fate seems to have been formed in the Stalin period. Olga Slavnikova's novel *2017* (2006) combines near-future science fiction with the folk traditions of miners in the Ural Mountains.

Freed from the pressure of Socialist Realism, many different forms of fiction have flourished in Russia. Boris Akunin (the pen name of Grigory Chkhartishvili) and Alexandra Marinina write popular and successful series of detective novels. Russian fantasy, which was restricted to children's literature in the Soviet period, emerged partly from reading J. R. R. Tolkien. However, it also takes inspiration from Russian folk mythology. Popular fantasy authors include Nik Perumov and Sergei Lukyanenko. Science fiction continues to be eagerly read, though many of the works are dark, in contrast with the optimism of most Soviet-era works.

Important Russian poets of the early 2000's include Arkadi Dragomoshchenko, Elena Fanailova, and Viktor Krivulin. The censorship of the Soviet period kept the classical forms of Russian poetry largely intact, but now a reader is able to find all kinds of formal variations, from Classical verse by Vladimir Gandelsman to free verse by Polina Barskova. Maria Stepanova has produced new developments in traditional poetic forms. Marianna Geide uses serious traditional language to explore modern topics.

Sibelan Forrester

Related articles in *World Book* include:

Biographies

Brodsky, Joseph	Pasternak, Boris
Bunin, Ivan	Pushkin, Alexander
Chekhov, Anton	Sholokhov, Mikhail
Dostoevsky, Fyodor	Solzhenitsyn, Alexander
Gogol, Nikolai	Tolstoy, Alexei
Gorki, Maxim	Tolstoy, Leo
Mayakovsky, Vladimir	Turgenev, Ivan
Nabokov, Vladimir	Yevtushenko, Yevgeny

Other related articles

Censorship	Realism
Classicism	Romanticism
Drama (Russian drama and Chekhov)	Russia (History)
Folklore	Russian language
Nihilism	Satire
Novel (Russia)	Science fiction
Poetry	Symbolism

Russian Revolution of 1917 was a series of rebellions against the Russian *czar* (emperor), Nicholas II. The revolution swept away the Russian monarchy and laid the foundation for the Union of Soviet Socialist Republics, also known as the Soviet Union. The Soviet Union ruled Russia and its neighboring republics for 70 years.

In March 1917 (February on the old Russian calendar, which was changed in 1918), the Russian people rebelled against Czar Nicholas II. He gave up his throne, and a *provisional* (temporary) government tried to administer the country. That government was unable to resolve the many challenges facing Russia. The October Revolution took place in November 1917, when the Bolshevik (later Communist) Party seized power. That takeover is sometimes called the October, Bolshevik, or Communist Revolution.

Background to the revolution. Russia experienced great changes in the latter half of the 1800's and in the early 1900's. The *serfs* (rural slaves) were freed in 1861. However, they received little land and were heavily in debt. In the towns and cities, industrialization altered the face of Russian society.

Discontented Russians formed a number of political organizations, all of which the government tried to repress. There were four broad types of groups, with some overlapping ideals. *Liberals* wanted democratic checks on the power of the czars. *Nationalists* sought greater independence from Moscow for populations in Eastern Europe, the Caucasus, and elsewhere. *Peasant socialists* sought to start a revolution among the Russian peasants. *Marxists* wanted a revolution among the city and town workers. The Marxists were heavily influenced by the teachings and ideas of the German social philosopher Karl Marx.

In 1898, the Marxists formed the Russian Social Democratic Labor Party. In 1903, it split into two groups. Vladimir Ilyich Ulyanov, better known as V. I. Lenin, argued that party membership should be limited to a small number of professional revolutionaries. His opponents supported fewer limitations on party membership. Lenin named his faction the Bolsheviks ("members of the majority") and his opponents the Mensheviks ("members of the minority").

The 1905 Revolution. In the early 1900's, Russia's economy slowed, the country waged an unsuccessful war with Japan, and social unrest grew. On Jan. 22, 1905, thousands of men, women, and children peacefully marched to Czar Nicholas's Winter Palace in St. Petersburg, the capital. Their intention was to deliver a petition asking for better working conditions and a democratically elected assembly. The czar's soldiers fired on the demonstrators, killing or wounding hundreds of them.

The "Bloody Sunday" shootings fueled even greater demonstrations. The liberals formed a Union of Unions to help coordinate strikes and protests by different groups. A wave of strikes that began in September grew into a huge general strike in mid-October. Nicholas then agreed to set up an elected lawmaking body, called the Duma (parliament), to advise him, but strikes continued. In St. Petersburg, revolutionaries set up a *soviet* (council) called the St. Petersburg Soviet of Workers' Deputies. In December 1905, the army crushed an uprising in Moscow and police arrested the members of the St. Petersburg Soviet, including revolutionary leader Leon Trotsky.

Nicholas and his officials refused to give up much power, and the Duma did not work in the way the liberals had hoped. The czar dissolved the first two Dumas (1906 and 1907) after only a few months. For the third Duma (1907-1912), Nicholas changed the election law so that fewer workers and peasants could vote and so that border regions lost some representation. The changes resulted in a Duma dominated by supporters of the czar.

World War I (1914-1918) highlighted the weakness of czarist rule. Germany declared war on Russia in August 1914. Soon afterward, Russia changed the German-sounding name of St. Petersburg to Petrograd. The Germans easily overwhelmed a Russian army that was poorly trained and badly led. The war strained the Russian economy. Shortages of food and fuel resulted, increasing the level of social discontent. Within the army, untrained soldiers became rebellious. Many Russian army units refused to go on fighting the war with Germany.

Meanwhile, Czar Nicholas and his wife were deeply influenced by the monk Grigori Rasputin. Under Rasputin's influence, Nicholas filled key posts with officials who were incompetent and unpopular. In December 1916, a group of Russian nobles loyal to the czar murdered Rasputin.

The February Revolution. On March 8, 1917 (February 25, on the old Russian calendar), strikes and riots over food and coal shortages broke out in Petrograd. This uprising became known as the February Revolution. Troops sent to stop the uprising joined the demonstrators instead.

In response, some moderate and liberal members of the Duma set up a provisional government. On March 15, 1917, the government forced Czar Nicholas to *abdicate* (resign his throne). Nicholas and his family were later taken into custody. The Bolsheviks killed them at Yekaterinburg in 1918.

Also in March 1917, leaders of several workers' groups, left-leaning members of the Duma, and some soldiers revived the Petrograd soviet that had been first set up in 1905. The new soviet—called the Soviet of Workers' and Soldiers' Deputies—opposed the provisional government. It became a model for other soviets that were soon set up throughout Russia.

This environment, in which both the provisional government and the Petrograd Soviet claimed authority, became known as "Dual Power." The provisional government drew support from business people, military officers, and government officials. The Soviet had support among industrial workers and enlisted soldiers.

Lenin, who had lived in Switzerland since 1914, returned to Petrograd in April 1917. There, he began calling for an overthrow of the provisional government. In July, soldiers began another uprising in Petrograd. Once order was restored, the provisional government ordered Lenin to be arrested as a German agent. Lenin fled to Finland. Other leading Bolsheviks escaped or were imprisoned. Later that month, the provisional government appointed the socialist Alexander Kerensky as prime minister.

In September 1917, General Lavr Kornilov, the army commander in chief, made a bid to seize power. As Kornilov advanced on Petrograd, Kerensky released the imprisoned Bolsheviks and allowed them to arm the workers. Kornilov's force broke up before reaching the capital, and the coup attempt ended without violence. With their popularity on the rise, especially among soldiers, the Bolsheviks won a majority in the Petrograd Soviet soon after the "Kornilov affair."

The October Revolution. Trotsky, who had escaped in 1907 and gone into exile, had returned to Petrograd in May 1917 and was chosen to head the soviet there in September. Soon after, Lenin returned from Finland and urged the Bolsheviks to take power from the provisional government. On Nov. 7, 1917 (Oct. 25, 1917, on the old calendar), a Bolshevik-led army of workers, soldiers, and sailors took control of key positions in Petrograd. That night, they captured the Winter Palace, which had become the headquarters of Kerensky's provisional government. Other cities, including Moscow, soon fell to the Bolsheviks.

On Nov. 8, 1917, the All-Russian Congress of Soviets authorized the Bolsheviks to set up a Council of People's Commissars to run the national government. The new government established a secret police force called the Cheka. Local soviets in towns and cities throughout Russia gave workers control of factories and confiscated the property of large landowners, the Russian Orthodox Church, and anyone who opposed the revolution.

The new government quickly withdrew Russia from the war with Germany. On Dec. 2, 1917, Russia negotiated a cease-fire. On March 3, 1918, the government signed the Treaty of Brest-Litovsk to prevent German invasion. Under this treaty, Russia lost a quarter of its territory. Ukraine and Finland became independent. Bessarabia (now mostly part of Moldova), Lithuania, Latvia, Estonia, and the Polish territory that had been ruled by Russia fell under German control. Russia lost many of its factories and about a third of its food-producing land.

In March 1918, the Bolshevik government moved the capital of Russia from Petrograd to Moscow. The Bolsheviks also altered the name of their Russian Social

Democratic Labor Party to the Russian Communist Party. It later became the Communist Party of the Soviet Union. In July 1918, a Soviet constitution went into effect.

Barely a month after the October Revolution, counterrevolutionaries—known as Whites—began organizing resistance. Trotsky organized the Red Army (named for the red of the Communist flag) to fight the counterrevolutionaries as well as foreign intervention. The Red (Communist) Russians, aided by the peasantry, fought a bloody civil war with the Whites for nearly three years. The Whites received support from several other countries, including Canada, France, Japan, the United Kingdom, and the United States. Foreign-led resistance to the government continued in eastern Siberia for almost two years. But by 1920, the Communists had won and the revolution was complete.

Aftermath. Communist Russia gradually transformed itself into the Soviet Union. It reconquered Ukraine, which it had lost in 1918, and Georgia and eastern Armenia, which it had lost during the period of civil war. Russia also suppressed nationalist movements in central Asia and what is now Belarus. In 1922, the Russian Communist government formed the Union of Soviet Socialist Republics, or Soviet Union. In April 1922, Joseph Stalin became general secretary of the Communist Party. From this position, he gained control of the Soviet Union after the death of Lenin in 1924. Stalin remained in power until his own death in March 1953.

At first, many foreign nations refused to recognize the new Soviet government. The United Kingdom recognized the Soviet Union in 1924, followed by the United States in 1933. The Communist system ended in Russia in 1991, two years after it had collapsed in the East European countries. The Soviet Union itself also broke up.

Andrew Barnes

Related articles in *World Book* include:

Bloody Sunday
Bolsheviks
Brest-Litovsk, Treaty of
Communism (Communism in the Soviet Union)
Kerensky, Alexander Feodorovich
Krupskaya, Nadezhda Konstantinovna
Lenin, V. I.
Marx, Karl
Mensheviks
Nicholas II
Rasputin, Grigori Efimovich
Reed, John
Russia (History)
Stalin, Joseph
Trotsky, Leon
Union of Soviet Socialist Republics
World War I (Revolution in Russia)

Russo-Finnish wars. During World War II (1939-1945), the Soviet Union and Finland fought each other in two wars. They battled in the brief Winter War of 1939-1940. The second war, called the Continuation War, took place from 1941 to 1944. Finland lost both wars.

The Winter War. Germany conquered Poland in 1939. The Soviet Union feared a German invasion by way of Finnish territory. It maintained that it needed Finland's Karelian Isthmus, only 25 miles (40 kilometers) from the Soviet city of Leningrad (now St. Petersburg), to protect its borders. The Soviet Union demanded that Finland surrender this territory and allow it to set up defenses along the Finnish coast. The Finns refused. After talks failed, the Soviets broke diplomatic ties with the Finns.

On Nov. 30, 1939, the Soviets attacked Finland without formally declaring war. At first, the Finns were able to use their country's rugged, forested terrain to their advantage. In a series of brilliant maneuvers, they stopped the first Soviet attacks. Several nations, including France and the United Kingdom, tried to send military supplies to the Finns. But most supplies arrived too late to use in battle. By February 1940, the larger, better equipped Soviet invaders overwhelmed the exhausted defenders.

A peace treaty signed in Moscow on March 13, 1940, imposed extremely harsh terms on Finland. The Soviets took more than they had first demanded. Finland lost a tenth of its area, including most of Karelia, the industrialized areas of Lake Ladoga, strategic islands in the Gulf of Finland, and the Petsamo region on Finland's Arctic coast near the Soviet port of Murmansk. The Soviets also received a 30-year lease on the Hangö Peninsula.

The Continuation War. In 1940 and 1941, Finland entered into agreements that allowed Nazi Germany to move troops across Finland, and to base troops on Finnish soil. In return, Germany provided the Finnish army with military equipment. The Finns rejected Nazism, but they cooperated with Germany because it was the only nation able to give them large-scale military aid. On June 22, 1941, Germany invaded the Soviet Union. Finland joined this invasion hoping to regain the territory it had lost in 1940. By late 1941, Finnish troops reoccupied southern Karelia and advanced into Soviet Karelia, where they established defensive positions.

The war, however, later turned against the Germans and the Finns. In September 1944, Finland accepted severe Soviet peace terms. The treaty restored the 1940 Finnish-Soviet border. The Finns lost the Arctic port of Petsamo and nearby nickel mines. They regained the Hangö Peninsula but had to grant the Soviets a 50-year lease on the Porkkala Peninsula, near Helsinki. Finland agreed to disarm the German troops in Finland and to pay the Soviets $300 million for war damages. The Soviet Union returned the Porkkala Peninsula to Finland early in 1956. In 1962, the Soviets agreed to lease to Finland part of the Saimaa Canal, which was lost to the Soviet Union in 1940. William R. Trotter

See also **Finland** (History).

Russo-Japanese War brought recognition to Japan as a major world power. Russia's poor showing in the war sharpened the dissatisfaction of its people with the Russian government. This discontent helped shape the course of the Russian Revolution of 1905. The Russo-Japanese War began on Feb. 8, 1904, when Japan attacked Lüshun (also called Port Arthur) in Manchuria. It ended on Sept. 5, 1905, with the signing of the Treaty of Portsmouth.

Underlying causes of the war were the conflicting ambitions of Russia and Japan. Russia had been expanding its holdings and interests in the Far East throughout the late 1800's. In 1891, Russia began to build the Trans-Siberian Railroad connecting Moscow and Vladivostok. In 1896, a treaty between Russia and China allowed Russia to build the Chinese Eastern Railway across Manchu-ria. In 1898, Russia leased the Liaodong Peninsula from China and built there the naval base of Lüshun and the commercial port of Dalian. As a result of the Boxer Rebellion in China (1900-1901), Russia increased its influence in Manchuria (see **Boxer Rebellion**). Russia also expanded its influence in Korea during these years.

These actions disturbed Japan, which also wanted to extend its power at the expense of China. After Japan defeated China in a war (1894-1895), it tried to seize the

Liaodong Peninsula. But Russia, Germany, and France prevented that move. Japan became angry when Russia leased Liaodong. The two nations were also rivals in Korea, whose location was important to them both. Japan wanted to control Korean trade and industry. It already owned the Korean railroads and had sent thousands of Japanese settlers to Korea.

Japan sought a settlement with Russia over their rival interests in Manchuria and Korea. But Russia rejected Japan's offers. The Japanese therefore made an alliance with Britain in 1902 and began to prepare for war.

Attack on Lüshun. Japan broke off diplomatic relations with Russia on Feb. 6, 1904. On February 8, Vice Admiral Heihachiro Togo's fleet attacked Russian ships at Lüshun without warning. Japan declared war against Russia on February 10. Russia seemed so much more powerful than Japan that most people expected Russia to win the war easily. But Russia had only 80,000 troops in the Far East when the war began. More soldiers and all supplies for the army had to be shipped over 5,000 miles (8,000 kilometers) from western Russia on the uncompleted Trans-Siberian Railroad. Also, Russia was weakened by social and political problems that would lead to a revolution in 1905.

Final battles. Japan had 200,000 troops in North China, and another large army nearby. Japan lay closer to the scene of the fighting, and its people supported the government. Japanese warships and mines soon bottled up in Lüshun most of Russia's Pacific squadron. The Japanese destroyed most of the Russian ships that tried to escape. They also defeated the Russians at Vladivostok in the Battle of the Sea of Japan. Russia then ordered its Baltic Fleet to the Far East. This fleet steamed from the Baltic Sea around Africa, across the Indian Ocean, and into the Korean Strait. But the Japanese nearly annihilated it in the Battle of Tsushima Straits.

The land war went just as badly for the Russians. The Russians were handicapped by poor leadership and a lack of troops and supplies. The Japanese were trained and well-organized and had modern equipment. Japanese forces gradually drove the Russian forces back into Manchuria and defeated them at the Battle of Mukden in 1905. After a two-month siege, Lüshun surrendered to Japan. By then, both countries were ready to stop the war. The Japanese were running out of war funds. The Russian government wanted to end an unpopular war because revolution had broken out at home.

Treaty at Portsmouth. In 1905, at the secret suggestion of Japan, President Theodore Roosevelt of the United States arranged a peace conference at Portsmouth, New Hampshire. The Treaty of Portsmouth gave southern Sakhalin Island to Japan and forced Russia to remove its troops from Manchuria. Russia had to give Lüshun and Dalian to Japan and also leave Korea for the Japanese. But Russia kept control of the Chinese Eastern Railway. Donald J. Raleigh

Russo-Turkish wars were a series of conflicts between the Russian Empire and the Ottoman Empire, which was based in what is now Turkey. From the 1400's to the 1900's, these two empires engaged in nearly constant warfare with each other. At first, they clashed over lands that were claimed by both the Russians and the Crimean Tatars, who were allies of the Ottomans. Most of these lands lie in what is now Ukraine. Beginning in the late 1600's, Russian advances into Ottoman territory on the Black Sea and in southeastern Europe caused further fighting between the empires.

Peter the Great and then Catherine the Great of Russia each fought successful wars against the Ottomans. During the late 1600's, Peter forced them out of most of present-day Ukraine. During the 1700's, Catherine's armies conquered the Crimea, a peninsula that extends from southern Ukraine, and completed the opening of the southern lands to Russian settlement. Catherine also forced the Ottomans to allow Russian merchant vessels to sail the Black Sea.

Russia and Austria allied themselves against the Ottoman Empire during a war fought from 1736 to 1739. They also formed an alliance against the Ottomans in the two Russo-Turkish wars (1768-1774 and 1787-1792) fought in the reign of Catherine the Great. Russia and the Ottomans were allies briefly in the early 1800's, but this unusual arrangement did not last.

During the 1800's, Russia and the Ottomans fought four wars against each other: 1806-1812, 1828-1829, 1853-1856, and 1877-1878. At the end of the first war, Russia acquired Bessarabia (now parts of Moldova and Ukraine). It also gained a special position in the Balkans, a region that included present-day Albania and Bulgaria and much of what became Yugoslavia. The second war gave Russia control of the eastern coast of the Black Sea. The Ottomans won the third war, known as the Crimean War. As a result, Russia lost its dominant position in the Balkans and Black Sea area. However, it regained these losses after the 1877-1878 war.

During World War I (1914-1918), the Ottomans fought on the side of Germany against Russia and the other Allies. Both the Russian and Ottoman empires were destroyed in the war. The nations that succeeded the Ottoman and Russian empires—Turkey and the Soviet Union, respectively—continued to oppose each other. The Soviet Union attempted to seize portions of the Turkish Republic after World War II ended in 1945. But firm Turkish refusal and an alliance between Turkey and the United States blocked the attempt. Justin McCarthy

See also **Berlin, Congress of; Crimea; Crimean War.**

Russwurm, John Brown (1799-1851), was an early spokesman against slavery and a major figure in a black American "back-to-Africa" movement. Russwurm expressed his antislavery views chiefly through *Freedom's Journal,* a newspaper he and Samuel Cornish started in New York City in 1827. The newspaper was the first in the United States to be owned and operated by blacks.

Russwurm was born in Jamaica on Oct. 1, 1799. He grew up in Maine and graduated from Bowdoin College. He soon came to believe that blacks could never gain full U.S. citizenship. In 1829, he moved to Liberia, in Africa. Liberia had been founded in 1822 as a place where free blacks from the United States could settle. He served as governor of a colony at Cape Palmas, Liberia. He died there on June 9, 1851. Robert A. Pratt

Rust is the common name of a group of diseases caused by fungi that are parasites on plants. Rusts are especially harmful to cereal crops. The rust diseases are named for the spores produced by the fungi. These spores are brownish and resemble iron rust. Rusts have special organs resembling threads that grow among the cells of the host plant and absorb the food of the plant cells. This action robs the plant of nutrients and may cause the leaves and stems to wither. Badly rusted crops produce shriveled and worthless grain. Rust-causing fungi also attack other types of plants. For example, *asparagus rust* damages asparagus, *blister rust* attacks white pine trees, and *cedar rust* harms apples.

Every species of rust-causing fungi goes through a certain life cycle. Each period or stage in this life cycle is marked by a different type of spore formation. Some rust-causing fungi have as many as five different types of spores, while others have only two or three. Some species of rust-causing fungi spend their entire life cycle on one host. These species are called *autoecious.* Other species must spend their life cycle on two different hosts. This type is called *heteroecious.* The second host is known as the *alternate host.*

A common heteroecious type of rust-causing fungus causes *black stem rust* of wheat plants. This species has five different kinds of spores and must live its life cycle on two hosts, the wheat plant and the American barberry plant (see **Barberry**). In the spring, small cups filled with spores appear on the lower side of the leaves of the barberry plant. These spores are carried by the wind and spread to wheat plants. The spores germinate and send out threads, which enter the tissues of the wheat plant. The threads produce reddish spores that are carried to other healthy wheat plants. Then in the fall, a growth of tiny black spores appears on the plants' stalks and stubble. These black spores sprout in the spring and produce small colorless spores called *sporidia.* Such sporidia are carried by the wind to the barberry plant, the only plant on which they can grow. Tiny yellow spores then develop on the upper surface of the barberry leaves. Later, yellow-orange cups containing spores appear on the undersurface of the barberry leaves. These spores are not able to infect the barberry plants. They must be carried on the wind to wheat plants. There the life cycle begins again.

One method of controlling a rust that grows on two hosts is to destroy the alternate host. In the case of black stem rust, wheat crops have been saved by destroying barberry plants. Another method is to breed rust-resistant plants. Rust is sometimes controlled by destroying or uprooting crops affected by the disease. Crop rotation also helps prevent rust. Joseph G. Hancock

Rust is a brownish-red substance that forms on the surface of iron or steel when it is exposed to damp air. The term used alone means *iron rust,* which consists mainly of hydrated iron oxide ($3Fe_2O_3 \cdot H_2O$). Rust is formed by the union of the oxygen of the air with the iron by a process called *oxidation* (see **Oxidation**).

Rust not only corrodes the surface but also weakens the metal. Long exposure to air and moisture will cause nails to rust off, and rust holes to form in sheet iron. Iron can be *alloyed* (mixed) with other chemical elements to create rust-resistant metals called *stainless steels.* Iron and steel that are not rust resistant should be kept dry or coated with some substance, such as chrome or paint, that will resist the action of oxygen. Polished tools may be easily protected if wiped with a cloth soaked in oil. Coating metal objects with heavy greases or spray-on plastics, or wrapping them in special chemically treated paper, also prevents rust.

A coat of rust may be removed by scrubbing in water or using a polishing powder. Removal of a thick coat requires use of an emery wheel, a grindstone, or a file. Acids also dissolve rust. Raymond E. Davis

See also **Corrosion; Stainless steel.**

Rustin, Bayard, *BY urd* (1912?-1987), was an American civil rights leader. A Quaker and a pacifist, he believed in achieving civil rights by nonviolent means. Rustin was the chief organizer of the 1963 March on Washington. About 250,000 people took part in the march to protest racial injustice in the United States. He also planned the organization of the Southern Christian Leadership Conference, led by Martin Luther King, Jr. In 1947, Rustin helped organize the first "freedom ride" into the South to protest racial discrimination. Because he was openly homosexual, Rustin was forced out of many leadership positions. But in 1964, he became executive director of the A. Philip Randolph Institute in New York City. This group works toward economic and social reforms to benefit Americans of all races. Rustin was born on March 17, 1910 or 1912, in West Chester, Pennsylvania. He died on Aug. 24, 1987. Robert A. Pratt

Rutabaga, *ROO tuh BAY guh,* is a plant with an edible root that tastes like a turnip. It is also called Swede, Swedish turnip, and Russian turnip. Rutabagas are hardier than turnips and so are usually harvested later in the year. The yellow roots are rich in vitamins and minerals. The blue-green leaves also may be eaten. They usually are harvested in early summer because they become spongy and bitter in hot weather. Albert Liptay

Scientific classification. Rutabaga's scientific name is *Brassica napus,* variety *napobrassica.*

WORLD BOOK illustration by Cy Baker, Wildlife Art Ltd.

The rutabaga has edible roots that are rich in vitamins and minerals. It tastes like a turnip.

Rutgers, the State University of New Jersey, has its main campus at New Brunswick and nearby Piscataway, New Jersey. It also has undergraduate colleges and graduate and professional schools in Newark and Camden. In addition, Rutgers offers extension courses throughout the state. The university's website at http://www.rutgers.edu offers additional information.

Rutgers was founded in 1766 as Queen's College. In 1825, the school was renamed Rutgers College. The first intercollegiate football game was played between Rutgers and Princeton in 1869. Rutgers became a university in 1924 and was designated as the state university of New Jersey by legislation in 1945 and 1956. The university's athletic teams are called the Scarlet Knights.

For some time, the main campus at Rutgers was divided into several individual colleges (in addition to Rutgers College), each with independent admissions policies and academic requirements. Douglass College, founded in 1918 as the New Jersey College for Women, admitted women students. University College, founded in 1934, served adult and part-time students. In 1969, Livingston College was founded as a coeducational and liberal arts college. In 2007, Douglass College was renamed Douglass Residential College. Douglass continued its mission of educating undergraduate women at Rutgers. However, admissions, academic requirements, and degrees for all the individual colleges were centralized under Rutgers University.

Critically reviewed by Rutgers, the State University of New Jersey

Ruth, Babe (1895-1948), was the first great home run hitter in baseball history. His batting ability and colorful personality attracted huge crowds. He made baseball more exciting by establishing homers as a common part of the game. Ruth had a .342 lifetime batting average.

George Herman Ruth was born on Feb. 6, 1895, in Baltimore. He began his baseball career in 1914 with the Baltimore Orioles, a minor league team at the time. Later that same year, he joined the Boston Red Sox as a pitcher. In the 1916 and 1918 World Series, Ruth pitched 29 ⅔ consecutive scoreless innings. He won 94 games and lost 46 in the major leagues. But Ruth had even greater talent as a hitter and began to play regularly in the outfield in 1918. That year also marked his first big home run season, when he hit 11. In 1920, the Red Sox sold Ruth to the New York Yankees. He attracted so many fans that Yankee Stadium, which opened in 1923, was nicknamed "the House That Ruth Built." Ruth led the American League in home runs 12 times, in runs batted in 6 times, and in runs scored 8 times. In 1924, he had the highest batting average (.378).

In 1927, Babe Ruth set a record of 60 home runs during a 154-game season. In 1961, Roger Maris hit 61 home runs during a 162-game season. Both feats were considered major league records until 1991, when Maris's 61 home runs were recognized as the sole record. Ruth hit 714 homers during his career, a record until Hank Aaron hit his 715th home run in 1974.

The Yankees released Ruth after the 1934 season, and he ended his playing career in 1935 with the Boston Braves. In the final game he started in the outfield for Boston, Ruth hit three home runs. In 1936, Ruth became one of the first five players elected to the National Baseball Hall of Fame. He died on Aug. 16, 1948.

Jack Lang

See also **Baseball** (The Babe Ruth Era; picture).

AP Photo

Babe Ruth was the first great home run hitter in major league baseball history and one of the sport's most popular players. Ruth hit 714 home runs during his career.

Ruth, Book of, is a book of the Hebrew Bible, or Old Testament. The story centers on the loving and loyal behavior of Ruth, a Moabite woman married to an Israelite. Left widowed and childless in Moab, Ruth resolves to leave her homeland and follow her mother-in-law, Naomi, to Bethlehem. When Naomi urges her to stay among her people, Ruth responds with the words "Where you go, I will go; ... your people shall be my people, and your God my God. Where you die, I will die—there will I be buried" (Ruth 1:16-17). Ruth manages to obtain food for herself and Naomi and to marry Boaz, a kinsman, and thus secure the family heritage.

The story of Ruth is a beautifully crafted piece of literature. It conveys the resources of individuals in dealing with life's problems. It shows Israelite openness to all peoples and the independent and courageous actions of women in ancient Israel. Since Ruth is portrayed as the great-grandmother of King David, the book links her to the genealogy of Israel's royal family. Carol L. Meyers

Ruthenia is a historic region in Ukraine. Ruthenia lies on the southern slopes of the Carpathian Mountains and on the nearby southwest highland. It covers about 4,940 square miles (12,800 square kilometers) and has about 1,257,000 people. Uzhhorod is the region's principal city.

In the 900's and 1000's, Ruthenia was part of Kievan Rus, the first state founded by the East Slavs. Ruthenia later came under the control of Magyar (Hungarian) landlords. In 1919, Ruthenia became a province of Czechoslovakia.

Ruthenia once had great strategic value because of its location near several countries. Germany, Hungary, Poland, and the Soviet Union all tried to gain control of the area in the 1930's. In 1939, Hungary took control of the entire region. The Soviet Union occupied Ruthenia in 1944, during World War II. It officially annexed the region in 1945. Ruthenia was made part of the Ukrainian Soviet Socialist Republic. In 1991, the republic became the independent country of Ukraine.

Ruthenium, *roo THEE nee uhm,* is a rare, silver-white metallic element. It is used mainly in jewelry as a hardener of the metals platinum and palladium. Alloys of ruthenium with those metals are highly resistant to wear and are used for electrical contacts in the ignition systems of some aircraft engines. Karl Klaus, a Russian chemist, discovered ruthenium in 1844. Ruthenium has an *atomic number* (number of protons in its nucleus) of 44. Its *relative atomic mass* is 101.07. An element's relative atomic mass equals its *mass* (amount of matter) divided by $\frac{1}{12}$ of the mass of carbon 12, the most abundant form of carbon. Ruthenium melts at about 2300 °C and boils at about 4000 °C. Its chemical symbol is Ru.

R. Craig Taylor

Rutherford, Ernest (1871-1937), a New Zealand-born British physicist, established the nuclear model of the atom in 1911. Later, he became the first person to break up the nucleus of an atom. Because of his many contributions, he is often called the father of nuclear science.

In the nuclear model, Rutherford theorized that atoms are constructed much like the solar system. That is, a heavy part, called the *nucleus,* forms the center of each atom. Particles with a negative electric charge, called *electrons,* form the outer part, most of which consists of empty space. In 1913, Niels Bohr combined this nuclear model of the atom with the quantum theory in the Bohr theory of atomic structure (see **Bohr, Niels**).

In 1902, Rutherford and the British chemist Frederick Soddy published their discovery of *atomic transmutation.* Their observations proved that radioactive elements give off electrically charged particles known as alpha and beta particles. This process changes the *parent* (original) atom into a *daughter* atom. The daughter atom is a different chemical element. This achievement won Rutherford the 1908 Nobel Prize in chemistry.

Rutherford produced the first artificial atomic transmutations in a series of experiments from 1917 to 1919. He bombarded nitrogen atoms with alpha particles. In rare collisions, an alpha particle pushed a *proton,* a positively charged particle, out of a nitrogen nucleus. At the same time, the nucleus absorbed the alpha particle, becoming an oxygen nucleus.

Rutherford was born on Aug. 30, 1871, in Nelson, New Zealand. He taught at McGill University in Montreal, the University of Manchester, and Cambridge University. In 1903, he was elected a Fellow of the Royal Society. He wrote several books, including *Radioactive Substances and Their Radiations* (1913). In 1931, he received the title of Baron Rutherford of Nelson. Rutherford died on Oct. 19, 1937. Roger H. Stuewer

See also **Atom** (The first descriptions of atomic structure).

Rutherfordium is an artificially produced radioactive element with 104 protons—that is, an *atomic number* of 104. Scientists have discovered many *isotopes* of rutherfordium. Isotopes of an element have the same number of protons but different numbers of neutrons. The most stable isotope of rutherfordium has an *atomic mass number* (total of protons and neutrons) of 261. This isotope has a *half-life* of 65 seconds—that is, due to radioactive decay, only half the atoms in a sample of isotope 261 would still be atoms of that isotope after 65 seconds.

In 1964, scientists at the Joint Institute for Nuclear Research in Dubna, near Moscow, claimed they had produced the element. Dubna was then part of the Soviet Union and is now in Russia. The Soviet scientists had bombarded plutonium, whose atomic number is 94, with neon, whose atomic number is 10. From 1966 to 1970, Dubna presented additional claims for the element. In 1969, scientists at the Lawrence Radiation Laboratory (now Lawrence Berkeley National Laboratory) in Berkeley, California, made a rival claim. The Americans had bombarded californium, whose atomic number is 98, with carbon, which has an atomic number of 6.

In 1986, the International Union of Pure and Applied Chemistry (IUPAC) and the International Union of Pure and Applied Physics formed a working group to review the histories of the elements with atomic numbers from 101 to 109. IUPAC is the recognized authority in crediting the discovery of elements and assigning names to them. The group concluded that the Berkeley claim and a 1969-1970 Dubna claim—but not the 1964 claim—were strong. In 1993, IUPAC accepted the group's recommendation that credit for the discovery be shared by the two institutions. Disagreements about what to name the element delayed an official naming until 1997, however.

Rutherfordium is named for the New Zealand-born physicist Ernest Rutherford. The symbol for rutherfordium is Rf. Before being named, rutherfordium was commonly referred to as *element 104.* Richard L. Hahn

Rutland (pop. 16,495) is the third largest city in Vermont. Only Burlington and South Burlington have more people. Rutland lies west of the Green Mountains in central Vermont (see **Vermont** [political map]). Industries in the Rutland area manufacture calcium carbonate products, iron lighting, jet engine parts, and wood products. Ski resorts are an important source of income in the area. Rutland is the home of the College of St. Joseph. The *Rutland Herald,* established in 1794, is Vermont's oldest continuously published newspaper. A mayor and board of aldermen govern Rutland.

John McCardell

Rutledge, Ann (1813-1835), became famous as Abraham Lincoln's first sweetheart. Romantic stories of their tragic love affair are based more on legend than on fact.

Ann Rutledge was born on Jan. 7, 1813, in Henderson County, Kentucky. She was the daughter of the innkeeper in New Salem, Illinois, where Lincoln lived for a time. She was engaged to John McNamar, a wealthy settler. He left for the East, and there was doubt that he would return to marry Ann. Meanwhile, she may have accepted a proposal of marriage from Lincoln. But she soon became ill and died on Aug. 25, 1835. Mark E. Neely, Jr.

Rutledge, Edward (1749-1800), a lawyer and statesman, was a South Carolina signer of the Declaration of Independence. He represented South Carolina in the First and Second Continental Congresses from 1774 to 1776. He defended American rights within the British Empire but accepted independence only reluctantly.

Rutledge was born in Charleston, South Carolina, on Nov. 23, 1749. He studied law in Britain. During the American Revolution (1775-1783), he was a captain of artillery. The British captured him when Charleston fell in 1780 and held him prisoner for about a year.

From 1782 to 1795, Edward Rutledge was a state representative. He served in the South Carolina Senate from 1796 to 1798 and was governor of South Carolina from 1798 to 1800. He died on Jan. 23, 1800. Robert M. Weir

Rutledge, John (1739-1800), was a South Carolina signer of the Constitution of the United States. At the Constitutional Convention of 1787, he favored efforts to develop a strong national government. Rutledge also helped convince Northern delegates that the Southern States would withdraw from the United States if the Constitution prohibited slavery.

Rutledge was born in Charleston in September 1739. He was educated in Charleston and London. He represented South Carolina in the First Continental Congress in 1774 and the Second Continental Congress in 1775. From 1776 to 1778, Rutledge was South Carolina's first executive, with the title of president. He was governor of South Carolina from 1779 to 1782. He served in the Congress of the Confederation from May 1782 to September 1783 and in the South Carolina House of Representatives from 1784 to 1790.

President George Washington appointed Rutledge an associate justice of the Supreme Court of the United States in 1789. But Rutledge served only a short time, and in 1791 became chief justice of South Carolina. In 1795, Washington nominated Rutledge as chief justice of the United States. Rutledge presided during the August term. But the U.S. Senate rejected his nomination, largely because of his opposition to the Jay Treaty of 1794. Rutledge died on July 18, 1800. Robert M. Weir

Ruysdael, Jacob van. See **Ruisdael, Jacob van.**

Rwanda, *roo WAHN duh,* is a small country in east-central Africa, just south of the equator. It is one of the poorest and most crowded countries on the continent. It has little industry and more people than the land can support. Kigali is Rwanda's capital and largest city.

Although Rwanda is near the equator, it has a cool, pleasant climate. It has cool weather because it lies on a high plateau along the western edge of the Great Rift Valley. Rwanda's landscape ranges from volcanic mountains to winding river valleys, and from beautiful lakes to grassy plains. Volcanoes National Park in the Virunga Mountains of northwestern Rwanda is a refuge for mountain gorillas, an endangered species.

Ethnic conflict has been a major part of Rwandan life. A large majority of Rwandans belong to the Hutu (also called the Bahutu) ethnic group. The Tutsi (also called the Batutsi or Watusi) form a minority. Before European colonization, the two groups lived together in relative peace. From the late 1890's until 1962, first Germany and then Belgium ruled Rwanda. Tensions between the Hutu and the Tutsi intensified because the colonial governments favored the Tutsi and helped them acquire power and wealth. In 1959, the Hutu rebelled against the Tutsi. After Rwanda became independent in 1962, the Hutu controlled the government. Ethnic violence and discrimination in the 1960's drove many Tutsi to flee into exile.

Rwanda gained international attention in 1994, when a bloody conflict between the two groups broke out. During this conflict, government-backed Hutu extremists massacred at least 500,000 Tutsi and moderate Hutu. The conflict ended after a Tutsi-controlled rebel group gained control of the government. See the *History* section of this article for details.

Government. In 2003, voters approved a new constitution for Rwanda. Under the Constitution, the president is the country's most powerful official. Voters elect the president to a five-year term. The president appoints a prime minister and Cabinet to help carry out government operations. Rwanda's legislature consists of an 80-member Chamber of Deputies and a 26-member Senate. Deputies serve five-year terms. Senators serve eight-year terms. Rwanda's main political party is the Rwandan Patriotic Front (RPF). The RPF, originally made up mainly of Tutsi, overthrew a Hutu-controlled government in 1994. The Constitution reserves seats in the legislature for women, representatives of a youth organization, and a representative for people with disabilities.

Rwanda

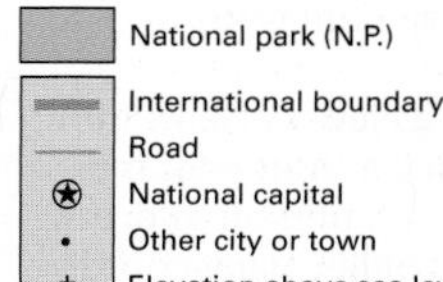

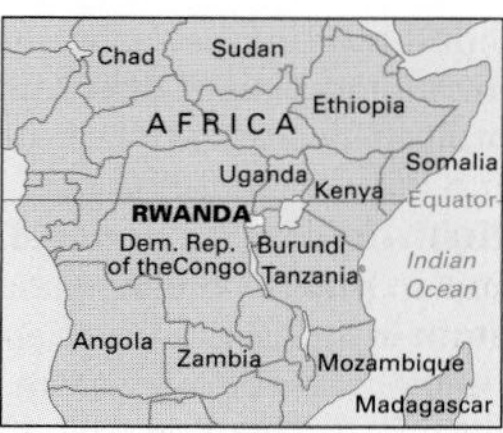

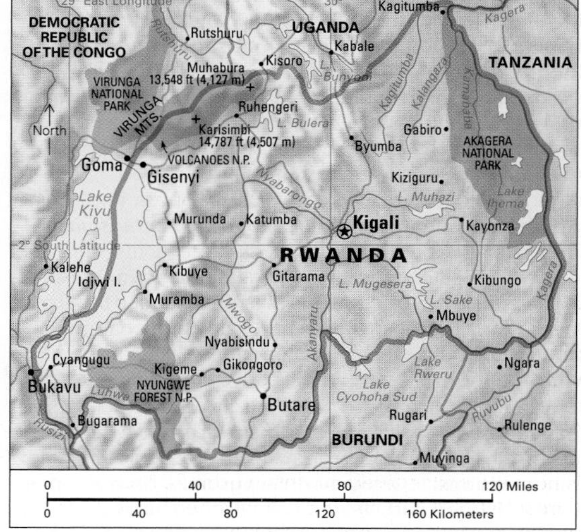

WORLD BOOK maps

People. About 85 percent of the people of Rwanda are Hutu, and about 15 percent are Tutsi. Historically, the Hutu have been farmers who raise crops to feed their families, and the Tutsi have raised cattle and goats and served as chiefs in business or government. Today, however, few obvious lifestyle differences exist between the Hutu and Tutsi. The groups generally share a common culture and live in integrated communities. Both groups speak Kinyarwanda, a Bantu language.

The Twa, a Pygmy group, make up less than 1 percent of Rwanda's population. They once made their living by hunting, but some now live and work in towns.

Kinyarwanda, English, and French are Rwanda's official languages. Most people speak Kinyarwanda. Over half of the people are Roman Catholics, and about a

Facts in brief

Capital: Kigali.
Official languages: English, French, and Kinyarwanda.
Official name: Rwandese Republic.
Area: 10,169 mi² (26,338 km²). *Greatest distances*—east-west, 145 mi (233 km); north-south, 110 mi (177 km).
Population: *Estimated 2022 population*—13,333,000; density, 1,311 per mi² (506 per km²); distribution, 83 percent rural, 17 percent urban. *2020 official government estimate*—12,663,116.
Chief products: *Agriculture*—bananas, beans, beef and dairy cattle, cassava, coffee, potatoes, sorghum, sweet potatoes, tea. *Mining*—niobium, tin, tungsten.
Flag: The flag has three horizontal stripes of blue, yellow, and green, with a yellow sun in the upper right corner. See **Flag** (picture: Flags of Africa).
Money: *Basic unit*—Rwandan franc.

third are Protestants. Many Christians also follow some traditional African religious practices. About 5 percent of Rwanda's people are Muslims. The Roman Catholic and Protestant churches operate most elementary and high schools. The National University of Rwanda operates in Butare, and several newer universities now operate in Kigali. Public education is free and required for children from ages 7 through 15. The majority of adult Rwandans can read and write.

Land. Much of Rwanda's land is rugged and mountainous. The country's highest mountains, in the northwest, were formed by volcanic activity. Lake Kivu and the Rusizi River form Rwanda's western border and are part of Africa's Great Rift Valley. The Kagera River forms the eastern border, and the Akanyaru River forms part of the southern border. The land rises sharply from Lake Kivu to about 9,000 feet (2,700 meters) above sea level, forming the continental divide between the Nile and Congo river valleys. The Virunga Mountains rise to 14,800 feet (4,510 meters) in the northwest.

A series of plateaus in eastern Rwanda range from 5,000 to 7,000 feet (1,500 to 2,100 meters) above sea level and slope down toward the east. Each plateau is bounded on the east by an *escarpment* (steep edge) with a marsh at its foot. Forests once covered the plateaus, but the majority of this land has been cleared for farming. Rwanda's wildlife refuges are popular tourist destinations. Volcanoes National Park in the northwest is home to endangered mountain gorillas. Nyungwe Forest National Park in the southwest has large troops of monkeys. Many large mammals inhabit Akagera National Park in the east.

The high-altitude areas in the west have an average annual temperature of 73 °F (23 °C) and an average annual rainfall of 30 inches (76 centimeters). The mountainous areas in the northwest have an average annual temperature of 63 °F (17 °C) and an average annual rainfall of 58 inches (147 centimeters). On the plateaus, the temperature averages 68 °F (20 °C) annually. Annual rainfall is about 47 inches (119 centimeters). Rwanda has two dry seasons and two rainy seasons.

Economy. Rwanda is a poor country, and many of its people live in poverty. Foreign aid is a helpful source of national income. Agriculture is the main economic activity in Rwanda. Many Rwandans are farmers who work their own land. Because the plots of land are small, many farmers grow only enough food to feed their families. Food crops include bananas, beans, cassava, corn, potatoes, sorghum, and sweet potatoes. Some rural people also raise beef and dairy cattle and goats.

Bernard Gerard, Explorer

Rwanda is a country in east-central Africa. Small towns, villages, and farms dot the country's landscape. This photograph shows a street scene in the town of Gitarama.

Coffee and tea are among the country's chief exports. Rwandan farmers grow both of the two main types of coffee plants, *Coffea arabica* and *Coffea robusta.* Most farmers in Rwanda have at least a few coffee trees. Tea is grown on large plantations.

Mined products, including niobium, tin, and tungsten, are also exported. Most manufacturing in Rwanda is for domestic consumption. Rwanda has no railroads. The country's main highways are paved, but many other roads are dirt. Kigali has an international airport.

Rwanda's chief trading partners include China, India, Kenya, Tanzania, Uganda, and the United Arab Emirates. Rwanda imports much more than it exports. Because the country is landlocked, it must transport goods over land, which increases their cost. The country's imports include food, machinery, petroleum products, and vehicles. Many of Rwanda's exports are shipped through Uganda to the port of Mombasa in Kenya, or through Burundi or Tanzania to the Tanzanian port of Dar es Salaam.

History. Twa hunters were the original inhabitants of what is now Rwanda. Small groups of farmers and cattle herders migrated into the area nearly 2,000 years ago. The ancestors of the Hutu and the Tutsi developed a common language and culture. Around the 1500's, the Tutsi established themselves as the elite, those who owned cattle and held political power in the Rwandan kingdom. Many Hutu farmers provided labor and military services to Tutsi landowners in return for cattle. Intermarriage between the groups was common, however, and people could change economic and social status.

Germany colonized the area that is now Rwanda and Burundi in the 1890's and ruled it as part of German East Africa. During World War I (1914-1918), Belgian troops occupied the area. After the war, the area, then called Ruanda-Urundi, became a *mandated territory* of Belgium—that is, a colony or territory placed under Belgium's administration. Under Belgian rule, inequalities between the Hutu and Tutsi intensified. The Belgians favored the Tutsi, who received greater employment and educational opportunities than the Hutu or Twa. The Belgians also formalized ethnic divisions by requiring all people to carry passes identifying themselves as Hutu, Tutsi, or Twa. In 1946, Ruanda-Urundi became a United Nations (UN) trust territory administered by Belgium.

The Tutsi King Mutara III died in 1959, and political unrest followed. Mutara's half-brother succeeded him as King Kigeli V (also spelled Kigeri), but the Belgian-controlled government overthrew Kigeli while he was out of the country. The Hutu rebelled against the Tutsi, and several thousand Tutsi died. Attacks against Tutsi continued until 1965. During this period, about 150,000 Tutsi fled to Burundi, Uganda, and Congo.

Elections held in 1960 gave the Hutu control of the government. Ruanda-Urundi became independent as two countries, Rwanda and Burundi, on July 1, 1962. The people of Rwanda elected Grégoire Kayibanda, a Hutu from the south of the country, as the first president.

In 1973, military leaders led by Major General Juvénal Habyarimana, a Hutu from northern Rwanda, overthrew Kayibanda. Habyarimana then became president. During the next several years, he established a single political party and imposed a new constitution.

In 1990, a growing number of Rwandans protested the Habyarimana regime and demanded democracy. Also in 1990, a rebel group called the Rwandan Patriotic Front (RPF) began launching attacks against the government. Most of the rebels were Tutsi. In 1993, the government and the RPF signed a peace agreement in which they agreed to share power in a democratic regime.

In April 1994, Habyarimana died after his airplane was shot down near Kigali. Hutu extremists in Rwanda's government began a campaign of violence against people they viewed as political opponents. Hutu militias, known as the Interahamwe, massacred thousands of Tutsi and moderate Hutu. From April to July, about 500,000 people, mostly Tutsi, were slaughtered. In response, the RPF launched military attacks against government forces. More than 2 million refugees, mostly Hutu, left Rwanda to escape RPF forces. Many refugees fled to Zaire (now the Democratic Republic of the Congo, or DRC).

The RPF defeated the Hutu forces by mid-July and took control of Rwanda's government. The RPF established a multiparty system that included some moderate Hutu officials. Pasteur Bizimungu, a Hutu from the RPF, was appointed president. In 1994, the UN created a special court of justice to prosecute the organizers of the *genocide* (systematic killing) of Tutsi and moderate Hutu. The RPF government emphasized building the economy and promoting reconciliation. However, ethnic tensions in Rwanda remained high. From 1994 to 1996, the former Hutu army remained in Zaire. Many Hutu soldiers lived in refugee camps. In 1996, the RPF began attacking refugee camps. Rwanda then aided rebels to overthrow the Zairian government in 1997. The fighting forced many Hutu refugees back to Rwanda. In 1998, Rwandan troops backed another group of Congolese rebels in a war against the new government of the DRC.

In 2000, Bizimungu resigned as president. Vice President Paul Kagame, a Tutsi and head of the RPF, succeeded him. In July 2002, Rwanda and the DRC signed a peace agreement. In 2003, Rwandan voters approved a new constitution. Later that year, Kagame was elected to a seven-year term as president, and the RPF won a large majority of seats in the Chamber of Deputies. Kagame was reelected in 2010. The RPF kept its majority in the Chamber of Deputies after elections in September 2013. In 2017, Kagame was elected to a third presidential term.

In 2007, Rwanda joined the East African Community (EAC). The EAC promotes economic and political cooperation among its members. Other member countries include Kenya, Tanzania, and Uganda. Timothy Longman

Related articles in *World Book* include:

Bantu	Hutu	Rwandan Genocide
Burundi	Kigali	Tutsi
Congo, Democratic Republic of the	Pygmies	

Rwandan Genocide refers to the mass killings of at least 500,000 Rwandans from April to July 1994. Most of the victims were Tutsi, an ethnic minority in Rwanda. The term *genocide* refers to the systematic destruction of an ethnic, racial, religious, or national group. Government forces carried out the genocide in the name of protecting the Hutu ethnic majority.

The Hutu and Tutsi generally speak the same language, live in the same areas, and follow similar traditions. But ethnicity has long caused social and political tensions in Rwanda. A critical period occurred under Belgian colonial rule in the early to mid-1900's. The Belgians initially favored the Tutsi, giving them more power in government administration and greater job and educational opportunities than the Hutu. The Belgians also formalized the ethnic divisions by requiring all people to carry passes identifying themselves as Hutu or Tutsi.

As Rwandans struggled for independence in the late 1950's and early 1960's, a violent reversal of the ethnic power structure took place. The period is called the "Hutu social revolution." In 1959, a Hutu uprising led to violence against the Tutsi. With Belgian help, Hutu elites took over the government. After Rwanda gained independence in 1962, Hutu secured the presidency. Violence during the uprising and the early years of independence resulted in the deaths of thousands of Tutsi. After independence, the Tutsi were subjected to discrimination and political repression. Hundreds of thousands of Tutsi fled to neighboring countries.

Beginning in 1990, a Uganda-based Tutsi-led rebel group, the Rwandan Patriotic Front (RPF), launched attacks against the Hutu-led government. In August 1993, the government signed a peace treaty with the RPF. But on April 6, 1994, Rwandan President Juvénal Habyarimana, a Hutu, was killed when his plane was shot down above Kigali, Rwanda's capital. Hutu extremists filled the power vacuum left by the president's assassination. The extremists immediately began a campaign of violence against people they viewed as political opponents.

Over the following three months, government forces with militia and civilian assistance massacred at least 500,000 people in one of the worst human rights violations of the 1900's. Most victims were Tutsi, but Hutu who opposed the violence also were killed.

Meanwhile, the RPF advanced against government forces, eventually defeating them and taking control of Rwanda's government. The RPF also committed human rights violations as they secured the country. More than 2 million refugees, mostly Hutu, left Rwanda to escape the RPF. Most refugees fled to Zaire (now the Democratic Republic of the Congo, or DRC), where violence between Hutu and Tutsi continued for years.

In late 1994, the United Nations created a special court of justice to prosecute the organizers of the genocide in Rwanda. The court convicted dozens of individuals. The RPF-led Rwandan government also tried hundreds of thousands of perpetrators in domestic courts and through a community justice program. Scott Straus

See also **Genocide; Rwanda** (History).

Rx. See ℞ (symbol) alphabetized between **R** and **Ra.**

Ryan, Nolan (1947-), ranks among baseball's greatest pitchers. In his major league career, Ryan struck out 5,714 batters, a record. In 1973, Ryan set a major league record of 383 strikeouts for a season. He pitched seven no-hit games in the major leagues. No other pitcher has more than four major league no-hitters. During his career, Ryan won 324 games. He is one of 24 pitchers in major league history to win 300 games. Ryan was especially noted for his blazing fast ball and his durability.

Lynn Nolan Ryan was born on Jan. 31, 1947, in Refugio, Texas. He began his major league career with the New York Mets in 1966 and pitched again for the Mets from 1968 to 1971. He played for the California Angels (now the Los Angeles Angels of Anaheim) from 1972 to 1979 and the Houston Astros from 1980 to 1988. He pitched for the Texas Rangers from 1989 until his retirement after the 1993 season. Ryan was elected to the National Baseball Hall of Fame in 1999. In 2008, he became president of the Rangers. In 2011, Ryan became chief executive officer. He retired in 2013. Donald Honig

See also **Baseball** (picture).

Ryan, Paul (1970-), an American politician, served as the speaker of the United States House of Representatives from 2015 to 2019. Ryan was the Republican nominee for vice president of the United States in 2012. Ryan and the Republican presidential nominee, Mitt Romney, lost to their Democratic opponents, President Barack Obama and Vice President Joe Biden, in the November election. Ryan represented southeastern Wisconsin in the U.S. House of Representatives from 1999 to 2019.

Early life and family. Paul Davis Ryan, Jr., was born in Janesville, Wisconsin, on Jan. 29, 1970. He was the youngest of four children. He was only 16 when his father, Paul Ryan, Sr., died of a heart attack.

Ryan graduated from Miami University, in Oxford, Ohio, in 1992 with a bachelor's degree in political science and economics. In 1991, while still a student, Ryan worked as an intern in the office of Senator Bob Kasten, a Wisconsin Republican. In 1993, Ryan went to work for Empower America, a center for conservative research based in Washington, D.C. Ryan married Janna Little, a former tax attorney and lobbyist, in 2000. The couple have three children: Elizabeth, Charles, and Samuel.

Career. In 1997, Ryan returned to Janesville. He worked for a short time as a marketing consultant for Ryan Incorporated Central, a construction firm started by his great-grandfather.

In 1998, at the age of 28, Ryan announced his candidacy for a seat in the U.S. House of Representatives. He supported tax cuts and greater rights for gun owners. He also spoke out strongly against abortion. He won the November election by a large margin.

As a congressman, Ryan sought to reduce the size of government. He proposed measures to partially *privatize* (shift from government to private ownership) Social Security and Medicare. Ryan also became known as an expert on the federal budget.

Ryan became chairman of the House Budget Committee in 2011. That year, Ryan issued "The Path to Prosperity," a budget plan that called for deep spending cuts in federal programs. The plan failed to pass the Democratic-controlled Senate, but the debates helped make Ryan a national figure. Ryan also became a senior member of the House Ways and Means Committee.

In August 2012, Mitt Romney, after becoming the Republican presidential nominee, selected Ryan to be his running mate. Romney and Ryan lost the election. Election law allowed Ryan to concurrently seek the vice presidency and reelection to the House. In October 2015, Ryan succeeded John Boehner as speaker of the House after Boehner retired. Ryan did not seek reelection in 2018.

Jeremy D. Mayer

U.S. House of Representatives

Paul Ryan

Rye is a cereal grain similar to wheat and barley. The plant has slender seed spikes with long, stiff *awns* (beards). The dark-colored grains grow in pairs. Rye flowers, unlike those of wheat, oats, and barley, open for pollination. The flowers shed their pollen into the air, and the pollen is spread by the wind. Rye is used to make bread and certain types of liquors. Rye probably originated from wild species in eastern Europe or Asia. Wild rye still grows in these regions and in northern Africa.

Production. Rye is a major crop in the cool climates of northern Europe, Asia, and North America. The leading rye-growing countries include Germany, Poland, and Russia. In North America, much of the rye is grown in central Canada, the Dakotas, Georgia, and Oklahoma. The world produces about 500 million bushels of rye annually. A bushel of rye weighs 56 pounds (25 kilograms).

Uses. In most countries, rye is used chiefly for human food. Its food value is nearly as great as that of wheat. But American farmers feed much of the grain to livestock. Rye hay and *middlings* (medium-sized particles that are a by-product of bran flour milling) are often used as livestock feed. Young rye plants make good pasture in spring and autumn. But sometimes, cows that graze on rye give milk with an unusually strong flavor.

Farmers frequently grow rye to improve or to protect the soil. For example, a crop of rye may be raised alternately with other crops to protect the soil. Then, it is called a *cover crop.* If it is plowed under before it matures, it is called a *green manure crop.*

The heavy, black bread of Europe is made from rye. Rye does not contain as much gluten as wheat. Because of this, yeast cannot raise rye dough as easily as wheat dough, and rye bread is heavier and more compact. In the United States, bakers usually add much wheat flour to the rye so that the bread is not so dark as the bread made in Europe. During the past few hundred years, wheat bread has become more popular than rye bread.

Distillers use malt made from rye for rye whiskey and Holland gin. Rye straw is long, smooth, and easy to bend. Packers use it in their work. Manufacturers use it for hats, paper, mats, and mattress stuffing. Rye straw is

WORLD BOOK illustration by John D. Dawson

A rye seed spike, *left,* has long, stiff beards. Rye grains, *right,* grow in pairs. Rye is a major crop in many countries.

Leading rye-growing countries

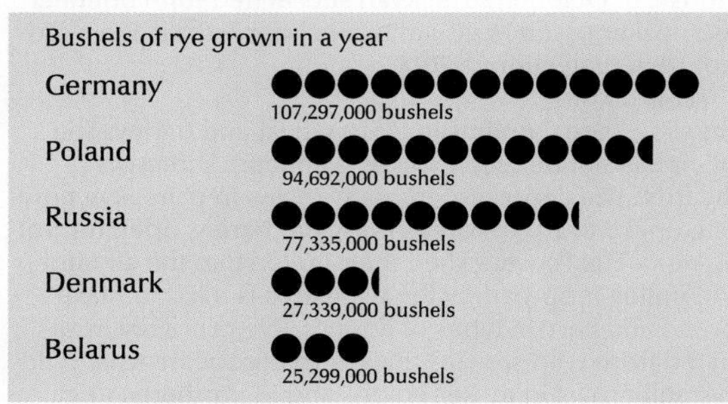

One bushel equals 56 pounds (25 kilograms).
Figures are for a three-year average, 2017-2019.
Source: FAOSTAT, Statistics Division, Food and Agriculture Organization of the UN. http://www.fao.org. Data accessed in 2021.

also used in European countries for thatched roofs because it decays less rapidly than most other straw.

Construction workers use rye to conserve soil. They plant rye in the raw soil along new roadbeds. The plants grow in the infertile subsoil and keep it from eroding.

Cultivation. Rye grows well in much poorer soils than those necessary for most cereal grains. Thus, it is an especially valuable crop in regions where the soil has sand or peat. Rye plants withstand cold better than other small grains do. Most farmers grow winter ryes, which are planted and begin to grow in autumn. In spring, the plants develop and produce their crop.

Like all cereal grains, rye plants are annuals, and new seeds must be planted each year. Most American farmers use grain drills to plant rye. These machines plant the seeds in rows 6 to 7 inches (15 to 18 centimeters) apart. About 84 to 112 pounds of seed are sown per acre (93 to 124 kilograms per hectare). In the United States, rye yields an average of about 30 bushels of grain per acre (75 bushels per hectare). In some European countries, the crop may yield two to three times this amount. Because of the low rye yields and a greater demand for wheat, U.S. farmers usually grow wheat instead of rye.

Ergot is a poisonous fungus that often destroys rye grain. Ergot replaces the grain with a hornlike blackish body several times longer than the normal grain. These ergot bodies poison livestock and human beings who eat the grain or products made from it. This disease is called *ergotism.* Doctors use small doses of drugs made from ergot to ease migraine headaches, to control bleeding, and to aid in childbirth. Robert D. Wych

Scientific classification. Rye's scientific name is *Secale cereale.*

See also Ergot.

Ryukyu Islands, *ree OO KYOO,* are a group of more than 100 islands in the North Pacific Ocean that belong to Japan. They stretch from the main islands of Japan to Taiwan. They have a land area of 1,205 square miles (3,120 square kilometers) and a population of about 1,500,000. Some islands have no people. The Ryukyus can be divided into five groups from north to south—(1) the Osumi Islands, (2) the Tokara Islands, (3) the central Ryukyus including the Amami Islands and Okinawa, (4) the Miyako Islands, and (5) the Yaeyama Islands.

People. Farming is the most important occupation of the islanders, though the soil is rocky and the landscape is hilly. The people grow rice, but their main food crop is sweet potatoes. They export sugar cane and pineapple. Many people work at hotels and resorts, which attract visitors from the Japanese mainland.

The Ryukyuans speak Japanese. Their religion has been influenced by both China and Japan. Burial of the dead in large family tombs and ceremonies honoring ancestors are important parts of the Ryukyuan religion. Ryukyuans also worship things connected with nature, such as trees and fire.

Land and climate. Most of the Ryukyu Islands are mountainous. The highest elevation above sea level, more than 6,000 feet (1,800 meters), is on Yaku Island. Some of the islands have active volcanoes. The Ryukyus have a warm, wet climate. The average temperature is about 70 °F (21 °C), and the annual rainfall ranges from 53 to 120 inches (135 to 305 centimeters). Typhoons bring damaging winds and rains in summer and fall. Winters are usually cloudy and chilly, with less rain.

History. Ancestors of the Ryukyuans probably came from Japan and Taiwan, and possibly from the Philippines. Some scientists believe that prehistoric people may have lived on the islands during the most recent ice age, which ended about 11,500 years ago. Chinese and Japanese expeditions stopped in the Ryukyu Islands as early as the A.D. 600's. During the 1400's and 1500's, Okinawa was part of a trade network that linked China, Japan, Korea, and Southeast Asia.

China and Japan both claimed the Ryukyus until 1874, when China recognized Japanese rule. In 1879, the islands became part of two *prefectures* (provinces) of Japan. After World War II (1939-1945), the United States took over the Ryukyus. In 1953, the islands north of Okinawa were returned to Japan. Okinawa and the southern Ryukyus were returned in 1972. David L. Howell

See also **Okinawa.**

Ryukyu Islands

WORLD BOOK maps

EAGLE PUBLIC LIBRARY
PO BOX 240 / 600 BROADWAY
EAGLE CO 81631 (970)328-8800